MW00744026

Principles of
International Criminal Law

Principles of
International Criminal Law

by

Gerhard Werle

Professor of German and International Criminal Law
Humboldt-Universität zu Berlin

in cooperation with

Florian Jessberger
Senior Research Fellow
Humboldt-Universität zu Berlin

Wulf Burchards
Senior Research Fellow
Humboldt-Universität zu Berlin

Volker Nerlich
Former Senior Research Fellow
Humboldt-Universität zu Berlin

Belinda Cooper
Senior Fellow
World Policy Institute
New York

T·M·C· ASSER PRESS

Published by T·M·C·ASSER PRESS
P.O.Box 16163, 2500 BD The Hague, The Netherlands
<www.asserpress.nl>

T·M·C·ASSER PRESS' English language books are distributed exclusively by:

Cambridge University Press, The Edinburgh Building, Shaftesbury Road,
Cambridge CB2 2RU, UK,
or
for customers in the USA, Canada and Mexico:
Cambridge University Press, 100 Brook Hill Drive, West Nyack, NY 10994-2133, USA
<www.cambridge.org>

Author:

Prof. Dr. Gerhard Werle
Lehrstuhl für deutsches und internationales Strafrecht,
Strafprozessrecht und Juristische Zeitgeschichte
Juristische Fakultät der Humboldt-Universität zu Berlin
Unter den Linden 6
10099 Berlin
Germany
Email: gerhard.werle@rewi.hu-berlin.de

ISBN 90-6704-202-1 ⎫ paperback
ISBN 9789067042024 ⎭

ISBN 90-6704-196-3 ⎫ hardcover
ISBN 9789067041966 ⎭

All rights reserved.
© 2005, T·M·C·ASSER PRESS, The Hague, The Netherlands and the Author

No part of the material protected by this copyright notice may be reproduced or utilized in any form or
by any means, electronic or mechanical, including photocopying, recording, or by any information
storage and retrieval system, without written permission from the copyright owner.

PRINTED IN THE NETHERLANDS

Preface

International criminal law has made immense strides in the recent past, from the creation of the Yugoslavia Tribunal in 1993 to the establishment of the International Criminal Court, which took up operations in 2003. While as recently as the early 1990s, the very existence of international criminal law was often called into question, the baseline today is clear: International criminal law is an integral part of international law, not simply law in the making. International criminal law is applied by international courts, states are called upon to assist in its implementation, and domestic incorporation processes are underway in many countries. The consequences for the study of international criminal law are obvious: Today, what is needed is not a merely historical presentation of the evolution of the subject, but an ordering and analysis of this body of law. In that spirit, this book undertakes a systematic survey of the foundations and general principles of substantive international criminal law and of the core crimes – that is, genocide, crimes against humanity, war crimes, and the crime of aggression.

The subject of this volume is the norms that form the basis for individual criminal responsibility under international law. The discussion includes both the Statute of the International Criminal Court and customary international criminal law. It is true that the Statute essentially embodies customary law, but it does not exhaust it; customary international criminal law goes beyond the Statute, especially in the criminalization of violations of international humanitarian law. The jurisprudence of international tribunals is included throughout the text as an authoritative source, particularly the case law of the Yugoslavia and Rwanda Tribunals, which has already contributed significantly to the development of international criminal law.

This volume is addressed to law students, academics and practitioners concerned with international criminal law, international humanitarian and human rights law, or application of international criminal law in a domestic context. The present edition is based on my book "Völkerstrafrecht," which was published in Germany in 2003 (publishers Mohr Siebeck, Tübingen). The text has been thoroughly updated and revised to meet the needs of an international, English-speaking audience; references to Germany and German-language sources have been retained where they are relevant to the international context. Scholarship and jurisprudence have been included through August 2004; later decisions and publications were incorporated to the extent permitted by the editing process.

I am grateful to the Berghof Stiftung für Konfliktforschung e.V. which generously funded this project. I would also like to sincerely thank a number of current and former researchers at Humboldt-Universität zu Berlin for their extraordinary dedication. Above all, my thanks go to Dr. Florian Jessberger, not only for his active involvement in the writing of the first two sections (Foundations and General Principles), but also for having contributed significantly to the overall concept of this book. I would also like to acknowledge the important contributions by Dr. Volker Nerlich (War Crimes and Aggression) and Dr. Wulf Burchards (War Crimes Against Persons and Use of Prohibited Methods of Warfare). Dr. Burchards was also in charge of revising the third and fourth sections (Genocide and Crimes Against Humanity); Dr. Stephan Meseke and Dr. Barbara Lüders made valuable contributions to the German versions of these chapters. Belinda Cooper's translation of the German text provided an important basis for this edition. She served as a competent and critical interlocutor in resolving numerous issues that arose in the course of the revisions, many of which went beyond linguistic details. My thanks extend also to Professor Horst Fischer for fruitful discussions on matters of international humanitarian law.

Gregoria Palomo Suarez, Ines Peterson, Camill Sander, Boris Burghardt, Stefan Langbein and Anja Schepke provided invaluable support in finding and analyzing cases and literature, as well as dealing with a variety of technical tasks. The appendices were compiled by Ines Peterson and Gregoria Palomo Suarez (Table of Cases, Table of Statutes and International Instruments), Dr. Wulf Burchards and Dr. Volker Nerlich (Index).

Berlin, January 2005   Gerhard Werle

Summary of Contents

	p.	*marg. no.*
Preface	V	
Table of Contents	IX	
Table of Abbreviations	XIX	
Part One: Foundations	1	1
A. Historical Evolution	2	2
B. Concepts, Tasks and Legitimacy	24	71
C. International Criminal Law and the International Legal Order	34	96
D. Sources and Interpretation	43	122
E. Universal Jurisdiction, the Duty to Prosecute, and Amnesty	57	168
F. Enforcement	66	193
G. Domestic Implementation	73	215
Part Two: General Principles	90	266
A. Towards a General Theory of Crimes Under International Law	91	271
B. Material Elements	96	285
C. Mental Element	99	293
D. Individual Criminal Responsibility	116	337
E. Superior Responsibility	128	367
F. Grounds for Excluding Criminal Responsibility	138	401
G. Inchoate Crimes	165	485
H. Omissions	170	502
I. Official Capacity and Immunity	172	509
J. Multiplicity of Offenses	178	527
K. Requirements for Prosecution	183	544
Part Three: Genocide	186	554
A. Introduction	188	555
B. Material Elements	193	571
C. Mental Element	206	610
D. Incitement to Commit Genocide	211	623
E. Multiplicity of Offenses	212	628
Part Four: Crimes Against Humanity	214	632
A. Introduction	216	633
B. Contextual Element (Attack on a Civilian Population)	221	646
C. Individual Acts	231	672
D. Multiplicity of Offenses	266	769

Part Five: War Crimes   267   772

A.   Introduction   269   773
B.   Overall Requirements   286   822
C.   War Crimes Against Persons   298   859
D.   War Crimes Against Property and Other Rights   334   986
E.   Employing Prohibited Methods of Warfare   341   1008
F.   Use of Prohibited Means of Warfare   368   1096
G.   War Crimes Against Humanitarian Operations   380   1133
H.   Multiplicity of Offenses   383   1144

Part Six: The Crime of Aggression   384   1147

A.   The Prohibition of Aggression Under International Law   386   1151
B.   Criminal Responsibility Under Customary International Law
     (War of Aggression)   390   1161
C.   The Crime of Aggression in the ICC Statute – Prospects   400   1184

Appendix 1: Materials   405
Appendix 2: Table of Cases   435
Appendix 3: Table of Statutes and International Instruments   451
Appendix 4: Index   469
Appendix 5: International Criminal Law in the World Wide Web   483

Table of Contents

	p.	*marg. no.*
Preface	V	
Summary of Contents	VII	
Table of Abbreviations	XIX	
Part One: Foundations	1	1
A. **Historical Evolution**	2	2
I. The Versailles Peace Treaty	3	6
II. The Law of Nuremberg and Tokyo	6	15
1. The Nuremberg Charter and Trial	7	17
a) Creation of the Nuremberg Tribunal	7	17
b) Provisions of the Nuremberg Charter	8	19
c) The Nuremberg Judgment	8	22
d) Contemporary and Current Assessments	9	25
2. The Tokyo Charter and Trial	11	30
3. Control Council Law No. 10	12	34
III. International Criminal Law During the Cold War	13	40
IV. The United Nations *ad hoc* Tribunals	15	45
1. The Yugoslavia Tribunal	16	48
2. The Rwanda Tribunal	18	54
V. The ICC Statute and the International Criminal Court	18	56
1. Previous Efforts to Create a Permanent International Criminal Court	18	57
2. The Conference of Plenipotentiaries in Rome	20	60
3. Significance of the ICC Statute	24	68
B. **Concepts, Tasks and Legitimacy**	24	71
I. The Notions of "International Criminal Law" and "Crimes Under International Law"	25	72
II. Protected Interests	27	77
III. The "International Element" of Crimes Under International Law	29	81
IV. Purposes of Punishment	30	85
V. The Principle of Legality in International Criminal Law *(Nullum Crimen, Nulla Poena Sine Lege)*	32	90
C. **International Criminal Law and the International Legal Order**	34	96
I. International Criminal Law and State Responsibility	35	97
II. Crimes Under International Law and Other International Crimes	36	100
III. International Criminal Law, Supranational Criminal Law, Co-operation in Criminal Matters, and Extraterritorial Jurisdiction	38	105
IV. International Criminal Law and Protection of Human Rights	39	109
1. Protection of Human Rights Through International Criminal Law	40	110

2. The Function of Human Rights in Limiting International Criminal
Law   42   117
V. International Criminal Law and the Law of International Criminal
Procedure   42   118

D.   Sources and Interpretation   43   122
I. Sources of Law   44   123
1. International Treaties   45   126
2. Customary International Law   46   128
3. General Principles of Law   47   134
II. Subsidiary Means for Determining the Law   48   136
III. Individual Sources   48   137
1. ICC Statute, Elements of Crimes, Rules of Procedure and Evidence 49 138
2. The ICTY and ICTR Statutes   50   142
3. The Nuremberg and Tokyo Charters   50   144
4. Control Council Law No. 10   51   146
5. Geneva Conventions, Genocide Convention, Hague Regulations   51   147
6. Decisions of International Courts and Tribunals   51   148
7. Resolutions of the UN General Assembly and the UN Security Council,
and Reports of the UN Secretary-General   52   150
8. International Law Commission Drafts and Comments   53   152
9. Drafts and Comments of International Scholarly Associations   53   153
10. Decisions of National Courts   53   154
11. National Legislation   54   156
12. Military Manuals   54   157
IV. Interpretation   54   158
V. Determining the Law Through the International Criminal Court   56   164

E.   Universal Jurisdiction, the Duty to Prosecute, and Amnesty   57   168
I. Universal Jurisdiction and the Power to Prosecute and Punish   58   169
II. The Duty to Prosecute   61   177
1. The Duty to Prosecute by the State of Commission   62   179
2. Do "Third States" Have a Duty to Prosecute?   63   182
III. Amnesties and Truth Commissions   65   188

F.   Enforcement   66   193
I. Direct and Indirect Enforcement   67   194
II. National and International Criminal Justice Systems   68   197
III. International Criminal Law in Action   70   201
1. The International Criminal Court   70   201
2. The Yugoslavia Tribunal   71   206
3. The Rwanda Tribunal   72   211

G.   Domestic Implementation   73   215
I. The Need for Implementation   74   217
II. Options for Implementation   75   220
1. Complete Incorporation   76   221
a) Direct Application   76   222
b) Reference   76   223
c) Copying   76   224
2. Non-Incorporation – Applying "Ordinary" Criminal Law   77   225
3. Modified Incorporation   77   228

4. Combinations	78	229
III. Forms of Incorporation	78	230
1. Amendment of Existing Laws	78	231
2. Self-Contained Codification	78	233
IV. Interpretation of International Criminal Law in a Domestic Context	79	235
V. The (German) Code of Crimes Against International Law	80	238
1. Historical Background	81	239
2. Aims	83	246
3. Structure	84	249
4. General Principles	84	250
5. Genocide	85	254
6. Crimes Against Humanity	85	255
7. War Crimes	85	256
8. Violations of Supervisory Responsibility	87	261
9. Aggression	87	263
10. Universal Jurisdiction	88	264
Part Two: General Principles	90	266
A. **Towards a General Theory of Crimes Under International Law**	91	271
I. The Concept of Crimes Under International Law	92	272
II. The Context of Organized Violence (International Element)	94	278
III. The Structure of Crimes Under International Law	95	279
1. Step One: Material Elements	95	280
2. Step Two: Mental Element	95	281
3. Step Three: Grounds for Excluding Responsibility	95	282
4. Requirements for Prosecution	96	284
B. **Material Elements**	96	285
I. Conduct	97	288
II. Consequence and Causation	97	289
III. Circumstances	98	291
C. **Mental Element**	99	293
I. International Case Law	101	296
II. Article 30 of the ICC Statute	102	298
1. Structure	102	299
2. Standard Requirements: "Intent and Knowledge"	104	304
a) Intent as Regards the Criminal Conduct	104	305
b) Intent and Knowledge as Regards the Consequences of the Conduct	104	306
c) Knowledge as Regards the Circumstances of the Crime	105	308
3. Departures From the Standard Requirements	106	310
a) Sources of Other Provisions Within the Meaning of Article 30	106	311
aa) "Otherwise provided" in the ICC Statute	106	311
bb) "Otherwise provided" in the Elements of Crimes and in Customary International Law	107	313
b) Effects of Other Provisions Within the Meaning of Article 30	109	317
aa) Affirmation and Clarification	109	318
bb) Expansion of Criminal Liability	109	319
cc) Narrowing of Criminal Liability	110	323

	4.	The Context of the Crime and the Mental Element	111	325
	5.	Recklessness and *Dolus Eventualis*	113	330

D. **Individual Criminal Responsibility** — 116 · 337

  I. Towards a Doctrine of Modes of Participation in International Criminal Law — 117 · 339
    1. International Case Law and Customary Law — 117 · 339
    2. ICC Statute — 119 · 343
  II. Commission — 120 · 345
    1. Commission as an Individual — 120 · 345
    2. Joint Commission — 120 · 346
    3. Commission Through Another Person — 123 · 353
  III. Encouragement — 124 · 356
    1. Ordering — 124 · 357
    2. Instigation — 125 · 358
  IV. Assistance — 125 · 360
    1. Assisting the (Primary) Perpetrator — 126 · 361
    2. Assisting the Commission of a Crime by a Group — 127 · 364

E. **Superior Responsibility** — 128 · 367

  I. Superior-Subordinate Relationship — 130 · 374
    1. Military Commanders — 131 · 377
    2. Civilian Superiors — 131 · 378
  II. Mental Element — 133 · 381
  III. Failure to Take Necessary Measures — 134 · 386
    1. Preventive Measures — 134 · 387
    2. Repressive Measures — 135 · 388
    3. Necessary and Reasonable Measures — 135 · 390
  IV. Commission of a Crime as a Result of Violation of the Duty of Control — 136 · 395

F. **Grounds for Excluding Criminal Responsibility** — 138 · 401

  I. Historical Development of Defenses in International Criminal Law — 138 · 402
    1. International Case Law — 138 · 402
    2. ICC Statute — 139 · 405
  II. Self-Defense — 139 · 407
    1. Self-Defense Situation — 141 · 410
      a) Use of Force — 141 · 411
      b) Defensible Interests — 141 · 412
    2. Self-Defense Measures — 142 · 416
    3. Mental Element — 142 · 417
    4. Individual Self-Defense and a State's Right of Self-Defense — 142 · 418
  III. Necessity and Duress — 143 · 420
    1. Threat to Life or Limb — 145 · 426
    2. Necessary and Reasonable Measures — 146 · 428
    3. Intention of Averting a Threat — 147 · 430
    4. Balancing of Interests — 147 · 431
    5. Self-Induced Necessity — 147 · 432
    6. Limits on Duress and Necessity in Cases of Special Duty to Assume Danger — 148 · 434
  IV. Mistake — 148 · 435
    1. Mistake of Fact — 150 · 439
    2. Mistake of Law — 151 · 443

V.	Superior Orders		152	448
	1.	Basic Positions	153	450
	2.	International Case Law and Customary International Law	154	454
	3.	Article 33 of the ICC Statute	156	460
VI.	Mental Disease or Defect		157	463
VII.	Intoxication		160	469
	1.	Destruction of the Capacity to Appreciate or Control Conduct	161	472
	2.	Exclusion of Responsibility for Voluntary Intoxication?	161	473
VIII.	Other Grounds for Excluding Responsibility		163	477

G.   Inchoate Crimes — 165 — 485

I.	Conspiracy	166	488
II.	Planning and Preparation	167	491
III.	Attempt	168	493
IV.	Abandonment	169	500

H.   Omissions — 170 — 502

I.   Official Capacity and Immunity — 172 — 509

I.	Immunity and International Criminal Law	172	510
II.	Irrelevance of Official Capacity	174	515
III.	(Limited) Immunity for Heads of State and Government, Foreign Ministers, and Diplomats	176	520
IV.	Summary	178	526

J.   Multiplicity of Offenses — 178 — 527

I.	International Case Law		179	530
II.	Same Conduct		179	531
	1.	Cumulative Charging	180	534
	2.	Multiple Convictions	180	535
III.	Sentencing		183	541

K.   Requirements for Prosecution — 183 — 544

Part Three: Genocide — 186 — 554

A.   Introduction — 188 — 555

I.	The Phenomenon of Genocide	188	555
II.	History of the Crime	190	560
III.	Structure of the Crime	191	563
IV.	Protected Interests	192	566

B.   Material Elements — 193 — 571

I.	Protected Groups		193	571
	1.	Criteria for Group Classification	194	573
	2.	National Groups	196	580
	3.	Ethnic Groups	196	581
	4.	Racial Groups	197	582
	5.	Religious Groups	197	583
	6.	Other Groups	198	585

II. Individual Acts 199 587
  1. Killing 200 589
  2. Causing Serious Bodily or Mental Harm 200 590
  3. Inflicting Destructive Conditions of Life 201 593
  4. Imposing Measures to Prevent Births 202 597
  5. Forcibly Transferring Children 203 598
  6. Is So-Called Ethnic Cleansing Genocide? 204 604
III. Destruction of the Group Required? 204 606

C. Mental Element 206 610
  I. Intent and Knowledge (Article 30 of the ICC Statute) 206 611
  II. Specific Intent to Destroy 207 615
    1. The Term "Intent" 207 616
    2. The Group as the Object of Destructive Intent 208 618
    3. Evidentiary Issues 210 622

D. Incitement to Commit Genocide 211 623
  I. Structure and Purpose of Punishment 211 623
  II. Material Elements 211 626
  III. Mental Element 212 627

E. Multiplicity of Offenses 212 628

Part Four: Crimes Against Humanity 214 632

A. Introduction 216 633
  I. The Phenomenon of Crimes Against Humanity 216 633
  II. History of the Crime 216 635
  III. Structure of the Crime 220 644
  IV. Protected Interests 220 645

B. Contextual Element (Attack on a Civilian Population) 221 646
  I. A Civilian Population as the Object of the Crime 221 647
  II. Widespread or Systematic Attack 224 652
    1. Attack 224 652
    2. Widespread or Systematic Character 225 654
  III. The "Policy Element" 226 658
    1. ICC Statute 226 658
    2. Customary International Law 229 666
  IV. Perpetrators 230 668
  V. Mental Element 230 669

C. Individual Acts 231 672
  I. Killing 232 674
  II. Extermination 234 678
  III. Enslavement 236 683
    1. Definition 237 685
    2. Forced Labor 238 690
    3. Trafficking in Persons 239 693
  IV. Deportation or Forcible Transfer of Population 240 695
  V. Imprisonment 243 704

VI. Torture 244 709
VII. Sexual Violence 247 721
    1. Rape 248 723
    2. Sexual Slavery 250 728
    3. Enforced Prostitution 251 729
    4. Forced Pregnancy 251 731
    5. Enforced Sterilization 252 733
    6. Other Forms of Sexual Violence 252 734
VIII. Persecution 253 735
    1. Material Elements 254 738
    2. Mental Element 257 745
      a) Political, Racial or Religious Grounds 258 747
      b) Other Grounds 258 749
IX. Enforced Disappearance 259 752
X. Apartheid 262 758
XI. Other Inhumane Acts 264 766

D.   **Multiplicity of Offenses** 266 769

Part Five: War Crimes 267 772

A.   **Introduction** 269 773
I. Historical Development 269 774
    1. Laws of War and International Humanitarian Law 270 775
    2. National Criminal Law to Implement International Humanitarian Law 276 795
    3. International Criminal Law and International Humanitarian Law 278 800
II. International Humanitarian Law and Criminal Sanctions 279 803
III. War Crimes in Non-International Armed Conflict 282 811
IV. Protected Interests 285 817
V. Categories of War Crimes 285 819

B.   **Overall Requirements** 286 822
I. Armed Conflict 286 822
    1. Inter-State Conflict 287 824
    2. Intra-State Conflict 288 825
    3. Applicability of the Law of War Crimes Despite No Use of Force 290 831
II. International or Non-International Conflict 290 833
    1. International Character of Inter-State Armed Conflicts 291 834
    2. Intra-State Armed Conflicts of an International Character 291 835
      a) Wars of National Liberation 291 836
      b) Other Intra-State Conflicts 292 837
    3. Mixed Armed Conflicts 293 842
III. Applicability of the Law of War Crimes, *Rationae Temporis* and *Loci* 294 844
IV. The Nexus Between the Individual Act and the Armed Conflict 294 846
    1. Perpetrator's Position 295 848
    2. Conduct of Private Persons 296 851
    3. Perpetrator's Motivation 297 853
V. Mental Element 297 854
    1. Perpetrator's Awareness of the Conflict 297 855
    2. Wilfulness in the Law of War Crimes 298 857

C. War Crimes Against Persons 298 859
  I. Victims of War Crimes Against Persons 298 859
    1. Persons Protected in the Geneva Conventions 299 860
      a) Protected Persons in International Conflicts 299 861
      b) Protected Persons in Non-International Conflicts 302 872
    2. Persons Protected by Other Provisions 302 874
  II. Killing 302 875
  III. Killing and Wounding Persons Not Involved in Combat 304 879
  IV. Offenses of Mistreatment 305 885
    1. Torture 305 887
    2. Causing Suffering or Injury to Health (International Conflict) 306 891
    3. Mutilation 307 895
    4. Biological, Medical or Scientific Experiments 308 898
    5. Inhuman or Cruel Treatment 310 903
  V. Sexual Violence 311 907
    1. Rape 313 912
    2. Other Serious Forms of Sexual Violence 313 914
  VI. Humiliating and Degrading Treatment 314 917
  VII. Compelled Service in Military Forces and Operations of War
    (International Conflict) 316 924
    1. Compelled Service in the Forces of a Hostile Power 316 924
    2. Compelled Participation in Operations of War 317 929
  VIII. Slavery 318 932
  IX. Forced Labor (International Conflict) 319 935
  X. Punishment Without Regular Trial 320 938
    1. International Conflict 320 938
    2. Non-International Conflict 322 944
  XI. Unlawful Confinement (International Conflict) 323 950
  XII. Delay in Repatriation (International Conflict) 325 955
  XIII. Hostage-Taking 325 958
  XIV. Deportation or Forcible Transfer 327 963
    1. International Conflict 327 964
    2. Non-International Conflict 328 968
  XV. Transfer of a Party's Own Civilian Population (International Conflict) 329 971
  XVI. Use of Child Soldiers 331 977

D. War Crimes Against Property and Other Rights 334 986
  I. Offenses of Expropriation 334 987
    1. Conduct 334 987
    2. Object of the Conduct 335 990
    3. Extent of Expropriation 336 994
    4. Mental Element 337 996
    5. Military Necessity 337 997
  II. Offenses of Destruction 338 1000
    1. Conduct 339 1002
    2. Object and Extent of the Offense and Military Necessity 340 1003
    3. Mental Element 340 1004
  III. Encroachments on Other Rights 340 1005

E. Employing Prohibited Methods of Warfare 341 1008
  I. Introduction 341 1008

1. Attacks on Non-Military Targets	341	1008
2. Other Prohibited Methods	342	1012
II. Attacks on Civilian Populations	343	1015
III. Terror Against a Civilian Population	344	1019
IV. Attacks on Civilian Objects	345	1024
1. International Conflict	345	1024
2. Non-International Conflict	346	1027
V. Attacks on Specially Protected Objects	346	1029
VI. Attacks on Persons and Objects Using the Emblems of the Geneva Conventions	348	1035
VII. Attacks Causing Disproportionate Incidental Damage	349	1039
1. International Conflict	350	1040
2. Non-International Conflict	352	1048
VIII. Attacks on Undefended Non-Military Objects	352	1049
1. International Conflict	352	1049
2. Non-International Conflict	354	1053
IX. Perfidious Killing or Wounding	354	1054
1. International Conflict	354	1054
2. Non-International Conflict	356	1059
X. Improper Use of Insignia	357	1061
1. International Conflict	357	1061
a) Improper Use of Flags of Truce	358	1064
b) Improper Use of Enemy Flags, Insignia, and Uniforms	358	1066
c) Improper Use of Protective Emblems of the Geneva Conventions	359	1068
d) Improper Use of Protected Insignia of the United Nations	359	1070
e) Serious Consequences	360	1072
2. Non-International Conflict	360	1073
XI. Giving No Quarter	360	1074
XII. Starvation of the Civilian Population	362	1080
1. International Conflict	362	1081
2. Non-International Conflict	365	1088
XIII. Use of Human Shields	365	1090
1. International Conflict	365	1090
2. Non-International Conflict	367	1095
F. Use of Prohibited Means of Warfare	368	1096
I. Introduction	368	1097
II. International Conflict (ICC Statute)	369	1100
1. Use of Poison or Poisoned Weapons	369	1100
a) The Term "Poison"	370	1103
b) Poison Gas as Poison?	371	1105
c) Chemical and Biological Weapons of Mass Destruction	371	1106
2. Use of Poison Gas and Similar Substances	372	1107
3. Use of Prohibited Ammunition	373	1111
4. The Catch-All Offense of Article 8(2)(b)(xx) of the ICC Statute	374	1114
III. International Conflict (Customary International Law)	375	1116
1. Nuclear Weapons	375	1118
2. Chemical Weapons	376	1119
3. Biological Weapons	377	1122
4. Conventional Weapons	377	1125
IV. Non-International Conflict (Customary International Law)	379	1127

G. War Crimes Against Humanitarian Operations   380   1133

H. Multiplicity of Offenses   383   1144

Part Six: The Crime of Aggression   384   1147

A. The Prohibition of Aggression Under International Law   386   1151
    I. Developments Prior to World War II   386   1151
    II. Current Status   389   1158

B. Criminal Responsibility Under Customary International Law
    (War of Aggression)   390   1161
    I. Nuremberg and the Criminality of Aggressive War   391   1162
    II. Material Elements   394   1168
        1. Aggressive War   394   1168
        2. Other Acts of Aggression   396   1175
        3. Perpetrators   397   1176
        4. Criminal Acts   398   1178
    III. Mental Element   399   1181
    IV. Jurisdiction   400   1182

C. The Crime of Aggression in the ICC Statute – Prospects   400   1184
    I. Definition of the Crime of Aggression   401   1187
    II. The Role of the UN Security Council   402   1188

Appendix 1: Materials   405
A. ICC Statute   406
B. ICTY Statute   418
C. ICTR Statute   420
D. London Agreement   422
E. Nuremberg Charter   423
F. Tokyo Charter   424
G. CCL No. 10   425
H. Nuremberg Principles   427
I. (German) Code of Crimes Against International Law   428

Appendix 2: Table of Cases   435

Appendix 3: Table of Statutes and International Instruments   451

Appendix 4: Index   469

Appendix 5: International Criminal Law in the World Wide Web   483

Table of Abbreviations

Additional Protocol I	*Protocol Additional to Geneva Conventions of August 12th, 1949, and Relating to the Protection of Victims of International Armed Conflicts*, of 8 June 1977, 1125 *UNTS* (1977), p. 3
Additional Protocol II	*Protocol Additional to the Geneva Conventions of 12 August 1949, and relating to the Protection of Victims of Non-International Armed Conflicts* of 8 June 1977, 1125 *UNTS* (1977), p. 609
Bundesgesetzblatt	(German) Federal Law Gazette
BGHSt	Decisions of the (German) Federal Supreme Court in Criminal Matters
BT-Drs.	Official Documents of the German Parliament *[Bundestags-Drucksache]*
Biotoxin Weapons Convention	*Convention on the Prohibition of the Development, Production and Stockpiling of Bacteriological (Biological) and Toxin Weapons and on their Destruction* of 10 April 1972, 1015 *UNTS* (1972), p. 163
CCL No. 10	Control Council Law No. 10, Official Gazette of the Control Council for Germany No. 3, 31 January 1945, pp. 50 et seq.
Chemical Weapons Convention	*Convention on the Prohibition of the Development, Production, Stockpiling and Use of Chemical Weapons and on their Destruction* of 13 January 1993, 1975 *UNTS* (1997), p. 469
Draft Code 1954	Draft Code of Offences against the Peace and Security of Mankind, Report of the International Law Commission covering the work of its sixth session (3 June-28 July 1954),UN Doc. A/2693, in: *Yearbook of the International Law Commission* 1954 II, p. 149
Draft Code 1991	Draft Code of Crimes against the Peace and Security of Mankind, Report of the International Law Commission on the work of its forty-third session (29 April-19 July 1991), UN Doc. A/46/10, in: *Yearbook of the International Law Commission* 1991 II, p. 79
Draft Code 1996	Draft Code of Crimes against the Peace and Security of Mankind, Report of the International Law Commission on the work of its forty-eighth session (6 May-26 July 1996), UN Doc. A/51/10, in: *Yearbook of the International Law Commission* 1996 II, p. 15
Draft ICC Statute (1998)	*Draft Statute for the International Criminal Court, Report of the Preparatory Committee on the Establishment of an International Criminal Court* of 14 April 1998, UN Doc. A/CONF.183/2/ Add.1, p. 14
EU	European Union
ETS	European Treaty Series
fn.	Footnote(s)
GAOR	UN General Assembly Official Records

Geneva Convention I	*Convention for the Amelioration of the Condition of the Wounded and Sick in Armed Forces in the Field* of 12 August 1949, 75 *UNTS* (1949), pp. 31 et seq.
Geneva Convention II	*Convention for the Amelioration of the Condition of the Wounded, Sick and Shipwrecked Members of in Armed Forces at Sea* of 12 August 1949, 75 *UNTS* (1949), pp. 85 et seq.
Geneva Convention III	*Convention relative to the Treatment of Prisoners of War* of 12 August 1949, 75 *UNTS* (1949), pp. 135 et seq.
Geneva Convention IV	*Convention relative to the Protection of Civilian Persons in Time of War* of 12 August 1949, 75 *UNTS* (1949), pp. 287 et seq.
Genocide Convention	*Convention on the Prevention and Punishment of the Crime of Genocide* of 9 December 1948, 78 *UNTS* (1949), p. 277
Hague Regulations	*Annex to Convention (IV) respecting the Laws and Customs of War on Land: Regulation concerning the Laws and Customs of War on Land* of 18 October 1907, the text of the treaty can be found at <http://www.icrc.org/ihl>
ICC	International Criminal Court
ICC Statute	*Rome Statute of the International Criminal Court* of 17 July 1998, 37 *ILM* (1998), pp. 999 et seq.
ICJ	International Court of Justice
ICJ Rep.	International Court of Justice, Reports of Judgments, Advisory Opinions and Orders
ICRC-Study on Art. 8 ICC Statute	Text prepared by the International Committee of the Red Cross on Article 8 of the Rome Statute, UN Doc. PCNICC/1999/WGEC/INF/2 and Add.1–Add.3
ICTR	International Criminal Tribunal for the Prosecution of Persons Responsible for Genocide and Other Serious Violations of International Humanitarian Law Committed in the Territory of Rwanda and Rwandan Citizens Responsible for Genocide and Other Such Violations Committed in the Territory of Neighbouring States between 1 January and 31 December 1994
ICTR Statute	*Statute for the International Criminal Tribunal for Rwanda*, UN Doc. S/RES/955 (1994).
ICTY	International Tribunal for the Prosecution of Persons Responsible for Serious Violations of International Humanitarian Law Committed in the Territory of the Former Yugoslavia since 1991
ICTY Statute	*Statute for the International Criminal Tribunal for the Former Yugoslavia*, UN Doc. S/RES/808 (1993)
ILA	International Law Association
ILC	International Law Commission
ILM	International Legal Materials
ILO	International Labour Organisation
ILR	International Law Reports
IMT	International Military Tribunal Nuremberg
IMT Charter	*Charter of the International Military Tribunal, Nuremberg*, in: 39 *American Journal of International Law* (1945), Suppl. pp. 257 et seq.

LNTS	League of Nations Treaty Series
NATO	North Atlantic Treaty Organisation
Nuremberg Charter	*Charter of the International Military Tribunal, Nuremberg*, in: 39 *American Journal of International Law* (1945), Suppl. pp. 257 et seq.
Nuremberg Principles	Principles of International Law Recognized in the Charter of the Nuremberg Tribunal and in the Judgment of the Tribunal, Report of the International Law Commission covering the work of its second session (5 June-29 July 1950), UN Doc. A/1316, in: *Yearbook of the International Law Commission* 1950 II, 374.
Nuremberg Tribunal	International Military Tribunal Nuremberg
OGHSt.	Decisions of the Supreme Court in the British Occupied Zone
para.(s.)	paragraph(s)
Poison Gas Protocol	*Protocol for the Prohibition of the Use in War of Asphyxiating, Poisonous or Other Gases, and of Bacteriological Methods of Warfare* of 17 June 1925, see <http://www.icrc.org/ihl>
Preparatory Commission	Preparatory Commission for the International Criminal Court
Preparatory Committee	Preparatory Committee on the Establishment of an International Criminal Court
Res.	Resolution
Reichsgesetzblatt	Law Gazette for the German Reich
Rwanda Tribunal	International Criminal Tribunal for the Prosecution of Persons Responsible for Genocide and Other Serious Violations of International Humanitarian Law Committed in the Territory of Rwanda and Rwandan Citizens Responsible for Genocide and Other Such Violations Committed in the Territory of Neighbouring States between 1 January and 31 December 1994
Supp(l).	Supplementum
TIAS	(US) Treaties and other International Acts
Tokyo Charter	*Charter of the International Military Tribunal for the Far East*, reprinted in: J. Pritchard and S.M. Zaide (eds.), *The Tokyo War Crimes Trial* (1981), Vol. 1
Tokyo Tribunal	International Military Tribunal for the Far East
UN	United Nations
UN Apartheid Convention	*International Convention on the Suppression and Punishment of the Crime of Apartheid* of 30 November 1973
UN Definition of Aggression	*UN General Assembly Resolution 3314 (XXIX)* of 14 December 1974
UN Doc.	Documents of the United Nations
UN GA	United Nations General Assembly
UN SCOR	United Nations Security Council Offical Records
UNTAET	United Nations Transitional Administration in East Timor
UNTS	United Nations Treaty Series

UNWCC

United Nations War Crimes Commission

Yugoslavia Tribunal

International Tribunal for the Prosecution of Persons Responsible for Serious Violations of International Humanitarian Law Committed in the Territory of the Former Yugoslavia since 1991

Part One: Foundations

Heiko Ahlbrecht: *Geschichte der völkerrechtlichen Strafgerichtsbarkeit im 20. Jahrhundert* (1999); **1**
Gary Jonathan Bass: *Stay the Hand of Vengeance, The Politics of War Crimes Tribunals* (2000), pp.
147 et seq.; M. Cherif Bassiouni: International Criminal Investigations and Prosecutions: From
Versailles to Rwanda, in M. Cherif Bassiouni (ed.), *International Criminal Law*, Vol. 3, 2nd edn.
(1999), pp. 31 et seq.; Adriaan Bos: From the International Law Commission to the Rome Con-
ference (1994–1998), in Antonio Cassese, Paola Gaeta and John R.W.D. Jones (eds.), *The Rome
Statute of the International Criminal Court: A Commentary*, Vol. 1 (2002), pp. 35 et seq.; Antonio
Cassese: *International Criminal Law* (2003), pp. 327 et seq.; Antonio Cassese: From Nuremberg to
Rome: International Military Tribunals to the International Criminal Court, in Antonio Cassese,
Paola Gaeta and John R.W.D. Jones (eds.), *The Rome Statute of the International Criminal Court: A
Commentary*, Vol. 1 (2002), pp. 3 et seq.; Lee A. Casey: The Case Against the International Crimi-
nal Court, 25 *Fordham International Law Journal* (2002), pp. 840 et seq.; James Crawford: The
Work of the International Law Commission, in Antonio Cassese, Paola Gaeta and John R.W.D.
Jones (eds.), *The Rome Statute of the International Criminal Court: A Commentary*, Vol. 1 (2002),
pp. 23 et seq.; Gerd Hankel: *Die Leipziger Prozesse* (2003); Robert Herde: *Command Responsibility,
Die Verfolgung der "Zweiten Garde" deutscher und japanischer Generäle im alliierten Prozeßprogramm
nach dem Zweiten Weltkrieg* (2001); Chihiro Hosoya et al. (eds.): *The Tokyo War Crimes Trial, An
International Symposium* (1986); Hans-Heinrich Jescheck: *Die Verantwortlichkeit der Staatsorgane
nach Völkerstrafrecht, Eine Studie zu den Nürnberger Prozessen* (1952), pp. 19 et seq.; Hans-
Heinrich Jescheck: The General Principles of International Criminal Law Set Out in Nuremberg
as Mirrored in the ICC Statute, 2 *Journal of International Criminal Justice* (2004), pp. 38 et seq.;
Susanne Jung: *Die Rechtsprobleme der Nürnberger Prozesse, dargestellt am Verfahren gegen Friedrich
Flick* (1992); Hans-Peter Kaul: Der Aufbau des Internationalen Strafgerichtshofs, Schwierigkeiten
und Fortschritte, *Vereinte Nationen* 2001, pp. 215 et seq.; Hans-Peter Kaul: Auf dem Weg zum
Weltstrafgerichtshof, Verhandlungsstand und Perspektiven, *Vereinte Nationen* 1997, pp. 177 et
seq.; Gabrielle Kirk McDonald: Contributions of the International Criminal Tribunals to the De-
velopment of Substantive International Humanitarian Law, in Sienho Yee and Wang Tieya (eds.),
International Law in the Post-Cold War World, Essays in Memory of Li Haopei (2001), pp. 446 et
seq.; Philippe Kirsch and Darryl Robinson: Reaching Agreement at the Rome Conference, in Antonio Cassese, Paola Gaeta and John R.W.D. Jones (eds.), *The Rome Statute of the International
Criminal Court: A Commentary*, Vol. 1 (2002), pp. 67 et seq.; Philippe Kirsch and Valerie
Oosterveld: The Post-Rome Conference Preparatory Commission, in Antonio Cassese, Paola
Gaeta and John R.W.D. Jones (eds.), *The Rome Statute of the International Criminal Court: A Com-
mentary*, Vol. 1 (2002), pp. 93 et seq.; Matthew Lippman: The Other Nuremberg: American Pros-
ecution of Nazi War Criminals in Occupied Germany, *Indiana International and Comparative Law
Review* 1992, pp. 1 et seq.; Reinhard Merkel: Das Recht des Nürnberger Prozesses, Gültiges,
Fragwürdiges, Überholtes, in Nürnberger Menschenrechtszentrum (ed.), *Von Nürnberg nach Den
Haag, Menschenrechtsverbrechen vor Gericht, Zur Aktualität des Nürnberger Prozesses* (1996), pp. 68
et seq.; Virginia Morris and Michael P. Scharf: *An Insider's Guide to the International Criminal Tri-
bunal for the Former Yugoslavia*, Vol. 1 (1995), pp. 17 et seq.; Virginia Morris and Michael P.
Scharf: *The International Criminal Tribunal for Rwanda*, Vol. 1 (1998), pp. 2 et seq.; Kai Müller:
Oktroyierte Siegerjustiz nach dem Ersten Weltkrieg, 39 *Archiv des Völkerrechts* (2001), pp. 202 et
seq.; Wolfgang Naucke: Bürgerliche Kriminalität, Staatskriminalität und Rückwirkungsverbot, in

Andreas Donatsch (ed.), *Festschrift für Trechsel* (2002), pp. 505 et seq.; Karin Oellers-Frahm: Das Statut des Internationalen Strafgerichtshofs zur Verfolgung von Kriegsverbrechen im ehemaligen Jugoslawien, 54 *Zeitschrift für ausländisches öffentliches Recht und Völkerrecht* (1994), pp. 416 et seq.; Philipp Osten: *Der Tokioter Kriegsverbrecherprozeß und die japanische Rechtswissenschaft* (2003); Philip R. Piccigallo: *The Japanese on Trial, Allied War Crimes Operations in the East, 1945– 1951* (1979); Herwig Roggemann: *Die internationalen Strafgerichtshöfe*, 2nd edn. (1998); Michael P. Scharf: *Balkan Justice* (1997); Walter Schwengler: *Völkerrecht, Versailler Vertrag und Auslieferungsfrage, Die Strafverfolgung wegen Kriegsverbrechen als Problem des Friedensschlusses 1919/20* (1982); Dirk von Selle: Prolog zu Nürnberg – Die Leipziger Kriegsverbrecherprozesse vor dem Reichsgericht, *Zeitschrift für Neuere Rechtsgeschichte* 1997, pp. 193 et seq.; Telford Taylor: *The Anatomy of the Nuremberg Trials: A Personal Memoir* (1993); Christian Tomuschat: Das Statut von Rom für den Internationalen Strafgerichtshof, 73 *Die Friedens-Warte* (1998), pp. 335 et seq.; Christian Tomuschat: Die Arbeit der ILC im Bereich des materiellen Völkerstrafrechts, in Gerd Hankel and Gerhard Stuby (eds.), *Strafgerichte gegen Menschheitsverbrechen, Zum Völkerstrafrecht 50 Jahre nach den Nürnberger Prozessen* (1995), pp. 270 et seq.; Otto Triffterer: Der ständige Internationale Strafgerichtshof – Anspruch und Wirklichkeit, Anmerkungen zum "Rome Statute of the International Criminal Court" vom 17. Juli 1998, in Karl Heinz Gössel and Otto Triffterer (eds.), *Gedächtnisschrift für Zipf* (1999), pp. 493 et seq.; Otto Triffterer: Der lange Weg zu einer internationalen Strafgerichtsbarkeit, 114 *Zeitschrift für die gesamte Strafrechtswissenschaft* (2002), pp. 321 et seq.; United Nations (ed.): *The United Nations and Rwanda 1993–1996* (1996); Ruth Wedgwood: The International Criminal Court: An American View, 10 *European Journal of International Law* (1999), pp. 93 et seq.; J.F. Willis: *Prologue to Nuremberg, The Politics and Diplomacy of Punishing War Criminals of the First World War* (1982); Andreas Zimmermann: Die Schaffung eines ständigen Internationalen Strafgerichtshofes, Perspektiven und Probleme vor der Staatenkonferenz in Rom, 58 *Zeitschrift für ausländisches öffentliches Recht und Völkerrecht* (1998), pp. 47 et seq.; Andreas Zimmermann and Holger Scheel: Zwischen Konfrontation und Kooperation, Die Vereinigten Staaten und der Internationale Strafgerichtshof, *Vereinte Nationen* 2002, pp. 137 et seq.

A. Historical Evolution

2   The idea of universal criminal justice has its roots far back in human history. But only in the 20th century did such ideas begin to be conceptualized as legal issues.[1] In the process, establishment of individual criminal responsibility under international law faced two main obstacles: first, in classical international law, states, not individuals, were the exclusive subjects. Therefore, establishment of criminal norms in international law first required the recognition of the individual as a subject of international law. Second, it was necessary to overcome states' defensive attitude towards outside interference, which was rooted in the concept of sovereignty.

3   Both obstacles were ultimately overcome. In the process, the development of international criminal law was fuelled by the general tendency of modern international law to strengthen the position of the individual. But it was the horror of Nazi tyranny that first brought about the acceptance of international criminal responsibility. Impunity for the

---

[1] On the origins of international criminal law, see M.C. Bassiouni, in M.C. Bassiouni (ed.), *International Criminal Law*, Vol. 3, 2nd edn. (1999), pp. 31 et seq.; A. Cassese, *International Criminal Law* (2003), pp. 15 et seq.; see also H. Ahlbrecht, *Geschichte der völkerrechtlichen Strafgerichtsbarkeit im 20. Jahrhundert* (1999), pp. 19 et seq.; H.-H. Jescheck, *Die Verantwortlichkeit der Staatsorgane nach Völkerstrafrecht* (1952), pp. 19 et seq.

perpetrators of Nazi atrocities was deemed unacceptable, and joint action was called for on the part of the international community. The victorious World War II powers responded to these demands by creating international criminal courts.

In the decades following the horrors of World War II and the genocide of the European Jews, the international public would be shocked again and again by major crimes that were ordered or covered up by governments. During the Cold War, however, a lack of political will prevented the use of penal sanctions against state-sponsored atrocities. Not until the end of the Cold War did the United Nations, spurred by the terrible crimes in former Yugoslavia and Rwanda, demonstrate renewed political will by creating the criminal Tribunals for Yugoslavia and Rwanda. Thus the evolution of international criminal law is a result of some of the darkest chapters in human history. In addition to these catastrophes, however, favorable political conditions were necessary before the idea of universal justice could be put into practice. **4**

Three milestones have marked the path of international criminal law. Immediately after World War II, international criminal law took shape in the "Nuremberg Principles," as enumerated in the *Charter of the International Military Tribunal at Nuremberg*, applied by the Nuremberg Tribunal and affirmed by the UN General Assembly. Since the mid-1990s, the work of the UN-created *ad hoc* Tribunals for the former Yugoslavia and Rwanda has reaffirmed the status of international criminal law as customary law. The high point, and for now the conclusion, of the crystallization of international criminal law is the *Rome Statute of the International Criminal Court* (ICC Statute), which came into force in 2002. The ICC Statute represents the first comprehensive codification of international criminal law, and it affirms and clarifies customary international criminal law. **5**

I. The Versailles Peace Treaty

The initial move towards the establishment of individual criminal responsibility under international law can be found in the *Versailles Peace Treaty* of 28 June 1919,[2] which states: "The Allied and Associated Powers publicly arraign William II of Hohenzollern, formerly German Emperor, for a supreme offence against international morality and the sanctity of treaties."[3] **6**

An international tribunal was to be set up to try the Kaiser.[4] In addition, the peace treaty stipulated the Allies' power to try persons before their military courts "for viola- **7**

---

[2] 11 *Martens Nouveau Récueil Général de Traités* (ser. 3 (1923), pp. 323 et seq. For greater detail, see M.C. Bassiouni, in M.C. Bassiouni (ed.), *International Criminal Law*, Vol. 3, 2nd edn. (1999), pp. 33 et seq.; W. Schwengler, *Versailler Vertrag und Auslieferungsfrage* (1982), pp. 71 et seq.; D. von Selle, *Zeitschrift für Neuere Rechtsgeschichte* 1997, pp. 193 et seq.; J.F. Willis, *Prologue to Nuremberg* (1982), pp. 65 et seq. During the war, a number of trials of German soldiers had already taken place before Allied military courts in which the "Law of Nations" had been applied on the basis of the territoriality and personality principles, see T.L.H. McCormack, in T.L.H. McCormack and G.J. Simpson (eds.), *The Law of War Crimes* (1997), p. 31 and p. 44.

[3] See Versailles Treaty, Art. 227(1).

[4] See Versailles Treaty, Art. 227(2). The Court itself was to have five judges, of which one each would be appointed by the United States, Great Britain, France, Italy and Japan.

tions of the laws and customs of war."[5] To make this possible, the peace treaty required the German government to hand over war criminals[6] and assist in their prosecution.[7]

8 The *Commission des Responsabilités des Auteurs de la Guerre et Sanctions*, created by the preliminary Paris Peace Conference of 25 January 1919, had done important preparatory work.[8] Its mandate included establishing the responsibility of the initiators of the war, determining violations of the laws and customs of war committed by German armed forces and their allies, assigning responsibility for those violations of the laws of war, and drafting proposals for the formation of a tribunal to try those responsible.[9] The elements of crimes developed by the commission included four groups of crimes:[10] crimes against the sanctity of treaties, crimes against international morality, violations of the laws of humanity, and "genuine" war crimes – that is, violations of the Hague Regulations, the Geneva Red Cross Convention of 1864 and the accepted rules of sea warfare. Crucial to the further development of international criminal law was, above all, the enumeration of individual war crimes, including murder and massacre, systematic terror, cruel treatment of the civilian population, intentional starvation of the civilian population, deportation of civilians, intentional bombardment of hospitals, and plundering. This list of violations of international humanitarian law was taken up in, for example, Article 6 (b) of the Nuremberg Charter.

9 However, the new and ambitious model of establishing individual criminal responsibility formulated in the Versailles Treaty was never implemented. No international tribunal was ever created. The former German Kaiser was granted asylum in the Netherlands,[11] and he never had to stand trial before a criminal court. Otherwise, the prosecution of war criminals by Allied military courts failed due to the Germans' stubborn refusal to surrender persons named by the Allies.[12]

---

[5] See Versailles Treaty, Art. 228(1) and Art. 229(1) and (2) provided for international military courts if crimes were committed against citizens of various countries.

[6] See Versailles Treaty, Art. 228(2). The extent to which the German Reich's treaty obligations could be fulfilled at all is questionable, given the German legal situation (Sec. 9 of the Reich Criminal Code prohibited the extradition of German citizens).

[7] See Versailles Treaty, Art. 230.

[8] The commission report is published in 14 *American Journal of International Law* (1920), pp. 95 et seq.; *Walter Schwengler* deserves credit for a comprehensive analysis of the commission material, which is not easily accessible, especially in *Versailler Vertrag und Auslieferungsfrage* (1982), pp. 90 et seq.; on the mandate and findings of the commission, see H. Ahlbrecht, *Geschichte der völkerrechtlichen Strafgerichtsbarkeit im 20. Jahrhundert* (1999), pp. 28 et seq.

[9] See W. Schwengler, *Versailler Vertrag und Auslieferungsfrage* (1982), p. 91.

[10] For details see H. Ahlbrecht, *Geschichte der völkerrechtlichen Strafgerichtsbarkeit im 20. Jahrhundert* (1999), pp. 32 et seq.

[11] The Netherlands, a strong promoter of international criminal law today and the site of the Yugoslavia Tribunal and the International Criminal Court, declared in connection with its refusal to extradite the German Kaiser: "If in the future an international jurisprudence should be created by the League of Nations that is authorized, in case of war, to administer justice which has been stamped as crimes and sanctioned as such by a previously-devised statute, then the Netherlands will join the new order of things." See "Antwortnote der niederländischen Regierung auf das Auslieferungsverlangen der Alliierten und Assoziierten Mächte betreffend den ehemaligen Deutschen Kaiser" of 21 January 1920, reprinted in W.G. Grewe (ed.), *Historiae Iuris Gentium*, Vol. 3/2 (1992), No. 95.

[12] The extradition list submitted to the German delegation in Paris on 3 February 1920 referred to some 900 people mentioned by name as responsible for the "most serious violations of the laws and customs of war," including numerous officers and troop commanders, see M.C. Bassiouni, in M.C. Bassiouni (ed.), *International Criminal Law*, Vol. 3, 2nd edn. (1999), p. 31 and p. 34. For discussion, especially on the domestic political background, see W. Schwengler, *Versailler Vertrag und Aus-*

The trials that were then held instead before the German Reichsgericht (Reich Su- **10**
preme Court) in Leipzig (the "Leipzig War Crimes Trials"[13]), to which the Allies had
reluctantly agreed,[14] were show trials to satisfy the victorious powers rather than serious
attempts to prosecute war crimes.[15] The results of the trials were correspondingly mea-
ger.

In December 1919, the German National Assembly adopted the *Law on Prosecution of War Crimes* **11**
and Offenses [Gesetz zur Verfolgung von Kriegsverbrechen und Kriegsvergehen] of 18 December
1919.[16] It made the Reichsgericht the one forum responsible for prosecuting crimes or misdemeanors committed by Germans inside or outside the country during the war, prior to 28 June
1919, against enemy citizens or enemy property (Section 1). A total of 907 proceedings were initiated before the Reichsgericht on the basis of the extradition list; the Reichsgericht took up an additional 837 proceedings on its own initiative.[17] Only 13, however, ever reached the trial stage. In
the nine trials that came to a judgment on the merits, six persons were convicted and six acquitted.
Even in those cases, none of the sentences was fully executed. As the victorious powers lost interest,
all further trials were suspended, and two of the defendants convicted were acquitted in a dubious
retrial.[18]

The Leipzig War Crimes Trials had only an indirect impact on the development of international **12**
criminal law,[19] since the basis for the trials before the Reichsgericht was German criminal law. In
the few cases that ended in a conviction, the Reichsgericht applied the definitions of crimes under
the Reich Criminal Code. Yet the Reichsgericht referred to international law to justify the illegality
of the acts.

Ultimately, there was essentially no criminal prosecution of international crimes commit- **13**
ted by Germans in World War I.[20] Nevertheless, the significance of the model provided
for in the Versailles Treaty should not be underestimated. For the first time, the idea of
individual criminal responsibility under international law was explicitly recognized in an

---

lieferungsfrage (1982), pp. 233 et seq.; see also D. von Selle, *Zeitschrift für Neuere Rechtsgeschichte*
1997, p. 193 at p. 194.

[13] For greater detail, see G. Hankel, *Die Leipziger Prozesse* (2003); W. Schwengler, *Versailler
Vertrag und Auslieferungsfrage* (1982), p. 317 and pp. 322 et seq.

[14] See H.-H. Jescheck, *Die Verantwortlichkeit der Staatsorgane nach Völkerstrafrecht* (1952), pp. 64
et seq.; K. Müller, 39 *Archiv des Völkerrechts* (2001), pp. 202 et seq.

[15] See also D. von Selle, *Zeitschrift für Neuere Rechtsgeschichte* 1997, p. 193 at p. 201.

[16] *Reichsgesetzblatt* 1919, p. 2125.

[17] See H. Ahlbrecht, *Geschichte der völkerrechtlichen Strafgerichtsbarkeit im 20. Jahrhundert* (1999),
pp. 42 et seq.

[18] Particular attention was paid to the trial of the sinking by the submarine U86 of the British
hospital ship "Llandovery Castle" and two lifeboats full of shipwrecked people who could have saved
themselves. The Reichsgericht sentenced the two officers on duty to four years' imprisonment as accessories to manslaughter. But in a retrial, after the commander of the submarine took "sole responsibility," they too were acquitted. See D. von Selle, *Zeitschrift für Neuere Rechtsgeschichte* 1997, p. 193 at
p. 199 and p. 201; H.-H. Jescheck, *Die Verantwortlichkeit der Staatsorgane nach Völkerstrafrecht*
(1952), pp. 65 et seq.

[19] For details, see D. von Selle, *Zeitschrift für Neuere Rechtsgeschichte* 1997, p. 193 at pp. 203 et
seq.

[20] See also H. Ahlbrecht, *Geschichte der völkerrechtlichen Strafgerichtsbarkeit im 20. Jahrhundert*
(1999), p. 44.

international treaty. This laid the groundwork upon which to build following the horrors of World War II.

14   Also largely unsuccessful were efforts at criminal prosecution for the mass deportation and murder of hundreds of thousands of Armenian Christians in Turkey beginning in 1915.[21] In 1915, the Allied powers had declared in unambiguous terms, "In view of those new crimes of Turkey against humanity and civilization, the Allied governments announce publicly to the Sublime-Porte that they will hold personally responsible [for] these crimes all members of the Ottoman government and those of their agents who are implicated in such massacres."[22] Accordingly, the Treaty of Sèvres,[23] which was signed in 1920 but never entered into force, explicitly envisaged a duty to surrender those responsible for these acts to an unspecified Allied or international court.[24] In the end, however, the Allies' vigorous proclamation remained without result.[25] Due to legal concerns[26] and political considerations,[27] there would be no joint action by the victorious powers or creation of an international court.

II. The Law of Nuremberg and Tokyo

15   The *Charter of the International Military Tribunal at Nuremberg* (Nuremberg Charter or IMT Charter), agreed upon along with the London Agreement on 8 August 1945 by the four victorious powers of World War II,[28] can be considered the birth certificate of international criminal law. The Charter's main statement was that crimes against peace, war crimes, and crimes against humanity entail individual responsibility under international law. This position was revolutionary. For the first time, individuals were actually held criminally accountable under international law. Perhaps the best-known passage in

---

[21] For details, see V.N. Dadrian, 14 *Yale Journal of International Law* (1989), pp. 221 et seq.; R. Herde, *Command Responsibility* (2001), pp. 58 et seq.

[22] See J.F. Willis, *Prologue to Nuremberg* (1982), p. 26.

[23] Reprinted in 15 *American Journal of International Law* (1921), Suppl. 179.

[24] See Art. 230.

[25] In contrast, the trials held by Turkey itself at first seemed promising, see T. Akçam, *Armenien und der Völkermord* (1996), pp. 77 et seq. The first trial of a group of former government officials (the so-called Talaat Pasha trial) began on 28 April 1919, before the War Crimes Court in Istanbul. The basis of the trial and the charge were general crimes under Ottoman criminal law. At the trial, a total of 17 death sentences were imposed for participation in atrocities against the Armenians, and three were carried out. In the so-called Yozgat trial of three political officials for the deportation and murder of over 30,000 Armenians in the Yozgat district, one death sentence was imposed, one defendant was sentenced to 15 years imprisonment, and a third escaped. However, the efforts at criminal prosecution in Turkey came to an abrupt end with the resurgence of the Turkish national movement in the early 1920s.

[26] Particularly controversial for legal experts dealing with the subject was the question whether the massacres were in fact war crimes; the view was widespread that it was an internal Turkish affair that was not open to judgment, let alone punishment, by outsiders. See the report in J.F. Willis, *Prologue to Nuremberg* (1982), p. 157.

[27] See J.F. Willis, *Prologue to Nuremberg* (1982), pp. 156 et seq. See also V.N. Dadrian, 14 *Yale Journal of International Law* (1989), p. 221 at pp. 281 et seq.

[28] *Agreement for the Prosecution and Punishment of the Major War Criminals of the European Axis*; the IMT Charter is included as an appendix to the Agreement. The text is reprinted in 39 *American Journal of International Law* (1945), Suppl. 257. Even before the end of the Nuremberg trial against the major war criminals, 19 more countries had signed the agreement, see K. Ipsen, in K. Ipsen, *Völkerrecht*, 5th edn. (2004), § 42 marginal no. 13.

the judgment of the International Military Tribunal commented on this: "Crimes against international law are committed by men, not by abstract entities, and only by punishing individuals who commit such crimes can the provisions of international law be enforced."[29]

The principles of the Nuremberg Charter were applied not only at Nuremberg, but **16** also at the war crimes trial in Tokyo,[30] and were tested and consolidated in numerous subsequent trials in the occupied zones. Today the Nuremberg principles are recognized as customary law, and they form the nucleus of substantive international criminal law.

1. The Nuremberg Charter and Trial

a) Creation of the Nuremberg Tribunal

The London Agreement concluded by the four victorious powers in 1945 provided for **17** the creation of an international military tribunal "for the trial of war criminals whose offenses have no particular geographical location."[31] These major war criminals were to be tried on the basis of the Nuremberg Charter, which was included as an appendix to the Agreement. War criminals whose crimes could be localized to a specific country's territory were to be prosecuted by the respective countries. Allied occupation courts *[Besatzungsgerichte]* would have jurisdiction over war crimes committed by Germans within the borders of the German Reich.[32]

The Allies had learned the lessons of the unsuccessful efforts to prosecute war crimes following **18** World War I. This time, prosecution by international courts was prepared well in advance and with the necessary energy.[33] An important basis for the trials held by the Allies after World War II was the result of investigations by the confusingly named (from today's point of view) United Nations War Crimes Commission (UNWCC),[34] created in 1942.[35] This internationally-staffed commission was mandated to collect evidence of the commission of war crimes. Furthermore, in

---

[29] IMT, judgment of 1 October 1946, in *The Trial of German Major War Criminals, Proceedings of the International Military Tribunal Sitting at Nuremberg, Germany*, Part 22, p. 447.

[30] The Charter of the International Military Tribunal for the Far East (Tokyo Charter) follows the IMT Charter almost word for word. It can be found in J. Pritchard and S.M. Zaide (eds.), *The Tokyo War Crimes Trial* (1981), Vol. 1.

[31] London Agreement, Art. 1. On the controversial legal nature of the International Military Tribunal, see H. Ahlbrecht, *Geschichte der völkerrechtlichen Strafgerichtsbarkeit im 20. Jahrhundert* (1999), pp. 69 et seq.; H.-H. Jescheck, *Die Verantwortlichkeit der Staatsorgane nach Völkerstrafrecht* (1952), pp. 148 et seq. and p. 168.

[32] Following the final declaration of the Potsdam Conference on 2 August 1945, the commanders in chief of the four occupying powers were authorized to exercise governmental authority in their respective zones of Germany. A joint Allied Control Council was formed, see Control Council Proclamation No. 1, 30 August 1945.

[33] On developments during the war, see H.-H. Jescheck, *Die Verantwortlichkeit der Staatsorgane nach Völkerstrafrecht* (1952), pp. 121 et seq.

[34] The name can be attributed to a conference that took place in Washington in 1942, at which the participating allies called themselves the United Nations. See H. Ahlbrecht, *Geschichte der völkerrechtlichen Strafgerichtsbarkeit im 20. Jahrhundert* (1999), p. 62.

[35] See M.C. Bassiouni, in M.C. Bassiouni (ed.), *International Criminal Law*, Vol. 3, 2nd edn. (1999), p. 31 at pp. 39 et seq.; H.-H. Jescheck, *Die Verantwortlichkeit der Staatsorgane nach Völkerstrafrecht* (1952), pp. 128 et seq.

the Moscow Declaration of German Atrocities,[36] Great Britain, the United States and the Soviet Union had already declared their firm intention of prosecuting enemy crimes: "Those German officers and men and members of the Nazi party who have been responsible for, or have taken a consenting part in the above atrocities, massacres and executions, will be sent back to the countries in which their abominable deeds were done in order that they may be judged and punished according to the laws of these liberated countries." Regarding the major perpetrators, the soon-to-be victorious powers also left no doubt as to their intentions: "The above declaration is without prejudice to the case of the major criminals, whose offences have no particular geographical localization and who will be punished by the joint decision of the Government of the Allies."

b) Provisions of the Nuremberg Charter

19   Crimes against peace are first among the crimes in Article 6 of the Nuremberg Charter. These concern the planning, preparation and waging of a war of aggression. The Charter renders violations of the laws and customs of war punishable as war crimes. While the criminalization of war crimes serves to protect the rights of foreign citizens, crimes against humanity include offenses against one's own citizens. Thus the domestic arena is also included in international law. Crimes against humanity are based on the idea that certain serious attacks on individuals gain an international dimension when they are systematically aimed at a specific civilian population. The most important example of this new type of crime was genocide, though it was not called this in either the Charter or the judgment of the Nuremberg Tribunal.

20   Not sustainable, in contrast, was the punishment of membership in organizations whose criminal character was established by the International Military Tribunal (Article 10 of the Nuremberg Charter). In any case, this was dubious because it tended to ignore the question of *individual* responsibility.

21   The Charter expressly emphasized that the domestic legality of a crime did not prevent its prosecution. Individual criminal responsibility did not depend on whether the act violated the laws of the country in which it was committed. Thus it was logical that, as provided by Article 7 of the Nuremberg Charter, the perpetrator's official capacity did not bar punishment. A further consequence was that acting upon orders did not protect against punishment, but could at most mitigate it.[37]

c) The Nuremberg Judgment

22   The trial before the International Military Tribunal "*against Göring et al.*" began on 20 November 1945 in Nuremberg, after opening in Berlin.[38] A total of 24 people were indicted, of whom only 21 could actually be brought to trial. Robert Ley eluded prosecution through suicide, Gustav Krupp was found unable to stand trial, and Martin Bormann had to be prosecuted *in absentia*. The Court consisted of one judge from each of the four victorious powers, with one alternate each (Article 2 of the Nuremberg Charter); the Court's decisions required a majority of its members, so

---

[36] Reprinted in 38 *American Journal of International Law* (1944), Suppl. 7.

[37] IMT Charter, Art. 8.

[38] The entire trial was officially recorded and published in a 23-volume documentation, see *The Trial of German Major War Criminals, Proceedings of the International Military Tribunal Sitting at Nuremberg, Germany* (1950). See also G. Ginsburgs and V.N. Kudriavtsev (eds.), *The Nuremberg Trial and International Law* (1990); T. Taylor, *The Anatomy of the Nuremberg Trials* (1993).

that three votes were necessary for a guilty verdict. The prosecution also consisted of one member of each of the four nations (Article 14 of the Nuremberg Charter). No appeal was possible from the decision of the Court (Article 26 of the Nuremberg Charter).

The International Military Tribunal announced its judgment on 30 September and 1 **23** October 1946. Even today, its findings are of paramount importance to both general history and international law.[39] On the basis of extensive evidence, the judgment provided a synopsis of the history of the Third Reich, and especially of the atrocities committed. At the same time, the judgment more precisely explained and refined the rules of international criminal law laid out in the Nuremberg Charter. A focus – and at the same time a weakness – of the judgment lay in its justification of the criminality of wars of aggression, essentially derived from the *Treaty Providing for the Renunciation of War as an Instrument of National Policy* of 27 August 1928 (the so-called Kellogg-Briand Pact).[40] On crimes against humanity, the Court stated that political opponents of the Nazis had been murdered and imprisoned even before the war, and in the process also referred to the persecution of the Jews. But based on the wording of Article 6(c) of the Nuremberg Charter ("in execution of or in connection with any crime within the jurisdiction of the Tribunal"), the Court required a link between crimes against humanity and war crimes or wars of aggression. Often this connection could not be proved for actions occurring before the start of the war.

In all, twelve defendants were sentenced to death (Göring, von Ribbentrop, Keitel, Kaltenbrunner, **24** Rosenberg, Frank, Frick, Streicher, Sauckel, Jodl, Seyss-Inquart, Bormann), three sentenced to life imprisonment (Hess, Funk, Raeder), and four sentenced to prison terms of between ten and 20 years (Dönitz, von Schirach, Speer, von Neurath); three defendants were acquitted (Schacht, von Papen, Fritsche). Four groups were declared to be criminal organizations.[41]

d) Contemporary and Current Assessments

In legal and political assessments, the victorious powers' course of action after World **25** War II was controversial.[42] The two central objections to the Nuremberg model questioned its political legitimacy, on the one hand, and its legal foundations, on the other. The accusation of victors' justice was nourished above all by the fact that no prosecutions for Allied war crimes ever took place.[43] Were the people bearing primary responsibility on the Axis side before the Court because they had started and waged an aggressive war – or only because they had lost it? From a legal point of view, the judgment was criticized

---

[39] The official version of the judgment is published in *The Trial of German Major War Criminals, Proceedings of the International Military Tribunal Sitting at Nuremberg, Germany.*

[40] The text of the treaty is published at <http://www.yale.edu/lawweb/avalon/imt/kbpact.htm>.

[41] These included the Nazi Party's political leadership corps and their staffs, the "Gestapo," the "Sicherheitsdienst" (SD) and the regular and "Waffen SS."

[42] For discussion of the objections, see H.-H. Jescheck, *Die Verantwortlichkeit der Staatsorgane nach Völkerstrafrecht* (1952), pp. 149 et seq.; see also M.C. Bassiouni, *Introduction to International Criminal Law* (2003), pp. 404 et seq. For a critical view, from today's perspective, on the prejudicial effects of the London Agreement and the Nuremberg judgment, see H. Ahlbrecht, *Geschichte der völkerrechtlichen Strafgerichtsbarkeit im 20. Jahrhundert* (1999), p. 96.

[43] See also M.C. Bassiouni, in M.C. Bassiouni (ed.), *International Criminal Law*, Vol. 3, 2nd edn. (1999), p. 31 and p. 45.

mainly for violating the prohibition on retroactive punishment, a principle fundamentally accepted by the Nuremberg Tribunal itself.[44]

26   Opinion remains divided as to whether all the crimes prosecuted before the International Military Tribunal had already been criminal under international law at the time they were committed.[45] However, it is indisputable that punishment of war crimes rested on a secure foundation in the law as it existed at the time they were committed. Regarding crimes against humanity, it was at least undisputed that the various crimes, such as murder, enslavement, torture, and rape, were illegal in virtually all legal systems at the time. Thus it was not the criminality of the acts themselves that offered a target for attack, but their prosecution under the legal heading of crimes against humanity and their direct criminalization under international law. Here too, however, one could argue that a recognized source of international law – general principles of law – could justify the punishment of crimes against humanity.[46]

27   Crimes against peace met with the strongest objections.[47] While the illegality of aggressive war under international law was justified convincingly by the Court, the leap from illegality to criminalization would have required a stronger foundation. The Court merely stated:

"In the opinion of the Tribunal, the solemn renunciation of war as an instrument of national policy necessarily involved the proposition that such a war was illegal in international law; and that those who planned and waged such a war, with its inevitable and terrible consequences, were committing a crime in so doing."[48]

It can at least be advanced, in support of this conclusion, that serious violations of the international laws of war had traditionally been considered criminal without the exist-

---

[44] See K. Ipsen, in K. Ipsen, *Völkerrecht*, 5th edn. (2004), § 42 marginal no. 22; R. Merkel, in Nürnberger Menschenrechtszentrum (ed.), *Von Nürnberg nach Den Haag* (1996), p. 68 at pp. 80 et seq.

[45] See also the discussion in M.C. Bassiouni, *Introduction to International Criminal Law* (2003), pp. 408 et seq.; K. Kittichaisaree, *International Criminal Law* (2001), p. 44.

[46] The British and French prosecutors at the Nuremberg Trials stated, "If murder, rapine, and robbery are indictable under the ordinary municipal laws of our countries, shall those who differ from the common criminal only by the extent and systematic nature of their offenses escape accusation?", see International Military Tribunal at Nuremberg, in *The Trial of German Major War Criminals, Proceedings of the International Military Tribunal Sitting at Nuremberg, Germany*, Part 2, p. 46. "I think . . . that this body of Crimes against Humanity constitutes, in the last analysis, nothing less than the perpetration for political ends and in a systematic manner, of common law crimes such as theft, looting, ill treatment, enslavement, murders, and assassinations, crimes that are provided for and punishable under the penal laws of all civilized states"; see International Military Tribunal at Nuremberg, in *The Trial of German Major War Criminals, Proceedings of the International Military Tribunal Sitting at Nuremberg, Germany*, Part 4, p. 34.

[47] See H.-H. Jescheck, *Die Verantwortlichkeit der Staatsorgane nach Völkerstrafrecht* (1952), p. 190: "Crimes against humanity and peace are the preliminary stage of true international criminal law, namely the criminalization by occupation law of violations of law that are recognized as such by international law." See also K. Kittichaisaree, *International Criminal Law* (2001), p. 44. For critical comment, see K. Ipsen, in R.D. Herzberg (ed.), *Festschrift für Oehler* (1985), p. 505 at p. 512.

[48] IMT judgment, 1 October 1946, in *The Trial of German Major War Criminals, Proceedings of the International Military Tribunal Sitting at Nuremberg, Germany*, Part 22, p. 445. For agreement, see G. Dahm, J. Delbrück and R. Wolfrum, *Völkerrecht*, Vol. I/3, 2nd edn. (2002), p. 1035: "The criminal prosecution of aggressive war is ultimately the logical consequence of the proscription of war."

ence of any express declaration of criminality, and that therefore waging an aggressive war was also criminal because of its illegality under international law.[49]

In the ensuing period, the principles applied and developed by the Nuremberg Tribu-   **28** nal were repeatedly confirmed to be part of international law. Therefore, the question whether Nuremberg simply confirmed existing law or created new law is of interest to-day only to the historian of international law. As far as the possible violation of the pro-hibition on retroactivity is concerned, from today's perspective it is agreed that the principle of non-retroactivity was not intended to shield from punishment abuses of power that violate international law.[50]

Today there is no doubt that the Nuremberg Principles are firmly established as cus-   **29** tomary international law. Nuremberg accomplished what had failed after World War I. The criminality of the worst violations of international law was from now on a firm component of the international legal system.

2. The Tokyo Charter and Trial

The international criminal law employed at Nuremberg was confirmed in the second   **30** trial of major World War II war criminals, which took place in Tokyo from 1946 to 1948.[51]

The subject of the trial was Japan's aggressive policies in the years before 1945. The defendants at   **31** this trial were the political and military elites, a total of 28 former Japanese generals and politi-cians. For political reasons, however, no indictment was brought against the Japanese Emperor.

The basis of the Tokyo war crimes trial was a directive from the commander-in-chief of   **32** the Allied forces, Douglas MacArthur, issued on 19 January 1946, which created the Tribunal and established its law (*Charter of the International Military Tribunal for the Far East*, Tokyo Charter or IMTFE Charter).[52] The Nuremberg Charter served as the model for the Tokyo Charter; the Nuremberg crimes – crimes against peace, war crimes, and crimes against humanity – were the centerpiece of the Charter.[53] The structure of the

---

[49] See marginal nos. 1161 et seq.

[50] See W. Naucke, in A. Donatsch (ed.), *Festschrift für Trechsel* (2002), p. 505 at p. 511; G. Werle, *Neue Juristische Wochenschrift* 2001, pp. 3001 et seq.

[51] Trial protocols and judgments are found in a 22-volume documentation, see J. Pritchard and S.M. Zaide (eds.), *The Tokyo War Crimes Trial*, Vol. 1 (1981). On the trial itself, see A. Brackman, *The Other Nuremberg* (1989); K. Ipsen, in R.D. Herzberg (ed.), *Festschrift für Oehler* (1985), pp. 505 et seq.; P.R. Piccigallo, *The Japanese on Trial* (1979); J. Pritchard, in M.C. Bassiouni (ed.), *International Criminal Law*, Vol. 3, 2nd edn. (1999), pp. 109 et seq.; B.V.A. Röling and A. Cassese, *The To-kyo Trial and Beyond* (1993); for summaries, see P. Osten, *Der Tokioter Kriegsverbrecherprozeß und die japanische Rechtswissenschaft* (2003), pp. 22 et seq.

[52] The proclamation determined that "the constitution, jurisdiction and functions of this Tribunal are those set forth in the Charter of the International Military Tribunal for the Far East, approved by me this day", see *Proclamation by the Supreme Commander for the Allied Powers* of 19 January 1946, reprinted in J. Pritchard and S.M. Zaide (eds.), *The Tokyo War Crimes Trial*, Vol. 1 (1981).

[53] IMTFE Statute, Art. 5 almost exactly echoes IMT Charter, Art. 6. On the differences, see H. Ahlbrecht, *Geschichte der völkerrechtlichen Strafgerichtsbarkeit im 20. Jahrhundert* (1999), pp. 107 et seq.

Tokyo Tribunal differed from that of the Nuremberg Tribunal in a number of ways; in particular, many more countries were represented on the judges' bench.[54]

33 The objections to the legal basis and the opinions of the tribunal, which were shared at this trial by several of the judges,[55] corresponded to those already raised against the Nuremberg trial.[56] The Tokyo trial ended with the conviction of all the defendants. In addition to seven death sentences, 16 sentences of life imprisonment were imposed, as well as one 20-year and one seven-year prison term.[57]

3. Control Council Law No. 10

34 In the post-war period, the law applied at Nuremberg and Tokyo was confirmed and stated more precisely in numerous trials before national courts and military tribunals.[58] Some of these trials are documented in an extensive collection published by the United Nations War Crimes Commission.[59]

35 As a common legal basis for the trials in the occupied zones, *Law No. 10 on the Punishment of Persons Guilty of War Crimes, Crimes Against Peace and Against Humanity* (CCL No. 10), issued by the Allied Control Council on 20 December 1945,[60] was of outstanding importance. With this law, the Allied Control Council accepted and improved upon the model of the Nuremberg war crimes trial. The law was intended to ensure that the subsequent trials in the four occupied zones would rest on a uniform legal basis.

---

[54] All states to which Japan had capitulated took part (in addition to the US and Great Britain, these included the Soviet Union, Australia, China, France, Canada, the Netherlands and New Zealand), along with India and the Philippines, which had suffered most from Japanese expansionism. The president of the Court, in contrast to Nuremberg, was not elected by its members, but designated by the commander-in-chief of the Allied forces (Art. 3). The same was true of the chief prosecutor, under Art. 8.

[55] The French, Indian and Dutch judges dissented from the judgment of the majority. Essentially, their objections related to what the minority believed was international law's lack of recognition of the legal bases of the judgment. Specifically, they found that crimes against peace were not punishable under existing law. For details, see H. Ahlbrecht, *Geschichte der völkerrechtlichen Strafgerichtsbarkeit im 20. Jahrhundert* (1999), pp. 120 et seq.

[56] Summarized in M.C. Bassiouni, in M.C. Bassiouni (ed.), *International Criminal Law*, Vol. 3, 2nd edn. (1999), p. 31 at pp. 47 et seq.; A. Cassese, *International Criminal Law* (2003), pp. 329 et seq.; P. Osten, *Der Tokioter Kriegsverbrecherprozeß und die japanische Rechtswissenschaft* (2003), pp. 129 et seq.

[57] The judgment is reprinted in J. Pritchard and S.M. Zaide (eds.), *The Tokyo War Crimes Trial*, Vol. 20 (1981).

[58] See also A. Rückerl, *NS-Verbrechen vor Gericht*, 2nd edn. (1984), pp. 98 et seq.; R. Herde, *Command Responsibility* (2001); on prosecution of war crimes in other East Asian countries, see P. Osten, *Der Tokioter Kriegsverbrecherprozeß und die japanische Rechtswissenschaft* (2003), pp. 22 et seq.

[59] See United Nations War Crimes Commission, *Law Reports of Trials of War Criminals*, 15 Volumes (1947–1949).

[60] CCL No. 10 (Official Gazette Control Council for Germany No. 3, 31 January 1945, pp. 50 et seq.) served to "give effect to the terms of the Moscow Declaration . . . and the London Agreement . . . and the Charter issued pursuant thereto and . . . to establish a uniform legal basis in Germany for the prosecution of war criminals and other similar offenders, other than those dealt with by the International Military Tribunal." To apply this law, military tribunals were set up in the occupied zones, see, e.g., Military Government in the American Zone, Ordinance No. 7 of 18 October 1946.

Following the model of the Nuremberg Charter, Article 2 of CCL No. 10 included **36** crimes against peace, war crimes and crimes against humanity. For crimes against humanity, it should be emphasized, CCL No. 10 included an improvement that still has an effect today: the nexus to war crimes or crimes against peace required by the Nuremberg Charter was eliminated.[61] The law was also applied by German courts when the Allied forces in the British, French and Soviet occupied zones granted them jurisdiction on the basis of Article 3 of CCL No. 10.

Of the numerous national trials, the twelve so-called Nuremberg follow-up trials[62] **37** held by US military tribunals until mid-1949 can be highlighted. Each of these twelve trials concentrated on a specific perpetrator group; among the defendants were top representatives of the medical and legal professions and the military, the economy, and industry, as well as high-ranking officials of the state and party. The judgments have been published in a separate collection[63] and continue to influence international criminal law to this day.

Specifically, the trials included the so-called Medical Trial (*Brandt* et al.), the trial of General Field **38** Marshal Erhard Milch for participation in the rearmament program, the so-called Justice Trial (*Altstötter* et al.), the trial of members of the economic and administrative department of the SS that included the administration of the concentration camps (*Pohl* et al.), the trial of the industrialists (*Flick* et al.), the so-called IG Farben Trial (*Krauch* et al.), the so-called Hostages Trial (*List* et al.), the trial of members of the Race and Settlement Main Office (RuSHA, *Greifelt* et al.), the so-called Einsatzgruppen Trial (*Ohlendorf* et al.), the trial of the industrialists *Krupp* et al., the so-called Ministries Trial against high officials of the Nazi state (*von Weizsäcker* et al.), and the so-called High Command Trial against top Wehrmacht officers (*von Leeb* et al.).

In addition, the judgments of the Supreme Court in the British Occupied Zone were **39** highly important for the development of international criminal law; in numerous decisions between 1948 and 1950, the Court contributed to the interpretation of CCL No. 10 and thus to the development of international criminal law.[64]

III. International Criminal Law During the Cold War

The crimes and principles formulated at Nuremberg were affirmed in subsequent years **40** and decades by numerous UN General Assembly resolutions, decisions of the International Court of Justice and reports and drafts by the UN International Law Commission.

In Resolution 95 of 11 December 1946, the UN General Assembly endorsed the principles of international criminal law laid down in the Nuremberg Charter and applied in the judgment of the **41**

---

[61] See marginal no. 637.

[62] See M. Lippman, 3 *Indiana International and Comparative Law Review* (1992), pp. 1 et seq.; see also H. Ahlbrecht, *Geschichte der völkerrechtlichen Strafgerichtsbarkeit im 20. Jahrhundert* (1999), pp. 98 et seq.

[63] *Trials of War Criminals Before the Nuremberg Military Tribunals Under Control Council Law No. 10.*

[64] For more on this, see H. Rüping, *Neue Zeitschrift für Strafrecht* 2000, pp. 355 et seq.

Nuremberg Tribunal.[65] In Resolution 177 of 21 November 1947, the International Law Commission[66] was charged with drafting a codification of international crimes and the principles contained in the Charter and judgment of Nuremberg. The report of the International Law Commission on the so-called Nuremberg Principles particularly highlighted their recognition as customary international law.[67] In 1954, the International Law Commission presented the first draft of a "Code of Crimes against the Peace and Security of Mankind." Further drafts followed in 1991, 1994 and 1996.[68]

42　At the same time, various elements of customary international criminal law were being adopted into international treaty law. Of particular importance were the *Convention on the Prevention and Punishment of the Crime of Genocide*[69] of 9 December 1948 and the four Geneva Conventions[70] of 12 August 1949, including the two Additional Protocols[71] of 8 June 1977.

43　The signals sent out at Nuremberg and Tokyo at first found little resonance in the practice of states and the community of nations.[72] International criminal courts would not

---

[65] See UN Doc. A/RES/1/95 (1946) ("The General Assembly . . . [a]ffirms the principles of international law recognized by the Charter of the Nuremberg Tribunal and the judgment of the Tribunal").

[66] Under Art. 13(1)(a) of the UN Charter, the General Assembly authorizes investigations and gives recommendations "encouraging the progressive development of international law and its codification." The International Law Commission created by the United Nations in 1947 was charged with codifying and further developing international law. Its 34 members are elected by the General Assembly. See C. Tomuschat, *Vereinte Nationen* 1988, pp. 180 et seq.

[67] International Law Commission, Principles of International Law Recognized in the Charter of the Nuremberg Tribunal and in the Judgment of the Tribunal, *Yearbook of the International Law Commission* 1950 II, pp. 374 et seq.

[68] For discussion of the International Law Commission's contribution to the development of international criminal law, see J. Crawford, in A. Cassese, P. Gaeta and J.R.W.D. Jones (eds.), *The Rome Statute of the International Criminal Court*, Vol. 1 (2002), pp. 23 et seq.; C. Tomuschat, in G. Hankel and G. Stuby (eds.), *Strafgerichte gegen Menschheitsverbrechen* (1995), pp. 270 et seq.

[69] 78 *UNTS* (1949), p. 277. The Convention entered into force on 12 January 1951. The generally accepted view holds that the Genocide Convention embodies customary international law. See ICJ, Advisory Opinion of 28 May 1951 (Reservations to the Convention on the Prevention and Punishment of the Crime of Genocide), *ICJ Rep.* 1951, p. 15 at p. 23.

[70] *Geneva Convention for the Amelioration of the Condition of the Wounded and Sick in Armed Forces in the Field* (Geneva Convention I; 75 *UNTS* (1949), p. 31); *Geneva Convention for the Amelioration of the Condition of Wounded, Sick and Shipwrecked Members of Armed Forces at Sea* (Geneva Convention II; 75 *UNTS* (1949), p. 85); *Geneva Convention Relative to the Treatment of Prisoners of War* (Geneva Convention III; 75 *UNTS* (1949), p. 135); *Geneva Convention Relative to the Protection of Civilian Persons in Time of War* (Geneva Convention IV; 75 *UNTS* (1949), p. 287).

[71] *Protocol Additional to the Geneva Conventions of 12 August 1949 and Relating to the Protection of Victims of International Armed Conflicts* (Protocol I; 1125 *UNTS* (1977), p. 3); *Protocol Additional to the Geneva Conventions of 12 August 1949 and Relating to the Protection of Victims of Non-international Armed Conflicts* (Protocol II; 1125 *UNTS* (1977), p. 609).

[72] See the sobering review by C. van den Wyngaert, in M.C. Bassiouni (ed.), *International Criminal Law*, Vol. 3, 2nd edn. (1999), pp. 217 et seq. On the few trials held as a result of US war crimes in the Vietnam War, for example, see H. Ahlbrecht, *Geschichte der völkerrechtlichen Strafgerichtsbarkeit im 20. Jahrhundert* (1999), pp. 152 et seq.

appear on the scene for decades, and the application of international criminal law by national courts remained a rare exception.[73]

Overall, the situation until the early 1990s of the past century was paradoxical. On the one hand, the legal basis of international criminal law was largely secure and the law of Nuremberg had been consolidated. On the other hand, the states and the community of nations lacked the will and ability to apply these principles. **44**

IV. The United Nations *ad hoc* Tribunals

At the beginning of the 1990s, following the end of the Cold War, the United Nations activated its peace enforcement mechanisms. This development triggered a renaissance of international criminal law, which many had thought a dead letter. The reasons for reactivating the Law of Nuremberg in practice were the serious violations of international humanitarian law committed on the territory of former Yugoslavia in the early 1990s and the massacre of the minority Tutsi in Rwanda in 1994. **45**

This time it was the United Nations, not the victorious powers at the end of a military conflict, that pushed for the enforcement of international criminal law. The UN Security Council created two international criminal Tribunals as "subsidiary organs,"[74] under the heading of measures to "maintain and restore international peace and international security."[75] Thus the legal basis of the tribunals, unlike that of the *ad hoc* Tribunal at Nuremberg, was not an international treaty, but a resolution of the UN Security **46**

---

[73] Such exceptions have included, for example, the Jerusalem trial of Adolf Eichmann (*Attorney General of the Government of Israel* v. *Adolf Eichmann*, District Court of Jerusalem, judgment of 12 December 1961, in 36 *ILR* (1968), pp. 5 et seq. and Supreme Court, judgment of 29 May 1962, in 36 *ILR* (1968), pp. 277 et seq.), the French trial of Klaus Barbie (*Féderation National des Déportées et Internés Resistants et Patriots* et al. v. *Barbie*, Cour de Cassation, judgments of 6 October 1983, 26 January 1984, 20 December 1985, in 78 *ILR* (1988), pp. 124 et seq. and Cour de Cassation, judgment of 3 June 1988, in 100 *ILR* (1995), pp. 331 et seq.), the Canadian trial of Imre Finta (*Regina* v. *Finta*, Ontario Court of Appeal, judgment of 20 April 1992, in 98 *ILR* (1994), pp. 520 et seq., Ontario High Court of Justice, judgment of 25 May 1990, in 82 *ILR* (1990), pp. 424 et seq., and Canada, Supreme Court, judgment of 24 March 1994, in 104 *ILR* (1997), pp. 284 et seq.) and the Australian Polyukhovich trial (*Polyukhovich* v. *Commonwealth of Australia and Another*, Australian High Court, judgment of 14 August 1991, in 91 *ILR* (1993), pp. 1 et seq.; 172 *Commonwealth Law Reports* (1991), p. 501).

[74] See UN Charter, Arts. 39 et seq., 29 and 7(2). The model for creation of international *ad hoc* tribunals under the UN umbrella continues to have currency. This is shown by the efforts to create special tribunals for Sierra Leone (see *Report of the Secretary-General on the Establishment of a Special Court for Sierra Leone*, UN Doc. S/2000/915 (2000), and M. Frulli, 11 *European Journal of International Law* (2000), pp. 857 et seq.), East Timor (see UNTAET, Reg. 2000/13, UN Doc. UNTAET/ REG/2000/15, and K. Ambos and S. Wirth, 13 *Criminal Law Forum* (2002), pp. 1 et seq.), and Cambodia (see *Group of Experts for Cambodia established Pursuant to GA Resolution 52/145*, UN Doc. A/53/850 (1999), Annex; *Draft Agreement between the United Nations and the Royal Government of Cambodia Concerning the Prosecution under Cambodian Law of Crimes Committed During the Period of Democratic Kampuchea* of 17 March 2003, UN Doc. A/57/806). Summarized in A. Cassese, *International Criminal Law* (2003), pp. 343 et seq. See also C. Kress, 13 *Criminal Law Forum* (2002), pp. 409 et seq.; S. Linthon, 84 *International Review of the Red Cross* (2002), pp. 93 et seq.; A. McDonald, 84 *International Review of the Red Cross* (2002), pp. 121 et seq.; P.F. Trotter, 7 *New England International and Comparative Law Annual* (2001), pp. 31 et seq. Regarding plans to create an international tribunal for Burma, see L. Rotroff, 9 *New England Journal of International and Comparative Law* (2003), pp. 491 et seq.

[75] See UN Charter, Art. 39.

Council on the basis of Chapter VII of the UN Charter.[76] A direct result of this approach is the Courts' strong position vis-à-vis the states: Article 25 of the UN Charter obligates every member state to co-operate with the Courts, and allows, where necessary, for the use of force. At the same time, the Tribunals' precedence over national judicial systems, especially those of the perpetrator states, is expressly provided for in their Statutes.[77]

47   The Statutes of the Yugoslavia and Rwanda Tribunals reiterates the customary law character of international criminal law.[78] Both Statutes claim to reflect the "hard core" of existing international criminal law.[79]

1. The Yugoslavia Tribunal

48   The increased tension between ethnic groups living in the Federal Republic of Yugoslavia after the death of Josip Broz Tito in 1980 escalated, following the collapse of the surrounding socialist states, into one of the worst conflicts on European soil in the past century. After Croatia and Slovenia declared their independence in 1991, the majority of Bosnians also voted in a referendum for independence from the Federal Republic of Yugoslavia. Until the signing of the Dayton Peace Accord in 1995, massive violations of international law were committed on the territory of former Yugoslavia; the terrible phrase "ethnic cleansing" and the cities of Sarajevo and Srebrenica gained tragic fame.[80] After 1998 the conflict spread to the Kosovo region, populated mainly by people of Albanian descent.

49   In Resolution 808 of 22 February 1993, the UN Security Council determined that the events in former Yugoslavia posed a threat to international peace. This was followed by a military intervention by NATO forces authorized by the United Nations. The opinion quickly prevailed in the Security Council that, in view of the atrocities committed, long-term stability in the region could only be achieved if military measures to restore peace were accompanied by punishment of the perpetrators of crimes under international law. On 3 May 1993, the UN Secretary-General submitted a report prepared at the request of the Security Council on the possibility of United Nations' creation of a criminal court.[81]

50   In Resolution 827 of 25 May 1993, the Security Council decided, "for the sole purpose of prosecuting persons responsible for serious violations of international humanitarian law committed in the territory of the former Yugoslavia between 1 January 1991 and

---

[76] On the sustainability of this legal basis, see *Prosecutor* v. *Tadić*, ICTY (Trial Chamber), decision of 10 August 1995, paras. 1 et seq.; *Prosecutor* v. *Tadić*, ICTY (Appeals Chamber), decision of 2 October 1995, paras. 9 et seq.; see also A. Cassese, *International Criminal Law* (2003), pp. 337 et seq.; C. Tomuschat, *Europa-Archiv* 1994, p. 61 at p. 64.

[77] See ICTY Statute, Art. 9 and ICTR Statute, Art. 8: "shall have primacy over national courts." See also *Prosecutor* v. *Tadić*, ICTY (Trial Chamber), decision of 10 August 1995, para. 41.

[78] See G. Werle, 109 *Zeitschrift für die gesamte Strafrechtswissenschaft* (1997), p. 808 at p. 814.

[79] According to a report by the UN Secretary-General of 3 May 1993 on the ICTY Statute, (only) the "rules of international humanitarian law which are beyond any doubt part of customary law" became elements of the ICTY Statute, see UN Doc. S/25704 (1993), para. 29; but see H. Ahlbrecht, *Die Geschichte der völkerrechtlichen Strafgerichtsbarkeit im 20. Jahrhundert* (1999), p. 329.

[80] On the background and course of the conflict, see, e.g., the summary in V. Morris and M.P. Scharf, *An Insider's Guide to the International Criminal Tribunal for the Former Yugoslavia*, Vol. 1 (1995), pp. 17 et seq.

[81] UN Doc. S/25704 (1993).

a date to be determined by the Security Council upon the restoration of peace . . . to adopt the Statute of the International Tribunal."[82]

Articles 2 to 5 of the ICTY Statute list crimes under international law that the Tribunal is authorized to prosecute and try. These include war crimes, genocide and crimes against humanity; of the so-called core crimes[83] under international law, only crimes against peace are omitted. In its general principles, the ICTY Statute largely adopts the provisions of the Nuremberg Charter. **51**

The Yugoslavia Tribunal has already contributed substantially to clarifying and further developing international criminal law. Most important to emphasize is the assimilation of the scope of criminal law applied in international and in non-international armed conflict.[84] In this context, the international laws of war are largely applied to civil wars as well.[85] For crimes against humanity, the Tribunal has confirmed that the link to war crimes still required in the Nuremberg Charter is not necessary under customary international law.[86] In addition, the Yugoslavia Tribunal has in many respects added precision to the definitions of crimes against humanity and genocide.[87] **52**

While the procedural and evidentiary rules of the Nuremberg Tribunal[88] contained only rudimentary – and to some extent legally questionable – rules (death penalty, no appeal, trials *in absentia*), the Yugoslavia Tribunal possesses a well-developed body of procedural law in accordance with rule of law principles. This is laid down in the ICTY Statute and is clarified in extensive procedural and evidentiary rules.[89] **53**

---

[82] In the resolution, the Security Council referred to the "widespread and flagrant violations of international humanitarian law occurring within the territory of the former Yugoslavia . . . including reports of mass killings, massive, organized and systematic detention and rape of women, and the continuance of the practice of 'ethnic cleansing.'" On the creation and work of the Yugoslavia Tribunal, see J.E. Ackerman and E. O'Sullivan, *Practice and Procedure of the International Criminal Tribunal for the Former Yugoslavia* (2000); M.C. Bassiouni and P. Manikas, *The Law of the International Criminal Tribunal for the Former Yugoslavia* (1996); J.R.W.D. Jones, *The Practice of the International Criminal Tribunals for the Former Yugoslavia and Rwanda* (1997); H. Roggemann, *Die internationalen Strafgerichtshöfe*, 2nd edn. (1998), pp. 60 et seq.; M.P. Scharf, *Balkan Justice* (1997).

[83] On this concept, see marginal no. 74.

[84] The leading case is *Prosecutor* v. *Tadić*, ICTY (Appeals Chamber), decision of 2 October 1995, paras. 96 et seq.

[85] See marginal no. 813 for discussion.

[86] New doubts were raised by the wording of Art. 5 of the ICTY Statute, according to which the Court has jurisdiction over crimes against humanity only "when committed in armed conflict." According to the Court's decisions, this addendum is to be understood such "that the act be linked geographically as well as temporally with the armed conflict." See *Prosecutor* v. *Kupreškić* et al., ICTY (Trial Chamber), judgment of 14 January 2000, para. 546; see also *Prosecutor* v. *Tadić*, ICTY (Appeals Chamber), judgment of 15 July 1999, para. 249.

[87] See B. Lüders, in M. Chiavario (ed.), *La Justice Pénale Internationale entre Passé et Avenir* (2003), pp. 223 et seq. and S. Meseke, in M. Chiavario (ed.), *La Justice Pénale Internationale entre Passé et Avenir* (2003), pp. 173 et seq. See also G. Kirk McDonald, in S. Yee and W. Tieya (eds.), *International Law in the Post-Cold War World* (2001), pp. 446 et seq.

[88] See IMT Charter, Arts. 16 et seq. and the Rules of Procedure of the International Military Tribunal of 29 October 1945.

[89] ICTY Statute, Arts. 15 et seq. However, the rules of procedure lack a degree of legitimacy because they were established by the Court itself and have been constantly revised.

2. The Rwanda Tribunal

54 In 1995, the UN Security Council established the Rwanda Tribunal with Resolution 955. This Court, like the Yugoslavia Tribunal, was created as a measure "to maintain [and] restore international peace and security" under Chapter VII of the UN Charter.[90] This was the international community's reaction to the genocide in Rwanda in 1994 that took the lives of some 800,000 people within a few months.[91] The Yugoslavia Tribunal was not only the model for the creation of the Rwanda Tribunal, but is also institutionally interconnected with it in many ways. Until 2003, there was only one prosecutor's office for both Tribunals,[92] and the members of the ICTY's Appeals Chamber also serve as members of the ICTR's Appeals Chamber.[93]

55   The Rwanda Tribunal's jurisdiction extends to the prosecution of genocide, crimes against humanity and war crimes committed between 1 January and 31 December 1994. The Court has done pioneering work, particularly in developing the definition of genocide.[94]

V. The ICC Statute and the International Criminal Court

56 The entry into force of the ICC Statute and the creation of the permanent International Criminal Court form what is, for now, the final milestone in the development of international criminal law.[95]

1. Previous Efforts to Create a Permanent International Criminal Court

57 Efforts to create a permanent international criminal court date back to the period before World War II. An initial attempt to create an international criminal court to prosecute terrorist crimes within the framework of the League of Nations failed in 1937. A *Convention pour la Création d'une Cour Pénale Internationale* of 16 November 1937 was

---

[90] On the creation and work of the Rwanda Tribunal, see V. Morris and M.P. Scharf, *The International Criminal Tribunal for Rwanda* (1998); H. Roggemann, *Die Internationalen Strafgerichtshöfe*, 2nd edn. (1998), pp. 156 et seq.

[91] See Human Rights Watch (ed.), *Leave None to Tell the Story, Genocide in Rwanda* (1999).

[92] See ICTR Statute, Art. 15(3).

[93] See ICTR Statute, Art. 13(4). According to ICTR Statute, Art. 13(3), the President of the ICTR assigns two of the ICTR's judges to be members of the Appeals Chamber of the ICTY.

[94] The leading case is *Prosecutor* v. *Akayesu*, ICTR (Trial Chamber), judgment of 2 September 1998. For details, see marginal nos. 555 et seq.

[95] Of the overwhelming amount of literature on the ICC Statute and the ICC, see the commentaries by A. Cassese, P. Gaeta and J.R.W.D. Jones (eds.), *The Rome Statute of the International Criminal Court* (2002) and O. Triffterer (ed.), *Commentary on the Rome Statute of the International Criminal Court* (1999). See also A. Cassese, *International Criminal Law* (2003), pp. 340 et seq.; L.N. Sadat, *The International Criminal Court and the Transformation of International Law* (2002); W.A. Schabas, *An Introduction to the International Criminal Court*, 2nd edn. (2004); C. Tomuschat, 73 *Die Friedens-Warte* (1998), pp. 335 et seq.; O. Triffterer, 114 *Zeitschrift für die gesamte Strafrechtswissenschaft* (2002), p. 321 at pp. 345 et seq.

signed by 13 countries, but never went into effect.[96] Only after World War II and the successful completion of the war crimes trials at Nuremberg and Tokyo did efforts to create an international criminal court gain renewed impetus.

The Genocide Convention of 1948 provided for the jurisdiction of an international criminal **58** court, in addition to prosecution by the country in which the crime was committed. Therefore, with the adoption of the Genocide Convention, the UN General Assembly authorized the International Law Commission "to study the desirability and possibility of establishing an international judicial organ for the trial of persons charged with genocide."[97] In 1951, following a positive vote by the International Law Commission,[98] a subcommittee of the General Assembly's Legal Committee submitted a Draft Statute for an International Criminal Court.[99] The Court would be responsible for prosecuting any cases presented to it by the contracting parties, through international treaties generally or through the submission of individual cases. In 1954, a revised version of the draft was put before the General Assembly. But the rapidly worsening international political climate prevented a continuation of this work.[100] On 11 December 1957, the General Assembly decided to postpone discussions on codification of international criminal law and the statute of an international criminal court until a definition of aggression could be found.[101] However, this did not occur until 1974.[102] The International Law Commission thereupon resumed its work on substantive international criminal law. In 1989, at the initiative of Trinidad and Tobago, the Commission was authorized by the General Assembly to again consider the creation of a permanent international criminal court.[103]

---

[96] The basis for the Convention was a draft developed by a Romanian international lawyer, Vespasian Pella, which provided for optional jurisdiction at first only for terrorist acts and the application by the Court primarily of the law of the state in which the act occurred. See H.-H. Jescheck, *Die Verantwortlichkeit der Staatsorgane nach Völkerstrafrecht* (1952), pp. 117 et seq. Between the two world wars, it was mainly scholarly associations, specifically the International Law Association and the Association International de Droit Pénal, that drove the movement to create a permanent international criminal court. For details on developments prior to Nuremberg, see H. Ahlbrecht, *Geschichte der völkerrechtlichen Strafgerichtsbarkeit im 20. Jahrhundert* (1999), pp. 46 et seq.; M.C. Bassiouni, *Introduction to International Criminal Law* (2003), p. 393.

[97] UN Doc. A/RES/3/260 (1948).

[98] UN Doc. GAOR, 5th Session, Suppl. 12 (A/1316, 1950).

[99] See United Nations Committee on International Criminal Jurisdiction, *Draft Statute for an International Criminal Court*, reprinted in 46 *American Journal of International Law* (1952), Suppl. 1 et seq. and in M.C. Bassiouni (ed.), *The Statute of the International Criminal Court* (1998), pp. 741 et seq.

[100] See H. Ahlbrecht, *Geschichte der völkerrechtlichen Strafgerichtsbarkeit im 20. Jahrhundert* (1999), pp. 143 et seq.

[101] UN Doc. A/RES/12/1186 (1957), stating: "The General Assembly, [C]onsidering that the draft Code of Offences against the Peace and Security of Mankind . . . raises problems related to that of the definition of aggression, . . . 1. Decides to defer the consideration of the question of the draft Code of Offences against the Peace and Security of Mankind until such time as the General Assembly takes up again the question of defining aggression". In Res. 12/1187, on the same day, the General Assembly decided accordingly in regard to the work toward creating an international criminal jurisdiction ("defer consideration of the question of an international criminal jurisdiction").

[102] UN Doc. A/RES/29/3314 (1974), Annex, esp. Art. 3. See also marginal no. 1160.

[103] UN Doc. A/RES/44/39 (1989): The General Assembly "[r]equests the International Law Commission, when considering at its forty-second session the item entitled 'Draft Code of Crimes against the Peace and Security of Mankind,' to address the question of establishing an international criminal court or other international criminal trial mechanism with jurisdiction over persons alleged to have committed crimes which may be covered under such a code of crimes, including persons engaged

59 Not until the international political climate improved with the end of the Cold War was it possible to make significant progress in the effort to create a permanent international criminal court. The International Law Commission had soon prepared a Draft Statute for an International Criminal Court,[104] which was presented to the General Assembly in 1994.[105] The General Assembly then appointed an *ad hoc* committee.[106] In 1995, the committee submitted a report in which, for the first time, the distinction between regulation of procedure and constitution of the court (in a "Statute") and substantive law (in a "Code") was abandoned. From then on, provisions on the creation and jurisdiction of the international criminal court and the definitions of crimes would be included in a single document. Following submission of the report of the *ad hoc* committee, a preparatory committee was created by the General Assembly and charged with drafting texts for a planned conference of states.[107] It submitted its report in 1996.[108]

2. The Conference of Plenipotentiaries in Rome

60 The United Nations held an international conference in Rome from 16 June to 17 July 1998 to hammer out a statute for an international criminal court.[109] More than 160 states were represented in Rome; 17 international organizations and over 250 non-governmental organizations attended and observed the proceedings. The subject of negotiations was the draft text prepared by

---

in illicit trafficking in narcotic drugs across national frontiers, and to devote particular attention to that question in its report on that session." See also UN Doc. A/RES/47/33 (1992) and A/RES/48/31 (1993).

[104] The draft text was adopted at the 46th session of the International Law Commission on 23 November 1994; see Report of the Commission to the General Assembly, *Yearbook of the International Law Commission* 1994 II, Part 2, pp. 18 et seq.; for details, see J. Crawford, in A. Cassese, P. Gaeta and J.R.W.D. Jones (eds.), *The Rome Statute of the International Criminal Court*, Vol. 1 (2002), pp. 23 et seq.

[105] See *Yearbook of the International Law Commission* 1994 II, Part 2, pp. 26 et seq.

[106] UN Doc. A/RES/49/53 (1994); 50/46 (1995) and 51/207 (1996). See the *Report of the ad hoc committee on the establishment of an international criminal court*, UN Doc. A/50/22 (1995) and A. Bos, in A. Cassese, P. Gaeta and J.R.W.D. Jones (eds.), *The Rome Statute of the International Criminal Court*, Vol. 1 (2002), pp. 35 et seq.

[107] The preparatory committee should not be confused with the Preparatory Commission; on this so-called "PrepCom," see marginal no. 67.

[108] *Report of the Preparatory Committee on the Establishment of an International Criminal Court*, A/RES/51/207 (1996), Annex. See H.-P. Kaul, *Vereinte Nationen* 1997, pp. 177 et seq. In the following two years, the text was frequently revised before the final version, which would form the basis of the Rome Conference, was achieved (Draft ICC Statute (1998), UN Doc. A/CONF.183/2/Add.1). The so-called Zupthen draft (UN Doc. A/AC.249/1998/L.13), worked out in January 1998 in preparation for the last session of the preparatory committee, should be mentioned. At the same time that the preparatory committee was working, a loose group of private organizations, specifically the Association International de Droit Pénal and the Max Planck Institute for Foreign and International Criminal Law in Freiburg, had developed an alternative draft, the so-called Siracusa draft (Draft Statute for an International Criminal Court – Suggested Modifications to the 1994 ILC-Draft, "Siracusa-Draft" of 31 July 1995), see K. Ambos, *Zeitschrift für Rechtspolitik* 1996, pp. 269 et seq.

[109] UN Doc. A/RES/52/160 (1997). For details on the negotiations in Rome, see P. Kirsch and D. Robinson, in A. Cassese, P. Gaeta and J.R.W.D. Jones (eds.), *The Rome Statute of the International Criminal Court*, Vol. 1 (2002), pp. 67 et seq.

the preparatory committee (Draft ICC Statute),[110] which provided in 116 articles, with 1,400 bracketed additions and almost 200 options, for the creation of a permanent international criminal court.

From the start, two camps faced off against each other.[111] The so-called like-minded states, a **61** group of court-friendly states that included Australia, Canada and Germany, called for rapid creation of a strong court that would be as independent as possible. Opposing them was a group of states that included the United States, India and China. Worried about their sovereignty and about protecting their own citizens, these states sought a weak and more symbolic court; according to this group, the court should be seen as a sort of at-the-ready *ad hoc* criminal court, which the UN Security Council could then activate in crisis situations.

In the course of the negotiations, substantive issues, especially the formulation of the **62** definitions of crimes, proved less controversial. The main reason for this was the early limitation of the substantive issues to the core crimes.[112] It also proved fortunate that the Nuremberg Charter and the Statutes of the Yugoslavia and Rwanda Tribunals provided models that had already been tested in practice. At the same time, it was not possible to achieve complete agreement on the definitions of offenses. Thus efforts to agree on a definition of the crime of aggression failed.[113]

The main areas of contention involved defining the Court's jurisdiction, especially **63** the question whether the Court would have automatic jurisdiction, the role and status of the prosecutor, and the Court's relationship with the United Nations, especially the Security Council.

Regarding the scope of the Court's jurisdiction, it was not possible for the pro-court states to **64** achieve their goal of extending the court's jurisdiction, under the principle of universal jurisdiction,[114] to all crimes under international law, regardless of where, by whom, or against whom they had been committed. The orientation toward the territoriality and personality principles that was ultimately enshrined as a compromise in the ICC Statute creates sensitive gaps in the Court's jurisdiction.[115]

---

[110] UN Doc. A/CONF.183/2/Add.1 of 14 April 1998.

[111] See H.-P. Kaul, *Vereinte Nationen* 1998, pp. 126 et seq.

[112] On the discussion of inclusion of additional crimes within the Court's jurisdiction, see A. Zimmermann, 58 *Zeitschrift für ausländisches öffentliches Recht und Völkerrecht* (1998), p. 47 at pp. 78 et seq. In the *Final Act of the United Nations Diplomatic Conference of Plenipotentiaries on the Establishment of an International Criminal Court*, Annex I, E (UN Doc. A/CONF.183/10 (1998), the delegates regretted that they were unable to agree on a definition of international drug crimes and terrorism. The preliminary drafts had included other crimes in addition to the core crimes; see, e.g., Art. 20(e) of the International Law Commission draft, which includes violations of the *Convention Against Torture and Other Cruel, Inhuman or Degrading Treatment or Punishment* of 10 December 1984 (1465 *UNTS* (1987), p. 112) and the *Convention Against Illicit Traffic in Narcotic Drugs and Psychotropic Substances* of 20 December 1988 (28 *ILM* (1989), p. 493).

[113] The crime of aggression is included in the Court's jurisdiction, but placed in a sort of limbo until a provision is adopted into the Statute "defining the crime and setting out the conditions under which the Court shall exercise jurisdiction with respect to this crime," ICC Statute, Art. 5(2). See marginal no. 1184.

[114] See marginal no. 171.

[115] See ICC Statute, Art. 12, 13. Thus the typical case in which a crime under international law is committed on the territory and by a national of a non-state party is only subject to the Court's jurisdiction if the Security Council reports the matter in a resolution under Chapter VII of the UN Char-

65 Also controversial to the end was the question of who should be empowered to initiate trials before the Court (trigger mechanisms); here the pro-court coalition was at least partially successful.[116] Under the provisions finally adopted in the ICC Statute, the prosecutor, like the Security Council and the parties to the treaty, has the right to initiate investigations.[117] As far as the Security Council is concerned, dominated as it is by the five veto powers, there were fears that giving it too strong a position would polarize the Court's work and call its overall credibility into question; on the other hand, the negotiators wished to make it possible for the veto powers to agree to the Statute. The prosecutor's right, corresponding to the powers of the prosecutor of the ICTY and ICTR, to initiate investigations of his or her own accord was viewed as an indispensable guarantor of the Court's independence.

66 On 17 July 1998, the Rome Statute of the International Criminal Court (ICC Statute)[118] was adopted in plenary session with 120 votes. Only seven states, namely the USA,[119] China, Israel, Iraq, Libya, Yemen and Qatar, voted against the Statute; 21 countries abstained. Only four years later, on 11 April 2002, Bosnia and Herzegovina, Bulgaria, Cambodia, the DR Congo, Ireland, Jordan, Mongolia, Niger, Romania and Slovakia deposited their ratifications in New York, thereby exceeding the 60 ratifications required under Article 126 of the ICC Statute; the Statute thus went into effect on 1

---

ter (ICC Statute, Arts. 13(b), Art. 12(2)) or if – which is very unlikely in practice – the state on whose territory the crime was committed accepts the Court's jurisdiction over the case. The demands of pro-court states that this gap be closed by allowing the Court to take jurisdiction if the custodial state is a party to the treaty were unsuccessful. Nevertheless, they did succeed in establishing, in Art. 12 of the ICC Statute, that each state party automatically accepts the jurisdiction of the Court. Much more restrictive models could not achieve a majority; they would have required, for example, the consent of affected states to every single trial ("state consent"), or provided for selective acceptance or rejection of jurisdiction for certain crimes ("opt in/opt out"). On the entire discussion, see H.-P. Kaul, in A. Cassese, P. Gaeta and J.R.W.D. Jones (eds.), *The Rome Statute of the International Criminal Court*, Vol. 1 (2002), pp. 583 et seq.

[116] See C. Kress, in H. Grützner and P.G. Pötz (eds.), *Internationaler Rechtshilfeverkehr in Strafsachen*, Vol. 4, 2nd edn. (2002), Vor III 26, marginal nos. 18 et seq.

[117] ICC Statute, Art. 15(1).

[118] 37 *ILM* (1998), p. 999; authentic versions of the text are available in the official languages of the United Nations.

[119] The US reservations are summarized in L.A. Casey, 25 *Fordham International Law Journal* (2002), pp. 840 et seq. und R. Wedgwood, 10 *European Journal of International Law* (1999), pp. 93 et seq. Since the Rome Conference, the United States has made numerous attempts to weaken the effectiveness of the International Criminal Court, summarized in A. Zimmermann and H. Scheel, *Vereinte Nationen* 2002, pp. 137 et seq. In this context, three main elements of US obstructionist policy should be emphasized. Security Council Resolution 1422, a US initiative, asked that in line with Article 16 of the ICC Statute, "if a case arises involving current or former officials or personnel from a contributing State not a Party to the Rome Statute over acts or omissions relating to a United Nations established or authorized operation, [the ICC] shall for a twelve-month period starting 1 July 2002 not commence or proceed with investigation or prosecution of any such case," see marginal no. 202. In Resolution 1487 of 12 June 2003, the Security Council extended Resolution 1422 for an additional year. In June 2004, however, the US abandoned its efforts to renew the resolution a second time due to strong opposition in the Security Council. A second element of US policy toward the ICC involves the (only partially successful) efforts by the US government to conclude bilateral agreements on non-extradition to the ICC, see marginal no. 524. Third, on 2 August 2002 the American Servicemembers' Protection Act (reprinted in 23 *Human Rights Law Journal* (2002), pp. 275 et seq.) went into effect; it also aims to remove US citizens from the jurisdiction of the ICC.

July 2002. By August 2004, 139 countries had signed the Statute and 97 had ratified it.[120] From 4 to 7 February 2003, the Assembly of States Parties elected 18 judges. On 11 March 2003, the International Criminal Court began operations in The Hague, Netherlands. On 21 April 2003 Luis Moreno Ocampo of Argentina was elected prosecutor by the Assembly of States Parties.

In the conference's final act, the Preparatory Commission ("PrepCom") was authorized to submit **67** recommendations to the Assembly of States Parties[121] on practical questions connected with the creation and work of the Court.[122] Among other things, it developed the financial rules as well as additional important bases for the work of the Court, the Rules of Procedure and Evidence and the Elements of Crimes as provided for in Article 9 of the ICC Statute.[123] At its first meeting in September 2002, the Assembly of States Parties approved the PrepCom's recommendations.

---

[120] These include all countries of the European Union and many South American and African countries. Asian representation has so far been comparatively weak. The following have ratified:
Afghanistan, Albania, Andorra, Antigua and Barbuda, Argentina, Australia, Austria, Barbados, Belgium, Belize, Benin, Bolivia, Bosnia and Herzegovina, Botswana, Brazil, Bulgaria, Burkina Faso, Burundi, Cambodia, Canada, Central African Republic, Colombia, Congo, Costa Rica, Croatia, Cyprus, Democratic Republic of Congo, Denmark, Djibouti, Dominica, East Timor, Ecuador, Estonia, Fiji, Finland, France, Gabon, Gambia, Georgia, Germany, Ghana, Greece, Guinea, Guyana, Honduras, Hungary, Iceland, Ireland, Italy, Jordan, Latvia, Lesotho, Liberia, Liechtenstein, Lithuania, Luxembourg, Malawi, Mali, Malta, Marshall Islands, Mauritius, Mongolia, Namibia, Nauru, Netherlands, New Zealand, Niger, Nigeria, Norway, Panama, Paraguay, Peru, Poland, Portugal, Republic of Korea, Romania, Saint Vincent and The Grenadines, Samoa, San Marino, Senegal, Serbia and Montenegro, Sierra Leone, Slovakia, Slovenia, South Africa, Spain, Sweden, Switzerland, Tajikistan, Tanzania, The Former Yugoslav Republic of Macedonia, Trinidad and Tobago, Uganda, United Kingdom, Uruguay, Venezuela, Zambia.
The following have only signed: Algeria, Angola, Armenia, Bahamas, Bahrain, Bangladesh, Cameroon, Cape Verde, Chad, Chile, Comoros, Côte d'Ivoire, Czech Republic, Dominican Republic, Egypt, Eritrea, Guinea-Bissau, Haiti, Iran, Israel, Jamaica, Kenya, Kuwait, Kyrgyzstan, Madagascar, Mexico, Monaco, Morocco, Mozambique, Oman, Philippines, Republic of Moldova, Russian Federation, St. Lucia, São Tomé and Príncipe, Seychelles, Solomon Islands, Sudan, Syrian Arabic Republic, Thailand, Ukraine, United Arab Emirates, Uzbekistan, Yemen and Zimbabwe. The US has rescinded President Clinton's signature. For the current status, see <http://www.un.org/law/icc>.
[121] ICC Statute, Art. 112. See D. Mundis, 97 *American Journal of International Law* (2003), pp. 132 et seq.
[122] See Final Act, Annex I, F., UN Doc. A/CONF.183/10 (1998). According to this, the "PrepCom's" task was to "prepare proposals for practical arrangements for the establishment and coming into operation of the Court, including the draft texts of: (a) Rules of Procedure and Evidence; (b) Elements of Crimes; (c) A relationship agreement between the Court and the United Nations; (d) Basic principles governing a headquarters agreement to be negotiated between the Court and the host country; (e) Financial regulations and rules; (f) An agreement on the privileges and immunities of the Court; (g) A budget for the first financial year; (h) The rules of procedure of the Assembly of States Parties; 6. The draft texts of the Rules of Procedure and Evidence and of the Elements of Crimes shall be finalized before 30 June 2000; 7. The Commission shall prepare proposals for a provision on aggression, including the definition and Elements of Crimes of aggression and the conditions under which the International Criminal Court shall exercise its jurisdiction with regard to this crime. The Commission shall submit such proposals to the Assembly of States Parties at a Review Conference, with a view to arriving at an acceptable provision on the crime of aggression for inclusion in this Statute. The provisions relating to the crime of aggression shall enter into force for the States Parties in accordance with the relevant provisions of this Statute; 8. The Commission shall remain in existence until the conclusion of the first meeting of the Assembly of States Parties."
[123] See, e.g., *Agreement on the Privileges and Immunities of the International Criminal Court* of 9 September 2002, entry into force on 22 July 2004 (ICC-ASP/1/3). For details on the work of the

3. Significance of the ICC Statute

68 In 128 articles, the ICC Statute regulates the creation of the International Criminal Court (Part 1), its constitution, administration and financing (Parts 4, 11, 12), procedure before the Court and co-operation with the Court (Parts 5 to 10). The Statute also enumerates the crimes over which the Court has jurisdiction, and contains general principles of criminal law (Parts 2 and 3).

69 The ICC Statute is the core document of international criminal law today. It sets out the legal bases of the International Criminal Court and develops its new brand of procedure. The ICC Statute was also a major step forward for substantive international criminal law. The four core crimes under international criminal law, the "classic" Nuremberg definitions plus the crime of genocide, are contained in Article 5. While there is still no definition of the crime of aggression, genocide, crimes against humanity and war crimes are subdivided into almost 70 subordinate crimes in Articles 6, 7 and 8 of the ICC Statute. Here the value of the ICC Statute lies mainly in collecting and consolidating scattered provisions of law.[124]

70 The ICC Statute has an especially innovative impact in the area of general principles of criminal law. While the Statute's predecessors contained only fragmentary provisions, the ICC Statute for the first time contains comprehensive rules on the "general principles" of international criminal law.[125]

B. Concepts, Tasks and Legitimacy

71 Payam Akhavan: Beyond Impunity: Can International Criminal Justice Prevent Future Atrocities?, 95 *American Journal of International Law* (2001), pp. 7 et seq.; Kai Ambos and Christian Steiner: Vom Sinn des Strafens auf innerstaatlicher und supranationaler Ebene, *Juristische Schulung* 2001, pp. 9 et seq.; M. Cherif Bassiouni: The Philosphy and Policy of International Criminal Justice, in Lal Chand Vohrah et al. (eds.), *Man's Inhumanity to Man* (2003), pp. 65 et seq.; M. Cherif Bassiouni: The Sources and Content of International Criminal Law: A Theoretical Framework, in M. Cherif Bassiouni (ed.), *International Criminal Law*, Vol. 1, 2nd edn. (1999), pp. 3 et seq.; Aline Bruer-Schäfer: *Der Internationale Strafgerichtshof, Die Internationale Strafgerichtsbarkeit im Spannungsfeld von Recht und Politik* (2001), pp. 21 et seq.; Antonio Cassese: *International Criminal Law* (2003), pp. 15 et seq.; Tom J. Farer: Restraining the Barbarians: Can International Criminal Law Help?, 22 *Human Rights Quarterly* (2000), pp. 90 et seq.; Herbert Jäger: Makroverbrechen als Gegenstand des Völkerstrafrechts, Kriminalpolitisch-kriminologische Aspekte, in Gerd Hankel and Gerhard Stuby (eds.), *Strafgerichte gegen Menschheitsverbrechen, Zum Völkerstrafrecht 50 Jahre nach den Nürnberger Prozessen* (1995), pp. 325 et seq.; Hans-Heinrich Jescheck: *Die Verantwortlichkeit der Staatsorgane nach Völkerstrafrecht, Eine Studie zu den Nürnberger Prozessen* (1952), pp. 190 et seq.; Hans-Heinrich Jescheck: International Crimes, in Rudolf Bernhardt (ed.), *Encyclopedia of Public International Law*, Vol. 2 (1995), pp. 1119 et seq.; Kriangsak Kittichaisaree: *International*

Preparatory Commission, see P. Kirsch and V. Oosterveld, in A. Cassese, P. Gaeta and J.R.W.D. Jones (eds.), *The Rome Statute of the International Criminal Court*, Vol. 1 (2002), pp. 93 et seq.

[124] See the comprehensive summary in C. Tomuschat, 73 *Die Friedens-Warte* (1998), p. 335 at pp. 337 et seq. On the relationship between statutory criminal law and customary international law, see marginal no. 139.

[125] See marginal no. 270.

Criminal Law (2001), pp. 3 et seq.; Kai-Michael König: *Die völkerrechtliche Legitimation der Strafgewalt internationaler Strafjustiz* (2003); Otto Lagodny: Legitimation und Bedeutung des Ständigen Internationalen Strafgerichtshofes, 113 *Zeitschrift für die gesamte Strafrechtswissenschaft* (2001), pp. 800 et seq.; Christina Möller: *Völkerstrafrecht und Internationaler Strafgerichtshof – kriminologische, straftheoretische und rechtspolitische Aspekte* (2003), pp. 413 et seq.; Patrick Robinson: The Missing Crimes, in Antonio Cassese, Paola Gaeta and John R.W.D. Jones (eds.), *The Rome Statute of the International Criminal Court, A Commentary*, Vol. 1 (2002), pp. 497 et seq.; William A. Schabas: *An Introduction to the International Criminal Court*, 2nd edn. (2004), pp. 26 et seq.; Georg Schwarzenberger: The Problem of an International Criminal Law, 3 *Current Legal Problems* (1950), pp. 263 et seq.; Sandra Szurek: Historique, La Formation du Droit International Pénal, in Hervé Ascensio, Emmanuel Decaux and Alain Pellet (eds.), *Droit International Pénal* (2000), pp. 7 et seq.; Otto Triffterer: *Dogmatische Untersuchungen zur Entwicklung des materiellen Völkerstrafrechts seit Nürnberg* (1966), pp. 25 et seq.; Otto Triffterer: Der ständige Internationale Strafgerichtshof – Anspruch und Wirklichkeit, in Karl Heinz Gössel and Otto Triffterer (ed.), *Gedächtnisschrift für Zipf* (1999), pp. 493 et seq.; Christian Tomuschat: Das Statut von Rom für den Internationalen Strafgerichtshof, 73 *Die Friedens-Warte* (1998), pp. 335 et seq.; Gerhard Werle: Menschenrechtsschutz durch Völkerstrafrecht, 109 *Zeitschrift für die gesamte Strafrechtswissenschaft* (1997), pp. 808 et seq.; Peter Wilkitzki: Die völkerrechtlichen Verbrechen und das staatliche Strafrecht (Bundesrepublik Deutschland), 99 *Zeitschrift für die gesamte Strafrechtswissenschaft* (1987), pp. 455 et seq.

I. The Notions of "International Criminal Law" and "Crimes Under International Law"

Crimes under international law are all crimes that involve direct individual criminal responsibility under international law. International criminal law encompasses all norms that establish, exclude or otherwise regulate responsibility for crimes under international law. **72**

In the terminology used here, international criminal law has the same meaning as "Völkerstrafrecht,"[126] "droit international pénal,"[127] and "derecho internacional penal."[128] Some authors use the term international criminal law in a broader sense,[129] which includes not only the **73**

---

[126] See G. Werle, *Völkerstrafrecht* (2003), marginal no. 71.

[127] See S. Szurek, in H. Ascensio, E. Decaux and A. Pellet (eds.), *Droit International Pénal* (2000), p. 7 at pp. 10 et seq.

[128] See A. Quintano Ripollès, *Tratado de Derecho Penal Internacional e Internacional Penal*, Vol. 1 (1955) and Vol. 2 (1957).

[129] See M.C. Bassiouni, *Introduction to International Criminal Law* (2004), pp. 1 et seq. and K. Kittichaisaree, *International Criminal Law* (2001), p. 3. Interpreted in this way, the term international criminal law corresponds to the German term "Internationales Strafrecht"; see G. Werle, *Völkerstrafrecht* (2003), marginal no. 106. For a middle ground between the expansive interpretation and the more narrow interpretation taken as a basis here, see A. Cassese, *International Criminal Law* (2003), p. 15 ("International criminal law is a body of international rules designed both to proscribe international crimes and to impose upon States the obligation to prosecute and punish at least some of those crimes"). G. Schwarzenberger, 3 *Current Legal Problems* (1950), p. 263 at pp. 264 et seq., distinguishes six meanings for the phrase "international criminal law." The interpretation of the term international criminal law used here corresponds to "international criminal law in the material sense of the word" ("such rules would be of a prohibitive character and would have to be strengthened by punitive sanctions of their own").

criminal aspects of international law, particularly crimes under international law, but also the international aspects of national criminal law, especially domestic rules on criminal jurisdiction over crimes with a foreign element.[130] The interpretation preferred here provides a single, handy term for the important area of prosecution of crimes under international law by international courts: international criminal law.

74 Crimes under international law are war crimes, crimes against humanity, genocide and the crime of aggression.[131] These so-called core crimes[132] are the "most serious crimes of concern to the international community"[133] and are subject to the jurisdiction of the International Criminal Court.[134] It is controversial whether other crimes, such as narcotics trafficking or terrorism, also involve direct individual criminal responsibility under international law; here the development of international law is in flux. Above all, the question whether and under what circumstances acts of terrorism can be judged international crimes has gained renewed currency. However, terrorism as such is not a crime under international law.[135] Efforts to extend the jurisdiction of the International Criminal

---

[130] For the difference between international criminal law in the sense used here and other areas of criminal law with international aspects, see marginal nos. 105 et seq.

[131] See I. Brownlie, *Principles of Public International Law*, 6th edn. (2003), pp. 559 et seq.; H.-H. Jescheck, in R. Bernhardt (ed.), *Encyclopedia of Public International Law*, Vol. 2 (1995), p. 1119 at pp. 1120 et seq.; O. Triffterer, in T. Vogler (ed.), *Festschrift für Jescheck* (1985), p. 1477 at p. 1485 ("classic offenses of international criminal law"). Using a broader concept of international criminal law, A. Cassese, *International Criminal Law* (2003), p. 24, includes, in addition to the crimes named in the text, torture outside of armed conflict or systematic attacks on civilian populations and state-sponsored forms of international terrorism.

[132] On the concept of "core crimes," see C. Kress, in H. Grützner and P.G. Pötz (eds.), *Internationaler Rechtshilfeverkehr in Strafsachen*, Vol. 4, 2nd edn. (2002), III 27 marginal no. 8 and A. Zimmermann, 58 *Zeitschrift für ausländisches öffentliches Recht und Völkerrecht* (1998), p. 47 at p. 48.

[133] See ICC Statute, Preamble (4) and (9) and Art. 5.

[134] The ICC's jurisdiction to try conduct against its own administration of justice (ICC Statute, Art. 70) appears, in contrast, to be an annexed power that expands on and ensures its core jurisdiction; in regard to procedure and standards for liability, it essentially follows other rules, see K. Harris in O. Triffterer (ed.), *Commentary on the Rome Statute of the International Criminal Court* (1999), Art. 70 marginal nos. 2 et seq. For the relevant rules in the ICTY Statute (Arts. 77, 91), see *Prosecutor v. Tadić*, ICTY (Appeals Chamber), judgment of 31 January 2000, paras. 13 et seq.: "The Tribunal does, however, possess an inherent jurisdiction, deriving from its judicial function, to ensure that its exercise of the jurisdiction which is expressly given to it by that Statute is not frustrated and that its basic judicial functions are safeguarded." Under some preliminary drafts of the ICC Statute, the Court's subject matter jurisdiction would have included other crimes in addition to the core crimes, see, e.g., *Draft Code* 1991, Arts. 15 et seq. ("colonial domination," "recruitment, use, financing and training of mercenaries," "international terrorism," "illicit traffic in narcotic drugs," see C. Tomuschat, in G. Hankel and G. Stuby (eds.), *Strafgerichte gegen Menschheitsverbrechen* (1995), p. 270 at pp. 278 et seq.). At the Rome Conference, the inclusion of terrorism and narcotics trafficking in the jurisdictional catalogue was discussed, but relevant proposals were ultimately unsuccessful. The final act merely states that extension of the Court's jurisdiction should be the subject of negotiations at a future "review conference" under Art. 123 of the ICC Statute, see P. Robinson, in A. Cassese, P. Gaeta and J.R.W.D. Jones (eds.), *The Rome Statute of the International Criminal Court*, Vol. 1 (2002), pp. 497 et seq.; A. Zimmermann in O. Triffterer (ed.), *Commentary on the Rome Statute of the International Criminal Court* (1999), Art. 5, marginal nos. 3 et seq.

[135] See S. Oeter, 76 *Die Friedens-Warte* (2001), pp. 11 et seq.; F. Jessberger, in Deutsches Institut für Menschenrechte (ed.), *Menschenrechtliche Erfordernisse bei der Bekämpfung des Terrorismus* (2002), pp. 22 et seq.; D.F. Vagts, 14 *European Journal of International Law* (2003), pp. 313 et seq.

Court to include terrorist acts failed to gain a majority at the Rome Conference.[136] But terrorist crimes will frequently fulfill the prerequisites of international core crimes, such as crimes against humanity or war crimes,[137] depending on the circumstances of the individual case.[138]

Beyond the definitions of crimes in the ICC Statute, there exists certain conduct that involves direct individual criminal responsibility under customary international law.[139] The ICC Statute expressly presumes that conduct can be characterized "as criminal under international law independently of this Statute" (Article 22(3)). This, however, refers not to other groups of crimes, but to certain subgroups of crimes or individual acts of war crimes or crimes against humanity. This is true, for example, for the criminality under customary law of certain conduct during civil wars that is not included in the ICC Statute.[140]   **75**

The norms of international law typically must possess universal validity; the core crimes are an example of this. But regionally-limited applicability of a norm of international criminal law is also conceivable, in accordance with general principles of international law.[141]   **76**

II. Protected Interests

International criminal law protects "peace, security and [the] well-being of the world"[142] as the fundamental values of the international community.[143]   **77**

The three protected values, peace, security and the well-being of the world, cannot be strictly separated from one another.[144] World peace and international security, the two   **78**

---

[136] See fn. 134.

[137] See P. Robinson, in A. Cassese, P. Gaeta and J.R.W.D. Jones (eds.), *The Rome Statute of the International Criminal Court*, Vol. 1 (2002), p. 497 at pp. 520 et seq.; O. Triffterer, 114 *Zeitschrift für die gesamte Strafrechtswissenschaft* (2002), p. 321 at p. 371.

[138] There are good reasons to define the terrorist attacks on the World Trade Center on 11 September 2001 as crimes against humanity; see also A. Cassese, 12 *European Journal of International Law* (2001), pp. 993 et seq.; C. Tomuschat, *Europäische Grundrechte-Zeitschrift* 2001, pp. 535 et seq.

[139] See also O. Triffterer, in K.H. Gössel and O. Triffterer (eds.), *Gedächtnisschrift für Zipf* (1999), p. 493 at p. 532 ("[the ICC Statute allocates to the Court] *some of* the crimes under international criminal law").

[140] See marginal no. 815.

[141] This is correctly stated in O. Triffterer, in T. Vogler (ed.), *Festschrift für Jescheck* (1985), p. 1477 at p. 1502.

[142] ICC Statute, Preamble (3) ("la paix, la sécurité et le bien-être du monde"). For more detail, see T.N. Slade and R.S. Clark, in R.S. Lee (ed.), *The International Criminal Court, The Making of the Rome Statute* (1999), p. 421 at p. 426. The reference to international peace and security is already found in the first drafts by the International Law Commission, where crimes "against the peace and security of mankind" are criminalized, see, e.g., *Draft Code* 1954, Art. 1 and *Draft Code* 1996, Art. 1 (1).

[143] See O. Triffterer, in O. Triffterer (ed.), *Commentary on the Rome Statute of the International Criminal Court* (1999), Preamble, marginal no. 9 ("international criminal law is . . . the criminal law of the community of nations, with the function of protecting the highest legal values of this community"). See also K. Ambos and C. Steiner, *Juristische Schulung* 2001, p. 9 at p. 13; M.C. Bassiouni, in L.C. Vohrah et al. (eds.), *Man's Inhumanity to Man* (2003), pp. 65 et seq.

[144] The same is true for the aims of the UN Charter, see R. Wolfrum, in B. Simma (ed.), *The Charter of the United Nations*, Vol. 1, 2nd edn. (2002), Art. 1, marginal nos. 4 et seq.

values of the international community that lie at the heart of international criminal law, are at the same time the main goals of the United Nations.[145] International criminal law is thus based on a broad concept of peace, which means not only the absence of military conflict between states, but also the conditions within a state.[146] Therefore, a threat to *world* peace can be presumed even as a result of massive violations of human rights within one state. In the Preamble of the ICC Statute, the well-being of the world appears as a separate object of protection next to peace and security; in this way, the allocation of the necessities of life is included as an additional guideline for the application and interpretation of the Statute.[147]

79   An attack on the fundamental values of the international community lends a crime an international dimension and turns it into a crime under international law. Such crimes under international law affect "the international community as a whole."[148] Punishment of international crimes is therefore the task of the international community, and for this reason the norms of international criminal law penetrate the "armor of state sovereignty."[149] Thus its link to the interests of the international community lends international criminal law its specific legitimacy.

80   Whether and to what extent international criminal law also protects individual rights is subject to debate.[150] Here one would have to distinguish between the various international crimes.[151]

---

[145] UN Charter, Art. 1(1); see also UN Charter Art. 2(6), Arts. 11, 12, 18, 39 et seq. The Charter provides for various collective measures in case of a threat to international peace and security, UN Charter, Art. 39. These may also include measures of criminal prosecution; see above, marginal no. 46.

[146] See UN Doc. S/RES/808 (1993), Security Council resolution on creation of the ICTY; UN Doc. S/RES/955 (1994), Security Council resolution on creation of the ICTR: "Expressing once again its grave concern at the reports indicating that genocide and other systematic, widespread and flagrant violations of international humanitarian law have been committed in Rwanda, [d]etermining that this situation continues to constitute a threat to international peace and security"; UN Doc. S/RES/1373 (2001), Security Council resolution on measures against the attacks of 11 September 2001; see also C. Tomuschat, in G. Hankel and G. Stuby (eds.), *Strafgerichte gegen Menschheitsverbrechen* (1995), p. 270 at p. 291.

[147] See O. Triffterer, in O. Triffterer (ed.), *Commentary on the Rome Statute of the International Criminal Court* (1999), Preamble, marginal no. 11.

[148] ICC Statute, Preamble (4) and (9), Art. 5(1) ("crimes of concern to the international community as a whole"). Without deviating from the issue, Art. 1 of the ICC Statute refers to "crimes of international concern." See also *Prosecutor v. Tadić*, ICTY (Appeals Chamber), decision of 2 October 1995, para. 59: The ". . . crimes which the International Tribunal has been called upon to try . . . affect the whole of mankind and shock the conscience of all nations of the world. There can therefore be no objection to an international tribunal properly constituted trying these crimes on behalf of the international community." See also K.M. König, *Die völkerrechtliche Legitimation der Strafgewalt internationaler Strafjustiz* (2003), p. 26; M.C. Bassiouni, in L.C. Vohrah et al. (eds.), *Man's Inhumanity to Man* (2003), pp. 65 et seq.

[149] "Panzer der staatlichen Souveränität"; see H.-H. Jescheck, *Die Verantwortlichkeit der Staatsorgane nach Völkerstrafrecht* (1952), p. 11; M.C. Bassiouni, in L.C. Vohrah et al. (eds.), *Man's Inhumanity to Man* (2003), pp. 65 et seq.

[150] According to O. Lagodny, 113 *Zeitschrift für die gesamte Strafrechtswissenschaft* (2001), p. 800 at pp. 803 et seq., crimes under international law apparently should only protect values transcending the individual. In contrast, O. Triffterer, in O. Triffterer (ed.), *Commentary on the Rome Statute of the International Criminal Court* (1999), Preliminary Remarks, marginal no. 21, presumes throughout the protection of individual rights as well. From this perspective, see also C. Tomuschat, in H.J. Cremer et al. (eds.), *Festschrift für Steinberger* (2002), p. 315 at p. 329: "Genocide is certainly the worst of all offenses against both human dignity and international peace and security."

[151] From this perspective, see also A. Gil Gil, 112 *Zeitschrift für die gesamte Strafrechtswissenschaft* (2000), p. 381 at pp. 382 et seq.; H. Vest, 113 *Zeitschrift für die gesamte Strafrechtswissenschaft* (2001), p. 457 at pp. 463 et seq.

III. The "International Element" of Crimes Under International Law

A connection to the most important values of the international community is established   **81**
for all crimes under international law through one common characteristic, the so-called
international element: all international crimes presume a context of systematic or large-
scale use of force. As a rule, it is a collective that is responsible for this use of force, typically a state.[152]

For crimes against humanity, this context of organized violence consists of a wide-   **82**
spread or systematic attack on a civilian population. This contextual element[153] is
formed from the sum of individual acts. For genocide, the context of organized violence
consists of the intentional destruction of a protected group in whole or in part. Here the
contextual element is shifted to the perpetrator's intent.

For war crimes, the context of organized violence consists of an armed conflict, in the   **83**
course of which the criminal act must have occurred. Armed conflict is made up of
criminal and non-criminal use of force. For the crime of aggression, the use of organized
violence as such is subject to criminalization.[154] Aggression is thus a "crime against
peace"[155] in its immediate sense.

The fundamental values of the international community – peace, security and well-   **84**
being – are protected by international criminal law against attacks from various directions. For genocide, the disruption of world peace lies in an (intentional) attack on the
physical or social existence of a particular group. For crimes against humanity, the threat
to peace, security and the well-being of the world consists of the systematic or widespread violation of the fundamental human rights of the civilian population.[156]
Criminalizing violations of the laws of war is intended to minimize the effects of armed
conflict as much as possible and help prevent escalation.[157] Armed conflicts between
states generally disrupt world peace; here criminality depends on whether behavior can
be found to have brought about aggressive war.

---

[152] See also K. Marxen, in K. Lüderssen (ed.), *Aufgeklärte Kriminalpolitik oder Kampf gegen das Böse*, Vol. 3 (1995), p. 220 at pp. 227 et seq.; H. Vest, 113 *Zeitschrift für die gesamte Strafrechtswissenschaft* (2001), p. 457 at pp. 458 et seq. ("collective commission"). The fact that crimes under international law typically involve "state-supported" criminality (W. Naucke) is a main reason for their widespread impunity. Their integration into the apparatus of state power and state sovereignty as a rule continues to protect perpetrators from punishment.

[153] The term "contextual element" corresponds to the German term "*Gesamttat*," see G. Werle, *Völkerstrafrecht* (2003), marginal no. 80. The German term makes possible a clear distinction between the individual act *("Einzeltat")*, such as the killing of a civilian by a soldier, and the context of the crime *("Gesamttat")*, such as the attack on a civilian population. A literal translation of "*Gesamttat*" would be "contextual act" or "overall act"; however, the term "contextual element" seems more appropriate. It should be noted, however, that what is called the "contextual element" here is not necessarily an element of the definition of the crime, e.g., as regards genocide.

[154] On the customary-law roots of the crime of aggression, see marginal nos. 1161 et seq.

[155] See IMT Charter, Art. 6(a).

[156] See G. Werle, 109 *Zeitschrift für die gesamte Strafrechtswissenschaft* (1997), p. 808 at pp. 814 et seq.

[157] See also marginal no. 818, and C. Tomuschat, in H.J. Cremer et al. (eds.), *Festschrift für Steinberger* (2002), p. 315 at p. 344 ("Internal violence [is] prone swiftly to spill over into other countries like a contagious disease.").

IV. Purposes of Punishment

85 While the connection to the international legal order is created by a relationship to the most important values of the international community, international criminal law gains its legitimacy as criminal law from the purposes of punishment, which can be transferred from domestic criminal law.[158] The Yugoslavia Tribunal explicitly confirmed the relevance of the traditional purposes of punishment:

"The Trial Chamber is of the view that, in general, retribution and deterrence are the main purposes to be considered when imposing sentences before the International Tribunal. . . . punishment for having violated international humanitarian law is, in the light of the serious nature of the crimes committed, a relevant and important consideration. As to the latter, the purpose is to deter the specific accused as well as others, which means . . . persons worldwide from committing crimes in similar circumstances against international humanitarian law. The Trial Chamber is further of the view that another relevant sentencing purpose is to show the people of not only former Yugoslavia, but of the world in general, that there is no impunity for these types of crimes. This should be done in order to strengthen the resolve of all involved not to allow crimes against international humanitarian law to be committed as well as to create trust and respect for the developing system of international criminal justice. The Trial Chamber also supports the purpose of rehabilitation for persons convicted . . . ."[159]

86 Elementary justice demands the punishment of crimes under international law. Also, the idea of retribution undeniably has its place.[160] However, the preventive effect of international criminal law is even more important (deterrence; norm stabilization). There is much to be said for the belief that the practice of impunity for human rights violations (a "culture of impunity") is an important reason for their persistent recurrence.[161] In this spirit, the UN Security Council declared, in connection with the creation of the Yugosla-

---

[158] See, e.g., T.J. Farer, 22 *Human Rights Quarterly* (2000), p. 90 at p. 91; G. Werle, 109 *Zeitschrift für die gesamte Strafrechtswissenschaft* (1997), p. 808 at pp. 821 et seq. It goes without saying that the concept of legitimacy is subject to the same fundamental objections, which will not be discussed further here, as in national law. But for arguments against transferrability, see H. Jäger, in G. Hankel and G. Stuby (eds.), *Strafgerichte gegen Menschheitsverbrechen* (1995), p. 325 at pp. 339 et seq., according to which "the theoretical justifications so far are not applicable at all [to crimes under international law] or may be transferred only in greatly modified form." For a comprehensive discussion, see C. Möller, *Völkerstrafrecht und Internationaler Strafgerichtshof* (2003), pp. 413 et seq.

[159] *Prosecutor* v. *Kupreškić* et al., ICTY (Trial Chamber), judgment of 14 January 2000, paras. 848 et seq. with additional notes; *Prosecutor* v. *Naletilić and Martinović*, ICTY (Trial Chamber), judgment of 31 March 2003, para. 739; most recently *Prosecutor* v. *Deronjić*, ICTY (Trial Chamber), judgment of 30 March 2004, paras. 142 et seq., and *Prosecutor* v. *Jokić*, ICTY (Trial Chamber), judgment of 18 March 2004, paras. 30 et seq.

[160] See G. Werle, 109 *Zeitschrift für die gesamte Strafrechtswissenschaft* (1997), p. 808 at p. 821; but see H. Jäger, in G. Hankel and G. Stuby (eds.), *Strafgerichte gegen Menschheitsverbrechen* (1995), p. 325 at p. 339; H.-H. Jescheck, *Die Verantwortlichkeit der Staatsorgane nach Völkerstrafrecht* (1952), p. 195 sees a justification from the point of view of atonement; see also O. Lagodny, 113 *Zeitschrift für die gesamte Strafrechtswissenschaft* (2001), p. 800 at p. 806, who however sees the justification for international criminal law in a "victim-oriented retributive concept embedded in human rights."

[161] See M.C. Bassiouni, in L.C. Vohrah et al. (eds.), *Man's Inhumanity to Man* (2003), p. 65 at pp. 119 et seq.; G. Werle, 109 *Zeitschrift für die gesamte Strafrechtswissenschaft* (1997), p. 808 at p. 821.

via Tribunal, that the prosecution and punishment of the guilty would contribute to preventing future human rights violations.[162]

The ICC Statute, too, emphasizes that punishment of those responsible for crimes **87** under international law will contribute to "prevention of such crimes."[163] This refers not only – and not even primarily – to the deterrent effect of international criminal law.[164] More important is the creation and reinforcement of an international awareness of law: the ability of international criminal law to contribute to stabilizing the norms of international law.[165] The punishment of the most serious crimes under international law should "make humankind conscious of the fact that international law is law and will be implemented against lawbreakers."[166] Finally, international criminal law may have a specific preventive effect on individual (potential) perpetrators.[167]

Two specific effects of the punishment of crimes under international law should also **88** be emphasized.[168] One is the trial's acknowledgment and truth-finding functions. The determination of a crime in itself has independent and far-reaching significance. Representatives of repressive systems typically deny that systematic violations of human rights have occurred. Judicial determination that crimes under international law have been committed confronts such denials. Convictions represent official acknowledgment of past injustices and the sufferings of the victims. They destroy the foundation for denial of atrocities and prevent falsification of history. A second is the individualization of accountability. Individual accountability makes it clear that it was not an abstract entity,

---

[162] UN Doc. S/RES/827 (1993).

[163] ICC Statute, Preamble (5).

[164] In view of the negative, general-preventive effect of international criminal law, its chronic enforcement deficit creates difficulties. The probability of actually having to answer to a court for a crime under international law remains small (H.-H. Jescheck, *Die Verantwortlichkeit der Staatsorgane nach Völkerstrafrecht* (1952), pp. 194 et seq. said this early: "At present, punishment still depends on military defeat." The International Law Association, *Final Report* (2000), pp. 3 et seq. accurately points out that neither the announcement by the Allies in the so-called Moscow Declaration of 1943 that all international criminals would be brought to trial, nor the corresponding announcement by the ICTY prosecution in 1990, kept the Nazis or the perpetrators in Kosovo from committing crimes under international law. In contrast, T.J. Farer, 22 *Human Rights Quarterly* (2000), p. 90 at p. 92 and p. 117 presumes "that the risk of criminal responsibility could weigh on the decisions of the principals to internal armed conflict."

[165] There is agreement today on this, see H.-H. Jescheck, *Die Verantwortlichkeit der Staatsorgane nach Völkerstrafrecht* (1952), p. 195. See also P. Akhavan, 95 *American Journal of International Law* (2001), p. 7 at p. 30; N. Roht-Arriaza, in N. Roht-Arriaza (ed.), *Punishment, Redress and Pardon* (1995), p. 13 at pp. 16 et seq.

[166] H.-H. Jescheck, *Die Verantwortlichkeit der Staatsorgane nach Völkerstrafrecht* (1952), p. 195; H. Jäger, in G. Hankel and G. Stuby (eds.), *Strafgerichte gegen Menschheitsverbrechen* (1995), p. 325 at p. 347, agrees. According to *Prosecutor* v. *Aleksovski*, ICTY (Appeals Chamber), judgment of 24 March 2000, para. 185, punishment shall, among other things, express "the outrage of the international community at these crimes." This apparently reflects a view of the Court in terms of positive general prevention, if punishment is also supposed to serve to "make plain the condemnation of the international community of the behaviour in question and show that the international community was not ready to tolerate serious violations of international humanitarian law and human rights law." See also *Prosecutor* v. *Niyitegeka*, ICTR (Appeals Chamber), judgment of 16 May 2003, para. 484.

[167] See O. Triffterer, 114 *Zeitschrift für die gesamte Strafrechtswissenschaft* (2002), p. 321 at pp. 334 et seq.; G. Werle, 109 *Zeitschrift für die gesamte Strafrechtswissenschaft* (1997), p. 808 at p. 821.

[168] See G. Werle, 109 *Zeitschrift für die gesamte Strafrechtswissenschaft* (1997), p. 808 at p. 822.

such as a state, that committed crimes under international law. Specific individuals worked together. They determined the victims and planned, organized and implemented the use of force. This individualization is important for the victims and their relatives, because they have a right to the whole truth. Individualization also confronts the perpetrators with their individual contributions to systematic crimes and thereby gives them an opportunity to come to terms with their responsibility.

89   The fact that the legitimacy of international criminal law derives mainly from its ability to stabilize the normative framework of international law (so-called positive general prevention) has direct consequences for the design of substantive and procedural international criminal law.[169] Only a punishment that is considered just and is imposed and executed after a trial recognized as fair can achieve the desired educational effect.

V. The Principle of Legality in International Criminal Law (*Nullum Crimen, Nulla Poena Sine Lege*)

90   Bruce Broomhall: Commentary on Art. 22 of the ICC Statute, in Otto Triffterer (ed.), *Commentary on the Rome Statute of the International Criminal Court, Observers' Notes, Article by Article* (1999), pp. 447 et seq.; Antonio Cassese: *International Criminal Law* (2003), pp. 139 et seq.; Mauro Catenacci: Nullum Crimen Sine Lege, in Flavia Lattanzi (ed.), *The International Criminal Court, Comments on the Draft Statute* (1998), pp. 159 et seq.; Kai-Michael König: *Die völkerrechtliche Legitimation der Strafgewalt internationaler Strafjustiz* (2003), pp. 185 et seq.; Susan Lamb: Nullum Crimen, Nulla Poena Sine Lege in International Criminal Law, in Antonio Cassese, Paola Gaeta and John R.W.D. Jones (eds.), *The Rome Statute of the International Criminal Court, A Commentary*, Vol. 1 (2002), pp. 733 et seq.; Raul C. Pangalangan: Commentary on Art. 24 of the ICC Statute, in Otto Triffterer (ed.), *Commentary on the Rome Statute of the International Criminal Court, Observers' Notes, Article by Article* (1999), pp. 467 et seq.; Per Saland: International Criminal Law Principles, in Roy S. Lee (ed.), *The International Criminal Court, The Making of the Rome Statute* (1999), pp. 189 et seq.; William A. Schabas: Commentary on Art. 23 of the ICC Statute, in Otto Triffterer (ed.), *Commentary on the Rome Statute of the International Criminal Court, Observers' Notes, Article by Article* (1999), pp. 463 et seq.; William A. Schabas: Perverse Effects of the Nulla Poena Principle: National Practice and the *Ad Hoc* Tribunals, 11 *European Journal of International Law* (2000), pp. 521 et seq.; Otto Triffterer: *Dogmatische Untersuchungen zur Entwicklung des materiellen Völkerstrafrechts seit Nürnberg* (1962), pp. 92 et seq.

91   At the time the crime was committed, a written or unwritten[170] norm must have existed upon which to base criminality under international law.[171] The principle of legality (*nullum crimen sine lege*) is part of customary international law.[172] Specifically, the prin-

---

[169] This is the accurate suggestion in H.-H. Jescheck, *Die Verantwortlichkeit der Staatsorgane nach Völkerstrafrecht* (1952), p. 196.

[170] For details on the use of unwritten customary law and general principles of law, see O. Triffterer, *Dogmatische Untersuchungen zur Entwicklung des materiellen Völkerstrafrechts seit Nürnberg* (1962), p. 124; see also S. Lamb, in A. Cassese, P. Gaeta and J.R.W.D. Jones (eds.), *The Rome Statute of the International Criminal Court*, Vol. 1 (2002), p. 746 at pp. 749 et seq.

[171] For details, see A. Cassese, *International Criminal Law* (2003), pp. 139 et seq.

[172] See M.C. Bassiouni, *Introduction to International Criminal Law* (2003), pp. 198 et seq.; B. Broomhall, in O. Triffterer (ed.), *Commentary on the Rome Statute of the International Criminal Court* (1999), Art. 22, marginal no. 15; H.-H. Jescheck, 2 *Journal of International Criminal Justice* (2004), p. 38 at pp. 40 et seq.; S. Lamb, in A. Cassese, P. Gaeta and J.R.W.D. Jones (eds.), *The Rome Statute*

ciple requires that the criminal behavior be laid down as clearly as possible in the definition of the crime; however, this standard is less rigid than is usually required in continental European law. In addition, the principle of legality forbids retroactive punishment or analogies as a basis for punishment.[173] The principle also extends to sanctions (*nulla poena sine lege*).[174] Here international criminal law is also less restrictive than some domestic legal systems,[175] which require a fairly narrow framework of sanctions, as found for example in the German concept of strict legality of penalties.[176]

The principle of legality played a major role at the Nuremberg trials. The International Military Tribunal took the defense's *ex post facto* argument as an opportunity to examine (and affirm) the criminal nature of crimes against peace at the time the acts were committed by the defendants.[177] The Yugoslavia and Rwanda Tribunals have frequently affirmed the validity of the principle.[178]   **92**

The principle of legality is now set out in Articles 22 to 24 of the ICC Statute, at the head of the general principles. The norms correspond with customary international law.[179]   **93**

---

of the International Criminal Court, Vol. 1 (2002), p. 734 at p. 756; D.L. Wade, in E.G. Schaffer and R.J. Snyder (eds.), *Contemporary Practice of Public International Law* (1997), p. 210. It is sometimes assumed that the validity of the principle arises not from customary law, but from general principles of law, see, e.g., *Prosecutor* v. *Mucić*, ICTY (Trial Chamber), judgment of 16 November 1998, para. 402; O. Triffterer, *Dogmatische Untersuchungen zur Entwicklung des materiellen Völkerstrafrechts seit Nürnberg* (1962), pp. 125 et seq.; in addition, see *Report of the Secretary-General Pursuant to Paragraph 2 of the Security Council Resolution 808*, UN Doc. S/25704 (1993), para. 34. The principle has been established in numerous agreements, see, e.g., *International Covenant on Civil and Political Rights* of 16 December 1966 (6 *ILM* (1967), p. 368), Art. 15; *European Convention on Human Rights and Fundamental Freedoms* of 4 November 1950 (*ETS* No. 5 (1950)), Art. 7; Geneva Convention III, Art. 99.

[173] For discussion, see A. Cassese, *International Criminal Law* (2003), pp. 145 et seq. For its development, see K.M. König, *Die völkerrechtliche Legitimation der Strafgewalt internationaler Strafjustiz* (2003), pp. 186 et seq.

[174] But see A. Cassese, *International Criminal Law* (2003), p. 157, who believes, based on an overly narrow conception of the principle, that *nulla poena* does not apply to international criminal law.

[175] For example, the ICC Statute threatens imprisonment of up to 30 years or life in prison; in addition, the International Criminal Court can impose a fine or order the confiscation of property acquired from the crime, see ICC Statute, Art. 77. However, Art. 23 of the ICC Statute rules out, for example, imposition of imprisonment of 40 years (as the ICTY imposed on Jelisić, see *Prosecutor* v. *Jelisić*, ICTY (Appeals Chamber), judgment of 5 July 2001), or of other sanctions not provided for in the ICC Statute.

[176] See, e.g., H.-H. Jescheck and T. Weigend, *Lehrbuch des Strafrechts*, 5th edn. (1996), pp. 133 et seq.

[177] IMT, judgment of 1 October 1946, in *The Trial of German Major War Criminals, Proceedings of the International Military Tribunal Sitting at Nuremberg, Germany*, Part 22, p. 444 ("In the first place, it is to be observed that the maxim *nullum crimen sine lege* is not a limitation of sovereignty, but is in general a principle of justice."). On the IMT's argumentation, see marginal no. 27.

[178] See, e.g., *Prosecutor* v. *Tadić*, ICTY (Appeals Chamber), decision of 2 October 1995, para. 92; *Prosecutor* v. *Jelisić*, ICTY (Trial Chamber), judgment of 14 December 1999, para. 61. Summarized in S. Lamb, in A. Cassese, P. Gaeta and J.R.W.D. Jones (eds.), *The Rome Statute of the International Criminal Court*, Vol. 1 (2002), p. 734 at pp. 742 et seq.

[179] For details on the history of the negotiations, see S. Lamb, in A. Cassese, P. Gaeta and J.R.W.D. Jones (eds.), *The Rome Statute of the International Criminal Court*, Vol. 1 (2002), p. 734 at pp. 746 et seq.

94 Article 22 of the ICC Statute anchors the principle *nullum crimen sine lege*. This states that conduct is criminal only if, at the time of commission, the conduct in question fits the definition of a crime under Article 5 of the ICC Statute. Article 22(2) further clarifies the principle. It forbids the use of analogy to define a crime. For necessary and permissible interpretations, Article 22(2) provides that definitions of crimes are to be narrowly construed. Article 22(3) makes it clear that characterizations of international crimes outside the Statute, particularly crimes under customary law, are not affected by the Statute's definitions of crimes.

95 Article 23 of the ICC Statute contains the principle of *nulla poena sine lege*. Article 24 regulates the temporal limits of criminal responsibility, which is a segment of the *nullum crimen* principle.[180] No retroactive punishment is permitted. The decisive question is the date on which the Statute entered into force, to be determined under Articles 11 and 126 of the ICC Statute. For prosecution of an offense by the International Criminal Court, the relevant point in time is normally 1 July 2002.[181] Under Article 24(2), if the legal situation changes between the time the crime is committed and the punishment of the perpetrator, the law more favorable to the defendant (*lex mitior*) applies.[182]

C. International Criminal Law and the International Legal Order

96 M. Cherif Bassiouni: The Prescribing Function of International Criminal Law in the Processes of International Protection of Human Rights, in Theo Vogler (ed.), *Festschrift für Jescheck*, Part 2 (1985), pp. 1453 et seq.; Jacob Katz Cogan: International Criminal Trials: Difficulties and Prospects, 27 *Yale Journal of International Law* (2002), pp. 111 et seq.; James Crawford: Revising the Draft Articles on State Responsibility, 10 *European Journal of International Law* (1999), pp. 435 et seq.; Vladimir-Djuro Degan: Responsibility of States and Individuals for International Crimes, in Sienho Yee and Wang Tieya (eds.), *International Law in the Post-Cold War World, Essays in Memory of Li Haopei* (2001), pp. 202 et seq.; Giorgio Gaja: Should all References to International Crimes Disappear from the ILC Draft Articles on State Responsibility?, 10 *European Journal of International Law* (1999), pp. 365 et seq.; Rainer Hofmann: Zur Unterscheidung von Verbrechen und Delikt im Bereich der Staatenverantwortlichkeit, 45 *Zeitschrift für ausländisches öffentliches Recht und Völkerrecht* (1985), pp. 195 et seq.; Hans-Heinrich Jescheck: Gegenstand und neueste Entwicklung des Internationalen Strafrechts, in Friedrich-Christian Schroeder and Heinz Zipf (ed.), *Festschrift für Maurach* (1972), pp. 579 et seq.; Richard B. Lillich: *International Human Rights, Problems of Law, Policy and Practice*, 2nd edn. (1991); Dominic McGoldrick: *The Human Rights Committee, Its Role in the Development of the International Covenant on Civil and Political Rights* (1994); Theodor Meron: The Convergence between Human Rights and Humanitarian Law, in Daniel Warner (ed.), *Human Rights and Humanitarian Law, The Quest for Universality* (1997), pp. 97 et seq.; Manfred Mohr: Strafrechtliche Verantwortlichkeit und Staatenverantwortlichkeit für internationale Verbrechen – Wechselwirkung statt Konfusion, in Gerd Hankel and Gerhard Stuby (ed.), *Strafgerichte gegen Menschheitsverbrechen, Zum Völkerstrafrecht 50 Jahre nach den Nürnberger Prozessen* (1995), pp. 401 et seq.; Manfred Nowak: *U.N. Covenant on Civil and Political Rights (CCPR Commentary)* (1993); Karl Josef Partsch: Human Rights and Humanitarian Law, in Rudolf Bernhardt (ed.), *Encyclopedia of Public International Law*, Vol. 2 (1995), pp.

---

[180] On the relationship between Art. 22(1) and Art. 24 of the ICC Statute, see B. Broomhall, in O. Triffterer (ed.), *Commentary on the Rome Statute of the International Criminal Court* (1999), Art. 22, marginal no. 51.

[181] For trial of international crimes committed on the territory or by nationals of a state that ratified the treaty only *after* 1 July 2002, the date the treaty went into force *for that state* is decisive.

[182] See also *Prosecutor* v. *Deronjić*, ICTY (Trial Chamber), judgment of 30 March 2004, paras. 167 et seq. and *Prosecutor* v. *Nikolić*, ICTY (Trial Chamber), judgment of 18 December 2003, paras. 157 et seq.

910 et seq.; Fausto Pocar: The Rome Statute of the International Criminal Court and Human Rights, in Mauro Politi and Giuseppe Nesi (ed.), *The Rome Statute of the International Criminal Court, A Challenge to Impunity* (2001), pp. 67 et seq.; Christoph Safferling: *Towards an International Criminal Procedure* (2001); Marco Sassòli: State Responsibility for Violations of International Humanitarian Law, 84 *International Review of the Red Cross* (2002), pp. 401 et seq.; Christian Tomuschat: *Gegenwartsprobleme der Staatenverantwortlichkeit in der Arbeit der Völkerrechtskommission der Vereinten Nationen* (1994); Andreas Zimmermann: Role and Function of International Criminal Law in the International System After Entry into Force of the Rome Statute of the International Criminal Court, 45 *German Yearbook of International Law* (2002), pp. 35 et seq.

I. International Criminal Law and State Responsibility

The addressee of international criminal law is the individual,[183] not the state. Thus international criminal law deviates from the traditional model of international law, according to which, under the rules of so-called state responsibility,[184] the consequences of conduct that violates international law can affect only a state, but not an individual. International criminal law "embodies the new quality of international law, which is no longer limited to the rules of true interstate matters, but reaches deep into the state's domestic sphere."[185]   **97**

Crimes under international law are committed by individuals; violations of international law that may result in state responsibility are committed by states.[186] Both concepts, "state responsibility" and "international criminal law," share the goal of implementing international law; however, the mechanisms they use to achieve this goal differ.   **98**

---

[183] There is no corporate liability in international law. Thus the personal jurisdiction of the ICC is limited to natural persons (ICC Statute Art. 25(1)). For details, see M.C. Bassiouni, in M.C. Bassiouni (ed.), *International Criminal Law*, Vol. 1, 2nd edn. (1999), pp. 17 et seq.; O. Triffterer, in K.H. Gössel and O. Triffterer (eds.), *Gedächtnisschrift für Zipf* (1999), p. 493 at pp. 505 et seq. The beginnings of corporate liability were found in Art. 9 of the IMT Charter, under which the International Military Tribunal could declare associations "[criminal] organizations." The purpose of this construction, however, was not to punish the organization, but to create a way of bringing (natural) persons to justice for membership in criminal organizations in the follow-up trials, without having to prove the existence of a criminal organization in every case (see IMT Charter, Art. 10).

[184] On the bases of state responsibility, see Art. 1 of the International Law Commission's *Draft Articles on Responsibility of States for Internationally Wrongful Acts* (UN Doc. A/CN.4/L.602/Rev.1 (2001): "Every internationally wrongful act of a State entails the international responsibility of that State." The International Law Commission has since moved away from the concept of "state criminal responsibility" for serious violations of international law that was provided for in earlier drafts, as well as the division of "international wrongful acts" into "international crimes" and "international delicts" (see *Draft Articles on State Responsibility* of 1976, Art. 19(4). On the entire issue, see I. Brownlie, *Principles of Public International Law*, 6th edn. (2003), pp. 419 et seq.; J. Crawford, 10 *European Journal of International Law* (1999), pp. 435 et seq.; M. Sassòli, 84 *International Review of the Red Cross* (2002), pp. 401 et seq.; C. Tomuschat, *Gegenwartsprobleme der Staatenverantwortlichkeit in der Arbeit der Völkerrechtskommission der Vereinten Nationen* (1994).

[185] C. Tomuschat, 73 *Die Friedens-Warte* (1998), p. 335 at p. 347 (author's translation). See also A. Zimmermann, 45 *German Yearbook of International Law* (2002), p. 35 at pp. 37 et seq.

[186] On the distinction, see A. Cassese, *International Law* (2003), pp. 271 et seq.; V.D. Degan, in S. Yee and W. Tieya (eds.), *International Law in the Post-Cold War World* (2001), pp. 202 et seq.; H.-H. Jescheck, in R. Bernhardt (ed.), *Encyclopedia of Public International Law*, Vol. 2 (1995), pp. 1119 et seq.

International criminal law takes account of the fact that every violation of international law can ultimately be ascribed to an individual person, and prevents the individual – even when acting, for example, as an organ of the state – from hiding behind the shield of state sovereignty. In contrast, the principles of state responsibility only apply to associatively-structured subjects of international law. All violations of international law attributable to the state create state responsibility. The laws of state responsibility and criminal law also differ in their sanctions: while the legal consequences under the law of state responsibility aim only to restore a situation that conforms with international law,[187] sanctions in international criminal law are of a punitive and preventive nature.

99 Crimes under international law typically, though not necessarily, presume state participation. Therefore, responsibility on the part of the state does not follow automatically from the commission of a crime under international law by one of its citizens or agents. Article 25(4) of the ICC Statute makes this clear: "No provision in this Statute relating to individual criminal responsibility shall affect the responsibility of States under international law." Conversely, liability of a state under the law of state responsibility does not automatically lead to individual criminal responsibility of any of its agents involved under international law.[188] But crimes under international law and wrongful acts by a state will often coincide. For example, the state-sponsored extermination of a group would justify both the criminal prosecution of the persons involved for genocide and the state's duty to compensate the victims or their relatives.[189]

II. Crimes Under International Law and Other International Crimes

100 Crimes under international law are part of what we will here call international crimes.[190] Crimes under international law differ from other international crimes in that they are

---

[187] See M. Sassòli, 84 *International Review of the Red Cross* (2002), p. 401 at pp. 418 et seq.; M.N. Shaw, *International Law*, 5th edn. (2003), pp. 715 et seq. Under Arts. 30 et seq. of the *Draft Articles* (fn. 184), the concept of state responsibility mainly creates duties to end behavior or situations violative of international law and to make reparation.

[188] Art. 58 of the *Draft Articles* (fn. 184) makes this explicit. It states that the principles of state responsibility are "without prejudice to any question of the individual responsibility under international law of any person acting on behalf of the state."

[189] See, e.g., *Bosnia and Herzegovina* v. *Yugoslavia*, ICJ, judgment of 11 July 1996 (Case Concerning Application on the Prevention and Punishment of the Crime of Genocide), *ICJ Rep.* 1996, paras. 13 et seq. Grave breaches of the Geneva Conventions also create state liability under the law of state responsibility and individual liability under criminal law; on the "dual nature" of international legal norms, see M. Mohr, in G. Hankel and G. Stuby (eds.), *Strafgerichte gegen Menschheitsverbrechen* (1995), pp. 401 et seq.; O. Triffterer, 30 *Zeitschrift für Rechtsvergleichung* (1989), p. 83 at p. 109.

[190] The language corresponds to that of the ICC Statute, which says that it is the duty of states to exercise their jurisdiction over persons responsible "for international crimes." This means other crimes beyond those under the jurisdiction of the International Criminal Court, crimes under international law; see ICC Statute, Preamble (5). The records of the negotiations show that the parties were thinking above all of the crimes of terrorism and narcotics trafficking; see O. Triffterer, in O. Triffterer (ed.), *Commentary on the Rome Statute of the International Criminal Court* (1999), Preamble, marginal no. 17. Bassiouni has investigated references to criminal law in international treaty law. He has identified 260 treaties with a relationship to criminal law; of these, 57 expressly declare behavior to be an (international) crime; 183 obligate a state to prosecute or punish the conduct; 85 treaties expressly provide for criminalization of the conduct; 32 refer expressly to international jurisdiction (in M.C. Bassiouni (ed.), *International Criminal Law*, Vol. 1, 2nd edn. (1999), p. 47).

directly punishable under international law.[191] In contrast, the basis for prosecution and punishment of other international crimes is not international law, but domestic (implementing) legislation; in such cases, international law, in particular international agreements, merely obligate states to declare certain offenses criminal.[192] In these cases, one may speak at most of *indirect* criminality under international law, mediated through the domestic legal system.[193] In contrast to crimes under international law, these other international crimes may be classified as treaty-based crimes.[194] These include, for example, crimes against air traffic[195] and maritime navigation,[196] certain forms of narcotics crimes,[197] acts of terrorism,[198] counterfeiting,[199] and torture[200].[201]

---

[191] Like the text, the following writers also distinguish between international crimes in the narrow sense (crimes under international law) and in the broad sense: H. Ascensio, E. Decaux and A. Pellet (eds.), *Droit International Pénal* (2000), pp. 249 et seq. ("les crimes contre la paix et la sécurité de l'humanité" and "les autres infractions internationalement définies"); see also H. Ahlbrecht, *Geschichte der völkerrechtlichen Strafgerichtsbarkeit* (1999), p. 11, fn. 14; L. Condorelli, in H. Ascensio, E. Decaux and A. Pellet (eds.), *Droit International Pénal* (2000), p. 241; C. Nill-Theobald, *"Defences" bei Kriegsverbrechen am Beispiel Deutschlands und der USA* (1998), p. 24; similarly, O. Triffterer, 30 *Zeitschrift für Rechtsvergleichung* (1989), p. 83 at pp. 95 et seq. ("international crimes *sensu lato*"); H.-H. Jescheck, in R. Bernhardt (ed.), *Encyclopedia of Public International Law*, Vol. 2 (1995), pp. 1119 et seq.

[192] See, e.g., Art. 4(1) of the *Convention Against Torture and Other Cruel, Inhuman or Degrading Treatment or Punishment* of 10 December 1984 (1465 *UNTS* (1987), p. 112): "Each State Party shall ensure that all acts of torture are offences under its criminal law."

[193] See also A. Verdross and B. Simma, *Universelles Völkerrecht*, 3rd edn. (1984), § 430; G. Schwarzenberger, 3 *Current Legal Problems* (1950), p. 264 at pp. 266 et seq. ("International Criminal Law in the Meaning of Internationally Prescribed/Authorized Municipal Criminal Law.")

[194] See, e.g., W.A. Schabas, *Introduction to the International Criminal Court*, 2nd edn. (2004), p. 21; C. Kress , 114 *Zeitschrift für die gesamte Strafrechtswissenschaft* (2002), p. 818 at p. 829.

[195] See the (so-called Tokyo) *Convention on Offenses and Certain Other Acts Committed on Board Aircraft* of 14 September 1963 (704 *UNTS* (1969), p. 219); (Hague) *Convention for the Suppression of Unlawful Seizure of Aircraft* of 16 December 1970 (10 *ILM* (1971), p. 133); (Montreal) *Convention for the Suppression of Unlawful Acts against the Safety of Civil Aviation* of 23 September 1971 (10 *ILM* (1971), p. 1151); on the entire issue, see J. Dugard, *International Law*, 2nd edn. (2000), p. 146.

[196] See the (Geneva) *Convention on the High Seas* of 29 April 1958 (450 *UNTS* (1958), p. 11); *United Nations Convention on the Law of the Sea* of 10 December 1982 (21 *ILM* (1982), p. 1261); *Convention on the Suppression of Unlawful Acts Against the Safety of Maritime Navigation* of 10 March 1988 (27 *ILM* (1988), p. 668). In contrast to most other international crimes, the crime of piracy is grounded not in international treaty law, but in customary law. See J. Dugard, *International Law*, 2nd edn. (2000), p. 143; H.-H. Jescheck, in R. Bernhardt (ed.), *Encyclopedia of Public International Law*, Vol. 2 (1995) at p. 1122.

[197] See the *Single Convention on Narcotic Drugs* of 30 March 1961 (520 *UNTS* (1961), p. 151), *Convention on Psychotropic Substances* of 21 February 1971 (10 *ILM* (1971), p. 261); *United Nations Convention Against Illicit Traffic in Narcotic Drugs and Psychotropic Substances* of 20 December 1988 (28 *ILM* (1989), p. 493). See J. Dugard, *International Law*, 2nd edn. (2000), p. 149.

[198] See the *Convention for the Prevention and Punishment of Crimes Against Internationally Protected Persons, Including Diplomatic Agents* of 14 December 1973 (13 *ILM* (1974), p. 41); for a purely regional convention aimed at improving co-operation, see the *European Convention on the Suppression of Terrorism* of 27 January 1977 (*ETS* No. 90 (1977). For more on the spread of terror through commission of crimes under international law, see marginal no. 74 und S. Oeter, 76 *Die Friedens-Warte* (2001), pp. 11 et seq.; on the latest developments at the EU level, see T. Stein and C. Meiser, 76 *Die Friedens-Warte* (2001), pp. 33 et seq.

[199] See *International Convention for the Suppression of Counterfeiting of* 20 April 1929 (112 *LNTS*, p. 371).

101 It is a specific link to the international community that turns a crime into an international crime – be it a crime under international law or another international crime. This link is created either by an attack on an "international" interest or by the cross-border nature of the crime, which as a rule makes co-ordinated interstate action necessary, or at least expedient.[202]

102 A link to the international community and the need to internationalize protective mechanisms can arise, first of all, from the nature of the affected interest where a common interest of all (or many) states is at stake. This is true, for example, of attacks on international peace or systematic violations of basic human rights. This category primarily includes crimes under international law, which affect the most important interests of the community of nations.

103 Internationalization can also be rooted in practical needs. Considerations of expediency may call for an internationalization of criminal law enforcement when isolated prosecution of certain crimes by an individual state has no prospect of success.[203] Here the particular characteristics of the crime, specifically its commission across borders, make it necessary for states to co-operate for effective prosecution. This aspect is most important for crimes such as cross-border narcotics trafficking.

104 Finally, the prerequisites for the first and second groups may coincide. This is true for "typical" state-supported macro-criminality, which is normally not satisfactorily investigated or prosecuted by the state involved in the crime itself. If the international community were to leave prosecution up to such states, it would be tantamount to prosecution of the perpetrator by the perpetrator.[204] Here both the affected interests *and* the particular mode of conduct bring international law into play.

III. International Criminal Law, Supranational Criminal Law, Co-operation in Criminal Matters, and Extraterritorial Jurisdiction

105 International criminal law must be distinguished from certain related disciplines that also share both international and criminal characteristics, though in different ways. These include supranational criminal law, the laws of international judicial assistance and co-operation in criminal matters, and the rules of extraterritorial jurisdiction.

106 International criminal law is most closely related to supranational criminal law. However, the latter is not based on interstate agreements or customary international law. Instead, supranational crimi-

---

[200] See *Convention Against Torture and Other Cruel, Inhuman or Degrading Treatment or Punishment* of 10 December 1984 (1465 *UNTS* (1987), p. 112); see also J. Dugard, *International Law*, 2nd edn. (2000), p. 146.

[201] See M.C. Bassiouni, in M.C. Bassiouni (ed.), *International Criminal Law*, Vol. 1, 2nd edn. (1999), pp. 32 et seq. distinguishes 25 categories of "international crimes": In addition to the core crimes, he includes crimes against the United Nations, unauthorized possession or use of weapons, theft of nuclear substances, acting as a mercenary, slavery, torture, piracy, hostage-taking, narcotics trafficking and trafficking in pornographic images.

[202] See W.A. Schabas, *Introduction to the International Criminal Court*, 2nd edn. (2004), p. 21.

[203] See B. Yarnold, in M.C. Bassiouni (ed.), *International Criminal Law*, Vol. 1, 2nd edn. (1999), p. 127 at pp. 131 et seq.

[204] See O. Lagodny, 113 *Zeitschrift für die gesamte Strafrechtswissenschaft* (2001), p. 800 at p. 804.

nal law is created directly by supranational institutions. Given the small number of genuine supranational institutions with their own legal authority and the competence to create criminal norms,[205] it is not surprising that supranational criminal law is barely developed today. The first serious beginnings of such criminal law may be discerned within the framework of the "Europeanization of criminal law."[206]

The law of international judicial assistance and co-operation in criminal matters includes **107** rules on cross-border enforcement of criminal law, especially on extradition, enforcement assistance, transfer of proceedings and other forms of legal assistance, such as mutual support in collection of evidence.[207] Unlike international criminal law, the rules are purely procedural and do not create individual criminal responsibility. Nevertheless, there are numerous points of overlap with international criminal law. Without an executive organ of their own, international criminal courts, in particular, are dependent on the co-operation of states (so-called vertical co-operation).[208] The majority of cases, however, concern cooperation between states (so-called horizontal co-operation). In such cases, the basis for legal assistance is often interstate agreements, which supplement domestic rules on international co-operation.

In contrast, rules on extraterritorial jurisdiction are purely domestic in nature. They **108** determine whether a case that involves a foreign element is subject to domestic criminal jurisdiction and which norms are to be applied.[209] Several principles of extraterritorial jurisdiction can be distinguished: the nationality or active personality principle, the passive personality principle, the protection principle, the principle of vicarious administration of justice and the universality principle.[210] The latter is also relevant in the context of international criminal law, since it establishes the jurisdiction of domestic courts to prosecute and punish crimes under international law.[211]

IV. International Criminal Law and Protection of Human Rights

The emergence and development of international criminal law and the protection of hu- **109** man rights are closely related. Their common root lies in international humanitarian law.[212] Human rights, which provide the basis for individual rights, and the norms of

---

[205] On the concept of supranational institutions, see V. Epping, in K. Ipsen, *Völkerrecht*, 5th edn. (2004), § 6, marginal no. 15 et seq.

[206] However, there is no European criminal law as yet, in the sense of supranational criminal law. On this issue as a whole, see G. Corstens and J. Pradel, *European Criminal Law* (2002); H. Satzger, *Europäisierung des Strafrechts* (2001), pp. 57 et seq.

[207] See the contributions of M.C. Bassiouni, D. Poncet, P. Gully-Hart, E. Muller-Rappard and D. Spinellis, in M.C. Bassiouni (ed.), *International Criminal Law*, Vol. 2, 2nd edn. (1999), pp. 191 et seq.

[208] See, e.g., ICC Statute, Arts. 86 et seq.

[209] See D. Oehler, *Internationales Strafrecht*, 2nd edn. (1983), esp. marginal nos. 111 et seq.

[210] For details see C.L. Blakesley, in M.C. Bassiouni (ed.), *International Criminal Law*, Vol. 2, 2nd edn. (1999), pp. 33 et seq.; A. Cassese, *International Criminal Law* (2003), pp. 277 et seq.

[211] See marginal nos. 169 et seq.

[212] On the relationship between human rights protection and humanitarian international law, which has not yet been fully clarified, see T. Meron, *The Convergence between Human Rights and Humanitarian Law* (1997), pp. 97 et seq.; K.J. Partsch, in R. Bernhardt (ed.), *Encyclopedia of Public International Law*, Vol. 2 (1995), pp. 910 et seq.

international criminal law, which ascribe individual responsibility, were originally alien to traditional, state-centered international law. Both international criminal law and human rights law achieved their breakthrough as a consequence of the catastrophe of World War II. As regards the position of the individual as subject, international criminal law and protection of human rights are two sides of the same coin: the individual human being becomes the addressee of both international (human) rights and duties, the latter including criminal responsibility for actions or omissions.

1. Protection of Human Rights Through International Criminal Law

110   International criminal law is, among other things, an instrument to protect human rights. It responds to massive violations of fundamental human rights.[213] International criminal law provides an answer to the failure of traditional mechanisms for protecting human rights.

111   Observing and enforcing human rights is mainly the task of the states: human rights are implemented within, not between states.[214] Although states use criminal law in the process, and although, under certain circumstances, they are even required to use it,[215] this does not change the fact that victims often remain unprotected, especially from the worst human rights violations. This is especially true when human rights violations are initiated by states themselves. In such cases, protection at the national level fails. The internationalization of human rights protection—for example through the creation of international monitoring systems – is a step towards ending this unfortunate state of affairs.[216]

112   In conflicts between state sovereignty and the protection of human rights, international criminal law intervenes on the side of humanity. In this way it supplements and safe-

---

[213] On the human rights aspects of international criminal law, see C. Tomuschat, in G. Hankel and G. Stuby (eds.), *Strafgerichte gegen Menschheitsverbrechen* (1995), p. 270 at p. 283 ("massive violations of the core values of the human being"); G. Werle, 109 *Zeitschrift für die gesamte Strafrechtswissenschaft* (1997), p. 808 at pp. 815 et seq.

[214] U. Fastenrath, in U. Fastenrath (ed.), *Internationaler Schutz der Menschenrechte* (2000), p. 9 at p. 39.

[215] It is widely accepted today that human rights protection instruments give rise to a duty of states not only to investigate serious violations of human rights (see F. Jessberger, *Kritische Justiz* 1996, p. 290), but also to punish perpetrators, see K. Ambos, *Straflosigkeit von Menschenrechtsverletzungen* (1997), pp. 163 et seq. For more on this, see marginal no. 181.

[216] See generally, on the juxtaposition of non-judicial, quasi-judicial and judicial protection systems, C. Pappa, *Das Individualbeschwerdeverfahren des Fakultativprotokolls zum Internationalen Pakt über Bürgerliche und Politische Rechte* (1996), pp. 6 et seq. Noteworthy are, first of all, the universal protective mechanisms of the UN Human Rights Committee, including reporting (*International Covenant on Civil and Political Rights* of 16 December 1966 (6 *ILM* (1967), p. 368), Arts. 28 et seq.) and individual complaints (see *Optional Protocol to the International Covenant on Civil and Political Rights* of 16 December 1966 (999 *UNTS* (1967), p. 171). There are, in addition, regional protective mechanisms, especially the European Court of Human Rights (*European Convention on Human Rights and Fundamental Freedoms* of 4 November 1950, Arts. 32 et seq., *ETS* No. 5 (1950), p. 14: state complaint procedures and individual complaint procedures) and the Inter-American Court of Human Rights (*American Convention on Human Rights* of 22 November 1969 (9 *ILM* (1970), p. 673), Arts. 33, 44 et seq.).

guards[217] other human rights protection mechanisms, and to this extent aids in the protection of human rights.[218] International criminal law is subsidiary here in two ways – first of all, vis-à-vis state mechanisms, and second of all, vis-à-vis mechanisms outside of criminal law.

The human rights-protecting function of international criminal law is especially clear **113** for crimes against humanity,[219] which criminalize systematic attacks on fundamental human rights, such as the rights to life and physical integrity, to freedom of movement and human dignity. The idea of humanity as the foundation of human rights protection and of international criminal law is visible here.[220] The broad concept of peace upon which international criminal law is based[221] also conveys the connection between human rights and the other crimes under international law.

It should be noted that the task of protecting human rights does not end with the implementation **114** of substantive international criminal law—that is, with the perpetrator's conviction. One should for example consider procedural protections for the victims in trials before an international court, or the possibility of determining reparations or restitution measures in the course of a trial under international law.[222]

This does not mean, however, that every violation of human rights, or even every serious **115** violation, is directly punishable under international law.[223] Instead, only a small sample of human rights are guaranteed the protection of international criminal law. The direct criminalization of its violation under international law is the highest level of protection that a human right can achieve.[224] In international law, too, the use of criminal law is only admissible as a last resort, that is, when all other (national and international) protective mechanisms fail.

---

[217] However, international criminal law and international criminal justice are not merely additions to existing protective mechanisms. Rather, existing monitoring mechanisms themselves gain new weight and "teeth" as a result of the possibility of forwarding their results to a criminal court. From this perspective, see F. Pocar, in M. Politi and G. Nesi (eds.), *The Rome Statute of the International Criminal Court* (2001), p. 67 at p. 73.

[218] See M.C. Bassiouni, in T. Vogler (ed.), *Festschrift für Jescheck* (1985), p. 1453 ("*ultima ratio* modality of protection"); T. Buergenthal, *International Human Rights* (1995), p. 271 ("giving it teeth"); F. Pocar, in M. Politi and G. Nesi (eds.), *The Rome Statute of the International Criminal Court* (2001), p. 67 at p. 70; O. Triffterer, 114 *Zeitschrift für die gesamte Strafrechtswissenschaft* (2002), p. 321 at pp. 341 et seq. For a skeptical view, see M. Köhler, in F. Jessberger and C. Kress, 113 *Zeitschrift für die gesamte Strafrechtswissenschaft* (2001), p. 827 at p. 866.

[219] In the *Draft Code* 1991, crimes against humanity were still titled "Article 21 – Systematic or mass violations of human rights."

[220] See T. Meron, *The Convergence between Human Rights and Humanitarian Law* (1997), p. 97 and p. 100.

[221] See marginal no. 78.

[222] See M.B. Dembour and E. Haslam, 15 *European Journal of International Law* (2004), pp. 151 et seq.; E.-C. Gillard, 85 *International Review of the Red Cross* (2003), pp. 529 et seq.; F. Rigaux, in L.C. Vohrah et al. (eds.), *Man's Inhumanity to Man* (2003), pp. 771 et seq.; C. Safferling, 115 *Zeitschrift für die gesamte Strafrechtswissenschaft* (2003), pp. 352 et seq.

[223] See K. Kittichaisaree, *International Criminal Law* (2001), p. 4. M.C. Bassiouni, in T. Vogler (ed.), *Festschrift für Jescheck* (1985), p. 1453 at pp. 1466 et seq., develops various criteria for judging whether human rights should be protected by criminal law.

[224] See M.C. Bassiouni, in T. Vogler (ed.), *Festschrift für Jescheck* (1985), p. 1453 at p. 1455, who distinguishes the various levels of human rights protection. At present, protection under criminal law

116   Yet to see the relationship between human rights and international criminal law as a
one-way street would be insufficient.[225] The development of international criminal law
also has an impact on the substance and the status of human rights guarantees. International criminal law thus contributes significantly to strengthening and further developing
the protection of human rights.[226]

2. The Function of Human Rights in Limiting International Criminal Law

117   Human rights protections legitimize international criminal law and at the same time
limit its application. Like national criminal law,[227] international criminal law is subject
to human rights limitations. This is true of the extension of penal authority in general.
But the limiting function of human rights comes into effect mainly in the design of procedure: even a suspect accused of a crime under international law has the right to a fair
trial that adheres to human rights principles and standards.

V. International Criminal Law and the Law of International Criminal Procedure

118   Like national criminal law, international law also distinguishes between substantive and
procedural norms. While substantive international criminal law establishes the conditions for culpability and punishment, as well as sentencing provisions, the international
law of criminal procedure sets rules to be followed in determining whether a person is
responsible for a crime under international law.[228] The rules of procedure for the Yugoslavia Tribunal and the Rwanda Tribunal largely follow the adversarial procedural
model;[229] the procedure developed for the ICC Statute, however, clearly possesses important elements of the inquisitorial model.[230]

---

is limited to so-called first generation human rights (on this concept, see V. Herdegen, *Völkerrecht*
(2000), § 47, marginal no. 6). For a critical view of the hierarchization of human rights, connected
with partial criminalization, see F. Pocar, in M. Politi and G. Nesi (eds.), *The Rome Statute of the International Criminal Court* (2001), p. 67 and p. 72.

[225] On the interactions between international criminal law and protection of human rights, see
also K. Kittichaisaree, *International Criminal Law* (2001), pp. 56 et seq.

[226] See F. Pocar, in M. Politi and G. Nesi (ed.), *The Rome Statute of the International Criminal
Court* (2001), pp. 67; C. Tomuschat, 73 *Die Friedens-Warte* (1998), p. 335 at p. 347 ("one [may]
consider the adoption of the Rome Statute a great victory for international efforts to strengthen the
rule of law and human rights"); see also T. Buergenthal, *International Human Rights in a Nutshell*, 2nd
edn. (1995), pp. 271 et seq. ("The caselaw [of the ICTR] will . . . strengthen the normative framework of this branch of international human rights law").

[227] See, e.g., H.-H. Jescheck and T. Weigend, *Lehrbuch des Strafrechts*, 5th edn. (1996), pp. 11 et
seq.

[228] On international criminal procedure, see A. Bruer-Schäfer, *Der Internationale Strafgerichtshof*
(2001), pp. 128 et seq.; A. Cassese, *International Criminal Law* (2003), pp. 389 et seq.; C. Safferling,
Towards an International Criminal Procedure (2001); J.K. Cogan, 27 *Yale Journal of International Law*
(2002), pp. 111 et seq.

[229] For discussion of the characteristics of this model and its adoption in international criminal
justice, see A. Cassese, *International Criminal Law* (2003), pp. 65 et seq.

[230] See A. Cassese, *International Criminal Law* (2003), pp. 386 et seq.

International criminal procedure aids in the implementation of substantive international criminal **119**
law, but the latter is by no means implemented solely through international criminal procedure.
The enforcement of substantive international criminal law is primarily the task of states.[231] Inves-
tigating facts, determining guilt, sentencing, and execution of sentences are all accomplished
through application of effective national rules. The only direct role played here by international
rules of criminal procedure involves at most the distribution of authority, as for example the
complementarity principle in Article 1 of the ICC Statute. The only area in which international
criminal procedure in its genuine sense is actually applicable is in trials before international courts.

The ICC Statute has also brought about significant progress in procedural law. Proce- **120**
dural[232] and substantive law are combined in a unified body of rules. The comprehensive Rules of Procedure and Evidence supplement and better define the Statute's
provisions. Within the international law of criminal procedure, we can distinguish between the areas of organization and administration of the courts; the law governing investigations, prosecution and trial procedures; and the law applicable to the enforcement
of sentences. Finally, the law of international co-operation in criminal matters is also ultimately procedural – as well as being of crucial significance to the functioning of international criminal law enforcement for the foreseeable future.[233]

Distinguishing between substantive and procedural norms in international criminal law is not al- **121**
ways easy. For example, the definitions of crimes in the ICC Statute, like the corresponding rules
in the Statutes of the Yugoslavia and Rwanda Tribunals, are by their wording jurisdictional
norms.[234] Nevertheless, they are correctly viewed as defining the crimes, because in establishing
grounds for jurisdiction, the substantive criminality of the conduct described is already presumed.[235]

D. Sources and Interpretation

Ian Brownlie: *Principles of Public International Law*, 6th edn. (2003), pp. 1 et seq.; Antonio **122**
Cassese: The Contribution of the International Criminal Tribunal for the former Yugoslavia to the
Ascertainment of General Principles of Law Recognized by the Community of Nations, in Sienho
Yee and Wang Tieya (eds.), *International Law in the Post-Cold War World, Essays in Memory of Li
Haopei* (2001), pp. 43 et seq.; Antonio Cassese: *International Criminal Law* (2003), pp. 25 et seq.;
Ida Caracciolo: Applicable Law, in Flavia Lattanzi and William A. Schabas (eds.), *Essays on the*

---

[231] See marginal nos. 195, 199 et seq.

[232] The rules concern all aspects of procedure: constitution of the Court (e.g., Art. 1, Art. 5,
Arts. 34 et seq.), investigation (Arts. 14 et seq., Arts. 53 et seq.), trial (Arts. 62 et seq.), appeal
(Arts. 81 et seq.), legal assistance and co-operation (Arts. 86 et seq.) and enforcement (Arts. 103 et
seq.).

[233] See, e.g., ICC Statute, Arts. 86 et seq.

[234] Thus ICC Statute, Art. 5(1) sentence 2 extends the "jurisdiction of the Court" to "the following crimes," see also ICC Statute, Arts. 1, 2 and 3: "shall have the power to exercise its jurisdiction
over persons."

[235] On classification of definitions of crimes in the ICC Statute, see, on the one hand, C.
Tomuschat, 73 *Die Friedens-Warte* (1998), p. 335 at p. 337: "the descriptions of crimes not only [de-
termine] the Court's jurisdiction, but are conceived as substantive criminal law"; on the other hand,
O. Triffterer, in K.H. Gössel and O. Triffterer (eds.), *Gedächtnisschrift für Zipf* (1999), p. 493 at
p. 532: "The Rome Statute does not create substantive international criminal law. It is the 'constitution of courts act' for the permanent International Criminal Court."

Rome Statute of the International Criminal Court (1999), pp. 211 et seq.; Ulrich Fastenrath: *Lücken im Völkerrecht, Zu Rechtscharakter, Quellen, Systemzusammenhang, Methodenlehre und Funktionen des Völkerrechts* (1991); Bing Bing Jia: Judicial Decisions as a Source of International Law and the Defence of Duress in Murder or Other Cases Arising from Armed Conflict, in Sienho Yee and Wang Tieya (eds.), *International Law in the Post-Cold War World, Essays in Memory of Li Haopei* (2001), pp. 77 et seq.; Kriangsak Kittichaisaree: *International Criminal Law* (2001), pp. 44 et seq.; Claus Kress: Zur Methode der Rechtsfindung im Allgemeinen Teil des Völkerstrafrechts, Die Bewertung von Tötungen im Nötigungsnotstand durch die Rechtsmittelkammer des Internationalen Straftribunals für das ehemalige Jugoslawien im Fall Erdemovic, 111 *Zeitschrift für die gesamte Strafrechtswissenschaft* (1999), pp. 597 et seq.; Theodor Meron: Crimes under the Jurisdiction of the International Criminal Court, in Herman von Hebel, Johan G. Lammers and Jolien Schukking (eds.), *Reflections on the International Criminal Court* (1999), pp. 47 et seq.; Theodor Meron: *Human Rights and Humanitarian Norms as Customary Law* (1989), pp. 1 et seq., pp. 136 et seq.; Theodor Meron: The Continuing Role of Custom in the Formation of International Humanitarian Law, 90 *American Journal of International Law* (1996), pp. 238 et seq.; Jordan Paust: Customary International Law: Its Nature, Source and Status as Law of the United States, 12 *Michigan Journal of International Law* (1990), pp. 59 et seq.; Alain Pellet: Applicable Law, in Antonio Cassese, Paola Gaeta and John R.W.D. Jones (eds.), *The Rome Statute of the International Criminal Court, A Commentary*, Vol. 2 (2002), pp. 1051 et seq.; Per Saland: International Criminal Law Principles, in Roy S. Lee (ed.), *The International Criminal Court, The Making of the Rome Statute* (1999), pp. 189 et seq.; William A. Schabas: *An Introduction to the International Criminal Court* , 2nd edn. (2004), pp. 90 et seq.; Bruno Simma and Andreas Paulus: Le Role Relatif Des Differentes Sources Du Droit International Pénal, in Hervé Ascensio, Emmanuel Decaux and Alain Pellet (eds.), *Droit International Pénal* (2001), pp. 55 et seq.; Alfred Verdross and Bruno Simma: *Universelles Völkerrecht*, 3rd edn. (1984), pp. 321 et seq.; Daniel L. Wade: A Basic Guide to the Sources of International Criminal Law, in Ellen G. Schaffer and Randall J. Snyder (eds.), *Contemporary Practice of Public International Law* (1997), pp. 189 et seq.

I. Sources of Law

123   As part of the international legal order, international criminal law originates from the same legal sources as international law.[236] These include international treaties, customary international law, and general principles of law recognized by the world's major legal systems.[237] Decisions of international courts and international legal doctrine can be used

---

[236] See A. Cassese, *International Criminal Law* (2003), p. 26; C. Kress, 111 *Zeitschrift für die gesamte Strafrechtswissenschaft* (1999), p. 597; B. Simma and A. Paulus, in H. Ascensio, E. Decaux and A. Pellet (eds.), *Droit International Pénal* (2001), p. 55; O. Triffterer, *Dogmatische Untersuchungen zur Entwicklung des materiellen Völkerstrafrechts seit Nürnberg* (1962), p. 35 and p. 128. See also *Prosecutor v. Furundžija*, ICTY (Trial Chamber), judgment of 10 December 1998, paras. 190 et seq.

[237] Art. 38(1) of the ICJ Statute lists the sources of international law. It provides that the International Court of Justice is to apply "a) international conventions . . ., b) international custom, as evidence of a general practice accepted as law, c) the general principles of law accepted by civilized nations [and] d) . . . judicial decisions and the teachings of the most highly qualified publicists of the various nations as subsidiary means for the determination of rules of law." See I. Brownlie, *Principles of International Law*, 6th edn. (2003), pp. 4 et seq.; W. Heintschel von Heinegg, in K. Ipsen, *Völkerrecht*, 5th edn. (2004), before § 9, marginal no. 2. According to accepted views, general principles as a source of international law are subsidiary to treaty and customary law and are only used when these sources provide no relevant guidelines, see I. Brownlie, *Principles of Public International Law*, 6th edn. (2003), p. 15; on the status of the debate, see G. Dahm, J. Delbrück and R. Wolfrum, *Völkerrecht*, Vol. I/1,

not as sources of law, but as subsidiary means for determining the law.[238] Decisions of national courts applying international law can also be referred to here.[239]

With the entry into force of the ICC Statute, doubts about whether the rules of inter- **124** national criminal law in fact satisfy the requirements of clarity and transparency under the principle of legality have lost their force. Today, the rules of international criminal law in the ICC Statute have been set out with a clarity approaching that of civil law systems. The provisions of the Statute have been further clarified by the Elements of Crimes and the Rules of Procedure and Evidence. In this way, international criminal law, which in terms of sources could be roughly described as a reciprocal mix of customary international law and partial codification by treaty, has reached a new level of consolidation.

The codification of unwritten customary criminal law marks a considerable advance for the clarity **125** and transparency of norms.[240] The greater ease with which the content and limits of written penal norms can now be determined easily compensates for the possible detriments to the development of international criminal law caused by the fixing of norms in the ICC Statute.[241]

1. International Treaties

Until the ICC Statute entered into force, international treaties were of lesser importance **126** for international criminal law. Today, the ICC Statute, a multilateral international treaty, is the main source of international criminal law.

There is a close connection in international criminal law between treaty law and customary law. **127** Numerous treaties in the area of international criminal law expressly or incidentally codify customary law; this is true, for example, of the definitions of crimes in the ICC Statute.[242] The treaty provisions clarify the contours of customary legal rules; in many instances, international treaties were the starting point for the formation of customary law norms. This is true, for example, of Common Article 3 of the Geneva Conventions.[243] Because of the interconnections between treaty and customary law, *both* sources of law must be kept in mind when applying international criminal law.

2nd edn. (1989), p. 63 and J. Kammerhofer, 15 *European Journal of International Law* (2004), p. 523 at pp. 541 et seq.

[238] See ICJ Statute, Art. 38(1)(d).

[239] See, e.g., *Prosecutor* v. *Kupreškić* et al., ICTY (Trial Chamber), judgment of 14 January 2000, para. 541.

[240] Nevertheless, A. Verdross and B. Simma, *Universelles Völkerrecht*, 3rd edn. (1984), § 593 seem quite justified in pointing out the limiting effect of this codification, through the "adoption of dilatory compromise wordings that are worthless as a matter of legal policy, and even dangerous." This holds true in particular with regard to some provisions of the ICC Statute. For a general discussion of the advantages and disadvantages of the codification of customary international law, see W. Heintschel von Heinegg, in K. Ipsen, *Völkerrecht*, 5th edn. (2004), § 16, marginal nos. 49 et seq. See also A. Cassese, *International Law* (2003), pp. 136 et seq.

[241] Especially since Art. 10 of the ICC Statute, under which the provisions of the Statute do not touch "existing or developing rules of international law for purposes other than this Statute," additionally reduces the danger of an "encrustation" of international criminal law.

[242] See marginal no. 135.

[243] See *Prosecutor* v. *Tadić*, ICTY (Appeals Chamber), decision of 2 October 1995, para. 98.

2. Customary International Law

128 In the absence of a global institution for creating law, customary law continues to play a crucial role in international criminal law, even after the ICC Statute's entry into force.[244] Under the classic definition, customary international law exists if actual practice *(consuetudo)* can be found, based on a sense of legal obligation *(opinio juris)*.[245]

129 The objective component of the emergence of customary law is state practice. This can be determined from the totality of states' official behavior.[246] Legislative measures must be considered, along with decisions of courts and official acts and declarations by state representatives. Relevant treaty practice may also be significant. Practice must be uniform, widespread, and also long-term.[247] Decisions of international courts and the practices of international organizations also provide indirect evidence of the practices and beliefs of states involved, and thus contribute to the formation of customary international law.[248]

130 State practice must be joined with a corresponding sense of legal obligation *(opinio juris)*.[249] The borderline between *opinio juris* and state practice has become fluid. In many cases, state conduct may be considered an indication of both practice and corresponding *opinio juris*. Objective and subjective components also merge when state practice is concluded from a state's articulation of *opinio juris*.[250]

---

[244] See A. Cassese, *International Criminal Law* (2003), p. 28; T. Meron, 90 *American Journal of International Law* (1996), p. 238 at pp. 244 et seq. An important example is the applicability of large portions of the international laws of war to civil wars, which was established in *Prosecutor* v. *Tadić*, ICTY (Appeals Chamber), decision of 2 October 1995. The principle of *nullum crimen sine lege* is not an obstacle to grounding criminality in customary law, see marginal no. 91. For a very critical view, see S. Estreicher, 44 *Virginia Journal of International Law* (2003), pp. 5 et seq.

[245] ICJ Statute, Art. 38(1)(b): "general practice accepted as law"; see A. Verdross and B. Simma, *Universelles Völkerrecht*, 3rd edn. (1984), §§ 549 et seq.; A.E. Roberts, 95 *American Journal of International Law* (2001), p. 757, is instructive on various trends in legal theory, some of which emphasize the objective components of its emergence and some of which concentrate on the legal beliefs of states.

[246] Here acts of any state authorities must be taken into account, in principle, see I. Brownlie, *Principles of Public International Law*, 6th edn. (2003), p. 6. On the role of non-state subjects of international law in the emergence of customary international law, see *Prosecutor* v. *Tadić*, ICTY (Appeals Chamber), decision of 2 October 1995, paras. 108 et seq.

[247] See I. Brownlie, *Principles of Public International Law*, 6th edn. (2003), pp. 6 et seq. and J. Kammerhofer, 15 *European Journal of International Law* (2004), p. 523 at pp. 525 et seq.

[248] See *Prosecutor* v. *Tadić*, ICTY (Appeals Chamber), decision of 2 October 1995, para. 133: "Of great relevance to the formation of opinio juris . . . are certain resolutions unanimously adopted by the Security Council." See also I. Brownlie, *Principles of Public International Law*, 6th edn. (2003), p. 15: "acceptance by a majority vote constitutes *evidence* of the opinions of governments in the widest forum for the expression of such opinions"; J.A. Frowein, 49 *Zeitschrift für ausländisches öffentliches Recht und Völkerrecht* (1989), pp. 78 et seq.; J. Paust, 12 *Michigan Journal of International Law* (1990), p. 59 at pp. 70 et seq.

[249] An example of *opinio juris* is the opinion presented by the US government as *amicus curiae* in the trial of Tadić before the ICTY: "That statement articulates the legal views of one of the permanent members of the Security Council on a delicate legal issue; on this score it provides the first indication of a possible change in *opinio juris* of States"; see *Prosecutor* v. *Tadić*, ICTY (Appeals Chamber), decision of 2 October 1995, para. 83. See also J. Kammerhofer, 15 *European Journal of International Law* (2004), p. 523 at pp. 532 et seq.

[250] See V. Herdegen, *Völkerrecht* (2000), § 16, marginal no. 3.

Judicial practice naturally has great significance for the formation of customary law in **131** the area of international criminal law. In addition, countries' verbal acts, expressed in official pronouncements, play an important role.[251] The Yugoslavia Tribunal explicitly emphasized this in its landmark decision in the *Tadić* case.[252]

The reason for the significance of verbal acts is that international criminal law continues to suffer **132** from a chronic lack of willingness on the part of states to not only acknowledge, but also to implement, its penal norms. A considerable discrepancy continues to exist between the declarations of states, often well-disposed toward international criminal law, and the generally much more reluctant practice of state prosecution. Not infrequently, commitment to a norm is accompanied by its widespread disregard in actual practice. However, one should not prematurely conclude from this that little customary law has been created in international criminal law because of a lack of state practice. Even state conduct that contradicts a rule can confirm it – for example, if the conduct is accompanied by attempts at justification.[253] In such a case, the state involved confirms the norm's validity and shows its own behavior to be a violation of the norm.

A verification procedure for determining the customary character of international crimi- **133** nal law can be found in the Yugoslavia Tribunal's decision in the *Krstić* case. The starting point for the chamber's discussion was the codification of customary law principles in international treaties. As a second step, it would consult international case law, for example that of the Rwanda Tribunal, relevant International Law Commission drafts ("particularly relevant source for the interpretation of Article 4 [of the ICTY Statute]"), the reports of other international institutions, such as the UN Human Rights Commission, the Elements of Crimes of the ICC Statute ("the [Rome Statute] is a useful key to the *opinio juris* of the States"), and finally, relevant domestic legislation.[254]

3. General Principles of Law

General principles of law are also of considerable significance to international criminal **134** law.[255] These are legal principles recognized by the world's major legal systems.[256] How-

---

[251] See C. Kress, 111 *Zeitschrift für die gesamte Strafrechtswissenschaft* (1999), p. 597 at p. 602; T. Meron, 90 *American Journal of International Law* (1996), p. 238 at p. 240; N. Roht-Arriaza, in N. Roht-Arriaza (ed.), *Impunity and Human Rights in International Law and Practice* (1995), p. 40; D.L. Wade, in E.G. Schaffer and R.J. Snyder, *Contemporary Practice of Public International Law* (1997), p. 208. However, reference to verbal acts is not generally sufficient, in itself, to prove corresponding state practice, see G.M. Danilenko, *Law-Making in the International Community* (1993), p. 91.

[252] See *Prosecutor* v. *Tadić*, ICTY (Appeals Chamber), decision of 2 October 1995, para. 99: "In appraising the formation of customary rules or general principles one should therefore be aware that, on account of the inherent nature of this subject matter, reliance must primarily be placed on such elements as official pronouncements of States, military manuals and judicial decisions."

[253] See I. Gross, *Humanitäres Völkerrecht-Informationsschriften* 2001, p. 162 at p. 166.

[254] See *Prosecutor* v. *Krstić*, ICTY (Trial Chamber), judgment of 2 August 2001, paras. 541 et seq.

[255] See A. Cassese, in S. Yee and W. Tieya (eds.), *International Law in the Post-Cold War World* (2001), pp. 43 et seq.

[256] See *Prosecutor* v. *Furundžija*, ICTY (Trial Chamber), judgment of 10 December 1998, para. 177; A. Cassese, *International Law* (2003), pp. 155 et seq.; K. Kittichaisaree, *International Criminal Law* (2001), pp. 46 et seq. Normally, Anglo-American common law and continental European civil law are the main systems consulted, see K. Ambos, *Der Allgemeine Teil des Völkerstrafrechts* (2002), p. 46.

ever, not every law found in several or all legal systems is automatically a general principle of law and therefore a component of the international legal order. The dual conditions are that the law represent a legal *principle* and that it be transferable to the international legal order.[257] The Yugoslavia Tribunal has stated the following in this regard:

"Whenever international criminal rules do not define a notion of criminal law, reliance upon national legislation is justified, subject to the following conditions: (i) . . . international courts must draw upon the general concepts and legal institutions common to all the major legal systems of the world [not only common-law or civil-law States] . . . ; (ii) . . . account must be taken of the specificity of international criminal proceedings when utilising national law notions. In this way a mechanical importation or transposition from national law into international criminal proceedings is avoided."[258]

135   Thus the elements of international criminal law are not all the legal norms upon which major legal systems agree as such, but only the general principles upon which these norms are based.[259] It is often difficult to distinguish between customary international law and general principles of law, as the development of state practice is in constant flux.[260]

II. Subsidiary Means for Determining the Law

136   Subsidiary means for determining international criminal law are primarily the decisions of international courts and legal scholarship. Information on the "teachings of the most highly qualified publicists" may be obtained mainly from the reports and statements of international law associations (such as the Institut du Droit International and International Law Association) and the United Nations International Law Commission. National court decisions may also be consulted.[261]

III. Individual Sources

137   The following will introduce the most important sources of law and means of determining rules of law in international criminal law.

---

[257] See A. Verdross and B. Simma, *Universelles Völkerrecht*, 3rd edn. (1984), § 602; A. Cassese, *International Law* (2003), p. 158, and C. Kress, 111 *Zeitschrift für die gesamte Strafrechtswissenschaft* (1999), p. 597 at p. 609, fn. 58.

[258] *Prosecutor* v. *Furundžija*, ICTY (Trial Chamber), judgment of 10 December 1998, para. 178.

[259] See A. Verdross and B. Simma, *Universelles Völkerrecht*, 3rd edn. (1984), § 602; G. Dahm, J. Delbrück and R. Wolfrum, *Völkerrecht*, Vol. I/1, 2nd edn. (1989), p. 64 ("a general principle that dominates the entire legal system").

[260] See O. Kimminich and S. Hobe, *Einführung in das Völkerrecht*, 7th edn. (2000), p. 185.

[261] On the authoritative nature of national decisions, see I. Brownlie, *Principles of Public International Law*, 6th edn. (2003), p. 22; U. Fastenrath, *Lücken im Völkerrecht* (1991), p. 122.

1. ICC Statute, Elements of Crimes, Rules of Procedure and Evidence

The ICC Statute is the central source of international criminal law. It is an international **138** treaty to which the general rules of interpretation apply. The Statute's provisions are supplemented by the Elements of Crimes[262] and the Rules of Procedure and Evidence.[263] The Elements of Crimes clarify the definitions of crimes in Articles 6 to 8. They aid the International Criminal Court in interpreting and applying those provisions ("shall assist the Court in the interpretation and application of article 6, 7 and 8," Article 9(1)).[264] The Rules of Procedure and Evidence supplement and clarify the rules of procedure contained in the Statute itself. The Rules of Procedure and Evidence are binding on the Court and all state parties.[265] If the Elements of Crimes or the provisions of the Rules of Procedure and Evidence contradict the Statute, the Statute takes precedence.[266]

The ICC Statute largely confirms and clarifies the criminal law that exists under cus- **139** tomary international law. But the Statute also to some extent goes beyond simply reflecting and systematizing customary law, and thus makes its own independent contribution to the development of international criminal law.[267] On the other hand, the Statute also in part lags behind the current state of customary law, especially as regards criminalizing prohibited methods of warfare in non-international armed conflicts.[268]

The Yugoslavia Tribunal summarized the significance of the ICC Statute as follows, **140** even before its entry into force:

"In many areas the Statute may be regarded as indicative of the legal views, i.e. *opinio juris* of a great number of States. Notwithstanding article 10 of the Statute, the purpose of which is to ensure that existing or developing law is not 'limited' or 'prejudiced' by the Statute's provisions, resort may be had *cum grano salis to* these provisions to help elucidate customary international law. Depending on the matter at issue, the Rome Statute may be taken to restate, reflect or clarify customary rules or crystallise them, whereas in some areas it creates new law or modifies existing law. At any event, the Rome Statute by and large may be taken as constituting an authoritative expression of the legal views of a great number of States."[269]

---

[262] See commentary on the provisions in R.S. Lee (ed.), *The International Criminal Court, Elements of Crimes and Rules of Procedure and Evidence* (2001).

[263] See commentary on the provisions in R.S. Lee (ed.), *The International Criminal Court, Elements of Crimes and Rules of Procedure and Evidence* (2001).

[264] The unusual combination of binding and non-binding elements of crimes are the result of differences of opinion at the Rome Conference on the degree of definitional precision required by the principle of *nullum crimen sine lege*. The concept of supplementing the definitions of crimes in the Statute with elements of crimes can be traced to a proposal by the US delegation, see E. Gadirov, in O. Triffterer (ed.), *Commentary on the Rome Statute of the International Criminal Court* (1999), Art. 9, marginal nos. 1 et seq.

[265] See B. Broomhall, in O. Triffterer (ed.), *Commentary on the Rome Statute of the International Criminal Court* (1999), Art. 51, marginal nos. 34 et seq.

[266] See ICC Statute, Art. 51(3) (for the procedural and evidentiary systems) and ICC Statute, Art. 9(3).

[267] See also R.S. Clark, in M. Politi and G. Nesi (eds.), *The Rome Statute of the International Criminal Court* (2001), p. 75 at p. 79.

[268] For more information, see marginal nos. 815 et seq.

[269] *Prosecutor* v. *Furundžija*, ICTY (Trial Chamber), judgment of 10 December 1998, para. 227.

141 Whether and to what extent the Statute's provisions create original treaty-based international law or are merely declarative determinations of preexisting customary law[270] is not merely of academic significance. If the norms possess customary law character, they represent general international law and apply even to non-state parties. Here, a distinction must be made: Where the rules of the ICC Statute can be attributed to preexisting customary international law, it may be assumed that they are declaratory determinations; this reflects the will of the contracting parties. The provisions involved are mainly the definitions of crimes and various aspects of general principles. Here the Statute's rules are evidence of what the parties believed to be customary international law. On the other hand, where there are no examples in customary international law, the Statute has a law-creating character; this is especially the case for the provisions on procedure. Furthermore, the provisions directly affecting the jurisdiction and organization of the International Criminal Court are also constitutive.

2. The ICTY and ICTR Statutes

142 The Statutes of the Yugoslavia and Rwanda Tribunals are bodies of rules determined by the UN Security Council, not by international treaties. They claim to embody customary international law, though they do not entirely live up to this claim. The Statutes' primary significance is naturally their function as the basis of judicial decisions in both *ad hoc* Tribunals. In addition, however, they can be viewed as determinations of customary international law, that is, as an expression of *opinio juris* on the part of the members of the UN Security Council.

143 *The Agreement between the United Nations and the Government of Sierra Leone on the Establishment of a Special Court for Sierra Leone* is a bilateral treaty with international criminal law as its subject.[271] In its content, the agreement – like the ICC Statute – can be classified partly as a confirmation of customary international law[272] and partly as original treaty-based law.

3. The Nuremberg and Tokyo Charters

144 To the extent they involved substantive international criminal law, the provisions of the Statutes of the International Military Tribunal at Nuremberg and the International Mili-

---

[270] The fact that it is not unusual for an international treaty to adopt customary-law norms, along with additional rules, is exemplified by the Hague Conventions of 1899 and 1907 and the Geneva Conventions of 1949. See A. Verdross and B. Simma, *Universelles Völkerrecht*, 3rd edn. (1984), §§ 589 et seq.

[271] UN-Doc. S/2000/915, Annex I.

[272] Here, too, this is mainly true for the definitions of crimes; see the *Report of the Secretary-General on the Establishment of a Special Court for Sierra Leone* of 4 October 2000, UN Doc. S/2000/915, 3: "In recognition of the principle of legality . . . the international crimes enumerated, are crimes considered to have had the character of customary international law at the time of the alleged commission of the crime." But see A. McDonald, 84 *International Review of the Red Cross* (2002), pp. 121 et seq.

tary Tribunal for the Far East embodied norms of customary international law (the Nuremberg Principles).[273]

Unlike the Tokyo Charter, one-sidedly imposed by the occupation authorities, the Nuremberg **145** Charter appended to the London Agreement was part of an international treaty.[274] This classification of the rules in the Nuremberg Charter as international treaty law is separate from the controversial question whether the fact that Germany was not included among the parties to the treaty rendered the International Military Tribunal merely an "occupation" court rather than a truly "international" court.[275]

4. Control Council Law No. 10

Control Council Law No. 10 was occupation law.[276] Nevertheless, its provisions, to the **146** extent they involve substantive international criminal law, are recognized as an expression of customary law.[277]

5. Geneva Conventions, Genocide Convention, Hague Regulations

The relevant provisions of the Hague Regulations of 18 October 1907, the Genocide **147** Convention of 9 December 1948, and the Geneva Conventions of 12 August 1949, including their Additional Protocols, are also important sources of international criminal law. Numerous penal norms contained in these treaties, for example in the Genocide Convention, are recognized today as customary international law.[278]

6. Decisions of International Courts and Tribunals

The decisions of international courts have left a lasting impression on the shape of exist- **148** ing international criminal law.[279] These especially include the decisions of the International Military Tribunal at Nuremberg, the International Military Tribunal for the Far

---

[273] The Yugoslavia Tribunal cites to the IMT Charter and the Tokyo Charter as "relevant practice," see *Prosecutor* v. *Tadić*, ICTY (Appeals Chamber), judgment of 15 July 1999, paras. 288 et seq.; *Prosecutor* v. *Furundžija*, ICTY (Trial Chamber), judgment of 10 December 1998, paras. 190 et seq. See also H.-H. Jescheck, *Die Verantwortlichkeit der Staatsorgane nach Völkerstrafrecht* (1952), p. 415. In the opinion of the Yugoslavia Tribunal, the Statute of the International Military Tribunal and CCL No. 10 are "treaty provisions which are at the very origin of the customary process," see *Prosecutor* v. *Tadić*, ICTY (Appeals Chamber), judgment of 15 July 1999, para. 290.

[274] See marginal no. 15.

[275] See fn. 31 in marginal no. 17.

[276] See H.-H. Jescheck, *Die Verantwortlichkeit der Staatsorgane nach Völkerstrafrecht* (1952), p. 178.

[277] See *Prosecutor* v. *Tadić*, ICTY (Appeals Chamber), judgment of 15 July 1999, paras. 288 et seq.; *Prosecutor* v. *Furundžija*, ICTY (Trial Chamber), judgment of 10 December 1998, paras. 190 et seq.

[278] See marginal no. 562.

[279] This is also emphasized in A. Cassese, *International Criminal Law* (2003), pp. 36 et seq. The decisions of the currently active tribunals may be accessed in their entirety on the Internet, see <http://www.un.org/law/icc>; <http://www.un.org/icty>; <http://www.ictr.org>.

East, and the Yugoslavia and Rwanda Tribunals. The decisions of these Courts are important means of determining international law.[280]

149 The extent to which courts are bound by their own decisions varies. The International Criminal Court can base its decisions on "principles and rules of law as interpreted in its previous decisions,"[281] but it is not required to do so. The Tribunals for Yugoslavia and Rwanda are bound more strongly by precedent. The Appeals Chamber of the Yugoslavia Tribunal has determined that "[in] the interests of certainty and predictability, the Appeals Chamber should follow its previous decisions, but should be free to depart from them for cogent reasons in the interest of justice."[282] The chamber was assuming a tendency among courts in all legal systems not to deviate, where possible, from their own earlier decisions.[283] As a rule, therefore, the Appeals Chamber will follow the *ratio decidendi* of its own earlier decisions. But the decisions of the Appeals Chamber are binding on the Trial Chambers.[284] These, in turn, are not bound by the decisions of the other Trial Chambers.[285] The decisions of other international courts, such as the International Military Tribunal at Nuremberg[286] or the International Court of Justice,[287] have no binding effect on the Yugoslavia and Rwanda Tribunals.

7. Resolutions of the UN General Assembly and the UN Security Council, and Reports of the UN Secretary-General

150 Decisions by international organizations express the *opinio juris* of the participating states and thus contribute to the emergence and confirmation of customary international law.[288] Resolution 95 of 11 December 1946, in which the UN General Assembly affirmed the Nuremberg Principles, is an important example.[289] Security Council resolutions are also expressions of its members' *opinio juris*. For international criminal law, the ICTY and ICTR Statutes, adopted by the UN Security Council, are particularly noteworthy. The statements of various members in connection with the adoption of the ICTY Statute, in the *travaux preparatoires*, can be consulted in interpreting the Statute's provisions.[290]

---

[280] See K. Ambos, *Der Allgemeine Teil des Völkerstrafrechts* (2002), p. 48; B.B. Jia, in S. Yee and W. Tieya (eds.), *International Law in the Post-Cold War World* (2001), p. 77 at pp. 93 et seq.; C. Kress, 111 *Zeitschrift für die gesamte Strafrechtswissenschaft* (1999), p. 597 at p. 603.

[281] ICC Statute Art. 21(2).

[282] *Prosecutor v. Aleksovski*, ICTY (Appeals Chamber), judgment of 24 March 2000, para. 107. See A. Cassese, *International Criminal Law* (2003), p. 37.

[283] *Prosecutor v. Aleksovski*, ICTY (Appeals Chamber), judgment of 24 March 2000, para. 97: "a general trend in both the common law and civil law systems, whereby the highest courts, whether as a matter of doctrine or of practice, will normally follow their previous decisions."

[284] *Prosecutor v. Aleksovski*, ICTY (Appeals Chamber), judgment of 24 March 2000, para. 113.

[285] *Prosecutor v. Aleksovski*, ICTY (Appeals Chamber), judgment of 24 March 2000, para. 113; *Prosecutor v. Kordić and Čerkez*, ICTY (Trial Chamber), judgment of 26 February 2001, para. 163.

[286] *Prosecutor v. Kupreškić* et al., ICTY (Trial Chamber), judgment of 14 January 2000, para. 540.

[287] *Prosecutor v. Mucić* et al., ICTY (Appeals Chamber), judgment of 20 February 2001, para. 24: "Although the Appeals Chamber will necessarily take into consideration other decisions of international courts, it may, after careful consideration, come to a different conclusion."

[288] See marginal no. 129.

[289] See fn. 65 to marginal no. 41.

[290] See *Prosecutor v. Tadić*, ICTY (Appeals Chamber), judgment of 15 July 1999, para. 303; *Prosecutor v. Mucić* et al., ICTY (Appeals Chamber), judgment of 20 February 2001, para. 131.

Furthermore, reports of the UN Secretary-General connected with the creation of the **151**
ad hoc Tribunals[291] are to be considered authentic interpretations in applying their Statutes, as long as they do not contradict the Statutes' provisions.[292]

8. International Law Commission Drafts and Comments

The reports and drafts of the United Nations International Law Commission[293] are aids **152**
in determining customary international law and general principles of law, and thus have
significant influence on the development of international criminal law. The various revisions of the *Draft Codes of Crimes against the Peace and Security of Mankind* have proved
particularly influential for substantive international criminal law. In the words of the Yugoslavia Tribunal, this is

"an authoritative international instrument which, depending upon the specific question at issue,
may (i) constitute evidence of customary law, or (ii) shed light on customary rules which are of
uncertain contents or are in the process of formation, or, at the very least, (iii) be indicative of the
legal views of eminently qualified publicists representing the major legal systems of the world."[294]

9. Drafts and Comments of International Scholarly Associations

Another important aid in determining the law is the work of private scholarly associa- **153**
tions in the fields of international and criminal law, such as the Association International
de Droit Pénal, the International Law Association, and the Institut de Droit International.

10. Decisions of National Courts

The function of national courts in determining international criminal law is twofold. **154**
First, as expressions of *opinio juris* and as state practice, they may confirm or create customary law and contribute to the formation of general principles of law. Second, national court decisions can serve as aids in recognizing law, helping to determine the
content of norms of international criminal law.[295]

Most important for the emergence of norms of international criminal law are the rare **155**
criminal trials by national courts that explicitly refer to international criminal law. Note-

---

[291] See, e.g., *Report of the Secretary-General* of 3 May 1993 (UN Doc. S/25704) and *Report of the
Secretary-General* of 4 October 2000 (UN Doc. S/2000/915); see also marginal no. 47.

[292] For details, see *Prosecutor* v. *Tadić*, ICTY (Appeals Chamber), judgment of 15 July 1999,
paras. 294 et seq. ("authoritative interpretation").

[293] On the mandate of the International Law Commission, see fn. 66 to marginal no. 41.

[294] *Prosecutor* v. *Furundžija*, ICTY (Trial Chamber), judgment of 10 December 1998, para. 227;
the remarks refer concretely to the *Draft Code* 1996.

[295] See *Prosecutor* v. *Furundžija*, ICTY (Trial Chamber), judgment of 10 December 1998,
paras. 190 et seq. However, the Court does note that "one should constantly be mindful of the need
for great caution in using national case law for the purpose of determining whether customary rules of
international criminal law have evolved in a particular matter." (para. 194).

worthy, among others, were the decisions by occupation courts and the Supreme Court in the British Occupied Zone in the immediate post-war period on the basis of CCL No. 10.[296] The later trials of *Eichmann, Barbie, Demjanjuk, Touvier* and *Finta* should also be noted.[297]

11. National Legislation

156   National legislative acts can also influence international criminal law as expressions of *opinio juris* as well as state practice – for example, in the form of an adoption of international penal norms as part of national law, such as the (German) Code of Crimes Against International Law [*Völkerstrafgesetzbuch,* VStGB] of 26 June 2002.[298]

12. Military Manuals

157   In the field of international criminal law, the military manuals used in many countries are important expressions of *opinio juris* as well as state practice.[299]

IV. Interpretation

158   The application of international treaty law always requires interpretation of the provisions to be applied. To this extent, international law is no different from statutory law in domestic legal systems. The core requirements for the interpretation of international treaties are contained in Articles 31 and 32 of the *Vienna Convention on the Law of Treaties* of 23 May 1969.[300] As expressions of customary law,[301] these rules of interpretation

---

[296] See marginal nos. 34 et seq.

[297] The subjects of these trials were crimes committed during the Third Reich: *Attorney-General of the Government of Israel* v. *Eichmann*, Israel, District Court of Jerusalem, judgment of 12 December 1961, in 36 *ILR* (1968), pp. 1 et seq., Supreme Court, judgment of 29 May 1962, in 36 *ILR* (1968), pp. 277 et seq.; *Fédération National des Déportés et Internés Résistants et al.* v. *Barbie*, France, Cour de Cassation, judgment of 6 October 1983, judgment of 26 January 1984, judgment of 20 December 1985 in 78 *ILR* (1988), pp. 125 et seq., Cour de Cassation, judgment of 3 June 1988 in 100 *ILR* (1995), pp. 330 et seq.; *Petrovsky* v. *Demjanjuk*, USA, Court of Appeals, decision of 31 October 1983 in 79 *ILR* (1989), pp. 534 et seq.; *Advocate General* v. *Touvier*, France, Cour d'Appel de Paris, judgment of 13 April 1992 in 100 *ILR* (1995), pp. 338 et seq., Cour de Cassation, judgment of 27 November 1992 in 100 *ILR* (1995), pp. 357 et seq.; *Regina* v. *Finta*, Canada, Ontario Court of Appeal, judgment of 29 April 1992 in 98 *ILR* (1994), pp. 520 et seq., Canada, Supreme Court, judgment of 24 March 1994 in 104 *ILR* (1997), pp. 284 et seq.

[298] See *Prosecutor* v. *Tadić*, ICTY (Appeals Chamber), decision of 2 October 1995, para. 132: "Attention should also be drawn to national legislation designed to implement the Geneva Conventions."

[299] See *Prosecutor* v. *Tadić*, ICTY (Appeals Chamber), decision of 2 October 1995, para. 83 ("German Military Manual"), paras. 130 et seq. On the legally binding nature of such military manuals, see L. Green, 27 *Canadian Yearbook of International Law* (1989), p. 167 at pp. 180 et seq.

[300] 1155 *UNTS* (1969), pp. 331 et seq. Art. 31: "1. A treaty shall be interpreted in good faith in accordance with the ordinary meaning to be given to the terms of the treaty in their context and in the light of its object and purpose. 2. The context for the purpose of the interpretation of a treaty shall comprise, in addition to the text, including its preamble and annexes: a) any agreement relating to the treaty which was made between all the parties in connection with the conclusion of the treaty; b) any

must be applied in interpreting not only the ICC Statute, but "any other norm-creating instrument,"[302] including the ICTY and ICTR Statutes.[303]

Accordingly, the classic[304] interpretive methods essentially also apply to international criminal **159** law.[305] The starting point for interpretation is the wording, that is, the "ordinary meaning." The systematic context must be considered; that is, other agreements or accords between the parties to the treaty, as well as the aim and purpose of the treaty rules and the treaty generally (Article 32 of the *Vienna Convention of the Law of Treaties*). In interpreting the ICC Statute, for example, the Elements of Crimes must be taken into account. Historical interpretation – that is, inclusion of the materials from negotiations, which are typically quite substantial in international law – is classed as a "supplementary means of interpretation" that is subsidiary to grammatical, teleological and systematic interpretation (Article 32 of the *Vienna Convention of the Law of Treaties*). It takes on independent significance only if other means of interpretation lead to an ambiguous or manifestly absurd or unreasonable result.

In addition to the more general interpretive criterion of *effet utile*, interpretation in light **160** of the purpose of the treaty and its furtherance,[306] international criminal law has two additional specific rules of interpretation: first, treaty provisions, to the extent they can be ascribed to a norm of customary law, are to be interpreted according to this corresponding norm of customary law (so-called interpretation in conformity with customary law).[307] In the words of the Yugoslavia Tribunal, "[i]n case of doubt and whenever the contrary is not apparent from the text of a statutory or treaty provision, such a provision must be interpreted in light of, and in conformity with, customary international law."[308]

Second, it is most important for war crimes law to take account of the prohibitions in **161** international law to which a penal norm can be ascribed. International humanitarian law

---

instrument which was made by one or more parties in connection with the conclusion of the treaty and accepted by the other parties as an instrument related to the treaty. . . . "; Art. 32: "Recourse may be had to supplementary means of interpretation, including the preparatory work of the treaty and the circumstances of its conclusion, in order to confirm the meaning resulting from the application of article 31, or to determine the meaning when the interpretation according to article 31: a) leaves the meaning ambiguous or obscure; or b) leads to a result which is manifestly absurd or unreasonable."

[301] On the significance of customary law, see *Iran* v. *USA*, ICJ, judgment of 12 December 1996 (Case Concerning Oil Platforms) *ICJ Rep.* 1996, p. 803 para. 23.

[302] *Prosecutor* v. *Tadić*, ICTY (Appeals Chamber), judgment of 15 July 1999, para. 303. K. Kittichaisaree, *International Criminal Law* (2001), p. 46.

[303] See, e.g., *Prosecutor* v. *Aleksovski*, ICTY (Appeals Chamber), judgment of 24 February 2000, para. 98; A. Cassese, *International Criminal Law* (2003), pp. 26 et seq.

[304] See H.-H. Jescheck and T. Weigend, *Lehrbuch des Strafrechts*, 5th edn. (1996), pp. 150 et seq.; W.R. LaFave, *Criminal Law*, 4th edn. (2003), pp. 85 et seq.

[305] Thus, for example, *Prosecutor* v. *Tadić*, ICTY (Appeals Chamber), decision of 2 October 1995, paras. 71 et seq., distinguishes between the "literal," "teleological," and "logical and systematic interpretation." *Prosecutor* v. *Mucić*, ICTY (Trial Chamber), judgment of 16 November 1998, paras. 158 et seq., uses the "literal rule," the "golden rule," and the "mischief rule of interpretation."

[306] See V. Herdegen, *Völkerrecht* (2000), § 15 marginal no. 32.

[307] See also K. Kittichaisaree, *International Criminal Law* (2001), p. 45.

[308] *Prosecutor* v. *Tadić*, ICTY (Appeals Chamber), judgment of 15 July 1999, para. 287. The authors of the ICTY Statute intended to remain within the framework of customary international law wherever they did not explicitly deviate from it. See *Prosecutor* v. *Tadić*, ICTY (Appeals Chamber), judgment of 15 July 1999, paras. 287, 296; K. Kittichaisaree, *International Criminal Law* (2001), p. 45.

and its prohibitions are relevant in interpreting war crimes law. Other aspects of international law, such as human rights law, may be relevant to other crimes.[309]

162 The linkage between prohibitions and penal norms is not always equally close. Whereas for crimes against humanity, the connections to the human rights on which they are based are only vaguely discernable, in the area of war crimes the close connection to international humanitarian law is obvious: many of the crimes (and the resulting prohibitions) have long been elements of positive law. Only the criminal consequences have been added.[310]

163 While interpretation is the challenge where treaty law is concerned, the difficulty in applying (unwritten) customary international law lies first of all in actually identifying the legal norms as such.[311]

V. Determining the Law Through the International Criminal Court

164 Article 21 of the ICC Statute makes special provision for determining the law through the International Criminal Court. This article establishes the type and order of priority of the sources to be applied by the Court.[312] Article 21 brings the legal sources of general international law into a hierarchy and adds some precision.[313]

165 Article 21 contains a dual hierarchy. First, in its instructions for application, it distinguishes between what "shall" (1) and what "may" (2) be used. Second, within Subsection 1, three groups of legal sources are listed according to rank. Finally, a general rule for interpretation and application is found in Subsection 3.

166 The main source of law according to Article 21 is the ICC Statute itself, supplemented by the Elements of Crimes and the Rules of Procedure and Evidence.[314] As ad-

---

[309] The close connection between international criminal law and protection of human rights (see marginal nos. 109 et seq.) is confirmed, though with slightly different nuance, in Art. 21(3) of the ICC Statute. It provides that the application and interpretation of international criminal law (or more precisely, "law pursuant to this article") "must be consistent with internationally recognized human rights." This provision is especially significant for the rights of the defendant, see W.A. Schabas, *Introduction to the International Criminal Court* (2001), p. 74.

[310] For details, see marginal nos. 504 et seq.

[311] The customary norm is also subject to interpretation, see U. Fastenrath, *Lücken im Völkerrecht* (1991), pp. 206 et seq., with additional notes.

[312] On its origins, see P. Saland, in R.S. Lee (ed.), *The International Criminal Court, The Making of the Rome Statute* (1999), p. 189 at pp. 213 et seq. However, whether Art. 21 of the ICC Statute embodies customary international law in the same way as Art. 38 of the ICJ Statute, that is, contains authoritative rules for international criminal law in general, is questionable. Taking this view, however, see M. McAuliffe de Guzman, in O. Triffterer (ed.), *Commentary on the Rome Statute of the International Criminal Court* (1999), Art. 21, marginal no. 6: "first codification of the sources of international *criminal law*." According to A. Cassese, *International Criminal Law* (2003), p. 26, the order of sources established in Art. 21 of the ICC Statute reflects the hierarchy that applies to international criminal law generally.

[313] See A. Pellet, in A. Cassese, P. Gaeta and J.R.W.D. Jones (eds.), *The Rome Statute of the International Criminal Court*, Vol. 2 (2002), p. 1051 at pp. 1076 et seq.

[314] The ICC Statute's primacy over the Elements of Crimes and the Rules of Procedure and Evidence does not, however, arise from Art. 21(1) of the ICC Statute, but from the overall context, see Art. 9(3) and Art. 51(5) of the ICC Statute; see also I. Caracciolo, in F. Lattanzi and W.A. Schabas

ditional sources, international criminal law is comprised of international treaties and other international law ("principles and rules of international law"),[315] including the law of armed conflict. Other international law in this sense includes primarily customary international law,[316] but not general principles of law.[317] Only in cases where the ICC Statute and other international treaty and customary law prove unhelpful ("Failing that") does Article 21(1)(c) also allow reference to national law. This occurs in the form of general principles of law "derived by the Court from national laws of legal systems of the world.[318] It particularly emphasizes laws of states that "would normally exercise jurisdiction over the crime."[319] A specification of which nations were meant,[320] contained in preliminary drafts, is lacking in the text of Article 21. Thus, according to generally recognized rules on criminal jurisdiction, the law of the state in which the crime occurred, as well as the laws of the states of residence of the perpetrator and victim, are to be drawn upon. Penal authority under the principle of universal jurisdiction is not sufficient.[321]

Article 21(2) of the ICC Statute clearly rejects the strict reliance on precedent (*stare decisis*) common to Anglo-American law. Under it, the Court *may*, but does not have to, rely on earlier decisions. Thus, decisions of the Court have no precedential effect in the strict sense.[322]   **167**

E. Universal Jurisdiction, the Duty to Prosecute, and Amnesty

Kai Ambos: *Straflosigkeit von Menschenrechtsverletzungen, Zur "impunidad" in südamerikanischen Ländern aus völkerstrafrechtlicher Sicht* (1997), pp. 161 et seq.; M. Cherif Bassiouni: Universal Jurisdiction for International Crimes: Historical Perspectives and Contemporary Practice, 42 *Vir-*   **168**

(eds.), *Essays on the Rome Statute of the International Criminal Court* (1999), p. 211 at p. 226; W.A. Schabas, *Introduction to the International Criminal Court* (2001), p. 72.

[315] The principles of international law referred to here must be distinguished from the "general principles of law recognized by all civilized nations" as meant by Art. 38(1)(c) of the ICJ Statute.

[316] See W.A. Schabas, *Introduction to the International Criminal Court* (2001), p. 73.

[317] Similarly, A. Pellet, in A. Cassese, P. Gaeta and J.R.W.D. Jones (eds.), *The Rome Statute of the International Criminal Court*, Vol. 2 (2002), p. 1051 at pp. 1071, 1073: "exclusively to customary international law," but see I. Caracciolo, in F. Lattanzi and W.A. Schabas (eds.), *Essays on the Rome Statute of the International Criminal Court* (1999), p. 211 at p. 227 and K. Ambos, *Der Allgemeine Teil des Völkerstrafrechts* (2002), p. 41, according to which general principles are contained in Art. 21(1)(b) of the ICC Statute.

[318] See M. McAuliffe de Guzman, in O. Triffterer (ed.), *Commentary on the Rome Statute of the International Criminal Court* (1999), Art. 21, marginal nos. 15 et seq. The significance of national law for ICC jurisprudence was a subject of great controversy at the plenipotentiary conference in Rome. See P. Saland, in R.S. Lee (ed.), *The International Criminal Court, The Making of the Rome Statute* (1999), p. 189 at pp. 213 et seq.

[319] The inconsistency with the postulated "general nature" of the principles created by this addition is a typical example of the compromise character of the ICC Statute, which has thus far existed at the expense of logical and systematic stringency.

[320] See M. McAuliffe de Guzman, in O. Triffterer (ed.), *Commentary on the Rome Statute of the International Criminal Court* (1999), Art. 21, marginal no. 19.

[321] Otherwise, any state would "normally" be authorized to prosecute, and Art. 21(1)(c) of the ICC Statute would come to nothing; thus M. McAuliffe de Guzman, in O. Triffterer (ed.), *Commentary on the Rome Statute of the International Criminal Court* (1999), Art. 21, marginal no. 19 is incorrect.

[322] On the binding nature of the decisions of the Yugoslavia Tribunal, see marginal no. 149.

ginia Journal of International Law (2001), pp. 81 et seq.; M. Cherif Bassiouni and Edward M. Wise: *Aut Dedere Aut Judicare, The Duty to Extradite or Prosecute in International Law* (1995); William Burke-White: Reframing Impunity: Applying Liberal International Law Theory to an Analysis of Amnesty Legislation, 42 *Harvard International Law Journal* (2001), pp. 467 et seq.; Antonio Cassese: *International Criminal Law* (2003), pp. 284 et seq.; John Dugard: Dealing with Crimes of a Past Regime. Is Amnesty still an Option?, 12 *Leiden Journal of International Law* (1999), pp. 1001 et seq.; Carla Edelenbos: Human Rights Violations: A Duty to Prosecute?, 7 *Leiden Journal of International Law* (1994), pp. 5 et seq.; Colleen Enache-Brown and Ari Fried: Universal Crime, Jurisdiction and Duty: The Obligation of Aut Dedere Aut Judicare in International Law, 43 *McGill Law Journal* (1998), pp. 613 et seq.; Albin Eser: National Jurisdiction over Extraterritorial Crimes within the Framework of International Complementarity, in Lal Chand Vohrah et al. (eds.), *Man's Inhumanity to Man* (2003), pp. 279 et seq.; Geoff Gilbert: *Transnational Fugitive Offenders in International Law, Extradition and Other Mechanisms* (1998), pp. 320 et seq.; Bernhardt Graefrath: Universal Jurisdiction and an International Criminal Court, 1 *European Journal of International Law* (1990), pp. 67 et seq.; International Law Association, Committee on International Human Rights Law and Practice: *Final Report on the Exercise of Universal Jurisdiction in Respect of Gross Human Rights Offences* (2000); Florian Jessberger: Von der Pflicht des Staates, Menschenrechtsverletzungen zu untersuchen, *Kritische Justiz* 1996, pp. 290 et seq.; Menno T. Kamminga: Lessons Learned from the Exercise of Universal Jurisdiction in Respect of Gross Human Rights Offenses, 23 *Human Rights Quarterly* (2001), pp. 940 et seq.; Claus Kress: Völkerstrafrecht und Weltrechtspflegeprinzip im Blickfeld des Internationalen Gerichtshofs, 114 *Zeitschrift für die gesamte Strafrechtswissenschaft* (2002), pp. 818 et seq.; Stephen Macedo (ed.): *Universal Jurisdiction* (2004); Diane F. Orentlicher: Settling Accounts: The Duty to Prosecute Human Rights Violations of a Prior Regime, 100 *Yale Law Journal* (1991), pp. 2537 et seq.; Keith Randall: Universal Jurisdiction under International Law, 66 *Texas Law Review* (1988), pp. 785 et seq.; Luc Reydams: *Universal Jurisdiction* (2002); Leila N. Sadat: International Criminal Law and Alternative Modes of Redress, in Andreas Zimmermann (ed.), *International Criminal Law and the Current Development of Public International Law* (2003), pp. 161 et seq.; Michael P. Scharf: The Amnesty Exception to the Jurisdiction of the International Criminal Court, 32 *Cornell International Law Journal* (1999), pp. 507 et seq.; Angelika Schlunck: *Amnesty versus Accountability, Third Party Intervention Dealing with Gross Human Rights Violations in Internal and International Conflicts* (2000); Christian Tomuschat: The Duty to Prosecute International Crimes Committed by Individuals, in Hans-Joachim Cremer et al. (eds.), *Festschrift für Steinberger* (2002), pp. 315 et seq.; Gerhard Werle: Alternativen zur Strafjustiz bei der Aufarbeitung von Systemunrecht – Die Amnestieverfahren der südafrikanischen Wahrheits- und Versöhnungskommission, in Hagen Hof and Martin Schulte (eds.), *Wirkungsforschung zum Recht*, Vol. III (2001), pp. 291 et seq.; Gerhard Werle: Neue Wege. Die südafrikanische Wahrheitskommission und die Aufarbeitung von schweren Menschenrechtsverletzungen, in Petra Bock and Edgar Wolfrum (eds.), *Umkämpfte Vergangenheit* (1999), pp. 269 et seq.; Rüdiger Wolfrum: The Decentralized Prosecution of International Offences Through National Courts, in Yoram Dinstein and Mala Tabory (eds.), *War Crimes in International Law* (1996), pp. 233 et seq.

I. Universal Jurisdiction and the Power to Prosecute and Punish

169   Crimes under international law are directed against the interests of the international community as a whole. It follows from this universal nature of international crimes that the international community is empowered to prosecute and punish these crimes, regardless of who committed them or against whom they were committed. Every legal system may defend itself with criminal sanctions against attacks on its elementary values.

Thus, as far as international law is concerned, the International Criminal Court could easily have **170** been equipped with worldwide jurisdiction on the basis of the principle of universal jurisdiction. But a proposal along these lines by the German delegation was unsuccessful at the Rome Conference.[323] Political rather than legal motives were decisive for the rejection of this proposal.

But it is not only the power to prosecute on the part of the international community as a **171** whole that arises from the nature of crimes under international law and their direct affiliation with the international legal order. Every country is allowed to prosecute criminals in all cases without restriction; it is not important where the conduct in question took place, who the victims were, or whether any other link[324] with the prosecuting state can be established.[325] The authority to punish derives here from the crime itself ("criminal jurisdiction is based solely on the nature of the crime"[326]). The effects of acts directed against the most important interests of the community of nations are by definition not limited to the domestic realm of the state where the crime was committed. International crimes are not domestic matters. As regards the prosecution of international crimes, the limits international law sets on the expansion of national criminal jurisdiction, particularly the prohibition on interference, are not affected. Thus, the principle of universal jurisdiction applies to crimes under international law.[327]

---

[323] See S.A. Williams, in O. Triffterer (ed.), *Commentary on the Rome Statute of the International Criminal Court* (1999), Art. 12, marginal nos. 6 et seq.; see also marginal no. 64.

[324] Universal jurisdiction does not require that the perpetrator be in the custody of the state exercising jurisdiction. On this controversial question, see C. Kress, 114 *Zeitschrift für die gesamte Strafrechtswissenschaft* (2002), p. 818 at pp. 840 et seq., analyzing the separate opinions in *DR Congo* v. *Belgium*, ICJ, judgment of 14 February 2002 (Case Concerning the Arrest Warrant of 11 April 2000).

[325] See, e.g., the contributions in S. Macedo (ed.), *Universal Jurisdiction* (2004), pp. 39 et seq.; A. Cassese, *International Criminal Law* (2003), p. 284; G. de La Pradelle, in H. Ascensio, E. Decaux and A. Pellet (eds.), *Droit International Pénal* (2000), pp. 905 et seq.; C. Kress, 30 *Israel Yearbook on Human Rights* (2001), p. 103 at p. 168; International Law Association, *Final Report* (2000), pp. 2 et seq.; G. Werle and F. Jessberger, *Juristische Schulung* 2001, p. 141 at p. 142; for discussion of the foundations of universal jurisdiction, see M.C. Bassiouni, 42 *Virginia Journal of International Law* (2001), p. 81 at pp. 96 et seq. In its decision of 2 October 1995 the Appeals Chamber of the ICTY approvingly cited a decision of the Italian Supreme Military Tribunal: "Norms prohibiting them [crimes against the laws and customs of war] have a universal character, not simply a territorial one. [Crimes against the laws and customs of war] concern all civilised states, and are to be opposed and punished, in the same way as the crimes of piracy, trade of women or minors and enslavement are to be opposed and punished, wherever they may have been committed." See *Prosecutor* v. *Tadić*, ICTY (Appeals Chamber), decision of 2 October 1995, para. 57. The International Court of Justice did not take advantage of the opportunity to express an opinion on the validity of universal jurisdiction, see DR *Congo* v. *Belgium*, ICJ, judgment of 14 February 2002 (Case Concerning the Arrest Warrant of 11 April 2000). But comments are found in the separate opinions; for discussion, see C. Kress, 114 *Zeitschrift für die gesamte Strafrechtswissenschaft* (2002), pp. 818 et seq.

[326] ". . . without regard to where the crime was committed, the nationality of the alleged or convicted perpetrator, the nationality of the victim, or any other connection to the state exercising such jurisdiction," as is correctly stated in Principle 1(1) of the *Princeton Principles on Universal Jurisdiction*, in S. Macedo (ed.), *Universal Jurisdiction* (2004), p. 21.

[327] It must be noted that the range of crimes that may be prosecuted under universal jurisdiction extends beyond crimes under international law. For example, worldwide authority has long been recognized under customary law to punish piracy and slave trade. Universal jurisdiction also applies to torture, see C.L. Blakesley, in M.C. Bassiouni (ed.), *International Criminal Law*, Vol. 2, 2nd edn. (1999), p. 33 at pp. 71 et seq.; D. Oehler, *Internationales Strafrecht*, 2nd edn. (1983), marginal nos. 878 et seq. In other words, universal jurisdiction applies to all crimes under international law, but

172   Essentially, the extent of national criminal jurisdiction is within each state's sovereign power to determine as a product of state authority . Each state is fundamentally free to establish the area of applicability and the scope of its own criminal law.[328] In doing so, states must abide by international obligations, which function in two main ways. On the one hand, the extension of national criminal jurisdiction is limited by international law, specifically by the prohibition on interference.[329] Under international law, the state may only extend its criminal jurisdiction to matters with which it can show some connection, for example through the site of the conduct in question, the nationality of the perpetrator or victim, or the protected interest involved.[330] On the other hand, it may be required to extend its national criminal jurisdiction – for example, because of an international duty to prosecute.[331]

173   Within this framework, the specific international obligations attached to national criminal jurisdiction may be more clearly defined in two steps. The first step is to determine the extent of national criminal jurisdiction for crimes under international law. In a second step, it must be asked if an additional duty exists to prosecute and punish international crimes. In this context, the admissibility of alternative models in dealing with crimes under international law must be determined.

174   The validity of the principle of universal jurisdiction under customary international law is generally acknowledged for genocide, war crimes in international armed conflicts, and crimes against humanity,[332] and is also accepted in regard to crimes in civil wars.[333] This

---

not all crimes to which universal jurisdiction applies are crimes under international law. For an overview, see M.C. Bassiouni, 42 *Virginia Journal of International Law* (2001), p. 81 at pp. 107 et seq.

[328] This has been recognized for national "jurisdiction to prescribe" since the decision of the Permanent Court of Justice in the Lotus case (*PCIJ Ser.* A, No. 10 (7 September 1927)): "It does not, however, follow that international law prohibits a State from exercising jurisdiction in its own territory, in respect of any case which relates to acts which have taken place abroad, and in which it cannot rely on some permissive rule of international law." "[A]ll that can be required of a State is that it should not overstep the limits which international law places upon its jurisdiction; within these limits, its title to exercise jurisdiction rests in its sovereignty." See also L. Reydams, *Universal Jurisdiction* (2002), pp. 11 et seq. and p. 21. But on more recent developments that call into question this international law position on the extent of national criminal jurisdiction, see C. Kress, 114 *Zeitschrift für die gesamte Strafrechtswissenschaft* (2002), p. 818 at pp. 831 et seq., citing to several separate opinions on the *DR Congo* v. *Belgium*, ICJ, judgment of 14 February 2002 (Case Concerning the Arrest Warrant of 11 April 2000).

[329] UN Charter, Art. 2(7).

[330] See D. Oehler, *Internationales Strafrecht*, 2nd edn. (1983), marginal nos. 111 et seq.

[331] See marginal nos. 177 et seq.

[332] See I. Brownlie, *Principles of Public International Law*, 6th edn. (2003), pp. 303 et seq. and p. 565; C. Kress, 114 *Zeitschrift für die gesamte Strafrechtswissenschaft* (2002), p. 818 at p. 836; C. Tomuschat, in H.J. Cremer et al. (eds.), *Festschrift für Steinberger* (2002), p. 315 at p. 340; G. Werle, 109 *Zeitschrift für die gesamte Strafrechtswissenschaft* (1997), p. 808 at p. 824; R. Wolfrum, in Y. Dinstein and M. Tabory (eds.), *War Crimes in International Law* (1996), p. 233 at pp. 237 et seq. See the overview of national laws in Amnesty International, *Universal Jurisdiction* (2001). The fact that the Genocide Convention explicitly grants jurisdiction to prosecute genocide only to "a competent tribunal of the State in the territory of which the act was committed" or "such international penal tribunal [to be created] as may have jurisdiction with respect to those Contracting Parties which shall have accepted its jurisdiction" (Genocide Convention, Art. VI) is not an obstacle to the customary-law application of the principle to genocide, see *Bosnia and Herzegovina* v. *Yugoslavia*, ICJ, judgment of 11 July 1996 (Application of the Convention on the Prevention and Punishment of the Crime of Genocide), *ICJ Rep.* 1996, p. 595, para. 31.

[333] Here doubts arise from the fact that the Geneva Conventions explicitly provide for universal jurisdiction only for war crimes in international armed conflict. But for applicability to civil wars un-

authorizes even third states – that is, states with no special connection to the crime – to prosecute these crimes. Some doubt exists where the crime of aggression is concerned.[334]

From a policy perspective, the application of the principle of universal jurisdiction is **175** welcome. Even after the creation of the International Criminal Court, after all, direct enforcement of international criminal law through international courts will remain the exception. The unrestricted applicability of universal jurisdiction raises the possibility of decentralized prosecution of international crimes by third states. This would create a comprehensive network of jurisdictional claims for international crimes and markedly improve the chances of ending widespread impunity for international crimes. Certain dangers, however, must not be ignored. For one, opening national legal systems to intervention from third states brings with it a significant potential for abuse.[335] For another, worldwide authority to prosecute will necessarily lead to a large number of competing prosecution claims.

Given the problems at least theoretically associated with universal jurisdiction (for example, forum **176** shopping), this is not the ideal solution; in a world in which impunity for international crimes remains the rule rather than the exception, however, such a situation should be seen as progress. From a policy perspective, the issue, for now, continues to be bringing those responsible to justice in the first place, rather than sensibly channeling competing national claims. The above-mentioned reservations are therefore not a reason to abandon universal jurisdiction, but they do argue caution in employing it.

II. The Duty to Prosecute

International law not only allows the international community and the states to pros- **177** ecute international crimes through universal jurisdiction, but even obligates them to do so under certain circumstances.

In the Preamble to the ICC Statute, the contracting parties emphasize that "the most **178** serious crimes of concern to the international community as a whole must not go unpunished and . . . their effective prosecution must be ensured by taking measures at the national level and by enhancing international cooperation." The parties recall that "it is the duty of every State to exercise its criminal jurisdiction over those responsible for international crimes," and underline their resolve "to these ends . . . to establish an independent permanent International Criminal Court."[336]

---

der customary law, see C. Kress, 30 *Israel Yearbook on Human Rights* (2001), p. 103 at pp. 169 et seq.; G. Werle 109 *Zeitschrift für die gesamte Strafrechtswissenschaft* (1997), p. 808 at pp. 818 et seq.

[334] See C. Tomuschat, in H.J. Cremer et al. (eds.), *Festschrift für Steinberger* (2002), p. 315 at pp. 341 et seq.

[335] See C. Tomuschat, in H.J. Cremer et al. (eds.), *Festschrift für Steinberger* (2002), p. 315 at p. 339 and p. 342. It has been suggested that, even for constellations that are today subject to universal jurisdiction, an additional link should be required with the forum state. A. Cassese, *International Criminal Law* (2003), pp. 289 et seq., also calls for restraint in the application of universal jurisdiction. See also N. Roth-Arriaza, 17 *Leiden Journal of International Law* (2004), pp. 375 et seq.

[336] ICC Statute, Preamble (4) and (6). This was already included in International Law Commission, *Principles of International Law Recognised in the Charter of the Nuremberg Tribunal and in the judgment of the Tribunal*, Principle I, *Yearbook of the International Law Commission* 1950 II, p. 364: "Crimes Against Humanity wherever they are committed, shall be subject to investigation and the per-

1. The Duty to Prosecute by the State of Commission

179 Customary international law today recognizes that the state in which a crime under international law is committed has a duty to prosecute.[337] This duty also exists under treaty law for genocide and war crimes in international armed conflicts.[338]

180 The "grave breaches" provisions of the Geneva Conventions obligate every state party to prosecute certain serious violations. The relevant acts include killing, serious bodily injury or unlawful confinement if committed against "protected persons." These protected persons generally include only foreign nationals. But Common Article 3 of the Geneva Conventions also protects a state's own nationals in non-international armed conflicts, and thus essentially turns them into protected persons as well. Only this interpretation of the Conventions does justice to the development of human rights protection in internal armed conflicts since 1949. The grave breaches provisions of the Geneva Conventions thus also include the crimes in internal armed conflicts listed in Common Article 3 of the Conventions.[339]

181 An academic debate in the 1990s, triggered by a 1988 decision by the Inter-American Court of Human Rights,[340] was also useful in demonstrating duties to prosecute. The participants in this debate presumed the existence of an obligation to prosecute any serious violation of fundamental human rights.[341] The Inter-American Court had decided that a state has a legal duty to prevent human rights violations, seriously investigate evidence of such violations, identify those responsible, impose suitable penalties and ensure suitable restitution to the victims. Under this interpretation of human rights instruments, which has since been affirmed by the European Court of Human Rights and the

---

sons against whom there is evidence . . . shall be subject to tracing, arrest, trial and, if found guilty, to punishment."

[337] See C. Kress, 30 *Israel Yearbook on Human Rights* (2001), p. 103 at p. 163 fn. 237; N. Roht-Arriaza, in D. Shelton (ed.), *International Crimes, Peace and Human Rights* (2000), p. 77 at p. 78; C. Tomuschat, in H.J. Cremer et al. (eds.), *Festschrift für Steinberger* (2002), p. 315 at pp. 342 et seq.; see also A. Schlunck, *Amnesty versus Accountability* (2000), p. 27; O. Triffterer, in O. Triffterer (ed.), *Commentary on the Rome Statute of the International Criminal Court* (1999), Preamble, marginal no. 17.

[338] See Genocide Convention, Art. IV; Geneva Convention III, Art. 129 and Geneva Convention IV, Art. 146; in addition, there is a treaty-based duty to prosecute if the crime under international law is based on torture; this derives from Art. 7 of the Torture Convention. For details on this area, see M. Schmidt, *Externe Strafpflichten* (2002), pp. 136 et seq.; see also A. Cassese, *International Criminal Law* (2003), pp. 302 et seq.; A. Eser, in L.C. Vohrah et al. (eds.), *Man's Inhumanity to Man* (2003), pp. 279 et seq.; C. Kress, 30 *Israel Yearbook on Human Rights* (2001), p. 103 at p. 162; N. Roht-Arriaza, in N. Roht-Arriaza (ed.), *Impunity and Human Rights* (1995), pp. 24 et seq.; M.P. Scharf, 32 *Cornell International Law Journal* (1999), p. 507 at p. 526.

[339] See K. Ambos, *Neue Zeitschrift für Strafrecht* 1999, p. 226 at pp. 228 et seq.; O. Triffterer, in G. Hankel and G. Stuby (eds.), *Strafgerichte gegen Menschheitsverbrechen* (1995), p. 169 at p. 181; R. Wolfrum, in D. Fleck (ed.), *The Handbook of Humanitarian Law in Armed Conflicts* (1999), no. 425; left open by the (German) Federal Supreme Court [Bundesgerichtshof], judgment of 21 February 2001, *BGHSt* 46, p. 292 at p. 302.

[340] *Velázquez Rodríguez*, Inter-American Court of Human Rights, judgment of 29 July 1988, Series C No. 4.

[341] A standard work is D.F. Orentlicher, 100 *Yale Law Journal* (1991), pp. 2537 et seq. See also M.C. Bassiouni, *Crimes Against Humanity* (1992), p. 503; C. Edelenbos, 7 *Leiden Journal of International Law* (1994), pp. 5 et seq.

UN Human Rights Committee,[342] the duty to prosecute follows from the duty of states to guarantee human rights and ensure effective legal protection.[343] An important instrument for guaranteeing human rights is the criminalization of their violation. Therefore, in the interests of effective legal protection and the duty to guarantee human rights, the above-mentioned Conventions entail a duty to prosecute on the part of the state of commission, though it is limited *ratione personae* to the state parties.[344]

2. Do "Third States" Have a Duty to Prosecute?

The practical effect of the duty to prosecute on the part of the state of commission is **182** limited. Crimes under international law are typically state crimes; leaving it up to the state of commission to prosecute international crimes would often mean making the perpetrators their own judges. Therefore, the question whether and to what extent there exists a duty to prosecute on the part of third states is of supreme legal and practical relevance.

The principle of universal jurisdiction gives only the *authority* to prosecute. A far **183** broader *duty* to prosecute crimes under international law committed outside a state's own territory by foreign nationals (so-called mandatory universal jurisdiction)[345] has so far been universally recognized only for war crimes in international armed conflicts. The Geneva Conventions form the basis for this customary law principle; they provide that the contracting states must either prosecute "grave breaches" themselves, regardless of where, by whom, or against whom they are committed, or "hand such persons over for trial to another High Contracting Party concerned."[346] This rule aims at the most complete possible prosecution of serious violations. Any custodial state is obligated to try perpetrators itself or hand them over to a state that is willing to prosecute (*aut dedere aut judicare*).[347] There is a genuine right to choose between the two alternatives.[348] The cus-

---

[342] For details, and with cites to current case law, see C. Tomuschat, in H.J. Cremer et al. (eds.), *Festschrift für Steinberger* (2002), p. 315 at pp. 320 et seq.

[343] The bases are primarily the "respect and ensure" clauses in the human rights conventions (e.g., *European Convention on Human Rights and Fundamental Freedoms* of 4 November 1950 (*ETS* No. 5 (1950)), Art. 1) and the guarantees of effective legal protection (e.g., *European Convention on Human Rights and Fundamental Freedoms* of 4 November 1950, *ETS* No. 5 (1950), Art. 13); for details, see K. Ambos, *Straflosigkeit von Menschenrechtsverletzungen* (1997), pp. 163 et seq.; N. Roht-Arriaza, in N. Roht-Arriaza (ed.), *Impunity and Human Rights* (1995), p. 24 at pp. 29 et seq.; A. Schlunck, *Amnesty versus Accountability* (2000), pp. 39 et seq.

[344] For discussion of the corresponding duty to investigate violations of human rights, see F. Jessberger, *Kritische Justiz* 1996, p. 290 at pp. 293 et seq.

[345] On this concept, see C. Tomuschat, in H.J. Cremer et al. (eds.), *Festschrift für Steinberger* (2002), p. 315 at pp. 327 et seq. (what is meant is the case in which "States are . . . not only empowered, but also enjoined, to prosecute and try alleged offenders under their jurisdiction, no matter where the crime concerned was committed.").

[346] Geneva Convention IV, Art. 146. See G. Dahm, J. Delbrück and R. Wolfrum, *Völkerrecht*, Vol. I/3, 2nd edn. (2002), p. 1008.

[347] For discussion, see M.C. Bassiouni and E.M. Wise, *Aut Dedere Aut Judicare* (1995), which provides numerous international treaties that include this principle.

[348] See G. Gilbert, *Transnational Fugitive Offenders* (1998), pp. 322 et seq. ("genuine choice"). In the so-called Lockerbie Case, Libya argued in this spirit before the ICJ that the Montreal Convention

todial state is even obligated in this way if no specific connection exists between the custodial state and the crime other than the presence of the suspect. The scope of the Geneva Conventions' provisions on "grave breaches" correctly also includes crimes committed in civil wars.[349]

184   Whether a third state also has a customary law duty to prosecute for genocide and crimes against humanity remains in dispute.[350] In any case, there is no treaty-based requirement.[351] The ICC Statute purposely leaves open the question whether third states are obligated to prosecute international crimes under the principle of universal jurisdiction.[352]

185   The principle of *aut dedere aut judicare* was provided for in the International Law Commission drafts for all crimes against international law, with customary law limitations for the crime of aggression.[353]

186   However, the relevant rules in the draft were not accepted and are not reflected in the ICC Statute. From the Preamble it follows only that prosecution of international crimes must be ensured by "taking measures at the national level and by enhancing international cooperation" and that "it is the duty of every State to exercise its criminal jurisdiction over those responsible for international crimes." But this only reinforces the duty to punish crimes committed on a state's own territory.[354] On the other hand, the fact that the International Criminal Court does not have universal jurisdiction, because the states

---

allows the custodial state the choice between prosecuting and extraditing. The ICJ did not decide this question. (*Libyan Arab Jamahiriya* v. *United Kingdom*, ICJ, judgment of 14 April 1992 (Case Concerning Questions of Interpretation and Application of the 1971 Montreal Convention Arising from Aerial Incident at Lockerbie), *ICJ Rep.* 1992, p. 3 at pp. 6 et seq.).

[349] See G. Werle, 109 *Zeitschrift für die gesamte Strafrechtswissenschaft* (1997), p. 808 at pp. 818 et seq., with additional notes and marginal nos. 811 et seq.

[350] For arguments against the existence of a duty under customary international law, see J. Dugard, in A. Cassese, P. Gaeta and J.R.W.D. Jones (eds.), *The Rome Statute of the International Criminal Court*, Vol. 1 (2002), p. 693 at p. 698; G. Gilbert, *Transnational Fugitive Offenders* (1998), p. 322; C. Tomuschat, in H.J. Cremer et al. (eds.), *Festschrift für Steinberger* (2002), p. 315 at pp. 337 et seq. In contrast, M.C. Bassiouni argues that the principle of *aut dedere aut judicare* has become a part of customary international law and applies to all crimes under international law, see M.C. Bassiouni and E.M. Wise, *Aut Dedere Aut Judicare* (1995), p. 21 at p. 24; M.C. Bassiouni, 42 *Virginia Journal of International Law* (2001), p. 81 at pp. 148 et seq. For a similar argument, see C. Enache-Brown, 43 *McGill Law Journal* (1998), p. 613 at pp. 625 et seq.

[351] On the scope of the duty to prosecute under the Genocide Convention, see, e.g., C. Tomuschat, in H.J. Cremer et al. (eds.), *Festschrift für Steinberger* (2002), p. 315 at p. 332. See also A. Eser, in L.C. Vohrah et al. (eds.), *Man's Inhumanity to Man* (2003), p. 279 at pp. 281 et seq.

[352] See A. Eser, in L.C. Vohrah et al. (eds.), *Man's Inhumanity to Man* (2003), p. 279 at pp. 281 et seq.; C. Kress, 30 *Israel Yearbook on Human Rights* (2001), p. 103 at p. 163; T.N. Slade and R.S. Clark, in R.S. Lee (ed.), *The International Criminal Court, The Making of the Rome Statute* (1999), p. 421 at p. 427 ("delightfully ambiguous"); O. Triffterer, in O. Triffterer (ed.), *Commentary on the Rome Statute of the International Criminal Court* (1999), Preamble, marginal no. 17 ("deliberately left ambiguous").

[353] See *Draft Code* 1991, Art. 6(1): "A State in whose territory an individual alleged to have committed a crime against the peace and security of mankind is present shall either try or extradite him." See also *Draft Code* 1996, Art. 9.

[354] See O. Triffterer, in O. Triffterer (ed.), *Commentary on the Rome Statute of the International Criminal Court* (1999), Preamble, marginal no. 17.

were unable to agree to it, cannot be advanced as an argument against a third-state duty to prosecute.[355]

Nor can one derive a third-state duty to prosecute from human rights treaties.[356] This duty's ac- **187** cessorial relationship to the violated human right stands against it.[357] All that can be inferred for the duty of prosecution from the triad "human rights-duty of protection-duty to prosecute" is that the state, to the extent it must guarantee human rights, is also obligated to guard against the most serious violations of such rights through appropriate penal norms. But the duty to prosecute cannot extend further than the duty to protect, and the latter ends at the borders of territorial sovereignty. For this reason, all that can be derived from human rights treaties for serious violations of human rights is a duty to prosecute on the part of the state of commission.[358]

III. Amnesties and Truth Commissions

The scope of the duty to prosecute has great practical significance, especially because the **188** duty to prosecute implies a prohibition on amnesty. The decision not to punish crimes under international law is nevertheless a typical phenomenon in the transition from macrocriminal systems to systems based on the rule of law.

No clear position on this has yet emerged in international (criminal) law.[359] It is **189** certain, at least, that an across-the-board exemption from criminal responsibility is unacceptable, to the extent that international law creates a duty to prosecute and punish.[360] This means that general amnesties for crimes under international law are impermissible under customary international law.[361] As a result, an amnesty in

---

[355] But this is the argument in C. Tomuschat, in H.J. Cremer et al. (eds.), *Festschrift für Steinberger* (2002), p. 315 at p. 339: "Under these circumstances it would be highly contradictory to construe a duty of prosecution."

[356] For the arguments, see marginal no. 181.

[357] See C. Tomuschat, in H.J. Cremer et al. (eds.), *Festschrift für Steinberger* (2002), p. 315 at p. 326 ("secondary obligation"); F. Jessberger, *Kritische Justiz* 1996, p. 290 at p. 298 ("annex duty").

[358] C. Tomuschat makes this argument convincingly in H.J. Cremer et al. (eds.), *Festschrift für Steinberger* (2002), p. 315 at p. 326: "No State can assume the burden of ensuring enjoyment of human rights in the territory of other States."

[359] For details, see G. Dahm, J. Delbrück and R. Wolfrum, *Völkerrecht*, Vol. I/3, 2nd edn. (2002), pp. 1014 et seq.; J. Dugard, in A. Cassese, P. Gaeta and J.R.W.D. Jones (eds.), *The Rome Statute of the International Criminal Court*, Vol. 1 (2002), p. 693 at pp. 695 et seq. See also J.M. Kamatali, 16 *Leiden Journal of International Law* (2003), pp. 115 et seq.

[360] See C. Tomuschat, in H.J. Cremer et al. (eds.), *Festschrift für Steinberger* (2002), p. 315 at p. 344; see also L.N. Sadat, in A. Zimmermann (ed.), *International Criminal Law and the Current Development of Public International Law* (2003), pp. 161 et seq.; for a more cautious view, see A. Cassese, *International Criminal Law* (2003), pp. 313 et seq. Seen correctly, Art. 6(5) of Protocol Additional II ("At the end of hostilities, the authorities in power shall endeavour to grant the broadest possible amnesty to persons who have participated in the armed conflict . . . ") involves only freedom from punishment for legal military operations, see C. Tomuschat, in H.J. Cremer et al. (eds.), *Festschrift für Steinberger* (2002), p. 315 at p. 348.

[361] See International Law Association, *Final Report on the Exercise of Universal Jurisdiction in Respect of Gross Human Rights Offences* (2000), pp. 15 et seq.; see also Art. 10 of the *Statute of the Special Court for Sierra Leone*, UN Doc. S/2000/915, Annex: "An amnesty granted to any person falling within the jurisdiction of the Special Court in respect of [crimes against humanity, violations of common art. 3, other serious violations of international humanitarian law] shall not be a bar to prosecu-

contravention of international law does not prevent prosecution by third states.[362]

190   On the other hand, international (criminal) law cannot completely block an amnesty that is necessary to restore peace.[363]

191   As a matter of fact, refraining from punishing crimes under international law can be necessary in individual cases to restore domestic peace and make national reconciliation possible.[364] This is the case, for example, if a civil war can only be ended at the cost of forgoing punishment. In such situations, deciding not to punish can be legitimized from the point of view of necessity.[365] Here the difficulty lies in finding sustainable criteria for the permissibility of an amnesty.[366]

192   The relationship between prosecution, on the one hand, and amnesties and truth commissions, on the other, is not addressed in the ICC Statute.[367] Whether a domestic amnesty stands in the way of a case's admissibility before the International Criminal Court is in dispute.[368] One must correctly make a distinction here: a general amnesty for crimes under international law does not affect the admissibility of a case before the ICC, see Article 17(1)(b), (2)(a). In all other cases, especially a nation's assignment of the task of "dealing with history" to a truth commission, the admissibility of a case to the ICC must be considered on a case-by-case basis.

F. Enforcement

193   Heiko Ahlbrecht: *Geschichte der völkerrechtlichen Strafgerichtsbarkeit im 20. Jahrhundert, Unter besonderer Berücksichtigung der völkerrechtlichen Straftatbestände und der Bemühungen um einen*

---

tion." See Principle 7 of the *Princeton Principles on Universal Jurisdiction*, in S. Macedo (ed.), *Universal Jurisdiction* (2004), p. 22: "1. Amnesties are generally inconsistent with the obligation of states to provide accountability for [war crimes, crimes against peace, crimes against humanity, genocide]."

[362] Amnesties in conformity with international law, in contrast, must be respected by third states as well as by the international community – that is, by the ICC – as correctly noted in C. Tomuschat, in H.J. Cremer et al. (eds.), *Festschrift für Steinberger* (2002), p. 315 at p. 347.

[363] What is of interest here is not so much the effectiveness and "sociopolitical desirability" of alternative response mechanisms as the amount of leeway that international law leaves to the states.

[364] See, e.g., J. Dugard, 12 *Leiden Journal of International Law* (1999), pp. 1001 et seq.

[365] See G. Werle, in H. Hof and M. Schulte (eds.), *Wirkungsforschung zum Recht*, Vol. III (2001), p. 291 at pp. 302 et seq. and G. Werle, in P. Bock and E. Wolfrum (eds.), *Umkämpfte Vergangenheit* (1999), p. 269 at pp. 274 et seq.

[366] See suggestions in I. Gross, *Humanitäres Völkerrecht-Informationsschriften* 2001, p. 162 at pp. 168 et seq.; M.P. Scharf, 32 *Cornell International Law Journal* (1999), pp. 507 et seq.

[367] On the history of the negotiations, see J.T. Holmes, in R.S. Lee (ed.), *The International Criminal Court, The Making of the Rome Statute* (1999), p. 41 at pp. 52 et seq.; N. Roht-Arriaza, in D. Shelton (ed.), *International Crimes, Peace and Human Rights* (2000), p. 77 at pp. 79 et seq.; M.P. Scharf, 32 *Cornell International Law Journal* (1999), pp. 507 et seq.

[368] See M. Bennouna, in L.C. Vohrah et al. (eds.), *Man's Inhumanity to Man* (2003), pp. 127 et seq.; G. Hafner et al., 10 *European Journal of International Law* (1999), pp. 108 et seq.; D. Momtaz, 78 *Die Friedens-Warte* (2003), pp. 53 et seq.; Y. Naqvi, 85 *International Review of the Red Cross* (2003), pp. 583 et seq.; F. Orrego Vicuna, in L.C. Vohrah et al. (eds.), *Man's Inhumanity to Man* (2003), pp. 641 et seq.; M.C.W. Pinto, in L.C. Vohrah et al. (eds.), *Man's Inhumanity to Man* (2003), pp. 481 et seq.; W.A. Schabas, 25 *Human Rights Quarterly* (2003), pp. 1035 et seq.; R. Wedgwood, 10 *European Journal of International Law* (1999), p. 93 at p. 95; for a detailed discussion, see J. Dugard, in A. Cassese, P. Gaeta and J.R.W.D. Jones (eds.), *The Rome Statute of the International Criminal Court*, Vol. 1 (2002), p. 693 at pp. 700 et seq.; see also G. Dahm, J. Delbrück and R. Wolfrum, *Völkerrecht*, Vol. I/3, 2nd edn. (2002), pp. 1017 et seq.

Ständigen Internationalen Strafgerichtshof (1999), pp. 232 et seq.; Payam Akhavan: The International Criminal Tribunal for Rwanda: The Politics and Pragmatics of Punishment, 90 *American Journal of International Law* (1996), pp. 501 et seq.; M. Cherif Bassiouni: The Philosophy and Policy of International Criminal Justice, in Lal Chand Vohrah et al. (eds.), *Man's Inhumanity to Man* (2003), pp. 65 et seq.; M. Cherif Bassiouni and Peter Manikas: *The Law of the International Criminal Tribunal for the Former Yugoslavia* (1996), pp. 775 et seq.; Paolo Benvenuti: Complementarity of the International Criminal Court to National Jurisdictions, in Flavia Lattanzi and William A. Schabas (eds.), *Essays on the Rome Statute of the International Criminal Court* (1999), pp. 21 et seq.; Paolo Benvenuti: The Repression of Crimes Against Humanity, War Crimes, Genocide Through National Courts, 46 *Jus Rivista di Scienze Giuridiche* (1999), pp. 145 et seq.; Bartram S. Brown: Primacy or Complementarity: Reconciling the Jurisdiction of National Courts and International Criminal Tribunals, 23 *Yale Journal of International Law* (1998), pp. 383 et seq.; Aline Bruer-Schäfer: *Der Internationale Strafgerichtshof, Die Internationale Strafgerichtsbarkeit im Spannungsfeld von Recht und Politik* (2001), pp. 128 et seq.; Antonio Cassese: *International Criminal Law* (2003), pp. 348 et seq.; Antonio Cassese: On the Current Trend Towards Criminal Prosecution and Punishment of Breaches of International Humanitarian Law, 10 *European Journal of International Law* (1998), pp. 1 et seq.; Florian Jessberger: Prosecuting International Crimes in Domestic Courts: A Look Back Ahead, 11 *Finnish Yearbook of International Law* (2002), pp. 281 et seq.; Florian Jessberger and Cathleen Powell: Prosecuting Pinochets in South Africa – Implementing the Rome Statute of the International Criminal Court, in 14 *South African Journal of Criminal Justice* (2001), pp. 344 et seq.; Hans-Peter Kaul: Der Internationale Strafgerichtshof – Eine Bestandsaufnahme, 78 *Die Friedens-Warte* (2003), pp. 11 et seq.; Madeleine Morris: Complementarity and its Discontents: States, Victims, and the International Criminal Court, in Dinah Shelton (ed.), *International Crimes, Peace and Human Rights* (2000), pp. 177 et seq.; Herwig Roggemann: *Die Internationalen Strafgerichtshöfe*, 2nd edn. (1998); Leila N. Sadat: *The International Criminal Court and the Transformation of International Law* (2002), pp. 225 et seq.; Jeremy Sarkin: The Necessity and Challenges of Establishing a Truth and Reconciliation Commission in Rwanda, 21 *Human Rights Quarterly* (1999), pp. 767 et seq.; Jeremy Sarkin: Promoting Justice, Truth and Reconciliation in Transitional Societies: Evaluating Rwanda's Approach in the New Millenium of Using Community Based Gacaca Tribunals to Deal With the Past, in *International Law Forum* (2000), pp. 112 et seq.; William A. Schabas: *An Introduction to the International Criminal Court*, 2nd edn. (2004), pp. 67 et seq.; Christian Tomuschat: Das Statut von Rom für den Internationalen Strafgerichtshof, 73 *Die Friedens-Warte* (1998), pp. 335 et seq.; Otto Triffterer: Der ständige Internationale Strafgerichtshof – Anspruch und Wirklichkeit, in Karl Heinz Gössel and Otto Triffterer (eds.), *Gedächtnisschrift für Zipf* (1999), pp. 493 et seq.; Ruth Wedgwood: National Courts and the Prosecution of War Crimes, in Gabrielle Kirk McDonald and Olivia Swaak-Goldman (eds.), *Substantive and Procedural Aspects of International Criminal Law*, Vol. 1 (2000), pp. 393 et seq.; Thomas Weigend: Völkerstrafrecht – Grundsatzfragen und aktuelle Probleme, in Günter Kohlmann et al. (eds.), *Entwicklungen und Probleme des Strafrechts an der Schwelle zum 21. Jahrhundert* (2003), pp. 11 et seq.; Christine Van den Wyngaert: War Crimes, Genocide and Crimes Against Humanity – Are States Taking National Prosecutions Seriously?, in M. Cherif Bassiouni (ed.), *International Criminal Law*, Vol. 3, 2nd edn. (1999), pp. 227 et seq.

I. Direct and Indirect Enforcement

194

International criminal law distinguishes between mechanisms for direct and indirect enforcement.[369] This refers to the prosecution of crimes under international law by

---

[369] See M.C. Bassiouni, *International Criminal Law: A Draft International Criminal Code* (1980), p. 187; M.C. Bassiouni: The Philosophy and Policy of International Criminal Justice, in L.C. Vohrah

international courts, on the one hand, and by national courts, on the other.

195   Until recently, international criminal law was almost entirely dependent on indirect enforcement mechanisms. With no permanent international criminal court, prosecution of international crimes occurred, if at all, in national courts.[370] Where direct enforcement of international criminal law did occur, mainly through the International Military Tribunal and the *ad hoc* UN Tribunals, the Court's jurisdiction *ratione temporis, loci,* and *materiae* was limited.

196   With the entry into force of the ICC Statute on 1 July 2002 and the creation of the International Criminal Court, a permanent forum for direct enforcement of international criminal law stands at the ready. The Court was not, it is true, conceived of as a world criminal court with universal responsibility, but as an emergency, standby court.[371] Therefore, the indirect enforcement of international criminal law through national prosecution will continue to be of preeminent importance.

II. National and International Criminal Justice Systems

197 The parallel existence of direct and indirect enforcement mechanisms can lead to situations in which national and international courts simultaneously claim jurisdiction to prosecute. This relationship between national and international criminal justice systems can be regulated in various ways.[372]

198   The Nuremberg Charter regulated the jurisdiction of the International Military Tribunal according to the principle of exclusivity, as far as trials of the major German war criminals of World War II were concerned.[373] Jurisdiction was only granted to the country of commission for other perpetrators.[374] In contrast, the ICTY and ICTR Statutes accept the concurrent jurisdiction of national courts.[375] Collisions are resolved according to the principle that international courts take precedence: "The International Tribunal shall have primacy over national courts. At any stage of the procedure, the International

---

et al. (eds.), *Man's Inhumanity to Man* (2003), p. 65 at p. 69. See also F. Jessberger and C. Powell, 14 *South African Journal of Criminal Justice* (2001), p. 344 at pp. 347 et seq.; T. Weigend, in G. Kohlmann et al. (eds.), *Entwicklungen und Probleme des Strafrechts an der Schwelle zum 21. Jahrhundert* (2003), p. 11 at p. 12.

[370] See, e.g., the sobering conclusions in C. Van den Wyngaert, in M.C. Bassiouni (ed.), *International Criminal Law*, Vol. 3, 2nd edn. (1999), pp. 341 et seq.; R. Wedgwood, in G. Kirk McDonald and O. Swaak-Goldman (eds.), *Substantive and Procedural Aspects of International Criminal Law*, Vol. 1 (2000), p. 393 at p. 404; see also F. Jessberger, 12 *Finnish Yearbook of International Law* (2001), pp. 307 et seq., T. Weigend, in G. Kohlmann et al. (eds.), *Entwicklungen und Probleme des Strafrechts an der Schwelle zum 21. Jahrhundert* (2003), p. 11 at p. 12.

[371] For more detailed discussion, see marginal no. 199.

[372] See A. Cassese, *International Criminal Law* (2003), pp. 348 et seq. and O. Triffterer, in K.H. Gössel and O. Triffterer (eds.), *Gedächtnisschrift für Zipf* (1999), p. 493 at pp. 516 et seq. The largely unresolved issues surrounding the concurrent jurisdiction of various countries for prosecuting crimes against international law are particularly sensitive.

[373] See Art. 1 of the London Agreement: "major criminals whose offenses have no particular geographic location"; IMT Charter, Art. 6; for discussion, see marginal no. 17.

[374] See Art. 4 of the London Agreement.

[375] See ICTY Statute, Art. 9(1); ICTR Statute, Art. 8(1).

Tribunal may formally request national courts to defer to the competence of the International Tribunal . . .."[376]

The ICC Statute is guided by the realistic assessment that direct enforcement of international criminal law through international courts will continue to be the exception even after the creation of the International Criminal Court.[377] The Statute's Preamble emphasizes that, for "the most serious crimes of concern to the international community as a whole," effective prosecution must be "ensured by taking measures at the national level and by enhancing international cooperation"; at the same time, it recalls that it is each state's duty to "exercise its criminal jurisdiction over those responsible for international crimes."[378] For the relationship between international and national criminal justice, the Statute therefore applies the principle of complementarity in the sense of the subsidiarity of the International Criminal Court.[379] International jurisdiction does not replace national jurisdiction, even for core crimes, but simply supplements it. National jurisdiction takes precedence as a rule, unless the state is unwilling or unable genuinely to carry out the investigation or prosecution.[380] Whether these prerequisites exist in an individual case is determined exclusively by the International Criminal Court itself.[381] **199**

The main burden of enforcing international criminal law will in future rest not with the International Criminal Court and probably not with the countries of commission, but with third states willing to prosecute.[382] **200**

---

[376] ICTY Statute, Art. 9(2); the same wording is found in ICTR Statute Art. 8(2). A historical survey of the relationship between national and international criminal jurisdiction is found in P. Benvenuti, in F. Lattanzi and W.A. Schabas (eds.), *Essays on the Rome Statute of the International Criminal Court* (1999), p. 21 at pp. 35 et seq. For a discussion of the primacy of the UN Tribunals over national courts, see B.S. Brown, 23 *Yale Journal of International Law* (1998), p. 383 at pp. 394 et seq. But see for recent trends to the contrary M. Bohlander, 14 *Criminal Law Forum* (2003), pp. 59 et seq.

[377] The activity of the Rwanda Tribunal dramatically demonstrates the limits on the capacity of international criminal justice. Since the Tribunal's creation, it has completed only 11 trials; at the same time, over 120,000 suspects are being held in "investigative detention" in Rwandan jails. For discussion, see J. Sarkin, 21 *Human Rights Quarterly* (1999), pp. 767 et seq. See also A. Cassese, 9 *European Journal of International Law* (1998), pp. 1 et seq.; F. Jessberger and C. Powell, 14 *South African Journal of Criminal Justice* (2001), p. 344 at p. 347.

[378] ICC Statute, Preamble, (4) and (6); on the effects on national law, see D. Robinson, in A. Cassese, P. Gaeta and J.R.W.D. Jones (eds.), *The Rome Statute of the International Criminal Court*, Vol. 2 (2002), pp. 1849 et seq.

[379] See ICC Statute, Art. 1, sentence 2, clause 2; ICC Statute, Preamble (10); for discussion, see P. Benvenuti, in F. Lattanzi and W.A. Schabas (eds.), *Essays on the Rome Statute of the International Criminal Court* (1999), pp. 21 et seq.; J.T. Holmes, in A. Cassese, P. Gaeta and J.R.W.D. Jones (eds.), *The Rome Statute of the International Criminal Court*, Vol. 1 (2002), pp. 667 et seq.; M. Morris, in D. Shelton (ed.), *International Crimes, Peace and Human Rights* (2000), pp. 177 et seq.; O. Solera, 84 *International Review of the Red Cross* (2002), pp. 145 et seq.

[380] See ICC Statute, Art. 17.

[381] On this important limitation on the "primacy" of states, see O. Triffterer, in K.H. Gössel and O. Triffterer (eds.), *Gedächtnisschrift für Zipf* (1999), p. 493 at p. 517.

[382] For discussion, see, e.g., F. Jessberger and C. Powell, 14 *South African Journal of Criminal Justice* (2001), pp. 347 et seq.; P. Sands, 16 *Leiden Journal of International Law* (2003), pp. 40 et seq.

III. International Criminal Law in Action

1. The International Criminal Court

201 The International Criminal Court came into being on 1 July 2002, when the ICC Statute entered into force. On 11 March 2003, it took up operations in The Hague. The Court is responsible for trying genocide, crimes against humanity, and war crimes committed after 1 July 2002[383] on the territory of a state party[384] or by a citizen of a state party.[385] If situations in which it "appears" that such crimes have been committed are referred to the prosecutor by the UN Security Council under Chapter VII of the UN Charter, the Court has jurisdiction over the crimes regardless of the place of commission or the nationality of the perpetrator.[386]

202 The Security Council has already made use of its authority under Article 16 of the ICC Statute, based on Chapter VII of the UN Charter, to postpone prosecution by the International Criminal Court for a (renewable) period of 12 months. UN Security Council Resolution 1422, adopted at the initiative of the United States, requests that the Court, "if a case arises involving current or former officials or personnel from a contributing State not a Party to the Rome Statute over acts or omissions relating to a United Nations established or authorized operation, shall for a twelve-month period starting 1 July 2002 not commence or proceed with investigation or prosecution of any such case, unless the Security Council decides otherwise."[387] At the same time, in this resolution the Security Council announced its intention to extend the request for 12 months every 1 July. This was done for the first time on 12 June 2003 with Resolution 1487. In June 2004, the United States abandoned its efforts to extend the resolution for a second time due to strong opposition in the Security Council.

203 The Court consists of a presidency and registry, prosecutor's office, appeals division, trial division, and pretrial division.[388] The president of the Court is Philippe Kirsch of Canada, and the chief prosecutor is Luis Moreno Ocampo of Argentina. The two deputy prosecutors are Fatou Bensouda of Gambia and Serge Brammertz of Belgium. Eighteen judges have been elected to terms of between three and 9 years. In October 2004, the Court had a staff of 250, and its budget for 2005 is around € 67 million.

---

[383] For states that accede to the Statute after it enters into force, the crucial point is when the Statute goes into effect for the state.

[384] For an overview of the state parties, see fn. 120 to marginal no. 66.

[385] See ICC Statute, Arts. 5 to 8, 11, 12, and 13. The state parties are thus equal to states that have accepted the jurisdiction of the Court, under Art. 12(3) of the ICC Statute, in regard to a specific crime. The Court will not exercise the jurisdiction granted over the crime of aggression in Art. 5 until the requirements provided for in Art. 5(2) of the ICC Statute are fulfilled. Art. 26 of the ICC Statute provides that the Court has no jurisdiction over persons younger than 18 at the time of the alleged commission of the crime.

[386] See ICC Statute, Art. 13(b). For the legal nature of the ICC, see S.R. Lüder, 84 *International Review of the Red Cross* (2002), pp. 79 et seq., and K.S. Gallant, 16 *Leiden Journal of International Law* (2003), pp. 553 et seq.

[387] UN Doc. S/RES/1422 (2002); for discussion, see R. Lavalle, 14 *Criminal Law Forum* (2003), pp. 195 et seq.; J. Mayerfeld, 25 *Human Rights Quarterly* (2003), pp. 93 et seq.

[388] See ICC Statute, Art. 34. L.N. Sadat, *The International Criminal Court and the Transformation of International Law* (2002), pp. 286 et seq., is instructive on the function of the individual bodies.

A trial before the Court can begin in three ways (so-called trigger mechanisms).[389] Any **204** state party can refer a situation to the prosecutor in which it "appears" that a crime falling within the Court's jurisdiction has been committed.[390] The UN Security Council can do the same, through a resolution under Chapter VII of the UN Charter.[391] Finally, the prosecutor can begin an investigation on his own initiative. In the subsequent pretrial procedure, the validity of the charges is reviewed first by the prosecutor, then by the pretrial chamber; most importantly, decisions are made on the admissibility[392] of a case before the Court as well as on arrest measures and other sanctions.[393] In a type of intermediate procedure, the pretrial chamber must confirm the charges in the indictment.[394] This is followed by a public trial before the Trial Chamber.[395] The Trial Chamber may admit any evidence it considers necessary and can impose prison sentences; additionally, it may order a fine or forfeiture.[396] If need be, this is followed by an appeal. The sentence is executed on the territory of a state party to the treaty, to be determined by the Court.[397]

In June 2004, the chief prosecutor announced his decision to investigate crimes allegedly commit- **205** ted on the territory of the Democratic Republic of Congo, in particular in the Ituri region, since 1 July 2002. This investigation, the first by the International Criminal Court, resulted from a referral by the government of the Democratic Republic of Congo. In July 2004, the prosecutor determined that there was also a reasonable basis to open an investigation into the situation in northern Uganda. This announcement again followed a referral of the situation by Uganda in December 2003.

2. The Yugoslavia Tribunal

The Yugoslavia Tribunal was created on the basis of Security Council Resolution 827 **206** and is located in The Hague.[398] It has jurisdiction to prosecute war crimes, genocide, and crimes against humanity committed after 1 January 1991 on the territory of former Yugoslavia.[399] The main focus of the Tribunal's activity until now has been crimes committed in Bosnia and Herzegovina and Kosovo.

The Tribunal consists of a prosecutor's office, the chambers, and a registry.[400] The President of **207**

---

[389] On the trigger mechanism and the ICC Prosecutor, see A. Marston Danner, 97 *American Journal of International Law* (2003), pp. 510 et seq. See also C.K. Hall, 17 *Leiden Journal of International Law* (2004), pp. 121 et seq.

[390] See ICC Statute, Arts. 13(a), 14.

[391] See ICC Statute, Art. 13(b).

[392] See ICC Statute, Art. 17.

[393] For details, see ICC Statute, Arts. 53 et seq., and the ICC Rules of Procedure and Evidence. Summarized in A. Cassese, *International Criminal Law* (2003), pp. 416 et seq.; L.N. Sadat, *The International Criminal Court and the Transformation of International Law* (2002), pp. 294 et seq.

[394] See ICC Statute, Art. 61.

[395] See ICC Statute, Arts. 62 et seq.

[396] See ICC Statute, Art. 77.

[397] See ICC Statute, Arts. 103 et seq.

[398] See marginal nos. 48 et seq.

[399] See ICTY Statute, Arts. 1 to 8.

[400] See ICTY Statute, Art. 11.

the Tribunal is the American Theodor Meron. At present, 16 judges are active on the Tribunal, as well as nine so-called *ad litem* judges brought in for specific trials. The prosecutor's office has been headed since 1999 by Carla del Ponte of Switzerland. Important functions are carried out by the registry, headed by Hans Holthuis of the Netherlands. This Tribunal's administrative unit is responsible, among other things, for looking after witnesses, executing sentences, and organizing the defense. At present, the Tribunal has a staff of over 1,200 from more than 80 countries. Its budget for 2004-2005 is around $270 million.

208   The trial process is established in Articles 18 et seq. of the ICTY Statute and clarified in the ICTY Rules of Procedure and Evidence.[401] The prosecutor's office leads the investigation, issues indictments and represents the prosecution at trial. Following confirmation of the indictment in an intermediate procedure, the public trial takes place before a Trial Chamber; appeals are brought before the Appeals Chamber.[402]

209   A review of the Tribunal's activity more than ten years after its creation seems disappointing if one looks only at the number of proceedings and defendants. By spring 2005, 109 defendants had appeared in proceedings before the Tribunal; 5 defendants had been acquitted. Terms of imprisonment imposed at trial have ranged from three to 40 years. Fourteen people are serving prison sentences, among them Dusko Tadić in Germany.

210   A total of 82 people have been (publicly[403]) indicted. In most cases, the charge is war crimes or crimes against humanity. Fifty-one indictees are currently in custody in The Hague, the most prominent being former Yugoslav prime minister Slobodan Milošević. Seventeen indictees remain at large, including the former president of Republika Srpska, Radovan Karadžić. A look at the number of trial days shows how complicated and protracted trials before the Tribunal can be: the trials held so far have ranged from ten to 239 days (*Prosecutor* v. *Kordić and Čerkez*). The average number of trial days in domestic criminal trials is much lower. So far, 55 persons received Trial Chamber judgment, and 33 persons have received final sentence. A lack of co-operativeness, especially on the part of the Federal Republic of Yugoslavia, has often made obtaining evidence very difficult, and sometimes impossible.

3. The Rwanda Tribunal

211   The Rwanda Tribunal, created by UN Security Council Resolution 955 and based in Arusha, Tanzania, has jurisdiction over genocide, crimes against humanity, and violations of Common Article 3 and Additional Protocol II of the Geneva Conventions committed in Rwanda between 1 January and 31 December 1994. In addition, its jurisdiction extends to crimes committed by Rwandan citizens within this period but on the territory of neighboring states.[404]

---

[401] See ICTY Statute, Art. 15.

[402] See ICTY Statute, Art. 25.

[403] ICTY Rules of Procedure and Evidence, Rule 53, foresees the possibility of non-public indictment of a suspect, in the hopes of preventing suspects from going underground after becoming aware of an indictment.

[404] See ICTR Statute, Art. 1. See also H. Ahlbrecht, *Geschichte der völkerrechtlichen Strafgerichtsbarkeit im 20. Jahrhundert* (1999), pp. 302 et seq.; H. Roggemann, *Die Internationalen Strafgerichtshöfe*, 2nd edn. (1998), pp. 156 et seq.

The organization and procedure of the Tribunal resemble the model of the Yugoslavia Tribunal. **212** In addition, there are organizational connections between the two Tribunals.[405] At present, the Tribunal employs a staff of over 1042 from 85 countries, including 14 judges. In 2004-2005, it had a budget of around $255 million. The President is Erik Møse of Norway; the chief of the registry is Adama Dieng of Senegal. The chief prosecutor is Hassan Bubacar Jallow of Gambia.

One difference from the Yugoslavia Tribunal arises from the fact that large numbers of **213** trials relating to the 1994 crimes have been held in Rwanda itself.[406] Over 100,000 suspects still await trial in Rwandan jails. At first the Rwandan government strongly supported creation of the Tribunal, but the relationship has cooled greatly since then.

Indictments have so far been issued against 70 people, of which 63 are in the Court's **214** custody. Trials have been completed against 23 people; one defendant was finally acquitted by the Appeals Chamber. Of particular importance were the trial of John Paul Akayesu,[407] in which an international court for the first time found a defendant guilty of genocide, and the conviction of Rwanda's former prime minister, Jean Kambanda.[408]

G. Domestic Implementation

Bruce Broomhall: The International Criminal Court: A Checklist for National Implementation, **215** 13 *Nouvelles Études Pénales* (1999), pp. 148 et seq.; Douglass Cassel: The ICC's New Legal Landscape: The Need to Expand United States Domestic Jurisdiction to Prosecute Genocide, War Crimes, and Crimes Against Humanity, 23 *Fordham International Law Journal* (1999), pp. 378 et seq.; Antonio Cassese: On the Current Trend towards Criminal Prosecution and Punishment of Breaches of International Humanitarian Law, 9 *European Journal of International Law* (1998), pp. 1 et seq.; Katherine L. Doherty and Timothy L.H. McCormack: Complementarity as a Catalyst for Comprehensive Domestic Penal Legislation, 5 *UC Davis Journal of International Law and Policy* (1999), pp. 147 et seq.; John Dugard: *International Law – A South African Perspective*, 2nd edn. (2000); Florian Jessberger and Cathleen Powell, Prosecuting Pinochets in South Africa, Implementing the Rome Statute of the International Criminal Court, 14 *South African Journal of Criminal Justice* (2001), pp. 344 et seq.; Claus Kress: *Vom Nutzen eines deutschen Völkerstrafgesetzbuchs* (2000), pp. 18 et seq.; Claus Kress and Flavia Lattanzi (eds.): *The Rome Statute and Domestic Legal Orders*, Vol. 1 (2000); Matthias Neuner (ed.): *National Codes on International Crimes* (2003); Kimmo Nuotio: Transforming International Law and Obligations into Finnish Criminal Legislation, 10 *Finnish Yearbook of International Law* (1999) pp. 325 et seq.; J. Peglau: Die Vorschriften zu Strafen und Strafzumessung für den Internationalen Strafgerichtshof und ihre Bedeutung für das nationale Strafrecht, *Humanitäres Völkerrecht-Informationsschriften* 2001, pp. 247 et seq.; Luc Reydam: Universal Criminal Jurisdiction: The Belgian State of Affairs, 11 *Criminal Law Forum* (2000), pp. 183 et seq.; William A. Schabas: Follow up to Rome: Preparing for Entry into Force of the International Criminal Court Statute, 20 *Human Rights Law Journal* (1999), pp. 157 et seq.; Hans Vest: Zum Handlungsbedarf auf dem Gebiet des Völkerstrafrechts –

---

[405] See marginal no. 54.

[406] For discussion of prosecution of crimes under international law in Rwanda and attempts to relieve the burden on the regular criminal justice system by creating so-called Gacaca tribunals, see J. Sarkin, 21 *Human Rights Quarterly* (1999), pp. 767 et seq.; J. Sarkin, 2 *International Law Forum* (2000), pp. 112 et seq.

[407] *Prosecutor* v. *Akayesu*, ICTR (Trial Chamber), judgment of 2 September 1998.

[408] *Prosecutor* v. *Kambanda*, ICTR (Trial Chamber), judgment of 4 September 1998, affirmed in *Prosecutor* v. *Kambanda*, ICTR (Appeals Chamber), judgment of 19 October 2000.

Elemente eines Gesetzgebungsvorschlags, 121 *Schweizerische Zeitschrift für Strafrecht* (2003), pp.
46 et seq.; Gerhard Werle: *Völkerstrafrecht und geltendes deutsches Strafrecht, Juristenzeitung*
2000, pp. 755 et seq.; Gerhard Werle: *Konturen eines deutschen Völkerstrafrechts, Juristenzeitung*
2001, pp. 885 et seq.; Gerhard Werle and Florian Jessberger: *Das Völkerstrafgesetzbuch,
Juristenzeitung* 2002, pp. 725 et seq.; Andreas Zimmermann: *Auf dem Weg zu einem deutschen
Völkerstrafgesetzbuch, Zeitschrift für Rechtspolitik* 2002, pp. 97 et seq.

216   In the process of ratifying the ICC Statute, several countries have reviewed their domestic laws to assess the need for adaptation. As a result, many states have taken the opportunity either to enact new legislation or to amend existing laws, incorporating the ICC
Statute's crimes and enabling the state to exercise extraterritorial jurisdiction.[409]

I. The Need for Implementation

217   Efforts to adapt domestic criminal law to international criminal law, and especially to the
ICC Statute, take into account that domestic prosecutions of crimes under international
law are vital to the international system of criminal justice.[410] The ICC Statute explicitly
acknowledges the idea of decentralized administration of justice. Under Article 1, the International Criminal Court "shall be complementary to national criminal jurisdictions."[411] The International Criminal Court will not replace but will complement the
efforts of national systems to bring to justice those responsible for crimes under international law. Hence, even after the establishment of the International Criminal Court, the
(indirect) enforcement of international criminal law through national courts will remain
the backbone of the international criminal justice system.

218   However, the ICC Statute does not establish any obligations regarding the incorporation of the Statute's substantive criminal law into national law.[412] In this respect it differs from most other international treaties in the field of criminal law.[413] Neither Statute
provisions nor the underlying principle of complementarity oblige states parties to enact
criminal legislation or even to "copy" the ICC Statute. In fact, national systems retain

---

[409] On the status of the implementation of the ICC Statute in Europe, see <http://
www.legal.coe.int/criminal/icc/>; see also D. Cassel, 23 *Fordham International Law Journal* (1999),
pp. 378 et seq.; K.L. Doherty and T.L.H. McCormack, 5 *UC Davis Journal of International Law and
Policy* (1999), pp. 147 et seq.; F. Jessberger and C. Powell, 14 *South African Journal of Criminal Justice*
(2001), pp. 344 et seq.; C. Kress and F. Lattanzi (eds.), *The Rome Statute and Domestic Legal Orders*,
Vol. 1 (2000); M. Neuner (ed.), *National Codes on International Crimes* (2003); K. Nuotio, 10 *Finnish
Yearbook of International Law* (1999), pp. 325 et seq.; L. Reydams, 11 *Criminal Law Forum* (2000)
pp. 183 et seq.; W.A. Schabas, 20 *Human Rights Law Journal* (1999), pp. 157 et seq.

[410] See F. Jessberger and C. Powell, 14 *South African Journal of Criminal Justice* (2001), p. 344 at
p. 347.

[411] On the principle of complementarity, see marginal no. 199.

[412] An exception exists to this rule for offenses against the administration of justice under Art. 70
of the ICC Statute. Art. 70(4) provides that each state party "shall extend its criminal laws . . . to
offences against the administration of justice referred to in this article." Apart from that, the ICC Statute contains obligations only with regard to cooperation and legal assistance to the Court. For details,
see part 9 of the ICC Statute.

[413] See, e.g., Geneva Convention IV, Art. 146 ("parties undertake to enact any legislation necessary to provide effective penal sanctions") and *Convention Against Torture and Other Cruel, Inhuman
or Degrading Treatment or Punishment* of 10 December 1984, 1465 *UNTS* (1987), p. 85, Art. 4.

their autonomy with regard to the provisions of their criminal law even after becoming party to the ICC Statute. The threshold test established by the Statute is willingness and ability of the state to prosecute.[414] As regards the quality of domestic substantive law, it is obvious that a certain amount of deviation in the definition of a crime under domestic law from the corresponding definition in the ICC Statute will not, in itself, prevent a state from prosecuting.[415] Thus the Statute allows flexibility on the extent to which states incorporate the definitions of crimes in their domestic law. Should punishment under domestic law be impossible or inadequate, however, the possible "sanction" is that the International Criminal Court may take over the case.[416]

While the ICC Statute does not oblige the states to enact domestic legislation pursu-   **219** ant to the Statute's prescriptions, it encourages them to do this.[417] In fact, the ultimate aim of the Statute is not to effect that crimes be tried by the International Criminal Court, but to provide a source of norms and legal standards that would provide states the basis to effectively investigate and prosecute the most serious crimes under international law themselves.[418] The message of the ICC Statute as regards the quality of domestic criminal legislation is that states should be both willing *and* able (through their domestic legislation) to prosecute genocide, crimes against humanity, and war crimes in a capacity similar to that of the International Criminal Court.

II. Options for Implementation

States have wide latitude in deciding how to adopt substantive international criminal   **220** law.

---

[414] See ICC Statute, Art. 17.

[415] At first sight, the mere fact that a state prosecutes an alleged war criminal "only" on a murder charge does not seem an appropriate reason to view the state as "unable" or even "unwilling" to prosecute the offender. However, the law and practice of the ICTY and ICTR appear to give some indication to the contrary. Under ICTY Statute, Art. 10(2)(a) and ICTR Statute, Art. 9(2)(a), the principle *ne bis in idem* does not apply even though a person has been tried by a national court, if the act for which he or she was tried "was characterised as an ordinary crime." In this case, the person may be tried again by the Tribunals. One example, suggested by V. Morris and M.P. Scharf, *The International Criminal Tribunal for Rwanda* (1998), p. 344, is conduct that "constitutes the ordinary crime of murder under national laws as well as the more serious crime of genocide under international law." The Commentary of the International Law Commission explains the corresponding rule in Art. 12 of the *Draft Code* 1996 by saying that "in such a case, the individual has not been tried or punished for the same crime but for a 'lesser crime' that does not encompass the full extent of his criminal conduct," see International Law Commission, Draft Code of Crimes Against the Peace and Security of Mankind [Commentary], 18 *Human Rights Law Journal* (1997), p. 102 at p. 119. Yet it is important to note that the corresponding rule in Art. 20 of the ICC Statute does *not* provide for an exception to the *ne bis in idem* principle in these cases.

[416] See ICC Statute, Art. 17.

[417] See B. Broomhall, 13 *Nouvelles Études Pénales* (1999), p. 113 at pp. 148 et seq.; D. Cassel, 35 *New England Law Review* (2001), p. 421 at p. 423; F. Jessberger and C. Powell, 14 *South African Journal of Criminal Justice* (2001), p. 344 at pp. 348 et seq.; H. Satzger, *Neue Zeitschrift für Strafrecht* 2002, p. 125 at p. 127; W.A. Schabas, 20 *Human Rights Law Journal* (1999), p. 157 at p. 160; G. Werle and F. Jessberger, *Juristenzeitung* 2002, p. 725 at p. 726; G. Werle, *Juristenzeitung* 2001, p. 885 at p. 886; A. Zimmermann, *Zeitschrift für Rechtspolitik* 2002, p. 97 at p. 98.

[418] See B. Broomhall, 13 *Nouvelles Études Pénales* (1999), p. 113 at p. 159.

1. Complete Incorporation

221   At least at first glance, the most international law-friendly solution lies in conforming domestic law completely to the substantive law of the ICC Statute. Such complete incorporation can be achieved in various ways: by directly applying customary international law (see a), by reference to the ICC Statute (see b), or by copying the provisions of the ICC Statute verbatim (see c).

a) Direct Application

222   Definitions of crimes under customary international law can be directly applicable to domestic law if, as in common law systems, criminality may be based not only on written but also on unwritten (customary) law.[419] Since the offenses in the ICC Statute embody customary international law, the conduct criminalized in Articles 6 to 8 could be punishable under existing domestic law, regardless of whether the Statute is ratified, as long as customary international law can be directly applied domestically without implementing legislation.[420] Notwithstanding this situation, courts in these legal systems are extraordinarily reluctant to apply customary law. Dormant customary law definitions of crimes are rarely revived without legislative activity.[421]

b) Reference

223   Complete adoption of international criminal law can also be achieved by reference to its relevant provisions and principles. Domestic law could conceivably refer to the provisions of the ICC Statute in conjunction with domestic regulations.[422] The reference might also extend further, for example to include all criminal law recognized under customary international law.[423] Reference, however, is precluded in legal systems with constitutions requiring written domestic legislation to establish individual criminal responsibility.

c) Copying

224   If both global reference to customary international criminal law and targeted reference to Statute offenses are precluded, complete incorporation can occur by adopting the offenses verbatim into

---

[419] Thus under South African law, for example, not all serious offenses are common law crimes, see J. Burchell and J. Milton, *Principles of Criminal Law*, 2nd edn. (1999), p. 28.

[420] Under Sec. 232 of the South African constitution, customary international law, including customary international criminal law, is part of South African law, see also Art. 25 sentence 1 of the (German) Basic Law [*Grundgesetz, GG*].

[421] On South Africa, see J. Dugard, *International Law*, 2nd edn. (2000), p. 141: "Most states, including South Africa, will not try a person for an international crime unless the conduct has been criminalized under municipal law"; see also S. Maqungo, in C. Kress and F. Lattanzi (eds.), *The Rome Statute and Domestic Legal Orders*, Vol. 1 (2000), p. 183 at p. 186.

[422] New Zealand moved in this direction in its International Crimes and International Criminal Court Act 2000; Sec. 9, for example, states: "Every person is liable on conviction on indictment . . . who, in New Zealand or elsewhere, commits genocide . . .. For the purpose of this section, genocide is an act referred to in article 6 of the [Rome] Statute [of the International Criminal Court]." The text of the Act can be found at <http://www.legislation.govt.nz>.

[423] This is the direction taken by the Canadian Crimes Against Humanity and War Crimes Act, *Canada Gazette*, Part III (2000), Vol. 23 No. 3, Ch. 24. Sec. 4(3) defines criminality for war crimes as follows: "War crime means any act or omission committed during an armed conflict, that at the time and in the place of its commission, constitutes a war crime according to customary international law or conventional international law applicable to armed conflicts." Sec 4(4) states: "Crimes described in Articles 6 and 7 and paragraph 2 of Article 8 of the Rome Statute are, as of July 17, 1998, crimes according to customary international law."

domestic law. Domestic law then becomes a reflection of international criminal law. The only domestic limits to this approach are encountered where a constitution prevents unaltered adoption of certain norms of international criminal law, for example if the constitution contains specific requirements for legal certainty.

2. Non-Incorporation – Applying "Ordinary" Criminal Law

A second option is not to incorporate international criminal law into domestic law at all. **225** In this "zero solution," states rely on ordinary criminal law to cover crimes under international law adequately, for example under the definitions of murder, deprivation of liberty, and the like. Whether and to what extent crimes under international law can be punished adequately will depend on the configuration of each legal system.

As pointed out, this solution is not precluded under the ICC Statute because there is no treaty **226** obligation. Therefore, no "sanctions" are foreseen for not adapting domestic criminal law to the Statute's standards. However, a state whose substantive criminal law does not provide for adequate punishment of crimes under international law must expect prosecutions to be taken up, if necessary, by the International Criminal Court. This would happen if national law leaves wide gaps in relation to the ICC Statute that result in a state's "inability" genuinely to carry out a prosecution.[424]

The legality under international law of this "zero solution" has undoubtedly facilitated **227** ratification of the ICC Statute, and this may have encouraged the Rome Conference to adopt such a comparatively "soft" approach. Ratifying states face no pressure to change their substantive criminal law; at least for the present, they may retain existing legal arrangements without violating the treaty. However, non-incorporation of international criminal law into domestic law is not a recommended long-term solution. To comply fully with the spirit and plan of the ICC Statute, states should adapt their substantive criminal law.

3. Modified Incorporation

A third method is to incorporate international criminal law by integrating its substance **228** into the national criminal law system.[425] In this case, international legal norms are adopted in principle; however, distinctive features of the national legal culture can be taken into account in the process of incorporation. In addition, modified incorporation provides an opportunity to formally document certain state conceptions of the scope and interpretation of international criminal law, for example by including certain crimes in domestic law that are part of customary law but are not included in the ICC Statute.[426]

---

[424] See ICC Statute, Art. 17(1)(a), (3).

[425] In Chapter 11 of the Finnish Criminal Code, e.g., genocide, crimes against humanity and war crimes have been punishable since 1995 – though in a version different from that of the ICC Statute. See K. Nuotio, 10 *Finnish Yearbook of International Law* (1999), pp. 325 et seq.

[426] Applicable customary international law is not restricted by the ICC Statute, see, e.g., ICC Statute, Art. 10.

4. Combinations

229   In domestic incorporation, the options listed will often come into play at the same time. Thus a state might conceivably apply ordinary domestic criminal law to general principles of criminal law and war crimes (non-incorporation), adopt genocide verbatim (complete incorporation), and incorporate the definition of crimes against humanity with some changes (modified incorporation).

III. Forms of Incorporation

230   If legislative action is required to implement a state's decision to incorporate international criminal law, the question arises as to what legislative form this incorporation should take. The possibilities are an amendment to existing laws (see 1) or creation of a separate law (codification, see 2).

1. Amendment of Existing Laws

231   Technically, the simplest way to incorporate international criminal law by legislation is to add relevant provisions to existing criminal codes. Depending on the scope and structure of the provisions to be added, the spectrum of possible methods can range from selective adaptation of specific provisions to the addition of a self-contained chapter.

232   Selective changes to existing laws will be considered in particular if a state is cautious about incorporating international criminal law but finds certain basic changes to domestic law necessary. Further, to close gaps between international and domestic criminal law, it may be necessary to integrate single offenses or parts of offenses under international law into existing law. The Federal Republic of Germany carried out this type of implementation in 1954 by adding the crime of genocide as Section 220a of the (German) Criminal Code [*Strafgesetzbuch, StGB*]. Similarly, crimes against humanity could be integrated into a criminal code. As an obvious alternative to isolated changes to an existing criminal code, provisions of international law could be brought together in a chapter on "crimes under international law."

2. Self-Contained Codification

233   The second form of implementing legislation is an independent codification of the substance of international criminal law. Such an international criminal law act or code contains all relevant crimes under international law, and at the same time makes it possible to accommodate necessary special provisions relating to general principles. This procedure will typically be considered in cases of complete incorporation of substantive international law through verbatim adoption into domestic law, since a separate body of law brings the international law basis into particularly sharp focus. But even an international law-friendly modified incorporation can employ this method without problem.

234   Advantages of codification include the possibility of compact consolidation and clarification of this comprehensive and sometimes obscure body of law.[427] A certain disadvantage lies in codification

---

[427] For discussion, see C. Kress, *Vom Nutzen eines deutschen Völkerstrafgesetzbuchs* (2000), pp. 18 et seq.

outside of the regular criminal code, which could give rise to the impression that a code of crimes under international law does not contain the "core of the core of criminal law," but rather rules for "subsidiary criminal law," or even that it is a politically-motivated "special law." However, this danger must be weighed against the heightened symbolic value of self-contained codification. There are important additional advantages, too, from an international perspective: A self-contained law increases the international accessibility of domestic international criminal law and thus the possibility that modified approaches, especially, will be acknowledged outside the state's own legal system. This also increases the chances of contributing to the progressive clarification and consolidation of international criminal law.

IV. Interpretation of International Criminal Law in a Domestic Context

In practice, international criminal law raises a host of novel and highly complex legal issues,[428] which have gained increased significance for domestic courts in the process of implementation. Most responsible for this are the collision between rules and principles of international and national criminal law, the interplay of various legal systems and legal cultures, and the parallel existence of international and national jurisdictions. The entry into force of the ICC Statute, and the fact that some states took this as an occasion to adapt their domestic criminal laws, will greatly strengthen both "vertical" interaction between national and international criminal justice and "horizontal" interaction between criminal justice administration in different states.[429] **235**

In this area, international criminal law exercises its primary influence on the interpretation of norms incorporated into national legal systems.[430] Although the rules of international criminal law adopted into national legislation are formally part of domestic law, their substantive origin is in international law. This is most clearly visible where the **236**

---

[428] For examples, see the report on the work of the Yugoslavia Tribunal by A. Cassese, 9 *European Journal of International Law* (1998), p. 1 at pp. 10 et seq.

[429] As an expression of German state practice and *opinio juris*, e.g., the (German) Code of Crimes Against International Law directly contributes to clarifying and consolidating existing international criminal law. See also Explanatory Memorandum of the (German) Code of Crimes Against International Law, *BT-Drs.* 14/8524, p. 12. The jurisprudence of international courts includes numerous decisions that refer to German criminal law and the opinions of German courts, as well as to the drafts of the (German) Code of Crimes Against International Law, see, e.g., *Prosecutor* v. *Krstić*, ICTY (Trial Chamber), judgment of 2 August 2001, para. 579; *DR Congo* v. *Belgium*, ICJ, judgment of 14 February 2002 (Case Concerning the Arrest Warrant of 11 April 2000), separate opinion of Judges Higgins, Kooijmans and Buergenthal, para. 20: "It should be noted, however, that the German Government on 16 January 2002 has submitted a legislative proposal to the German Parliament, section 1 of which provides: [text of (German) Code of Crimes Against International Law, Sec. 1]."

[430] Correctly, the Explanatory Memorandum of the (German) Code of Crimes Against International Law emphasizes the necessity, for interpretation, of consulting relevant international law and the decisions of international courts. Thus, for example, it states, "[i]n order to interpret the element of an 'attack on the civilian population,' we must look at the legal definition in Article 7 Subsection 2 Letter a) of the ICC Statute," see Explanatory Memorandum of the (German) Code of Crimes Against International Law, *BT-Drs.* 14/8524, p. 20. In interpreting the factual alternatives for enslavement under Sec. 7(1) no. 3 of the (German) Code of Crimes Against International Law [*Völkerstrafgesetzbuch*, *VStGB*], "it is necessary to consider the *Supplementary Convention on the Abolition of Slavery, the Slave Trade and Institutions and Practices Similar to Slavery* of 7 September 1956 [226 *UNTS* (1956), p. 3] and the precedents of the International Criminal Tribunal for the former Yugoslavia," see Explanatory Memorandum of the (German) Code of Crimes Against International Law, *BT-Drs.* 14/8524, p. 20.

implementing legislation explicitly refers to international law.[431] But even more generally, recognized methods of interpretation make it necessary to consider the norms of the ICC Statute and customary international law in interpreting implementing legislation.[432]

237   In sum, it is necessary to start with an interpretation of the implementing legislation that is favorable to international criminal law.[433] Domestic courts must consider the "parent norms" of international law and their interpretation by international and, where relevant, foreign courts.

V. The (German) Code of Crimes Against International Law

238   Kai Ambos and Steffen Wirth: Genocide and War Crimes in the Former Yugoslavia before German Criminal Courts, in Horst Fischer, Claus Kress and Sascha R. Lüder (eds.), *International and National Prosecution of Crimes under International Law, Current Developments* (2001), pp. 769 et seq.; Bundesministerium der Justiz (ed.): *Arbeitsentwurf eines Gesetzes zur Einführung des Völkerstrafgesetzbuchs mit Begründung* (2001); Frank Dietmeier: Völkerstrafrecht und deutscher Gesetzgeber – Kritische Anmerkungen zum Projekt eines "Deutschen Völkerstrafgesetzbuchs", in Eva Graul and Gerhard Wolf (Hrsg.), *Gedächtnisschrift für Meurer* (2002), pp. 333 et seq.; Albin Eser: Völkermord und deutsche Strafgewalt, in Albin Eser et al. (eds.), *Festschrift für Meyer-Goßner* (2001), pp. 3 et seq.; Helmut Gropengießer und Helmut Kreicker: Deutschland, in Albin Eser und Helmut Kreicker (eds.), *National Prosecution of International Crimes*, Vol. 1 (2003), pp. 21 et seq.; Willibald Hermsdörfer: Auswirkungen der Errichtung des Internationalen Strafgerichtshofs auf das deutsche Recht, *Deutsche Richterzeitung* 2000, pp. 70 et seq.; Florian Jessberger: Prosecuting International Crimes in Domestic Courts, A Look Back Ahead, 12 *Finnish Yearbook of International Law* (2001), pp. 307 et seq.; Claus Kress: Völkerstrafrecht in Deutschland, *Neue Zeitschrift für Strafrecht* 2000, pp. 617 et seq.; Claus Kress: *Vom Nutzen eines deutschen Völkerstrafgesetzbuchs* (2000); Jan MacLean: Gesetzentwurf über die Zusammenarbeit mit dem Internationalen Strafgerichtshof, *Zeitschrift für Rechtspolitik* 2002, pp. 260 et seq.; Jörg Meissner: Die Zusammenarbeit Deutschlands mit dem Internationalen Strafgerichtshof, *Humanitäres Völkerrecht-Informationsschriften* 2002, pp. 35 et seq.; Helmut Satzger, Internationales und Europäisches Strafrecht (2005), pp. 220 et seq.; Helmut Satzger: Das neue Völkerstrafgesetzbuch, Eine kritische

---

[431] See, e.g., (German) Code of Crimes Against International Law [*Völkerstrafgesetzbuch, VStGB*], Sec. 7(1) no. 5 ("internationally admissible sanctions") and Sec. 9(1) ("in violation of international law").

[432] For greater detail, see G. Werle and F. Jessberger, *Juristenzeitung* 2002, p. 725 at pp. 733 et seq. The (German) Federal Supreme Court [*Bundesgerichtshof*] has cited decisions of the Yugoslavia Tribunal repeatedly, see Bundesgerichtshof, judgment of 30 April 1999, BGHSt 45, p. 64 at p. 69; Bundesgerichtshof, judgment of 21 February 2001, BGHSt 46, p. 292 at pp. 299 et seq. (on the character of armed conflict and on the concept of torture). See also the (German) Federal Constitutional Court [*Bundesverfassungsgericht*], decision of 12 December 2002, *Neue Juristische Wochenschrift* 2001, pp. 1848 et seq.

[433] For details, see G. Werle and F. Jessberger, *Juristenzeitung* 2002, p. 725 at pp. 733 et seq.; see also J. Peglau, *Humanitäres Völkerrecht-Informationsschriften* 2001, p. 247 at p. 248; A. Zimmermann, *Zeitschrift für Rechtspolitik* 2002, p. 97 at p. 99. Under the decisions of the (German) Federal Constitutional Court [*Bundesverfassungsgericht*], laws are to be interpreted and applied in accordance with Germany's international obligations, "for it cannot be assumed that the legislature, if it did not clearly announce this, wished to deviate from Germany's international obligations or make possible the violation of these obligations," see Bundesverfassungsgericht, decision of 31 March 1987, BVerfGE 75, p. 1 at p. 18. On the principle of "pro-international law interpretation," see C. Tomuschat, in J. Isensee and P. Kirchhof (eds.), *Handbuch des Staatsrechts der Bundesrepublik Deutschland*, Vol. 7 (1992), § 172, marginal nos. 27 et seq.

Würdigung, *Neue Zeitschrift für Strafrecht* 2002, pp. 125 et seq.; Stephanie Scholz: *Die Zulieferung an den Jugoslawien-Strafgerichtshof* (1998), pp. 97 et seq.; Wolfgang Schomburg: Gesetz über die Zusammenarbeit mit dem Internationalen Strafgerichtshof für das ehemalige Jugoslawien, in Wolfgang Schomburg and Otto Lagodny (eds.), *Internationale Rechtshilfe in Strafsachen, Kommentar*, 3rd edn. (1998), pp. 1187 et seq.; Wolfgang Schomburg: Jugoslawien-Strafgerichtshof-Gesetz, *Neue Zeitschrift für Strafrecht* 1995, pp. 428 et seq.; Hans Vest: Zum Handlungsbedarf auf dem Gebiet des Völkerstrafrechts – Elemente eines Gesetzgebungsvorschlags, 121 *Schweizerische Zeitschrift für Strafrecht* (2003), pp. 46 et seq.; Gerhard Werle: Anmerkung zum Urteil des BGH vom 30. April 1999, *Juristenzeitung* 1999, pp. 1181 et seq.; Gerhard Werle: Der Holocaust als Gegenstand der bundesdeutschen Strafjustiz, *Neue Juristische Wochenschrift* 1992, pp. 2529 et seq.; Gerhard Werle: Völkerstrafrecht und geltendes deutsches Strafrecht, *Juristenzeitung* 2000, pp. 755 et seq.; Gerhard Werle: Konturen eines deutschen Völkerstrafrechts, *Juristenzeitung* 2001, pp. 885 et seq.; Gerhard Werle and Florian Jessberger: Das Völkerstrafgesetzbuch, *Juristenzeitung* 2002, pp. 725 et seq.; Gerhard Werle and Florian Jessberger: International Criminal Justice is Coming Home: The New German Code of Crimes Against International Law, 13 *Criminal Law Forum* (2002), pp. 191 et seq.; Gerhard Werle and Volker Nerlich: Die Strafbarkeit von Kriegsverbrechen nach deutschem Recht, *Humanitäres Völkerrecht-Informationsschriften* 2002, pp. 124 et seq.; Peter Wilkitzki: The Contribution of the Federal Republic of Germany and the German Laender to the Work of the ICTY, in Lal Chand Vohrah (ed.), *Man's Inhumanity to Man* (2003), pp. 923 et seq.; Andreas Zimmermann: Die Auslieferung Deutscher an Staaten der Europäischen Union und internationale Strafgerichtshöfe, *Juristenzeitung* 2001, pp. 233 et seq.; Andreas Zimmermann: Auf dem Weg zu einem deutschen Völkerstrafgesetzbuch, *Zeitschrift für Rechtspolitik* 2002, pp. 97 et seq.; Andreas Zimmermann: Role and Function of International Criminal Law in the International System After the Entry into Force of the Rome Statute of the International Criminal Court, 45 *German Yearbook of International Law* (2002), pp. 35 et seq.; Andreas Zimmermann: Bestrafung völkerrechtlicher Verbrechen durch deutsche Gerichte nach Inkrafttreten des Völkerstrafgesetzbuches, *Neue Juristische Wochenschrift* 2002, pp. 3068 et seq.

1. Historical Background

The origins and development of international criminal law are closely connected with **239** Germany and the Germans. In particular, the Law of Nuremberg can only be understood as a reaction to the Nazi crimes committed in Germany's name, to which the Nuremberg Charter provided a legal response. The attitude of West Germans, and later the Federal Republic of Germany, toward international criminal law was at first skeptical, if not hostile.[434] The accusation of one-sided victors' justice played the most important part in the public debate. Tellingly, prosecution of Nazi crimes by the West German criminal justice system was not based on the Nuremberg Principles.[435]

---

[434] See G. Werle and F. Jessberger, *Juristenzeitung* 2002, pp. 725 et seq.; A. Zimmermann, 45 *German Yearbook of International Law* (2002), p. 35 at pp. 49 et seq. In the former German Democratic Republic, in contrast, the Nuremberg Principles were accepted without reservation, and trials were held on that basis. After the cancellation of CCL No. 10, the Nuremberg crimes were at first applied directly. Later, the definitions of crimes under international law were adopted into the Criminal Code of the former German Democratic Republic. At the same time, the law of Nuremberg was misused by the East German regime to commit new human rights violations. This was true, for example, in the so-called Waldheim trials in 1950, which blatantly ignored basic procedural rules. See K. Marxen, in K. Marxen, K. Miyazawa and G. Werle (eds.), *Der Umgang mit Kriegs- und Besatzungsunrecht in Japan und Deutschland* (2001), p. 159 at pp. 169 et seq.

[435] Summarized in G. Werle, in K. Marxen, K. Miyazawa and G. Werle (eds.), *Der Umgang mit Kriegs- und Besatzungsunrecht in Japan und Deutschland* (2001), pp. 137 et seq.

240   In addition to this basic, overwhelmingly skeptical attitude, however, there were trends more favorable to international criminal law even in the early Federal Republic, such as Germany's accession to the Geneva Conventions and the Genocide Convention and the incorporation of the crime
of genocide into the Criminal Code.

241   The resistance to international criminal law has since given way to active promotion of
and participation in a "globalized" criminal law. Today, the German attitude is pro-international criminal law. The Federal Republic of Germany strongly supports the enforcement of international criminal law.

242   The German criminal justice system had an opportunity to demonstrate its new determination to
contribute to the enforcement of international criminal law in connection with the prosecution of
crimes under international law committed on the territory of former Yugoslavia.[436] Between 1996
and 2001, the German judiciary complied with some 500 requests for judicial assistance from the
Yugoslavia Tribunal; in the same period, over 100 investigations were initiated in Germany in connection with the events in former Yugoslavia.[437] Several convictions were obtained, including
some for genocide.[438]

243   In the negotiations on the ICC Statute, Germany belonged to the group of like-minded
states, and many German proposals found their way into the ICC Statute.[439] Germany
signed the ICC Statute on 9 December 1998 and ratified it on 11 December 2000.[440]
The ICC Statute Ratification Act [*Gesetz zum Römischen Statut des Internationalen
Strafgerichtshofes*] of 4 December 2000 set the stage for the ICC Statute's entry into force
in Germany.[441] A change to Article 16(2) of the Basic Law [*Grundgesetz, GG*], the German constitution, ensured that Germany may surrender German citizens to the International Criminal Court.[442] On 1 July 2002, simultaneously with the ICC Statute, the
ICC Statute Implementation Act [*Gesetz zur Ausführung des Römischen Statuts des*

---

[436] In connection with the criminal prosecution of East German crimes, in 1995 the (German)
Federal Supreme Court [*Bundesgerichtshof*] for the first time made an explicit commitment to international criminal law, see Bundesgerichtshof, judgment of 20 March 1995, *BGHSt* 41, p. 101 at p. 109.
In this case, the Court determined that its judgment of the shootings at the Berlin Wall "further developed the substantive legal foundations of the judgment of the Nuremberg Tribunal, on which it was
based, for a special case."

[437] See K. Ambos and S. Wirth, in H. Fischer, C. Kress and S.R. Lüder (eds.), *International and
National Prosecution of Crimes under International Law* (2001), pp. 769 et seq.; P. Wilkitzki, in L.C.
Vohrah (ed.), *Man's Inhumanity to Man* (2003), p. 923 at pp. 926 et seq.

[438] See, e.g., Bundesgerichtshof, judgment of 21 February 2001, *BGHSt* 46, p. 292; Bundesgerichtshof, judgment of 30 April 1999, *BGHSt* 45, p. 64, and Bundesverfassungsgericht, decision of 12
December 2000, *Neue Juristische Wochenschrift* 2001, p. 1848; Bundesgerichtshof, decision of 11 December 1998, *Neue Zeitschrift für Strafrecht* 1999, p. 236; Bayerisches Oberstes Landesgericht, judgment of 23 May 1997, *Neue Juristische Wochenschrift* 1998, p. 392; Bundesgerichtshof, decision of 13
February 1994, *Neue Zeitschrift für Strafrecht* 1994, pp. 232 et seq.

[439] See H.-P. Kaul, in G. Baum, E. Riedel and M. Schaefer (eds.), *Menschenrechtsschutz in der
Praxis der Vereinten Nationen* (1998), pp. 273 et seq.

[440] See summary of the implementation process in C. Kress, in H. Grützner and P.G. Pötz (eds.),
Internationaler Rechtshilfeverkehr in Strafsachen, Vol. 4, 2nd edn. (2002), Vor III 26, marginal nos. 266
et seq.

[441] *Bundesgesetzblatt* 2000 II, p. 1393.

[442] *Bundesgesetzblatt* 2000 I, p. 1633; see H. Satzger, *Internationales und Europäisches Strafrecht*
(2005), pp. 220 et seq.; A. Zimmermann, *Juristenzeitung* 2001, pp. 209 et seq.

Internationalen Strafgerichtshofes] of 21 June 2002 went into effect.[443] It contains the necessary regulations for cooperation with the International Criminal Court.

The (German) Code of Crimes Against International Law [*Völkerstrafgesetzbuch*, **244** *VStGB*] of 26 June 2002[444] went into effect on 30 June 2002, one day before the ICC Statute.[445] The law adapts substantive German law to the provisions of the ICC Statute.

When the German government signed the ICC Statute, it was already its declared intention to **245** work on adapting existing German criminal law to the Statute's provisions. To accomplish this, in October 1999 the Federal Ministry of Justice established an expert working group. In May 2001, the group submitted a "Working Draft of a Law for the Introduction of a Code of Crimes Against International Law."[446] On 22 March 2002, the government's bill, which adhered closely to the working draft, underwent its first reading in the Bundestag. After taking account of minor changes recommended by the law committee, on 25 April 2002 the Bundestag adopted the law unanimously.

2. Aims

The Code of Crimes Against International Law has four aims.[447] First, it is meant **246** to comprehend the "specific wrong of crimes against international law"; at the same time, it aims to avoid gaps between German criminal law and international criminal law.

German criminal law as it existed before the creation of the Code of Crimes Against International **247** Law contained significant deficiencies in regard to inclusion of crimes under international law.[448] In the majority of cases, crimes under international law were criminal under German law, but the international element, which lends the crimes an international dimension,[449] was not apparent. In

---

[443] *Bundesgesetzblatt* 2002 I, p. 2144. See J. MacLean, *Zeitschrift für Rechtspolitik* 2002, pp. 260 et seq.; J. Meissner, *Humanitäres Völkerrecht-Informationsschriften* 2002, pp. 35 et seq.

[444] *Bundesgesetzblatt* 2002 I, p. 2254.

[445] For further discussion, see G. Werle and F. Jessberger, 13 *Criminal Law Forum* (2002), p. 191 at pp. 214 et seq.; see also H. Gropengiesser and H. Kreicker, in A. Eser and H. Kreicker (eds.), *National Prosecution of International Crimes*, Vol. 1 (2003), pp. 21 et seq.; G. Werle and F. Jessberger, *Juristenzeitung* 2002, pp. 725 et seq.; A. Zimmermann, *Neue Juristische Wochenschrift* 2002, pp. 3068 et seq.; on the preparatory work, see C. Kress, *Vom Nutzen eines deutschen Völkerstrafgesetzbuchs* (2000); H. Satzger, *Neue Zeitschrift für Strafrecht* 2002, pp. 125 et seq.; G. Werle, *Juristenzeitung* 2001, pp. 885 et seq.

[446] Bundesministerium der Justiz (ed.), *Arbeitsentwurf eines Gesetzes zur Einführung des Völkerstrafgesetzbuchs mit Begründung* (2001). See G. Werle, *Juristenzeitung* 2001, pp. 885 et seq.

[447] On the following, see Explanatory Memorandum of the (German) Code of Crimes Against International Law, *BT-Drs.* 14/8524, p. 12.

[448] For specifics, see G. Werle, *Juristenzeitung* 2000, p. 755 at pp. 756 et seq.; see also F. Jessberger, 12 *Finnish Yearbook of International Law* (2001), pp. 307 et seq.; H. Satzger, *Internationales und Europäisches Strafrecht* (2005), pp. 222 et seq. It would have made sense, in the early fifties at the latest, to incorporate the crimes in the IMT Charter, which were also laid down in CCL No. 10, into German criminal law. In 1953 the federal government had already stated, in the explanation of a draft law on Germany's accession to the four Geneva Conventions, "the crucial criminal law provisions of the Conventions make it necessary to partly adapt German domestic law." Yet the legislature did nothing. In 1980 the Ministry of Justice did submit a preliminary draft of a law to punish violations of the international laws of war, but it went no further. For details, see C. Kress, *Vom Nutzen eines deutschen Völkerstrafgesetzbuchs* (2000), pp. 4 et seq.

[449] See marginal no 79.

addition, some gaps were conceivable that might have led to an act being criminalized under international law but not under German law. Further significant deficiencies were found as regards the extraterritorial scope of German criminal law.

248   Second, the collection of international criminal laws into one unified code is intended to promote "legal clarity and practical application." A third aim, with regard to the principle of complementarity, is to ensure "that Germany is always in a position to prosecute crimes over which the ICC has jurisdiction."[450] Fourth, creation of the Code is intended to contribute to the promotion and spread of international humanitarian law.

3. Structure

249   Part 1 of the Code contains several general principles applicable to the crimes. Crimes under international law, specifically genocide, crimes against humanity, war and civil war crimes are contained in Part 2. In addition to the special penal norms, definitions of crimes under ordinary criminal law remain essentially applicable; as a rule, however, under the principle of lesser included offenses, they usually take second place to the norms in the Code of Crimes Against International Law.

4. General Principles

250   The Code of Crimes Against International Law includes general principles (Sections 1 to 5) that concentrate only upon the essentials. Section 2 of the Code provides for the application of ordinary criminal law, in particular the (German) Criminal Code [*Strafgesetzbuch, StGB*], when no special rules are created by the Code of Crimes Against International Law. Thus general rules apply, such as those for the mental element, mistake, self-defense, modes of participation, and omission.

251   Section 2 reflects a basic decision by German lawmakers to incorporate the provisions on crimes against international law into the tried and tested system and the existing doctrinal framework of German criminal law. The establishment of a second or parallel set of general principles – the first one for ordinary crimes, the second one for crimes under international law – would have led to unforeseeable difficulties in the application of the law. The underlying idea was that, as a rule, the application of the general principles of German law will lead to results that are both appropriate and consistent with the ICC Statute. Accordingly, the Code of Crimes Against International Law makes no special provisions as regards most of the general principles contained in Articles 22 to 33 of the ICC Statute. Only where the norms of the ICC Statute differ significantly from general German criminal law were special provisions tracking the prescriptions of the ICC Statute included in the Code. Whether they differ may in some cases be a matter of debate.

252   One important example relates to the mental element. According to German doctrine, *dolus eventualis* meets the requirements of Section 15 of the (German) Criminal Code [*Strafgesetzbuch, StGB*] providing for *mens rea*. Pursuant to Section 2 of the Code of Crimes Against International

---

[450] Explanatory Memorandum of the (German) Code of Crimes Against International Law, *BT-Drs.* 14/8524, p. 12.

Law, Section 15 is applicable to crimes under the Code of Crimes Against International Law. Whether *dolus eventualis* meets the standard established under Article 30(1) of the ICC Statute is, however, a matter of debate.[451] Another example relates to the criminalization of omissions. Here, the applicability of Section 13 of the Criminal Code[452] results in the general criminalization of the failure to act.[453]

The few special provisions included in the Code of Crimes Against International Law **253** relate to the responsibility of military commanders and others in authority (Sections 4, 13 and 14), the absence of a statutory limitation for crimes under international law (Section 5) and acting upon orders (Section 3). In these respects the provisions of the Code of Crimes Against International Law take precedence over the corresponding rules of the Criminal Code.

5. Genocide

In Section 6 of the Code of Crimes Against International Law, the first chapter of Part 2 **254** incorporates the crime of genocide from the Criminal Code (former Section 220(a)). Its minor deviations function as clarifications. While Article 6(a), (b), and (e) of the ICC Statute require that "members" of a group be affected, Section 6 of the Code of Crimes Against International Law requires that "a member" of the group be affected. This wording conforms to the international interpretation of the norm.

6. Crimes Against Humanity

Section 7 defines crimes against humanity; the provision closely tracks Article 7 of the **255** ICC Statute.[454] In formulating the individual offenses, the legislature sought to maintain the substance of the international "primary norms" and at the same time to do justice to the constitutional requirements of the principle of legality. Thus there are a number of clarifications that to some extent narrow the scope of criminal behavior in comparison with the ICC Statute.[455]

7. War Crimes

The second chapter (Sections 8 to 12) governs war crimes and civil war crimes, that is, **256** crimes committed in connection with international or non-international armed conflicts.[456]

---

[451] See marginal nos. 331 et seq.

[452] Section 13 of the (German) Criminal Code [*Strafgesetzbuch, StGB*] (commission by omission) reads as follows:
"Whoever fails to avert a result that is an element of a penal norm shall only be punishable under this law if he is legally responsible for the fact that the result does not occur, and if the omission is equivalent to the realization of the statutory elements of the crime through action . . .."

[453] For the position of international criminal law, see marginal nos. 503 et seq.

[454] For greater detail, see marginal nos. 644 et seq.

[455] On the tension between friendliness toward international criminal law and the principle of legality, see H. Satzger, *Neue Zeitung für Strafrecht* 2002, p. 125 at p. 131; G. Werle and F. Jessberger, *Juristenzeitung* 2002, p. 725 at p. 730.

[456] For discussion, see G. Werle and V. Nerlich, *Humanitäres Völkerrecht-Informationsschriften* 2002, pp. 124 et seq.; see also marginal nos. 811 et seq.

257 Here, the Code not only incorporates the offenses contained in Article 8(2) of the ICC Statute, but additionally satisfies the obligations, assumed in 1991 with German ratification of Additional Protocol I, to criminalize the grave breaches listed therein.[457] In addition, the chapter on war crimes is completely restructured compared to the ICC Statute. As far as possible, related offenses are combined in a single provision.[458] This is especially true for war crimes and civil war crimes with the same or similar targets of attack: Whether a conflict is of an international or non-international character is immaterial to these offenses.[459] Offenses are further tightened through uniform wordings. Some differences were already smoothed over in the German translation of the ICC Statute.[460] In some places, the German legislation restored similar wordings in the ICC Statute to their common core.

258 However, the Code is not limited to collecting identical or similar rules from the ICC Statute on international and non-international armed conflicts. In many cases, offenses that were only applicable to international armed conflicts under the ICC Statute have been extended to non-international armed conflicts. As a result, most of the acts included in the Code of Crimes Against International Law are criminal in both international and civil wars. Only where current customary international law does not permit equal treatment of international and non-international armed conflicts is a distinction made within individual provisions between types of conflicts.

259 Heading the second chapter are war crimes against persons. Section 8(1) applies to international and non-international armed conflicts and includes, as separate acts, killing (no. 1), taking of hostages (no. 2), cruel or inhuman treatment (no. 3), sexual violence (no. 4), forced conscription and use of child soldiers (no. 5), expulsion (no. 6), punishment without proper trial (no. 7), medical experiments and removal of organs (no. 8), and humiliating or degrading treatment (no. 9). To further tighten the law of war crimes, Article 8(1) and (3) of the Code of Crimes Against International Law use the phrase "persons to be protected under international humanitarian law." This phrase is defined in section 8(6).[461] Section 8(3) contains the few acts that can only be committed in in-

---

[457] See Additional Protocol I, Art. 85(1) in conjunction with Geneva Convention I, Art. 49(1), Geneva Convention II, Art. 50(1), Geneva Convention III, Art. 129(1), Geneva Convention IV, Art. 146(1), since not all the grave breaches in Additional Protocol I were incorporated into the ICC Statute. Germany ratified Additional Protocols I and II on 14 February 1991. For discussion, see A. Zimmermann, *Zeitschrift für Rechtspolitik* 2002, p. 97 at pp. 98 et seq.

[458] A helpful tabular list of the norms of the international criminal laws of war included in the (German) Code of Crimes Against International Law and the underlying international legal rules is found in the Explanatory Memorandum of the (German) Code of Crimes Against International Law, *BT-Drs.* 14/8524, p. 24.

[459] Thus it is not necessary, as a rule, to determine whether the conflict was international or non-international in character, as long as it is an armed conflict; on this distinction, see *Prosecutor* v. *Tadić*, ICTY (Appeals Chamber), judgment of 15 July 1999, paras. 83 et seq.; H. Fischer, in G. Kirk McDonald and O. Swaak-Goldman (eds.), *Substantive and Procedural Aspects of International Criminal Law*, Vol. 1 (2000), p. 67 at pp. 78 et seq. The distinction can be important if the conflict only reaches minor intensity; see marginal no. 816.

[460] Thus, for example, ICC Statute, Art. 8(2)(a)(i) ("wilful killing"/"l'homocide intentionnel"/ "vorsätzliche Tötung"), Art. 8(2)(b)(vi) ("killing"/"le fait de tuer"/"Tötung"), and Art. 8(2)(c)(i) ("murder"/"le meurtre"/"vorsätzliche Tötung") are combined in (German) Code of Crimes Against International Law, Sec. 8(1) no. 1 as "töte[n]" (killing).

[461] (German) Code of Crimes Against International Law, Sec. 8(6) no. 1, contains a reference to persons protected by the Geneva Conventions and Additional Protocol I. This ensures that German law is completely in accord with the provisions of international law. The purpose of (German) Code

ternational armed conflicts. They include delayed repatriation of prisoners of war (no. 1), transfer of the occupying power's civilian population (no. 2), forced conscription into the enemy's armed forces (no. 3), and forcing the commission of acts of war against one's own country (no. 4). Sections 9 and 10 concern war crimes against property and other rights, as well as war crimes against humanitarian operations and insignia.

A significant body of Hague law is regulated under Section 11, which criminalizes **260** prohibited methods of warfare. Paragraph 1, which applies to international and non-international conflicts equally, criminalizes attacks on civilians (no. 1) and civilian objects (no. 2), as well as attacks that cause disproportionate civilian harm (no. 3). Also included are use of persons as human shields (no. 4), starvation of the civilian population (no. 5), ordering or threatening to give no quarter (no. 6), and perfidious killing or wounding of enemy combatants and fighters (no. 7). War crimes involving the use of prohibited means of warfare, a further central aspect of Hague law, are included in Section 12. Regardless of whether harm occurs in the individual case, it criminalizes the use of poison and poisoned weapons (no. 1), biological and chemical weapons (no. 2), and dum dum bullets (no. 3).

8. Violations of Supervisory Responsibility

In Sections 13 and 14, violations of supervisory responsibility and failure to report a **261** crime are made punishable. These two provisions, together with Section 4, serve to implement the rules on command responsibility in Article 28 of the ICC Statute.

Article 28 of the ICC Statute has been split into three separate provisions.[462] Section 13 of the **262** Code of Crimes Against International Law provides for a separate definition of infringement of supervisory duties, taking into account the varying grades of guilt in cases where the superior knew nothing about the impending commission of the crime by the subordinate. Section 14 provides for the punishment of a superior for not reporting a crime under international law committed by a subordinate. Section 4 clarifies that a superior who is vested with the appropriate supervisory powers and who does not hinder a subordinate from the commission of genocide, a crime against humanity or a war crime shall be punished in the same way as a perpetrator of the offense committed by the subordinate.

9. Aggression

The crime of aggression was not included in the Code of Crimes Against International **263** Law. However, Section 80 of the (German) Criminal Code [*Strafgesetzbuch, StGB*] crim-

---

of Crimes Against International Law, Sec. 8(6) no. 2, is to define the class of people to be protected in non-international armed conflict, closely following the class of people protected in international armed conflict; see Explanatory Memorandum of the (German) Code of Crimes Against International Law, *BT-Drs.* 14/8524, p. 30. This includes the wounded, sick, and shipwrecked, as well as all persons not directly participating in hostilities and found in the hands of the enemy party. (German) Code of Crimes Against International Law, Sec. 8(6) no. 3 protects persons *hors de combat*. See generally, for thorough discussion, G. Werle and V. Nerlich, *Humanitäres Völkerrecht-Informationsschriften* 2002, p. 124 at pp. 130 et seq.

[462] For the reasons, see T. Weigend, in B. Schünemann et al. (eds.), *Festschrift für Roxin* (2001), p. 1375 at p. 1397.

inalizes preparation of aggressive war.[463] Section 80 does not regulate a crime under international law, but contains a so-called state protection offense that protects the Federal Republic's peaceful relations with other nations and its internal security.[464] Not included are aggressive wars in which Germany does not participate. Criminal prosecution of the crime of aggressive war by Germany as a third state is thus impossible. So far, this criminal offense has had little practical significance.[465]

10. Universal Jurisdiction

264   Section 1 of the Code of Crimes Against International Law decrees the applicability of the universality principle, hitherto applicable only to genocide and war crimes,[466] to all crimes[467] defined in the Code, "even when the offence was committed abroad and bears no relation to Germany." Thus German criminal law is always applicable to crimes under international law, regardless of where, by whom or against whom these acts were committed. The only "link" necessary for the applicability of German criminal law is the crime itself, which affects the international community as a whole. Thus the (German) Federal Supreme Court's [*Bundesgerichtshof*] different opinion on universal jurisdiction under former Section 6(1) of the (German) Criminal Code [*Strafgesetzbuch, StGB*][468] is irrelevant to the applicability of the Code of Crimes Against International Law.

265   The "pure" universal jurisdiction provided for in Section 1 of the Code of Crimes Against International Law is flanked by a novel procedural rule:[469] Section 153f of the Code of Criminal Procedure [*Strafprozessordnung, StPO*][470] provides for a duty of inves-

---

[463] For details see G. Werle, *Völkerstrafrecht* (2003), marginal nos. 1179 et seq.

[464] See, e.g., K. Lackner and K. Kühl, *Strafgesetzbuch mit Erläuterungen*, 24th edn. (2001), Sec. 80, marginal no. 1.

[465] In the only decision so far, the Landgericht Köln, *Neue Zeitschrift für Strafrecht* 1981, p. 261, explained that aggressive war, as used in (German) Criminal Code, Secs. 80, 80a, and (German) Basic Law [*Grundgesetz, GG*], Art. 26(1), means "armed aggression contrary to international law." However, the Court left unanswered the underlying question of what constitutes aggressive conduct.

[466] (German) Criminal Code, former Sec. 6 no. 1 and Sec. 6 no. 9 of the (German) Criminal Code, in conjunction with the Geneva Conventions. On the extent to which Sec. 6 no. 9 of the (German) Criminal Code includes crimes committed in civil wars, see G. Werle, *Juristenzeitung* 2000, p. 755 at p. 759. For discussion of the insufficiency of the prior legal situation (which continues to be applicable for prosecution of international crimes committed before the (German) Code of Crimes Against International Law went into effect), see F. Jessberger, 12 *Finnish Yearbook of International Law* (2001), p. 307 at pp. 320 et seq.

[467] (German) Code of Crimes Against International Law, Sec. 1, does not apply to the offenses in Secs. 13 and 14 of the (German) Code of Crimes Against International Law.

[468] See Bundesgerichtshof, judgment of 30 April 1999, *BGHSt* 45, p. 64 at p. 66, with a dismissive discussion by A. Eser, in A. Eser et al. (eds.), *Festschrift für Meyer-Gossner* (2001), pp. 3 et seq., and G. Werle, *Juristenzeitung* 1999, p. 1181 at p. 1182; see also G. Werle and F. Jessberger, *Juristische Schulung* 2001, p. 141 at p. 142.

[469] See Art. 3 of the (German) Act to Introduce the Code of Crimes against International Law of 26 June 2002 [*Gesetz zur Einführung des Völkerstrafgesetzbuchs*], *Bundesgesetzblatt* 2002 I, 2254. See W. Beulke, in Löwe-Rosenberg, *Die Strafprozeßordnung*, 25th edn. (2002), Nachtr. § 153f marginal nos. 1 et seq.; G. Werle and F. Jessberger, *Juristenzeitung* 2002, p. 725 at pp. 732 et seq.

[470] Section 153f of the (German) Code of Criminal Procedure [*Strafprozessordnung, StPO*] reads as follows:

tigation and prosecution even for international crimes committed abroad. This can be dismissed only if there is no domestic connection to the act or if superordinate jurisdiction, such as the International Criminal Court, comes into play.

"(1) In the cases referred to under Section 153c subsection (1), numbers 1 and 2, the public prosecution office may dispense with prosecuting an offence punishable pursuant to sections 6 to 14 of the Code of Crimes against International Law, if the accused is not present in Germany and such presence is not to be anticipated. If in the cases referred to under Section 153c subsection (1), number 1, the accused is a German, this shall however apply only where the offence is being prosecuted before an international court or by a State on whose territory the offence was committed or whose national was harmed by the offence.

(2) In the cases referred to under Section 153c subsection (1), numbers 1 and 2, the public prosecution office may dispense with prosecuting an offence punishable pursuant to sections 6 to 14 of the Code of Crimes against International Law, in particular if

1. there is no suspicion of a German having committed such offence,

2. such offence was not committed against a German,

3. no suspect in respect of such offence is residing in Germany and such residence is not to be anticipated and

4. the offence is being prosecuted before an international court or by a State on whose territory the offence was committed, whose national is suspected of its commission or whose national was harmed by the offence. The same shall apply if a foreigner accused of an offence committed abroad is present in Germany but the requirements pursuant to the first sentence, numbers 2 and 4, have been fulfilled and transfer to an international court or extradition to the prosecuting state is permissible and is intended."

Part Two: General Principles

266   Until the entry into force of the ICC Statute, general principles were of secondary importance in efforts to codify international criminal law. What was important in practice took precedence: the definition of criminal conduct of crimes under international law.

267   A look at the Nuremberg Charter and the Statutes of the international criminal Tribunals created by the UN Security Council illuminates the subordinate status of general principles. The few special rules placed "outside the brackets" of the definitions of crimes neither possess substantive similarities with general norms of accountability in domestic legal systems nor claim, like these, to comprehensively regulate general principles. On the contrary, a need for rules was seen only in those areas where traditional rules for allocating criminal liability threatened to fail in face of the peculiarities of collective, typically state-sponsored conduct. In fact, the Statutes contain only provisions on the (general) irrelevance of acting under orders or in an official capacity, as well as on the criminal liability of superiors for criminal behavior by their subordinates.[1]

268   This approach, of not encumbering the early stages of an emerging body of international criminal law with the formulation of general rules of criminal responsibility, proved uncomplicated in international practice. A survey of this practice confirms that there was at first no need to develop a comprehensive set of general principles for international criminal law. Where necessary, the international criminal Tribunals turned to rules common to domestic legal systems.[2] Since national courts were anyway responsible for implementing international criminal law, the application of national "general principles" was to be expected.

269   Part 3 of the ICC Statute now contains comprehensive provisions on "general principles of criminal law" that form the nucleus of a self-contained set of general principles of international criminal law.[3] They are modeled, in part, on customary international law and general principles of law recognized by civilized nations (Article 38(1)(b), (c) of the ICJ Statute); in other cases, however, the Statute stakes out new territory. Against this background, the ICC Statute is without question the high point of efforts at codification of general principles of international criminal law. For the first time, general questions of law have been separated from the definitions of crimes. Thus statutory criminal law, supplemented by the rich case law of the Yugoslavia and Rwanda Tribunals, forms the starting point for the following discussion, which will also illuminate the relationship

---

[1] For details see marginal nos. 455 et seq., 372. See also H.-H. Jescheck, 2 *Journal of International Criminal Justice* (2004), pp. 38 et seq.

[2] For a summary of case law, see K. Ambos, *Der Allgemeine Teil des Völkerstrafrechts* (2002), pp. 125 et seq., pp. 159 et seq., and pp. 253 et seq.

[3] Part 3 of the ICC Statute contains numerous rules on general principles that the ICC can apply, but not all of them. They are to be supplemented especially by rules that are part of general international law, ICC Statute, Art. 21.

between the law laid out in the ICC Statute and customary international law.

A direct consequence of the recent codification of general rules of criminal responsi- **270** bility is the limited "doctrinal maturity" of some of the general principles in the ICC Statute. One of the central challenges is to clarify them further.[4] This task is made more difficult by the fact that norm creation and determination of law in the area of general principles – in contrast to definitions of crimes – occurs within a thicket of parallel national laws. Every legal system has written or unwritten rules concerning general principles of criminal law; every lawyer reads the provisions of international criminal law first and foremost through the lens of familiar national terminology and doctrine. In addition, most of the provisions in Part 3 of the ICC Statute form an "unsystematic conglomeration from a variety of legal traditions."[5] Elements frequently can be traced to national legal systems. Sometimes the conceptual (and in reality often merely apparent) similarity of international criminal rules to models in domestic law can prove deceptive. Therefore, discussing the general principles of international criminal law requires freeing oneself from the ways of thinking and the doctrinal concepts of one's own domestic law.[6] The Rome Conference showed how difficult this can be.[7]

A. Towards a General Theory of Crimes Under International Law

Kai Ambos: General Principles of Criminal Law in the Rome Statute, 10 *Criminal Law Forum* **271** (1999), pp. 1 et seq.; Kai Ambos: *Der Allgemeine Teil des Völkerstrafrechts* (2002), pp. 539 et seq.; Antonio Cassese: *International Criminal Law* (2003), pp. 136 et seq., p. 222; Roger S. Clark: The Mental Element in International Criminal Law: The Rome Statute of the International Criminal Court and the Elements of Offences, 12 *Criminal Law Forum* (2001), pp. 291 et seq.; Yoram Dinstein: Defences, in Gabrielle Kirk McDonald and Olivia Swaak-Goldman (eds.), *Substantive and Procedural Aspects of International Criminal Law, The Experience of International and National Courts*, Vol. 1 (2000), pp. 371 et seq.; Albin Eser: Die Unterscheidung von Rechtfertigung und Entschuldigung: Ein Schlüsselproblem des Verbrechensbegriffs, in Raimo Lahti and Kimmo Nuotio (eds.), *Strafrechtstheorie im Umbruch, Finnische und vergleichende Perspektiven* (1992), pp. 301 et seq.; Albin Eser: "Defences" in Strafverfahren wegen Kriegsverbrechen, in Kurt Schmoller (ed.), *Festschrift für Triffterer* (1996), pp. 755 et seq.; Albin Eser: Commentary on ICC Statute, Article 31, in Otto Triffterer (ed.), *Commentary on the Rome Statute of the International Criminal Court, Observers' Notes, Article by Article* (1999), pp. 537 et seq.; Maria Kelt and Herman von Hebel: General Principles of Criminal Law and Elements of Crimes, in Roy S. Lee (ed.), *The International Criminal Court, Elements of Crimes and Rules of Procedure and Evidence* (2001),

---

[4] On an initial attempt at "doctrinalization" ("Dogmatisierung"), see K. Ambos, *Der Allgemeine Teil des Völkerstrafrechts* (2002).

[5] A. Eser, in K. Schmoller (ed.), *Festschrift für Triffterer* (1996), p. 755 at p. 775.

[6] The Yugoslavia Tribunal correctly stated: "[A] simple semantic approach . . . can only lead to confusion or a fruitless search for an elusive commonality. In any national legal system, terms are utilised in a specific legal context and are attributed to their own specific connotations by the jurisprudence of that system. Such connotations may not necessarily be relevant when these terms are applied in an international jurisdiction." See *Prosecutor* v. *Mucić et al.*, ICTY (Trial Chamber), judgment of 16 November 1998, para. 431.

[7] The description in R.S. Clark, 12 *Criminal Law Forum* (2001), p. 291 at p. 302, fn. 37 is representative ("breakdown in communication"); see also M. Kelt and H. von Hebel, in R.S. Lee (ed.), *The International Criminal Court, Elements of Crimes and Rules of Procedure and Evidence* (2001), p. 13 at p. 22.

pp. 19 et seq.; Claus Kreß: Die Kristallisation eines Allgemeinen Teils des Völkerstrafrechts: Die Allgemeinen Prinzipien des Strafrechts im Statut des Internationalen Strafgerichtshofs, *Humanitäres Völkerrecht-Informationsschriften* 1999, pp. 4 et seq.; Claus Kreß: Kommentierung III 26, in Heinrich Grützner and Paul-Günter Pötz (eds.), *Internationaler Rechtshilfeverkehr in Strafsachen*, Vol. 4 (2002); Otto Lagodny: Legitimation und Bedeutung des Ständigen Internationalen Strafgerichtshofes, 113 *Zeitschrift für die gesamte Strafrechtswissenschaft* (2001), pp. 800 et seq.; Stefano Manacorda: Die allgemeine Lehre von der Straftat in Frankreich, Besonderheiten oder Lücken in der französischen Strafrechtswissenschaft, *Goltdammer's Archiv für Strafrecht* 1998, pp. 124 et seq.; Klaus Marxen: Beteiligung an schwerem systematischen Unrecht, Bemerkungen zu einer völkerstrafrechtlichen Straftatlehre, in Klaus Lüderssen (ed.), *Aufgeklärte Kriminalpolitik oder Kampf gegen das "Böse"*, Vol. 3: Makrokriminalität (1998), pp. 220 et seq.; Reinhard Merkel: Gründe für den Ausschluss der Strafbarkeit im Völkerstrafrecht, 114 *Zeitschrift für die gesamte Strafrechtswissenschaft* (2002), pp. 437 et seq.; Christiane Nill-Theobald: *"Defences" bei Kriegsverbrechen am Beispiel Deutschlands und der USA, Zugleich ein Beitrag zum Allgemeinen Teil des Völkerstrafrechts* (1998), pp. 57 et seq.; Donald K. Piragoff: Commentary on ICC Statute, Article 30, in Otto Triffterer (ed.), *Commentary on the Rome Statute of the International Criminal Court, Observers' Notes, Article by Article* (1999), pp. 527 et seq.; Leila N. Sadat: *The International Criminal Court and the Transformation of International Law, Justice for the New Millenium* (2002), pp. 213 et seq.; Massimo Scaliotti: Defences before the International Criminal Court: Substantive grounds for excluding criminal responsibility, Part 1, 1 *International Criminal Law Review* (2001), pp. 111 et seq.; Part 2, 2 *International Criminal Law Review* (2002), pp. 1 et seq.; William A. Schabas: Commentary on ICC Statute, Article 66, in Otto Triffterer (ed.), *Commentary on the Rome Statute of the International Criminal Court, Observers' Notes, Article by Article* (1999), pp. 833 et seq.; John C. Smith and Brian Hogan: *Criminal Law*, 9th edn. (1999), pp. 28 et seq., pp. 189 et seq.; Joachim Vogel: Elemente der Straftat, Bemerkungen zur französischen Straftatlehre und zur Straftatlehre des common law, *Goltdammer's Archiv für Strafrecht* 1998, pp. 127 et seq.; Thomas Weigend: Zur Frage eines "internationalen" Allgemeinen Teils, in Bernd Schünemann et al. (eds.), *Festschrift für Roxin* (2001), pp. 1375 et seq.

I. The Concept of Crimes Under International Law

272   Only a rough outline has thus far emerged of a specific doctrine of international crimes. Such a doctrine would need to provide general standards of liability for crimes under international law[8] by systematically recording and classifying the structural elements common to all such crimes.

273   The practice of the international criminal Tribunals has been geared toward a two-pronged concept of crime that is widespread in common law.[9] It distinguishes, as a starting point, between offenses that create grounds for criminal liability, consisting of a

---

[8] On the tasks of a general doctrine of criminal law, see G. Jakobs, *Strafrecht Allgemeiner Teil*, 2nd edn. (1993), pp. 125 et seq.; H.-H. Jescheck and T. Weigend, *Lehrbuch des Strafrechts, Allgemeiner Teil*, 5th edn. (1996), p. 194; and specifically for crimes under international law, see K. Marxen, in K. Lüderssen (ed.), *Aufgeklärte Krimimalpolitik oder Kampf gegen das "Böse"?*, Vol. 3 (1998), pp. 220 et seq.

[9] See K. Ambos, *Der Allgemeine Teil des Völkerstrafrechts* (2002), p. 361 and pp. 539 et seq.; for discussion of the common law's doctrine of crimes from a civil law perspective, see J. Vogel, *Goltdammer's Archiv für Strafrecht* 1998, p. 127 at pp. 136 et seq. This model is sometimes also described as a three-pronged concept of crime (*actus reus*, *mens rea*, and *defenses*), see J.C. Smith and B. Hogan, *Criminal Law*, 9th edn. (1999), pp. 28 et seq. and p. 189.

material element (*actus reus*) and a mental element (*mens rea*),[10] on the one hand, and defenses that rule out liability, on the other.[11] The latter include not only substantive grounds for excluding criminal responsibility (such as self-defense and necessity), but also procedural obstacles to prosecution (such as incapacity and statutes of limitations).[12]

The Yugoslavia and Rwanda Tribunals distinguish between the crime and the individual criminal responsibility of the defendant. The latter is seen as a separate category, involving the establishment of a mode of participation in particular. Both categories, the crime and the individual criminal responsibility, possess both material elements and a mental element.   **274**

The ICC Statute emphasizes the independence of international criminal law and grounds it in a foundation of its own. This concept contains elements of common law and civil law doctrine, but combines them into a specific concept of crimes under international law.[13]   **275**

The ICC Statute largely refrains from applying well-established terminology from the major legal systems.[14] This approach is correct, in that using technical terms that are already "taken" often   **276**

---

[10] *"Actus non facit reum nisi mens sit rea."* See Y. Dinstein, in G. Kirk McDonald and O. Swaak-Goldman (eds.), *Substantive and Procedural Aspects of International Criminal Law*, Vol. 1 (2000), p. 371.

[11] This tendency becomes clear primarily in regard to the design of criminal proceedings. The real characteristic of the concept of crime in the common law tradition is that different standards of proof are associated with offenses and defenses, see J. Herrmann, 93 *Zeitschrift für die gesamte Strafrechtswissenschaft* (1981), p. 615 at pp. 653 et seq.; J. Vogel, *Goltdammer's Archiv für Strafrecht* 1998, p. 127 at p. 137. Very roughly, it is up to the prosecution to prove the elements of crime, while the defendant must show the presence of the conditions for a defense, see W.R. LaFave, *Criminal Law*, 4th edn. (2003), pp. 55 et seq. In *Prosecutor* v. *Mucić* et al., ICTY (Trial Chamber), judgment of 16 November 1998, paras. 1157 et seq., the Trial Chamber referred to the "general principle that the burden of proof . . . is on the person . . . who raises the defence." See also ICTY Rules of Procedure, Rule 67(A)(ii)(b): "[T]he defence shall notify the Prosecutor of its intent to offer . . . any special defence, including that of diminished or lack of mental responsibility; in which case the notification shall specify the names and addresses of witnesses and any other evidence upon which the accused intends to rely to establish the special defence."

[12] See A. Ashworth, *Principles of Criminal Law*, 3rd edn. (1999), p. 209; Y. Dinstein, in G. Kirk McDonald and O. Swaak-Goldman (eds.), *Substantive and Procedural Aspects of International Criminal Law* (2000), p. 371 at pp. 372 et seq.; W.R. LaFave, *Criminal Law*, 4th edn. (2003), p. 57; M. Scaliotti, 1 *International Criminal Law Review* (2001), p. 111 at p. 112.

[13] See also C. Kress, *Humanitäres Völkerrecht-Informationsschriften* 1999, p. 4 at p. 5. While the title of Part 3 ("General Principles of Criminal Law") suggests a certain linguistic affinity to common law, the designation of grounds for excluding punishment ("Grounds for Excluding Criminal Responsibility," ICC Statute, Art. 31) is closer to the continental European conceptual terminology, see A. Eser, in O. Triffterer (ed.), *Commentary on the Rome Statute of the International Criminal Court* (1999), Art. 31, marginal no. 15. Use of the terms "élément materiel" and "élément psychologique" in ICC Statute, Art. 30 also recalls the use of continental European, specifically common French, terminology, see S. Manacorda, *Goltdammer's Archiv für Strafrecht* 1998, p. 124 at p. 125.

[14] For example, the Statute does not use the paired terms *actus reus/mens rea*. While the preliminary drafts by the UN International Law Commission, alluding to the common law concepts, did speak of *actus reus* and *mens rea* (see *Draft Code* 1994), at the Rome Conference the terms "physical element" and "objective elements" were at first used instead, see R.S. Clark, 12 *Criminal Law Forum* (2001), p. 291 at p. 299, fn. 25. Ultimately it was the editing committee that replaced the term "physical element" with "material element," see K. Ambos, *Der Allgemeine Teil des Völkerstrafrechts*

leads to the interpretation of such concepts in national law being "brought along" as well. The price paid for this restraint in using existing, tested legal concepts is that many rules require further clarification through practice.

277 The ICC Statute distinguishes first of all between crimes, grounds for individual criminal responsibility, and grounds to exclude it. The definitions of crimes are found in Articles 6, 7, and 8 of the ICC Statute. Each contains material elements and a mental element. For the mental element, Article 30 of the ICC Statute formulates general requirements that are applicable, except where other rules apply. The grounds for individual criminal responsibility are found in Articles 25 and 28 of the ICC Statute. Article 25(2) deals with the general principles of individual criminal liability. Article 25(3) enumerates the various modes of participation. Article 28 expands this list to include superior responsibility. How the forms of criminal responsibility relate to the definitions of the offenses is unclear even within the structure of the ICC Statute and will require further clarification. Article 31 enumerates grounds for excluding criminal responsibility.

II. The Context of Organized Violence (International Element)

278 It is possible to consider the peculiarities of macrocriminality in terms of the three elements of a crime under international law. In addition to the individual act ("any of the following acts"),[15] the classification also requires a context of organized violence (contextual element or contextual circumstances).[16] The connection to this context turns an ordinary crime into a crime under international law.[17] The contextual element comes into play, depending on the crime, as either a material or a mental element of the crime. For genocide, the context, the destruction of a protected group, is included in the mental element of the crime;[18] the destruction of the group or of a part of the group must be the perpetrator's aim. In contrast, for crimes against humanity, war crimes and the crime of aggression, contextual elements concern the objective conditions. For crimes against humanity, a widespread or systematic attack on a civilian population is, like armed conflict

---

(2002), p. 762. Nor were the terms *offense/defense* used. Here the adoption of common law terminology might have been misunderstood as a reference to the applicability of the pragmatic-procedural model of distributing the burden of proof that is common to the adversarial criminal trial. But this was specifically not reflected in the ICC Statute, see ICC Statute, Art. 54(1)(a): "The Prosecutor shall . . . in doing so, investigate incriminating and exonerating circumstances equally"; Art. 66(2): "The onus is on the Prosecutor to prove the guilt of the accused"; Art. 67(1)(i): "[The accused shall be entitled] not to have imposed on him or her any reversal of the burden of proof or any onus of rebuttal." For discussion, see W.A. Schabas, in O. Triffterer (ed.), *Commentary on the Rome Statute of the International Criminal Court* (1999), Art. 66, marginal nos. 18 et seq.

[15] ICC Statute, Art. 6, Art. 7(1), Art. 8(2)(b), (c).

[16] Elements of Crimes for the ICC Statute, General Introduction, num. 7. See also Elements of Crimes for Article 7 ICC Statute, Introduction, num. 2: "The last two elements for each crime against humanity describe the context in which the conduct must take place." For discussion of the term "contextual element", see marginal no. 82, fn. 153.

[17] See marginal no. 81.

[18] See marginal no. 82.

for war crimes, part of the material elements of the crime. Organized use of force is also a material element of the crime of aggression.

III. The Structure of Crimes Under International Law

The test of liability under international criminal law can be made according to the fol- **279**
lowing three-pronged scheme:[19]

1. Step One: Material Elements

As a first step, it must be examined whether the suspect fulfilled the material elements of **280**
a crime ("*element materiel du crime*").[20] These include conduct, consequence, and any
other accompanying circumstance contained in the definition of a crime under international law.[21] For crimes against humanity and war crimes, attacks on a civilian population or armed conflict must be emphasized as essential circumstances.[22] Conduct,
consequences and circumstances also become the reference points for the mental element
of the crimes.[23]

2. Step Two: Mental Element

The mental element requires that the perpetrator commits the material elements of the **281**
act "with intent and knowledge" (ICC Statute, Article 30). For some crimes under international law, these requirements are less strict; for others, the conditions are stricter or
additional subjective elements are included.

3. Step Three: Grounds for Excluding Responsibility

As a third step, it must be asked whether circumstances are present that exclude indi- **282**
vidual criminal responsibility on the part of the perpetrator. Technically, the ICC Statute distinguishes three groups of grounds for excluding criminal responsibility. Exclusion
of responsibility for reasons of mental disease, intoxication, self-defense or necessity and

---

[19] See also C. Kress, *Humanitäres Völkerrecht-Informationsschriften* 1999, p. 4 at p. 5.

[20] The term is found in Art. 30 of the ICC Statute and in the Elements of Crimes for the ICC
Statute, General Introduction. It describes the "specific elements of the definition of the crimes as defined in articles 5 to 8" of the ICC Statute, see D.K. Piragoff, in O. Triffterer (ed.), *Commentary on
the Rome Statute of the International Criminal Court* (1999), Art. 30, marginal no. 6. For discussion,
see K. Ambos, *Der Allgemeine Teil des Völkerstrafrechts* (2002), pp. 762 et seq.

[21] The question whether material elements include not only the objective characteristics in the
definitions of crimes, but also all other material conditions for criminal liability, especially the (lack of)
exclusionary grounds, must be answered in the negative. It can be inferred from ICC Statute, Art.
30(2) that the objective conditions for liability include only conduct, consequences and circumstances,
see K. Ambos, *Der Allgemeine Teil des Völkerstrafrechts* (2002), pp. 762 et seq.

[22] See marginal no. 202.

[23] See ICC Statute, Art. 30; see M. Kelt and H. von Hebel, in R.S. Lee (ed.), *The International
Criminal Court, Elements of Crimes and Rules of Procedure and Evidence* (2001), p. 13 at p. 26.

duress is covered by Article 31(1) of the ICC Statute. Separate provision is made for exclusion of responsibility because of mistake or acting pursuant to superior orders (ICC Statute, Articles 32 and 33).[24] Additional reasons for excluding responsibility may arise from international legal sources outside the Statute.[25] If the conditions for exclusion of responsibility are present, the person is "not criminally responsible" (ICC Statute, Article 31(1)).[26]

283   The distinction between justification (of the act) and excuse (for the perpetrator) has hitherto been alien to international criminal law.[27] However, we must note the insistent efforts on the part of criminal law scholars with a civil law background to anchor the distinction between unlawfulness and guilt in international criminal law.[28]

4. Requirements for Prosecution

284   This three-pronged test establishes whether there is individual criminal responsibility under international law. However, though the perpetrator may be fully criminally responsible, punishment may be impossible because obstacles to prosecution exist. Such obstacles to criminal prosecution are external to the definitions of crimes, as they concern not the criminality of the conduct, but merely the admissibility of prosecution; at issue are requirements for trial and elements of procedural law. Relevant provisions are found in the ICC Statute on prohibition of double jeopardy in Article 20(1), on minors in Article 26, on immunity in Article 27(2), and on statutes of limitations in Article 29.[29]

B. Material Elements

285   K. Ambos: *Der Allgemeine Teil des Völkerstrafrechts, Ansätze einer Dogmatisierung* (2002), pp. 764 et seq.; Maria Kelt and Herman von Hebel: General Principles of Criminal Law and Elements of Crimes, in Roy S. Lee (ed.), *The International Criminal Court, Elements of Crimes and Rules of Procedure and Evidence* (2001), pp. 13 et seq.; Geert-Jan Knoops: *Defenses in Contemporary International Criminal Law* (2001), pp. 9 et seq.; Claus Kreß: Die Kristallisation eines Allgemeinen Teils des Völkerstrafrechts: Die Allgemeinen Prinzipien des Strafrechts im Statut des Internationalen

---

[24] It follows explicitly from ICC Statute, Art. 31, that the rule is not exclusive: "In addition to other grounds for excluding criminal responsibility provided for in this Statute . . . ".

[25] See ICC Statute, Art. 31(3): "At trial, the Court may consider a ground for excluding criminal responsibility other than those referred to in paragraph 1 where such a ground is derived from applicable law as set forth in article 21."

[26] In this context, the Statute uses various terms, though this does not constitute a substantive difference: "excluding criminal responsibility"; "a person shall not be criminally responsible" (Art. 31); Arts. 22(1), 24(1), "exempt from criminal responsibility" (Art. 27(1)); "relieve that person of criminal responsibility" (Art. 33).

[27] For detail, see A. Cassese, *International Criminal Law* (2003), p. 222.

[28] See K. Ambos, *Der Allgemeine Teil des Völkerstrafrechts* (2002), pp. 826 et seq.; A. Eser, in O. Triffterer (ed.), *Commentary on the Rome Statute of the International Criminal Court* (1999), Art. 31, marginal no. 2; L.N. Sadat, *The International Criminal Court and the Transformation of International Law* (2002), pp. 213 et seq.; on the difference between justification and excuse, see generally A. Eser, in Raimo Lahti and Kimmo Nuotio (eds.), *Strafrechtstheorie im Umbruch, Finnische und vergleichende Perspektiven* (1992), pp. 301 et seq.

[29] See also marginal nos. 545 et seq.

Strafgerichtshofs, *Humanitäres Völkerrecht-Informationsschriften* 1999, pp. 4 et seq.; Donald K. Piragoff: Commentary on ICC Statute, Article 30, in Otto Triffterer (ed.), *Commentary on the Rome Statute of the International Criminal Court, Observers' Notes, Article by Article* (1999), pp. 527 et seq.; Per Saland: International Criminal Law Principles, in Roy S. Lee (ed.), *The International Criminal Court, The Making of the Rome Statute* (1999), pp. 189 et seq.

The material elements of crimes under international law include all conditions that de- **286**
termine the external appearance of the act. These objective elements can be descriptive or normative, concerned with the act or with the perpetrator. Unlike the mental element, no general provision on material elements of crimes is found in the ICC Statute.[30]

The ICC Statute distinguishes between three aspects of the material elements.[31] The **287**
starting point is the conduct described in the definition of the crime; most definitions of crimes additionally require the occurrence of a specific consequence of this conduct, as well as the presence of other circumstances that concern neither the conduct nor the consequences.

I. Conduct

Objectively, every international crime presumes some conduct[32] that is more precisely **288**
delineated in the definition of the crime. This can consist of an action or – to the extent this is provided for in the definition[33] – an omission.[34]

II. Consequence and Causation

Most crimes under international law require not only incriminating behavior, but also a **289**
specific consequence of this behavior. Consequences in this sense include all effects of

---

[30] Art. 28 of the Draft ICC Statute (1998), although it was still contained in the conference submission (though generally "bracketed"), was ultimately eliminated due to differences of opinion on the validity and scope of the liability for omissions provided for in its subsection 2. See marginal nos. 507 et seq.

[31] ICC Statute, Art. 30(2). See K. Ambos, *Der Allgemeine Teil des Völkerstrafrechts* (2002), pp. 764 et seq.; R.S. Clark, 12 *Criminal Law Forum* (2001), p. 291 at pp. 306 et seq.; M. Kelt and H. von Hebel, in R.S. Lee (ed.), *The International Criminal Court, Elements of Crimes and Rules of Procedure and Evidence* (2001), p. 13 at p. 14, and p. 26; D.K. Piragoff, in O. Triffterer (ed.), *Commentary on the Rome Statute of the International Criminal Court* (1999), Art. 30, marginal no. 6. The distinction between conduct, consequences and circumstances arises from a common law doctrine, see A. Eser, in A. Cassese, P. Gaeta and J.R.W.D. Jones (eds.), *The Rome Statute of the International Criminal Court*, Vol. 1 (2002), p. 889 at pp. 911 et seq., and is of great significance mainly because each requires something different of the mental element, see ICC Statute, Art. 30(2) and the detailed marginal nos. 299 et seq.

[32] The preliminary drafts still spoke of "act or omission", see Draft ICC Statute (1998), Art. 28. See P. Saland, in R.S. Lee (ed.), *The International Criminal Court, The Making of the Rome Statute* (1999), p. 189 at p. 212.

[33] See marginal nos. 503 et seq. Examples include ICC Statute, Art. 28 (command responsibility) and Art. 8(2)(b)(xxv) ("Intentionally using starvation of civilians as a method of warfare by depriving them of objects indispensable to their survival.").

[34] See K. Ambos, *Der Allgemeine Teil des Völkerstrafrechts* (2002), p. 765 ("act and omission"); A. Eser, in A. Cassese, P. Gaeta and J.R.W.D. Jones (eds.), *The Rome Statute of the International Criminal Court*, Vol. 1 (2002), p. 889 at p. 913; M. Kelt and H. von Hebel, in R.S. Lee (ed.), *The International Criminal Court, Elements of Crimes and Rules of Procedure and Evidence* (2001), p. 13 at p. 26.

the criminal conduct;[35] even so-called conduct crimes may have "consequences." The consequence can consist of harm that has actually occurred (such as causing great physical suffering to the victim),[36] or merely of danger to a protected right (such as seriously endangering the health of the victim[37]).[38]

290 If a crime under international law requires a specific consequence, it is necessary, for it to be criminal, that a causal link exist between the perpetrator's conduct and the consequence, so that the concrete consequence can be seen as having been caused by the perpetrator.[39] Under customary law, the requirement of a causal connection between conduct and consequence is recognized as a precondition of criminality. Reference to a causation requirement is found even in the Nuremberg judgment.[40] The Supreme Court in the British Occupied Zone considered questions of causation in detail,[41] and the opinions of the Yugoslavia Tribunal also contain remarks on causation.[42] No explicit provision on the causation requirement was ultimately included in the ICC Statute, although it was provided for in the draft version;[43] implicitly, however, it arises out of Article 30 of the ICC Statute,[44] and, in addition, frequently follows from the definition of a crime itself.[45]

III. Circumstances

291 In addition to conduct and consequences, crimes under international law normally require the presence of additional circumstances.[46] Objective circumstances can be of a

---

[35] See A. Eser, in A. Cassese, P. Gaeta and J.R.W.D. Jones (eds.), *The Rome Statute of the International Criminal Court*, Vol. 1 (2002), p. 889 at p. 914: "all definitional effects which may ensue from the prohibited conduct."

[36] See ICC Statute, Art. 8(2)(a)(ii).

[37] See ICC Statute, Art. 8(2)(b)(x).

[38] See M. Kelt and H. von Hebel, in R.S. Lee (ed.), *The International Criminal Court, Elements of Crimes and Rules of Procedure and Evidence* (2001), p. 13 at p. 15.

[39] However, under the ICC Statute, the causal connection between conduct and consequences is not an element "in itself"; it must, correctly, be examined in connection with discussion of the consequences, see R.S. Clark, 12 *Criminal Law Forum* (2001), p. 291 at p. 372 and p. 304.

[40] For greater detail, see K. Ambos, *Der Allgemeine Teil des Völkerstrafrechts* (2002), pp. 87 et seq. and pp. 125 et seq.

[41] See, e.g., Supreme Court in the British Occupied Zone, *OGHSt* 2, p. 291 at pp. 295 et seq., on the question of the causal nature of the racist film "Jud Süss," commissioned by Goebbels, in regard to the attacks on Jews and thus its assessment as a crime against humanity. For details, see K. Ambos, *Der Allgemeine Teil des Völkerstrafrechts* (2002), pp. 167 et seq.

[42] See, e.g., *Prosecutor v. Mucić* et al., ICTY (Trial Chamber), judgment of 16 November 1998, para. 424: "the conduct of the accused must be a substantial cause of the death of the victim."

[43] Draft ICC Statute (1998), Art. 28(3) states: "A person is only criminally responsible under this Statute for committing a crime if the harm required for the commission of the crime is caused by and [accountable] [attributable] to his or her act or omission."

[44] See ICC Statute, Art. 30(2)(b): "that person means to cause that consequence or is aware that it will occur in the ordinary course of events"; see also G.-J. Knoops, *Defenses in Contemporary International Criminal Law* (2001), p. 11.

[45] See, e.g., ICC Statute, Art. 7(1)(k): "Other inhumane acts of a similar character intentionally causing great suffering . . .."

[46] In common law, "circumstances" are normally understood to mean facts arising from legally established factual requirements, and do not describe the conduct itself or the consequences of the act, see K. Ambos, *Der Allgemeine Teil des Völkerstrafrechts* (2002), p. 766.

factual nature, such as the fact that the victim is younger than 15 years old,[47] or they can concern normative characteristics, for example that the victim is a person protected under the Geneva Conventions[48].[49]

In classifying conduct as a crime under international law, circumstances play a key **292** role in the crime of aggression, crimes against humanity, and war crimes.[50] Here so-called contextual circumstances[51] or elements[52] constitute the objective requirement that lend individual acts an international dimension.[53] For the crime of aggression, organized use of force constitutes the core element for criminality. For crimes against humanity and war crimes, the contextual elements arise directly from the definitions of the crimes: crimes against humanity require that actual conduct take place in the context of a widespread or systematic attack on a civilian population; war crimes require that "the conduct took place in the context of and was associated with an international armed conflict."[54] The crime of genocide, in contrast, does not require the objective presence of a context of organized violence; here, this context is shifted entirely onto the subjective element. To the extent the Elements of Crimes objectively require a context of further genocidal conduct according to the same pattern,[55] under a correct interpretation this affects only the jurisdiction of the International Criminal Court, but not the substantive criminality of genocide.[56]

C. Mental Element

Kai Ambos: Some Preliminary Reflections on the Mens Rea Requirements of the ICC Statute and **293** the Elements of Crimes, in Lal Chand Vohrah et al. (eds.), *Man's Inhumanity to Man* (2003), pp. 11 et seq.; Kai Ambos: *Der Allgemeine Teil des Völkerstrafrechts, Ansätze einer Dogmatisierung* (2002), pp. 757 et seq.; K. Ambos: General Principles of Criminal Law in the Rome Statute, 10 *Criminal Law Forum* (1999), pp. 1 et seq.; Roberta Arnold: The Mens Rea of Genocide under the Statute of the International Criminal Court, 14 *Criminal Law Forum* (2003), pp. 127 et seq.; Antonio Cassese: *International Criminal Law* (2003), pp. 159 et seq.; Roger S. Clark: The Mental Element in International Criminal Law: The Rome Statute of the International Criminal Court and the Elements of Offences, 12 *Criminal Law Forum* (2001), pp. 291 et seq.; Catherine Elliott: The French Law of Intent and Its Influence on the Development of International Criminal Law, 11 *Criminal Law Forum* (2000), pp. 35 et seq.; Albin Eser: Mental Elements – Mistake of Fact and Mistake of Law, in Antonio Cassese, Paola Gaeta and John R.W.D. Jones (eds.), *The Rome Statute*

---

[47] See ICC Statute, Art. 8(2)(b)(xxvi).

[48] See ICC Statute, Art. 8(2)(a).

[49] M. Kelt and H. von Hebel, in R.S. Lee (ed.), *The International Criminal Court, Elements of Crimes and Rules of Procedure and Evidence* (2001), p. 13 at p. 15 and p. 27.

[50] On the dispute over the classification of the contextual elements at the Rome Conference, see marginal no. 326.

[51] See Elements of Crimes for the ICC Statute, General Introduction, num. 7.

[52] See M. Kelt and H. von Hebel, in R.S. Lee (ed.), *The International Criminal Court, Elements of Crimes and Rules of Procedure and Evidence* (2001), p. 13 at p. 15.

[53] For the notion of contextual element ("Gesamttat"), see marginal nos. 81 et seq.

[54] See, e.g., Elements of Crimes for Article 8(2)(a)(i) ICC Statute, num. 5.

[55] See Elements of Crimes for Article 6(a) ICC Statute, num. 4: "took place in the context of a manifest pattern of similar conduct directed against that group or was conduct that could itself effect such destruction."

[56] For discussion, see marginal no. 609.

of the International Criminal Court: A Commentary, Vol. 1 (2002), pp. 889 et seq.; George Fletcher: *Rethinking Criminal Law* (2000), pp. 443 et seq.; Hans-Heinrich Jescheck: *Die Verantwortlichkeit der Staatsorgane nach Völkerstrafrecht, Eine Studie zu den Nürnberger Prozessen* (1952), pp. 375 et seq.; Maria Kelt and Herman von Hebel: General Principles of Criminal Law and Elements of Crimes, in Roy S. Lee (ed.), *The International Criminal Court, Elements of Crimes and Rules of Procedure and Evidence* (2001), pp. 13 et seq.; Claus Kress: Die Kristallisation eines Allgemeinen Teils des Völkerstrafrechts: Die Allgemeinen Prinzipien des Strafrechts im Statut des Internationalen Strafgerichtshofs, *Humanitäres Völkerrecht-Informationsschriften* 1999, pp. 4 et seq.; Wayne R. LaFave: *Criminal Law*, 4th edn. (2003), pp. 239 et seq.; Donald K. Piragoff: ICC Statute, Article 30, in Otto Triffterer (ed.), *Commentary on the Rome Statute of the International Criminal Court, Observers' Notes, Article by Article* (1999), pp. 527 et seq.; Leila N. Sadat: *The International Criminal Court, and the Transformation of International Law: Justice for the New Millenium* (2002), pp. 208 et seq.; Per Saland: International Criminal Law Principles, in Roy S. Lee (ed.), *The International Criminal Court, The Making of the Rome Statute* (1999), pp. 189 et seq.; William A. Schabas: *Introduction to the International Criminal Court*, 2nd edn. (2004), pp. 108 et seq.; William A. Schabas: General Principles of Criminal Law in the International Criminal Court Statute (Part III), 4 *European Journal of Crime, Criminal Law and Criminal Justice* (1998), pp. 400 et seq.; Ellies van Sliedregt, *The Criminal Responsibility of Individuals for Violations of International Humanitarian Law* (1985), pp. 48 et seq.; Otto Triffterer: Bestandsaufnahme zum Völkerstrafrecht, in Gerd Hankel and Gerhard Stuby (eds.), *Strafgerichte gegen Menschheitsverbrechen, Zum Völkerstrafrecht 50 Jahre nach den Nürnberger Prozessen* (1995), p. 169 at pp. 223 et seq.; Otto Triffterer: ICC Statute, Article 32, in Otto Triffterer (ed.), *Commentary on the Rome Statute of the International Criminal Court, Observers' Notes, Article by Article* (1999), pp. 555 et seq.; Otto Triffterer: Kriminalpolitische Überlegungen zum Entwurf gleichlautender "Elements of Crimes" für alle Tatbestände des Völkermordes, in Bernd Schünemann et al. (eds.), *Festschrift für Roxin* (2001), pp. 1415 et seq.; Hans Vest: Humanitätsverbrechen – Herausforderung für das Individualstrafrecht?, 113 *Zeitschrift für die gesamte Strafrechtswissenschaft* (2001), pp. 457 et seq.; Thomas Weigend: Zwischen Vorsatz und Fahrlässigkeit, 93 *Zeitschrift für die gesamte Strafrechtswissenschaft* (1981), pp. 657 et seq.; Thomas Weigend: Zur Frage eines "internationalen" Allgemeinen Teils, in Bernd Schünemann et al. (eds.), *Festschrift für Roxin* (2001), pp. 1375 et seq.; Thomas Weigend, 19 *Nouvelles Études Pénales* (2004), pp. 319 et seq.; Johan D. van der Vyver, 23 *Fordham International Law Journal* (1999), pp. 286 et seq.; Gerhard Werle and Florian Jessberger: Das Völkerstrafgesetzbuch, *Juristenzeitung* 2002, pp. 725 et seq.

294   Under international criminal law, individual criminal responsibility requires a certain state of mind on the part of the perpetrator, which must accompany the act or omission as specified in the definition of the crime. The requirement of a mental element as a prerequisite for criminal responsibility is generally recognized.

295   In the customary law definitions of crimes under international law, the subjective elements are clarified separately for each crime.[57] Neither the Nuremberg Charter nor the Statutes of the Yugoslavia or Rwanda Tribunals include general provisions on requirements for the mental element. However, subjective prerequisites for criminality can be found in the definitions of crimes; for example, for the crime of genocide ("intent . . . to

---

[57] See R.S. Clark, 12 *Criminal Law Forum* (2001), 291 at pp. 295 et seq.; A. Eser, in A. Cassese, P. Gaeta and J.R.W.D. Jones (eds.), *The Rome Statute of the International Criminal Court*, Vol. 1 (2002), p. 889 at pp. 893 et seq.: "the concept of mens rea though not explicitly mentioned in either the Nuremberg Charter nor in other conventions in international crimes may be required by the very nature of the crimes concerned."; W.A. Schabas, 4 *European Journal of Crime, Criminal Justice and Criminal Law* (1998), p. 400 at p. 419.

destroy . . . a group," Article 4(2) of the ICTY Statute) or for certain war crimes ("wilful killing" or "wilfully causing great suffering," Article 2(a) and (c) of the ICTY Statute).[58] Additionally, it is recognized as a general principle of law that the material elements of an act and a subjective element related to the perpetrator's perceptions (mental element) must coincide in order to constitute a crime. On this, the Yugoslavia Tribunal has stated:

"It is apparent that it is a general principle of law that the establishment of criminal culpability requires an analysis of two aspects. The first of these may be termed the *actus reus* – the physical act necessary for the offence. . . . The second aspect . . . relates to the necessary mental element, or *mens rea*."[59]

Article 30 of the ICC Statute now provides a general rule, applicable in principle to all crimes under international law, on the subjective requirements for criminality.

I. International Case Law

In international case law, the subjective requirements for criminality have been devel- **296** oped on a case-by-case basis, as needed, for the various crimes.[60] The spectrum of subjective requirements is broad. While some crimes require purpose or knowledge of the material circumstances, for others, recklessness is sufficient.[61] Negligence can only form a basis for criminal liability in exceptional cases.[62] Furthermore, the distinction between general intent, as a common requirement for all crimes, and specific intent is widely acknowledged.[63] The latter requires an additional mental attitude that goes beyond simply

---

[58] It would be wrong to assume that, in those places where the definitions of crimes do not explicitly include a subjective element, it may be dispensed with. The reason for the selective mention of subjective elements in the definitions of crimes lies particularly in the incorporation of penal norms from the rules of international humanitarian law.

[59] *Prosecutor* v. *Mucić* et al., ICTY (Trial Chamber), judgment of 16 November 1998, paras. 424 et seq. See also IMT, judgment of 1 October 1946, in *The Trial of German Major War Criminals. Proceedings of the International Military Tribunal Sitting at Nuremberg, Germany*, Part 22, p. 507. The defendant Schacht was acquitted by the IMT because "this necessary inference [that Schacht had knowledge about the attacking plans] has not been established beyond reasonable doubt."; see also US Military Tribunal, Nuremberg, judgment of 10 April 1948 (*Ohlendorf* et al., so-called Einsatzgruppen Trial), *Trials of War Criminals* IV, p. 470: "intent is a basic prerequisite to responsibility for crime"; see also A. Cassese, *International Criminal Law* (2003), pp. 159 et seq.

[60] See the detailed analysis of the IMT judgment and the Nuremberg follow-up trials in H.-H. Jescheck, *Die Verantwortlichkeit der Staatsorgane nach Völkerstrafrecht* (1952), pp. 375 et seq.; see also K. Ambos, *Der Allgemeine Teil des Völkerstrafrechts* (2002), pp. 107 et seq.; A. Cassese, *International Criminal Law* (2003), pp. 159 et seq.

[61] For example, the crime against humanity of killing under Art. 5(a) of the ICTY Statute requires either "intent to kill" or at least "intent to inflict serious injury in reckless disregard of human life," see *Prosecutor* v. *Kupreškić* et al., ICTY (Trial Chamber), judgment of 14 January 2000, para. 561. Under Art. 2(b), among others, the war crime of torture presumes that the injury was caused "intentionally," *Prosecutor* v. *Mucić* et al., ICTY (Trial Chamber), judgment of 16 November 1998, para. 494. See also marginal no. 334.

[62] But see marginal nos. 381 et seq.

[63] See A. Cassese, *International Criminal Law* (2003), pp. 167 et seq.

reflecting the material elements of the crime. Such specific intent must be present for certain international crimes,[64] such as genocide.

297 A comparative analysis of the categories of *mens rea*, mental element or fault applied in a domestic context reveals a sometimes confusing diversity of concepts and terms.[65] As will be shown, the language of Article 30 of the ICC Statute adds to this confusion. Where necessary, this book refers to the language used by the Model Penal Code, which distinguishes four levels of the mental element ("minimum requirements of culpability"):[66] purpose, knowledge, recklessness, and negligence. The traditional civil law concepts of *dolus directus in the first degree* (purpose), *dolus directus in the second degree* (knowledge), and *dolus eventualis* (recklessness) are used interchangebly.[67]

II. Article 30 of the ICC Statute

298 Article 30 of the ICC Statute now establishes subjective requirements for individual criminal responsibility that apply in principle to all crimes included in the ICC Statute.[68]

1. Structure

299 Article 30 of the ICC Statute consists of three subsections. Subsection 1 contains the general principle under which criminal responsibility requires that the material elements of the crime must be committed with intent and knowledge, unless otherwise provided. The "intent and knowledge" elements distinguish cognitive from voluntative conditions of criminality; their cumulative presence at the time of the conduct[69] is necessary for liability. The points of reference for both elements – intent and knowledge – are the material elements of the crime. Subsections 2 and 3 further elaborate on the elements of this principle, in particular by defining what is meant by intent and knowledge. Three crucial points can be made if Article 30(1) is read together with Article 30(2) and (3) of the ICC Statute.

300 First, Article 30(1) of the ICC Statute cannot be interpreted as requiring that *all* material elements must be committed with intent *and* knowledge. This follows from subsec-

---

[64] See marginal no. 615.

[65] See, e.g., A. Ashworth, *Principles of Criminal Law*, 4th edn. (2003), pp. 198 et seq.

[66] See Sec. 2.02(1) Model Penal Code. Practice and scholarship contributions typically rely on the categories of Anglo-American law; see also A. Ashworth, *Principles of Criminal Law*, 4th edn. (2003), pp. 173 et seq.; T. Weigend, 93 *Zeitschrift für die gesamte Strafrechtswissenschaft* (1981), pp. 673 et seq., as well as overviews in A. Cassese, *International Criminal Law* (2003), p. 161, and A. Eser, in A. Cassese, P. Gaeta and J.R.W.D. Jones (eds.), *The Rome Statute of the International Criminal Court*, Vol. 1 (2002), p. 889 at pp. 905 et seq.

[67] For these concepts, see H.-H. Jescheck and T. Weigend, *Lehrbuch des Strafrechts, Allgemeiner Teil*, 5th edn. (1996), pp. 297 et seq. On the similarities and differences between *dolus eventualis* and recklessness in particular, see marginal no. 330.

[68] On the history of the rule, see R.S. Clark, 12 *Criminal Law Forum* (2001), p. 291 at pp. 296 et seq.; A. Eser, in A. Cassese, P. Gaeta and J.R.W.D. Jones (eds.), *The Rome Statute of the International Criminal Court*, Vol. 1 (2002), p. 889 at pp. 894 et seq.

[69] Both conditions must be present at the time of the act's commission; *dolus antecedens* or *dolus subsequens* are insufficient, see A. Eser, in A. Cassese, P. Gaeta and J. R.W.D. Jones (eds.), *The Rome Statute of the International Criminal Court*, Vol. 1 (2002), p. 889 at p. 930.

tions (2) and (3); under these provisions, the intent requirement relates to conduct and consequences only, while the knowledge requirement relates to circumstances and consequences only. Therefore, the intent of the perpetrator need not cover the circumstances of the crime, while his or her knowledge need not cover the criminal conduct. The only material element that must be covered by both intent and knowledge is the consequence of a crime.

This interpretation is in line with the Introduction to the Elements of Crimes, which states that where "no reference is made in the Elements of Crimes to a mental element for any particular conduct, consequence or circumstance listed, it is understood that the relevant mental element, i.e. *intent, knowledge or both*, set out in article 30 applies" (emphasis added). Together with Article 30(1) of the ICC Statute, this wording can only be understood to mean that Article 30 demands either "intent" or "knowledge" or both, depending on the material element. In addition, our interpretation does not conflict with the fact that the wording of Article 30(1) was changed at the last moment from "intent *or* knowledge" to "intent *and* knowledge."[70] While the "or" would have suggested two alternative standards of *mens rea*, the "and" appears to refer to a concept of intent and knowledge as recognized under civil law systems: that is, the distinction between a voluntative and a cognitive element. It fully corresponds to our understanding that the perpetrator must in fact possess both intent and knowledge. **301**

Second, intent and knowledge have differing meanings depending on the material element in question. This requires a careful distinction between the various material elements[71] – that is, the conduct, its consequences and any circumstances.[72] **302**

Third, Article 30 of the ICC Statute explicitly allows differing or supplementary rules ("unless otherwise provided"), which take precedence over the mental element as established in Article 30 itself. It follows that the standard of *mens rea* established by Article 30(1) to (3) of the ICC Statute must be distinguished from the *mens rea* requirements that arise from "other provisions." **303**

---

[70] The wording "intent and knowledge" was a subject of intense disagreement right up to the end of the negotiations in Rome, see D.K. Piragoff, in O. Triffterer (ed.), *Commentary on the Rome Statute of the International Criminal Court* (1999), Art. 30, marginal no. 10; P. Saland, in R.S. Lee (ed.), *The International Criminal Court, The Making of the Rome Statute* (1999), p. 189 at 205. It was mainly at France's instigation that the word "and" was accepted in place of the word "or" included in the draft, see R.S. Clark, 12 *Criminal Law Forum* (2001), p. 291 at p. 302. On the drafting history of the rule, see generally R.S. Clark, 12 *Criminal Law Forum* (2001), p. 291 at p. 296; A. Eser, in A. Cassese, P. Gaeta and J.R.W.D Jones (eds.), *The Rome Statute of the International Criminal Court*, Vol. 1 (2002), p. 889 at pp. 894 et seq.

[71] For the distinction between material elements, see K. Ambos, *Der Allgemeine Teil des Völkerstrafrechts* (2002), pp. 764 et seq.; R.S. Clark, 12 *Criminal Law Forum* (2001), p. 291 at p. 306; M. Kelt and H. von Hebel, in R.S. Lee (ed.), *The International Criminal Court, Elements of Crimes and Rules of Procedure and Evidence* (2001), p. 13 at p. 14 and p. 26; D.K. Piragoff, in O. Triffterer (ed.), *Commentary on the Rome Statute of the International Criminal Court* (1999), Art. 30, marginal no. 6; The distinction between conduct, consequences and circumstances arises from common law doctrine, see A. Eser, in A. Cassese, P. Gaeta and J. R.W.D. Jones (eds.), *The Rome Statute of the International Criminal Court*, Vol. 1 (2002), p. 889 at pp. 911 et seq.

[72] Thus, for example, in shooting someone to death, which constitutes the crime against humanity of killing, the conduct required under ICC Statute, Article 30(2)(a) occurs (only) in pulling the weapon's trigger, while the fact that the victim was hit by the bullet and dies as a result is a "consequence," to which different subjective requirements apply, see R.S. Clark, 12 *Criminal Law Forum* (2001), p. 291 at p. 306. For the various material elements, see marginal nos. 286 et seq.

2. Standard Requirements: "Intent and Knowledge"

304 Article 30 of the ICC Statute sets a standard for the mental element of crimes under international law that is applicable in all cases where no rules specifically regulate the *mens rea*.

a) Intent as Regards the Criminal Conduct

305 Under Article 30(1) and (2)(a) of the ICC Statute, a person is criminally liable only if he or she "means to engage in the conduct" described in the definition of the crime. Thus the conduct must be the result of a voluntary action on the part of the perpetrator.[73] Automatism, such as the behavior following an attack by a swarm of bees, prevents criminal responsibility for crimes under international law.

b) Intent and Knowledge as Regards the Consequences of the Conduct

306 If the definition of the crime requires that the perpetrator's conduct cause a specific consequence, such as the death of the victim, the perpetrator must either "mean to cause that consequence" or[74] at least, in committing the act, must be "aware that it will occur in the ordinary course of events." This follows from Article 30(1), (2)(b), and (3) of the ICC Statute. Under this definition, the minimum requirement for criminal liability is awareness of the probable occurrence of the consequence.[75] This means that, in the perpetrator's perception at the time of the act, carrying out the conduct would cause the consequence, unless extraordinary circumstances intervened. Thus it is not enough for the perpetrator to merely anticipate the possibility that his or her conduct would cause the consequence. This follows from the words "will occur"; after all, it does not say "may occur."[76]

307   This interpretation of Article 30(2)(b) and (3) of the ICC Statute, which appears to be shared by most commentators,[77] has a critical effect: It establishes a standard of *mens rea* that is apparently stricter than the one applied by both domestic and international courts.[78] There, under the concepts of recklessness or *dolus eventualis*, the perpetrator's

---

[73] See A. Eser, in A. Cassese, P. Gaeta and J. R.W.D. Jones (eds.), *The Rome Statute of the International Criminal Court*, Vol. 1 (2002), p. 889 at p. 913; D.K. Piragoff, in O. Triffterer (ed.), *Commentary on the Rome Statute of the International Criminal Court* (1999), Art. 30, marginal no. 19. But see, K. Ambos, *Der Allgemeine Teil des Völkerstrafrechts* (2002), p. 767.

[74] But see, K. Ambos, *Der Allgemeine Teil des Völkerstrafrechts* (2002), p. 770, who argues that the perpetrator must mean to cause the consequence *and* be aware that it will occur.

[75] For example, a soldier who aims to destroy a building, while not wishing to kill civilians he knows are in the building, may be liable for a war crime under Article 8(2)(a)(i) of the ICC Statute if the building is in fact destroyed and the civilians killed.

[76] In fact, the wording of Art. 30(2)(b) of the ICC Statute corresponds to the text in the English Draft Criminal Code Bill, which was presented to the British Parliament by the Law Commission in 1989, but has never been implemented. Under Sec. 18(b)(ii) of that Draft Bill a person acts "intentionally" – as distinguished from "recklessly" – with respect to a result when he acts either in order to bring it about or with awareness that it will occur in the ordinary course of events; see The Law Commission, *A Criminal Code for England and Wales, Vol 1: Report and Draft Criminal Code Bill* (1989).

[77] See marginal no. 331, fn. 134. Remarkably, the few commentators who advocate the inclusion of recklessness and *dolus eventualis* in the standard set by Art. 30 of the ICC Statute rarely give any reasons for their position.

[78] For details see marginal no. 330.

awareness merely of the risk that a particular consequence may occur is generally suffi-cient to establish criminal responsibility.[79] In fact, domestic legislation implementing the provisions of the ICC Statute usually extends the standard of *mens rea* applicable to "or-dinary" crimes, which includes recklessness or *dolus eventualis* to include genocide, crimes against humanity, and war crimes.[80] And why should the standard of *mens rea* under the ICC Statute be stricter than the standard applied by the Yugoslavia or the Rwanda Tribunals or national courts in prosecuting crimes under international law? One possibility of resolving this tension could be a more extensive interpretation of Article 30 of the ICC Statute; here the point of departure could be the wording "in the *ordinary course of events*" (emphasis added). However, such an extensive interpretation of Article 30(2)(b) and (3) of the ICC Statute, which might easily conflict with the principle of strict construction,[81] may not be necessary if – as will be demonstrated shortly[82] – there is a smoother way of bringing the law under the ICC Statute in line with customary in-ternational law and domestic legislation.

c) Knowledge as Regards the Circumstances of the Crime

To the extent that the crime presumes additional objective elements aside from conduct and specific consequences, it suffices for liability if the perpetrator has "awareness that a circumstance exists."[83]   **308**

Where Article 30 of the ICC Statute requires knowledge of a material element, be it a consequence or a circumstance, a distinction must be made. In regard to the descriptive criteria of a crime, knowledge means the perpetrator's sensory perceptions. In regard to the normative criteria – that is, those whose presence presumes a value judgment – it is sufficient in principle if the perpetrator knows of the fundamental factual circumstances and comprehends the significance of the incriminating conduct that is described by those criteria.[84] It is immaterial, in principle, whether the perpetrator's legal assessment is correct.[85] For the criterion "protected persons" in Article 8(2)(a) of the ICC Statute,   **309**

---

[79] For details see marginal no. 330.

[80] See, e.g., Sec. 2 of the (German) Code of Crimes against International Law [*Völkerstrafgesetz-buch, VStGB*] and marginal nos. 250, 330; for discussion see G. Werle and F. Jessberger, 13 *Criminal Law Forum* (2002), p. 191 at p. 202.

[81] See ICC Statute, Art. 22(2).

[82] See marginal no. 252.

[83] See ICC Statute, Art. 30(3).

[84] See also Elements of Crimes for the ICC Statute, General Introduction, num. 4: "With respect to mental elements associated with elements involving value judgment, such as those using the terms 'inhumane' or 'severe,' it is not necessary that the perpetrator personally completed a particular value judgment, unless otherwise indicated." See M. Kelt and H. von Hebel, in R.S. Lee (ed.), *The Interna-tional Criminal Court, Elements of Crimes and Rules of Procedure and Evidence* (2001), p. 13 at p. 34. See also K. Ambos, *Der Allgemeine Teil des Völkerstrafrechts* (2002), pp. 786 et seq.; A. Eser, in A. Cassese, P. Gaeta and J.R.W.D. Jones (eds.), *The Rome Statute of the International Criminal Court*, Vol. 1 (2002), p. 889 at p. 925; O. Triffterer, in O. Triffterer (ed.), *Commentary on the Rome Statute of the International Criminal Court* (1999), Art. 32, marginal nos. 16, 32.

[85] However, there are exceptions to this principle; for example, under ICC Statute, Art. 8(2)(b)(iv), it is required that the perpetrator realize that the harm caused by his or her attack was unmistakably out of proportion to the expected military advantage. On this, the Elements state the following: "As opposed to the general rule set forth in paragraph 4 of the General Introduction, this knowledge element requires that the perpetrator make the value judgment as described therein," see Elements of Crimes for Article 8(2)(b)(iv) ICC Statute, num. 3, fn. 37.

this means the following: it is not necessary for the perpetrator to have correctly assessed the protected status of a person, for example a "civilian" or "wounded combatant," under international humanitarian law; it suffices for him or her to have been aware of the factual circumstances upon which the legally protected status was based, for example non-participation in combat (for civilians) or inability to continue participating in combat (for wounded combatants).[86] Nor does the perpetrator need to have correctly classified the armed conflict as international or non-international.[87]

3. Departures From the Standard Requirements

310   Article 30 of the ICC Statute establishes the requirements for the subjective elements only "unless otherwise provided." "Otherwise provided" as used in Article 30(1) of the ICC Statute may encompass provisions arising from the Statute itself, from the Elements of Crimes, and from other sources of international law under Article 21 of the ICC Statute, in particular from customary international law. This category of provisions on the mental element may work in various ways.[88] They may confirm or clarify the subjective requirements as established in Article 30 of the ICC Statute for a specific crime; but they may also bring about a departure from the standard requirements by broadening or narrowing criminal responsibility.

a)   Sources of Other Provisions Within the Meaning of Article 30
aa) "Otherwise provided" in the ICC Statute

311   The ICC Statute itself contains elements that concern the perpetrator's perceptions, especially in the definitions of crimes. The terms "intent," "intentional," and "intentionally,"[89] "wilful," "wilfully,"[90] and "wantonly"[91] are frequently employed.[92] Whether the

---

[86] This is confirmed in the Elements of Crimes: "The perpetrator was aware of the factual circumstances that established the protected status of the person," see Elements of Crimes for Article 8(2)(a)(i) ICC Statute, num. 3.

[87] See M. Kelt and H. von Hebel, in R.S. Lee (ed.), *The International Criminal Court, Elements of Crimes and Rules of Procedure and Evidence* (2001), p. 13 at p. 35. For a critical assessment, see K. Ambos, *Der Allgemeine Teil des Völkerstrafrechts* (2002), p. 788.

[88] See also K. Ambos, *Der Allgemeine Teil des Völkerstrafrechts* (2002), p. 805; R.S. Clark, 12 *Criminal Law Forum* (2001), p. 291 at p. 321; A. Eser, in A. Cassese, P. Gaeta and J.R.W.D. Jones (eds.), *The Rome Statute of the International Criminal Court*, Vol. 1 (2002), p. 889 at p. 898; D.K. Piragoff, in O. Triffterer (ed.), *Commentary on the Rome Statute of the International Criminal Court* (1999), Art. 30, marginal no. 14.

[89] "[I]ntent to destroy" (genocide, ICC Statute, Art. 6); "intentionally causing great suffering" (crime against humanity of inhuman treatment, ICC Statute, Art. 7(1)(k)); "intentional infliction of conditions of life" (crime against humanity of extermination, ICC Statute, Art. 7(2)(b)); "intentional infliction of severe pain" (crime against humanity of torture, ICC Statute, Art. 7(2)(e)); "intent of affecting the ethnic population" (crime against humanity of forced pregnancy, ICC Statute, Art. 7(2)(f)); "intention of maintaining that regime" (crime against humanity of apartheid, ICC Statute, Art. 7(2)(h)); "intention of removing them from the protection of law" (crime against humanity of enforced disappearance, ICC Statute, Art. 7(2)(i)); "intentionally directing attacks" (war crime of attack on civilian population, civilian objects, protected buildings, and humanitarian missions, ICC Statute, Art. 8(2)(b)(i), (ii), (iii), (ix), (xxiv) and (e)(i), (ii), (iii), (iv)); "intentionally launching an attack" (war crime of disproportionate damage, ICC Statute, Art. 8(2)(b)(iv)); "intentionally using starvation" (war crime of starvation of civilians, ICC Statute, Art. 8(2)(b)(xxv)).

different wordings involve a departure from the standard laid down in Article 30 of the ICC Statute must be determined on a case-to-case basis.[93]

The multiplicity of special rules is less a result of a consciously varying assessment of the subjective **312** requirements for criminality by the creators of the Statute than it is a consequence of the literal incorporation of "parent norms" into the Statute. In the area of war crimes, the frequent use of such additional elements arises from the fact that the ICC Statute has absorbed the corresponding rules of international humanitarian law. This regulatory technique cannot be faulted in principle. It avoids leveling and leaves room for nuanced treatment, as well as recourse to "parent norms," such as those of the Geneva Conventions. On occasion, however, noteworthy textual differences may emerge: for example, when "causing great suffering" must occur "wilfully" as a war crime (Article 8(2)(a)(iii) of the ICC Statute), but "intentionally" as a crime against humanity (Article 7(1)(k) of the ICC Statute). Another reason for the variety of subjective elements in the ICC Statute might be that the general principles, including Article 30 of the ICC Statute, on the one hand, and the definitions of crimes, on the other, were formulated by different working groups, between which the necessary communication did not always take place.[94]

bb) "Otherwise provided" in the Elements of Crimes and in Customary International Law

The Elements of Crimes, too, contain numerous provisions concerning the offender's **313** state of mind. Among others, the following wordings are used: "knew or should have known,"[95] "was aware of,"[96] "intended,"[97] and "in order to."[98] In addition, rules on the

---

[90] "[W]ilful killing" (war crime of killing, ICC Statute, Art. 8(2)(a)(i)); "wilfully causing great suffering" (war crime of causing great suffering, ICC Statute, Art. 8(2)(a)(iii)); "wilfully depriving a ... protected person of the rights of a fair and regular trial" (war crime of deprivation of the right to a fair trial, ICC Statute, Art. 8(2)(a)(vi)); "wilfully impeding relief supplies" (war crime of starvation of civilians, ICC Statute, Art. 8(2)(b)(xxv)).

[91] "[D]estruction . . . carried out unlawfully and wantonly" (war crime of destruction and appropriation of property, ICC Statute, Art. 8(2)(a)(iv)).

[92] Additional examples of subjective characteristics in the ICC Statute are: "should have known," Art. 28(a)(i); "for the purpose of," ICC Statute, Art. 25(3)(c); "killing or wounding treacherously," ICC Statute, Art. 8(2)(b)(xi), (e)(ix).

[93] Similarly, see K. Ambos, *Der Allgemeine Teil des Völkerstrafrechts* (2002), pp. 797 et seq.; A. Eser, in A. Cassese, P. Gaeta and J.R.W.D. Jones (eds.), *The Rome Statute of the International Criminal Court*, Vol. 1 (2002), p. 889 at p. 901. It would be too much of a generalization to see the use of "intentional(ly)" in the Statute as merely a declaratory confirmation of the general requirement of intent, but see, from this perspective, D.K. Piragoff, in O. Triffterer (ed.), *Commentary on the Rome Statute of the International Criminal Court* (1999) Art. 30, marginal no. 12; T. Weigend, in B. Schünemann et al. (eds.), *Festschrift für Roxin* (2001), p. 1375 at p. 1389, fn. 57; see also M. Kelt and H. von Hebel, in R.S. Lee (ed.), *The International Criminal Court, Elements of Crimes and Rules of Procedure and Evidence* (2001), p. 13 at p. 33.

[94] R.S. Clark, 12 *Criminal Law Forum* (2001), p. 291 at pp. 313 et seq.

[95] E.g., Elements of Crimes for Article 6(e) ICC Statute, num. 6 (genocide by forcible transfer of children); Elements of Crimes for Article 8(2)(b)(vii) ICC Statute, -1, -2, -4, num. 3 (war crime of improper use of insignia); Elements of Crimes for Article 8(2)(e)(vii) ICC Statute, num. 3 (war crime of use of child soldiers).

[96] Here the wording is often used: "The perpetrator was aware of the factual circumstances that established . . .," e.g., referring to "the gravity of the conduct" (Elements of Crimes for Article 7(1)(e) ICC Statute, num. 3; crime against humanity of deprivation of liberty); "the character of the act" (Elements of Crimes for Article 7(1)(k) ICC Statute, num. 3; crime against humanity of inhumane treatment); "[the] protected status [of the victim]" and "the existence of an armed conflict" (Elements of

mental element are also found in customary international law, in particular as applied by the Yugoslavia and Rwanda Tribunals.[99] Whether these rules are "other provisions" within the meaning of Article 30(1) of the ICC Statute is, however, a matter of controversy.[100]

314   Taking Article 21(1) of the ICC Statute into account, one would correctly conclude that the "unless otherwise provided" clause allows modification of the subjective requirements laid out in Article 30 of the ICC Statute through both the Elements of Crimes and customary international law. According to Article 21(1), the Court shall apply the Statute and the Elements of Crimes, but also, secondarily, customary international law.[101] It cannot be gathered from Article 30 of the ICC Statute that – in contrast to this general rule – only provisions of the Statute itself can be "other provisions." On the contrary, comparison with other wording in the Statute suggests that the range of norms referred to is much wider. Thus a comparable clause in Article 31(1) of the ICC Statute on grounds for exclusion from punishment explicitly refers to "other grounds for excluding criminal responsibility *provided for in this Statute.*"[102]

315   Admittedly, it might be argued that the principle of legality requires that any expansions of the definition of the mental element in Article 30 of the ICC Statute would have to be found in the Statute itself, not in outside sources.[103] But what might be a cherished and fundamental principle in a domestic context should not necessarily be transferred literally to international criminal law. There can be no doubt that customary international law is a source of international criminal law.[104] And there is no reason why this should not hold true in principle in relation to the mental element of crimes under international law. In addition, a strong argument may be made in favor of uniform interpretation and application of the ICC Statute and customary international law.[105]

Crimes for Article 8 (2)(a)(i) ICC Statute, num. 3 and num. 5; war crime of killing; a large number of other Elements of Crimes for war crimes are consistent with this).

[97] E.g., Elements of Crimes for Article 8(2)(b)(i), (ii), (iii) ICC Statute, in each case num. 3 (war crimes through attack on nonmilitary targets); Elements of Crimes for Article 8(2)(b)(xvi) ICC Statute, num. 2 (war crime of plundering); Elements of Crimes for Article 8(2)(b)(xxiii) ICC Statute, num. 2 (war crime of using human shields).

[98] E.g., Elements of Crimes for Article 8(2)(b)(vii) ICC Statute, -1, num. 2, (war crime of improper use of a flag of truce; Elements of Crimes for Article 8(2)(b)(xii) ICC Statute, num. 2 (giving no quarter).

[99] See the examples at marginal nos. 322, 334, 613, 676, 878.

[100] Pro, see A. Cassese, *International Criminal Law* (2003), p. 176; R.S. Clark, 12 *Criminal Law Forum* (2001), p. 291 at p. 321; M. Kelt and H. von Hebel, in R.S. Lee (ed.), *The International Criminal Court, Elements of Crimes and Rules of Procedure and Evidence* (2001), p. 13 at pp. 29 et seq.; D.K. Piragoff, in O. Triffterer (ed.), *Commentary on the Rome Statute of the International Criminal Court* (1999), Art. 30, marginal no. 14; M. Politi, in A. Cassese, P. Gaeta and J.R.W.D. Jones (eds.), *The Rome Statute of the International Criminal Court* Vol. 1 (2002), p. 443 at p. 461. But see, K. Ambos, *Der Allgemeine Teil des Völkerstrafrechts* (2002), p. 789 (departures from Art. 30 can only arise directly from Arts. 6–8); A. Eser, in A. Cassese, P. Gaeta and J.R.W.D. Jones (eds.), *The Rome Statute of the International Criminal Court*, Vol. 1 (2002), p. 889 at p. 898 and p. 933; T. Weigend, 19 *Nouvelles Études Pénales* (2004), p. 319 at pp. 326 et seq.

[101] For details and for the status of Article 21 of the ICC Statute as the authoritative rule on the sources of international criminal law, see marginal nos. 164 et seq.

[102] Emphasis added.

[103] See T. Weigend, 19 *Nouvelles Études Pénales* (2004), p. 319 at p. 327.

[104] See marginal nos. 128 et seq.

[105] See marginal no. 127.

This warrants an interpretation of the provisions of the ICC Statute that is as far as possible in line with customary international law. As a result, customary international law may often be relevant even in interpreting other provisions explicitly included in the ICC Statute. For example, in determining what *mens rea* is required for a "wilful killing" under Article 8(2)(a)(i) of the ICC Statute, the corresponding rules of international humanitarian law, such as Article 147 of Geneva Convention IV, and their interpretation by international courts play a key role.

Finally, our reasoning is not altered by the fact that Article 9 of the ICC Statute requires **316** the Elements of Crimes to be compatible with the Statute. What is important under this provision is the compatibility of the Elements of Crimes with the definitions of the crimes. But Article 30 of the ICC Statute explicitly permits differing provisions. From the point of view of Article 30, therefore, differing provisions in the Elements of Crimes are to be treated identically to differing provisions in the Statute itself. The question of compatibility is thus posed only if the definition of a crime in the Statute contains a subjective element that is modified in the Elements of Crimes.

b) Effects of Other Provisions Within the Meaning of Article 30
Other provisions within the meaning of Article 30(1) of the ICC Statute may work in **317** various ways.[106] Whether another provision in fact causes a departure from the standard of *mens rea* established under Article 30 must be examined separately for each provision.

aa) Affirmation and Clarification
The effect of "otherwise provided" can first of all be affirmation of the subjective ele- **318** ments established in Article 30 of the ICC Statute. For example, Article 7(1) of the ICC Statute explicitly provides, in the case of crimes against humanity, that the perpetrator must act "with knowledge of the attack" on the civilian population; without this addition to the definition of crimes, the requirement of knowledge of the attack would arise from Article 30(3) of the ICC Statute.[107]

bb) Expansion of Criminal Liability
Under some other provisions within the meaning of Article 30(1) of the ICC Stat- **319** ute, the requirements of the mental element are lowered in comparison to the standard of Article 30. The spectrum ranges from recklessness and *dolus eventualis* to negligence.

A significant lowering of the standard requirements for the mental element as laid **320** down in Article 30 is effected by Article 28 of the ICC Statute.[108] Under Article 28(a)(i), sufficient grounds exist to find criminal liability of a military commander for the crimes of a subordinate if he or she, "owing to the circumstances at the time, should

---

[106] See also T. Weigend, 19 *Nouvelles Études Pénales* (2004), p. 319 at p. 327.

[107] See K. Ambos, *Der Allgemeine Teil des Völkerstrafrechts* (2002), p. 774; T. Weigend, in B. Schünemann et al. (eds.), *Festschrift für Roxin* (2001), p. 1375 at p. 1389, fn. 57; see also marginal no. 326.

[108] See M. Kelt and H. von Hebel, in R.S. Lee (ed.), *The International Criminal Court, Elements of Crimes and Rules of Procedure and Evidence* (2001), p. 13 at p. 21. On the customary international law standard of the *mens rea* of superior responsibility, see *Prosecutor* v. *Mucić* et al., ICTY (Appeals Chamber), judgment of 20 February 2001, para. 241, and K. Keith, 14 *Leiden Journal of International Law* (2001), pp. 617 et seq.

have known" that the subordinate was committing or was about to commit the crime. The frequently used term "wanton" also reduces the requirements, for example for the war crime of destruction of property under Article 8(2)(a)(iv) of the ICC Statute; here recklessness is sufficient.[109] The same can be presumed for "wilfulness," which is often required for war crimes; to this extent, reckless conduct is usually sufficient.[110]

321   In the Elements of Crimes, too, numerous provisions may be found that expand liability under Article 30 of the ICC Statute into the realm of negligence liability. For instance, when applying Article 30(3) of the ICC Statute, the perpetrator of the war crime of using child soldiers must, according to Article 8(2)(b)(xxvi) of the ICC Statute, have positive knowledge ("knowledge means awareness that a circumstance exists") of the soldier's minor status; but under the Elements of Crimes, it is enough that he or she "should have known" they were minors. In the same way, it is sufficient under the Elements of Crimes if the perpetrator of a war crime under Article 8(2)(b)(vii) of the ICC Statute (making improper use of a flag of truce or of the flag of the enemy or of the United Nations) "should have known" that this use of the flag was not permitted.

322   Finally, important departures from the *mens rea* established by Article 30 of the ICC Statute emerge under customary international law.[111] This is mainly true of killings, to the extent that they fulfill other requirements of a crime under international law. Here it is sufficient if the perpetrator, with reckless disregard for human life, consciously causes harm.[112]

cc) Narrowing of Criminal Liability

323   "Otherwise provided" can also have a liability-limiting effect, by either strengthening subjective elements or adding further subjective requirements.

324   Numerous provisions of the ICC Statute include additional subjective requirements which – unlike "intent and knowledge" under Article 30 of the ICC Statute – do not necessarily refer to a material element of the crime, such as conduct, consequence or circumstance.[113] The most important example concerns the "intent to destroy" element of genocide pursuant to Article 6 of the ICC Statute. Here, the perpetrator must not only act with intent and knowledge in relation to the material elements of the crime, such as

---

[109] See J. Allain and J.R.W.D. Jones, 8 *European Journal of International Law* (1997), p. 100 at p. 106; A. Eser, in A. Cassese, P. Gaeta and J.R.W.D. Jones (eds.), *The Rome Statute of the International Criminal Court*, Vol. 1 (2002), p. 889 at p. 899. For more on recklessness, see marginal no. 330.

[110] Whether this reduction affects all violations of international humanitarian law punishable as grave breaches has not yet been definitively determined; for discussion see marginal nos. 857 et seq.; from the inconsistent jurisprudence of the Yugoslavia Tribunal, see, on the one hand, *Prosecutor* v. *Blaškić*, ICTY (Trial Chamber), judgment of 3 March 2000, para. 152: "the *mens rea* constituting all the violations of Article 2 of the Statute includes both guilty intent and recklessness which may be likened to serious criminal negligence," and para. 181; but note that the decision of the Trial Chamber has been overruled in significant part by *Prosecutor* v. *Blaškić*, ICTY (Appeals Chamber), judgment of 29 July 2004, paras. 34 et seq.; on the other hand, *Prosecutor* v. *Aleksovski*, ICTY (Trial Chamber), judgment of 25 June 1999, para. 56: "Recklessness cannot suffice," and *Prosecutor* v. *Vasiljević*, ICTY (Trial Chamber), judgment of 29 November 2002, para. 194. But A. Eser, in A. Cassese, P. Gaeta and J.R.W.D. Jones (eds.), *The Rome Statute of the International Criminal Court*, Vol. 1 (2002), p. 889 at p. 899, is incorrect in stating that the addition "wilful" is supposed to constantly *increase* the subjective requirements.

[111] For details see marginal nos. 334 et seq.

[112] For details, see marginal nos. 334, 613, 676, 878.

[113] See also K. Ambos, *Der Allgemeine Teil des Völkerstrafrechts* (2002), pp. 789 et seq.

the killing of a member of a protected group, but in addition he or she must aim to destroy the group as such.[114] The requirement of specific discriminatory grounds for the crime against humanity of persecution pursuant to Article 7(1)(h) of the ICC Statute can also narrow liability.[115] Additional examples include the intent of affecting the ethnic composition of any population, which is required for the crime against humanity of forced pregnancy pursuant to Article 7(1)(g), (2)(f) of the ICC Statute, as well as the treacherous killing or wounding of hostile forces pursuant to Article 8(2)(b)(xi) and (e)(ix) of the ICC Statute. Other cases include the intent to facilitate the commission of a crime under Article 25(3)(c) of the ICC Statute ("for the purpose of facilitating"). Limitations on liability also arise from the Elements of Crimes. Thus, for example, under the Elements of Crimes for Article 8(2)(a)(viii) and (c)(iii), the war crime of hostage-taking requires a coercive intent that is not (explicitly) provided for in the text of the Statute – that is, that the perpetrator "intended to compel a State . . . to act or refrain from acting . . .."[116]

4. The Context of the Crime and the Mental Element

One critical and controversial issue relates to whether and to what extent the specific context[117] that elevates a crime to an international crime, such as a "widespread or systematic attack" or an "armed conflict," must be reflected in the offender's state of mind.   **325**

At the Rome Conference, this question was controversial in regard to the chapeau of Article 7, crimes against humanity, and the requirement of an armed conflict for war   **326** crimes.[118] The view was advocated that these characteristics were merely so-called jurisdictional elements,[119] which involved only the Court's jurisdiction and did not require any knowledge on the part of the perpetrators. However, this view cannot be reconciled with the principles of individual responsibility and culpability. Therefore, one would correctly have to assume that the context elements of crimes against humanity and war crimes involve "circumstances" that are, within the scope of Article 30 of the ICC Statute, in principle subjects of the mental element.[120] After long discussion, a nuanced solution prevailed in Rome. Technically, this solution was made possible by adopting

---

[114] See K. Ambos, in L.C. Vohrah et al. (eds.), *Man's Inhumanity to Man* (2003), p. 11 at pp. 18 et seq.; J. van der Vyver, 23 *Fordham International Law Journal* (1999), p. 286 at p. 308. This is also clearly warranted by the jurisprudence of the Tribunals, summarized by C. Aptel, 13 *Criminal Law Forum* (2002), p. 273 at pp. 277 et seq.; R. Arnold, 14 *Criminal Law Forum* (2003), p. 127 at pp. 138 et seq. But see O. Triffterer, 14 *Leiden Journal of International Law* (2001), p. 399 at pp. 404 et seq., and marginal no. 615.

[115] For the "specific intent to discriminate," see *Prosecutor* v. *Blaškić*, ICTY (Appeals Chamber), judgment of 29 July 2004, para. 164, see also marginal nos. 745 et seq.

[116] Additional examples in M. Kelt and H. von Hebel, in R.S. Lee (ed.), *The International Criminal Court, Elements of Crimes and Rules of Procedure and Evidence* (2001), p. 13 at p. 32.

[117] For the context element ("Gesamttat"), see marginal no. 278.

[118] For details, see K. Ambos, *Der Allgemeine Teil des Völkerstrafrechts* (2002), pp. 774 et seq.; M. Kelt and H. von Hebel, in R.S. Lee (ed.), *The International Criminal Court, Elements of Crimes and Rules of Procedure and Evidence* (2001), p. 13 at pp. 34 et seq.

[119] See, e.g., L.N. Sadat, *The International Criminal Court and the Transformation of International Law* (2002), p. 208, fn. 140 ("jurisdictional requirements").

[120] See also T. Weigend, in B. Schünemann et al. (eds.), *Festschrift für Roxin* (2001), p. 1375 at p. 1389, fn. 57.

separate provisions for each crime in the Elements.[121]

For crimes against humanity, Article 7(1) of the ICC Statute explicitly provides that
327   the perpetrator must act "with knowledge of the attack" against the civilian population.[122] This involves a clarification and confirmation of the *mens rea* already required by
Article 30 of the ICC Statute.[123] It suffices that the offender was aware of the relevant
factual background (the context) of the crime; he or she was not required to come to the
normative conclusion that the attack was indeed widespread or systematic.[124] For war
crimes, unlike crimes against humanity, there is no reference in the ICC Statute itself to
the idea that the perpetrator's perceptions must include the context of organized violence, that is, the presence of an armed conflict. Here, however, it follows from Article
30 that the perpetrator must recognize the presence of an armed conflict.[125] This result
is confirmed by the Elements of Crimes; they demand across the board that the perpetrator "was aware of factual circumstances that established the existence of an armed conflict."[126]

In contrast, the threshold clause in Article 8(1) of the ICC Statute involves a jurisdictional element
328   only, that is, a requirement for jurisdiction that need not be present in the perpetrator's mind.[127]
Under this provision, the Court has jurisdiction over war crimes, "in particular when committed as
part of a plan or policy or as part of a large-scale commission of such crimes." Here, a particular
quality of war crime is made a requirement for jurisdiction of and prosecution by the International
Criminal Court. This threshold clause, however, is not a limitation of the substantive requirements
for liability.

Unlike crimes against humanity and war crimes, the crime of genocide does not require

---

[121] See T. Weigend, 19 *Nouvelles Études Pénales* (2004), p. 319 at pp. 327 et seq.

[122] In the Elements of Crimes for the different sub-categories of crimes, this requirement is consistently clarified such that "the perpetrator knew that the conduct was part of or intended the conduct
to be part of a widespread or systematic attack against a civilian population." This requirement, however, is immediately qualified by underlining that the requirement "should not be interpreted as requiring proof that the perpetrator had knowledge of all characteristics of the attack or the precise
details of the plan or policy of the State or organization. In the case of an emerging widespread or
systematic attack against a civilian population, the intent clause of the last element indicates that this
mental element is satisfied if the perpetrator intended to further such an attack." See Elements of
Crimes for Article 7 ICC Statute, Introduction. The legal situation under the Statute corresponds to
customary law. See *Prosecutor* v. *Tadić*, ICTY (Trial Chamber), judgment of 7 May 1997, para. 656:
"perpetrator must know of the broader context"; see also H. Vest, 113 *Zeitschrift für die gesamte
Strafrechtswissenschaft* (2001), p. 457 at p. 475.

[123] See also R.S. Clark, 12 *Criminal Law Forum* (2001), p. 291 at p. 315; and marginal no. 669.

[124] See T. Weigend, in B. Schünemann et al. (eds.), *Festschrift für Roxin* (2001), p. 1375 at p. 1389.

[125] See K. Ambos, *Der Allgemeine Teil des Völkerstrafrechts* (2002), pp. 778 et seq.; A. Eser, in A.
Cassese, P. Gaeta and J.R.W.D. Jones (eds.), *The Rome Statute of the International Criminal Court*,
Vol. 1 (2002), p. 889 at p. 898, pp. 928 et seq.

[126] This requirement is clarified in three ways: "There is no requirement for a legal evaluation by
the perpetrator as to the existence of an armed conflict or its character as international or non-international; in that context there is no requirement for awareness by the perpetrator of the facts that established the character of the conflict as international or non-international; there is only a requirement
for the awareness of the factual circumstances that established the existence of an armed conflict that is
implicit in the terms, took place in the context of and was associated with."

[127] See also K. Ambos, in L.C. Vohrah et al. (eds.), *Man's Inhumanity to Man* (2003), p. 11 at
pp. 32 et seq.

that the single act objectively take place within a broader context of organized vio- **329**
lence.[128] Instead the perpetrator must act with the purpose of destroying a group, according to Article 6 of the ICC Statute.[129] The requirement established by the Elements
of Crimes that the individual act of genocide must have occurred within a context of
comparable acts ("took place in the context of a manifest pattern of similar conduct"),
does not add a material element to the crime of genocide. This requirement only affects
the Court's jurisdiction; it is thus not required that the perpetrator was aware that his or
her act took place within a context of comparable acts.[130]

5. Recklessness and *Dolus Eventualis*

In many if not most domestic systems, a *mens rea* lower than *dolus directus* or purpose **330**
and knowledge warrants full criminal responsibility on the part of the offender. Common standards are recklessness and *dolus eventualis*.[131] A person acts with *dolus eventualis*
– as distinguished from *dolus directus* on the one hand and negligence on the other – if
he is aware that a material element included in the definition of a crime (such as the
death of a person) may result from his conduct and "reconciles himself" or "makes
peace" with this fact.[132] Recklessness, particular to the common law tradition, is also located somewhere between (direct) intention and negligence. Under this concept, an offender is held liable for consciously creating a risk that is realized through the
commission of the crime.[133]

---

[128] For details see marginal nos. 606 et seq.

[129] The Elements of Crimes for Article 6 ICC Statute state explicitly: "Notwithstanding the normal requirement for a mental element provided for in article 30, and recognizing that knowledge of
the circumstances will usually be addressed in proving genocidal intent, the appropriate requirement,
if any, for a mental element regarding this circumstance will need to be decided by the Court on a
case-by-case basis."

[130] See also R.S. Clark, 12 *Criminal Law Forum* (2001), p. 291 at p. 326, and marginal no. 609.

[131] On the similarities and differences between *dolus eventualis* and recklessness, see T. Weigend,
93 *Zeitschrift für die gesamte Strafrechtswissenschaft* (1981), p. 657 at pp. 688 et seq. Some authors and
courts place recklessness and *dolus eventualis* on a comparable level of culpability, see, e.g., B. Huber,
in A. Eser et al. (eds.), *Einzelverantwortung und Mitverantwortung im Strafrecht* (1998), p. 79 at p. 80;
D. Neressian, 37 *Texas International Law Journal* (2002), p. 231 at p. 263; *Prosecutor* v. *Stakić*, ICTY
(Trial Chamber), judgment of 31 July 2003, para. 587; see also marginal no. 294; others locate recklessness closer to an aggravated modality of negligence common to civil law systems ("bewusste
Fahrlässigkeit"), see, e.g., G. Fletcher, *Rethinking Criminal Law* (2000), p. 443; for a similar view, see
Prosecutor v. *Blaškić*, ICTY (Appeals Chamber), judgment of 29 July 2004, para. 152: "recklessness
which may be likened to serious criminal negligence."

[132] For discussion of the various requirements of *dolus eventualis*, see H.-H. Jescheck and T.
Weigend, *Lehrbuch des Strafrechts, Allgemeiner Teil*, 5th edn. (1996), pp. 299 et seq.

[133] See, e.g., Sec. 2.02(2)(c) Model Penal Code: "A person acts recklessly . . . when he consciously
disregards a substantial and unjustifiable risk that the material element [of the offense] exists or will
result from his conduct. The risk must be of such a nature and degree that, considering the nature and
purpose of the actor's conduct and the circumstances known to him, its disregard involves a gross deviation from the standard of conduct that a law-abiding person would observe in the actor's situation."
See W. Eser, *Criminal Law*, 4th edn. (2003), pp. 261 et seq., p. 267. See also Sec. 18(c) of the (English) Draft Criminal Code Bill (1989): "A person acts 'recklessly' with respect to (i) a circumstance
when he is aware of a risk that it exists or will exist; (ii) a result when he is aware of a risk that it will
occur; and it is in the circumstances known to him, unreasonable to take the risk."

331   Whether and to what extent recklessness or *dolus eventualis* is sufficient to establish criminal responsibility under the provisions of the ICC Statute is subject to dispute.[134] In any event, the fact that a definition of recklessness provided for in the Draft ICC Statute[135] was removed during the negotiations in Rome does not militate against including recklessness.[136] The simple reason for the removal of the provision was that the concept did not appear in the final text of the Statute, specifically in the definitions of crimes; thus adopting a definition would have made no sense.[137]

332   To answer the question in dispute, a distinction must be made. To the extent they are not "otherwise provided," Article 30 of the ICC Statute leaves no room for *dolus eventualis* or recklessness. As already mentioned, the requirement that the perpetrator be aware that the consequence will occur in the ordinary course of events or that he mean to cause that consequence (Article 30(2)(b) of the ICC Statute) excludes both forms of subjective accountability.[138] It thus follows from the wording of Article 30(2)(b) that recklessness and *dolus eventualis* do not meet the requirements.

333   To the extent they are otherwise provided for the mental element, however, *dolus eventualis* or recklessness may legitimately be made the basis for individual criminal responsibility. Whether *dolus eventualis* or recklessness applies must be decided for each "other provision" separately. Appropriate provisions can be found in the Statute and in the Elements of Crimes; but as argued above, "other provisions" in customary international law must also be considered. A main source of subjective conditions of liability under customary international law is the jurisprudence of the Yugoslavia and the Rwanda Tribunals. According to their case law, recklessness and *dolus eventualis* may be sufficient to meet the requirements of the mental elements of several crimes.

---

[134] For advocates of inclusion of *dolus eventualis*, see H.-H. Jescheck, 2 *Journal of International Criminal Justice* (2004), p. 38 at p. 45; G.-J. Knoops, *Defenses in Contemporary International Criminal Law* (2001), pp. 11 et seq.; F. Mantovani, 1 *Journal of International Criminal Justice* (2003), p. 26 at p. 32; D.K. Piragoff, in O. Triffterer (ed.), *Commentary on the Rome Statute of the International Criminal Court* (1999), Art. 30, marginal no. 22; for a more nuanced view, A. Eser, in A. Cassese, P. Gaeta and J.R.W.D. Jones (eds.), *The Rome Statute of the International Criminal Court*, Vol. 1 (2002), p. 767 at pp. 932 et seq.; against inclusion, see K. Ambos, *Der Allgemeine Teil des Völkerstrafrechts* (2002), p. 804; C. Kress, in H. Grützner and P. Pötz (eds.), *Internationaler Rechtshilfeverkehr in Strafsachen*, Vol. 4, 2nd edn. (2002), Vor III 26, marginal no. 52; L.N. Sadat, *The International Criminal Court and the Transformation of International Law* (2002), pp. 208 et seq.; W. Schabas, *Introduction to the International Criminal Court*, 2nd edn. (2004), pp. 108 et seq.; T. Weigend, in B. Schünemann et al. (eds.), *Festschrift für Roxin* (2001), p. 1375 at p. 1390, fn. 58.

[135] Art. 29(4) Draft ICC Statute (1998) states: "For the purposes of this Statute and unless otherwise provided, where this Statute provides that a crime may be committed recklessly, a person is reckless with respect to a circumstance or a consequence if: (a) the person is aware of a risk that the circumstance exists or that the consequence will occur; (b) the person is aware that the risk is highly unreasonable to take; [and] [(c) the person is indifferent to the possibility that the circumstance exists or that the consequence will occur.]" The concept of *dolus eventualis* disappeared from the written documents even before the start of the Rome Conference, see R.S. Clark, 12 *Criminal Law Forum* (2001), p. 291 at p. 301.

[136] Though this is apparently the view of K. Ambos, 10 *Criminal Law Forum* (1999), p. 1 at p. 21.

[137] See also W. Schabas, 4 *European Journal of Crime, Criminal Justice and Criminal Law* (1998), p. 400 at p. 420.

[138] See marginal nos. 313 et seq., and T. Weigend, 19 *Nouvelles Études Pénales* (2004), p. 319 at pp. 326 et seq.; A. Eser, in A. Cassese, P. Gaeta and J.R.W.D. Jones (eds.), *The Rome Statute of the International Criminal Court*, Vol. 1 (2002), p. 889 at pp. 898, 945 et seq.

The Tribunals have frequently referred to the concept of recklessness, sometimes ex- **334**
plicitly, sometimes not. For example, the subjective requirements of the war crime of
killing are fulfilled if a person causes considerable injury to the victim with "reckless disregard of human life."[139] The same is true of killing as a crime against humanity.[140] This
consideration, developed for intentional killing in the course of an armed conflict or a
widespread or systematic attack on a civilian population, can sensibly be transferred by
way of interpretation of customary international law to other types of intentional killing,
such as similar individual acts in the course of genocide. Another example is liability in
the course of participation in a criminal enterprise. This presumes that it was predictable
that a member of the group would commit the crime and that the perpetrator "willingly
took that risk."[141] Most recently, the *Blaškić* appeals judgment extensively discussed the
question with reference to the *mens rea* required for ordering a crime under Article 7(1)
of the ICTY Statute.[142] After a comparative analysis of the standards of *mens rea* in some
common law and civil law systems, the Appeals Chamber concluded that the requisite
mens rea for establishing liability pursuant to Article 7(1) of the ICTY Statute required
that the "person . . . orders an act or omission with the awareness of a substantial likelihood that a crime will be committed in the execution of that order," adding that "ordering with such awareness has to be regarded as accepting the crime."[143]

The concept of *dolus eventualis* was referred to for the first time in international **335**
criminal law jurisprudence in the *Stakić* trial judgment. The Trial Chamber held that
"both a *dolus directus* and a *dolus eventualis* are sufficient to establish the crime of murder
under Article 3"[144] of the ICTY Statute. The Chamber explicitly referred to the standard
of *mens rea* required for homicide under German law. The Chamber also noted that
"large scale killings that would be classified as reckless murder in the United States would
meet the continental criteria of *dolus eventualis*."[145] However, the Chamber emphasized
that negligence on the part of the perpetrator does not suffice to meet the requirements
of the mental element of the war crime of murder. The Chamber set the same standard –
dolus eventualis as a minimum requirement – for the crime against humanity of extermination.[146] Here, it concurred with the *Kayishema* judgment. In that case, the Rwanda
Tribunal stipulated that "the act(s) or omission(s) may be done with intention, recklessness, or gross negligence."[147]

---

[139] *Prosecutor* v. *Mucić* et al., ICTY (Trial Chamber), judgment of 16 November 1998, para. 439;
see also marginal no. 878.

[140] See *Prosecutor* v. *Kupreskić* et al., ICTY (Trial Chamber), judgment of 14 January 2000, para.
561; *Prosecutor* v. *Musema*, ICTR (Trial Chamber), judgment of 27 January 2000, para. 215: "At the
time of the killing the Accused or a subordinate had the intention to kill or inflict grievous bodily
harm on the deceased having known that such bodily harm is likely to cause the victim's death, and is
reckless as to whether or not death ensues." See also marginal no. 676.

[141] *Prosecutor* v. *Tadić*, ICTY (Appeals Chamber), judgment of 15 July 1999, paras. 227 et seq.;
see also A. Cassese, *International Criminal Law* (2003), p. 169.

[142] *Prosecutor* v. *Blaškić*, ICTY (Appeals Chamber), judgment of 29 July 2004, paras. 34 et seq.

[143] *Prosecutor* v. *Blaškić*, ICTY (Appeals Chamber), judgment of 29 July 2004, para. 42.

[144] *Prosecutor* v. *Stakić*, ICTY (Trial Chamber), judgment of 31 July 2003, para. 587.

[145] *Prosecutor* v. *Stakić*, ICTY (Trial Chamber), judgment of 31 July 2003, para. 587.

[146] *Prosecutor* v. *Stakić*, ICTY (Trial Chamber), judgment of 31 July 2003, para. 642.

[147] *Prosecutor* v. *Kayishema and Ruzindana*, ICTR (Trial Chamber), judgment of 21 May 1999,
para. 146.

336   Apparently, international jurisprudence has not yet developed consistent and general
guidelines for the requirements of the mental element under customary international
law. Taking the above decisions into account, however, it seems safe to say that international tribunals frequently apply a standard of *mens rea* that is lower than the standard
established in Article 30 of the ICC Statute – be it recklessness or *dolus eventualis*.[148]
Through the "unless otherwise provided" clause, this case law also determines the subjective requirements of crimes under Articles 6 to 8 of the ICC Statue. Given the considerable number of "other provisions" in customary international law in particular, the
rule-exception relationship envisaged by Article 30 of the ICC Statute is in fact reversed.

D. Individual Criminal Responsibility

337   Kai Ambos: *Der Allgemeine Teil des Völkerstrafrechts, Ansätze einer Dogmatisierung* (2002), pp. 543
et seq.; K. Ambos: General Principles of Criminal Law in the Rome Statute, 10 *Criminal Law Forum* (1999), pp. 1 et seq.; Kai Ambos: ICC Statute, Art. 25, in Otto Triffterer (ed.), *Commentary
on the Rome Statute of the International Criminal Court, Oberservers' Notes, Article by Article* (1999),
pp. 475 et seq.; Antonio Cassese: *International Criminal Law* (2003), pp. 179 et seq.; Andrew
Clapman: On Complicity, in Marc Henzelin and Robert Roth (eds.), *Le Droit Penal A L'Epreuve
de L'Internationalisation* (2002), pp. 241 et seq.; Albin Eser: Individual Criminal Responsibility, in
Antonio Cassese, Paola Gaeta and John R.W.D. Jones (eds.), *The Rome Statute of the International
Criminal Court: A Commentary*, Vol. 1 (2002), pp. 767 et seq.; Günter Heine: Täterschaft und
Teilnahme in staatlichen Machtapparaten, NS- und DDR-Unrecht im Vergleich der Recht-
sprechung, *Juristenzeitung* 2000, pp. 920 et seq.; Herbert Jäger: Menschheitsverbrechen und die
Grenzen des Kriminalitätskonzeptes, Theoretische Aspekte der Einsetzung eines UN-Kriegs-
verbrechertribunals, 76 *Kritische Vierteljahresschrift für Gesetzgebung und Rechtswissenschaft* (1993),
pp. 259 et seq.; Hans-Heinrich Jescheck: *Die Verantwortlichkeit der Staatsorgane nach Völker-
strafrecht, Eine Studie zu den Nürnberger Prozessen* (1952), pp. 268 et seq.; Kriangsak Kittichaisaree:
International Criminal Law (2001), pp. 233 et seq.; Claus Roxin: Probleme von Täterschaft und
Teilnahme bei der organisierten Kriminalität, in Erich Samson et al. (eds.), *Festschrift für Gerald
Grünwald* (1999), pp. 549 et seq.; Per Saland: International Criminal Law Principles, in Roy S.
Lee (ed.), *The International Criminal Court, The Making of the Rome Statute* (1999), pp. 189 et
seq.; William A. Schabas: *An Introduction to the International Criminal Court*, 2nd edn. (2004),
pp. 101 et seq.; Kurt Seelmann: *Kollektive Verantwortung im Strafrecht* (2002); Otto Triffterer:
Bestandsaufnahme zum Völkerstrafrecht, in Gerd Hankel and Gerhard Stuby (eds.), *Strafgerichte
gegen Menschheitsverbrechen, Zum Völkerstrafrecht 50 Jahre nach den Nürnberger Prozessen* (1995),
pp. 169 et seq.; Hans Vest: *Genozid durch organisatorische Machtapparate, An der Grenze von
individueller und kollektiver Verantwortlichkeit* (2002); Hans Vest: Verantwortlichkeit für
wirtschaftliche Betätigung im Völkerstrafrecht, 119 *Schweizerische Zeitschrift für Strafrecht* (2001),
pp. 238 et seq.; Joachim Vogel: Individuelle Verantwortlichkeit im Völkerstrafrecht, Zugleich ein
Beitrag zu den Regelungsmodellen der Beteiligung, 113 *Zeitschrift für die gesamte Strafrechtswissenschaft* (2002), pp. 404 et seq.; Thomas Weigend: Article 3: Responsibility and Punishment, in Cherif M. Bassiouni (ed.), *Commentaries on the International Law Commission's 1991
Draft Code of Crimes against the Peace and Security of Mankind* (1993), pp. 113 et seq.

338   Typically, a large number of persons co-operate in committing crimes under international law. This generally occurs by way of a more or less established network, which is

---

[148] See also E. van Sliedregt, *The Criminal Responsibility of Individuals for Violations of International Humanitarian Law* (1985), p. 48 at p. 49.

often part of the state or the military, but is in any case organized. However, the collective nature of crimes under international law does not absolve us of the need to determine individual responsibility.[149] In this process, international criminal law faces more than the task of establishing individual contributions to crimes within a network of collective action. A major additional challenge is weighing the individual contribution to the crime. It must be kept in mind that the degree of criminal responsibility does not diminish as distance from the actual act increases; in fact, it frequently grows.[150] A typical example is the case of armchair killer Adolf Eichmann, who sent thousands to their deaths without ever laying a hand on a single victim himself. The Yugoslavia Tribunal vividly summarized the problem:

"Most of these crimes do not result from the criminal propensity of single individuals but constitute manifestations of collective criminality: the crimes are often carried out by groups of individuals acting in pursuance of a common criminal design. Although some members of the group may physically perpetrate the criminal act (murder . . .), the participation and contribution of the other members of the group is often vital in facilitating the commission of the offence in question. It follows that the moral gravity of such participation is often no less – or indeed no different – from that of those actually carrying out the acts in question."[151]

I. Towards a Doctrine of Modes of Participation in International Criminal Law

1. International Case Law and Customary Law

The same holds true for the modes of participation under international criminal law as **339** for the general principles of international criminal law as a whole: the rules governing modes of participation were at first only rudimentary and fragmentary.[152]

The Nuremberg Charter contained rather archaic-sounding regulations on complic-   **340** ity.[153] Some modes of participation were included directly in the definitions of crimes.

---

[149] This poses the question whether traditional models of participation fail in the area of international criminal law; suggestions include replacing the distinction between principal and accessorial liability with a three-fold model of complicity (leading perpetrator, organizational perpetrator, execution perpetrator). For thorough discussion, see H. Vest, *Genozid durch organisatorische Machtapparate* (2002), pp. 240 et seq.; K. Ambos, *Der Allgemeine Teil des Völkerstrafrechts* (2002), pp. 614 et seq.; K. Hamdorf, *Beteiligungsmodelle im Strafrecht* (2002), pp. 359 et seq.; K. Marxen and G. Werle, *Die strafrechtliche Aufarbeitung von DDR-Unrecht* (1999), p. 243; K. Seelmann, *Kollektive Verantwortung im Strafrecht* (2002); J. Vogel, 114 *Zeitschrift für die gesamte Strafrechtswissenschaft* (2002), p. 403 at p. 420; G. Werle, 109 *Zeitschrift für die gesamte Strafrechtswissenschaft* (1997) p. 808 at p. 822.

[150] It is thus consistent for 145(2)(b) of the ICC Rules of Procedure and Evidence to establish "[A]buse of power or official capacity" as grounds for harsher punishment.

[151] *Prosecutor* v. *Tadić*, ICTY (Appeals Chamber), judgment of 15 July 1999, para. 191.

[152] See K. Ambos, *Der Allgemeine Teil des Völkerstrafrechts* (2002), p. 615; A. Cassese, *International Criminal Law* (2003), p. 180; A. Eser, in A. Cassese, P. Gaeta and J.R.W.D. Jones (eds.), *The Rome Statute of the International Criminal Court*, Vol. 1 (2002), p. 767 at pp. 784 et seq. See also A. Clapman, in M. Henzelin and R. Roth (eds.), *Le Droit Penal A L'Epreuve de L'Internationalisation* (2002), pp. 241 et seq.

[153] For details, see A. Eser, in A. Cassese, P. Gaeta and J.R.W.D. Jones (eds.), *The Rome Statute of the International Criminal Court*, Vol. 1 (2002), p. 767 at p. 784; O. Triffterer, in G. Hankel and G. Stuby (eds.), *Strafgerichte gegen Menschheitsverbrechen* (1995), p. 169 at p. 227.

For example, "participation in a common plan or conspiracy" to wage a war of aggression was a crime.[154] Under Article 6(c) of the Nuremberg Charter, "leaders, organizers, instigators and accomplices" who took part in the formulation or execution of a common plan or conspiracy to commit a crime against international law were responsible even for acts performed by others in execution of the plan.[155] The International Law Commission's Nuremberg Principles state that complicity in a crime against international law is itself a crime against international law.[156]

341   A relatively nuanced provision was found in Article II(2) of Control Council Law No. 10. It distinguished between "principals" and "accessories." An accessory was one who assisted in the commission of a crime, ordered or abetted it, took a consenting part in it, was connected with its planning or execution, or belonged to an organization connected with its commission. In addition, liability for crimes against peace extended to people who held high political, civil or military positions in Germany or in one of its Allies, co-belligerents or satellites or held high positions in the financial, industrial or economic life of such countries. Early adjudicators of international criminal law were correspondingly reluctant to make distinctions.[157] The evident goal of the Nuremberg Trial and the subsequent trials was to subject those responsible to criminal prosecution, and to do this as comprehensively as possible.

342   This rough concept of different modes of participation under international criminal law was first refined in the International Law Commission drafts and the Statutes of the *ad hoc* Tribunals.[158] The breakthrough to a more nuanced doctrine was ultimately achieved by the Yugoslavia Tribunal.[159] Today, various modes of criminal participation are recognized under customary law.[160] Other forms have been established in addition to sole re-

---

[154] Nuremberg Charter, Art. 6(a); Tokyo Charter, Art. 5(a).

[155] See IMT, judgment of 1 October 1946, in *The Trial of German Major War Criminals. Proceedings of the International Military Tribunal Sitting at Nuremberg, Germany*, Part 22, p. 449.

[156] Nuremberg Principle VII.

[157] In the trials before the Nuremberg Tribunal and in the subsequent trials, no distinction was made between forms of participation, in accordance with the so-called unified perpetrator model. The guiding principle was that any actual and legal support or promotion of the act was to be considered criminal participation. Thus participation in war crimes and crimes against humanity was present, under the Nuremberg judgment, if there was a "direct connection" between an act and the crimes. If several people worked together in committing a crime, reciprocal accountability was presumed if the contributions to the crime were functionally linked based on a common purpose or plan ("common design"). For details, see K. Ambos, *Der Allgemeine Teil des Völkerstrafrechts* (2002), pp. 362 et seq.

[158] Art. 7(1) of the ICTY Statute and Art. 6(1) of the ICTR Statute state: "1. A person who planned, instigated, ordered, committed or otherwise aided and abetted in the planning, preparation or execution of a crime referred to in . . . the present Statute, shall be individually responsible for the crime." See also Art. 3 *Draft Code* 1991; see A. Eser, in A. Cassese, P. Gaeta and J.R.W.D. Jones (eds.), *The Rome Statute of the International Criminal Court*, Vol. 1 (2002), p. 767 at pp. 785 et seq.

[159] See *Prosecutor* v. *Tadić*, ICTY (Appeals Chamber), judgment of 15 July 1999, paras. 185 et seq.

[160] See *Prosecutor* v. *Mucić* et al., ICTY (Trial Chamber), judgment of 16. November 1998, para. 321: "That under Article 7(1) ICTY Statute individuals may be held criminally responsible for their participation in the commission of offences in any of several further capacities is in clear conformity with general principles of criminal law. . . . there can be no doubt that this corresponds to the position under customary international law." For thorough discussion of the "basic forms of criminal participation," see K. Ambos, *Der Allgemeine Teil des Völkerstrafrechts* (2002), pp. 543 et seq. For a critical view of the "expansion of the set of perpetrators" associated with distinguishing between forms of participation, see C. Tomuschat, in G. Hankel and G. Stuby (eds.), *Strafgerichte gegen Menschheitsverbrechen* (1995), p. 270 at pp. 286 et seq.

sponsibility.[161] These include joint commission, causing a third party to commit a crime under international law by ordering or inciting, and abetting a third party in the commission of a crime under international law. Customary law modes of participation have been lent more precise contours, mainly through the jurisprudence of the Yugoslavia Tribunal.

2. ICC Statute

Article 25(3) of the ICC Statute now regulates in detail the modalities of individual **343** criminal responsibility and distinguishes several modes of criminal participation; special rules apply to the crime of aggression, which is a "leadership crime" and thus subject to limitations with regard to perpetrators and conduct.[162] Article 25(3) almost entirely embodies customary international law.[163] This provision for the first time systematizes the modalities of participation recognized under customary international law, while cautiously supplementing and modifying them. It affirms individual commission, joint perpetration and participation in the forms of ordering, inducing or abetting the commission of a crime under international law. In contrast, there is no direct basis in customary international law for the concept of perpetration-by-means, which is now included in Article 25(3)(a) of the ICC Statute;[164] the same is true of the provision on participation in a collectivity,[165] which is included as a disguised "conspiracy" rule.[166] It is not clear whether a basis exists in customary law for the fact that, throughout Article 25, accessorial liability, such as inciting or supporting, is derivative of the criminal liability of the perpetrator.[167] Specifically, in cases in which criminal responsibility exists for inciting or supporting another's crimes, Article 25 of the ICC Statute requires that the crime itself actually have been committed, or at least attempted.[168]

If the requirements for a form of participation are present, the legal consequence un- **344** der Article 25(3) is that the perpetrator shall be "criminally responsible and liable for

---

[161] On the not always uniform language of the ICTY, see *Prosecutor* v. *Mucić* et al., ICTY (Trial Chamber), judgment of 16 November 1998, para. 351, and *Prosecutor* v. *Kvočka* et al., ICTY (Trial Chamber), judgment of 2 November 2001, para. 242. In the common terminology, an *accomplice* is anyone who did not participate in the crime as a *principal offender* or *perpetrator*, that is, for example, *co-perpetrators* and *accessories*, see G. Fletcher, *Rethinking Criminal Law* (2000), p. 637. For further distinctions, see *Prosecutor* v. *Krnojelac*, ICTY (Trial Chamber), judgment of 15 March 2002, para. 76.

[162] Agreement on the principles of criminal participation doctrine enshrined in Art. 25(3) of the ICC Statute created considerable difficulty at the Rome Conference. For detail, see P. Saland, in R.S. Lee (ed.), *The International Criminal Court, The Making of the Rome Statute* (1999), p. 189 at p. 198. On the crime of aggression, see marginal nos. 1176 et seq.

[163] On the ICC Statute's departures from the corresponding provisions of the ICTY Statute, see K. Kittichaisaree, *International Criminal Law* (2001), pp. 235 et seq.

[164] See ICC Statute, Art. 25(3)(a), third alternative. For the concept of perpetration-by-means, see G. Fletcher, *Rethinking Criminal Law* (2000), p. 639.

[165] See ICC Statute, Art. 25(3)(d).

[166] Conspiracy to commit a crime under international law, in contrast, was not adopted into the Statute's rules. For additional information, see marginal nos. 488 et seq.

[167] For thorough discussion, see K. Ambos, *Der Allgemeine Teil des Völkerstrafrechts* (2002), pp. 616 et seq.

[168] An exception is made only for incitement to genocide under Art. 25(3)(e) of the ICC Statute; but this is an independent offense which is included incorrectly, from a structural point of view, in the provision on modes of participation; see marginal nos. 623 et seq.

punishment."[169] No gradations in the degree of criminal liability are provided for in Article 25, but they may be taken into account in sentencing.[170]

II. Commission

1. Commission as an Individual

345 One who, under Article 25(3)(a), first alternative, of the ICC Statute, fulfills the requirements of a crime against international law in his or her own person, and thus "commits a crime as an individual," is clearly liable under international criminal law.[171] This conforms to customary international law.[172]

2. Joint Commission

346 If several people act together in committing a crime under international law ("jointly with another"), each one is individually responsible.[173] This is established by Article 25(3)(a), second alternative, of the ICC Statute, in conformity with customary international law.[174] The basic outlines of joint commission have been developed, above all, in the case law of the Yugoslavia Tribunal.[175]

---

[169] Art. 25(3) of the ICC Statute does not explicitly distinguish between perpetration and (simple) accessorial liability. To this extent, the Statute – like the Charter of the Nuremberg Tribunal and the Statutes of the ICTY and ICTR – seems to be based on a certain affinity with the unified perpetrator model, on this term, see A. Eser, in A. Cassese, P. Gaeta and J.R.W.D. Jones (eds.), *The Rome Statute of the International Criminal Court*, Vol. 1 (2002), p. 767 at pp. 781 et seq. In regard to the requirements for accessory, however, echoes of a nuanced participation model can be recognized. In the literature, the rule is not uniformly classified: Ambos sees a trend toward a differentiation model, see K. Ambos, *Der Allgemeine Teil des Völkerstrafrechts* (2002), pp. 543 et seq., and probably also H. Vest, *Genozid durch organisatorische Machtapparate* (2002), p. 181. In contrast, an interpretation in the spirit of the uniform system is found in C. Kress, *Humanitäres Völkerrecht-Informationsschriften* 1999, p. 4 at p. 9, and K. Hamdorf, *Beteiligungsmodelle im Strafrecht* (2002), p. 396.

[170] See ICC Statute, Art. 78(1); under ICC Rule of Procedure and Evidence 145(1)(c), the ICC is to consider in particular "the degree of participation of the convicted person."

[171] See A. Eser, in A. Cassese, P. Gaeta and J.R.W.D. Jones (eds.), *The Rome Statute of the International Criminal Court*, Vol. 1 (2002), p. 767 at p. 789. According to ICTY case law, the commission of a crime under international law is the "physical perpetration of a crime by the offender himself, or the culpable omission of an act," see *Prosecutor* v. *Tadić*, ICTY (Appeals Chamber), judgment of 15 July 1999, para. 188; *Prosecutor* v. *Kvočka* et al., ICTY (Trial Chamber), judgment of 2 November 2001, para. 243; *Prosecutor* v. *Kajelijeli*, ICTR (Trial Chamber), judgment of 1 December 2003, para. 764.

[172] See also Nuremberg Charter, Art. VI; Tokyo Charter, Art. 5; ICTY Statute, Art. 1(1); ICTR Statute, Art. 1(1); and Genocide Convention, Art. 2.

[173] See in detail K. Ambos, *Der Allgemeine Teil des Völkerstrafrechts* (2002), pp. 548 et seq.; A. Cassese, *International Criminal Law* (2003), pp. 181 et seq.; K. Kittichaisaree, *International Criminal Law* (2001), p. 237.

[174] See *Prosecutor* v. *Tadić*, ICTY (Appeals Chamber), judgment of 15 July 1999, paras. 194 et seq.; K. Ambos, *Der Allgemeine Teil des Völkerstrafrechts* (2002), p. 363. Despite the roots of the joint liability model in many legal systems of the world, the ICTY Appeals Chamber explicitly sees insufficient evidence that would allow it to presume such a general principle of law, see *Prosecutor* v. *Tadić*, ICTY (Appeals Chamber), judgment of 15 July 1999, paras. 224 et seq.

[175] See *Prosecutor* v. *Tadić*, ICTY (Appeals Chamber), judgment of 15 July 1999, paras. 194 et seq., summary in para. 227. See also *Prosecutor* v. *Vasiljević*, ICTY (Trial Chamber), judgment of 29

The Yugoslavia Tribunal bases joint liability on the legal concept of participation in a **347** "joint criminal enterprise."[176] In the Tribunal's view, this is grounded in post-war jurisprudence, which has become part of customary international law.[177] The doctrine of the joint criminal enterprise is of great relevance to the work of the Yugoslavia Tribunal. It has since also been adopted by other international criminal courts.[178]

The difference between joint commission and mere participation lies largely in the **348** subjective sphere. The key to joint commission is the "common plan, design or purpose." This must be aimed at committing one or more crimes against international law.[179] However, the plan need not be formed before the act is committed; it can also be spontaneous. Its presence may be deduced from the cooperation of several persons to carry out a criminal undertaking.[180]

November 2002, paras. 63 et seq.; *Prosecutor* v. *Furundžija*, ICTY (Appeals Chamber), judgment of 21 July 2000, para. 119; *Prosecutor* v. *Kvočka* et al., ICTY (Trial Chamber), judgment of 2 November 2001, paras. 265 et seq., 312. The development of these principles continues without a special rule on joint liability being provided in the ICTY Statute. Under ICTY case law, co-perpetratorship is implicitly included in Article 7(1) of the ICTY Statute, see *Prosecutor* v. *Tadić*, ICTY (Appeals Chamber), judgment of 15 July 1999, paras. 188 et seq., citing to teleological and historical interpretation: "the commission of one of the crimes . . . might also occur through participation in the realisation of a common design or purpose."

[176] See *Prosecutor* v. *Vasiljević*, ICTY (Trial Chamber), judgment of 29 November 2002, para. 67: " . . . all of the participants in a joint criminal enterprise are equally guilty of the committed crime regardless of the part played by each in its commission."

[177] The doctrine of the joint criminal enterprise can be traced to *Prosecutor* v. *Tadić*, ICTY (Appeals Chamber), judgment of 15 July 1999, paras. 194 et seq. See also *Prosecutor* v. *Vasiljević*, ICTY (Trial Chamber), judgment of 29 November 2002, paras. 63 et seq.; *Prosecutor* v. *Furundžija*, ICTY (Appeals Chamber), judgment of 21 July 2000, para. 119; *Prosecutor* v. *Kvočka* et al., ICTY (Trial Chamber), judgment of 2 November 2001, paras. 265 et seq., 312.

[178] See, e.g., the indictment before the Special Court for Sierra Leone, *Prosecutor* v. *Charles Ghankay Taylor*, indictment of 7 March 2003, paras. 23 et seq.: "The RUF and the AFRC shared a common plan, purpose or design (joint criminal enterprise) which was to take any actions necessary to gain and exercise political power and control over the territory of Sierra Leone, in particular the diamond mining areas. . . . The crimes alleged in this Indictment, including unlawful killings, abductions, forced labour, physical and sexual violence, use of child soldiers, looting and burning of civilian structures, were either actions within the joint criminal enterprise or were a reasonably foreseeable consequence of the joint criminal enterprise. . . . The Accused participated in this joint criminal enterprise." The doctrine of the joint criminal enterprise has hardly been applied so far by the Rwanda Tribunal. This may be due mainly to the fact that Art. 2(3)(b) of the ICTR Statute encompasses conspiracy to commit genocide, so that, in many cases, there is no need for recourse to the principle of the joint criminal enterprise.

[179] *Prosecutor* v. *Tadić*, ICTY (Appeals Chamber), judgment of 15 July 1999, para. 188; *Prosecutor* v. *Kupreškić* et al., ICTY (Appeals Chamber), judgment of 14 January 2000, para. 772: "Co-perpetration requires a plurality of persons, the existence of a common plan, design or purpose which amounts to or involves the commission of a crime provided for in the Statute and participation of the accused in the common design."

[180] *Prosecutor* v. *Tadić*, ICTY (Appeals Chamber), judgment of 15 July 1999, para. 227: "There is no necessity for this plan, design or purpose to have been previously arranged or formulated. The common plan or purpose may materialize extemporaneously and be inferred from the fact that a plurality of persons acts in unison to put into effect a joint criminal enterprise."

349   The notion of a joint criminal enterprise encompasses three different categories, according to the judgments of the Yugoslavia Tribunal.[181] The first category includes cases in which a group of persons possesses shared intent to commit a crime under international law and the crime is carried out according to a "common design." The joint perpetrators can play various roles. It is not necessary for each perpetrator to be seeking to carry out the plan for the same reason.[182] To establish joint responsibility, a significant and causal contribution to the accomplishment of a common design is necessary. The contribution to the crime need not be related to execution,[183] but can consist of any kind of assistance ("assistance in, or contribution to, the execution of the common plan or purpose").[184] Contributions even at the planning stage are sufficient.[185] It is not necessary for the joint perpetrators to be organized in a military, political or administrative unit.[186]

350   So-called concentration camp cases make up the second category of joint criminal enterprises. These include crimes committed by several persons, especially members of military or administrative units, as part of "systems of ill-treatment." To find joint commission, from an objective point of view, it is necessary to show the existence of a system for mistreating prisoners and for committing crimes under international law. The perpetrator must actively participate in the implementation of this repressive system. This participation can usually be deduced from a defendant's position and specific tasks.[187] Subjectively, the perpetrator must be aware of the character of the system and act with intent to further the system of mistreatment. This intent can also generally be derived from the defendant's position of authority.[188]

351   Under both categories of joint criminal enterprise, the participants are responsible for all crimes contained within the framework of the common plan.[189] The third and broad-

---

[181] *Prosecutor* v. *Tadić*, ICTY (Appeals Chamber), judgment of 15 July 1999, para. 195.

[182] *Prosecutor* v. *Krnojelac*, ICTY (Appeals Chamber), judgment of 17 September 2003, para. 100: "The Appeals Chamber agrees with the Prosecution that shared criminal intent does not require the co-perpetrator's personal satisfaction or enthusiasm or his personal initiative in contributing to the joint enterprise."

[183] A. Eser, in A. Cassese, P. Gaeta and J.R.W.D. Jones (eds.), *The Rome Statute of the International Criminal Court*, Vol. 1 (2002), p. 767 at pp. 791 et seq.

[184] See *Prosecutor* v. *Tadić*, ICTY (Appeals Chamber), judgment of 15 July 1999, paras. 196 et seq., 227. Under these principles, the high-ranking officer Krstić, for example, was convicted as a joint perpetrator, although he "did not conceive the plan to kill the men, nor did he kill them personally. However, he fulfilled a key coordinating role in the implementation of the killing campaign," see *Prosecutor* v. *Krstić*, ICTY (Trial Chamber), judgment of 2 August 2001, para. 644.

[185] *Prosecutor* v. *Tadić*, ICTY (Appeals Chamber), judgment of 15 July 1999, para. 192: "Under these circumstances, to hold criminally liable as a perpetrator only the person who materially performs the criminal act would disregard the role as co-perpetrators of all those who in some way made it possible for the perpetrator physically to carry out that criminal act. At the same time, depending upon the circumstances, to hold the latter liable only as aiders and abettors might understate the degree of their criminal responsibility."

[186] *Prosecutor* v. *Tadić*, ICTY (Appeals Chamber), judgment of 15 July 1999, para. 227.

[187] *Prosecutor* v. *Tadić*, ICTY (Appeals Chamber), judgment of 15 July 1999, paras. 202 et seq.

[188] *Prosecutor* v. *Tadić*, ICTY (Appeals Chamber), judgment of 15 July 1999, para. 203.

[189] The Yugoslavia Tribunal defined the second category of joint criminal enterprise as a variant of the first category: The defendants, it said, were considered joint perpetrators because they held objective "position[s] of authority" and did not attend sufficiently to the welfare of the prisoners, although

est category ("extended joint criminal enterprise"),[190] in contrast, concerns cases in which one joint perpetrator commits excesses that go beyond the framework of the common plan. A participant in a criminal undertaking who wishes to take part in a scheme based on a common plan can nevertheless be held accountable for consequences not included in the plan if they are the "natural and foreseeable consequence" of the plan's execution. Subjectively, the participant must have consciously accepted, or been indifferent to, the risk of the consequence occurring.[191]

Although the Yugoslavia Tribunal in its decisions on joint criminal enterprise referred to Article **352** 25(3)(d) of the ICC Statute,[192] it remains to be seen whether the International Criminal Court will adopt the doctrine. The question arises especially in light of the fact that the Yugoslavia Tribunal, in the *Stakić* judgment, recently pointed out that the legal concept of the joint criminal enterprise is only one of several ways of constructing joint commission. But, the Court added, a more literal interpretation of its Statute, and one more oriented toward national legal systems, had to take precedence, because of the danger that the joint criminal enterprise might wrongly be seen to define a new offense.[193]

3. Commission Through Another Person

If the perpetrator uses another person as a tool to commit a crime under international **353** law – that is, if he or she commits the crime "through another person" – this is a basis for criminal liability under Article 25(3)(a), third alternative, of the ICC Statute. In this form of participation, the perpetrator-by-means typically holds a superior position.[194]

The idea of a perpetrator-by-means is recognized by the world's major legal systems.[195] However, **354** before the ICC Statute entered into force, it had neither been regulated by international criminal law nor dealt with by international courts. Thus the Statute provision has no model in customary law.

---

the prisoners were in their hands, see *Prosecutor* v. *Tadić*, ICTY (Appeals Chamber), judgment of 15 July 1999, para. 203.

[190] *Prosecutor* v. *Stakić*, ICTY (Trial Chamber), judgment of 31 July 2003, para. 436.

[191] *Prosecutor* v. *Tadić*, ICTY (Appeals Chamber), judgment of 15 July 1999, paras. 204, 206, 228: ". . . responsibility for a crime other than the one agreed upon in the common plan arises only if, under the circumstances of the case, (i) it was foreseeable that such a crime might be perpetrated by one or other members of the group and (ii) the accused willingly took that risk."

[192] *Prosecutor* v. *Tadić*, ICTY (Appeals Chamber), judgment of 15 July 1999, paras. 222 et seq.

[193] *Prosecutor* v. *Stakić*, ICTY (Trial Chamber), judgment of 31 July 2003, para. 441: "The Trial Chamber is aware that the end result of its definition of co-perpetration approaches that of the aforementioned joint criminal enterprise and even overlaps in part. However, the Trial Chamber opines that this definition is closer to what most legal systems understand as 'committing' and avoids the misleading impression that a new crime not foreseen in the Statute of this Tribunal has been introduced through the backdoor."

[194] See also A. Eser, in A. Cassese, P. Gaeta and J.R.W.D. Jones (eds.), *The Rome Statute of the International Criminal Court*, Vol. 1 (2002), p. 767 at p. 793.

[195] Sec. 2.06(2) Model Penal Code, for example, states: "A person is legally accountable for the conduct of another person when: (a) . . . he causes on innocent or irresponsible person to engage in such conduct . . . .." For detail see K. Ambos, *Der Allgemeine Teil des Völkerstrafrechts* (2002), pp. 568 et seq.; G. Fletcher, *Rethinking Criminal Law* (2000), p. 639; see also marginal nos. 356 et seq.

355   Criminal responsibility under Article 25(3)(a), third alternative, of the ICC Statute is independent of whether the direct perpetrator is liable him or herself ("regardless of whether that other person is criminally responsible"). This addition clarifies matters in two ways: first, it acknowledges the concept of the "perpetrator behind the perpetrator" (*"Täter hinter dem Täter"*),[196] since the addition expressly does not rule out the possibility that the direct perpetrator can be manipulated, even if he or she is also fully responsible for the crime. Second, it establishes that a perpetrator-by-means can also be liable – indeed is most likely to be – if the direct perpetrator is not responsible, for example if he or she is not yet of legal age (Article 26 of the ICC Statute) or because a ground for exclusion of responsibility works in his or her favor.

III. Encouragement

356   Under Article 25(3)(b) of the ICC Statute, a person who does not commit a crime under international law him or herself, but encourages another to do so, is also responsible under international law.[197] It is possible to distinguish between ordering a crime under international law and inducing someone to commit such a crime. Incitement to genocide, which is incorrectly regulated under Article 25(3)(e) of the ICC Statute, is not a modality of participation but a crime in itself.[198]

1. Ordering

357   Anyone who orders the commission of a crime against international law is criminally liable.[199] This provision of Article 25(3)(b), first alternative, of the ICC Statute embodies customary international law.[200] An order assumes the existence of a – typically military – relationship of subordination between the one giving and the one receiving the order. The perpetrator uses his or her authority to cause another person to commit a crime.[201]

---

[196] See also A. Eser, in A. Cassese, P. Gaeta and J.R.W.D. Jones (eds.), *The Rome Statute of the International Criminal Court*, Vol. 1 (2002), p. 767 at pp. 794 et seq.; J. Vogel, 114 *Zeitschrift für die gesamte Strafrechtswissenschaft* (2002), p. 404 at p. 427. Thus the doctrine of the "perpetrator behind the perpetrator" that was developed by C. Roxin, *Golddammer's Archiv für Strafrecht* 1963, pp. 193 et seq., in connection with the *Eichmann* trial – that is, in an international criminal law context – and has since considerably influenced German criminal jurisprudence, has been affirmed for international criminal law. It is doubtful, however, whether it is at the same time established that German doctrine on acting through an organizational power structure can be translated into international criminal law; but see K. Ambos, in O. Triffterer (ed.), *Commentary on the Rome Statute of the International Criminal Court* (1999), Art. 25, marginal no. 8; for a skeptical view, see H. Vest, *Genozid durch organisatorische Machtapparate* (2002), p. 185.

[197] See K. Ambos, *Der Allgemeine Teil des Völkerstrafrechts* (2002), pp. 644 et seq.

[198] For more, see marginal nos. 623 et seq.

[199] See A. Cassese, *International Criminal Law* (2003), p. 194; A. Eser, in A. Cassese, P. Gaeta and J.R.W.D. Jones (eds.), *The Rome Statute of the International Criminal Court*, Vol. 1 (2002), p. 767 at p. 796.

[200] See also ICTY Statute, Art. 7(1); ICTR Statute, Art. 6(1); Geneva Convention III, Art. 129(1); Geneva Convention IV, Art. 146(1).

[201] See *Prosecutor* v. *Krstić*, ICTY (Trial Chamber), judgment of 2 August 2001, para. 601: "person in a position of authority using that position to convince another to commit an offence"; *Prosecutor* v. *Naletilić and Martinović*, ICTY (Trial Chamber), judgment of 31 March 2003, para. 61;

2. Instigation

A person who "solicits" or "induces" another to commit a crime against international law **358** is also criminally liable under international law.[202] The provisions of Article 25(3)(b), second and third alternatives, of the ICC Statute reflect customary law. According to ICTY jurisprudence, one who "prompts" another, by action or omission,[203] to commit a crime against international law is an instigator.[204] As a rule, this results from psychological pressure; however, physical inducements are also conceivable.[205] Even a primary perpetrator who has already decided to act may be induced to act.[206] A chain of inducements is possible.[207] The instigator is not liable for the excesses of a person who acts at his instigation.[208]

Subjectively, instigation requires that the perpetrator wished to "provoke or induce" **359** the commission of the crime or that he or she was aware of the "substantial likelihood" that the commission of the crime would result from his or her conduct.[209]

IV. Assistance

In addition, assisting the (primary) perpetrator can also suffice as a basis for criminal re- **360** sponsibility.[210] This is recognized under customary international law and affirmed in Article 25(3)(c) and (d) of the ICC Statute.

Prosecutor v. Stakić, ICTY (Trial Chamber), judgment of 31 July 2003, paras. 444 et seq.; *Prosecutor v. Semanza*, ICTR (Trial Chamber), judgment of 15 May 2003, para. 382; *Prosecutor v. Kamuhanda*, ICTR (Trial Chamber), judgment of 22 January 2004, para. 594. On the responsibility of superiors, see also marginal nos. 368 et seq.

[202] Without changing the substance, Art. 25(3)(b), second and third alternatives, of the ICC Statute use the terms "solicits or induces" ("*sollicite ou encourage*"). See also K. Ambos, *Der Allgemeine Teil des Völkerstrafrechts* (2002), p. 664; A. Eser, in A. Cassese, P. Gaeta and J.R.W.D. Jones (eds.), *The Rome Statute of the International Criminal Court*, Vol. 1 (2002), p. 767 at p. 796.

[203] See *Prosecutor v. Blaškić*, ICTY (Trial Chamber), judgment of 3 March 2000, para. 280.

[204] See *Prosecutor v. Krstić*, ICTY (Trial Chamber), judgment of 2 August 2001, para. 601; *Prosecutor v. Kvočka* et al., ICTY (Trial Chamber), judgment of 2 November 2001, para. 243, with additional notes; most recently *Prosecutor v. Naletilić and Martinović*, ICTY (Trial Chamber), judgment of 31 March 2003, para. 60; *Prosecutor v. Akayesu*, ICTR (Appeals Chamber), judgment of 1 June 2001, paras. 478 et seq.; *Prosecutor v. Semanza*, ICTR (Trial Chamber), judgment of 15 May 2003, para. 381.

[205] See K. Ambos, in O. Triffterer (ed.), *Commentary on the Rome Statute of the International Criminal Court* (1999), Art. 25, marginal no. 13.

[206] See *Prosecutor v. Kvočka* et al., ICTY (Trial Chamber), judgment of 2 November 2001, para. 252; *Prosecutor v. Kordić and Čerkez*, ICTY (Trial Chamber), judgment of 26 February 2001, para. 387. But see *Prosecutor v. Blaškić*, ICTY (Trial Chamber), judgment of 3 March 2000, para. 278, under which a causal connection between the act of incitement and the commission of the crime must be shown.

[207] See A. Eser, in A. Cassese, P. Gaeta and J.R.W.D. Jones (eds.), *The Rome Statute of the International Criminal Court*, Vol. 1 (2002), p. 767 at p. 796.

[208] See A. Eser, in A. Cassese, P. Gaeta and J.R.W.D. Jones (eds.), *The Rome Statute of the International Criminal Court*, Vol. 1 (2002), p. 767 at p. 798.

[209] See *Prosecutor v. Kvočka* et al., ICTY (Trial Chamber), judgment of 2 November 2001, para. 252, with additional cites; *Prosecutor v. Naletilić and Martinović*, ICTY (Trial Chamber), judgment of 31 March 2003, para. 60; A. Eser, in A. Cassese, P. Gaeta and J.R.W.D. Jones (eds.), *The Rome Statute of the International Criminal Court*, Vol. 1 (2002), p. 767 at p. 797, requires dual intention on the part of the instigator.

[210] See A. Eser, in A. Cassese, P. Gaeta and J.R.W.D. Jones (eds.), *The Rome Statute of the International Criminal Court*, Vol. 1 (2002), p. 767 at pp. 798 et seq.

1. Assisting the (Primary) Perpetrator

361 Anyone who "aids, abets or otherwise assists" in the commission or the attempted commission of a crime under international law is criminally liable.[211] Liability for assisting the primary perpetrator has been clarified in judgments of the Yugoslavia Tribunal.[212]

362 The assistance need not be given at the location or at the time[213] the main crime is committed; it is enough for it to facilitate the crime or otherwise have a substantial[214] effect on it ("practical assistance, encouragement or moral support which has substantial effect on the commission of the crime").[215] Encouraging the perpetrator or granting other moral support, in some circumstances even mere presence at the scene of the crime, can suffice.[216] It is not necessary for the assistance to be causally connected to the crime.[217] A typical form of assistance, expressly mentioned in Article 25(3)(c) of the ICC Statute, is "providing the means for its commission."

---

[211] "Aiding" here includes acts in support, while "abetting" is "being sympathetic" to another, see *Prosecutor* v. *Akayesu*, ICTR (Trial Chamber), judgment of 2 September 1998, para. 484; *Prosecutor* v. *Semanza*, ICTR (Trial Chamber), judgment of 15 May 2003, para. 384; *Prosecutor* v. *Kvočka* et al., ICTY (Trial Chamber), judgment of 2 November 2001, para. 254.

[212] For a summary of the requirements, see *Prosecutor* v. *Vasiljević*, ICTY (Appeals Chamber), judgment of 25 February 2004, para. 102; *Prosecutor* v. *Blaškić*, ICTY (Appeals Chamber), judgment of 29 July 2004, para. 45; *Prosecutor* v. *Naletilić and Martinović*, ICTY (Trial Chamber), judgment of 31 March 2003, para. 63; *Prosecutor* v. *Krnojelac*, ICTY (Trial Chamber), judgment of 15 March 2002, paras. 88 et seq.; *Prosecutor* v. *Kvočka* et al., ICTY (Trial Chamber), judgment of 2 November 2001, paras. 253 et seq. See also K. Ambos, *Der Allgemeine Teil des Völkerstrafrechts* (2002), pp. 619 et seq.; a thorough analysis of the state of customary law is found in *Prosecutor* v. *Furundžija*, ICTY (Trial Chamber), judgment of 10 December 1998, paras. 192 et seq.

[213] See *Prosecutor* v. *Blaškić*, ICTY (Trial Chamber), judgment of 3 March 2000, para. 285, with additional citations, and *Prosecutor* v. *Semanza*, ICTR (Trial Chamber), judgment of 15 May 2003, para. 385. However, the ICC Statute does not expressly determine that abetting can lead to liability even after completion of the crime. A footnote to Art. 23 of the Draft ICC Statute (1998) states: "This presumption [that successive assistance can be enough for liability] was questioned in the context of the ICC. If aiding, etc., *ex post facto* were deemed necessary to be criminalized, an explicit provision would be needed." A. Eser, in A. Cassese, P. Gaeta and J.R.W.D. Jones (eds.), *The Rome Statute of the International Criminal Court*, Vol. 1 (2002), p. 767 at p. 807, also supports the inclusion of "successive assistance."

[214] This requirement, developed by the *ad hoc* Tribunals in 1996 pursuant to the *Draft Code* 1996 and since then applied consistently in their cases, is not found in Art. 25(3)(c) of the ICC Statute. In fact, however, it is reasonable to exclude quite distant assistance. See also A. Eser, in A. Cassese, P. Gaeta and J.R.W.D. Jones (eds.), *The Rome Statute of the International Criminal Court*, Vol. 1 (2002), p. 767 at p. 800.

[215] See *Prosecutor* v. *Krnojelac*, ICTY (Trial Chamber), judgment of 15 March 2002, para. 88; see also J. Vogel, 114 *Zeitschrift für die gesamte Strafrechtswissenschaft* (2002), p. 404 at pp. 426 et seq.

[216] See *Prosecutor* v. *Kvočka* et al., ICTY (Trial Chamber), judgment of 2 November 2001, para. 257; *Prosecutor* v. *Kamuhanda*, ICTR (Trial Chamber), judgment of 22 January 2004, para. 600, see also K. Ambos, *Der Allgemeine Teil des Völkerstrafrechts* (2002), p. 363. *Tadić*, the convicted defendant, was present while third parties committed crimes under international law. In contrast to earlier occasions, *Tadić* himself did not take actual part, see *Prosecutor* v. *Tadić*, ICTY (Trial Chamber), judgment of 7 May 1997, para. 690. *Aleksovski* did nothing when a subordinate badly abused prisoners not far from his office, see *Prosecutor* v. *Aleksovski*, ICTY (Trial Chamber), judgment of 25 June 1999, para. 88. See also A. Clapman, in M. Henzelin and R. Roth (eds.), *Le Droit Penal A L'Epreuve de L'Internationanisation* (2002), p. 241 at pp. 252 et seq.

[217] See *Prosecutor* v. *Blaškić*, ICTY (Appeals Chamber), judgment of 29 July 2004, para. 48; *Prosecutor* v. *Kvočka* et al., ICTY (Trial Chamber), judgment of 2 November 2001, para. 255, with addi-

From a subjective point of view, the person giving the assistance must be aware that his or **363** her contribution is supporting the commission of the crime.[218] Article 25(3)(c) of the ICC Statute additionally requires that the assistance be afforded "for the purpose of facilitating the commission" of the crime.[219] But the person assisting need not share the particular intent on the part of the primary perpetrator, if required, such as the intent to destroy required for genocide.[220] Knowledge of the primary perpetrator's intent is sufficient.

2. Assisting the Commission of a Crime by a Group

Article 25(3)(d) of the ICC Statute regulates a new form of criminal participation: Con- **364** tributing to the commission of a crime or an attempted crime by a group creates criminal liability. The provision incorporates a rule from the 1997 *International Convention for the Suppression of Terrorist Bombings* into general international criminal law.[221] There is no model for this in customary international law. The provision is the result of complicated negotiations at the Rome Conference on the inclusion of conspiracy.[222]

As an objective requirement, responsibility is connected to the commission or at- **365** tempted commission of a crime under international law by a group. A group is any association of at least three persons[223] who act in furtherance of a "common purpose." Any contribution to the group crime ("in any other way contributes") not covered by another form of participation, especially assistance, establishes the criminal responsibility of the accessory.[224] This catch-all rule includes supplying weapons, financing, and other forms of indirect support for crimes against international law.[225]

---

tional citations: "no requirement that the aider or abettor have a causal effect on the act of the principal"; *Prosecutor* v. *Blaškić*, ICTY (Trial Chamber), judgment of 3 March 2000, para. 285. See also A. Eser, in A. Cassese, P. Gaeta and J.R.W.D. Jones (eds.), *The Rome Statute of the International Criminal Court*, Vol. 1 (2002), p. 767 at pp. 799 et seq.; K. Kittichaisaree, *International Criminal Law* (2001), p. 243.

[218] See *Prosecutor* v. *Aleksovski*, ICTY (Appeals Chamber), judgment of 24 March 2000, para. 162; *Prosecutor* v. *Vasiljević*, ICTY (Trial Chamber), judgment of 29 November 2002, para. 71; recently *Prosecutor* v. *Vasiljević*, ICTY (Appeals Chamber), judgment of 25 February 2004, para. 102. This is the most important limiting criterion for joint liability, see *Prosecutor* v. *Tadić*, ICTY (Appeals Chamber), judgment of 15 July 1999, para. 229; A. Clapman, in M. Henzelin and R. Roth (eds.), *Le Droit Penal A L'Epreuve de L'Internationanisation* (2002), p. 241 at p. 250; K. Kittichaisaree, *International Criminal Law* (2001), p. 245.

[219] This requirement is also taken from Sec. 2.06 Model Penal Code.

[220] See *Prosecutor* v. *Vasiljević*, ICTY (Trial Chamber), judgment of 29 November 2002, para. 71; *Prosecutor* v. *Krnojelac*, ICTY (Appeals Chamber), judgment of 17 September 2003, para. 52: the aider and abetter "need not to share the intent but he must be aware of the discriminatory context in which the crime is to be committed and know that his support or encouragement has a substantial effect." K. Kittichaisaree, *International Criminal Law* (2001), p. 244, with additional citations.

[221] Art. 2(3)(c) of the 15 December 1997 Convention (UN Doc. A/RES/52/164).

[222] See P. Saland, in R.S. Lee (ed.), *The International Criminal Court, The Making of the Rome Statute* (1999), p. 199; A. Eser, in A. Cassese, P. Gaeta and J.R.W.D. Jones (eds.), *The Rome Statute of the International Criminal Court*, Vol. 1 (2002), p. 767 at p. 802. See also marginal no. 490.

[223] See A. Eser, in A. Cassese, P. Gaeta and J.R.W.D. Jones (eds.), *The Rome Statute of the International Criminal Court*, Vol. 1 (2002), p. 767 at p. 802.

[224] But see J. Vogel, 114 *Zeitschrift für die gesamte Strafrechtswissenschaft* (2002), p. 404 at p. 421, according to whom ICC Statute, Art. 25(3)(d), relates to a special case of joint liability that primarily forms a basis for including liability for excesses.

[225] See J. Vogel, 114 *Zeitschrift für die gesamte Strafrechtswissenschaft* (2002), p. 404 at p. 421.

366 Additional requirements for the mental element provide something of a counter-weight to the relatively few objective requirements here. Specifically, the contribution to the crime must be made either with the aim of furthering the group's criminal activity or common purpose, to the extent these relate to commission of the crime under international law, or with knowledge of the group's intent to commit the crime.[226]

E. Superior Responsibility

367 Kai Ambos: *Der Allgemeine Teil des Völkerstrafrechts, Ansätze einer Dogmatisierung* (2002), pp. 666 et seq.; Kai Ambos: Superior Responsibility, in Antonio Cassese, Paola Gaeta and John R.W.D. Jones (eds.), *The Rome Statute of the International Criminal Court: A Commentary*, Vol. 1 (2002), pp. 823 et seq.; Ilias Bantekas: The Contemporary Law of Superior Responsibility, 93 *American Journal of International Law* (1999), pp. 573 et seq.; Sonia Boelaert-Suominen: Prosecuting Superiors for Crimes Committed by Subordinates: A Discussion of the First Significant Case Law Since the Second World War, 41 *Virginia Journal of International Law* (2001), pp. 747 et seq.; Antonio Cassese: *International Criminal Law* (2003), pp. 203 et seq.; Kirsten Keith: Superior Responsibility applied before the ICTY, *Humanitäres Völkerrecht-Informationsschriften* 2001, pp. 98 et seq.; Maria Nybondas: Civilian Responsibility in the *Kordić* Case, 50 *Netherlands International Law Review* (2003), pp. 59 et seq.; Greg R. Vetter: Command Responsibility of Non-Military Superiors in the International Criminal Court (ICC), 25 *Yale Journal of International Law* (2000), pp. 89 et seq.; Thomas Weigend: Zur Frage eines "internationalen" Allgemeinen Teils, in Bernd Schünemann et al. (eds.), *Festschrift für Claus Roxin* (2001), pp. 1375 et seq.; Zhu Wenqi: The Doctrine of Command Responsibility as Applied to Civilian Leaders: The ICTR and the Kayishema Case, in Sienho Yee and Wang Tieya (eds.), *International Law in the Post-Cold War World: Essays in Memory of Li Haopei* (2001), pp. 373 et seq.; Jamie A. Williamson: Command Responsibility in the Case Law of the International Tribunal for Rwanda, 13 *Criminal Law Forum* (2002), pp. 365 et seq.

368 The concept of superior responsibility is "an original creation of international criminal law"[227] for which there are no paradigms in national legal systems. Under superior responsibility, military commanders or civilian superiors can be made criminally liable for crimes under international law committed by their subordinates. Superiors must answer for the crimes of subordinates[228] if they culpably violate the duties of control assigned to them.

369 Given the extension of this basic idea to non-military contexts as well,[229] which has meanwhile been generally recognized, the idea of "superior responsibility" is now preferable to the more nar-

---

[226] The fact that the contribution to the crime must be "intentional" is merely a declaratory allusion to the general subjective requirements under ICC Statute, Art. 30; see also K. Ambos, in O. Triffterer (ed.), *Commentary on the Rome Statute of the International Criminal Court* (1999), Art. 25, marginal no. 22.

[227] See K. Ambos, *Der Allgemeine Teil des Völkerstrafrechts* (2002), p. 667.

[228] See K. Ambos, *Der Allgemeine Teil des Völkerstrafrechts* (2002), p. 667, vividly calls this prerequisite a "basic crime"; see also S. Boelaert-Suominen, 41 *Virginia Journal of International Law* (2001), p. 747 at pp. 760 et seq., p. 772, which further points out that no conviction of the subordinate is necessary.

[229] See *Prosecutor* v. *Mucić* et al., ICTY (Trial Chamber), judgment of 16 November 1998, para. 333; W.J. Fenrick, in O. Triffterer (ed.), *Commentary on the Rome Statute of the International Criminal*

row concept of "command responsibility."[230] This terminology also reflects Article 28 of the ICC Statute ("Responsibility of Commanders and Other Superiors").

The need for this expansion of the criminal liability of superiors is rooted in the hierar-   **370**
chical organizational structure that typically characterizes the environment in which crimes under international law occur. This environment first of all makes it far more difficult to prove direct involvement in the crime, although the degree of responsibility often increases in inverse proportion to a person's distance from the actual commission of the crime. Here the concept of superior responsibility acts as a safety net when evidence of direct criminal responsibility on the part of the superior is absent. Second of all, conduct below the threshold of direct participation in the crime also represents a serious potential danger, especially in the form of "looking the other way" or "looking on without acting" on the part of superiors with command authority.

Doctrinally, the concept of superior responsibility can be located between omission and complic-   **371**
ity. This may on occasion raise difficult issues of line drawing for certain modes of participation. Article 28 of the ICC Statute, by its wording, applies "in addition to other grounds"; the provision thus takes account especially of Article 25(2) and (3) of the Statute. If a superior participates in the crimes of a subordinate, the question may arise whether he or she is liable under the concepts of joint commission, ordering or instigating the crime, or under the principle of superior responsibility. According to ICTY judgments, liability based on direct participation in a crime takes precedence over liability under the doctrine of superior responsibility.[231]

The principle of superior responsibility is today anchored firmly in customary interna-   **372**
tional law.[232] Although neither the Nuremberg nor the Tokyo Charters contained such a rule, international courts began early on to rely on this principle as grounds to hold military commanders as well as civilian superiors criminally liable.[233] Its practical signifi-

---

Court (1999), Art. 28, marginal no. 1; K. Kittichaisaree, *International Criminal Law* (2001), p. 252; see also K. Ambos, *Der Allgemeine Teil des Völkerstrafrechts* (2002), p. 666.

[230] See also K. Ambos, *Der Allgemeine Teil des Völkerstrafrechts* (2002), p. 666; S. Boelaert-Suominen, 41 *Virginia Journal of International Law* (2001), p. 747 at p. 750.

[231] See *Prosecutor* v. *Naletilić and Martinović*, ICTY (Trial Chamber), judgment of 31 March 2003, paras. 78 et seq.; *Prosecutor* v. *Krstić*, ICTY (Trial Chamber), judgment of 2 August 2001, para. 605.

[232] See, e.g., *Prosecutor* v. *Mucić* et al., ICTY (Appeals Chamber), judgment of 20 February 2001, para. 195. For command responsibility in international armed conflict, see recently *Prosecutor* v. *Hadžihasanović* et al., ICTY (Appeals Chamber), decision on Interlocutory Appeal Challenging Jurisdiction in Relation to Command Responsibility of 16 July 2003, paras. 11 et seq.

[233] The concept achieved a breakthrough with the conviction of the Japanese general *Yamashita* by the US Military Tribunal in Manila, reprinted in United Nations War Crimes Commission, *Law Reports of Trials of War Criminals* IV, pp. 1 et seq. See O. Triffterer, in C. Prittwitz et al. (eds.), *Festschrift für Lüderssen* (2002), p. 437 at p. 439. See also US Military Tribunal, Nuremberg, judgment of 20 August 1947 (*Brandt* et al., so-called Medical Trial), in *Trials of War Criminals* II, pp. 187 et seq., p. 212; US Military Tribunal, Nuremberg, judgment of 19 February 1948 (*List* et al., so-called Hostages Trial), in *Trials of War Criminals* XI, pp. 1236 et seq.; US Military Tribunal, Nuremberg, judgment of 28 October 1948 (*von Leeb* et al., so-called High Command Trial), in *Trials of War Criminals* XI, pp. 542 et seq. See generally G.R. Vetter, 25 *Yale Journal of International Law* (2000), p. 89 at pp. 105 et seq.

cance has been affirmed in the case law of both *ad hoc* Tribunals.[234] Both Courts have been able to rely on corresponding provisions of their Statutes.[235] In Article 28 of the ICC Statute, superior responsibility is now comprehensively regulated in a way that further clarifies earlier provisions. The provision largely reflects the current state of customary international law.

373   Four elements must be distinguished in determining superior responsibility: a superior-subordinate relationship must exist (see I); the superior must know or negligently fail to know that the subordinate is about to commit or has committed a crime under international law (see II); and finally, the superior must fail to take necessary and reasonable measures to prevent the commission of the crime or initiate criminal prosecution of the perpetrator (see III). It is not clear how to classify the requirement in Article 28(a) and (b) of the ICC Statute that the crime be committed "as a result of [the superior's] failure to exercise control properly over [the subordinate]" (see IV).

I. Superior-Subordinate Relationship

374   The basic requirement for criminal responsibility is the existence of a superior-subordinate relationship. Superiors are liable for the acts of their subordinates. Today, this liability no longer concerns only military commanders, but also all others, especially civilian superiors, who exercise similar control.

375   The core element of a superior-subordinate relationship is a position of effective control on the part of the superior vis-à-vis the subordinate.[236] Evidence of this control, according to judgments of the Yugoslavia Tribunal, is the person's "material ability to prevent and punish commission of the offences."[237] This control can exist *de jure* and be conveyed, for example, through a legal relationship; but it is sufficient if the superior exercises only *de facto* effective control.

---

[234] See *Prosecutor* v. *Mucić* et al., ICTY (Trial Chamber), judgment of 16 November 1998, paras. 330 et seq.; *Prosecutor* v. *Aleksovski*, ICTY (Trial Chamber), judgment of 25 June 1999, paras. 90 et seq.; *Prosecutor* v. *Blaškić*, ICTY (Trial Chamber), judgment of 3 March 2000, paras. 289 et seq.; *Prosecutor* v. *Aleksovski*, ICTY (Appeals Chamber), judgment of 24 March 2000, paras. 69 et seq.; *Prosecutor* v. *Mucić* et al., ICTY (Appeals Chamber), judgment of 20 February 2001, paras. 182 et seq.; *Prosecutor* v. *Akayesu*, ICTR (Trial Chamber), judgment of 2 September 1998, paras. 487 et seq.; *Prosecutor* v. *Kambanda*, ICTR (Trial Chamber), judgment of 4 September 1998, para. 40; *Prosecutor* v. *Serushago*, ICTR (Trial Chamber), judgment of 5 February 1999, paras. 28 et seq.; *Prosecutor* v. *Kayishema and Ruzindana*, ICTR (Trial Chamber), judgment of 21 May 1999, paras. 209 et seq.; *Prosecutor* v. *Semanza*, ICTR (Trial Chamber), judgment of 15 May 2003, paras. 399 et seq.

[235] ICTY Statute, Art. 7(3); ICTR Statute, Art. 6(3).

[236] See *Prosecutor* v. *Mucić* et al., ICTY (Appeals Chamber), judgment of 20 February 2001, para. 196; Prosecutor v. *Blaškić*, ICTY (Appeals Chamber), judgment of 29 July 2004, para. 67; *Prosecutor* v. *Semanza*, ICTR (Trial Chamber), judgment of 15 May 2003, para. 402; *Prosecutor* v. *Ntagerura* et al., ICTR (Trial Chamber), judgment of 25 February 2004, para. 628; K. Ambos, *Der Allgemeine Teil des Völkerstrafrechts* (2002), p. 676.

[237] See *Prosecutor* v. *Mucić* et al., ICTY (Trial Chamber), judgment of 16 November 1998, para. 378; *Prosecutor* v. *Mucić* et al., ICTY (Appeals Chamber), judgment of 20 February 2001, para. 256. See also *Prosecutor* v. *Semanza*, ICTR (Trial Chamber), judgment of 15 May 2003, para. 402.

As a rule, superiors cannot limit their responsibility by delegating their duties of control and super-   **376**
vision. This is certainly the case if the delegation is merely formal and does not affect the superior's
effective control.[238]

1. Military Commanders

Military commanders are persons with command authority within a military organiza-   **377**
tion.[239] Command authority exists if the person in question is actually capable, by virtue
of the authority vested in him or her and/or because of his or her actual position, of in-
fluencing the conduct of subordinates through orders.[240] Thus a position as commander
can, on the one hand, be created by a legal grant of authority to a person. On the other
hand, however, a lack of formal authority does not *per se* rule out superior responsibility,[241] because grounds for classification as a superior can also be established by considering the *de facto* command relationships in the specific case.[242] A requirement for liability
in *de facto* superior-subordinate relationships is a degree of stability of command and
control that is independent of the concrete situation.

2. Civilian Superiors

The basic concept of superior responsibility is applicable to all non-military superiors   **378**
possessing supervisory authority that is equal to – that is, as effective as – command au-

---

[238] See I. Bantekas, 93 *American Journal of International Law* (1999), p. 573 at p. 585: "Command responsibility cannot be avoided"; K. Ambos, *Der Allgemeine Teil des Völkerstrafrechts* (2002),
p. 681.

[239] No compact definition is yet available in the case law or the literature. The beginnings of a
definition that corresponds to the one given here is found, *inter alia*, in *Prosecutor* v. *Mucić* et al.,
ICTY (Trial Chamber), judgment of 16 November 1998, paras. 354, 365 et seq. See also *Prosecutor* v.
Blaškić, ICTY (Trial Chamber), judgment of 3 March 2000, paras. 300 et seq.; *Prosecutor* v. *Mucić* et
al., ICTY (Appeals Chamber), judgment of 20 February 2001, para. 196; *Prosecutor* v. *Musema*, ICTR
(Trial Chamber), judgment of 27 January 2000, para. 148; W.J. Fenrick, in O. Triffterer (ed.), *Com-
mentary on the Rome Statute of the International Criminal Court* (1999), Art. 28, marginal no. 4; S.
Boelaert-Suominen, 41 *Virginia Journal of International Law* (2001), p. 747 at pp. 761 et seq.

[240] See *Prosecutor* v. *Mucić* et al., ICTY (Trial Chamber), judgment of 16 November 1998, para.
378; *Prosecutor* v. *Blaškić*, ICTY (Trial Chamber), judgment of 3 March 2000, para. 302; K. Ambos,
Der Allgemeine Teil des Völkerstrafrechts (2002), p. 677; I. Bantekas, 93 *American Journal of International Law* (1999), p. 573 at pp. 580, 582 et seq.; W.J. Fenrick, in O. Triffterer (ed.), *Commentary on
the Rome Statute of the International Criminal Court* (1999), Art. 28, marginal no. 7. See also US Military Tribunal, Nuremberg, judgment of 10 April 1948 (*Ohlendorf* et al., so-called Einsatzgruppen
Trial), in *Trials of War Criminals* IV, p. 480.

[241] In particular, the applicability of the concept of superior responsibility is not limited to certain
levels of hierarchy. This is well illustrated in I. Bantekas, 93 *American Journal of International Law*
(1999), p. 573 at pp. 578 et seq. See also *Prosecutor* v. *Češić*, ICTY (Trail Chamber), judgment of 11
March 2004, para. 37.

[242] For the basic principle, see *Prosecutor* v. *Mucić* et al., ICTY (Trial Chamber), judgment of 16
November 1998, para. 354. Similarly, *Prosecutor* v. *Mucić* et al., ICTY (Appeals Chamber), judgment
of 20 February 2001, para. 193. See also I. Bantekas, 93 *American Journal of International Law* (1999),
p. 573 at pp. 578, 581 et seq.), which attempts to systematize factors upon which to base a presumption of *de facto* command authority. See also *Prosecutor* v. *Kamuhanda*, ICTR (Trial Chamber), judgment of 22 January 2004, para. 607.

thority within a military organization.[243] This is expressly recognized in Article 28(b) of the ICC Statute.[244] But Article 28(b) at the same time offers a new rule by separating the responsibility of civilian superiors from that of military commanders and establishing somewhat different requirements for accountability, especially in regard to the mental element.[245]

379   The necessary effective control can be present within a national government, in particular, examples provided in court judgments and in the literature are members of government, mayors, and chiefs of police.[246] But it is also conceivable in non-state arenas, on the part of persons holding positions in organizations such as parties or unions, or in businesses or corporations.[247] For civilian superiors, too, such control authority need not be *de jure*, but can also be based on the *de facto* ability to influence the conduct of subordinates through the issuing of instructions.[248] But it is also necessary in the case of civilian superiors to show that the *de facto* control is of a permanent character.

380   For civilian superiors, Article 28(b)(ii) of the ICC Statute further limits the range of conduct on the part of subordinates for which the superior can be held criminally accountable. These must be acts that "were within the effective responsibility and control of the superior." This wording was intended to make clear that the control authority of a civilian superior, unlike that of a military commander, is normally limited in place and time to his or her official function.[249] There is thus

---

[243] See *Prosecutor* v. *Mucić* et al., ICTY (Trial Chamber), judgment of 16 November 1998, paras. 356, 363; *Prosecutor* v. *Aleksovski*, ICTY (Appeals Chamber), judgment of 24 March 2000, para. 76; *Prosecutor* v. *Ntakirutimana*, ICTR (Trial Chamber), judgment of 21 February 2003, paras. 819 et seq.; M. Nybondas, 50 *Netherlands International Law Review* (2003), p. 59 at p. 63; J.A. Williamson, 13 *Criminal Law Forum* (2002), p. 365 at pp. 366 et seq.; W.J. Fenrick, in O. Triffterer (ed.), *Commentary on the Rome Statute of the International Criminal Court* (1999), Art. 28, marginal nos. 15, 18; US Military Tribunal, Nuremberg, judgment of 11 April 1949 (*von Weizsäcker* et al., so-called Ministries Trial), in *Trials of War Criminals* XIV, pp. 308 et seq.

[244] See S. Boelaert-Suominen, 41 *Virginia Journal of International Law* (2001), p. 747 at pp. 765, 769; K. Ambos, *Der Allgemeine Teil des Völkerstrafrechts* (2002), pp. 675 et seq., W.J. Fenrick, in O. Triffterer (ed.), *Commentary on the Rome Statute of the International Criminal Court* (1999), Art. 28, marginal no. 15; G.R. Vetter, 25 *Yale Journal of International Law* (2000), p. 89 at p. 104; K. Kittichaisaree, *International Criminal Law* (2001), p. 251.

[245] See marginal nos. 384 et seq.

[246] See *Prosecutor* v. *Kayishema and Ruzindana*, ICTR (Trial Chamber), judgment of 21 May 1999, paras. 217 et seq. (Prefect); *Prosecutor* v. *Kambanda*, ICTR (Trial Chamber), judgment of 4 September 1999, para. 39 (Prime Minister); see also K. Kittichaisaree, *International Criminal Law* (2001), p. 252; G.R. Vetter, 25 *Yale Journal of International Law* (2000), p. 89 at p. 95; S. Boelaert-Suominen, 41 *Virginia Journal of International Law* (2001), p. 748.

[247] *Prosecutor* v. *Musema*, ICTR (Trial Chamber), judgment of 27 January 2000, paras. 868 et seq. (director of a tea factory); *Prosecutor* v. *Nahimana*, ICTR (Trial Chamber), judgment of 3 December 2003, paras. 970 et seq. (leading position in the management of a radio station); W.J. Fenrick, in O. Triffterer (ed.), *Commentary on the Rome Statute of the International Criminal Court* (1999), Art. 28, marginal nos. 15 et seq.

[248] See K. Ambos, *Der Allgemeine Teil des Völkerstrafrechts* (2002), pp. 675 et seq.; W.J. Fenrick, in O. Triffterer (ed.), *Commentary on the Rome Statute of the International Criminal Court* (1999), Art. 28, marginal nos. 15, 18; M. Nybondas, 50 *Netherlands International Law Review* (2003), p. 59 at pp. 64 et seq.; J.A. Williamson, 13 *Criminal Law Forum* (2002), p. 365 at pp. 368 et seq. An example for the basis of such control authority is found in *Prosecutor* v. *Musema*, ICTR (Trial Chamber), judgment of 27 January 2000, paras. 878 et seq.

[249] For a doubtful view, however, see G.R. Vetter, 25 *Yale Journal of International Law* (2000), p. 89 at pp. 119 et seq., who also raises the possibility of interpreting it as a causality requirement.

no criminal liability on the part of a civilian superior under Article 28 if the subordinate commits the crime outside the scope of his or her duties.[250]

II. Mental Element

In conformity with customary international law,[251] a superior can only be made accountable for the crime of a subordinate under Article 28 of the ICC Statute if he or she knew or "should have known" about it. This distinctly lowers Article 30's requirements for the mental element.[252]   **381**

Liability of superiors for negligence was found in the Nuremberg follow-up trials,[253] later in Article 86(2) of Additional Protocol I, and finally in Article 7(3) of the ICTY Statute and Article 6(3) of the ICTR Statute. Though they largely agree on substance, each chose a different wording from that of Article 28 of the ICC Statute. Both Article 7(3) of the ICTY Statute and Article 6(3) of the ICTR Statute use the phrase "had reason to know."[254]   **382**

Court judgments have used different criteria to determine the conditions under which superiors should have known of the imminent commission of a crime. In the view of the Yugoslavia Tribunal, current customary international law allows a presumption of negligent lack of knowledge if the superior had information "which would have put him on notice of offences committed by subordinates."[255]   **383**

---

[250] See W.J. Fenrick, in O. Triffterer (ed.), *Commentary on the Rome Statute of the International Criminal Court* (1999), Art. 28, marginal nos. 19, 22.

[251] See the information in marginal nos. 381 et seq., esp. fns. 252 et seq.

[252] See, e.g., *Prosecutor* v. *Kordić and Čerkez*, ICTY (Trial Chamber), judgment of 26 February 2001, para. 427; M. Nybondas, 50 *Netherlands International Law Review* (2003), p. 59 at pp. 67 et seq.; J.A. Williamson, 13 *Criminal Law Forum* (2002), p. 365 at pp. 373 et seq. See also marginal no. 320. In contrast, it remains unclear which additional subjective requirements apply, especially concerning violation of the duty of supervision and failure to take necessary and reasonable measures.

[253] See US Military Tribunal, Nuremberg, judgment of 19 February 1948 (*List* et al, so-called Hostages Trial), in *Trials of War Criminals* XI, pp. 1236 et seq.; US Military Tribunal, Nuremberg, judgment of 3 November 1947 (*Pohl* et al.), in *Trials of War Criminals* V, pp. 1054 et seq.

[254] Additional Protocol I, Art. 86(2), requires that the superior could "infer it under the given circumstances on the basis of information available to him." On the various interpretations of this wording, see K. Ambos, *Der Allgemeine Teil des Völkerstrafrechts* (2002), pp. 697 et seq.; I. Bantekas, 93 *American Journal of International Law* (1999), p. 573, pp. 589 et seq.; G.R. Vetter, 25 *Yale Journal of International Law* (2000), p. 89 at pp. 109 et seq. For a critical view from the ICTR Appeals Chamber concerning the terminology of negligence – "References to negligence in the context of superior responsibility are likely to lead to confusion of thought" – see *Prosecutor* v. *Bagilishema*, ICTR (Appeals Chamber), judgment of 3 July 2002, para. 35.

[255] *Prosecutor* v. *Mucić* et al., ICTY (Appeals Chamber), judgment of 20 February 2001, paras. 241 and 238: "For instance, a military commander who has received information that some of the soldiers under his command have a violent or unstable character, or have been drinking prior to being sent to a mission, may be considered as having the required knowledge." See also *Prosecutor* v. *Krnojelac*, ICTY (Appeals Chamber), judgment of 17 September 2003, para. 59: " . . . the information he received from detainees was enough to constitute 'alarming information' requiring him, as superior, to launch an investigation or make inquiries." But the Appeals Chamber finds that the information "need not to contain specific details on the unlawful acts . . ." (para. 155). *Prosecutor* v. *Blaškić*, ICTY (Appeals Chamber), judgment of 29 July 2004, para. 62; *Prosecutor* v. *Bagilishema*, ICTR (Appeals Chamber), judgment of 3 July 2002, para. 28.

384   The standard for negligence is clarified with greater precision in the ICC Statute. Under Article 28(a)(i), for military commanders it is sufficient that the superior, "owing to the circumstances at the time, should have known" that the subordinate would commit a crime. It is thus crucial to determine whether the superior, in the proper exercise of his duties, would have gained knowledge of the commission of the crime by his or her subordinate.[256]

385   For civilian superiors, Article 28(b)(i) of the ICC Statute also sets requirements that are lower than those in Article 30. In contrast to the requirements for military commanders, however, here culpable lack of knowledge is insufficient. It is instead required that the superior "consciously disregarded information which clearly indicated . . . that the subordinates were committing or about to commit such crimes." This calls for a greater degree of negligence.[257]

III. Failure to Take Necessary Measures

386 A key factor in determining individual criminal responsibility is the superior's failure to take "necessary and reasonable measures."[258] Only failure to take measures in breach of a duty can form a basis for criminal liability. The superior's duty to act creates a basis for liability for omission in two ways: if a crime has not yet been committed, he or she must take measures to prevent its commission. If a crime has already been committed by a subordinate, but the superior cannot be accused of derelict failure to act, the superior is obligated either to punish those responsible himself or to report the matter to the responsible authorities. The superior's obligation to initiate preventive or repressive countermeasures is limited to those that are necessary and reasonable in the concrete case.

1. Preventive Measures

387 The first point of reference for the charge of failure to take action is the superior's failure, in breach of duty, to "prevent or repress" commission of the crime.[259] Preventive measures are of course only possible before the crime has been completed. The superior is required to prevent the crime if his subordinates are "about to commit"[260] such a crime;

---

[256] But not merely "could have gained knowledge." See *Prosecutor* v. *Mucić* et al., ICTY (Trial Chamber), judgment of 16 November 1998, paras. 388 et seq.; *Prosecutor* v. *Bagilishema*, ICTR (Appeals Chamber), judgment of 3 July 2002, para. 35.

[257] Gradations extend from recklessness to wilful blindness, see K. Ambos, *Der Allgemeine Teil des Völkerstrafrechts* (2002), p. 706; G.R. Vetter, 25 *Yale Journal of International Law* (2000), p. 89 at p. 124.

[258] See ICC Statute, Art. 28(a)(ii), (b). See for Art. 7(3) of the ICTY Statute, M. Nybondas, 50 *Netherlands International Law Review* (2003), p. 59 at pp. 68 et seq.; see for Art. 6(3) of the ICTR Statute, J.A. Williamson, 13 *Criminal Law Forum* (2002), p. 365 at pp. 380 et seq. See also *Prosecutor* v. *Kamuhanda*, ICTR (Trial Chamber), judgment of 22 January 2004, para. 601. On the question whether command responsibility exists for crimes committed before the superior-subordinate relationship, see *Prosecutor* v. *Hadžihasanović* et al., ICTY (Appeals Chamber), decision on Interlocutory Appeal Challenging Jurisdiction in Relation to Command Responsibility of 16 July 2003, paras. 37 et seq.

[259] The wording in Art. 7(3) of the ICTY Statute and 6(3) of the ICTR Statute is "to prevent such acts."

[260] See Art. 28(a)(i) and (b)(i) of the ICC Statute: "the forces/subordinates were . . . about to commit such crimes."

this phase stretches from the preparation to the complete execution of the crime.[261] If the superior fails to take the necessary preventive countermeasures, he or she is responsible for the crime under international law.

2. Repressive Measures

Once the crime has been committed by the subordinate, preventive countermeasures are **388** no longer possible. Here the derelict failure to punish or to initiate a prosecution becomes the reference point for the charge of failure to take action. If the superior does not initiate the necessary investigation with the aim of punishing the perpetrator, he or she is liable for the crime. Article 28 of the ICC Statute requires that the superior "submit the matter to the competent authorities for investigation and prosecution."[262]

The retroactive initiation of investigative or punitive measures does not, however, free the superior **389** from liability for derelict failure to take preventive measures.[263] If, in subjective and objective dereliction of duty, he failed to take preventive measures, he remains responsible for his subordinates' crimes against international law, even if he later makes efforts to punish the perpetrators.

3. Necessary and Reasonable Measures

No charge of failure to take action may be made against a superior if he or she was un- **390** able to prevent the crime or prosecute the perpetrator, or if he or she took all necessary and reasonable measures but the crime took place nevertheless. The superior must actually have the opportunity to prevent the crime or initiate prosecution.[264] This is affirmed in Article 28(a)(ii) and (b)(iii) of the ICC Statute, under which the superior must (only) take all measures "within his or her power."

---

[261] See K. Ambos, *Der Allgemeine Teil des Völkerstrafrechts* (2002), pp. 691 et seq. It is also criminal to fail to take necessary measures before the commission of the crime, making it impossible for the superior to prevent it when it is being committed. See I. Bantekas, 93 *American Journal of International Law* (1999), p. 573 at pp. 591, 593; W.J. Fenrick, in O. Triffterer (ed.), *Commentary on the Rome Statute of the International Criminal Court* (1999), Art. 28, marginal no. 12.

[262] See ICTY Statute, Art. 7(3); ICTR Statute, Art. 6(3). The Yugoslavia and Rwanda Statutes refer to the failure to "to punish the perpetrators."

[263] See *Prosecutor* v. *Blaškić*, ICTY (Trial Chamber), judgment of 3 March 2000, para. 336; S. Boelaert-Suominen, 41 *Virginia Journal of International Law* (2001), p. 747 at pp. 783, 785; W.J. Fenrick, in O. Triffterer (ed.), *Commentary on the Rome Statute of the International Criminal Court* (1999), Art. 28, marginal no. 13.

[264] *Prosecutor* v. *Mucić* et al., ICTY (Trial Chamber), judgment of 16 November 1998, para. 395: "[I]nternational law cannot oblige a superior to perform the impossible. Hence, a superior may only be held criminally responsible for failing to take such measures that are within his powers." *Prosecutor* v. *Mucić* et al., ICTY (Appeals Chamber), judgment of 20 February 2001, paras. 197 et seq.; *Prosecutor* v. *Aleksovski*, ICTY (Appeals Chamber), judgment of 24 March 2000, para. 76; *Prosecutor* v. *Blaškić*, ICTY (Trial Chamber), judgment of 3 March 2000, para. 335; *Prosecutor* v. *Kayishema and Ruzindana*, ICTR (Trial Chamber), judgment of 21 May 1999, para. 217; *Prosecutor* v. *Stakić*, ICTY (Trial Chamber), judgment of 31 July 2003, para. 461; S. Boelaert-Suominen, 41 *Virginia Journal of International Law* (2001), p. 747 at pp. 780 et seq.

391   The standard for determining which measures are "necessary and reasonable" is inter-national humanitarian law.[265] Such measures are necessary if they would have served, from an objective *ex ante* point of view, to prevent the commission of the crime by the subordinate or to initiate prosecutorial measures. These include instruction in the principles of international humanitarian law, for example, or creation of systems of reporting, supervision and threat of sanction.[266]

392   The decisive factor is thus not the rules of the organization or association of which the superior is a part. Otherwise, these rules would negate the force of the concept of superior responsibility. A superior's plea of lack of authority to take the necessary measures under internal regulations does not generally free him or her from criminal responsibility.[267]

393   Disagreement exists over whether measures should be considered necessary and reason-able only if the superior's failure to take them is causally connected to the subordinate's commission of the crime. The *ad hoc* Tribunals have rejected this view; they are supported, in particular, by the fact that failure to initiate prosecutorial measures, since it occurs after the actual crime, obviously cannot be brought into accord with such a cau-sality requirement.[268]

394   It is not possible to generalize as to what measures are reasonable. Most important is the extent of control and influence that the superior has at his or her disposal in dealing with subordinates ("commander's degree of effective control").[269] This, in turn, deter-mines the extent to which the superior is able to prevent or punish violations of the law by subordinates.[270] The degree of effective control is thus the crucial factor in determin-ing superior responsibility: it is a constitutive element not only for the presumption of a superior-subordinate relationship, but also for the substance and scope of the superior's duties of command and control.

IV. Commission of a Crime as a Result of Violation of the Duty of Control

395   Article 28 of the ICC Statute adds a fourth element to superior responsibility. It requires that the crime committed by the subordinate be a result of the failure of the superior "to

---

[265] These standards should be applied by analogy for civilian superiors, if they do not already ap-ply directly, see W.J. Fenrick, in O. Triffterer (ed.), *Commentary on the Rome Statute of the Interna-tional Criminal Court* (1999), Art. 28, marginal no. 9; see also Additional Protocol I, Art. 87.

[266] See W.J. Fenrick, in O. Triffterer (ed.), *Commentary on the Rome Statute of the International Criminal Court* (1999), Art. 28, marginal no. 9; I. Bantekas, 93 *American Journal of International Law* (1999), p. 573 at pp. 591 et seq. However, no generally applicable catalogue of duties can be formu-lated for superiors, see *Prosecutor* v. *Mucić* et al., ICTY (Trial Chamber), judgment of 16 November 1998, para. 394.

[267] See similarly *Prosecutor* v. *Mucić* et al., ICTY (Trial Chamber), judgment of 16 November 1998, para. 395; I. Bantekas, 93 *American Journal of International Law* (1999), p. 573 at p. 593.

[268] *Prosecutor* v. *Mucić* et al., ICTY (Trial Chamber), judgment of 16 November 1998, paras. 396 et seq.; recently *Prosecutor* v. *Blaškić*, ICTY (Appeals Chamber), judgment of 29 July 2004, para. 77.

[269] See *Prosecutor* v. *Blaškić*, ICTY (Trial Chamber), judgment of 3 March 2000, para. 335; *Pros-ecutor* v. *Aleksovski*, ICTY (Trial Chamber), judgment of 25 June 1999, para. 81.

[270] See marginal no. 375.

exercise control properly" over his or her subordinate. This makes violation of the duty of control and supervision a central element of superior responsibility, alongside failure, in dereliction of duty, to prevent or prosecute the crime of a subordinate. There is no precedent for this in customary international law. The significance of this additional element and its place in the overall structure of Article 28 are not yet clear.[271]

The main difficulty of establishing a violation of the duty of control lies in determining its relationship to the offense of not preventing or reporting. Closer examination reveals that, in contrast to the meaning suggested by the wording of Article 28 of the ICC Statute, the violation of the duty of control only gains independent significance in connection with the failure to report. If, however, the superior fails to prevent his or her subordinates from committing a crime under international law, this automatically entails a failure to exercise proper control. It is not necessary to find an additional violation of the duty of control.   **396**

This is the only way to prevent absurd results, as illustrated by the following case: A superior who finds out, through his excellent reporting system, that some of his subordinates are about to commit a crime under international law and who, through his organizational safeguards, could prevent the subordinates from committing the crime, nevertheless does nothing. This failure to act is a sufficient basis for the superior's criminal responsibility. It would make no sense to negate superior responsibility by arguing that the superior cannot be accused of any additional violation of the duty of control.   **397**

In cases of non-reporting, however, the requirement of proper control gains importance. It is true that failure to submit the matter to the competent authorities for investigation and prosecution can be considered a failure to exercise proper control in the broadest sense. But it goes without saying that a crime by a subordinate that has already been committed can never be "a result of" a failure of proper control understood in this way. In this case, the wording of Article 28 of the ICC Statute can only be accommodated if the superior can be accused of an additional violation of the duty of control *before* the crime was committed.   **398**

In addition, Article 28 of the ICC Statute requires that the subordinate's commission of the crime be a "result" of the violation of the duty of control. It is an open question whether this is a causality requirement (which has been rejected by the *ad hoc* Tribunals[272]).[273]   **399**

Another open question is whether, and in what form, the violation of the duty of control is subject to the mental element; this depends on whether Article 30 of the ICC Statute is to be applied, that is, whether the elements in Article 28 comprise "material elements" of the crime.[274]   **400**

---

[271] See T. Weigend, in B. Schünemann et al. (eds.), *Festschrift für Roxin* (2001), p. 1375 at p. 1397 ("unable to be resolved even with great dogmatic acumen").

[272] See marginal no. 393.

[273] See also O. Triffterer, in C. Prittwitz et al. (eds.), *Festschrift für Lüderssen* (2002), p. 437 at p. 445.

[274] See T. Weigend, in B. Schünemann et al. (eds.), *Festschrift für Roxin* (2001), p. 1375 at p. 1397, fn. 85.

F. Grounds for Excluding Criminal Responsibility

401 Kai Ambos: *Der Allgemeine Teil des Völkerstrafrechts, Ansätze einer Dogmatisierung* (2002), pp. 825 et seq.; Kai Ambos: Defences, in Antonio Cassese, Paola Gaeta and John R.W.D. Jones (eds.), *The Rome Statute of the International Criminal Court: A Commentary*, Vol. 1 (2002), pp. 949 et seq.; Antonio Cassese: *International Criminal Law* (2003), pp. 219 et seq.; Yoram Dinstein: Defences, in Gabrielle Kirk McDonald and Olivia Swaak-Goldman (eds.), *Substantive and Procedural Aspects of International Criminal Law, The Experience of International and National Courts*, Vol. 1 (2000), pp. 369 et seq.; Georg Dahm, Jost Delbrück and Rüdiger Wolfrum: *Völkerrecht*, Vol. I/3, 2nd edn. (2002), pp. 1124 et seq.; Albin Eser: "Defences" in Strafverfahren wegen Kriegsverbrechen, in Kurt Schmoller (ed.), *Festschrift für Otto Triffterer* (1996), pp. 755 et seq.; Albin Eser: ICC Statute, Article 31, in Otto Triffterer (ed.), *Commentary of the Rome Statute of the International Criminal Court* (1999), pp. 537 et seq.; Hans-Heinrich Jescheck: *Die Verantwortlichkeit der Staatsorgane nach Völkerstrafrecht, Eine Studie zu den Nürnberger Prozessen* (1952), pp. 328 et seq.; Geert-Jan Knoops: *Defenses in Contemporary International Criminal Law* (2001); Claus Kress: Die Kristallisation eines Allgemeinen Teils des Völkerstrafrechts: Die Allgemeinen Prinzipien des Strafrechts im Statut des Internationalen Strafgerichtshofs, *Humanitäres Völkerrecht-Informationsschriften* 1999, pp. 4 et seq.; Claus Kress: War Crimes Committed in Non-International Armed Conflict and the Emerging System of International Criminal Justice, 30 *Israel Yearbook on Human Rights* (2001), pp. 103 et seq.; Reinhard Merkel: Gründe für den Ausschluss der Strafbarkeit im Völkerstrafrecht, 114 *Zeitschrift für die gesamte Strafrechtswissenschaft* (2002), pp. 437 et seq.; Christiane Nill-Theobald: *"Defences" bei Kriegsverbrechen am Beispiel Deutschlands und der USA* (1998); Massimo Scaliotti: Defences before the International Criminal Court: Substantive Grounds for Excluding Criminal Responsibility, Part 1, 1 *International Criminal Law Review* (2001), pp. 111 et seq.; Part 2, 2 *International Criminal Law Review* (2002), pp. 1 et seq.

I. Historical Development of Defenses in International Criminal Law

1. International Case Law

402 Defenses at first played only a marginal role in the practice of international and national courts. At the start, the greatest challenge for practical international criminal law consisted in finding a legal basis for individual criminal liability under international law.[275] Thus no grounds for excluding criminal responsibility were provided for in the Nuremberg Charter; in consequence, the lawyers for defendants who found themselves in the sights of international criminal justice took aim, at first, primarily at the international community's authority to punish and the legitimacy of international justice as such.

403   Only as the principle of individual criminal responsibility took firmer root in international law did various grounds for excluding responsibility move to the center of defense efforts. As early as the Nuremberg successor trials, but especially in the trials before the Yugoslavia and Rwanda Tribunals, defenses played a greater role. The establishment of conditions for excluding criminal responsibility, however, remained up to the Courts: no defenses are contained in the Statutes of either the Yugoslavia or the Rwanda Tribunals.[276]

---

[275] See marginal nos. 2 et seq.

[276] See ICTY Statute, Art. 7(4). Some progress was made in the International Law Commission's drafts, which recognized that exclusion of responsibility was possible in principle in international

In practice, the main area where grounds for excluding responsibility play a role is **404** war crimes, with its broad range of offenses. In contrast, for genocide and crimes against humanity, exclusion from liability can be presumed only in extraordinary cases.[277] In the jurisprudence of international courts thus far, acting upon orders and duress have been most significant.[278]

2. ICC Statute

Grounds for excluding responsibility is another area in which the ICC Statute makes **405** great strides in the direction of a fully-developed system of criminal law. Part 3 for the first time comprehensively codifies the scope of, and conditions for, the most important grounds for excluding criminal responsibility in international criminal law.

The starting point in the ICC Statute is Article 31, which summarizes various **406** grounds for excluding responsibility (mental disease or defect, intoxication, self-defense, duress and necessity).[279] Under Article 31(3), the Court may also "consider a ground for excluding criminal responsibility other than those referred to in paragraph 1."[280] Such other grounds are found, first of all, in the Statute itself (mistake, acting upon orders or instructions, abandonment). Also noteworthy are grounds for exclusion of responsibility that arise from other sources of law, as referred to in Article 21 of the ICC Statute, especially from customary international law or general principles of law (military necessity, reprisal).

II. Self-Defense

Kai Ambos: *Der Allgemeine Teil des Völkerstrafrechts, Ansätze einer Dogmatisierung* (2002), pp. 830 **407** et seq.; Antonio Cassese: The Statute of the International Criminal Court: Some Preliminary Re-

---

criminal law. In this regard, Art. 14 of the 1996 *Draft Code* stated that "defences" were to be determined by the Court "in accordance with the general principles of law, in the light of the character of each crime."

[277] See also A. Zimmermann, 58 *Zeitschrift für ausländisches öffentliches Recht und Völkerrecht* (1998), p. 47 at p. 83; however, he sees little scope for applicability even for war crimes. See also C. Kress, 30 *Israel Yearbook on Human Rights* (2001), p. 103 at p. 151.

[278] See K. Ambos, *Der Allgemeine Teil des Völkerstrafrechts* (2002), p. 514.

[279] On the development of Art. 31 of the ICC Statute, see A. Eser, in O. Triffterer (ed.), *Commentary on the Rome Statute of the International Criminal Court* (1999), Art. 31, marginal no. 3.

[280] See A. Eser, in O. Triffterer (ed.), *Commentary on the Rome Statute of the International Criminal Court* (1999), Art. 31, marginal nos. 5 et seq. The question whether the Statute should contain a complete and enumerative list or simply an "open list" was the subject of intense controversy in Rome, see M. Scaliotti, 1 *International Criminal Law Review* (2001), p. 111 at p. 119. Art. 34 of the Draft ICC Statute (1998) still contained the following rule: "1. At trial the Court may consider a ground for excluding criminal responsibility not specifically enumerated in this part if the ground: (a) is recognized [in general principles of criminal law common to civilized nations] [in the State with the most significant contacts to the crime] with respect to the type of conduct charged; and (b) deals with a principle clearly beyond the scope of the grounds for excluding criminal responsibility enumerated in this part and is not otherwise inconsistent with those or any other provisions of the Statute. 2. The procedure for asserting such a ground for excluding criminal responsibility shall be set forth in the Rules of Procedure and Evidence."

flections, 10 *European Journal of International Law* (1999), pp. 144 et seq.; Antonio Cassese: *International Criminal Law* (2003), pp. 222 et seq.; Georg Dahm, Jost Delbrück and Rüdiger Wolfrum: *Völkerrecht*, Vol. I/3, 2nd edn. (2002), pp. 1124 et seq.; Yoram Dinstein: *War, Aggression and Self-Defence*, 3rd edn. (2001); Albin Eser: "Defences" in Strafverfahren wegen Kriegsverbrechen, in Kurt Schmoller (ed.), *Festschrift für Otto Triffterer* (1996), pp. 755 et seq.; Albin Eser: ICC Statute, Article 31, in Otto Triffterer (ed.), *Commentary on the Rome Statute of the International Criminal Court, Observers' Notes, Article by Article* (1999), pp. 573 et seq.; Hans-Heinrich Jescheck: *Die Verantwortlichkeit der Staatsorgane nach Völkerstrafrecht, Ein Studie zu den Nürnberger Prozessen* (1952), pp. 328 et seq.; Geert-Jan Knoops: *Defenses in Contemporary International Criminal Law* (2001), pp. 73 et seq.; Claus Kress: War Crimes Committed in Non-International Armed Conflict and the Emerging System of International Criminal Justice, 30 *Israel Yearbook on Human Rights* (2001), pp. 103 et seq.; Reinhard Merkel: Gründe für den Ausschluss der Strafbarkeit im Völkerstrafrecht, 114 *Zeitschrift für die gesamte Strafrechtswissenschaft* (2002), pp. 437 et seq.; Christiane Nill-Theobald: *"Defences" bei Kriegsverbrechen am Beispiel Deutschlands und der USA* (1998), pp. 358 et seq.; Per Saland: International Criminal Law Principles, in Roy S. Lee (ed.), *The International Criminal Court, The Making of the Rome Statute* (1999), pp. 189 et seq.; Massimo Scaliotti: Defences before the International Criminal Court: Substantive Grounds for Excluding Criminal Responsibility, Part 1, 1 *International Criminal Law Review* (2001), pp. 111 et seq.

408 Although self-defense has hitherto played only a subordinate role in the practice of international courts,[281] it has long been recognized in customary international law.[282] The conditions for self-defense are now governed by Article 31(1)(c) of the ICC Statute;[283] the provision reflects customary international law.[284] According to this provision, appropriate defense measures are permissible against an imminent and unlawful use of force.

409 In the trial of *Kordić and Čerkez*, the Yugoslavia Tribunal most recently dealt in detail with the applicability and scope of the right of self-defense in international criminal law. The judgment is significant in two respects. First, the principles laid out in Article 31(1)(c) of the ICC Statute were applied for the first time, if only indirectly; it was explicitly stated that the rule embodied customary international law. Second, the judgment proves that the adoption of a self-defense provision in the ICC Statute was justified: cases in which self-defense plays a role are conceivable.

---

[281] See K. Ambos, *Der Allgemeine Teil des Völkerstrafrechts* (2002), p. 830; A. Eser, in K. Schmoller (ed.), *Festschrift für Triffterer* (1996), p. 755 at p. 766.

[282] For details, see *Prosecutor* v. *Kordić and Čerkez*, ICTY (Trial Chamber), judgment of 26 February 2001, para. 451: "The principle of self-defence enshrined in [Art. 31 of the ICC Statute] reflects provisions found in most national criminal codes and may be regarded as constituting a rule of customary international law"; C. Kress, 30 *Israel Yearbook on Human Rights* (2001), p. 103 at p. 151; G.-J. Knoops, *Defenses in Contemporary International Criminal Law* (2001), p. 75; M. Scaliotti, 1 *International Criminal Law Review* (2001), p. 111 at pp. 158, 160 et seq. The principle of self-defense is also an inherent part of domestic criminal law systems, see the comparative survey in M. Scaliotti, 1 *International Criminal Law Review* (2001), p. 111 at p. 161; thus there is good reason to view this as a general principle of law.

[283] For details on the substantive problems dealt with in the negotiations at and leading up to Rome (including provocation of a self-defense situation by the perpetrator, putative self-defense, defense against threats), see M. Scaliotti, 1 *International Criminal Law Review* (2001), p. 111 at pp. 164 et seq.

[284] See *Prosecutor* v. *Kordić and Čerkez*, ICTY (Trial Chamber), judgment of 26 February 2001, para. 451.

1. Self-Defense Situation

A self-defense situation is based on an "imminent and unlawful use of force" against certain protected interests.   **410**

a) Use of Force

"Use of force" includes not only physical but also psychological attacks, particularly   **411**
threats, where these create an immediate, coercive situation.[285] The use of force must be
"unlawful"; in particular, it may not be covered by grounds for excluding responsibility.[286] The use of force is "imminent" if it is immediately impending or has already begun and is ongoing.[287]

b) Defensible Interests

Self-defense is only admissible if the use of force is directed against the life, bodily integrity or freedom of movement of the defender or a third party.[288] While this conclusively   **412**
describes the extent of defensible interests for genocide, crimes against humanity, and aggression, Article 31(1)(c) of the ICC Statute additionally allows the commission of war
crimes to defend against attacks on specific material interests ("property").

The inclusion of property on the list of interests in defense of which, if necessary, international   **413**
crimes may be committed was very controversial at the negotiations on the ICC Statute.[289] The
nuanced rule that was finally included in the Statute as a compromise is based on the presumption
that the seriousness of the act in certain cases of war crimes can be less than for genocide or crimes
against humanity.[290]

The requirement is that the defended property be either "essential for the survival of the   **414**
person or another person" or "essential for accomplishing a military mission."[291]

The extension of the right of self-defense to the defense of things "essential for accomplishing a   **415**
military mission" must be viewed in the context of the "military necessity" grounds for excluding

---

[285] See A. Eser, in O. Triffterer (ed.), *Commentary on the Rome Statute of the International Criminal Court* (1999), Art. 31, marginal no. 29, fn. 50.

[286] See A. Eser, in O. Triffterer (ed.), *Commentary on the Rome Statute of the International Criminal Court* (1999), Art. 31, marginal no. 29.

[287] See K. Ambos, *Der Allgemeine Teil des Völkerstrafrechts* (2002), p. 850; A. Eser, in O. Triffterer (ed.), *Commentary on the Rome Statute of the International Criminal Court* (1999), Art. 31, marginal no. 29; C. Kress, 30 *Israel Yearbook on Human Rights* (2001), p. 103 at p. 151.

[288] The limitation to protected interests of the person arises from the fact that self-defense must occur in order to "defend himself or herself or another person," see Art. 31(1)(c) of the ICC Statute. See A. Eser, in O. Triffterer (ed.), *Commentary on the Rome Statute of the International Criminal Court* (1999), Art. 31, marginal no. 29.

[289] See P. Saland, in R.S. Lee (ed.), *The International Criminal Court, The Making of the Rome Statute* (1999), p .189 at pp. 207 et seq.; M. Scaliotti, 1 *International Criminal Law Review* (2001), p. 111 at pp. 166 et seq.

[290] See P. Saland, in R.S. Lee (ed.), *The International Criminal Court, The Making of the Rome Statute* (1999), p. 189 at p. 208.

[291] For criticism of this extension, see A. Cassese, 10 *European Journal of International Law* (1999), p. 144 at pp. 154 et seq. See also M. Scaliotti, 1 *International Criminal Law Review* (2001), p. 111 at p. 167.

responsibility,[292] which must be taken account of under customary international law, albeit within narrow limits.[293] Here, Article 31(1)(c), sentence 2, of the ICC Statute must be taken into account: participation in a military defense operation alone does not in itself rule out liability.

2. Self-Defense Measures

416 If a self-defense situation exists, the right of self-defense permits "reasonable" measures that must be "proportionate" to the degree of danger threatening the person or thing.[294] The right of self-defense therefore allows the killing of a person as a last resort, for example if the defender is threatened with death or serious bodily harm.[295]

3. Mental Element

417 For the mental element of self-defense, it is necessary that the defensive act be committed with intent "to defend himself or herself or another person or, in the case of war crimes, property" for it to release a person from criminal responsibility under Art. 31(1)(c) of the ICC Statute.[296]

4. Individual Self-Defense and a State's Right of Self-Defense

418 Crimes under international law are frequently committed within the framework of a military conflict between states. This is literally true for war crimes; here the presence of an armed conflict is even a requirement for liability. These cases raise the question of the relationship between lawfulness or unlawfulness of the use of force between states, on the one hand, and criminal responsibility on the other.[297]

419 Any state's right to defend itself against attacks that violate international law is recognized as part of customary international law.[298] Article 51 of the UN Charter underscores the "inherent right of individual or collective self-defense" against armed attack.[299]

---

[292] See marginal no. 479.

[293] See C. Kress, 30 *Israel Yearbook on Human Rights* (2001), p. 103 at p. 151.

[294] The cumbersome doubling of proportionality in the text should be understood correctly as a uniform proportionality requirement; see C. Kress, 30 *Israel Yearbook on Human Rights* (2001), p. 103 at p. 152; A. Eser, in O. Triffterer (ed.), *Commentary on the Rome Statute of the International Criminal Court* (1999), Art. 31, marginal nos. 32 et seq. According to A. Cassese, *International Criminal Law* (2003), p. 222, the act of self-defense must be the *only* way of ending the attack.

[295] See A. Eser, in O. Triffterer (ed.), *Commentary on the Rome Statute of the International Criminal Court* (1999), Art. 31, marginal no. 33.

[296] In contrast, K. Ambos, *Der Allgemeine Teil des Völkerstrafrechts* (2002), p. 831, would consider mere knowledge of the emergency situation to be sufficient.

[297] Attempts to defend against the charge of committing crimes under international law by pointing to participation in a (supposedly legal) war of self-defense were made especially by defendants at the Nuremberg trials and the follow-up trials. See K. Ambos, *Der Allgemeine Teil des Völkerstrafrechts* (2002), p. 121; A. Cassese, *International Criminal Law* (2003), p. 223.

[298] See Y. Dinstein, *War, Aggression and Self-Defence*, 3rd edn. (2001), pp. 159, 226; G.-J. Knoops, *Defenses in Contemporary International Criminal Law* (2001), pp. 197 et seq.; M. Scaliotti, 1 *International Criminal Law Review* (2001), p. 111 at p. 158.

[299] See I. Brownlie, *Principles of Public International Law*, 6th edn. (2003), p. 701.

It is not individuals, but the affected state, that is thereby permitted to take defensive measures. Therefore, individual self-defense must be strictly distinguished from a state's right of self-defense.[300] This is made explicit in Article 31(1)(c), sentence 2, of the ICC Statute.[301] Here, involvement "in a defensive operation conducted by forces shall not in itself" lead to exclusion of criminal responsibility.[302] This, too, reflects customary international law.

III. Necessity and Duress

Kai Ambos: *Der Allgemeine Teil des Völkerstrafrechts, Ansätze einer Dogmatisierung* (2002), pp. 837   **420** et seq.; Kai Ambos: Other Grounds for Excluding Criminal Responsibility, in Antonio Cassese, Paola Gaeta and John R.W.D. Jones (eds.), *The Rome Statute of the International Criminal Court: A Commentary*, Vol. 2 (2002), pp. 1003 et seq.; Antonio Cassese: *International Criminal Law* (2003), pp. 242 et seq.; Georg Dahm, Jost Delbrück and Rüdiger Wolfrum: *Völkerrecht*, Vol. I/3, 2nd edn. (2002), pp. 1124 et seq.; Yoram Dinstein: *War, Aggression and Self-Defence*, 3rd edn. (2001); Yoram Dinstein: Defences, in Gabrielle Kirk McDonald and Olivia Swaak-Goldman (eds.), *Substantive and Procedural Aspects of International Criminal Law, The Experience of International and National Courts*, Vol. 1 (2000), pp. 369 et seq.; Albin Eser: "Defences" in Strafverfahren wegen Kriegsverbrechen, in Kurt Schmoller (ed.), *Festschrift für Otto Triffterer* (1996), pp. 755 et seq.; Albin Eser: ICC Statute, Art. 31, in Otto Triffterer (ed.), *Commentary on the Rome Statute of the International Criminal Court, Observers' Notes, Article by Article* (1999), pp. 537 et seq.; George Fletcher: *Basic Concepts of Criminal Law* (1998), pp. 130 et seq.; Hans-Heinrich Jescheck: *Die Verantwortlichkeit der Staatsorgane nach Völkerstrafrecht, Eine Studie zu den Nürnberger Prozessen* (1952), pp. 328 et seq.; Geert-Jan Knoops: *Defenses in Contemporary International Criminal Law* (2001), pp. 55 et seq.; Claus Kress: Die Kristallisation eines Allgemeinen Teils des Völkerstrafrechts: Die Allgemeinen Prinzipien des Strafrechts im Statut des Internationalen Strafgerichtshofs, *Humanitäres Völkerrecht-Informationsschriften* 1999, pp. 4 et seq.; Claus Kress: Zur Methode der Rechtsfindung im Allgemeinen Teil des Völkerstrafrechts, 111 *Zeitschrift für die gesamte Strafrechtswissenschaft* (1999), pp. 597 et seq.; *Enrico Mezzetti*: Grounds for Excluding Criminal Responsibility, in Flavia Lattanzi (ed.), *The International Criminal Court, Comments on the Draft Statute* (1998), pp. 147 et seq.; Jan Christoph Nemitz and Steffen Wirth: Legal Aspects of the Appeal Decision in the Erdemovic case: The Plea of Guilty and Duress in International Humanitarian Law, *Humanitäres Völkerrecht-Informationsschriften* 1999, pp. 43 et seq.; Christiane Nill-Theobald: *"Defences" bei Kriegsverbrechen am Beispiel Deutschlands und der USA* (1998), pp. 171 et seq.; Per Saland: International Criminal Law Principles, in Roy S. Lee (ed.), *The International Criminal Court, The Making of the Rome Statute* (1999), pp. 189 et seq.; Massimo Scaliotti: Defences before the International Criminal Court: Substantive Grounds for Excluding Criminal Responsibility, Part 1: 1 *International Criminal Law Review* 2001, pp. 111 et seq.

---

[300] See also M. Scaliotti, 1 *International Criminal Law Review* (2001), p. 111 at p. 159.

[301] The relationship between state self-defense and individual self-defense was a subject of debate at the Rome Conference, see M. Scaliotti, 1 *International Criminal Law Review* (2001), p. 111 at p. 166. The inclusion of sentence 2 was largely a result of the concern of several states that sentence 1, specifically the clause "property which is essential for accomplishing a military mission," would extend the authority to act in self-defense too far.

[302] See also *Prosecutor* v. *Kordić and Čerkez*, ICTY (Trial Chamber), judgment of 26 February 2001, para. 452: "[M]ilitary operations in self-defence do not provide a justification for serious violations of international humanitarian law"; K. Ambos, 10 *Criminal Law Forum* (1999), p. 1 at p. 27; M. Scaliotti, 1 *International Criminal Law Review* (2001), p. 111 at p. 166.

421   While duress and necessity may be recognized, as in traditional common law, as two separate defenses, international criminal law does not consider it necessary to distinguish between the two.[303]

422   Necessity refers to threats to life and limb emanating from objective circumstances, in particular forces of nature. This defense is based on a choice of evils.[304] In contrast, for duress, the perpetrator is compelled to commit the crime by a threat to life and limb coming from another person.[305]

423   The ICC Statute lumps both defenses together as one ground for excluding criminal responsibility under Article 31(1)(d). This provision[306] takes up elements of necessity and duress and combines them into a uniform rule.[307] The agreed-upon rule is no doubt an expression of a general principle of law; that is the conclusion of a comprehensive comparative legal analysis undertaken by the Appeals Chamber of the Yugoslavia Tribunal.[308] Necessity and duress have also become an element of customary international law as grounds for excluding responsibility.[309] Article 31(1)(d) reflects the state of customary law.[310]

---

[303] See K. Ambos, in A. Cassese, P. Gaeta and J.R.W.D. Jones (eds.), *The Rome Statute of the International Criminal Court* (2002), Vol. 1, p. 1003 at p. 1035. In modern common law, especially in US criminal law, the distinction is leveled in favor of a general choice of evils defense, see, e.g., Sec. 3.02 Model Penal Code, W.R. LaFave, *Criminal Law*, 4th edn. (2003), pp. 523 et seq. On the confusing terminology at the Nuremberg successor trials, see K. Ambos, *Der Allgemeine Teil des Völkerstrafrechts* (2002), pp. 119 et seq.; C. Nill-Theobald, *"Defences" bei Kriegsverbrechen am Beispiel Deutschlands und der USA* (1998), pp. 179 et seq., 184, 187, 205 et seq.

[304] See A. Cassese, *International Criminal Law* (2003), p. 242; K. Ambos, in A. Cassese, P. Gaeta and J.R.W.D Jones (eds.), *The Rome Statute of the International Criminal Court* (2002), Vol. 1, p. 1003 at p. 1036.

[305] See W.A. Schabas, *Introduction to the International Criminal Court*, 2nd edn. (2004), p. 113.

[306] On its history, see Y. Dinstein, in G. Kirk McDonald and O. Swaak-Goldman (eds.), *Substantive and Procedural Aspects of International Criminal Law*, Vol. 1 (2000), p. 369 at p. 373; A. Eser, in O. Triffterer (ed.), *Commentary on the Rome Statute of the International Criminal Court* (1999), Art. 31, marginal no. 35; P. Saland, in R.S. Lee (ed.), *The International Criminal Court, The Making of the Rome Statute* (1999), p. 189 at p. 208; M. Scaliotti, 1 *International Criminal Law Review* (2001), p. 111 at pp. 150 et seq.

[307] In the preliminary drafts, the two forms were still regulated separately; see Draft ICC Statute (1998), Art. 31(1).

[308] *Prosecutor* v. *Erdemović*, ICTY (Appeals Chamber), judgment of 7 October 1997, separate opinion of Judges Kirk McDonald and Vohrah, paras. 59 et seq.; M. Scaliotti, *International Criminal Law Review* 1 (2001), p. 111 at pp. 143 et seq.

[309] See A. Cassese, *International Criminal Law* (2003), pp. 242 et seq.; M. Scaliotti, 1 *International Criminal Law Review* (2001), p. 111 at p. 142. A clear summary of the requirements of the defense of duress under customary international law is found in the separate opinion of Judge Cassese, see *Prosecutor* v. *Erdemović*, ICTY (Appeals Chamber), judgment of 7 October 1997, separate opinion of Judge Cassese, para. 16: "(i) the act charged was done under an immediate threat of severe and irreparable harm to life or limb; (ii) there was no adequate means of averting such evil; (iii) the crime committed was not disproportionate to the evil threatened . . . ; (iv) the situation leading to duress must not have been voluntarily brought about by the person coerced." See also *Prosecutor* v. *Erdemović*, ICTY (Appeals Chamber), judgment of 7 October 1997, separate opinion of Judge Li, para. 5: "As a general rule, duress can be a complete defence if the following requirements are met, (a) the act was done to avoid an immediate danger both serious and irreparable, (b) there was no other adequate means to escape, and (c) the remedy was not disproportionate to the evil." Elements of an international criminal law concept of necessity are also presented in C. Nill-Theobald, *"Defences" bei Kriegsverbrechen am Beispiel Deutschlands und der USA* (1998), p. 230.

In comparison to other grounds for excluding responsibility, this defense plays a **424** prominent role in international case law,[311] as illustrated by the large number of relevant court decisions. In the trials of Nazi criminals before national and international courts, the defendants frequently argued the presence of a situation of necessity or duress.[312] Duress, in the form of superior orders, took on particular importance.[313] With a few exceptions, this defense was recognized in principle in the judgments, but they generally denied that its requirements were actually present.[314]

The conditions for exclusion of responsibility under Article 31(1)(d) of the ICC Stat- **425** ute are a threat to life or limb, reasonable response measures, and the intention of avoiding the threat. Under Article 31(1)(d), an additional subjective requirement is that the person did not intend to cause greater harm than what he or she sought to avoid.

1. Threat to Life or Limb

This ground for excluding criminal responsibility is based on the presence of a threat to **426** the life or bodily integrity of the actor or another person. A threat to bodily integrity is only understood here, in limited fashion, as a threat of serious bodily harm.[315] Danger to other protected interests, such as freedom or property, may not be averted using this ground for excluding responsibility.[316]

The perpetrator must be "caused by duress" to commit the crime under international **427** law through the "threat of imminent death" or a "threat of continuing or imminent serious bodily harm." The threat may be made by another person or constituted by other circumstances.[317] States of psychological coercion are included only if they threaten imminent serious physical consequences to life or limb.[318] Continuing threats, in which the

---

[310] See A. Cassese, *International Criminal Law* (2003), p. 251.

[311] See A. Eser, in K. Schmoller (ed.), *Festschrift für Triffterer* (1996), p. 755 at p. 765; A. Zimmermann, 58 *Zeitschrift für ausländisches öffentliches Recht und Völkerrecht* (1998), p. 41 at p. 83.

[312] A thorough survey of these trials is found in M. Scaliotti, 1 *International Criminal Law Review* (2001), p. 111 at pp. 147 et seq.

[313] See C. Nill-Theobald, *"Defences" bei Kriegsverbrechen am Beispiel Deutschlands und der USA* (1998), pp. 245 et seq. For discussion of the effect of obeying orders on exclusion of responsibility, see marginal nos. 449 et seq.

[314] For more on this, see H.-H. Jescheck, *Die Verantwortlichkeit der Staatsorgane nach Völkerstrafrecht* (1952), p. 395; C. Nill-Theobald, *"Defences" bei Kriegsverbrechen am Beispiel Deutschlands und der USA* (1998), p. 188. Occasionally, however, exclusion of responsibility due to necessity was affirmed, see, e.g., US Military Tribunal, Nuremberg, judgment of 22 December 1947 (*Flick* et al., so-called Flick Trial), in *Trials of War Criminals*, VI, pp. 1196 et seq.

[315] See A. Eser, in O. Triffterer (ed.), *Commentary on the Rome Statute of the International Criminal Court* (1999), Art. 31, marginal no. 37.

[316] There was no majority for the inclusion of freedom and property, despite relevant proposals in Rome. For more on the debate, see P. Saland, in R.S. Lee (ed.), *The International Criminal Court, The Making of the Rome Statute* (1999), p. 189 at p. 208; M. Scaliotti, 1 *International Criminal Law Review* (2001), p. 111 at pp. 150 et seq.

[317] See ICC Statute, Art. 31(1)(d), sentence 2.

[318] See K. Ambos, *Der Allgemeine Teil des Völkerstrafrechts* (2002), p. 849; A. Eser, in O. Triffterer (ed.), *Commentary on the Rome Statute of the International Criminal Court* (1999), Art. 31, marginal no. 29.

violation of protected interests may occur at any time, are also included.[319] A mere higher general probability of harm, such as the "omnipresence of the Gestapo" in the Third Reich, is not enough.

2. Necessary and Reasonable Measures

428 The actor must act "necessarily and reasonably."[320] An action is necessary if it is the only possibility of immediately eliminating the threat. It is reasonable if it is generally appropriate to avert the danger and causes no disproportionate consequences.

429 Under these conditions, even killing under duress may be grounds for excluding responsibility.[321] The ICC Statute here stakes out a position that has long been a subject of debate.[322] Following disputes[323] at the Rome Conference, the Statute adopted the continental European criminal law tradition, under which killing a person out of duress or necessity as a last resort can go unpunished. In contrast, in common law, the killing of innocent civilians is always criminal;[324] the presence of a situation of necessity or duress can at most lead to mitigation of punishment. Following this approach, the Yugoslavia Tribunal, in a close majority decision in the trial of Drazen Erdemović, refused to accept duress as grounds for excluding responsibility for the killing of innocent people: "[D]uress does not afford a complete defense to a soldier charged with a crime against humanity and/or a war crime involving the killing of innocent human beings."[325]

---

[319] See K. Ambos, *Der Allgemeine Teil des Völkerstrafrechts* (2002), p. 850.

[320] See A. Eser, in O. Triffterer (ed.), *Commentary on the Rome Statute of the International Criminal Court* (1999), Art. 31, marginal no. 39.

[321] See K. Ambos, *Der Allgemeine Teil des Völkerstrafrechts* (2002), pp. 859 et seq.; A. Eser, in O. Triffterer (ed.), *Commentary on the Rome Statute of the International Criminal Court* (1999), Art. 31, marginal no. 40; M. Scaliotti, 1 *International Criminal Law Review* (2001), p. 111 at pp. 146 et seq.

[322] For in-depth discussion of international criminal law in practice, see A. Cassese, *International Criminal Law* (2003), pp. 246 et seq.

[323] See P. Saland, in R.S. Lee (ed.), *The International Criminal Court, The Making of the Rome Statute* (1999), p. 189 at p. 208. Art. 31(1)(d) of the Draft ICC Statute (1998) included (though still in brackets) the addition: "provided that the person's action causes/was not intended to cause (n)either death."

[324] For example, Rule 916(h) of the US Rules of Courts-Martial contains the "defence of coercion or duress to any offence except killing an innocent person"; see also *Prosecutor* v. *Erdemović*, ICTY (Appeals Chamber), judgment of 7 October 1997, separate opinion of Judge Stephen, paras. 23 et seq., and separate opinion of Judges Kirk McDonald and Vohrah, para. 49; Y. Dinstein, in G. Kirk McDonald and O. Swaak-Goldman (eds.), *Substantive and Procedural Aspects of International Criminal Law*, Vol. 1 (2000), p. 369 at p. 375. In the meantime, however, common law, specifically US criminal law, has moved closer to continental European criminal law on this issue, see W.R. LaFave, *Criminal Law*, 4th edn. (2003), pp. 497 et seq.

[325] *Prosecutor* v. *Erdemović*, ICTY (Appeals Chamber), judgment of 7 October 1997, para. 17. See also *Prosecutor* v. *Mrđa*, ICTY (Trial Chamber), judgment of 31 March 2004, paras. 59 et seq. For agreement, see C.K. Hall, in F. Lattanzi (ed.), *The International Criminal Court* (1998), p. 19 at pp. 46 et seq.; E. Mezzetti, in F. Lattanzi (ed.), *The International Criminal Court* (1998), p. 148 at pp. 152 et seq. But a critical view is found in the separate opinions of Judges Cassese, Li, and Stephen in *Prosecutor* v. *Erdemović*, ICTY (Appeals Chamber), judgment of 7 October 1997, and G.-J. Knoops, *Defenses in Contemporary International Criminal Law* (2001), pp. 59 et seq.; K. Oellers-Frahm and B. Specht, 58 *Zeitschrift für ausländisches öffentliches Recht und Völkerrecht* (1998), p. 389

3. Intention of Averting a Threat

Exclusion of responsibility under Article 31(1)(d) of the ICC Statute also requires that **430** the perpetrator act to avert the threat. Other motives on his or her part are harmless as long as the actor's intent, above and beyond awareness of the threatening situation, is ultimately aimed at averting the danger.[326] This relatively strict subjective requirement is based on well-established international case law[327] and is appropriate in view of the seriousness of crimes under international law.

4. Balancing of Interests

In addition to intent to avert the threat, Article 31(1)(d) of the ICC Statute requires that **431** the actor "not intend to cause a greater harm than the one sought to be avoided." Making the requirement of proportionality subjective, as an element of the perpetrator's perceptions, is new to international criminal law.[328] The objective requirement of balancing interests[329] must also be reflected in the perpetrator's mind. There is much to be said for the view that no secure foundation exists in customary international law for this criterion. The only requirement for this defense in customary international law is an objective balancing test, specifically that "the crime committed was not disproportionate to the evil threatened"; that is, "the crime committed under duress must be, on balance, the lesser of two evils."[330]

5. Self-Induced Necessity

It is not possible to argue necessity or duress if the perpetrator caused the danger him or **432**

---

at pp. 407 et seq. For the difficult issues involved, see R. Ehrenreich Brooks, 43 *Virginia Journal of International Law* (2003), pp. 860 et seq. Drazen Erdemović was tried for crimes against humanity before the Yugoslavia Tribunal. He was accused of taking part in the shooting of Muslim men and boys in July 1995 as a member of the Bosnian Serb army. When he refused to take part in executing the prisoners, his superior threatened that he would be shot if he continued to refuse. According to his own testimony, Erdemović then shot some 70 people.

[326] See K. Ambos, *Der Allgemeine Teil des Völkerstrafrechts* (2002), pp. 852 et seq.

[327] See, e.g., Supreme Court in the British Occupied Zone, in *OGHSt* 1, p. 310 at p. 313; *Prosecutor* v. *Erdemović*, ICTY (Appeals Chamber), judgment of 7 October 1997, separate opinion of Judge Li, para. 5.

[328] See K. Ambos, *Der Allgemeine Teil des Völkerstrafrechts* (2002), p. 853. In both English and US criminal law, however, a large number of grounds for excluding responsibility are defined based on the perpetrator's perceptions. Thus the issue is not whether a criminal attack or a danger was actually present, but only whether the perpetrator believed this was so ("if the actor believes"). See K. Ambos, *Der Allgemeine Teil des Völkerstrafrechts* (2002), pp. 853 et seq.

[329] See marginal no. 428 and C. Kress, *Humanitäres Völkerrecht-Informationsschriften* 1999, p. 4 at p. 7. A. Eser, in O. Triffterer (ed.), *Commentary on the Rome Statute of the International Criminal Court* (1999), Art. 31, marginal no. 40, incorrectly states that it is not necessary for the perpetrator *objectively* to cause a lesser harm through his action than that which threatens from the source of the danger.

[330] *Prosecutor* v. *Erdemović*, ICTY (Appeals Chamber), judgment of 7 October 1997, separate opinion of Judge Cassese, para. 16, with numerous case citations.

herself.[331] According to Article 31(1)(d)(ii) of the ICC Statute, this limitation comes into play when it is determined that a situation of necessity can only arise out of "circumstances beyond that person's control." The defense is not available if the perpetrator was responsible for bringing about the danger. However, some remote contribution that may only have a distant causal relationship to the existence of the threat does not rule out the exclusionary ground.

433 A related question, especially relevant to the area of war crimes, is whether voluntary exposure to the danger should negate this ground for excluding responsibility.[332] Here the answer is still unclear. An exclusionary clause was included in Article 31(1)(d) of the Draft ICC Statute (1998): "if the person has [knowingly] [recklessly] exposed him or herself to a situation which was likely to lead to the threat, the person shall remain responsible." In Rome, however, it was agreed that the decision should be left to the Court.

6. Limits on Duress and Necessity in Cases of Special Duty to Assume Danger

434 A further limitation on necessity and duress can arise from the perpetrator's position or function.[333] Certain activities and duties create a higher level of accepted risk. This is true, for example, for members of armed forces.[334] In specific dangerous situations, a higher degree of risk-taking is to be expected of soldiers who have been trained for life-threatening situations. The activity-specific risk to soldiers consists in the danger of being wounded or killed in battle. In determining the duty to assume danger, the perpetrator's position in the military hierarchy must be taken into account.[335]

IV. Mistake

435 Kai Ambos: *Der Allgemeine Teil des Völkerstrafrechts* (2002), pp. 805 et seq.; Antonio Cassese: *International Criminal Law* (2003), pp. 251 et seq.; Yoram Dinstein: Defences, in Gabrielle Kirk

---

[331] This restriction is based both on a broad comparative legal basis and on a firm foundation in international case law. In his separate opinion to the *Erdemović* judgment of the ICTY Appeals Chamber, Judge Cassese also mentioned self-induced necessity as a reason to exclude the defense of duress in international criminal law, see *Prosecutor* v. *Erdemović*, ICTY (Appeals Chamber), judgment of 7 October 1997, separate opinion of Judge Cassese, paras. 16, 41, 50. See also K. Ambos, *Der Allgemeine Teil des Völkerstrafrechts* (2002), pp. 855 et seq.; Y. Dinstein, in G. Kirk McDonald and O. Swaak-Goldman (eds.), *Substantive and Procedural Aspects of International Criminal Law*, Vol. 1 (2000), p. 369 at p. 374; G.-J. Knoops, *Defenses in Contemporary International Criminal Law* (2001), pp. 61 et seq.; M. Scaliotti, 1 *International Criminal Law Review* (2001), p. 111 at p. 144.

[332] See also K. Ambos, *Der Allgemeine Teil des Völkerstrafrechts* (2002), p. 858 et seq.

[333] See *Prosecutor* v. *Erdemović*, ICTY (Appeals Chamber), judgment of 7 October 1997, separate opinion of Judge Cassese, para. 16; K. Ambos, *Der Allgemeine Teil des Völkerstrafrechts* (2002), p. 856; G.-J. Knoops, *Defenses in Contemporary International Criminal Law* (2001), p. 68.

[334] See, e.g., Sec. 6 of the German Military Criminal Code [*Wehrstrafgesetz, WStG*]: "Fear of personal danger does not excuse an act if a soldier's duty requires that the danger be faced." See also K. Ambos, *Der Allgemeine Teil des Völkerstrafrechts* (2002), p. 856; K. Oellers-Frahm and B. Specht, 58 *Zeitschrift für ausländisches öffentliches Recht und Völkerrecht* (1998), p. 389 at p. 408; C. Nill-Theobald, *"Defences" bei Kriegsverbrechen am Beispiel Deutschland und der USA* (1998), pp. 252 et seq.

[335] See *Prosecutor* v. *Erdemović*, ICTY (Appeals Chamber), judgment of 7 October 1997, separate opinion of Judge Cassese, para. 51; G.-J. Knoops, *Defenses in Contemporary International Criminal Law* (2001), p. 61 at p. 68.

McDonald and Olivia Swaak-Goldman (eds.), *Substantive and Procedural Aspects of International Criminal Law, The Experience of International and National Courts*, Vol. 1 (2000), pp. 377 et seq.; Albin Eser: "Defences" in Strafverfahren wegen Kriegsverbrechen, in Kurt Schmoller (ed.), *Festschrift für Otto Triffterer* (1996), pp. 755 et seq.; Albin Eser: Mental Elements – Mistake of Fact and Mistake of Law, in Antonio Cassese, Paola Gaeta and John R.W.D. Jones (eds.), *The Rome Statute of the International Criminal Court: A Commentary*, Vol. 1 (2002), pp. 889 et seq.; Hans-Heinrich Jescheck: *Die Verantwortlichkeit der Staatsorgane nach Völkerstrafrecht, Eine Studie zu den Nürnberger Prozessen* (1952), pp. 375 et seq.; Christiane Nill-Theobald: *"Defences" bei Kriegsverbrechen am Beispiel Deutschlands und der USA* (1998), pp. 342 et seq.; Massimo Scaliotti: Defences before the International Criminal Court: Substantive Grounds for Excluding Criminal Responsibility, Part 2, 2 *International Criminal Law Review* (2002), pp. 1 et seq.; Otto Triffterer: ICC Statute, Article 32, in Otto Triffterer (ed.), *Commentary on the Rome Statute of the International Criminal Court, Observers' Notes, Article by Article* (1999), pp. 555 et seq.; Thomas Weigend: Zur Frage eines "internationalen" Allgemeinen Teils, in Bernd Schünemann et al. (eds.), *Festschrift für Claus Roxin* (2001), pp. 1375 et seq.

The ICC Statute is the first international instrument to regulate the conditions under **436** which a mistake by the perpetrator can exclude his or her criminal responsibility,[336] a matter which is quite relevant to the practice of international criminal law.[337] Article 32 distinguishes mistake of fact from mistake of law. Both types of mistake exclude individual criminal responsibility if the subjective requirements of the crime are not met on account of the mistake. Exclusion of liability may therefore also be derived from Article 30 of the ICC Statute. Article 32 thus has no independent significance.[338]

Under Article 32 of the ICC Statute, the relevance of a mistake depends on whether a mistaken **437** perception eliminates the subjective conditions of liability. This link may suggest that the issue of mistake should be dealt with as part of the subjective requirements for responsibility, the mental element.[339] But the better reasoning argues for classifying mistake by the perpetrator as grounds for excluding responsibility, in line with the heretofore prevalent view in international criminal law

---

[336] On the history of this provision, see A. Eser, in A. Cassese, P. Gaeta and J.R.W.D. Jones (eds.), *The Rome Statute of the International Criminal Court*, Vol. 1 (2002), p. 889 at pp. 896 et seq.; M. Scaliotti, 2 *International Criminal Law Review* (2002), p. 1 at pp. 8 et seq.

[337] See O. Triffterer, in O. Triffterer (ed.), *Commentary on the Rome Statute of the International Criminal Court* (1999), Art. 32, marginal no. 4. An example of the relevance of mistake issues was provided by the International Military Tribunal at Nuremberg, judgment of 20 August 1947 (*Brandt* et al., so-called Medical Trial), in *Trials of War Criminals* II, pp. 2712 et seq. Of note was the (non-refutable) defense argument by three doctors that they had assumed that, regarding the medical experiments performed on concentration camp inmates, the prisoners they were shown were criminals condemned to death and would be granted clemency if they survived the experiments.

[338] Similarly, K. Ambos, *Der Allgemeine Teil des Völkerstrafrechts* (2002), pp. 806 et seq.; A. Eser, in A. Cassese, P. Gaeta and J.R.W.D. Jones (eds.), *The Rome Statute of the International Criminal Court*, Vol. 1 (2002), p. 889 at p. 934; T. Weigend, in B. Schünemann et al. (eds.), *Festschrift für Roxin* (2001), p. 1375 at p. 1391.

[339] See K. Ambos, *Der Allgemeine Teil des Völkerstrafrechts* (2002), p. 757; A. Eser, in A. Cassese, P. Gaeta and J.R.W.D. Jones (eds.), *The Rome Statute of the International Criminal Court*, Vol. 1 (2002), pp. 889 et seq. See also T. Weigend, in B. Schünemann et al. (eds.), *Festschrift für Roxin* (2001), p. 1375 at pp. 1390 et seq., who finds that the "controversial question internationally" has been decided in this spirit, through the fact that mistake was not included in the catalogue in Art. 31 of the ICC Statute. But see A. Eser, in K. Schmoller (ed.), *Festschrift für Triffterer* (1996), p. 755 at pp. 768 et seq.

and in conformity with the common law legal tradition. In Article 32 of the ICC Statute, any relevant mistake is explicitly defined as a "ground for excluding criminal responsibility."

438 Article 32 of the ICC Statute at its core embodies customary international law.[340] This is true, first of all, of the distinction between mistake of fact and mistake of law; second of all, the provision that mistake about the factual requirements for responsibility leads, in principle, to exclusion from criminal responsibility is securely grounded in customary law. At most, doubt may exist as to the customary law upon which the treatment of mistake of law is based; customary law has not yet formulated a clear position on this. In the end, however, here too, the proposition of Article 32(2) that a mistake of law shall not, as a rule, exclude criminal responsibility conforms to customary law.

1. Mistake of Fact

439 If the perpetrator makes a mistake of fact, criminal liability is excluded under Article 32(1) of the ICC Statute if this mistaken perception affects the material elements and thereby negates the subjective conditions for liability. Mistake about facts relevant to the definition of the crime is thus a ground for excluding responsibility.

440   A requirement for exclusion of responsibility in this case is, first of all, that the perpetrator's mistaken perception refer to the facts underlying the material elements of the crime. This is the case, for example, if the perpetrator shoots at a Red Cross vehicle[341] because he assumes, due to bad visibility, that it is an enemy tank.[342] The facts do not include the elements that determine the legal basis for liability. Thus it is not a mistake of fact if the perpetrator's mistaken perception concerns (normative) elements of the definition of the crime, the determination of which would require a legal judgment.[343] In such cases, the perpetrator is mistaken as to the legal requirements of liability, and the provision on mistake of law applies.[344] Thus if the perpetrator in the above example recognizes that the vehicle is a Red Cross vehicle, but erroneously assumes that, under law, he is permitted to attack such a vehicle if it has not formally registered its passage in advance, this is not a mistake of fact but an (irrelevant) mistake of law.

---

[340] On the state of customary law, see K. Ambos, *Der Allgemeine Teil des Völkerstrafrechts* (2002), pp. 805 et seq.; A. Cassese, *International Criminal Law* (2003), pp. 251, 256; M. Scaliotti, 2 *International Criminal Law Review* (2002), p. 1 at pp. 2 et seq., with additional notes. O. Triffterer, in O. Triffterer (ed.), *Commentary on the Rome Statute of the International Criminal Court* (1999), Art. 32, marginal no. 4. Aside from the special case of acting under orders, there were no provisions in the statutes to be applied by the courts on treatment of mistake. The practice of international criminal law was oriented towards traditional common law.

[341] See ICC Statute, Art. 8(2)(b)(iii).

[342] See for additional examples A. Eser, in A. Cassese, P. Gaeta and J.R.W.D. Jones (eds.), *The Rome Statute of the International Criminal Court*, Vol. 1 (2002), p. 889 at p. 938.

[343] On the normative elements of crimes and their treatment with regard to the subjective aspect, see marginal no. 309.

[344] See T. Weigend, in B. Schünemann et al. (eds.), *Festschrift für Roxin* (2001), p. 1375 at p. 1391.

The mistake must lead to the loss of the subjective requirements of responsibility. **441** This is normally the case if the perpetrator's mistaken perception concerns a material element of the definition of the crime.

This requirement is not fulfilled, in contrast, if the mistake concerns the factual re- **442** quirements of the grounds for excluding responsibility, for example, self-defense or necessity. If the perpetrator, for example, erroneously assumes that a prisoner of war is reaching into his pocket to pull a weapon, and he therefore shoots him, no grounds for excluding responsibility due to mistake of fact under Article 32(1) of the ICC Statute are available. Here, however, it may be argued that this unsatisfying result should be corrected.[345] The reason (and possibly also the methodological starting point) for this correction is the observation that in such constellations, national legal systems uniformly do not punish.[346] Thus a general principle of law might be presumed to this extent.

2. Mistake of Law

Unlike mistake of fact, under the Statute the relevant mistake of law has only a narrow **443** scope of application. If the perpetrator's mistaken perception concerns the legal requirements of liability ("law"), under Article 32(2), this only leads to exclusion of responsibility if the mistake either negates the subjective conditions of liability or, under the conditions in Article 33, concerns superior orders.[347]

It follows that ignorance of the law is not, in principle, a ground for excluding crimi- **444** nal responsibility; nor is a perpetrator's mistaken assumption that his act does not fall under the jurisdiction of the International Criminal Court.[348] In these cases, only mitigation of punishment is possible.

---

[345] K. Ambos, *Der Allgemeine Teil des Völkerstrafrechts* (2002), pp. 808 et seq., and A. Eser, in A. Cassese, P. Gaeta and J.R.W.D. Jones (eds.), *The Rome Statute of the International Criminal Court*, Vol. 1 (2002), pp. 889 at 945, suggest analogous application of Art. 32 of the ICC Statute to these cases; similarly, O. Triffterer, in O. Triffterer (ed.), *Commentary on the Rome Statute of the International Criminal Court* (1999), Art. 32, marginal no. 14. See also M. Scaliotti, 2 *International Criminal Law Review* (2002), p. 1 at p. 14.

[346] It conforms to the Anglo-American criminal law tradition that self-defense and necessity are defined based on the perpetrator's perceptions. Thus a person who (perhaps in error) believed that an attack or a danger was really present would not be punished, see marginal no. 431, fn. 328. Under civil law doctrine, e.g., German law, a mistake about the factual requirements of a ground for excluding criminal responsibility ("*Erlaubnistatbestandsirrtum*") may also exclude criminal responsibility, see H.-H. Jescheck and T. Weigend, *Lehrbuch des Strafrechts, Allgemeiner Teil*, 5th edn. (1996), pp. 462 et seq.

[347] The wording "may" in sentence 2 should not be understood to make exclusion of responsibility optional. The text here makes reference to the absolute irrelevance of certain types of mistake of law provided for in sentence 1. For a correct approach, see T. Weigend, in B. Schünemann et al. (eds.), *Festschrift für Roxin* (2001), p. 1375 at p. 1391, fn. 66; but see K. Ambos, *Der Allgemeine Teil des Völkerstrafrechts* (2002), p. 811; A. Eser, in A. Cassese, P. Gaeta and J.R.W.D. Jones (eds.), *The Rome Statute of the International Criminal Court*, Vol. 1 (2002), p. 889 at pp. 941 et seq.; O. Triffterer, in O. Triffterer (ed.), *Commentary on the Rome Statute of the International Criminal Court* (1999), Art. 32, marginal no. 38.

[348] See ICC Statute, Art. 32(2), sentence 1; K. Ambos, *Der Allgemeine Teil des Völkerstrafrechts* (2002), pp. 816 et seq.; T. Weigend, in B. Schünemann et al. (eds.), *Festschrift für Roxin* (2001), p. 1375 at p. 1391.

445 The Statute does not even allow for a defense if the ignorance of the law could not have been avoided. This may amount to a violation of the principle of individual criminal responsibility.[349] This is especially true as regards to war crimes law, with its manifold regulations.[350]

446 A mistake of law can be relevant if it concerns normative elements of a crime under international law. It is decisive here whether the perpetrator recognized the significance of the normative element.[351] A mistaken legal assessment on the part of the perpetrator is no bar to liability if he or she is aware of the underlying facts (otherwise there is mistake of fact) and of the meaning of the legal definition of the crime (otherwise, relevant mistake of law is present).[352] A relevant mistake of law is present, for example, if a perpetrator holding a trial of a prisoner of war considers an objectively insufficient hearing of the defendant to be sufficient.[353] In such a case, the perpetrator is not responsible for a war crime under Article 8(2)(a)(vi) of the ICC Statute.

447 An exception to the principle that ignorance of the law is no excuse (*"ignorantia legis non excusat"*) is made in Article 32(2), sentence 2, through reference to Article 33 of the ICC Statute, where ignorance of the law meets duress: a mistake about the unlawfulness of a superior order to commit a war crime that is not manifestly illegal can be a relevant mistake of law under Article 32(2) of the Statute.

V. Superior Orders

448 Kai Ambos: *Der Allgemeine Teil des Völkerstrafrechts, Ansätze einer Dogmatisierung* (2002), pp. 832 et seq.; Cherif M. Bassiouni and Peter Manikas: *The Law of the International Criminal Tribunal for the former Yugoslavia* (1996), pp. 374 et seq.; Antonio Cassese: *International Criminal Law* (2003), pp. 231 et seq.; Yoram Dinstein: *The Defence of "obedience to superior orders" in International Law* (1965); Albin Eser: "Defences" in Strafverfahren wegen Kriegsverbrechen, in Kurt Schmoller (ed.), *Festschrift für Otto Triffterer* (1996), pp. 755 et seq.; Paola Gaeta: The Defence of Superior Orders: The Statute of the International Criminal Court versus Customary International Law, 10 *European Journal of International Law* (1999), pp. 172 et seq.; Leslie C. Green: Superior Orders and the Rea-

---

[349] See A. Eser, in A. Cassese, P. Gaeta and J.R.W.D. Jones (eds.), *The Rome Statute of the International Criminal Court*, Vol. 1 (2002), p. 889 at p. 945; T. Weigend, in B. Schünemann et al. (eds.), *Festschrift für Roxin* (2001), p. 1375 at pp. 1392 et seq. Art. 30 of the Draft ICC Statute (1998) still included the following rule, as Option 1: "Unavoidable mistake of fact or of law shall be a ground for excluding criminal responsibility provided that the mistake is not inconsistent with the nature of the alleged crime. Avoidable mistake of fact or of law may be considered in mitigation of punishment." For a thorough discussion of the debate in Rome, see M. Scaliotti, 2 *International Criminal Law Review* (2002), p. 1 at p. 5. Not taken into account – but equally suitable as a corrective to the rigid Statute rule – is the consideration, developed in the modern Anglo-American doctrine of mistake, of the extent to which the perpetrator's mistaken perception is "honest" or "reasonable." See W.R. LaFave, *Criminal Law*, 4th edn. (2003), pp. 290 et seq.

[350] See A. Cassese, *International Criminal Law* (2003), pp. 257 et seq.; A. Eser, in A. Cassese, P. Gaeta and J.R.W.D. Jones (eds.), *The Rome Statute of the International Criminal Court*, Vol. 1 (2002), p. 889 at p. 945.

[351] See also marginal no. 309.

[352] See also A. Eser, in A. Cassese, P. Gaeta and J.R.W.D. Jones (eds.) *The Rome Statute of the International Criminal Court*, Vol. 1 (2002), p. 889 at p. 941.

[353] See T. Weigend, in B. Schünemann et al. (eds.), *Festschrift für Roxin* (2001), p. 1375 at pp. 1391 et seq.

sonable Man, 8 *Canadian Yearbook of International Law* (1970), pp. 61 et seq.; Leslie C. Green: *Superior orders in national and international law* (1976); James B. Insco: Defence of Superior Orders Before Military Commissions, 13 *Duke Journal of Comparative and International Law* (2003), pp. 389 et seq.; Hans-Heinrich Jescheck: *Die Verantwortlichkeit der Staatsorgane nach Völkerstrafrecht, Eine Studie zu den Nürnberger Prozessen* (1952), pp. 385 et seq.; Christiane Nill-Theobald: *"Defences" bei Kriegsverbrechen am Beispiel Deutschlands und der USA* (1998), pp. 65 et seq.; Massimo Scaliotti: Defences before the international criminal court, Substantive grounds for excluding criminal responsibility, Part 1, 1 *International Criminal Law Review* (2001), pp. 111 et seq.; William A. Schabas: *Genocide in International Law* (2000), pp. 331 et seq.; Günter Stratenwerth: *Verantwortung und Gehorsam, Zur strafrechtlichen Wertung hoheitlich gebotenen Handelns* (1958); Otto Triffterer: ICC Statute, Article 33, in Otto Triffterer (ed.), *Commentary on the Rome Statute of the International Criminal Court, Oberservers' Notes, Article by Article* (1999), pp. 573 et seq.; Andreas Zimmermann: Superior Orders, in Antonio Cassese, Paola Gaeta and John R.W.D. Jones (eds.), *The Rome Statute of the International Criminal Court: A Commentary*, Vol. 1 (2002), pp. 957 et seq.

Crimes under international law are often committed pursuant to the orders of a (military **449** or civilian) superior. The perpetrators are frequently integrated into a hierarchically structured collective, such as an army or police force.[354] Such systems of orders and obedience are essential in some areas. To function, they require a basic duty of obedience on the part of the persons receiving the orders. In the process, subordinates must be able to trust the binding character of the orders and instructions they are given; thus they experience a degree of protection from personal responsibility in carrying out those orders.[355] The central question from the perspective of international criminal law is whether this protection can go so far as to create grounds for excluding the responsibility of subordinates even for crimes against international law.

1. Basic Positions

On the question of the responsibility of the obedient perpetrator, the following basic po- **450** sitions may be distinguished.[356]

Under the principle of *respondeat superior*, which applied until World War II, supe- **451** rior orders always completely excluded criminal liability on the part of a subordinate who acted under those orders. Only the superior would be liable.[357] The main purpose of this approach, developed to fit the context of military orders, was to ensure the unlimited obedience of those receiving orders. This model is outdated today. It is obvious that un-

---

[354] See marginal nos. 81 et seq.

[355] For basic discussion, see G. Stratenwerth, *Verantwortung und Gehorsam, Zur strafrechtlichen Wertung hoheitlich gebotenen Handelns* (1958); see also Y. Dinstein, *The Defence of "obedience to superior orders" in International Law* (1965).

[356] See also Y. Dinstein, in G. Kirk McDonald and O. Swaak-Goldman (eds.), *Substantive and Procedural Aspects of International Criminal Law*, Vol. 1 (2000), p. 371 at pp. 379 et seq.; A. Eser, in K. Schmoller (ed.), *Festschrift für Triffterer* (1996), p. 755 at pp. 760 et seq.; P. Gaeta, 10 *European Journal of International Law* (1999), p. 172 at pp. 174 et seq.; J.B. Insco, 13 *Duke Journal of Comparative and International Law* (2003), p. 389 at pp. 390 et seq.; A. Zimmermann, in A. Cassese, P. Gaeta and J.R.W.D. Jones (eds.), *The Rome Statute of the International Criminal Court*, Vol. 1 (2002), p. 957 at pp. 958 et seq.

[357] On superior responsibility, see marginal nos. 368 et seq.

conditionally allowing the obedient subordinate to go unpunished would have unacceptable consequences. In the extreme case, criminal responsibility would remain concentrated at the top of the chain of command, perhaps in one person ("It was all Hitler's fault").

452   According to the opposing position, the fact that the perpetrator committed the crime under orders or instructions does not affect his or her liability (the absolute liability principle).

453   Under a third, intermediate position, orders do in principle have the effect of excluding responsibility, but not if the perpetrator knew the order was illegal or if it was manifestly illegal (the manifest illegality principle).[358] Here, the question arises whether an order to commit genocide, a crime against humanity, or a war crime is not always manifestly illegal, given the severity of these crimes.[359]

2. International Case Law and Customary International Law

454   Under customary international law, acting under orders or instructions cannot in principle free a person from criminal liability for crimes under international law.[360] Obeying orders can only play a role within the context of general grounds for excluding responsibility, especially duress and mistake of law.[361] In addition, it is established under customary law that obeying orders may work in the perpetrator's favor in setting punishment.[362]

455   The Nuremberg and Tokyo Charters, as well as Control Council Law No. 10, explicitly stated that acting under the orders of a government or a superior did not release the perpetrator from responsibility.[363] The Nuremberg Tribunal rightly stated: "That a sol-

---

[358] The so-called *mens rea* principle developed by Dinstein generally leads to the same results as the *manifest illegality* principle. According to this principle, orders are not classed as independent grounds for excluding responsibility. The situation of superior orders comes into play, however, in the context of the general exclusionary grounds of necessity and mistake, where this excludes the subjective element. For details, see Y. Dinstein, *The Defence of "obedience to superior orders" in International Law* (1965); see also M.C. Bassiouni and P. Manikas, *The Law of the International Criminal Tribunal for the former Yugoslavia* (1996), pp. 384 et seq.

[359] See ICC Statute, Art. 33(2), and marginal no. 461. In H.-H. Jescheck's opinion, Art. 8 of the Nuremberg Charter is a specially-created rule that, in regard to the conviction of the top war criminals, creates the irrefutable presumption that the crimes for which these people were charged were manifestly illegal, see H.-H. Jescheck, *Die Verantwortlichkeit der Staatsorgane nach Völkerstrafrecht* (1952), p. 386.

[360] For thorough discussion of international criminal law practice, see A. Cassese, *International Criminal Law* (2003), pp. 234 et seq.; Y. Dinstein, in G. Kirk McDonald and O. Swaak-Goldman (eds.), *Substantive and Procedural Aspects of International Criminal Law*, Vol. 1 (2000), p. 371 at p. 379.

[361] See also K. Ambos, *Der Allgemeine Teil des Völkerstrafrechts* (2002), p. 833, p. 836; A. Zimmermann, in A. Cassese, P. Gaeta and J.R.W.D. Jones (eds.), *The Rome Statute of the International Criminal Court*, Vol. 1 (2002), p. 957 at p. 966; W.A. Schabas, *Genocide in International Law* (2000), p. 331.

[362] See Y. Dinstein, in G. Kirk McDonald and O. Swaak-Goldman (eds.), *Substantive and Procedural Aspects of International Criminal Law*, Vol. 1 (2000), p. 371 at p. 379.

[363] Nuremberg Charter, Art. 8; Tokyo Charter, Art. 6; CCL No. 10, Art. II(4)(b). See also ILC, Principles of International Law Recognised in the Charter of the Nuremberg Tribunal and in the

dier was ordered to kill or torture in violation of the international law of war has never been recognised as a defense to such acts of brutality, though . . . the order may be urged in mitigation of the punishment."[364] This position was affirmed in numerous follow-up trials.[365]

The provisions may be understood either as an expression of the absolute liability principle or, reflecting the manifest illegality principle, as establishing the irrefutable presumption that an order to commit crimes against peace, crimes against humanity, or war crimes is always manifestly illegal.[366] Given the monstrosity of the crimes in question, the possibility of considering obeying orders to be a mitigating circumstance, explicitly permitted by the rules, was not utilized by the Nuremberg Tribunal.[367]   **456**

The Statutes of the Yugoslavia and Rwanda Tribunals adopted the rules in the Nuremberg Charter, with minor alterations.[368] Obeying orders has so far played no role in the practice of the international Tribunals.[369]   **457**

No clear position can be found in customary law on how to handle cases in which a subordinate is mistaken about the legality of an order that is not manifestly illegal.[370] It remains unclear whether   **458**

---

judgment of the Tribunal, Principle IV, in *Yearbook of the International Law Commission* 1950 II, p. 364 at p. 375.

[364] IMT, judgment of 1 October 1946, in *The Trial of German Major War Criminals. Proceedings of the International Military Tribunal Sitting at Nuremberg, Germany*, Part 22, p. 447.

[365] See, e.g., US Military Tribunal, Nuremberg, judgment of 19. February 1948 (*List* et al., so-called Hostages Trial), in *Trials of War Criminals* XI, pp. 1236 et seq.; US Military Tribunal, Nuremberg, judgment of 10 April 1948 (*Ohlendorf* et al., so-called Einsatzgruppen Trial), in *Trials of War Criminals* IV, pp. 470 et seq.; US Military Tribunal, Nuremberg, judgment of 28 October 1948 (*von Leeb* et al., so-called High Command Trial), in *Trials of War Criminals* XI, pp. 507 et seq. Overview in A. Zimmermann, in A. Cassese, P. Gaeta and J.R.W.D. Jones (eds.), *The Rome Statute of the International Criminal Court*, Vol. 1 (2002), p. 957 at pp. 963 et seq. The law of Nuremberg was most recently affirmed in connection with the prosecution of crimes under international law in East Timor, see UNTAET, Regulation 15/2000 of 6 June 2000.

[366] Contrary to the wording of CCL No. 10, many successor trials were oriented around the manifest illegality principle. See the analysis in H.-H. Jescheck, *Die Verantwortlichkeit der Staatsorgane nach Völkerstrafrecht* (1952), pp. 255 et seq.

[367] On this, the Nuremberg Tribunal stated: "Superior orders, even to a soldier, cannot be considered in mitigation where crimes as shocking and extensive have been committed consciously, ruthlessly and without military excuse or justification," IMT, judgment of 1 October 1946, in *The Trial of German Major War Criminals. Proceedings of the International Military Tribunal Sitting at Nuremberg, Germany*, Part 22, p. 493.

[368] ICTY Statute, Art. 7(4); ICTR Statute, Art. 6(4). An important guide to application of these rules is found in the UN Secretary-General's report on Resolution 808. It states that acting under orders must be considered in the context of other grounds for excluding responsibility; see Report of the Secretary-General pursuant to paragraph 2 of Security Council Resolution 808, UN Doc. S/25704, para. 57; see also A. Zimmermann, in A. Cassese, P. Gaeta and J.R.W.D. Jones (eds.), *The Rome Statute of the International Criminal Court*, Vol. 1 (2002), p. 957 at p. 961.

[369] *Obiter dicta* are found in two separate opinions on the decision in the *Erdemović* case, see the joint separate opinion of Judges Kirk McDonald and Vohrah to *Prosecutor* v. *Erdemović*, ICTY (Appeals Chamber), judgment of 7 October 1997, paras. 34 et seq.; separate opinion of Judge Cassese to *Prosecutor* v. *Erdemović*, ICTY (Appeals Chamber), judgment of 7 October 1997, para. 15.

[370] On the debate over whether the absolute liability principle has advanced to the status of customary law, see, on the one hand, A. Zimmermann, in A. Cassese, P. Gaeta and J.R.W.D. Jones

it is even conceivable under customary international law for an order to commit a crime under international law not to be manifestly illegal. On the basis of the absolute liability principle, only general rules of mistake would be applicable here. The consequences of applying the manifest illegality principle depend on whether one always classifies orders to commit crimes against international law as manifestly illegal or whether one can imagine "simple" illegality here.

459 Presumption of conditional responsibility under a manifest illegality principle is widespread in national legal systems.[371] National courts tend to presume the manifest illegality of orders aimed at the commission of crimes under international law.[372]

3. Article 33 of the ICC Statute

460 The starting point of Article 33 of the ICC Statute corresponds to the undisputed core of customary law: the existence of an order does not, in principle, absolve the perpetrator of criminal responsibility. This is true regardless of whether the order came from a government, a military or a civilian superior.[373] An order can only lead to freedom from responsibility in exceptional cases, namely if the perpetrator had a legal duty to obey the order, if he or she did not know that the order was unlawful, and if the unlawfulness of the order was not manifest.[374] The applicability of general grounds for excluding responsibility is unaffected by Article 33 of the ICC Statute.[375] Here the ICC Statute decides in principle for the manifest illegality principle.

461 The manifest illegality principle is, however, interpreted by the Statute in such a way that it results in partial conformity with the absolute liability principle, a type of compromise between the opposing positions at the Rome Conference.[376] Under Article 33(2) of the ICC Statute, orders to commit genocide or crimes against humanity are al-

---

(eds.), *The Rome Statute of the International Criminal Court*, Vol. 1 (2002), p. 957 at p. 965 (according to which the absolute liability principle is not customary law), on the other hand, A. Cassese, *International Criminal Law* (2003), pp. 231 et seq., and P. Gaeta, 10 *European Journal of International Law* (1999), p. 172: "the customary rule on superior orders upholds the absolute liability approach."

[371] See P. Gaeta, 10 *European Journal of International Law* (1999), p. 172 at pp. 177 et seq.; L.C. Green, *Superior orders in national and international law* (1976), pp. 17 et seq.; C. Nill-Theobald, *"Defences" bei Kriegsverbrechen am Beispiel Deutschlands und der USA* (1998), pp. 108 et seq.; A. Zimmermann, in A. Cassese, P. Gaeta and J.R.W.D. Jones (eds.), *The Rome Statute of the International Criminal Court*, Vol. 1 (2002), p. 957 at p. 965.

[372] See P. Gaeta, 10 *European Journal of International Law* (1999), p. 172, fn. 32.

[373] This includes national laws that prescribe crimes contained in the ICC Statute, see O. Triffterer, in O. Triffterer (ed.), *Commentary on the Rome Statute of the International Criminal Court* (1999), Art. 33, marginal nos. 13, 17 et seq. On the concepts, see A. Zimmermann, in A. Cassese, P. Gaeta and J.R.W.D. Jones (eds.), *The Rome Statute of the International Criminal Court*, Vol. 1 (2002), p. 957 at pp. 968 et seq.

[374] For greater detail, see O. Triffterer, in O. Triffterer (ed.), *Commentary on the Rome Statute of the International Criminal Court* (1999), Art. 33, marginal nos. 13 et seq.; A. Zimmermann, in A. Cassese, P. Gaeta and J.R.W.D. Jones (eds.), *The Rome Statute of the International Criminal Court*, Vol. 1 (2002), p. 957 at pp. 968 et seq.

[375] See K. Ambos, *Der Allgemeine Teil des Völkerstrafrechts* (2002), p. 837.

[376] On the negotiations, see P. Gaeta, 10 *European Journal of International Law* (1999), p. 172 at pp. 188 et seq.; M. Scaliotti, 1 *International Criminal Law Review* (2001), p. 111 at pp. 135 et seq.; O. Triffterer, in O. Triffterer (ed.), *Commentary on the Rome Statute of the International Criminal Court* (1999), Art. 33, marginal nos. 8 et seq.; A. Zimmermann, in A. Cassese, P. Gaeta and J.R.W.D. Jones (eds.), *The Rome Statute of the International Criminal Court*, Vol. 1 (2002), p. 957 at p. 967.

ways manifestly illegal. To this extent, therefore, the Statute presumes that the illegality of such orders is obvious to the average observer using objective *ex ante* judgment.[377] In its practical consequences, this result corresponds to the absolute liability principle. The Statute thus only leaves room for exclusion of responsibility in case of orders to commit war crimes.[378] This new distinction is justified with the argument that, given the varied forms that war crimes take and their varying degrees of severity, it is in this area that exclusion from responsibility can most readily be considered.

The elements of the absolute liability and manifest illegality principles employed in the Statute are, **462** as such, familiar to customary international law. What is new, however, is the normative interpretation of the manifest illegality principle. This interpretation of customary international law operates, within a narrow scope, as a clarification in the perpetrator's favor: If the subordinate is mistaken about the lawfulness of an order that is not manifestly illegal, this is a special case of mistake of law (Article 32(2) of the ICC Statute), which can lead to exclusion of responsibility within the framework of the above explanation. The possibility of mitigation of sentence is not explicitly regulated in the Statute, however, it arises out of Article 78 of the ICC Statute.[379]

VI. Mental Disease or Defect

Kai Ambos: Other Grounds for Excluding Criminal Responsibility, in Antonio Cassese, Paola Gaeta **463** and John R.W.D. Jones (eds.), *The Rome Statute of the International Criminal Court: A Commentary*, Vol. 1 (2002), pp. 1003 et seq.; Kai Ambos: General Principles of Criminal Law in the Rome Statute, 10 *Criminal Law Forum* (1999), pp. 1 et seq.; Antonio Cassese: *International Criminal Law* (2003), pp. 224 et seq.; Albin Eser: ICC Statute, Article 31, in Otto Triffterer (ed.), *Commentary on the Rome Statute of the International Criminal Court, Observers' Notes, Article by Article* (1999), pp. 537 et seq.; Kriangsak Kittichaisaree: *International Criminal Law* (2001), pp. 261 et seq.; Geert-Jan Knoops: *Defenses in Contemporary International Criminal Law* (2001), pp. 108 et seq.; Claus Kress: Die Kristallisation eines Allgemeinen Teils des Völkerstrafrechts: Die Allgemeinen Prinzipien des Strafrechts im Statut des Internationalen Strafgerichtshofs, *Humanitäres Völkerrecht-Informationsschriften* 1999, pp. 4 et seq.; Peter Krug: The Emerging Mental Incapacity Defense in International Criminal Law: Some Initial Questions of Implementation, 94 *American Journal of International Law* (2000), pp. 317 et seq.; Ronald D. Mackay: *Mental Condition Defences in the Criminal Law* (1995); Christiane Nill-Theobald: *"Defences" bei Kriegsverbrechen am Beispiel Deutschlands und der USA* (1998), pp. 383 et seq.; Per Saland: International Criminal Law Principles, in Roy S. Lee (ed.), *The International Criminal Court, The Making of the Rome Statute* (1999), pp. 189 et seq.; Massimo Scaliotti: Defences before the international criminal court, Substantive grounds for excluding criminal responsibility, Part 1, 1 *International Criminal Law Review* (2001), pp. 111 et seq.; Part 2, 2 *International Criminal Law Review* (2002), pp. 1 et seq.; William A. Schabas: General Principles of Criminal Law in the International Criminal Court Statute (Part III), *European Journal of Crime, Criminal Law and Criminal Justice* 1998, pp. 399 et seq.

---

[377] On the standard of measurement, see A. Zimmermann, in A. Cassese, P. Gaeta and J.R.W.D. Jones (eds.), *The Rome Statute of the International Criminal Court*, Vol. 1 (2002), p. 957 at p. 970.

[378] See P. Gaeta, 10 *European Journal of International Law* (1999), p. 172 at pp. 189 et seq.; A. Zimmermann, in A. Cassese, P. Gaeta and J.R.W.D. Jones (eds.), *The Rome Statute of the International Criminal Court*, Vol. 1 (2002), p. 957 at p. 971, fn. 70. The same is true for the crime of aggression, but for now the rule has no practical value, see marginal nos. 1184 et seq.

[379] See also O. Triffterer, in O. Triffterer (ed.), *Commentary on the Rome Statute of the International Criminal Court* (1999), Art. 33, marginal no. 24. A footnote to Art. 32(2) of the Draft ICC Statute (1998) expressly states: "For the question of mitigating circumstances, see Part 7."

464 Exclusion of criminal liability due to mental disease or defect, provided for in most domestic legal systems, applies in international criminal law as well.[380] Although this ground for excluding responsibility has hitherto achieved little significance in the practice of international courts,[381] it is confirmed and clarified by Article 31(1)(a) of the ICC Statute. As a condition for excluding responsibility, the presence of a "mental disease or defect" is required that "at the time of that person's conduct . . . destroys that person's capacity to appreciate the unlawfulness or nature of his or her conduct, or capacity to control his or her conduct to conform to the requirements of law."[382]

465 The Court can bring in experts to establish mental disease or defect.[383] Although the ICC Statute contains no explicit rule regarding expert testimony, its admissibility is presumed. This arises from numerous provisions, of which Articles 48(4) and 100(1)(d) are the most explicit.[384] In contrast, how to deal with persons who have been freed from responsibility due to mental disease or defect is completely unregulated. Neither the ICC Statute nor the Rules of Procedure and Evidence provide a means for committing mentally disturbed perpetrators to treatment facilities.[385]

---

[380] See *Prosecutor* v. *Mucić* et al., ICTY (Appeals Chamber), judgment of 20 February 2001, para. 582: "plea of insanity is a complete defence"; the Yugoslavia Tribunal defined insanity as "such a defect of reason, from disease of the mind, as not to know the nature and quality of his act or, if [the perpetrator] did know it, that [the perpetrator] did not know that what he was doing was wrong"; "lack of mental responsibility" is also expressly described as a "defence" in ICTY Rule of Procedure 67(A)(ii)(b). However, ICTY case law leaves open the question whether this ground for exclusion of responsibility is an element of customary international law or if it claims a place in international criminal law as a general principle of law. But Cassese expressly counts this ground for exclusion of responsibility as part of customary international criminal law, see A. Cassese, in A. Cassese, P. Gaeta and J.R.W.D. Jones (eds.), *The Rome Statute of the International Criminal Court*, Vol. 1 (2002), p. 951 at p. 954; see also K. Kittichaisaree, *International Criminal Law* (2001), p. 261; M. Scaliotti, 2 *International Criminal Law Review* (2002), p. 1 at pp. 16 et seq. Following the terminology of common law, this ground for excluding responsibility is also known as insanity (defense) or incapacity, see L.N. Sadat, *The International Criminal Court and the Transformation of International Law* (2002), p. 189 at p. 212; W.A. Schabas, *European Journal of Crime, Criminal Law and Criminal Justice* 1998, p. 399 at p. 422; A. Eser, in O. Triffterer (ed.), *Commentary on the Rome Statute of the International Criminal Court* (1999), Art. 30, marginal no. 20.

[381] When the Tribunals have found reason to consider the defendant's mental state at the time of the crime, they have generally refused to exclude criminal responsibility, see, e.g., *Prosecutor* v. *Mucić* et al., ICTY (Trial Chamber), judgment of 16 November 1998, paras. 1156 et seq.; *Prosecutor* v. *Todorović*, ICTY (Trial Chamber), judgment of 31 July 2001, paras. 93 et seq.; additional examples in A. Cassese, *International Criminal Law* (2003), p. 225.

[382] For thorough discussion of this rule, see G.J. Knoops, *Defenses in Contemporary International Criminal Law* (2001), p. 114; A. Eser, in O. Triffterer (ed.), *Commentary on the Rome Statute of the International Criminal Court* (1999), Art. 31, marginal no. 20.

[383] See, e.g., *Prosecutor* v. *Mucić* et al., ICTY (Trial Chamber), judgment of 16 November 1998, paras. 1170, 1173 et seq.; *Prosecutor* v. *Banović*, ICTY (Trial Chamber), judgment of 28 October 2003, para. 77.

[384] Here experts are mentioned explicitly. See also ICC Statute, Arts. 56(2)(c); 93(1)(b), (c), (2); 100(1)(a). See *Prosecutor* v. *Mucić* et al., ICTY (Trial Chamber), judgment of 16 November 1998, para. 1186, and G.J. Knoops, *Defenses in Contemporary International Criminal Law* (2001), p. 114.

[385] For details, see W.A. Schabas, *European Journal of Crime, Criminal Law and Criminal Justice* 1998, p. 399 at p. 423.

The prerequisite for exclusion from responsibility is the presence of a "mental disease or **466** defect"[386] in the perpetrator at the time the act was committed.[387] This includes, in principle, any mental defect that achieves a degree of severity and permanence and can disrupt the perpetrator's ability to appreciate or control his or her conduct.[388] In exceptional cases, exclusion from responsibility may be considered even for the commission of a crime under international law in the heat of passion. This does not apply, however, to merely temporary states of exhaustion or excitement.[389] In addition, psychological disturbances on the part of the perpetrator that are merely emotional, such as deep sorrow or blind rage, are not included.[390]

Only mental disturbances that destroy the perpetrator's capacity to appreciate or con- **467** trol his or her conduct lead to exclusion of responsibility.[391] Article 31(1)(a) of the ICC Statute distinguishes between three effects of mental disease or defect, each of which can lead to exclusion of responsibility:[392] destruction of the capacity to appreciate the unlawfulness of conduct; destruction of the capacity to appreciate the nature of conduct; and destruction of the capacity to control one's own conduct to conform to the requirements of law.

---

[386] ICC Statute, Art. 31(1)(a). A uniform, internationally recognized key to understanding the phrase is provided by the International Classification of Disease (ICD) published by the World Health Organization, see World Health Organization (ed.), *International Statistical Classification of Diseases and related Health Problems, ICD-10* (1992-1994). In the trial of *Mucić* et al. before the ICTY, the experts referred to the ICD, see *Prosecutor* v. *Mucić* et al., ICTY (Trial Chamber), judgment of 16 November 1998, para. 1178.

[387] See also *Prosecutor* v. *Mucić* et al., ICTY (Trial Chamber), judgment of 16 November 1998, para. 1156; *Prosecutor* v. *Mucić* et al., ICTY (Appeals Chamber), judgment of 20 February 2001, para. 582 ("disease of mind"); K. Kittichaisaree, *International Criminal Law* (2001), p. 261.

[388] See A. Eser, in O. Triffterer (ed.), *Commentary on the Rome Statute of the International Criminal Court* (1999), Art. 31, marginal no. 21; G.J. Knoops, *Defenses in Contemporary International Criminal Law* (2001), p. 114.

[389] See *Prosecutor* v. *Mucić* et al., ICTY (Trial Chamber), judgment of 16 November 1998, para. 1166; A. Eser, in O. Triffterer (ed.), *Commentary on the Rome Statute of the International Criminal Court* (1999), Art. 31, marginal no. 21; G.-J. Knoops, *Defenses in Contemporary International Criminal Law* (2001), p. 114.

[390] See A. Eser, in O. Triffterer (ed.), *Commentary on the Rome Statute of the International Criminal Court* (1999), Art. 31, marginal no. 21; G.-J. Knoops, *Defenses in Contemporary International Criminal Law* (2001), p. 114.

[391] See *Prosecutor* v. *Mucić* et al., ICTY (Appeals Chamber), judgment of 20 February 2001, para. 582.

[392] See K. Ambos, 10 *Criminal Law Forum* (1999), p. 1 at pp. 24 et seq.; A. Eser, in O. Triffterer (ed.), *Commentary on the Rome Statute of the International Criminal Court* (1999), Art. 31, marginal no. 22; G.-J. Knoops, *Defenses in Contemporary International Criminal Law* (2001), p. 114. By including three effects, the Statute brings together the basic positions of common law and civil law. Both recognize that the inability of a perpetrator to recognize the criminality of an act due to mental disease can be a ground to exclude responsibility. But while common law is geared in addition toward the inability to recognize the significance of one's conduct due to illness (on the so-called M'Naghten Rule, see *Prosecutor* v. *Mucić* et al., ICTY (Appeals Chamber), judgment of 20 February 2001, para. 582; also Sec. 4.01 Model Penal Code, many continental European criminal law systems also include inability to control behavior (see, e.g., German Criminal Code [*Strafgesetzbuch, StGB*], Sec. 20); for details, see W.A. Schabas, *European Journal of Crime, Criminal Law and Criminal Justice* 1998, p. 399 at p. 423.

468　　If these abilities are impaired but not completely destroyed, there is no way to avoid responsibility.[393] The ICC Statute contains no explicit provision regarding mere diminished capacity. The possibility remains, however, of considering mitigation of punishment within the framework of the general sentencing provisions of Article 78 of the ICC Statute.[394]

VII. Intoxication

469　　Kai Ambos: *Der Allgemeine Teil des Völkerstrafrechts, Ansätze einer Dogmatisierung* (2002), pp. 158 et seq.; Kai Ambos: Other Grounds for Excluding Criminal Responsibility, in Antonio Cassese, Paola Gaeta and John R.W.D. Jones (eds.), *The Rome Statute of the International Criminal Court: A Commentary*, Vol. 1 (2002), pp. 1003 et seq.; K. Ambos: General Principles of Criminal Law in the Rome Statute, 10 *Criminal Law Forum* (1999), pp. 1 et seq.; Antonio Cassese: *International Criminal Law* (2003), pp. 228 et seq.; Albin Eser: ICC Statute, Article 31, in Otto Triffterer (ed.), *Commentary on the Rome Statute of the International Criminal Court, Observers' Notes, Article by Article* (1999), pp. 537 et seq.; Kriangsak Kittichaisaree: *International Criminal Law* (2001), p. 261; Geert-Jan Knoops: *Defenses in Contemporary International Criminal Law* (2001), pp. 108 et seq.; Claus Kress: Die Kristallisation eines Allgemeinen Teils des Völkerstrafrechts: Die Allgemeinen Prinzipien des Strafrechts im Statut des Internationalen Strafgerichtshofs, *Humanitäres Völkerrecht-Informationsschriften* 1999, pp. 4 et seq.; Christiane Nill-Theobald: *"Defences" bei Kriegsverbrechen am Beispiel Deutschlands und der USA* (1998), pp. 383 et seq.; Per Saland: International Criminal Law Principles, in Roy S. Lee (ed.), *The International Criminal Court, The Making of the Rome Statute* (1999), pp. 189 et seq.; William A. Schabas: General Principles of Criminal Law in the International Criminal Court Statute (Part III), *European Journal of Crime, Criminal Law and Criminal Justice* 1998, pp. 399 et seq.

470　　Article 31(1)(b) of the ICC Statute regulates exclusion of criminal liability for commission of a crime under international law in a state of intoxication.[395] A person who, due to intoxication, is unable to "appreciate the unlawfulness or nature of his or her conduct, or . . . control his or her conduct to conform to the requirements of law" when committing the act will not be punished. But no exclusion of responsibility is possible, under the ICC Statute, if the perpetrator became "voluntarily intoxicated under such circumstances that the person knew, or disregarded the risk, that, as a result of the intoxication, he or she was likely to engage in conduct constituting a crime within the jurisdiction of the Court."[396]

---

[393] See ICC Statute, Art. 31(1)(a) ("destroy"); *Prosecutor* v. *Mucić* et al., ICTY (Appeals Chamber), judgment of 20 February 2001, para. 587; A. Eser, in O. Triffterer (ed.), *Commentary on the Rome Statute of the International Criminal Court* (1999), Art. 31, marginal no. 22.

[394] See also *Prosecutor* v. *Banović*, ICTY (Trial Chamber), judgment of 28 October 2003, paras. 79 et seq.; *Prosecutor* v. *Češić*, ICTY (Trial Chamber), judgment of 11 March 2004, paras. 88 et seq.

[395] Summarized in A. Eser, in O. Triffterer (ed.), *Commentary on the Rome Statute of the International Criminal Court* (1999), Art. 31, marginal no. 25; G.-J. Knoops, *Defenses in Contemporary International Criminal Law* (2001), p. 117. One consequence of the separate regulation of intoxication in Art. 31(1)(b) of the ICC Statute is that the presumption of mental defect might be ruled out as a basis for exclusion of responsibility in cases where the perpetrator used intoxicating substances; see K. Ambos, in A. Cassese, P. Gaeta and J.R.W.D. Jones (eds.), *The Rome Statute of the International Criminal Court*, Vol. 1 (2002), p. 1003 at p. 1020.

[396] See ICC Statute, Art. 31(1)(b), clause 2.

The provisions of the ICC Statute that lead to exclusion of responsibility if the perpetrator did not **471** voluntarily become intoxicated – that is, for example, if he was not aware of imbibing an intoxicating substance or was forced to imbibe it[397] – reflect general principles of law.[398] This is probably not the case for exclusion of responsibility for voluntary intoxication. Given the varying treatment of such cases in domestic legal systems, it appears that in this case the Statute's rule finds no support in general principles of law, nor is there evidence of any corresponding rule of customary international law.

1. Destruction of the Capacity to Appreciate or Control Conduct

Exclusion from responsibility presumes the presence of a state of intoxication caused by **472** imbibing substances with toxic effects.[399] Most significant from a practical point of view are alcohol and drugs. The perpetrator must lose the ability to appreciate or control his or her conduct due to the state of intoxication. It is not possible to state a general rule on when to infer a state of intoxication that would free a perpetrator from criminal liability – for example, on the basis of a certain concentration of an intoxicating substance in his or her blood. Most important are the circumstances of the individual case. A simple diminution of the ability to appreciate or control conduct is not enough to exclude responsibility.[400]

2. Exclusion of Responsibility for Voluntary Intoxication?

The question of criminal liability of perpetrators whose inability to appreciate or control **473** their behavior is the result of voluntary intoxication is a question of extreme practical significance, and is also particularly sensitive with regard to legal policy.[401]

While states at the Rome Conference quickly agreed to recognize involuntary intoxication as a basis **474** for exclusion of responsibility, the question whether and to what extent voluntary intoxication

---

[397] See G.-J. Knoops, *Defenses in Contemporary International Criminal Law* (2001), pp. 119 et seq.

[398] According to A. Cassese, in A. Cassese, P. Gaeta and J.R.W.D. Jones (eds.), *The Rome Statute of the International Criminal Court*, Vol. 1 (2002), p. 951 at p. 954, they are even part of customary law.

[399] See A. Eser, in O. Triffterer (ed.), *Commentary on the Rome Statute of the International Criminal Court* (1999), Art. 31, marginal no. 25; G.-J. Knoops, *Defenses in Contemporary International Criminal Law* (2001), p. 117. Conduct based on endogenous causes is not included within Art. 31(b)(a) of the ICC Statute, but may be considered in the context of Art. 31(a)(1).

[400] See A. Eser, in O. Triffterer (ed.), *Commentary on the Rome Statute of the International Criminal Court* (1999), Art. 31, marginal no. 26; G.-J. Knoops, *Defenses in Contemporary International Criminal Law* (2001), p. 118. As with the reduced ability to appreciate and control conduct because of mental defect, however, the punishment may be mitigated. See also marginal no. 468. In the relatively few cases in which international courts have considered the legality of acts committed when intoxicated, they have generally approached it only from the perspective of whether mitigation of punishment is in order. For details, see K. Ambos, *Der Allgemeine Teil des Völkerstrafrechts* (2002), pp. 158 et seq.

[401] The commission of crimes under international law not infrequently occurs under the influence of intoxicating substances. For example, it was reported of the internment camps in Bosnia that the tormentors were generally under the influence of alcohol or drugs, see R. Gutman in T. Zülch (ed.), *"Ethnische Säuberung" – Völkermord für "Großserbien"* (1993), p. 105 at p. 121; C. Nill-Theobald, *"Defences" bei Kriegsverbrechen am Beispiel Deutschlands und der USA* (1998), p. 383.

should free the perpetrator from responsibility caused conflict until the very end.[402] The background to the discussion was the differing treatment of these cases in national legal systems. Some legal systems reject the exclusion of criminal responsibility for voluntary intoxication in principle.[403] Sometimes, consumption of alcohol before commission of a crime is even considered an aggravating circumstance.[404] In other legal systems, on the other hand, even voluntary intoxication can be a reason to exclude responsibility or mitigate punishment.[405]

475 Article 31(1)(b), clause 2, of the ICC Statute charts a middle course. Voluntary intoxication does not rule out exclusion of responsibility across the board, but only if the perpetrator, when becoming intoxicated, knew for certain that he would commit a crime under international law while intoxicated or disregarded the risk of committing such a crime. It is necessary for the perpetrator to have been aware of the risk of his conduct while intoxicated, but to have acted nevertheless. Thus to rule out the defense of intoxication, an aggravated form of negligence is sufficient in regard to the commission of the crime under international law.[406]

476 The result is that a loss of capacity to appreciate or control one's conduct through voluntary intoxication only works to free the perpetrator from responsibility if he or she was not aware of the risk of committing a crime under international law while intoxicated.[407] In any case, the provision makes it impossible to exclude the criminal responsibility of perpetrators who become voluntarily intoxicated to free themselves from inhibitions in order to commit crimes. Fears that the Statute's rule would make it impos-

---

[402] See A. Eser, in O. Triffterer (ed.), *Commentary on the Rome Statute of the International Criminal Court* (1999), Art. 31, marginal no. 24; P. Saland, in R.S. Lee (ed.), *The International Criminal Court, The Making of the Rome Statute* (1999), p. 189 at pp. 206 et seq. On the preliminary drafts, see W.A. Schabas, *European Journal of Crime, Criminal Law and Criminal Justice* 1998, p. 399 at p. 423. The compromise ultimately agreed upon came about only with the elimination of a footnote in the Draft ICC Statute (1998) under which exclusion of responsibility would have been impossible generally for genocide and crimes against humanity. See K. Ambos, in A. Cassese, P. Gaeta and J.R.W.D. Jones (eds.) *The Rome Statute of the International Criminal Court*, Vol. 1 (2002), p. 1003 at p. 1030.

[403] Such a regulation is found, for example, in the US Rules of Courts Martial, see Rule 916k(2): "Voluntary intoxication, whether caused by alcohol or drugs, is not a defense. However, evidence of any degree of voluntary intoxication may be introduced for the purpose of raising a reasonable doubt as to the existence of actual knowledge, specific intent, wilfulness, or a premeditated design to kill." See also Sec. 2.08 Model Penal Code; Art. 20(2) of the Spanish Criminal Code; see also K. Ambos, in A. Cassese, P. Gaeta and J.R.W.D. Jones (eds.), *The Rome Statute of the International Criminal Court*, Vol. 1 (2002), p. 1003 at p. 1030; W.A. Schabas, *European Journal of Crime, Criminal Law and Criminal Justice* 1998, p. 399 at pp. 423 et seq.

[404] See *Prosecutor* v. *Kvočka* et al., ICTY (Trial Chamber), judgment of 2 November 2001, para. 706: "While a state of intoxication could constitute a mitigating circumstance if it is forced or coerced, the Trial Chamber cannot accept Zigić's contention that an intentionally procured diminished mental state could result in a mitigated sentence. Indeed, the Trial Chamber considers that, particularly in contexts where violence is the norm and weapons are carried, intentionally consuming drugs or alcohol constitutes an aggravating rather than a mitigating factor."

[405] See K. Ambos, 10 *Criminal Law Forum* (1999), p. 1 at p. 25.

[406] See also the French ("qu'elle savait que . . . elle risquait d'adopter . . . un crime . . . ou qu'elle n'ait tenu aucun compte de ce risque") and Spanish ("a sabiendas de que . . . probablemente incurriria en una . . . crimen . . . o haya hecho caso omiso del riesgo de que ello ocurriere") original texts.

[407] See also A. Eser, in O. Triffterer (ed.), *Commentary on the Rome Statute of the International Criminal Court* (1999), Art. 31, marginal no. 27.

sible to punish a large number of war crimes and crimes against humanity[408] appear to be unjustified.[409]

VIII. Other Grounds for Excluding Responsibility

Antonio Cassese: Justifications and Excuses in International Criminal Law, in Antonio Cassese, **477** Paola Gaeta and John R.W.D. Jones (eds.), *The Rome Statute of the International Criminal Court: A Commentary*, Vol. 1 (2002), pp. 951 et seq.; Albin Eser: ICC Statute, Article 31, in Otto Triffterer (ed.), *Commentary on the Rome Statute of the International Criminal Court, Observers' Notes, Article by Article* (1999), pp. 537 et seq.; Hans-Heinrich Jescheck: *Die Verantwortlichkeit der Staatsorgane nach Völkerstrafrecht, Eine Studie zu den Nürnberger Prozessen* (1952), pp. 395 et seq.; Christiane Nill-Theobald: *"Defences" bei Kriegsverbrechen am Beispiel Deutschlands und der USA* (1998), pp. 281 et seq., pp. 350 et seq.; Stefan Oeter: Reprisals, in Dieter Fleck (ed.), *The Handbook of Humanitarian Law in Armed Conflict* (1999), marginal nos. 476 et seq.

The discussion so far has been limited to grounds for excluding responsibility that are **478** regulated in the ICC Statute. But other circumstances in addition to these may lead to exclusion of responsibility under international criminal law.[410] This is confirmed by Article 31(3) of the ICC Statute, under which the Court may take into consideration other grounds for exclusion of responsibility in addition to those provided for in Article 31(1) or elsewhere in the Statute, "where such a ground is derived from applicable law as set forth in article 21."

Most significant, especially where the laws of war are concerned, are reprisals and **479** military necessity.[411] A reprisal is conduct that violates international law and is used by a

---

[408] Footnote 24 to Art. 31 of the Draft ICC Statute (1998) still stated: "If this text [the rule in the later Art. 31(1)(b) second clause of the ICC Statute] were to be retained, the ground for excluding criminal responsibility would apply in all cases of voluntary intoxication except for those in which the person became intoxicated in order to commit the crime in an intoxicated condition (*actio libera in causa*). This would probably lead to a great number of war crimes and crimes against humanity going unpunished." See also A. Eser, in O. Triffterer (ed.), *Commentary on the Rome Statute of the International Criminal Court* (1999), Art. 31, marginal no. 27 and K. Ambos, in A. Cassese, P. Gaeta and J.R.W.D. Jones (eds.), *The Rome Statute of the International Criminal Court*, Vol. 1 (2002), p. 1003 at pp. 1030 et seq.

[409] The circumstances, e.g., overseers in an internment camp getting drunk together, would often reveal that an awareness of the risk must have been present.

[410] See A. Cassese, in A. Cassese, P. Gaeta and J.R.W.D. Jones (eds.), *The Rome Statute of the International Criminal Court*, Vol. 1 (2002), p. 951 at pp. 953 et seq.; A. Eser, in A. Cassese, P. Gaeta and J.R.W.D. Jones (eds.), *The Rome Statute of the International Criminal Court*, Vol. 1 (2002), p. 767 at p. 773. From a structural point of view, abandonment is also a ground for exclusion of responsibility. Given the close substantive connection, this is treated together with attempts, see marginal nos. 500 et seq.

[411] At first, the intention was to regulate reprisals and military necessity in the ICC Statute as grounds for exclusion of responsibility. A note to Art. 33 of the Draft ICC Statute (1998) states on the issue: "It was questioned whether such grounds as military necessity could be dealt with in connection with the definition of war crimes." Given the highly disparate positions on reprisals and military necessity as grounds for exclusion of responsibility, no such provision was ultimately adopted into the Statute. Summarized by P. Saland, in R.S. Lee (ed.), *The International Criminal Court, The Making of the Rome Statute* (1999), p. 189 at p. 209 and R. Boed, 3 *Yale Human Rights and Development Law Journal* (2000), pp. 1 et seq.

subject of international law as a coercive measure, in response to conduct by another subject of international law that also violates international law.[412] An example is the use of prohibited weapons in response to serious violations of international humanitarian law committed by the opposing side.[413]

480 It is generally believed that the permissibility of reprisals can only be considered in connection with an armed conflict. Thus they do not come into play at all as a justification for genocide or crimes against humanity committed in peacetime. But even in connection with war crimes, reprisals may only function as a basis for excluding responsibility within narrow parameters. Reprisals must be ordered by the top government or military leadership, their use must be proportional, they may only be used as a last resort and not in retaliation, and finally, considerations of humanity must be taken into account. Today, therefore, this legal concept is granted at most only a narrow scope of application.[414] Developments in international humanitarian law suggest that reprisals will ultimately be deemed completely inadmissible.

481 We speak of military necessity when one state commits a violation of international law vis-à-vis another state in order to defend itself against a military threat.[415] Military necessity can lead to exclusion of responsibility for crimes under international law in exceptional cases – specifically, when the definition of the crime makes liability dependent on whether the conduct was justified by military necessity. This is the case for several war crimes, such as destruction and appropriation of property under Article 8(2)(a)(iv) and (e)(xii) of the ICC Statute, and destruction and devastation of cities, towns or villages under Article 3(b) of the ICTY Statute and Article 6(b) of the Nuremberg Charter.[416]

482 The victim's consent does not free a perpetrator of responsibility for crimes under international law.[417] Crimes under international law target interests beyond those of the

---

[412] For more on reprisals as a ground for exclusion of responsibility and its requirements, see *Prosecutor* v. *Kupreškić* et al., ICTY (Trial Chamber), judgment of 14 January 2000, paras. 527 et seq.; A. Cassese, in A. Cassese, P. Gaeta and J.R.W.D. Jones (eds.), *The Rome Statute of the International Criminal Court*, Vol. 1 (2002), pp. 951 et seq.; C. Greenwood, 20 *Netherlands Yearbook of Humanitarian Law* (1989), pp. 47 et seq.; F. Kalshoven, in L.C. Vohrah et al. (eds.), *Man's Inhumanity to Man* (2003), pp. 481 et seq.; S. Oeter, in D. Fleck (ed.), *The Handbook of Humanitarian Law in Armed Conflicts* (1999), marginal no. 476.

[413] See A. Cassese, in A. Cassese, P. Gaeta and J.R.W.D. Jones (eds.), *The Rome Statute of the International Criminal Court*, Vol. 1 (2002), pp. 951 et seq.

[414] *Prosecutor* v. *Kupreškić* et al., ICTY (Trial Chamber), judgment of 14 January 2000, para. 530: "[W]hile reprisals have had a modicum of justification in the past, when they constituted practically the only effective means of compelling the enemy to abandon unlawful acts of warfare to comply in future with international law at present they can no longer be justified in this manner." Explanatory Memorandum of the (German) Code of Crimes Against International Law [*Völkerstrafgesetzbuch, VStGB*], BT-Drs. 14/8524, pp. 15 et seq. See also F. Kalshoven, in L.C. Vohrah et al. (eds.), *Man's Inhumanity to Man* (2003), p. 481 at pp. 483 et seq.

[415] See I. Brownlie, *Principles of Public International Law*, 6th edn. (2003), p. 448; A. Cassese, *International Law* (2001), pp. 195 et seq.; M.N. Shaw, *International Law*, 5th edn. (2003), pp. 1031 et seq.

[416] See marginal nos. 997 et seq., 1003.

[417] See A. Eser, in K. Schmoller (ed.), *Festschrift für Triffterer* (1996), p. 755 at pp. 768 et seq. The defendants' claim that the victims consented was dealt with by the courts as early as the Nuremberg follow-up trials; see US Military Tribunal, Nuremberg, judgment of 17 April 1947 (*Milch*, so–called

individual, which the individual has no power to surrender. However, the victim's consent is always taken into account if the definition of the crime itself makes the victim's objection a prerequisite for liability.[418] Still, the voluntary nature of the victim's agreement in such cases must always be carefully examined.[419]

When duties collide, the perpetrator can fulfill only one of two conflicting obligations.[420] Exclusion of responsibility for conflicting obligations was accepted, in principle, in connection with the punishment of the so-called "euthanasia doctors."[421] **483**

A plea of *tu quoque* does not lead to exclusion of responsibility. A perpetrator's conduct in violation of international law cannot be justified by pointing to conduct by his or her opponent that also violated international law.[422] No basis is found in either customary international law or treaty law for taking this as grounds for exclusion. Since the end of World War II, courts confronted with such a defense plea have rightly refused to accept it as a reason to exclude liability.[423] **484**

G. Inchoate Crimes

Kai Ambos: *Der Allgemeine Teil des Völkerstrafrechts, Ansätze einer Dogmatisierung* (2002), pp. 707 et seq.; Antonio Cassese: *International Criminal Law* (2003), pp. 190 et seq.; Albin Eser: Individual Criminal Responsibility, in Antonio Cassese, Paola Gaeta and John R.W.D. Jones (eds.), *The Rome Statute of the International Criminal Court: A Commentary*, Vol. 1 (2002), pp. 767 et seq.; Otto Triffterer: Bestandsaufnahme zum Völkerstrafrecht, in Gerd Hankel and Gerhard Stuby (eds.), *Strafgerichte gegen Menschheitsverbrechen, Zum Völkerstrafrecht 50 Jahre nach den Nürnberger Prozessen* (1995), pp. 169 et seq. **485**

Milch Trial), in *Trials of War Criminals* II, pp. 775 et seq.; US Military Tribunal, Nuremberg, judgment of 30 July 1948 (*Krauch* et al., so-called IG Farben Trial), in *Trials of War Criminals* VIII, p. 1170; for discussion, see H.-H. Jescheck, *Die Verantwortlichkeit der Staatsorgane nach Völkerstrafrecht* (1952), pp. 335 et seq.

[418] See, e.g., the crime against humanity of forced pregnancy (Art. 7(1)(g), (2)(f) of the ICC Statute).

[419] See A. Eser, in K. Schmoller (ed.), *Festschrift für Triffterer* (1996), p. 755 at p. 769. Special care is required in judging voluntariness in cases of sexual violence. In this connection, ICTY Rule of Procedure and Evidence 96 establishes that "In cases of sexual assault: . . . (ii) consent shall not be allowed as a defence if the victim (a) has been subjected to or threatened with or has had reason to fear violence, duress, detention or psychological oppression, or (b) reasonably believed that if the victim did not submit, another might be so subjected, threatened or put in fear."

[420] See C. Nill-Theobald, *"Defences" bei Kriegsverbrechen am Beispiel Deutschlands und der USA* (1998), pp. 352 et seq.; H.-H. Jescheck, *Die Verantwortlichkeit der Staatsorgane nach Völkerstrafrecht* (1952), pp. 395 et seq.

[421] See Supreme Court in the British Occupied Zone, in *OGHSt* 1, p. 321 at p. 335; for detail, see C. Nill-Theobald, *"Defences" bei Kriegsverbrechen am Beispiel Deutschlands und der USA* (1998), p. 352, with additional notes.

[422] See C. Nill-Theobald, *"Defences" bei Kriegsverbrechen am Beispiel Deutschlands und der USA* (1998), pp. 365 et seq., p. 371. The Nuremberg Tribunal did not view the sinking of enemy ships by the German U-boot fleet without prior warning as a war crime, among other things "[i]n view of . . . an order of the British Admiralty announced on the 8th May, 1940, according to which all vessels should be sunk at sight in the Skagerrak," see IMT, judgment of 1 October 1946, in *The Trial of German Major War Criminals. Proceedings of the International Military Tribunal Sitting at Nuremberg, Germany*, Part 22, p. 509.

[423] For details, see *Prosecutor* v. *Kupreškić* et al., ICTY (Trial Chamber), judgment of 14 February 2000, para. 516; A. Eser, in K. Schmoller (ed.), *Festschrift für Triffterer* (1996), p. 755 at p. 771.

486   Carrying out the decision to commit a crime under international law may be considered a criminal plan or attempt even if not all the elements of the crime are executed. Attempts are explicitly made criminal in Article 25(3)(f) of the ICC Statute. Planning and preparing a crime under international law, however, is not criminal under the provisions of the ICC Statute.[424] The zone of criminality only begins once the perpetrator has taken a significant step toward carrying out the crime.[425] In contrast, customary international law provides that certain conduct occurring long before the actual execution of the crime may be criminal. Here we must distinguish between conspiracy to commit a crime, planning to commit a crime, and preparing a crime under international law.

487   The Nuremberg and Tokyo Charters already extended criminality to preliminary conduct engaged in long before the crime began to be executed. In addition to the actual "waging" of war, Article 6(a) of the Nuremberg Charter also criminalized not only "planning, preparation, initiation" of a war of aggression, but also "participation in a common plan or conspiracy for the accomplishment" of such a crime.[426] In addition, Article 6 of the Nuremberg Charter provided that anyone participating in the "formulation" of such a plan or in a conspiracy to commit a crime was responsible for all acts performed in the execution of the plan. Article 7(1) of the ICTY Statute and Article 6(1) of the ICTR Statute provide a basis for criminal responsibility for acts before the start of an attempt. They criminalize anyone who has "planned" or "otherwise" taken part in the "planning [or] preparation" of the crime.

I. Conspiracy

488   Criminality is shifted farthest back in time through the concept of conspiracy.[427] It penalizes mere agreement between two or more persons to commit a crime. The commission of the intended crime is not necessarily required. The justification for this is largely preventive, since it enables the justice system to intervene before any harm has been inflicted.[428] From a doctrinal perspective, conspiracy lies somewhere between the doctrines of participation and criminal preparation, and is normally seen as a crime in its own right.[429]

489   The Genocide Convention, as well as the ICTR and ICTY Statutes, explicitly criminalize conspiracy to commit genocide.[430] These provisions reflect customary international law.[431] In light of the Nuremberg judgment, there is good reason to assume that under customary international law, conspiracy to commit a crime of aggression is a

---

[424] Under Art. 23(7)(e) of the Draft ICC Statute (1998), anyone who "[intentionally] [participates in planning] [plans] to commit such a crime which in fact occurs or is attempted" is subject to criminal sanction.

[425] See marginal no. 495.

[426] See also CCL No. 10, Art. II(1)(a), (2).

[427] The concept of "conspiracy" is found in many national legal systems, above all in those following the penal tradition of the common law, see, e.g., G. Fletcher, *Rethinking Criminal Law* (2000), pp. 646 et seq.

[428] See A. Ashworth, *Principles of Criminal Law*, 4th edn. (2003), p. 455.

[429] For a decisive view, see G. Fletcher, *Rethinking Criminal Law* (2000), pp. 646 et seq.

[430] Genocide Convention, Art. III(b); ICTY Statute, Art. 4(3)(b); ICTR Statute, Art. 2(3)(b).

[431] See A. Cassese, *International Criminal Law* (2003), p. 197; K. Kittichaisaree, *International Criminal Law* (2001), pp. 248 et seq.

crime as well; its requirements were further clarified by the Nuremberg Tribunal.[432] There is no basis in customary international law, however, for the crime of conspiracy to commit a war crime or a crime against humanity.[433] In the view of the Nuremberg Tribunal, which was repeatedly affirmed in subsequent jurisprudence on the basis of Control Council Law No. 10, criminality under the Nuremberg Charter did not extend to cover conspiracy to commit war crimes or crimes against humanity.[434]

After intensive debates, the delegates to the Rome Conference decided not to adopt the stipulations on conspiracy contained in the Nuremberg Charter and the ICTY and ICTR Statutes. The ICC Statute's surrogate for the crime of conspiracy is Article 25(3)(d).[435] **490**

II. Planning and Preparation

Planning is defined as the design of the commission of a specific crime under international law.[436] Preparation is any dangerous conduct intended to further the planned crime. **491**

Under customary international law, planning and preparation of a crime under international law are definitely criminal only with regard to the crime of aggression.[437] However, in light of the provisions of the ICTY Statute and the ICTY's judgments, there is a great deal of evidence that planning and preparation of genocide, crimes against humanity, and war crimes are also criminal under customary international law.[438] The ICC Statute did not adopt this shift of criminality to the preparatory phase. **492**

---

[432] See IMT, judgment of 1 October 1946, in *The Trial of German Major War Criminals. Proceedings of the International Military Tribunal Sitting at Nuremberg, Germany*, Part 22, pp. 447 et seq.

[433] See also A. Cassese, *International Criminal Law* (2003), p. 191.

[434] See IMT, judgment of 1 October 1946, in *The Trial of German Major War Criminals. Proceedings of the International Military Tribunal Sitting at Nuremberg, Germany*, Part 22, p. 449; US Military Tribunal, Nuremberg, judgment of 26 August 1947 (*Brandt* et al., so-called Medical Trial), in *Trials of War Criminals* II, p. 173; US Military Tribunal, Nuremberg, judgment of 28 October 1948 (*von Leeb* et al., so-called High Command Trial), in *Trials of War Criminals* XI, pp. 482 et seq.; US Military Tribunal, Nuremberg, judgment of 3 November 1947 (*Pohl* et al.), in *Trials of War Criminals* V, pp. 961 et seq.

[435] See marginal no. 364.

[436] See *Prosecutor v. Krstić*, ICTY (Trial Chamber), judgment of 2 August 2001, para. 601, with additional citations: "'planning' means that one or more persons design the commission of a crime at both the preparatory and execution phases"; *Prosecutor v. Stakić*, ICTY (Trial Chamber), judgment of 31 July 2003, para. 443; See also A. Cassese, *International Criminal Law* (2003), p. 192. There is disagreement over whether the criminality of planning requires the actual commission of the crime, see *Prosecutor v. Kordić and Čerkez*, ICTY (Trial Chamber), judgment of 26 February 2001, para. 386, on the one hand, (no accessory), and *Prosecutor v. Rutaganda*, ICTR (Trial Chamber), judgment of 6 December 1999, para. 34, on the other hand; see A. Cassese, *International Criminal Law* (2003), pp. 192 et seq.

[437] See also marginal nos. 1178 et seq.

[438] See *Prosecutor v. Mucić* et al., ICTY (Trial Chamber), judgment of 16 November 1998, para. 321: "participation . . . in any of several capacities [under Article 7(1)] is in clear conformity with general principles of criminal law"; *Prosecutor v. Tadić*, ICTY (Trial Chamber), judgment of 7 May 1997, para. 669; A. Cassese, *International Criminal Law* (2003), p. 193; and marginal no. 487.

III. Attempt

493 Article 25(3)(f) of the ICC Statute criminalizes the attempt to commit a crime under international law.[439] Liability for attempt begins as soon as the perpetrator has taken a substantial step toward carrying out the crime.

494 At its core, this provision reflects customary international law. For although the law of attempts has heretofore played no independent role in the practice of international criminal law, and no general rules on attempts have been found in codifications of international criminal law,[440] it has generally been assumed that the crime of attempt is part of international criminal law.[441] It is generally noted in this regard that it would be inconsistent to punish even earlier preparatory actions, such as preparing a war of aggression or participating in a common plan or conspiracy to commit a crime under international law, while leaving unpunished attempts to commit the crime.[442] At the same time, it must be assumed that the law of attempts claims a place in international law as a general principle of law.[443]

495 Criminal responsibility for attempt requires, under Article 25(3)(f) of the ICC Statute, the undertaking of conduct that "commences" the execution of a crime against international law "by means of a substantial step." Under this unfortunate wording,[444] the line between preparatory actions, which are not criminal under the ICC Statute, and criminal attempts is crossed if the perpetrator has begun to execute the crime and a material element of the definition of the crime is already in place.[445] In addition, however, conduct taking place before the actual execution may also be criminal.[446] A "substantial step" is present if the perpetrator's purpose has been reinforced or corroborated.[447]

---

[439] For more on these provisions, see K. Ambos, *Der Allgemeine Teil des Völkerstrafrechts* (2002), pp. 707 et seq.

[440] Art. III(d) of the Genocide Convention is an exception; the criminality of attempted genocide is also established under ICTY Statute, Art. 4(3)(d), and ICTR Statute, Art. 2(3)(d).

[441] See A. Cassese, *International Criminal Law* (2003), pp. 194 et seq.; A. Eser, in A. Cassese, P. Gaeta and J.R.W.D. Jones (eds.), *The Rome Statute of the International Criminal Court*, Vol. 1 (2002), p. 767 at p. 807.

[442] See A. Eser, in A. Cassese, P. Gaeta and J.R.W.D. Jones (eds.), *The Rome Statute of the International Criminal Court*, Vol. 1 (2002), p. 767 at pp. 807 et seq.

[443] See O. Triffterer, in G. Hankel and G. Stuby (eds.), *Strafgerichte gegen Menschheitsverbrechen* (1995), p. 169 at p. 233.

[444] To separate criminal attempt and mere non-criminal preparation, the provision connects two criteria that are otherwise usually applied in the alternative: "commencement of execution," a criterion borrowed from French criminal law, and a "substantial step" toward carrying out the crime, according to the model of US law. See K. Ambos, in O. Triffterer (ed.), *Commentary on the Rome Statute of the International Criminal Court* (1999), Art. 25, marginal no. 32. See also Sec. 5.01 of the Model Penal Code; T. Weigend, in M.C. Bassiouni (ed.), *Commentaries on the International Law Commission's 1991 Draft Code of Crimes against the Peace and Security of Mankind* (1993), p. 113 at p. 117.

[445] See A. Eser, in A. Cassese, P. Gaeta and J.R.W.D. Jones (eds.), *The Rome Statute of the International Criminal Court*, Vol. 1 (2002), p. 767 at p. 812; K. Ambos, in O. Triffterer (ed.), *Commentary on the Rome Statute of the International Criminal Court* (1999), Art. 25, marginal no. 32.

[446] See A. Eser, in A. Cassese, P. Gaeta and J.R.W.D. Jones (eds.), *The Rome Statute of the International Criminal Court*, Vol. 1 (2002), p. 767 at p. 812.

[447] See Sec. 5.01(2) of the Model Penal Code: "when it is strongly corroborative of the actor's criminal purpose."

Under Article 25(3)(f), sentence 1, clause 2, if the crime is not carried out, this must be a result of **496**
"circumstances independent of the person's intentions." This unfortunate clause turns the
perpetrator's abandonment of the crime into a negative element of the definition of attempt.[448]

Participating in an attempt is criminal, as is an ineffective attempt.[449] The Statute makes **497**
no explicit provision for mitigation of punishment for attempted crimes under international law, but mitigation is easily possible within the framework of the sentencing rules.

The Statute's rules leave many questions unanswered. It is not clear when an attempt **498**
begins if more than one person is involved, or whether attempted participation is a
crime.[450] Explicit provision is made only for the crime of public incitement to genocide,
found in Article 25(3)(e).

If we recall the complex questions raised by attempt and abandonment in domestic **499**
criminal law, it becomes clear how much doctrinal effort is still needed to clarify the requirements for attempt and abandonment, which will be discussed below. However, it
remains to be seen to what extent attempt and abandonment will actually play a significant role in the work of international courts. The concentration on the most serious
crimes affecting the international community as a whole makes it likely that the focus
will continue to be on prosecution of fully executed crimes.[451]

IV. Abandonment

Under Article 25(3)(f), sentence 2 of the ICC Statute, a person is not guilty of at- **500**
tempt if he or she "abandons the effort to commit the crime or otherwise prevents
the completion of the crime . . . if that person completely and voluntarily gave up
the criminal purpose."

The rule in Article 25(3)(f) contains a partial error. It can be gathered from sentence 1 of this **501**
norm that no criminal liability arises for attempt if the crime fails to be carried out because of circumstances dependent on the person's intentions. Under sentence 2, there is no liability if a person
"abandons the effort to commit the crime or otherwise prevents the completion of the crime" and
in the process "completely and voluntarily gave up the criminal purpose." This repetition of the
rule on abandonment has been blamed on an editing error,[452] and it does not affect the result: if a
person abandons his or her efforts to commit the crime, there is no criminal liability.[453] However,
it remains unclear whether abandonment negates the offense or if it simply functions as grounds

---

[448] See marginal no. 501.

[449] For more, see K. Ambos, *Der Allgemeine Teil des Völkerstrafrechts* (2002), p. 488; A. Eser, in A.
Cassese, P. Gaeta and J.R.W.D. Jones (eds.), *The Rome Statute of the International Criminal Court*,
Vol. 1 (2002), p. 767 at p. 813.

[450] See K. Ambos, *Der Allgemeine Teil des Völkerstrafrechts* (2002), pp. 745 et seq.

[451] For a critical view of the inclusion of attempt in the *Draft Code* 1996 for this reason, see C.
Tomuschat, in G. Hankel and G. Stuby (eds.), *Strafgerichte gegen Menschheitsverbrechen* (1995), p. 270
at p. 288.

[452] See K. Ambos, *Der Allgemeine Teil des Völkerstrafrechts* (2002), pp. 709 et seq., with additional
citations; A. Eser, in A. Cassese, P. Gaeta and J.R.W.D. Jones (eds.), *The Rome Statute of the International Criminal Court*, Vol. 1 (2002), p. 767 at p. 815.

[453] See K. Ambos, in O. Triffterer (ed.), *Commentary on the Rome Statute of the International
Criminal Court* (1999), Art. 25, marginal no. 34.

for excluding responsibility. This could have an effect on the possibility of participation in an attempted crime under international law, which is explicitly recognized by the ICC Statute in Article 25(3)(b), (c), and (d).

H. Omissions

502 Kai Ambos: *Der Allgemeine Teil des Völkerstrafrechts, Ansätze einer Dogmatisierung* (2002), pp. 667 et seq.; Antonio Cassese: *International Criminal Law* (2003), pp. 200 et seq.; Claus Kress: Die Kristallisation eines Allgemeinen Teils des Völkerstrafrechts: Die Allgemeinen Prinzipien des Strafrechts im Statut des Internationalen Strafgerichtshofs, *Humanitäres Völkerrecht-Informationsschriften* 1999, pp. 4 et seq.; Per Saland: International Law Principles, in Roy S. Lee (ed.), *The International Criminal Court, The Making of the Rome Statute* (1999), pp. 189 et seq.

503 In certain circumstances, a mere omission can amount to a crime under international criminal law.[454] This is clearly the case where the definitions of offenses explicitly criminalize the omission of certain conduct. In such cases, the criminal conduct consists in the very fact that the perpetrator failed to act.

504 An example is starvation of civilians in armed conflict under Article 8(2)(b)(xxv) of the ICC Statute. Here the criminal conduct consists in the fact that the perpetrator deprives civilians of food necessary for survival.[455] "The deprivation of access to food and medicine" is expressly included in connection with the crime against humanity of extermination in Article 7(1)(b) and (2)(b).[456] A further example relates to command responsibility under Article 28;[457] the basis for criminal liability in this case is the failure to prevent or to report a crime under international law.

505 For numerous other crimes, the equation of acting and not acting arises not from a codified definition of the crime, but from customary international law. This has been affirmed in various decisions by both the Yugoslavia and the Rwanda Tribunals. Examples are the war crimes of killing,[458] torture,[459] and wilfully causing great suffering.[460] The Rwanda Court additionally found that accessorial liability, in the form of aiding and abetting, may also include omissions.[461]

506 It is a matter of dispute whether a general liability for omissions, beyond these areas, can be incorporated into international criminal law – that is, whether even in cases in

---

[454] See, e.g., *Prosecutor* v. *Tadić*, ICTY (Appeals Chamber), judgment of 15 July 1999, para. 188: Art. 7(1) of the ICTY Statute "covers first and foremost the physical perpetration of a crime by the offender himself, or the culpable omission of an act that was mandated by a rule of criminal law."

[455] See marginal nos. 1083 et seq.

[456] See marginal no. 679.

[457] For thorough discussion, see marginal nos. 386 et seq.

[458] See *Prosecutor* v. *Mucić* et al., ICTY (Trial Chamber), judgment of 16 November 1998, para. 424; *Prosecutor* v. *Kordić and Čerkez*, ICTY (Trial Chamber), judgment of 26 February 2001, para. 236.

[459] *Prosecutor* v. *Mucić* et al., ICTY (Trial Chamber), judgment of 16 November 1998, para. 494.

[460] *Prosecutor* v. *Mucić* et al., ICTY (Trial Chamber), judgment of 16 November 1998, para. 511.

[461] *Prosecutor* v. *Akayesu*, ICTR (Trial Chamber), judgment of 2 September 1998, para. 548: "aiding and abetting may consist in failing to act or refraining from action."

which conduct is formulated actively in the definition of the crime, violation of a corresponding duty to act is always a crime as well.[462]

No general liability norm similar to that found in Article 86 of Additional Protocol I ("failure to act when under a duty to do so") was included in the ICC Statute;[463] France, especially, expressed serious reservations about establishing general liability for omissions.[464] Given the varying situations in the major systems of criminal law, it is not possible to presume the existence of a corresponding general principle of law.[465] **507**

All the same, there are good reasons to presume that general criminal liability for omission is anchored in customary law. The lack of a general provision equating action and failure to act is not a convincing objection.[466] The aforementioned decisions of the international Tribunals, in particular, support the adoption of general liability for omission, at least if it causes a consequence prescribed by the definition of the crime. Some of the Nuremberg follow-up trials also recognized criminal responsibility for omission.[467] Ulti- **508**

---

[462] Rejecting this, see K. Ambos, *Der Allgemeine Teil des Völkerstrafrechts* (2002), p. 667; but see, e.g., A. Cassese, *International Criminal Law* (2003), p. 201: "It may therefore seem warranted to hold that [Additional Protocol I, Art. 86(1)] also crystallized a general principle on criminal liability for omission."

[463] Art. 28 of the Draft ICC Statute (1998) still provided for the following: "1. Conduct for which a person may be criminally responsible and liable for punishment as a crime can constitute either an act or an omission, or a combination thereof. 2. Unless otherwise provided and for the purposes of paragraph 1, a person may be criminally responsible and liable for punishment for an omission where the person [could] [has the ability], [without unreasonable risk of danger to him/herself or others,] but intentionally [with the intention to facilitate a crime] or knowingly fails to avoid the result of an offence where: (a) the omission is specified in the definition of the crime under this Statute; or (b) in the circumstances, [the result of the omission corresponds to the result of a crime committed by means of an act] [the degree of unlawfulness realized by such omission corresponds to the degree of unlawfulness to be realized by the commission of such act], and the person is [either] under a pre-existing [legal] obligation under this Statute to avoid the result of such crime [or creates a particular risk or danger that subsequently leads to the commission of such crime]."

[464] For thorough discussion, see P. Saland, in R.S. Lee (ed.), *The International Criminal Court, The Making of the Rome Statute* (1999), p. 189 at p. 212. At the same time, however, it is also reported that the majority of the negotiating delegations apparently assumed that in certain cases – some already addressed in the text – omissions should be criminal, see R.S. Clark, 12 *Criminal Law Forum* (2001), p. 291 at p. 303.

[465] See also C. Kress, *Humanitäres Völkerrecht-Informationsschriften* 1999, p. 4 at p. 9. French law, specifically, and legal systems that follow it recognize no general liability for omissions; for more information, see J. Pradel, *Droit Penal Comparé* (1995), p. 236.

[466] The report by Saland, chairman of the working group that drafted the general principles at the Rome Conference, points out: "Lengthy discussions in Rome showed that . . . it would be almost impossible to negotiate a solution [regarding the problem of criminal responsibility for omission] acceptable to all. I therefore made the suggestion of not having a general provision on omission at all. This was after all the situation in some legal systems . . . which does not prevent courts from construing criminal responsibility from omission under certain circumstances. . . . As a result, the issue of omission will be left to the Court's case law"; see P. Saland, in R.S. Lee (ed.), *The International Criminal Court, The Making of the Rome Statute* (1999), p. 189 at pp. 212 et seq.

[467] See, e.g., US Military Tribunal, Nuremberg, judgment of 20 August 1947 (*Brandt* et al., so-called Medical Trial), in *Trials of War Criminals* II, p. 193 (supervisory duty of head doctors in regard to their assistants' acts); US Military Tribunal, Nuremberg, judgment of 17 April 1947 (*Milch*, so-called Milch Trial), in *Trials of War Criminals* II, pp. 774 et seq.; US Military Tribunal, Nuremberg,

mately, it will be up to the International Criminal Court to decide the extent to which crimes under international law can be caused by omission as well as commission.

I. Official Capacity and Immunity

509 Dapo Akande: International Law Immunities and the International Criminal Court, 98 *American Journal of International Law* (2004), pp. 407 et seq.; Kai Ambos: Der Fall Pinochet und das anwendbare Recht, *Juristenzeitung* 1999, pp. 564 et seq.; Andrea Bianci: Immunity versus Human Rights: The Pinochet Case, 10 *European Journal of International Law* (1999), pp. 237 et seq.; Michael Bothe: Die strafrechtliche Immunität fremder Staatsorgane, 31 *Zeitschrift für ausländisches öffentliches Recht und Völkerrecht* (1971), pp. 246 et seq.; Antonio Cassese: *International Criminal Law* (2003), pp. 264 et seq.; Antonio Cassese: When may Senior State Officials be Tried for International Crimes? Some Comments on the Congo v. Belgium Case, 13 *European Journal of International Law* (2002), pp. 853 et seq.; J.-P. Fonteyne: Acts of State, in Rudolph Bernhardt (ed.), *Encyclopedia of Public International Law*, Vol. 1 (1992), pp. 17 et seq.; Hazel Fox: Enforcement Jurisdiction, Foreign State Property and Diplomatic Immunity, 34 *International and Comparative Law Quarterly* (1985), pp. 115 et seq.; Paola Gaeta: Official Capacity and Immunities, in A. Cassese, P. Gaeta and John R.W.D. Jones (eds.), *The Rome Statute of the International Criminal Court: A Commentary*, Vol. 1 (2002), pp. 975 et seq.; Claus Kress: Der Internationale Gerichtshof im Spannungsfeld von Völkerstrafrecht und Immunitätsschutz, Besprechung von IGH, Urteil vom 14. 2. 2002 (Demokratische Republik Kongo gegen Belgien), *Goltdammer's Archiv für Strafrecht* 2003, pp. 25 et seq.; Christiane Nill-Theobald: *"Defences" bei Kriegsverbrechen am Beispiel Deutschlands und der USA* (1998), pp. 372 et seq.; Matthias Ruffert: Pinochet Follow Up: The End of Sovereign Immunity?, 48 *Netherlands International Law Review* (2001), pp. 171 et seq.; Per Saland: International Criminal Law Principles, in Roy S. Lee (ed.), *The International Criminal Court, The Making of the Rome Statute* (1999), p. 189 at pp. 202 et seq.; Philippe Sands: International Law Transformed? From Pinochet to Congo . . . ?, 16 *Leiden Journal of International Law* (2003), pp. 37 et seq.; William A. Schabas: *An Introduction to the International Criminal Court*, 2nd edn. (2004), pp. 114 et seq.; Jill M. Sears: Confronting the "Culture of Impunity": Immunity of Heads of State from Nuremberg to *ex parte* Pinochet, 42 *German Yearbook of International Law* (1999), pp. 125 et seq.; Helmut Steinberger: State Immunity, in Rudolph Bernhardt (ed.), *Encyclopedia of Public International Law*, Vol. 4 (2000), pp. 615 et seq.; Otto Triffterer: ICC Statute, Article 27, in Otto Triffterer (ed.), *Commentary on the Rome Statute of the International Criminal Court, Observers' Notes, Article by Article* (1999), pp. 501 et seq.; Arthur Watts: The Legal Position in International Law of Heads of States, Heads of Governments and Foreign Ministers, 247 *Recueil des Cours*, Vol. III (1994), pp. 19 et seq.

I. Immunity and International Criminal Law

510 In international law, certain official acts and certain officials are granted immunity before foreign courts, especially foreign criminal courts. This immunity is particularly relevant to international criminal law because of the typical level of state involvement in crimes under international law.[468] A high degree of immunity could ultimately protect the most powerful authors of crimes under international law.

---

judgment of 28 October 1948 (*von Leeb* et al., so-called High Command Trial), in *Trials of War Criminals* XI, pp. 542 et seq.; See also K. Ambos, *Der Allgemeine Teil des Völkerstrafrechts* (2002), p. 138.

[468] See, e.g., A. Cassese, 13 *European Journal of International Law* (2002), p. 853 at p. 873; H.-H. Jescheck, *Die Verantwortlichkeit der Staatsorgane nach Völkerstrafrecht* (1952), p. 164; see also P. Gaeta,

Immunity under international law is based on two fundamental concepts. First, the principle of **511**
the sovereign equality of all states dictates that no state sit in judgment over another (*par in parem
non habet iudicium*).[469] Second, a minimum amount of transborder movement and action is required for the effective functioning of interstate relations.[470]

Traditionally, a distinction is made between (functional) immunity *ratione materiae* and (per- **512**
sonal) immunity *ratione personae*, based on their scope and effect.[471] Immunity *ratione materiae*
affects all official acts. These acts are ascribed to the state; only the state is responsible for them
under international law, not the official who carries them out. If a perpetrator is acting in an official capacity, for example as a minister, police officer or soldier, immunity *ratione materiae* would
thus prevent any individual criminal responsibility from accruing;[472] functional immunity therefore affects substantive law.

In contrast, international law grants immunity *ratione personae* to a limited group of state offi- **513**
cials whose freedom of action in international intercourse is especially important to the functioning of their state. These include heads of state[473] and diplomats,[474] as well as heads of government
and foreign ministers.[475] Personal immunity does not prevent criminal liability as such, but only

---

in A. Cassese, P. Gaeta and J.R.W.D. Jones (eds.), *The Rome Statute of the International Criminal
Court*, Vol. 1 (2002), pp. 975 et seq.; C. Kress, *Goltdammer's Archiv für Strafrecht* 2003, p. 25 at
pp. 30, 31, with additional citations.

[469] See *Prosecutor* v. *Blaškić*, ICTY (Appeals Chamber), judgment (on the Request of the Republic
Croatia for Review of the Decision of Trial Chamber II of 18 July 1997) of 29 October 1997, paras.
38, 41. All acts involving the exercise of sovereign power *(acta jure imperii)* are the subject of this state
immunity, but not other acts of state, especially economic actions *(acta jure gestionis)*. Immunities under international law must be distinguished from immunities and privileges granted by a state to its
employees on the *national level*. On the significance of these immunities in international criminal law,
see marginal no. 522, fn. 490.

[470] See A. Cassese, *International Criminal Law* (2003), p. 265.

[471] For more information, see A. Cassese, 13 *European Journal of International Law* (2002), p. 853
at pp. 862 et seq. This system of immunity under international law is addressed in Art. 27 of the ICC
Statute, see P. Gaeta, in A. Cassese, P. Gaeta and J.R.W.D. Jones (eds.), *The Rome Statute of the International Criminal Law*, Vol. 1 (2002), p. 975 at p. 978. Article 27(1) concerns the (lack of) a *substantive* legal effect of acts in an official capacity; Article 27(2) concerns immunities or procedural
regulations connected with official capacities, that is, provisions of *procedural law*. See also D. Akande,
98 *American Journal of International Law* (2004), p. 407 at pp. 419 et seq.

[472] See A. Cassese, 13 *European Journal of International Law* (2002), p. 853 at p. 863: "individual
criminal responsibility does not even arise," and *Prosecutor* v. *Blaškić*, ICTY (Appeals Chamber), judgment (on the Request of the Republic Croatia for Review of the Decision of Trial Chamber II of 18
July 1997) of 29 October 1997, para. 38. See also H. Fox, in L.C. Vohrah et al. (eds.), *Man's Inhumanity to Man* (2003), p. 297 at pp. 299 et seq.

[473] For thorough discussion, see C. Tangermann, *Die völkerrechtliche Immunität von Staatsober-
häuptern* (2002), pp. 104 et seq.

[474] See the *Vienna Convention on Diplomatic Relations* of 1961, 500 *UNTS* (1961), p. 95,
and especially Arts. 31 and 39. Consular officials enjoy only limited protection in the state of
residence; they can be prosecuted especially for serious crimes. See Arts. 41, 43 of the *Vienna
Convention on Consular Relations* of 1963, 596 *UNTS* (1963), p. 261. Other high representatives of a state can be exempted from the host states' jurisdiction for the period of an official
visit abroad, but no general immunity exists for them. See Arts. 21, 31 of the *Convention on
Special Missions* of 1969, UN Doc. A/RES/24/2530. For the privileges and immunities of the
ICC, see *Agreement of the Privileges and Immunities of the International Criminal Court* of 9 September 2002 (ICC-ASP/1/3), entry into force 22 July 2004.

[475] See *DR Congo* v. *Belgium*, ICJ, judgment of 14 February 2002 (Case Concerning the Arrest
Warrant of 11 April 2000), paras. 51, 53 et seq.; C. Kress, *Goltdammer's Archiv für Strafrecht* 2003,
p. 25 at pp. 31 et seq., is instructive.

creates an obstacle to prosecution.[476] Unlike functional immunity, it ends with the official's tenure in office. A former official may subsequently be taken to court for private acts even in other countries, even if these acts occurred during his or her tenure in office. For official acts, however, as with "simple" officials, immunity *ratione materiae* continues to apply, with no temporal limits.[477] Here functional and personal immunity overlap.[478]

514 Modern international law has resolved the tension[479] between immunity and international criminal law almost exclusively in favor of international criminal law. Except for some narrow areas in which certain important state dignitaries are protected from prosecution under international criminal law, the interests in protecting state sovereignty and maintaining the effective functioning of interstate relations have taken second place to the most effective and thorough possible prosecution of crimes under international law.

II. Irrelevance of Official Capacity

515 The fact that a perpetrator acts in his or her official capacity does not affect his or her responsibilities under international criminal law. Immunity *ratione materiae* thus does not affect the commission of crimes under international law. This view of immunity under international law is recognized in customary international law.[480] Indeed, the fact

---

[476] See A. Cassese, 13 *European Journal of International Law* (2002), p. 853 at pp. 864 et seq. ("procedural defence"). The ICJ correctly determined, in regard to personal immunity (of a foreign minister): "Jurisdictional immunity may well bar prosecution for a certain period or for certain offences; it cannot exonerate the person to whom it applies from all criminal responsibility," see *DR Congo v. Belgium*, ICJ, judgment of 14 February 2002 (Case Concerning the Arrest Warrant of 11 April 2000), para. 60. See also H. Fox, in L.C. Vohrah et al. (eds.), *Man's Inhumanity to Man* (2003), p. 297 at p. 301.

[477] See *Vienna Convention on Diplomatic Relations* of 1961, 500 *UNTS* (1961), p. 95, Art. 39(2), and *Vienna Convention on Consular Relations* of 1963, 596 *UNTS* (1963), p. 261, Art. 53 Abs. 4.

[478] See A. Cassese, *International Criminal Law* (2003), p. 267.

[479] See A. Cassese, 13 *European Journal of International Law* (2002), p. 853 at p. 854.

[480] See *Prosecutor v. Blaškić*, ICTY (Appeals Chamber), judgment (on the Request of the Republic Croatia for Review of the Decision of Trial Chamber II of 18 July 1997) of 29 October 1997, para. 41: "The general rule under discussion [that the individual organ may not be held accountable for acts or transactions performed in its official capacity] is well established in international law . . . . The few exceptions . . . arise from the norms of international criminal law prohibiting war crimes, crimes against humanity and genocide. Under these norms, those responsible for such crimes cannot invoke immunity from national or international jurisdiction even if they perpetrated such crimes while acting in their official capacity"; *Prosecutor v. Furundžija*, ICTY (Trial Chamber), judgment of 10 December 1998, para. 140; A. Cassese, *International Criminal Law* (2003), p. 267; H. Fox, in L.C. Vohrah et al. (eds.), *Man's Inhumanity to Man* (2003), p. 297 at p. 300; O. Triffterer, in O. Triffterer (ed.), *Commentary on the Rome Statute of the International Criminal Court* (1999), Art. 27, marginal no. 12. In part, the irrelevance of functional immunity is justified by the fact that international crimes are always "private" acts; thus there is from the start no place for a presumption of functional immunity. In this spirit, see, e.g., *DR Congo v. Belgium*, ICJ, judgment of 14 February 2002 (Case Concerning the Arrest Warrant of 11 April 2000), separate opinion of Judges Higgins, Kooijmans, and Buergenthal, para. 85 and separate opinion of Judge van den Wyngaert, para. 36. For a rightly very skeptical view, see A. Cassese, 13 *European Journal of International Law* (2002), p. 853 at pp. 866 et seq. The fact, above all, that it declares the most serious crimes of international concern to be private matters militates against this view.

that the crime is committed in the exercise of sovereign functions is often an aggravating circumstance.[481]

Article 27(1) of the ICC Statute affirms that official capacity neither exempts from criminal responsibility nor in and of itself constitutes a ground for reduction of sentence. The ICC Statute thus follows corresponding provisions of the Nuremberg and Tokyo Charters and the ICTY and ICTR Statutes.[482] The Nuremberg Tribunal explicitly established the irrelevance of functional immunity:

516

"The principle of international law, which under certain circumstances, protects the representatives of a state, cannot be applied to acts which are condemned as criminal by international law. The authors of these acts cannot shelter themselves behind their official position in order to be freed from punishment in appropriate proceedings. . . . [I]ndividuals have international duties which transcend the national obligations of obedience imposed by the individual State. He who violates the laws of war cannot obtain immunity while acting in pursuance of the authority of the State if the State in authorising action moves outside its competence under international law."[483]

517

Article 27(1) of the ICC Statute clarifies these prior rules by listing (though not exclusively)[484] various state officials whose actions are, in principle, granted immunity *ratione materiae*, but not for crimes under the Statute. These include heads of state and government, members of government or parliament, and other elected representatives or officials of a government.

518

In the case of crimes under international law, immunity *ratione materiae* is inapplicable not only to trials before international courts,[485] but also vis-à-vis state judiciaries. This, too, is today anchored in customary international law.[486] This development gained

519

---

[481] See O. Triffterer, in O. Triffterer (ed.), *Commentary on the Rome Statute of the International Criminal Court* (1999), Art. 27, marginal no. 20.

[482] Nuremberg Charter, Art. 7; Tokyo Charter, Art. 6. These rules were affirmed by the ILC in 1946 as the third Nuremberg Principle. See also CCL No. 10, Art. II No. 4(a); Genocide Convention, Art. IV; ICTY Statute, Art. 7(2); ICTR Statute, 6(2); see *Prosecutor* v. *Blaškić*, ICTY (Appeals Chamber), judgment (on the Request of the Republic Croatia for Review of the Decision of Trial Chamber II of 18 July 1997) of 29 October 1997, para. 41; *Prosecutor* v. *Furundžija*, ICTY (Trial Chamber), judgment of 10 December 1998, para. 140. Summarized in P. Gaeta, in A. Cassese, P. Gaeta and J.R.W.D. Jones (eds.), *The Rome Statute of the International Criminal Court*, Vol. 1 (2002), p. 975 at pp. 979 et seq.; O. Triffterer, in O. Triffterer (ed.), *Commentary on the Rome Statute of the International Criminal Court* (1999), Art. 27, marginal nos. 1 et seq.

[483] IMT, judgment of 1 October 1946, in *The Trial of German Major war Criminals. Proceedings of the International Military Tribunal Sitting at Nuremberg, Germany,* Part 22, p. 447.

[484] See O. Triffterer, in O. Triffterer (ed.), *Commentary on the Rome Statute of the International Criminal Court* (1999), Art. 27, marginal nos. 14 et seq.; D. Akande, 98 *American Journal of International Law* (2004), p. 407 at pp. 419 et seq.

[485] Thus the irrelevance of functional immunity already arises from the fact that genuine supranational jurisdiction *per definitionem* supersedes state governments and penal authority; see G. Dahm, J. Delbrück and R. Wolfrum, *Völkerrecht*, Vol. I/3, 2nd edn. (2002), p. 1018. To the extent that international jurisdiction is treaty-based, such as in the case of the International Criminal Court, the treaty parties have partially given up state immunity; thus this does not stand in the way of prosecution before the ICC. For immunities before the international Tribunals, see D. Akande, 98 *American Journal of International Law* (2004), p. 407 at pp. 415 et seq.

[486] See A. Cassese, 13 *European Journal of International Law* (2002), p. 853 at p. 870, with numerous examples from state practice; see also P. Gaeta, in A. Cassese, P. Gaeta and J.R.W.D. Jones (eds.)

significant momentum as a result of the decisions of the British House of Lords in the *Pinochet* case.[487]

III. (Limited) Immunity for Heads of State and Government, Foreign Ministers, and Diplomats

520 The personal immunity enjoyed by heads of state and government, foreign ministers, and diplomats only stands in the way of prosecution for crimes under international law for the duration of their tenure in office, and only in regard to state criminal courts.

521 Because the protective effect of personal immunity lasts only until the end of the official's tenure in office,[488] the obstacle to prosecution falls away as soon as this tenure ends. Former heads of state and government, foreign ministers, and diplomats may then be prosecuted without restriction.[489]

522 Distinctions must be made for persons holding office: The effect of immunity on trials falls away completely in the case of prosecution by an international court. This is now underscored in Article 27(2) of the ICC Statute for prosecution of crimes under international law by the International Criminal Court.[490] There is good reason also to presume

---

The Rome Statute of the International Criminal Court, Vol. 1 (2002), p. 975 at pp. 979 et seq.; P. Sands, 16 *Leiden Journal of International Law* (2003), pp. 37 et seq. Here the ICJ's *obiter dictum* is misleading: it finds prosecution of another country's former foreign minister possible if, among other things, the case involves "private" acts during his tenure in office, see *DR Congo* v. *Belgium*, ICJ, judgment of 14 February 2002 (Case Concerning the Arrest Warrant of 11 April 2000), para. 61. This passage of the opinion can only be brought into conformity with the generally-accepted thesis of the penetration of functional immunity if one either denies that international crimes ever have the quality of official acts or does not see the constellation presented by the Court in which prosecution may be possible to be exclusive. In this context, A. Cassese, 13 *European Journal of International Law* (2002), p. 853 at p. 876, points to the press release by the President of the Court, Guillaume, in which he states that this passage in the judgment should only be understood "by way of example," see ICJ, Press Statement of Judge Gilbert Guillaume, 14 February 2002.

[487] During a visit to London in 1998, Augusto Pinochet was arrested on the basis of a Spanish arrest warrant and later a deportation request. On final appeal, the Law Lords found that Pinochet was not protected by immunity from arrest and deportation, see In re *Augusto Pinochet Ugarte*, High Court of Justice, judgment of 28 October 1998, in 38 *ILM* (1999), pp. 68 et seq.; *Regina* v. *Bartle* and *Evans*, ex parte *Pinochet*, House of Lords, judgment of 25 November 1998, in 37 *ILM* (1998), pp. 1302 et seq.; judgment of 24 March 1999, in 38 *ILM* (1999), pp. 581 et seq.; For details, see A. Bianci, 10 *European Journal of International Law* (1999), pp. 239 et seq.; M. Byers, 10 *Duke Journal of Comparative and International Law* (2002), pp. 415 et seq.; M. Ruffert, 48 *Netherlands International Law Review* (2001), p. 171 at pp. 178 et seq.; P. Sands, 16 *Leiden Journal of International Law* (2003), p. 37 at pp. 45 et seq.

[488] See marginal no. 513.

[489] Among the most important practical examples are the trial of Hitler's successor Admiral Karl Dönitz before the Nuremberg Tribunal and the trial of the former Rwandan head of government Jean Kambanda before the Rwanda Tribunal; see *Prosecutor* v. *Kambanda*, ICTR (Trial Chamber), judgment of 4 September 1998; IMT, judgment of 1 October 1946, in *The Trial of German Major war Criminals. Proceedings of the International Military Tribunal Sitting at Nuremberg, Germany*, Part 22, p. 507.

[490] See C. Kress, in H. Grützner and P.G. Pötz (eds.), *Internationaler Rechtshilfeverkehr in Strafsachen*, Vol. 4, 2nd edn. (2002), Vor III 26 at marginal no. 61. According to this, obstacles to prosecution connected with a person's official capacity are irrelevant, regardless of whether they arise from international law or are provided for by domestic law.

a corresponding rule of customary international law.[491] The exclusion of immunity in customary international law will henceforth be significant primarily in regard to the possible trial of top representatives of non-party states by the International Criminal Court.

Article 98 of the ICC Statute only appears to conflict with the uncompromising stance manifested by Article 27 of the ICC Statute.[492] Article 98 does not allow the Court to request legal assistance from a state if this would require the state to act contrary to its immunity obligations with respect to other states.[493] The provision was meant only to take account of existing interstate agreements, to assure that they would not hinder ratification. **523**

Against this background, it is highly problematic for states like the United States to attempt to avoid the jurisdiction of the International Criminal Court by subsequently concluding bilateral non-extradition treaties. The United States has meanwhile concluded bilateral immunity agreements with over 80 countries that strictly bar the custodial state from surrendering its citizens to the International Criminal Court.[494] These treaties have caused serious misgivings, particularly in regard to states that are also parties to the Statute (such as Romania and Afghanistan), because such treaties are contrary to the purposes of the ICC Statute. **524**

Note must be taken, however, of the personal immunity of officeholders before domestic courts. Here, immunity *ratione personae* creates an obstacle to prosecution; without corresponding state practice, no exception for the prosecution of crimes under international law can be assumed.[495] **525**

---

[491] The question is disputed in the literature, see P. Gaeta, in A. Cassese, P. Gaeta and J.R.W.D. Jones (eds.), *The Rome Statute of the International Criminal Court*, Vol. 1 (2002), p. 975 at pp. 988, 995, 1000, sees no basis in customary law, but calls *de lege ferenda* for a presumption that immunity can be overcome at least if "it appears to be legally impossible or most unlikely for the alleged perpetrator to ever be brought to justice"; P. Sands, 16 *Leiden Journal of International Law* (2003), p. 37 at p. 38. See also *Prosecutor* v. *Milošević*, ICTY (Trial Chamber), decision of 8 November 2001, paras. 26 et seq., 33. Before the ICC Statute went into force, the irrelevance of procedural immunity was inferred as a corollary to the exclusion of substantive immunity: "The absence of any procedural immunity with respect to prosecution or punishment in appropriate judicial proceedings is an essential corollary of the absence of any substantive immunity or defence. It would be paradoxical to prevent an individual from invoking his official position to avoid responsibility for a crime only to permit him to invoke this consideration to avoid the consequences of this responsibility." See *Draft Code* 1996, commentary to Art. 7.

[492] See P. Gaeta, in A. Cassese, P. Gaeta and J.R.W.D. Jones (eds.), *The Rome Statute of the International Criminal Court*, Vol. 1 (2002), p. 975 at p. 992.

[493] Art. 98(1) of the ICC Statute lists the state and diplomatic immunities that may need to be considered. Art. 98(2) of the ICC Statute refers to other treaties, such as agreements on stationing troops for international operations (SOFAs). In cases under Art. 98, before making a request for surrender to the custodial state, the International Criminal Court must obtain a waiver of immunity from third states (such as the perpetrator's home country). The ICC Statute thus differs from the Statutes of the Yugoslavia and Rwanda Tribunals, which represent Security Council measures on the basis of Chapter VII of the UN Charter and with which all UN member states are therefore obliged to cooperate, see P. Gaeta, in A. Cassese, P. Gaeta and J.R.W.D. Jones (eds.), *The Rome Statute of the International Criminal Court*, Vol. 1 (2002), p. 975 at p. 989.

[494] In these agreements, the parties agree, "bearing in mind Article 98 of the Rome Statute," not to surrender government officials, employees, military personnel or nationals of a treaty party to the International Criminal Court or "any other entity or third country . . . for the purpose of surrender to or transfer to the International Criminal Court."

[495] See *DR Congo* v. *Belgium*, ICJ, judgment of 14 February 2002 (Case Concerning the Arrest Warrant of 11 April 2000), para. 56; A. Cassese, 13 *European Journal of International Law* (2002),

IV. Summary

526 In principle, neither immunity under national law nor immunity under international law prevents prosecution of crimes under international law. The only exception is prosecution of heads of state and government, foreign ministers, and diplomats while they are in office (immunity *ratione personae*), and only for prosecution by states. Prosecution by international courts is always possible; in the case of the International Criminal Court, this is true even when the perpetrator derives his or her immunity from a non-state party.

J. Multiplicity of Offenses

527 Gilbert Bitti: Two Bones of Contention Between Civil and Common Law: The Record of the Proceedings and the Treatment of a Concursus Delictorum, in Horst Fischer, C. Kress and Sascha R. Lüder (eds.), *International and National Prosecution of Crimes Under International Law, Current Developments* (2001), pp. 273 et seq.; Antonio Cassese: *International Criminal Law* (2003), pp. 212 et seq.; Richard May and Marieke Wierda: Is There a Hierarchy of Crimes in International Law?, in Lal Chand Vohrah et al. (eds.), *Man's Inhumanity to Man* (2003), pp. 511 et seq.; Olaoluwa Olusanya: *Double Jeopardy Without Parameters* (2004); William A. Schabas: Penalties, in Antonio Cassese, Paola Gaeta, and John R.W.D. Jones (eds.), *The Rome Statute of the International Criminal Court: A Commentary*, Vol. 2 (2002), pp. 1497 et seq.; Friedrich Stuckenberg: Multiplicity of Offences: Concursus Delictorum, in Horst Fischer, C. Kress and Sascha R. Lüder (eds.), *International and National Prosecution of Crimes Under International Law, Current Developments* (2001), pp. 559 et seq.; Susanne Walther: Cumulation of Offences, in Antonio Cassese, Paola Gaeta and John R.W.D. Jones (eds.), *The Rome Statute of the International Criminal Court: A Commentary*, Vol. 1 (2002), pp. 475 et seq.

528 It is often the case in international criminal law that a single perpetrator's conduct meets the definitions of several crimes. This occurs, first of all, because crimes under international law often overlap. This is true of killings, for example; depending on the elements present, they may be prosecuted simultaneously as genocide, crimes against humanity, and war crimes. Another phenomenon creates even more difficult issues of *concursus delictorum*. Crimes under international law are typically committed not through the individual acts of a single person (a blow, a shot), but through numerous individual acts by numerous individuals. Definitions of crimes like genocide or crimes against humanity describe entire complexes of crimes and can comprise conduct stretching over a long period of time, in some cases even several years. This raises the question whether and to what extent a perpetrator's individual acts should be classified as various independent crimes or as a single crime.

---

pp. 865 et seq.; P. Gaeta, in A. Cassese, P. Gaeta and J.R.W.D. Jones (eds.), *The Rome Statute of the International Criminal Court*, Vol. 1 (2002), p. 975 at pp. 984 et seq.; for discussion, see C. Kress, *Goltdammer's Archiv für Strafrecht* 2003, p. 25 at p. 33. But see *DR Congo* v. *Belgium*, ICJ, judgment of 14 February 2002 (Case Concerning the Arrest Warrant of 11 April 2000), separate opinion of Judge Al-Khasawneh (para. 7) and separate opinion Judge Van den Wyngaert (paras. 27 et seq.). This has been affirmed in the few trials of foreign heads of state still in office that have been held before national courts; see the trial of *Qaddafi* before the French Cour de Cassation, *Bulletin des arrets de la Cour de Cassation* (2001), p. 218; see S. Zappalá, 12 *European Journal of International Law* (2001), p. 595; additional examples in A. Cassese, *International Criminal Law* (2003), p. 866, fn. 37.

No rules exist to resolve such problems of multiplicity of offenses in either the **529** Nuremberg Charter or the Statutes of the *ad hoc* Tribunals.[496] The ICC Statute merely presumes the obvious possibility of a person being found guilty of more than one crime by providing in Article 78(3): "When a person has been convicted of more than one crime, the Court shall pronounce a sentence for each crime and a joint sentence specifying the total period of imprisonment. This period shall be no less than the highest individual sentence pronounced . . .."

I. International Case Law

Courts have dealt pragmatically with the issue of multiplicity of offenses. The Nurem- **530** berg Tribunal, for example, convicted numerous defendants of war crimes and crimes against humanity for the same acts, without any legal discussion of *concursus delictorum*. The first serious efforts to develop international legal rules on handling competing crimes were undertaken by the Yugoslavia Tribunal.[497] This case law has grown since then to the point that certain basic principles of an international doctrine of *concursus delictorum* may today be considered well-established. The methodological starting point is a distillation of general legal principles taken from the corresponding rules of national legal systems.[498]

II. Same Conduct

Where several individual acts are present that fulfill the definition of a crime, it must be **531** examined whether, in light of the applicable crime, they comprise the same conduct in a legal sense.[499]

Certain definitions of crimes explicitly link a variety of individual acts into a single unit. For geno- **532** cide, for example, conduct that meets the definition of the crime and is carried out as part of the same intent to commit genocide is combined into one act for legal purposes.[500] For crimes against humanity, a widespread or systematic attack on a civilian population presumes a large number of

---

[496] Indications are however also found in ICTY Rules of Procedure and Evidence 87 and 101.

[497] See the overview of developments in the case law of the Yugoslavia Tribunal in F. Stuckenberg, in H. Fischer, C. Kress and S.R. Lüder (eds.), *International and National Prosecution of Crimes under International Law* (2001), pp. 573 et seq.

[498] Treatment of the problem of multiple offenses in common law and civil law legal circles differs less in outcome than in form; see discussion in S. Walther, in A. Cassese, P. Gaeta and J.R.W.D. Jones (eds.), *The Rome Statute of the International Criminal Court*, Vol. 1 (2002), p. 475 at pp. 478 et seq.; on US law, see F. Stuckenberg, 113 *Zeitschrift für die gesamte Strafrechtswissenschaft* (2001), pp. 146 et seq.

[499] In place of "same conduct," there may also be "same act or transaction," see *Prosecutor* v. *Kunarac* et al., ICTY (Appeals Chamber), judgment of 12 June 2002, para. 173. "Same conduct" apparently will always be present if the allegations relate to the "the same set of facts," see *Prosecutor* v. *Musema*, ICTR (Appeals Chamber), judgment of 16 November 2001, para. 358; see also *Prosecutor* v. *Vasiljević*, ICTY (Trial Chamber), judgment of 29 November 2002, para. 266: "There is, therefore, no issue of cumulative conviction arising in relation to those two Counts as they are not based upon the same facts."

[500] For more information, see marginal no. 630.

individual acts; here, too, various types of conduct by a perpetrator that fulfill the definition of the crime can be combined to form a single act.[501] In contrast, the presence of an armed conflict is not sufficient to combine multiple war crimes into one crime for legal purposes.[502]

533 If an assessment of the conduct indicates the presence of several legally separate acts, the indictment and conviction for each separate act will occur based on the definition of the crime for each case.[503] If, however, it turns out that the perpetrator has become liable for the same conduct, the indictment, conviction, and sentencing occur according to the following rules.

1. Cumulative Charging

534 Cumulative charging for several crimes under international law committed through the same conduct is always permissible, according to the judgments of the Yugoslavia and Rwanda Tribunals: "[P]rior to the presentation of all of the evidence, it is not possible to determine to a certainty which of the charges brought against an accused will be proven."[504]

2. Multiple Convictions

535 The Yugoslavia Tribunal first considered the issue of multiple offenses in depth in the trial of *Kupreškić* et al.[505] The practice is guided today by the so-called Čelebići test,[506] developed in the trial of *Mucić* et al.[507] by the Appeals Chamber of the Yugoslavia Tribunal.[508] Under this test, competing crimes are to be eliminated from the verdict only under the following, narrow conditions:

---

[501] For more information, see marginal no. 770.

[502] For more information, see marginal no. 1146.

[503] See *Prosecutor* v. *Vasiljević*, ICTY (Trial Chamber), judgment of 29 November 2002, para. 266. See also A. Cassese, *International Criminal Law* (2003), p. 213.

[504] *Prosecutor* v. *Mucić* et al., ICTY (Appeals Chamber), judgment of 20 February 2001, para. 400; *Prosecutor* v. *Musema*, ICTR (Appeals Chamber), judgment of 16 November 2001, para. 369; *Prosecutor* v. *Naletilić and Martinović*, ICTY (Trial Chamber), judgment of 31 March 2003, para. 718; *Prosecutor* v. *Ntakirutimana*, ICTR (Trial Chamber), judgment of 21 February 2003, paras. 862 et seq.; *Prosecutor* v. *Semanza*, ICTR (Trial Chamber), judgment of 15 May 2003, paras. 408 et seq. But see R. May and M. Wierda, in L.C. Vohrah et al. (eds.), *Man's Inhumanity to Man* (2003), p. 511 at pp. 539 et seq.

[505] *Prosecutor* v. *Kupreškić* et al., ICTY (Trial Chamber), judgment of 14 February 2000, paras. 668 et seq.; even prior to this, see *Prosecutor* v. *Akayesu*, ICTR (Trial Chamber), judgment of 2 September 1998, para. 468; on the development of the case law, see S. Walther, in A. Cassese, P. Gaeta and J.R.W.D. Jones (eds.), *The Rome Statute of the International Criminal Court*, Vol. 1 (2002), p. 475 at p. 492.

[506] The term is based on the name of a former Yugoslav People's Army base ("Čelebići camp") at which the defendants in the *Mucić* et al. case committed their crimes, see *Prosecutor* v. *Mucić* et al., ICTY (Appeals Chamber), judgment of 20 February 2001, para. 1. See also *Prosecutor* v. *Kamuhanda*, ICTR (Trial Chamber), judgment of 22 January 2004, paras. 577 et seq.

[507] *Prosecutor* v. *Mucić* et al., ICTY (Appeals Chamber), judgment of 20 February 2001, paras. 412 et seq.

[508] See also *Prosecutor* v. *Jelisić*, ICTY (Appeals Chamber), judgment of 5 July 2001, paras. 78 et seq.; *Prosecutor* v. *Kunarac* et al., ICTY (Appeals Chamber), judgment of 12 June 2002, para. 168;

"Multiple criminal convictions entered under different statutory provisions but based on the same **536** conduct are permissible only if each statutory provision involved has a materially distinct element not contained in the other. An element is materially distinct from another if it requires proof of a fact not required by the other. Where this test is not met, the Chamber must decide in relation to which offence it will enter a conviction. This should be done on the basis of the principle that the conviction under the more specific provision should be upheld. Thus, if a set of facts is regulated by two provisions, one of which contains an additional materially distinct element, then a conviction should be entered only under that provision."[509]

As a first step, therefore, the two relevant provisions must be compared to determine if **537** each of them requires proof of at least one element that the other does not require. All elements of the definition of the crime must be taken into account, especially contextual elements.[510] If this test is positive, both definitions of crimes may be employed simultaneously and both will be listed in the verdict. If the test results are negative – that is, if the competing rules either have identical requirements or one rule is completely included in the other – a second step is needed to determine which of the two is the more specific rule. Only this one will be included in the verdict. The suppressed norm is subsidiary. Here a principle that is widespread in most legal systems has been recognized by international criminal law.[511] The Čelebići test has meanwhile been applied frequently by the Yugoslavia and Rwanda Tribunals, and in this way the following principles have developed.

As regards the relationship between the various crimes under international law, **538** crimes against humanity can coincide with both war crimes[512] and genocide. The long-

---

Prosecutor v. Naletilić and Martinović, ICTY (Trial Chamber), judgment of 31 March 2003, para. 718; most recently *Prosecutor v. Krstić*, ICTY (Appeals Chamber), judgment of 19 April 2004, para. 218. See also A. Cassese, *International Criminal Law* (2003), pp. 214 et seq.

[509] *Prosecutor v. Mucić* et al., ICTY (Appeals Chamber), judgment of 20 February 2001, paras. 412 et seq.

[510] See *Prosecutor v. Musema*, ICTR (Appeals Chamber), judgment of 16 November 2001, para. 363.

[511] See, e.g., *Prosecutor v. Kunarac* et al., ICTY (Appeals Chamber), judgment of 12 June 2002, para. 170, according to which this principle is an "established principle of both civil and common law"; *Prosecutor v. Kamuhanda*, ICTR (Trial Chamber), judgment of 22 January 2004, paras. 577 et seq. See also A. Cassese, *International Criminal Law* (2003), p. 216; F. Stuckenberg, in H. Fischer, C. Kress and S.R. Lüder (eds.), *International and National Prosecution of Crimes under International Criminal Law* (2001), pp. 586 et seq.

[512] *Prosecutor v. Kunarac* et al., ICTY (Appeals Chamber), judgment of 12 June 2002, para. 176: "crimes against humanity constitute crimes distinct from crimes against the laws or customs of war [under ICTY Statute, Art. 3] in that each contains an element that does not appear in the other"; referring to the *Prosecutor v. Kupreškić* et al., ICTY (Appeals Chamber), judgment of 23 October 2001, para. 388, and *Prosecutor v. Jelisić*, ICTY (Appeals Chamber), judgment of 5 July 2001, para. 82. See also *Prosecutor v. Češić*, ICTY (Trial Chamber), judgment of 11 March 2004, paras. 32 et seq.; *Prosecutor v. Galić*, ICTY (Trial Chamber), judgment of 5 December 2003, para. 163; *Prosecutor v. Stakić*, ICTY (Trial Chamber), judgment of 31 July 2003, para. 874. See also G. Mettraux, 43 *Harvard International Law Journal* (2002), p. 302. In contrast (crime against humanity of killing supersedes the corresponding war crime), see *Prosecutor v. Kupreškić* et al., ICTY (Trial Chamber), judgment of 14 January 2000, para. 701. But see R. May and M. Wierda, in L.C. Vohrah et al. (eds.), *Man's Inhumanity to Man* (2003), pp. 511 et seq., 528 et seq.

debated[513] question whether genocide is *lex specialis* – this is, the more specific crime under the Čelibići test – vis-à-vis crimes against humanity has been answered in the negative by the Appeals Chamber.[514] On the basis of this case law, war crimes and genocide may also be applied simultaneously.

539 As regards the relationships between various individual acts, torture and rape can coincide as crimes against humanity,[515] as can torture and rape as war crimes.[516] The same is true of rape and enslavement as crimes against humanity[517] and of extermination and murder.[518] The crime against humanity of inhuman treatment is subsidiary to other individual crimes against humanity.[519] If the crime of persecution is committed by way of killing, torture, deprivation of liberty or other inhuman treatment, it supersedes, through specificity, the corresponding crimes against humanity (killing, torture, deprivation of liberty, inhuman treatment).[520]

540 As a less specific form of participation, superior responsibility is subsidiary to the (direct) commission of a crime under international law by a superior.[521] Executing a crime takes precedence over planning it.[522]

---

[513] For the subsidiarity of crimes against humanity in relation to genocide, see *Prosecutor* v. *Krstić* ICTY, judgment of 2 August 2001, paras. 682 et seq.; See also *Prosecutor* v. *Kayishema and Ruzindana*, ICTR (Trial Chamber), judgment of 21 May 1999, para. 648 ("subsumed fully").

[514] See *Prosecutor* v. *Musema*, ICTR (Appeals Chamber), judgment of 16 November 2001, paras. 366 et seq.; *Prosecutor* v. *Ntakirutimana*, ICTR (Trial Chamber), judgment of 21 February 2003, para. 864; recently *Prosecutor* v. *Krstić*, ICTY (Appeals Chamber), judgment of 19 April 2004, paras. 222 et seq.; earlier, opposing specificity of genocide, *Prosecutor* v. *Akayesu*, ICTR (Trial Chamber), judgment of 2 September 1998 para. 469. See also E. Fronza, in F. Lattanzi and W.A. Schabas (eds.), *Essays on Rome Statute of the International Criminal Court*, Vol. 1 (1999), p. 105 at pp. 117 et seq.; A. Gil Gil, 112 *Zeitschrift für die gesamte Strafrechtswissenschaft* (2000), p. 381 at pp. 396 et seq.; S. Walther, in A. Cassese, P. Gaeta and J.R.W.D. Jones (eds.), *The Rome Statute of the International Criminal Court*, Vol. 1 (2002), p. 475 at p.491. But see R. May and M. Wierda, in L.C. Vohrah et al. (eds.), *Man's Inhumanity to Man* (2003), p. 511 at p. 531.

[515] *Prosecutor* v. *Kunarac* et al., ICTY (Appeals Chamber), judgment of 12 June 2002, para. 179: "an element of the crime of rape is penetration, whereas an element for the crime of torture is a prohibited purpose."

[516] *Prosecutor* v. *Kunarac* et al., ICTY (Appeals Chamber), judgment of 12 June 2002, paras. 181 et seq.

[517] *Prosecutor* v. *Kunarac* et al., ICTY (Appeals Chamber), judgment of 12 June 2002, para. 186.

[518] *Prosecutor* v. *Stakić*, ICTY (Trial Chamber), judgment of 31 July 2003, paras. 876 et seq.: " . . . to reflect the totality of the accussed's culpable conduct directed both at individual victims and at groups of victims on a large scale, it is in principle permissible to enter for extermination and murder." (para. 877).

[519] *Prosecutor* v. *Kvočka* et al., ICTY (Trial Chamber), judgment of 2 November 2001, para. 217 ("subsidiary nature"); *Prosecutor* v. *Krstić*, ICTY (Appeals Chamber), judgment of 19 April 2004, para. 231.

[520] See *Prosecutor* v. *Kvočka* et al., ICTY (Trial Chamber), judgment of 2 November 2001, para. 220 (killing), 227 (torture, inhuman treatment); *Prosecutor* v. *Kronjelac*, ICTY (Trial Chamber), judgment of 15 March 2002, para. 503 (deprivation of liberty, inhuman treatment); *Prosecutor* v. *D. Nikolić*, ICTY (Trial Chamber), judgment of 18 December 2003, para. 119; *Prosecutor* v. *Krstić*, ICTY (Appeals Chamber), judgment of 19 April 2004, para. 231; *Prosecutor* v. *Stakić*, ICTY (Trial Chamber), judgment of 31 July 2003, paras. 879 et seq.

[521] For a summary of ICTY views, see *Prosecutor* v. *Naletilić and Martinović*, ICTY (Trial Chamber), judgment of 31 March 2003, para. 78 et seq.; *Prosecutor* v. *Blaškić*, ICTY (Appeals Chamber), judgment of 29 July 2004, para. 91; *Prosecutor* v. *Stakić*, ICTY (Trial Chamber), judgment of 31 July 2003, paras. 463 et seq.; see also marginal no. 371.

[522] *Prosecutor* v. *Naletilić and Martinović*, ICTY (Trial Chamber), judgment of 31 March 2003, para. 59; *Prosecutor* v. *Stakić*, ICTY (Trial Chamber), judgment of 31 July 2003, para. 443.

III. Sentencing

If an individual is convicted under the above principles for multiple crimes, the further **541** question is raised of how sentencing is affected.[523]

The practice of the international Tribunals on this issue is not consistent.[524] In some **542** cases, individual sentences have been imposed and combined into an overall sentence;[525] in others, a single sentence has been imposed.[526] According to the jurisprudence of the Appeals Chamber of the Yugoslavia Tribunal, both methods are permissible; it is up to the respective Trial Chamber to decide which method to employ:

"It is within a Trial Chamber's discretion to impose sentences which are either global, concurrent or consecutive, or a mixture of concurrent or consecutive. In terms of the final sentence imposed, however, the governing criteria is that it should reflect the totality of the culpable conduct (the "totality" principle), or generally, that it should reflect the gravity of the offences and the culpability of the offender so that it is both just and appropriate."[527]

Under Article 78(3) of the ICC Statute, a separate sentence shall be pronounced for each **543** crime, and several individual sentences can then be combined into a joint sentence. The only guidance provided by the Statute as to what principles to use in determining the joint sentence is the provision that the joint sentence shall be no less than the highest individual sentence.[528]

K. Requirements for Prosecution

Antonio Cassese: *International Criminal Law* (2003), pp. 316 et seq.; William A. Schabas: *Intro-* **544** *duction to the International Criminal Court*, 2nd edn. (2004), pp. 114 et seq.; William A. Schabas: ICC Statute, Article 29, in Otto Triffterer (ed.), *Commentary on the Rome Statute of the International Criminal Court, Observers' Notes, Article by Article* (1999), pp. 523 et seq.; Christine Van den Wyngaert and John Dugard: Non-Applicability of Statute of Limitations, in Antonio Cassese, Paola Gaeta and John R.W.D. Jones (eds.), *The Rome Statute of the International Criminal Court: A Commentary*, Vol. 1 (2002), pp. 873 et seq.

The requirements for prosecution are entirely external to the concept of crimes under in- **545** ternational law.[529] They are by nature part of international criminal procedure, and concern not criminality, but admissibility of criminal prosecution. If a requirement for prosecution is not present, no trial may be held.

---

[523] See also S. Walther, in A. Cassese, P. Gaeta and J.R.W.D. Jones (eds.), *The Rome Statute of the International Criminal Court*, Vol. 1 (2002), p. 475 at p. 488.

[524] See F. Stuckenberg, in H. Fischer, C. Kress and S.R. Lüder (eds.), *International and National Prosecution of Crimes under International Law* (2001), p. 585.

[525] See, e.g., *Prosecutor* v. *Kupreškić* et al., ICTY (Trial Chamber), judgment of 14 January 2000, paras. 864 et seq.

[526] See, e.g., *Prosecutor* v. *Blaškić*, ICTY (Trial Chamber), judgment of 3 March 2000, paras. 805 et seq.; *Prosecutor* v. *Vaslijević*, ICTY (Trial Chamber), judgment of 29 November 2002, para. 269.

[527] *Prosecutor* v. *Mucić* et al., ICTY (Appeals Chamber), judgment of 20 February 2001, para. 429.

[528] See also W.A. Schabas, in A. Cassese, P. Gaeta and J.R.W.D. Jones (eds.), *The Rome Statute of the International Criminal Court*, Vol. 2 (2002), p. 1497, pp. 1529 et seq.

[529] See marginal no. 284.

546   One requirement for prosecution before the International Criminal Court, for example, is that the crime not have already been tried before the Court (*ne bis in idem*, Article 20 of the ICC Statute). Article 20(3) extends the prohibition of double jeopardy to all cases in which the perpetrator has been acquitted or convicted by the courts of any state.

547   Prosecution of a crime under international law before the International Criminal Court further requires that the defendant be at least 18 years of age at the time the crime was committed (Article 26 of the ICC Statute).

548   For genocide and war crimes, the ICC Statute and the Elements of Crimes contain specific requirements for prosecution. This is intended to ensure that the International Criminal Court concentrates on the most serious cases.

549   The so-called threshold clause for war crimes, for example, is a jurisdictional element of this sort that does not need to be part of the perpetrator's perceptions. Under Article 8(1), clause 2, of the ICC Statute, the Court is responsible for war crimes, "in particular when committed as part of a plan or policy or as part of a large-scale commission of such crimes." Here, as a reasonable legal policy, a war crime must achieve a certain degree of severity to be subject to ICC jurisdiction. The threshold clause is not a limitation on the substantive requirements for criminality.

550   The same is true where the Elements of Crimes require a "context of a manifest pattern of similar conduct" for genocide.[530] Correctly interpreted, this concerns only the jurisdiction of the International Criminal Court, not the substantive criminality of genocide.[531]

551   Finally, of considerable practical significance are the ICC Statute's provisions under which statutes of limitations and immunity do not prevent prosecution before the International Criminal Court. Thus statutes of limitations and immunity are no bar to trial.[532]

552   Under Article 27(2) of the ICC Statute, the perpetrator's procedural immunity, which might arise, for example, from his position as head of state or government, is no bar to trial before the International Criminal Court.[533]

553   Article 29 of the ICC Statute establishes that crimes under international law, as the most serious international crimes, are not subject to statutes of limitations.[534] There are no models for this in the Nuremberg Charter or the Statutes of the Yugoslavia and Rwanda Tribunals.[535] During the negotiations in Rome, the inapplicability of statutes of limitations to war crimes was the most controversial point.[536] It has not been conclusively determined whether and to what extent the inapplicability of statutes of limitations

---

[530] See Elements of Crimes for Article 6 ICC Statute, num. 4.

[531] For discussion, see marginal no. 329 and marginal nos. 606 et seq.

[532] For immunity see marginal nos. 510 et seq.

[533] For discussion, see marginal nos. 520 et seq.

[534] See W.A. Schabas, *Introduction to the International Criminal Court*, 2nd edn. (2004), p. 115.

[535] See W.A. Schabas, in O. Triffterer (ed.), *Commentary on the Rome Statute of the International Criminal Court* (1999), Art. 29, marginal no. 1, sees the lack of statute-of-limitation rules in the Nuremberg and Tokyo Charters and the Statutes of the ICTY and ICTR as evidence that crimes under international law are not subject to statutes of limitations.

[536] On the history of the negotiations, see W.A. Schabas, in O. Triffterer (ed.), *Commentary on the Rome Statute of the International Criminal Court* (1999), Art. 29, marginal nos. 4 et seq.

to crimes under international law has become part of customary international law.[537] There is little state practice in this area. International treaties provide for the inapplicability of statutes of limitations, but states have heretofore been reluctant to adopt them.[538]

---

[537] See W.A. Schabas, *Introduction to the International Criminal Court*, 2nd edn. (2004), pp. 115 et seq. On inapplicability of statutes of limitations, see C. Van den Wyngaert and J. Dugard, in A. Cassese, P. Gaeta and J.R.W.D. Jones (eds.), *The Rome Statute of the International Criminal Court*, Vol. 1 (2002), p. 873 at p. 887; for genocide, crimes against humanity and torture, see also A. Cassese, *International Criminal Law* (2003), p. 319; for torture, see also *Prosecutor* v. *Furundžija*, ICTY (Trial Chamber), judgment of 10 December 1998, para. 157. See also Princeton Project on Universal Jurisdiction (ed.), *The Princeton Principles on Universal Jurisdiction* (2001), Principle 6: "Statutes of limitations or other forms of prescription shall not apply to [war crimes, crimes against peace, crimes against humanity and genocide . . .]"; See also Cour de Cassation, judgment of 26 January 1984 (*Féderation National des Deportées et Internés Resistants et Patriots* et al. v. *Barbie*), in 78 *ILR* (1988), p. 126: "This rule [that prosecution is not subject to statutory limitation] was applicable to such crimes by virtue of the principles of law recognized by the community of nations." But for denial of the existence of a corresponding provision of customary law, see C. Kress, in H. Grützner and P.G. Pötz (eds.), *Internationaler Rechtshilfeverkehr in Strafsachen*, Vol. 4, 2nd edn. (2002), III 26, marginal no. 62, fn. 163; H. Kreicker, *Neue Zeitschrift für Strafrecht* 2002, p. 281, pp. 284 et seq.

[538] See *UN Convention on the Non-Applicability of Statutory Limitations to War Crimes and Crimes Against Humanity* of 16 November 1968, reprinted in 8 *ILM* (1969), p. 68; it has so far been ratified by only 43 states; die *European Convention on the Non-Applicability of Statutory Limitation to Crimes Against Humanity and War Crimes* of 25 January 1974, *ETS* No. 82, has been signed by only four states and ratified only by the Netherlands and Romania.

Part Three: Genocide

554 Diane Marie Amann: Prosecutor v. Akayesu ICTR-96–4-T, 93 *American Journal of International Law* (1999), pp. 195 et seq.; Cécile Aptel: The Intent to Commit Genocide in the Case Law of the International Criminal Tribunal of Rwanda, 13 *Criminal Law Forum* (2002), pp. 273 et seq.; Roberta Arnold: The Mens Rea of Genocide under the Statute of the International Criminal Court, 14 *Criminal Law Forum* (2003), pp. 127 et seq.; Kelly Dawn Askin: Sexual Violence in Decisions and Indictments of the Yugoslav and Rwandan Tribunals: Current Status, 93 *American Journal of International Law* (1999), pp. 97 et seq.; Howard Ball: *Prosecuting War Crimes and Genocide, The Twentieth-Century Experience* (1999); Christopher R. Browning: *Nazi Policy, Jewish Workers, German Killers* (2000); Micha Brumlik: Zu einer Theorie des Völkermords, *Blätter für deutsche und internationale Politik* 2004, pp. 923 et seq.; Bryant Bunyan and Robert H. Jones: Comment – The United States and the Genocide Convention, 16 *Harvard International Law Journal* (1975), pp. 683 et seq.; Antonio Cassese: Genocide, in Antonio Cassese, Paola Gaeta and John R.W.D. Jones (eds.): *The Rome Statute of the International Criminal Court*, Vol. 1 (2002), pp. 335 et seq.; Antonio Cassese: *International Criminal Law* (2003), pp. 96 et seq.; Frank Chalk and Kurt Jonassohn: *The History and Sociology of Genocide* (1990); Roger S. Clark: Does the Genocide Convention Go Far Enough? Some Thoughts on the Nature of Criminal Genocide in the Context of Indonesia's Invasion of East Timor, 8 *Ohio Northern University Law Review* (1981), pp. 321 et seq.; Howard J. De Nike, John Quigley and Kenneth J. Robinson (eds.): *Genocide in Cambodia, Documents from the Trial of Pol Pot and Ieng Sary* (2000); Pieter N. Drost: *The Crime of State, Vol. II: Genocide* (1959); Emanuela Fronza: Genocide in the Rome Statute, in Flavia Lattanzi and William A. Schabas (eds.), *Essays on the Rome Statute of the International Criminal Court*, Vol. 1 (1999), pp. 105 et seq.; Alicia Gil Gil: Die Tatbestände der Verbrechen gegen die Menschlichkeit und des Völkermordes im Römischen Statut des Internationalen Strafgerichtshofs, 112 *Zeitschrift für die gesamte Strafrechtswissenschaft* (2000), pp. 381 et seq.; Stephen Gorove: The Problem of "Mental Harm" in the Genocide Convention, *Washington University Law Quarterly* 1951, pp. 174 et seq.; Alexander K.A. Greenawalt: Rethinking Genocidal Intent: The Case for a Knowledge-Based Interpretation, 99 *Columbia Law Review* (1999), pp. 2264 et seq.; Hurst Hannum: International Law and Cambodian Genocide: The Sounds of Silence, 11 *Human Rights Quarterly* (1989), pp. 82 et seq.; Hans Joachim Heintze: Zur Durchsetzung der UN-Völkermordkonvention, *Humanitäres Völkerrecht-Informationsschriften* 2000, pp. 225 et seq.; Raul Hilberg: *The Destruction of the European Jews*, 3rd edn. (2003); Burkhard Jähnke: Commentary on Section § 220a StGB, in Burkhard Jähnke, Heinrich-Wilhelm Laufhütte, Walter Odersky (eds.), *StGB (Strafgesetzbuch, German Criminal Code), Leipziger Kommentar, Großkommentar: Sections 220a-222; 234–238*, 11th edn. (1999); Hans-Heinrich Jescheck: Die internationale Genocidium-Konvention vom 9. Dezember 1948 und die Lehre vom Völkerstrafrecht, 66 *Zeitschrift für die gesamte Strafrechtswissenschaft* (1954), pp. 193 et seq.; John R.W.D. Jones: Whose intent is it anyway? – Genocide and the Intent to Destroy a Group, in Lal Chand Vohrah et al. (eds.), *Man's Inhumanity to Man* (2003), pp. 467 et seq.; Magdalini Karagiannakis: The Definition of Rape and Its Characterization as an Act of Genocide – A Review of the Jurisprudence of the International Criminal Tribunals for Rwanda and the Former Yugoslavia; 12 *Leiden Journal of International Law* (1999), pp. 479 et seq.; Kriangsak Kittichaisaree: *International Criminal Law* (2001), pp. 67 et seq.; Josef L. Kunz: The United Nations Convention on Genocide, 43 *American Journal of International Law* (1949), pp. 738 et seq.; Leo Kuper: *The Prevention of Genocide* (1985); Leo Kuper: *Genocide* (1981); Lawrence

J. LeBlanc: The Intent to Destroy Groups in the Genocide Convention: The Proposed US Under-standing, 78 *American Journal of International Law* (1984), pp. 369 et seq.; Roy S. Lee: The Rwanda Tribunal, 9 *Leiden Journal of International Law* (1996), pp. 37 et seq.; Lutz Lehmler: *Die Strafbarkeit von Vertreibungen aus ethnischen Gründen in bewaffneten nicht-internationalen Konflikten* (1999); Raphael Lemkin: *Axis Rule in Occupied Europe, Laws of Occupation, Analysis of Government, Proposal for Redress* (1973); Natan Lerner: Ethnic Cleansing, 24 *Israel Yearbook on Human Rights* (1994), pp. 103 et seq.; Matthew Lippman: Genocide, in M. Cherif Bassiouni (ed.), *International Criminal Law*, Vol. 1, 2nd edn. (1999), pp. 589 et seq.; Matthew Lippman: The Convention on the Prevention and Punishment of the Crime of Genocide: Fifty Years Later, 15 *Arizona Journal of International and Comparative Law* (1998), pp. 415 et seq.; Matthew Lippman: The Drafting of the 1948 Convention on the Prevention and Punishment of the Crime of Geno-cide, 65 *Boston University International Law Journal* (1985), pp. 1 et seq.; Barbara Lüders: *Die Strafbarkeit von Völkermord nach dem Römischen Statut für den Internationalen Strafgerichtshof* (2004); Barbara Lüders: L'incrimination de génocide dans la jurisprudence des Tribunaux pénaux internationaux pour lèx-Yougoslavie et le Rwanda, in Mario Chiavario (ed.), *La justice pénale internationale entre passé et avenir* (2003), pp. 223 et seq.; David Marcus: Famine Crimes in Inter-national Law, 97 *American Journal of International Law* (2003), pp. 245 et seq.; Jamie Frederic Metzl: Rwandan Genocide and the International Law of Radio Jamming, 91 *American Journal of International Law* (1997), pp. 628 et seq.; Christina Möller: *Völkerstrafrecht und Internationaler Strafgerichtshof – kriminologische, straftheoretische und rechtspolitische Aspekte* (2003); Virginia Mor-ris and Michael Scharf: *The International Criminal Tribunal for Rwanda*, Vol. 1 (1998); Virginia Morris and Michael Scharf: *An Insider's Guide to the International Criminal Tribunal for the Former Yugoslavia – A Documentary History and Analysis*, Vol. 1 (1995); David D. Nersessian: The Con-tours of Genocidal Intent: Troubling Jurisprudence from the International Criminal Tribunals, 37 *Texas International Law Journal* (2002), pp. 231 et seq.; Daniel D. Ntanda Nsereko: Genocide: A Crime against Mankind, in Gabrielle Kirk McDonald and Olivia Swaak-Goldman (ed.), *Substan-tive and Procedural Aspects of International Criminal Law, The Experiences of International and Na-tional Courts*, Vol. 1 (2000), pp. 117 et seq.; Daniel D. Ntanda Nsereko: Genocidal Conflict in Rwanda and the ICTR, *Netherlands International Law Review* 2001, pp. 31 et seq.; Helena Nygren Krug: Genocide in Rwanda: Lessons Learned and Future Challenges to the UN Human Rights System, 67 *Nordic Journal of International Law* (1998), pp. 165 et seq.; Philip B. Perlman: The Genocide Convention, 30 *Nebraska Law Review* (1950), pp. 1 et seq.; Drazen Petrovic: Ethnic Cleansing – An Attempt at Methodology, 5 *European Journal of International Law* (1994), pp. 343 et seq.; Erich H. Pircher: *Der vertragliche Schutz ethnischer, sprachlicher und religiöser Minderheiten im Völkerrecht* (1979); Antonio Planzer: *Le crime de genocide* (1956); Samantha Powers: *A Problem from Hell: America in the Age of Genocide* (2003); Nehemia Robinson: *The Genocide Convention, A Commentary* (1960); Wiebke Rückert and Georg Witschel: Genocide and Crimes Against Human-ity in the Elements of Crimes, in Horst Fischer, Claus Kress and Sascha Rolf Lüder (eds.), *Interna-tional and National Prosecution of Crimes under International Law – Current Developments* (2001), pp. 59 et seq.; Beth van Schaack: The Crime of Political Genocide: Repairing the Genocide Convention's Blind Spot, 106 *Yale Law Journal* (1997), pp. 2259 et seq.; William A. Schabas: *Genocide in International Law, The Crime of Crimes* (2000); William A. Schabas: Hate Speech in Rwanda: The Road to Genocide, 46 *McGill Law Journal* (2000), pp. 141 et seq.; William A. Schabas: The *Jelisic* Case and the *Mens Rea* of the Crime of Genocide, 14 *Leiden Journal of Interna-tional Law* (2000), pp. 125 et seq.; William A. Schabas: International Decisions, Mugesera v. Min-ister of Citizenship and Immigration, Nov. 1998, 93 *American Journal of International Law* (1999), pp. 529 et seq.; William A. Schabas: ICC Statute, Art. 6, in Otto Triffterer (ed.), *Com-mentary on the Rome Statute of the International Criminal Court* (1999), pp. 107 et seq.; Frank Selbmann: *Der Tatbestand des Genozids im Völkerstrafrecht* (2002); Malcolm N. Shaw: Genocide and International Law, in Yoram Dinstein (ed.), *International Law at a Time of Perplexity* (1989), pp. 797 et seq.; Kurt Stillschweig: Das Abkommen zur Bekämpfung von Genocide, *Die Friedens-*

Warte 1949, pp. 93 et seq.; Yves Ternon: *Der verbrecherische Staat, Völkermord im 20. Jahrhundert* (1996); Cécile Tournaye: Genocidal Intent before the ICTY, 52 *International and Comparative Law Quarterly* (2003), pp. 447 et seq.; Otto Triffterer: Kriminalpolitische und dogmatische Überlegungen zum Entwurf gleichlautender "Elements of Crimes" für alle Tatbestände des Völkermordes, in Bernd Schünemann et al. (eds.), *Festschrift für Roxin* (2001), pp. 1415 et seq.; Otto Triffterer: Die Bestrafung von Vertreibungsverbrechen, in Dieter Blumenwitz (ed.), *Flucht und Vertreibung* (1987), pp. 259 et seq.; Guglielmo Verdirame: The Genocide Convention in the Jurisprudence of the ad hoc Tribunals, 49 *International and Comparative Law Quarterly* (2000), pp. 578 et seq.; Hans Vest: Humanitätsverbrechen – Herausforderung für das Individualstrafrecht, 113 *Zeitschrift für die gesamte Strafrechtswissenschaft* (2001), pp. 457 et seq.; Hans Vest: Die bundesrätliche Botschaft zum Beitritt der Schweiz zur Völkermordkonvention – kritische Überlegungen zum Entwurf eines Tatbestandes für den Völkermord, 117 *Schweizer Zeitschrift für Strafrecht* (1999), pp. 351 et seq.; Hans Vest: *Genozid durch organisatorische Machtapparate, An der Grenze von individueller und kollektiver Verantwortlichkeit* (2002); Johan D. van den Vyver: Prosecution and Punishment of the Crime of Genocide, 23 *Fordham Journal of International Law* (1999), pp. 286 et seq.; John Webb: Genocide Treaty – Ethnic Cleansing – Substantive and Procedural Hurdles in the Application of the Genocide Convention to Alleged Crimes in the Former Yugoslavia, 23 *Georgia Journal of International and Comparative Law* (1993), pp. 377 et seq.

A. Introduction

I. The Phenomenon of Genocide

555 The systematic annihilation of entire groups of people has cut a broad swathe of blood through human history. The manifestations of the crime are as varied as the motives for it and the events that have triggered it.[1] Genocides particularly marked the face of the 20th century. At the start of World War I, Armenians living in Turkey were the victims of an extermination campaign in which the estimated number of dead ranged from 500,000 to a million.[2] The tragic climax of the history of genocide was the Holocaust, the Nazi extermination of the European Jews.

556 More than six million Jews fell victim to the extermination policies of the Third Reich initiated by Hitler. After Hitler's seizure of power in 1933, Jews in Germany were first gradually deprived of their rights and ostracized from society. Jewish institutions were attacked and Jews arbitrarily arrested and interned in concentration camps. During World War II, the Nazis waged a campaign of annihilation against the Jewish population of Europe. SS Einsatzgruppen killed Jews as they followed the Wehrmacht's advance into the Soviet Union. In larger cities, Jews were forced into ghettoes and deported to concentration and extermination camps. Many did not survive the transports

---

[1] See summary in F. Chalk and K. Jonassohn (eds.), *The History and Sociology of Genocide* (1990); L. Kuper, *Genocide* (1981); Y. Ternon, *Der verbrecherische Staat* (1996); see also C. Möller, *Völkerstrafrecht und Internationaler Strafgerichtshof* (2003), pp. 19 et seq.

[2] See F. Chalk and K. Jonassohn (eds.), *The History and Sociology of Genocide* (1990), pp. 249 et seq.; L. Kuper, *Genocide* (1981), pp. 105 et seq.; C. Möller, *Völkerstrafrecht und Internationaler Strafgerichtshof* (2003), pp. 50 et seq.; A. Ohandjanian, *Armenien: der verschwiegene Völkermord* (1989); Y. Ternon, *Der verbrecherische Staat* (1996), pp. 139 et seq. For a classification of the German Imperial Army's actions against the Herero in Namibia as genocide, see Y. Ternon, *Der verbrecherische Staat* (1996), p. 256; F. Chalk and K. Jonassohn (eds.), *The History and Sociology of Genocide* (1990), p. 230.

or died from inhuman conditions in the camps or as a result of forced labor. Millions were killed in the gas chambers. It was not only the number of victims but the manner of their killing, the bureaucratically-planned and, from start to finish, industrial extermination, that made this crime unique.[3]

The *Convention on the Prevention and Punishment of the Crime of Genocide* was **557** adopted on 9 December 1948 as a reaction to the Nazi genocide. But the experience of World War II and the proscription of genocide were not sufficient deterrent. Thus in the late 1960s, the world was shaken by tragic events in Nigeria. After a wave of massacres of members of the Ibo group, the eastern part of the country, with a majority Ibo population, sought independence. In July 1967, civil war broke out between the government and the eastern region, in the course of which the Ibo were targeted by a campaign of extermination: between 600,000 and a million members of the group lost their lives. Many were massacred or died as a result of intentionally-created famine.[4] The terrible experiences of Bangladesh,[5] Burundi,[6] Ethiopia,[7] and Guatemala[8] must also be noted.[9]

Toward the end of the 20th century, atrocities in Rwanda and on the territory of **558** former Yugoslavia jolted world public opinion. In Rwanda, civil war broke out in April 1994 after the Rwandan prime minister was killed in a plane crash. In the following months, thousands of Hutu took up arms to exterminate the Tutsi, led by the military and militias and goaded by the media. Tutsi and moderate Hutu were singled out at roadblocks and often killed on the spot. Villagers were driven together and liquidated. Within three months, according to various estimates, between 500,000 and a million people died. Genocide was also committed during the war in Bosnia, according to the Yugoslavia Tribunal.[10] In July 1995, Bosnian Serb units took over the enclave of Srebre-

---

[3] See generally R. Hilberg, The Destruction of the European Jews, 3rd edn. (2003). See also C.R. Browning, *Nazi Policy, Jewish Workers, German Killers* (2000).

[4] See O. Balogun, *The Tragic Years: Nigeria in Crisis 1966–1970* (1973); L. Kuper, *Genocide* (1981), pp. 74 et seq.; Y. Ternon, *Der verbrecherische Staat* (1996), pp. 258 et seq.

[5] See F. Chalk and K. Jonassohn (eds.), *The History and Sociology of Genocide* (1990), pp. 394 et seq.; Y. Ternon, *Der verbrecherische Staat* (1996), pp. 243 et seq.

[6] See F. Chalk and K. Jonassohn (eds.), *The History and Sociology of Genocide* (1990), pp. 384 et seq.

[7] See Y. Ternon, *Der verbrecherische Staat* (1996), p. 267.

[8] On the events in Guatemala, see C. Tomuschat, 74 *Die Friedens-Warte* (1999), pp. 433 et seq. and Commission for Historical Clarification, Report: Guatemala – Memory of Silence, Conclusions and Recommendations, 74 *Die Friedens-Warte* (1999), pp. 511 et seq.

[9] The mass killings in Cambodia under Pol Pot and in the Soviet Union under Stalin have been mentioned frequently in this context. However, it is doubtful whether these events constituted genocide. On Cambodia, see, e.g., A. Barth and T. Terzani, *Holocaust in Kambodscha* (1980), pp. 7 et seq.; F. Chalk and K. Jonassohn (eds.), *The History and Sociology of Genocide* (1990), pp. 398 et seq.; H.J. De Nike, J. Quigley and K.J. Robinson, *Genocide in Cambodia* (2000); for the view that it did constitute genocide, see H. Hannum, 11 *Human Rights Quarterly* (1989), pp. 82 et seq.; Y. Ternon, *Der verbrecherische Staat* (1996), pp. 158 et seq.; for the opposing view, see H. Vest, 117 *Schweizerische Zeitschrift für Strafrecht* (1999), p. 351 at p. 356; H. Vest, 113 *Zeitschrift für die gesamte Strafrechtswissenschaft* (2001), p. 457 at p. 478. On the mass murders in the Stalinist Soviet Union, see Y. Ternon, *Der verbrecherische Staat* (1996), pp. 196 et seq., sees genocide only in the treatment of the kulaks. On the decimation of the North American Indians and the Australian aboriginals, see F. Chalk and K. Jonassohn (eds.), *The History and Sociology of Genocide* (1990), pp. 173 et seq., 204 et seq.; D. Stannard, *American Holocaust* (1992), pp. 57 et seq.; R. Thornton, *American Indian Holocaust and Survival* (1987).

[10] See, e.g., *Prosecutor* v. Krstić, ICTY (Trial Chamber), judgment of 2 August 2001.

nica in Bosnia and Herzegovina, which had been declared a UN safe area and where numerous Muslims had sought refuge from the fighting. The Muslims were split up,
women, children, and old people deported, and men of military age executed.[11]

559   The history of the criminal prosecution of genocide on the international level can be
quickly told.[12] In the trial of the major German war criminals before the Nuremberg
Tribunal, the crimes against the European Jews played only a subordinate role.[13] Despite
the adoption of the Genocide Convention in 1948, 50 years would pass before an international court, the Yugoslavia Tribunal, would be created to prosecute genocide, though
with temporal and territorial limitations. Shortly thereafter, the UN Security Council
created the Rwanda Tribunal to deal specifically with the genocide in Rwanda.[14] With
the creation of the International Criminal Court, there is now for the first time an international institution that can punish genocide anywhere in the world.[15]

II. History of the Crime

560 The term "genocide" was coined by Polish lawyer Raphael Lemkin during World War II
to describe the crimes committed against the Jews by the Nazis. The word is formed
from the Greek *genos*, for race, and the Latin *caedere*, for killing.[16] Lemkin defined genocide as different actions aiming at the destruction of essential foundations of the life of a
group and guided by a plan to annihilate the group.[17] More years would pass before the
international community could agree on a corresponding definition of the crime in the
Genocide Convention.

561 The trial of the major war criminals before the Nuremberg Tribunal focused on the war of aggression undertaken by the Nazis and their violations of the laws and customs of war.[18] The Nazi
genocide was not included as such, but as a war crime and a crime against humanity, in particular
as "extermination" and "persecution."[19] After the trial, efforts to promote the development of international criminal law intensified. In Resolution 96(I) of 11 December 1946,[20] the UN General
Assembly for the first time defined the crime of genocide and determined it to be a crime under
international law. The UN Economic and Social Council was authorized to draft a proposal for

---

[11] See, e.g., J. Bogoeva and C. Fetscher (eds.), *Srebrenica, Ein Prozess* (2002). On the events in
former Yugoslavia, see also, e.g., M.C. Bassiouni and P. Manikas, *The Law of the International Criminal Tribunal for the Former Yugoslavia* (1996), pp. 48 et seq., pp. 608 et seq.
[12] J.D. van den Vyver, 23 *Fordham Journal of International Law* (1999), pp. 286 et seq.
[13] See marginal nos. 19, 23.
[14] See D.D.N. Nsereko, *Netherlands International Law Review* 2001, pp. 31 et seq.; R.S. Lee, 9
Leiden Journal of International Law (1996), p. 37; V. Morris and M. Scharf, *The International Criminal Tribunal for Rwanda* (1998). On the Tribunals' jurisprudence, see G. Verdirame, 49 *International
and Comparative Law Quarterly* (2000), p. 578.
[15] For an overview of national prosecutions based on the Genocide Convention, see G. Dahm, J.
Delbrück and R. Wolfrum, *Völkerrecht*, Vol. I/3, 2nd edn. (2002), pp. 1075 et seq.
[16] R. Lemkin, *Axis Rule in Occupied Europe* (1973), p. 79. See also G. Dahm, J. Delbrück and R.
Wolfrum, *Völkerrecht*, Vol. I/3, 2nd edn. (2002), p. 1073.
[17] R. Lemkin, *Axis Rule in Occupied Europe* (1973), p. 79.
[18] See marginal no. 23.
[19] IMT, judgment of 1 October 1946, in *The Trial of German Major War Criminals. Proceedings
of the International Military Tribunal Sitting at Nuremberg, Germany*, Part 22, pp. 463 et seq.
[20] UN Doc. A/RES/1/96 (1946).

the formulation of a Genocide Convention. A group of experts, including Lemkin, drew up an initial draft convention, together with the Human Rights Division of the Office of the Secretary-General. It was presented to the Economic and Social Council, which then formed an *ad hoc* committee that thoroughly revised the draft and returned it to the Council. The draft was passed on to the Sixth Committee, the Legal Committee.[21] There, the text was again modified and finally presented to the General Assembly, which unanimously adopted the draft in Resolution 260 A(III) on 9 December 1948.[22]

Article II of the *Convention on the Prevention and Punishment of the Crime of Genocide*[23] **562** marked the first time the crime was formulated in an international legal instrument.[24] Today, the substance of Article II is part of customary international law[25] and *jus cogens*.[26] The wording of the crime in the Genocide Convention was adopted verbatim into Article 4(2) of the ICTY Statute and Article 2(2) of the ICTR Statute. At the negotiations on the Statute of the International Criminal Court, efforts were made to include political and social groups in the definition; however, the majority of delegates preferred not to tamper with the definition recognized under customary international law.[27] Thus Article 6 of the ICC Statute repeats Article II of the Genocide Convention verbatim.

III. Structure of the Crime

Conduct is punishable as genocide if it aims to destroy in whole or in part a national, **563** ethnic, racial or religious group. The group's physical and social existence receive primary protection; the victims' dignity is also protected.

Genocide requires the commission of one of the acts specified in Article 6(a) to (e) of **564** the ICC Statute. This includes acts against the physical or psychological integrity of members of the group or its existence or biological continuity. Article 6(e) additionally defines a form of cultural genocide. The target of the act is the individual member of the group. The material element of genocide does not require that the individual act be part

---

[21] The drafts are reprinted in W.A. Schabas, *Genocide in International Law* (2000), pp. 553 et seq.

[22] RES 3/260, UN GA (1948).

[23] 78 *UNTS* (1949), p. 277. The Convention has been ratified by 133 states. Current numbers can be found at <http://www.preventgenocide.org>.

[24] On the history of the Genocide Convention, see P.N. Drost, *The Crime of State, Vol. II: Genocide* (1959), pp. 1 et seq.; H.-H. Jescheck, 66 *Zeitschrift für die gesamte Strafrechtswissenschaft* (1954), pp. 193 et seq.; J.L. Kunz, 43 *American Journal of International Law* (1949), pp. 489 et seq.; L. Kuper, *Genocide* (1981), pp. 19 et seq.; M. Lippman, 65 *Boston University International Law Journal* (1985), pp. 1 et seq.; N. Robinson, *The Genocide Convention, A Commentary* (1960), pp. 17 et seq.; W.A. Schabas, *Genocide in International Law* (2000), pp. 14 et seq., 51 et seq.; K. Stillschweig, *Die Friedens-Warte* 1949, pp. 93 et seq.; Y. Ternon, *Der verbrecherische Staat* (1996), pp. 17 et seq., 34 et seq.

[25] See *Prosecutor* v. *Akayesu*, ICTR (Trial Chamber), judgment of 2 September 1998, para. 495; *Prosecutor* v. *Krstić*, ICTY (Trial Chamber), judgment of 2 August 2001, para. 541; A. Cassese, *International Criminal Law* (2003), pp. 96, 98.

[26] See ICJ, Advisory Opinion of 28 May 1951 (Reservation to the Convention on the Prevention and Punishment of Genocide), *ICJ Rep.* 1951, p. 23; A. Cassese, *International Criminal Law* (2003), pp. 96, 98.

[27] See W.A. Schabas, in O. Triffterer (ed.), *Commentary on the Rome Statute of the International Criminal Court* (1999), Art. 6, marginal no. 6.

of a systematic or widespread attack on a group, although this will typically be the case.[28]

565   The mental element of genocide requires that the material elements of the crime are committed with "intent and knowledge" (ICC Statute, Article 30).[29] In addition, genocide requires the specific intent to destroy in whole or in part a national, ethnic, racial or religious group as such; therefore purpose on the part of the perpetrator to destroy the group or a part of it is a precondition for individual criminal responsibility. The actual destruction of the group or a part of it is not necessary. The intent to destroy simultaneously embodies the systematic element of genocide, which lends the crime its international dimension.

IV. Protected Interests

566   The criminalization of genocide seeks to protect certain groups' right to exist.[30] This is evident in particular from the history of the Genocide Convention. Thus in Resolution 96(1) in 1946, the General Assembly defined genocide as "denial of the right of existence of entire human groups in the same way as homicide is the denial of the right to live for individual human beings."[31]

567   The definition of the crime protects not only the physical but also the social existence of the group.[32] The destruction of a group "as such" can also be accomplished by de-

---

[28] See marginal no. 606.

[29] See marginal no. 304

[30] See ICJ, Advisory Opinion of 28 May 1951 (Reservation to the Convention on the Prevention and Punishment of Genocide), *ICJ Rep.* 1951, p. 23; *Prosecutor* v. *Akayesu*, ICTR (Trial Chamber), judgment of 2 September 1998, para. 469; *Prosecutor* v. *Jelisić*, ICTY (Trial Chamber), judgment of 14 December 1999, paras. 69 et seq., under the heading "Groups protected by Article 4 of the [ICTY] Statute"; *Prosecutor* v. *Krstić*, ICTY (Trial Chamber), judgment of 2 August 2001, paras. 551 et seq. See also *Attorney-General of the Government of Israel* v. *Eichmann*, District Court of Jerusalem, judgment of 12 December 1961, paras. 190 et seq., 36 *ILM* (1968), pp. 232 et seq., on "crimes against the Jewish people," a concept borrowed from the definition of the crime of genocide; *Draft Code* 1996, Commentary on Art. 17, paras. 6 et seq.; P. Drost, *The Crime of State, Vol. II: Genocide* (1959), pp. 84 et seq.; E. Fronza, in F. Lattanzi and W.A. Schabas (eds.), *Essays on the Rome Statute of the International Criminal Court*, Vol. 1 (1999), p. 105 at pp. 118 et seq.; A. Gil Gil, 112 *Zeitschrift für die gesamte Strafrechtswissenschaft* (2000), p. 381 at p. 393; K. Kittichaisaree, *International Criminal Law* (2001), p. 69; L. Kuper, *Genocide* (1981), p. 30; N. Robinson, *The Genocide Convention, A Commentary* (1960), p. 58; W.A. Schabas, in O. Triffterer (ed.), *Commentary on the Rome Statute of the International Criminal Court* (1999), Art. 6, marginal no. 6; O. Triffterer, in B. Schünemann et al. (eds.), *Festschrift für Roxin* (2001), p. 1415 at pp. 1432 et seq., who believes individual values are also protected by the norm. See also H. Vest, *Genozid durch organisatorische Machtapparate* (2002), p. 99: "group variety and thus immediately the constitution of humanity".

[31] UN Doc. A/RES/1/96 (1946), which also says: "such denial of the right of existence . . . results in great losses to humanity in the form of cultural and other contributions represented by these human groups . . . ."

[32] See E. Fronza, in F. Lattanzi and W.A. Schabas (eds.), *Essays on the Rome Statute of the International Criminal Court*, Vol. 1 (1999), p. 105 at pp. 118 et seq.; H.-H. Jescheck, 66 *Zeitschrift für die gesamte Strafrechtswissenschaft* (1954), p. 193 at p. 213; B. Lüders, *Die Strafbarkeit von Völkermord nach dem Römischen Statut für den Internationalen Strafgerichtshof* (2004), pp. 45 et seq.; O. Triffterer, in B. Schünemann et al. (eds.), *Festschrift für Roxin* (2001), p. 1415 at p. 1433; H. Vest, 113 *Zeitschrift für die gesamte Strafrechtswissenschaft* (2001), p. 457 at p. 476; H. Vest, *Genozid durch organisatorische Machtapparate* (2002), p. 99.

stroying group identity,[33] because, like physical extermination, this leads to the demise of the group and its loss to humankind.

The idea that physical existence alone is protected by the criminalization of genocide is therefore **568** too narrow.[34] The objection, in particular, that inclusion of the social existence of the group within the norm's protective scope violates the principle of *nullum crimen sine lege*[35] does not hold: to satisfy the principle, it suffices that the social existence of the group is only protected against attacks laid out in the definition of the crime. Attacks aimed at annihilating only the cultural identity of the group (so-called cultural genocide) were purposely left out of the definition.

Whether the criminalization of genocide additionally protects the individual rights of **569** members of the group is subject to dispute. Individual members of a group are usually targets of attack, but injury or danger to individual rights is only governed by international law if the individual is attacked specifically because of his or her membership in the group. Only the intended result, the destruction of the group as such, turns harm to individual rights into the international crime of genocide.[36]

At the same time, however, it cannot be denied that victims of a genocidal attack en- **570** dure serious violations of their human dignity: the individual is a victim of the crime solely because of his or her membership in a specific group, and is thus depersonalized and reduced to a mere object. Therefore, in addition to the primary protected right, the existence of the group, the human dignity of the individual victim is also protected.[37]

B. Material Elements

I. Protected Groups

Only groups constituted through "national," "ethnic," "racial" or "religious" characteris- **571** tics are protected under the definition of the crime. This list is exclusive;[38] the drafters of

---

[33] The destruction of the social existence of a group is conceivable through, for example, expulsion and dispersal of the members of a group, through systematic destruction of their awareness of belonging together, or through elimination of the group's intellectual or political leadership.

[34] But see *Prosecutor* v. *Krstić*, ICTY (Trial Chamber), judgment of 2 August 2001, para. 580.

[35] See *Prosecutor* v. *Krstić*, ICTY (Trial Chamber), judgment of 2 August 2001, paras. 574 et seq., 580.

[36] See *Prosecutor* v. *Jelisić*, ICTY (Trial Chamber), judgment of 14 December 1999, para. 66. The ICTR also stated in the *Akayesu* decision: "The perpetration of the act charged therefore extends beyond its actual commission, for example, the murder of a particular individual, for the realisation of an ulterior motive, which is to destroy, in whole or in part, the group of which the individual is just one element," see *Prosecutor* v. *Akayesu*, ICTR (Trial Chamber), judgment of 2 September 1998, para. 522.

[37] Fronza also advocates the protection of individual interests, in F. Lattanzi and W.A. Schabas (eds.), *Essays on the Rome Statute of the International Criminal Court*, Vol. 1 (1999), p. 105 at p. 119; A. Planzer, *Le crime de genocide* (1956), pp. 79 et seq., saying that genocide violates both the group's right to exist and the elementary rights of the individual; C. Tomuschat, in H.J. Cremer et al. (eds.), *Festschrift für Steinberger* (2002), p. 315 at p. 329: "Genocide is certainly the worst of all offenses against both human dignity and international peace and security." Triffterer defined the individual rights as protection of life, bodily integrity, psychological health and the individual freedom to join a group, see O. Triffterer, in B. Schünemann et al. (eds.), *Festschrift für Roxin* (2001), p. 1415 at pp. 1432 et seq.

[38] *Prosecutor* v. *Krstić*, ICTY (Trial Chamber), judgment of 2 August 2001, para. 554. See also G. Dahm, J. Delbrück and R. Wolfrum, *Völkerrecht*, Vol. I/3, 2nd edn. (2002), pp. 1077 et seq.; P. Drost,

the Genocide Convention purposely limited Article II to protection of the four named groups.[39] Common to the protected groups is the fact that group membership is generally determined by birth and is of a permanent and stable nature.

572 A clear distinction between the various groups is not possible, since social perceptions are ultimately decisive in the constitution of groups; the definitions of groups will frequently overlap. Thus the group under attack may possess the characteristics of several groups. Because all the groups included in the definition of the crime are equally protected, there is no need definitively to assign one group of victims a particular common characteristic. Nor must all members belong to the group on the basis of the same characteristic.[40]

1. Criteria for Group Classification

573 The classification of a set of persons as a national, ethnic, racial or religious group can be accomplished from a variety of perspectives. The first criteria that come to mind are of an objective nature, such as common customs, language or religion or visible physical characteristics such as skin color or stature. But it is also possible to see group characteristics subjectively and rely on social ascription processes – that is, a group's self-perception or its perception by others as a national, ethnic, racial or religious group. Both approaches can be found in the judgments of the international Tribunals.

574   In its first major decision on the crime of genocide, the *Akayesu* decision, the Rwanda Tribunal took a firmly objective approach.[41]

575 In that judgment, the Tribunal came to the remarkable interim conclusion that the Tutsi did not constitute a group explicitly included in the definition of genocide. The Tutsi and Hutu, it said, were perceived by the Rwandan population to be separate ethnic entities,[42] but this was difficult to justify through objective observation. Specifically, Tutsi and Hutu speak the same language, share the same religion, and have a common cultural identity. Classification as "Tutsi" or "Hutu" is thus

---

The Crime of State, Vol. II: Genocide (1959), p. 80; W.A. Schabas, *Genocide in International Law* (2000), pp. 102, 130. For another view, see *Prosecutor* v. *Akayesu*, ICTR (Trial Chamber), judgment of 2 September 1998, para. 701: "protection of any stable and permanent group"; Audiencia Nacional, judgment of 5 November 1998, section 5, available at <http://www.ua.es/up/pinochet/documentos/chile.htm>; B. van Schaack, 106 *Yale Law Journal* (1997), p. 2259 at pp. 2282 et seq.; J.D. van den Vyver, 23 *Fordham Journal of International Law* (1999), p. 286 at pp. 303 et seq.

[39] This decision was based on the determination that in the past these groups in particular had been the repeated targets of hostility and that they were defined by homogeneity, involuntariness of membership, and permanence. See M. Lippman, in M.C. Bassiouni (ed.), *International Criminal Law*, 2nd edn. (1999), p. 589 at p. 597.

[40] See B. Jähnke, in B. Jähnke et al. (eds.), *StGB (Strafgesetzbuch, German Criminal Code), Leipziger Kommentar*, 11th edn. (1999), Sec. 220a, marginal no. 9. According to Schabas, the four groups' characteristics not only overlap, they help to clarify each other and essentially make up the four pillars that support the norm's protected zone, see W.A. Schabas, *Genocide in International Law* (2000), pp. 111 et seq. See also M.N. Shaw, in Y. Dinstein (ed.), *International Law at the Time of Perplexity* (1989), p. 797 at pp. 807.

[41] *Prosecutor* v. *Akayesu*, ICTR (Trial Chamber), judgment of 2 September 1998, paras. 510 et seq. A. Cassese, *International Criminal Law* (2003) at p. 101, speaks in regard to the *Akayesu* judgment of a combination of objective and subjective criteria; G. Dahm, J. Delbrück and R. Wolfrum, *Völkerrecht*, Vol. I/3, 2nd edn. (2002) at p. 1078 in contrast, share the view presented here.

[42] See *Prosecutor* v. *Akayesu*, ICTR (Trial Chamber), judgment of 2 September 1998, para. 702.

less the result of the application of objective criteria than the result of a social ascription process. The Tribunal acknowledged this social ascription process, but did not find it decisive for the constitution of the group. Ultimately, the chamber simply extended the definition of genocide to cover all "stable groups," including those not explicitly named,[43] a result that is incompatible with the principle of legality (*nullum crimen sine lege*),[44] which also applies to international law.[45]

In the *Kayishema and Ruzindana* judgment, Trial Chamber II of the Rwanda Tribunal **576** did not follow the purely objective approach of the *Akayesu* judgment, declaring social ascription processes relevant in determining the concept of the ethnic group, along with objective characteristics: "An ethnic group is one whose members share a common language and culture; or, a group which distinguishes itself, as such (self identification); or, a group identified as such by others, including perpetrators of the crimes (identification by others)."[46]

In the decisions of Trial Chamber I of the Rwanda Tribunal, too, subjective elements have increas- **577** ingly been taken into consideration. Thus the significance of subjective elements was acknowledged in the *Rutaganda* and later in the *Musema* judgments; however, the Chamber continues to adhere to the view that social ascription processes alone are not sufficient for classification as an ethnic group. The authors of the Genocide Convention, in this view, intended to limit the definition to stable groups.[47] It is therefore not possible to dispense with objective criteria.[48] In *Bagilishema*, the Chamber stated that, given the lack of a universally-accepted definition, the concept of the group must be understood in light of the respective political, social, historical, and cultural context. In the Court's view, therefore, the objective element of membership in a specific group also took on a subjective dimension.[49] In *Semanza*, the Rwanda Tribunal's Trial Chamber III took an approach based on both objective and subjective criteria.[50]

The Yugoslavia Tribunal has so far taken a clear position: The "group" is a social con- **578** struction, and therefore its characteristics must be determined from the respective sociohistorical context. Perception of a set of people as a particular group is decisive, because the group is not amenable to objective scientific definition. To classify a group as national, ethnic, racial, or religious, therefore, what is most important is the characteristics upon which perpetrators or third parties base their perceptions.[51]

---

[43] *Prosecutor v. Akayesu*, ICTR (Trial Chamber), judgment of 2 September 1998, paras. 511, 516, 701 et seq.

[44] See marginal nos. 91 et seq.

[45] For a critical view, see also A. Cassese, *International Criminal Law* (2003), pp. 96, 101 ("unconvincing").

[46] *Prosecutor v. Kayishema and Ruzindana*, ICTR (Trial Chamber), judgment of 21 May 1999, para. 98.

[47] For a critical view of this "impermissible narrowing" of the crime, see G. Dahm, J. Delbrück and R. Wolfrum, *Völkerrecht*, Vol. I/3, 2nd edn. (2002), p. 1079.

[48] See *Prosecutor v. Rutaganda*, ICTR (Trial Chamber), judgment of 9 December 1999, paras. 56 et seq.; *Prosecutor v. Musema*, ICTR (Trial Chamber), judgment of 27 January 2000, paras. 162 et seq.

[49] *Prosecutor v. Bagilishema*, ICTR (Trial Chamber), judgment of 7 June 2001, para. 65.

[50] *Prosecutor v. Semanza*, ICTR (Trial Chamber), judgment of 15 May 2003, para. 317: "The Chamber finds that the determination of a protected group is to be made on a case-by-case basis." Trial Chamber II concurred in this view, see *Prosecutor v. Kamuhanda*, ICTR (Trial Chamber), judgment of 22 January 2004, para. 630.

[51] *Prosecutor v. Jelisić*, ICTY (Trial Chamber), judgment of 14 December 1999, para. 70; *Prosecutor v. Krstić*, ICTY (Trial Chamber), judgment of 2 August 2001, para. 557.

579   The international Courts' retreat from an exclusively objective designation of group characteristics is welcome.[52] For ultimately, social perceptions determine the classification of a group as national, ethnic, racial or religious. The starting point for determining group characteristics for purposes of defining genocide must therefore be the ascriptions of group members as well as outsiders; in particular, perpetrators usually define the victim group themselves. However, it must be noted that the definition of the group is a material element of the crime, and cannot be determined arbitrarily. Thus the only ascriptions to be taken into account are those indicating that a set of people, defined as a national, ethnic, racial or religious group, is a concrete entity.

2. National Groups

580   The element that connects a national group, above all, is shared nationality.[53] Additional elements to consider are a common history, customs, culture, and language.[54] Typical examples of national groups are so-called national minorities; political or social groups are not included.[55]

3. Ethnic Groups

581   By including ethnic groups in the definition, the authors of the Genocide Convention intended to include groups similar or identical in nature to national, racial or religious groups. Thus some believed that ethnic groups were a subcategory of national groups; another view held that the concept of ethnicity was identical with that of race.[56] An ethnic group is distinguished in particular by a specific cultural tradition and a common

---

[52] A subjective approach is also advocated by D.M. Amann, 93 *American Journal of International Law* (1999), p. 195 at p. 198; E. Fronza, in F. Lattanzi and W.A. Schabas (eds.), *Essays on the Rome Statute of the International Criminal Court*, Vol. 1 (1999), p. 105 at pp. 118 et seq.; B. Lüders, *Die Strafbarkeit von Völkermord nach dem Römischen Statut für den Internationalen Strafgerichtshof* (2004), pp. 60 et seq.; F. Selbmann, *Der Tatbestand des Genozids im Völkerstrafrecht* (2002), pp. 187 et seq.; G. Verdirame, 49 *International and Comparative Law Quarterly* (2000), p. 578 at pp. 588 et seq., 592. See also H. Vest, 117 *Schweizerische Zeitschrift für Strafrecht* (1999), p. 351 at pp. 357 et seq. A purely objective approach, in contrast, is advocated by E.H. Pircher, *Der vertragliche Schutz ethnischer, sprachlicher und religiöser Minderheiten im Völkerrecht* (1979), p. 230; W.A. Schabas, *Genocide in International Law* (2000), pp. 109 et seq., finding that the group is a material element of the crime and must therefore be objectively determined. The perpetrator's perceptions cannot alone determine whether the group is to be included in the protective scope of the norm.

[53] See *Prosecutor* v. *Akayesu*, ICTR (Trial Chamber), judgment of 2 September 1998, para. 512.

[54] See D.D. Nsereko, in G. Kirk McDonald and O. Swaak-Goldman (eds.), *Substantive and Procedural Aspects of International Criminal Law*, Vol. 1 (2000), p. 117 at p. 131; A. Planzer, *Le crime de genocide* (1956), p. 97.

[55] See W.A. Schabas, *Genocide in International Law* (2000), pp. 114 et seq. In contrast, in the view of the Spanish Audiencia Nacional, ultimately all political and social groups within a state are "national" groups according to the definition of the crime; this includes, in addition to members of political groups, AIDS patients, old people, or simply "the powerful." See Audiencia Nacional, judgment of 5 November 1998, Sec. 5, available at <http://www.ua.es/up/pinochet/documentos/chile.htm>. This view explodes the definition of the crime; it violates both its wording and its historical meaning, see B. Lüders, *Die Strafbarkeit von Völkermord nach dem Römischen Statut für den Internationalen Strafgerichtshof* (2004), p. 74.

[56] *Study on the Question of the Prevention and Punishment of the Crime of Genocide*, prepared by Mr Nicodeme Ruhashyankiko, Special Rapporteur (1978), UN Doc. E/CN.4/Sub.2/416, para. 69.

history. The members of the group speak the same language, have the same customs and traditions and share a common way of life.[57] The group can frequently be found in a specific geographical region. Common "racial" characteristics are not necessary for the existence of an ethnic group.[58]

4. Racial Groups

The concept of race, which is not unproblematic given its abusive usage, is employed to **582** describe social groups whose members exhibit the same inherited, visible physical traits, such as skin color or physical stature.[59] Tribal groups also fall into this category.[60]

5. Religious Groups

Religious groups were already included in General Assembly Resolution 96(I) of 1946 as **583** a group that could fall victim to genocide,[61] and religious groups also appeared in all the draft attempts to formulate the crime.[62] The authors of the Convention assumed that, even if membership is voluntary, religious groups evolved historically in the same way as national and ethnic groups, demonstrate consistent characteristics, and thus have a stable character.[63]

The members of a religious community are of the same faith, believe in the same **584** spiritual paradigm,[64] and share a common spiritual idea[65] or similar forms of religious practice.[66] Small religious groups and sects[67] meet this definition as well as larger ones.

---

[57] See *Prosecutor* v. *Akayesu*, ICTR (Trial Chamber), judgment of 2 September 1998, para. 513; *Prosecutor* v. *Kayishema and Ruzindana*, ICTR (Trial Chamber), judgment of 21 May 1999, para. 98; M. Lippman, 15 *Arizona Journal of International and Comparative Law* (1998), p. 415 at p. 456; A. Planzer, *Le crime de genocide* (1956), p. 97.

[58] But see D.D.N. Nsereko, in G. Kirk McDonald and O. Swaak-Goldman (eds.), *Substantive and Procedural Aspects of International Criminal Law*, Vol. 1 (2000), p. 117 at p. 131.

[59] See *Prosecutor* v. *Akayesu*, ICTR (Trial Chamber), judgment of 2 September 1998, para. 514; K. Kittichaisaree, *International Criminal Law* (2001), p. 69; M. Lippman, in Bassiouni (ed.), *International Criminal Law*, Vol. 1, 2ⁿᵈ edn. (1999), p. 589 at p. 598; D.D.N. Nsereko, in G. Kirk McDonald and O. Swaak-Goldman (eds.), *Substantive and Procedural Aspects of International Criminal Law*, Vol. 1 (2000), p. 117 at pp. 131 et seq.; W.A. Schabas, *Genocide in International Law* (2000), p. 123.

[60] *Draft Code* 1996, Commentary to Art. 17, para. 9. See also A. Planzer, *Le crime de genocide* (1956), p. 97.

[61] UN Doc. A/RES/1/96 (1946).

[62] Various drafts are reprinted in W.A. Schabas, *Genocide in International Law* (2000), pp. 553 et seq.

[63] See W.A. Schabas, *Genocide in International Law* (2000), p. 127.

[64] See M. Lippman, 15 *Arizona Journal of International and Comparative Law* (1998), p. 415 at pp. 456 et seq.; A. Planzer, *Le crime de genocide* (1956), p. 98.

[65] See A. Planzer, *Le crime de genocide* (1956), p. 98.

[66] See *Prosecutor* v. *Akayesu*, ICTR (Trial Chamber), judgment of 2 September 1998, para. 515; similarly *Prosecutor* v. *Kayishema and Ruzindana*, ICTR (Trial Chamber), judgment of 21 May 1999, para. 98.

[67] See D.D.N. Nsereko, in G. Kirk McDonald and O. Swaak-Goldman (eds.), *Substantive and Procedural Aspects of International Criminal Law*, Vol. 1 (2000), p. 117 at p. 132; M.N. Shaw, in Y. Dinstein (ed.), *International Law at the Time of Perplexity* (1989), p. 797 at p. 807.

Atheistic groups are not included,[68] since the freedom not to practice a religion is not protected.[69] Nor can political convictions be equated with religious faith; otherwise, political groups could be classified as religious groups through the backdoor.[70]

6. Other Groups

585 Groups other than those named explicitly in the definition of the crime are not protected by either international treaty or customary law. The limitation of the scope of the crime of genocide to the groups listed above can be explained, first of all, by the fact that these groups' members are in greatest need of protection. At least where national, racial or ethnic groups are concerned, individuals cannot separate themselves from the group by merely distancing themselves from it; the fate of the individual is indissolubly linked with the fate of the group. Second of all, such stable communities are relatively easy to distinguish, while political, social, economic and other comparable groups constantly change their composition and are therefore not protected as such.[71] From a legal policy perspective, the failure to include political groups, in particular, is controversial.[72]

586   The definition of genocide encompasses only "stable groups," but not all of them. In contrast, the Rwanda Tribunal attempted, in the aforementioned *Akayesu* judgment,[73] to include all groups possessing a permanent character for which membership was determined by birth.[74] This interpretation rightly failed to be affirmed in subsequent case law. The inclusion of all stable groups does not conform to the wording of Article 6 of

---

[68] For a different view see M. Lippman, 15 *Arizona Journal of International and Comparative Law* (1998), p. 415 at p. 456.

[69] M.N. Shaw, in Y. Dinstein (ed.), *International Law at a Time of Perplexity* (1989), p. 797 at p. 807, points out that atheist groups are often precisely the political groups that do not enjoy the protection of the genocide norm. In addition, atheist groups are not clearly definable.

[70] See E.H. Pircher, *Der vertragliche Schutz ethnischer, sprachlicher und religiöser Minderheiten im Völkerrecht* (1979), p. 37.

[71] On this argument, see L.J. LeBlanc, 13 *Yale Journal of International Law* (1988), p. 268 at pp. 273 et seq.; D.D.N. Nsereko, in G. Kirk McDonald and O. Swaak-Goldman (eds.), *Substantive and Procedural Aspects of International Criminal Law*, Vol. 1 (2000), p. 117 at p. 130.

[72] On the discussion of the inclusion of political groups in Art. II of the Genocide Convention, see P.N. Drost, *The Crime of State, Vol. II: Genocide* (1959), pp. 60 et seq.; L. Kuper, *Genocide* (1981), pp. 24 et seq.; B. van Schaack, 106 *Yale Law Journal* (1997), p. 2259 at pp. 2262 et seq.; W.A. Schabas, *Genocide in International Law* (2000), pp. 134 et seq.; H. Vest, *Genozid durch organisatorische Machtapparate* (2002), p. 129. The inclusion of political and other groups was discussed again at the Rome Conference, and ultimately rejected, see W.A. Schabas, in O. Triffterer (ed.), *Commentary on the Rome Statute of the International Criminal Court* (1999), Art. 6, marginal no. 6.

[73] See marginal nos. 574 et seq.

[74] See *Prosecutor* v. *Akayesu*, ICTR (Trial Chamber), judgment of 2 September 1998, paras. 511, 516, 701 et seq. For this expansion of genocide, the Tribunal relied on the history of the Genocide Convention: "On reading through the *travaux préparatoires* of the Genocide Convention, it appears that the crime of genocide was allegedly perceived as targeting only stable groups, constituted in a permanent fashion and membership of which is determined by birth" (para. 511); "the Chamber considered whether the groups protected by the Convention . . ., should be limited to only the four groups expressly mentioned and whether they should not also include any group which is stable and permanent like the said four groups. . . ., it is particularly important to respect the intention of the drafters of the Genocide Convention, which according to the *travaux préparatoires*, was patently to ensure the protection of any stable and permanent group" (para. 516).

the ICC Statute and therefore violates the principle of legality (*nullum crimen sine lege*). The history of the Genocide Convention also argues against such an expansive interpretation, as the crime was purposely limited to the specific "stable groups" listed above.[75]

II. Individual Acts

The various forms of physical genocide encompass the acts of killing under Article 6(a)   **587** of the ICC Statute, causing serious bodily or mental harm under Article 6(b), and inflicting destructive conditions of life on a group under Article 6(c). Measures intended to prevent births within a group, which are criminalized in Article 6(d), can be considered a form of biological genocide, while Article 6(e), on forcible transfer of children from the group to another group, represents a special form of cultural genocide that is not otherwise punished.[76]

The targets of attack are always individual members of the group, whose physical in-   **588** tegrity or social existence are violated or endangered.[77] This follows in part directly from the text of the norm.[78] But even where the definition requires conduct against the "group,"[79] this conduct is conveyed through attacks on individual group members. Although Article 6(a), (b), (d), and (e) use the plural form and speak of "members" as victims, the requirement is already fulfilled if a single member of the group is affected by the conduct.[80] In addition, the victim must actually, not merely putatively, belong to the group that has been selected for extermination.[81] Otherwise, the act can only constitute an attempt.[82]

---

[75] See also W.A. Schabas, *Genocide in International Law* (2000), pp. 109 et seq., pp. 130 et seq.

[76] For more information, see marginal no. 599.

[77] See, e.g., P.N. Drost, *The Crime of State, Vol. II: Genocide* (1959), p. 86; A. Gil Gil, 112 *Zeitschrift für die gesamte Strafrechtswissenschaft* (2000), p. 381 at p. 396; O. Triffterer, in B. Schünemann et al. (eds.), *Festschrift für Roxin* (2001), p. 1415 at p. 1433.

[78] See ICC Statute, Art. 6(a), (b), (e).

[79] See ICC Statute, Art. 6(c), (d).

[80] See P.N. Drost, *The Crime of State, Vol. II: Genocide* (1959), pp. 85 et seq.; A. Gil Gil, 112 *Zeitschrift für die gesamte Strafrechtswissenschaft* (2000), p. 381 at pp. 395 et seq., with additional cites; H.-H. Jescheck, 66 *Zeitschrift für die gesamte Strafrechtswissenschaft* (1954), p. 193 at pp. 212 et seq.; N. Robinson, *The Genocide Convention, A Commentary* (1960), pp. 62 et seq.; W.A. Schabas, *Genocide in International Law* (2000), p. 158; O. Triffterer, in B. Schünemann et al. (eds.), *Festschrift für Roxin* (2001), p. 1415 at p. 1433; G. Dahm, J. Delbrück and R. Wolfrum, *Völkerrecht*, Vol. I/3, 2nd edn. (2002), p. 1080. For the corresponding rule in German law see marginal no. 254.

[81] Elements of Crimes for ICC Statute, Art. 6(a) to (e), no. 2; *Prosecutor* v. *Akayesu*, ICTR (Trial Chamber), judgment of 2 September 1998, para. 712: The Tribunal found genocide only if the victim was Tutsi. See also W.A. Schabas, *Genocide in International Law* (2000), p. 158. In the ICTR's *Bagilishema* judgment, the Trial Chamber presented a different view, see *Prosecutor* v. *Bagilishema*, ICTR (Trial Chamber), judgment of 7 June 2001, para. 65: "A group may not have precisely defined boundaries and there may be occasions when it is difficult to give a definitive answer as to whether or not a victim was a member of a protected group. Moreover, the perpetrators of genocide may characterize the targeted group in ways that do not fully correspond to conceptions of the group shared generally, or by other segments of society. In such a case, the Chamber is of the opinion that, on the evidence, if a victim was perceived by a perpetrator as belonging to a protected group, the victim could be considered by the Chamber as a member of the protected group, for the purposes of genocide."

[82] B. Jähnke, in B. Jähnke et al. (eds.), *StGB (Strafgesetzbuch, German Criminal Code), Leipziger Kommentar*, 11th edn. (1999), Sec. 220a, marginal no. 10.

1. Killing

589   Article 6(a) of the ICC Statute requires the perpetrator to have caused the death of at least one member of the group.

2. Causing Serious Bodily or Mental Harm

590   Article 6(b) of the ICC Statute requires the perpetrator to have caused serious bodily or mental harm to at least one member of the group.[83] International case law interprets serious bodily harm to mean serious damage to health, causing disfigurement, and serious injuries to external or internal organs or senses.[84] As examples of conduct under this article, the *Akayesu* judgment listed, among other things, mutilation and use of force, beating with rifle butts, and injuries inflicted with a machete.[85] The definition also specifically includes sexual violence, which causes serious bodily and, generally, also mental injury.[86]

591   Causing serious mental harm does not require a physical attack or any physical effects of mental harm.[87] This interpretation is supported, first of all, by the wording of the definition, which places the two modalities of conduct on an equal footing. Second of all, causing serious mental harm to members of the group can have a significant effect on the group's social existence.[88] Thus the Rwanda Tribunal has rightly assumed that the

---

[83] The inclusion of mental harm was controversial in the negotiations on Art. II of the Genocide Convention, see S. Gorove, *Washington University Law Quarterly* 1951, p. 174; W.A. Schabas, *Genocide in International Law* (2000), p. 160. The initiative to include mental harm came from China. This criterion was intended especially to cover administration of drugs.

[84] See *Prosecutor* v. *Kayishema and Ruzindana*, ICTR (Trial Chamber), judgment of 21 May 1999, para. 109; *Prosecutor* v. *Akayesu*, ICTR (Trial Chamber), judgment of 2 September 1998, paras. 504, 711, 720 et seq.; *Prosecutor* v. *Krstić*, ICTY (Trial Chamber), judgment of 2 August 2001, para. 543, pointing to the remarks on crimes against humanity in paras. 507 et seq., 513.

[85] *Prosecutor* v. *Akayesu*, ICTR (Trial Chamber), judgment of 2 September 1998, paras. 706 et seq. (mutilation), para. 720 (interrogation involving threat of death or violence), para. 711 (beating with rifle butts), para. 722 (wounding with machete).

[86] *Prosecutor* v. *Akayesu*, ICTR (Trial Chamber), judgment of 2 September 1998, paras. 706, 731. In Rwanda in 1994, Tutsi women in particular were victims of widespread sexual violence. The women were raped and sexually abused repeatedly, frequently by different men and often publicly. The Tribunal determined that this conduct represented the worst kind of harm to physical and mental integrity, as the victims were harmed both physically and mentally. On the crime of sexual violence, see also K.D. Askin, 93 *American Journal of International Law* (1999), pp. 97 et seq.; K. Karagiannakis, 12 *Leiden Journal of International Law* (1999), pp. 479 et seq.; W.A. Schabas, *Genocide in International Law* (2000), pp. 161 et seq.; G. Verdirame, 49 *International and Comparative Law Quarterly* (2000), p. 578 at pp. 594 et seq.; P. Viseur Sellers, in G. Kirk McDonald and O. Swaak-Goldman (eds.), *Substantive and Procedural Aspects of International Criminal Law*, Vol. 1 (2000), pp. 263 et seq.

[87] D. Petrovic, 5 *European Journal of International Law* (1994), p. 342 at p. 357. But see D.D.N. Nsereko, in G. Kirk McDonald and O. Swaak-Goldman (eds.), *Substantive and Procedural Aspects of International Criminal Law*, Vol. 1 (2000), p. 117 at p. 129.

[88] See B. Bryant and R.H. Jones, 16 *Harvard International Law Journal* (1975), p. 682 at p. 694; P.N. Drost, *The Crime of State, Vol. II: Genocide* (1959), p. 81. "The insertion 'mental harm' was meant to protect the psychological integrity of human beings"; W.A. Schabas, *Genocide in International Law* (2000), pp. 160 et seq.

criterion of mental harm possesses its own separate scope.[89] The destructive psychological effects of crimes of sexual violence are thus granted the same importance as the physical consequences of the acts.[90]

Causing "serious" bodily or mental harm does not require that the harm be permanent or irreversible.[91] A merely temporary physical or mental impairment, however, is insufficient. It must involve damage "that results in a grave and long-term disadvantage to a person's ability to lead a normal and constructive life."[92] Whether this is the case must be decided by taking account of all circumstances surrounding the individual case.[93]   **592**

3. Inflicting Destructive Conditions of Life

Article 6(c) of the ICC Statute covers the infliction of conditions of life on a group that are calculated to bring about its physical destruction, in whole or in part. The provision prohibits so-called slow death measures – that is, conduct that does not immediately kill, but that can (and is intended to) bring about the death of group members over the long term.[94]   **593**

In formulating this provision of the Genocide Convention, the authors had in mind specific manifestations of the Nazi genocide of the European Jews. These included forced labor, deportations in which people were penned together in trains for days, and imprisonment in extermination and concentration camps, in which inmates were denied the necessities of life and forced to live in degrading conditions.   **594**

Possible conduct includes withholding necessities such as food, clothing, shelter and medicine, as well as *de facto* enslavement through forced labor.[95] Deportations, including   **595**

---

[89] *Prosecutor* v. *Kayishema and Ruzindana*, ICTR (Trial Chamber), judgment of 21 May 1999, paras. 110 et seq.

[90] *Prosecutor* v. *Akayesu*, ICTR (Trial Chamber), judgment of 2 September 1998, para. 731.

[91] See *Prosecutor* v. *Akayesu*, ICTR (Trial Chamber), judgment of 2 September 1998, para. 502; concurring: *Prosecutor* v. *Kayishema and Ruzindana*, ICTR (Trial Chamber), judgment of 21 May 1999, para. 108; *Prosecutor* v. *Krstić*, ICTY (Trial Chamber), judgment of 2 August 2001, para. 513; B. Bryant and R.H. Jones, 16 *Harvard International Law Journal* (1975), p. 682 at pp. 693 et seq.; G. Dahm, J. Delbrück and R. Wolfrum, *Völkerrecht*, Vol. I/3, 2nd edn. (2002), p. 1080; J. Webb, 23 *Georgia Journal of International and Comparative Law* (1993), p. 377 at p. 393.

[92] *Prosecutor* v. *Krstić*, ICTY (Trial Chamber), judgment of 2 August 2001, para. 513.

[93] *Prosecutor* v. *Kayishema and Ruzindana*, ICTR (Trial Chamber), judgment of 21 May 1999, para. 113.

[94] This covers "extermination through slow death," see F. Selbmann, *Der Tatbestand des Genozids im Völkerstrafrecht* (2002), p. 161.

[95] *Prosecutor* v. *Kayishema and Ruzindana*, ICTR (Trial Chamber), judgment of 21 May 1999, para. 115. See also Elements of Crimes for ICC Statute, Art. 6(c), no. 3, fn. 4: "The term 'conditions of life' may include, but is not necessarily restricted to, deliberate deprivation of resources indispensable for survival, such as food or medical services, or systematic expulsion from homes"; *Prosecutor* v. *Akayesu*, ICTR (Trial Chamber), judgment of 2 September 1998, para. 506; *Prosecutor* v. *Karadžić and Mladić*, ICTY (Trial Chamber), decision of 11 July 1996, paras. 94 et seq.; *Attorney-General of the Government of Israel* v. *Eichmann*, District Court of Jerusalem, judgment of 12 December 1961, paras. 190 et seq., 36 *ILM* (1968), pp. 235 et seq.; P.N. Drost, *The Crime of State, Vol. II: Genocide* (1959),

so-called ethnic cleansing,[96] are not included as such, but they are included if – as will usually be the case in systematic expulsions – they are combined with the withholding of food, medical care, shelter, etc., and are thus calculated to physically exterminate group members.[97] Mass rapes are not "conditions of life" as such, but they become so if inflicted systematically and repeatedly, perhaps in connection with other measures.[98] The conditions of life must only be calculated to physically exterminate part of the group;[99] thus the death of individual members as a result is not a necessary element of the crime. As only partial destruction is necessary, it is enough if only a part of the group is subject to destructive conditions of life.

596   The subjective requirement "deliberately" makes it clear that the perpetrator must employ the conduct as a means to physically exterminate the group. No requirement of prior planning can be derived from this criterion.[100]

4. Imposing Measures to Prevent Births

597   Article 6(d) of the ICC Statute encompasses the imposition of measures aimed at preventing births within the group and thereby targeting its continued biological existence. This conduct includes, for example, sterilization, forced birth control, prohibitions on marriage and segregation of the sexes.[101] Rape can fit the definition, for example if it causes the victim to decide not to reproduce because of the trauma suffered.[102] The Tribunals have also included rape with the purpose of changing the ethnic composition of a group; this can be the case, for example, in patriarchal societies where children are counted as belonging to the father's ethnic group.[103] The measures imposed must be forcible;[104] merely permitting abortions is not sufficient. In any case, the measures taken by various heavily populated countries – such as China – to forcibly lower the birth rate for social, economic or other reasons do not reflect genocidal intent.

---

p. 87; D. Petrovic, 5 *European Journal of International Law* (1994), p. 342 at p. 357; N. Robinson, *The Genocide Convention, A Commentary* (1960), pp. 63 et seq. On famine crimes as genocide, see D. Marcus, 97 *American Journal of International Law* (2003), p. 245 at pp. 262 et seq.

[96] See marginal no. 605.

[97] See W.A. Schabas, *Genocide in International Law* (2000), p. 168; the Elements of Crimes should also be read with this clarification ("systematic expulsion from home"), see marginal no. 595, fn. 95.

[98] See B. Jähnke, in B. Jähnke et al. (eds), *StGB (Strafgesetzbuch, German Criminal Code), Leipziger Kommentar*, 11th edn. (1999), Sec. 220a, marginal no. 11.

[99] See *Prosecutor v. Akayesu*, ICTR (Trial Chamber), judgment of 2 September 1998, para. 505. Similarly, *Prosecutor v. Kayishema and Ruzindana*, ICTR (Trial Chamber), judgment of 21 May 1999, para. 116; M. Lippman, 15 *Arizona Journal of International and Comparative Law* (1998), p. 415 at p. 456; O. Triffterer, in D. Blumenwitz (ed.), *Flucht und Vertreibung* (1987), p. 259 at p. 283.

[100] But in favor of a requirement of prior planning, see N. Robinson, *The Genocide Convention, A Commentary* (1960), p. 60. See also K. Ambos, *Der Allgemeine Teil des Völkerstrafrechts* (2002), p. 796, according to which the term "deliberately" refers only to the general reqirement of "intent and knowledge" under ICC Statute, Art. 30.

[101] See *Prosecutor v. Akayesu*, ICTR (Trial Chamber), judgment of 2 September 1998, para. 507.

[102] See *Prosecutor v. Akayesu*, ICTR (Trial Chamber), judgment of 2 September 1998, para. 508.

[103] See *Prosecutor v. Akayesu*, ICTR (Trial Chamber), judgment of 2 September 1998, para. 507; *Prosecutor v. Karadžić and Mladić*, ICTY (Trial Chamber), decision of 11 July 1996, para. 94.

[104] See *Draft Code* 1996, Commentary on Art. 17, para. 16.

5. Forcibly Transferring Children

Article 6(e) of the ICC Statute comprises the forcible transfer of children from one group to another group. **598**

Early drafts of the Genocide Convention included so-called cultural genocide – the destruction of a group's specific characteristics, such as its language or cultural traditions. The forcible transfer of children to another group was the first of five subcategories of cultural genocide. Cultural genocide as such was not adopted into the Genocide Convention, nor is it recognized as a crime under customary international law; but the forcible transfer of children to another group, a specific form of cultural genocide, did become part of the definition of the crime.[105] **599**

This encompasses permanent transfer done with the specific intent of destroying the group's existence. When transferred to another group, children cannot grow up as part of their group, or they become estranged from their cultural identity. The language, traditions, and culture of their group become or remain alien to the children. This conduct therefore endangers the group's social existence. In addition, it endangers the group's biological existence, as those involved generally will not reproduce within their own group.[106] **600**

This provision seeks to prevent children from being torn from their group and thus estranged from it. An essential element of the criminal conduct, therefore, is separation of children from their group; this in itself necessarily places the children in another group.[107] According to the Elements of Crimes for Article 6(e), children, as referred to in the definition, are members of the group under 18 years of age.[108] **601**

The transfer of children must be forcible. This force can be physical or psychological, as the Elements of Crimes for Article 6(e) make clear: **602**

"The term forcibly is not restricted to physical force, but may include threat of force or coercion, such as that caused by fear of violence, duress, detention, psychological oppression or abuse of power, against such person or persons or another person, or by taking advantage of a coercive environment."[109] **603**

---

[105] See P.N. Drost, *The Crime of State, Vol. II: Genocide* (1959), p. 87; D.D.N. Nsereko, in G. Kirk McDonald and O. Swaak-Goldman (eds.), *Substantive and Procedural Aspects of International Criminal Law*, Vol. 1 (2000), p. 117 at p. 130; N. Robinson, *The Genocide Convention, A Commentary* (1960), p. 64; K. Stillschweig, *Die Friedens-Warte* 1949, p. 93 at p. 98; C. Tournaye, 52 *International and Comparative Law Quarterly* (2003), p. 447 at pp. 453 et seq. For a thorough history of the Genocide Convention with regard to "cultural genocide," see W.A. Schabas, *Genocide in International Law* (2000), pp. 179 et seq.

[106] See B. Lüders, *Die Strafbarkeit von Völkermord nach dem Römischen Statut für den Internationalen Strafgerichtshof* (2004), pp. 198 et seq.

[107] See B. Jähnke, in B. Jähnke et al. (eds), *StGB (Strafgesetzbuch, German Criminal Code), Leipziger Kommentar*, 11th edn. (1999), Sec. 220a, marginal no. 11.

[108] Elements of Crimes for ICC Statute, Art. 6(e), no. 5. Schabas correctly argues that the age limit is too high, as it is generally impossible to estrange people who are almost adults from their group, see W.A. Schabas, *Genocide in International Law* (2000), p. 176.

[109] Elements of Crimes for ICC Statute, Art. 6(e), no. 1 fn. 5. The Trial Chamber of the ICTR had also stated: "the objective is not only to sanction a direct act of forcible physical transfer, but also to sanction acts of threats or trauma which would lead to the forcible transfer of children from one group to another," *Prosecutor v. Akayesu*, ICTR (Trial Chamber), judgment of 2 September 1998,

6. Is So-Called Ethnic Cleansing Genocide?

604 The term "ethnic cleansing" was used in connection with the war in former Yugoslavia[110] and referred to the practice by Serb forces in Bosnia and Herzegovina of forcing Muslims and Croats out of their traditional areas of settlement. This expulsion policy aimed to create a region occupied solely by Serbs, which would then be united with Serbia to form a "Greater Serbia." In the course of such "cleansing operations," civilians were massacred and mistreated, acts of sexual violence committed, cities bombarded, places of worship destroyed and property confiscated. The expression "ethnic cleansing" is thus not a legal term. It instead describes a complex criminal phenomenon, a policy whose implementation is accompanied by serious human rights violations geared toward forcing an ethnic group out of a certain region in order to change the ethnic composition of the population.[111]

605 Whether and to what extent so-called ethnic cleansing can be classified as genocide depends on the individual circumstances of the case. The blanket classification of ethnic cleansing as genocide that one occasionally encounters is incorrect.[112] Classification as genocide can fail because the primary aim of "ethnic cleansing" is expulsion of a population group, not its extermination. Also, not all conduct that takes place in the course of ethnic cleansing can be subsumed under the heading of genocide; this is the case, for example, of the destruction of houses or churches and pillaging and destruction of property. But there is no doubt that "ethnic cleansing" frequently exhibits genocidal features, and in such cases it can be punished as genocide. Thus the extent of killing operations and the choice of victims based on ethnicity can suggest that the perpetrators' purpose is not just expulsion, but also extermination of the group. Even acts that do not fall under the definition of the crime can be important evidence of the presence of genocidal intent.[113]

III. Destruction of the Group Required?

606 While crimes against humanity require the actual existence of a systematic attack against a civilian population, the crime of genocide has a different structure.[114] Here, the con-

---

para. 509. For a concurring opinion, see *Prosecutor* v. *Kayishema and Ruzindana*, ICTR (Trial Chamber), judgment of 21 May 1999, para. 118.

[110] See, e.g., J. Webb, 23 *Georgia Journal of International and Comparative Law* (1993), pp. 377 et seq.

[111] On the relevant events in the Yugoslavia conflict, see, e.g., M.C. Bassiouni and P. Manikas, *The Law of the International Criminal Tribunal for the Former Yugoslavia* (1996), pp. 48 et seq., pp. 608 et seq.; D. Petrovic, 5 *European Journal of International Law* (1994), p. 342 at pp. 344 et seq., and *Prosecutor* v. *Karadžić and Mladić*, ICTY (Trial Chamber), decision of 11 July 1996, para. 94.

[112] See also A. Cassese, *International Criminal* Law (2003), p. 96 at pp. 99 et seq. For a nuanced treatment, see also G. Dahm, J. Delbrück and R. Wolfrum, *Völkerrecht*, Vol. I/3, 2nd edn. (2002), pp. 1082 et seq.

[113] See *Prosecutor* v. *Karadžić and Mladić*, ICTY (Trial Chamber), decision of 11 July 1996, para. 94.

[114] See *Prosecutor* v. *Kayishema and Ruzindana*, ICTR (Trial Chamber), judgment of 21 May 1999, para. 94; *Prosecutor* v. *Jelisić*, ICTY (Trial Chamber), judgment of 14 December 1999, para. 100; A. Cassese, in A. Cassese, P. Gaeta and J.R.W.D. Jones (eds.), *The Rome Statute of the Interna-*

textual element is shifted to the *mens rea* – genocidal intent. From a purely terminological point of view, therefore, even an isolated individual acting with specific intent can, through his or her individual conduct, be guilty of the crime of genocide.[115]

This clear position in customary international law, reflected in Article 6 of the ICC **607** Statute, is called into question by the Elements of Crimes for the ICC Statute. The elements provide that "the conduct took place in the context of a manifest pattern of similar conduct directed against that group or was conduct that could itself effect such destruction."[116] The Elements thus promote the misunderstanding that the total or partial destruction of the group, or at least the launching of a systematic genocidal attack against a protected group, is necessary for genocide, in the same way as an attack on a civilian population is necessary for crimes against humanity.

The terms "in the context of" and "manifest" were interpreted more precisely in the **608** Elements of Crimes for Article 6: "The term 'in the context of' would include the initial acts in an emerging pattern. The term 'manifest' is an objective qualification."[117]

The Elements of Crimes here leave open whether these contextual requirements are **609** material elements of the crime that must be reflected in the perpetrator's state of mind, or merely so-called jurisdictional requirements about which the perpetrator need not have knowledge. The former (restrictive) position clearly contradicts the text of the Statute and must therefore be rejected; the Elements of Crimes cannot have the effect of limiting the material elements, in opposition to the wording of the Statute and to customary international law.[118] The standards of the Elements of Crimes are therefore to be under-

---

tional Criminal Court, Vol. 1 (2002), p. 335 at pp. 349 et seq.; G. Dahm, J. Delbrück and R. Wolfrum, *Völkerrecht*, Vol. I/3, 2nd edn. (2002), p. 1077; H.-H. Jescheck, 66 *Zeitschrift für die gesamte Strafrechtswissenschaft* (1954), p. 193 at p. 212; V. Morris and M.P. Scharf, *The International Criminal Tribunal for Rwanda*, Vol. 1 (1998), pp. 168 et seq.; O. Triffterer, in B. Schünemann et al. (eds.), *Festschrift für Roxin* (2001), p. 1415 at p. 1434. However, the presence of a contextual act is essential evidence of acting with genocidal intent, see, e.g., *Prosecutor* v. *Jelisić*, ICTY (Appeals Chamber), judgment of 5 July 2001, para. 48; *Prosecutor* v. *Krstić*, ICTY (Trial Chamber), judgment of 2 August 2001, para. 572; A. Cassese, in A. Cassese, P. Gaeta and J.R.W.D. Jones (eds.), *The Rome Statute of the International Criminal Court*, Vol. 1 (2002), p. 335 at p. 349.

[115] See *Prosecutor* v. *Kayishema and Ruzindana*, ICTR (Trial Chamber), judgment of 21 May 1999, para. 94; *Prosecutor* v. *Jelisić*, ICTY (Trial Chamber), judgment of 14 December 1999, paras. 100 et seq. ("Such a case is theoretically possible"); O. Triffterer, in B. Schünemann et al. (eds.), *Festschrift für Roxin* (2001), p. 1415 at p. 1434. However, this case is unlikely to have practical significance, as the criminal acts will typically be part of a systematic attack.

[116] Elements of Crimes for ICC Statute, Art. 6(a), (b), no. 4; Elements of Crimes for ICC Statute, Art. 6(c), (d), no. 5; Elements of Crimes for ICC Statute, Art. 6(e), no. 7; similarly, *Prosecutor* v. *Krstić*, ICTY (Trial Chamber), judgment of 2 August 2001, para. 682.

[117] Elements of Crimes for ICC Statute, Art. 6, Introduction. It also states: "Notwithstanding the normal requirement for a mental element provided for in article 30, and recognizing that knowledge of the circumstances will usually be addressed in proving genocidal intent, the appropriate requirement, if any, for a mental element regarding this circumstance will need to be decided by the Court on a case-by-case basis." The requirements mentioned are classified by some as criteria of the material element, to which the perpetrator's intent must refer, see O. Triffterer, in B. Schünemann et al. (eds.), *Festschrift für Roxin* (2001), p. 1415 at p. 1442, by others as objective requirements for criminality, see K. Ambos, *Neue Juristische Wochenschrift* 2001, p. 405 at p. 406.

[118] On the relationship between the Elements of Crimes and the Statute's norms, see marginal no. 138; E. Fronza, in F. Lattanzi and W.A. Schabas (eds.), *Essays on the Rome Statute of the International Criminal Court*, Vol. 1 (1999), p. 105 at pp. 114 et seq.; E. Gadirov, in O. Triffterer (ed.), *Commentary on the Rome Statute of the International Criminal Court* (1999), Art. 9, marginal nos. 30, 32;

stood as procedural requirements that limit the jurisdiction of the International Criminal Court to cases of genocide in which a systematic attack has actually been carried out.[119] This does not affect the substantive criminality of genocide.

C. Mental Element

610 The mental element of genocide requires that the material elements of the crime committed with "intent and knowledge" (ICC Statute, Article 30), as well as the specific intent to destroy a protected group as such in whole or in part.

I. Intent and Knowledge (Article 30 of the ICC Statute)

611 A first subjective requirement is that the perpetrator carry out the material elements of genocide with intent and knowledge. The standard here is Article 30 of the ICC Statute.[120]

612 Where Article 6(c) of the ICC Statute requires that destructive conditions of life be inflicted "deliberately," it does not deviate from the general requirements of the mental element, as provided by Article 30. Article 6(d), under which measures calculated to prevent births must be "intended," is also merely an affirmation of the general subjective requirement.

613 For some individual acts of genocide, however, lower requirements for the mental element – as compared to Article 30 of the ICC Statute – arise from the Elements of Crimes and customary law.[121] This is the case, first of all, for killings undertaken with the specific intent to destroy under Article 6(a). Here there is much evidence that the requirements developed for the mental element in killings undertaken in the course of an attack against a civilian population or in the course of an armed conflict[122] also set the standard for killing with specific intent to destroy.[123] While the courts have yet to find a relevant provision of customary law, it is not clear what reason there would be to find a different subjective requirement. This means that the infliction of serious injury with reckless disregard for human life, committed with specific intent to destroy, is punishable as genocide under Article 6.

614 The Elements of Crimes for Article 6(e), number 6, provide for a lower intent requirement than Article 30 of the ICC Statute, under which – unlike Article 30(3), which

---

O. Triffterer, in B. Schünemann et al. (eds.), *Festschrift für Roxin* (2001), p. 1415 at pp. 1425, 1443.

[119] In the *Krstić* judgment, the ICTY used and explained the wording of the Elements of Crimes: ". . . acts of genocide must be committed in the context of a manifest pattern of similar conduct, or themselves constitute a conduct that could in itself effect the destruction of the group, in whole or part, as such," see *Prosecutor* v. *Krstić*, ICTY (Trial Chamber), judgment of 2 August 2001, para. 682.

[120] For thorough discussion of the general requirements of the mental element, see marginal nos. 294.

[121] On the relationship between Art. 30, the Elements of Crimes and customary law, see marginal nos. 313 et seq.

[122] For thorough discussion, see marginal nos. 676, 878; see also marginal no. 334.

[123] However, G. Dahm, J. Delbrück and R. Wolfrum, *Völkerrecht*, Vol. I/3, 2nd edn. (2002), p. 1083, go too far in their view that *dolus eventualis* is enough without more for all acts of genocide.

requires the perpetrator's knowledge of the circumstances – it is enough that the perpetrator "should have known" that the victims transferred to another group were minors.

II. Specific Intent to Destroy

In addition to "intent and knowledge" as regards the material elements of the crime, the **615** mental element of the crime of genocide also requires that the perpetrator have acted with specific intent to destroy a protected group as such in whole or in part.[124] The requirement of intent to destroy restricts the scope of criminality in a way that is expressly permitted by Article 30.[125]

1. The Term "Intent"

The intent to destroy a group as such in whole or in part, as required for the mental **616** element, should be understood as specific intent. The destruction of the group in whole or in part must be the perpetrator's (preliminary) goal.[126] Only if the individual act is, in the perpetrator's mind, a step toward this desired destruction of the group does the act gain an international dimension as a threat to world peace. It is sufficient for the destructive intent to be present at the time of the execution of the criminal act; no prior planning on the perpetrator's part is necessary.[127] The perpetrator's knowledge that he or she

---

[124] See in particular the foundational judgment of *Prosecutor* v. *Akayesu*, ICTR (Trial Chamber), judgment of 2 September 1998, paras. 497 et seq., 517 et seq., and, following upon it, *Prosecutor* v. *Kayishema and Ruzindana*, ICTR (Trial Chamber), judgment of 21 May 1999, paras. 89, 91; *Prosecutor* v. *Jelisić*, ICTR (Trial Chamber), judgment of 14 December 1999, para. 66, 108; *Prosecutor* v. *Jelisić*, ICTY (Appeals Chamber), judgment of 5 July 2001, paras. 45, 50 et seq. See also *Draft Code* 1996, Commentary on Art. 17, para. 5; C. Aptel, 13 *Criminal Law Forum* (2002), pp. 273 et seq.; R. Arnold, 14 *Criminal Law Forum* (2003), pp. 127 et seq.; M.C. Bassiouni and P. Manikas, *The Law of the International Criminal Tribunal for the Former Yugoslavia* (1996), p. 527 at p. 529; E. Fronza, in F. Lattanzi and W.A. Schabas (eds.), *Essays on the Rome Statute of the International Criminal Court*, Vol. 1 (1999), p. 105 at p. 127; R.W.D. Jones, in L.C. Vohrah et al. (eds.), *Man's Inhumanity to Man* (2003), pp. 467 et seq.; W.A. Schabas, *Genocide in International Law* (2000), p. 214 at pp. 217 et seq.; C. Tournaye, 52 *International and Comparative Law Quarterly* (2003), pp. 447 et seq.

[125] See marginal nos. 310 et seq.

[126] *Prosecutor* v. *Akayesu*, ICTR (Trial Chamber), judgment of 2 September 1998, para. 520; *Prosecutor* v. *Rutaganda*, ICTR (Trial Chamber), judgment of 6 December 1999, para. 59; *Prosecutor* v. *Bagilishema*, ICTR (Trial Chamber), judgment of 7 June 2001, para. 61; *Prosecutor* v. *Jelisić*, ICTY (Trial Chamber), judgment of 14 December 1999, para. 86; *Prosecutor* v. *Jelisić*, ICTY (Appeals Chamber), judgment of 5 July 2001, paras. 46, 50 et seq.; *Prosecutor* v. *Krstić*, ICTY (Trial Chamber), judgment of 2 August 2001, para. 550. In the literature, see, e.g., K. Ambos, *Der Allgemeine Teil des Völkerstrafrechts* (2002), p. 411; R.S. Clark, 114 *Zeitschrift für die gesamte Strafrechtswissenschaft* (2002), p. 372 at p. 396; P.N. Drost, *The Crime of State, Vol. II: Genocide* (1959), p. 82; A. Gil Gil, 112 *Zeitschrift für die gesamte Strafrechtswissenschaft* (2000), p. 381 at pp. 393 et seq.; B. Lüders, *Die Strafbarkeit von Völkermord nach dem Römischen Statut für den Internationalen Strafgerichtshof* (2004), pp. 106 et seq.; W.A. Schabas, in O. Triffterer (ed.), *Commentary on the Rome Statute of the International Criminal Court* (1999), Art. 6, marginal no. 4; W.A. Schabas, *Genocide in International Law* (2000), p. 227; C. Tournaye, 52 *International and Comparative Law Quarterly* (2003), p. 447 at p. 453.

[127] See *Prosecutor* v. *Krstić*, ICTY (Trial Chamber), judgment of 2 August 2001, para. 572; P.N. Drost, *The Crime of State, Vol. II: Genocide* (1959), p. 82; M. Lippman, 15 *Arizona Journal of International and Comparative Law* (1998), p. 415 at p. 455; N. Robinson, *The Genocide Convention, A Com-*

is participating in an extermination campaign against a group cannot replace the specific intent (purpose), but can indicate its presence.[128] However, it is always necessary to determine that the perpetrator him or herself acted with intent to destroy.[129]

617 Some authors have argued that genocidal intent already exists if the perpetrator knew of the attempt to exterminate the group.[130] This view is justified by the features of the systematic acts typical of genocide. In systematic crimes, the argument runs, the goals, preconditions and effects cannot be distinguished. In this constellation, therefore, the perpetrator's certain knowledge of the specific intent of the main or organizational perpetrators should be sufficient to find the requisite mental element. Furthermore, a perpetrator who knows for certain that he or she will exterminate the group is far more dangerous to the protected rights than one who intends to destroy but is not certain if he or she can actually achieve his goal. It may be possible to bring this interpretation into conformity with the text of the norm, but not with the historical meaning of the crime. The only cases intended to be included were precisely those in which the perpetrator aimed at destruction of the group in whole or in part.[131]

2. The Group as the Object of Destructive Intent

618 The object of the perpetrator's destructive intent is the national, ethnic, racial or religious group "as such." This addition makes the reference point of the intent to destroy more precise by requiring that the perpetrator's desire to kill the victim be based specifically on his or her membership in the group.[132] The perpetrator's interest must be in destroying the group, not the individuality of the victim. However, it is not necessary for the perpetrator to act for discriminatory reasons.[133] The intent to commit individual discriminatory acts against members of the group is not sufficient.[134]

---

mentary (1960), p. 60. For a different view, see *Prosecutor* v. *Kayishema and Ruzindana*, ICTR (Trial Chamber), judgment of 21 May 1999, para. 91.

[128] See German Federal Supreme Court, decision of 21 February 2001, in *Neue Juristische Wochenschrift* 2001, pp. 2732 et seq.

[129] See *Prosecutor* v. *Krstić*, ICTY (Trial Chamber), judgment of 2 August 2001, para. 549: "As a preliminary, the Chamber emphasises the need to distinguish between the individual intent of the accused and the intent involved in the conception and commission of the crime. The gravity and the scale of the crime of genocide ordinarily presume that several protagonists were involved in its perpetration. Although the motive of each participant may differ, the objective of the criminal enterprise remains the same. In such cases of joint participation, the intent to destroy, in whole or in part, a group as such must be discernible in the criminal act itself, apart from the intent of particular perpetrators. It is then necessary to establish whether the accused being prosecuted for genocide shared the intention that a genocide be carried out."

[130] See A.K.A. Greenawalt, 99 *Columbia Law Review* (1999), p. 2259 at pp. 2265 et seq.; O. Triffterer, in B. Schünemann et al. (eds.), *Festschrift für Roxin* (2001), p. 1415 at pp. 1440 et seq.; H. Vest, 113 *Zeitschrift für die gesamte Strafrechtswissenschaft* (2001), p. 457 at pp. 482 et seq.; H. Vest, *Genozid durch organisatorische Machtapparate* (2002), pp. 104 et seq., 107. For a similar approach, see R.W.D. Jones, in L.C. Vohrah et al. (eds.), *Man's Inhumanity to Man* (2003), p. 467 at pp. 471 et seq.

[131] See C. Aptel, 13 *Criminal Law Forum* (2002), p. 272 at pp. 277 et seq.; R. Arnold, 14 *Criminal Law Forum* (2003), p. 127 at pp. 132 et seq.; B. Lüders, in M. Chiavario (ed.), La justice pénale internationale entre passé et avenir (2003), p. 223 at pp. 249 et seq.

[132] See H. Vest, 117 *Schweizerische Zeitschrift für Strafrecht* (1999), p. 351 at pp. 356 et seq. See also *Prosecutor* v. *Bagilishema*, ICTR (Trial Chamber), judgment of 7 June 2001, para. 61.

[133] See *Prosecutor* v. *Jelisić*, ICTY (Appeals Chamber), judgment of 5 July 2001, para. 49, according to which the reason for criminality is not significant. See also P.N. Drost, *The Crime of State, Vol.*

Since the group is protected precisely because of its specific character as a national, ethnic, racial or **619**
religious group, it is not enough for the perpetrator to attack people of the same nationality,
ethnicity, etc., who are linked by certain additional traits.[135] For example, the crimes of the
Khmer Rouge in Cambodia did not possess the specific intent required for genocide. Membership
in the Khmer ethnic group was not decisive for the choice of victims, but rather, among other
things, the victim's social position or level of education, or simple arbitrariness.[136]

The perpetrator must act with intent to destroy the group "in whole or in part." What **620**
comprises the group as a whole, and thus the actual target of the crime, is determined by
the perpetrator's perceptions. Therefore, the targeted group can be part of a larger entity.
A genocidal act can be aimed, for example, against those members of a larger group who
live in a particular area.[137]

It is sufficient for the perpetrator to aim at exterminating a substantial part of the **621**
group.[138] In the persuasive opinion of the Yugoslavia Tribunal, the criterion "substantial" can be understood both quantitatively and qualitatively.[139] Intent to destroy a nu-

---

II: Genocide (1959), pp. 83 et seq.; E. Fronza, in F. Lattanzi and W.A. Schabas (eds.), *Essays on the
Rome Statute of the International Criminal Court*, Vol. 1 (1999), p. 105 at p. 129; H. Hannum, 11
Human Rights Quarterly (1989), p. 82 at p. 108; M. Lippman, 15 *Arizona Journal of International and
Comparative Law* (1998), p. 415 at p. 454; A. Planzer, *Le crime de genocide* (1956), pp. 94 et seq.; H.
Vest, 117 *Schweizerische Zeitschrift für Strafrecht* (1999), p. 351 at p. 355. For a different view, see
Prosecutor v. *Kayishema and Ruzindana*, ICTR (Trial Chamber), judgment of 21 May 1999, para. 98:
"on these discriminatory grounds"; see generally W.A. Schabas, *Genocide in International Law* (2000),
pp. 253 et seq.

[134] *Prosecutor* v. *Jelisić*, ICTY (Trial Chamber), judgment of 14 December 1999, para. 79; *Prosecutor* v. *Krstić*, ICTY (Trial Chamber), judgment of 2 August 2001, para. 553; *Draft Code* 1996, Commentary on Art. 17, para. 7.

[135] But see the view of the Spanish Audiencia Nacional in the *Pinochet* case, see Audiencia
Nacional, judgment of 5 November 1998, section 5, available at <http://www.ua.es/up/pinochet/
documentos/chile.htm>.

[136] See H. Vest , 117 *Schweizerische Zeitschrift für Strafrecht* (1999), p. 351 at p. 356; H. Vest, 113
Zeitschrift für die gesamte Strafrechtswissenschaft (2001), p. 457 at p. 478. For a different view, see H.
Hannum, 11 *Human Rights Quarterly* (1989), p. 82 at pp. 111 et seq.; Y. Ternon, *Der verbrecherische
Staat* (1996), pp. 158 et seq., esp. pp. 167 et seq.

[137] See *Prosecutor* v. *Jelisić*, ICTY (Trial Chamber), judgment of 14 December 1999, para. 83. See
also *Prosecutor* v. *Krstić*, ICTY (Trial Chamber), judgment of 2 August 2001, para. 590.

[138] See *Prosecutor* v. *Kayishema and Ruzindana*, ICTR (Trial Chamber), judgment of 21 May
1999, paras. 96 et seq.; *Prosecutor* v. *Jelisić*, ICTY (Trial Chamber), judgment of 14 December 1999,
para. 82; *Prosecutor* v. *Krstić*, ICTY (Trial Chamber), judgment of 2 August 2001, para. 634; *Prosecutor* v. *Semanza*, ICTR (Trial Chamber), judgment of 15 May 2003, para. 316; *Prosecutor* v.
Kamuhanda, ICTR (Trial Chamber), judgment of 22 January 2004, para. 628; *Draft Code* 1996,
Commentary on Art. 17, para. 8; D.D.N. Nsereko, in G. Kirk McDonald and O. Swaak-Goldman
(eds.), *Substantive and Procedural Aspects of International Criminal Law*, Vol. 1 (2000), p. 117 at
p. 125; N. Robinson, *The Genocide Convention, A Commentary* (1960), p. 63; W.A. Schabas, in O.
Triffterer (ed.), *Commentary on the Rome Statute of the International Criminal Court* (1999), Art. 6,
marginal no. 5.

[139] *Prosecutor* v. *Jelisić*, ICTY (Trial Chamber), judgment of 14 December 1999, para. 82: "A targeted part of a group would be classed as substantial either because the intent sought to harm a large
majority of the group in question or the most representative members of the targeted community. . . .
Genocidal intent may therefore be manifest in two forms. It may consist of desiring the extermination
of a very large number of the members of the group, in which case it would constitute an intention to
destroy a group en masse. However it may also consist of the desired destruction of a more limited
number of persons selected for the impact that their disappearance would have upon the survival of
the group as such."

merically significant part of the group is thus sufficient, as is the intent to exterminate a representative part of the group, such as its intellectual leaders. The crucial question is the effect the extermination of the part is intended to have upon the existence of the group as a whole.[140]

3. Evidentiary Issues

622   In practice, proving specific intent to destroy is difficult. According to international case law, substantial evidence includes the existence of a plan, a large number of victims, choice of victims based on their membership in the group, and the perpetrator's bearing when committing the crime.[141] Acts that are not covered by the definition of the crime, such as the destruction of cultural institutions, monuments, religious sites or buildings, can be evidence of genocidal intent.[142]

---

[140] In the *Krstić* judgment, the ICTY determined in regard to the Srebrenica massacre: "[O]nly the men of military age were systematically massacred, but it is significant that these massacres occurred at a time when the forcible transfer of the rest of the Bosnian Muslim population was well under way. The Bosnian Serb forces could not have failed to know, by the time they decided to kill all the men, that this selective destruction of the group would have a lasting impact upon the entire group . . . , the Bosnian Serb forces had to be aware of the catastrophic impact that the disappearance of two or three generations of men would have on the survival of a traditionally patriarchal society . . . , " see *Prosecutor* v. *Krstić*, ICTY (Trial Chamber), judgment of 2 August 2001, para. 595.

[141] See *Prosecutor* v. *Akayesu*, ICTR (Trial Chamber), judgment of 2 September 1998, para. 523; *Prosecutor* v. *Kayishema and Ruzindana*, ICTR (Trial Chamber), judgment of 21 May 1999, paras. 93, 527 et seq.; *Prosecutor* v. *Bagilishema*, ICTR (Trial Chamber), judgment of 7 June 2001, para. 63; *Prosecutor* v. *Jelisić*, ICTY (Appeals Chamber), judgment of 5 July 2001, paras. 47 et seq.; *Prosecutor* v. *Krstić*, ICTY (Trial Chamber), judgment of 2 August 2001, paras. 572, 592, 595; *Prosecutor* v. *Semanza*, ICTR (Trial Chamber), judgment of 15 May 2003, paras. 313, 314. See also C. Aptel, 13 *Criminal Law Forum* (2002), p. 273 at pp. 287 et seq.; M.C. Bassiouni and P. Manikas, *The Law of the International Criminal Tribunal for the Former Yugoslavia* (1996), pp. 527 et seq.; D.D.N. Nsereko, in G. Kirk McDonald and O. Swaak-Goldman (eds.), *Substantive and Procedural Aspects of International Criminal Law*, Vol. 1 (2000), p. 117 at pp. 126 et seq.; W.A. Schabas, *Genocide in International Law* (2000), p. 222. On the establishment of an intent to destroy in crimes of sexual violence, see *Prosecutor* v. *Akayesu*, ICTR (Trial Chamber), judgment of 2 September 1998, para. 731: "Sexual violence was an integral part of the process of destruction, specifically targeting Tutsi women and specifically contributing to their destruction and to the destruction of the Tutsi group as a whole." See also para. 732: "Sexual violence was a step in the process of destruction of the Tutsi group – destruction of the spirit, of the will to live, and of life itself."

[142] Thus in the case of *Karadžić and Mladić* the ICTY stated, in connection with the legal assessment of the ethnic cleansing actions in Bosnia by Serb units: ". . . certain methods used for implementing the project of 'ethnic cleansing' appear to reveal an aggravated intent as, for example, the massive scale of the effect of destruction. . . . The destruction of mosques or Catholic churches is designed to annihilate the centuries-long presence of the group or groups; the destruction of the libraries is intended to annihilate a culture which was enriched through the participation of the various national components of the population," see *Prosecutor* v. *Karadžić and Mladić*, ICTY (Trial Chamber), decision of 11 July 1996, para. 94. See also *Prosecutor* v. *Kayishema and Ruzindana*, ICTR (Trial Chamber), judgment of 21 May 1999, para. 93, and W.A. Schabas, *Genocide in International Law* (2000), pp. 223 et seq.

D. Incitement to Commit Genocide

I. Structure and Purpose of Punishment

Incitement to commit genocide was already prohibited by the Genocide Convention. **623** The provision was adopted into the ICC Statute word for word as Article 25(3)(e).[143] It provides a separate ground for criminalizing a separate form of complicity, namely inducing – or even merely attempting to induce – others to commit genocide. A completed genocide is not required.[144]

Public incitement creates, or significantly increases, the risk of an uncontrollable mass **624** crime against members of the group under attack. Because the addressees of the incitement cannot be identified by the perpetrator, he or she has no control from the outset over the progress of events.[145]

A recent example of the significance and effect of incitement on genocide was pro- **625** vided by the events in Rwanda during the 1994 civil war.[146] Even before the outbreak of the conflict, extremist Hutu had taken control of the radio stations and used them to conduct an extremely effective hate campaign against the Tutsi. The ICTR has convicted a number of defendants of incitement to genocide. In the *Ruggiu* case, one of them was convicted solely because of his statements.[147]

II. Material Elements

The criminal act is direct, public incitement to commit genocide. This criminal incite- **626** ment requires that the perpetrator call for commission of genocide; provocative expressions alone are insufficient.[148] "Direct" incitement includes cases in which the perpe-

---

[143] See Genocide Convention, Art. III(c), ICTY Statute, Art. 4(3)(c), ICTR Statute, Art. 2(3)(c), and ICC Statute, Art. 25(3)(e).

[144] See *Prosecutor v. Akayesu*, ICTR (Trial Chamber), judgment of 2 September 1998, paras. 561 et seq.; *Prosecutor v. Ruggiu*, ICTR (Trial Chamber), judgment of 1 June 2000, para. 16; D.D.N. Nsereko, in G. Kirk McDonald and O. Swaak-Goldman (eds.), *Substantive and Procedural Aspects of International Criminal Law*, Vol. 1 (2000), p. 117 at p. 133; W.A. Schabas, *Genocide in International Law* (2000), p. 257 at pp. 266, 292; N. Robinson, *The Genocide Convention, A Commentary* (1960), p. 67.

[145] See *Prosecutor v. Akayesu*, ICTR (Trial Chamber), judgment of 2 September 1998, para. 562: "such acts are in themselves particularly dangerous because of the high risk they carry for society, even if they fail to produce results"; K. Ambos, in O. Triffterer (ed.), *Commentary on the Rome Statute of the International Criminal Court* (1999), Art. 15, marginal no. 29. See also *Draft Code* 1996, Commentary on Art. 2, para. 16.

[146] See, e.g., J.F. Metzl, 91 *American Journal of International Law* (1997) p. 628; W.A. Schabas, 46 *McGill Law Journal* (2000), p. 141; W.A. Schabas, 93 *American Journal of International Law* (1999), p. 529.

[147] *Prosecutor v. Ruggiu*, ICTR (Trial Chamber), judgment of 1 June 2000. Other defendants are being tried by the ICTR on the charge of incitement. See also the Rwanda Tribunal's judgment in the so-called Media Trial, in which all defendants were convicted on the charge of incitement to genocide, *Prosecutor v. Nahimana* et al., ICTR (Trial Chamber), judgment of 3 December 2003.

[148] For more information, see V. Morris and M.P. Scharf, *The International Criminal Tribunal for Rwanda*, Vol. I (1998), p. 183; D.D.N. Nsereko, in G. Kirk McDonald and O. Swaak-Goldman (eds.), *Substantive and Procedural Aspects of International Criminal Law*, Vol. 1 (2000), p. 117 at

trator does not call for commission of genocide expressly, but does so in a way that is unmistakable to the addressee;[149] in fact, perpetrators frequently use euphemistic, metaphorical or otherwise coded language that is nevertheless perfectly clear to their audience.[150] "Public" means, in particular, an appeal made in a public place or through a medium targeted at the public.[151] The deciding factor is that the appeal be aimed at a non-individualizable audience and thus create or enhance the danger of uncontrolled commission of the crime.

III. Mental Element

627   The mental element of incitement to genocide requires that the perpetrator intentionally and knowingly commit the material elements of crime (ICC Statute, Article 30) and act with intent to destroy a group in whole or in part.[152]

E. Multiplicity of Offenses

628   Typically, numerous acts are involved in carrying out the crime of genocide, each of which in itself fulfills the requirements for genocide. It is necessary to decide whether these individual acts should be seen as legally separate crimes or as one single crime.

629   On the one hand, it is conceivable to see each act that meets the definition of the crime as a separate act of genocide. Another completely opposite solution could consist in combining into a single unit all genocidal acts flowing from the intent to destroy a certain group. Such an "overall crime" could, in extreme cases, even constitute a sort of "world crime" made up of genocidal acts committed in various countries at various times.

---

pp. 132 et seq. See also *Prosecutor* v. *Akayesu*, ICTR (Trial Chamber), judgment of 2 September 1998, para. 555: ". . . Civil law systems punish direct and public incitement assuming the form of provocation, which is defined as an act intended to directly provoke another to commit a crime or a misdemeanour through speeches, shouting or threats, or any other means of audiovisual communication. Such a provocation, as defined under Civil law, is made up of the same elements as direct and public incitement to commit genocide covered by Article 2 of the Statute . . .. "

[149] See *Prosecutor* v. *Akayesu*, ICTR (Trial Chamber), judgment of 2 September 1998, paras. 557 et seq.; *Prosecutor* v. *Ruggiu*, ICTR (Trial Chamber), judgment of 1 June 2000, para. 17; W.A. Schabas, *Genocide in International Law* (2000), p. 277.

[150] The former Rwandan prime minister, Jean Kambanda, made such an appeal to the Hutu population: "You refuse to give your blood to your country and the dogs drink it for nothing." With this statement, Kambanda called on Hutu to participate in the battle against the Tutsi, proclaimed to be "dogs," and to give their blood for the country, see *Prosecutor* v. *Kambanda*, ICTR (Trial Chamber), judgment of 4 September 1998. The Appeals Chamber affirmed the perpetrator's conviction, see *Prosecutor* v. *Kambanda*, ICTR (Appeals Chamber), judgment of 19 October 2000.

[151] See *Prosecutor* v. *Akayesu*, ICTR (Trial Chamber), judgment of 2 September 1998, para. 556; *Prosecutor* v. *Niyitegaka*, ICTR (Trial Chamber), judgment of 16 May 2003, para. 431.

[152] See *Prosecutor* v. *Akayesu*, ICTR (Trial Chamber), judgment of 2 September 1998, para. 560; *Prosecutor* v. *Ruggiu*, ICTR (Trial Chamber), judgment of 1 June 2000, para. 14; W.A. Schabas, *Genocide in International Law* (2000), p. 275; K. Ambos, in O. Triffterer (ed.), *Commentary on the Rome Statute of the International Criminal Court* (1999), Art. 15, marginal no. 30.

The applicable standard is a limited cumulative approach. Essentially, a number of indi- **630** vidual acts, such as killing or serious bodily harm, form a single crime of genocide if the acts flowed from destructive intent aimed at the same group.[153] The formation of such a single crime takes into account the fact that for genocide, the protection of a value that transcends the individual – the existence of the group – is paramount. At the same time, "outsized or temporally endless sets of acts"[154] must be avoided. Thus acts aimed at the same group can form a single crime only if they occurred in the same context of place and time.[155]

A genocidal act can at the same time constitute a war crime and a crime against hu- **631** manity. The relevant norms are then applied simultaneously.[156] Genocide is not a *lex specialis* in relation to crimes against humanity.[157] An analysis of the requirements of the crimes indicates significant differences: crimes against humanity require an actual attack on a civilian population, which is not required by the definition of genocide. In contrast, for genocide, specific intent must be proven to destroy a group in whole or in part. Though it is true that genocidal acts will often fulfill the requirements of crimes against humanity, genocide is not a special case of crimes against humanity. Rather, the two offenses function like two overlapping circles.[158] Thus conviction is necessary for both crimes in order to comprehend the wrongfulness of the acts to the fullest extent. This is also true for the relationship of genocide and the crime against humanity of persecution.

---

[153] See *Prosecutor* v. *Kayishema and Ruzindana*, ICTR (Trial Chamber), judgment of 21 May 1999, paras. 517 et seq. On Sec. 220a of the (German) Criminal Code [*Strafgesetzbuch, StGB*] (old version), see German Federal Supreme Court, judgment of 30 April 1999, *BGHSt* 45, p. 64 at p. 88. For a concurring view, see A. Gil Gil, 112 *Zeitschrift für die gesamte Strafrechtswissenschaft* (2000), p. 381 at pp. 396 et seq.; G. Werle, *Juristenzeitung* 1999, p. 1181 at p. 1184.

[154] See German Federal Supreme Court, judgment of 30 April 1999, *BGHSt* 45, p. 64 at p. 88.

[155] But see K. Ambos, *Neue Zeitschrift für Strafrecht* 1999, p. 404.

[156] *Prosecutor* v. *Krstić*, ICTY (Trial Chamber), judgment of 2 August 2001, para. 681. See also marginal no. 538.

[157] The Rwanda Tribunal has made this clear, see *Prosecutor* v. *Musema*, ICTR (Appeals Chamber), judgment of 16 November 2001, paras. 366 et seq.; but see F. Selbmann, *Der Tatbestand des Genozids im Völkerstrafrecht* (2002), p. 207, who classifies the crime of genocide as a *lex specialis* in relationship to crimes against humanity. See also marginal no. 538.

[158] This is the accurate image in G. Dahm, J. Delbrück and R. Wolfrum, *Völkerrecht*, Vol. I/3, 2nd edn. (2002), p. 1073; similarly, A. Cassese, in A. Cassese, P. Gaeta and J.R.W.D. Jones (eds.), *The Rome Statute of the International Criminal Court*, Vol. 1 (2002), p. 335 at p. 339 and A. Cassese, *International Criminal Law* (2003), p. 96 at p. 106.

Part Four: Crimes Against Humanity

632 Kai Ambos and Steffen Wirth: The Current Law of Crimes Against Humanity, 13 *Criminal Law Forum* (2002), pp. 1 et seq.; Eugène Aroneanu: *Le crime contre l'humanité* (1961); Kelly Dawn Askin: Crimes Within the Jurisdiction of the International Criminal Court, 10 *Criminal Law Forum* (1999), pp. 33 et seq.; M. Cherif Bassiouni: *Crimes Against Humanity in International Criminal Law*, 2nd edn. (1999); M. Cherif Bassiouni: Crimes against Humanity: The Need for a Specialized Convention, 31 *Columbia Journal of Transnational Law* (1994), pp. 457 et seq.; Astrid Becker: *Der Tatbestand des Verbrechens gegen die Menschlichkeit – Überlegungen zur Problematik eines völkerrechtlichen Strafrechts* (1996); Machteld Boot: *Genocide, Crimes against Humanity, War Crimes: Nullum Crimen Sine Lege and the Subject Matter Jurisdiction of the International Criminal Court* (2002); James T. Brand: Crimes against Humanity and the Nürnberg Trials, 28 *Oregon Law Review* (1949), pp. 93 et seq.; Antonio Cassese: Crimes against Humanity, in Antonio Cassese, Paula Gaeta and John R.W.D. Jones (eds.), *The Rome Statute of the International Criminal Court: A Commentary*, Vol. 1 (2002), pp. 353 et seq.; Antonio Cassese: *International Criminal Law* (2003), pp. 64 et seq.; Simon Chesterman: An altogether different Order: Defining the Elements of Crimes against Humanity, 10 *Duke Journal of Comparative and International Law* (2000), pp. 307 et seq.; Roger S. Clark: Crimes against Humanity at Nuremberg, in George Ginsburgs and V.N. Kudriavtsev (eds.), *The Nuremberg Trial and International Law* (1990), pp. 177 et seq.; Roger S. Clark: Crimes Against Humanity and the Rome Statute of the International Criminal Court, in Mauro Politi and Giuseppe Nesi (eds.), *The Rome Statute of the International Criminal Court, A challenge to impunity* (2001), pp. 75 et seq.; Mireille Delmas-Marty: Le crime contre l'humanité, les droits de l'homme et l'irréductible humain, 11 *Revue de science criminelle et de droit pénal comparé* (1994), pp. 477 et seq.; Yoram Dinstein: Crimes against Humanity, in Jerzy Makarczyk (ed.), *Theory of International Law at the Threshold of the 21st Century: Essays in Honour of Krzysztof Skubiszewski* (1996), pp. 891 et seq.; Yoram Dinstein: Crimes against Humanity after Tadić, 13 *Leiden Journal of International Law* (2000), pp. 373 et seq.; David Donat-Cattin: Crimes against Humanity, in Flavia Lattanzi (ed.), *The International Criminal Court, Comments on the Draft Statute* (1998), pp. 49 et seq.; David Donat-Cattin: A General Definition of Crimes against Humanity under International Law: The Contribution of the Rome Statute of the International Criminal Court, *L'Astree, Revue de Droit Penal et des Droits de l'Homme* (1999), pp. 83 et seq.; Alicia Gil Gil: Die Tatbestände der Verbrechen gegen die Menschlichkeit und des Völkermordes im Römischen Statut des Internationalen Strafgerichtshofs, 112 *Zeitschrift für die gesamte Strafrechtswissenschaft* (2000), pp. 381 et seq.; Jean Graven: Les crimes contre l'humanité, 76 *Recueil des Cours de l'Académie de Droit International de la Haye* (1950-I), pp. 429 et seq.; Herman von Hebel and Darryl Robinson: Crimes within the Jurisdiction of the Court, in Roy S. Lee (ed.), *The International Criminal Court, The Making of the Rome Statute* (1999), pp. 79 et seq., pp. 90 et seq.; Phyllis Hwang: Defining Crimes against Humanity in the Rome Statute of the International Criminal Court, 22 *Fordham International Law Journal* (1998), pp. 457 et seq.; Heinrich Jagusch: Das Verbrechen gegen die Menschlichkeit in der Rechtsprechung des Obersten Gerichtshofs für die Britische Zone, *Süddeutsche Juristenzeitung* 1949, columns 620 et seq.; Hans-Heinrich Jescheck: Gegenstand und neueste Entwicklung des internationalen Strafrechts, in Friedrich-Christian Schroeder and Heinz Zipf (eds.), *Festschrift für Maurach* (1972), pp. 579 et seq.; Bing Bing Jia: The Differing Concepts of War Crimes and Crimes against Humanity in International Criminal Law, in Guy S. Goodwin-Gill and Stefan Talmon (eds.), *The Reality of Inter-*

national Law, Essays in Honour of Ian Brownlie (1999), pp. 243 et seq.; Kriangsak Kittichaisaree: *International Criminal Law* (2001), pp. 85 et seq.; Ernst-Joachim Lampe: Verbrechen gegen die Menschlichkeit, in Hans-Joachim Hirsch et al. (eds.), *Festschrift für Kohlmann* (2003), pp. 147 et seq.; Richard Lange: Die Rechtsprechung des Obersten Gerichtshofes für die Britische Zone zum Verbrechen gegen die Menschlichkeit, *Süddeutsche Juristenzeitung* 1948, columns 655 et seq.; Flavia Lattanzi: Crimes Against Humanity in the Jurisprudence of the International Criminal Tribunals for the Former Jugoslavia and Rwanda, in Horst Fischer, Claus Kress and Sascha Rolf Lüder (eds.), *International and National Prosecution of Crimes under International Law – Current Developments* (2001), pp. 491 et seq.; Matthew Lippman: Crimes against humanity, 17 *Boston College Third World Law Journal* (1997), pp. 171 et seq.; David Luban: A Theory of Crimes Against Humanity, 29 *Yale Journal of International Law* (2004), pp. 85 et seq.; Gisela Manske: *Verbrechen gegen die Menschlichkeit als Verbrechen gegen die Menschheit* (2003); David Marcus: Famine Crimes in International Law, 97 *American Journal of International Law* (2003), pp. 245 et seq.; Margaret McAuliffe de Guzman: The Road from Rome: The Developing Law of Crimes against Humanity, 22 *Human Rights Quarterly* (2000), pp. 335 et seq.; Stephan Meseke: La contribution de la jurisprudence des tribunaux pénaux internationaux pour l'ex-Yugoslavie et le Rwanda à la concrétisation de l'incrimination du crime contre l'humanité, in Mario Chiavario (ed.), *La justice pénale internationale entre passé et avenir* (2003), pp. 173 et seq.; Stephan Meseke: *Der Tatbestand der Verbrechen gegen die Menschlichkeit nach dem Römischen Statut des Internationalen Strafgerichtshofs* (2004); Henri Meyrowitz: *La répression des crimes contre l'humanité par les tribunaux allemands en application de la loi no. 10 du Conseil de Contrôle Allié* (1960); Guénael Mettraux: Crimes against Humanity in the Jurisprudence of the International Criminal Tribunals for the former Yugoslavia and for Rwanda, 43 *Harvard International Law Journal* (2002), pp. 237 et seq.; Philipp Osten: *Der Tokioter Kriegsverbrecherprozeß und die japanische Rechtswissenschaft* (2003); Gustav Radbruch: Zur Diskussion über das Verbrechen gegen die Menschlichkeit, *Süddeutsche Juristenzeitung* 1947, columns 131 et seq.; Darryl Robinson: Defining Crimes against Humanity at the Rome Conference, 93 *American Journal of International Law* (1999), pp. 43 et seq.; Darryl Robinson: Crimes Against Humanity: Reflections on State Sovereignty, Legal Precision and the Dictates of the Public Conscience, in Flavia Lattanzi and William A. Schabas (eds.), *Essays on the Rome Statute of the International Criminal Court*, Vol. 1 (1999), pp. 139 et seq.; Darryl Robinson: The Elements of Crimes Against Humanity, in Roy S. Lee (ed.), *The International Criminal Court, Elements of Crimes and Rules of Procedure and Evidence* (2001), pp. 57 et seq.; Wiebke Rückert and Georg Witschel: Genocide and Crimes Against Humanity in the Elements of Crimes, in Horst Fischer, Claus Kress and Sascha Rolf Lüder (eds.), *International and National Prosecution of Crimes under International Law – Current Developments* (2001), pp. 59 et seq.; Leila N. Sadat: The Interpretation of the Nuremberg Principles by the French Court of Cassation: From Touvier to Barbie and Back Again, 32 *Columbia Journal of Transnational Law* (1994), pp. 289 et seq.; Elena Martin Salgado: The Judgment of the International Criminal Tribunal for the former Yugoslavia in the Vasiljević Case, 16 *Leiden Journal of International Law* (2003), pp. 321 et seq.; Beth van Schaack: The Definition of Crimes against Humanity: Resolving the Incoherence, 37 *Columbia Journal of Transnational Law* (1999), pp. 787 et seq.; Egon Schwelb: Crimes against Humanity, 23 *British Yearbook of International Law* (1946), pp. 178 et seq.; Olivia Swaak-Goldman: Crimes against humanity, in Gabrielle Kirk McDonald and Olivia Swaak-Goldman (eds.), *Substantive and Procedural Aspects of International Criminal Law, The Experience of International and National Courts*, Vol. 1 (2000), pp. 141 et seq.; Hans Vest: Humanitätsverbrechen – Herausforderung für das Individualstrafrecht, 113 *Zeitschrift für die gesamte Strafrechtswissenschaft* (2001), pp. 457 et seq.; Hellmuth von Weber: Das Verbrechen gegen die Menschlichkeit in der Rechtsprechung, *Monatsschrift für Deutsches Recht* 1949, pp. 261 et seq.; Günter Wieland: Ahndung von NS-Verbrechen in Ostdeutschland 1945–1990, *Neue Justiz* 1991, pp. 49 et seq.; Georg Witschel and Wiebke Rückert: The Elements of Crimes against Humanity, in Roy S. Lee (ed.), *The International Criminal Court, Elements of Crimes and Rules of Procedure and Evidence* (2001), pp. 94 et seq. Additional cites to the literature can be found for the crimes of killing (marginal no. 674); enslavement (marginal no. 683); expulsion or forcible transfer (marginal no. 695); torture (marginal no. 709); sexual violence (marginal no. 721), persecution (marginal no. 735) and the crime of apartheid (marginal no. 758).

A. Introduction

I. The Phenomenon of Crimes Against Humanity

633 Crimes against humanity are mass crimes committed against a civilian population. Most serious is the killing of entire groups of people, which is also characteristic of genocide.[1] Thus the genocide of the European Jews was seen and punished as a crime against humanity by the Nuremberg Tribunal. However, crimes against humanity are broader than genocide: they need not target a specific group, but a civilian population in general. Thus they also include crimes against political or other groups. Also, unlike genocide, it is not necessary for the perpetrator to intend to destroy a group, as such, in whole or in part.

634 In addition to the most serious cases – killing and extermination – crimes against humanity include manifestations also deriving from sad historical experience: enslavement through forced labor, expulsion of people from their native regions, arbitrary imprisonment or torture of political opponents, mass rape of defenseless women, forced disappearance,[2] and persecution through discriminatory laws and measures. The crime of apartheid is addressed in the latter context, as an institutionalized form of racial oppression.[3]

II. History of the Crime

635 Crimes against humanity were first explicitly formulated as a category of crimes in Article 6(c) of the Nuremberg Charter. The Charter defined as crimes "murder, extermination, enslavement, deportation, and other inhumane acts committed against any civilian population, before or during the war; or persecutions on political, racial or religious grounds in execution of or in connection with any crime within the jurisdiction of the Tribunal, whether or not in violation of the domestic law of the country where perpetrated."[4] This category of crimes, unlike war crimes, also included crimes against the perpetrator's own citizens if they systematically targeted a specific civilian population.

---

[1] On the manifestations of genocide, see marginal nos. 555 et seq.

[2] See, e.g., *Report of the Chilean National Commission on Truth and Reconciliation*, Vols. 1 and 2 (1993), pp. 136 et seq. and pp. 495 et seq.; *Nunca Mas (Never Again) – Report of Conadep (National Commission on the Disappearance of Persons)* (1984).

[3] See, e.g., *Truth and Reconciliation Commission of South Africa Report* (1998), Vol. 1, pp. 94 et seq.

[4] Nuremberg Charter, Art. 6(c). See E. Schwelb, 23 *British Yearbook of International Law* (1946), pp. 178 et seq. and R.S. Clark, in G. Ginsburgs and V.N. Kudriavtsev (eds.), *The Nuremberg Trial and International Law* (1990), pp. 177 et seq. On the role of crimes against humanity in the Nuremberg judgment, see G. Manske, *Verbrechen gegen die Menschlichkeit als Verbrechen gegen die Menschheit* (2003), pp. 52 et seq.

In describing the history of crimes against humanity, it is first necessary to mention the Preamble **636** to the Hague Regulations of 1899 and 1907.[5] A general provision in these Conventions obligated the belligerent parties to obey the "laws of humanity." The idea of criminalizing violations of such laws of humanity, however, was not yet hinted at in the Martens Clause,[6] the application of which was limited to wartime. The term "crimes against humanity" was coined in 1915: France, the United Kingdom and Russia used it to refer to the massacres of the Armenian population in Turkey.[7] After World War I, there was talk of prosecuting "offenses against humanity," but this was never accomplished.[8]

Crimes against humanity were also included in Article 5(c) of the Tokyo Charter.[9] In **637** contrast to the Nuremberg trial, however, no one was convicted of crimes against humanity in Tokyo.[10] Control Council Law No. 10 also included crimes against humanity, with some supplements and an essential change: While the Nuremberg and Tokyo Charters required that crimes against humanity evidence a connection to aggressive war or war crimes, this supplementary requirement was left out of Control Council Law No. 10.[11]

The judgments at the Nuremberg successor trials, however, mainly interpreted Control Council **638** Law No. 10 in light of the Nuremberg judgment, and therefore did not punish crimes against humanity committed before the outbreak of World War II.[12] The Supreme Court for the British Occupied Zone proceeded differently, extending the definition of the crime, commensurate with its wording, to acts outside the context of war.[13]

---

[5] *Second Convention with Respect to the Laws and Customs of War on Land* of 29 July 1899 and *Fourth Convention respective the Laws and Customs of War on Land and its Annex: Regulation concerning the Laws and Customs of War on Land* of 18 October 1907, respectively see <http://www.icrc.org/ihl>.

[6] On the "Martens Clause," see A. Cassese, 11 *European Journal of International Law* (2000), pp. 187 et seq.; T. Meron, 94 *American Journal of International Law* (2000), pp. 78 et seq.

[7] Declaration of 28 May 1915, reprinted in United Nations War Crimes Commission (ed.), *History of the United Nations War Crimes Commission and the Development of the Laws of War* (1948), p. 35. On the history of the term, see also D. Luban, 29 *The Yale Journal of International Law* (2004), p. 85 at pp. 86 et seq.

[8] On developments prior to World War II, see marginal nos. 6 et seq.; M.C. Bassiouni, *Crimes against Humanity*, 2nd edn. (1999), pp. 60 et seq.

[9] Tokyo Statute, Art. 5(c): "Crimes against Humanity: Namely, murder, extermination, enslavement, deportation, and other inhumane acts committed before or during the war, or persecutions on political or racial grounds in execution of or in connection with any crime within the jurisdiction of the Tribunal, whether or not in violation of the domestic law of the country where perpetrated."

[10] See, e.g., P. Osten, *Der Tokioter Kriegsverbrecherprozeß und die japanische Rechtswissenschaft* (2003).

[11] CCL No. 10, Art. II(1)(c): "Crimes against Humanity. Atrocities and offenses, including but not limited to murder, extermination, enslavement, deportation, imprisonment, torture, rape, or other inhumane acts committed against any civilian population, or persecutions on political, racial or religious grounds whether or not in violation of the domestic laws of the country where perpetrated."

[12] On crimes against humanity in the judgments of the Nuremberg successor trials, see J.T. Brand, 28 *Oregon Law Review* (1949), pp. 93 et seq.

[13] On crimes against humanity in the judgments of the Supreme Court in the British Occupied Zone, see H. Jagusch, *Süddeutsche Juristenzeitung* 1949, columns 620 et seq.; R. Lange, *Süddeutsche Juristenzeitung* 1948, columns 655 et seq. See also H. Meyrowitz, *La répression des crimes contre l'humanité par les tribunaux allemands* (1960), pp. 213 et seq.

639 Like the Nuremberg Principles generally, criminal liability for crimes against humanity under customary international law has since been frequently affirmed and acknowledged.[14] Thus the crime was included in the 1954 *Draft Code of Offences against the Peace and Security of Mankind* and was also contained in all successive International Law Commission drafts.[15] The criminal status of crimes against humanity was further assumed in conventions that nullified the statutes of limitations for these crimes or dealt with new ways in which they could be committed.[16]

640 The practice of prosecuting crimes against humanity has been weaker. No trials before international criminal courts were held subsequent to the Nuremberg trials until the early 1990s. However, the prosecution of crimes against humanity did not come to a complete standstill. The trial of Adolf Eichmann in Israel[17] and the conviction of Klaus Barbie in France should be noted.[18] Trials for crimes against humanity also took place in the Netherlands, East Germany[19] and Canada.[20] However, the only defendants were Nazi criminals whose crimes had occurred years in the past, despite the existence of numerous other cases of serious crimes against humanity.[21] This situation changed only upon creation of the Yugoslavia and Rwanda Tribunals.[22]

641 The Statutes of the Yugoslavia and Rwanda Tribunals have reaffirmed the customary law character of crimes against humanity. However, there are considerable differences between the texts of the relevant provisions. These deviations are not expressions of uncertainty about the scope of the crime; they can be explained by the situational nature of

---

[14] See M. Lippman, 17 *Boston College Third World Law Journal* (1997), pp. 171 et seq.; B. van Schaack, 37 *Columbia Journal of Transnational Law* (1999), pp. 787 et seq. and marginal nos. 40 et seq.

[15] See 1954 *Draft Code*, Art. 2(11); 1991 *Draft Code*, Art. 21 and 1996 *Draft Code*, Art. 18.

[16] See, e.g., *Convention on the Non-Applicability of Statutory Limitations to War Crimes and Crimes Against Humanity*, adopted in General Assembly Resolution 2391 (XXIII) of 26 November 1968; *International Convention on the Suppression and Punishment of the Crime of Apartheid*, adopted in General Assembly Resolution 3068 (XXVIII) of 30 November 1973.

[17] *Attorney-General of the Government of Israel* v. *Eichmann*, District Court of Jerusalem, judgment of 12 December 1961, in 36 *ILR* (1968), pp. 18 et seq.; *Attorney-General of the Government of Israel* v. *Eichmann*, Supreme Court of Israel, judgment of 29 May 1962, in 36 *ILR* (1968), pp. 277 et seq.

[18] *Féderation National des Deportées et Internés Resistants et Patriots* et al. v. *Barbie*, Cour de Cassation, judgment of 20 December 1985, in 78 *ILR* (1988), pp. 136 et seq.; *Advocate General* v. *Barbie*, Cour de Cassation, judgment of 3 June 1988, in 100 *ILR* (1995), pp. 330 et seq. Summarized in L.N. Sadat, 32 *Columbia Journal of Transnational Law* (1994), pp. 289 et seq.

[19] In contrast to West Germany, East Germany consistently tried Nazi criminals in accordance with the definition of crimes against humanity under customary international law, see, e.g., the judgment against Hans Globke, Supreme Court of the GDR, judgment of 23 July 1963, in *Neue Justiz* 1963, p. 449 at pp. 507 et seq.; the judgment against Horst Fischer, Supreme Court of the GDR, judgment of 25 March 1966, in *Neue Justiz* 1966, p. 193 at pp. 203 et seq. Subsequently, this crime was included in the East German Criminal Code. Summarized in G. Wieland, *Neue Justiz* 1991, pp. 49 et seq.

[20] *Regina* v. *Finta*, Ontario Court of Appeal, judgment of 29 April 1992, in 98 *ILR* (1994), pp. 520 et seq.; Canada Supreme Court, judgment of 24 March 1994, in 104 *ILR* (1997), pp. 284 et seq.

[21] For a summary of national prosecutions of crimes against humanity, see the forthcoming dissertation by S. Meseke, *Der Tatbestand der Verbrechen gegen die Menschlichkeit nach dem Römischen Statut des Internationalen Strafgerichtshofs* (2004), pp. 44 et seq.

[22] On this issue, see marginal nos. 45 et seq.

the Statutes. When the ICTY Statute states, in Article 5, that a crime must occur "in armed conflict, whether international or internal in character,"[23] it is simply drawing a connection in place and time to the Yugoslavia conflict. This is by no means a reintroduction of the long-abandoned supplementary requirement of the Nuremberg Charter.[24] Article 3 of the ICTR Statute includes crimes against humanity without requiring a link to armed conflict, and thus avoids any misunderstanding: crimes against humanity provisions apply regardless of the presence of armed conflict. But the ICTR Statute requires, not only for the crime of persecution but for all crimes against humanity, that they be committed "on national, political, ethnic, racial or religious grounds."[25] This, too, should not be seen as a requirement that limits the definition of the crime, but as a means of restricting the Tribunal's jurisdiction to those crimes against humanity typical of the Rwanda case.[26]

Two years after the adoption of the ICTR Statute by the Security Council, the International Law Commission issued a *Draft Code of Crimes against the Peace and Security of Mankind*, which included a further definition of crimes against humanity that would play an important part in the negotiations on the ICC Statute.[27] **642**

---

[23] See ICTY Statute, Art. 5: "The International Tribunal shall have the power to prosecute persons responsible for the following crimes when committed in armed conflict, whether international or internal in character, and directed against any civilian population . . ." On the definition of crimes against humanity in the judgments of the Yugoslavia Tribunal, see F. Lattanzi, in H. Fischer, C. Kress and S.R. Lüder (eds.), *International and National Prosecution of Crimes under International Law – Current Developments* (2001), pp. 491 et seq.; G. Mettraux, 43 *Harvard International Law Journal* (2002), pp. 237 et seq.

[24] *Prosecutor* v. *Tadić*, ICTY (Appeals Chamber), judgment of 15 July 1999, paras. 249 and 251; *Prosecutor* v. *Kunarac* et al., ICTY (Appeals Chamber), judgment of 12 June 2002, para. 83: "purely jurisdictional prerequisite." See also S. Chesterman, 10 *Duke Journal of Comparative and International Law* (2002), p. 307 at pp. 311 et seq.

[25] See ICTR Statute, Art. 3: "The International Tribunal for Rwanda shall have the power to prosecute persons responsible for the following crimes when committed as part of a widespread or systematic attack against any civilian population on national, political, ethnic, racial or religious grounds . . .." On the definition of crimes against humanity in the judgments of the Rwanda Tribunal, see F. Lattanzi, in H. Fischer, C. Kress and S.R. Lüder (eds.), *International and National Prosecution of Crimes under International Law – Current Developments* (2001), pp. 491 et seq.; G. Mettraux, 43 *Harvard International Law Journal* (2002), pp. 237 et seq.

[26] *Prosecutor* v. *Akayesu*, ICTR (Appeals Chamber), judgment of 1 June 2001, para. 465: "[T]he Security Council did not depart from international humanitarian law nor did it change the legal ingredients required under international humanitarian law with respect to crimes against humanity. It limited at the very most the jurisdiction of the Tribunal to a sub-group of such crimes, which in actuality may be committed in a particular situation"; see also para. 464: "This is to say that the Security Council intended thereby that the Tribunal should not prosecute perpetrators of other possible crimes against humanity."

[27] See 1996 *Draft Code*, Art. 18: "A crime against humanity means any of the following acts, when committed in a systematic manner or on a large scale and instigated or directed by a government or by any organization or group: a) murder; b) extermination; c) torture; d) enslavement; e) persecution on political, racial, religious or ethnic grounds; f) institutionalized discrimination on racial, ethnic, or religious grounds involving the violation of fundamental human rights and freedoms and resulting in seriously disadvantaging a part of the population; g) arbitrary deportation or forcible transfer of population; h) arbitrary imprisonment; i) forced disappearance of persons; j) rape, enforced prostitution and other forms of sexual abuse; k) other inhumane acts which severely damage physical or mental integrity, health or human dignity, such as mutilation and severe bodily harm." See C. Tomuschat, *Europäische Grundrechte-Zeitschrift* 1998, pp. 5 et seq.

643   During the negotiations in Rome, there was agreement that crimes against humanity should be included in the list of core crimes. In spite of this broad consensus, formulating crimes against humanity proved to be a difficult undertaking. Ultimately, however, it was possible to work out a relatively precise definition in Article 7 of the ICC Statute, utilizing earlier definitions and especially the case law of the Yugoslavia Tribunal.[28]

III. Structure of the Crime

644   The material elements of crimes against humanity require the commission of one of the individual acts described more precisely in Article 7(1). These individual acts become crimes against humanity when they are committed in the course of a widespread or systematic attack on a civilian population. The attack on a civilian population represents the contextual element[29] of the crime. The mental element requires intent and knowledge (Article 30 of ICC Statute) regarding the material elements of the crime, including the contextual element.

IV. Protected Interests

645   For crimes against humanity, the threat to peace, security and well-being of the world consists in the systematic or widespread attack on the fundamental human rights of a civilian population.[30] This context of organized violence calls into question humanity as such[31] – in the sense of a "minimal standard of the rules of human coexistence."[32] The crime thus affects not only the individual victim, but also the international community as a whole.[33] In addition to these values, which transcend the individual, the norm pro-

---

[28] On the negotiations on Art. 7 of the ICC Statute, see especially D. Robinson, 93 *American Journal of International Law* (1999), pp. 43 et seq.; D. Robinson, in F. Lattanzi and W.A. Schabas (eds.), *Essays on the Rome Statute of the International Criminal Court*, Vol. 1 (1999), pp. 139 et seq. See also R.S. Clark, in M. Politi and G. Nesi (eds.), *The Rome Statute of the International Criminal Court, A challenge to impunity* (2001), pp. 75 et seq.; D. Donat-Cattin, *L'Astree, Revue de Droit Penal et des Droits de l'Homme* (1999), pp. 83 et seq.; P. Hwang, 22 *Fordham International Law Journal* (1998), pp. 457 et seq.; M. McAuliffe de Guzman, 22 *Human Rights Quarterly* (2000), pp. 335 et seq.

[29] For discussion of the term "contextual element" see marginal no. 82, fn. 153.

[30] On the interests protected by international criminal law, see marginal nos. 77 et seq.

[31] For an instructive discussion of the interpretation of humanity as a legal concept, see G. Radbruch, *Süddeutsche Juristenzeitung* 1947, columns 131 et seq.; see also A. Cassese, in A. Cassese, P. Gaeta and J.R.W.D. Jones (eds.), *The Rome Statute of the International Criminal Court*, Vol. 1 (2002), p. 353 at p. 360: "constitute a serious attack on human dignity"; A. Cassese, *International Criminal Law* (2003), p. 65: "constitute an attack on humanity"; S. Meseke, *Der Tatbestand der Verbrechen gegen die Menschlichkeit nach dem Römischen Statut des Internationalen Strafgerichtshofs* (2004), pp. 117 et seq.

[32] Stated explicitly by H.-H. Jescheck, in F.C. Schroeder and H. Zipf (eds.), *Festschrift für Maurach* (1972), p. 579 at p. 590.

[33] See *Prosecutor* v. *Erdemović*, ICTY (Appeals Chamber), judgment of 7 October 1997, separate opinion of Judges Kirk McDonald and Vohrah, para. 21: "[R]ules proscribing crimes against humanity address the perpetrator's conduct not only towards the immediate victim but also towards the whole of humankind. . . . It is therefore the concept of humanity as victim which essentially characterises crimes against humanity. . . . Because of their heinousness and magnitude they constitute an egregious attack on human dignity, on the very notion of humaneness. They consequently affect, or

tects individual rights: that is, the individual victim's life, health, freedom and dignity.[34]

B. Contextual Element (Attack on a Civilian Population)

Crimes against humanity under Article 7(1) of the ICC Statute comprise only those **646** crimes listed in the definition that are committed "as part of a widespread or systematic attack directed against any civilian population." Only if these elements, which can be taken together as a contextual element of the crime, are present can one presume the existence of a crime against humanity. According to the definition in Article 7(2)(a), an "attack on a civilian population" means "a course of conduct involving the multiple commission of acts referred to in paragraph 1 against any civilian population, pursuant to or in furtherance of a State or organizational policy to commit such attack." The following text first analyzes the material elements of the contextual element – that is, the term "civilian population," the requirement of "widespread or systematic attack," and the meaning of the "policy element" in Article 7(2)(a). It will then discuss the range of potential perpetrators and the question of whether and how the mental element refers to the attack on a civilian population.

I. A Civilian Population as the Object of the Crime

Crimes against humanity are directed against a civilian population as such, not merely at **647** an individual. This does not mean, however, that the entire population of a state or territory must be affected by the attack. Rather, this criterion emphasizes the collective nature of the crime, thus ruling out attacks against individuals and isolated acts of violence.[35] The crime can occur both in war and in peacetime. In contrast to war crimes, the definition protects not only civilians from the opposing side, but also, and specifically, the ci-

---

should affect, each and every member of mankind, whatever his or her nationality, ethnic group and location. . . . This aspect of crimes against humanity as injuring a broader interest than that of the immediate victim . . . is shown by the intrinsic elements of the offence. . . ."

[34] For a correct view of the issue, see H.J. Lampe, in H.J. Hirsch et al. (eds.), *Festschrift für Kohlmann* (2003), p. 147 at pp. 153 et seq.; see also H. Vest, 113 *Zeitschrift für die gesamte Strafrechtswissenschaft* (2001), p. 457 at pp. 463 et seq. The international character of the crime is missed if it is reduced to a violation of "individual legal rights," as is the case in A. Gil Gil, 112 *Zeitschrift für die gesamte Strafrechtswissenschaft* (2000), p. 381 at p. 382. On post-World War II jurisprudence relating to this question, see G. Manske, *Verbrechen gegen die Menschlichkeit als Verbrechen gegen die Menschheit* (2003), pp. 176 et seq.

[35] See the precedent in *Prosecutor* v. *Tadić*, ICTY (Trial Chamber), judgment of 7 May 1997, para. 644: "The requirement . . . 'population' does not mean that the entire population of a given State or territory must be victimised by these acts in order for the acts to constitute a crime against humanity. Instead the 'population' element is intended to imply crimes of a collective nature and thus exclude single or isolated acts which, although possibly constituting war crimes or crimes against national penal legislation, do not rise to the level of crimes against humanity. [T]he requirement . . . 'directed against any civilian population' ensures that what is to be alleged will not be one particular act but, instead, a course of conduct. . . . Thus the emphasis is not on the individual victim but rather on the collective, the individual being victimised not because of his individual attributes but rather because of his membership of a targeted civilian population." See also *Prosecutor* v. *Kunarac* et al., ICTY (Appeals Chamber), judgment of 12 June 2002, para. 90.

vilian population of the perpetrator's state.[36] Neither the victim's nor the perpetrator's nationality plays any role. Also, the presence of soldiers among an attacked civilian population does not negate its civilian character.[37]

648   The "attack" must target a civilian population, while the individual crime must target civilians. The "civilian" character of the attacked population and persons applies both in war and in peacetime. Therefore, the distinction cannot be made solely by applying the terms of international humanitarian law. However, these terms, if correctly employed, can supply useful guidelines for more precisely defining the scope of crimes against humanity in general:[38] international humanitarian law specifically protects anyone not or no longer participating in hostilities.[39]

649   Most important in demonstrating membership in a civilian population is the victims' need for protection, which follows from their defenselessness vis-à-vis state, military or other organized force.[40] Therefore, anyone who is not part of the organized power using force should be considered a civilian. What is crucial is not formal status, such as membership in specific military forces or units, but the person's actual role at the time of commission of the crime.[41] This therefore includes members of military forces who have

---

[36] *Prosecutor* v. *Tadić*, ICTY (Trial Chamber), judgment of 7 May 1997, para. 635: "The inclusion of the word 'any' makes it clear that crimes against humanity can be committed against civilians of the same nationality as the perpetrator or those who are stateless, as well as those of a different nationality."

[37] See Additional Protocol I to the Geneva Conventions of 1949, Art. 50(3); *Prosecutor* v. *Tadić*, ICTY (Trial Chamber), judgment of 7 May 1997, para. 638: "[T]he targeted population must be of predominantly civilian nature" and para. 643: "[T]he presence of those actively involved in the conflict should not prevent the characterisation of a population as civilian"; affirmed in *Prosecutor* v. *Jelisić*, ICTY (Trial Chamber), judgment of 14 December 1999, para. 54; *Prosecutor* v. *Kupreškić* et al., ICTY (Trial Chamber), judgment of 14 January 2000, para. 549; *Prosecutor* v. *Blaškić*, ICTY (Trial Chamber), judgment of 3 March 2000, paras. 211 and 214: "[T]he presence of soldiers within an intentionally targeted civilian population does not alter the civilian nature of that population"; *Prosecutor* v. *Kunarac* et al., ICTY (Trial Chamber), judgment of 22 February 2001, para. 425; *Prosecutor* v. *Kordić and Čerkez*, ICTY (Trial Chamber), judgment of 26 February 2001, para. 180; also *Prosecutor* v. *Akayesu*, ICTR (Trial Chamber), judgment of 2 September 1998, para. 582; *Prosecutor* v. *Kayishema and Ruzindana*, ICTR (Trial Chamber), judgment of 21 May 1999, para. 128.

[38] *Prosecutor* v. *Tadić*, ICTY (Trial Chamber), judgment of 7 May 1997, para. 639: "[T]his definition of civilians contained in Common Article 3 is not immediately applicable to crimes against humanity because it is a part of the laws or customs of war and can only be applied by analogy. The same applies to the definition contained in Protocol I and the Commentary, Geneva Convention IV, on the treatment of civilians, both of which advocate a broad interpretation of the term 'civilian.'"

[39] For details, see marginal nos. 774 et seq.; *Prosecutor* v. *Kunarac* et al., ICTY (Trial Chamber), judgment of 22 February 2001, para. 425: "all persons who are civilians as opposed to members of the armed forces and other legitimate combatants."

[40] For an accurate discussion of the purpose of the norm, see K. Ambos and S. Wirth, 13 *Criminal Law Forum* (2002), p. 1 at pp. 22 et seq.

[41] *Prosecutor* v. *Blaškić*, ICTY (Trial Chamber), judgment of 3 March 2000, para. 214: "It also follows that the specific situation of the victim at the moment the crimes were committed, rather than his status, must be taken into account in determining his standing as a civilian." See also O. Swaak-Goldman, in G. Kirk McDonald and O. Swaak-Goldman (eds.), *Substantive and Procedural Aspects of International Criminal Law*, Vol. 1 (2000), p. 141 at p. 154: "Thus, a formalistic distinction based upon membership in the armed forces no longer suffices for deciding whether a prohibited act against a certain victim qualifies as a war crime or as a crime against humanity. Rather, a more flexible approach toward civilian status is required."

laid down their arms or are no longer participating in hostilities, commensurate with the idea behind Common Article 3 of the Geneva Conventions. The same is true in international armed conflict for soldiers no longer participating in hostilities or for prisoners of war, who are specifically protected by international humanitarian law.[42]

In contrast to international humanitarian law, it is not important to the protected status of civilians whether they are under the control of their own side or the opposing side. Hence present or former members of one's own armed forces, in particular, who are not protected by international humanitarian law can become direct objects of a crime against humanity.[43] In this way, such people are given protection not offered by international humanitarian law. This interpretation of Article 7 of the ICC Statute corresponds to the state of customary international law.[44]   **650**

Outside of armed conflicts, crimes against humanity are generally characterized by one-sided acts on the part of the state or other organized armed groups against a civilian population. Here holders of state or other organized power are not included under the heading of civilian population, if they wield this power against the civilian population. Examples are members of a state police apparatus[45] or of non-governmental organizations endowed with comparable *de facto* authority. The entire population of a geographical entity in which an attack is taking place need not be subject to the attack. It is   **651**

---

[42] *Prosecutor v. Blaškić*, ICTY (Trial Chamber), judgment of 3 March 2000, para. 214: "Crimes against humanity therefore do not mean only acts committed against civilians in the strict sense of the term, but include also crimes against two categories of people: those who were members of a resistance movement and former combatants – regardless of whether they wore uniforms or not – but who were no longer taking part in hostilities when the crimes were perpetrated because they had either left army or were no longer bearing arms or, ultimately, had been placed *hors de combat*, in particular, due to their wounds or their being detained." For an explicitly "broad" interpretation of the term "civilian population", see *Prosecutor v. Tadić*, ICTY (Trial Chamber), judgment of 7 May 1997, para. 643; *Prosecutor v. Jelisić*, ICTY (Trial Chamber), judgment of 14 December 1999, para. 54; *Prosecutor v. Kupreškić* et al., ICTY (Trial Chamber), judgment of 14 January 2000; *Prosecutor v. Blaškić*, ICTY (Trial Chamber), judgment of 3 March 2000, para. 210; *Prosecutor v. Kordić and Čerkez*, ICTY (Trial Chamber), judgment of 26 February 2001, para. 180. For a summary of judgments, see K. Ambos and S. Wirth, 13 *Criminal Law Forum* (2002), p. 1 at pp. 22 et seq.; S. Meseke, in M. Chiavario (ed.), *La justice pénale internationale entre passé et avenir* (2003), p. 173 at pp. 197 et seq.

[43] The judgments of the Supreme Court in the British Occupied Zone also applied the definition of crimes against humanity when the victims were members of the armed forces, see, e.g., Supreme Court in the British Occupied Zone, *OGHSt* 1, pp. 45 et seq.; *OGHSt* 2, pp. 231 et seq.

[44] On the scope of the definition of crimes against humanity under customary international law, see *Prosecutor v. Kupreškić* et al., ICTY (Trial Chamber), judgment of 14 January 2000, para. 547: "One fails to see why only civilians and not also combatants should be protected by these rules . . ., given that these rules may be held to possess a broader humanitarian scope and purpose than those prohibiting war crimes. [T]he explicit limitation . . . constitutes a departure from customary international law."

[45] *Prosecutor v. Kayishema and Ruzindana*, ICTR (Trial Chamber), judgment of 21 May 1999, para. 127: "The Trial Chamber considers that a wide definition of civilian is applicable and, in the context of Kibuye *Prefecture* where there was no armed conflict, includes all persons *except* those who have the duty to maintain public order and have the legitimate means to exercise force. Non-civilians would include, for example, members of the . . . police and the Gendarmerie Nationale." It is however problematic that the decision, at least in its wording, focuses only on formal membership in the armed forces; for a critical analysis, see K. Ambos and S. Wirth, 13 *Criminal Law Forum* (2002), p. 1 at pp. 25 et seq.

sufficient that a relevant number of individuals – though not merely a few randomly selected persons – be attacked.[46]

II. Widespread or Systematic Attack

1. Attack

652 The "attack" element describes a course of conduct involving the commission of acts of violence.[47] Such a course of conduct must include the "multiple commission" of acts listed in Article 7(1) of the ICC Statute. Multiple commission is a lesser requirement than a "widespread" attack.[48] Multiple commission is present both if the same act is committed many times and if different acts are committed. The perpetrator does not need to act repeatedly him or herself. A single act of intentional killing can constitute a crime against humanity if the single act fits within the overall context.[49] A vivid historical example is the denunciation of a single Jew to the Gestapo, which was part of the process of excluding German Jews from cultural and economic life in the Third Reich.[50]

653 A military attack is not necessary, as the Elements of Crimes explicitly state ("the acts need not constitute a military attack").[51] Nor is use of force against the civilian population required.[52] The concept of "attack" encompasses any mistreatment of the civilian population.[53]

---

[46] *Prosecutor v. Kunarac* et al., ICTY (Appeals Chamber), judgment of 12 June 2002, para. 90; *Prosecutor v. Naletilić and Martinović*, ICTY (Trial Chamber), judgment of 31 March 2003, para. 235; *Prosecutor v. Bagilishema*, ICTR (Trial Chamber), para. 80.

[47] *Prosecutor v. Naletilić and Martinović*, ICTY (Trial Chamber), judgment of 31 March 2003, para. 233.

[48] See D. Robinson, 93 *American Journal of International Law* (1999), p. 43 at p. 48; H. von Hebel and D. Robinson, in R.S. Lee (ed.), *The International Criminal Court, The Making of the Rome Statute* (1999), p. 79 at p. 96.

[49] Making this explicit, see *Prosecutor v. Tadić*, ICTY (Trial Chamber), judgment of 7 May 1997, para. 649: "Clearly, a single act by a perpetrator taken within the context of a widespread or systematic attack against a civilian population entails individual criminal responsibility and an individual perpetrator need not commit numerous offences to be held liable. [T]hus, '[e]ven an isolated act can constitute a crime against humanity if it is the product of a political system based on terror or persecution.'"

[50] See, e.g., Supreme Court in the British Occupied Zone, *OGHSt* 1, pp. 6 et seq.; pp. 19 et seq.; pp. 91 et seq.; pp. 105 et seq.; pp. 122 et seq.; pp. 141 et seq. On Nazi denunciations in the judgments of the Supreme Court in the British Occupied Zone, see, e.g., T. Klefisch, *Monatsschrift für Deutsches Recht* 1949, pp. 324 et seq.

[51] According to the ICTY even before adoption of the Elements of Crimes, see *Prosecutor v. Kunarac* et al., ICTY (Trial Chamber), judgment of 22 February 2001, para. 416.

[52] See *Prosecutor v. Akayesu*, ICTR (Trial Chamber), judgment of 2 September 1998, para. 581: "An attack may also be non-violent in nature, like imposing a system of apartheid, . . . or exerting pressure on the population to act in a particular manner, may come under the purview of an attack, if orchestrated on a massive scale or in a systematic manner." See also *Prosecutor v. Rutaganda*, ICTR (Trial Chamber), judgment of 6 December 1999, para. 68 and *Prosecutor v. Musema*, ICTR (Trial Chamber), judgment of 27 January 2000, para. 205.

[53] *Prosecutor v. Kunarac* et al., ICTY (Trial Chamber), judgment of 12 June 2002, para. 86; affirmed in *Prosecutor v. Stakić*, ICTY (Trial Chamber), judgment of 31 July 2003, para. 623; *Prosecutor v. Semanza*, ICTR (Trial Chamber), judgment of 15 May 2003, para. 327; *Prosecutor v. Kajelijeli*, ICTR (Trial Chamber), judgment of 1 December 2003, para. 868.

2. Widespread or Systematic Character

At the negotiations on the ICC Statute, it was soon agreed that the criteria of "widespread" and **654** "systematic" would be included in the definition of the crime. However, there was disagreement over whether these two criteria should be alternative or cumulative. The group of "like-minded states" advocated an alternative relationship.[54] But a large number of the remaining delegations believed that the criteria had to be cumulative. In the end, an alternative linkage was accepted, but with the proviso that the definition "attack on a civilian population" – including the policy element it contained – would be adopted into Article 7(2)(a).[55]

The criterion of "widespread" describes a quantitative element.[56] The widespread nature **655** of the attack can be derived in particular from the number of victims, as clarified in the International Law Commission's commentary on the corresponding article in the 1996 *Draft Code*.[57] International case law has followed this view.[58] The widespread nature of the attack can also be derived from its extension over a broad geographic area, but this is not necessary to satisfy this requirement. Rather, a widespread attack can consist even of a single act, if a large number of civilians fall victim to it.[59]

The criterion of a "systematic" attack is qualitative in nature.[60] It refers to "the orga- **656** nized nature of the acts of violence and the improbability of their random occurrence."[61]

---

[54] In this spirit, see also ICTR Statute, Art. 3. The two criteria are not contained in Art. 5 of the ICTY Statute. The interpretation in the report of the UN Secretary-General at the creation of the ICTY, however, was that crimes against humanity "refer to inhumane acts of a very serious nature . . . committed as part of a widespread or systematic attack against any civilian population," see *Report of the Secretary-General Pursuant to Paragraph 2 of Security Council Resolution 808 (1993)*, UN Doc. S/25704, para. 48. See, finally, *Prosecutor v. Tadić*, ICTY (Trial Chamber), judgment of 7 May 1997, para. 646: "While this issue has been the subject of considerable debate, it is now well established that the requirement that the acts be directed against a civilian 'population' can be fulfilled if the acts occur on either a widespread or systematic manner. Either one of these is sufficient to exclude isolated or random acts." This idea was already contained in the 1996 *Draft Code*, commentary on Art. 18, paras. 3, 4: ". . . that the act was 'committed in a systematic manner or on a large scale' . . . consists of two alternative requirements. . . . Consequently, an act could constitute a crime against humanity if either of these conditions is met."

[55] On the history of the negotiations on the ICC Statute, Art. 7, see D. Robinson, 93 *American Journal of International Law* (1999), p. 43 at pp. 47 et seq.; D. Robinson, in F. Lattanzi and W.A. Schabas (eds.), *Essays on the Rome Statute of the International Criminal Court*, Vol. 1 (1999), p. 139 at pp. 151 et seq.; H. von Hebel and D. Robinson, in R.S. Lee (ed.), *The International Criminal Court, The Making of the Rome Statute* (1999), p. 79 at pp. 94 et seq. See also marginal nos. 658 et seq.

[56] H. Vest, 113 *Zeitschrift für die gesamte Strafrechtswissenschaft* (2001), p. 457, esp. p. 468 is instructive.

[57] See 1996 *Draft Code*, commentary on Art. 18, para. 4: "The . . . alternative requires the inhumane acts be committed on a large scale meaning that the acts are directed against a multiplicity of victims."

[58] See, e.g., *Prosecutor v. Tadić*, ICTY (Trial Chamber), judgment of 7 May 1997, para. 648; *Prosecutor v. Kunarac et al.*, ICTY (Trial Chamber), judgment of 22 February 2001, para. 428; see also *Prosecutor v. Akayesu*, ICTR (Trial Chamber), judgment of 2 September 1998, para. 580: "The concept of 'widespread' may be defined as massive, frequent, large scale action, carried out collectively with considerable seriousness and directed against a multiplicity of victims."

[59] See 1996 *Draft Code*, commentary on Art. 18, para. 4; *Prosecutor v. Blaškić*, ICTY (Trial Chamber), judgment of 3 March 2000, para. 206.

[60] See H. Vest, 113 *Zeitschrift für die gesamte Strafrechtswissenschaft* (2001), p. 457 at pp. 468 et seq.

[61] *Prosecutor v. Kunarac et al.*, ICTY (Appeals Chamber), judgment of 12 June 2002, para. 94.

It requires that the individual act follow a predetermined plan or policy. This interpretation is based on the International Law Commission's commentary on the corresponding criterion included there.[62] The *ad hoc* tribunals' case law has followed this correct approach and has always emphasized the necessity of a plan or policy.[63]

657 Under Article 7(1) of the ICC Statute, the criteria "widespread" and "systematic" need only be present in the alternative, but in practice, both are generally satisfied.[64]

III. The "Policy Element"

1. ICC Statute

658 At the negotiations in Rome, the price for an alternative, rather than cumulative, relationship between the requirements "widespread" and "systematic" was the inclusion of a definition of "attack on a civilian population." This contains a "policy element" that applies to both widespread and systematic attacks: Article 7(2)(a) of the ICC Statute requires that the attack on a civilian population be carried out "pursuant to or in furtherance of a State or organizational policy to commit such attack."[65] The formulation of this "policy element" was inspired in particular by the 1996 *Draft Code*, in which incitement or support of the crime by a government, organization or group was a requirement for criminality.[66]

---

[62] See 1996 *Draft Code*, commentary on Art. 18, para. 3: "The . . . alternative requires that the inhumane acts be committed in a systematic manner meaning pursuant to a preconceived plan or policy."

[63] The foundational case is *Prosecutor* v. *Akayesu*, ICTR (Trial Chamber), judgment of 2 September 1998, para. 580 (". . . there must however be some kind of preconceived plan or policy"); see also *Prosecutor* v. *Tadić*, ICTY (Trial Chamber), judgment of 7 May 1997, para. 648 ("pattern or methodological plan"); *Prosecutor* v. *Kayishema and Ruzindana*, ICTR (Trial Chamber), judgment of 21 May 1999, para. 123 ("preconceived policy or plan"); *Prosecutor* v. *Kunarac* et al., ICTY (Trial Chamber), judgment of 22 February 2001, para. 429. In certain cases, however, the requirements for the presence of a plan or policy are wrongly increased, see *Prosecutor* v. *Blaškić*, ICTY (Trial Chamber), judgment of 3 March 2000, para. 203: ". . . the perpetration of a criminal act on a very large scale against a group of civilians or the repeated and continuos commission of inhumane acts linked to one another; the preparation and use of significant financial public or private resources, whether military or other." For justified criticism, see K. Ambos and S. Wirth, 13 *Criminal Law Forum* (2002), p. 1 at pp. 19 et seq.

[64] *Prosecutor* v. *Blaškić*, ICTY (Trial Chamber), judgment of 3 March 2000, para. 207: "The fact still remains however that, in practice, these two criteria will often be difficult to separate since a widespread attack targeting, a large number of victims generally relies on some form of planning or organisation." See also *Prosecutor* v. *Jelisić*, ICTY (Trial Chamber), judgment of 14 December 1999, para. 53; *Prosecutor* v. *Bagilishema*, ICTR (Trial Chamber), judgment of 7 June 2001, para. 77: "The criteria which allow one or other of the aspects to be established partially overlap."

[65] For a critical view, see R.S. Clark, in M. Politi and G. Nesi (eds.), *The Rome Statute of the International Criminal Court, A challenge to impunity* (2001), p. 75 at p. 91: "something close to widespread and systematic seems to be required by the very definition of 'attack'"; see also M. Boot, *Genocide, Crimes Against Humanity, War Crimes: Nullum Crime Sine Lege* (2002), pp. 481 et seq.; P. Hwang, 22 *Fordham International Law Journal* (1998), p. 457 at pp. 502 et seq.

[66] This rule was intended to make clear that isolated crimes by individuals were not included in the definition of the crime, see 1996 *Draft Code*, commentary on Art. 18, para. 5: "This alternative is intended to exclude the situation in which an individual commits an inhumane act while acting on his own initiative pursuant to his own criminal plan in the absence of any encouragement or direction

Earlier definitions, such as Article 6(c) of the Nuremberg Charter, made do without this element,[67] since the criteria "civilian population" and "widespread or systematic" already contained minimum quantitative and qualitative requirements.[68] Thus crimes against humanity tried earlier were also based on criminal state policies:[69] The presence of a specific policy was the typical manifestation of crimes against humanity, even though neither the policy element, nor even government participation, was a requirement.[70] **659**

The "policy" criterion does not require a formal programmatic determination. The term is instead interpreted in a broad sense as a planned, directed or organized crime, as opposed to spontaneous, isolated acts of violence.[71] Thus in the *Tadić* judgment, the Trial Chamber stated: **660**

---

from either a Government or a group or organization. This type of isolated criminal conduct on the part of a single individual would not constitute a crime against humanity."

[67] See also CCL No. 10, Art. II(1)(c); ICTY Statute, Art. 5; ICTR Statute, Art. 3.

[68] See *Prosecutor* v. *Bagilishema*, ICTR (Trial Chamber), judgment of 7 June 2001, para. 78: ". . . either of the requirements of widespread or systematic will be enough to exclude acts not committed as part of a broader policy or plan. Also the requirement that the attack must be committed against a 'civilian population' presupposes a kind of plan. Thus the policy element can be seen to be an inherent feature of the attack, whether the attack be characterised as widespread or systematic."

[69] See, e.g., IMT, judgment of 1 October 1946, in *The Trial of German Major War Criminals. Proceedings of the International Military Tribunal sitting at Nuremberg, Germany*, Part 22, p. 468: "With regard to crimes against humanity, there is no doubt whatever that political opponents were murdered in Germany before the war, and that many of them were kept in concentration camps in circumstances of great horror and cruelty. The policy of terror was certainly carried out on a vast scale, and in many cases was organized and systematic. The policy of persecution, repression and murder of civilians in Germany before the war of 1939, who were likely to be hostile to the Government, was most ruthlessly carried out." See also *Public Prosecutor* v. *Menten*, Supreme Court of the Netherlands, judgment of 13 January 1981, in 75 *ILR* (1987), p. 336 at pp. 362 et seq.: "Crimes against humanity in Art. 6(c) of the London Charter should be understood in the restrictive sense that the crimes formed part of a system based on terror, or constituted a link in a consciously pursued policy directed against particular groups of people." Supporting a "policy element," see *Prosecutor* v. *Tadić*, ICTY (Trial Chamber), judgment of 7 May 1997, paras. 644, 653: "[T]he reason that crimes against humanity so shock the conscience of mankind and warrant intervention by the international community is because they are not isolated, random acts of individuals but rather result from a deliberate attempt to target a civilian population. Traditionally this requirement was understood to mean that there must be some form of policy to commit these acts." See also *Prosecutor* v. *Kupreškić* et al., ICTY (Trial Chamber), judgment of 14 January 2000, paras. 551 et seq.; *Prosecutor* v. *Blaškić*, ICTY (Trial Chamber), judgment of 3 March 2000, paras. 203 et seq., 254 and 257; *Prosecutor* v. *Akayesu*, ICTR (Trial Chamber), judgment of 2 September 1998, para. 580; *Prosecutor* v. *Kayishema and Ruzindana*, ICTR (Trial Chamber), judgment of 21 May 1999, para. 124.

[70] See, e.g., *Prosecutor* v. *Kordić and Čerkez*, ICTY (Trial Chamber), judgment of 26 February 2001, paras. 181 et seq.: "[T]he existence of a policy should be better regarded as indicative of the systematic character of offences charged as crimes against humanity." For a concurring opinion, see *Prosecutor* v. *Krnojelac*, ICTY (Trial Chamber), judgment of 15 March 2002, para. 58; this is also implicit in *Prosecutor* v. *Blaškić*, ICTY (Trial Chamber), judgment of 3 March 2000, para. 203. For detail, see G. Mettraux, 43 *Harvard International Law Journal* (2002), p. 237 at pp. 281 et seq.

[71] See D. Robinson, 93 *American Journal of International Law* (1999), p. 43 at p. 51; D. Robinson, in F. Lattanzi and W.A. Schabas (eds.), *Essays on the Rome Statute of the International Criminal Court*, Vol. 1 (1999), p. 139 at p. 161; H. von Hebel and D. Robinson, in R.S. Lee (ed.), *The International Criminal Court, The Making of the Rome Statute* (1999), p. 79 at p. 97.

"[S]uch a policy need not be formalized and can be deduced from the way in which the acts occur. Notably, if the acts occur on a widespread or systematic basis that demonstrates a policy to commit those acts, whether formalized or not."[72]

661 The policy need not be explicit or clearly and precisely stipulated. Nor is it necessary that it be decided upon at the highest levels.[73] The presence of the policy element can be gathered from the totality of the circumstances. Significant evidence includes actual events, political platforms or writings, public statements or propaganda programs and the creation of political or administrative structures.[74]

662 The body responsible for the policy must be a specific entity, a state or organization. The term "state" is understood in the functional sense and, aside from the 192 states in the world, also includes forces that control an area *de facto* and exercise governmental functions there.[75]

663 The term "organization" certainly includes groups of persons that govern a specific territory, or in any case can move freely there.[76] But this territorial element is not necessary. Ultimately, any group of people can be categorized as an organization if it has at its disposal, in material and personnel, the potential to commit a widespread or systematic attack on a civilian population.[77] In addition to paramilitary units, this particularly includes terrorist organizations.

664 The view that no violation of human rights has occurred if it is not possible to attribute the act to a state entity[78] may be correct, but it is not a convincing objection. Threats to values protected by international law, especially to world peace, can certainly arise from non-state actors or private persons. The victims' need for protection does not depend on the classification of a serious attack as a

---

[72] *Prosecutor* v. *Tadić*, ICTY (Trial Chamber), judgment of 7 May 1997, para. 653.

[73] See *Prosecutor* v. *Blaškić*, ICTY (Trial Chamber), judgment of 3 March 2000, paras. 204 et seq.

[74] For details, see *Prosecutor* v. *Blaškić*, ICTY (Trial Chamber), judgment of 3 March 2000, para. 204: "[T]he general historical circumstances and the overall political background against which the criminal acts are set; the establishment and implementation of autonomous political structures at any level of authority in a given territory; the general content of a political programme, as it appears in the writings and speeches of its authors; media propaganda; the establishment and implementation of autonomous military structures; the mobilisation of armed forces; temporally and geographically repeated and co-ordinated military offensives; links between the military hierarchy and the political structure and its political programme; alterations to the 'ethnic' composition of populations; discriminatory measures, whether administrative or other . . .; the scale of the acts of violence perpetrated – in particular, murders and other physical acts of violence, rape, arbitrary imprisonment, deportations and expulsions or the destruction of non-military property, in particular sacral sites."

[75] In the ICTY Rules of Procedure, Rule 2, the term "state" is defined as follows: "(i) A State Member or non-Member of the United Nations; . . . or (iii) a self-proclaimed entity de facto exercising governmental functions, whether recognised as a State or not."

[76] The leading case is *Prosecutor* v. *Tadić*, ICTY (Trial Chamber), judgment of 7 May 1997, para. 654: ". . . the law in relation to crimes against humanity has developed to take into account forces, which although not those of the legitimate government, have de facto control over . . . or are able to move freely within, defined territory . . . without international recognition or formal status of a *de jure* state." Affirmed in *Prosecutor* v. *Kupreškić* et al., ICTY (Trial Chamber), judgment of 14 January 2000, para. 552; *Prosecutor* v. *Blaškić*, ICTY (Trial Chamber), judgment of 3 March 2000, para. 205.

[77] See, e.g., 1991 *Draft Code*, commentary on Art. 21, para. 5: "private individuals with de facto power or organized in criminal gangs or groups."

[78] See K. Ambos and S. Wirth, 13 *Criminal Law Forum* (2002), p. 1 at pp. 30 et seq.

violation of human rights, but on the magnitude of the attack. As with genocide, in crimes against humanity the participation of states or state-like entities is the rule in practice, but not a legal requirement. This leads to the conclusion that, in order to classify the attacks on the New York World Trade Center and the Pentagon on 11 September 2001 as crimes against humanity, it does not matter whether the acts can be ascribed to a terrorist organization alone or also to a state or state-like entity.

The policy of a state or organization can consist of taking a leading role in commission **665** of the crime, but also in actively promoting the crime or in merely tolerating it. The Elements of Crimes are too narrow in requiring that the state or organization "actively" promote or encourage the attack on the civilian population.[79] The text of the ICC Statute gives no cause for such a limitation; in a number of decisions, international criminal courts have permitted tolerating to be sufficient to satisfy the requirements of the crime.[80] Indeed, the purpose of the norm supports the inclusion of tolerance: the very act of a state looking away, refusing to take measures to protect the population, and failing to prosecute perpetrators can be effective tools in a policy of terror and extermination.[81]

2. Customary International Law

The requirement of a "widespread or systematic attack on a civilian population" embodies   **666** the contextual element required by customary international law. No additional "policy" element to limit the definition is called for under customary law. The Yugoslavia Tribunal clearly stated this, after initial hesitance,[82] in the *Kunarac* et al. judgment.[83]

---

[79] Elements of Crimes for Art. 7 ICC Statute, Introduction: "3. . . . It is understood that 'policy to commit such attack' requires that the State or organization *actively* (author's emphasis) promote or encourage such an attack against a civilian population". However, fn. 6, added as a compromise, somewhat weakens this statement: "A policy which has a civilian population as the objective of the attack would be implemented by State or organizational action. Such a policy may, in exceptional circumstances, be implemented by a deliberate failure to take action, which is consciously aimed at encouraging such attack. The existence of such a policy cannot be inferred solely from the absence of governmental or organizational action."

[80] *Prosecutor* v. *Kupreškić* et al., ICTY (Trial Chamber), judgment of 14 January 2000, para. 552 ("at least tolerated"); *Prosecutor* v. *Tadić*, ICTY (Appeals Chamber), judgment of 31 January 2000, para. 14; also 1954 *Draft Code,* Art. 2 para. 11; *Final Report of the Commission of Experts Established Pursuant To Security Council Resolution 780 (1992)*, UN Doc. S/1994/674, Annex II: Rape and Sexual Assault: A Legal Study, 27 May 1994, p. 8, para. 33: "It also has proven . . . that the state is involved. This can be concluded from state tolerance."

[81] See K. Ambos and S. Wirth, 13 *Criminal Law Forum* (2002), p. 1 at pp. 30 et seq.

[82] See *Prosecutor* v. *Kunarac* et al., ICTY (Trial Chamber), judgment of 22 February 2001, para. 432; *Prosecutor* v. *Kordić and Čerkez*, ICTY (Trial Chamber), judgment of 26 February 2001, paras. 181 et seq.; *Prosecutor* v. *Krnojelac*, ICTY (Trial Chamber), judgment of 15 March 2002, para. 58; *Prosecutor* v. *Kupreškić* et al., ICTY (Trial Chamber), judgment of 14 January 2000, para. 551:"[A]lthough the concept of crimes against humanity implies a policy element, there is some doubt as to whether it is strictly a *requirement* as such, for crimes against humanity."; *Prosecutor* v. *Galić*, ICTY (Trial Chamber), judgment of 5 December 2003, para. 147.

[83] *Prosecutor* v. *Kunarac* et al., ICTY (Appeals Chamber), judgment of 12 June 2002, para. 98: "There was nothing in . . . in customary international law . . . which required proof of the existence of a plan or policy to commit these crimes. . . . [P]roof that the attack was directed against a civilian

This view is correct; since Nuremberg, most definitions of crimes against humanity have not contained an additional policy element.[84] Elements of planning are already required for the (systematic) attack on a civilian population. To prove this contextual element, it is usually helpful to show evidence of a corresponding policy. But that does not make the policy element a criterion of the offense.[85]

667 Ultimately, the International Criminal Court will have to determine whether the policy element in the ICC Statute will restrict liability in comparison with customary international law. If interpreted broadly, as suggested here, the ICC Statute's policy element is essentially nothing more than an illustration of the requirements for the contextual element of a widespread or systematic attack on a civilian population.

IV. Perpetrators

668 Perpetrators need not be members of the state or organization involved in the crime, but can include all persons who act to implement or support the policy of the state or the organization. Typical examples of commission of a crime by private persons are denunciations that lead to deprivation of liberty or to the death of the victim.[86]

V. Mental Element

669 In accordance with customary international law,[87] Article 7(1) of the ICC Statute explicitly provides that the perpetrator must act "with knowledge" of the attack on the civilian

---

population and that it was widespread or systematic, are legal elements of the crime. But to prove these elements, it is not necessary to show that they were the result of the existence of a policy or plan. It may be useful in establishing that the attack was directed against a civilian population and that it was widespread or systematic (especially the latter) to show that there was in fact a policy or plan, but it may be possible to prove these things by reference to other matters. Thus, the existence of a policy or plan may be evidentially relevant, but it is not a legal element of the crime."

[84] See Nuremberg Charter, Art. (6)(c); CCL No. 10, Art. II(1)(c); ICTY Statute, Art. 5 and ICTR Statute, Art. 3.

[85] See also *Prosecutor* v. *Simić* et al., ICTY (Trial Chamber), judgment of 17 October 2003, para. 44: "There is no requirement in customary international law that the acts which form the attack be connected to a policy or plan. However, a plan or policy may be relevant in an evidential sense, in proving whether or not the attack is properly characterised as either 'widespread' or 'systematic', and whether the acts of the accused were part of that attack." See also *Prosecutor* v. *Semanza*, ICTR (Trial Chamber), judgment of 15 May 2003, para. 329; *Prosecutor* v. *Kamuhanda*, ICTR (Trial Chamber), judgment of 22 January 2004, para. 665.

[86] See marginal no. 652.

[87] The foundational judgment is *Prosecutor* v. *Tadić*, ICTY (Trial Chamber), judgment of 7 May 1997, para. 659. See also *Prosecutor* v. *Tadić*, ICTY (Appeals Chamber), judgment of 15 July 1999, para. 248; *Prosecutor* v. *Jelisić*, ICTY (Trial Chamber), judgment of 14 December 1999, para. 56; *Prosecutor* v. *Kupreškić* et al., ICTY (Trial Chamber), judgment of 14 January 2000, para. 556; *Prosecutor* v. *Blaškić*, ICTY (Trial Chamber), judgment of 3 March 2000, paras. 246 et seq.; *Prosecutor* v. *Kunarac* et al., ICTY (Trial Chamber), judgment of 22 February 2001, para. 434; *Prosecutor* v. *Kordić and Čerkez*, ICTY (Trial Chamber), judgment of 26 February 2001, para. 185; *Prosecutor* v. *Krstić*, ICTY (Trial Chamber), judgment of 2 August 2001, para. 482; *Prosecutor* v. *Kvočka* et al., ICTY (Trial Chamber), judgment of 2 November 2001, para. 127, *Prosecutor* v. *Krnojelac*, ICTY (Trial Chamber), judgment of 15 March 2002, para. 59.

population. This is a merely declaratory reference to Article 30's general requirement for the mental element.[88] As a "circumstance," the attack is in any case an aspect of the mental element under Article 30(3).[89]

Thus the perpetrator must be aware that a (widespread or systematic) attack on a ci-   **670** vilian population is taking place and that his action is part of this attack.[90] However, it is not necessary that the perpetrator be aware of the details of the state's or organization's plan or policy.[91]

Additional subjective criteria for crimes against humanity are found neither in cus-   **671** tomary international law nor in the ICC Statute's definition of the crime. In particular, crimes against humanity do not require that the perpetrator act out of discriminatory motives, as required by Article 3 of the ICTR Statute[92] and by early decisions on Article 5 of the ICTY Statute.[93] Discriminatory intent is required only for the act of persecution, one of the possible individual acts in the definition.[94]

C. Individual Acts

The following text analyzes the individual acts of crimes against humanity in the order in   **672** which they are contained in the ICC Statute. No distinction is made between the categories "inhuman acts" ("murder type") and "acts of persecution" ("persecution type").

---

[88] See marginal nos. 325 et seq. and K. Ambos, *Der Allgemeine Teil des Völkerstrafrechts* (2002), p. 774; D. Robinson, 93 *American Journal of International Law* (1999), p. 43 at pp. 51 et seq.

[89] The view still advocated in Rome that the attack on a civilian population represented only a *jurisdictional element* can therefore no longer be justified today, see marginal nos. 326 et seq.

[90] See *Prosecutor* v. *Kunarac* et al., ICTY (Trial Chamber), judgment of 22 February 2001, para. 434. Affirmed in *Prosecutor* v. *Kunarac* et al., ICTY (Appeals Chamber), judgment of 12 June 2002, para. 121; K. Ambos, *Der Allgemeine Teil des Völkerstrafrechts* (2002), p. 778; H. von Hebel and D. Robinson, in R.S. Lee (ed.), *The International Criminal Court, The Making of the Rome Statute* (1999), p. 98, fn. 55; D. Robinson, 93 *American Journal of International Law* (1999), p. 43 at pp. 51 et seq.; D. Robinson, in F. Lattanzi and W.A. Schabas (eds.), *Essays on the Rome Statute of the International Criminal Court*, Vol. 1 (1999), p. 139 at pp.164 et seq.

[91] See Elements of Crimes for Art. 7 ICC Statute, Introduction: "[The] element should not be interpreted as requiring proof that the perpetrator had knowledge of all characteristics of the attack or the precise details of the plan or policy of the State or organization. In the case of an emerging widespread or systematic attack against a civilian population . . . this mental element is satisfied if the perpetrator intended to further such an attack."

[92] See marginal no. 641.

[93] *Prosecutor* v. *Tadić*, ICTY (Trial Chamber), judgment of 7 May 1997, para. 652: ". . . discriminatory intent as an additional requirement for all crimes against humanity was not included in the Statute. . . . Nevertheless, because the requirement of discriminatory intent on national, political, ethnic, racial or religious grounds for all crimes against humanity was included in the Report of the Secretary-General, and since several Security Council members stated that they interpreted Article 5 as referring to acts taken on a discriminatory basis, the Trial Chamber adopts the requirement of discriminatory intent for all crimes against humanity under Article 5."

[94] A leading case is *Prosecutor* v. *Tadić*, ICTY (Appeals Chamber), judgment of 15 July 1999, paras. 273 et seq. and finally *Prosecutor* v. *Akayesu*, ICTR (Appeals Chamber), judgment of 1 June 2001, paras. 464 et seq. Affirmed in *Prosecutor* v. *Kupreškić* et al., ICTY (Trial Chamber), judgment of 14 January 2000, para. 558; *Prosecutor* v. *Blaškić*, ICTY (Trial Chamber), judgment of 3 March 2000, para. 260; *Prosecutor* v. *Kordić and Čerkez*, ICTY (Trial Chamber), judgment of 26 February 2001, para. 186. See ICC Statute, Art. 7(1)(h). See also S. Chesterman, 10 *Duke Journal of Comparative and International Law* (2002), p. 307 at pp. 326 et seq.

673   The distinction between crimes against humanity of the *murder type* and of the *persecution type* is
common because it is the basis of Article 6(c) of the Nuremberg Charter. In contrast, the 1991
Draft Code and the 1996 *Draft Code* did not make this distinction, nor do the Statutes of the
ICTY, ICTR and ICC. The separation into *murder type* and *persecution type* crimes against humanity can be explained primarily by the fact that the mental element of crimes of persecution requires
discriminatory motives, which are not necessary for crimes of the *murder type*.[95] This aspect, however, can be taken into account in interpreting the individual definitions of crimes of persecution;
there is no need to base such a classification of offenses upon it.

I. Killing

674   Günter Heine and Hans Vest: Murder/Wilful Killing, in Gabrielle Kirk McDonald and Olivia
Swaak-Goldman (eds.), *Substantive and Procedural Aspects of International Criminal Law – The Ex-
perience of International and National Courts*, Vol. 1 (2000), pp. 175 et seq.; Albin Eser and Hans
Georg Koch: Die vorsätzlichen Tötungstatbestände, 92 *Zeitschrift für die gesamte Strafrechts-
wissenschaft* (1980), pp. 491 et seq.; Justin Hogan-Doran: Murder as a Crime under International
Law and the Statute of the International Criminal Tribunal for the Former Yugoslavia: Of Law,
Legal Language and a Comparative Approach to Legal Meaning, 11 *Leiden Journal of International
Law* (1998), pp. 165 et seq.

675   Article 7(1)(a) of the ICC Statute encompasses the individual act of murder. The provision is based on Article 6(c) of the Nuremberg Charter, Article II(1)(c) of Control
Council Law No. 10, Article 5(c) of the Tokyo Charter, Article 5(a) of the ICTY Statute
and Article 3(a) of the ICTR Statute. At the negotiations on the ICC Statute, murder
was seen as a crime that is clearly defined in all national legal systems.[96] According to the
Elements of Crimes,[97] the material element requires the perpetrator to have caused the
death of another through his or her conduct.[98] This corresponds to the requirements for

---

[95] The discrimination upon which persecution is based is emphasized by A. Cassese, in A. Cassese,
P. Gaeta and J.R.W.D. Jones (eds.), *The Rome Statute of the International Criminal Court*, Vol. 1
(2002), p. 353 at p. 361.

[96] 1996 *Draft Code*, commentary on Art. 18(a), para. 7: "Murder is a crime that is clearly understood and well defined in the national law of every State. This prohibited act does not require any
further explanation." On the sometimes significant differences among national criminal law systems in
the definition of intentional killing, see A. Eser and H.-G. Koch, 92 *Zeitschrift für die gesamte
Strafrechtswissenschaft* (1980), pp. 491 et seq.; C.K. Hall, in O. Triffterer (ed.), *Commentary on the
Rome Statute of the International Criminal Court* (1999), Art. 7, marginal no. 19; G. Heine and H.
Vest, in G. Kirk McDonald and O. Swaak-Goldman (eds.), *Substantive and Procedural Aspects of International Criminal Law*, Vol. 1 (2000), pp. 175 et seq.; J. Hogan-Doran, 11 *Leiden Journal of Interna-
tional Law* (1998), pp. 165 et seq.

[97] Elements of Crimes for Art. 7(1)(a) ICC Statute: "1. The perpetrator killed (fn. 7: The term
'killed' is interchangeable with the term 'caused death.' This fn. applies to all elements which use either of these concepts) one or more persons."

[98] A leading case is *Prosecutor* v. *Akayesu*, ICTR (Trial Chamber), judgment of 2 September 1998,
para. 588; see also *Prosecutor* v. *Rutaganda*, ICTR (Trial Chamber), judgment of 6 December 1999,
para. 79; *Prosecutor* v. *Musema*, ICTR (Trial Chamber), judgment of 27 January 2000, para. 214;
Prosecutor v. *Jelisić*, ICTY (Trial Chamber), judgment of 14 December 1999, para. 51; *Prosecutor* v.
Kupreškić et al., ICTY (Trial Chamber), judgment of 14 January 2000, para. 560; *Prosecutor* v. *Blaškić*,
ICTY (Trial Chamber), judgment of 3 March 2000, para. 216; *Prosecutor* v. *Kordić and Čerkez*, ICTY
(Trial Chamber), judgment of 26 February 2001, para. 235; *Prosecutor* v. *Krstić*, ICTY (Trial Cham-

killing in genocide,[99] as well as in war crimes in international armed conflict (wilful killing) and in non-international armed conflict (murder).[100]

From a subjective point of view, unlike the standard requirements of Article 30,[101] it **676** is sufficient here that the perpetrator caused the victim serious injury with reckless disregard for human life.[102]

Because of the French version of the crime against humanity of killing ("*assassinat*") and **677** Article 6(c) of the Nuremberg Charter, as well as Article 5(a) of the ICTY Statute and Article 3(a) of the ICTR Statute, it was long unclear whether the mental element of the crime required premeditation. Given this background, the international criminal Tribunals at first had difficulty[103] in clearly delineating the mental element of killing in accordance with customary international law.[104] Well-established case law now presumes that, despite the French wording ("*assassinat*"), only the French term "*meurtre*" correctly characterizes customary international law.[105] Thus it is not necessary for the perpetrator to have acted with premeditation.[106]

---

ber), judgment of 2 August 2001, para. 485; *Prosecutor v. Kvočka* et al., ICTY (Trial Chamber), judgment of 2 November 2001, para. 132; *Prosecutor v. Krnojelac*, ICTY (Trial Chamber), judgment of 15 March 2002, para. 324.

[99] ICC Statute, Art. 6(a); see marginal no. 579.

[100] See ICC Statute, Art. 8(2)(a)(i), ICC Statute, Art. 8(2)(c)(i) (see marginal nos. 875 et seq.) and *Prosecutor v. Jelisić*, ICTY (Trial Chamber), judgment of 14 December 1999, para. 51; *Prosecutor v. Kordić and Čerkez*, ICTY (Trial Chamber), judgment of 26 February 2001, para. 236; *Prosecutor v. Krnojelac*, ICTY (Trial Chamber), judgment of 15 March 2002, para. 323.

[101] On the general requirements of Art. 30 of the ICC Statute and on the provision's receptiveness to customary international law, see marginal nos. 294 et seq. and marginal nos. 313 et seq.

[102] See *Prosecutor v. Kupreškić* et al., ICTY (Trial Chamber), judgment of 14 January 2000, para. 561; *Prosecutor v. Musema*, ICTR (Trial Chamber), judgment of 27 January 2000, para. 215; *Prosecutor v. Stakić*, ICTY (Trial Chamber), judgment of 31 July 2003, para. 150.

[103] For an analysis of early ICTY judgments on intentional killing, see J. Hogan-Doran, 11 *Leiden Journal of International Law* (1998), pp. 165 et seq.

[104] For a detailed discussion of this issue, see G. Heine and H. Vest, in G. Kirk McDonald and O. Swaak-Goldman (eds.), *Substantive and Procedural Aspects of International Criminal Law*, Vol. 1 (2000), pp. 175 et seq.

[105] A leading case is *Prosecutor v. Akayesu*, ICTR (Trial Chamber), judgment of 2 September 1998, para. 588; see also *Prosecutor v. Rutaganda*, ICTR (Trial Chamber), judgment of 6 December 1999, para. 79; *Prosecutor v. Musema*, ICTR (Trial Chamber), judgment of 27 January 2000, para. 214; *Prosecutor v. Jelisić*, ICTY (Trial Chamber), judgment of 14 December 1999, para. 51; *Prosecutor v. Blaškić*, ICTY (Trial Chamber), judgment of 3 March 2000, para. 216; *Prosecutor v. Kordić and Čerkez*, ICTY (Trial Chamber), judgment of 26 February 2001, para. 235; *Prosecutor v. Krstić*, ICTY (Trial Chamber), judgment of 2 August 2001, para. 485; *Prosecutor v. Kvočka* et al., ICTY (Trial Chamber), judgment of 2 November 2001, para. 132.

[106] The requirement of "premeditation" is actually a unique feature of Romance legal systems and the legal orders influenced by them. From a comparative perspective, however, such a requirement of cold-blooded planning is not sufficiently widespread, H. Vest, 113 *Zeitschrift für die gesamte Strafrechtswissenschaft* (2001), p. 458 at p. 472; but see *Prosecutor v. Kayishema and Ruzindana*, ICTR (Trial Chamber), judgment of 21 May 1999, para. 139: "When murder is considered along with assassinat . . . the standard of mens rea required is intentional and premeditated killing. The result is premeditated when the actor formulated his intent to kill after a cool moment of reflection. The result is intended when it is the actor's purpose, or the actor is aware that it will occur in the ordinary course of events."; see also *Prosecutor v. Bagilishema*, ICTR (Trial Chamber), judgment of 7 June 2001, paras. 84 et seq. *Prosecutor v. Semanza*, ICTR (Trial Chamber), judgment of 15 May 2003, para. 339. This is left open in *Prosecutor v. Kupreškić* et al., ICTY (Trial Chamber), judgment of 14 January 2000, para. 561. On the discussion see also S. Chesterman, 10 *Duke Journal of Comparative and International Law* (2002), p. 307 at pp. 332 et seq.

II. Extermination

678 Article 7(1)(b) of the ICC Statute governs the crime of extermination. The provision is based on Article 6(c) of the Nuremberg Charter, Article II(1)(c) of Control Council Law No. 10, Article 5(c) of the Tokyo Charter, Article 5(b) of the ICTY Statute and Article 3(b) of the ICTR Statute. At the Nuremberg trial, the genocide committed against the European Jews, in particular, was considered the crime against humanity of extermination. In contrast to the crime of genocide, however, no specific group must be attacked, but only a civilian population as such. Mass killing of political opponents or annihilating attacks on cultural, social or economic groups cannot be considered genocide, but they can be considered a crime against humanity: that of extermination.[107]

679 Under Article 7(2)(b) of the ICC Statute, which borrows from the crime of genocide,[108] "'[e]xtermination' includes the intentional infliction of conditions of life, *inter alia* the deprivation of access to food and medicine,[109] calculated to bring about the destruction of part of a population." Contrasting with the wording of Article 7(2)(b), under the Elements of Crimes[110] extermination requires, from an objective point of view, that the perpetrator cause the death of one or more persons, a view that was quite controversial at the beginning of the discussions on the Elements of Crimes.[111] Further, according to the Elements of Crimes, these killings must be part of a mass killing. The Elements of Crimes are largely based on the case law of the Rwanda Tribunal.[112]

---

[107] 1996 *Draft Code*, commentary on Art. 18(b), para. 8: ". . . extermination is closely related to the crime of genocide in that both crimes are directed against a large number of victims. However, the crime of extermination would apply to situations that differ from those covered by the crime of genocide. Extermination covers situations in which a group of individuals who do not share any common characteristics are killed. It also applies to situations in which some members of a group are killed while others are spared." See also *Prosecutor* v. *Vasiljević*, ICTY (Trial Chamber), judgment of 29 November 2002, para. 227.

[108] See ICC Statute, Art. 6(c).

[109] This example added to the definition of genocide stemmed from a proposal made by Cuba, see H. von Hebel and D. Robinson, in R.S. Lee (ed.), *The International Criminal Court, The Making of the Rome Statute* (1999), p. 99.

[110] Elements of Crimes for Art. 7(1)(b) ICC Statute: "1. The perpetrator killed (fn. 8: . . . either directly or indirectly) one or more persons, including by inflicting conditions of life calculated to bring about the destruction of part of a population. (fn. 9: The infliction of such conditions could include the deprivation of access to food and medicine.) 2. The conduct constituted, or took place as part of (fn. 10: The term 'as part of' would include the initial conduct in a mass killing.) a mass killing of members of a civilian population."

[111] See, e.g., the draft of the Elements of Crimes, UN Doc. PCNICC/1999/L.5/Rev.1/Add.2, 22 December 1999. Its fn. 6 still states: "Some delegations believe that death is not required . . ." In the course of the discussions, however, this view was not adopted, see W. Rückert and G. Witschel, in H. Fischer, C. Kress and S.R. Lüder (eds.), *International and National Prosecution of Crimes under International Law – Current Developments* (2001), p. 59 at pp. 75 et seq.

[112] A leading case is *Prosecutor* v. *Akayesu*, ICTR (Trial Chamber), judgment of 2 September 1998, para. 591: "Extermination differs from murder in that it requires an element of mass destruction which is not required for murder"; *Prosecutor* v. *Kayishema and Ruzindana*, ICTR (Trial Chamber), judgment of 21 May 1999, para. 142: "the difference between murder and extermination is the scale; extermination can be said to be murder on a massive scale"; *Prosecutor* v. *Rutaganda*, ICTR (Trial Chamber), judgment of 6 December 1999, para. 82; *Prosecutor* v. *Musema*, ICTR (Trial Chamber), judgment of 27 January 2000, paras. 217 et seq. From the period before adoption of the Elements of Crimes, see *Prosecutor* v. *Bagilishema*, ICTR (Trial Chamber), judgment of 7 June 2001, paras. 86 et

The crime of extermination includes direct and "indirect" causing of death.[113] The **680** latter was described by the Rwanda Tribunal as the infliction of conditions of life calculated to bring about the destruction of a part of the population.[114] As possible examples of indirect causing of death, the Tribunal mentioned imprisoning a large group of people while depriving them of necessities,[115] or infecting such a group with a deadly virus while withholding medical care.[116] However, the Tribunal found that it could also include cases in which an individual perpetrator caused the death of only a few people or even merely a single person. The decisive point was whether the death was caused as part of a mass killing.[117]

The Yugoslavia Tribunal at first largely affirmed this interpretation,[118] but in the **681** *Krstić* case the Tribunal stipulated that the conduct must cause the death of a "numerically significant part of the population."[119] The Yugoslavia Tribunal has meanwhile further tightened the requirements of the customary law crime of extermination and has advocated the view that the perpetrator him or herself must, directly or indirectly, be responsible for the death of a large number of people.[120] The ICTR has now concurred in this view.[121]

---

seq. These judgments are oriented towards the 1996 *Draft Code*, commentary on Art. 18(b), para. 8: "[Murder and extermination] consist of distinct and yet closely related criminal conduct which involves taking the lives of innocent human beings . . . the act used to carry out the offence of extermination involves an element of mass destruction which is not required for murder."

[113] *Prosecutor* v. *Rutaganda*, ICTR (Trial Chamber), judgment of 6 December 1999, para. 84: "[The] act or omission includes but is not limited to the direct act of killing. It can be any act or omission, or cumulative acts or omissions, that cause the death of the targeted group of individuals"; see also *Prosecutor* v. *Musema*, ICTR (Trial Chamber), judgment of 27 January 2000, para. 219.

[114] *Prosecutor* v. *Kayishema and Ruzindana*, ICTR (Trial Chamber), judgment of 21 May 1999, para. 144: ". . . The actor participates in the mass killing of others or in the creation of conditions of life that lead to the mass killing of others, through his act(s) or omission(s)."

[115] On famine crimes as crimes against humanity, see D. Marcus, 97 *American Journal of International Law* (2003), p. 245 at pp. 271 et seq.

[116] *Prosecutor* v. *Kayishema and Ruzindana*, ICTR (Trial Chamber), judgment of 21 May 1999, para. 146.

[117] *Prosecutor* v. *Kayishema and Ruzindana*, ICTR (Trial Chamber), judgment of 21 May 1999, para. 147: "An actor may be guilty of extermination if he kills, or creates the conditions of life that kills, a single person providing the actor is aware that his act(s) or omission(s) forms part of a mass killing event. For a single killing to form part of extermination, the killing must actually form part of a mass killing event. An 'event' exists when the (mass) killings have close proximity in time and place."

[118] *Prosecutor* v. *Krstić*, ICTY (Trial Chamber), judgment of 2 August 2001, paras. 490 et seq.; *Prosecutor* v. *Vasiljević*, ICTY (Trial Chamber), judgment of 29 November 2002, paras. 216 et seq.

[119] *Prosecutor* v. *Krstić*, ICTY (Trial Chamber), judgment of 2 August 2001, para. 503. But see, e.g., G. Mettraux, 43 *Harvard International Law Journal* (2002), p. 237 at p. 285; see also *Prosecutor* v. *Kayishema and Ruzindana*, ICTR (Trial Chamber), judgment of 21 May 1999, para. 145: "The term 'mass,' which may be understood to mean 'large scale,' does not command a numerical imperative but may be determined on a case by case basis using a common sense approach."

[120] See *Prosecutor* v. *Vasiljević*, ICTY (Trial Chamber), judgment of 29 November 2002, para. 227: ". . . responsibility for extermination only attaches to those individuals responsible for a large number of deaths, even if their part therein was remote or indirect. Responsibility for one or for a limited number of such killings is insufficient." See also E.M. Salgado, 16 *Leiden Journal of International Law* (2003), p. 321 at pp. 326 et seq.

[121] *Prosecutor* v. *Ntakirutimana*, ICTR (Trial Chamber), judgment of 21 February 2003, paras. 813 et seq.; *Prosecutor* v. *Semanza*, ICTR (Trial Chamber), judgment of 15 May 2003, para. 340;

682   For the mental element of extermination, Article 30 of the ICC Statute applies.[122] Article 7(2)(b)'s provision that inflicting destructive conditions of life must be "intentional" is no different from the general requirement for the mental element. The perpetrator must be aware that his or her conduct is part of a mass killing.[123] The act must in addition be "calculated" to bring about the destruction of a part of the population. The term "calculated" is sometimes[124] interpreted subjectively as purpose on the part of the perpetrator to destroy a population in whole or in part. Such an intent requirement, however, has been correctly rejected by the international criminal Tribunals,[125] and there is no basis for it in the text of the ICC Statute.

III. Enslavement

683   M. Cherif Bassiouni: Enslavement as an International Crime, 23 *New York University Journal of International Law and Politics* (1991), pp. 445 et seq.; Janie Chuang: Redirecting the Debate over Trafficking in Women: Definitions, Paradigms and Contexts, 11 *Harvard International Law Journal* (1998), pp. 65 et seq.; A. Yasmine Rassam: Contemporary Forms of Slavery and the Evolution of the Prohibition of Slavery and Slave Trade Under Customary International Law, 39 *Virginia Journal of International Law* (1999), pp. 303 et seq.; Stephanie Farrior: The International Law on Trafficking in Women and Children for Prostitution: Making it Live up to its potential, 10 *Harvard Human Rights Journal* (1997), pp. 213 et seq.; Anne Gallagher: Human Rights and the New UN Protocols on Trafficking and Migrant Smuggling: A Preliminary Analysis, 23 *Human Rights Quarterly* (2001), pp. 975 et seq.

684   Article 7(1)(c) of the ICC Statute, enslavement, comprises a classic crime against humanity. Such a stipulation is found in Article 6(c) of the Nuremberg Charter, Article II(1)(c) of Control Council Law No. 10, Article 5(c) of the Tokyo Charter, Article 5(c) of the ICTY Statute and Article 3(c) of the ICTR Statute.

Prosecutor v. Kajelijeli, ICTR (Trial Chamber), judgment of 1 December 2003, para. 893; *Prosecutor v. Kamuhanda*, ICTR (Trial Chamber), judgment of 22 January 2004, para. 691.

[122] See marginal no. 304 and *Prosecutor v. Akayesu*, ICTR (Trial Chamber), judgment of 2 September 1998, para. 592; *Prosecutor v. Kayishema and Ruzindana*, ICTR (Trial Chamber), judgment of 21 May 1999, paras. 144, 146; *Prosecutor v. Rutaganda*, ICTR (Trial Chamber), judgment of 6 December 1999, para. 83; *Prosecutor v. Musema*, ICTR (Trial Chamber), judgment of 27 January 2000, para. 218; *Prosecutor v. Bagilishema*, ICTR (Trial Chamber), judgment of 7 June 2001, para. 89 and *Prosecutor v. Krstić*, ICTY (Trial Chamber), judgment of 2 August 2001, para. 495.

[123] *Prosecutor v. Kayishema and Ruzindana*, ICTR (Trial Chamber), judgment of 21 May 1999, para. 144.

[124] See K. Ambos, *Der Allgemeine Teil des Völkerstrafrechts* (2002), p. 798: "Thus it is a question of the general intentional infliction of conditions of life with the intent to destroy a specific group in whole or in part."

[125] *Prosecutor v. Krstić*, ICTY (Trial Chamber), judgment of 2 August 2001, para. 500; *Prosecutor v. Vasiljević*, ICTY (Trial Chamber), judgment of 29 November 2002, para. 227. At times even negligence is found to be sufficient, see *Prosecutor v. Kayishema and Ruzindana*, ICTR (Trial Chamber), judgment of 21 May 1999, para. 146: "The act(s) or omission(s) may be done with intention, recklessness, or gross negligence"; see also *Prosecutor v. Bagilishema*, ICTR (Trial Chamber), judgment of 7 June 2001, para. 89.

1. Definition

Under Article 7(2)(c) of the ICC Statute, enslavement is "the exercise of any or all of the **685** powers attaching to the right of ownership over a person." This wording[126] was borrowed from the *Slavery Convention* of 25 September 1926[127] and corresponds to the definition under customary international law.[128] In addition, it is made clear that enslavement also includes "the exercise of such power in the course of trafficking in persons, in particular women and children." The Elements of Crimes expand the definition with a list of examples of additional manifestations of enslavement, including purchasing, selling, lending or bartering a person or persons or "similar" deprivation of liberty.[129]

By referring to "similar" deprivation of liberty, the Elements of Crimes suggest that **686** the crime should not be limited to traditional manifestations of enslavement such as "slavery" and the "slave trade," as defined in relevant treaties.[130] Such traditional manifestations of slavery, in which perpetrators treat victims as "chattel,"[131] rarely occur today.[132] The term "enslavement" used in the ICC Statute should thus not be limited to slavery in the traditional sense, but should be interpreted in a functional legal sense that includes institutions and practices that do not fall under the formal heading of slavery.[133]

The Yugoslavia Tribunal has moved in this direction, and in the *Kunarac* et al. case it **687** clarified the requirements for slavery.[134] According to the facts upon which the judgment was based, the defendants kept two young women prisoner for months in an abandoned house, completely controlled their lives, and among other things, repeatedly raped them. In the judgment, the Yugoslavia Tribunal set forth the conditions under which conduct can be classified as enslavement. Essential indications include controlling the

---

[126] On the history of the negotiations on Art. 7(1)(c) of the ICC Statute, see H. von Hebel and D. Robinson, in R.S. Lee (ed.), *The International Criminal Court, The Making of the Rome Statute* (1999), p. 99.

[127] 212 *UNTS* (1955), p. 17.

[128] *Prosecutor* v. *Kunarac* et al., ICTY (Trial Chamber), judgment of 22 February 2001, para. 539; *Prosecutor* v. *Krnojelac*, ICTY (Trial Chamber), judgment of 15 March 2002, para. 350. Affirmed in *Prosecutor* v. *Kunarac* et al., ICTY (Appeals Chamber), judgment of 12 June 2002, para. 124.

[129] On deprivation of liberty, Elements of Crimes for Art. 7(1)(c) ICC Statute, fn. 11 states: "It is understood that such deprivation of liberty may, in some circumstances, include exacting forced labour or otherwise reducing a person to a servile status as defined in the Supplementary Convention on the Abolition of Slavery, the Slave Trade, and Institutions and Practices Similar to Slavery of 1956."

[130] See Art. 1 of the *Slavery Convention* of 25 September 1926 in the version of the amendment protocols of 7 December 1953, 212 *UNTS* (1955), p. 17, and Art. 7 of the *Supplementary Convention on the Abolition of Slavery, the Slave Trade, and Institutions and Practices Similar to Slavery* of 7 September 1956, 226 *UNTS* (1956), p. 3.

[131] "Chattel slavery," see *Prosecutor* v. *Kunarac* et al., ICTY (Appeals Chamber), judgment of 12 June 2002, para. 117.

[132] See A.Y. Rassam, 39 *Virginia Journal of International Law* (1999), p. 303 at p. 321.

[133] See *Supplementary Convention on the Abolition of Slavery, the Slave Trade, and Institutions and Practices Similar to Slavery* of 7 September 1956, 226 *UNTS* (1956), p. 3, esp., Art. 1(a) and (b) (serfdom, debt bondage).

[134] *Prosecutor* v. *Kunarac* et al., ICTY (Trial Chamber), judgment of 22 February 2001, paras. 515 et seq. The Appeals Chamber affirmed the judgment, see *Prosecutor* v. *Kunarac* et al., ICTY (Appeals Chamber), judgment of 12 June 2002, paras. 106 et seq.

victim's freedom of movement, acting against the victim's will, and economic control or exploitation.[135] The Court stated:

"[I]ndications of enslavement include elements of control and ownership; the restriction or control of an individual's autonomy, freedom of choice or freedom of movement; and, often, the accruing of some gain to the perpetrator. The consent or free will of the victim is absent. It is often rendered impossible or irrelevant by, for example, the threat or use of force or other forms of coercion; the fear of violence, deception or false promises; the abuse of power; the victim's position of vulnerability; detention or captivity, psychological oppression or socio-economic conditions. Further indications of enslavement include exploitation; sex; prostitution . . . The 'acquisition' or 'disposal' of someone for monetary or other compensation, is not a requirement for enslavement. Doing so, however, is a prime example of the exercise of the right of ownership over someone. The duration of the suspected exercise of powers attaching to the right of ownership is another factor that may be considered when determining whether someone was enslaved; however, its importance in any given case will depend on the exercise of other indications of enslavement."[136]

688 The Appeals Chamber subsequently made clear that neither a specific length of time nor the victim's opposition are necessary requirements for a presumption of slavery.[137]

689   For the mental element of enslavement, Article 30 of the ICC Statute applies.[138]

2. Forced Labor

690 "Forced labor"[139] is not addressed by the ICC Statute and the Elements of Crimes as a separate form of enslavement. However, in accordance with customary international law, it is classified as enslavement if it is accompanied by the exercise of supposed property rights in the person affected.[140] At the Nuremberg trials, forced labor was the most important example of the crime of enslavement, which was included in the Nuremberg Charter as a crime against humanity.

691 During the Nazi period and World War II, some eight million forced laborers were employed in the German Reich and in the territories occupied by Germany. The Nuremberg Tribunal con-

---

[135] *Prosecutor* v. *Kunarac* et al., ICTY (Trial Chamber), judgment of 22 February 2001, para. 542.

[136] A leading case is *Prosecutor* v. *Kunarac* et al., ICTY (Trial Chamber), judgment of 22 February 2001, para. 542; see also *Prosecutor* v. *Krnojelac*, ICTY (Trial Chamber), judgment of 15 March 2002, para. 359; *Prosecutor* v. *Kunarac* et al., ICTY (Appeals Chamber), judgment of 12 June 2002, para. 119.

[137] *Prosecutor* v. *Kunarac* et al., ICTY (Appeals Chamber), judgment of 12 June 2002, paras. 120 et seq.

[138] On the general requirements of the mental element, see marginal nos. 294 et seq., esp. marginal nos. 304 et seq. See also *Prosecutor* v. *Kunarac* et al., ICTY (Trial Chamber), judgment of 22 February 2001, para. 540; affirmed in *Prosecutor* v. *Kunarac* et al., ICTY (Appeals Chamber), judgment of 12 June 2002, para. 122; see also *Prosecutor* v. *Krnojelac*, ICTY (Trial Chamber), judgment of 15 March 2002, para. 350.

[139] For basic discussion, see H. Bülck, *Die Zwangsarbeit im Friedensvölkerrecht* (1953).

[140] On the definition of forced or compulsory labor, see Art. 2 of the *Convention Concerning Forced or Compulsory Labor* (ILO Convention 29) of 28 June 1930, 39 *UNTS* (1949), p. 55 and Art. 1 of the *Abolition of Forced Labor Convention* (ILO Convention 105) of 25 June 1957, 320 *UNTS* (1957), p. 291; see also Art. 8(3) International Covenant on Civil and Political Rights of 16 December 1966, 6 *ILM* (1967), p. 368, and Art. 4(3) of the *European Convention for the Protection of Human Rights and Fundamental Freedoms* of 4 November 1950, *ETS* No. 5 (1950).

victed the defendant *von Schirach* for the crime against humanity of enslavement alone; most of the major war criminals, in contrast, were convicted for both deportations to slave labor as a war crime and for enslavement as a crime against humanity. At the Nuremberg successor trials, US military courts also convicted various perpetrators for both crimes. Particularly noteworthy is the Court's reasoning in the *Milch* Trial.[141]

The Yugoslavia Tribunal, too, has recognized forced labor as one possible crime against humanity and has clarified the requirements.[142]   **692**

3. Trafficking in Persons

Practices similar to enslavement include "trafficking in persons, in particular women and   **693**
children." Here, international treaty law until recently had included trafficking only for purposes of prostitution.[143] An example is the *Convention for the Suppression of the Traffic in Persons and of the Exploitation of the Prostitution of Others* of 21 March 1950.[144] More recent international treaties, such as the *Convention on the Elimination of all Forms of Discrimination Against Women* of 18 December 1979[145] and the *Convention on the Rights of the Child* of 20 November 1989,[146] have abandoned the link between trafficking and prostitution. This is also the position of the ICC Statute.

The *Convention Against Transnational Organized Crime* of 15 November 2000 did   **694**
not come into existence until after the adoption of the ICC Statute. An additional protocol explicitly regulates trafficking, especially in women and children, and for the first time in international treaty law contains a definition of trafficking in persons.[147]

---

[141] See the section "Slave Labor Policy," IMT, judgment of 1 October 1946, in *The Trial of German Major War Criminals. Proceedings of the International Military Tribunal Sitting at Nuremberg, Germany*, Part 22, pp. 460 et seq., and the explanations of the judgments of *von Schirach* and *Göring, Keitel, Kaltenbrunner, Rosenberg, Frank, Frick, Funk, Saukel, Jodl, Seyss-Inquart* and *Speer*, and US Military Tribunal, Nuremberg, judgment of 17 April 1947 (*Milch*, so-called Milch Trial), in *Trials of War Criminals* II, p. 773 at p. 789.

[142] *Prosecutor* v. *Kunarac* et al., ICTY (Trial Chamber), judgment of 22 February 2001, para. 542 and *Prosecutor* v. *Krnojelac*, ICTY (Trial Chamber), judgment of 15 March 2002, paras. 358 et seq. In adjudging the slave labor of inmates in a concentration camp, for example, the Yugoslavia Tribunal took into account the following objective circumstances of the crime: "the substantially uncompensated aspect of the labour performed, the vulnerable position in which the detainees found themselves, the allegations that detainees who were unable or unwilling to work were either forced to or put in solitary confinement, claims of longer term consequences of the labour, the fact of detention . . .," see *Prosecutor* v. *Krnojelac*, ICTY (Trial Chamber), judgment of 15 March 2002, para. 373.

[143] For a critical view, see J. Chuang, 11 *Harvard International Law Journal* (1998), pp. 64 et seq.; C.K. Hall, in O. Triffterer (ed.), *Commentary on the Rome Statute of the International Criminal Court* (1999), Art. 7, marginal no. 96.

[144] 96 *UNTS* (1950), p. 271.

[145] 1249 *UNTS* (1984), p. 13. Art. 6 provides that: "The treaty states will take all suitable measures, including legislative measures, to abolish any form of trafficking in women and exploitation of the prostitution of women."

[146] 1577 *UNTS* (1990), p. 43. Art. 11 provides that: "(1) The treaty states will take measures to combat the illegal transport of children abroad and illegally refusing to return them."

[147] See Art. 3(a), *Protocol to Prevent, Suppress and Punish Trafficking in Persons, Especially Women and Children*, supplementing the *United Nations Convention against Transnational Organized Crime, Report of the Ad Hoc Committee on the Elaboration of a Convention against Transnational Organized*

IV. Deportation or Forcible Transfer of Population

695 Jean Marie Henckaerts: *Mass Expulsion in Modern International Law and Practice* (1995); Jean Marie Henckaerts: Deportation and Transfer of Civilians in Time of War, 26 *Vanderbilt Journal of Transnational Law* (1993), pp. 469 et seq.; Lutz Lehmler: *Die Strafbarkeit von Vertreibungen aus ethnischen Gründen im bewaffneten nicht-internationalen Konflikt* (1999); Theodor Meron: Deportation of Civilians as a War Crime under Customary International Law, in Theodor Meron (ed.), *War Crimes Law Comes of Age* (1998), pp. 142 et seq.; Michael P. Roch: Forced displacement in the former Yugoslavia: A crime under international law?, 14 *Dickinson Journal of International Law* (1995), pp. 1 et seq.; Otto Triffterer: Die Bestrafung von Vertreibungsverbrechen, in Dieter Blumenwitz (ed.), *Flucht und Vertreibung* (1987), pp. 259 et seq.; Alfred de Zayas: International Law and Mass Population Transfers, 16 *Harvard International Law Journal* (1975), pp. 207 et seq.

696 Article 7(1)(d) of the ICC Statute deals with deportation or forcible transfer of population. The crime of deportation is based on Article 6(c) of the Nuremberg Charter, Article II(1)(c) of Control Council Law No. 10, Article V(c) of the Tokyo Charter, Article 5(d) of the ICTY Statute and Article 3(d) of the ICTR Statute. "Forcible transfer of population" as a crime against humanity is not contained in these instruments[148] and is based on Article 18(g) of the 1996 *Draft Code*.

697 Article 7(2)(d) of the ICC Statute defines deportation and forcible transfer of population as the "forced displacement of the persons concerned by expulsion or other coercive acts from the area in which they are lawfully present, without grounds permitted under international law." In both cases, the material element thus requires the transfer of persons from one territory to another (forced displacement). The Elements of Crimes establish that the transfer of even one person from a territory can be sufficient.[149]

698 The difference between deportation and forcible transfer of population lies only in whether a border is crossed. Deportation means the transfer of one or more persons from one state's territory to another state's territory; that is, a state border is crossed.[150] In

---

Crime on the work of its first to eleventh sessions, UN Doc. A/55/383 (2000), Annex II. See generally A. Gallagher, 23 *Human Rights Quarterly* (2001), 975 et seq.

[148] According to M.P. Roch, 14 *Dickinson Journal of International Law* (1995), pp. 1 et seq., the "forcible transfer of population" was not included in the definition of expulsion as a crime against humanity in Art. 5(d) of the ICTY Statute. However, enforced transfer of population was already contained as a war crime in a variety of international legal instruments, see Geneva Convention IV, Art. 147; Additional Protocol I, Art. 87(4)(a) and Additional Protocol II, Art. 17. On ICC Statute, Art. 8(2)(a)(vii), (b)(viii) and (e)(viii), see also marginal nos. 964 et seq.

[149] See Elements of Crimes for Art. 7(1)(d) ICC Statute: "1. The perpetrator deported of forcibly transferred, without grounds permitted under international law, one or more persons to another State of location by expulsion or other coercive acts." See also, in the same vein, Sec. 7(1) No. 4 (German) Code of Crimes against International Law *[Völkerstrafgesetzbuch, VStGB]*, and Explanatory Memorandum of the (German) Code of Crimes against International Law *[Begründung zum Völkerstrafgesetzbuch, VStGB]*, BT-Drs. 14/8524, p. 21.

[150] *Prosecutor* v. *Krstić*, ICTY (Trial Chamber), judgment of 2 August 2001, para. 521: "Deportation presumes transfer beyond State borders." Affirmed in *Prosecutor* v. *Krnojelac*, ICTY (Trial Chamber), judgment of 15 March 2002, para. 474. See also *Draft Code* 1996, commentary on Art. 18, para. 13: "[D]eportation implies expulsion from the national territory." A similar definition is found in the literature: "Deportation is the forced removal of people from one country to another," see M.C. Bassiouni, *Crimes against Humanity* (1999), p. 312; C.K. Hall, in O. Triffterer (ed.), *Commentary on the Rome Statute of the International Criminal Court* (1999), Art. 7, marginal nos. 31, 34; J.M.

contrast, forcible transfer means the transfer of one or more persons within the same state's territory.[151]

The transfer of the persons involved must occur through expulsion or other coercive **699** acts. The Elements of Crimes employ a broad interpretation of the term "coercion."[152] A characteristic element is the "involuntariness" of the transfer. Thus, for example, exchanges of population on the basis of bilateral treaties with "opt out" clauses are not included.[153] Nor does the flight of a civilian population from a territory for fear of discrimination satisfy the definition of the crime.[154]

In every case, the transfer of the persons involved from a specific territory must be **700** impermissible under international law. Thus, for example, deportation and other coercive measures necessary to protect national security, public order or public health are not included in the definition of the crime.[155] The total or partial evacuation of an area during armed conflict can also be called for to protect the civilians involved or for compelling military reasons.[156] However, the civilian population must be returned to its home territory immediately upon cessation of hostilities. In such cases, it must be ensured, as far as possible, that the civilian population finds suitable conditions in the place of recep-

---

Henckaerts, 26 *Vanderbilt Journal of Transnational Law* (1993), p. 269 at p. 472; O. Triffterer, in D. Blumenwitz (ed.), *Flucht und Vertreibung* (1987), p. 259 at pp. 265 et seq.

[151] A leading case is *Prosecutor* v. *Krstić*, ICTY (Trial Chamber), judgment of 2 August 2001, para. 521: "[F]orcible transfer relates to displacements within a State." Affirmed in *Prosecutor* v. *Krnojelac*, ICTY (Trial Chamber), judgment of 15 March 2002, para. 474. See also 1996 *Draft Code*, commentary on Art. 18, para. 13: "[F]orcible transfer of population could occur wholly within the frontiers of one and the same State." A similar definition is found in the literature, see M.C. Bassiouni, *Crimes against Humanity* (1999), p. 312; C.K. Hall, in O. Triffterer (ed.), *Commentary on the Rome Statute of the International Criminal Court* (1999), Art. 7, marginal nos. 31, 34; J.M. Henckaerts, 26 *Vanderbilt Journal of Transnational Law* (1993), p. 269 at p. 472; O. Triffterer, in D. Blumenwitz (ed.), *Flucht und Vertreibung* (1987), p. 259 at pp. 265 et seq.

[152] The Elements of Crimes for Art. 7(1)(d) ICC Statute, fn. 12 provide: "The term 'forcibly' is not restricted to physical force, but may include threat of force or coercion, such as, that caused by fear of violence, duress, detention, psychological oppression or abuse of power, against such person or another person, or by taking advantage of a coercive environment." Affirmed in *Prosecutor* v. *Krstić*, ICTY (Trial Chamber), judgment of 2 August 2001, para. 529; *Prosecutor* v. *Krnojelac*, ICTY (Trial Chamber), judgment of 15 March 2002, para. 475. See also C.K. Hall, in O. Triffterer (ed.), *Commentary on the Rome Statute of the International Criminal Court* (1999), Art. 7, marginal no. 100: "Considering the recent history of internal displacement of people, 'expulsion or other coercive acts' must include the full range of coercive pressures on people to flee their homes, including death threats, destruction of their homes, and other acts of persecution, such as depriving members of a group of employment, denying them access to schools and forcing them to wear a symbol of their religious identity."

[153] A. de Zayas, 16 *Harvard International Law Journal* (1975), p. 207 at pp. 246 et seq.

[154] *Prosecutor* v. *Krstić*, ICTY (Trial Chamber), judgment of 2 August 2001, para. 528.

[155] See also *International Covenant on Civil and Political Rights*, Art. 12(3); *European Convention for the Protection of Human Rights and Fundamental Freedoms*, Protocol No. 4, Art. 2(3); *American Convention on Human Rights*, Art. 22(3) and (4); *African (Banjul) Charter on Human and Peoples' Rights*, Art. 12(2).

[156] *Prosecutor* v. *Krstić*, ICTY (Trial Chamber), judgment of 2 August 2001, para. 524. See Geneva Convention IV, Art. 49 for cases of deportation from "an occupied territory" by an "Occupying Power." On transfer of a civilian population for reasons connected with a non-international armed conflict, see ICC Statute, Art. 8(2)(e)(viii), see also Additional Protocol II, Art. 17(1).

tion in regard to accommodation, cleanliness, hygiene, security and food.[157] Assistance by humanitarian agencies does not render a displacement lawful.[158]

701   The crime requires that the civilians involved be residing legally in the territory from which they are deported or forcibly transferred. The standard for the lawfulness of their residence is set by international law. A forcible measure on the basis of a national law contravening international law, such as the deportation of a citizen,[159] is therefore impermissible.[160] The same is true for the collective deportation of foreign nationals.[161] However, individual foreign nationals may in certain cases be transferred out of a state's territory.[162]

702   The ICC Statute's criminalization of (intrastate) forcible transfer is not new in relation to customary international law.[163] Under customary international law, forcible transfer of persons within the same state's territory is not yet classified as deportation, but it is included as other inhumane conduct of a similar nature.[164] The ICC Statute clarifies customary international law by classifying forced transfer of persons within a state as forcible transfer, and thus, quite correctly, placing it on an equal footing with the crime against humanity of deportation.

703   The mental element must encompass the fact that the victim will not return to the place of his or her origin (ICC Statute, Article 30).[165]

---

[157] See Geneva Convention IV, Art. 49, see also Additional Protocol II, Art. 17(1).

[158] *Prosecutor* v. *Stakić*, ICTY (Trial Chamber), judgment of 31 July 2003, para. 683.

[159] C.K. Hall, in O. Triffterer (ed.), *Commentary on the Rome Statute of the International Criminal Court* (1999), Art. 7, marginal nos. 98, 101.

[160] *International Covenant on Civil and Political Rights*, Art. 12(4) provides: "No one shall be arbitrarily deprived of the right to enter his own country." See also Art. 3 of Protocol No. 4 of the *European Convention for the Protection of Human Rights and Fundamental Freedoms*: "(1) No one shall be expelled, by means either of an individual or of a collective measure, from the territory of the State of which he is a national. (2) No one shall be deprived of the right to enter the territory of the State of which he is a national." See also Art. 22(5) *American Convention on Human Rights*: "No one can be expelled from the territory of the state of which he is a national or be deprived of the right to enter it."

[161] Art. 4 of Protocol No. 4 of the *European Convention for the Protection of Human Rights and Fundamental Freedoms* provides: "Collective expulsion of aliens is prohibited." See also *American Convention on Human Rights*, Art. 22(9); *African (Banjul) Charter on Human and Peoples' Rights*, Art. 12(5).

[162] For aliens, Art. 13 *International Covenant on Civil and Political Rights* provides: "An alien lawfully in the territory of a State Party to the present Covenant may be expelled therefrom only in pursuance of a decision reached in accordance with law and shall, except where compelling reasons of national security otherwise require, be allowed to submit the reasons against his expulsion and to have his case reviewed by, and be represented for the purpose before, the competent authority or a person or persons especially designated by the competent authority"; see also *American Convention on Human Rights*, Art. 22(6), *African (Banjul) Charter on Human and Peoples' Rights*, Art. 12(4).

[163] *Prosecutor* v. *Stakić*, ICTY (Trial Chamber), judgment of 31 July 2003, paras. 673 et seq., 684: "The Trial Chamber emphasizes that the underlying act – i.e. irrespective of whether the displacement occurred across an internationally recognized border or not – was already punishable under public international law by the time relevant to the present case."

[164] See *Prosecutor* v. *Krstić*, ICTY (Trial Chamber), judgment of 2 August 2001, para. 523.

[165] Prosecutor v. *Naletilić and Martinović*, ICTY (Trial Chamber), judgment of 31 March 2003, paras. 520, 1362. On the general requirements for the mental element, see marginal nos. 294 et seq., esp. nos. 304 et seq.

V. Imprisonment

Article 7(1)(e) of the ICC Statute encompasses "imprisonment or other severe depriva-   **704**
tion of physical liberty in violation of fundamental rules of international law." This provision is based on Article II(1)(c) of Control Council Law No. 10, Article V(e) of the
ICTY Statute, and Article 3(e) of the ICTR Statute. The Elements of Crimes require
that the perpetrator have imprisoned one or more persons or deprived them of their liberty of movement.

The term *imprisonment* includes cases in which a person is, literally, "imprisoned" in   **705**
an enclosed space and thus prevented from moving to another place.[166] Cases classed as
other severe deprivations of physical liberty include those in which a person can continue
to move in a specific area, for example within a ghetto or concentration camp.[167] House
arrest may also fall under this definition.[168] Deprivation of liberty for a short period of
time should not be viewed as "severe" in terms of Article 7(1)(e) of the ICC Statute.

Imprisonment achieves the status of a crime under international law only through its   **706**
violation of the "fundamental rules" of international law. This criterion was first set out
by the Yugoslavia Tribunal in the *Kordić and Čerkez* case. Under customary international
law, the crucial issue is the "arbitrariness" of the deprivation of liberty. This is present if
there was no proper legal procedure. The judgment states:

"The term imprisonment . . . should be understood as arbitrary imprisonment, that is to say, the
deprivation of liberty of the individual without due process of law. . . . In that respect the Trial
Chamber will have to determine the legality of imprisonment as well as the procedural safeguards
pertaining to the subsequent imprisonment of the person or group of persons in question."[169]

The cases that come into play here are especially those involving deprivation of liberty   **707**
without any legal basis or without regard for elementary rules of procedure.[170]

For the mental element, Article 30 of the ICC Statute applies.[171]   **708**

---

[166] C.K. Hall, in O. Triffterer (ed.), *Commentary on the Rome Statute of the International Criminal Court* (1999), Art. 7, marginal no. 38.

[167] See also 1996 *Draft Code*, commentary on Art. 18, para. 14: "The present sub-paragraph would cover systematic and large scale instances of arbitrary imprisonment such as concentration camps or detention camps or other forms of long term detention."

[168] See, e.g., C.K. Hall, in O. Triffterer (ed.), *Commentary on the Rome Statute of the International Criminal Court* (1999), Art. 7, marginal no. 38.

[169] See *Prosecutor* v. *Kordić and Čerkez*, ICTY (Trial Chamber), judgment of 26 February 2001, para. 302; affirmed in *Prosecutor* v. *Krnojelac*, ICTY (Trial Chamber), judgment of 15 March 2002, para. 110; see also 1996 *Draft Code*, Art. 18(h): "arbitrary imprisonment," and 1996 *Draft Code*, commentary on Art. 18, para. 14: "The term 'imprisonment' encompasses deprivation of liberty of the individual and the term 'arbitrary' establishes the requirement that the deprivation be without due process of law."

[170] *Prosecutor* v. *Krnojelac*, ICTY (Trial Chamber), judgment of 15 March 2002, para. 113; see also Commission on Human Rights, Question of the human rights of all persons subjected to any form of detention or imprisonment, *Report of the Working Group on Arbitrary Detention*, UN Doc.E/CN.4/1998/44, 19 December 1997, Annex I, para. 8. *Prosecutor* v. *Krnojelac*, ICTY (Trial Chamber), judgment of 15 March 2002, para. 115: "no legal basis can be invoked to justify the deprivation of liberty. . . ."

[171] On the general requirements for the mental element, see marginal nos. 294 et seq., esp. nos. 304 et seq. See also *Prosecutor* v. *Krnojelac*, ICTY (Trial Chamber), judgment of 15 March 2002,

VI. Torture

709 Andrew Byrnes: Torture and Other Offences Involving the Violation of the Physical or Mental Integrity of the Human Person, in Gabrielle Kirk McDonald and Olivia Swaak-Goldman (eds.), *Substantive and Procedural Aspects of International Criminal Law – The Experience of International and National Courts*, Vol. 1 (2000), pp. 197 et seq.; Jasper M. Wauters: Torture and Related Crimes – A Discussion of the Crimes Before the International Criminal Tribunal for the former Yugoslavia, 11 *Leiden Journal of International Law* (1998), pp. 155 et seq.

710 The crime against humanity of torture is covered by Article 7(1)(f) of the ICC Statute. The provision is based on Article II(1)(c) of Control Council Law No. 10, Article V(f) of the ICTY Statute and Article 3(f) of the ICTR Statute. The Elements of Crimes[172] additionally set forth that torture of even a single person fits the definition of the crime.

711 Article 7(2)(e) of the ICC Statute contains the definition of torture as a crime against humanity. Under this provision, "'Torture' means the intentional infliction of severe pain or suffering, whether physical or mental, upon a person in the custody or under the control of the accused; except that torture shall not include pain or suffering arising only from, inherent in or incidental to, lawful sanctions." This definition takes up wording in the *Convention on Torture and Other Cruel, Inhuman or Degrading Treatment or Punishment* of 10 December 1984,[173] but does not adopt the means-ends relationship it contains. Under the ICC Statute, torture therefore includes pain caused even without a particular purpose, for example for purely arbitrary reasons. In a further deviation from the Torture Convention, participation by someone acting in an official capacity is not necessary.

712 The definitions of torture under international criminal law and in the Torture Convention thus differ significantly. Therefore, it is impossible to avoid a separate definition of the crime against humanity of torture. In fashioning this definition, however, international human rights law must be considered the standard, to the extent that its guiding considerations can be transferred to international criminal law.[174]

---

para. 115: "intent to deprive the individual arbitrarily of his or her physical liberty or in the reasonable knowledge that his or her act or omission is likely to cause arbitrary deprivation of physical liberty." The Elements of Crimes for Art. 7(1)(e) of the ICC Statute provide: "3. The perpetrator was aware of the factual circumstances that established the gravity of the conduct."

[172] On the history of negotiations on the Elements of Crimes for Art. 7(1)(f) ICC Statute, see D. Robinson, in R.S. Lee (ed.), *Elements of Crimes and Rules of Procedure* (2001), pp. 90 et seq.

[173] 1465 *UNTS* (1987), p. 112. Art. 1(1) of the Torture Convention provides: "(1) For the purposes of this Convention, the term 'torture' means any act by which severe pain or suffering, whether physical or mental, is intentionally inflicted on a person for such purposes as obtaining from him or a third person information or a confession, punishing him for an act he or a third person has committed or is suspected of having committed, or intimidating or coercing him or a third person, or for any reason based on discrimination of any kind, when such pain or suffering is inflicted by or at the instigation of or with the consent or acquiescence of a public official or other person acting in an official capacity. It does not include pain or suffering arising only from, inherent in or incidental to lawful sanctions."

[174] In various judgments, the ICTY has considered in detail the significance of international human rights law for structuring the crime against humanity of torture. The first leading case was *Prosecutor* v. *Kunarac* et al., ICTY (Trial Chamber), judgment of 22 February 2001, para. 482: "[T]he definition of torture contained in the Torture Convention cannot be regarded as the definition of tor-

The characteristic objective criterion for torture as a crime against humanity is the infliction of severe physical or mental pain or suffering. This criterion is also a core element of the "human rights" definition of torture. Therefore, in their interpretations, the international criminal Tribunals consider, for example, reports by the UN Human Rights Committee or relevant case law from international courts on the prohibition of torture.[175] These provide that all the circumstances of the individual case should be considered, especially the duration of the abuse and its physical and mental effects. While it is not possible to formulate a complete catalogue of torture practices,[176] the following conduct is, as a rule, classified as torture *per se*:[177]   **713**

Pulling out teeth, fingernails or toenails; electric shocks to sensitive parts of the body; blows to the ears   **714**
that cause the eardrums to burst; breaking bones; burning parts of the body; spraying eyes or other sensitive parts of the body with acid; hanging from a pole; submersion in water until symptoms of drowning occur; plugging nose and mouth to cause asphyxiation; causing hypothermia with strong fans; administration of medication (psychotropic drugs); withholding food, water or sleep; rape.

Severe mental pain or suffering also fits the definition of the crime, such as forcing a per-   **715**

---

ture under customary international law which is binding regardless of the context in which it is applied. The definition of the Torture Convention was meant to apply at an inter-state level and was, for that reason, directed at the states' obligations. The definition was also meant to apply only in the context of that Convention, and only to the extent that other international instruments or national laws did not give the individual a broader or better protection. . . . [T]he definition of torture contained in Article 1 of the Torture Convention can only serve . . . as an interpretational aid." This was largely affirmed, but with greater nuance, in *Prosecutor* v. *Kunarac* et al., ICTY (Appeals Chamber), judgment of 12 June 2002, para. 147: " . . . the definition of torture in the Torture Convention reflects customary international law as far as the obligation of States is concerned, must be distinguished from an assertion that this definition wholly reflects customary international law regarding the meaning of the crime of torture generally." In contrast, early judgments referred directly to the UN definition of torture, see *Prosecutor* v. *Akayesu*, ICTR (Trial Chamber), judgment of 2 September 1998, para. 593, and considered the UN definition of torture above and beyond this, more generally, to be customary international law, see *Prosecutor* v. *Mucić* et al., ICTY (Trial Chamber), judgment of 16 November 1998, para. 459: "reflects a consensus which the Trial Chamber considers to be representative of customary international law"; *Prosecutor* v. *Furundžija*, ICTY (Trial Chamber), judgment of 10 December 1998, para. 160: "An extra-conventional effect may however be produced to the extent that the definition at issue codifies, or contributes to developing or crystallising customary international law"; *Prosecutor* v. *Furundžija*, ICTY (Appeals Chamber), judgment of 21 July 2000, para. 111: "takes the view that the definition given in Article 1 reflects customary international law."

[175] See, e.g., *Prosecutor* v. *Mucić* et al., ICTY (Trial Chamber), judgment of 16 November 1998, paras. 461 et seq.; *Prosecutor* v. *Kvočka* et al., ICTY (Trial Chamber), judgment of 2 November 2001, paras. 142 et seq.

[176] See *Prosecutor* v. *Mucić* et al., ICTY (Trial Chamber), judgment of 16 November 1998, paras. 461, 469: "It is difficult to articulate with any degree of precision the threshold level of suffering. . . . However the existence of such a grey area should not be seen as an invitation to create an exhaustive list of acts constituting torture, in order to neatly categorise the prohibition." See also *Prosecutor* v. *Kvočka* et al., ICTY (Trial Chamber), judgment of 2 November 2001, para. 147: "Clearly, an exhaustive list of torturous practices is impossible to devise"; *Prosecutor* v. *Kunarac* et al., ICTY (Appeals Chamber), judgment of 12 June 2002, para. 149: "there are no more specific requirements which allow an exhaustive classification and enumeration of acts which may constitute torture. Existing case law has not determined the absolute degree of pain required for an act to amount to torture."

[177] See, e.g., *Prosecutor* v. *Kvočka* et al., ICTY (Trial Chamber), judgment of 2 November 2001, para. 144.

son to be present during torture of a family member[178] or simulating execution. However, the methods of torture need not lead to permanent damage to health.[179]

716   The definition of torture in Article 7(2)(e) of the ICC Statute clearly goes farther than the definition in the Torture Convention.[180] The conduct need not be carried out by a public official or other person acting in an official capacity, nor at their instigation or with their express or implicit consent. Such a requirement would be contrary to both the ICC Statute and customary international law.[181] Thus torture by non-state organizations and even private individuals is included.[182]

717   Torture does not include pain or suffering arising only from, inherent in, or incidental to lawful sanctions. However, legalization by the state does not automatically make torture "lawful;" the decisive factor is the international law standard.[183]

718   For the mental element of torture Article 30 of the ICC Statute applies.[184] The provision in Article 7(2)(e) that infliction of pain be "intentional" is not a deviation from the general requirements of the mental element. Pursuance of a goal beyond the infliction of severe physical or mental pain or suffering is not necessary. The Elements of Crimes make this explicit.[185]

719   International courts have created additional subjective requirements that borrow from the Torture Convention.[186] According to the Rwanda and the Yugoslavia Tribunal's

---

[178] *Prosecutor* v. *Furundžija*, ICTY (Trial Chamber), judgment of 10 December 1998, para. 267; *Prosecutor* v. *Kvočka* et al., ICTY (Trial Chamber), judgment of 2 November 2001, para. 149.

[179] *Prosecutor* v. *Kvočka* et al., ICTY (Trial Chamber), judgment of 2 November 2001, para. 148: "Although such torture practices often cause permanent damage to the health of the victims, permanent injury is not a requirement for torture."

[180] See marginal no. 711.

[181] *Prosecutor* v. *Kunarac* et al., ICTY (Trial Chamber), judgment of 22 February 2001, paras. 495, 496: "The characteristic trait of the offence is to be found in the nature of the act committed rather than in the status of the person who committed it"; *Prosecutor* v. *Kvočka* et al., ICTY (Trial Chamber), judgment of 2 November 2001, para. 139; *Prosecutor* v. *Krnojelac*, ICTY (Trial Chamber), judgment of 15 March 2002, para. 187. This view has since been expressly affirmed by the Appeals Chamber of the Yugoslavia Tribunal, see *Prosecutor* v. *Kunarac* et al., ICTY (Appeals Chamber), judgment of 12 June 2002, para. 148. See also *Prosecutor* v. *Semanza*, ICTR (Trial Chamber), judgment of 15 May 2003, paras. 342 et seq. This can be contrasted with *Prosecutor* v. *Akayesu*, ICTR (Trial Chamber), judgment of 2 September 1998, para. 594; *Prosecutor* v. *Furundžija*, ICTY (Trial Chamber), judgment of 10 December 1998, para. 162; *Prosecutor* v. *Furundžija*, ICTY (Appeals Chamber), judgment of 21 July 2000, para. 111.

[182] This is the conclusion in C.K. Hall, in O. Triffterer (ed.), *Commentary on the Rome Statute of the International Criminal Court* (1999), Art. 7, marginal no. 107: "Thus, torture in peacetime by members of armed political groups not connected to any State would be included."

[183] See *Report of the Special Rapporteur to the Commission on Human Rights Peter Kooijmans*, UN Doc. E/CN.4/1988/17 (1988), para. 42: ". . . sanctions are accepted under domestic law does not necessarily make them 'lawful sanctions' in the sense of art. 1 of the Convention against Torture. . . . It is international law and not domestic law which ultimately determines whether a certain practice may be regarded as 'lawful.'"

[184] For detail on the general requirements of the mental element, see marginal nos. 294 et seq., esp. nos. 304 et seq. See also *Prosecutor* v. *Kunarac* et al., ICTY (Trial Chamber), judgment of 22 February 2001, para. 497: "[I]n the field of international humanitarian law, the elements of the offence of torture, under customary international law are as follows . . . (ii) The act or omission must be intentional."

[185] In the Elements of Crimes for Art. 7(1)(f) ICC Statute, fn. 14 states: "It is understood that no specific purpose need be proved for this crime."

[186] See marginal no. 711.

judgments, the crime must be committed to obtain a statement or confession from a person or a third person, in order to punish a person, for an act actually or supposedly committed by that person, or a third person, or to intimidate or coerce that person or a third person, or on another ground based on any type of discrimination.[187] These grounds have even attained the status of customary international law.[188]

Under these judgments, at least until the adoption of the ICC Statute, a purpose or **720** motivation beyond the infliction of pain was required. This was in accordance with the Torture Convention. The new definition in the ICC Statute, however, points to a development that could lead to a retreat from such additional subjective elements even under customary international law. Otherwise, one should not overestimate the practical effects of these divergences. The purpose or motivation required by the judgments is already so broadly conceived that few cases can be imagined in which it is not present. Therefore, one would generally achieve the same outcome based on the case law of the Yugoslavia Tribunal as on the Statute.

VII. Sexual Violence

Kelly Dawn Askin: Sexual Violence in Decisions and Indictments of the Yugoslav and Rwandan **721** Tribunals: Current Status, 93 *American Journal of International Law* (1999), pp. 97 et seq.; Christine M. Chinkin: Women's International Tribunal on Japanese Military Sexual Slavery, 95 *American Journal of International Law* (2001), pp. 335 et seq.; Nora V. Demleitner: Forced Prostitution: Naming an International Offense, 18 *Fordham International Law Journal* (1994), pp. 163 et seq.; Eve La Haye: The Elements of War Crimes – Rape, Sexual Slavery, Enforced Prostitution, Forced Pregnancy, Enforced Sterilisation, and Sexual Violence, in Roy S. Lee (ed.), *The International Criminal Court, Elements of Crimes and Rules of Procedure and Evidence* (2001), pp. 184 et seq.;

---

[187] *Prosecutor v. Akayesu*, ICTR (Trial Chamber), judgment of 2 September 1998, para. 594; *Prosecutor v. Mucić* et al., ICTY (Trial Chamber), judgment of 16 November 1998 paras. 470 et seq.; *Prosecutor v. Kunarac* et al., ICTY (Trial Chamber), judgment of 22 February 2001, para. 497; *Prosecutor v. Kvočka* et al., ICTY (Trial Chamber), judgment of 2 November 2001, para. 141; *Prosecutor v. Krnojelac*, ICTY (Trial Chamber), judgment of 15 March 2002, para. 179. Some decisions consider the purpose of humiliating the victim as sufficient, see, e.g., *Prosecutor v. Furundžija*, ICTY (Trial Chamber), judgment of 10 December 1998, para. 162; *Prosecutor v. Kvočka* et al., ICTY (Trial Chamber), judgment of 2 November 2001, para. 152.

[188] For an explicit statement of the customary international law status of the listed purposes of torture, see *Prosecutor v. Kunarac* et al., ICTY (Trial Chamber), judgment of 22 February 2001, paras. 485, 497; *Prosecutor v. Krnojelac*, ICTY (Trial Chamber), judgment of 15 March 2002, para. 185. In contrast, "other" grounds ("humiliating") have not yet attained the status of customary international law, see *Prosecutor v. Krnojelac*, ICTY (Trial Chamber), judgment of 15 March 2002, para. 186; but see *Prosecutor v. Furundžija*, ICTY (Trial Chamber), judgment of 10 December 1998, para. 162; *Prosecutor v. Kvočka* et al., ICTY (Trial Chamber), judgment of 2 November 2001, paras. 141, 152. The listed purposes or grounds need not dominate; it is sufficient for them to be part of the motivation, see *Prosecutor v. Mucić* et al., ICTY (Trial Chamber), judgment of 16 November 1998, para. 470; *Prosecutor v. Kunarac* et al., ICTY (Trial Chamber), judgment of 22 February 2001, para. 486; *Prosecutor v. Kvočka* et al., ICTY (Trial Chamber), judgment of 2 November 2001, para. 153; *Prosecutor v. Krnojelac*, ICTY (Trial Chamber), judgment of 15 March 2002, para. 184: "There is no requirement under customary international law that the conduct must be solely perpetrated for one of the prohibited purposes. . . . the prohibited purpose must simply be part of the motivation behind the conduct and need not be the predominating or sole purpose." Affirmed in *Prosecutor v. Kunarac* et al., ICTY (Appeals Chamber), judgment of 12 June 2002, para. 155.

Patricia Viseur Sellers: The Context of Sexual Violence: Sexual Violence as Violations of International Humanitarian Law, in Gabrielle Kirk McDonald and Olivia Swaak-Goldman (eds.), *Substantive and Procedural Aspects of International Criminal Law – The Experience of International and National Courts*, Vol. 1 (2000), pp. 263 et seq.

722 Crimes against humanity through sexual violence were not contained as such in the Nuremberg Charter, but could be incorporated by way of the catch-all clause of "other inhuman acts." Rape was soon after explicitly included in Control Council Law No. 10 and is also contained in the ICTY and ICTR Statutes as a separate crime. Other forms of sexual violence, however, are not mentioned in these instruments and can only be incorporated as other crimes against humanity or through the catch-all clause of "other inhuman acts." Article 7(1)(g) of the ICC Statute here effects a significant clarification by bundling the crimes of sexual violence. The ICC Statute encompasses rape, sexual slavery, enforced prostitution, forced pregnancy, enforced sterilization, and any other form of sexual violence of comparable gravity.[189]

1. Rape

723 Article 7(1)(g) first alternative of the ICC Statute deals with the crime against humanity of rape. The provision is based on Article II(1)(c) of Control Council Law No. 10, Article 5(g) of the ICTY Statute and Article 3(g) of the ICTR Statute.

724   No definition of the crime had yet been developed at the start of the negotiations on the ICC Statute. Thus the Elements of Crimes[190] for the first time provide a more specific definition of the criminal conduct. The material element requires an invasion of the victim's body by the perpetrator, which must result in penetration. This is understood to be gender-neutral, as both men and women can be victims of rape. Rape does not include only forced sex (penetration of the male penis into the vagina); the crime also includes sexual conduct connected with the insertion of the perpetrator's sexual organ into other body cavities (oral and anal penetration). Finally, the insertion of other parts of the perpetrator's body or of objects into the vagina or other parts of the body is included. The definition of the crime also requires the use of violence or the threat of violence or force.

---

[189] The perseverance of The Women's Caucus for Gender Justice in the International Criminal Court during the negotiating process on the Rome Statute played a large part in this development, see K.D. Askin, 10 *Criminal Law Forum* (1999), p. 33 at p. 45. Art. 2(g) of the Statute of the Special Court for Sierra Leone adopted the rule in the ICC Statute. On the identical definition of sexual violence in war crimes law, see marginal nos. 908 et seq.

[190] The Elements of Crimes for Art. 7(1)(g)-1 ICC Statute provide: "1. The perpetrator invaded (fn. 15: The concept of 'invasion' is intended to be broad enough to be gender-neutral) the body of a person by conduct resulting in penetration, however slight, of any part of the body of the victim or of the perpetrator with a sexual organ, or of the anal or genital opening of the victim with any object or any other part of the body. 2. The invasion was committed by force, or by threat of force or coercion, such as that caused by fear of violence, duress, detention, psychological oppression or abuse of power, against such person or another person, or by taking advantage of a coercive environment, or the invasion was committed against a person incapable of giving genuine consent. (fn. 16: It is understood that a person may be incapable of giving genuine consent if affected by natural, induced or age-related incapacity. This fn. also applies to the corresponding elements of Article 7(1)(g)-3, -5 and -6)."

The elements of the crime were formulated to reflect the case law of the international **725** criminal Tribunals.[191] In the *Akayesu* case, the Rwanda Tribunal defined rape as a physical invasion of a sexual nature that must be accompanied by coercion,[192] while the Yugoslavia Tribunal, in the *Furundžija* case, first characterized rape as (i) sexual penetration of a bodily cavity of the victim (ii) using coercion or force or threat of force against the victim or a third person.[193] However, in the *Kunarac* et al. case, the Trial Chamber of the Yugoslavia Tribunal found this emphasis on the coercive element too restrictive. In the Court's view, a comprehensive comparison of the world's national criminal law systems shows that the accent has been less on the exercise of coercion or use of force than on whether it occurred against the victim's will.[194] Element (ii) was therefore reformulated.[195] The Appeals Chamber has since affirmed the *Kunarac* definition.[196] The result is that the focus of the definition of rape has shifted from the perpetrator's objective behavior to the victim's opposing will.[197]

---

[191] On the history of the negotiations on the Elements of Crimes for Art. 7(1)(g)-1 of the ICC Statute, see E. La Haye, in R.S. Lee (ed.), *The International Criminal Court, Elements of Crimes and Rules of Procedure and Evidence* (2001), pp. 184 et seq. A detailed overview of the jurisprudence of the ICTY and ICTR on sexual violence is provided in K.D. Askin, 93 *American Journal of International Law* (1999), pp. 97 et seq.; C. Möller, in J. Hasse, E. Müller and P. Schneider (eds.), Humanitäres Völkerrecht (2001), p. 280 at pp. 288 et seq., and P. Viseur Sellers, in G. Kirk McDonald and O. Swaak-Goldman (eds.), *Substantive and Procedural Aspects of International Criminal Law*, Vol. 1 (2000), pp. 263 et seq.

[192] A leading case is *Prosecutor* v. *Akayesu*, ICTR (Trial Chamber), judgment of 2 September 1998, paras. 598 and 688: "a physical invasion of a sexual nature, committed on a person under circumstances which are coercive"; affirmed in *Prosecutor* v. *Mucić* et al., ICTY (Trial Chamber), judgment of 16 November 1998, paras. 478 et seq., and *Prosecutor* v. *Musema*, ICTR (Trial Chamber), judgment of 27 January 2000, para. 229.

[193] *Prosecutor* v. *Furundžija*, ICTY (Trial Chamber), judgment of 10 December 1998, para. 185: "(i) the sexual penetration, however slight: (a) of the vagina or anus of the victim by the penis of the perpetrator or any other object used by the perpetrator; or (b) of the mouth of the victim by the penis of the perpetrator; (ii) by coercion or force or threat of force against the victim or a third person."

[194] For detailed discussion, see *Prosecutor* v. *Kunarac* et al., ICTY (Trial Chamber), judgment of 22 February 2001, paras. 441 et seq.

[195] *Prosecutor* v. *Kunarac* et al., ICTY (Trial Chamber), judgment of 22 February 2001, para. 460: ". . . where such penetration occurs without the consent of the victim. Consent must be given voluntarily, as a result of the victim's free will, assessed in the context of the surrounding circumstances." But see *Prosecutor* v. *Kvočka* et al., ICTY (Trial Chamber), judgment of 2 November 2001, para. 177: "(i) the sexual activity must be accompanied by force or threat of force to the victim or a third party; (ii) the sexual activity must be accompanied by force or a variety of other specified circumstances which made the victim particularly vulnerable or negated her ability to make an informed refusal; or (iii) the sexual activity must occur without the consent of the victim."

[196] See *Prosecutor* v. *Kunarac* et al., ICTY (Appeals Chamber), judgment of 12 June 2002, para. 128.

[197] However, the approaches taken in both judgments will usually lead to the same results. From this perspective, see *Prosecutor* v. *Kunarac* et al., ICTY (Appeals Chamber), judgment of 12 June 2002, para. 129; *Prosecutor* v. *Kunarac* et al., ICTY (Trial Chamber), judgment of 22 February 2001, para. 458: "In practice, the absence of genuine and freely given consent or voluntary participation may be evidenced by the presence of the various factors . . . such as force, threats of force, or taking advantage of a person who is unable to resist." and para. 459: "Given that it is evident from the *Furundžija* case that the terms coercion, force, or threat of force were not to be interpreted narrowly and that coercion in particular would encompass most conduct which negates consent, [*Kunarac*] does not differ substantially from the *Furundžija* definition."

726   In armed conflict in which armed forces are present, a nearly universal situation of coercion exists, such that as a rule no genuine consent on the part of the victim can be assumed.[198] This is even more true if the victim is held captive.[199] This interpretation also forms the basis of the ICC Rules of Procedure.[200]

727   For the mental element of rape, Article 30 of the ICC Statute applies.[201]

2. Sexual Slavery

728 Sexual slavery is, in substance, a specific manifestation of enslavement.[202] This is made clear in the Elements of Crimes, in that they take up the criteria of slavery. In addition, the perpetrator must cause the victim to engage in sexual acts.[203] Examples of sexual sla-

---

[198] *Prosecutor* v. *Akayesu*, ICTR (Trial Chamber), judgment of 2 September 1998, para. 688: "Coercive circumstances need not be evidenced by a show of physical force . . . and coercion may be inherent in certain circumstances, such as armed conflict or the military presence."; similarly, *Prosecutor* v. *Mucić* et al., ICTY (Trial Chamber), judgment of 16 November 1998, para. 495; *Prosecutor* v. *Kvočka* et al., ICTY (Trial Chamber), judgment of 2 November 2001, para. 178. Affirmed in *Prosecutor* v. *Kunarac* et al., ICTY (Appeals Chamber), judgment of 12 June 2002, para. 130: "[M]ost cases charged as either war crimes or crimes against humanity will be almost universally coercive. That is to say, true consent will not be possible." See also *Contemporary Forms of Slavery, Systematic Rape, Sexual Slavery and Slavery-like Practices During Armed Conflict, Final Report submitted by Ms. Gay J. McDougall, Special Rapporteur*; UN Doc. E/CN.4/Sub.2/1998/13, 22 June 1998, para. 24: "The manifestly coercive circumstances that exist in all armed conflict situations establish a presumption of non-consent and negates the need for the prosecution to establish a lack of consent as an element of the crime."

[199] *Prosecutor* v. *Furundžija*, ICTY (Trial Chamber), judgment of 10 December 1998, para. 271: "any form of captivity vitiates consent"; similarly, with comparative legal cites, *Prosecutor* v. *Kunarac* et al., ICTY (Appeals Chamber), judgment of 12 June 2002, para. 131.

[200] ICC Rule of Procedure 70 (Principles of evidence in cases of sexual violence) provides: "In cases of sexual violence, the Court shall be guided by and where appropriate, apply the following principles: (a) Consent cannot be inferred by reason of any words or conduct of a victim where force, threat of force, coercion or taking an advantage of a coercive environment undermined the victim's ability to give voluntary and genuine consent; (b) Consent cannot be inferred by reason of any words or conduct of a victim where the victim is incapable of giving genuine consent; (c) Consent cannot be inferred by reason of the silence of, or lack of resistance by, a victim to the alleged sexual violence; (d) Credibility, character or predisposition to sexual availability of a victim or witness cannot be inferred by reason of the sexual nature of the prior or subsequent conduct of a victim or witness."

[201] On the general requirements of the mental element, see marginal nos. 294 et seq., esp. nos. 304 et seq. See also *Prosecutor* v. *Kunarac* et al., ICTY (Trial Chamber), judgment of 22 February 2001, para. 460: "intention to effect this sexual penetration and the knowledge that it occurs without the consent of the victim."

[202] See *Contemporary Forms of Slavery, Systematic Rape, Sexual Slavery and Slavery-like Practices During Armed Conflict, Final Report submitted by Ms. Gay J. McDougall, Special Rapporteur*; UN Doc. E/CN.4/Sub.2/1998/13, 22 June 1998, para. 30: "The term 'sexual' is used . . . as an adjective to describe a form of slavery, not to denote a separate crime." For a critical view of its status as a separate crime, see also M. Boot, in O. Triffterer (ed.), *Commentary on the Rome Statute of the International Criminal Court* (1999), Art. 7, marginal no. 47: "it should be considered as a particular form of enslavement which includes various forms of slavery." See also marginal nos. 684 et seq.

[203] The Elements of Crimes for Art. 7(1)(g)-2 ICC Statute provide: "2. The perpetrator caused such person or persons to engage in one or more acts of a sexual nature."

very are the "comfort stations" set up by the Japanese army during World War II[204] and the "rape camps" that existed during the Yugoslavia conflict.[205]

3. Enforced Prostitution

"Enforced prostitution" has long been explicitly forbidden by a number of instruments **729** of international humanitarian law.[206] The ICC Statute for the first time recognizes it as a separate crime against humanity.[207] According to the Elements of Crimes, the material element requires that the perpetrator cause one or more persons to engage in sexual acts through the exercise of force or threat of force or coercion. The perpetrator or another person must receive or expect financial or other advantages in exchange for or in connection with the sexual act.[208]

Enforced prostitution will typically fit the definition of enslavement during armed conflict.[209] The **730** creation of coerced brothels frequently serves not to make a profit, but to "strengthen the morale" of the troops.

4. Forced Pregnancy

"Forced pregnancy" as a crime against humanity is a unique feature of the ICC Statute. **731** According to the definition in Article 7(2)(f) of the ICC Statute, the material element requires the illegal imprisonment of a forcibly impregnated woman. To complete the crime, it is sufficient if the perpetrator holds prisoner a woman who has been impregnated by someone else. The definition makes clear that domestic laws that prohibit abor-

---

[204] See *The Prosecutors and the Peoples of Asia-Pacific Region* v. *Emperor Hirohito et al. and the Government of Japan*, Women's International War Crimes Tribunal 2000 for the Trial of Japanese Military Sexual Slavery, judgment of 12 December 2000. See also C. Chinkin, 95 *American Journal of International Law* (2001), pp. 335 et seq.

[205] See *Prosecutor* v. *Kunarac* et al., ICTY (Trial Chamber), judgment of 22 February 2001.

[206] See Geneva Convention IV, Art. 27(2); Additional Protocol I, Arts. 75(2)(b) and 76(1); and Additional Protocol II, Art. 4(2)(e), see marginal nos. 914 et seq.

[207] Enforced prostitution was also contained in 1996 *Draft Code*, Art. 18(j) as a crime against humanity. See also N.V. Demleitner, 18 *Fordham International Law Journal* (1994), pp. 163 et seq.

[208] The Elements of Crimes for Art. 7(1)(g)-3 ICC Statute provide: "1. The perpetrator caused one or more persons to engage in one or more acts of a sexual nature by force, or by threat of force or coercion, such as that caused by fear of violence, duress, detention, psychological oppression or abuse of power, against such person or persons or another person, or by taking advantage of a coercive environment or such person's or persons' incapacity to give genuine consent. 2. The perpetrator or another person obtained or expected to obtain pecuniary or other advantage in exchange for or in connection with the acts of a sexual nature."

[209] *Contemporary Forms of Slavery, Systematic Rape, Sexual Slavery, and Slavery-Like Practices During Armed Conflict, Final Report submitted by Ms. Gay J. McDougall, Special Rapporteur*; UN Doc. E/CN.4/Sub.2/1998/13, 22 June 1998, para. 33: "As a general principle it would appear that in situations of armed conflict, most factual scenarios that could be described as forced prostitution would also amount to sexual slavery and could more appropriately and more easily be characterized and prosecuted as slavery." See also marginal no. 687.

tion are not included. This obviated concerns that would have made the negotiations on forced pregnancy more difficult.[210]

732   From a subjective point of view, forced pregnancy first of all requires that the material elements of the crime are committed with intent and knowledge (ICC Statute, Article 30).[211] In addition, the perpetrator must act with the purpose of affecting the ethnic composition of any population or carrying out other grave violations of international law. This is found in Article 7(2)(f) of the ICC Statute.

5. Enforced Sterilization

733   Enforced sterilization is listed for the first time in the ICC Statute as a special manifestation of a crime against humanity. The ICC Statute contains no definition of enforced sterilization. According to the Elements of Crimes,[212] the perpetrator must permanently deprive at least one person of his or her biological reproductive capacity. Exceptions are cases of medically necessary treatment. Classic examples of relevant criminal acts were the forced sterilizations in the Third Reich to ensure so-called "racial hygiene" and the medical experiments on inmates in the Nazi concentration camps.[213]

6. Other Forms of Sexual Violence

734   The inclusion of other forms of sexual violence of comparable gravity has a catch-all character. According to the Elements of Crimes,[214] the perpetrator must commit an act of a sexual nature against one or more persons or cause such person or persons to engage in an act of a sexual nature by force, threat of force or coercion. The conduct must be comparable in gravity to the acts listed in Article 7(1)(g) of the ICC Statute. The Elements of Crimes are based on the judgment of the Rwanda Tribunal in the *Akayesu*

---

[210] On the negotiations, see H. von Hebel and D. Robinson, in R.S. Lee (ed.), *The International Criminal Court, The Making of the Rome Statute* (1999), p. 79 at p. 100; K.D. Askin, 10 *Criminal Law Forum* (1999), p. 33 at p. 46.

[211] On the general requirements for the mental element, see marginal nos. 294 et seq., esp. nos. 304 et seq.

[212] Elements of Crimes for Art. 7(1)(g)-5 ICC Statute: "1. The perpetrator deprived one or more persons of biological reproductive capacity. (fn. 19: The deprivation is not intended to include birth-control measures which have a non-permanent effect in practice.) 2. The conduct was neither justified by the medical or hospital treatment of the person or persons concerned nor carried out with their genuine consent. (fn. 20: It is understood that 'genuine consent' does not include consent obtained through deception.)."

[213] See US Military Tribunal, Nuremberg, judgment of 20 August 1947 (*Brandt* et al., so-called Medical Trial), in *Trials of War Criminals* II, pp. 171 et seq.

[214] Elements of Crimes for Art. 7(1)(g)-6 ICC Statute: "1. The perpetrator committed an act of a sexual nature against one or more persons or caused such person or persons to engage in an act of a sexual nature by force, or by threat of force or coercion, such as that caused by fear of violence, duress, detention, psychological oppression or abuse of power, against such person or persons or another person, or by taking advantage of a coercive environment or such person's or persons' incapacity to give genuine consent. 2. Such conduct was of a gravity comparable to the other offences in Article 7, paragraph 1(g) of the Statute."

case.[215] The Tribunal applied this concept to the order to strip a female student and force her to perform gymnastics naked before a large crowd of people.[216]

VIII. Persecution

Stephan Meseke: *Der Tatbestand der Verbrechen gegen die Menschlichkeit nach dem Römischen Statut* **735** *des Internationalen Strafgerichtshofs* (2004), pp. 238 et seq.; Olivia Swaak-Goldman: Persecution, in Gabrielle Kirk McDonald and Olivia Swaak-Goldman (eds.), *Substantive and Procedural Aspects of International Criminal Law – The Experience of International and National Courts*, Vol. 1 (2000), pp. 247 et seq.; Olivia Swaak-Goldman: The Crime of Persecution in International Criminal Law, 11 *Leiden Journal of International Law* (1998), pp. 145 et seq.

Article 7(1)(h) of the ICC Statute deals with the crime against humanity of persecution. **736** The crime of persecution has been included in all relevant international criminal law instruments since Nuremberg, specifically in Article 6(c) of the Nuremberg Charter, Article II(1)(c) of Control Council Law No. 10, Article 5(c) of the Tokyo Charter, Article 5(h) of the ICTY Statute and Article 3(h) of the ICTR Statute. However, none of these instruments contained as detailed a definition of the crime of persecution as the one that can be derived from Article 7(1)(h), in conjunction with the definition of "persecution" and the term "gender" in Article 7(2)(g) and (3) of the ICC Statute.

The negotiators on the ICC Statute faced the problem that no definition of persecution existed.[217] **737** While the definition of "persecution" is at times borrowed from international refugee law or human rights law, the international criminal Tribunals have explicitly rejected such an analogy.[218] The definition of persecution in Article 7(2)(g) of the ICC Statute is based on the precedent set by the Yugoslavia Tribunal in the *Tadić* case and is oriented around Article 18 of the 1996 *Draft Code*. The judgments of the Yugoslavia Tribunal have since succeeded in further clarifying the characteristics of the crime of persecution under customary international law.[219]

---

[215] *Prosecutor* v. *Akayesu*, ICTR (Trial Chamber), judgment of 2 September 1998, para. 598: "any act of a sexual nature which is committed on a person under circumstances which are coercive."

[216] *Prosecutor* v. *Akayesu*, ICTR (Trial Chamber), judgment of 2 September 1998, para. 688.

[217] On this review, see *Prosecutor* v. *Tadić*, ICTY (Trial Chamber), judgment of 7 May 1997, para. 694; *Prosecutor* v. *Kupreškić* et al., ICTY (Trial Chamber), judgment of 14 January 2000, para. 567; *Prosecutor* v. *Blaškić*, ICTY (Trial Chamber), judgment of 3 March 2000, para. 219; *Prosecutor* v. *Kordić and Čerkez*, ICTY (Trial Chamber), judgment of 26 February 2001, para. 192.

[218] See *Prosecutor* v. *Kupreškić* et al., ICTY (Trial Chamber), judgment of 14 January 2000, para. 589: "The definition stemming from international refugee law or human rights law cannot . . . be followed here."

[219] See judgments following adoption of the ICC Statute: *Prosecutor* v. *Kupreškić* et al., ICTY (Trial Chamber), judgment of 14 January 2000, paras. 567 et seq.; *Prosecutor* v. *Blaškić*, ICTY (Trial Chamber), judgment of 3 March 2000, paras. 218 et seq.; *Prosecutor* v. *Kordić and Čerkez*, ICTY (Trial Chamber), judgment of 26 February 2001, paras. 188 et seq.; *Prosecutor* v. *Krstić*, ICTY (Trial Chamber), judgment of 2 August 2001, paras. 533 et seq.; *Prosecutor* v. *Kvočka* et al., ICTY (Trial Chamber), judgment of 2 November 2001, paras. 184 et seq.; *Prosecutor* v. *Krnojelac*, ICTY (Trial Chamber), judgment of 15 March 2002, paras. 431 et seq.; *Prosecutor* v. *Vasiljević*, ICTY (Trial Chamber), judgment of 29 November 2002, paras. 244 et seq.; *Prosecutor* v. *Simić* et al., ICTY (Trial Chamber), judgment of 17 October 2003, paras. 47 et seq.; *Prosecutor* v. *Stakić*, ICTY (Trial Chamber), judgment of 31 July 2003, paras. 732 et seq.; *Prosecutor* v. *Semanza*, ICTR (Trial Chamber), judgment of 15 May 2003, paras. 347 et seq.

1. Material Elements

738   The material element requires the persecution of an identifiable group or community. The group as such can be the object of persecution, for example when laws discriminate against specific groups. But the definition also includes acts aimed at individuals as representatives of a group. The kind of group or collectivity that may be involved can be derived from the motives required for the perpetrator's conduct. In contrast to genocide, here it is clear from the start that only the perpetrator's identification of the group is decisive.[220]

739   According to the definition in Article 7(2)(g) of the ICC Statute, persecution is the intentional and severe deprivation of fundamental rights contrary to international law by reason of the identity of the group or collectivity. This definition is based on the judgments of the Yugoslavia Tribunal, especially the leading *Tadić* case,[221] and is also geared toward Article 18 of the 1996 *Draft Code*.[222] It can be determined from this context that the term "fundamental rights" refers to the rights set out, for example, in the *Universal Declaration of Human Rights* and the *International Covenant on Civil and Political Rights*. From among these fundamental rights, the Yugoslavia Tribunal especially emphasized the right to life, the right to physical and mental inviolability, and the right to personal freedom.[223] The Elements of Crimes make it clear that deprivation of the rights of a single person is enough to satisfy the requirements of the definition.

740   Under the wording of Article 7(2)(g) of the ICC Statute, it would be possible to include only a formal deprivation of rights in regard to a group, such as legal measures that abrogate certain rights based on group identity. However, the judgments of the Yugosla-

---

[220] *Prosecutor* v. *Naletilić and Martinović*, ICTY (Trial Chamber), judgment of 31 March 2003, para. 636: "The targeted group must be interpreted broadly, and may, in particular, include such persons who are defined by the perpetrator as belonging to the victim group due to their close affiliations or sympathies for the victim group."

[221] See *Prosecutor* v. *Tadić*, ICTY (Trial Chamber), judgment of 7 May 1997, para. 697: "[W]hat is necessary is some form of discrimination that is intended to be and results in an infringement of an individual's fundamental rights. . . . It is the violation of the right to equality in some serious fashion that infringes on the enjoyment of a basic or fundamental right that constitutes persecution." After adoption of the Rome Statute, the Yugoslavia Tribunal further clarified the customary international law definition, see *Prosecutor* v. *Kupreškić* et al., ICTY (Trial Chamber), judgment of 14 January 2000, para. 621: "gross or blatant denial, on discriminatory grounds, of a fundamental right, laid down in international customary or treaty law, reaching the same level of gravity as the other acts prohibited in Article 5" of the ICTY Statute. Affirmed in *Prosecutor* v. *Kordić and Čerkez*, ICTY (Trial Chamber), judgment of 26 February 2001, para. 195; *Prosecutor* v. *Krstić*, ICTY (Trial Chamber), judgment of 2 August 2001, para. 534; *Prosecutor* v. *Kvočka* et al., ICTY (Trial Chamber), judgment of 2 November 2001, para. 184; *Prosecutor* v. *Krnojelac*, ICTY (Trial Chamber), judgment of 15 March 2002, para. 434; *Prosecutor* v. *Simić* et al., ICTY (Trial Chamber), judgment of 17 October 2003, para. 47.

[222] See 1996 *Draft Code*, commentary on Art. 18, para. 11: "denial of the human rights and fundamental freedoms to which every individual is entitled without distinction as recognized in the Charter of the United Nations (Arts. 1, 55) and the International Covenant of Civil and Political Rights (Art. 2)."

[223] *Prosecutor* v. *Blaškić*, ICTY (Trial Chamber), judgment of 3 March 2000, para. 220: "the elementary and inalienable rights of man, which are 'the right to life, liberty and security of person,' the rights not to be 'held in slavery or servitude,' the right not to 'be subjected to torture or to cruel, inhuman or degrading treatment or punishment' and the right not to 'be subjected to arbitrary arrest, detention or exile' as affirmed in Articles 3, 4, 5 and 9 of the Universal Declaration of Human Rights".

via Tribunal upon which the ICC Statute is based confirm that the acts making up the crime of persecution can take numerous forms. Acts that violate fundamental human rights should be included, whether these acts are of a physical, economic or legal nature.[224] The decisive aspect is always the objectively discriminatory, rights-affecting character of the violation.[225] Hate speech can also meet the requirements of persecution.[226]

Following the judgments of the Yugoslavia Tribunal, two categories of violations may **741** be distinguished. The first category contains behaviors that are relevant in and of themselves to international criminal law, because they satisfy the definition of a war crime or genocide[227] or another separate crime against humanity.[228] The second category contains behaviors that do not in themselves satisfy the listed definitions.[229] Not every impairment is included as an act of persecution, but only "severe" deprivation of fundamental rights. This "threshold clause" can be explained as part of the effort to bring the dynamic development of human rights into conformity with the principle of legality (*nullum crimen sine lege*).[230] The standard for severity is the other individual crimes against humanity. Deprivation of rights should not be considered in isolation; it

---

[224] *Prosecutor* v. *Tadić*, ICTY (Trial Chamber), judgment of 7 May 1997, para. 710: "[P]ersecution encompasses a variety of acts, including, *inter alia,* those of a physical, economic or judicial nature, that violate an individual's right to the equal enjoyment of his basic rights."

[225] Explicitly developed in *Prosecutor* v. *Krnojelac*, ICTY (Trial Chamber), judgment of 15 March 2002, para. 431: "discriminates in fact and which denies or infringes upon a fundamental right laid down in international customary or treaty law (the actus reus)."; similarly, *Prosecutor* v. *Tadić*, ICTY (Trial Chamber), judgment of 7 May 1997, para. 707: "[P]ersecution can take numerous forms, so long as the common element of discrimination in regard to the enjoyment of a basic or fundamental right is present and persecution does not necessarily require a physical element"; *Prosecutor* v. *Kordić and Čerkez*, ICTY (Trial Chamber), judgment of 26 February 2001, para. 189: "discriminatory act or omission."

[226] *Prosecutor* v. *Nahimana* et al., ICTR (Trial Chamber), judgment of 3 December 2003, paras. 1070 et seq.

[227] See *Prosecutor* v. *Tadić*, ICTY (Trial Chamber), judgment of 7 May 1997, para. 700; *Prosecutor* v. *Kupreškić* et al., ICTY (Trial Chamber), judgment of 14 January 2000, para. 617; *Prosecutor* v. *Kordić and Čerkez*, ICTY (Trial Chamber), judgment of 26 February 2001, paras. 201 et seq.; *Prosecutor* v. *Krstić*, ICTY (Trial Chamber), judgment of 2 August 2001, para. 535; *Prosecutor* v. *Kvočka* et al., ICTY (Trial Chamber), judgment of 2 November 2001, para. 185; *Prosecutor* v. *Krnojelac*, ICTY (Trial Chamber), judgment of 15 March 2002, para. 433.

[228] For a leading case, see *Prosecutor* v. *Kupreškić* et al., ICTY (Trial Chamber), judgment of 14 January 2000, paras. 593 et seq., 617; affirmed in *Prosecutor* v. *Blaškić*, ICTY (Trial Chamber), judgment of 3 March 2000, paras. 220 et seq.; *Prosecutor* v. *Kordić and Čerkez*, ICTY (Trial Chamber), judgment of 26 February 2001, para. 201; *Prosecutor* v. *Krstić*, ICTY (Trial Chamber), judgment of 2 August 2001, para. 535; *Prosecutor* v. *Kvočka* et al., ICTY (Trial Chamber), judgment of 2 November 2001, para. 185; *Prosecutor* v. *Krnojelac*, ICTY (Trial Chamber), judgment of 15 March 2002, para. 433.

[229] For a leading case, see *Prosecutor* v. *Tadić*, ICTY (Trial Chamber), judgment of 7 May 1997, paras. 703 et seq.; affirmed in *Prosecutor* v. *Kupreškić* et al., ICTY (Trial Chamber), judgment of 14 January 2000, paras. 614, 617; *Prosecutor* v. *Blaškić*, ICTY (Trial Chamber), judgment of 3 March 2000, para. 233; *Prosecutor* v. *Kordić and Čerkez*, ICTY (Trial Chamber), judgment of 26 February 2001, para. 193; *Prosecutor* v. *Krstić*, ICTY (Trial Chamber), judgment of 2 August 2001, para. 535; *Prosecutor* v. *Kvočka* et al., ICTY (Trial Chamber), judgment of 2 November 2001, para. 185; *Prosecutor* v. *Krnojelac*, ICTY (Trial Chamber), judgment of 15 March 2002, para. 433.

[230] See *Prosecutor* v. *Kupreškić* et al., ICTY (Trial Chamber), judgment of 14 January 2000, para. 618: "Although the realm of human rights is dynamic and expansive, not every denial of human right may constitute a crime against humanity."

is typically an expression of discriminatory policies and must be appreciated in its overall context.[231] The persecutor act or omission must have discriminatory consequences.[232]

742 A classic example of the second category of persecution is the persecution policies of the Third Reich, with the numerous anti-Jewish laws, edicts and measures decreed by its leadership. The Reich Citizenship Law,[233] for example, decreed that only "citizens of German or related blood" could be citizens of the Reich and thus "bearers of full political rights." Other measures in legal form excluded Jews from access to public offices and professions, interfered with their property and family life, and limited their freedom of movement.[234]

743 It is unclear to what extent violations of property rights can be classified as acts of persecution. In the *Flick* trial, for example, the Court decided that violation of property rights through forcible seizure of industrial assets was not a crime against humanity.[235] Under the new international case law, a distinction must rightly be made based on the type and severity of the attack on property. Thus the destruction of a single piece of property does not become a crime of persecution simply because of the presence of discriminatory intent. In contrast, a crime of persecution can be presumed if attacks on property are serious enough to destroy the economic livelihood of a part of the population.[236] This

---

[231] *Prosecutor* v. *Kupreškić* et al., ICTY (Trial Chamber), judgment of 14 January 2000, paras. 622, 615: "Acts of persecution must not be considered in isolation, but examined in their context and weighed for their cumulative effect. . . . Although individual acts may not be inhumane, their overall consequences must offend humanity in such way that they may be termed 'inhumane'"; see also *Prosecutor* v. *Kordić and Čerkez*, ICTY (Trial Chamber), judgment of 26 February 2001, para. 199; *Prosecutor* v. *Krstić*, ICTY (Trial Chamber), judgment of 2 August 2001, para. 535; *Prosecutor* v. *Kvočka* et al., ICTY (Trial Chamber), judgment of 2 November 2001, para. 185; *Prosecutor* v. *Krnojelac*, ICTY (Trial Chamber), judgment of 15 March 2002, para. 434.

[232] *Prosecutor* v. *Vasiljević*, ITCY (Trial Chamber), judgment of 29 November 2002, para. 245; *Prosecutor* v. *Stakić*, ICTY (Trial Chamber), judgment of 31 July 2003, para. 733.

[233] (German) Reich Citizenship Law *[Reichsbürgergesetz]*, 15 September 1935, Reichsgesetzblatt 1935 I, 1146.

[234] See the collection of sources in J. Walk (ed.), *Das Sonderrecht für die Juden im NS-Staat*, 2nd edn. (1996) sowie IMT, judgment of 1 October 1946, in *The Trial of German Major War Criminals. Proceedings of the International Military Tribunal Sitting at Nuremberg*, Germany, Part 22, pp. 463 et seq.

[235] US Military Tribunal, Nuremberg, judgment of 22 December 1947 (*Flick* et al., so-called Flick Trial), in *Trials of War Criminals* VI, pp. 1215 et seq.; see also US Military Tribunal, Nuremberg, judgment of 30 July 1948 (*Krauch* et al., so-called IG Farben Trial), in *Trials of War Criminals* VIII, pp. 1129 et seq.

[236] For a leading case, see *Prosecutor* v. *Kupreškić* et al., ICTY (Trial Chamber), judgment of 14 January 2000, para. 631: "[A]ttacks on property can constitute persecution. To some extent this may depend on the type of property. . . . There may be certain types of property whose destruction may not have a severe enough impact on the victim as to constitute a crime against humanity, even if such a destruction is perpetrated on discriminatory grounds: an example is the burning of someone's car (unless the car constitutes an indispensable and vital asset to the owner). [T]he comprehensive destruction of homes and property . . . constitutes a destruction of the livelihood of a certain population. This may have the same inhumane consequences as a forced transfer or deportation. Moreover, the burning of a residential property may often be committed with a recklessness towards the lives of its inhabitants." See also *Prosecutor* v. *Tadić*, ICTY (Trial Chamber), judgment of 7 May 1997, para. 707: "[E]conomic measures of a personal, as opposed to an industrial type, can constitute persecutory acts."; *Prosecutor* v. *Blaškić*, ICTY (Trial Chamber), judgment of 3 March 2000, para. 233; *Prosecutor* v. *Kordić and Čerkez*, ICTY (Trial Chamber), judgment of 26 February 2001, para. 205.

allows for the inclusion of targeted destruction, plundering or confiscation of private property, even in peacetime.[237] Forced sale at less than a fair price or expropriation without compensation can constitute a crime. An example would be the systematic attacks on Jewish property and assets in the Nazi period.

The ICC Statute deals with persecution only if it is committed "in connection with" **744** any act referred to in paragraph 1 or any crime within the jurisdiction of the Court. The requirement of a connection was intended to take account of concerns about the breadth of the crime of persecution.[238] With this accessorial design, the ICC Statute lags behind customary international law, since the crime of persecution, like crimes against humanity, has developed into an independent crime.[239]

2. Mental Element

From a subjective point of view, persecution requires that the material elements of the **745** crime be committed with intent and knowledge (ICC Statute, Article 30).[240] Article 7(2)(g)'s determination that deprivation of rights must be "intentional" is not a deviation from the general requirements for the mental element. In addition, the crime must be committed for discriminatory reasons, specifically "on political, racial, national, ethnic, cultural, religious, gender as defined in paragraph 3, or other grounds that are universally recognized as impermissible under international law." The crime of persecution thus differs here from all other crimes against humanity.[241] The perpetrator must either target a group or collectivity as such, or attack a person specifically because of his or her membership in this group or collectivity. In the latter case, the individual is attacked as a representative of the group.[242] For the perpetrator, then, the issue must always be discrimination against the group or collectivity as such.

---

[237] On war crimes against property, see marginal nos. 986 et seq.

[238] See M. Boot, in O. Triffterer (ed.), *Commentary on the Rome Statute of the International Criminal Court* (1999), Art. 7, marginal no. 112.

[239] See *Prosecutor* v. *Kupreškić* et al., ICTY (Trial Chamber), judgment of 14 January 2000, paras. 580 et seq.: "[T]he Statute of the ICC may be indicative of the opinio juris of many States, Article 7[(1)](h) is not consonant with customary international law. . . . Accordingly, the Trial Chamber rejects the notion that persecution must be linked to crimes found elsewhere in the Statute of the International Tribunal. It notes that in any case no such requirement is imposed on it by the Statute. . . . For agreement, see also *Prosecutor* v. *Kordić and Čerkez*, ICTY (Trial Chamber), judgment of 26 February 2001, para. 194. Sec. 7(1) No. 10 (German) Code of Crimes Against International Law *[Völkerstrafgesetzbuch, VStGB]* has also taken on this view, see Explanatory Memorandum of the (German) Code of Crimes against International Law *[Begründung zum Völkerstrafgesetzbuch, VStGB]*, BT-Drs. 14/8524, p. 22.

[240] On the general requirements for the mental element, see marginal nos. 294 et seq., esp. no. 304.

[241] *Prosecutor* v. *Kupreškić* et al., ICTY (Trial Chamber), judgment of 14 January 2000, para. 607: "Although the *actus reus* of persecution may be identical to other crimes against humanity, what distinguishes the crime of persecution is that it is committed on discriminatory grounds"; affirmed in *Prosecutor* v. *Kordić and Čerkez*, ICTY (Trial Chamber), judgment of 26 February 2001, para. 217. See also marginal no. 661; *Prosecutor* v. *Simić* et al., ICTY (Trial Chamber), judgment of 17 October 2003, para. 51.

[242] Elements of Crimes for Art. 7(1)(h) of the ICC Statute: "2. The perpetrator targeted such person or persons by reason of the identity of a group or collectivity or targeted the group or collectivity as such. 3. Such targeting was based on political, racial, national, ethnic, cultural, religious, gender as

746   It is sufficient for the perpetrator to act out of one of the listed motivations;[243] specific objecticiable group-constitutive characteristics that connect the members of a group or collectivity in at least rudimentary fashion are not necessary.

a) Political, Racial or Religious Grounds

747   Classic features of the crime of persecution include the perpetrator's political, racial or religious motivations. These features are also found in Article 6(c) of the Nuremberg Statute, Article II(1)(c) of Control Council Law No. 10, Article 5(h) of the ICTY Statute and Article 3(h) of the ICTR Statute. Only Article 5(c) of the Tokyo Statute did not include religious grounds.

748   A perpetrator acts on political grounds if he or she discriminates against the victim because of his or her political beliefs.[244] The victim is not required to be a member of a political party or group. If the perpetrator discriminates against the victim because the victim is of a certain race, he or she is acting on racial grounds.[245] If the perpetrator discriminates against the victim because of the victim's specific religious faith, he or she is acting on religious grounds.[246]

b) Other Grounds

749   The ICC Statute is the first international instrument to include other discriminatory grounds, going beyond the scope of customary international law. They include acts of persecution on national, ethnic, and cultural grounds, grounds of gender, or other grounds universally recognized as impermissible under international law.[247]

750   A perpetrator is acting on "national" grounds if he or she discriminates against a victim because of the victim's nationality or membership in a national minority.[248] Discrimination on the grounds of "ethnic" identity most likely has little independent scope

---

defined in Article 7, paragraph 1 of the Statute, or other grounds that are universally recognized as impermissible under international law." See also *Prosecutor* v. *Blaškić*, ICTY (Trial Chamber), judgment of 3 March 2000, para. 235: "[T]he perpetrator of the acts of persecution does not initially target the individual but rather membership in a specific racial, religious or political group."

[243] *Prosecutor* v. *Tadić*, ICTY (Trial Chamber), judgment of 7 May 1997, paras. 712 et seq.

[244] *Prosecutor* v. *Akayesu*, ICTR (Trial Chamber), judgment of 2 September 1998, para. 583: "Discrimination on the basis of a person's political ideology satisfies the requirement of 'political' grounds."; M. Boot and C.K. Hall, in O. Triffterer (ed.), *Commentary on the Rome Statute of the International Criminal Court* (1999), Art. 7, marginal no. 64.

[245] *Prosecutor* v. *Tadić*, ICTY (Trial Chamber), judgment of 7 May 1997, para. 711: "persecution undertaken on the basis of race."

[246] *Prosecutor* v. *Tadić*, ICTY (Trial Chamber), judgment of 7 May 1997, para. 711: "persecution undertaken on the basis of . . . religion"; see also M. Boot and C.K. Hall, in O. Triffterer (ed.), *Commentary on the Rome Statute of the International Criminal Court* (1999), Art. 7, marginal no. 69. See also remarks on the characteristics of "racial" and "religious" groups in genocide, see marginal nos. 582 et seq.

[247] Persecution on "cultural grounds" was already contained in 1954 *Draft Code*, Art. 2(11) and 1991 *Draft Code*, Art. 21. Persecution on "ethnic grounds," in contrast, was first contained in 1996 *Draft Code*, Art. 18(e).

[248] M. Boot and C.K. Hall, in O. Triffterer (ed.), *Commentary on the Rome Statute of the International Criminal Court* (1999), Art. 7, marginal no. 66: "The concept of 'national' is broader than citizenship and includes attributes of a group which considers that it is a nation even though the members of the group are located in more than one State."

outside racial grounds.[249] The term "cultural" is used in a variety of international instruments, but no final definition has been arrived at.[250] This term should be interpreted in a broad sense, including a specific group's language, customs, art, architecture, etc. An example would be discrimination because of a specific native language.

Grounds of gender refers, according to the legal definition in Article 7 (3) of the ICC **751** Statute, "to the two sexes, male and female, within the context of society." It should be noted that the term "gender" comprehends both biological and sociological differences.[251] *The Convention on the Elimination of All Forms of Discrimination against Women*[252] is to be used as a basis for interpretation in cases of discrimination against women. The criterion "other grounds that are universally recognized as impermissible under international law" makes reference to customary international law,[253] and thus leaves room for further development of customary international law in a direction favorable to human rights. Persecution on grounds of sexual orientation (homosexuality) cannot yet be included, as no such prohibition has thus far been established in customary international law.[254] Further grounds, for example of a social or economic nature,[255] were purposely not recognized by the ICC Statute.[256]

IX. Enforced Disappearance

Reed Brody and Felipe Gonzalez: Nunca Más: An Analysis of International Instruments on "Dis- **752** appearances", 19 *Human Rights Quarterly* (1997), pp. 365 et seq.; Matthew Lippman: Disappear-

---

[249] Therefore it makes no difference that the term "ethnic" used in the official English text (ICC Statute, Art. 7(1)(h)) will be narrower than the term "ethnical" in genocide, see M. Boot and C.K. Hall, in O. Triffterer (ed.), *Commentary on the Rome Statute of the International Criminal Court* (1999), Art. 7, marginal no. 67. For additional information on conduct on "national" and "ethnic" grounds, see the remarks on corresponding group characteristics in marginal nos. 580 et seq.

[250] See M. Boot and C.K. Hall, in O. Triffterer (ed.), *Commentary on the Rome Statute of the International Criminal Court* (1999), Art. 7, marginal no. 68 with additional notes. On "cultural genocide," see also marginal no. 586.

[251] M. Boot, in O. Triffterer (ed.), *Commentary on the Rome Statute of the International Criminal Court* (1999), Art. 7, marginal no. 128. On the discussion surrounding the term "gender" at the negotiations on the Rome Statute, see C. Steains, in R.S. Lee (ed.), *The International Criminal Court, The Making of the Rome Statute* (1999), p. 357 at p. 374.

[252] Of 18 December 1979, 1249 *UNTS* (1984), p. 13. Art. 1 defines the term "discrimination against women" as "any distinction, exclusion or restriction made on the basis of sex which has the effect or purpose of impairing or nullifying the recognition, enjoyment or exercise by women, irrespective of their marital status, on a basis of equality of men and women, of human rights and fundamental freedoms in the political, economic, social, cultural, civil or any other field."

[253] From this perspective, see M. Boot and C.K. Hall, in O. Triffterer (ed.), *Commentary on the Rome Statute of the International Criminal Court* (1999), Art. 7, marginal no. 71: "widely recognised"; M. Boot, *Genocide, Crimes against Humanity, War Crimes: Nullum Crimen Sine Lege* (2002), p. 521: "recognized as impermissible under customary international law."

[254] See Explanatory Memorandum of the (German) Code of Crimes against International Law *[Begründung zum Völkerstrafgesetzbuch, VStGB], BT-Drs.* 14/8524, p. 22.

[255] See explanatory fn. 15 on "other similar grounds" in the Draft ICC Statute (1998). Persecution on "social grounds," however, was contained in 1954 *Draft Code,* Art. 2(11) and 1991 *Draft Code,* Art. 21.

[256] See M. Boot, *Genocide, Crimes against Humanity, War Crimes: Nullum Crimen Sine Lege* (2002), p. 522.

ances: Towards a Declaration on the Prevention and Punishment of the Crime of Enforced or Involuntary Disappearances, 4 *Connecticut Journal of International Law* (1988), pp. 121 et seq.

753   Article 7(1)(i) of the ICC Statute deals with the crime against humanity of enforced disappearance. The policy of disappearance, particularly widespread in Latin America,[257] was already classified as a crime against humanity in the 1994 *Inter-American Convention on the Forced Disappearance of Persons*[258] and soon after became part of the 1996 *Draft Code*.[259] By the end of the negotiations in Rome, the view prevailed that enforced disappearance, hitherto dealt with only as a deprivation of freedom or an inhuman act, should be regulated as a separate crime against humanity.[260]

754   According to the definition in Article 7(2)(i) of the ICC Statute, "'Enforced disappearance of persons' means the arrest, detention or abduction of persons by, or with the authorization, support or acquiescence of, a State or a political organization, followed by a refusal to acknowledge that deprivation of freedom or to give information on the fate or whereabouts of those persons, with the intention of removing them from the protection of the law for a prolonged period of time." This definition is based on the Preamble of the *Declaration on the Protection of All Persons from Enforced Disappearance*.[261] The extensive Elements of Crimes add precision to the complex definition of the crime.[262] Ob-

---

[257] On "impunidad" for the policy of disappearance in Latin American countries from an international criminal law perspective, see K. Ambos, *Straflosigkeit von Menschenrechtsverletzungen* (1997), pp. 23 et seq. The phenomenon of disappearance had already appeared in the Third Reich in Hitler's "Night and Fog" decree. The Nuremberg Tribunal convicted the defendant Wilhelm Keitel for war crimes on this basis, see IMT, judgment of 1 October 1946, in *The Trial of German Major War Criminals. Proceedings of the International Military Tribunal Sitting at Nuremberg, Germany*, Part 22, p. 493; see also US Military Tribunal, Nuremberg, judgment of 4 December 1947 (*Altstötter* et al., so-called Justice Trial), in *Trials of War Criminals* III, pp. 1031 et seq.

[258] Of 9 June 1994, reprinted in 33 *ILM* (1994), p. 1529. Art. II contains the following definition: "For the purpose of this Convention, forced disappearance is considered to be the act of depriving a person or persons of his or their freedom, in whatever way, perpetrated by agents of the state or by persons or groups of persons acting with the authorization, support, or acquiescence of the state, followed by an absence of information or a refusal to acknowledge that deprivation of freedom or to give information on the whereabouts of that person, thereby impeding his or her recourse to the applicable legal remedies and procedural guarantees." See also R. Brody and F. Gonzalez, 19 *Human Rights Quarterly* (1997), pp. 365 et seq.

[259] See 1996 *Draft Code*, commentary on Art. 18(i), para. 15: "Although this type of criminal conduct is a relatively recent phenomenon, the present Code proposes its inclusion as a crime against humanity because if its cruelty and gravity."

[260] On the negotiations, see H. von Hebel and D. Robinson, in R.S. Lee (ed.), *The International Criminal Court, The Making of the Rome Statute* (1999), p. 79 at p. 102; D. Robinson, 93 *American Journal of International Law* (1999), pp. 55 et seq.

[261] Adopted in General Assembly Resolution 47/133 of 18 December 1992, UN Doc. A/47/49 (1992), p. 207. "Preamble: Deeply concerned that in many countries, often as a persistent manner, enforced disappearances occur in the sense that persons are arrested, detained or abducted against their will or otherwise deprived of their liberty by officials of different branches or levels of Government, or by organized groups or private individuals acting on behalf of, or with the support, direct or indirect, consent or acquiescence of the Government, followed by a refusal to disclose the fate or whereabouts of the persons concerned or a refusal to acknowledge the deprivation of their liberty, which places such persons outside the protection of law."

[262] Elements of Crimes for Art. 7(1)(i) ICC Statute: "1. The perpetrator: a) Arrested, detained (fn. 25: The word 'detained' would include a perpetrator who maintained an existing detention.), (fn. 26:

jectively, the definition distinguishes between two alternative types of conduct: deprivation of liberty and withholding information.

Deprivation of liberty must occur at the behest of or with the approval of a state or **755** political organization. In addition, it is necessary that no immediate information be provided upon request, for example by the victim's relatives, on the fate and whereabouts of the victim. The simple failure to provide information even without a request is not enough. Purposely providing false information is considered a refusal to provide information. The perpetrator of the deprivation of liberty need not be the one who withholds information.

The second type of conduct deals with the refusal to immediately provide informa- **756** tion after an abduction or serious deprivation of liberty. This always requires that an inquiry first be made. Withholding information is in a sense the mirror image of the first type of conduct, so that the above explanations essentially also apply. However, the second type of conduct is only satisfied if information is withheld at the behest of a state or a political organization, or if the perpetrator voluntarily takes part in a state policy of disappearance, on his own and without orders, and in the process also violates an existing legal duty to provide information. Approval by the state or a political organization is not sufficient.

For the mental element, Article 30 of the ICC Statute applies.[263] For the first alterna- **757** tive type of conduct, intent (ICC Statute, Article 30(2)) must extent to the failure to provide the information in question. For the second alternative type of conduct, the perpetrator must be aware of the fact that the victim about whose fate information has been withheld was first abducted in accordance with the first alternative, or otherwise deprived of liberty. In addition, the perpetrator must act with the "intention" (purpose) of removing the person from the protection of the law for a prolonged period of time.[264] This is derived from Article 7(2)(i) of the ICC Statute.

It is understood that under certain circumstances an arrest or detention may have been lawful) or abducted one or more persons; or b) Refused to acknowledge the arrest, detention or abduction, or to give information on the fate or whereabouts of such person or persons. 2. a) Such arrest, detention or abduction was followed or accompanied by a refusal to acknowledge that deprivation of freedom or to give information on the fate or whereabouts of such person or persons; or b) such refusal was preceded or accompanied by that deprivation of freedom. 3. The perpetrator was aware that: a) Such arrest, detention or abduction would be followed in the ordinary course of events by a refusal to acknowledge that deprivation of freedom or to give information on the fate or whereabouts of such person or persons; (fn. 28: It is understood that, in the case of a perpetrator who maintained an existing detention, this element would be satisfied if the perpetrator was aware that such refusal had already taken place) or b) Such refusal was preceded or accompanied by that deprivation of freedom. 4. Such arrest, detention or abduction was carried out by, or with the authorization, support or acquiescence of, a State or a political organization. 5. Such refusal to acknowledge that deprivation of freedom or to give information on the fate or whereabouts of such person or persons was carried out by, or with the authorization or support of, such State or political organization. 6. The perpetrator intended to remove such person or persons from the protection of the law for a prolonged period of time." On the negotiations on these Elements of Crimes, see W. Rückert and G. Witschel, in R.S. Lee (ed.), *The International Criminal Court, Elements of Crimes and Rules of Procedure and Evidence* (2001), pp. 98 et seq.

[263] On the general requirements of the mental element, see marginal nos. 294 et seq., esp. nos. 304 et seq.

[264] This narrows the scope of criminality, which is explicitly permitted by Art. 30 ICC Statute, see marginal nos. 310 et seq.

X. Apartheid

758 Roger S. Clark: Apartheid, in M. Cherif Bassiouni (ed.), *International Criminal Law*, Vol. 1, 2nd edn. (1999), pp. 643 et seq.; Bernhard Graefrath: Apartheid – ein internationales Verbrechen, *Neue Justiz* 1974, pp. 192 et seq.; Ronald C. Slye: Apartheid as a Crime against Humanity: A submission to the South African Truth and Reconciliation Commission, 20 *Michigan Journal of International Law* (1999), pp. 267 et seq.

759 Article 7(1)(j) of the ICC Statute deals with the crime of apartheid. The term "apartheid" (Afrikaans for "separateness") stands for the policy of racial segregation and discrimination pursued in South Africa after 1948.

760 Apartheid was already described as a crime against humanity in a range of international legal instruments. Article 1(b) of the *Convention on the Non-Applicability of Statutory Limitations to War Crimes and Crimes Against Humanity*[265] explicitly extends crimes against humanity to include "inhuman acts resulting from the policy of apartheid." The *International Convention on the Suppression and Punishment of the Crime of Apartheid* (UN Apartheid Convention)[266] holds that "apartheid is a crime against humanity."[267] The 1991 *Draft Code* included apartheid as an independent crime, and the 1996 *Draft Code* formulated the crime against humanity of institutionalized discrimination.[268] The inclusion of the crime in the ICC Statute grew out of a proposal by South Africa.[269] Because the South African apartheid regime has been abolished, the creation of an independent crime of humanity of apartheid has primarily symbolic significance at present.

761 The material element is delineated in the definition in Article 7(2)(h) of the ICC Statute. It requires "inhumane acts of a character similar to those referred to in paragraph 1, committed in the context of an institutionalized regime of systematic oppression and domination by one racial group over any other racial group or groups." This definition first of all covers all conduct already included as such in Article 7(1)(a)-(i) and (k).[270] In addition, "inhuman acts of a similar character" encompass acts similar in nature and severity to those listed in Article 7(1).[271] This criterion can be interpreted using

---

[265] Adopted by General Assembly Resolution 2391 (XXIII) of 26 November 1968.

[266] Adopted by General Assembly Resolution 3068 (XXVIII) of 30 November 1973. On the history of the UN Apartheid Convention, see, e.g., B. Graefrath, *Neue Justiz* 1974, p. 192.

[267] See Art. I and III of the UN Apartheid Convention. The preamble refers to the fact that the General Assembly had already adopted a series of resolutions condemning apartheid as a crime against humanity.

[268] See 1991 *Draft Code*, Art. 20 and 1996 *Draft Code*, Art. 18(f).

[269] On the history of the negotiations, see H. von Hebel and D. Robinson, in R.S. Lee (ed.), *The International Criminal Court, The Making of the Rome Statute* (1999), p. 79 at p. 102. See also D. Robinson, 93 *American Journal of International Law* (1999), p. 55.

[270] The Elements of Crimes for Art. 7(1)(j) ICC Statute provide: "2. Such act was an act referred to in Article 7, paragraph 1, of the Statute or was an act of a character similar to any of those acts." Given the wording of the Statute ("act *similar* to"), doubt is expressed in C.K. Hall, in O. Triffterer (ed.), *Commentary on the Rome Statute of the International Criminal Court* (1999), Art. 7, marginal no. 116.

[271] Elements of Crimes for Art. 7(1)(j) ICC Statute, fn. 29 provides: "It is understood that 'character' refers to the nature and gravity of the act."

Article II of the UN Apartheid Convention.[272] The following can be considered specific manifestations of the crime of apartheid:

"Any legislative measures and other measures calculated to prevent a racial group or groups from participation in the political, social, economic and cultural life of the country and the deliberate creation of conditions preventing the full development of such a group or groups, in particular by denying to members of a racial group or groups basic human rights and freedoms, including the right to work, the right to form recognized trade unions, the right to education, the right to leave and to return to their country, the right to a nationality, the right to freedom of movement and residence, the right to freedom of opinion and expression, and the right to freedom of peaceful assembly and association,"[273] or "[a]ny measures, including legislative measures, designed to divide the population along racial lines by the creation of separate reserves and ghettos for the members of a racial group or groups, the prohibition of mixed marriages among members of various racial groups, the expropriation of landed property belonging to a racial group or groups or to members thereof."[274]

762

An "institutionalized regime" of systematic[275] oppression and domination of one or more other racial groups exists in particular when oppression and domination are anchored in domestic law.[276] The prime example of this was South African apartheid legislation.[277]

763

The crime of apartheid requires no particular perpetrator qualifications. In contrast to Article 20(1) of the 1991 *Draft Code* ("leader or organizer"),[278] the crime is not designed as one of leadership. However, it is usually political or governmental leaders who will be responsible for perpetrating this crime. The crime of apartheid is closely related to the crime of persecution, but unlike the latter, it does not require behavior to be based specifically on discriminatory grounds.[279]

764

For the mental element, Article 30 of the ICC Statute applies.[280] In addition, the perpetrator must act with the intention (purpose) of maintaining an institutionalized regime

765

---

[272] See C.K. Hall, in O. Triffterer (ed.), *Commentary on the Rome Statute of the International Criminal Court* (1999), Art. 7, marginal no. 116; K. Kittichaisaree, *International Criminal Law* (2001), p. 125: "illustration".

[273] UN Apartheid Convention, Art. II(c).

[274] UN Apartheid Convention, Art. II(d).

[275] The criterion of "systematic" oppression and domination is probably superfluous against the background of the contextual act that is always required, see C.K. Hall, in O. Triffterer (ed.), *Commentary on the Rome Statute of the International Criminal Court* (1999), Art. 7, marginal no. 119: "a double requirement of systematic does not make sense."

[276] For example, 1996 *Draft Code*, commentary on Article 18(f), para. 12 mentions "a series of legislative measures denying individuals who are members of a particular racial . . . group of their human rights or freedoms."

[277] See survey in *Truth and Reconciliation Commission of South Africa Report* (1998), Vol. 1, pp. 448 et seq.

[278] See 1991 *Draft Code*, commentary on Art. 20, para. 3: "The Commission has restricted the scope . . . to leaders or organizers – an approach it has also adopted in relation to other crimes such as aggression.. . . It has thereby sought to make criminally liable only those who are in a position to use the State apparatus for the planning, organization or perpetration of the crime."

[279] In contrast, Art. 18(f) of the 1996 *Draft Code* requires conduct "on racial, ethnic or religious grounds."

[280] On the general requirements for the mental element, see marginal nos. 294 et seq., esp. nos. 304 et seq.

of systematic oppression and domination over one or more other racial groups.[281] This arises from Article 7(2)(h) ICC Statute. In conformity with the definition of "racial discrimination" in the *International Convention on the Elimination of All Forms of Racial Discrimination* of 7 March 1966,[282] the term "racial group" is to be broadly interpreted.[283]

XI. Other Inhumane Acts

766 Article 7(1)(k) of the ICC Statute criminalizes "other inhumane acts of a similar character." Such a catch-all crime is found in all previous relevant instruments.[284] At the negotiations on the ICC Statute, it was agreed that it would continue to be impossible to enumerate all behaviors deserving of punishment as crimes against humanity.[285] The ICC Statute seeks to take account of reservations about the imprecision of a general-clause type of catch-all provision[286] by making the provision more precise than earlier rules.

767 Article 7(1)(k) of the ICC Statute requires that the perpetrator commit "other inhumane acts of a similar character," which cause "great suffering, or serious injury to body or to mental or physical health." Only an act that attains the same degree of severity is "similar" to the other individual crimes. In this spirit, the Elements of Crimes make clear that the necessary conduct must be comparable in "nature and severity" with the other acts listed in Article 7(1).[287] The international criminal Tribunals have taken the same

---

[281] This narrows the zone of criminality, which is explicitly permitted by Art. 30 ICC Statute, see marginal nos. 310 et seq.

[282] 660 *UNTS*, p. 195.

[283] According to Art. 1, the term "racial discrimination" refers to "any distinction, exclusion, restriction or preference based on race, colour, descent, or national or ethnic origin which has the purpose or effect of nullifying or impairing the recognition, enjoyment or exercise, on an equal footing, of human rights and fundamental freedoms in the political, economic, social, cultural or any other field of public life." From this, C.K. Hall, in O. Triffterer (ed.), *Commentary on the Rome Statute of the International Criminal Court* (1999), Art. 7, marginal no. 120 concludes: "that the crime will involve domination by a broad range of groups other than those which would fall within a narrow definition of race . . . ." The same direction is taken in 1996 *Draft Code,* Art. 18(f), which includes: "institutionalized discrimination on racial, ethnic or religious grounds involving the violation of fundamental human rights and freedoms and resulting in seriously disadvantaging a part of the population."

[284] See Nuremberg Charter, Art. 6(c), CCL No. 10, Art. II(1)(c), Tokyo Charter, Art. 5(c), ICTY Statute, Art. 5(i) and ICTR Statute, Art. 3(i).

[285] From this perspective, see 1996 *Draft Code,* commentary on Art. 18(k), para. 17: "[I]t was impossible to establish an exhaustive list of the inhumane acts which might constitute crimes against humanity." On the ICTY Statute, see also *Prosecutor* v. *Kupreškić* et al., ICTY (Trial Chamber), judgment of 14 January 2000, para. 563: "The phrase 'other inhumane acts' was deliberately designed as a residual category, as it was felt to be undesirable for this category to be exhaustively enumerated."

[286] See M. Boot, in O. Triffterer (ed.), *Commentary on the Rome Statute of the International Criminal Court* (1999), Art. 7, marginal no. 87; see also, with reference to Art. 5(i) of the ICTY Statute, *Prosecutor* v. *Kupreškić* et al., ICTY (Trial Chamber), judgment of 14 January 2000, para. 563: "There is a concern that this category lacks precision and is too general to provide a safe yardstick . . . hence, that it is contrary to the principle of the specificity of criminal law. It is thus imperative to establish what is included within this category."

[287] The Elements of Crimes for Art. 7(1)(k) ICC Statute state: "2. Such act was of a character similar to any other act referred to in Article 7, paragraph 1, of the Statute. (fn. 30: It is understood

position, with more recent judgments referring to Article 7(1)(k) of the ICC Statute.[288] According to established case law, a comparison of severity must not be schematic, but must always consider the circumstances of the individual case.[289] Taking this as a starting point, the Yugoslavia Tribunal subsumed under the catch-all clause of the ICTY Statute a range of acts that are now dealt with as independent crimes under Article 7(1) of the ICC Statute, such as forcible transfer of population,[290] enforced prostitution and enforced disappearance of persons.[291] In addition, serious bodily injury is classified as a concrete case to which the clause will be applied.[292] The offense additionally includes undertaking biological, medical or scientific experiments on human beings[293] in peacetime.[294]

For the mental element, Article 30 of the ICC Statute applies.[295] Article 7(1)(k)'s **768** provision that the infliction of pain must be "intentional" is not a deviation from the general requirements for the mental element. The intent requirement (Article 30(2)) is satisfied where the perpetrator, at the time of the act or omission, had the "intention to inflict serious physical or mental suffering or to commit a serious attack upon the human dignity of the victim, or where he knew that his or her act or omission was likely to cause serious physical or mental suffering or a serious attack on human dignity."[296]

---

that 'character' refers to the nature and gravity of the act.)" See also 1996 *Draft Code*, commentary on Art. 18(k), para. 17.

[288] See *Prosecutor v. Kayishema and Ruzindana*, ICTR (Trial Chamber), judgment of 21 May 1999, paras. 149 et seq., 154; *Prosecutor v. Kupreškić* et al., ICTY (Trial Chamber), judgment of 14 January 2000, paras. 562 et seq.; *Prosecutor v. Musema*, ICTR (Trial Chamber), judgment of 27 January 2000, paras. 230 et seq.; *Prosecutor v. Blaškić*, ICTY (Trial Chamber), judgment of 3 March 2000, paras. 239 et seq.; *Prosecutor v. Kordić and Čerkez*, ICTY (Trial Chamber), judgment of 26 February 2001, paras. 269 et seq.; *Prosecutor v. Bagilishema*, ICTR (Trial Chamber), judgment of 7 June 2001, paras. 91 et seq.; *Prosecutor v. Kvočka* et al., ICTY (Trial Chamber), judgment of 2 November 2001, para. 206. From the period before adoption of the ICC Statute, see *Prosecutor v. Tadić*, ICTY (Trial Chamber), judgment of 7 May 1997, para. 729.

[289] See *Prosecutor v. Kayishema and Ruzindana*, ICTR (Trial Chamber), judgment of 21 May 1999, para. 151; *Prosecutor v. Musema*, ICTR (Trial Chamber), judgment of 27 January 2000, para. 233; *Prosecutor v. Blaškić*, ICTY (Trial Chamber), judgment of 3 March 2000, para. 243; *Prosecutor v. Kordić and Čerkez*, ICTY (Trial Chamber), judgment of 26 February 2001, para. 271; *Prosecutor v. Bagilishema*, ICTR (Trial Chamber), judgment of 7 June 2001, para. 92; *Prosecutor v. Kvočka* et al., ICTY (Trial Chamber), judgment of 2 November 2001, para. 206.

[290] *Prosecutor v. Kupreškić* et al., ICTY (Trial Chamber), judgment of 14 January 2000, para. 566; *Prosecutor v. Krstić*, ICTY (Trial Chamber), judgment of 2 August 2001, para. 523.

[291] *Prosecutor v. Kupreškić* et al., ICTY (Trial Chamber), judgment of 14 January 2000, para. 566.

[292] *Prosecutor v. Blaškić*, ICTY (Trial Chamber), judgment of 3 March 2000, para. 239: "serious physical or mental injury."

[293] See US Military Tribunal, Nuremberg, judgment of 20 August 1947 (*Brandt* et al., so-called Medical Trial), in *Trials of War Criminals* II, p. 171 at p. 183; see also M.C. Bassiouni, *Crimes against Humanity*, 2nd edn. (1999), pp. 338 et seq.

[294] On the corresponding conduct in wartime, see marginal nos. 898 et seq.

[295] On the general requirements of the mental element, see marginal nos. 294 et seq., esp. nos. 304 et seq.

[296] *Prosecutor v. Galić*, ICTY (Trial Chamber), judgment of 5 December 2003, para. 154; *Prosecutor v. Vasiljević*, ICTY (Trial Chamber), judgment of 29 November 2002, para. 236; *Prosecutor v. Kayishema and Ruzindana*, ICTR (Trial Chamber), judgment of 21 May 1999, para. 154.

D. Multiplicity of Offenses

769   Conduct that constitutes a crime under Article 7 of the ICC Statute may also satisfy the requirements of genocide or war crimes.[297] The definitions of crimes against humanity and genocide may then be applied simultaneously.[298] In relation to crimes against humanity, genocide is not a *lex specialis*.[299] The same is true if the perpetrator fulfills the requirements of a war crime.[300] The individual crimes contained in both Article 7 and Article 8 of the ICC Statute – killing,[301] torture,[302] rape,[303] and deprivation of liberty[304] – can therefore be applied simultaneously.

770   As with genocide,[305] it is typical of crimes against humanity that a large number of criminal acts are usually present, each of which alone would satisfy the requirements of the definition of the crime. For criminal acts that are connected in substance, time and place, the functional link to the same contextual act creates the presumption that they form a single crime consisting of numerous individual acts.[306]

771   According to the judgments of the international criminal Tribunals, the various offenses that make up a crime against humanity may in principle be applied simultaneously.[307] The legal situation differs only in regard to the crime of persecution: if an individual crime of persecution is committed through the commission of another crime against humanity, such as persecution through killing, torture or deprivation of liberty, the Tribunals have usually found the crime of persecution to be a *lex specialis*.[308]

---

[297] See also marginal no. 528.

[298] See *Prosecutor* v. *Musema*, ICTR (Appeals Chamber), judgment of 16 November 2001, paras. 366 et seq.; see also marginal no. 538.

[299] An analysis of the definitions of crimes shows that the requirements for criminal liability differ significantly. Crimes against humanity require an actual attack on a civilian population, which the definition of genocide does not require. In contrast, for genocide, intent must be proven to destroy a group in whole or in part.

[300] See, e.g., *Prosecutor* v. *Jelisić*, ICTY (Appeals Chamber), judgment of 5 July 2001, para. 82; *Prosecutor* v. *Kupreškić* et al., ICTY (Appeals Chamber), judgment of 23 October 2001, para. 388; *Prosecutor* v. *Kunarac* et al., ICTY (Appeals Chamber), judgment of 12 June 2002, para. 176.

[301] *Prosecutor* v. *Jelisić*, ICTY (Appeals Chamber), judgment of 5 July 2001, para. 82.

[302] *Prosecutor* v. *Kunarac* et al., ICTY (Trial Chamber), judgment of 22 February 2001, para. 556.

[303] *Prosecutor* v. *Kunarac* et al., ICTY (Trial Chamber), judgment of 22 February 2001, para. 556.

[304] *Prosecutor* v. *Kordić and Čerkez*, ICTY (Trial Chamber), judgment of 26 February 2001, para. 824.

[305] See marginal nos. 628 et seq.

[306] See also marginal no. 630.

[307] For "torture through rape," see *Prosecutor* v. *Kunarac* et al., ICTY (Appeals Chamber), judgment of 12 June 2002, para. 179; for "enslavement through rape," *Prosecutor* v. *Kunarac* et al., ICTY (Appeals Chamber), judgment of 12 June 2002, para. 186. See also marginal no. 539.

[308] For killing, see: *Prosecutor* v. *Krstić*, ICTY (Trial Chamber), judgment of 2 August 2001, para. 675; for torture: *Prosecutor* v. *Kvočka* et al., ICTY (Trial Chamber), judgment of 2 November 2001, para. 227; for deprivation of liberty: *Prosecutor* v. *Krnojelac*, ICTY (Trial Chamber), judgment of 15 March 2002, para. 503.

Part Five: War Crimes

Georges Abi-Saab and Rosemary Abi-Saab: Les Crimes de Guerre, in Hervé Ascensio, Emmanuel **772** Decaux and Alain Pellet (eds.), *Droit International Pénal* (2000), pp. 265 et seq.; George H. Aldrich: Violations of the Laws or Customs of War, in Gabrielle Kirk McDonald and Olivia Swaak-Goldman (eds.), *Substantive and Procedural Aspects of International Criminal Law, The Experience of International and National Courts*, Vol. 1 (2000), pp. 95 et seq.; Hans Boddens Hosang, Knut Dörmann, Daniel Frank, Charles Garraway, Hermann von Hebel, Eve La Haye and Didier Pfirter: The Elements of War Crimes, in Roy S. Lee (ed.), *The International Criminal Court, Elements of Crimes and Rules of Procedure and Evidence* (2001), pp. 109 et seq.; Michael Bothe: War Crimes, in Antonio Cassese, Paola Gaeta and John R.W.D. Jones (eds.), *The Rome Statute of the International Criminal Court: A Commentary*, Vol. 1 (2002), pp. 379 et seq.; Michael Bothe: War Crimes in Non-International Armed Conflicts, 24 *Israel Yearbook on Human Rights* (1994), pp. 241 et seq.; Michael Bothe, Karl Josef Partsch and Waldemar A. Solf: *New Rules for Victims of Armed Conflicts* (1982); François Bugnion: Droit de Genève et Droit de La Haye, 83 *International Review of the Red Cross* (2001), pp. 901 et seq.; François Bugnion: Guerre Juste, Guerre D'Aggression et Droit International Humanitaire, 84 *International Review of the Red Cross* (2002), pp. 523 et seq.; Antonio Cassese: On the Current Trends towards Criminal Prosecution and Punishment of Breaches of International Humanitarian Law, 9 *European Journal of International Law* (1998), pp. 2 et seq.; Antonio Cassese: *International Criminal Law* (2003), pp. 47 et seq.; Luigi Condorelli: War Crimes and Internal Conflicts in the Statute of the International Criminal Court, in Mauro Politi and Giuseppe Nesi (eds.), *The Rome Statute of the International Criminal Court, A Challenge to Impunity* (2001), pp. 107 et seq.; Michael Cottier, William J. Fenrick, Patricia Viseur Sellers and Andreas Zimmermann: Commentary on Art. 8 ICC Statute, in Otto Triffterer (ed.), *Commentary on the Rome Statute of the International Criminal Court, Oberservers' Notes, Article by Article* (1999), pp. 181 et seq.; Isabelle Daoust, Robin Coupland and Rikke Ishoey: New wars, new weapons? The obligation of States to assess the legality of means and methods of warfare, 84 *International Review of the Red Cross* (2002), pp. 345 et seq.; Eric David: *Principes de droit des conflits armés*, 3rd edn. (2002); Ingrid Detter: *The Law of War*, 2nd edn. (2000); Knut Dörmann: *Elements of War Crimes under the Rome Statute of the International Criminal Court* (2002); Knut Dörmann: Preparatory Commission for the International Criminal Court: the Elements of War Crimes, 82 *International Review of the Red Cross* (2000), pp. 771 et seq.; Knut Dörmann: Preparatory Commission for the International Criminal Court: the Elements of War Crimes, 83 *International Review of the Red Cross* (2001), pp. 461 et seq.; Knut Dörmann: War Crimes in the Elements of Crimes, in Horst Fischer, Claus Kress and Sascha Rolf Lüder (eds.), *International and National Prosecution of Crimes Under International Law* (2001), pp. 95 et seq.; Louise Doswald-Beck and Sylvain Vité: International Humanitarian Law and Human Rights Law, 75 *International Review of the Red Cross* (1993), pp. 94 et seq.; G.I.A.D. Draper: The relationship between the human rights regime and the law of armed conflict, 1 *Israel Yearbook on Human Rights* (1971), pp. 191 et seq.; John Dugard: Bridging the gap between human rights and humanitarian law: The punishment of offenders, 80 *International Review of the Red Cross* (1998), pp. 445 et seq.; Horst Fischer: Grave Breaches of the 1949 Geneva Conventions, in Gabrielle Kirk McDonald and Olivia Swaak-Goldman (eds.), *Substantive and Procedural Aspects of International Criminal Law, The Experience of International and National Courts*, Vol. 1 (2000), pp. 63 et seq.; Dieter Fleck (ed.): *The Handbook of Humanitarian Law in Armed Conflicts* (1999); Hans-Peter Gasser: Acts of terror, "terrorism" and international humanitarian law, 84 *International Review of the Red Cross* (2002), pp. 547 et seq.; Gerhard von Glahn: *The Occupation of Enemy Territory* (1957); Thomas Graditzky: Individual criminal responsibility for violations of international humanitarian law committed in non-international armed conflicts, 80 *International Review of the Red Cross* (1998), pp. 29 et seq.; Leslie Claude Green: International Regulation of Armed Conflicts, in M. Cherif Bassiouni (ed.), *International Criminal Law*, Vol. 2, 2nd edn. (1999), pp. 355 et seq.; Leslie Claude Green: *The Contemporary Law of Armed Conflict*, 2nd edn. (2000); Christopher Greenwood: Current Issues in the Law of Armed Conflict: Weapons, Targets and International Criminal Liability, 1 *Singapore Journal of International & Comparative Law* (1997), pp. 441 et seq.; Christopher Greenwood: International Humanitarian Law and the Tadic Case, 7 *European Journal of International Law* (1996), pp. 265 et seq.; Christopher Greenwood: The Relationship of Ius ad Bellum and Ius in Bello, 9 *Review of International Studies* (1983), pp. 221 et seq.; Martin Hoch: Krieg und Politik im 21. Jahrhundert, 20 *Aus Politik und Zeitgeschichte* (2001), pp. 17 et seq.; Knut Ipsen: Bewaffneter Konflikt und Neutralität, in Knut Ipsen, *Völkerrecht*, 5th edn. (2004), pp. 1195 et seq.; Chris Jochnick and Roger Normand: The Legitimation of Violence, 35 *Harvard International Law Journal* (1994), pp. 49 et seq.; Kriangsak Kittichaisaree: *International Criminal Law* (2001), pp. 129 et seq.; Claus Kress: War Crimes Committed in Non-International Armed Conflict and the Emerging System of International Criminal Justice, 30 *Israel Yearbook on Human Rights* (2001), pp. 103 et seq.; Edward Kwakwa: *The International Law of Armed Conflict: Personal and Material Fields of Application* (1992); Howard S. Levie: *Terrorism in War – The Law of War Crimes* (1993); Howard S. Levie: The Modern Pattern of War Criminality, in Yoram Dinstein and Mala Tabory (eds.), *War Crimes in International Law* (1996), pp. 123 et seq.; Hilaire McCoubrey and Nigel D. White: *International Law and Armed Conflict* (1992); Myres McDougal and Florentino P. Feliciano: *The International Law of War* (1994); Juan E. Méndez: International Human Rights Law, International Humanitarian Law, and International Criminal Law and Procedure: New Relationships, in Dinah Shelton (ed.), *International Crimes, Peace and Human Rights: The Role of the International Criminal Court* (2000), pp. 65 et seq.; Theodor Meron: International Criminalization of Internal Atrocities, 89 *American Journal of International Law* (1995), pp. 554 et seq.; Theodor Meron: Is International Law Moving towards Criminalization?, 87 *American Journal of International Law* (1993), pp. 424 et seq.; Theodor Meron: *Human Rights and Humanitarian Norms as Customary Law* (1989); Theodor Meron: The Continuing Role of Custom in the Formation of International Humanitarian Law, 90 *American Journal of International Law* (1996), pp. 238 et seq.; Theodor Meron: The Geneva Conventions as Customary Law, 81 *American Journal of International Law* (1987), pp. 348 et seq.; Theodor Meron: The Humanization of Humanitarian Law, 9 *European Journal of International Law* (1998), pp. 18 et seq.; Jean S. Pictet: *Geneva Convention I, Commentary* (1952); Jean S. Pictet: *Geneva Convention II, Commentary* (1960); Jean S. Pictet: *Geneva Convention III, Commentary* (1960); Jean S. Pictet: *Geneva Convention IV, Commentary* (1958); Darryl Robinson and Hermann von Hebel: War Crimes in Internal Conflicts: Article 8 of the ICC Statute, 2 *Yearbook of International Humanitarian Law* (1999), pp. 139 et seq.; Peter Rowe: *Defence: the Legal Implications – Military Law and the Laws of War* (1987); Yves Sandoz: Le demi-siècle des Conventions de Genève, 81 *International Review of the Red Cross* (1999), pp. 241 et seq.; Yves Sandoz: Penal Aspects of International Humanitarian Law, in M. Cherif Bassiouni (ed.), *International Criminal Law*, Vol. 2, 2nd edn. (1999), pp. 393 et seq.; Yves Sandoz, Christophe Swinarski and Bruno Zimmermann: *Commentary on the Additional Protocols of 8 June 1977 to the Geneva Conventions of 12 August 1949* (1987); Marco Sassòli: La première décision de la chambre d'appel, *Revue Général de Droit International Public*, Vol. C (1996), pp. 103 et seq.; Marco Sassòli and Laura M. Olson: The judgment of the ICTY Appeals Chamber on the merits in the Tadic case, 82 *International Review of the Red Cross* (2000), pp. 733 et seq.; William A. Schabas: *An Introduction to the International Criminal Court*, 2nd edn. (2004), pp. 51 et seq.; Gabriella Venturini: War Crimes, in Flavia Lattanzi and William A. Schabas (eds.), *Essays on the Rome Statute of the International Criminal Court*, Vol. 1 (1999), pp. 171 et seq.; Gabriella

Venturini: War Crimes in International Armed Conflicts, in Mauro Politi and Giuseppe Nesi (eds.), *The Rome Statute of the International Criminal Court, A Challenge to Impunity* (2001), pp. 95 et seq.; Michel Veuthey: Non-International Armed Conflict and Guerilla Warfare, in M. Cherif Bassiouni (ed.), *International Criminal Law*, Vol. 2, 2nd edn. (1999), pp. 417 et seq.; Kenneth Watkin: Controlling the Use of Force: A Role for Human Rights Norms in Contemporary Armed Conflict, 98 *American Journal of International Law* (2004), pp. 1 et seq. Further references can be found under the separate crimes of sexual violence (marginal no. 907), deportation of a civilian population (marginal no. 963), use of child soldiers (marginal no. 977), attack involving disproportionate collateral damage (marginal no. 1039), starving a civilian population (marginal no. 1080), use of forbidden weapons (marginal no. 1096) and attacks on humanitarian operations (marginal no. 1139).

A. Introduction

The term "war crimes" is used in various and sometimes contradictory ways. Some see **773** war crimes very generally, as criminal conduct committed in the course of war or other armed conflict. Others apply the term to all violations of international humanitarian law, regardless of whether they are criminal.[1] The term is used to describe crimes under international law committed in connection with armed conflict, even if the individual case is a crime against humanity or genocide.[2] The following discussion is based on a more narrow, legally precise definition: a war crime is a violation of a rule of international humanitarian law that creates direct criminal responsibility under international law.[3] This body of law can also be termed the law of war crimes or the international criminal law of war.[4] The law of war crimes extends not only to international armed conflict, but, as the international criminal law of civil war, to internal armed conflicts as well, if they achieve a certain degree of intensity and duration. The law of war crimes does not cover the initiation of war; here the crime of aggression applies.[5]

I. Historical Development

The definition of war crimes as criminal violations of rules of international humanitarian **774** law illuminates the close connection between the law of war crimes and international hu-

---

[1] *United States Army Military Manual, The Law of Land Warfare* (1956), Section 499, FM 27–10; reprinted in H.S. Levie, *Terrorism in War* (1993), p. 2. See also J.S. Pictet (ed.), *Geneva Convention I, Commentary* (1957), pp. 351 et seq.

[2] The *London International Assembly* recommended using the term in this sense in connection with the Statute of the International Military Tribunal. See Y. Sandoz, in M.C. Bassiouni (ed.), *International Criminal Law*, Vol. 1, 2nd edn. (1999), p. 393 at p. 401. See also, e.g., K.D. Askin, *War Crimes Against Women* (1997), which deals not only with violations of the laws of war, but also with other crimes under international law. The name of the Yugoslavia Tribunal itself – *International Tribunal for the Prosecution of Persons Responsible for Serious Violations of International Humanitarian Law Committed in the Territory of the Former Yugoslavia since 1991* – points in this direction. While this description speaks to the Tribunal's prosecution of violations of humanitarian law – which, as we shall see, points to war crimes – the Tribunal also has jurisdiction to prosecute crimes against humanity and genocide.

[3] See, aptly, G. Abi-Saab and R. Abi-Saab, in H. Ascensio, E. Decaux and A. Pellet (eds.), *Droit International Pénal* (2000), Chapter 21, marginal no. 42.

[4] It should be noted that the international law of war applies not only to war, but to armed conflicts in general; on terminology, see marginal nos. 822 et seq.

[5] See marginal nos. 1148 et seq.

manitarian law. International humanitarian law is rooted in the 19th century and strives to ameliorate the conditions of those affected by acts of war.[6]

1. Laws of War and International Humanitarian Law

775   At the beginning of the 20th century, war was still considered a legitimate means of achieving political, economic and religious goals.[7] Even today, the use of military force is compatible with international law under certain conditions.[8] In wartime, prohibitions that are elementary for human coexistence, such as the prohibition of killing, are suspended; normally, those who take part in combat may not be punished under either international or domestic law.[9] Nevertheless, war is not a legal vacuum. In war and other armed conflict, *jus in bello* must be obeyed as part of international law.[10] This body of law declares certain behaviors impermissible, in order to limit the harmful effects of armed conflicts on participants and non-participants alike.

776   Certain behavior in armed conflict was already forbidden in antiquity. For example, in the Old Testament we find a prohibition on killing prisoners of war, who are to be released from captivity at the end of the war.[11] The siege of a city was permitted only if its population was first given the opportunity to surrender; women and children were not to be killed after the fall of the city, though the men could be.[12] The Odyssey describes how the use of poison arrows could call up the

---

[6] See C. Greenwood, in D. Fleck (ed.), *The Handbook of Humanitarian Law in Armed Conflicts* (1999), no. 102. The term "international humanitarian law" refers only to those international legal rules applicable to armed conflicts that involve humanitarian aspects. Other laws of war that do not pursue this goal (for example, the rules about declarations of war in the *Hague Convention (III) Relative to the Opening of Hostilities* of 1907 (see <http://www.icrc.org/ihl>), are not elements of international humanitarian law.

[7] See, e.g., I. Brownlie, *Principles of Public International Law*, 6th edn. (2003), p. 697.

[8] The right to resort to military force is regulated by so-called *jus ad bellum*. On the development of the prohibition of war, see also L.C. Green, *The Contemporary Law of Armed Conflict*, 2nd edn. (2000), p. 2. On the prohibition of use of force and self-defense in current international law, see I. Brownlie, *Principles of Public International Law*, 6th edn. (2003), pp. 699 et seq.; M.N. Shaw, *International Law*, 5th edn. (2003), pp. 1013 et seq.; On the crime of aggression, see marginal nos. 1148 et seq.

[9] See also K. Ipsen, in D. Fleck (ed.), *The Handbook of Humanitarian Law in Armed Conflicts* (1999), no. 302.

[10] On the relationship between *jus ad bellum* and *jus in bello*, see C. Greenwood, in D. Fleck (ed.), *The Handbook of Humanitarian Law in Armed Conflicts* (1999), nos. 101, 103.

[11] 2 Kings VI: "21. And the king of Israel said unto Elisha, when he saw them, My father, shall I smite them? shall I smite them? 22. And he answered, Thou shalt not smite them: wouldest thou smite those whom thou hast taken captive with thy sword and with thy bow? set bread and water before them, that they may eat and drink, and go to their master. 23. And he prepared great provision for them: and when they had eaten and drunk, he sent them away, and they went to their master. So the bands of Syria came no more into the land of Israel."

[12] 5 Moses XX: "10. When thou comest nigh unto a city to fight against it, then proclaim peace unto it. 11. And it shall be, if it make thee answer of peace, and open unto thee, then it shall be, that all the people that is found therein shall be tributaries unto thee, and they shall serve thee. 12. And if it will make no peace with thee, but will make war against thee, then thou shalt besiege it. 13. And when the LORD thy God hath delivered it into thine hands, thou shalt smite every male thereof with the edge of the sword: 14. But the women, and the little ones, and the cattle, and all that is in the city, even all the spoil thereof, shalt thou take unto thyself; and thou shalt eat the spoil of thine enemies,

gods' fury.[13] In ancient Greece, temples and priests were inviolable, and mercy was to be shown to prisoners. The Roman Empire, too, had rules to moderate the effects of war.[14]

In the course of the Middle Ages, behavioral standards were developed for armed conflict, in **777** part under the influence of the Church. Certain weapons and methods of warfare were outlawed.[15] Thus the Second Lateran Council in 1139 forbade the use of crossbows and bows, finding that they were not compatible with the will of God. The use of poison was condemned by the Church, as it was thought to be connected with witchcraft and black magic. At the same time, the use of poisoned weapons and the poisoning of an opponent's wells were normal methods of medieval warfare. A code of conduct developed within the knighthood that prohibited, for example, killing the wounded or the unarmed. This code of conduct only applied to battles among knights, however; others involved in battle, especially non-Christians, were killed without scruple.[16] Only in the course of the Middle Ages did rules develop for armed conflict that also applied to other military forces.[17]

Rules of conduct in armed conflicts were not limited to European cultures, but could be **778** found throughout the world. Thus in the 7th century, Caliph Abu Bakr ordered that women, children and the elderly be spared in wartime and that homes and fields not be destroyed.[18] Other examples of early laws of war may be found in India,[19] Japan and Africa.[20]

The laws of war developed further during the Age of Enlightenment, following the terrible **779** atrocities of the Thirty Years' War (1618 to 1648). The emergence of state structures also led to a different view of war. While in the past, anyone could wage war and soldiers were bound personally to their respective lords, now the waging of belligerent conflict became a "public" matter; only states were given the right to wage war. Wars were waged against other countries and between armies.[21] But now that attacker and attacked were states, the protection of the individual gained new meaning. In 1762, Jean Jacques Rousseau stated in "The Social Contract": "War then is a relation, not between

---

which the LORD thy God hath given thee. 15. Thus shalt thou do unto all the cities which are very far off from thee, which are not of the cities of these nations."

[13] Homer, *Odyssey* (trans. Samuel Butler), Book I, lines 260–263: "He was then coming from Ephyra, where he had been to beg poison for his arrows from Ilus, son of Mermerus. Ilus feared the ever-living gods and would not give him any . . .."

[14] See L.C. Green, *The Contemporary Law of Armed Conflict*, 2nd edn. (2000), pp. 21 et seq. For additional examples of rules of means and methods of warfare in ancient times, see C. Greenwood, in D. Fleck (ed.), *The Handbook of Humanitarian Law in Armed Conflicts* (1999), no. 107.

[15] See, e.g., on the portrayal of medieval laws of war in Shakespeare's *Henry V.*, T. Meron, 86 *American Journal of International Law* (1992), pp. 1 et seq.

[16] On this and on the cruelty of the orders of knights during the Crusades, see G.I.A.D. Draper, 5 *International Review of the Red Cross* (1965), p. 3 at pp. 10 et seq., and pp. 20 et seq.

[17] L.C. Green, *The Contemporary Law of Armed Conflict*, 2nd edn. (2000), pp. 24 et seq.

[18] C. Greenwood, in D. Fleck (ed.), *The Handbook of Humanitarian Law in Armed Conflicts* (1999), no. 108. On laws of war in Islam, see also H. Mneimneh and K. Makiya, *New York Review of Books*, 17 January 2002, Vol. 1, pp. 18 et seq.

[19] In the *Mahabharata*, a Sanskrit epic recorded between 200 B.C. and 200 A.D. It forbade, for example, the killing of the mentally or physically disabled, women, children and old people; see L.C. Green, *The Contemporary Law of Armed Conflict*, 2nd edn. (2000), p. 21.

[20] On the rules of the various cultures, see C. Greenwood, in D. Fleck (ed.), *The Handbook of Humanitarian Law in Armed Conflicts* (1999), nos. 107 et seq.

[21] L.C. Green, *The Contemporary Law of Armed Conflict*, 2nd edn. (2000), pp. 28 et seq. However, this was not true of armed conflicts fought by European states in their colonies or against non-European states, see M. Hoch, 20 *Aus Politik und Zeitgeschichte* (2001), p. 17 at p. 18.

man and man, but between State and State, and individuals are enemies only acciden-
tally, not as men, nor even as citizens, but as soldiers; not as members of their country,
but as its defenders."[22]

780   As a result, a right to kill soldiers of a hostile state only existed as long as they continued to fight. Afterwards, however, they "become once more merely men, whose life no
one has any right to take."[23] The duty to protect persons not participating in hostilities
was still the basis of international humanitarian law.[24]

781   The laws of war were first codified in military manuals in the 19th century.[25] Of particular significance was the so-called Lieber Code for the armed forces of the United
States of America. In 1863, German-American law professor Franz Lieber (1800-1872),
by order of the American President Abraham Lincoln, prepared guidelines for armed
conflict for the US Army.[26] They were declared to be binding during the American Civil
War.[27] The Lieber Code's 158 articles contained rules of conduct for the American military that, among other things, addressed treatment of prisoners and prohibited attacks
on hospitals and cultural property.

782   On the international level, too, early efforts were made to codify and further develop
the laws of war. Influenced by the terrible suffering of soldiers wounded in the battle of
Solferino between an Austrian and a French-Sardinian army (1859), Henry Dunant of
Switzerland worked to found the International Committee of the Red Cross.[28] In 1864,
the first Geneva Convention was adopted.[29] This agreement forms the cornerstone of
the so-called "law of Geneva," the primary purpose of which is to protect persons not or
no longer taking part in hostilities.

783   The most important rules applicable today under the law of Geneva were established
by the four Geneva Conventions of 1949 and the two Additional Protocols of 1977.
Geneva Convention I protects the sick and wounded in armed forces in wartime[30] and
further developed the Geneva Agreement of 1864, which had been revised in 1906[31] and

---

[22] J.-J. Rousseau, *The Social Contract* (<http://www.constitution.org/jjr/socon_01.htm# 003>),
pp. 12 et seq.

[23] See J.-J. Rousseau, The Social Contract (<http://www.constitution.org/jjr/socon_01.htm#
003>), pp. 13 et seq.: "The object of the war being the destruction of the hostile State, the other side
has a right to kill its defenders, while they are bearing arms; but as soon as they lay them down and
surrender, they cease to be enemies or instruments of the enemy, and become once more merely men,
whose life no one has any right to take."

[24] C. Greenwood, in D. Fleck (ed.), *The Handbook of Humanitarian Law in Armed Conflicts*
(1999), no. 113.

[25] L.C. Green, *The Contemporary Law of Armed Conflict*, 2nd edn. (2000), pp. 29 et seq.

[26] C. Greenwood, in D. Fleck (ed.), *The Handbook of Humanitarian Law in Armed Conflicts*
(1999), no. 116.

[27] *Instructions for the Government of Armies of the United States in the Field*, Prepared by Francis
Lieber, promulgated as General Orders no. 100 by President Lincoln, 24 April 1863, reprinted in D.
Schindler and J. Toman (eds.), *The Laws of Armed Conflicts* (1973), pp. 3 et seq.

[28] See the impressive description of this battle and the suffering of the wounded by H. Dunant, *A
Memory of Solferino* (1947).

[29] *Convention for the Amelioration of the Condition of the Wounded in Armies in the Field*, 22 August 1864, reprinted in D. Schindler and J. Toman (eds.), *The Laws of Armed Conflicts* (1973),
pp. 203 et seq.

[30] *Convention for the Amelioration of the Condition of the Wounded and Sick in Armed Forces in the
Field* (Geneva Convention I) of 12 August 1949, 75 *UNTS* (1949), p. 31.

[31] *Convention for the Amelioration of the Condition of the Wounded and Sick in Armies in the Field*
of 6 July 1906, 11 *LNTS*, p. 440.

1929.[32] Geneva Convention II[33] further developed Hague Convention X[34] (1907); it regulates the protection of the sick and wounded in warfare at sea. *Geneva Convention III* regulates the status and protection of prisoners of war, and goes beyond the 1929 Geneva Convention for the protection of prisoners of war.[35] *Geneva Convention IV* for the first time comprehensively codified the protection of civilians in wartime.[36]

The four Conventions contain some congruent provisions. The introductory article **784** common to all four instruments regulates the Conventions' applicability to international armed conflict. Common Article 3 contains minimum standards for non-international armed conflict, especially civil wars. It is also known as a "convention in miniature."[37] For the first time, it established rules that were also binding for these types of armed conflicts.

The 1977 Additional Protocols to the Geneva Conventions aimed to adapt interna- **785** tional humanitarian law to changing circumstances and new forms of conflict. Additional Protocol I[38] regulates the protection of persons in international armed conflict, which now also includes wars of national liberation in exercise of the right of self-determination of peoples.[39] It includes additional groups within the protective scope of international law and takes account of new developments in warfare. Additional Protocol II[40] expands the provisions of Common Article 3 of the Geneva Conventions of 1949 and establishes comprehensive regulations for non-international armed conflicts.

The so-called law of The Hague emerged alongside the law of Geneva. Intended **786** mainly to protect soldiers, it prohibits means and methods of warfare that are particularly atrocious or dangerous. The starting point for this development was the St. Petersburg Declaration of 1868,[41] in which the parties pledged to refrain from employing certain ammunition that was particularly devastating for soldiers. The preamble of the St. Petersburg Declaration was especially groundbreaking. The parties determined "that the only legitimate object which States should endeavor to accomplish during war is to

---

[32] *Convention for the Amelioration of the Condition of the Wounded and Sick in Armies in the Field* of 27 July 1929, 118 *LNTS*, p. 304.

[33] *Convention for the Amelioration of the Condition of Wounded, Sick and Shipwrecked Members of Armed Forces at Sea* (Geneva Convention II) of 12 August 1949, 75 *UNTS* (1949), p. 85.

[34] *Convention (X) for the Adaptation to Maritime Warfare of the Principles of the Geneva Convention* of 18 October 1907, reprinted in D. Schindler and J. Toman (eds.), *The Laws of Armed Conflicts* (1973), pp. 235 et seq.

[35] *Convention Relative to the Treatment of Prisoners of War* (Geneva Convention III) of 12 August 1949, 75 *UNTS* (1949), p. 135; and *Convention Relative to Treatment of Prisoners of War*, 27 July 1929, 118 *LNTS*, p. 343.

[36] *Convention Relative to the Protection of Civilian Persons in Time of War* (Geneva Convention IV) of 12 August 1949, 75 *UNTS* (1949), p. 287.

[37] See J.S. Pictet (ed.), *Geneva Convention IV, Commentary* (1958), p. 34.

[38] *Protocol Additional to the Geneva Conventions of 12 August 1949, and relating to the Protection of Victims of International Armed Conflicts (Protocol I)*, 8 June 1977, 1125 *UNTS* (1977), p. 3.

[39] Additional Protocol I, Art. 1(4). See K. Ipsen, in K. Ipsen, *Völkerrecht*, 5th edn. (2004), § 66 marginal nos. 15 et seq. On national liberation movements, see A. Cassese, *International Law* (2001), pp. 75 et seq.

[40] *Protocol Additional to the Geneva Conventions of 12 August 1949, and relating to the Protection of Victims of Non-International Armed Conflicts (Protocol II)*, 8. June 1977, 1125 *UNTS* (1977), p. 609.

[41] *Declaration Renouncing the Use, in Times of War, of Explosive Projectiles under 400 Grammes Weight* of 29 November/11 December 1868, reprinted in D. Schindler and J. Toman (eds.), *The Laws of Armed Conflicts* (1973), pp. 95 et seq.

weaken the military forces of the enemy."[42] The St. Petersburg Declaration was followed, at the invitation of Czar Alexander II of Russia, by conferences in Brussels (1874)
and The Hague (1899 and 1907).[43]

787 The most important outcome of these conferences was the Hague Regulations of
1899 and 1907,[44] which adopted comprehensive rules regarding permissible methods of
warfare.[45] The treaty parties recognized that "[t]he right of belligerents to adopt means
of injuring the enemy is not unlimited."[46] This statement stood in contrast to the traditional view that anything was permitted in war that would contribute to victory, and was
thus a decisive step in the development of international humanitarian law.[47] The provisions on means and methods of warfare were subsequently adapted to developments in
warfare,[48] for example in the Gas Protocol of 1925, adopted in response to the devastating effect of the use of poison gas in World War I, which reinforced the already-existing
prohibition on the use of poison gas.[49] The Hague Regulations and the other rules on
means and methods of warfare are termed "the law of The Hague."

788 The law of The Hague was expanded after World War II and adapted to new developments. Of note are the *Convention for the Protection of Cultural Property in the Event of
an Armed Conflict* of 14 May 1954,[50] the *Convention on the Prohibition of the Development, Production and Stockpiling of Bacteriological (Biological) and Toxin Weapons and on
their Destruction*[51] of 10 April 1972, the *Convention on Prohibitions or Restrictions on the
Use of Certain Conventional Weapons which may be Deemed to Be Excessively Injurious or to
have Indiscriminate Effects,*[52] adopted on 10 October 1980, and its four protocols, the
*Convention on the Prohibition of the Use, Stockpiling, Production and Transfer of Anti-Per-
sonnel Mines and on their Destruction,*[53] of 18 September 1997, and the *Convention on
the Prohibition of the Development, Production, Stockpiling and Use of Chemical Weapons
and on their Destruction*[54] of 13 January 1993. The titles of these Conventions themselves provide a sense of the subjects they regulate.

789 The fundamental separation into the law of Geneva and the law of The Hague continues to this day, despite growing substantive similarities and overlaps.[55]

---

[42] See C. Greenwood, in D. Fleck (ed.), *The Handbook of Humanitarian Law in Armed Conflicts*
(1999), no. 119.

[43] L.C. Green, *The Contemporary Law of Armed Conflict,* 2nd edn. (2000), pp. 31 et seq.

[44] Annexed to *Convention (II) with Respect to the Laws and Customs of War on Land* of 29 July
1899, and *Convention (IV) with Respect to the Laws and Customs of War on Land* of 18 October 1907,
see <http://www.icrc.org/ihl>.

[45] See Hague Regulations, Section II, Chapter I.

[46] See Hague Regulations, Art. 22.

[47] Y. Sandoz, in M.C. Bassiouni (ed.), *International Criminal Law,* Vol. 1, 2nd edn. (1999), p. 393
at p. 396.

[48] See also marginal no. 788.

[49] *Protocol for the Prohibition of the Use in War of Asphyxiating, Poisonous or Other Gases, and of
Bacteriological Methods of Warfare* of 17 June 1925, see <http://www.icrc.org/ihl>.

[50] 249 *UNTS* (1955), p. 215.

[51] 1015 *UNTS* (1972), p. 163.

[52] 1342 *UNTS* (1980), p. 137.

[53] 2056 *UNTS* (1999), p. 241.

[54] 1975 *UNTS* (1997), p. 469.

[55] For criticism of this distinction, see K. Ipsen, in K. Ipsen, *Völkerrecht,* 5th edn. (2004), § 63
marginal no. 8 with additional cites.

International humanitarian law has largely attained the character of customary international law.[56] This was established for the law of The Hague by the Nuremberg Tribunal.[57] The customary law status of the provisions of the Geneva Conventions is also beyond question.[58] The most important regulations in international humanitarian law thus apply independently of the treaty obligations of parties taking part in hostilities,[59] so that even if a state were to withdraw from the Geneva Conventions,[60] it would not be freed from its obligations to protect the wounded, prisoners of war, civilians, etc.[61] **790**

In addition, customary international humanitarian law exists that is not codified in the Conventions. This is recognized in the Martens Clause, adopted in the preamble to Hague Convention IV in 1907 and named for Professor Friedrich von Martens, the delegate of Czar Nicholas II.[62] Under its terms, even if an act of war is not expressly forbidden by an international treaty, it is not necessarily permitted. Rather, "civilians and combatants remain under the protection and authority of the principles of international law derived from established custom, from the principles of humanity and from the dictates of public conscience."[63] **791**

In summary, international humanitarian law can be reduced to a few basic principles. Only combatants, especially members of the armed forces, are authorized to undertake belligerent activity.[64] As long as they behave according to the rules of international humanitarian law, they cannot be held accountable by the parties for participating in armed conflict. As a rule, only combatants may be the targets of attack. No one who is not or is no longer participating in armed conflict because of wounding, illness, shipwreck or prisoner of war status is a legitimate target of attack, and such people must be protected.[65] When attacks on legitimate targets cause incidental consequences for protected persons, these must be limited to the extent possible. If an attack would lead to disproportionate **792**

---

[56] On the significance of customary international law for the development of international humanitarian law, see T. Meron, 90 *American Journal of International Law* (1996), pp. 238 et seq.

[57] IMT, judgment of 1 October 1946, in *The Trial of German Major War Criminals. Proceedings of the International Military Tribunal Sitting at Nuremberg, Germany*, Part 22, pp. 449 et seq.

[58] By April 2003, the four Geneva Conventions had been ratified by 190 states. On the validity of the provisions of the Geneva Convention as customary international law, see *Report of the Secretary-General pursuant to Paragraph 2 of Security Council Resolution 808* (1993), UN Doc. S/25704, para. 37: "the core of the customary law applicable in international armed conflict"; C. Greenwood, in D. Fleck (ed.), *The Handbook of Humanitarian Law in Armed Conflicts* (1999), no. 125; T. Meron, 81 *American Journal of International Law* (1987), pp. 348 et seq.

[59] On the question of the customary law status of the Additional Protocols to the Geneva Conventions, see, e.g., C. Greenwood, in A.J.M. Delissen and G.J. Tanja (eds.), *Humanitarian Law of Armed Conflict* (1991), pp. 93 et seq.; see also A. Cassese, 3 *UCLA Pacific Basin Law Journal* (1984), pp. 55 et seq.

[60] Withdrawal from the Convention is possible under Geneva Convention I, Art. 63; Geneva Convention II, Art. 62; Geneva Convention III, Art. 142; Geneva Convention IV, Art. 158.

[61] See T. Meron, 81 *American Journal of International Law* (1987), p. 348 at p. 349.

[62] See C. Greenwood, in D. Fleck (ed.), *The Handbook of Humanitarian Law in Armed Conflicts* (1999), no. 129.

[63] See Additional Protocol I, Art. 1(2), which adopts the Marten's Clause.

[64] See Additional Protocol I, Art. 43(2).

[65] At the same time, these persons may not take part in hostilities, even if they are capable of it. See, e.g., Additional Protocol I, Art. 43(2), under which (only) combatants are entitled to take direct part in hostilities.

incidental consequences, it may not be carried out. When engaging in a legitimate attack, parties must refrain from using means and methods that would cause unnecessary suffering.[66]

793   The central challenge for international humanitarian law is to adapt these basic principles to rapidly-changing situations. The laws of Geneva and The Hague originally applied only to wars between states. Since the end of World War II, however, new forms of conflict have emerged to which the "classic" rules are no longer tailored.[67] In contrast to Rousseau's depiction of the 18th century,[68] states no longer only have states as enemies. Of particular note are civil wars and wars of national liberation, which are carried out essentially among residents of one state on its own territory. This in itself already presents manifold challenges to international humanitarian law. Who should be granted combatant status? Do rebels have a claim to treatment as prisoners of war after their capture? To what extent are non-state troops bound by international humanitarian law? Some answers to these questions were provided by Common Article 3 of the Geneva Conventions, and especially by the 1977 Additional Protocols.[69]

794   But further difficult challenges lie ahead for international humanitarian law: What about attacks by private organizations? Is international humanitarian law applicable there? Can acts of terrorism be war crimes?[70] Or does only domestic law apply, especially domestic criminal law? These questions about international humanitarian law and the law of war crimes have called for answers since well before the events of 11 September 2001.[71]

2. National Criminal Law to Implement International Humanitarian Law

795   The objective of international humanitarian law is to limit the effects of armed conflicts. International humanitarian law is addressed first of all to states, as the classic bearers of international legal rights and obligations.[72] Every state is forbidden to wage war or

---

[66] See K. Kittichaisaree, *International Criminal Law* (2001), p. 129; S. Oeter, in D. Fleck (ed.), *The Handbook of Humanitarian Law in Armed Conflicts* (1999), no. 401.

[67] C. Daase, in J. Hasse, E. Müller and P. Schneider (eds.), *Humanitäres Völkerrecht* (2001), p. 132 at pp. 143 et seq.

[68] See J.-J. Rousseau, *The Social Contract* (trans. G.D.H. Cole, 1762) (<http://www.constitution. org/jjr/socon.htm>): "Finally, each State can have for enemies only other States, and not men; for between things disparate in nature there can be no real relation."

[69] On the question of war crimes committed in non-international conflicts, see marginal nos. 811 et seq.

[70] See L. Martinez, 34 *Rutgers Law Journal* (2002-2003), p. 1 at pp. 41 et seq.

[71] On the questions raised by the terrorist attacks on 11 September 2001, see, e.g., A. Cassese, 12 *European Journal of International Law* (2001), pp. 993 et seq.; R. Dolzer, 28 *The Yale Journal of International Law* (2003), pp. 337 et seq.; H.-P. Gasser, 84 *International Review of the Red Cross* (2002), pp. 547 et seq.; D. Jinks, 28 *Yale Journal of International Law* (2003), pp. 8 et seq.; J. Klabbers, 14 *European Journal of International Law* (2003), pp. 299 et seq.; J.J. Paust, 28 *Yale Journal of International Law* (2003), pp. 325 et seq.; M. Schneider, *Humanitäres Völkerrecht-Informationsschriften* 2001, pp. 222 et seq.; W.H. Taft, 28 *The Yale Journal of International Law* (2003), pp. 319 et seq.; C. Tomuschat, *Europäische Grundrechte-Zeitschrift* 2001, pp. 535 et seq. See also marginal no. 75; for a political science view, see H. Münkler, 85 *International Review of the Red Cross* (2003), pp. 7 et seq.

[72] On the subjects of international law, see I. Brownlie, *Principles of Public International Law*, 6th edn. (2003), pp. 57 et seq.

armed conflict in a manner that violates international humanitarian law. The duty of states is not limited to refraining from violations. They must also ensure that individuals under their control adhere to the provisions of international humanitarian law. Here domestic criminal law can function to deter individuals from violating international humanitarian law and punish those violations that do occur.[73]

At the state level, criminal sanctions on violations of the laws of war have a long history. Many states have adopted codes of military justice and claimed the right to try and punish members of enemy forces, after hostilities ceased, for violations of the laws of war. One example was Article 44 of the American *Lieber Code* of 1863,[74] which forbade murder, rape, bodily injury, robbery and pillaging and punished them with the death penalty. As a rule, the crimes were defined in domestic law,[75] except for some legal systems that took international law as the direct basis for criminal liability,[76] and trials took place before national (military) courts.   **796**

On the international level, too, the significance of criminal sanctions was recognized as a guarantor of international humanitarian law. While early agreements regarding international humanitarian law contained no statements on the criminal status of violations, hints were found in the 1906 Geneva Convention.[77] In Article 28 of the Convention, the parties obligated themselves to adapt their codes of military justice to the requirements of the Convention. Plundering and abuse of the wounded, as well as improper use of the insignia of the Red Cross, were required to be criminalized under   **797**

---

[73] See Y. Sandoz, in M.C. Bassiouni (ed.), *International Criminal Law,* Vol. 1, 2nd edn. (1999), p. 393 at pp. 402 et seq. On other possibilities of guaranteeing adherence to international humanitarian law, see H.-P. Gasser, in H. Fox and M.A. Meyer (eds.), *Armed Conflict and the New Law,* Vol. 2 (1993), pp. 15 et seq., and A. Cassese, 9 *European Journal of International Law* (1998), p. 2 at pp. 3 et seq. The use of criminal law to prevent violations of international humanitarian law is connected with the ever more broadly accepted prohibition on responding to violations of the laws of war with retaliatory action or reprisals, that is, with new violations of international humanitarian law. Where retaliation and reprisals were once seen as legitimate means of enforcing international humanitarian law, this function is now to be taken over by criminal law. See S.E. Nahlik, in A.J.M. Delissen and G.J. Tanja (eds.), *Humanitarian Law of Armed Conflict: Challenges Ahead* (1991), pp. 165 et seq. On the ICTY's opinions, see *Prosecutor* v. *Kupreškić* et al., ICTY (Trial Chamber), judgment of 14 January 2000, paras. 527 et seq., according to which retaliatory measures are impermissible under current customary international law, see paras. 531 et seq. with additional cites. See also marginal no. 479.

[74] See marginal no. 781.

[75] A state can use general definitions of crimes or create special crimes tailored to war crimes law. On the possibilities for implementation with regard to the ICC Statute, see marginal nos. 220 et seq.

[76] See A. D'Amato, in M.C. Bassiouni (ed.), *International Criminal Law,* Vol. 3, 2nd edn. (1999), p. 217 at p. 218. In this case, however, the order to apply the law is part of domestic law. On the applicability of crimes under international law in South African law, see V. Nerlich, *Apartheidkriminalität vor Gericht* (2002), pp. 81 et seq. On the prosecution of war crimes and other international crimes connected with World War II in Canada, Australia and Great Britain, see C.F. Amerasinghe, in M.C. Bassiouni (ed.), *International Criminal Law,* Vol. 3, 2nd edn. (1999), pp. 243 et seq.; G.T. Blewitt, in M.C. Bassiouni (ed.), *International Criminal Law,* Vol. 3, 2nd edn. (1999), pp. 301 et seq.; W. Burchards, *Die Verfolgung völkerrechtlicher Verbrechen durch Drittstaaten: Das kanadische Beispiel* (2005); J. Garwood-Cutler, in M.C. Bassiouni (ed.), *International Criminal Law,* Vol. 3, 2nd edn. (1999), pp. 325 et seq.; L.S. Wexler, in M.C. Bassiouni (ed.), *International Criminal Law,* Vol. 3, 2nd edn. (1999), pp. 273 et seq.

[77] On this development, see J.S. Pictet (ed.), *Geneva Convention I, Commentary* (1957), pp. 352 et seq.

domestic law. The use of criminal law was intended to ensure compliance with the Convention.[78]

798   The significance of criminal law for preventing violations of international humanitarian law became especially clear in the provisions on grave breaches of the Geneva Conventions of 1949.[79] To prevent particularly serious infractions of the Geneva Conventions, known as "grave breaches," the parties agreed to a special enforcement mechanism. They took on a duty to ensure penal sanction of grave breaches of the Conventions under domestic law,[80] to search for suspected perpetrators, and to try those suspected of committing grave breaches or hand them over to another state at its request (*aut dedere aut judicare*).[81] The principle of universal jurisdiction applies to grave breaches of the Geneva Conventions, giving any state the right to punish grave breaches regardless of the location of the crime or the nationality of the perpetrator or victim.[82] Domestic criminal law is thus expected to ensure compliance with international humanitarian law.[83]

799   The parties are also obligated to prevent other violations of the Conventions.[84] Additional Protocol I supplements the grave breaches provisions of the Geneva Conventions.[85]

3. International Criminal Law and International Humanitarian Law

800   Violations of international humanitarian law are also punished at the international

---

[78] See Y. Sandoz, in M.C. Bassiouni (ed.), *International Criminal Law*, Vol. 1, 2nd edn. (1999), p. 393 at p. 397.

[79] On grave breaches, see J.S. Pictet (ed.), *Geneva Convention I, Commentary* (1957), pp. 357 et seq.; H. Fischer, in G. Kirk McDonald and O. Swaak-Goldman (eds.), *Substantive and Procedural Aspects of International Criminal Law*, Vol. 1 (2000), pp. 67 et seq.

[80] See Geneva Convention I, Art. 49(1); Geneva Convention II, Art. 50(1); Geneva Convention III, Art. 129(1); Geneva Convention IV, Art. 146(1). In its *Loi du 16 juin 1993 relative à la répression des infractions graves aux conventions internationales de Genève du 12 août 1949 et aux protocoles I et II du 8 juin 1977, additionnels à ces conventions*, in the version of the *Loi relative à la répression des violations graves de droit international humanitaire, 10 février 1999*, Belgium provided a noteworthy example of the implementation of war crimes law in national law. On the *US War Crimes Act* of 1996, which allows US courts to prosecute grave breaches of the Geneva Conventions if the victims are members of the US armed forces or American citizens, see M.S. Zaid, in M.C. Bassiouni (ed.), *International Criminal Law*, Vol. 3, 2nd edn. (1999), pp. 331 et seq.

[81] See Geneva Convention I, Art. 49(2); Geneva Convention II, Art. 50(2); Geneva Convention III, Art. 129(2); Geneva Convention IV, Art. 146(2), and M.C. Bassiouni and E.M. Wise, *Aut Dedere Aut Judicare* (1995).

[82] G. Abi-Saab and R. Abi-Saab, in H. Ascensio, E. Decaux and A. Pellet (eds.), *Droit International Pénal* (2000), chapter 21 marginal no. 54, start with the assumption that the principle of universal jurisdiction applies to all war crimes, not only grave breaches of the Geneva Conventions and Additional Protocol I. While universal jurisdiction grants states the authority, the principle of *aut dedere aut judicare* obligates them. On universal jurisdiction, see marginal nos. 169 et seq.

[83] Y. Sandoz, in M.C. Bassiouni (ed.), *International Criminal Law*, Vol. 1, 2nd edn. (1999), p. 393 at pp. 415 et seq.

[84] See Geneva Convention I, Art. 49(3); Geneva Convention II, Art. 50(3); Geneva Convention III, Art. 129(3); Geneva Convention IV, Art. 146(3).

[85] See Additional Protocol I, Art. 11(4), Arts. 85 et seq.

level.[86] Article 229(2) of the *Treaty of Versailles* of 28 June 1919[87] already provided for the trial of German war criminals before courts consisting of judges from various allied states, if nationals of more than one state had been the victims of the crimes. However, this early attempt to internationalize criminal prosecution of war crimes was unsuccessful.[88]

After World War II, the victorious powers resolved to try at least the major war criminals from the Axis powers not before domestic courts, but before an international tribunal. In Article 6(b) of the Nuremberg Charter, the basis for the Nuremberg war crimes trials, the International Military Tribunal was granted jurisdiction over "violations of the laws and customs of war"; the Nuremberg and Tokyo Tribunals found a number of defendants guilty of war crimes on the basis of international law. This was a crucial innovation; for the first time, international courts held individuals directly accountable for war crimes under international law.[89]   **801**

After a long hiatus during which violations of international humanitarian law were only punished domestically,[90] this development continued with the creation of the Yugoslavia Tribunal, and shortly thereafter the Rwanda Tribunal. These Courts, too, have punished war crimes as crimes under international law and significantly clarified and developed the law of war crimes.[91] Under Article 8(1) of its Statute, the International Criminal Court has jurisdiction over war crimes. Thus today, the law of war crimes has achieved great significance in the enforcement of international humanitarian law. International criminal law is employed to prevent, or at least to punish, violations of international humanitarian law.[92] Those who violate international humanitarian law in armed conflicts must now expect to be held accountable before not only national but also international courts.[93]   **802**

II. International Humanitarian Law and Criminal Sanctions

International humanitarian law contains a large number of quite technical rules, not every violation of which is criminal. Determining which violations of international hu-   **803**

---

[86] Grotius already recognized the criminal status of violations of the laws of war under international law, see H.-H. Jescheck, *Die Verantwortlichkeit der Staatsorgane nach Völkerstrafrecht* (1952), p. 180. The trial of the knight Peter von Hagenbach in connection with the siege of the city of Breisach in 1474 is often mentioned as an early example of international prosecution of war crimes, see L.C. Green, *The Contemporary Law of Armed Conflict*, 2nd edn. (2000), p. 288; L.S. Sunga, *Individual Responsibility in International Law for Serious Human Rights Violations* (1992), pp. 18 et seq.

[87] 11 *Martens Nouveau Recueil Général des Traités* (ser. 3 (1923)), p. 323.

[88] See marginal no. 9.

[89] See marginal nos. 15 et seq.

[90] Though on the domestic level, too, trials for violations of international humanitarian law were rare, T. Meron, 89 *American Journal of International Law* (1995), p. 554 at pp. 555 et seq.

[91] For details, see marginal nos. 45 et seq.

[92] On the significance of this development for protection of human rights, see J. Dugard, 80 *International Review of the Red Cross* (1998), pp. 445 et seq.

[93] On the repressive and preventive function of international criminal law, see O. Triffterer, in M. Politi and G. Nesi (eds.), *The Statute of the International Criminal Court* (1998), pp. 137 et seq., and marginal nos. 85 et seq.

manitarian law create individual criminal liability is one of the principal challenges facing the law of war crimes.[94]

804   The structure of war crimes norms differs from those of crimes against humanity and
genocide. The latter are established as independent crimes under international law. A
war crime, however, is based on a violation of a rule of international humanitarian law.[95]
A provision of humanitarian law is supplemented by criminal sanction of its violation,
on the basis of an international treaty or customary international law.[96] Criminal sanction is linked to international humanitarian law.

805   But what are the rules of international humanitarian law that are subject to criminal
sanction? No definitive international codification exists of the substantive law of war
crimes. Important progress has now been made, however, in Article 8(2) of the ICC
Statute. This article lists the core crimes of the law of war crimes, which also embody
customary international law.[97] However, Article 8(2) is not exhaustive, and other war
crimes can exist under customary international law.[98] It should be noted that the International Criminal Court does not have jurisdiction over any war crimes that are not included in Article 8(2) of the ICC Statute.[99] The issue to be discussed below is mainly
relevant for the Yugoslavia and Rwanda Tribunals, or for states wishing to implement
war crimes law beyond the provisions of the ICC Statute.

806   In its *Tadić* decision of 2 October 1995, the Yugoslavia Tribunal dealt with the question of how to determine the criminal status, under customary law, of violations of international humanitarian law. The Appeals Chamber had to determine what requirements
needed to be fulfilled in order for a norm of international humanitarian law to be included in Article 3 of the ICTY Statute and for its violation to be prosecuted by the Tribunal. The decision pertained primarily to the Tribunal's jurisdiction, rather than to the
substantive criminality of violations of international humanitarian law, but it allowed in-
ferences to be made about substantive criminal law, since acceptance of jurisdiction over
crimes assumes their existence.

807   The Tribunal formulated the following requirements for jurisdiction:

"(i) the violation must constitute an infringement of a rule of international humanitarian law;
(ii) the rule must be customary in nature or, if it belongs to treaty law, the required conditions
must be met . . . ;
(iii) the violation must be 'serious,' that is to say, it must constitute a breach of a rule protecting
important values, and the breach must involve grave consequences for the victim. Thus, for in-

---

[94] See H.-H. Jescheck, *Die Verantwortlichkeit der Staatsorgane nach Völkerstrafrecht* (1952), p. 181.
See also A. Cassese, *International Criminal Law* (2003), pp. 50 et seq.

[95] An exception is represented by the rules on grave breaches of the Geneva Conventions; the acts
they cover are to be punished by the states. Thus the provisions bear a similarity to definitions of
crimes.

[96] G. Abi-Saab and R. Abi-Saab, in H. Ascensio, E. Decaux and A. Pellet (eds.), *Droit International Pénal* (2000), chapter 21 marginal nos. 44 et seq., speak of legal consequences as secondary
norms whose existence must be proven. At the Nuremberg trial, they say, this did not happen sufficiently, as the IMT limited itself to showing generally that crimes under international law are committed by individuals and must therefore be punished.

[97] See marginal no. 139.

[98] See ICC Statute, Art. 10 and marginal no. 139.

[99] This follows from the wording of the introductory sentence of Article 8(2) of the ICC Statute
("[f]or the purpose of the Statute 'war crimes' means . . .").

stance, the fact of a combatant simply appropriating a loaf of bread in an occupied village would not amount to a 'serious violation of international humanitarian law' although it may be regarded as falling foul of the basic principle laid down in Article 46, paragraph 1, of the Hague Regulations (and the corresponding rule of customary international law) whereby 'private property must be respected' by any army occupying an enemy territory;

(iv) the violation of the rule must entail, under customary or conventional law, the individual criminal responsibility of the person breaching the rule."[100]

Requirement (i) makes clear that the act in question must be inconsistent with international humanitarian law.[101] This expresses more than just a matter of course, for it means that war crimes law always makes reference to international humanitarian law. The substantive law involved is not autonomous law that happens to be based on international humanitarian law, but is accessorial to this body of law.[102] War crimes must thus be interpreted with an eye to the international humanitarian law upon which they are based. Also, as in (ii) in the above cite, all requirements for application of the norm must be met – in particular, where treaty law is concerned, the instrument in question must be binding on the states involved. **808**

Under requirement (iii), only serious violations of international humanitarian law can be war crimes. According to the Appeals Chamber, this derives above all from the ICTY's mandate to try only serious violations of international humanitarian law. But this can be no different for the international law of war in general.[103] The example given by the Appeals Chamber of the theft of a loaf of bread does not affect the interests of the international community, even if committed in an armed conflict. Only significant violations of international humanitarian law are criminal under international law.[104] It is not always easy to determine when this threshold for criminal sanction is reached. The Yugoslavia and Rwanda Tribunals have held that the rule of humanitarian law in question must protect important values, and that its breach must involve grave consequences for the victim.[105] If a person's bodily integrity is seriously violated or his or her life endangered, this must always be assumed to be a significant violation of international humanitarian law, since in such cases the acts are similar in severity to grave breaches of the Geneva Conventions.[106] For harm to property, an act is only criminal under interna- **809**

---

[100] *Prosecutor* v. *Tadić*, ICTY (Appeals Chamber), decision of 2 October 1995, para. 94.

[101] This is already assumed in the term "war crimes" as used here.

[102] This dependency of the law of war crimes is addressed elsewhere in the decision: contrary to the view of the Trial Chamber in *Prosecutor* v. *Tadić*, ICTY (Trial Chamber), decision of 10 August 1995, para. 53, the grave breaches provisions of the Geneva Conventions cannot be applied to non-international armed conflicts, see *Prosecutor* v. *Tadić*, ICTY (Appeals Chamber), decision of 2 October 1995, para. 81.

[103] T. Meron, 9 *European Journal of International Law* (1998), p. 18 at p. 24.

[104] Of course, the state retains the right to criminalize or otherwise sanction even minor violations of international humanitarian law, see G. Abi-Saab and R. Abi-Saab, in H. Ascensio, E. Decaux and A. Pellet (eds.), *Droit International Pénal* (2000), chapter 21 marginal no. 43. However, a state cannot refer to universal jurisdiction in prosecuting these violations.

[105] See *Prosecutor* v. *Tadić*, ICTY (Appeals Chamber), decision of 2 October 1995, para. 94; *Prosecutor* v. *Kunarac* et al., ICTY (Appeals Chamber), judgment of 12 June 2002, para. 66; *Prosecutor* v. *Akayesu*, ICTR (Trial Chamber), judgment of 2 September 1998, para. 616; *Prosecutor* v. *Rutaganda*, ICTR (Trial Chamber), judgment of 6 December 1999, para. 106.

[106] See also *Prosecutor* v. *Aleksovski*, ICTY (Appeals Chamber), judgment of 24 March 2000, para. 37.

tional law if more than insignificant amounts are involved. The decision is more difficult if an act results in no concrete harm or threat to individual rights. It must then be decided case by case, by analyzing the purpose of the norm's protections.

810   Requirement (iv) arises from the character of international humanitarian law as part of the international legal order, which is addressed primarily to states.[107] The breach of a rule of international humanitarian law can only be punished if the rule also creates norms of behavior for individuals.[108] For some rules, such as the grave breaches provisions of the Geneva Conventions, the obligations of individuals are particularly clearly drawn. A number of norms of international humanitarian law, however, are primarily addressed to states. But violations are possible by individuals even in these cases, if they make decisions for the states that are thus obligated. An example is the obligation, contained in Articles 15 and 26 of Geneva Convention III, to provide sufficient food to prisoners of war. This duty applies first of all to the custodial state.[109] But if the state's military leaders order that prisoners of war should not be provided with sufficient food, those responsible violate Article 26 of Geneva Convention III. The decision is made on behalf of the custodial state, and the actors are obligated to adhere to the norms addressed to the state. However, if an individual soldier refuses some rations to prisoners of war without the approval of the state, Article 26 of Geneva Convention III is not violated. In this case, the perpetrator is not acting for the custodial state.[110] Thus the question whether a rule of international humanitarian law imposes duties on individuals frequently can only be decided on a case-by-case basis, taking into account the actor's position and function.

III. War Crimes in Non-International Armed Conflict

811 Civil wars have traditionally been viewed as domestic matters, to which the prohibition on intervention applies. In Article 3 common to all the Geneva Conventions of 1949, international law for the first time created rules for non-international armed conflict. These rules are expanded in Additional Protocol II, but the rules are far less elaborate and comprehensive than in Additional Protocol I, which is applicable in international armed conflict only. Thus it is not surprising that the criminality under international law of violations of international humanitarian law applicable to non-international armed conflict long went unrecognized. As late as March 1993, in a commentary to the ICTY Statute, the International Committee of the Red Cross concluded that the concept of war crimes was limited to international armed conflict.[111]

---

[107] On the criminalization of violations of provisions of international humanitarian law under customary international law, see also A. Cassese, *International Criminal Law* (2003), pp. 50 et seq.

[108] T. Meron, 9 *European Journal of International Law* (1998), p. 18 at p. 24. See also E. David, *Principes de droit des conflits armés*, 3rd edn. (2002), marginal nos. 1.195 et seq.; C. Greenwood, in D. Fleck (ed.), *The Handbook of Humanitarian Law in Armed Conflicts* (1999), no. 133, is of the opinion that all norms of international humanitarian law place duties on individuals.

[109] J.S. Pictet (ed.), *Geneva Convention III, Commentary* (1960), p. 196.

[110] The situation is different if, for example, withholding food seriously harms the health of prisoners of war. This may constitute a grave breach of Geneva Convention III, for which individuals can be held accountable.

[111] Quoted in T. Meron, 89 *American Journal of International Law* (1995), p. 554 at p. 559 with additional citations; see also R. Boed, 13 *Criminal Law Forum* (2003), p 293 at p. 299.

Only in 1994, with the creation of the International Criminal Tribunal for **812** Rwanda,[112] did the international community apply international criminal law to an armed conflict with few international aspects.[113] The genocide was committed against Rwandans by Rwandans in Rwanda. This was irrelevant to the punishment of crimes against humanity or genocide committed during the conflict, since those crimes no longer required a connection to an international armed conflict.[114] But the ICTR Statute also permitted punishment of violations of international humanitarian law, among other things because they are easier to prove, and in order to close legal loopholes.[115] Thus it was decided to grant the ICTR, in Article 4, jurisdiction over violations of Common Article 3 of Geneva Conventions I to IV, as well as Article 4(2) of Additional Protocol II.[116] This marked a decisive step in the direction of international legal sanction of crimes committed in civil wars.

Also groundbreaking was the *Tadić* decision by the ICTY Appeals Chamber on 2 Oc- **813** tober 1995.[117] This decision is highly significant for two reasons. First, the Court determined that a range of provisions of international humanitarian law – such as the prohibition of treacherous killing, attacks on civilian populations, and the use of certain weapons – also extend under customary international law to non-international armed conflicts.[118] The Court referred to corresponding state practice and emphasized protection of the victims.[119] It found that acts that are inhuman and therefore forbidden in international armed conflict cannot be viewed as permissible in civil wars.[120] The Yugoslavia Tribunal has made clear that international humanitarian law reaches farther in non-international armed conflict than the provisions of Common Article 3 of the

---

[112] It was created on the basis of UN Security Council Resolution 955 of 8 November 1994. The ICTY Statute contains no express reference to Article 3 of Geneva Conventions I-IV, although the conflicts it addressed were, in part, of a non-international character. The conflict in former Yugoslavia was considered international by the Security Council, see T. Meron, 89 *American Journal of International Law* (1995), p. 554 at p. 556. On the significance of ICTY jurisprudence, see marginal nos. 813 et seq.

[113] For discussion of the criminalization of crimes in civil wars, see T. Meron, 89 *American Journal of International Law* (1995), pp. 554 et seq. See also R. Abi-Saab, in A.J.M. Delissen and G.J. Tanja (eds.), *Humanitarian Law of Armed Conflict* (1991), pp. 209 et seq.; T. Graditzky, 80 *International Review of the Red Cross* (1998), pp. 29 et seq.

[114] For crimes against humanity, see marginal nos. 637, 641.

[115] T. Meron, 89 *American Journal of International Law* (1995), p. 554 at p. 558.

[116] Not contained in ICTR Statute, Art. 4 is the prohibition against slavery and the slave trade (Additional Protocol II, Art. 4(2)(f)). Instead of the comprehensive legal guarantees for trials in Additional Protocol II, Art. 6, Art. 4(g) of the ICTR Statute adopts the general wording of Art. 3(1)(d) of Geneva Conventions I–IV.

[117] On this decision, see M. Cottier, in I. Erberich et al. (eds.), *Frieden und Recht* (1998), p. 183 at pp. 201 et seq.; W. Heintschel von Heinegg, in A. Zimmermann (ed.), *International Criminal Law, the Current Development of Public International Law* (2003), p. 27 at pp. 35 et seq.; C. Kress, *Europäische Grundrechte-Zeitschrift* 1996, pp. 638 et seq.; T. Meron, 90 *American Journal of International Law* (1996), pp. 238 et seq.; M. Sassòli, *Revue Général de Droit International Public*, Vol. C (1996), pp. 103 et seq.

[118] *Prosecutor* v. *Tadić*, ICTY (Appeals Chamber), decision of 2 October 1995, paras. 120 et seq.

[119] *Prosecutor* v. *Tadić*, ICTY (Appeals Chamber), decision of 2 October 1995, paras. 96 et seq. On protection of victims, see also G. Werle, 109 *Zeitschrift für die gesamte Strafrechtswissenschaft* (1997), p. 808 at p. 818.

[120] *Prosecutor* v. *Tadić*, ICTY (Appeals Chamber), decision of 2 October 1995, para. 119.

Geneva Conventions and Additional Protocol II, even if the overall number of rules continues to be fewer than for international armed conflicts.[121]

814   Second, the Tribunal found that violations of international humanitarian law applicable to non-international armed conflict can be criminal under customary international law.[122] This is logical, since there is no valid reason that the rules applicable to the criminalization of violations in non-international armed conflict should be different from those applicable to international conflict. The Yugoslavia Tribunal found criminal liability in internal armed conflicts based on the seriousness of the violations of international humanitarian law, and referred to the principles of the Nuremberg judgment: crimes under international law are committed by people, not states; only by punishing those responsible can international law prevail.[123] Thus the extension of the international laws of war to internal conflicts corresponds to an extension of the law of war crimes. The Yugoslavia Tribunal referred to state practice: in numerous legal systems, violations of international humanitarian law are punished even if committed in non-international armed conflict.[124] Therefore, the following is true not only for international, but also for non-international armed conflicts: In case of serious violations of international humanitarian law, the perpetrator is criminally liable under customary international law.[125]

815   The ICC Statute follows this development only in part. In Article 8(2)(c), the ICC Statute declares violations of Common Article 3 of the Geneva Conventions to be criminal. In Article 8(2)(e), these rules are supplemented by additional provisions that protect individuals and are based primarily on Additional Protocol II. The result is that, under the ICC Statute and in accordance with customary international law, protection of persons in non-international armed conflict is largely comparable to their protection in international armed conflict.[126] Regarding prohibition of forbidden means and methods of

---

[121] *Prosecutor* v. *Tadić*, ICTY (Appeals Chamber), decision of 2 October 1995, para. 126. In *Prosecutor* v. *Kupreškić* et al., ICTY (Trial Chamber), judgment of 14 January 2000, paras. 521 et seq., paras. 527 et seq., the Tribunal affirmed the customary law extension of certain provisions of international humanitarian law to non-international armed conflicts, and made especially clear that, in the area of international humanitarian law, *opinio juris* is more important than state practice in determining customary international law. See also Excerpt from the Report prepared by the International Committee of the Red Cross for the 28th International Conference of the Red Cross and the Red Crescent, Geneva, December 2003, 86 *International Review of the Red Cross* (2004), p 213 at pp. 228 et seq.

[122] *Prosecutor* v. *Tadić*, ICTY (Appeals Chamber), decision of 2 October 1995, paras. 128 et seq. The ICTR followed the ICTY in regard to the criminality of violations of the international humanitarian law applicable to non-international conflicts, see *Prosecutor* v. *Kanyabashi*, ICTR (Trial Chamber), decision of 18 June 1997, paras. 33 et seq.; *Prosecutor* v. *Akayesu*, ICTR (Trial Chamber), judgment of 2 September 1998, paras. 611 et seq.

[123] *Prosecutor* v. *Tadić*, ICTY (Appeals Chamber), decision of 2 October 1995, para. 128; see also marginal no. 15.

[124] *Prosecutor* v. *Tadić*, ICTY (Appeals Chamber), decision 2 October 1995, paras. 131 et seq.

[125] The criminal status of comparable violations in international conflicts is important evidence of their punishability in non-international conflicts as well.

[126] However, other legal consequences connected with the system of grave breaches should be distinguished from criminality under international law, especially the application of universal jurisdiction and the principle of *aut dedere aut judicare*. With regard to universal jurisdiction, a tendency can be observed to apply it to crimes in civil wars, see T. Meron, 9 *European Journal of International Law* (1998), p. 18 at p. 29; see also marginal no. 174.

warfare, however, the ICC Statute contains no rules and thus lags behind customary international law. Under customary international law, certain means and methods of warfare are often also prohibited in non-international conflicts, and violations of these prohibitions are criminal.[127] The German Code of Crimes against International Law takes account of this situation and, in accordance with customary international law, criminalizes the use of prohibited methods and means of warfare in non-international as well as international conflicts.[128]

In summary, it may be said that violations of international humanitarian law applicable to non-international armed conflict can entail criminal liability under customary international law. However, the scope of criminal conduct in non-international armed conflict is to some extent narrower than in international conflict, because not all rules of international humanitarian law apply to non-international armed conflict. The rules of international humanitarian law that apply to different types of conflict will be discussed under each individual crime. **816**

IV. Protected Interests

The law of war crimes protects fundamental individual rights in armed conflict. This is particularly clear in the grave breaches provisions of the Geneva Conventions. Protected persons are exposed to specific dangers in armed conflict; at least the most important rights, such as dignity, life and bodily integrity, are to remain inviolate.[129] The protection of individual rights is not as apparent in crimes based on the law of The Hague. But here, too, individual legal interests are protected: certain means and methods of warfare are forbidden because they cause unnecessary suffering.[130] **817**

In addition, the law of war crimes protects values that transcend individual rights. Like the other core crimes under international law,[131] the law of war crimes serves to protect world peace. This statement may seem contradictory at first glance; after all, peace has already been violated if war crimes are being committed. Nevertheless, it is the goal of the law of war crimes to limit the disruption of peace and security and to make it easier to restore peace and live together after the conflict ends.[132] **818**

V. Categories of War Crimes

The ICC Statute consolidates war crimes in Article 8. The Statute's organizing principle is the distinction between crimes in international and in non-international armed con- **819**

---

[127] For details, see marginal nos. 1008 et seq., 1097 et seq.

[128] See (German) Code of Crimes Against International Law [*Völkerstrafgesetzbuch, VStGB*], Sections 11 and 12 and the Explanatory Memorandum of the (German) Code of Crimes Against International Law, *BT-Drs.* 14/8524, pp. 32 et seq., which emphasizes that the (German) Code of Crimes Against International Law [*Völkerstrafgesetzbuch, VStGB*] merely adopts customary international law.

[129] O. Triffterer, *Dogmatische Untersuchungen zur Entwicklung des materiellen Völkerstrafrechts seit Nürnberg* (1966), p. 200.

[130] See generally, on the increased significance of individual rights in international humanitarian law, T. Meron, 94 *American Journal of International Law* (2000), pp. 239 et seq.

[131] See marginal nos. 77 et seq.

[132] J.S. Pictet (ed.), *Geneva Convention I, Commentary* (1957), p. 361.

flict. Article 8(2)(a) of the ICC Statute adopts the rules on grave breaches of the Geneva Conventions. Article 8(2)(b), on "other serious violations of the laws and customs" of war, covers all crimes arising from other sources of law and applicable to international armed conflict.[133] Article 8(2)(c) contains the crimes found in Article 3 of Geneva Conventions I to IV, while Article 8(2)(e) encompasses the crimes arising from sources other than the Geneva Conventions and applicable to non-international armed conflict.

820   Overall, the structure of Article 8(2) of the ICC Statute is complicated and to some extent conceals the relationships between the various crimes. In addition, as the laws applicable to international and non-international conflicts increasingly converge, distinguishing by types of conflict has become rather antiquated. It makes more sense to categorize the different crimes from a substantive point of view. Particularly useful would be a distinction between protection of persons and property, on the one hand (essentially the law of Geneva), and forbidden means and methods of warfare on the other (essentially the law of The Hague). Such a content-oriented structure, similar to the one upon which the German Code of Crimes Against International Law is based,[134] will be employed in the following text.[135] This structure results in classification of war crimes against persons (C), war crimes against property and other rights (D), war crimes involving use of prohibited methods of warfare (E), war crimes involving use of prohibited means of warfare (F), and war crimes against humanitarian operations (G).

821   The explanations within each section begin with the provisions of the ICC Statute, almost all of which embody customary international law. Discrepancies between statute law and customary international law will be pinpointed. Distinctions based on the type of conflict will only be made where different rules apply.

B. Overall Requirements

I. Armed Conflict

822   International humanitarian law, and thus also the laws of war, may as a rule[136] be applied only to armed conflict. The ICTY Appeals Chamber, in its judgment of 2 October 1995, defined armed conflict as follows: "[W]e find that an armed conflict exists when-

---

[133] However, the language employed in Art. 8(2)(b) of the ICC Statute sometimes deviates in details from the norms of international humanitarian law on which it is based, see G. Venturini, in F. Lattanzi and W.A. Schabas (eds.), *Essays on the Rome Statute of the International Criminal Court*, Vol. 1 (1999), p. 171 at p. 175. Some of the crimes mentioned in Art. 8 of the ICC Statute have no correspondence in traditional international humanitarian law. Worth note in particular are Art. 8(2)(b)(iii) and Art. 8(2)(e)(iii) of the ICC Statute, which criminalize attacks on humanitarian operations and peacekeeping missions. These provisions are based on the *Convention on the Safety of United Nations and Associated Personnel* of 9 December 1994, 2051 *UNTS* (1999), p. 391, and reflect the need for protection in such operations, which became clear as a result of attacks on humanitarian operations in the 1990s. For detail, see below, marginal nos. 1134 et seq.; Z. Galicki, in H. Ascensio, E. Decaux and A. Pellet (eds.), *Droit International Pénal* (2000), p. 493.

[134] See G. Werle, *Juristenzeitung* 2001, p. 885 at pp. 893 et seq.; G. Werle and F. Jessberger, *Juristenzeitung* 2002, p. 725 at p. 728; G. Werle and V. Nerlich, *Humanitäres Völkerrecht-Informationsschriften* 2002, p. 124 and marginal nos. 234 et seq.

[135] Similarly, A. Cassese, *International Criminal Law* (2003), pp. 54 et seq.

[136] On the exceptions, see marginal nos. 831 et seq.

ever there is a resort to armed force between States or protracted armed violence between governmental authorities and organized armed groups or between such groups within a State."[137]

Therefore, it is necessary to distinguish between armed conflicts waged directly be- **823** tween two states, usually by their armies or other armed forces (hereinafter "inter-state conflicts"), and conflicts within a state between government forces and other armed groups or between such groups (hereinafter "intra-state conflicts"). Intra-state conflicts do not involve two states facing each other (directly) as parties to a conflict. This distinction, as we shall see, is largely, though not entirely, the same as the distinction between international and non-international conflict.[138]

1. Inter-State Conflict

An inter-state armed conflict exists if a state employs armed force directly against the in- **824** ternationally protected territory of another state.[139] The magnitude of the use of force is irrelevant; international humanitarian law, and thus also the law of war crimes, is applicable even to minor skirmishes ("first shot").[140] It is not necessary for the parties to the conflict to see it as, or to call it, a war.[141] A state that employs armed force cannot pre-

---

[137] *Prosecutor* v. *Tadić*, ICTY (Appeals Chamber), decision of 2 October 1995, para. 70. Affirmed in *Prosecutor* v. *Mucić* et al., ICTY (Trial Chamber), judgment of 16 November 1998, para. 183; *Prosecutor* v. *Furundžija*, ICTY (Trial Chamber), judgment of 10 December 1998, para. 59; *Prosecutor* v. *Naletilić and Martinović*, ICTY (Trial Chamber), judgment of 31 March 2003, para. 177.

[138] On terminology, see E. David, *Principes de droit des conflits armés*, 3rd edn. (2002), marginal no. 1.46.

[139] See C. Greenwood, in D. Fleck (ed.), *The Handbook of Humanitarian Law in Armed Conflicts* (1999), no. 202.

[140] See E. David, *Principes de droit des conflits armés*, 3rd edn. (2002), marginal no. 1.51; J.S. Pictet (ed.), *Geneva Convention IV, Commentary* (1958), p. 20; more narrowly, C. Greenwood, in D. Fleck (ed.), *The Handbook of Humanitarian Law in Armed Conflicts* (1999), no. 202.

[141] Originally, the law of war crimes applied only to wars initiated by declarations of war, conditional ultimatums or the opening of hostilities with the intention of bringing about a state of war. See also W. Meng, in R. Bernhardt (ed.), *Encyclopedia of Public International Law*, Vol. IV (2000), p. 1334 at p. 1339. Further, the state of war had to be accepted by the opposing side, see J.S. Pictet (ed.), *Geneva Convention I, Commentary* (1957), p. 28. As late as 1978, the (German) Federal Social Security Court [*Bundessozialgericht*] declared, in connection with classification of the Spanish Civil War, that for a state of war to exist, international law required a war waged between two states or groups of states, characterized as a rule by the breaking off of diplomatic relations, suspension of general peacetime international law, and at least the willingness to use force, see (German) Federal Social Security Court, 47 *BSGE*, p. 263 at p. 265. Limiting the scope of international humanitarian law to war proved problematic after World War II, since states now used military force without first declaring war or allowing all the legal consequences of war to occur; see C. Greenwood, in D. Fleck (ed.), *The Handbook of Humanitarian Law in Armed Conflict* (1999), no. 203, with examples of armed conflicts that were not wars in the international legal sense. The law of war crimes, and especially international humanitarian law, had to take account of this development, as states repeatedly refused to apply international humanitarian law, under the pretext that a conflict was an armed conflict and not a war, since the state waging war did not recognize the hostile government, see J.S. Pictet (ed.), *Geneva Convention I, Commentary* (1957), p. 28. In the Geneva Conventions of 1949, the term "armed conflict" was already employed in Common Article 2, in order to prevent this sort of argument. As soon as an armed conflict is present, the parties to the conflict are bound to adhere to international humanitarian law. In

vent application of international humanitarian law by referring to its use of armed force as a police action.[142] Mere threats of military force or other activities that do not reach the threshold of armed force, in particular economic sanctions, are not considered armed conflict.[143]

2. Intra-State Conflict

825   The scope of international humanitarian law has been extended to intra-state conflicts through Common Article 3 of the Geneva Conventions, and especially through the detailed provisions of Additional Protocol II, as well as the extension of Additional Protocol I to cover wars of national liberation.[144] The law of war crimes can also be applied, as already discussed, to intra-state conflicts.[145] This constitutes a considerable infringement of the sovereignty of the state affected and is only justified if the intra-state conflict is comparable to an inter-state conflict.[146] Article 8(2)(d) and (f) of the ICC Statute attempts to distinguish intra-state armed conflicts from other intra-state conflicts that do not reach the threshold of armed conflict.

826   According to Article 8(2)(d) and (f), sentence 1, of the ICC Statute, "internal disturbances and tensions, such as riots, isolated and sporadic acts of violence or other acts of a similar nature" are not armed conflicts.[147] This statement corresponds to Article 1(2) of Additional Protocol II and functions only as a clarification.[148]

827   Article 8(2)(f), sentence 2, of the ICC Statute further specifies what is to be understood by non-international armed conflict: It requires that the conflict take place "between governmental authorities and organized armed groups or between such groups."[149] This wording arises out of the aforementioned judgment of the Yugoslavia

---

contrast to other legal consequences of war or armed conflict, such as for example the breaking off of diplomatic relations between the parties, the validity of international humanitarian law is not at the disposition of the parties, see K. Ipsen, in K. Ipsen, *Völkerrecht*, 5th edn. (2004), § 65 marginal no. 11. Here it is clear that the provisions of international humanitarian law – including those anchored in treaties – have developed from mutual treaty obligations into general rules of law that are merely officially confirmed in treaties, see J.S. Pictet (ed.), *Geneva Convention I, Commentary* (1957), p. 28. I. Detter, *The Law of War*, 2nd edn. (2000), pp. 17 et seq., suggests adapting the definition of war to these changed circumstances, rather than dodging them with the concept of armed conflict. For the applicability of the provisions of "Hague law," too, the touchstone is no longer a state of war, but the presence of an armed conflict, see C. Greenwood, in D. Fleck (ed.), *The Handbook of Humanitarian Law in Armed Conflicts* (1999), no. 202.

[142] J.S. Pictet (ed.), *Geneva Convention IV, Commentary* (1958), p. 20.

[143] K. Ipsen, in K. Ipsen, *Völkerrecht*, 5th edn. (2004), § 66, marginal no. 5 et seq. On "economic warfare", see K. Zemanek, in R. Bernhardt (ed.), *Encyclopedia of Public International Law*, Vol. II (1995), pp. 38 et seq.

[144] See Additional Protocol I, Art. 1(4), see marginal no. 836.

[145] See marginal nos. 811 et seq.

[146] See also J.S. Pictet (ed.), *Geneva Convention II, Commentary* (1960), p. 33.

[147] See also J.S. Pictet (ed.), *Geneva Convention II, Commentary* (1960), p. 33.

[148] A. Zimmermann, in O. Triffterer (ed.), *Commentary on the Rome Statute of the International Criminal Court* (1999), Art. 8 marginal no. 286. See also S.S. Junod, in Y. Sandoz, C. Swinarski and B. Zimmermann, *Commentary on the Additional Protocols* (1987), marginal no. 4472.

[149] On additional requirements of a "sustained" conflict, see marginal no. 828.

Tribunal[150] and clarifies that the parties participating in the conflict must achieve a certain degree of organization.[151]

The language chosen in the ICC Statute is not as narrow as the definition in Article 1(1) of Additional Protocol II, which demands an accountable military leadership as well as the ability, resulting from the occupation of part of the state territory, to carry out a "sustained" and "concerted" military operation. In particular, the requirement of occupying part of a territory proved too narrow, because this only covered "classic" civil wars, such as the American Civil War (1861-1865), but not modern guerrilla wars.[152] In contrast to Article 1(1) of Additional Protocol II, Article 8(2)(f) of the ICC Statute includes conflicts in which no government forces are involved.[153] **828**

Article 8(2)(f), sentence 2, of the ICC Statute additionally requires that the conflict be "protracted," again conforming to the judgment of the Yugoslavia Tribunal. However, this should not be understood as a purely temporal component. Instead, the fact that the conflict is protracted is often an indicator of its intensity.[154] It must be a more serious conflict that affects the interests of the international community and thus justifies interference with state sovereignty.[155] One-time eruptions of violence do not satisfy these requirements. Article 8(2)(f), sentence 2, of the ICC Statute, if understood in this way, does not alter the threshold of armed conflict as stipulated in Article 8(2)(c) and (f), sentence 1, but only renders the concept of non-international armed conflict more precisely. There are good reasons to assume that non-international armed conflicts under Article 8(2)(c) must also meet the criteria of Article 8(2)(f), sentence 2, allowing for a uniform definition of non-international armed conflict under the ICC Statute.[156] **829**

In summary, it may be said that international humanitarian law, and especially the law of war crimes, can only come into play if an intra-state conflict is comparable to an **830**

---

[150] *Prosecutor* v. *Tadić*, ICTY (Appeals Chamber), decision of 2 October 1995, para. 70.

[151] If, for example, a demonstration is followed by spontaneous battles between police and demonstrators, the "demonstrators," as parties to the conflict, lack the necessary level of organization, and it is not an armed conflict, see S.S. Junod, in Y. Sandoz, C. Swinarski and B. Zimmermann, *Commentary on the Additional Protocols* (1987), marginal no. 4474.

[152] E. David, *Principes de droit des conflits armés*, 3rd edn. (2002), marginal no. 1.75. A. Zimmermann, in O. Triffterer (ed.), *Commentary on the Rome Statute of the International Criminal Court* (1999), Art. 8 marginal no. 338. The ICTR, in contrast, in *Prosecutor* v. *Akayesu*, ICTR (Trial Chamber), judgment of 2 September 1998, para. 619, adhered to the requirement of territorial control.

[153] A. Zimmermann, in O. Triffterer (ed.), *Commentary on the Rome Statute of the International Criminal Court* (1999), Art. 8, marginal nos. 335 et seq. The limitation to conflicts with state participation in Additional Protocol II does not extend to Art. 3 of the Geneva Conventions, so that the wording in the ICC Statute is not a further development, but rather the adoption of the already-existing concept of intra-state armed conflict in the Geneva Conventions, see S.S. Junod, in Y. Sandoz, C. Swinarski and B. Zimmermann (eds.), *Commentary on the Additional Protocols* (1987), marginal no. 4461. See also E. David, *Principes de droit des conflits armés*, 3rd edn. (2002), marginal no. 1.71 et seq.

[154] This is also the sense in which the *Prosecutor* v. *Tadić*, ICTY (Trial Chamber), judgment of 7 May 1997, para. 562, interprets the requirement of a sustained conflict.

[155] The crimes contained in ICC Statute, Art. 8(2)(c) are based on Geneva Conventions I-IV, Art. 3; there, too, an armed conflict requires a minimum level of organization of the parties to the conflict and a degree of intensity, see E. David, *Principes de droit des conflits armés*, 3rd edn. (2002), marginal nos. 1.71 et seq.

[156] Similarly, C. Kress, 30 *Israel Yearbook on Human Rights* (2001), p. 103 at p. 118.

inter-state conflict, due to the organization of the parties and the increased power and amenability to control of the belligerents connected with it, and regardless of whether state troops are involved in the conflict.[157] This also explains the increased intensity that an intra-state conflict must exhibit. While in an inter-state conflict, in which two armies generally face each other, the danger of an escalation with incalculable consequences begins "with the first shot," scattered outbreaks of violence in intra-state conflicts do not endanger world peace.

3. Applicability of the Law of War Crimes Despite No Use of Force

831 In some cases, international humanitarian law, and thus the law of war crimes, are applicable although no use of force has actually occurred. This could be the case, first of all, if a declaration of war is not followed by acts of war.[158] Here international humanitarian law would apply, for example, in regard to treatment of interned members of the hostile state, for this would be a case of declared war under Common Article 2(1) of the Geneva Conventions.[159]

832 Second, according to Article 2(2), the Geneva Conventions apply even if the partial or complete occupation of an enemy state is not met with armed force.[160] In such cases, it is doubtful whether this can even be termed an armed conflict, or whether it does not more accurately fall within the scope of international humanitarian law outside of armed conflict. The latter is suggested by the wording of Common Article 2 of the Geneva Conventions. The Elements of Crimes for the ICC Statute, in contrast, include occupation under the heading of armed conflict.[161] Yet ultimately, this is essentially a terminological question without substantive consequences. As long as the definition of the crime does not require the use of armed force, war crimes can be committed without any prior armed action.[162]

II. International or Non-International Conflict

833 An armed conflict can have a non-international as well as an international character.

---

[157] See J.S. Pictet (ed.), *Geneva Convention III, Commentary* (1960), pp. 36 et seq.

[158] Such a situation existed in World War II in Latin American states, which declared war on the Axis powers but were not involved in actual hostilities, see C. Greenwood, in D. Fleck (ed.), *The Handbook of Humanitarian Law in Armed Conflicts* (1999), no. 202.

[159] See C. Greenwood, in D. Fleck (ed.), *The Handbook of Humanitarian Law in Armed Conflicts* (1999), no. 202.

[160] Geneva Convention I-IV, Art. 2(2). The term "occupation" is understood broadly and also covers cases in which enemy troops enter a foreign state's territory without the intention of staying for a longer period and exercising occupation powers, see J.S. Pictet (ed.), *Geneva Convention IV, Commentary* (1958), p. 60. An area is considered occupied if it is under the actual control of an occupying power. For thorough discussion, see *Prosecutor* v. *Naletilić and Martinović*, ICTY (Trial Chamber), judgment of 31 March 2003, paras. 210 et seq.

[161] See Elements of Crimes for Article 8(2)(a)(i) ICC Statute, num. 34. See also K. Dörmann, E. la Haye and H. von Hebel, in R.S. Lee (ed.), *The International Criminal Court, Elements of Crimes and Rules of Procedure and Evidence* (2001), p. 112 at p. 115.

[162] This is true only for inter-state conflicts, however. In intra-state conflicts, the conflict must always demonstrate the minimum level of intensity.

Classification of the conflict is important because international humanitarian law is applicable in its entirety only to international armed conflicts.[163] In addition, Article 8 of the ICC Statute also distinguishes between crimes in international and non-international armed conflicts.

1. International Character of Inter-State Armed Conflicts

International armed conflicts are primarily conflicts waged between two or more states – **834** that is, inter-state conflicts in the above-mentioned sense.[164] Conflicts also have an international character if international organizations such as the United Nations participate in them, and international humanitarian law is applicable.[165] Essentially, this involves parties fighting on an equal footing and not, as is often the case in non-international conflicts, one state exercising its state power against rebels.[166]

2. Intra-State Armed Conflicts of an International Character

Under certain circumstances, intra-state armed conflicts can take on an international **835** character.

a) Wars of National Liberation
Through Article 1(4) of Additional Protocol I, the concept of international armed con- **836** flict was extended to situations in which "peoples are fighting against colonial domination and alien occupation and against racist regimes in the exercise of their right of self-determination,"[167] despite the fact that only one state is involved in such conflicts. For this reason, it is uncertain whether this concept can be transferred to the ICC Statute, or whether such situations should be viewed as non-international armed conflicts for purposes of international criminal law.[168] The latter would mean that such conflicts would have to be treated as international for purposes of the application of international humanitarian law but as non-international for the law of war crimes. Because the law of war crimes serves to enforce international humanitarian law, this result would make little sense. Thus it is preferable also to consider such situations international armed conflicts for purposes of war crimes law.[169]

---

[163] E. David, *Principes de droit des conflits armés*, 3rd edn. (2002), marginal no. 1.40.

[164] On the concept of the state in international law, see I. Brownlie, *Principles of Public International Law*, 6th edn. (2003), pp. 69 et seq.; A. Cassese, *International Law* (2001), pp. 46 et seq.

[165] For details, see K. Ipsen, in K. Ipsen, *Völkerrecht*, 5th edn. (2004), § 67 marginal no. 5.

[166] S.S. Junod, in Y. Sandoz, C. Swinarski and B. Zimmermann (eds.), *Commentary on the Additional Protocols* (1987), marginal no. 4458.

[167] For details, see B. Zimmermann, in Y. Sandoz, C. Swinarski and B. Zimmermann (eds.), *Commentary on the Additional Protocols* (1987), marginal nos. 66 et seq.

[168] A. Zimmermann, in O. Triffterer (ed.), *Commentary on the Rome Statute of the International Criminal Court* (1999), Art. 8, marginal nos. 249 et seq.

[169] See A. Zimmermann, in O. Triffterer (ed.), *Commentary on the Rome Statute of the International Criminal Court* (1999), Art. 8, marginal no. 250.

b) Other Intra-State Conflicts

837 Finally, we must consider conflicts that may be limited to one state's territory, but in which other states support the belligerent parties, for example with weapons, though without themselves being militarily active. These can only be considered international conflicts if the acts of a party to the civil war may be ascribed to the supporting state. This belligerent would then function essentially as that state's proxy. This raises the question of when the conduct of individuals can be ascribed to a state if the individuals do not act *de jure* as its organs (armed forces, police, etc.), but are only *de facto* related to it.

838   International humanitarian law provides no definitive answer. Article 4(A)(2) of Geneva Convention III grants prisoner of war status even to members of militias, volunteer corps, and organized resistance movements, as long as they are "part of" one of the parties. But this does not resolve the crucial question of when an organization is "part of" one of the parties.[170] The Appeals Chamber of the Yugoslavia Tribunal dealt in detail with the requirements for imputation in its judgment of 15 July 1999. The Court found that the criteria developed by the International Court of Justice in its Nicaragua decision,[171] according to which the state's effective control of the individual conduct is required, were in part too narrow.[172]

839   Instead, the Appeals Chamber made the following distinction: Where the conduct in question was committed by militarily-organized groups, it is enough for the state to have overall control of the group.[173] It is not sufficient for the state to supply the group with equipment and weapons, or to finance it; rather, the Tribunal deemed it necessary for the state to co-ordinate military operations or support the general planning. However, it is not obligatory for the state to order a commander or individual members to commit specific acts that violate international law.[174] If acts are committed by individuals or groups that are not militarily organized, it is, on the other hand, not sufficient for the state to have overall control of the person or group. For such cases to lend the conflict an international character, it is necessary for the state to issue specific instructions regarding the individual conduct or to publicly endorse it after the fact.[175]

840 The Yugoslavia Tribunal thus placed militarily-organized groups on a par with state armed forces, at least in part, so that their conduct may also be imputed to the state in question. The Appeals

---

[170] *Prosecutor* v. *Tadić*, ICTY (Appeals Chamber), judgment of 15 July 1999, para. 93.

[171] *Nicaragua* v. *USA*, ICJ, judgment of 27 June 1986 (Case Concerning Military and Paramilitary Activities in and Against Nicaragua), *ICJ Rep.* 1986, p. 14, para. 115.

[172] *Prosecutor* v. *Tadić*, ICTY (Appeals Chamber), judgment of 15 July 1999, para. 117. In the judgment reviewed by the Appeals Chamber, the Trial Chamber relied essentially on the criteria developed by the ICJ in the Nicaragua decision, *Prosecutor* v. *Tadić*, ICTY (Trial Chamber), judgment of 7 May 1997, paras. 582 et seq. For a critical view of the underlying criteria developed in the Nicaragua decision, see T. Meron, 92 *American Journal of International Law* (1998), pp. 236 et seq.

[173] *Prosecutor* v. *Tadić*, ICTY (Appeals Chamber), judgment of 15 July 1999, para. 137.

[174] *Prosecutor* v. *Tadić*, ICTY (Appeals Chamber), judgment of 15 July 1999, para. 131.

[175] *Prosecutor* v. *Tadić*, ICTY (Appeals Chamber), judgment of 15 July 1999, para. 137. If a state only endorses an act retrospectively, it is doubtful whether this can support the assumption that an armed conflict exists. Especially if the conduct in question is a war crime only in international armed conflict, the perpetrator would be punished retroactively, as the conflict was not of an international nature at the time of the commission of the act.

Chamber justified this with reference to the hierarchical structure that prevails in such groups. Individual group members generally do not act on their own, but rather follow the orders of their leaders. Thus it is enough for a state to exercise overall control over a militarily organized group, even if individual group members act against instructions.[176] If a state enjoys the advantages of a military structure, it must also take responsibility for its consequences.[177] If acts by non-state organizations or even individuals cannot be imputed to a state, there is no international armed conflict (aside from the above-mentioned exception for struggles against colonial domination or racist regimes), not even if the conflict crosses borders.[178]

In summary, it may be said that an armed conflict is international if it involves an inter-   **841**
state conflict, that is, a confrontation between at least two states or a state and an international organization. An intra-state armed conflict is international even if only one state is involved in the conflict, but the conduct of another, non-state party to the conflict must be imputed to a second state, which thus itself becomes a party. Further, conflicts classified as struggles against colonial domination or racist regimes also have an international character.

3. Mixed Armed Conflicts

In the *Tadić* decision of 2 October 1995, the Appeals Chamber of the Yugoslavia Tribu-   **842**
nal determined that several partial conflicts of different natures may take place on a single territory. The characterization of the overall conflict as exclusively international or non-international would lead to inconsistencies and gaps in accountability.[179]

In such constellations, there is no general test for whether an armed conflict exists   **843**
and whether this conflict is international or non-international in nature. Rather, functionally, the act in question must be taken into account, along with the context in which it was committed. It is necessary to consider whether the act was part of an international or a non-international conflict. This depends primarily on the belligerent party to which the perpetrator belonged and the conflict situation as part of which the act was committed. If, for example, conflicts with another state are occurring on the territory of one state, along with conflicts between that state and a non-state organization, it must be determined which party the perpetrator belonged to, and as part of which conflict the act was committed. Only in this way can it be determined whether the act was committed in connection with an international or a non-international conflict and which set of rules of war crimes law applies.

---

[176] *Prosecutor* v. *Tadić*, ICTY (Appeals Chamber), judgment of 15 July 1999, paras. 120 et seq.

[177] *Prosecutor* v. *Tadić*, ICTY (Appeals Chamber), judgment of 15 July 1999, para. 121. The criteria developed by the Appeals Chamber were affirmed in *Prosecutor* v. *Blaškić*, ICTY (Trial Chamber), judgment of 3 March 2000, paras. 95 et seq.; *Prosecutor* v. *Aleksovski*, ICTY (Appeals Chamber), judgment of 24 March 2000, para. 134; and in *Prosecutor* v. *Naletilić and Martinović*, ICTY (Trial Chamber), judgment of 31 March 2003, paras. 181 et seq. It should be noted, however, that in such situations, the conflict remains an inter-state conflict, and thus the threshold for such conflicts must be met, as discussed above (marginal no. 824); but see also J.G. Stewart, 85 *International Review of the Red Cross* (2003), p. 313 at pp. 329 et seq.

[178] C. Greenwood, in D. Fleck (ed.), *The Handbook of Humanitarian Law in Armed Conflicts* (1999), no. 202.

[179] *Prosecutor* v. *Tadić*, ICTY (Appeals Chamber), decision of 2 October 1995, paras. 76 et seq.

III. Applicability of the Law of War Crimes, *Rationae Temporis* and *Loci*

844 In regard to the time and place in which international humanitarian law, and thus also the law of war crimes, can be applied, the Appeals Chamber of the Yugoslavia Tribunal found:

"International humanitarian law applies from the initiation of such armed conflicts and extends beyond the cessation of hostilities until a general conclusion of peace is reached; or, in the case of internal conflicts, a peaceful settlement is achieved. Until that moment, international humanitarian law continues to apply in the whole territory of the warring States or, in the case of internal conflicts, the whole territory under the control of a party, whether or not actual combat takes place there."[180]

845 This means that war crimes need not be committed only at the scene of, and during, actual fighting. Their temporal and geographic scope must be determined depending on the crime and with reference to the pertinent norm of international humanitarian law. By their wording, some war crimes can be committed only in direct relation to the time and place of actual hostilities.

IV. The Nexus Between the Individual Act and the Armed Conflict

846 A war crime is present only if the criminal conduct has a functional relationship ("nexus") to the armed conflict.[181] The Yugoslavia Tribunal found: "It is necessary to conclude that the act, which could well be committed in the absence of a conflict, was perpetrated against the victim(s) concerned because of the conflict at issue."[182]

847   Thus the conduct must be committed because of the conflict. The Yugoslavia Tribunal has clarified this requirement in various decisions, finding that the conduct must be "closely"[183] or "obvious[ly]"[184] related to the armed conflict. The existence of an armed conflict must play a "substantial part in the perpetrator's ability to commit it, his decision to commit it, the manner in which it was committed or the purpose for which it was committed."[185] This can be found without question if the act was committed in the course of fighting or during the takeover of a locality.[186] The nexus is especially apparent

---

[180] *Prosecutor* v. *Tadić*, ICTY (Appeals Chamber), decision of 2 October 1995, para. 70.

[181] *Prosecutor* v. *Mucić* et al., ICTY (Trial Chamber), judgment of 16 November 1998, para. 193. The Elements of Crimes for the definitions in the ICC Statute formulate the respective requirements as follows: "The conduct took place in the context of and was associated with an (international) armed conflict." The question of the context of the act refers primarily to the scope of the international law of war as to time and place (see marginal nos. 844 et seq.), while the second part of the sentence addresses the question that interests us here of the act's nexus to armed conflict, see K. Dörmann, 82 *International Review of the Red Cross* (2000), p. 771 at pp. 779 et seq.

[182] *Prosecutor* v. *Aleksovski*, ICTY (Trial Chamber), judgment of 25 June 1999, para. 45.

[183] *Prosecutor* v. *Tadić*, ICTY (Appeals Chamber), decision of 2 October 1995, para. 70; *Prosecutor* v. *Tadić*, ICTY (Trial Chamber), judgment of 7 May 1997, para. 573.

[184] *Prosecutor* v. *Mucić* et al., ICTY (Trial Chamber), judgment of 16 November 1998, para. 193.

[185] *Prosecutor* v. *Kunarac* et al., ICTY (Appeals Chamber), judgment of 12 June 2002, para. 58; affirmed in *Prosecutor* v. *Vasiljević*, ICTY (Trial Chamber), judgment of 29 November 2002, para. 25.

[186] *Prosecutor* v. *Mucić* et al., ICTY (Trial Chamber), judgment of 16 November 1998, para. 193.

in the case of violations of prohibitions on means and methods of warfare; here the perpetrators frequently could not have committed the act in this way in peacetime.[187] It is not necessary that the parties to the conflict have ordered the conduct or even tolerated it.[188] Nor is it relevant whether the perpetrator committed the act to achieve the goals of a party to the conflict or was pursuing personal goals: the functional relationship to the armed conflict must be objectively determined.[189]

1. Perpetrator's Position

The functional relationship between the act and the armed conflict can arise from the perpetrator's relationship to a belligerent party. In a judgment of 2 September 1998, the Rwanda Tribunal stated: **848**

"Hence, the Prosecutor will have to demonstrate to the Chamber and prove that Akayesu was either a member of the armed forces under the military command of either of the belligerent parties, or that he was legitimately mandated and expected, as a public official or agent or person otherwise holding public authority or de facto representing the Government, to support or fulfill the war efforts. Indeed, the Chamber recalls that Article 4 of the Statute also applies to civilians."[190]

The Appeals Chamber of the Rwanda Tribunal clarified that the position of the perpetrator in relation to the belligerent party was not a separate condition for war crimes, but was indicative of the nexus between the crime and the armed conflict.[191] A connection to an armed conflict thus exists if the act can be imputed to a party to the conflict, for that party is the primary addressee of international humanitarian law. At the least, acts of members of its armed forces must be imputed to it. This was already evidenced by Article 3, sentence 2, of Hague Convention IV (1907). The same is true of members of militias and volunteer corps.[192] Here, existing rules of international humanitarian law may be employed. **849**

In line with the jurisprudence of the Rwanda Tribunal, the rules of international humanitarian law can also be applied to persons who may not belong to the armed forces of a party to the conflict, but who undertake important wartime tasks for it. Under Article 29 of Geneva Convention IV, the parties to a conflict are responsible for the conduct of their "agents." As used in this provision, "agents" refers not only to members of the armed forces and similar organizations, but also to officials, judges and other persons act- **850**

---

[187] See H. Fischer, in G. Kirk McDonald and O. Swaak-Goldman (eds.), *Substantive and Procedural Aspects of International Criminal Law*, Vol. 1 (2000), p. 67 at pp. 81 et seq.

[188] *Prosecutor* v. *Tadić*, ICTY (Trial Chamber), judgment of 7 May 1997, para. 573.

[189] The Elements of Crimes make clear that the perpetrator's intent need only relate to the existence of an armed conflict, see K. Dörmann, E. La Haye and H. von Hebel, in R.S. Lee (ed.), *The International Criminal Court, Elements of Crimes and Rules of Procedure and Evidence* (2001), pp. 121 et seq.

[190] *Prosecutor* v. *Akayesu*, ICTR (Trial Chamber), judgment of 2 September 1998, para. 640; see also *Prosecutor* v. *Kayishema and Ruzindana*, ICTR (Trial Chamber), judgment of 21 May 1999, paras. 174 et seq.

[191] *Prosecutor* v. *Akayesu*, ICTR (Appeals Chamber), judgment of 1 June 2001, para. 444; see also R. Boed, 13 *Criminal Law Forum* (2003), p. 293 at pp. 311 et seq.

[192] See marginal no. 838.

ing on behalf of the state.[193] If they commit acts within the scope of their duties that meet the definitions of war crimes, the link between their acts and the armed conflict can be affirmed, regardless of whether the acts reflect the official policies of a party to the conflict or are directly linked to the place or time of the actual fighting.[194]

2. Conduct of Private Persons

851 The perpetrator's position is not the only circumstance that can establish a functional relationship between the act and the armed conflict. It has been recognized at least since World War II that civilians can also commit war crimes.[195] A functional relationship exists, for example, if an act is ordered or tolerated by a party to the conflict,[196] for this indicates that the parties to the conflict have made such conduct a part of their policy.[197]

852 Since World War II, however, persons have also been convicted of crimes that were neither ordered nor tolerated by parties to the conflict.[198] Here the connection between the act and the conflict cannot be explained by imputation of the act to a belligerent party. It is not enough that the parties to the conflict did nothing to prevent the act.[199] Such an omission does not allow imputation of the perpetrator's conduct to the party.[200] However, it must be considered that a range of provisions in international humanitarian law directly bind individuals. Therefore, even without imputing the act to a party to the conflict, in certain cases a functional relationship can be found between the act and the conflict.[201]

---

[193] See J.S. Pictet (ed.), *Geneva Convention IV, Commentary* (1958), pp. 211 et seq. This includes both state organs and persons entrusted with the exercise of public functions without being organs of the state.

[194] In this way, war crimes also differ from crimes against humanity, which require a widespread and systematic attack. The principles developed by the ICTY for determining the link between the individual act and the overall crime for crimes against humanity (see marginal nos. 646 et seq.) thus cannot be carried over to war crimes. The fact that a war crime need not be in conformity with the official policies of the party to the conflict is also indicated by Art. 8(1) of the ICC Statute, which grants the International Criminal Court jurisdiction over prosecution of war crimes even if they are not "part of a plan or policy."

[195] See H.S. Levie, *Terrorism in War* (1993), pp. 433 et seq.; see also K. Kittichaisaree, *International Criminal Law* (2001), p. 133; see also *Prosecutor v. Akayesu*, ICTR (Appeals Chamber), judgment of 1 June 2001 , paras. 425 et seq. Here the Tribunal made it clear that war crimes may also be committed by private persons.

[196] J.S. Pictet (ed.), *Geneva Convention IV, Commentary* (1958), p. 212. See generally, on states' responsibility for the behavior of private persons, K. Zemanek, in R. Bernhardt (ed.), *Encyclopedia of Public International Law*, Vol. IV (2000), p. 219 at pp. 224 et seq.; G. Sperduti, in R. Bernhardt (ed.), *Encyclopedia of Public International Law*, Vol. IV (2000), p. 216.

[197] *Prosecutor v. Tadić*, ICTY (Trial Chamber), judgment of 7 May 1997, paras. 574 et seq. As a rule, perpetrators in such cases are agents as defined in Geneva Convention IV, Art. 29, so that the connection between the act and the armed conflict already arises from this.

[198] See especially British Military Court, Essen, judgment of 22 December 1945 (*Heyer* et al., so-called Essen Lynching Trial), in United Nations War Crimes Commission, *Law Reports of Trials of War Criminals* I, pp. 88 et seq. In this trial, three civilians who killed Allied prisoners of war without being ordered to do so were convicted of war crimes.

[199] See J.S. Pictet (ed.), *Geneva Convention IV, Commentary* (1958), p. 213.

[200] See K. Ipsen, in K. Ipsen, *Völkerrecht*, 5th edn. (2004), § 40 marginal no. 33.

[201] *Prosecutor v. Kayishema and Ruzindana*, ICTR (Trial Chamber), judgment of 21 May 1999, para. 188, held that the nexus must be established factually on a case-by-case basis. For the view that

3. Perpetrator's Motivation

There is no agreement on the rule to apply if the perpetrator acts out of purely personal   **853**
motives that would eclipse the connection to the armed conflict.[202] This question arises,
for example, if a guard kills a prisoner of war out of jealousy. Here, too, the crucial issue
is the functional relationship between the act and the armed conflict: the specific danger
to which a prisoner of war is exposed comes into play even if the guard has personal reasons for harming the prisoner.[203] The purpose of war crimes law is to protect persons
from the specific dangers arising out of situations of armed conflict.

V. Mental Element

854

For the mental element of war crimes, Article 30 of the ICC Statute applies. Thus it is
required that the material elements of the crimes are committed with intent and knowledge, unless otherwise provided.[204]

1. Perpetrator's Awareness of the Conflict

The Elements of Crimes on the requirements for war crimes make clear that the perpe-   **855**
trator must be aware of the actual circumstances from which the existence of an armed
conflict can be deduced. However, no legal evaluation of these circumstances by the perpetrator is necessary.[205] The existence of an armed conflict is not only an objective condition for criminality and a requirement for the jurisdiction of the International
Criminal Court, it must also be reflected in the perpetrator's mind.[206]

In contrast, it is not necessary for the perpetrator to be aware of the circumstances   **856**
that determine the international or non-international character of an armed conflict, or
for him or her to be able to classify the conflict correctly from a legal point of view.[207]
This is especially significant in cases in which the international character of a conflict
arises from the support given to a party to the conflict by a third state, which may not be
obvious.

---

international humanitarian law is binding on individuals, see, e.g., Geneva Convention II, Art. 18(2),
sentence 2; see also E. David, *Principes de droit des conflits armés*, 3rd edn. (2002), marginal nos. 1.195,
and 4.65. R. Boed, 13 *Criminal Law Forum* (2003), p. 293 at p. 318.

[202] See K. Dörmann, in H. Fischer, C. Kress and S.R. Lüder (eds.) *International and National
Prosecution of Crimes Under International Law* (2001), p. 95 at p. 103; H. Fischer, in G. Kirk
McDonald and O. Swaak-Goldman (eds.), *Substantive and Procedural Aspects of International Criminal
Law*, Vol. 1 (2000), p. 67 at p. 82.

[203] For a different view, see K. Dörmann, 82 *International Review of the Red Cross* (2000), p. 771
at p. 780.

[204] See marginal nos. 294, esp. marginal nos. 304 et seq.

[205] See Elements of Crimes for Article 8 ICC Statute, Introduction.

[206] K. Dörmann, 82 *International Review of the Red Cross* (2000), p. 771 at pp. 779 et seq. The
ICTY interprets the presence of an armed conflict as a condition for its jurisdiction rather than as an
element of the crime to which the perpetrator's intent must relate; see, e.g., the wording in *Prosecutor
v. Tadić*, ICTY (Trial Chamber), judgment of 7 May 1997, para. 572.

[207] See K. Dörmann, E. La Haye and H. von Hebel, in R.S. Lee (ed.), *The International Criminal
Court, Elements of Crimes and Rules of Procedure and Evidence* (2001), p. 112 at p. 122; and marginal
no. 309.

2. Wilfulness in the Law of War Crimes

857   A range of provisions of international humanitarian law use the term wilfulness to characterize the mental element;[208] the ICC Statute adopted this wording in some of its provisions.[209] Wilfulness is interpreted broadly in international humanitarian law, and also includes cases of recklessness.[210] This interpretation is essentially authoritative in the law of war crimes as well. If the definition of a war crime requires wilfulness, recklessness generally suffices. This has been recognized by the *ad hoc* Tribunals for the war crime of killing, in particular.[211]

858   However, a schematic approach is unworkable. For a range of war crimes, the structure and wording of the definitions show recklessness to be insufficient. This is especially true of crimes that involve direct attacks on nonmilitary targets.[212] Although here the underlying provisions of international humanitarian law use the term wilfulness,[213] purposeful action is generally required.[214] On the other hand, even if the term wilfulness is not used in ICC provisions, recklessness may suffice if this derives from the underlying norm of international humanitarian law. An example is the killing or wounding of defenseless persons under Article 8(2)(b)(vi) of the ICC Statute.[215]

C. War Crimes Against Persons

I. Victims of War Crimes Against Persons

859   International law permits killing or wounding in military conflicts, as long as the rules of international humanitarian law are complied with. Thus definitions of crimes under international law must establish the requirements under which killing and wounding are forbidden and criminal. This determination occurs primarily by establishing the persons to be protected from harmful conduct.

---

[208] See Geneva Convention III, Art. 130: "wilful killing," "wilfully causing great suffering or serious injury to body or health," "wilfully depriving a prisoner of war of the rights of fair and regular trial"; Additional Protocol I, Art. 11(4): "any wilful act or omission which seriously endangers the physical or mental health or integrity of any person"; Additional Protocol I, Art. 85(3), (4): "the following shall be regarded as grave breaches of this Protocol, when committed wilfully".

[209] See ICC Statute, Art. 8(2)(a)(i), (iii), (vi).

[210] See Y. Sandoz, C. Swinarski and B. Zimmermann (eds.), *Commentary on the Additional Protocols* (1987), marginal no. 3474. For details, see marginal nos. 320, 330 et seq.

[211] See marginal no. 878. The Trial Chamber of the Yugoslavia Tribunal decided in the *Blaškić* case that recklessness was sufficient for all crimes based on the grave breaches provisions of the Geneva Conventions and their Common Article 3, see *Prosecutor* v. *Blaškić*, ICTY (Trial Chamber), judgment of 3 March 2000, paras. 151, 182. Thus it was irrelevant whether the term wilfulness was used in the definition of a crime. Further judgments by the Yugoslavia Tribunal have affirmed this position, but it has also met with skepticism, see *Prosecutor* v. *Kordić and Čerkez*, ICTY (Trial Chamber), judgment of 26 February 2001, para. 260; *Prosecutor* v. *Vasiljević*, ICTY (Trial Chamber), judgment of 29 November 2002, para. 194.

[212] See marginal nos. 1018, 1026, 1028, 1034.

[213] See Additional Protocol I, Introduction, Art. 85(3).

[214] For detail, see marginal no. 1018.

[215] See marginal no. 882.

1. Persons Protected in the Geneva Conventions

War crimes based in the law of Geneva, that is, the four Geneva Conventions and the **860** Additional Protocols, can generally be committed only against persons who are not, or are no longer, participating in hostilities.

a) Protected Persons in International Conflicts

In the area of international armed conflict, the Geneva Conventions uniformly use the **861** term "protected persons" to describe those persons particularly in need of protection, who can therefore become victims of "grave breaches" of the Conventions. Who counts as a protected person in the individual case, however, is not uniform for all the Conventions, but depends separately on the respective purpose of each Convention.[216]

The rules of Geneva Conventions I to III protect the sick, wounded and shipwrecked **862** soldiers and prisoners of war. Only those who are, first of all, members of the armed forces or otherwise permitted to take part in military action, and second of all, especially in need of protection, can be protected persons within the meaning of these Conventions.

Armed forces are "units and associations created through a legal or actual act of orga- **863** nization that are militarily structured, armed and are characterized by a distinctive sign (e.g., uniforms, armbands or other clearly visible distinctive marks)."[217] Members of militias and volunteer corps are also allowed to participate in hostilities, as long as they fulfill certain requirements that render them comparable to normal armed forces, as are civilians who take up arms spontaneously and without the time to organize in order to face an advancing enemy (so-called *levée en masse*). Persons who accompany the armed forces without belonging to them,[218] and are therefore not permitted to take part in hostilities,[219] as well as medical personnel, chaplains and members of aid organizations,[220] are also to some extent considered protected persons under Geneva Conventions I to III.

Additional requirements must also be satisfied, depending on the Convention, to jus- **864** tify a need for special protection. To be counted as a protected person for purposes of each Convention, the person must be wounded or sick (Geneva Conventions I and II, Article 13) or shipwrecked (Geneva Convention II, Article 13), or must have fallen into the hands of the enemy (Geneva Convention III, Article 4A).[221] Geneva Convention III also grants prisoner of war (and thus protected) status to (former) members of the armed forces who have been interned in occupied or neutral countries.

Geneva Convention IV protects persons who find themselves in the hands of a hostile **865** party to the conflict (Geneva Convention IV, Article 4(1)). This requirement should be understood broadly. Even persons who have never had contact with the opposing party

---

[216] See especially Geneva Convention I, Art. 13; Geneva Convention II, Art. 13; Geneva Convention III, Art. 4; Geneva Convention IV, Art. 13.

[217] See K. Ipsen, in K. Ipsen, *Völkerrecht*, 5th edn. (2004), § 68 marginal no. 34.

[218] See Geneva Convention I and II, Art. 13(4), (5); Geneva Convention III, Art. 4(4), (5).

[219] Under Additional Protocol I, Art. 43(2), all members of the armed forces, with the exception of medical personnel and chaplains, are authorized to take part in hostilities.

[220] See Geneva Convention I, Arts. 24–26.

[221] The wounded, sick and shipwrecked are to be protected even if they are not yet in the hands of the opposing party, see J.S. Pictet (ed.), *Geneva Convention I, Commentary* (1957), p. 135.

to the conflict may find themselves in that party's hands if they are located in territory it controls.[222]

866   Not protected by Geneva Convention IV, on the other hand, are people already counted as protected persons under one of the other three Geneva Conventions. It is irrelevant to protection under Geneva Convention IV whether the person took part in hostilities. Even so-called "unlawful combatants" – that is, persons who take up arms without being permitted to do so under the laws of war – are protected by Geneva Convention IV.[223] However, their protection is modified. As long as they participate in hostilities, they may be the target of attack, though with account taken of the rule that civilians are to be protected and losses among the civilian population kept as low as possible.[224] Should they fall into the hands of the hostile party, they have no claim to treatment as prisoners of war. In particular, they can be held accountable for participating in armed conflict. However, they do not lose their status as protected persons under Geneva Convention IV, and in particular retain the right to a fair trial.[225]

867   Caution is advisable in applying Article 8(2)(a) of the ICC Statute. The provision lists all the grave breaches covered in the Geneva Conventions and states in its chapeau that these acts constitute war crimes if committed against protected persons. This terminology is liable to misunderstanding. Not all of the acts listed in Article 8(2)(a)(i) to (viii) of the ICC Statute are grave breaches of all of the four Conventions. Thus, for example, unlawful confinement and taking of hostages[226] are only grave breaches under Geneva Convention IV. It is necessary that the particular Convention that protects the victim classify the act as a grave breach.[227]

868   The rules on protected persons are clearly geared towards inter-state conflicts; for civilians, nationality generally determines whether a person belongs to one of the parties to the conflict. The Balkan conflict from 1992 to 1994 was yet another example of the way

---

[222] *Prosecutor* v. *Tadić*, ICTY (Trial Chamber), judgment of 7 May 1997, para. 579; *Prosecutor* v. *Mucić* et al., ICTY (Trial Chamber), judgment of 16 November 1998, para. 246; *Prosecutor* v. *Naletilić and Martinović*, ICTY (Trial Chamber), judgment of 31 March 2003, para. 203; J.S. Pictet (ed.), *Geneva Convention IV, Commentary* (1958), p. 47. See also H. Fischer, in G. Kirk McDonald and O. Swaak-Goldman (eds.), *Substantive and Procedural Aspects of International Criminal Law*, Vol. 1 (2000), p. 67 at pp. 86 et seq.

[223] See K. Dörmann, 85 *International Review of the Red Cross* (2003), pp. 45 et seq.; J.S. Pictet (ed.), *Geneva Convention IV, Commentary* (1958), pp. 50 et seq.; C. Pilloud and J.S. Pictet, in Y. Sandoz, C. Swinarski and B. Zimmermann (eds.), *Commentary on the Additional Protocols* (1987), marginal no. 2909. On the protected status of persons detained in connection with the Afghanistan conflict since 2001, see Y. Naqvi, 84 *International Review of the Red Cross* (2002), pp. 571 et seq.; on the protected status of journalists in armed conflict, see A. Balguy-Gallois, 86 *International Review of the Red Cross* (2004), pp. 37 et seq.

[224] See H.-P. Gasser, in D. Fleck (ed.), *The Handbook of Humanitarian Law in Armed Conflicts* (1999), no. 501.

[225] See H.-P. Gasser, in D. Fleck (ed.), *The Handbook of Humanitarian Law in Armed Conflicts* (1999), no. 501. This arises conversely from Geneva Convention IV, Art. 5 and Additional Protocol I, Art. 45(3), which also provides that persons not protected by Geneva Convention IV have at least a claim to minimum protection under Additional Protocol I, Art. 75.

[226] See ICC Statute, Art. 8(2)(a)(vii) and (viii).

[227] Similarly, W.J. Fenrick, in O. Triffterer (ed.), *Commentary on the Rome Statute of the International Criminal Court* (1999), Art. 8, marginal no. 7. Like ICC Statute, Art. 8(2)(a), the Elements of Crimes also fail to clarify the differing levels of protection.

in which the nationality criterion becomes unworkable in conflicts among ethnic groups. Thus the Appeals Chamber of the Yugoslavia Tribunal rightly held early on, in its decision of 2 October 1995, that looking solely at the nationality of the victim would deny Bosnian Serbs the status of protected persons under Geneva Convention IV vis-à-vis the Bosnian government, because they are Bosnian nationals.[228]

In a judgment of 15 July 1999, the Tribunal explained that this result does not correspond to the reality of modern armed conflict, and that another criterion must be found to determine the class of protected persons: **869**

"While previously wars were primarily between well-established States, in modern inter-ethnic armed conflicts such as that in the former Yugoslavia, new States are often created during the conflict and ethnicity rather than nationality may become the grounds for allegiance. Or, put another way, ethnicity may become determinative of national allegiance. Under these conditions, the requirement of nationality is even less adequate to define protected persons. In such conflicts, not only the text and the drafting history of the Convention but also, and more importantly, the Convention's object and purpose suggest that allegiance to a Party to the conflict and, correspondingly, control by this Party over persons in a given territory, may be regarded as the crucial test."[229]

In consequence, the Trial Chamber declared in a judgment of 3 March 2000 that, in interethnic conflicts, ethnic background would be the decisive factor in determining a person's status as a protected person: "In an inter-ethnic armed conflict, a person's ethnic background may be regarded as a decisive factor in determining to which nation he owes his allegiance and may thus serve to establish the status of the victims as protected persons."[230] **870**

The Tribunal thus succeeded in adapting the rules of international humanitarian law to new realities.[231] Its approach can be applied to other constellations. For example, it would seem logical to look at the participants' religious orientation if this is crucial to the conflict. **871**

---

[228] *Prosecutor* v. *Tadić*, ICTY (Appeals Chamber), decision of 2 October 1995, para. 76.

[229] *Prosecutor* v. *Tadić*, ICTY (Appeals Chamber), judgment of 15 July 1999, para. 166; confirmed by *Prosecutor* v. *Aleksovski*, ICTY (Appeals Chamber), judgment of 24 March 2000, paras. 151 et seq.

[230] *Prosecutor* v. *Blaškić*, ICTY (Trial Chamber), judgment of 3 March 2000, para. 127; confirmed by *Prosecutor* v. *Blaškić*, ICTY (Appeals Chamber), judgment of 29 July 2004, paras. 167 et seq.

[231] See also *Prosecutor* v. *Mucić* et al., ICTY (Trial Chamber), judgment of 16 November 1998, paras. 247 et seq.; *Prosecutor* v. *Aleksovski*, ICTY (Appeals Chamber), judgment of 24 March 2000, paras. 150 et seq.; *Prosecutor* v. *Mucić* et al., ICTY (Appeals Chamber), judgment of 20 February 2001, paras. 83 et seq.; *Prosecutor* v. *Naletilić and Martinović*, ICTY (Trial Chamber), judgment of 31 March 2003, paras. 204 et seq.; *Prosecutor* v. *Blaskić*, ICTY (Appeals Chamber), judgment of 29 July 2004, paras. 167 et seq. On the development of ICTY case law, see T. Meron, 94 *American Journal of International Law* (2000), p. 239 at pp. 256 et seq.; see also N. Wagner, 85 *International Review of the Red Cross* (2003), p. 351 at pp. 371 et seq. If the ICTY had classified the conflict as non-international, the class of protected persons would have been oriented around Geneva Conventions I-IV, Art. 3, which is not geared toward the nationality of the victims. The adaptation of the concept of the protected person was thus also owing to the broad concept of international armed conflict advocated by the ICTY. On the problems that may arise from the broad interpretation of the concept of the protected persons, see M. Sassòli and L.M. Olson, 82 *International Review of the Red Cross* (2000), p. 733 at pp. 743 et seq.

b) Protected Persons in Non-International Conflicts

872   For non-international armed conflicts, Article 3(1) of Geneva Conventions I to IV determines that "persons taking no active part in the hostilities, including members of armed
forces who have laid down their arms and those placed *hors de combat* by sickness,
wounds, detention, or any other cause," shall be protected. Article 4(1) of Additional
Protocol II contains a similar rule. This broad definition of persons to be protected is
especially appropriate to modern armed conflicts.

873   The ICC Statute adopted this definition in Article 8(2)(c). Surprisingly, the Elements
of Crimes for this provision only take up this definition in part: "Such person or persons
were either *hors de combat*, or were civilians, medical personnel or religious personnel
taking no active part in the hostilities."[232] This seems to leave unprotected members of
the armed forces who "have laid down their arms"[233] or "have ceased to take part in hostilities,"[234] where these persons cannot in the individual case be considered civilians. Ultimately, however, the broader provision of the ICC Statute takes precedence over the
Elements of Crimes.

2. Persons Protected by Other Provisions

874   War crimes that are not based in the law of Geneva often protect only specific groups of
people.[235] The scope of the definitions, however, is far easier to determine, because the
definitions themselves conclusively describe the possible objects of the crime.

II. Killing

875   Killings of protected persons committed during international armed conflict are criminal
under Article 8(2)(a)(i) of the ICC Statute. This is considered a grave breach as defined
in all four Geneva Conventions.[236] A corresponding crime for non-international conflicts is contained in Article 8(2)(c)(i) of the ICC Statute, which is based in Common
Article 3 of the Geneva Conventions.[237] Although the wording of Article 3 ("murder")
differs from that of the grave breaches provisions of the Geneva Conventions, which
speak of "wilful killing," the substance of the crime is the same.[238] The requirements for

---

[232] Elements of Crimes for Article 8(2)(c)(i) to (iv) ICC Statute.

[233] Geneva Conventions I-IV, Art. 3(1).

[234] Additional Protocol II, Art. 4(1).

[235] See, e.g., ICC Statute, Art. 8(2)(b)(x): ". . . Persons who are in the power of an adverse party
. . ."

[236] See Geneva Convention I, Art. 50; Geneva Convention II, Art. 51; Geneva Convention III,
Art. 130; Geneva Convention IV, Art. 147. See also ICTY Statute, Art. 2(a).

[237] Geneva Conventions I-IV, Art. 3(1)(a). See also ICTR Statute, Art. 4(a).

[238] See *Prosecutor* v. *Mucić* et al., ICTY (Trial Chamber), judgment of 16 November 1998, paras.
420 et seq.; affirmed in *Prosecutor* v. *Naletilić and Martinović*, ICTY (Trial Chamber), judgment of
31 March 2003, para. 248. The purpose of Geneva Conventions I-IV, Art. 3, the Tribunal said, is the
extension of the principle of humanity to non-international conflicts. Different terminology thus cannot justify any substantive differences.

the crime are also identical with those of wilful killing under the provisions of crimes against humanity.[239]

In international armed conflict, the material elements, according to the Elements of Crimes for the ICC Statute, require killing a person under the protection of the Geneva Conventions or causing the death of such a person.[240] For non-international armed conflict, the wording is the same, aside from the definition of the possible victims.[241] In what way and with what means the killing is carried out are irrelevant, as long as the death can be attributed to the perpetrator's conduct (*substantial cause*).[242] **876**

Typical criminal acts in international armed conflict are the killing of prisoners of war or interned civilians without a prior fair trial, the reduction of rations for prisoners of war, resulting in starvation, and mistreatment of prisoners of war, leading to death.[243] The same is true for the killing of captured fighters in non-international armed conflict. However, killings of combatants by other combatants during hostilities do not satisfy the definition of the crime because combatants are not protected persons under the Geneva Conventions and because fighters are not protected in either non-international or international armed conflict. **877**

With regard to the mental element, and in a departure from the general requirements of Article 30 of the ICC Statute, it is sufficient here if the perpetrator seriously harms the victim with "reckless disregard of human life."[244] This interpretation is based on the underlying norms of international humanitarian law.[245] **878**

---

[239] See ICC Statute, Art. 7(1)(a), and *Prosecutor* v. *Mucić* et al., ICTY (Trial Chamber), judgment of 16 November 1998, para. 422; *Prosecutor* v. *Kordić and Čerkez*, ICTY (Trial Chamber), judgment of 26 February 2001, para. 236. For details, see marginal nos. 675 et seq.

[240] See Elements of Crimes for Article 8(2)(a)(i) ICC Statute, num. 1 and Elements of Crimes for Article 8(2)(c)(i) ICC Statute, num. 1. The terms "killing" and "causing death" were both adopted into the Elements of Crimes to make clear that indirect killing, such as killing through undernourishment of prisoners of war, can also satisfy the definition of the crime, see K. Dörmann, in R.S. Lee (ed.), *The International Criminal Court, Elements of Crimes and Rules of Procedure and Evidence* (2001), p. 124, which also refers to the fact that both terms appear in the judgments of the *ad hoc* Tribunals, for example in *Prosecutor* v. *Mucić* et al., ICTY (Trial Chamber), judgment of 16 November 1998, para. 424 on the one hand, and in *Prosecutor* v. *Blaškić*, ICTY (Trial Chamber), judgment of 3 March 2000, para. 153 on the other. On the concept of protected persons, see marginal nos. 859 et seq.

[241] See marginal nos. 872 et seq.

[242] *Prosecutor* v. *Mucić* et al., ICTY (Trial Chamber), judgment of 16 November 1998, para. 424

[243] See K. Kittichaisaree, *International Criminal Law* (2001), p. 142.

[244] See *Prosecutor* v. *Mucić* et al., ICTY (Trial Chamber), judgment of 16 November 1998, para. 439. Under the case law of the Rwanda Tribunal, the perpetrator must have known that the harm inflicted on the victim would probably cause his or her death, see *Prosecutor* v. *Akayesu*, ICTR (Trial Chamber), judgment of 2 September 1998, para. 589. This departure from the general mental requirements is expressly permitted by ICC Statute, Art. 30, see marginal nos. 310 et seq. For killings in international conflicts, the criterion "wilful" (ICC Statute, Art. 8(2)(a)(i) remains an indicator for this interpretation that conforms with the underlying norm of international humanitarian law and customary international law. According to *Prosecutor* v. *Blaškić*, ICTY (Trial Chamber), judgment of 3 March 2000, para. 182, recklessness is also sufficient for a violation of Geneva Convention I-IV, Common Art. 3; see also *Prosecutor* v. *Stakić*, ICTY (Trial Chamber), judgment of 31 July 2003, para. 587, in which the Tribunal held that, with regard to the mental element of the crime of murder under Common Art. 3 of the Geneva Conventions, *dolus eventualis* would suffice. It was likened to the concept of recklessness in US criminal law. See also marginal nos. 857 et seq.

[245] See, e.g., B. Zimmermann, in Y. Sandoz, C. Swinarski and B. Zimmermann (eds.), *Commentary on the Additional Protocols* (1987), marginal no. 3474.

III. Killing and Wounding Persons Not Involved in Combat

879 Article 8(2)(b)(vi) of the ICC Statute criminalizes the killing or wounding of people who have laid down their arms and surrendered at discretion in international armed conflict. The provision is based on Article 23(c) of the Hague Regulations. The law of Geneva also contains relevant prohibitions. Article 41 of Additional Protocol I prescribes that persons *hors de combat* may not be attacked. Under Article 85(3)(e) of Additional Protocol I, such attacks are grave breaches of the Protocol. All these rules are based on the principle that the only legitimate goal of warfare is to weaken the opponent's military strength. The prohibition ultimately benefits both parties, since troops that cannot expect to be left unharmed after laying down their weapons will be more likely to fight to the death.[246]

880   Under the ICC Statute, combatants are protected if they have laid down their weapons or are defenseless and have surrendered at discretion. A person has surrendered his or her weapons within the meaning of Article 8(2)(b)(vi) of the ICC Statute if he or she has ceased fighting and indicated the intention of ceasing hostilities, especially by surrendering control over his or her weapons. A person is defenseless within the meaning of the provision if he or she is no longer in a position to offer armed resistance, especially because he or she no longer has control over his or her weapons. A person surrenders at discretion if he or she wishes to cease hostilities and no longer resists being taken into custody by opposing forces.[247]

881 In doubtful cases, Article 41 of Additional Protocol I can be consulted to aid in interpretation. This provision speaks of persons *hors de combat*, but the term corresponds substantively with the description in the ICC Statute.[248] Under Article 41(2) of Additional Protocol II, a person is *hors de combat* if he or she is in the power of the opposing party, has clearly expressed the intention of surrendering, or is incapable of defending him or herself due to unconsciousness, wounding or sickness, assuming that this person abstains from any hostile acts and does not attempt to escape.

882 The mental element requires at least recklessness on the part of the perpetrator. This derives, first of all, from Article 85(3)(e) of Additional Protocol I, which provides a comparable rule, using the term "wilful" to describe the mental element.[249] Second, the similarity of this crime to the general war crime of killing suggests that here, too, under customary international law the requirements for the mental element of the act are lower than under Article 30 of the ICC Statute.[250]

883   The prohibition on killing and wounding persons *hors de combat* has no temporal limits, so that prisoners of war are also included within its protections[251] and the prohi-

---

[246] See M. Cottier, in O. Triffterer (ed.), *Commentary on the Rome Statute of the International Criminal Court* (1999), Art. 8, marginal no. 58.

[247] See M. Cottier, in O. Triffterer (ed.), *Commentary on the Rome Statute of the International Criminal Court* (1999), Art. 8, marginal nos. 61 et seq.

[248] See M. Cottier, in O. Triffterer (ed.), *Commentary on the Rome Statute of the International Criminal Court* (1999), Art. 8, marginal no. 60.

[249] On the concept of "wilfulness," see marginal nos. 857 et seq.

[250] On the subjective requirements for the crime of killing, see marginal no. 878; on the general requirements for the mental element under ICC Statute, Art. 30 and on possible deviations by way of customary international law or the Elements of Crimes, see marginal nos. 310 et seq.

[251] See J. de Preux, in Y. Sandoz, C. Swinarski and B. Zimmermann (eds.), *Commentary on the Additional Protocols* (1987), marginal no. 1602.

bition overlaps the rules of Geneva law.[252] The rule discussed here has separate signifi-cance primarily in protecting persons in the intermediate stage between combatant status and the secure status of prisoner of war.

The ICC Statute contains no independent rules on the crime for non-international **884** armed conflict. However, the killing or wounding of persons who have laid down their arms or otherwise ceased to take part in hostilities is criminal as a violation of Common Article 3 of the Geneva Conventions under Article 8(2)(c)(i) of the ICC Statute, so an equivalent protection exists for non-international conflict.

IV. Offenses of Mistreatment

The Yugoslavia Tribunal combined the war crimes of torture, wilfully causing great suf- **885** fering, serious injury to bodily integrity or health, and cruel or inhuman treatment under the heading of offenses of mistreatment not leading to death.[253] Closely related to these crimes are mutilation and performing medical or scientific experiments. There is broad overlap within this group of offenses.

Offenses of mistreatment are found in Article 8(2)(a)(ii) and (iii), (b)(x), (c)(i) and **886** (e)(xi) of the ICC Statute. In applying the definitions of the offenses, the protected class of persons involved, which varies gradually, must be determined in each case.[254]

1. Torture

Of the offenses of mistreatment, torture is the most specifically defined.[255] Torture is **887** prohibited by the grave breaches provisions of all four Geneva Conventions as well as by Common Article 3. The requirements are identical in all cases.[256] In the ICC Statute, the war crime of torture is regulated in Article 8(2)(a)(ii), first alternative, for interna-tional armed conflicts, and in Article 8(2)(c)(i), fourth alternative, for non-international armed conflicts.

---

[252] On the underlying rule of Additional Protocol I, see J. de Preux, in Y. Sandoz, C. Swinarski and B. Zimmermann (eds.), *Commentary on the Additional Protocols* (1987), marginal no. 1605. Kill-ing and wounding of prisoners of war, in particular, are already covered by the crimes of wilful killing and intentional infliction of great suffering or serious injury to body integrity or health. There are also overlaps with ICC Statute, Art. 8(2)(b)(xii) (giving no quarter). The majority of post-World War II jurisprudence on this crime refers to the killing of prisoners of war criminalized by Art. 23(c) of the Hague Regulations; see, e.g., British Military Court Hamburg, judgment of 3 September 1947 (*Max Wielen*, so-called Stalag Luft III Trial), in United Nations War Crimes Commission, *Law Reports of Trials of War Criminals* XI, pp. 30 et seq.; Canadian Military Court Aurich, judgment of 28 Decem-ber 1945 (*Kurt Meyer*, so-called Abbaye Ardenne Trial), in United Nations War Crimes Commission, *Law Reports of Trials of War Criminals* IV, pp. 97 et seq. There have been no decisions on this crime by the UN criminal Tribunals to date.

[253] *Prosecutor* v. *Mucić* et al., ICTY (Trial Chamber), judgment of 16 November 1998, paras. 440 et seq.

[254] For details, see marginal nos. 859 et seq.

[255] *Prosecutor* v. *Mucić* et al., ICTY (Trial Chamber), judgment of 16 November 1998, para. 442.

[256] See *Prosecutor* v. *Mucić* et al., ICTY (Trial Chamber), judgment of 16 November 1998, paras. 442 et seq., 452 et seq.; *Prosecutor* v. *Musema*, ICTR (Trial Chamber), judgment of 27 January 2000, para. 285. See also ICTY Statute, Art. 2(b); ICTR Statute, Art. 4(a).

888   Torture is the infliction of severe physical or mental pain.[257] This definition corresponds to Article 1(1) of the *Convention against Torture and Other Cruel, Inhuman or Degrading Treatment or Punishment* of 10 December 1984.[258] In contrast to the Torture Convention, it is not necessary for the perpetrator to act in an official capacity.[259] This mirrors the legal status of torture as a crime against humanity under Article 7(1)(f) of the ICC Statute.[260]

889   To be punishable as the war crime of torture, the mistreatment must also serve specific purposes, in conformity with Article 1(1) of the Torture Convention. This distinguishes torture as a war crime from torture as a crime against humanity.[261] Whether the purposes listed in the Torture Convention are conclusive has not been uniformly determined in Tribunal judgments.[262] The wording of the Elements of Crimes argues against a conclusive listing.[263] The listed purposes of torture need not be the perpetrator's sole or primary motive. It is enough for them to be a part of a bundle of motivations.[264]

890   Article 30 of the ICC Statute governs the mental element, with regard to the prohibited conduct and its consequences.[265]

2. Causing Suffering or Injury to Health (International Conflict)

891   The war crime of wilfully causing great suffering or serious injury to body or health,

---

[257] On details of torture as a crime against humanity, see marginal nos. 710 et seq. See also Elements of Crimes for Article 8(2)(a)(ii) ICC Statute, -1, num. 1, 2.

[258] 1465 *UNTS* (1987), p. 112.

[259] *Prosecutor* v. *Kunarac* et al., ICTY (Trial Chamber), judgment of 22 February 2001, para. 496. Affirmed in *Prosecutor* v. *Kunarac* et al., ICTY (Appeals Chamber), judgment of 12 June 2002, para. 148. Nor is the requirement of official capacity included in the Elements of Crimes, as it was feared that this would too greatly narrow the scope of the crime, see K. Dörmann, *Elements of War Crimes* (2002), pp. 45 et seq. In earlier decisions, the ICTY had affirmed the requirement of acting in an official capacity. Its case law, however, also included situations in which official functionaries acted passively and omitted to criminally prosecute torture, see *Prosecutor* v. *Mucić* et al., ICTY (Trial Chamber), judgment of 16 November 1998, para. 474. In non-international armed conflicts, agents of non-state parties to the conflict are also included, see *Prosecutor* v. *Mucić* et al., ICTY (Trial Chamber), judgment of 16 November 1998, para. 473.

[260] See marginal no. 716.

[261] See marginal no. 711.

[262] In the *Akayesu* judgment, the Rwanda Tribunal assumed it was a conclusive list, see *Prosecutor* v. *Akayesu*, ICTR (Trial Chamber), judgment of 2 September 1998, para. 594. In contrast, the Yugoslavia Tribunal recognizes as a purpose of torture not only the victim's punishment, but also his or her humiliation, see *Prosecutor* v. *Furundžija*, ICTY (Trial Chamber), judgment of 10 December 1998, para. 162. For the view that this is not a conclusive list, see also *Prosecutor* v. *Mucić* et al., ICTY (Trial Chamber), judgment of 16 November 1998, para. 470.

[263] The Elements of Crimes for Article 8(2)(a)(i) ICC Statute, -1, num. 2 do carry over the list from the Torture Convention, but introduce it with the words "such as" or "notamment."

[264] See *Prosecutor* v. *Mucić* et al., ICTY (Trial Chamber), judgment of 16 November 1998, para. 470; *Prosecutor* v. *Kunarac* et al., ICTY (Trial Chamber), judgment of 22 February 2001, para. 486.

[265] On the general requirements of the mental element, see marginal nos. 294 et seq., esp. 304 et seq. See also *Prosecutor* v. *Kunarac* et al., ICTY (Appeals Chamber), judgment of 12 June 2002, para. 153, where the Appeals Chamber of the ICTY held that it is decisive "whether a perpetrator intended to act in a way which, in the normal course of events, would cause severe suffering."

regulated in Article 8(2)(a)(iii) of the ICC Statute, has been defined by the Yugoslavia Tribunal as an intentional act or omission that causes serious mental or physical pain or suffering.[266] Only persons protected under the Geneva Conventions can be considered victims. The victim must experience great suffering[267] and suffer long-term consequences in regard to his or her ability to lead a normal, constructive life.[268] However, the harm to the victim need not be irreparable.[269]

This offense differs from the war crime of torture mainly in that the perpetrator need **892** not have any particular purpose in inflicting the suffering. Thus any war crime of torture also satisfies the definition of wilful infliction of great suffering.[270] However, acts that only violate the victim's dignity do not fall within this definition.[271] Examples of acts include the mutilation of the wounded, inflicting unnecessary and senseless suffering on prisoners of war,[272] and rape.[273] However, the crime includes not only physical but also mental suffering, so that impermissible disciplinary measures or solitary confinement can also be punished as inflictions of great suffering.[274]

The mental element requires at least recklessness.[275] This is inferred from the use of **893** the term "wilful" in the definition of the crime.[276]

The crime is only applicable to international armed conflict. In non-international **894** armed conflict, comparable cases are subsumed under the catch-all offense of cruel treatment.[277]

3. Mutilation

Criminal liability for physical mutilation of persons in the power of one of the parties to **895** a conflict is regulated for international armed conflict in Article 8(2)(b)(x) and for non-international armed conflict in Article 8(2)(c)(i) and Article 8(2)(e)(xi) of the ICC Stat-

---

[266] *Prosecutor* v. *Mucić* et al., ICTY (Trial Chamber), judgment of 16 November 1998, para. 511, in reference to ICTY Statute, Art. 2(c). Affirmed in Elements of Crimes for Article 8(2)(a)(iii) ICC Statute, num. 1.

[267] *Prosecutor* v. *Mucić* et al., ICTY (Trial Chamber), judgment of 16 November 1998, para. 510.

[268] *Prosecutor* v. *Krstić*, ICTY (Trial Chamber), judgment of 2 August 2001, para. 513, with an eye to the statements in the ICTR's *Akayesu* judgment on methods of causing serious physical or mental harm as part of the crime of genocide. The ICTY assumed this approach could be carried over to war crimes, see *Prosecutor* v. *Naletilić and Martinović*, ICTY (Trial Chamber), judgment of 31 March 2003, para. 342.

[269] *Prosecutor* v. *Akayesu*, ICTR (Trial Chamber), judgment of 2 September 1998, para. 502.

[270] *Prosecutor* v. *Mucić* et al., ICTY (Trial Chamber), judgment of 16 November 1998, para. 442.

[271] *Prosecutor* v. *Kordić and Čerkez*, ICTY (Trial Chamber), judgment of 26 February 2001, para. 245.

[272] Examples by W.J. Fenrick, in O. Triffterer (ed.), *Commentary on the Rome Statute of the International Criminal Court* (1999), Art. 8, marginal no. 13.

[273] K. Kittichaisaree, *International Criminal Law* (2001), p. 147.

[274] R. Wolfrum, in D. Fleck (ed.), *The Handbook of Humanitarian Law in Armed Conflicts* (1999), no. 1209.

[275] On the general requirements for the mental element under the ICC Statute, Art. 30 and on possible deviations by way of customary international law or the Elements of Crimes, see marginal nos. 294 et seq.

[276] On the concept of wilfulness in the law of war crimes, see marginal nos. 857 et seq.

[277] See marginal no. 903.

ute.[278] The provisions are based on the Additional Protocols to the Geneva Conventions.[279] The prohibition on physical mutilation is also found in Common Article 3 of Geneva Conventions I to IV, as well as Article 13(1) of Geneva Convention III and Article 32 of Geneva Convention IV. Mutilation within the meaning of these provisions is present in particular if the perpetrator permanently disfigures the victim or removes an organ or appendage or permanently disables him or her.[280] The concept of mutilation thus includes any severe encroachment on bodily integrity that causes permanent harm.[281] The victim's permission does not vitiate criminal liability.[282]

896   In international armed conflict, the definition protects "persons who are in the power of an adverse party,"[283] that is, primarily prisoners of war and civilians in occupied territories, but not members of one's own population. In non-international armed conflict, reference should be had to Common Article 3 of the Geneva Conventions.[284]

897   As to the mental element, Article 30 of the ICC Statute applies.[285]

4. Biological, Medical or Scientific Experiments

898   Under Article 8(2)(a)(ii) of the ICC Statute, carrying out biological experiments is a subset of inhuman treatment. The provision is based on the Geneva Conventions' grave breaches provisions. The concept of biological experiments is not defined, however, in either the Geneva Conventions or the ICC Statute or the Elements of Crimes. It is in any case necessary that the experiment not serve therapeutic goals and not be carried out in the victim's interests.[286] This is the case if a medical intervention is not required by the victim's state of health or if the intervention does not meet generally accepted medical standards that would be applied in comparable circumstances to citizens of the side in whose power the victim is found.[287] The victim's permission for the experiment is irrelevant.[288] The Elements of Crimes clarify the threshold for international criminal liabil-

---

[278] Although Art. 8(2)(c)(i) ICC Statute does not speak of *physical* mutilation, there is no difference in meaning, as mutilation by definition requires an action upon the body of the victim, see also A. Zimmermann, in O. Triffterer (ed.), *Commentary on the Rome Statute of the International Criminal Court* (1999), Art. 8, marginal no. 273.

[279] See Art. 11(2)(a), (b) in connection with Additional Protocol I, Art. 11(4) and Additional Protocol II, Art. 4(2)(a) and 5(2)(e). Under Additional Protocol I, Art. 11(4), any intentional act or omission that seriously endangers the physical or mental health or integrity of a person in the power of an adverse party is punishable as a grave breach of the Protocol. Mutilation is also included in ICTR Statute, Art. 4(a).

[280] Elements of Crimes for Article 8(2)(b)(x) ICC Statute, -1, num. 1. Art. 2(b) ICTY Statute also includes biological experiments.

[281] R. Wolfrum, in D. Fleck (ed.), *The Handbook of Humanitarian Law in Armed Conflicts* (1999), no. 1209.

[282] See Elements of Crimes for Article 8(2)(e)(xi) ICC Statute, -1, num. 3, fn. 68.

[283] ICC Statute, Art. 8(2)(b)(x).

[284] For details, see marginal nos. 872 et seq.

[285] See generally, on the subjective requirements, marginal nos. 294 et seq.

[286] Elements of Crimes for Article 8(2)(a)(ii) ICC Statute, -3, num. 3.

[287] See, e.g., Geneva Convention III, Art. 13; Additional Protocol I, Art. 11. These explanations unfortunately were not adopted into the Elements of Crimes, see M. Bothe, in A. Cassese, P. Gaeta and J.R.W.D. Jones (eds.), *The Rome Statute of the International Criminal Court*, Vol. 1 (2002), p. 379 at p. 393.

[288] K. Kittichaisaree, *International Criminal Law* (2001), p. 146.

ity: experiments of this nature are criminal only if they seriously endanger the physical or mental health or integrity of the victim.[289]

Article 8(2)(b)(x) and Article 8(2)(e)(xi) of the ICC Statute contain similar provisions. There, the undertaking of medical and scientific experiments on persons in the power of the opposing party can be punished. This is a form of the war crime of inhuman or cruel treatment,[290] so that this crime is also one of mistreatment. **899**

The carrying out of medical and scientific experiments is illegal if they serve no therapeutic purpose, but only that of gaining medical or scientific knowledge.[291] The distinction from biological experiments is unclear. In the ICC Statue and the Elements of Crimes, the terminology is explained no more clearly for these than for biological experiments. Relevant court decisions are found only in the immediate post-war years. Thus, for example, the carrying out of castrations and sterilizations, premature abortions of pregnancies, hormonal treatments,[292] and experiments with malarial agents, poison, typhus agents, high pressure, extreme temperatures and mustard gas were criminally prosecuted.[293] **900**

The act must cause the death of the victim or seriously endanger his or her physical or mental health. This threshold is part of the statutory definition of the crime itself, in contrast to the crime of biological experiments under Article 8(2)(a)(ii) of the ICC Statute, for which the threshold is only introduced in the Elements of Crimes. No actual injury to the victim is required, but only a concrete danger to health of some severity. The bases for such an assessment are the foreseeable consequences to the victim's health.[294] It is necessary that the danger be caused by the perpetrator. Acts that have actually caused harm to the victim are of course included under this definition.[295] The line between criminal medical experiments and necessary medical care is frequently problematic.[296] The decisive factor is which measures may be undertaken in the medical care of one's own civilians.[297] **901**

---

[289] Elements of Crimes for Article 8(2)(a)(ii) ICC Statute, -3, num. 2.

[290] A. Zimmermann, in O. Triffterer (ed.), *Commentary on the Rome Statute of the International Criminal Court* (1999), Art. 8, marginal no. 100.

[291] A. Zimmermann, in O. Triffterer (ed.), *Commentary on the Rome Statute of the International Criminal Court* (1999), Art. 8, marginal no. 108. On the war crime of carrying out medical experiments, see US Military Tribunal, Nuremberg, judgment of 20 August 1947 (*Brandt* et al., so-called Medical Trial), in *Trials of War Criminals* II, pp. 171 et seq.

[292] See *Prosecutor v. Hoess*, Supreme National Tribunal of Poland, judgment of 2 April 1947, in United Nations War Crimes Commission, *Law Reports of Trials of War Criminals* VII, p. 11 at pp. 14 et seq.

[293] See US Military Tribunal, Nuremberg, judgment of 17 April 1947 (*Milch*, so-called Milch Trial), in *Trials of War Criminals* VII, pp. 355 et seq.; US Military Tribunal Nuremberg, judgment of 20 August 1947 (*Brandt* et al., so-called Medical Trial), in *Trials of War Criminals* II, pp. 171 et seq.

[294] Y. Sandoz, in Y. Sandoz, C. Swinarski and B. Zimmermann (eds.), *Commentary on the Additional Protocols* (1987), marginal no. 493.

[295] A. Zimmermann, in O. Triffterer (ed.), *Commentary on the Rome Statute of the International Criminal Court* (1999), Art. 8, marginal no. 111.

[296] Thus, for example, an amputation can represent a justified mutilation required by the victim's state of health, see Y. Sandoz, in Y. Sandoz, C. Swinarski and B. Zimmermann (eds.), *Commentary on the Additional Protocols* (1987), marginal no. 480.

[297] R. Wolfrum, in D. Fleck (ed.), *The Handbook of Humanitarian Law in Armed Conflicts* (1999), no. 1209.

902   The perpetrator must act at least recklessly. The mental element thus requires less
than what is necessary under Article 30(2) of the ICC Statute.[298] This arises out of Article 11(4) of Additional Protocol I, which uses the term "wilfulness" and upon which
the definitions in the ICC Statute are based. Despite the fact that the term is not carried
over into Article 8(2)(a)(ii) or (2)(b)(x) of the ICC Statute, the underlying provisions of
Additional Protocol I, which embody customary international law,[299] must be respected.

5. Inhuman or Cruel Treatment

903   Inhuman or cruel treatment is criminalized for international armed conflict by Article
8(2)(ii), second alternative, of the ICC Statute, and for non-international armed conflict
by Article 8(2)(c)(i), third alternative. This war crime is based on the grave breaches provisions of the four Geneva Conventions as well as their Common Article 3. Despite terminological differences between Article 8(2)(a)(ii), second alternative ("inhuman
treatment") and Article 8(2)(c)(i), third alternative ("cruel treatment"), the two crimes
have the same requirements.[300]

904   Inhuman treatment is a catch-all crime that covers various other serious injuries.[301]
Thus it comes into play, for example, when an act does not entirely satisfy the definition
of torture.[302] In addition to all types of torture, the definition also includes all crimes of
intentional infliction of great suffering or serious injury to bodily integrity or health, as
provided in Article 8(2)(a)(iii) of the ICC Statute, and additionally, and especially, attacks on human dignity.[303] In the view of the Yugoslavia Tribunal, a smaller amount of
physical or psychological suffering is required as a result of inhuman or cruel treatment
than is the case for the crime of torture; the consequences of the act correspond in their
intensity to the consequences of causing great suffering.[304]

905   In contrast to torture, human rights instruments contain no definition of inhuman
treatment. The Yugoslavia Tribunal thus first interpreted inhuman treatment on the basis of the provisions of the Geneva Convention that prohibit inhuman acts.[305] The tri-

---

[298] On the general requirements for the mental element under ICC Statute, Art. 30 and on possible deviations by way of customary international law or the Elements of Crimes, see marginal
nos. 294 et seq., 313 et seq.

[299] On the concept of "wilfulness" in the law of war crimes, see marginal nos. 857 et seq., and K.
Dörmann, *Elements of War Crimes* (2002), pp. 74 and 239.

[300] *Prosecutor* v. *Mucić* et al., ICTY (Trial Chamber), judgment of 16 November 1998, para. 551;
Prosecutor v. *Naletilić and Martinović*, ICTY (Trial Chamber), judgment of 31 March 2003, para. 246;
A. Zimmermann, in O. Triffterer (ed.), *Commentary on the Rome Statute of the International Criminal
Court* (1999), Art. 8, marginal no. 274. ICTY Statute, Art. 2(b) covers inhuman treatment; ICTR
Statute, Art. 4(a) covers cruel treatment.

[301] *Prosecutor* v. *Mucić* et al., ICTY (Trial Chamber), judgment of 16 November 1998, paras. 442,
543 et seq. (in-depth discussion of the definitions of crimes in paras. 512 et seq.); affirmed in *Prosecutor* v. *Blaškić*, ICTY (Trial Chamber), judgment of 3 March 2000, paras. 154 et seq.

[302] *Prosecutor* v. *Mucić* et al., ICTY (Trial Chamber), judgment of 16 November 1998, para. 542.
Torture is the severest form of inhuman treatment.

[303] *Prosecutor* v. *Mucić* et al., ICTY (Trial Chamber), judgment of 16 November 1998, para. 544.

[304] *Prosecutor* v. *Naletilić and Martinović*, ICTY (Trial Chamber), judgment of 31 March 2003, para.
246; *Prosecutor* v. *Kvočka* et al., ICTY (Trial Chamber), judgment of 2 November 2001, para. 161.

[305] See, e.g., Geneva Convention II, Art. 12; Geneva Convention III, Arts. 13, 20, 46; Geneva
Convention IV, Arts. 27, 32; Geneva Convention I-IV, Art. 3; Additional Protocol I, Art. 75(1) and
Additional Protocol II, Arts. 4(1) and 7(2).

bunal described humanity as the basic pillar of the Geneva Conventions.[306] It stated that acts or omissions that cause serious mental or physical suffering,[307] represent a serious attack on bodily or psychological integrity, or otherwise contravene the principle of humanity are inhuman and inconsistent with the concept of humanity.[308] This includes violations of human dignity. A perpetrator is also guilty of inhuman treatment if he subjects his victims to inhuman conditions.[309] What sorts of conditions count as inhuman cannot, however, be generalized, but must be determined in light of the circumstances of the individual case.[310]

For the mental element, Article 30 of the ICC Statute applies.[311]

906

V. Sexual Violence

Kelly Dawn Askin: *War Crimes Against Women* (1997); Christine Chinkin: Rape and Sexual Abuse **907** of Women in International Law, 5 *European Journal of International Law* (1994), pp. 326 et seq.; Rhodna Copelon: Gender Crimes as War Crimes: Integrating Crimes Against Women into International Criminal Law, 46 *McGill Law Journal* (2000-2001), pp. 217 et seq.; Rosalind Dixon: Rape as a Crime in International Humanitarian Law: Where to from Here?, 13 *European Journal of International Law* (2002), pp. 697 et seq.; Helen Durham: Women, armed conflict and international law, 84 *International Review of the Red Cross* (2002), pp. 655 et seq.; Kate Fitzgerald: Problems of Prosecution and Adjudication of Rape and Other Sexual Assaults under International Law, 8 *European Journal of International Law* (1997), pp. 336 et seq.; Gabrielle McDonald: Crimes of Sexual Violence: The Experience of the International Criminal Tribunal, 39 *Columbia Journal of Transnational Law* (2000-2001), pp. 1 et seq.; Eve La Haye: The Elements of War Crimes – Rape, Sexual Slavery, Enforced Prostitution, Forced Pregnancy, Enforced Sterilisation, and Sexual Violence, in Roy S. Lee (ed.), *The International Criminal Court, Elements of Crimes and Rules of Procedure and Evidence* (2001), pp. 184 et seq.; Theodor Meron: Rape as a Crime under International Humanitarian Law, 87 *American Journal of International Law* (1993), pp. 424 et seq.; Navanethem Pillay: The Role of International Humanitarian Jurisprudence in Redressing Crimes of Sexual Violence, in Lal Chand Vohrah et al. (eds.), *Man's Inhumanity to Man* (2003), pp. 685 et seq.; Patricia Viseur Sellers: The Context of Sexual Violence: Sexual Violence as Violations of International Humanitarian Law, in Gabrielle Kirk McDonald and Olivia Swaak-Goldman (eds.), *Substantive and Procedural Aspects of International Criminal Law – The Experience of International and National Courts*, Vol. 1 (2000), pp. 263 et seq.

---

[306] *Prosecutor* v. *Mucić* et al., ICTY (Trial Chamber), judgment of 16 November 1998, para. 532. See also R. Wolfrum, in D. Fleck (ed.), *The Handbook of Humanitarian Law in Armed Conflicts* (1999), no. 1209: "The obligation of humane treatment is practically a guiding theme for the four Geneva Conventions."

[307] Similarly, Elements of Crimes for Article 8(2)(a)(ii) ICC Statute, -2, num. 1.; Elements of Crimes for Article 8(2)(c)(i) ICC Statute, -3, num. 1.

[308] *Prosecutor* v. *Aleksovski*, ICTY (Trial Chamber), judgment of 25 June 1999, paras. 56 et seq.; affirmed in *Prosecutor* v. *Naletilić and Martinović*, ICTY (Trial Chamber), judgment of 31 March 2003, para. 246.

[309] *Prosecutor* v. *Mucić* et al., ICTY (Trial Chamber), judgment of 16 November 1998, para. 558.

[310] *Prosecutor* v. *Mucić* et al., ICTY (Trial Chamber), judgment of 16 November 1998, para. 544; affirmed in *Prosecutor* v. *Blaškić*, ICTY (Trial Chamber), judgment of 3 March 2000, para. 155.

[311] On the general requirements for the mental element, see marginal nos. 294 et seq., esp. 304 et seq. See also K. Dörmann, *Elements of War Crimes* (2002), pp. 69 et seq.

908 Article 8(2)(b)(xxii) of the ICC Statute covers, for international armed conflict, rape, sexual slavery, forced prostitution, enforced pregnancy, forced sterilization, and other forms of sexual violence that represent grave breaches of the Geneva Conventions. A comparable rule for non-international armed conflict is contained in Article 8(2)(e)(vi) of the ICC Statute, which includes the same specific methods of commission as well as every other form of sexual violence that represents a serious violation of Article 3 of the Geneva Conventions.

909 Although crimes of sexual violence were employed repeatedly in the past as methods of warfare, international treaty law before the creation of the ICC did not treat sexual violence as a separate war crime, but merely as an attack on personal honor or dignity. This classification failed to do justice to the physical and psychological injury to the victim.[312] Article 27(2) of Geneva Convention IV, Articles 75(2) and 76(1) of Additional Protocol I, and Article 4(2)(e) of Additional Protocol II classified rape, enforced prostitution, and "any other form of indecent assault" as attacks on the victim's honor; they were not specifically classified as grave breaches of the Geneva Conventions or their Additional Protocols.

910 The ICTR Statute took up this approach and classified rape, enforced prostitution and other forms of sexual violence as outrages upon personal dignity.[313] The ICTY Statute gave the Yugoslavia Tribunal no express authority at all to prosecute crimes of sexual violence as war crimes,[314] although sexual violence was employed as a method of warfare during the Bosnia conflict. The Tribunal has therefore been forced to prosecute sexual violence as a war crime on the basis of the grave breaches provisions of the Geneva Conventions or other violations of the laws and customs of war.[315]

911 The incorporation of separate provisions on crimes of sexual violence into the section of the ICC Statute on war crimes expressly recognizes that these crimes, committed in a context of organized violence, count among the most serious of crimes.[316] Under the ICC Statute, it is no longer necessary to fall back on less-suitable definitions in order to prosecute sexual crimes.[317]

---

[312] M. Cottier, in O. Triffterer (ed.), *Commentary on the Rome Statute of the International Criminal Court* (1999), Art. 8, marginal nos. 200 et seq.

[313] See ICTR Statute, Art. 4(e).

[314] However, the Tribunal can prosecute sexual violence as crimes against humanity, see ICTY Statute, Art. 5(g).

[315] See, e.g., *Prosecutor* v. *Furundžija*, ICTY (Trial Chamber), judgment of 10 December 1998, para. 172, in which the Tribunal recognizes that, in addition to being a crime against humanity and an act of genocide, rape can embody both a grave breach of the Geneva Conventions and a violation of the laws and customs of war. See also *Prosecutor* v. *Mucić* et al., ICTY (Trial Chamber), judgment of 16 November 1998, paras. 476 et seq. (rape as torture).

[316] E. La Haye, in R.S. Lee (ed.), *The International Criminal Court, Elements of Crimes and Rules of Procedure and Evidence* (2001), pp. 185 et seq.

[317] Possibilities include, in particular, the prohibition of inhuman treatment or torture (ICC Statute, Art. 8(2)(a)(ii)), the prohibition on intentional infliction of great suffering or serious injury to bodily integrity or health (ICC Statute, Art. 8(2)(a)(iii)), and the prohibition of outrages against personal dignity (ICC Statute, Art. 8(2)(b)(xxi), Art. 8(2)(c)(ii)).

1. Rape

The definition of rape as a war crime differs from the definition of rape as a crime **912** against humanity only in terms of the context in which the crime is committed.[318] Therefore, the above explanations may be referred to for the various requirements of the crime.[319]

With regard to the mental element, Article 30 of the ICC Statute applies.[320]   **913**

2. Other Serious Forms of Sexual Violence

Aside from the context in which they are committed, the definitions of other forms of **914** sexual violence punishable as war crimes (enforced prostitution, forced pregnancy, enforced sterilization) match those of the relevant crimes against humanity. This is also expressed in the Elements of Crimes, which are completely identical except for the context of the act. Thus here, too, the above explanations may be referred to.[321]

Misunderstanding may be caused by the wording of the catch-all clause that includes **915** "any other form of sexual violence" under Article 8(2)(b)(xxii), last alternative, and Article 8(2)(e)(vi) of the ICC Statute. It is necessary for the act also to constitute "a grave breach of the Geneva Conventions" or "a serious violation of Article 3 common to the four Geneva Conventions." This seems to call into question the emancipation of the crime of sexual violence; apparently, it always requires examination of whether the sexual violence may also be considered a violation of the Geneva Conventions. But such an interpretation would fail to do justice to the Statute's intentions, and the Elements of Crimes also point in a different direction. The reference to the Geneva Conventions is merely a means of ensuring that only comparably severe forms of sexual violence will be punished as war crimes.[322] This interpretation is confirmed by a comparison with Article 7(1)(g), last alternative, of the ICC Statute: even as crimes against humanity, other forms of sexual violence are only punishable if they are "of comparable gravity" to the sexual offenses expressly listed in the definition.[323]

As to the mental element, Article 30 of the ICC Statute applies.[324]   **916**

---

[318] See K. Kittichaisaree, *International Criminal Law* (2001), p. 182.

[319] See marginal no. 723.

[320] On the general requirements of the mental element, see marginal nos. 294 et seq., esp. 304 et seq.

[321] See marginal nos. 729 et seq.

[322] Elements of Crimes for Article 8(2)(b)(xxii) ICC Statute, -6, num. 2; Elements of Crimes for Article 8(2)(e)(vi) ICC Statute, -6, num. 2. See also M. Cottier, in O. Triffterer (ed.), *Commentary on the Rome Statute of the International Criminal Court* (1999), Art. 8, marginal nos. 207 et seq., which points out that limiting this provision to acts that are simultaneously grave breaches would contradict the intention of the Statute's authors to subject sexual crimes to prosecution independently of the grave breaches provisions. For a different view in regard to Art. 8(2)(e)(vi), see A. Zimmermann, in O. Triffterer (ed.), *Commentary on the Rome Statute of the International Criminal Court* (1999), Art. 8, marginal no. 302, which requires that there be conduct actually punishable under Geneva Conventions I-IV, Art. 3.

[323] See marginal no. 734.

[324] On the general requirements for the mental element, see marginal nos. 294 et seq., esp. 304 et seq.

VI. Humiliating and Degrading Treatment

917 Article 8(2)(b)(xxi) of the ICC Statute includes outrages upon personal dignity committed in international armed conflict, especially humiliating and degrading treatment. Article 8(2)(c)(ii) of the ICC Statute provides a similar rule for non-international armed conflict.[325] The requirements are identical for both types of conflicts.[326] The status of humiliating and degrading treatment as a war crime is recognized under customary international law.[327]

918 The definition is based on Common Article 3(1)(c) of Geneva Conventions I-IV. Article 75(2)(b) of Additional Protocol I and Article 4(2)(e) of Additional Protocol II also contain prohibitions on humiliating and degrading treatment.[328] Protection of human dignity is the purpose of Article 27(1) of Geneva Convention IV. This provision requires respect for one's person, honor, family rights, and religious convictions and practices. The right to respect for one's person is understood broadly and covers all rights that are inseparable from human existence, especially the right to physical, moral and intellectual integrity.[329] It follows that there are many ways of committing this crime.[330]

919 According to the Elements of Crimes, the definition is satisfied if a person humiliates, degrades, or in another fashion violates a person's dignity.[331] It is not necessary for the victim to be aware of the violation of his or her dignity; the dignity of a deceased person is also protected. The violation must be of such severity as to be generally recognized as an outrage.[332]

920 Suffering lasting over a long period of time is not a necessary condition of the crime, according to the Yugoslavia Tribunal. For serious humiliating or degrading treatment, the definition is satisfied even if the victim overcomes the consequences relatively quickly.[333] Omissions with the purpose of humiliating the victim or exposing him or her to ridicule also satisfy the definition, according to ICTY judgments.[334] In the *Musema*

---

[325] See also ICTR Statute, Art. 4(e).

[326] A. Zimmermann, in O. Triffterer (ed.), *Commentary on the Rome Statute of the International Criminal Court* (1999), Art. 8, marginal no. 276.

[327] See P. Viseur Sellers, in O. Triffterer (ed.), *Commentary on the Rome Statute of the International Criminal Court* (1999), Art. 8, marginal no. 192.

[328] Geneva Conventions I-IV, Art. 3(1)(c) contains a prohibition on "outrages upon personal dignity, in particular humiliating and degrading treatment"; in addition to humiliating and degrading treatment, the wording in the Additional Protocols includes, as examples of prohibited acts, enforced prostitution and any form of indecent assault.

[329] See J.S. Pictet (ed.), *Geneva Convention IV, Commentary* (1958), p. 201.

[330] See P. Viseur Sellers, in O. Triffterer (ed.), *Commentary on the Rome Statute of the International Criminal Court* (1999), Art. 8, marginal nos. 195 et seq.

[331] Elements of Crimes for Article 8(2)(b)(xxi) ICC Statute, num. 1; Elements of Crimes for Article 8(2)(c)(ii) ICC Statute, num. 1. Similarly, *Prosecutor* v. *Kunarac* et al., ICTY (Trial Chamber), judgment of 22 February 2001, para. 507.

[332] Elements of Crimes for Article 8(2)(b)(xxi) ICC Statute, num. 2; Elements of Crimes for Article 8(2)(c)(ii) ICC Statute, num. 2.

[333] *Prosecutor* v. *Kunarac* et al., ICTY (Trial Chamber), judgment of 22 February 2001, paras. 501, 503. In contrast, see *Prosecutor* v. *Aleksovski*, ICTY (Trial Chamber), judgment of 25 June 1999, para. 56.

[334] *Prosecutor* v. *Aleksovski*, ICTY (Trial Chamber), judgment of 25 June 1999, paras. 55 et seq.

decision, the Rwanda Tribunal defined humiliating or degrading treatment as acts that undermine self-respect. Injury to personal dignity can be viewed as a preliminary stage of torture.[335]

As to the mental element, Article 30 of the ICC Statute applies.[336] No specific intent **921** to humiliate is required.[337]

The relationship between the crime and other, similar crimes, especially offenses of mistreatment, **922** is unclear. In connection with Article 75(2)(b) of Additional Protocol I, some suggest that humiliating and degrading treatment "refers to acts which, without directly causing harm to the integrity and physical and mental well-being of persons, are aimed at humiliating or ridiculing them, or even forcing them to perform degrading acts."[338] If this concept were to be carried over to the law of war crimes, the definition would not be satisfied by the use of physical force. But such a view cannot be derived from the jurisprudence of the Yugoslavia and Rwanda Tribunals, which have taken positions on the crime in various rulings.[339] In fact, in the *Aleksovski* decision, the Yugoslavia Tribunal emphasized that the overall aim of Article 3(1) of Geneva Conventions I-IV is to protect dignity and ensure humane treatment.[340] The Tribunal viewed humiliating and degrading treatment as a case of inhuman treatment that causes particularly severe suffering and can be accompanied by physical violence.[341]

---

[335] *Prosecutor* v. *Musema*, ICTR (Trial Chamber), judgment of 25 June 1999, para. 285.

[336] *Prosecutor* v. *Kunarac* et al., ICTY (Trial Chamber), judgment of 22 February 2001, para. 514. It is sufficient for the perpetrator to be aware that his act could humiliate his victim, see *Prosecutor* v. *Kunarac* et al., ICTY (Trial Chamber), judgment of 22 February 2001, paras. 512 et seq. See also K. Dörmann, *Elements of War Crimes* (2002), pp. 323 et seq.; on the general requirements for the mental element, see marginal nos. 294 et seq., esp. 304 et seq.

[337] *Prosecutor* v. *Kunarac* et al., ICTY (Trial Chamber), judgment of 22 February 2001, para. 509.

[338] C. Pilloud and J.S. Pictet, in Y. Sandoz, C. Swinarski and B. Zimmermann (eds.), *Commentary on the Additional Protocols* (1987), marginal no. 3047.

[339] The Statute of the Yugoslavia Tribunal does not expressly contain a provision on humiliating or degrading treatment, but the Tribunal can, in the view of the Appeals Chamber, prosecute it as a crime against Article 3 of Geneva Conventions I-IV under Article 3 of its Statute, which gives the Tribunal the jurisdiction to prosecute violations of the laws and customs of war, see *Prosecutor* v. *Tadić*, ICTY (Appeals Chamber), decision of 2 October 1995, paras. 65 et seq. ICTR Statute, Art. 4(e) contains the crime, which, following the wording of the Additional Protocols, lists crimes of sexual violence as examples of forms of commission along with humiliating and degrading treatment. In the ICC Statute, on the other hand, crimes of sexual violence are included as separate provisions, see Art. 8(2)(b)(xxii).

[340] *Prosecutor* v. *Aleksovski*, ICTY (Trial Chamber), judgment of 25 June 1999, para. 49.

[341] *Prosecutor* v. *Aleksovski*, ICTY (Trial Chamber), judgment of 25 June 1999, para. 56. The Tribunal took the view that the crime had to be based on the perpetrator's contempt for the victim's dignity. Direct attacks on the physical or mental well-being of the victim were not necessary; it was sufficient that the act caused actual, continuing suffering in the victim as a result of humiliation or ridicule. So as not to make its criminal status entirely dependent on the perceptions of the victim, which will vary depending on his or her psychological makeup, the act must be considered an outrage by a reasonable observer. The special gravity of the act could arise from the fact that an act that would not be an outrage in itself is repeated more than once. Additionally, the type of violence, the duration of the act, and the degree of suffering caused are crucial in determining whether humiliating treatment reaches the threshold of criminality, see *Prosecutor* v. *Aleksovski*, ICTY (Trial Chamber), judgment of 25 June 1999, para. 57. The Tribunal found the circumstances in prison camps, characterized by physical violence, and the use of prisoners as human shields and to dig trenches in dangerous areas, to be serious violations of personal dignity, see *Prosecutor* v. *Aleksovski*, ICTY (Trial Chamber), judgment of 25 June 1999, paras. 228 et seq.; affirmed by the Appeals Chamber as follows: "Under any circum-

923   The offense's relationship to crimes of sexual violence is also unclear. The Yugoslavia Tribunal found sexual violence to be included in the crime of humiliating and degrading treatment.[342] The Rwanda Tribunal found in the *Akayesu* decision that any coerced sexual act satisfied the definition of the crime.[343] Whether this jurisprudence will be adopted by the ICC is questionable. Unlike the Statutes of the *ad hoc* Tribunals, the ICC Statute contains separate provisions for the war crimes of sexual violence and rape. These provisions are more specific than those for the crimes of humiliating and degrading treatment.[344]

VII. Compelled Service in Military Forces and Operations of War (International Conflict)

1. Compelled Service in the Forces of a Hostile Power

924 Article 8(2)(a)(v) of the ICC Statute covers compelling protected persons[345] to serve in the forces of a hostile power. The scope of the provision overlaps in particular with the war crime of compelled participation in operations of war.[346] In conformity with customary international law, the provision only extends to international armed conflict.[347] It is based on Article 23(h) of the Hague Regulations, which prohibited parties to a conflict from forcing members of the opposing party to participate in "the operations of war directed against their own country." Under Article 130 of Geneva Convention III and Article 147 of Geneva Convention IV, it is a grave breach of the Geneva Conventions to force prisoners of war or persons protected under Geneva Convention IV to serve in the forces of a hostile power.

925   The Elements of Crimes for the ICC Statute clarify the definition: first, forcing protected persons to serve in hostile armed forces is criminal;[348] second, forcing them to participate in military operations against their own country is criminal, regardless of whether this includes integration into hostile forces.[349] The aim of this provision is to

---

stances, the outrages upon personal dignity that the victims in this instance suffered would be serious. The victims were not merely inconvenienced or made uncomfortable – what they had to endure, under the prevailing circumstances, were physical and psychological abuse and outrages that any human being would have experienced as such," see *Prosecutor* v. *Aleksovski*, ICTY (Appeals Chamber), judgment of 24 March 2000, para. 37.

[342] *Prosecutor* v. *Furundžija*, ICTY (Trial Chamber), judgment of 10 December 1998, para. 183.

[343] *Prosecutor* v. *Akayesu*, ICTR (Trial Chamber), judgment of 2 September 1998, para. 688.

[344] See also P. Viseur Sellers, in O. Triffterer (ed.), *Commentary on the Rome Statute of the International Criminal Court* (1999), Art. 8, marginal nos. 195 et seq.

[345] On the concept of the protected person, see marginal nos. 859 et seq.

[346] See marginal nos. 929 et seq.

[347] Thus the German implementation of the ICC Statute is based on the assumption that criminality is limited to international armed conflicts, see Sec. 8(3) no. 3 (German) Code of Crimes Against International Law [*Völkerstrafgesetzbuch, VStGB*] and Explanatory Memorandum of the (German) Code of Crimes Against International Law, *BT-Drs.* 14/8524, p. 29. The provision is also contained in ICTY Statute, Art. 2(e).

[348] Under Additional Protocol I, Art. 43, the armed forces include "all organized armed forces, groups and units which are under a command responsible to that Party for the conduct of its subordinates," see also W.J. Fenrick, in O. Triffterer (ed.), *Commentary on the Rome Statute of the International Criminal Court* (1999), Art. 8, marginal no. 15.

[349] Elements of Crimes for Article 8(2)(a)(v) ICC Statute, num. 1.

protect persons in the power of the opposing side from conflicts of loyalty.[350] The recruitment of prisoners of war is not prohibited if they volunteer to take part in the fight against their country of origin.[351]

It is disputed whether compelling persons to merely perform services for the hostile **926** forces, without integrating them into those forces, satisfies the definition of the crime. The explanatory note to the German Code of Crimes against International Law assumes that compelling assistance in the transport of military materiel, without actual integration into the armed forces, is not sufficient to satisfy the definition of the crime.[352] But others argue that the crucial issue is the main idea behind Article 52 of the Hague Regulations, under which the population of an occupied territory may not be forced to participate in "military operations against their own country," which includes forced labor for military purposes.[353]

The answer may be derived from the provisions of the Geneva Conventions on which **927** the statutory provision is based. The starting point is the recognition that the Geneva Conventions only permit a requirement of service under specified circumstances. Under Article 49 et seq. of Geneva Convention III, the custodial state may require certain types of work from prisoners of war; a similar rule is found in Article 51 of Geneva Convention IV for civilians in occupied territories. Article 50(f) of Geneva Convention III provides that prisoners of war may be used only for public services not of a military character or designation,[354] and under Article 51 of Geneva Convention IV, an occupying power may not force protected persons to serve in its armed forces or in military operations.[355] It follows that forced labor serving military purposes can satisfy this provision. If, however, the use for labor is covered by the Geneva Conventions, it does not constitute punishable compulsion to participate in military operations.

As to the mental element, Article 30 of the ICC Statute applies.[356]　　　**928**

2. Compelled Participation in Operations of War

Article 8(2)(b)(xv) of the ICC Statute covers compelling persons belonging to the hostile **929**

---

[350] M. Bothe, in A. Cassese, P. Gaeta and J.R.W.D. Jones (eds.), *The Rome Statute of the International Criminal Court*, Vol. 1 (2002), p. 379 at p. 394.

[351] US Military Tribunal, Nuremberg, judgment of 14 April 1949 (*von Weizsäcker* et al., so-called Ministries Trial), in *Trials of War Criminals* XIV, pp. 308 et seq.

[352] Explanatory Memorandum of the (German) Code of Crimes Against International Law, *BT-Drs.* 14/8524, p. 29. Such acts can at most be covered by the war crime of forced participation in operations of war, see marginal nos. 929 et seq.

[353] R. Wolfrum, in D. Fleck (ed.), *The Handbook of Humanitarian Law in Armed Conflicts* (1999), no. 1209.

[354] While public services of a military character are those that are carried out under the command of a military authority, there is no uniform definition of services with a military purpose. In any case, prisoners of war may not be used for activities that serve exclusively military interests, while they may be used for jobs that under normal circumstances would serve to maintain civilian life, even if military units happen to profit from them, see J.S. Pictet (ed.), *Geneva Convention III, Commentary* (1960), pp. 267 et seq.

[355] For details on this rule, see in *Prosecutor* v. *Naletilić and Martinović*, ICTY (Trial Chamber), judgment of 31 March 2003, paras. 250 et seq.

[356] On the general requirements for the mental element, see marginal nos. 294 et seq., esp. 304 et seq. See also K. Dörmann, *Elements of War Crimes* (2002), p. 99.

party to take part in operations of war against their own country. Compulsion may not be exercised even if the victim already belonged to the forces of the party to the conflict before the outbreak of war. The purpose of this provision, which applies only to international armed conflict, is also to prevent conflicts of loyalty. The provision is based directly on Article 23, sentence 2, of the Hague Regulations.

930   The prohibition protects all members of a hostile party located in territory controlled by a party to the conflict. It is immaterial whether they are prisoners of war or civilians, and whether they are from the occupied state or another party to the conflict.[357] There is disagreement on whether the provision also covers compelling acts that are not directly part of military operations. In the literature, the view is advocated that the prohibition extends at least to types of work directly connected to the war effort,[358] but the Preparatory Commission assumed that penalization was limited to compelling participation in military operations.[359] Thus the Elements of Crimes correctly require a compulsion, based on an act or a threat, to engage in military operations against one's own country or armed forces.[360]

931   As to the mental element, Article 30 of the ICC Statute applies.[361]

VIII. Slavery

932   Under Article 4(2)(d) of Additional Protocol II, "slavery and slave trade in all their forms" are prohibited. The prohibition of slavery in Article 4(2)(d) applies to "[a]ll persons who do not take a direct part or who have ceased to take part in hostilities, whether or not their liberty has been restricted."[362] Although Additional Protocol II only applies to non-international armed conflict, slavery is prohibited in international armed conflict as well, as it would infringe upon the fundamental principle of humane treatment, stipulated for example in Common Article 3 of the Geneva Conventions, Article 13 of Geneva Convention III, Article 27 of Geneva Convention IV, and Article 4(1) of Additional Protocol II.[363]

933   In light of the fundamental character of the prohibition of slavery, the Yugoslavia Tribunal in its judgment of 15 March 2002 held that slavery committed in the context of armed conflict could be penalized as a war crime.[364] As to the elements of the war crime, the Yugoslavia Tribunal found them to be the same as the elements of the crime

---

[357] M. Cottier, in O. Triffterer (ed.), *Commentary on the Rome Statute of the International Criminal Court* (1999), Art. 8, marginal no. 164.

[358] M. Cottier, in O. Triffterer (ed.), *Commentary on the Rome Statute of the International Criminal Court* (1999), Art. 8, marginal no. 165.

[359] H. Boddens Hosang, in R.S. Lee (ed.), *The International Criminal Court, Elements of Crimes and Rules of Procedure and Evidence* (2001), p. 174 at p. 175.

[360] Elements of Crimes for Article 8(2)(b)(xv) ICTY Statute, num. 1.

[361] On the general requirements for the mental element, see marginal nos. 294 et seq., esp. 304 et seq.

[362] Article 4(1) of Additional Protocol II. See S.S. Junod, in Y. Sandoz, C. Swinarski and B. Zimmermann (eds.), *Commentary on the Additional Protocols* (1987), marginal no. 4520.

[363] See S.S. Junod, in Y. Sandoz, C. Swinarski and B. Zimmermann (eds.), *Commentary on the Additional Protocols* (1987), marginal no. 4523.

[364] See *Prosecutor* v. *Krnojelac*, ICTY (Trial Chamber), judgment of 15 March 2002, paras. 351 et seq.

against humanity of enslavement;[365] thus, reference can be made to the discussion of that crime.[366]

Article 8(2) of the ICC Statute does not provide for the war crime of slavery as such. **934** However, as enslavement is "the exercise of any or all of the powers attaching to the right of ownership over a person,"[367] such conduct could qualify as a manifestation of "outrages upon personal dignity," a war crime under Article 8(2)(b)(xxi) and (c)(ii) of the ICC Statute.[368]

IX. Forced Labor (International Conflict)

Forced labor by prisoners of war or civilians is not entirely prohibited by humanitarian **935** law.[369] Article 51 of Geneva Convention IV stipulates the conditions under which an occupying power may compel civilians to work. Article 49 et seq. of Geneva Convention III contains detailed rules governing labor by prisoners of war. These provisions are applicable only in international armed conflict. Forced labor as such is not a war crime under Article 8 of the ICC Statute.

In its decision of 31 March 2003, the Yugoslavia Tribunal found that forced labor by **936** protected persons is a war crime under customary international law. The Tribunal opined that all breaches of the provisions in Geneva Conventions III and IV on compelled labor entailed individual criminal responsibility.[370] In view of the very technical nature of some of these provisions – for example, Article 51(3), sentence 4, of Geneva Convention IV stipulates that the occupied country's legislation concerning preliminary training shall be applicable – this finding is not entirely persuasive.[371]

However, the Tribunal was convincing in its conviction of the accused on the **937** grounds that they had forced prisoners of war "to perform military support tasks in extremely dangerous conditions, such as digging trenches near the confrontation line, sealing exposed windows or areas with sandbags, or other forms of fortification labor."[372] Such treatment would qualify as compelling protected persons to serve in the forces of a hostile power, a war crime under Article 8(2)(a)(v) of the ICC Statute.[373] The Tribunal also found the accused guilty of the war crime of forced labor for compelling prisoners of war to participate in the looting of houses, during which they were made to carry furniture, household appliances, and the like,[374] and for forcing them over a period of over

---

[365] See *Prosecutor* v. *Krnojelac*, ICTY (Trial Chamber), judgment of 15 March 2002, para. 356.

[366] See marginal nos. 684 et seq.

[367] See ICC Statute, Art. 7(2)(c).

[368] See marginal nos. 917 et seq.

[369] It should be noted that not every form of forced labor amounts to slavery; see marginal nos. 667 et seq.

[370] See *Prosecutor* v. *Naletelić and Martinović*, ICTY (Trial Chamber), judgment of 31 March 2003, para. 250.

[371] On the criteria for individual criminal responsibility for breaches of rules of humanitarian law, see marginal nos. 803 et seq. See also A. Cassese, *International Criminal Law* (2003), p. 51: "the simple equation, breach of international law equals a war crime, may not suffice."

[372] *Prosecutor* v. *Naletelić and Martinović* , ICTY (Trial Chamber), judgment of 31 March 2003, paras. 268, 302.

[373] See marginal nos. 924 et seq.

[374] *Prosecutor* v. *Naletelić and Martinović*, ICTY (Trial Chamber), judgment of 31 March 2003, paras. 307 et seq. In para. 308 of that decision, the Trial Chamber held that in any event consent of

two months to dig a trench for a water pipeline in the private garden of the accused under very difficult conditions, with little water and food and no pay.[375] Such behavior might not always qualify as a war crime under Article 8(2) of the ICC Statute[376] and it is open to question whether such acts are serious enough to be comparable to grave breaches of the Geneva Conventions.[377]

X. Punishment Without Regular Trial

1. International Conflict

938 Article 8(2)(a)(vi) of the ICC Statute ensures the right of prisoners of war and other protected persons to a fair and regular trial. The provision is based on Article 130 of Geneva Convention III and Article 147 of Geneva Convention IV; Article 2(f) of the ICTY Statute also contains such a rule. The deprivation of "the rights of fair and regular trial prescribed in this Convention" is a grave breach of the Conventions. This principle was extended to all protected persons within the meaning of Geneva Conventions I-IV through Article 85(4)(e) of Additional Protocol I. In defining the right to fair trial, the Elements of Crimes refer to the guarantees laid down in Geneva Conventions III and IV.[378]

939 These include the right to an independent and impartial court (Article 84(2) of Geneva Convention III), the right to timely notification by the detaining power about any planned trial of a prisoner of war (Article 104 of Geneva Convention III), the right to immediate information on the charges (Article 104 of Geneva Convention III and Article 71(2) of Geneva Convention IV), the prohibition of collective punishment (Article 87(3) of Geneva Convention III and Article 33 of Geneva Convention IV), the principle of legality (Article 99(1) of Geneva Convention III,[379] Ar-

---

the prisoners of war to assist in the looting would have been irrelevant, as "[t]he commission of looting being a crime in itself, the consent of prisoners may not render the labour lawful." This argumentation is not convincing, as it is not the purpose of the provisions on compelled labor in Geneva Conventions III and IV to prevent protected persons from voluntarily participating in crime. If one followed the Chamber's arguments, any voluntary participation in an illegal activity by a protected person would render the principal perpetrator of that activity liable for the war crime of forced labor.

[375] *Prosecutor* v. *Naletelić and Martinović*, ICTY (Trial Chamber), judgment of 31 March 2003, paras. 322 et seq.

[376] In particular, the war crime of outrages upon personal dignity (ICC Statute, Art. 8(2)(b)(xxi) and (c)(ii) could be considered; see marginal nos. 917 et seq.

[377] See also marginal no. 809.

[378] See Elements of Crimes for Article 8(2)(a)(vi) ICC Statute. The wording ("in particular") of the Elements of Crimes for Article 8(2)(a)(vi) ICC Statute, num. 1, makes it clear that other internationally recognized procedural guarantees must be included even beyond the law of the Geneva Conventions, see K. Kittichaisaree, *International Criminal Law* (2001), p. 151. Provisions to be considered include the guarantees in Additional Protocol I (such as the principle of innocence until proven guilty) and the various human rights treaties (e.g., *International Covenant on Civil and Political Rights, European Convention on Human Rights and Fundamental Freedoms, American Convention on Human Rights*).

[379] Under Geneva Convention III, Art. 99(1) no prisoner of war may be prosecuted or convicted of an act that was not, at the time it was committed, expressly forbidden by existing laws of the custodial state or international law. Such a rule is also found in Geneva Convention IV, Art. 67.

ticle 67 of Geneva Convention IV), the *ne bis in idem* principle (Article 86 of Geneva Convention III, Article 117(3) of Geneva Convention IV), the right to information on the possibility of appeal or petition (Article 106 of Geneva Convention III, Article 73 of Geneva Convention IV), the possibility of presenting a defense and having the assistance of qualified counsel (Article 99(3) of Geneva Convention III), the right to receive the charges and other trial documents in good time and in understandable language (Article 105(4) of Geneva Convention III), the right of an accused prisoner of war to assistance by one of his prisoner comrades (Article 105(1) of Geneva Convention III), the defendant's right to representation by an advocate of his own choice (Article 105(1) of Geneva Convention III, Article 72(1) of Geneva Convention IV),[380] the right of the defendant to present necessary evidence, and especially to call and question witnesses (Article 105(1) of Geneva Convention III, Article 72(1) of Geneva Convention IV), and the right to the services of an interpreter (Article 105(1) of Geneva Convention III, Article 72(3) of Geneva Convention IV). Further, the death penalty may only be imposed under specific circumstances (Article 100 of Geneva Convention III, Article 68 of Geneva Convention IV), and prisoners of war must be tried in the same courts and according to the same procedure as members of the armed forces of the detaining power (Article 102 of Geneva Convention III). A listing of generally recognized principles of regular trials that must be observed by impartial judges, going in part beyond the provisions of the Geneva Conventions, is contained in Article 75(3) and (4) of Additional Protocol I.[381]

940 The criminal status under international law of the deprivation of elementary procedural rights was recognized in various post-war trials. Defendants were convicted as war criminals for their responsibility for trials that operated with false accusations and faked evidence, or in which the accused were denied the right to defense lawyers or interpreters.[382] The Nuremberg Justice Trial should be noted in this context.[383] The issue at that trial, among others, was the deportation of civilians from territory occupied by Germany to the territory of the Reich, where arbitrary trials were then held that often ended in death sentences and executions.

941 In the judgment in the Justice Trial, the Court explained why such trials could not be considered regular trials:

"The trials . . . did not approach even a semblance of fair trial or justice. The accused . . . were arrested and secretly transported to Germany and other countries for trial. They were denied the right to introduce evidence, to be confronted by witnesses against them, or to present witnesses in their own behalf. They were tried secretly and denied the right of counsel of their own choice, and occasionally denied aid of any counsel. No indictment was served in many instances and the accused learned only a few moments before the trial of the nature of the alleged crime for which he was to be tried. The entire proceedings from beginning to end were secret and no public record was allowed to be made of them."[384]

---

[380] Under Geneva Convention IV, Art. 72(2), the defendant must at least be provided with court-appointed counsel. The defense lawyer must be granted access to the defendant and witnesses.

[381] W.J. Fenrick, in O. Triffterer (ed.), *Commentary on the Rome Statute of the International Criminal Court* (1999), Art. 8, marginal no. 16, suggests including all the principles listed there. But this must be rejected to the extent that the list goes beyond the provisions of the Geneva Conventions, as Art. 8(2)(a)(vi) of the ICC Statute does not refer to Additional Protocol I.

[382] US Military Commission Shanghai, judgment of 15 April 1946 (*Sawada*), United Nations War Crimes Commission, *Law Reports of Trials of War Criminals* V, p. 1 at pp. 12 et seq.

[383] US Military Tribunal Nuremberg, judgment of 4 December 1947 (*Altstötter* et al., so-called Justice Trial), *Trials of War Criminals* III, p. 954 at pp. 1046 et seq.

[384] US Military Tribunal Nuremberg, judgment of 4 December 1947 (*Altstötter* et al., so-called Justice Trial), *Trials of War Criminals* III, pp. 954 et seq.

942   It is not necessary to the commission of the crime that the perpetrator's actions be the cause of the imposition of a punishment on a protected person. Thus the definition is also satisfied if the victim commits suicide before the execution of the sentence.[385] If, on the other hand, the defendant is acquitted despite the errors in the trial, the definition is not satisfied. In such cases, the act does not attain the degree of severity necessary for a crime under international law.[386]

943   The mental element requires at least recklessness, as indicated by the use of the term "wilful."[387]

2. Non-International Conflict

944   Article 8(2)(c)(iv) of the ICC Statute covers "the passing of sentences and the carrying out of executions without previous judgement pronounced by a regularly constituted court, affording all judicial guarantees which are generally recognized as indispensable," in connection with non-international armed conflicts.[388] This provision is based on Common Article 3(1)(d) of Geneva Conventions I to IV.[389]

945   The Elements of Crimes distinguish the three separate criminal acts of execution without trial, passing of sentence by a court not regularly constituted, and violation of significant judicial guarantees.[390] The trial must generally appear unfair, taking account of all the circumstances.[391] The Elements of Crimes point out that the ICC Statute's rules regarding the various forms of participation remain unaffected, so that the perpetrator need not have imposed the sentence him or herself.[392]

946   There is a need to clarify the generally recognized legal guarantees at a trial. These cannot be derived from the Elements of Crimes. However, because its wording is almost identical, Article 6(2) of Additional Protocol II may be consulted to interpret Common Article 3(1)(d) of the Geneva Conventions, and thus also Article 8(2)(c)(iv) of the ICC Statute.[393] Article 6(2) of Additional Protocol II contains a non-exclusive list of minimum guarantees that must be observed even in non-international armed conflicts before imposing a punishment or execution. It includes the following guarantees: immediate

---

[385] K. Dörmann, in R.S. Lee (ed.), *The International Criminal Court, Elements of Crimes and Rules of Procedure and Evidence* (2001), p. 124 at pp. 135 et seq.

[386] A comparison with Art. 8(2)(c)(iv) ICC Statute, which also criminalizes violations of legal rights, supports this interpretation, since that provision requires at least a conviction.

[387] On the concept of wilfulness, see marginal nos. 857 et seq. See also marginal no. 320. On the general requirements for the mental element under ICC Statute, Art. 30, and on possible deviations by way of customary international law or the Elements of Crimes, see marginal nos. 294 et seq., esp. 304 et seq.

[388] See also ICTR Statute, Art. 4(b) and (g).

[389] The only difference in wording consists in the fact that the Geneva Conventions refer to the legal guarantees recognized by "civilized peoples." This wording was found to be antiquated during the drafting of the ICC Statute and was therefore replaced, see E. La Haye, in R.S. Lee (ed.), *The International Criminal Court, Elements of Crimes and Rules of Procedure and Evidence* (2001), p. 207 at p. 212.

[390] Elements of Crimes for Article 8(2)(c)(iv) ICC Statute, num. 4.

[391] Elements of Crimes for Article 8(2)(c)(iv) ICC Statute, num. 5, fn. 59.

[392] Elements of Crimes for Article 8(2)(c)(iv) ICC Statute, num. 1, fn. 58.

[393] See C. Pilloud and J.S. Pictet, in Y. Sandoz, C. Swinarski and B. Zimmermann (eds.), *Commentary on the Additional Protocols* (1987), marginal no. 3084; A. Zimmermann, in O. Triffterer (ed.), *Commentary on the Rome Statute of the International Criminal Court* (1999), Art. 8, marginal no. 282.

notification of the accused of the particulars of the alleged offense, provision of all rights and means of defense, prohibition of collective punishment, prohibition of retroactive punishment, the presumption of innocence until proven guilty, the right to be present at trial, and the right not to be forced to testify against oneself.

Like Article 3(1)(d) of Geneva Conventions I-IV, Article 8(2)(c)(iv) of the ICC Stat- **947** ute requires a regularly constituted court. Special *ad hoc* courts are prohibited.[394] The wording creates problems when non-state parties to a conflict, such as rebel groups, are affected, as they can rarely set up regular courts.[395] Instead of a regularly-constituted court, Article 6 of Additional Protocol II requires a court that assures the essential guarantees of independence and impartiality.[396] Unfortunately, these provisions were not incorporated into the ICC Statute.

State authorities retain the right to criminally prosecute fighters or civilians for crimes **948** they commit in connection with (internal) armed conflicts.[397] They may also impose the death penalty, where applicable domestic law permits it and the death penalty is not forbidden under international law in the particular case.[398]

As with the war crime in international armed conflict, the mental element requires at **949** least recklessness.[399]

XI. Unlawful Confinement (International Conflict)

Unlawful confinement of protected persons is covered by Article 8(2)(a)(vii), third alter- **950** native, of the ICC Statute. The crime is based on various provisions of Geneva Convention IV. Under Article 147 of Geneva Convention IV, unlawful confinement of civilians is a grave breach of the Convention. In non-international armed conflict, unlawful confinement is not a war crime under either the ICC Statute or customary international law.[400]

Geneva Conventions I to III also contain detailed rules that prohibit the confinement of protected **951** persons.[401] However, violating these provisions is not a grave breach of the Conventions. Thus

---

[394] See H.-P. Gasser, in D. Fleck (ed.), *The Handbook of Humanitarian Law in Armed Conflicts* (1999), no. 576.

[395] See A. Zimmermann, in O. Triffterer (ed.), *Commentary on the Rome Statute of the International Criminal Court* (1999), Art. 8, marginal no. 281.

[396] See S.S. Junod, in Y. Sandoz, C. Swinarski and B. Zimmermann (eds.), *Commentary on the Additional Protocols* (1987), marginal no. 4600.

[397] See S.S. Junod, in Y. Sandoz, C. Swinarski and B. Zimmermann (eds.), *Commentary on the Additional Protocols* (1987), marginal no. 4597.

[398] An example of a prohibition of the death penalty under international law is found in Additional Protocol II, Art. 6(4), which prohibits imposition of the death penalty on persons who were younger than 18 at the time of the crime and the execution of the death penalty on mothers of small children or pregnant women. Geneva Conventions I-IV, Art. 3 contains no such prohibition.

[399] See marginal no. 943.

[400] Explanatory Memorandum of the (German) Code of Crimes Against International Law, *BT-Drs.* 14/8524, p. 28.

[401] Both the conditions of confinement and the rights guaranteed to the prisoner are regulated. Under Geneva Convention I, Art. 28, chaplains and medical personnel from the opposing side may only be retained if the state of health, spiritual needs and the number of prisoners of war require it. In

unlawful confinement of protected persons as defined in the three Conventions – that is, the wounded, sick and prisoners of war – is not criminalized under Article 8(2)(a)(vii) of the ICC Statute.[402]

952   In its *Mucić* judgment, the Yugoslavia Tribunal interpreted unlawful confinement in light of the relevant provisions of Geneva Convention IV.[403] The Tribunal found that the definition covers two cases. First, the confinement of protected persons can itself be unlawful and entail criminal liability. In principle, after all, the personal freedom of civilians is to be assured even in armed conflicts. However, in certain circumstances, the confinement of protected persons could be justified, if for example a civilian threatens a party to the conflict with his or her behavior, or if there is probable cause to believe that he or she might do so.[404] But here, too, confinement is only permitted as a last resort.[405] Under no circumstances may a civilian be interned solely because of his or her political opinion, nationality or gender, nor may internment be used as a collective punishment.[406] Second, the definition is satisfied if, during lawful confinement, the procedural rights of the person involved are violated.[407] Article 43 of Geneva Convention IV provides for a system of regular review of detention, which is a main pillar of the Convention.[408]

953   The Elements of Crimes for Article 8(2)(a)(vii), third alternative, of the ICC Statute are also to be understood in light of the *Mucić* et al. judgment. The Elements make it clear that not only unlawful confinement, but also maintaining confinement, can satisfy the definition of the crime. The second alternative refers especially to cases of violation of procedural rights following confinement.[409] Thus if the original reason for the confine-

---

any case, they must be returned "as soon as a route for their return is open and military considerations permit" (Art. 32). Geneva Convention I, Art. 32, prohibits retaining medical personnel from neutral states. Under Geneva Convention II, Art. 36, religious, medical and hospital personnel of hospital ships and their crews may not be taken prisoner. If they are captured nevertheless, the persons involved must be returned as soon as possible under Art. 37. Geneva Convention III contains detailed rules on the confinement of prisoners of war. Art. 21 permits internment of prisoners of war but forbids holding them in close confinement unless this is necessary to safeguard their health. Under Art. 22, internment may take place only in facilities on land, which afford every guarantee of hygiene and healthfulness. Art. 118 establishes that, following cessation of hostilities, prisoners of war must be released and repatriated without delay.

[402] See also marginal nos. 955 et seq.

[403] See esp. the provisions of Geneva Convention IV, Arts. 5, 27, 41–43, 78.

[404] *Prosecutor* v. *Mucić* et al., ICTY (Trial Chamber), judgment of 16 November 1998, para. 576. In the Tribunal's view, these sorts of activities include primarily sabotage and spying.

[405] *Prosecutor* v. *Mucić* et al., ICTY (Trial Chamber), judgment of 16 November 1998, para. 576. W.J. Fenrick, in O. Triffterer (ed.), *Commentary on the Rome Statute of the International Criminal Court* (1999), Art. 8, marginal no. 18, assumes that, because of the discretion left to the parties to the conflict, the crime of unlawful confinement is difficult to prove.

[406] *Prosecutor* v. *Mucić* et al., ICTY (Trial Chamber), judgment of 16 November 1998, paras. 567, 577.

[407] *Prosecutor* v. *Mucić* et al., ICTY (Trial Chamber), judgment of 16 November 1998, paras. 583, 1135.

[408] *Prosecutor* v. *Mucić* et al., ICTY (Trial Chamber), judgment of 16 November 1998, paras. 579 et seq., esp. paras. 1135 and 1141.

[409] See H. von Hebel, in R.S. Lee (ed.), *The International Criminal Court, Elements of Crimes and Rules of Procedure and Evidence* (2001), p. 138.

ment later ceases to exist and the confinement continues nevertheless, this may entail criminal liability.

As to the mental element, Article 30 of the ICC Statute applies.[410]   **954**

XII. Delay in Repatriation (International Conflict)

Under Article 85(4)(b) of Additional Protocol I, it is a grave breach of the Protocol, and   **955** therefore a war crime, to unjustifiably delay repatriation of prisoners of war and civilians in international armed conflicts. This provision was not incorporated into the ICC Statute. However, cases of unjustifiable delay in repatriating civilians may often be considered[411] unlawful confinement.[412] The delayed repatriation of prisoners of war is nevertheless not covered by any provision of the ICC Statute;[413] here the Statute lags behind customary international law. In non-international armed conflict, there is no such war crime under customary international law.[414]

Article 85(4)(b) of Additional Protocol I follows from provisions of the Geneva Con-   **956** ventions. Article 109(1) of Geneva Convention III requires the parties to the conflict to repatriate badly wounded and seriously ill prisoners of war. Under Article 118(1) of Geneva Convention III, all prisoners of war are to be repatriated once hostilities end; a similar rule for interned civilians is found in Article 134 of Geneva Convention IV. Under Article 35(1) of Geneva Convention IV, civilians located on the territory of the hostile party to the conflict may not be refused permission to leave this territory. If this provision is violated without justification, the definition of delayed repatriation is satisfied.[415]

The mental element requires at least recklessness, as the use of the term "wilful" in   **957** Article 85(4) of Additional Protocol I indicates.[416]

XIII. Hostage-Taking

Hostage-taking is covered by Article 8(2)(a)(viii) of the ICC Statute for international   **958**

---

[410] On the general requirements of the mental element, see marginal nos. 294 et seq., esp. 304 et seq.

[411] Explanatory Memorandum of the (German) Code of Crimes Against International Law, *BT-Drs.* 14/8524, p. 29.

[412] See above, marginal no. 950.

[413] Neither is the delayed repatriation of prisoners of war included in ICC Statute, Art. 8(2)(a)(vii), alternative 3 (unlawful confinement), as this provision only protects civilians. Geneva Convention III does not recognize unlawful confinement as a grave breach, see W.J. Fenrick, in O. Triffterer (ed.), *Commentary on the Rome Statute of the International Criminal Court* (1999), Art. 8, marginal no. 7; on the different German rule, see Explanatory Memorandum of the (German) Code of Crimes Against International Law, *BT-Drs.* 14/8524, p. 29.

[414] For this reason, delayed repatriation is criminal only in international conflicts under the (German) Code of Crimes Against International Law [*Völkerstrafgesetzbuch, VStGB*] as well, see Explanatory Memorandum of the (German) Code of Crimes Against International Law, *BT-Drs.* 14/8524, p. 28.

[415] B. Zimmermann, in Y. Sandoz, C. Swinarski and B. Zimmermann (eds.), *Commentary on the Additional Protocols* (1987), marginal no. 3508.

[416] On the concept of wilfulness, see marginal nos. 857 et seq. On the general requirements for the mental element under ICC Statute, Art. 30 and on possible deviations by way of customary international law or the Elements of Crimes, see marginal nos. 304 et seq., 313 et seq.

armed conflict and Article 8(2)(c)(iii) for non-international armed conflict. The requirements are the same for both types of conflicts.[417]

959 Article 34(4) of Geneva Convention IV and Article 75(2)(c) of Additional Protocol I contain a prohibition on taking hostages in connection with international armed conflict. Under Article 147 of Geneva Convention IV, such hostage-taking is a grave breach of the Convention. Common Article 3 of Geneva Conventions I-IV and Article 4(2)(c) of Additional Protocol II also forbid hostage-taking in non-international conflicts. Originally, only the killing of hostages was viewed as a war crime,[418] and one which could even be justified under certain circumstances.[419] In Geneva Convention IV, however, the taking of hostages itself was described as a grave breach of the Convention.[420] This wording was adopted in Article 75 of Additional Protocol I. The Yugoslavia Tribunal, too, in the *Blaškić* case, convicted the defendant not only because of the killing of hostages, but because of the hostage-taking itself, which occurred with the intention of extorting the release of prisoners and forcing the opponent to cease military operations.[421]

960 Under the Elements of Crimes, the offense requires that the perpetrator seize one or more people and hold them prisoner or take them hostage in another way.[422] The hostage-taking need not necessarily be against the hostage's will, as long as only the party to the conflict has control of the hostage and intends in this way to force concessions from the opposing party.[423] In international armed conflicts, it is primarily civilians who are protected, as hostage-taking is only a grave breach of Geneva Convention IV. The class of protected persons in non-international conflicts is determined by Common Article 3 of Geneva Conventions I to IV, and is thus, surprisingly, broader, since it also includes former fighters.[424]

961 In addition, the perpetrator must threaten to kill or injure the victim or to maintain his or her imprisonment.

962 Beyond the general mental requirements regarding the material elements of the crime (Article 30 of the ICC Statute),[425] the mental element requires, as a specific subjective criterion, purpose on part of the perpetrator to coerce a state, international organization,

---

[417] See also ICTY Statute, Art. 2(h) and ICTR Statute, Art. 4(c). The Yugoslavia Tribunal described the requirements for both types of conflict as "similar," see *Prosecutor* v. *Blaškić*, ICTY (Trial Chamber), judgment of 3 March 2000, para. 158. A. Zimmermann, in O. Triffterer (ed.), *Commentary on the Rome Statute of the International Criminal Court* (1999), Art. 8 marginal no. 277, too, looks to ICC Statute, Art. 8(2)(a)(viii) for the requirements of ICC Statute, Art. 8(2)(c)(iii). The Elements of Crimes are identical for both crimes, aside from the protected group.

[418] See IMT Statute, Art. 6(b). The IMT described the prohibition as part of the laws and customs of war expressed in Art. 46 of the Hague Regulations; on this and on the development of the provision, see K. Kittichaisaree, *International Criminal Law* (2001), p. 155.

[419] See US Military Tribunal Nuremberg, judgment of 19 February 1948 (*List* et al., so-called Hostage Trial), in *Trials of War Criminals* XI, pp. 1248 et seq.

[420] See also J.S. Pictet (ed.), *Geneva Convention IV, Commentary* (1958), pp. 600 et seq., which makes it clear that hostage-taking itself is a serious act.

[421] *Prosecutor* v. *Blaškić*, ICTY (Trial Chamber), judgment of 3 March 2000, para. 701.

[422] It should be noted that confinement of protected persons can be lawful under certain circumstances, such as to protect civilians or as a security measure, see *Prosecutor* v. *Blaškić*, ICTY (Trial Chamber), judgment of 3 March 2000, para. 158.

[423] See C. Pilloud and J.S. Pictet, in Y. Sandoz, C. Swinarski and B. Zimmermann (eds.), *Commentary on the Additional Protocols* (1987), marginal nos. 3051 et seq.

[424] See marginal nos. 872 et seq.

[425] On the general requirements of the mental element, see marginal nos. 294 et seq., esp. 304 et seq.

natural or legal person or group of people to act or fail to act in a certain way as an express or implicit condition for the safety, continued bodily integrity,[426] or release of the victims.[427] Thus the perpetrator must expect to obtain a concession or gain an advantage in this way.[428] This special subjective criterion arises not from the text of the Statute itself, but from the Elements of Crimes, which in turn follow Article 1(1) of the *International Convention Against the Taking of Hostages* of 17 December 1979.[429]

XIV. Deportation or Forcible Transfer

Jean Marie Henckaerts: Deportation and Transfer of Civilians in Time of War, 26 *Vanderbilt* **963** *Journal of Transnational Law* (1993), pp. 469 et seq.; Theodor Meron: Deportation of Civilians as a War Crime under Customary Law, in Theodor Meron, *War Crimes Law Comes of Age* (1998), pp. 142 et seq.

1. International Conflict

Article 8(2)(a)(vii), first and second alternatives, of the ICC Statute create criminal liabil- **964** ity for unlawful deportation or transfer of protected persons. This is a grave breach of Geneva Convention IV,[430] so that only civilians, not prisoners of war or the wounded, are protected. A rule with the same content is found in Article 8(2)(b)(viii), second alternative, of the ICC Statute.[431] The provisions closely parallel the crime against humanity of deportation or forcible transfer of population (Art. 7(1)(d) of the ICC Statute)[432] and were adopted in reaction to the deportations of World War II.[433] The crime is primarily relevant where a party to the conflict is occupying territory.[434]

---

[426] See W.J. Fenrick, in O. Triffterer (ed.), *Commentary on the Rome Statute of the International Criminal Court* (1999), Art. 8, marginal no. 19.

[427] Elements of Crimes for Article 8(2)(a)(viii) ICC Statute, num. 1 et seq. Elements of Crimes for Article 8(2)(c)(iii) ICC Statute, num. 1 et seq. Here the Elements of Crimes narrow the scope of the crime, as specifically permitted by ICC Statute, Art. 30, see marginal nos. 310 et seq.

[428] See *Prosecutor* v. *Blaškić*, ICTY (Trial Chamber), judgment of 3 March 2000, para. 158.

[429] 18 *ILM* (1979), p. 1456. This Convention did not arise in the context of international humanitarian law and is generally not viewed as part of customary international law, see K. Dörmann, in R.S. Lee (ed.), *The International Criminal Court, Elements of Crimes and Rules of Procedure and Evidence* (2001), pp. 138 et seq. Art. 1(1) of the Convention reads: "Any person who seizes or detains and threatens to kill, to injure or to continue to detain another person (hereinafter referred to as the 'hostage') in order to compel a third party, namely, a State, an international intergovernmental organization, a natural or juridical person, or a group of persons, to do or abstain from doing any act as an explicit or implicit condition for the release of the hostage commits the offence of taking of hostages ('hostage-taking') within the meaning of this Convention."

[430] See Geneva Convention IV, Art. 147. See also ICTY Statute, Art. 2(g), first alternative.

[431] This provision is based on Additional Protocol I, Art. 85(4)(a), under which resettlement of a party's own population is declared a grave breach (see marginal nos. 971 et seq.), but also the expulsion or transfer of the population of the opposing party is once again proscribed, though this rule does not differ from the rule in Geneva Convention IV, see B. Zimmermann, in Y. Sandoz, C. Swinarski and B. Zimmermann (eds.), *Commentary on the Additional Protocols* (1987), marginal nos. 3503 et seq. This also explains the repetition of the provision in ICC Statute, Art. 8(2)(a) and (b).

[432] See marginal nos. 696 et seq.

[433] See J.S. Pictet (ed.), *Geneva Convention IV, Commentary* (1958), p. 599.

[434] See W.J. Fenrick, in O. Triffterer (ed.), *Commentary on the Rome Statute of the International Criminal Court* (1999), Art. 8, marginal no. 17.

965   The concepts of both deportation and transfer denote involuntary, unlawful movement of protected persons out of their home territory: to a place outside the state's borders, for deportation, and within the state's borders, for transfer.[435] The deportation or
transfer of a single person is enough to satisfy the definition of the crime.[436] When a
deportation or transfer is to be considered unlawful and when it can be justified in exceptional cases can be determined in particular from Articles 45 and 49 of Geneva Convention IV. If the transferred persons give their consent, there may be no grounds for
criminal liability. However, given the accompanying circumstance of armed conflict, it is
always necessary to carefully examine whether the victim was really in a position to give
his or her consent.[437]

966   Under Article 45(1) and (2) of Geneva Convention IV, protected persons may not be surrendered
to a power that is not a party to the Convention, unless this is a repatriation to the country of
settlement following the end of hostilities. Protected persons may only be surrendered to other
treaty parties if the custodial state has made certain of "the willingness and ability of such trans-
feree power to apply the present Convention" (Article 45(3)). Under no circumstances may protected persons be transferred to a state in which they would have reason to fear persecution for
their political or religious beliefs (Article 45(4)). According to Article 49(1) of Geneva Convention
IV, "individual or mass forcible transfers, as well as deportations of protected persons from occupied territory to the territory of the Occupying Power or to that of any other country, occupied or
not, are prohibited, regardless of their motive." Under Article 49(2), however, "total or partial
evacuation of a given area" is permitted if it protects the security of the population or is required
for imperative military reasons. Once these grounds are no longer present, the population must be
transferred back immediately. Further, under Article 49(3) of Geneva Convention IV, in case of
such temporary evacuations, the occupying power must ensure proper accommodation, hygienic
conditions, security and nutrition.

967   As to the mental element, Article 30 of the ICC Statute applies.[438]

2. Non-International Conflict

968   Article 8(2)(e)(viii) of the ICC Statute covers, as a crime in non-international armed
conflict, "ordering the displacement of the civilian population for reasons related to the
conflict, unless the security of the civilians involved or imperative military reasons so demand." This provision was derived directly from Article 17(1) of Additional Protocol II
and is based on the principles underlying Article 49(2) of Geneva Convention IV. Article
17(2) of Additional Protocol II additionally contains a prohibition on forcing civilians to
leave their territory because of the conflict. The broad wording of Article 8(2)(e)(viii) of

---

[435] *Prosecutor* v. *Krstić*, ICTY (Trial Chamber), judgment of 2 August 2001, para. 521.

[436] See Elements of Crimes for Article 8(2)(a)(vii) ICC Statute, -1, num. 1.

[437] *Prosecutor* v. *Naletilić and Martinović*, ICTY (Trial Chamber), judgment of 31 March 2003,
para. 519.

[438] On the general requirements of the mental element, see marginal nos. 294 et seq., esp. 304 et
seq. A lowering of the subjective requirements in comparison with Article 30 does not arise from the
use of the term "wilful" in Article 85(4) of Additional Protocol I, see *Prosecutor* v. *Naletilić and
Martinović*, ICTY (Trial Chamber), judgment of 31 March 2003, paras. 520 et seq.; on the concept of
wilfulness see marginal nos. 857 et seq.

the ICC Statute also encompasses this prohibition.[439] In contrast to international armed conflicts, in civil wars only an order to transfer populations is criminalized, not the transfer itself.[440] Transfer is the forcible resettlement of a population.[441] The definition only includes orders to acts that lead directly to removal of a population from a territory. Acts that aim only indirectly at expulsion of a civilian population, such as starvation with the intention of causing the population to leave the territory, are not included.[442] As the use of the term "civilian population" indicates, the definition is only satisfied if the transfer of a number of civilians is ordered.[443]

As to the mental element, Article 30 of the ICC Statute applies.[444] **969**

An order to transfer a civilian population is only justified in exceptional cases: it may **970** occur only to protect the security of the civilian population or for imperative military reasons. If the transfer is ordered for reasons not connected with the armed conflict, such as natural disaster or epidemic, the definition is not satisfied.[445]

XV. Transfer of a Party's Own Civilian Population (International Conflict)

The transfer by an occupying power of parts of its own civilian population to territory it **971** occupies is criminalized under Article 8(2)(b)(viii), first alternative, of the ICC Statute. This is a war crime under customary international law;[446] its penalization extends only to international armed conflict.[447]

A prohibition on an occupying power's sending or transporting part of its own civil- **972** ian population into occupied territories is already contained in Article 49(6) of Geneva Convention IV; however, a violation is not a grave breach of the Convention. The prohibition is a response to the practice of several states during World War II of transferring parts of their own populations into occupied territories in order to colonize them. These measures were an existential threat to those already living there.[448] Article 85(4)(a) of Additional Protocol I, created in part based on the experience of Israeli settlement poli-

---

[439] A. Zimmermann, in O. Triffterer (ed.), *Commentary on the Rome Statute of the International Criminal Court* (1999), Art. 8, marginal no. 313.

[440] The limitation of conduct to orders is also clear from the Elements of Crimes for Article 8(2)(e)(viii) ICC Statute, num. 1 and 3. The (German) Code of Crimes Against International Law [*Völkerstrafgesetzbuch, VStGB*], Sec. 8(1) no. 6 takes a different tack, criminalizing deportation or transfer even in non-international armed conflicts.

[441] See S.S. Junod, in Y. Sandoz, C. Swinarski and B. Zimmermann (eds.), *Commentary on the Additional Protocols* (1987), marginal nos. 4851 et seq.

[442] See A. Zimmermann, in O. Triffterer (ed.), *Commentary on the Rome Statute of the International Criminal Court* (1999), Art. 8, marginal no. 310.

[443] See A. Zimmermann, in O. Triffterer (ed.), *Commentary on the Rome Statute of the International Criminal Court* (1999), Art. 8, marginal no. 312.

[444] On the general requirements of the mental element, see marginal nos. 294 et seq., esp. 304 et seq.

[445] See A. Zimmermann, in O. Triffterer (ed.), *Commentary on the Rome Statute of the International Criminal Court* (1999), Art. 8, marginal nos. 315 et seq.

[446] See M. Cottier, in O. Triffterer (ed.), *Commentary on the Rome Statute of the International Criminal Court* (1999), Art. 8, marginal no. 86.

[447] See Explanatory Memorandum of the (German) Code of Crimes Against International Law, *BT-Drs.* 14/8524, p. 29.

[448] See J.S. Pictet (ed.), *Geneva Convention IV, Commentary* (1958), p. 283.

cies in the occupied Palestinian territories,[449] declares that "the transfer by the Occupying Power of parts of its own civilian population into the territory it occupies . . . in violation of Article 49 of the Fourth Convention" is a grave breach of the Protocol due to the severe consequences to the local population.[450] The ICC Statute adopted the provision with minor modifications. The ICC Statute makes clear that transfer can be direct or indirect;[451] it does not explicitly refer to Article 49 of Geneva Convention IV.

973   The provision aims to prevent a party to the conflict from changing the demographic and political realities on the territory of the opposing party by settling parts of its own population there, in order to create or consolidate political or territorial claims over an occupied territory.[452] In addition, such settlement makes the return of refugees and the restitution of confiscated property more difficult.[453] It also violates a basic principle of international humanitarian law: the limited duration of an occupying power's rule,[454] which is accompanied by greatly limited rights of sovereignty. As the norm protects only the population living in the occupied territory, it is irrelevant whether the population is resettled by force or voluntarily.[455] Further, transfer of only a small number of persons is sufficient.[456] The motive for the resettlement is irrelevant.[457]

974   Action by the occupying power is a necessary requirement: the transfer of persons must be imputable to the government of the occupying state. The term "transfer" is to be interpreted in light of international humanitarian law.[458] While a direct transfer can be seen in the settlement of part of the population by the government of the occupying power, indirect transfer can take various forms. The government can provide financial incentives such as subsidies or tax breaks for settlement in occupied territories. Discrimi-

---

[449] For details, see K. Partsch, in M. Bothe, K. Partsch and W.A. Solf (eds.), *New Rules for Victims of Armed Conflicts* (1982), Art. 85 Additional Protocol I, marginal no. 2.19.

[450] See B. Zimmermann, in Y. Sandoz, C. Swinarski and B. Zimmermann (eds.), *Commentary on the Additional Protocols* (1987), marginal no. 3504.

[451] This, however, is seen by most states not as an expansion of the scope, but only as a clarification, see H. von Hebel, in R.S. Lee (ed.), *The International Criminal Court, Elements of Crimes and Rules of Procedure and Evidence* (2001), p. 158 at pp. 159 et seq.

[452] A territory is considered occupied under Hague Regulations, Art. 42, if it is actually in the hands of the opposing forces. It is conditioned on whether the occupying power can actually exercise occupation authority, see H.-P. Gasser, in D. Fleck (ed.), *The Handbook of Humanitarian Law in Armed Conflicts* (1999), no. 526.

[453] M. Cottier, in O. Triffterer (ed.), *Commentary on the Rome Statute of the International Criminal Court* (1999), Art. 8, marginal no. 95.

[454] See, e.g., H.-P. Gasser, in D. Fleck (ed.), *The Handbook of Humanitarian Law in Armed Conflicts* (1999), nos. 531 and 552.

[455] See M. Cottier, in O. Triffterer (ed.), *Commentary on the Rome Statute of the International Criminal Court* (1999), Art. 8, marginal no. 96.

[456] See Explanatory Memorandum of the (German) Code of Crimes Against International Law, *BT-Drs.* 14/8524, p. 29; K. Kittichaisaree, *International Criminal Law* (2001), p. 169.

[457] See M. Cottier, in O. Triffterer (ed.), *Commentary on the Rome Statute of the International Criminal Court* (1999), Art. 8, marginal no. 95.

[458] Elements of Crimes for Article 8(2)(b)(viii) ICC Statute, num. 1 (a), fn. 44. Primarily at issue are the provisions of Geneva Convention IV and Additional Protocol I, see H. von Hebel, in R.S. Lee (ed.), *The International Criminal Court, Elements of Crimes and Rules of Procedure and Evidence* (2001), p. 158 at p. 162.

natory administrative practice that disadvantages the resident population, for example in the distribution of official permits, can also be seen as indirect transfer.[459]

An exception to the prohibition on transfer of a party's own civilian population is for- **975** mulated in Additional Protocol I, Article 78, which permits the sending of children to foreign countries and occupied territories, under strict conditions, for health or medical reasons.

With regard to the mental element, recklessness can suffice, as indicated by the use of **976** the term "wilfulness" in the definition of the crime.[460] Recklessness will be most relevant in cases of indirect transfer of a civilian population.

XVI. Use of Child Soldiers

Geraldine van Bueren: The International Legal Protection of Children in Armed Conflicts, 43 *In-* **977** *ternational and Comparative Law Quarterly* (1994), pp. 809 et seq.; Daniel Helle: Optional Protocol on the involvement of children in armed conflict to the Convention on the rights of the child, 82 *International Review of the Red Cross* (2000), pp. 797 et seq.; Sandrine Valentin: Trafficking of Child Soldiers: Expanding the United Nations Convention on the Rights of the Child and its Optional Protocol on the Involvement of Children in Armed Conflicts, 9 *New England Journal of International and Comparative Law* (2003), pp. 109 et seq.; Sarah L. Wells: Crimes Against Child Soldiers in Armed Conflict Situations: Application and Limits of International Humanitarian Law, 12 *Tulane Journal of International and Comparative Law* (2004), pp. 287 et seq.

Article 8(2)(b)(xxvi) of the ICC Statute covers conscripting or enlisting children under **978** fifteen in armed forces or using them to participate actively in hostilities during international armed conflicts; Article 8(2)(e)(vii) of the ICC Statute provides a corresponding rule for non-international conflicts. This is the first time this conduct has been expressly criminalized under international law. The prohibition is, however, based on existing provisions of international humanitarian and human rights law. It is unclear whether this criminalization under the ICC Statute fully reflects customary international law, or whether the scope of the crime under customary international law is limited to particularly serious recruitment methods and use of child soldiers.[461] Given the severe consequences normally suffered by children used as soldiers, however, it should be assumed that customary international law comprehensively criminalizes the recruitment and use of child soldiers.[462]

---

[459] See M. Cottier, in O. Triffterer (ed.), *Commentary on the Rome Statute of the International Criminal Court* (1999), Art. 8, marginal no. 97.

[460] On the term wilfulness, see marginal nos. 857 et seq. On the general requirements for the mental element under ICC Statute, Art. 30 and on possible deviations by way of customary international law or the Elements of Crimes, see marginal nos. 304 et seq., and nos. 313 et seq.

[461] See the statement of the UN Secretary-General on the Statute of the Sierra Leone Tribunal, UN Doc. S/2000/915, paras. 17 et seq.; K. Kittichaisaree, *International Criminal Law* (2001), p. 187. The Appeals Chamber of the Special Court for Sierra Leone, however, held that child recruitment had been criminalized under customary international law by November 1996, if not earlier, see *Prosecutor v. Norman*, Special Court for Sierra Leone (Appeals Chamber), decision of 31 May 2004, para. 53; see also *Prosecutor v. Norman*, Special Court for Sierra Leone (Appeals Chamber), decision of 31 May 2004, dissenting opinion of Justice Robertson, para. 47, who opined that "the crime of non-forcible child enlistment did not enter international criminal law until the Rome Treaty in July 1997."

[462] On the criteria for criminality of violations of international humanitarian law under customary international law, see marginal nos. 806 et seq.

979   Article 77(2) of Additional Protocol I and Article 4(3)(c) of Additional Protocol II forbid the treaty parties from enlisting children under age 15 in their armed forces or permitting them to take part in hostilities.[463] Article 38(3) of the *Convention on the Rights of the Child* of 20 November 1989[464] affirms this prohibition. As the Convention has been ratified by 191 states, the prohibition on the use of child soldiers has now become customary international law. The *Optional Protocol to the Convention on the Rights of the Child* adopted in 2000[465] raised the age limit for the participation of children in armed conflict to 18.[466] However, this rule has yet to achieve customary law status and was therefore not incorporated into the ICC Statute.[467]

980   The prohibition on using child soldiers was included in the ICC Statute for various reasons. First, children's participation in armed conflicts causes particularly severe trauma. Their willingness to use violence is greatly increased, their education interrupted.[468] The provision thus protects children from reckless recruitment by their own state.[469] Second, child soldiers represent a particular danger to other people, since children are often unpredictable.[470]

981   As to the objective elements, Article 8(2)(b)(xxvi) and (e)(vii) of the ICC Statute cover both forced conscription and voluntary enlistment of children into the armed forces.[471] National armed forces, as referred to in Article 8(2)(b)(xxvi) of the ICC Statute, are a country's official forces; here Article 43 of Additional Protocol I can be called upon for reference.[472] In non-international armed conflict, Article 8(2)(e)(vii) of the ICC Statute covers the conscription or enlistment into any armed force or group. This is in line with the language used in Article 4(3) of Additional Protocol II and ensures that the recruitment of child soldiers by insurgents is also a crime.[473]

982   The crime's third alternative, the use of children for active participation in hostilities, is somewhat problematic. It is, for one, unclear what is meant by "participat[ing] ac-

---

[463] Should the parties to the conflict recruit young people between 15 and 18 years of age, they are obligated under Additional Protocol I, Art. 77(2), sentence 2, to enlist the oldest first, wherever possible. This requirement, however, is accompanied by no penal sanction.

[464] 1577 *UNTS* (1990), p. 43.

[465] UN Doc. A/RES/54/263.

[466] See D. Helle, 82 *International Review of the Red Cross* (2000), pp. 797 et seq.

[467] See K. Kittichaisaree, *International Criminal Law* (2001), p. 187.

[468] See M. Cottier, in O. Triffterer (ed.), *Commentary on the Rome Statute of the International Criminal Court* (1999), Art. 8, marginal no. 225.

[469] See C. Pilloud and J.S. Pictet, in Y. Sandoz, C. Swinarski and B. Zimmermann (eds.), *Commentary on the Additional Protocols* (1987), marginal no. 3191.

[470] See C. Pilloud and J.S. Pictet, in Y. Sandoz, C. Swinarski and B. Zimmermann (eds.), *Commentary on the Additional Protocols* (1987), marginal no. 3183.

[471] See M. Cottier, in O. Triffterer (ed.), *Commentary on the Rome Statute of the International Criminal Court* (1999), Art. 8, marginal no. 228; C. Garraway, in R.S. Lee (ed.), *The International Criminal Court, Elements of Crimes and Rules of Procedure and Evidence* (2001), p. 205.

[472] See M. Cottier, in O. Triffterer (ed.), *Commentary on the Rome Statute of the International Criminal Court* (1999), Art. 8, marginal no. 231; H. von Hebel and D. Robinson, in: R.S. Lee (ed.), *The International Criminal Court, The Making of the Rome Statute* (1999), p. 79 at p. 118.

[473] See A. Zimmermann, in O. Triffterer (ed.), *Commentary on the Rome Statute of the International Criminal Court* (1999), Art. 8, marginal no. 306; H. von Hebel and D. Robinson, in R.S. Lee (ed.), *The International Criminal Court, The Making of the Rome Statute* (1999), p. 79 at p. 119.

tively" in hostilities. In the view of the Preparatory Commission, this term includes both direct participation in hostilities and active participation in other military activities that are closely connected with hostilities, such as, for example, acting as decoys or couriers or at military checkpoints or in connection with intelligence, espionage, or sabotage. Direct support, such as transport of supplies or other activities at the front, would be included as well. In contrast, activities with no connection to hostilities, such as delivery of food to an air force base or performance of housework in an officer's quarters, would not be included, in the view of the Preparatory Commission.[474]

The Rwanda Tribunal, in contrast, has defined the concept of active participation in a different **983** context, based on the concept of direct participation under Article 3 of Geneva Conventions I to IV, and thus more narrowly.[475] In the Tribunal's view, active participation includes acts that, because of their nature and purpose, are likely to harm the personnel or equipment of the enemy armed forces.[476] Whether this decision can also be applied to the offense of using child soldiers is doubtful, however.[477] If a more narrow concept of direct participation is used with regard to Common Article 3, it helps to protect children by broadening the group protected by Common Article 3 (civilians). In contrast, for the crime of using child soldiers, a narrow concept of active participation limits the protection of children – a result that can hardly reflect the purpose of the provision.

In addition, it is doubtful whether cases are also included in which children voluntarily **984** take an active part in hostilities, so that they are not "used" in the narrow sense of the term. But such a narrow interpretation of the term is contradicted by the fact that the prohibition in Article 4(3)(c) of Additional Protocol II on participation by children in hostilities is understood to be absolute,[478] and the parties to the conflict are normally obligated under Article 77(2) of Additional Protocol I to prevent the voluntary participation of children in military operations.[479] Finally, military commanders have a duty to bar children from hostilities or direct support activities;[480] otherwise, they may be charged with an omission.

As to the mental element, both the enlistment of children in armed forces and the use **985** of children in military operations require the perpetrator's knowledge that the child is under 15 years old. According to the Elements of Crimes, potential knowledge is sufficient.[481] Thus those who purposely close their eyes to a child's age are also acting intentionally – for example, by failing to make inquiries about the child's age even though the

---

[474] See fn. 12 to Draft ICC Statute (1998), Art. 5.

[475] *Prosecutor* v. *Akayesu,* ICTR (Trial Chamber), judgment of 2 September 1998, para. 629, on Additional Protocol II, Art. 4(1).

[476] *Prosecutor* v. *Rutaganda,* ICTR (Trial Chamber), judgment of 6 December 1999, para. 100.

[477] But see K. Kittichaisaree, *International Criminal Law* (2001), p. 187.

[478] See S.S. Junod, in Y. Sandoz, C. Swinarski and B. Zimmermann (eds.), *Commentary on the Additional Protocols* (1987), marginal no. 4557.

[479] For details see C. Pilloud and J.S. Pictet, in Y. Sandoz, C. Swinarski and B. Zimmermann (eds.), *Commentary on the Additional Protocols* (1987), marginal nos. 3184 et seq.

[480] See M. Cottier, in O. Triffterer (ed.), *Commentary on the Rome Statute of the International Criminal Court* (1999), Art. 8, marginal no. 232.

[481] See Elements of Crimes for Article 8(2)(b)(xxvi) ICC Statute, num. 3; Elements of Crimes for Article 8(2)(e)(ii) ICC Statute, num. 3.

child could, by his or her appearance, be younger than 15.[482] Thus the Elements of Crimes lower the subjective requirements in comparison with the general rule of Article 30 of the ICC Statute.[483]

D. War Crimes Against Property and Other Rights

986   Five of the provisions of the ICC Statute directly criminalize the expropriation or destruction of property.[484] Under Article 8(2)(a)(iv) of the ICC Statute, in international armed conflict the "extensive destruction and appropriation of property, not justified by military necessity and carried out unlawfully and wantonly," is subject to criminal sanction. This provision is based on the grave breaches provisions of the Geneva Conventions. Also for international armed conflict, Article 8(2)(b)(xiii) of the ICC Statute covers "destroying or seizing the enemy's property unless such destruction or seizure be imperatively demanded by the necessities of war." This prohibition is repeated almost word for word in Article 8(2)(e)(xii) for non-international armed conflict. Finally, Article 8(2)(b)(xvi) of the ICC Statute criminalizes pillaging of towns and places in international armed conflict, and Article 8(2)(e)(v) does the same for non-international armed conflict. Article 8(2)(b)(xiv) of the ICC Statute covers curtailing the rights and claims of nationals of the hostile party.

I. Offenses of Expropriation

1. Conduct

987   War crimes under Article 8(2)(a)(iv), second alternative, Article 8(2)(b)(xiii), second alternative, Article 8(2)(e)(xii), second alternative, and finally Article 8(2)(b)(xvi) and (2)(e)(v) of the ICC Statute are offenses of expropriation. The conduct is described, depending on the provision, as appropriation, confiscation or pillaging.

988   There is no substantive difference between appropriation and confiscation. Necessary for both appropriation and confiscation are the removal of something from the possession of an entitled person, for a not insignificant period of time, and against that person's will or without his or her agreement.[485] For the war crime of appropriation, it is not necessary for the perpetrator also to take possession of the expropriated thing, or in any case to intend to do so. Such a distinction between confiscation and appropriation is

---

[482] M. Cottier, in O. Triffterer (ed.), *Commentary on the Rome Statute of the International Criminal Court* (1999), Art. 8, marginal no. 232.

[483] On the general requirements for the mental element under ICC Statute, Art. 30 and on possible deviations by way of customary international law or the Elements of Crimes, see marginal nos. 304 et seq., esp. 313 et seq.

[484] A range of other offenses protect property at least indirectly. They include in particular the war crime of attacks on non-military targets and certain buildings (see Art. 8(2)(b)(ii), (iii), (iv), (v), (ix) and (xxiv), (2)(e)(ii)). For these offenses, protection of property is not of foremost importance; the incriminated conduct is a prohibited method of warfare. On these offenses, see marginal nos. 1008 et seq. See also ICTY Statute, Art. 2(d), 3(e) and ICTR Statute, 4(f).

[485] See K. Kittichaisaree, *International Criminal Law* (2001), p. 148; ICRC Study on ICC Statute, Art. 8(2)(a)(iv), p. 18, pp. 21 et seq.

questionable, since in international humanitarian law the two are often used synonymously.[486] Substantively, too, such a distinction would be contradictory. Appropriation, as a grave breach under Article 8(2)(a)(iv), second alternative, of the ICC Statute, requires that the act be committed "extensively." In contrast, confiscation under Article 8(2)(b)(xiii), second alternative, of the ICC Statute is punishable without having to satisfy this requirement,[487] although if one wished to distinguish the two as suggested, confiscation interferes less seriously than appropriation with the victim's right of disposition.

Pillaging differs from appropriation and confiscation only in regard to the per- **989** petrator's intention to obtain the property for private or personal use.[488] Thus the mental requirements are increased in comparison with Article 30 of the ICC Statute.[489] The Yugoslavia Tribunal also indicated that for pillaging, an element of force must be present.[490]

2. Object of the Conduct

Expropriation offenses in the law of war crimes are limited to specific objects that are **990** especially endangered and in need of protection. The provisions at issue choose varying ways of limiting the class of objects of the conduct. Article 8(2)(a)(iv) of the ICC Statute, applicable only to international armed conflict, is based on the grave breaches provisions of Geneva Conventions I, II and IV.[491] The objects of the conduct can only be protected property as defined in these Conventions. Objects especially protected under Geneva Conventions I, II and IV are hospitals, hospital ships and planes, and other material necessary for medical care.[492]

The property of prisoners of war is not an appropriate object of this crime.[493] While **991** Article 18 of Geneva Convention III protects the personal possessions of prisoners of war, Article 130 of Geneva Convention III, which defines grave breaches, does not refer to property violations, unlike the same provisions of the other Conventions.[494] For this reason, it is also doubtful whether property belonging to interned civilians is protected. Article 97 of Geneva Convention IV does establish rules for the handling of the personal possessions of internees, but the fact that this provision corresponds to Article 18 of

---

[486] See, e.g., K. Kittichaisaree, *International Criminal Law* (2001), p. 148; J.S. Pictet (ed.), *Geneva Convention II, Commentary* (1960), p. 269.

[487] But see marginal nos. 994 et seq.

[488] See Elements of Crimes for Article 8(2)(b)(xvi) ICC Statute, num. 2; see also H. Boddens Hosang, in R.S. Lee (ed.), *The International Criminal Court, Elements of Crimes and Rules of Procedure and Evidence* (2001), p. 176 at p. 177, fn. 99.

[489] On the narrowing of the zone of criminality by the Elements of Crimes, see marginal nos. 324 et seq.

[490] *Prosecutor* v. *Mucić* et al., ICTY (Trial Chamber), judgment of 16 November 1998, para. 591.

[491] See Geneva Convention I, Art. 50, Geneva Convention II, Art. 51 and Geneva Convention IV, Art. 147.

[492] See esp. Geneva Convention I, Arts. 19, 20, 33–36, Geneva Convention II, Arts. 22–28, 38, 39, Geneva Convention IV, Arts. 18, 21, 22.

[493] For a different view, see K. Dörmann, in R.S. Lee (ed.), *The International Criminal Court, Elements of Crimes and Rules of Procedure and Evidence* (2001), p. 124 at p. 132.

[494] The fact that the term "protected property" nevertheless appears in Geneva Convention III, Art. 130, sentence 1, is an editing error, see J.S. Pictet (ed.), *Geneva Convention III, Commentary* (1960), p. 626.

Geneva Convention III argues against including these possessions under the heading of protected property.

992   Confiscation as a war crime under Article 8(2)(b)(xiii) or (2)(e)(xiii) is also limited to specific objects. Only enemy property is protected, and therefore not property belonging to the perpetrator's side in the conflict or to third states. However, both state and private enemy property are protected, though here too the degree of protection varies. Property on the territory of the country in question is not protected even if it belongs to a member of the opposing party, as neither Hague law nor the Geneva Conventions contain such a provision.[495]

993   The crime of pillaging includes no explicit restrictions on possible objects. Nevertheless, here, too, property owned by persons on the perpetrator's own side is not protected. This arises from the protective purpose of the underlying international humanitarian law, which protects only the enemy party; aside from a few exceptions,[496] direct protection of the perpetrator party's interests is not its goal.

3. Extent of Expropriation

994   It is only Article 8(2)(a)(iv) of the ICC Statute that explicitly requires appropriation to be "extensive." But even with regard to the other war crimes of expropriation, occasional violations of property rights do not suffice.[497] For pillaging, this is clear from the wording of the provision itself. It requires that a town or place must be pillaged; if only a house is pillaged, the requirements for pillaging are not satisfied. Neither is an individual violation sufficient for seizure under Article 8(2)(b)(xiii), second alternative, or (2)(e)(xii) of the ICC Statute. This is not immediately apparent from the provision, but it is clear from the structure of the ICC Statute. Under Article 5(1), sentence 1, of the ICC Statute, the ICC's jurisdiction is limited to "the most serious crimes of concern to the international community as a whole." A single illegal seizure does not satisfy this requirement.[498] The act does violate international humanitarian law and may be criminal under domestic law. But the interests of the international community are not affected by it.

995   In this context, the Yugoslavia Tribunal found that, in judging the seriousness of a violation, the consequences for the victim must be considered. The Tribunal found it had no jurisdiction over the theft of jewelry, money and other valuables in a camp in Bosnia, as the consequences for those affected were not significant.[499] On the basis of this judgment, the requirements for the extent of the property violation are comparatively high. It is irrelevant whether the perpetrator committed the act for personal gain or

---

[495] See A. Zimmermann, in O. Triffterer (ed.), *Commentary on the Rome Statute of the International Criminal Court* (1999), Art. 8, marginal no. 144.

[496] To be noted here is the prohibition on the use of child soldiers, which aims above all to protect children regardless of whether they belong to one of the parties to a conflict. See also marginal nos. 978 et seq.

[497] Similarly, G. Dahm, J. Delbrück and R. Wolfrum, *Völkerrecht*, Vol. I/3, 2nd edn. (2002), p. 1064.

[498] On the same questions regarding ICTY Statute, Art. 3, see *Prosecutor* v. *Tadić*, ICTY (Appeals Chamber), decision of 2 October 1995, para. 94. The ICTY found that "theft of a loaf of bread," for example, did not fall under its jurisdiction.

[499] *Prosecutor* v. *Mucić* et al., ICTY (Trial Chamber), judgment of 16 November 1998, para. 1154.

whether it was part of the systematic economic exploitation of an occupied territory.[500] However, in the latter case, the necessary extent of the violation is likely to be attained more quickly.

4. Mental Element

The mental element in international armed conflict requires at least recklessness.[501] The **996** lower subjective requirements compared to Article 30 of the ICC Statute arise from the use of the term "wantonly" in Article 8(2)(a)(iv) of the ICC Statute.[502] This assessment applies to all crimes of expropriation. Whether the lowering of the subjective requirements also applies in non-international armed conflict is not yet certain.[503]

5. Military Necessity

The seizure of foreign property in armed conflicts is not forbidden under all circum- **997** stances. Thus, for example, an occupying power itself is permitted in principle to use the opposing party's weapons, ammunition and other munitions of war.[504] The use of private property is also allowed by international law under certain circumstances, and therefore not punishable as a war crime. This is also expressed in the wording of the provisions of the ICC Statute. Expropriations are not criminal under Article 8(2)(a)(iv) or Article 8(2)(b)(xiii) of the ICC Statute as long as they are "justified by military necessity" or "imperatively demanded by the necessities of war." In addition, the introductory sentence of Article 8(2)(b) of the ICC Statute makes the connection to the laws and customs applicable to armed conflict. This framework must be considered in interpreting the various offenses.[505]

Whether an expropriation is allowed by international humanitarian law must be veri- **998** fied in a two-step process. It must first be determined whether the conduct in question can be permissible at all. This is not the case, for example, with pillaging, which is expressly forbidden without exception under Article 47 of the Hague Regulations. Here there is no possible justification on the basis of military necessity.[506] The same is true for confiscation of important cultural property, against which, under Article 53(a) of Additional Protocol I and Article 16 of Additional Protocol II, no "acts of hostility" may be

---

[500] *Prosecutor* v. *Mucić* et al., ICTY (Trial Chamber), judgment of 16 November 1998, para. 590.

[501] On the general requirements of the mental element, see marginal nos. 294 et seq., esp. 304 et seq.

[502] See in *Prosecutor* v. *Naletilić and Martinović*, ICTY (Trial Chamber), judgment of 31 March 2003, para. 577; A. Eser, in A. Cassese, P. Gaeta and J.R.W.D. Jones (eds.), *The Rome Statute of the International Criminal Court*, Vol. 1 (2002), p. 889 at p. 899; see also marginal no. 320. For a different view, see W.J. Fenrick, in O. Triffterer (ed.), *Commentary on the Rome Statute of the International Criminal Court* (1999), Art. 8, marginal no. 14.

[503] For a lower threshold even for non-international armed conflicts, see *Prosecutor* v. *Blaškić*, ICTY (Trial Chamber), judgment of 3 March 2000, para. 182.

[504] See Hague Regulations, Art. 53, which presupposes this right on the part of the occupying power.

[505] On military necessity, see generally marginal nos. 479 et seq.

[506] Thus Art. 8(2)(b)(xvi) and Art. 8(2)(e)(v) of the ICC Statute do not refer to the military necessity of pillaging.

directed.[507] Civilian hospitals may only be seized in exceptional cases (see Article 57 of Geneva Convention IV).[508] Under Article 46(2) of the Hague Regulations, private property may not be confiscated by the occupying power. However, though it appears so at first sight, this prohibition is not absolute, as becomes clear from the subsequent provisions of the Hague Regulations. Under Article 53(2), certain privately-owned property of importance to the war effort may be confiscated. Private property that is not important to the war effort, however, is absolutely protected.

999   If the confiscation of property is not already prohibited by a specific provision, it must be examined, in a second step, whether the expropriation is justified by military necessity. The wordings of Article 8(2)(iv) and (2)(b)(xiii) or (2)(e)(xii) of the ICC Statute differ by degrees. While in the former case, simple "military necessity" is mentioned, the latter provisions speak of "imperatively demanded . . . necessities of the conflict." This linguistic difference does not reflect a substantive one, since both cases merely adopted the wordings of the underlying provisions of international humanitarian law.[509] Substantively, these requirements are frequently concretized in specific rules of international humanitarian law; here there is a degree of overlap with the previously-discussed question of the fundamental permissibility of certain conduct. It should be kept in mind that not every measure that seems militarily reasonable, for example because it increases the security of the armed forces, can therefore be considered a military necessity. The condition, rather, is that it be a last resort in meeting the requirements of military necessity.[510]

II. Offenses of Destruction

1000   The destruction of property is also penalized through offenses that cover methods of warfare.[511] Nevertheless, overlap is largely nonexistent. Article 8(2)(a)(iv) of the ICC Statute limits criminal liability to protected property within the meaning of the Geneva Conventions. Of particular significance is Article 53 of Geneva Convention IV, which forbids the destruction not only of civilian but also of state property. However, the provision only applies to the extent a party to the conflict occupies a territory. Thus, for example, air raids on civilian targets are not criminal as grave breaches of the Geneva Conventions, since the party to the conflict does not occupy the attacked territory.[512] However, if the attack is directed against targets such as hospitals, which are protected as

---

[507] See K.-J. Partsch, in D. Fleck (ed.), *The Handbook of Humanitarian Law in Armed Conflicts* (1999), nos. 919 et seq. This absolute prohibition on confiscation, like attacks on cultural property, is found alongside the prohibition on using cultural property for military purposes, see Additional Protocol I, Art. 53 (b); Additional Protocol II, Art. 16.

[508] On the entire issue, see H.-P. Gasser, in D. Fleck (ed.), *The Handbook of Humanitarian Law in Armed Conflicts* (1999), nos. 556 et seq.

[509] Geneva Convention I, Art. 50; Geneva Convention II, Art. 51 and Geneva Convention IV, Art. 147 on the one hand, and Hague Regulations, Art. 23(g) on the other.

[510] See A. Zimmermann, in O. Triffterer (ed.), *Commentary on the Rome Statute of the International Criminal Court* (1999), Art. 8, marginal no. 155.

[511] See marginal nos. 1008 et seq.

[512] See J.S. Pictet (ed.), *Geneva Convention IV, Commentary* (1958), p. 601. However, such attacks can for example be punishable as attacks on civilian objects (ICC Statute, Art. 8(2)(b)(ii)).

such regardless of the presence of an occupation, overlaps may exist with other offenses.[513]

The scope of the war crime of destruction under Article 8(2)(b)(xiii) and (2)(e)(xii) of **1001** the ICC Statute is unclear. The wording covers all destruction or confiscation of enemy property, if not imperatively required. However, Article 23(g) of the Hague Regulations, on which the offense is based, is found in the section on the carrying out of hostilities, suggesting that the scope could be limited to destruction or expropriation in the context of military operations. It has, however, been suggested that the scope of the provision be limited to cases in which the property is in the hands of the party to which the perpetrator belongs.[514] This view should be affirmed. If the scope were to be extended to military operations, overlap would often occur with the offenses relating to forbidden targets of attack.[515] The (German) Code of Crimes Against International Law [*Völkerstrafgesetzbuch, VStGB*] therefore limited this offense to property found in the hands of the party to the conflict.[516]

1. Conduct

Article 8(2)(a)(iv), first alternative, Article 8(2)(b)(xiii), first alternative, and Article **1002** 8(2)(e)(xii), first alternative, of the ICC Statute all include the destruction of property as criminal conduct. Only destruction of property, not merely damage to it, is covered. It is true that French courts after World War II viewed damage to property as a war crime, but these decisions were reached on the basis of French law, which also punishes damage.[517] Therefore, these decisions cannot lead to any conclusions for the interpretation of the ICC Statute.

---

[513] Overlaps with war crimes involving attacks on civilian objects, in particular, are conceivable. See also *Prosecutor v. Kordić and Čerkez*, ICTY (Trial Chamber), judgment of 26 February 2001, paras. 335 et seq.; *Prosecutor v. Naletilić and Martinović*, ICTY (Trial Chamber), judgment of 31 March 2003, para. 575. The German (German) Code of Crimes Against International Law [*Völkerstrafgesetzbuch, VStGB*] makes overlaps with these offenses largely impossible because (German) Code of Crimes Against International Law [*Völkerstrafgesetzbuch, VStGB*] § 9(1) only punishes destruction of objects in the hands of the perpetrator's own side. Attacks from a distance are thus excluded, see Explanatory Memorandum of the (German) Code of Crimes Against International Law, *BT-Drs.* 14/8524, p. 31.

[514] See A. Zimmermann, in O. Triffterer (ed.), *Commentary on the Rome Statute of the International Criminal Court* (1999), Art. 8, marginal nos. 141 et seq. This is also the direction taken in (German) Code of Crimes Against International Law [*Völkerstrafgesetzbuch, VStGB*] § 9(1). But see *Prosecutor v. Kordić and Čerkez* (Trial Chamber), judgment of 26 February 2001, paras. 346 et seq.; *Prosecutor v. Naletilić and Martinović*, ICTY (Trial Chamber), judgment of 31 March 2003, para. 580, where the ICTY extended the protection to property not under control of the perpetrator with regard to the crime of wanton destruction under ICTY Statute, Art. 3(d).

[515] See A. Zimmermann, in O. Triffterer (ed.), *Commentary on the Rome Statute of the International Criminal Court* (1999), Art. 8, marginal no. 143.

[516] See (German) Code of Crimes Against International Law [*Völkerstrafgesetzbuch, VStGB*], Sec. 9(1) and Explanatory Memorandum of the (German) Code of Crimes Against International Law, *BT-Drs.* 14/8524, p. 31.

[517] See ICRC Study on Art. 8(2)(a)(iv), p. 20.

2. Object and Extent of the Offense and Military Necessity

1003   The above discussion may be referred to with regard to the protected objects and the extent of the offense. Only destruction of protected property is criminal; the destruction must also achieve a certain degree of extensiveness. On the question of military necessity, meanwhile, account should be taken of the rules of international humanitarian law, some of which establish an absolute prohibition. Thus, for example, medical units are always protected under Article 19(1) of Geneva Convention I. Their destruction cannot be justified with reference to military necessity.[518] The principle that military necessity can justify destruction of certain property is expressed, for example, in Article 53 of Geneva Convention IV, which permits destruction of enemy (state and private) property if this is absolutely necessary. However, if the military goal could be achieved through confiscation or similar means, destruction is not permitted, as it is disproportionate.

3. Mental Element

1004   Article 30 of the ICC Statute is essentially decisive for the mental element.[519] If the destruction of property occurs in international armed conflict, recklessness suffices ("reckless disregard of the likelihood of its destruction").[520] Whether the lowering of the requirements for the mental element also applies to destruction in non-international armed conflict has yet to be determined.[521]

III. Encroachments on Other Rights

1005   Under Article 8(2)(b)(xiv) of the ICC Statute, "declaring abolished, suspended or inadmissible in a court of law the rights and actions of the nationals of the hostile party" is a criminal offense. The provision adopts the wording of Article 23(h) of the Hague Regulations. The scope and the exact meaning of the offense are unclear; this unclarity is not dispelled by the Elements of Crimes.

1006   This provision aims, on the one hand, to prevent the complete or partial suspension of the judiciary in occupied territories.[522] However, it should be kept in mind that an occupying power has access to wide-ranging authority in administering occupied terri-

---

[518] On additional provisions, see J.S. Pictet (ed.), *Geneva Convention I, Commentary* (1957), p. 372; ICRC Study on Art. 8(2)(a)(iv), p. 19.

[519] For detail on the general requirements, see marginal nos. 294 et seq.

[520] See *Prosecutor* v. *Naletilić and Martinović*, ICTY (Trial Chamber), judgment of 31 March 2003, para. 577, on ICTY Statute, Art. 2(d). The starting point for the establishment of subjective requirements which differ from ICC Statute, Art. 30 (see marginal nos. 310 et seq.) is the criterion "wantonly" in ICC Statute, Art. 8(2)(a)(iv). See also A. Eser, in A. Cassese, P. Gaeta and J.R.W.D. Jones (eds.), *The Rome Statut of the International Criminal Court*, Vol. 1 (2002), p. 889 at p. 899. On possible deviations from Art. 30 of the ICC Statute by way of customary international law or the Elements of Crimes, see marginal nos. 313 et seq.

[521] See e.g., *Prosecutor* v. *Blaškić*, ICTY (Trial Chamber) judgment of 3 March 2000, paras. 151, 182.

[522] M. Cottier, in O. Triffterer (ed.), *Commentary on the Rome Statute of the International Criminal Court* (1999), Art. 8, marginal no. 159.

tory, which also extends to the judiciary.[523] Whether, on the other hand, interference with the right to bring suit or the property rights of nationals of the enemy state on the state territory of the belligerent party is itself criminal is doubtful, and, in regard to Article 23(h) of the Hague Regulations, controversial.[524] The provision's wording nevertheless permits this broad interpretation, and the criminal nature of such conduct cannot be denied. Thus it may be assumed that the offense extends to such cases. In any case, the violation must be quite extensive, since minor interference with property rights[525] can hardly be considered among "the most serious crimes of concern to the international community as a whole."[526]

As to the mental element, Article 30 of the ICC Statute applies.[527]   **1007**

E. Employing Prohibited Methods of Warfare

I. Introduction

1. Attacks on Non-Military Targets

A first group of war crimes involving the employment of prohibited methods of warfare **1008** consists of attacks on non-military targets. Article 8(2)(b)(i), (ii), (ix) and (xxiv), as well as Article 8(2)(e)(i), (ii), and (iv) of the ICC Statute create liability for direct attacks on civilians and civilian objects and comparable targets. Article 8(2)(b)(iv) of the ICC Statute covers disproportionate incidental damage. Attacking undefended places[528] is a special case of attacks on non-military objects. The offenses in Articles 8(2)(b)(iii) and (e)(iii) of the ICC Statute, which criminalize attacks on humanitarian aid missions and UN peacekeeping missions, are closely related to the crimes to be discussed here.[529]

The prohibition on harming civilians and non-military objects is one of the oldest, **1009** most basic laws of war.[530] Harm to the enemy must be limited to what is militarily necessary (limited warfare). The medieval Scholastics already made a distinction between combatants and civilians and demanded broad protection of the civilian population.[531]

---

[523] See H.-P. Gasser, in D. Fleck (ed.), *The Handbook of Humanitarian Law in Armed Conflicts* (1999), nos. 547 et seq.

[524] For details, see G. von Glahn, *The Occupation of Enemy Territory* (1957), pp. 108 et seq.; M. Cottier, in O. Triffterer (ed.), *Commentary on the Rome Statute of the International Criminal Court* (1999), Art. 8, marginal no. 157; and the explanation in the ICRC Study on ICC Statute, Art. 8(2)(b)(xiii), pp. 58 et seq.

[525] This is made clear in the (German) Code of Crimes Against International Law [*Völkerstrafgesetzbuch, VStGB*]: The cancellation or suspension of claims is only criminal under the (German) Code of Crimes Against International Law [*Völkerstrafgesetzbuch, VStGB*], Sec. 9(2) if it affects all, or a significant number, of members of the hostile party. See also Explanatory Memorandum of the (German) Code of Crimes Against International Law, *BT-Drs.* 14/8524, p. 31.

[526] ICC Statute, Art. 5(1) sentence 1.

[527] On the general requirements of the mental element, see marginal nos. 294 et seq., esp. 304 et seq.

[528] ICC Statute, Art. 8(2)(b)(v); for thorough discussion, see below, marginal nos. 1049 et seq.

[529] For thorough discussion of this offense, see marginal nos. 1134 et seq.

[530] C. Pilloud and J.S. Pictet, in Y. Sandoz, C. Swinarski and B. Zimmermann (eds.), *Commentary on the Additional Protocols* (1987), marginal no. 1863.

[531] On the historical development, see I. Detter, *The Law of War*, 2nd edn. (2000), pp. 286 et seq.; S. Oeter, in D. Fleck (ed.), *The Handbook of Humanitarian Law in Armed Conflicts* (1999), nos. 401

Since the 19th century, the imperative of discriminating warfare has been recognized as part of customary international law.[532] This principle was codified in Article 48 of Additional Protocol I:

"In order to ensure respect for and protection of the civilian population and civilian objects, the Parties to the conflict shall at all times distinguish between the civilian population and combatants and between civilian objects and military objectives and accordingly shall direct their operations only against military objectives."

1010 The principle gained further contours in Articles 50 et seq. of Additional Protocol I. The Geneva Conventions and Additional Protocols, as well as a range of other provisions of international humanitarian law, contain similar protective provisions for a range of persons and objects.[533] Here, too, the issue is the protection of persons and objects that are not military targets. These are particular refinements of the general principle that civilians and civilian objects should not be attacked.

1011 The protection of civilians and civilian objects from military operations is not absolute, however. Attacks made against military targets that lead to incidental damage to civilians or civilian objects are not absolutely prohibited.[534] However, they are subject to the principle of proportionality. Only if this so-called civilian collateral damage is not unreasonably heavy in relation to the military advantage gained through the attack is the attack permitted. This basic principle is expressed in Article 57(2) and (3) of Additional Protocol I.

2. Other Prohibited Methods

1012 Other war crimes relating to employment of prohibited methods of warfare involve the means of warfare in a more narrow sense. The criminality of treacherous killing and the improper use of insignia are based on the prohibition of perfidy. This prohibition is based in medieval codes of chivalry.[535] It forbids breaches of trust committed in order to achieve military advantage.[536] The purpose of the prohibition on perfidy is, indirectly, the protection of the rules of international humanitarian law. Permissible subterfuges of warfare must be carefully distinguished from perfidious acts prohibited under international law.

---

et seq.; C. Pilloud and J.S. Pictet, in Y. Sandoz, C. Swinarski and B. Zimmermann (eds.), *Commentary on the Additional Protocols* (1987), marginal nos. 1822 et seq.

[532] See S. Oeter, in D. Fleck (ed.), *The Handbook of Humanitarian Law in Armed Conflicts* (1999), nos. 401 and 404.

[533] For details, see marginal nos. 1017, 1030 et seq., 1036 et seq.

[534] W.J. Fenrick, in O. Triffterer (ed.), *Commentary on the Rome Statute of the International Criminal Court* (1999), Art. 8, marginal nos. 24 et seq.

[535] See J. de Preux, in Y. Sandoz, C. Swinarski and B. Zimmermann (eds.), *Commentary on the Additional Protocols* (1987), marginal nos. 1485, 1498; S. Oeter, in D. Fleck (ed.), *The Handbook of Humanitarian Law in Armed Conflicts* (1999), no. 472; M. Cottier, in O. Triffterer (ed.), *Commentary on the Rome Statute of the International Criminal Court* (1999), Art. 8, marginal no. 114.

[536] See M. Cottier, in O. Triffterer (ed.), *Commentary on the Rome Statute of the International Criminal Court* (1999), Art. 8, marginal no. 118.

The threat or order of warfare without quarter is also a "classic" war crime under Article 8(2)(b)(xii) of the ICC Statute. Such order or threat increases the danger that the wounded and others unable to fight will be killed, and terrorizes the enemy.[537]   **1013**

Article 8(2)(b)(xxv) and Article 8(2)(b)(xxiii) of the ICC Statute concern starvation of the civilian population and use of human shields, methods of warfare that mainly affect persons not involved in hostilities.   **1014**

II. Attacks on Civilian Populations

Article 8(2)(b)(i) of the ICC Statute, following customary international law, deals with attacks on civilian populations as such or on individual civilians not involved in hostilities. For non-international armed conflicts, Article 8(2)(e)(i) of the ICC Statute provides an identical rule.   **1015**

The offense is based on Article 51(2) of Additional Protocol I and Article 13(2) of Additional Protocol II. Under Article 85(3)(a) of Additional Protocol I, attacks on civilian populations or on individual civilians are grave breaches of the Additional Protocol if they cause death or serious injury to the victim. Launching the attack is sufficient for criminal liability under the ICC Statute.[538]   **1016**

The material element requires an attack against civilians. An attack, under Article 49(1) of Additional Protocol I, is any offensive or defensive use of violence against an adversary. However, this definition refers only to military operations;[539] as derives from Article 49(3) of Additional Protocol I, which speaks of "warfare." Who is a civilian can be determined using the relevant rules of international humanitarian law. According to Article 50(2) of Additional Protocol I, the term "civilian population" includes all civilians. According to Article 50(1), a civilian is any person who is not a combatant.[540] Finally, Article 50(3) establishes that the presence of some combatants does not change the fact that a group of civilians must be considered a civilian population. Only if a person takes part in hostilities does he or she lose civilian status.[541] In contrast to Article 4(1) of Geneva Convention IV, which defines protected persons for purposes of that Convention, Article 51 of Additional Protocol I is not concerned with the victim's nationality.[542]   **1017**

The mental element requires that the perpetrator act with the purpose of attacking civilians.[543] This can be determined not only from the wording of the criteria of the of-   **1018**

---

[537] See M. Cottier, in O. Triffterer (ed.), *Commentary on the Rome Statute of the International Criminal Court* (1999), Art. 8, marginal no. 134.

[538] See K. Dörmann, 83 *International Review of the Red Cross* (2001), p. 461 at p. 467; D. Frank, in R.S. Lee (ed.), *The International Criminal Court, Elements of Crimes and Rules of Procedure and Evidence* (2001), p. 140 at p. 142.

[539] C. Pilloud and J.S. Pictet, in Y. Sandoz, C. Swinarski and B. Zimmermann (eds.), *Commentary on the Additional Protocols* (1987) marginal no. 1880, speak of "combat action."

[540] See also, in this vein, *Prosecutor* v. *Blaškić*, ICTY (Trial Chamber), judgment of 3 March 2000, para. 180; *Prosecutor* v. *Kayishema and Ruzindana*, ICTR (Trial Chamber), judgment of 21 May 1999, para. 179.

[541] See Additional Protocol I, Art. 51(3).

[542] See C. Pilloud and J.S. Pictet, in Y. Sandoz, C. Swinarski and B. Zimmermann (eds.), *Commentary on the Additional Protocols* (1987), marginal no. 1909.

[543] ICC Statute, Art. 30 permits different provisions for the requirements of the mental element to be created by the Statute and the Elements of Crimes, see marginal nos. 310 et seq.

fense ("intentionally") and the Elements of Crimes ("intended"),[544] but primarily from the interplay between the norms that criminalize direct attacks on non-military objects and war crimes under Article 8(2)(b)(iv) of the ICC Statute. The latter provision criminalizes excessive incidental damage to non-military objects. If an attack leads to incidental damage that is not excessive, Article 8(2)(b)(iv) of the ICC Statute does not apply.[545] This result, which reflects a principle of international humanitarian law, would be contradicted if non-purposeful incidental damage to non-military targets were criminalized under the norms to be considered here.[546]

III. Terror Against a Civilian Population

1019   Under Article 51(2), sentence 2, of Additional Protocol I and Article 13(2), sentence 2, of Additional Protocol II, "[a]cts or threats of violence the primary purpose of which is to spread terror among the civilian population are prohibited" in international and non-international armed conflict. These provisions do not directly correspond to any crime enumerated in Article 8(2) of the ICC Statute.

1020   In the *Galić* case, the Trial Chamber of the Yugoslavia Tribunal addressed the question of whether and under which conditions terror against a civilian population was a war crime over which the Tribunal had jurisdiction under Article 3 of the ICTY Statute.[547] The majority of the Trial Chamber held that terror against a civilian population entailed individual criminal responsibility, at least where acts of violence were committed (as opposed to mere threats of violence) and resulted in the death or serious injury to body or health of civilians. With the latter, the Trial Chamber took up the language of the grave breaches in Article 85(3) of Additional Protocol I. In the *Galić* judgment the Trial Chamber set out the elements of the war crime of terror against a civilian population as follows:

"1. Acts of violence directed against the civilian population or individual civilians not taking direct part in hostilities causing death or serious injury to body or health within the civilian population.
2. The offender wilfully made the civilian population or individual civilians not taking direct part in hostilities the object of those acts of violence.
3. The above offence was committed with the primary purpose of spreading terror among the civilian population."[548]

1021   Judge Nieto-Navia, dissenting, opined that the majority of the Trial Chamber had failed

---

[544] See K. Ambos, *Der Allgemeine Teil des Völkerstrafrechts* (2002), pp. 803 et seq.

[545] For details, see marginal nos. 1040 et seq.

[546] But see *Prosecutor* v. *Galić*, ICTY (Trial Chamber), judgment of 5 December 2003, para. 55, in which the Tribunal held that it would suffice if the perpetrator should have been aware of the civilian status of the object of the attack. It should be noted that the Tribunal – in accordance with Additional Protocol I, Art. 85(3)(a) – required the attack to result in serious consequences. This justifies the lowering of requirements with regard to the mental element. As ICC Statute, Art. 8(2)(b)(iv) does not require such serious consequences, lowering the requirements of the mental element would be inappropriate. But see W.J. Fenrick, in O. Triffterer (ed.), *Commentary on the Rome Statute of the International Criminal Court* (1999), Art. 8, marginal no. 21. On the concept of "wilfulness," see marginal nos. 857 et seq.

[547] See *Prosecutor* v. *Galić*, ICTY (Trial Chamber), judgment of 5 December 2003, paras. 63-138.

[548] *Prosecutor* v. *Galić*, ICTY (Trial Chamber), judgment of 5 December 2003, para. 133.

to establish that breaches of Article 51(2), sentence 2, of Additional Protocol I and 13(2), sentence 2, of Additional Protocol II incurred individual criminal liability under customary international law, and that references to conventional international law could not be the basis for such a finding.[549]

In view of the restrictive definition of the crime suggested by the Trial Chamber, the **1022** arguments of the majority are persuasive. The fact that the Trial Chamber equated the crime with the grave breaches provisions of Article 85 of Additional Protocol I, the criminal status of which is beyond any doubt, argues strongly in favor of such an assessment. In any event, the acceptance of such a war crime would have only limited repercussions for the prosecution of breaches of humanitarian law. The scope of the crime overlaps to a large extent with the crime of directing attacks against the civilian population as such or against individual civilians, as stipulated in Article 8(2)(b)(i) and (e)(i) of the ICC Statute. As long as the "acts of violence" are carried out by military means (as was the case in *Galić*), the conduct would also qualify as "attacks" within the meaning of these provisions of the ICC Statute.[550] However, the war crime of terror against a civilian population, as interpreted by the ICTY Trial Chamber, has additional elements, namely the death or serious injury of civilians as a consequence of the prohibited conduct and – as a specific mental element – the primary purpose of spreading terror. This led the Trial Chamber in the *Galić* case to dismiss the charges of attacks against civilians, as it found the crime of terror against a civilian population to be more specific.[551] Acts of violence inflicted upon a civilian population other then military attacks[552] would often qualify as war crimes against persons,[553] and thus also would not go unpunished.

It should be noted that acts of violence against a civilian population as such cannot be **1023** charged as war crimes in proceedings before the International Criminal Court; as noted above, the crime is not included in the conclusive list in Article 8(2) of the ICC Statute.

IV. Attacks on Civilian Objects

1. International Conflict

Article 8(2)(b)(ii) of the ICC Statute, closely related to Article 8(2)(b)(i) of the ICC Stat- **1024** ute, deals with intentional attacks on civilian objects. This war crime is based on Article 52(1) of Additional Protocol I, under which "civilian objects shall not be the object of

---

[549] *Prosecutor* v. *Galić*, ICTY (Trial Chamber), judgment of 5 December 2003, separate and partially dissenting opinion of Judge Nieto-Naiva, paras. 108 et seq.

[550] See marginal no. 1025.

[551] See *Prosecutor* v. *Galić*, ICTY (Trial Chamber), judgment of 5 December 2003, paras. 162 and 769. On multiple charges and convictions, see above, marginal nos. 528 et seq.

[552] Such acts could, for example, consist in torture of civilians; see the example cited in *Prosecutor* v. *Galić*, ICTY (Trial Chamber), judgment of 5 December 2003, para. 114: "repeated, regular and lengthy torture and/or ill-treatment."

[553] In such cases, the victims generally would find themselves in the hands of the enemy party and would thus be protected under the grave breaches provisions of Geneva Convention IV and the corresponding provisions of Article 8(2)(a) ICC Statute.

attack or of reprisals." However, violations of this prohibition, unlike attacks on the civilian population, are not grave breaches of the Protocol.

1025   The objective element requires an attack on civilian objects, as defined in Article
49(1) of Additional Protocol I. These are, under Article 52(1), sentence 2, of the Protocol, all objects that are not military targets. Article 52(2) defines military targets.[554] Difficulties of definition exist especially for objects that can be, or are, used for both civilian
and military purposes, such as bridges or power plants.[555] Here account must be taken
of the object's use and its military significance in the individual case.[556] In case of doubt,
the object is considered civilian under Article 52(3) of the Protocol.

1026   The mental element requires purposeful action.[557]

2. Non-International Conflict

1027   The ICC Statute contains no provision corresponding to Article 8(2)(b)(ii) for non-international armed conflict. This can be attributed to the fact that Additional Protocol II
contains no provisions comparable to Article 52(1) of Additional Protocol I, so that, at
the Rome Conference, it seemed doubtful that the prohibition on attacking civilian objects in non-international conflicts possessed customary law status.[558] This limitation,
however, lags behind the current state of customary international law. The Yugoslavia
Tribunal has emphasized the importance of the protection of civilians and civilian objects in international as well as non-international armed conflict; it has established an absolute prohibition on attacks on these objects.[559]

1028   The mental element requires purposeful action.[560]

V. Attacks on Specially Protected Objects

1029   A special case of attacks on civilian objects under Article 8(2)(b)(ii) of the ICC Statute,
placed separately under criminal sanction because of the particular significance of the

---

[554] For more information, see C. Pilloud and J.S. Pictet, in Y. Sandoz, C. Swinarski and B.
Zimmermann (eds.), *Commentary on the Additional Protocols* (1987), marginal nos. 2021 et seq.

[555] For details, see I. Detter, *The Law of War*, 2nd edn. (2000), pp. 280 et seq.; Excerpt of the Report prepared by the International Committee of the Red Cross for the 28th International Conference
of the Red Cross and the Red Crescent, Geneva, December 2003, 86 *International Review of the Red
Cross* (2004), p. 213 at pp. 222 et seq.; S. Oeter, in D. Fleck (ed.), *The Handbook of Humanitarian
Law in Armed Conflicts* (1999), nos. 442 et seq.

[556] See C. Pilloud and J.S. Pictet, in Y. Sandoz, C. Swinarski and B. Zimmermann (eds.), *Commentary on the Additional Protocols* (1987), marginal nos. 2021 et seq.

[557] See marginal no. 1018; this departure from the lower general subjective requirements is expressly permitted by ICC Statute, Art. 30, see marginal nos. 310 et seq.

[558] A. Zimmermann, in O. Triffterer (ed.), *Commentary on the Rome Statute of the International
Criminal Court* (1999), Art. 8, marginal no. 292; D. Frank, in R.S. Lee (ed.), *The International Criminal Court, Elements of Crimes and Rules of Procedure and Evidence* (2001), p. 140 at p. 143.

[559] *Prosecutor* v. *Kupreškić* et al., ICTY (Trial Chamber), judgment of 14 January 2000, paras. 521 et
seq. In accordance with this case law, the (German) Code of Crimes Against International Law [*Völkerstrafgesetzbuch, VStGB*] has extended the scope of this war crime to non-international armed conflict.

[560] See marginal no. 1018; this departure from the lower general subjective requirements is expressly permitted by ICC Statute, Art. 30, see marginal nos. 310 et seq.

values protected,[561] is covered by Article 8(2)(b)(ix) of the ICC Statute, embodying customary international law. These specially protected objects include buildings "dedicated to religion, education, art, science or charitable purposes, historic monuments, hospitals and places where the sick and wounded are collected." This protection through criminal sanction does not apply if an object is considered a military target under international humanitarian law.

Hospitals and artworks were already afforded protection under Article 35 of the *Lieber Code* of 1863.[562] The offense in its modern form is based primarily on Articles 27 and 56 of the Hague Regulations. The former provides that, during sieges and bombardments, buildings dedicated to religion, art, science or charitable causes, historical monuments, hospitals and places where the sick and wounded are collected enjoy special protection, unless they are used for military purposes. The besieged are obligated to place signs on the buildings or collection points and to notify the enemy in advance. Under Article 56 of the Regulations, seizure, intentional destruction or damage to institutions dedicated to religion, charity, education, art or science as well as historical monuments or artistic or scientific works are prohibited. The prohibition is a part of customary international law.[563] In addition, the offense is based in the provisions of the Geneva Conventions and its Additional Protocol I that regulate the protection of hospitals and places where the sick and wounded are collected.[564] Article 3(d) of the ICTY Statute contains a similar provision. **1030**

Article 53(a) of Additional Protocol I prohibits acts of hostility against historical monuments, works of art or places of worship "that constitute the cultural or spiritual heritage of peoples."[565] Under Article 85(4)(d) of Additional Protocol I, attacks that cause extensive destruction to historic monuments, works of art or places of worship are grave breaches of the Protocol, as long as the objects are not used for military purposes and are not located in immediate proximity to military targets. Even more detailed rules on protection of cultural property are provided in the *Convention for the Protection of Cultural Property in the Event of Armed Conflict* of 14 May 1954 and its protocols.[566] In Article 4(1) of the Convention, the parties agree to respect cultural property and especially to refrain from hostile action against such property.[567] Under Article 4(2), exceptions to the **1031**

---

[561] D. Pfirter, in R.S. Lee (ed.), *The International Criminal Court, Elements of Crimes and Rules of Procedure and Evidence* (2001), p. 162; similarly G. Dahm, J. Delbrück and R. Wolfrum, *Völkerrecht*, Vol. I/3, 2nd edn. (2002), p. 1062.

[562] *Instructions for the Government of Armies of the United States in the Field*, Prepared by Francis Lieber, promulgated as General Orders No. 100 by President Lincoln, of 24 April 1863, reprinted in D. Schindler and J. Toman (eds.), *The Laws of Armed Conflicts* (1973), pp. 3 et seq. For more information on the Lieber Code, see marginal no. 781.

[563] ICRC Study on ICC Statute, Art. 8(2)(b)(ix), p. 36.

[564] Specifically, these are Geneva Convention I, Arts. 19 to 23; Geneva Convention II, Arts. 22, 23, 24 and 35; Geneva Convention IV, Arts. 14, 18 and 19; Additional Protocol I, Arts. 12 and 85(4).

[565] See C.F. Wenger, in Y. Sandoz, C. Swinarski and B. Zimmermann (eds.), *Commentary on the Additional Protocols* (1987), marginal nos. 2063 et seq. Because of the limited applicability of the Convention on Cultural Property, a need was seen during the drafting of the Additional Protocol to include this material, and thus help it to achieve broad applicability, see K.-J. Partsch, in D. Fleck (ed.), *The Handbook of Humanitarian Law in Armed Conflicts* (1999), before no. 901.

[566] 249 *UNTS* (1955), p. 215.

[567] In Art. 1 of the Convention, cultural property is defined as "moveable or immoveable property of great importance to the cultural heritage of every people, such as monuments of architecture, art or history, whether religious or secular; archaeological sites, groups of buildings which, as a whole, are of historical or artistic interest; works of art; manuscripts, books and other objects of artistic, historical or archaeological interest; as well as scientific collections and important collections of books or archives or of reproductions." Also falling under the definition are buildings whose "main and effective pur-

prohibition are only possible in cases of imperative military necessity. Article 6(a) of the Second Protocol to the Convention of 26 March 1999 further limited this exception. Only if the cultural property is used for military purposes and no feasible alternative exists to achieve the desired military advantage shall an attack be permissible.[568]

1032 The objective element requires an attack on one of the objects enumerated. Here, too, the term "attack" must be based on Article 49(2) of Additional Protocol I. The object may not be a military target. Reference may be had to the above discussion on the distinction between civilian objects and military targets.[569]

1033   Article 8(2)(e)(iv) of the ICC Statute contains an identical provision for non-international armed conflict. Although the Hague Regulations are not applicable to civil wars, their rules regarding attacks on protected objects were incorporated into the *Convention of Protection of Cultural Property in the Event of Armed Conflict*, which also applies to non-international armed conflict. In addition, Article 11 of Additional Protocol II protects medical units and transports. Article 16 of the Protocol prohibits hostile acts against historic monuments, works of art or places of worship "which constitute the cultural or spiritual heritage of peoples" in non-international armed conflict. The ICC Statute thus introduces an important innovation by explicitly defining such attacks as war crimes for the first time.[570] The provision reflects customary international law.

1034   The mental element requires purpose on the part of the perpetrator in both international and non-international conflicts.[571]

VI. Attacks on Persons and Objects Using the Emblems of the Geneva Conventions

1035 Article 8(2)(b)(xxiv) of the ICC Statute criminalizes intentional attacks in international armed conflict on persons or objects using the distinguishing emblems of the Geneva Conventions in accordance with international law. Article 8(2)(e)(ii) of the ICC Statute contains an identical provision for non-international armed conflict. The term "attack"

---

pose is to preserve or exhibit cultural property, such as museums, large libraries and depositories of archives, and refuges intended to shelter cultural property in the event of armed conflict; also, monument centers containing a large amount of cultural property." The parties to the conflict are also obligated to protect cultural property by refraining from using this property, facilities for its protection, and its immediate surroundings for purposes that could expose it to destruction or damage in the event of an armed conflict. The purpose of this is to prevent attacks on cultural property in which the cultural property is used as a shield.

[568] Art. 15(1) of this Protocol criminalizes attacks on cultural property and creates a duty in member states to prosecute. This applies, under Art. 15(1)(a), to objects under enhanced protection. A limited category of cultural property can be placed under special protection, such as refuges (Art. 1(b) of the Cultural Property Convention), monument centers (Art. 1(c) of the Convention) and immoveable cultural property "of very great importance" (Art. 8 of the Convention). For more information, see V. Mainetti, 86 *International Review of the Red Cross* (2004), pp. 337 et seq.; K.-J. Partsch, in D. Fleck (ed.), *The Handbook of Humanitarian Law in Armed Conflicts* (1999), nos. 905 et seq.

[569] See marginal no. 1025.

[570] See A. Zimmermann, in O. Triffterer (ed.), *Commentary on the Rome Statute of the International Criminal Court* (1999), Art. 8, marginal no. 297.

[571] See marginal no. 1018; this departure from the general requirements of ICC Statute, Art. 30 is permitted, see marginal nos. 310 et seq.

corresponds to the offense of attacks on a civilian population. When an object may lawfully have such an emblem affixed to it is regulated in detail in the Geneva Conventions and in Additional Protocol I.[572]

The recognized emblems are listed in Article 38 of Geneva Convention I: they are the **1036** emblem of the Red Cross, which is the reverse of the Swiss coat of arms; the red crescent; and the red lion and red sun.[573] The red star of David used by Israel is *de facto* accepted, but is not recognized as an official fourth emblem.[574] Additional Protocol I introduces additional identifying symbols and methods for identifying protected objects, such as the blue light for ambulances and other beacons and radio signals as well as electronic identification.[575]

Those authorized to bear such protective emblems under the Geneva Conventions are medical per- **1037** sonnel, administrators of medical units and facilities, chaplains, workers for national organizations of the Red Cross or Red Crescent and employees of aid organizations from neutral states, and members of the armed forces trained as orderlies. Objects and institutions that may be so identified include medical facilities and equipment, such as hospitals, medical vehicles, medical ships and aircraft, hospital ships and coastal rescue craft.[576] Under Article 12 of Additional Protocol II, the protective emblems are also applicable to non-international armed conflict; Article 11(1) of Additional Protocol II prohibits attacks on medical units and medical transports.[577] According to the Elements of Crimes for Article 8(2)(b)(xxiv) of the ICC Statute, the offense requires that the perpetrator attack persons, buildings, medical units, transports or other objects that are identified as protected objects in conformity with international law through a protective emblem under the Geneva Conventions or through another method of identification.[578] The identification methods provided for in Additional Protocol I are thus also taken into account.[579]

The mental element is the same as for other offenses of attack.[580]   **1038**

VII. Attacks Causing Disproportionate Incidental Damage

Leslie Claude Green: The Environment and the Law of Conventional Warfare, 29 *Canadian Year-* **1039** *book of International Law* (1991), pp. 222 et seq.; Matthias Reichart: *Umweltschutz durch*

---

[572] See, e.g., Geneva Convention I, Arts. 24–27, 36, 39–44; Geneva Convention II, Arts. 42–44; Geneva Convention IV, Arts. 18–22.

[573] Illustrations of the emblems can be found in Art. 3 of the Annex I to Additional Protocol I.

[574] See W. Rabus, in D. Fleck (ed.), *The Handbook of Humanitarian Law in Armed Conflicts* (1999), no. 637.

[575] See Additional Protocol I, Arts. 12 et seq., 15, 18, 23 and 24, in conjunction with Arts. 5–8 of Annex 1 of Additional Protocol I.

[576] See W.J. Fenrick, in O. Triffterer (ed.), *Commentary on the Rome Statute of the International Criminal Court* (1999), Art. 8, marginal nos. 212 et seq.

[577] See A. Zimmermann, in O. Triffterer (ed.), *Commentary on the Rome Statute of the International Criminal Court* (1999), Art. 8, marginal nos. 293 et seq.

[578] Elements of Crimes for Article 8(2)(b)(xxiv) ICC Statute, nums. 1 et seq.

[579] D. Pfirter, in R.S. Lee (ed.), *The International Criminal Court, Elements of Crimes and Rules of Procedure and Evidence* (2001), pp. 201 et seq.

[580] See marginal no. 1018. The structure of the Elements of Crimes for Article 8(2)(b)(xxiv) ICC Statute differs from the Elements of Crimes for the other offenses of attack. This does not lead to a substantive change in regard to the subjective requirements; it is probably an editing error, see K. Dörmann, 83 *International Review of the Red Cross* (2001), p. 461 at pp. 479 et seq.

völkerrechtliches Strafrecht (1999); Heike Spieker (ed.), *Naturwissenschaftliche und völkerrechtliche Perspektiven für den Schutz der Umwelt im bewaffneten Konflikt* (1996).

1. International Conflict

1040   Article 8(2)(b)(iv) of the ICC Statute covers launching an attack with knowledge that it will cause harm to civilians or civilian objects or widespread, long-term and severe damage to the natural environment that is clearly excessive in relation to the concrete and direct overall military advantage anticipated. The actual occurrence of such damage will be the normal situation in practice, but is not absolutely required by the offense.[581] In contrast to the offenses relating to attacks on non-military targets,[582] this provision does not require that a non-military object be directly targeted. It covers, in particular, cases in which a perpetrator attacked a military target with the certain expectation of excessive incidental damage. Whereas for targeted attacks on civilians or non-military objects, the extent of the damage is immaterial, this provision only takes effect if excessive incidental harm is expected to civilians or civilian objects.

1041   This provision combines elements of Articles 35(3), 51(4) and (5), 55(1), 83(3)(b) and 85(3)(b) of Additional Protocol I. The major similarity is to the last-mentioned provision, which defines indiscriminate attacks as grave breaches of Additional Protocol I if these are launched with knowledge that they will cause excessive harm to civilians or damage to civilian objects. Unlike Article 85(3)(b), however, Article 8(2)(b)(iv) of the ICC Statute requires that the expected damage be "clearly" excessive in relation to the "overall" military advantage anticipated.[583]

1042   The provision also includes (anticipated) destruction and harm to the environment if it is widespread, long-term and severe. The use of methods and means of warfare that could bring about such environmental damage is prohibited under Article 35(3) of Additional Protocol I; this prohibition is affirmed in Article 55 of Additional Protocol I.[584] Under customary international law, too, parties to a conflict are forbidden to cause excessive damage to the environment through military operations.[585]

1043   The terminology used in Additional Protocol I and in Article 8(2)(b)(iv) of the ICC Statute is based on the *Convention on the Prohibition of Military or Any Other Hostile Use of Environmental Modification Techniques* (ENMOD) of 10 December 1976.[586] Article I of this Convention prohibits the use as means of warfare of environmental modification techniques that have widespread,

---

[581] On discussion of this issue during the drafting of the Elements of Crimes, see K. Dörmann, 83 *International Review of the Red Cross* (2001), p. 461 at pp. 470 et seq.

[582] See ICC Statute, Art. 8(2)(b)(i), (ii), (iii), (xxiv) and Art. 8(2)(e)(i), (ii), (iii), (iv).

[583] For a critical view of this high threshold for criminality, see A. Cassese, *International Criminal Law* (2003), pp. 60 et seq.

[584] See S. Oeter, in D. Fleck (ed.), *The Handbook of Humanitarian Law in Armed Conflicts* (1999), no. 403; J. de Preux, in Y. Sandoz, C. Swinarski and B. Zimmermann (eds.), *Commentary on the Additional Protocols* (1987), marginal nos. 1440 et seq.

[585] ICRC Study on ICC Statute, Art. 8(2)(b)(iv), p. 14; L.C. Green, *Canadian Yearbook of International Law* 1991, pp. 222 et seq.; G. Dahm, J. Delbrück and R. Wolfrum, *Völkerrecht*, Vol. I/3, 2nd edn. (2002), p. 1060, however, doubt that damage to the environment is criminal under customary international law as it stands today.

[586] 16 *ILM* (1977), p. 88.

long-lasting or severe effects on the environment. The UN Disarmament Committee further clarified this concept: Environmental damage is widespread if it affects an area of several hundred square kilometers. Long-term damage is damage lasting for a period of several months, or approximately a season. Finally, effects are severe if they cause serious or significant disruption or damage to human life, natural or economic resources, or other assets.[587]

Damage to the environment under Article 8(2)(b)(iv) of the ICC Statute is only criminal **1044** if "widespread, long-term and severe damage" can be anticipated. Article 35(3) of Additional Protocol I also contains this high threshold, in contrast to Article 1 of ENMOD. This can be explained by the fact that the provisions of the ICC Statute and Additional Protocol I also cover incidental damage to the environment.[588] Since environmental damage can be expected as a collateral consequence in any type of warfare, the requirements were raised in comparison to those of ENMOD.[589] Article 8(2)(b)(iv) of the ICC Statute combines the prohibition contained in the provisions of the Additional Protocol with the principle of proportionality.[590]

The terms "civilian population," "civilian objects," and "attack" do not differ from **1045** the corresponding criteria for war crimes under Article 8(2)(b)(i) and (ii) of the ICC Statute, so that the above discussion may be referred to in this regard. The offense does not require that the anticipated damage actually occur.[591]

The requirement of proportionality refers to all three variants of the offense.[592] The **1046** anticipated harm to the civilian population, civilian objects or the environment must be "clearly excessive in relation to the concrete and direct overall military advantage anticipated." Thus the requirement of proportionality is clearly heightened in comparison to the underlying norm in Additional Protocol I, and covers only particularly egregious violations of the principle of proportionality.[593] The Elements of Crimes make clear that the military advantage need not be connected temporally or territorially with the object of attack.[594] Rather, it must be considered with regard to military actions in general, above and beyond the concrete attack.[595]

---

[587] UN Doc. CCD/520 of 3 September 1976, Annex A. See also S. Oeter, in D. Fleck (ed.), *The Handbook of Humanitarian Law in Armed Conflicts* (1999), no. 403.

[588] J. de Preux, in Y. Sandoz, C. Swinarski and B. Zimmermann (eds.), *Commentary on the Additional Protocols* (1987), marginal no. 1453.

[589] S. Oeter, in D. Fleck (ed.), *The Handbook of Humanitarian Law in Armed Conflicts* (1999), no. 403, regarding the provisions of Additional Protocol I.

[590] It is not clear whether this results in the offense being limited vis-à-vis Additional Protocol I, Art. 35(3). It is doubtful that widespread, long-term and severe damage to the environment can ever be justified by military advantage.

[591] See marginal no. 1017 and D. Pfirter, in R.S. Lee (ed.), *The International Criminal Court, Elements of Crimes and Rules of Procedure and Evidence* (2001), p. 147 at p. 149; K. Kittichaisaree, *International Criminal Law* (2001), p. 164.

[592] This is established in Elements of Crimes for Article 8(2)(b)(iv) ICC Statute, num. 2.

[593] See Additional Protocol I, Art. 51(5)(b) and Additional Protocol I, 57(2)(a)(iii), which require no clear-cut violation of the principle of proportionality. W.J. Fenrick, in O. Triffterer (ed.), *Commentary on the Rome Statute of the International Criminal Court* (1999), Art. 8, marginal no. 51, takes the view that the scope of the provision is hardly narrowed as a result, since in any case only particularly clear violations of the principle of proportionality would be prosecuted.

[594] Elements of Crimes for Article 8(2)(b)(iv) ICC Statute, num. 2, fn. 36.

[595] Various state signatories to Additional Protocol I advocated this interpretation during the drafting of the Elements of Crimes, see D. Pfirter, in R.S. Lee (ed.), *The International Criminal Court,*

1047   For the mental element, Article 30 of the ICC Statute is determinative.[596] The perpetrator must have intended to attack a particular target and have acted with knowledge
that he or she would cause excessive damage of the type addressed by the definition of
the offense, which would be "clearly excessive" in relation to the anticipated military advantage.[597] To the extent Article 8(2)(b)(iv) of the ICC Statute requires the perpetrator
to have acted "intentionally," it does not deviate from the standard requirements of the
mental element.

2. Non-International Conflict

1048 Under customary international law, causing disproportionate incidental damage to civilians or civilian objects is also a crime in non-international armed conflict; only the crime
of causing disproportionate damage to the environment is limited to international armed
conflict. The ICC Statute has no corresponding provision for non-international armed
conflict, and thus in part lags behind customary law.[598]

VIII. Attacks on Undefended Non-Military Objects

1. International Conflict

1049 Article 8(2)(b)(v) of the ICC Statute covers "attacking or bombarding, by whatever
means, towns, villages, dwellings or buildings which are undefended and which are not
military objectives." Article 3(c) of the ICTY Statute contains a similar provision. The
provision, with the exception of the added qualifier "which are not military objectives,"
is taken from Article 25 of the Hague Regulations. Article 59(1) of Additional Protocol I
prohibits attacks on undefended places. The purpose of the provision is to prevent attacks on places that, because they are undefended, could be occupied by the enemy without first being attacked; the use of military force would be disproportionate. This
connection is made clear in the Elements of Crimes.[599]

1050 When a place should be considered undefended can be gathered from Article 59(2) of Additional
Protocol I. The place must be inhabited, located in a war zone, and open to occupation by an
adverse party.[600] If necessary, practical measures must be taken to make such an occupation pos-

---

Elements of Crimes and Rules of Procedure and Evidence (2001), p. 147 at p. 148; but see also Excerpt of
the Report prepared by the International Committee of the Red Cross for the 28th International Conference of the Red Cross and the Red Crescent, Geneva, December 2003, 86 *International Review of
the Red Cross* (2004), p. 213 at p. 224.

[596] On the general requirements, see marginal nos. 294 et seq., esp. 304 et seq.

[597] See Explanatory Memorandum of the (German) Code of Crimes Against International Law,
BT-Drs. 14/8524, p. 34.

[598] See Explanatory Memorandum of the (German) Code of Crimes Against International Law,
BT-Drs. 14/8524, pp. 33 et seq.

[599] Elements of Crimes for Article 8(2)(b)(v) ICC Statute, num. 2.

[600] Additional Protocol I, Art. 59(2)(a) to (d) enumerates the requirements that must be satisfied.
All combatants, moveable weapons and moveable military equipment must be removed from the
place. Existing immoveable military installations or facilities may not be used for hostile action; offi-

sible for the adverse party; for example, barriers or mines must be removed.[601] Article 59(2) of Additional Protocol I additionally provides for a declaration by the authorities to the enemy that the locality is undefended.[602] Under Article 59(3) of the Protocol, a place can be considered undefended even if persons are present who are entitled to special protection under the Geneva Conventions and Additional Protocol I, or if police forces remain there for purposes of maintaining law and order.[603] This clarification refers primarily to wounded or sick members of the armed forces and prisoners of war being treated in medical facilities. Military medical personnel and chaplains are covered by this rule. Uniformed police forces are part of the armed forces under Article 43(1) of Additional Protocol I, so that a clarification was necessary here.[604]

Places not located in the direct zone of combat or nearby do not count as undefended localities, as they cannot easily be occupied by the enemy.[605] Thus attacks on objects behind enemy lines do not satisfy the definition of the offense.[606] If, for example, a place in the hinterland is attacked from the air, this is not an attack on an undefended locality; however, the act can be punishable in other ways, for example as an attack on a civilian object. Under Article 8(2)(b)(v) of the ICC Statute, undefended locations may not be military objects.[607] This criterion should most likely be ascribed little independent significance, however:[608] Undefended locations usually are not military objects to begin with, as the enemy has exempted them from its military efforts, and the desired military success could in addition be achieved through simple occupation.[609] Under Article 49 of Additional Protocol I, any offensive or defensive use of force against the enemy counts as an attack. From the wording "by whatever means," it is clear that Article 8(2)(b)(v) of the ICC Statute also covers, for example, attacks from the air, as long as they target unprotected locations.[610]   **1051**

Unlike other war crimes provisions that punish direct attacks on non-military targets, here neither the ICC Statute itself nor the Elements of Crimes require that the perpetra-   **1052**

---

cials and the population may not conduct hostile acts. Finally, no activities may be conducted to support the war effort, for example through munitions production, or merely telecommunications and transport services, see S. Oeter, in D. Fleck (ed.), *The Handbook of Humanitarian Law in Armed Conflicts* (1999), no. 459.

[601] C. Pilloud and J.S. Pictet, in Y. Sandoz, C. Swinarski and B. Zimmermann (eds.), *Commentary on the Additional Protocols* (1987), marginal no. 2268.

[602] Official declarations have only a declaratory function; the protection takes effect even without them if the listed requirements are satisfied, see S. Oeter, in D. Fleck (ed.), *The Handbook of Humanitarian Law in Armed Conflicts* (1999), no. 459.

[603] This clarification was also adopted into the Elements of Crimes for Article 8(2)(b)(v) ICC Statute, fn. 38.

[604] C. Pilloud and J.S. Pictet, in Y. Sandoz, C. Swinarski and B. Zimmermann (eds.), *Commentary on the Additional Protocols* (1987), marginal no. 2278.

[605] S. Oeter, in D. Fleck (ed.), *The Handbook of Humanitarian Law in Armed Conflicts* (1999), no. 459.

[606] D. Pfirter, in R.S. Lee (ed.), *The International Criminal Court, Elements of Crimes and Rules of Procedure and Evidence* (2001), p. 147 at p. 152.

[607] The concept of military objects is to be interpreted as in ICC Statute, Art. 8(2)(b)(ii).

[608] Nevertheless, this criterion is once again referred to in the Elements of Crimes for Article 8(2)(b)(v) ICC Statute, num. 3.

[609] S. Oeter, in D. Fleck (ed.), *The Handbook of Humanitarian Law in Armed Conflicts* (1999), no. 458.

[610] See ICRC Study on ICC Statute, Art. 8(2)(b)(v), p. 18.

tor purposely target undefended places. Thus the standard for the mental element remains the general requirements of Article 30 of the ICC Statute.[611]

2. Non-International Conflict

1053   The ICC Statute contains no provision similar to Article 8(2)(b)(v) relating to non-international armed conflict. Here the Statute lags behind the current state of customary international law. The Yugoslavia Tribunal has emphasized the importance of protecting civilians and civilian objects in international as well as non-international conflict and the absolute prohibition on attacks on these objects.[612] In conformity with this case law, the (German) Code of Crimes Against International Law [*Völkerstrafgesetzbuch, VStGB*] extends the scope of the crime to non-international armed conflict.[613]

IX. Perfidious Killing or Wounding

1. International Conflict

1054   Article 8(2)(b)(xi) of the ICC Statute covers "treacherously" killing or wounding members of a hostile nation or army in international armed conflict. This provision embodies customary international law.[614] The rule incorporated into the ICC Statute is based essentially on Article 23(b) of the Hague Regulations and Article 37 of Additional Protocol I; the wording itself is borrowed from the Hague Regulations.[615]

---

[611] See in detail marginal nos. 294 et seq., esp. 304 et seq.

[612] *Prosecutor* v. *Kupreškić* et al., ICTY (Trial Chamber), judgment of 14 January 2000, paras. 521 et seq.

[613] See (German) Code of Crimes Against International Law [*Völkerstrafgesetzbuch, VStGB*], Sec. 11(1) no. 2. The explanation of the law also refers to the *UN Resolution on the Protection of the Civilian Population in Armed Conflicts* of 17 September 1999, UN Doc. S/RES/1265, which links the protection of civilian objects with the protection of the civilian population for all types of conflicts, see Explanatory Memorandum of the (German) Code of Crimes Against International Law, *BT-Drs.* 14/8524, p. 33.

[614] See, e.g., *Prosecutor* v. *Tadić*, ICTY (Appeals Chamber), decision of 2 October 1995, para. 125.

[615] C. Garraway, in R.S. Lee (ed.), *The International Criminal Court, Elements of Crimes and Rules of Procedure and Evidence* (2001), pp. 167 et seq. There are two major differences between the provisions of the ICC Statute and Additional Protocol I, Art. 37(1). First, the provisions of the Additional Protocol criminalize not only the killing or wounding of the victim, but also his or her capture. The failure to incorporate this variant of the offense into the prohibition of perfidy in ICC Statute, Art. 8(2)(b)(xi), can be explained mainly by the fact that only the most serious crimes under international law were to be included in the Statute, see C. Garraway, in R.S. Lee (ed.), *The International Criminal Court, Elements of Crimes and Rules of Procedure and Evidence* (2001), p. 167 at p. 168. Second, the criminal status of attempts related to treacherous killing and wounding was still controversial. The controversy resulted from the unclear wording of Additional Protocol I, Art. 37(1), under which only "kill[ing], injur[ing] or captur[ing]" were criminal. For historical reasons, some concluded that attempts did not fall under the prohibition on perfidy, see S. Oeter, in D. Fleck (ed.), *The Handbook of Humanitarian Law in Armed Conflicts* (1999), no. 472. Those holding the opposite view, referring to the purpose of the norm, advocated including attempts, see K. Ipsen, in R. Bernhardt (ed.), *Encyclopedia of Public International Law*, Vol. 3 (1997), p. 978 at pp. 979 et seq.; J. de Preux, in Y. Sandoz, C. Swinarski and B. Zimmermann (eds.), *Commentary on the Additional Protocols* (1987), marginal no. 1492. ICC Statute, Art. 25(3)(f), has now made clear that attempting this war crime is also criminal.

The Elements of Crimes speak of two variants of deception covered by the offense: **1055** the perpetrator must deceive the victim into thinking either that he or she is obligated, under international law applicable to the conflict,[616] to respect a claim to protection, or that the victim him- or herself has a claim to protection.[617] Primarily relevant in practice are cases in which the perpetrator claims a right to protection for him or herself – for example as a supposedly wounded person.[618]

Thus not every deception of the opponent is prohibited, but only the abuse of trust fraudulently **1056** obtained through specific acts contrary to international law.[619] The crucial element is the perpetrator's deception of the enemy by pretending to the existence of a state of protection under international law. This can be gathered directly from the purpose of the norm itself. The prohibition protects elementary rules of international law;[620] only deception in connection with these elementary rules is a criminal offense. Other deceptions – so-called ruses of war – are permitted.[621] This term includes, for example, deceiving the enemy about one's troop strength or the location of military units, simulating an attack or retreat, erecting fake fortified positions, and planting false information in the enemy's information network.[622] These measures may fool the enemy into incautious or overhasty action and thus disadvantage him, but they do not constitute forbidden perfidy.[623] The use of spies or secret agents does not fall under the prohibition of perfidy, as these

---

[616] Included in the international law applicable to armed conflicts are, in particular, all relevant international treaties as well as the rules of customary international law; that is, for example, the provisions of the Geneva Conventions and their Additional Protocols, the Hague Regulations, the *Convention for the Protection of Cultural Property in the Event of an Armed Conflict* of 14 May 1954, 249 *UNTS* (1955), p. 215 (marginal no. 1031), and the ICC Statute, where they establish an individual claim to protection.

[617] Elements of Crimes for Article 8(2)(b)(xi) ICC Statute, num. 1; see, in addition, the commentary to Additional Protocol I, Art. 37(1) by K. Ipsen, in M. Bothe, K. Ipsen and K.J. Partsch, 38 *Heidelberg Journal of International Law* (1978), p. 1 at pp. 24 et seq. The last-mentioned variant of the offense refers above all to cases in which the perpetrator pretends to the victim that he or she will respect the victim's existing right to protection. Here there will be frequent overlap with other war crimes.

[618] See Additional Protocol I, Art. 37. Special forms of the prohibition on perfidy include the prohibition on improperly using recognized protective emblems and the uniforms of neutral states and flags of truce, see K. Ipsen, in M. Bothe, K. Ipsen and K.J. Partsch, 38 *Heidelberg Journal of International Law* (1978), p. 1 at pp. 24 et seq. This conduct is regulated separately in the ICC Statute in Art. 8(2)(b)(vii), see marginal no. 1064.

[619] See Explanatory Memorandum of the (German) Code of Crimes Against International Law, *BT-Drs.* 14/8524, pp. 34 et seq.

[620] See S. Oeter, in D. Fleck (ed.), *The Handbook of Humanitarian Law in Armed Conflicts* (1999), no. 472.

[621] Additional Protocol I, Art. 37(2), sentence 2, defines permissible ruses of war as "acts which are intended to mislead an adversary or to induce him to act recklessly but which infringe no rule of international law applicable in armed conflict and which are not perfidious because they do not invite the confidence of an adversary with respect to protection under that law"; see also Hague Regulations, Art. 24; M. Cottier, in O. Triffterer (ed.), *Commentary on the Rome Statute of the International Criminal Court* (1999), Art. 8, marginal no. 119.

[622] Additional Protocol I, Art. 37(2) lists, as classic examples of ruses of war, camouflage, decoys, mock operations and misinformation. See J. de Preux, in Y. Sandoz, C. Swinarski and B. Zimmermann (eds.), *Commentary on the Additional Protocols* (1987), marginal nos. 1520 et seq.; L.C. Green, *The Contemporary Law of Armed Conflict*, 2nd edn. (2000), pp. 146 et seq.

[623] This shall also apply if the enemy at first (only) finds himself in an unfavorable tactical situation because of the ruse, but the situation later results in killing or wounding; see also K. Ipsen, in M.

methods of obtaining information are recognized under international law.[624] Nor does the use of propaganda to demoralize the enemy violate the prohibition.[625] Finally, special rules apply to the use of false colors in wars at sea.[626]

1057 Potential victims under the ICC Statute are members of the enemy nation or army – that is, both civilians and combatants.[627] The perpetrator must have killed or wounded the victim by exploiting his trust or belief in a state of protection under international law.[628]

1058 Article 8(2)(b)(xi) of the ICC Statute contains a specific intent requirement that goes beyond the general requirement of intent in Article 30 of the ICC Statute.[629] According to the Elements of Crimes, the offense requires that the perpetrator act with intent to violate the trust inspired in the enemy.[630] It is immaterial whether the perpetrator intended to exploit this trust from the beginning or only developed this intention after the act that created the trust, as both cases pose an equal threat of disregard for elementary protective rules of international law. A person does not commit a war crime if he or she pretends to be dead or to be a member of an enemy force in order to escape alive from an enemy attack or to escape a prisoner of war camp.[631]

2. Non-International Conflict

1059 Article 8(2)(e)(ix) of the ICC Statute covers treacherous killing and wounding committed in non-international armed conflict. The essential difference from its criminal status in international armed conflict exists in regard to the class of protected persons: in non-

---

Bothe, K. Ipsen and K.J. Partsch, 38 *Heidelberg Journal of International Law* (1978), p. 1 at p. 25; J. de Preux, in Y. Sandoz, C. Swinarski and B. Zimmermann (eds.), *Commentary on the Additional Protocols* (1987), marginal no. 1492.

[624] See Hague Regulations, Art. 24 (". . . the employment of measures necessary for obtaining information about the enemy and the country are considered permissible"), and Additional Protocol I, Art. 39(3). See also J. de Preux, in Y. Sandoz, C. Swinarski and B. Zimmermann (eds.), *Commentary on the Additional Protocols* (1987), marginal no. 1766 and H. McCoubrey and N.D. White, *International Law and Armed Conflict* (1992), p. 229. The admissibility of national criminal law governing treason or espionage is unaffected by this.

[625] See I. Detter, *The Law of War*, 2nd edn. (2000), p. 306; M. Gimmerthal, *Kriegslist und Perfidieverbot* (1990), pp. 170 et seq.; S. Oeter, in D. Fleck (ed.), *The Handbook of Humanitarian Law in Armed Conflicts* (1999), no. 474.

[626] See Additional Protocol I, Art. 39(3); for more information, see M. Gimmerthal, *Kriegslist und Perfidieverbot* (1990), pp. 173 et seq.; L.C. Green, *The Contemporary Law of Armed Conflict*, 2nd edn. (2000), pp. 177 et seq.; I. Detter, *The Law of War*, 2nd edn. (2000), pp. 304 et seq., with additional references.

[627] Elements of Crimes for Article 8(2)(b)(xi) ICC Statute, num. 5.

[628] Elements of Crimes for Article 8(2)(b)(xi) ICC Statute, num. 3 and 4.

[629] Here the Elements of Crimes provide for a permissible deviation from ICC Statute, Art. 30(1); see marginal nos. 310 et seq.

[630] Elements of Crimes for Article 8(2)(b)(xi) ICC Statute, num. 2.

[631] See M. Cottier, in O. Triffterer (ed.), *Commentary on the Rome Statute of the International Criminal Court* (1999), Art. 8, marginal no. 130; K. Ipsen, in R. Bernhardt (ed.), *Encyclopedia of Public International Law*, Vol. 3 (1997), p. 978 at p. 980; S. Oeter, in D. Fleck (ed.), *The Handbook of Humanitarian Law in Armed Conflicts* (1999), no. 472; J. de Preux, in Y. Sandoz, C. Swinarski and B. Zimmermann (eds.), *Commentary on the Additional Protocols* (1987), marginal no. 1502.

international armed conflict, the prohibition on perfidy extends only to combatants for the enemy party, but not to civilians.[632]

Particular practical problems arise in connection with the prohibition on perfidy in **1060** non-international armed conflict in regard to guerrilla wars. In such conflicts, the distinction between fighters and civilians is especially difficult, as guerrilla troops are generally not transparently-structured units and there is no duty under international law to wear a uniform. Since guerrilla fighters are frequently indistinguishable from civilians, guerrilla fighters who kill or wound an opponent would constantly be guilty of forbidden perfidy by pretending to civilian status. To avoid this result, Article 44(3) of Additional Protocol I established that guerrilla fighters are not guilty of perfidious conduct if they carry their weapons openly during any military action, including preparation of attacks.[633] This position is also relevant when applying the prohibition on perfidy in non-international conflict.

X. Improper Use of Insignia

1. International Conflict

Article 8(2)(b)(vii) of the ICC Statute covers improper use of flags of truce, the flag or **1061** military insignia and uniform of the enemy or of the United Nations, and the distinctive emblems of the Geneva Conventions, if this results in death or serious injury. The provision is a special form of the war crime of perfidy in Article 8(2)(b)(xi). The criminal status of the misuse of emblems protected under international law reflects customary international law.[634]

The Statute provision is based in Article 23(f) of the Hague Regulations, which already prohibited **1062** improper use of all objects listed in Article 8(2)(b)(vii) of the ICC Statute, with the exception of UN insignia. Improper use of UN insignia was prohibited by Articles 37(1)(d), 38(2) and 85(3)(f) of Additional Protocol I. Improper use of the Red Cross emblem, use of which is regulated in numerous provisions of the Geneva Conventions, is a grave breach of Additional Protocol I under its Article 85(3)(f) if a person is killed or seriously wounded as a result. However, improper use of enemy insignia, emblems or uniforms under Article 39(2) of Additional Protocol I is not a grave breach of the Protocol or the Geneva Conventions.

The offense of improper use of a protective emblem in any case covers its treacherous use **1063** as defined in Article 37 of Additional Protocol I.[635] What conduct otherwise represents improper use can only be determined individually with regard to the various protected insignia. A distinction must be made between the prohibition on improper use of a flag

---

[632] For an example of a case of perfidy in internal armed conflict, see *Prosecutor* v. *Pius Nwaoga*, Supreme Court of Nigeria, judgment of 3 March 1972, in 52 *ILR* (1979), pp. 494 et seq.

[633] On this issue, see especially J. de Preux, in Y. Sandoz, C. Swinarski and B. Zimmermann (eds.), *Commentary on the Additional Protocols* (1987), marginal nos. 1506 et seq.

[634] See M. Cottier, in O. Triffterer (ed.), *Commentary on the Rome Statute of the International Criminal Court* (1999), Art. 8, marginal no. 70; C. Greenwood, in D. Fleck (ed.), *The Handbook of Humanitarian Law in Armed Conflicts* (1999), no. 230, on the misuse of flags of truce.

[635] See K. Kittichaisaree, *International Criminal Law* (2001), p. 166.

of truce and international emblems, on the one hand, and the improper use of enemy insignia on the other. The former prohibition is concerned not only with the threat to human life in the concrete case, but with the danger that the general acceptance and validity of these emblems could be undermined. The protection lent by these emblems to certain operations would be lost as a result. This concern plays no part in the improper use of enemy insignia.[636]

a) Improper Use of Flags of Truce

1064 Envoys – that is, persons authorized to negotiate with the enemy – have a right to inviolability under Article 32, sentence 2, of the Hague Regulations and may not be attacked or taken prisoner. They identify themselves by a white flag, signaling a willingness to negotiate. The offense forbids attacking an enemy while the attacker displays a flag of truce.[637]

1065 As to the mental element, Article 30 of the ICC Statute applies.[638] A modification is made in two directions. First, the Elements of Crimes establish that it is sufficient if a perpetrator should have recognized the prohibited use of the flag of truce.[639] Second, the Elements of Crimes require that the perpetrator act "in order to" simulate a willingness to negotiate.[640] In both cases, these deviations from the general requirements are permissible under Article 30(1) of the ICC Statute.[641]

b) Improper Use of Enemy Flags, Insignia, and Uniforms

1066 The international law of war does not prohibit the improper use of enemy flags, insignia and uniforms with the same strictness as the improper use of international protective emblems. Article 39(2) of Additional Protocol I forbids "mak[ing] use of the flags or military emblems, insignia or uniforms of adverse Parties while engaging in attacks or in order to shield, favour, protect or impede military operations." Under customary law, their direct use in military operations, at least, is prohibited, but the use of enemy insignia in the lead-up to hostilities is sometimes viewed as permissible.[642] Thus the Elements of Crimes also limit the offense to an improper use that is committed during an attack in a manner contrary to the international law of war.

1067 As to the mental element, Article 30 of the ICC Statute applies.[643] The Elements of Crimes specify that the perpetrator must have or should have recognized that the use of the enemy insignia was forbidden.[644] Unlike the war crime of improper use of a flag of truce, criminality here does not require intent to deceive on the part of the perpetrator.

---

[636] See M. Cottier, in O. Triffterer (ed.), *Commentary on the Rome Statute of the International Criminal Court* (1999), Art. 8, marginal nos. 72 et seq.

[637] See Elements of Crimes for Article 8(2)(b)(vii) ICC Statute, -1, num. 1, 2.

[638] For details on the general requirements for the mental element, see marginal nos. 294 et seq., esp. 304 et seq.

[639] See Elements of Crimes for Article 8(2)(b)(vii) ICC Statute, -1, num. 3.

[640] See Elements of Crimes for Article 8(2)(b)(vii) ICC Statute, -1, num. 2.

[641] See marginal nos. 310 et seq.

[642] See M. Cottier, in O. Triffterer (ed.), *Commentary on the Rome Statute of the International Criminal Court* (1999), Art. 8, marginal nos. 81 et seq.

[643] See marginal nos. 294 et seq., esp. 304 et seq.

[644] Elements of Crimes for Article 8(2)(b)(vii) ICC Statute, -2, num. 3.

c) Improper Use of Protective Emblems of the Geneva Conventions

The recognized protective emblems of the Geneva Conventions are, under Article 38 of **1068** Geneva Convention I, the red cross, red crescent, and the red lion and red sun, all on a white background.[645] These signs mark medical and spiritual personnel as well as medical facilities and transports, medical zones and medical equipment.[646] Thus the protective emblems may in principle be used only by persons who do not themselves participate in hostilities, but instead perform humanitarian tasks.[647] The specific conditions under which the use of protective emblems is permitted can be found in the relevant provisions of the Geneva Conventions and Additional Protocol I.[648] The Elements of Crimes clarify the offense such that the improper use must serve military purposes.[649]

As to the mental element, what has already been said in regard to the previously dis- **1069** cussed variants of the offense applies,[650] except that, unlike the war crime of misuse of a flag of truce, criminality here does not require intent to deceive on the part of the perpetrator.

d) Improper Use of Protected Insignia of the United Nations

Improper use of insignia of the United Nations particularly affects the interests of the **1070** international community. The offense is closely linked to criminal attacks on UN peacekeeping missions.[651] The insignia include the blue UN flag and other insignia and uniforms of the UN and its subsidiary organizations. According to the Elements of Crimes for Article 8(2)(b)(vii) of the ICC Statute, these insignia must be used in a manner forbidden by the international laws of war.[652] According to the wording of the provision, only UN military insignia are included. However, this is viewed as an editorial error, attributable to the combining of improper use of international emblems and enemy insignia in one offense. It cannot be assumed that the drafters of the ICC Statute would have wanted to exclude insignia used by the personnel of non-military operations from the scope of the offense.[653] Articles 37(1)(d) and 38(2) of Additional Protocol I, on which the ICC Statute provision is based, do not distinguish between military and non-military insignia.

---

[645] Illustrations of the protective emblems are found in Art. 3 of Annex I to Additional Protocol I. The emblem of the red lion and red sun, introduced by the Shah of Iran, has not been used since the 1980 Iranian Revolution, see W. Rabus, in D. Fleck (ed.), *The Handbook of Humanitarian Law in Armed Conflicts* (1999), no. 637, fn. 55.

[646] See W. Rabus, in D. Fleck (ed.), *The Handbook of Humanitarian Law in Armed Conflicts* (1999), no. 637.

[647] See J. de Preux, in Y. Sandoz, C. Swinarski and B. Zimmermann (eds.), *Commentary on the Additional Protocols* (1987), marginal no. 1538.

[648] See the listing in J. de Preux, in Y. Sandoz, C. Swinarski and B. Zimmermann (eds.), *Commentary on the Additional Protocols* (1987), marginal nos. 1528 et seq.

[649] See Elements of Crimes for Article 8(2)(b)(vii) ICC Statute, -4, num. 2. Under fn. 42 of the Elements of Crimes, this means use in direct connection with military operations.

[650] Here, too, the Elements of Crimes contain a reference to the requirement that the perpetrator knew or should have known of the improper use, see Elements of Crimes for Article 8(2)(b)(vii) ICC Statute, -4, num. 3.

[651] See marginal nos. 1134 et seq.

[652] See Elements of Crimes for Article 8(2)(b)(vii) ICC Statute, -3, num. 1, 2.

[653] See M. Cottier, in O. Triffterer (ed.), *Commentary on the Rome Statute of the International Criminal Court* (1999), Art. 8, marginal no. 76.

1071   As to the mental element, Article 30 of the ICC Statute applies.[654] The Elements of Crimes establish that the perpetrator must have been aware of the forbidden use of the insignia.[655] This requirement distinguishes this variant from the other variants of the offense, where it is sufficient that the perpetrator "should have known." This takes account of the fact that the provisions on the use of United Nations insignia are not always easily accessible to those outside the UN system.[656]

e) Serious Consequences

1072   The conduct described above is only criminal under Article 8(2)(b)(vii) of the ICC Statute if it led to a person's death or serious injury. A person is seriously injured if his or her physical integrity is impaired critically or for a long period.[657] The victim need not be a member of the opposing armed forces; the definition of the offense can also be satisfied by the killing or wounding of civilians or other persons *hors de combat*.[658] However, generally one's own nationals are not part of the class of protected persons, since there is no such prohibition under the international law of war.[659]

2. Non-International Conflict

1073   The ICC Statute limits criminality to international armed conflict; under customary international law, however, the improper use of recognized protected emblems is also criminal in non-international armed conflict. For improper use of emblems, state practice makes no distinction based on the type of conflict. This is shown, for example, by the unanimous condemnation of attacks on humanitarian missions, which occurs regardless of the type of conflict.[660] Therefore, the (German) Code of Crimes Against International Law [*Völkerstrafgesetzbuch, VStGB*] rightly also criminalizes improper use of recognized protective emblems in non-international armed conflict.[661]

XI. Giving No Quarter

1074   Article 8(2)(b)(xii) of the ICC Statute criminalizes a declaration that no quarter will be given in connection with an international armed conflict. The wording of the provision

---

[654] For details on the general requirements for the mental element, see marginal nos. 294 et seq., esp. 304 et seq.

[655] See Elements of Crimes for Article 8(2)(b)(vii) ICC Statute, -3, num. 3.

[656] See C. Garraway, in R.S. Lee (ed.), *The International Criminal Court, Elements of Crimes and Rules of Procedure and Evidence* (2001), p. 154 at p. 158.

[657] See B. Zimmermann, in Y. Sandoz, C. Swinarski and B. Zimmermann (eds.), *Commentary on the Additional Protocols* (1987), marginal no. 3474.

[658] See M. Cottier, in O. Triffterer (ed.), *Commentary on the Rome Statute of the International Criminal Court* (1999), Art. 8, marginal no. 84.

[659] But see also marginal nos. 869 et seq.

[660] See UN Doc. S/PRST/2000/4 of 9 February 2000 and the underlying debate on protection of humanitarian relief personnel, UN Doc. A/RES/52/167 of 16 December 1997. The *Convention on the Safety of United Nations and Associated Personnel* of 9 December 1994, 2051 *UNTS* (1999), p. 391, also makes no distinction based on the type of conflict.

[661] See (German) Code of Crimes Against International Law [*Völkerstrafgesetzbuch, VStGB*], Sec. 10(2) and Explanatory Memorandum of the (German) Code of Crimes Against International Law, *BT-Drs.* 14/8524, pp. 32.

corresponds to Article 23(d) of the Hague Regulations. A similar provision is found in Article 40 of Additional Protocol I.[662] Although Additional Protocol II has no analogous provision, Article 8(2)(e)(x) of the ICC Statute includes an identical provision for non-international armed conflict.[663] The Statute rules reflect customary international law.

The offense covers "take no prisoners" warfare. Another view has it that a situation in **1075** which no quarter is given already exists if a belligerent party uses a weapon that leaves the enemy no chance of survival; this is considered analogous to denying quarter.[664] But this interpretation confuses criteria of proportionality with the requirements of this specific offense. The prevailing view, as well as state practice, holds that combatants are not required to provide opposing fighters with the opportunity to surrender.[665]

The overly broad wording of Article 8(2)(b)(xii) of the ICC Statute prohibits "declar- **1076** ing" that no quarter will be given. The Elements of Crimes clarify the offense by requiring that a commander ("the perpetrator was in a position of effective command or control over the subordinate forces") give a "declaration or order."[666] Only under these precise circumstances does the offense become criminal under international law, as a methodical use of ruthless warfare.[667] The threat of warfare without quarter made by a simple soldier, or even a civilian, does not create criminal liability.

Article 8(2)(b)(xii) of the ICC Statute deals with two possible constellations. Either **1077** the declaration is made openly (for example, a public threat), or it remains an internal matter (for example, an order within a unit of the armed forces).[668] In the former case,

---

[662] For more, see J. de Preux, in Y. Sandoz, C. Swinarski and B. Zimmermann (eds.), *Commentary on the Additional Protocols* (1987), marginal nos. 1588 et seq.

[663] The offense has already achieved practical significance: after the end of World War II, a number of German officers were convicted in military trials for waging war without quarter, see British Military Court Hamburg, judgment of 20 October 1945 (*Eck* et al., so-called Peleus Trial), in United Nations War Crimes Commission, *Law Reports of Trials of War Criminals* I, pp. 1 et seq.; on this case, see also K. Zemanek, in R. Bernhardt (ed.), *Encyclopedia of Public International Law*, Vol. 4 (2000), pp. 977 et seq. See also United States Military Commission Rome, judgment of 12 October 1945 (*Dostler*), in United Nations War Crimes Commission, *Law Reports of Trials of War Criminals* I, pp. 22 et seq.; Canadian Military Court Aurich, judgment of 28 December 1945 (*Meyer*, so-called Abbaye-Ardenne Trial), in United Nations War Crimes Commission, *Law Reports of Trials of War Criminals* IV, pp. 97 et seq.

[664] See J. de Preux, in Y. Sandoz, C. Swinarski and B. Zimmermann (eds.), *Commentary on the Additional Protocols* (1987), marginal no. 1598.

[665] See M. Cottier, in O. Triffterer (ed.), *Commentary on the Rome Statute of the International Criminal Court* (1999), Art. 8, marginal no. 136.

[666] The Elements of Crimes for Article 8(2)(b)(xii) ICC Statute, num. 1, 2 and 3 each contain the words "declaration or order." See also the formulation "Anordnung oder Androhung" in (German) Code of Crimes Against International Law [*Völkerstrafgesetzbuch, VStGB*], Sec. 11(1) no. 6. The explanation of the law indicates that this was an intentional deviation from the wording of the ICC Statute for purposes of precision, see Explanatory Memorandum of the (German) Code of Crimes Against International Law, *BT-Drs.* 14/8524, p. 34.

[667] The (German) Code of Crimes Against International Law also limits the offense to orders by commanders, see (German) Code of Crimes Against International Law [*Völkerstrafgesetzbuch, VStGB*], Sec. 11(1) no. 6 and Explanatory Memorandum of the (German) Code of Crimes Against International Law, *BT-Drs.* 14/8524, p. 34.

[668] See Additional Protocol I, Art. 40, under which it is prohibited both to threaten the opponent with a declaration of ruthless warfare and to *conduct hostilities in this way*. This interpretation cannot be found directly in the ICC Statute, but was adopted into num. 2 of the Elements of Crimes for Article 8(2)(b)(xii) ICC Statute.

the aim is to terrorize and demoralize the opponent through particular ruthlessness. Terrorizing the opponent in this way is impermissible in international law.[669] In addition, the enemy is likely to resist all the more fiercely, which can lead to unnecessary victims.[670] In the second case, the situation is different. The enemy is not terrorized, as the declaration does not become public. The enemy will find out at best indirectly about the order to give no quarter. Here the criminal act is the instigation of the perpetrator's own soldiers to kill people who are *hors de combat* and violate international humanitarian law.[671]

1078　The crime of giving no quarter is satisfied once the relevant declaration is made or the order given. If no quarter is actually given, and if, consequently, persons no longer engaging in combat are killed, criminal liability can arise with regard to the relevant offenses, especially Article 8(2)(b)(vi) of the ICC Statute.

1079　As to the mental element, Article 30 of the ICC Statute applies with regard to the declaration or order and the perpetrator's authority.[672] In addition, the Elements of Crimes[673] require that the declaration be made with intent to ("in order to") threaten the enemy or to carry out hostilities on this basis.[674]

XII. Starvation of the Civilian Population

1080　Waldemar Solf: Siege, in Rudolf Bernhardt (ed.), *Encyclopedia of Public International Law*, Vol. 4 (2000), pp. 414 et seq.

1. International Conflict

1081　Article 8(2)(b)(xxv) of the ICC Statute covers starvation of civilians as a method of waging war. The rule is based primarily on Article 54 of Additional Protocol I and reflects customary international law.[675] However, it is not a grave breach of Additional Protocol I or the Geneva Conventions.

1082　Articles 23 and 55 of Geneva Convention IV should also be noted in this context. Article 23 establishes that all shipments of medicines, medical personnel and necessary objects of worship destined for the civilian population, as well as essential foodstuffs, clothing and tonics intended for groups

---

[669] See S. Oeter, in D. Fleck (ed.), *The Handbook of Humanitarian Law in Armed Conflicts* (1999), no. 450.

[670] See M. Cottier, in O. Triffterer (ed.), *Commentary on the Rome Statute of the International Criminal Court* (1999), Art. 8, marginal no. 134.

[671] See also the comparable arguments by the prosecution in Canadian Military Court Aurich, judgment of 28 December 1945 (*Meyer*, so-called Abbaye-Ardenne Trial), in United Nations War Crimes Commission, *Law Reports of Trials of War Criminals* IV, p. 97 at p. 100.

[672] On the general requirements of the mental element, see marginal nos. 294 et seq., esp. 304 et seq.

[673] Elements of Crimes for Article 8(2)(b)(xii) ICC Statute, num. 2.

[674] See C. Garraway, in R.S. Lee (ed.) *The International Criminal Court, Elements of Crimes and Rules of Procedure and Evidence* (2001), p. 167 at p. 170. On deviations from Art. 30 of the ICC Statute, see marginal nos. 310 et seq.

[675] See M. Cottier, in O. Triffterer (ed.), *Commentary on the Rome Statute of the International Criminal Court* (1999), Art. 8, marginal no. 214; D. Frank, in R.S. Lee (ed.), *The International Criminal Court, Elements of Crimes and Rules of Procedure and Evidence* (2001), p. 203.

in need of special protection, are to be guaranteed safe passage.[676] Article 55 obligates an occupying power to ensure the population's supply of foodstuffs and medicines.[677] This duty is extended by Articles 69 to 71 of Additional Protocol I to additional objects for satisfaction of essential needs, including materials for sleeping and emergency accommodation. The occupying power is obligated to bring such supplies to the occupied territory, if they are not already available in sufficient quantity.[678] In addition, Article 23(g) of the Hague Regulations and Article 53 of Geneva Convention IV forbid the destruction of moveable or immoveable property. These rules are expressions of the principle that the civilian population and individual civilians enjoy general protection from dangers arising from military operations. Facilities, equipment and objects indispensable to the survival of the civilian population are to be maintained.

The term "starvation" first of all requires more precise definition. Under a literal interpretation, only the withholding of food would apply. But the wording of the offense indicates that it cannot be based on such a narrow concept of starvation. Article 8(2)(b)(xxv) of the ICC Statute also covers the withholding of indispensable objects, such as medicines, blankets or clothing.[679] It is not necessary that civilians actually be harmed, or even endangered, through the withholding of these supplies, though that will generally be the case. **1083**

Article 8(2)(b)(xxv) of the ICC Statute can be fulfilled in various ways. The definition of the offense is satisfied if the perpetrator removes or destroys essential supplies.[680] If food is meant for civilians as well as for the enemy military, attacking it is forbidden if this would endanger the survival of the civilian population, unless the attack is required by imperative military necessity.[681] In case of doubt, it must be assumed that the supplies in question are to be used by the civilian population. **1084**

Preventing production of food by destroying cropland, agricultural areas, or other facilities is also covered if the population's nutrition would be endangered by these actions.[682] This criminalizes so-called "scorched earth" tactics, in which a passing army **1085**

---

[676] These rules were primarily inspired by the events of World War II, during which, although there were provisions for the protection of prisoners of war and civilian internees, there were no rules that would have authorized relief supplies for civilians in occupied territories, see J.S. Pictet (ed.), *Geneva Convention IV, Commentary* (1958), pp. 319 et seq.

[677] This is a major advance over Hague Regulations, Art. 43, which merely obligates the occupying power to maintain public security and order, see J.S. Pictet (ed.), *Geneva Convention IV, Commentary* (1958), p. 309.

[678] See Y. Sandoz, in Y. Sandoz, C. Swinarski and B. Zimmermann (eds.), *Commentary on the Additional Protocols* (1987), marginal no. 2779.

[679] See D. Frank, in R.S. Lee (ed.), *The International Criminal Court, Elements of Crimes and Rules of Procedure and Evidence* (2001), p. 203 at p. 204; M. Cottier, in O. Triffterer (ed.), *Commentary on the Rome Statute of the International Criminal Court* (1999), Art. 8, marginal no. 218.

[680] See Art. 54(2) Additional Protocol I, which covers all imaginable effects on food and other provisions, see C. Pilloud and J. de Preux, in Y. Sandoz, C. Swinarski and B. Zimmermann (eds.), *Commentary on the Additional Protocols* (1987), marginal no. 2101.

[681] This derives from Art. 54(3) and (5) of Additional Protocol I and from the principle of proportionality. On the exception in Art. 54(5), see C. Pilloud and J. de Preux, in Y. Sandoz, C. Swinarski and B. Zimmermann (eds.), *Commentary on the Additional Protocols* (1987), marginal nos. 2104 et seq.; M. Cottier, in O. Triffterer (ed.), *Commentary on the Rome Statute of the International Criminal Court* (1999), Art. 8, marginal no. 221. The situation is different for the destruction of provisions meant only for the enemy military. These are a legitimate military target.

[682] These examples are enumerated in Additional Protocol I, Art. 54(2); on the history of the Elements of Crimes, in which the broad concept of starvation was originally to be emphasized in a sepa-

destroys all food supplies.[683] An additional variant of the offense is referred to in Article 8(2)(b)(xxv) of the ICC Statute: impeding relief supplies as provided for under the Geneva Conventions.[684] Finally, not fulfilling a duty under international law to provide supplies can constitute an offense. In drafting the Elements of Crimes, the Preparatory Commission emphasized the importance of criminalizing omissions.[685] This variant of the offense is especially significant in occupations of foreign territory, since Article 69 of Additional Protocol I imposes upon an occupier the duty to ensure the provision of supplies to the civilian population of an occupied territory.[686]

1086   In addition to the general requirements for the mental element (Article 30 of the ICC Statute),[687] the perpetrator must have "intended to starve civilians as a method of warfare."[688] In other words, it must have been the perpetrator's purpose to use starvation as a weapon against the population. Thus cases in which destruction of foodstuffs is merely a secondary consequence of an otherwise legal military action are not criminalized, as the perpetrator in such cases does not act for the required purpose.[689]

1087   The starvation of civilians by destroying facilities, equipment or objects necessary for survival can also, in certain cases, satisfy the definition of an attack on the civilian population.[690] In such constellations, Article 8(2)(b)(xxv) of the ICC Statute is a more specific provision than Article 8(2)(b)(i) of the ICC Statute. Overlap is also possible with, for example, wilful infliction of great suffering or serious injury to physical integrity or

---

rate footnote, see D. Frank, in R.S. Lee (ed.), *The International Criminal Court, Elements of Crimes and Rules of Procedure and Evidence* (2001), p. 203.

[683] According to Additional Protocol I, Art. 54(5), however, this does not affect cases in which one party to an armed conflict clears a part of its own territory. In case of "imperative military necessity," scorched earth tactics also continue to be permissible under the provisions of Additional Protocol I, see L.C. Green, *The Contemporary Law of Armed Conflict*, 2nd edn. (2000), p. 144; C. Pilloud and J. de Preux, in Y. Sandoz, C. Swinarski and B. Zimmermann (eds.), *Commentary on the Additional Protocols* (1987), marginal nos. 2118 et seq.; W.A. Solf, in R. Bernhardt (ed.), *Encyclopedia of Public International Law*, Vol. 4 (2000), p. 414 at p. 415; for a skeptical view, see K. Kittichaisaree, *International Criminal Law* (2001), p. 186.

[684] The most important provision to be noted in this context is Geneva Convention IV, Arts. 59–62, which obligates the occupying power to ensure safe passage to relief consignments supplying civilians in occupied territories. See, in detail, J.S. Pictet (ed.), *Geneva Convention IV, Commentary* (1958), pp. 319 et seq. Additional Protocol I, Art. 70 has the same purpose. Its provisions contain, among other things, the duty to allow safe passage to neutral humanitarian relief supplies, see in detail Y. Sandoz, in Y. Sandoz, C. Swinarski and B. Zimmermann (eds.), *Commentary on the Additional Protocols* (1987), marginal nos. 2823 et seq. Geneva Convention IV, Art. 23 also contains special rules on medical relief supplies and relief for children and pregnant women. If such a supply consignment is held up by a party to the conflict, this satisfies the material element of the offense of starvation.

[685] See D. Frank, in R.S. Lee (ed.), *The International Criminal Court, Elements of Crimes and Rules of Procedure and Evidence* (2001), p. 203 at p. 204; for an express affirmation of the criminality of omissions, see also M. Cottier, in O. Triffterer (ed.), *Commentary on the Rome Statute of the International Criminal Court* (1999), Art. 8, marginal no. 223.

[686] For detail, see Y. Sandoz, in Y. Sandoz, C. Swinarski and B. Zimmermann (eds.), *Commentary on the Additional Protocols* (1987), marginal nos. 2779 et seq.

[687] On the general requirements of the mental element, see marginal nos. 294 et seq., esp. 304 et seq.

[688] See Elements of Crimes for Article 8(2)(b)(xxv) ICC Statute, num. 2.

[689] See D. Frank, in R.S. Lee (ed.), *The International Criminal Court, Elements of Crimes and Rules of Procedure and Evidence* (2001), p. 203 at p. 205.

[690] R. Wolfrum, in D. Fleck (ed.), *The Handbook of Humanitarian Law in Armed Conflicts* (1999), no. 1209.

health under Article 8(2)(a)(iii) of the ICC Statute, or with war crimes against property.[691]

2. Non-International Conflict

Starvation of the civilian population in the course of non-international armed conflict is **1088** not covered by the provisions of the ICC Statute, although at the negotiations in Rome many delegations advocated extending the crime of starvation to non-international armed conflict.[692] This limitation of the provision cannot be justified substantively,[693] and it lags behind the latest customary international law.[694] Most recently, in numerous demands, the international community has expressed its legal opinion that affected civilian populations must unconditionally be given access to relief supplies even in non-international armed conflict.[695] Therefore, the (German) Code of Crimes Against International Law [*Völkerstrafgesetzbuch, VStGB*] provides a uniform regulation for the criminality of starvation of a civilian population in both types of conflicts.[696]

Article 14 of Additional Protocol II prohibits the destruction, removal or rendering useless of food- **1089** stuffs, agricultural areas for the production of foodstuffs, crops, livestock, drinking water installations and supplies and irrigation works. This enumeration indicates that the term "starvation" must be viewed more narrowly in non-international armed conflicts than in international armed conflicts. Article 14 of Additional Protocol II only covers acts that expose civilians to famine, but not the withholding of other essential supplies.[697]

XIII. Use of Human Shields

1. International Conflict

Under Article 8(2)(b)(xxiii) of the ICC Statute, it is criminal to use civilians and other **1090** protected persons as human shields. The provision is based on Article 23(1) of Geneva

---

[691] M. Cottier, in O. Triffterer (ed.), *Commentary on the Rome Statute of the International Criminal Court* (1999), Art. 8, marginal no. 217.

[692] During the negotiations preceding adoption of the Statute, many delegations advocated an extension of the Statute's provisions on starvation to cover non-international armed conflicts, see M. Cottier, in O. Triffterer (ed.), *Commentary on the Rome Statute of the International Criminal Court* (1999), Art. 8, marginal no. 216.

[693] See also Art. 14 Additional Protocol II and, for discussion of this provision, S.S. Junod, in Y. Sandoz, C. Swinarski and B. Zimmermann (eds.), *Commentary on the Additional Protocols* (1987), marginal nos. 4790 et seq.

[694] See Explanatory Memorandum of the (German) Code of Crimes Against International Law, *BT-Drs.* 14/8524, p. 34.

[695] See UN Doc. A/RES/54/179 of 17 December 1999 (Congo); UN Doc. A/RES/54/185 of 17 December 1999 (Afghanistan); see also Explanatory Memorandum of the (German) Code of Crimes Against International Law, *BT-Drs.* 14/8524, p. 34.

[696] See (German) Code of Crimes Against International Law [*Völkerstrafgesetzbuch, VStGB*], Sec. 11(1) no. 5.

[697] In this direction, see also S.S. Junod, in Y. Sandoz, C. Swinarski and B. Zimmermann (eds.), *Commentary on the Additional Protocols* (1987), marginal no. 4791.

Convention III, Article 28 of Geneva Convention IV, and Article 51(7) of Additional Protocol I. The Statute's provision is oriented primarily around the latter norm,[698] but it combines all the provisions, particularly with regard to the persons protected by the norm.[699] The use of human shields is not a grave breach of the Geneva Conventions or the Additional Protocol.

1091 As a rule, protected persons may not be attacked. The offense in question here also serves to protect the civilian population and other persons in need of protection. At the same time, the offense is the reverse of the rules that directly protect civilians. This protection may not be misused for military purposes. The use of human shields does not relieve the opposing party of the duty to uphold the rules of international humanitarian law. In particular, in attacking an object surrounded by human shields, a party is bound by the principle of proportionality, so that the killing or wounding of an excessive number of civilians could in turn satisfy the definition of a war crime.[700] Isolated incidents of the misuse of civilians as shields already occurred during World War II;[701] more recently, especially in the conflict in former Yugoslavia, the offense has taken on drastic proportions. Several people have been prosecuted before the Yugoslavia Tribunal for using people as human shields.[702] In the 1991 Gulf War, too, protected persons were placed in strategic locations by the Iraqi army in order to prevent attacks on these targets.[703]

1092 Article 8(2)(b)(xxiii) of the ICC Statute lists as an offense the use of the presence of civilians or other protected persons to keep certain points, areas or military forces free of military operations. With the term "protected persons," the offense adopts the terminology of the Geneva Conventions and Additional Protocol I. Unlike the offenses under Article 8(2)(a) of the ICC Statute, however, it does not expressly refer to these Conventions. The Elements of Crimes speak of persons protected by international humanitarian law.[704] Protected status will also normally arise from the relevant provisions of the Geneva Conventions and Additional Protocol I, and in certain cases other provisions of international humanitarian law may also come into play.[705]

---

[698] See D. Frank, in R.S. Lee (ed.), *The International Criminal Court, Elements of Crimes and Rules of Procedure and Evidence* (2001), p. 199 at p. 201. The Elements of Crimes largely reflect the wording of Art. 51(7) of Additional Protocol I.

[699] See W.J. Fenrick, in O. Triffterer (ed.), *Commentary on the Rome Statute of the International Criminal Court* (1999), Art. 8, marginal no. 211. Thus Geneva Convention III, Art. 23 refers only to protection of prisoners of war, while Geneva Convention IV, Art. 28 affects protected persons under this Convention, and Additional Protocol I, Art. 51(7) affects the civilian population. For more, see C. Pilloud and J. de Preux, in Y. Sandoz, C. Swinarski and B. Zimmermann (eds.), *Commentary on the Additional Protocols* (1987), marginal nos. 1986 et seq.

[700] See W.J. Fenrick, in O. Triffterer (ed.), *Commentary on the Rome Statute of the International Criminal Court* (1999), Art. 8, marginal no. 211.

[701] See J.S. Pictet (ed.), *Geneva Convention IV, Commentary* (1958), p. 208; see also *Prosecutor v. Student*, British Military Court Lüneburg, trial of 6–10 May 1946, in United Nations War Crimes Commission, *Law Reports of Trials of War Criminals* IV, pp. 118 et seq.

[702] *Prosecutor v. Karadžić and Mladić*, ICTY (Trial Chamber), indictment of 24 July 1995, paras. 46 et seq.; *Prosecutor v. Blaškić*, ICTY (Trial Chamber), judgment of 3 March 2000, paras. 709 et seq.

[703] See H.-P. Gasser, in D. Fleck (ed.), *The Handbook of Humanitarian Law in Armed Conflicts* (1999), no. 506.

[704] Elements of Crimes for Article 8(2)(b)(xxiii) ICC Statute, num. 1.

[705] W.J. Fenrick, in O. Triffterer (ed.), *Commentary on the Rome Statute of the International Criminal Court* (1999), Art. 8, marginal no. 210, supports the view that even protected medical equipment cannot be used as a shield. This extension of the provision is not acceptable.

Article 51(7) of Additional Protocol I distinguishes between two situations. In one, **1093** objects that may be considered military targets may not be placed in protected surroundings with the intention of turning the prohibition on attacking protected persons to the perpetrator's military advantage. In the second, civilians may not be employed as shields in front of a possible military target or to shield military operations. Thus it does not matter whether the perpetrator places an object that he or she wishes to protect in a protected area or whether he or she brings protected persons to the object. This is reflected in the Elements of Crimes.[706] The definition of the offense is satisfied even if protected persons move of their own volition, and are then used by one side for protective purposes.[707] This can be the case, for example, if large groups of civilians flee a war zone, and military organizations use the train of refugees as cover from the enemy.

As to the mental element, Article 30 of the ICC Statute applies with regard to the **1094** material elements of the offense.[708] In addition, the perpetrator must act to protect, aid or prevent a military objective or military operation.[709] Proof of this purpose will not always be easy to obtain. Often, military command centers or war industries are found in civilian population centers, and military forces are frequently sent through cities in times of conflict.[710]

2. Non-International Conflict

The ICC Statute does not criminalize the use of human shields in non-international armed **1095** conflict. There is, however, no apparent justification for this differing treatment of the two types of conflict, given the latest developments in customary international law. These developments seek to protect civilians comprehensively in all types of conflicts.[711] The Yugoslavia Tribunal has rightly found the use of human shields to be criminal under customary international law even in non-international armed conflict.[712] The (German) Code of Crimes

---

[706] On this, the Elements of Crimes for Article 8(2)(b)(xxiii) ICC Statute, num. 1 state: "The perpetrator moved or otherwise took advantage of the location of one or more civilians . . . "; see D. Frank, in R.S. Lee (ed.), *The International Criminal Court, Elements of Crimes and Rules of Procedure and Evidence* (2001), p. 199 at p. 200.

[707] Here the ICC Statute, through the Elements of Crimes, takes up Additional Protocol I, Art. 51(7), which also covers the movement of the civilian population of its own volition, see D. Frank, in R.S. Lee (ed.), *The International Criminal Court, Elements of Crimes and Rules of Procedure and Evidence* (2001), p. 199 at p. 200; on Additional Protocol I, Art. 51(7), see C. Pilloud and J.S. Pictet, in Y. Sandoz, C. Swinarski and B. Zimmermann (eds.), *Commentary on the Additional Protocols* (1987), marginal no. 1988.

[708] On the general requirements of the mental element, see marginal nos. 294 et seq., esp. 304 et seq.

[709] Elements of Crimes for Article 8(2)(b)(xxiii) ICC Statute, num. 2. See D. Frank, in R.S. Lee (ed.), *The International Criminal Court, Elements of Crimes and Rules of Procedure and Evidence* (2001), p. 199 at pp. 200 et seq. In any case, however, the earlier rules in Additional Protocol I and the Geneva Conventions underlie the intent requirements. This narrows the zone of criminality, as permitted under ICC Statute, Art. 30 (see marginal nos. 323 et seq.).

[710] See W.J. Fenrick, in O. Triffterer (ed.), *Commentary on the Rome Statute of the International Criminal Court* (1999), Art. 8, marginal no. 210.

[711] See marginal nos. 812 et seq.

[712] *Prosecutor* v. *Blaškić*, ICTY (Trial Chamber), judgment of 3 March 2000, paras. 709 et seq.

Against International Law [*Völkerstrafgesetzbuch, VStGB*] has therefore extended the criminality of the use of human shields to non-international armed conflict.[713]

F. Use of Prohibited Means of Warfare

1096 Michael Bothe: Chemical Warfare, in Rudolf Bernhardt (ed.), *Encyclopedia of Public International Law*, Vol. 1 (1992), pp. 566 et seq.; Michael Bothe: *Das völkerrechtliche Verbot des Einsatzes chemischer und biologischer Waffen* (1973); Yoram Dinstein: Ratification and Universality, in Daniel Bardonnet (ed.), *La Convention sur l'Interdiction et l'Elimination des Armes Chimiques* (1995), pp. 151 et seq.; Jozef Goldblat: The Biological Weapons Convention – An overview, 79 *International Review of the Red Cross* (1997), pp. 251 et seq.; Josef L. Kunz: Gaskrieg und Völkerrecht, 6 *Archiv des Öffentlichen Rechts* (1927), pp. 73 et seq.; Elmar Rauch: Biological Warfare, in Rudolf Bernhardt (ed.), *Encyclopedia of Public International Law*, Vol. 1 (1992), pp. 404 et seq.; Dietrich Rauschning: Nuclear Warfare and Weapons, in Rudolf Bernhardt (ed.), *Encyclopedia of Public International Law*, Vol. 3 (1997), pp. 730 et seq.; Natalino Ronzitti: Relations between the Chemical Weapons Convention and Other Relevant International Norms, in Daniel Bardonnet (ed.), *La Convention sur l'Interdiction et l'Elimination des Armes Chimiques* (1995), pp. 167 et seq.

I. Introduction

1097 Even in the early stages of the development of international humanitarian law, states recognized that, while certain weapons and methods of warfare might be useful in effectively fighting the enemy, the consequences of their use for the affected soldiers or the population were so grave that their use should be restricted.[714] In addition to prohibitions on specific weapons that are regulated in numerous treaties,[715] general principles were developed on forbidden methods of warfare: if their use leads to unnecessary suffering or they act indiscriminately by nature – if their consequences, that is, cannot be limited to enemy combatants – they may not be utilized. These rules were codified in Article 23(e) of the Hague Regulations and Articles 35(2) and 51(4)(b) of Additional Protocol I.

1098 The provisions of the ICC Statute on the war crime of using prohibited means of warfare are the result of political compromise. During the negotiations on the ICC Statute, it was especially disputed whether the use of nuclear weapons and chemical and bio-

---

[713] See (German) Code of Crimes Against International Law [*Völkerstrafgesetzbuch, VStGB*], Sec. 11(1) no. 4 and Explanatory Memorandum of the (German) Code of Crimes Against International Law, *BT-Drs.* 14/8524, p. 34.

[714] See marginal nos. 776 et seq.

[715] See, e.g., the St. Petersburg Declaration of 1868 (*Declaration Renouncing the Use, in Times of War, of Explosive Projectiles under 400 Grammes Weight* of 29 November/11 December 1868, reprinted in D. Schindler and J. Toman (eds.), *The Laws of Armed Conflicts* (1973), pp. 95 et seq.; see also <http://www.icrc.org/ihl>; the Poison Gas Protocol of 1925 (*Protocol for the Prohibition of the Use in War of Asphyxiating, Poisonous or Other Gases, and of Bacteriological Methods of Warfare* of 17 June 1925, see <http://www.icrc.org/ihl>); the Biotoxin Weapons Convention of 1972 (*Convention on the Prohibition of the Development, Production and Stockpiling of Bacteriological (Biological) and Toxin Weapons and on Their Destruction* of 10 April 1972, 1015 *UNTS* (1972), p. 163) and the UN Weapons Convention and its four protocols (*Convention on Prohibitions or Restrictions on the Use of Certain Conventional Weapons Which May Be Deemed to be Excessively Injurious or to Have Indiscriminate Effects*, 1342 *UNTS* (1980), p. 137).

logical weapons of mass destruction should be forbidden.[716] Ultimately it was decided to forbid only the use of poison,[717] poison gas,[718] and certain types of ammunition.[719] These provisions reflect long-recognized prohibitions on means of warfare under international law. Article 8(2)(b)(xx) of the ICC Statute additionally criminalizes the use of means of warfare of a nature to cause superfluous injury or unnecessary suffering or which are inherently indiscriminate, and thus adopts the aforementioned general rule. But an additional requirement under Article 8(2)(b)(xx) is that these means of warfare be contained in a list, to be issued by the Assembly of States Parties. Thus this offense has more or less been put on hold until a prohibited list can be adopted[720] through the Statute's long and complicated amendment process.[721]

All the provisions mentioned have in common the fact that the mere use of forbidden **1099** means of warfare is criminalized. Criminal liability does not depend on the killing or wounding of persons or their endangerment in individual cases. All the provisions on prohibited means of warfare are limited in the ICC Statute to international armed conflict, and thus lag behind customary international law (see III).

II. International Conflict (ICC Statute)

1. Use of Poison or Poisoned Weapons

Article 8(2)(b)(xvii) of the ICC Statute criminalizes the use of poison or poisoned weap- **1100** ons. Article 3(a) of the ICTY Statute contains a similar provision. The wording of the provision is based on Article 23(a) of the Hague Regulations. It criminalizes any use of poison in armed conflict. It is immaterial whether the poison is employed as such or in connection with a weapon, for example if it is carried by bullets or in ammunition.[722] All that matters for criminal liability under international criminal law is the "whether," not the "how," of the use of poison by the perpetrator. The production and storage of poison is not covered by the offense.

There are no exceptions to the prohibition created by Article 8(2)(b)(xvii) of the ICC **1101** Statute. Use of poison is criminal even if the enemy and the civilian population are warned and endangerment is unlikely.[723] Nor can the use of poison be justified with reference to military necessity.[724]

---

[716] For details, see H. von Hebel and D. Robinson, in R.S. Lee (ed.), *The International Criminal Court, The Making of the Rome Statute* (1999), p. 79 at pp. 113 et seq.; P. Kirsch and J.T. Holmes, 93 *American Journal of International Law* (1999), p. 2 at pp. 7 et seq.; M. Cottier, in O. Triffterer (ed.), *Commentary on the Rome Statute of the International Criminal Court* (1999), Art. 8, marginal nos. 179 et seq.

[717] See ICC Statute, Art. 8(2)(b)(xvii).

[718] See ICC Statute, Art. 8(2)(b)(xviii).

[719] See ICC Statute, Art. 8(2)(b)(xix).

[720] For a critical view, see A. Cassese, *International Criminal Law* (2003), p. 60.

[721] ICC Statute, Arts. 121 and 123.

[722] See Elements of Crimes for Article 8(2)(b)(xvii) ICC Statute, num. 1: "The perpetrator employed a substance or a weapon that releases a substance . . .."

[723] *British Military Manual, The Law of War on Land being Part III of the Manual of Military Law* (1958), p. 42; K. Kittichaisaree, *International Criminal Law* (2001), p. 177; for a more skeptical view, see M. McDougal and F.P. Feliciano, *The International Law of War* (1994), pp. 619 et seq.

[724] See also marginal no. 479.

1102   As to the mental element, Article 30 of the ICC Statute applies.[725]

a) The Term "Poison"

1103   The Elements of Crimes define "poison" as substances that cause death or serious damage to health in the ordinary course of events because of their toxic properties.[726] Here the Elements of Crimes employ a narrow concept of poison: it does not include substances that may only have harmful effects on the environment or on animals, or substances that cause only less serious damage to health.[727]

1104   This limitation is not uncontroversial with regard to the underlying norm of international humanitarian law.[728] Some advocate a broader concept of poison that would also include substances that cause only short-term or minor harm to people (such as so-called incapacitating agents or tear gas) or damage to the environment.[729] Because violations of the prohibition on the use of poison gas are punished with severe penalties as crimes under international law, the restrictive interpretation in the Elements of Crimes must be affirmed.[730] Also, limiting the definition to substances that cause serious consequences takes account of the principle of legality.[731] Additionally, substances that are not toxic, but instead work physiothermally or through radiation, are not included under the term "poison."[732] Nor are weapons included under the prohibition if their poisonous effect is only an unintentional incidental effect, which is insignificant in comparison with the weapon's main effect.[733]

---

[725] On the general requirements of the mental element, see marginal nos. 294 et seq., esp. 304 et seq.

[726] Elements of Crimes for Article 8(2)(b)(xvii) ICC Statute, num. 2.

[727] For a more sceptical view, see M. Bothe, in A. Cassese, P. Gaeta and J.R.W.D. Jones (eds.), *The Rome Statute of the International Criminal Court*, Vol. 1 (2002), p. 379 at p. 407.

[728] *Convention on the Prohibition of the Development, Production, Stockpiling and Use of Chemical Weapons and on their Destruction* of 13 January 1993, 1975 *UNTS* (1997), p. 469, Art. 2(2), includes as poison substances with a toxic effect (only) on animals.

[729] See, e.g., M. Bothe, *Das völkerrechtliche Verbot des Einsatzes chemischer und biologischer Waffen* (1973), pp. 16 et seq.; but see, e.g., M. McDougal and F.P. Feliciano, *The International Law of War* (1994), pp. 636 et seq.; H. Meyrowitz, 10 *Annuaire Français de Droit International* (1964), pp. 89 et seq.

[730] On the negotiations on the Elements of Crimes regarding this issue, see K. Dörmann, in H. Fischer, C. Kress and S.R. Lüder (eds.), *International and National Prosecution of Crimes under International Law* (2001), p. 95 at pp. 128 et seq.

[731] See C. Garraway, in R.S. Lee (ed.), *The International Criminal Court, Elements of Crimes and Rules of Procedure and Evidence* (2001), p. 178.

[732] On the issue of nuclear weapons, see ICJ, advisory opinion of 8 July 1996 (Legality of the Threat or Use of Nuclear Weapons), *ICJ Rep.* 1996, p. 226, para. 55; see also the discussion in marginal no. 1118.

[733] See S. Oeter, in D. Fleck (ed.), *The Handbook of Humanitarian Law in Armed Conflicts* (1999), no. 434. A special case, increasingly discussed today, is the use of armor-piercing ammunition containing uranium. The depleted uranium in these projectiles is suspected of causing long-term damage to persons who come in contact with them. The poisonous effect of these weapons has not been proven with sufficient certainty as yet. For this reason alone, use of uranium-containing ammunition cannot be criminalized. In any case, however, it is unlikely that such weapons would qualify as poison within the meaning of ICC Statute, Art. 8(2)(b)(xvii), as the main purpose of the projectiles is not to poison people, but to be used against armor. As explained above, mere secondary effects of ammunition are not enough to classify a weapon as poisonous.

b) Poison Gas as Poison?

There is no agreement on whether the prohibition on the use of poison also extends to   **1105**
the use of poison gas. At first glance, there seems little doubt that these substances cause
toxicological damage to the body. The argument for excluding poison gas is mainly historical. The prohibition on poison in Article 23(a) of the Hague Regulations codified
customary international law, which could not have contained any rules about modern
methods of warfare like poison gas, since these were still unknown.[734] The question is
ultimately irrelevant to international criminal law, since Article 8(2)(b)(xviii) of the ICC
Statute creates a special rule for the use of poison gas ("Employing . . . poisonous . . .
gases"). Thus the offense in Article 8(2)(b)(xvii) extends to the poisoning of foodstuffs or
ammunition or similar approaches, while Article 8(2)(b)(xviii) covers the use of poison
gas.[735]

c) Chemical and Biological Weapons of Mass Destruction

Clarification is needed on whether chemical and biological weapons of mass destruc-   **1106**
tion[736] are covered by the prohibition on the use of poison. The ICC Statute contains
no express prohibition, although the Rome Conference was offered proposals for provisions[737] that referred to the Chemical Weapons Convention of 1993[738] and the Biological and Toxin Weapons Convention of 1972.[739] Instead, weapons of mass destruction
are covered by Article 8(2)(b)(xx) of the ICC Statute, which criminalizes the use of
weapons with indiscriminate effect, but which is not yet in force. The provision is based
on a compromise among the negotiating parties: because a prohibition on the use of
nuclear weapons failed due to the resistance of the nuclear powers, the use of other weapons of mass destructions would also not be directly criminalized. Instead, it was decided
that the question of the criminality of the use of weapons of mass destruction would be
dealt with later.[740] Thus it would contradict the structure and the negotiating history of
Article 8(2)(b) of the ICC Statute for the use of chemical and biological weapons of mass

---

[734] See the comprehensive evidence in M. Bothe, *Das völkerrechtliche Verbot des Einsatzes
chemischer und biologischer Waffen* (1973), pp. 5 et seq., and I. Detter, *The Law of War*, 2nd edn.
(2000), pp. 252 et seq.; see also S. Oeter, in D. Fleck (ed.), *The Handbook of Humanitarian Law in
Armed Conflicts* (1999), no. 434, which sees in the Poison Gas Protocol merely the confirmation of an
already-existing prohibition on poison gas.

[735] The provision in the (German) Code of Crimes Against International Law [*Völkerstrafgesetzbuch, VStGB*] is clearer, distinguishing in Sec. 12(1) nos. 1 and 2 between the use of poison gas and
the employment of biological and chemical weapons; see G. Werle and V. Nerlich, *Humanitäres
Völkerrecht-Informationsschriften* 2002, p. 124 at p. 133.

[736] On the concept of weapons of mass destruction, see I. Detter, *The Law of War*, 2nd edn.
(2000), pp. 234 et seq.

[737] See the evidence in H. von Hebel and D. Robinson, in R.S. Lee (ed.), *The International Criminal Court, The Making of the Rome Statute* (1999), p. 79 at pp. 113 et seq.

[738] *Convention on the Prohibition of the Development, Production, Stockpiling and Use of Chemical
Weapons and on their Destruction* of 13 January 1993, 1975 *UNTS* (1997), p. 469. On this Convention, see also marginal no. 1119.

[739] *Convention on the Prohibition of the Development, Production and Stockpiling of Bacteriological
(Biological) and Toxin Weapons and on Their Destruction* of 10 April 1972, 1015 *UNTS* (1972),
p. 163. On this Convention, see also marginal no. 1120.

[740] See H. von Hebel and D. Robinson, in R.S. Lee (ed.), *The International Criminal Court, The
Making of the Rome Statute* (1999), p. 79 at p. 116.

destruction to be included under Article 8(2)(b)(xvii). This outcome is regrettable from the standpoint of international legal policy, but unavoidable. The use of biological or chemical weapons of mass destruction is, however, criminal under customary international law.[741]

2. Use of Poison Gas and Similar Substances

1107   Article 8(2)(b)(xviii) of the ICC Statute is based on the Geneva Poison Gas Protocol of 1925[742] and prohibits the use of means of warfare that are asphyxiating, poisonous or act in similar ways. The Elements of Crimes bring the offense closer to the prohibition on the use of poison. The perpetrator must use gases, liquids or other materials that cause death or serious damage to health due to their asphyxiating or toxic properties.[743] Thus it is not criminal to use irritant gases, as long as they cause no significant health damage. This limiting interpretation is controversial with regard to the underlying provision of the Geneva Poison Gas Protocol of 1925,[744] but it is proper under international criminal law, since we are speaking here not merely of a norm addressed to states, but of a criminal prohibition.

1108   For this offense, too, the question arises whether it includes the use of modern chemical weapons. Once again, historical and structural reasons militate against undermining the compromise made in Article 8(2)(b)(xx) of the ICC Statute. However, the clear wording of Article 8(2)(b)(xviii) of the ICC Statute and the uncontroversial broad interpretation of the underlying Poison Gas Protocol of 1925[745] do not permit the exclusion of modern weapons.[746] The compromise achieved at the Rome Conference is thus essentially nullified.[747]

---

[741] See marginal nos. 1119 et seq.

[742] *Protocol for the Prohibition of the Use in War of Asphyxiating, Poisonous or Other Gases, and of Bacteriological Methods of Warfare* of 17 June 1925, see <http://www.icrc.org/ihl>.

[743] Elements of Crimes for Article 8(2)(b)(xviii) ICC Statute, num. 2.

[744] See I. Detter, *The Law of War*, 2nd edn. (2000), pp. 255 et seq.; A. Boserup, in Stockholm International Peace Research Institute (ed.), *The Problem of Chemical and Biological Warfare*, Vol. 3 (1973), pp. 57 et seq.; N. Ronzitti, in D. Bardonnet (ed.), *La Convention sur l'Interdiction et l'Elimination des Armes Chimiques* (1995) p. 167 at p. 173. The use of tear gas in armed conflict is expressly forbidden at least under Art. 1(5) in conjunction with Art. 2(7) of the Chemical Weapons Convention. A prohibition of the use of irritant gases is also found in a General Assembly resolution of 16 December 1969, UN Doc. A/RES/24/2603. A footnote to the Elements of Crimes makes it clear that the interpretation chosen there should not interfere with the further development of prohibitions on weapons. This took account of corresponding reservations among some of the delegations, see C. Garraway, in R.S. Lee (ed.), *The International Criminal Court, Elements of Crimes and Rules of Procedure and Evidence* (2001), p. 179 at p. 180.

[745] See M. Bothe, *Das völkerrechtliche Verbot des Einsatzes chemischer und biologischer Waffen* (1973), pp. 23 et seq.; K. Dörmann, in H. Fischer, C. Kress and S.R. Lüder (eds.), *International and National Prosecution of Crimes under International Law* (2001), p. 95 at pp. 128 et seq.; C. Garraway, in R.S. Lee (ed.), *The International Criminal Court, Elements of Crimes and Rules of Procedure and Evidence* (2001), p. 179.

[746] Similarly M. Bothe, in A. Cassese, P. Gaeta and J.R.W.D. Jones (eds.), *The Rome Statute of the International Criminal Court*, Vol. 1 (2002), p. 379 at p. 407; M. Cottier, in O. Triffterer (ed.), *Commentary on the Rome Statute of the International Criminal Court* (1999), Art. 8, marginal no. 183. The German legislation also assumes that ICC Statute, Art. 8(2)(b)(xviii) covers chemical weapons, see Ex-

Whether, on the other hand, biological weapons are covered by Article 8(2)(b)(xviii) **1109** of the ICC Statute is doubtful. It is true that the Poison Gas Protocol of 1925 extended the use of poison gas to bacteriological warfare.[748] However, this passage of the Protocol was not incorporated into the ICC Statute. Considering the history and structure of the overall regulatory system, therefore, bacteriological and other biological weapons must be excluded from the scope of Article 8(2)(b)(xviii).[749]

As to the mental element, Article 30 of the ICC Statute applies.[750] **1110**

3. Use of Prohibited Ammunition

Article 8(2)(b)(xix) of the ICC Statute criminalizes the use of bullets that expand or flat- **1111** ten easily in the human body. Examples of prohibited ammunition are bullets with a hard envelope that does not entirely cover the core or is pierced with incisions (so-called dum dum bullets). The provision is based on the *Declaration on the Use of Bullets Which Expand or Flatten Easily in the Human Body* of 29 July 1899.[751] Whether the ammunition as such is produced with these technical characteristics, or if conventional ammunition is later prepared manually, is immaterial.[752] The crucial point is solely the increased ability to wound in comparison to normal bullets that is created by the prohibited bullets. The provision is a form of the general prohibition on means of warfare that cause unnecessary suffering.[753]

Other than the examples listed in Article 8(2)(b)(xix) of the ICC Statute, there is of- **1112** ten disagreement on what ammunition is subject to the prohibition.[754] In applying the provision, it must be determined in the individual case whether the ammunition used causes the results described and whether a prohibition of the ammunition involved can be found under international law.[755]

---

planatory Memorandum of the (German) Code of Crimes Against International Law, *BT-Drs.* 14/8524, p. 35.

[747] M. Cottier, in O. Triffterer (ed.), *Commentary on the Rome Statute of the International Criminal Court* (1999), Art. 8, marginal no. 183, suspects that some delegations at the Rome Conference were unaware of this interpretation of the Poison Gas Protocol of 1925.

[748] See Poison Gas Protocol of 1925, para. 5.

[749] See M. Cottier, in O. Triffterer (ed.), *Commentary on the Rome Statute of the International Criminal Court* (1999), Art. 8, marginal no. 183, fn. 311. Here the German legislation took a different direction in (German) Code of Crimes Against International Law [*Völkerstrafgesetzbuch, VStGB*], Sec. 12(1) no. 2, with reference to customary international law (see below, marginal no. 1116); see also Explanatory Memorandum of the (German) Code of Crimes Against International Law, *BT-Drs.* 14/8524, p. 35.

[750] On the general requirements of the mental element, see marginal nos. 294 et seq., esp. 304 et seq.

[751] See <http://www.icrc.org/ihl>.

[752] See M. Cottier, in O. Triffterer (ed.), *Commentary on the Rome Statute of the International Criminal Court* (1999), Art. 8, marginal no. 184.

[753] See M. Bothe, in A. Cassese, P. Gaeta and J.R.W.D. Jones (eds.), *The Rome Statute of the International Criminal Court*, Vol. 1 (2002), p. 379 at p. 408; S. Oeter, in D. Fleck (ed.), *The Handbook of Humanitarian Law in Armed Conflicts* (1999), no. 407.

[754] Doubtful cases involve, for example, the use of pellet ammunition or of so-called high-velocity bullets, see I. Detter, *The Law of War*, 2nd edn. (2000), pp. 231 et seq.; S. Oeter, in D. Fleck (ed.), *The Handbook of Humanitarian Law in Armed Conflicts* (1999), no. 407.

[755] See also K. Dörmann, *Elements of War Crimes* (2002), pp. 295 et seq.

1113   As to the mental element, Article 30 of the ICC Statute applies.[756] The subjective requirements are further clarified in the Elements of Crimes. They require that the perpetrator be aware of the particularly dangerous nature of the ammunition.[757]

4. The Catch-All Offense of Article 8(2)(b)(xx) of the ICC Statute

1114 The prohibition on means of warfare in Article 8(2)(b)(xvii) to (xix) of the ICC Statute is based on a single underlying idea: the use of means of warfare that cause unnecessary suffering, or that are uncontrollable and therefore act with indiscriminate effect, is impermissible in international armed conflict. These basic prohibitions of international humanitarian law have been expressed, in particular, in Article 23(e) of the Hague Regulations, Articles 35(2) and 51(4) of Additional Protocol I, and Article 3(a) of the ICTY Statute, and are taken up in Article 8(2)(b)(xx) of the ICC Statute, which covers the use of such means of warfare in a catch-all offense. This clause defines as a war crime "employing weapons, projectiles and material and methods of warfare which are of a nature to cause superfluous injury or unnecessary suffering or which are inherently indiscriminate in violation of the international law of armed conflict."[758]

1115   The prohibition of means of warfare that cause particular suffering primarily protects those directly involved in hostilities, while the prohibition on weapons with indiscriminate effect primarily protects non-participants. Which means of warfare are included in this prohibition must be examined on a case-by-case basis. The resulting indeterminacy of the offense is mitigated by the ICC Statute in that, under Article 8(2)(b)(xx), it provides for a list in which prohibited means of warfare are to be enumerated. As a result, however, the offense will not be capable of application for the foreseeable future, since the list must be enacted using the complicated process for amending the Statute.[759] A further requirement of Article 8(2)(b)(xx) of the ICC Statute is that the means of warfare employed be the "subject of a comprehensive prohibition." The significance of this criterion is unclear. Placing a means of warfare on the list of prohibited means of warfare should be sufficient indication of a comprehensive prohibition.[760]

---

[756] On the general requirements of the mental element, see marginal nos. 294 et seq., esp. 304 et seq.

[757] Elements of Crimes for Article 8(2)(b)(xix) ICC Statute, num. 3: "The perpetrator was aware that the nature of the bullets was such that their employment would uselessly aggravate suffering or the wounding effect." For details, see C. Garraway, in R.S. Lee (ed.), *The International Criminal Court, Elements of Crimes and Rules of Procedure and Evidence* (2001), p. 182. It is to be prevented, in particular, that soldiers are held liable for using prohibited ammunition that they have been issued without knowing its properties, see K. Kittichaisaree, *International Criminal Law* (2001), p. 179.

[758] M. Bothe, in A. Cassese, P. Gaeta and J.R.W.D. Jones (eds.), *The Rome Statute of the International Criminal Court*, Vol. 1 (2002), p. 379 at pp. 408 et seq.; M. Cottier, in O. Triffterer (ed.), *Commentary on the Rome Statute of the International Criminal Court* (1999), Art. 8, marginal no. 186.

[759] Under ICC Statute, Art. 121(1), such proposals cannot be submitted until seven years after the ICC Statute entered into force, that is, not until after 30 June 2009. The adoption of the list also requires, under ICC Statute, Art. 121(2) to 4, a qualified majority and is only binding on the state parties when seven-eighths of the state parties have ratified the list.

[760] M. Cottier, in O. Triffterer (ed.), *Commentary on the Rome Statute of the International Criminal Court* (1999), Art. 8, marginal no. 187.

III. International Conflict (Customary International Law)

The ICC Statute does not cover all cases of criminal use of means of warfare in interna- **1116** tional armed conflicts. This is the result primarily of the fact that the catch-all offense of Article 8(2)(b)(xx) of the ICC Statute, as explained above, is not yet applicable. This poses the question of how far the use of other means of warfare in international conflicts is criminal under customary international law.

The starting point for such an assessment is the prohibition discussed above of weap- **1117** ons that have an indiscriminate effect and cause unnecessary suffering, as codified in Article 23(e) of the Hague Regulations and Article 35(2) and 51(4)(b) of Additional Protocol I. These rules are very generally worded and not useful for purposes of criminal law. The prohibitions have been made more concrete for a variety of means of warfare. In the following we will discuss, for the most important weapons, whether criminal liability for their use can be established under customary international law. The test proceeds in two steps: first of all, it is necessary to examine whether a prohibition exists in regard to specific weapons, deriving from customary international law or an international treaty. Second, the question must be addressed whether the violation of such a prohibition is criminal under customary international law.[761]

1. Nuclear Weapons

The prohibition under international law of the use of nuclear weapons is highly contro- **1118** versial. The starting point for a possible prohibition is the prohibition of poison in the Hague Regulations and the Poison Gas Protocol of 1925.[762] Also, numerous international treaties limit the proliferation and production of nuclear weapons.[763] Nevertheless, the nuclear powers insist that the use of these weapons is not subject *per se* to a

---

[761] On the structure of war crimes, see generally marginal no. 803.

[762] The ICJ does not consider the poison or poison gas prohibition to be involved, as the primary effect of nuclear weapons is not aimed at poisoning, see ICJ, advisory opinion of 8 July 1996 (Case Concerning the Legality of the Threat or Use of Nuclear Weapons), *ICJ Rep.* 1996, p. 226, para. 55; see also D. Rauschning, in R. Bernhardt (ed.), *Encyclopedia of Public International Law*, Vol. 4 (2000), p. 730 at pp. 733 et seq.

[763] For example, the *Treaty Banning Nuclear Weapon Tests in the Atmosphere, Outer Space and Under Water* of 5 August 1963, 480 *UNTS* (1963), p. 43; the *Treaty on Principles Governing the Activities of States in the Exploration and Use of Outer Space, Including the Moon and Other Celestial Bodies* (Outer Space Treaty) of 27 January 1967, 610 *UNTS* (1967), p. 205; the *Treaty for the Prohibition of Nuclear Weapons in Latin America* of 14 February 1967, 6 *ILM* (1967), p. 521; the *Treaty on the Non-Proliferation of Nuclear Weapons* of 1 July 1968, 729 *UNTS* (1968), p. 169; the *Treaty on the Prohibition of the Emplacement of Nuclear Weapons and Other Weapons of Mass Destruction on the Sea Bed and the Ocean-Floor and in the Subsoil thereof* (Sea Bed Treaty) of 11 February 1971, 955 *UNTS* (1971), p. 115; the *South Pacific Nuclear Free Zone Treaty* of 6 August 1985, 24 *ILM* (1985), p. 1440; the *Treaty Between The United States of America and The Union of Soviet Socialist Republics on the Elimination of Their Intermediate-Range and Shorter-Range Missiles* (INF Treaty) of 8 December 1987, 27 *ILM* (1987), p. 84; the *Treaty on the Final Settlement with respect to Germany* (2+4 Treaty) of 12 September 1990, 29 *ILM* (1990), p. 1186; the *Treaty on the Reduction and Limitation of American and Soviet Strategic Offensive Arms* (START I Treaty) of 31 July 1991; see <http://www.state.gov/documents/organization/27360.pdf>, and its "Lisbon" Protocol of 23 May 1992, see <http://www.state.gov/documents/organization/27389.pdf>.

prohibition under international law. In a controversial advisory opinion, the International Court of Justice concluded in 1996 that the use of nuclear weapons can be permissible under limited circumstances.[764] Thus no comprehensive ban on the use of nuclear weapons may be assumed to be recognized under customary international law. However, the use of nuclear weapons will usually violate the prohibition on the use of weapons with indiscriminate effect, and will for this reason be criminal. The prohibitions on means of warfare recognized under customary international law are applicable in principle to nuclear weapons.[765]

2. Chemical Weapons

1119   Under Article 1(1)(c) of the *Convention on the Prohibition of the Development, Production, Stockpiling and Use of Chemical Weapons and on their Destruction* (Chemical Weapons Convention) of 13 January 1993,[766] the use of chemical weapons is prohibited under any circumstances. The Chemical Weapons Convention was signed by 176 states and ratified by 151 states, including the United States and Russia;[767] it embodies customary international law.[768] Thus there is no doubt as to the validity of the primary norm, the prohibition under international law of the use of chemical weapons.

1120   In regard to the secondary norm, criminal liability for use of chemical weapons under customary international law, the legal situation is also clear. True, the states were unable to agree on inclusion of the use of chemical weapons at the Rome Conference, as discussed above.[769] But at the conference, the actual point of contention was not criminal liability under customary international law for use of chemical weapons, but rather the International Criminal Court's jurisdiction to try such crimes. Additionally, Article 7(1)(a) of the Chemical Weapons Convention obligates the treaty parties to ensure adherence to the Convention through criminal penalty. As discussed earlier, the use of chemical weapons can anyway be included in the prohibition of the use of poison gas. Finally, the above-listed criteria for criminalizing violations of international humanitarian law militate in favor of criminal liability under customary international law for use of

---

[764] ICJ, advisory opinion of 8 July 1996 (Case Concerning the Legality of the Threat or Use of Nuclear Weapons), *ICJ Rep.* 1996, p. 226.

[765] See ICJ, advisory opinion of 8 July 1996 (Case Concerning the Legality of the Threat or Use of Nuclear Weapons), *ICJ Rep.* 1996, p. 226, paras. 85 et seq.; see also S. Oeter, in D. Fleck (ed.), *The Handbook of Humanitarian Law in Armed Conflicts* (1999), nos. 428 et seq., with additional cites; C. Pilloud and J.S. Pictet, in Y. Sandoz, C. Swinarski and B. Zimmermann (eds.), *Commentary on the Additional Protocols* (1987), marginal no. 1843.

[766] 1975 *UNTS* (1997), p. 469.

[767] As of 23 April 2003.

[768] See Y. Dinstein, in D. Bardonnet (ed.), *La Convention sur l'Interdiction et l'Elimination des Armes Chimiques* (1995), p. 151 at pp. 162 et seq.; for the legal situation before the entry into force of the Chemical Weapons Convention, see S. Oeter, in D. Fleck (ed.), *The Handbook of Humanitarian Law in Armed Conflicts* (1999), nos. 434 et seq.

[769] See marginal no. 1098 and M. Cottier, in O. Triffterer (ed.), *Commentary on the Rome Statute of the International Criminal Court* (1999), Art. 8, marginal no. 181; H. von Hebel and D. Robinson, in R.S. Lee (ed.), *The International Criminal Court, The Making of the Rome Statute* (1999), p. 79 at pp. 115 et seq.

chemical weapons, since large numbers of persons are normally concretely endangered by the use of chemical weapons.[770]

A mental element is required under customary international law. Negligence is not sufficient.[771]   **1121**

3. Biological Weapons

Biological weapons are also subject to a comprehensive prohibition. The *Convention on the Prohibition of the Development, Production and Stockpiling of Bacteriological (Biological) and Toxin Weapons and on Their Destruction* (Biotoxin Weapons Convention) of 10 April 1972[772] prohibits all treaty parties from developing, producing, stockpiling or obtaining biological or toxin weapons.[773] However, the Biotoxin Weapons Convention does not contain an express prohibition on use. This results only indirectly from the prohibition on possessing biological weapons.[774] The preamble of the Biotoxin Weapons Convention also addresses the prohibition on use as the purpose of the Convention.[775] Finally, the Poison Gas Protocol of 1925 prohibits the use of bacteriological weapons. The use of biological weapons is thus forbidden by international law.[776]   **1122**

Nor is there any serious doubt that their use is criminalized under customary international law. The prohibition on the use of biological weapons was not adopted into the ICC Statute only because the parties could not agree in their assessment of the use of nuclear weapons.[777]   **1123**

A mental element is required under customary international law. Negligence is not sufficient.[778]   **1124**

4. Conventional Weapons

With the exception of the prohibition on dum dum bullets in Article 8(2)(b)(xix), the ICC Statute contains no prohibitions on conventional weapons; attempts to criminalize the use of anti-personnel mines and blinding laser weapons in the ICC Statute were unsuccessful.[779] But some conventional weapons are also subject to international legal pro-   **1125**

---

[770] See marginal no. 809.

[771] On the requirements for the mental element, see marginal nos. 294 et seq., esp. 304 et seq.

[772] 1015 *UNTS* (1972), p. 163.

[773] Biotoxin Weapons Convention, Art. 1; see J. Goldblat, 79 *International Review of the Red Cross* (1997), p. 251 at pp. 253 et seq.

[774] I. Detter, *The Law of War*, 2nd edn. (2000), p. 260.

[775] Biotoxin Weapons Convention, Preamble, paras. 9, 10.

[776] See also S. Oeter, in D. Fleck (ed.), *The Handbook of Humanitarian Law in Armed Conflicts* (1999), no. 438. In addition, the use of biological weapons would violate the prohibition against indiscriminate warfare, as the effect of contagious biological substances cannot normally be limited in target or number of victims, see S. Oeter, in J. Hasse, E. Müller and P. Schneider (eds.), *Humanitäres Völkerrecht* (2001), p. 78 at p. 101.

[777] See the relevant discussions of the criminality of the use of chemical weapons, marginal nos. 1119 et seq.

[778] For details on the requirements for the mental element, see marginal nos. 294 et seq., esp. 304 et seq.

[779] See *Decisions taken by the Preparatory Committee at its Session held from 11 to 21 February 1997*, UN Doc. A/AC.249/1997/L.5, pp. 10 et seq.; *Decisions taken by the Preparatory Committee at its Session held from 1 to 12 December 1997*, UN Doc. A/AC.249/1997/L.9/Rev.1, pp. 8 et seq.; *Report of the*

hibitions. First of all, there is the *Convention on Prohibitions or Restrictions on the Use of Certain Conventional Weapons Which May be Deemed to be Excessively Injurious or to Have Indiscriminate Effects* (UN Weapons Convention) of 10 October 1980.[780] In the four protocols to the UN Weapons Convention, specific groups of weapons are prohibited: Protocol I prohibits weapons whose primary effect is to create fragments that cannot be detected by X-rays in the human body and therefore cannot be removed.[781] Protocol II limits the use of mines and other booby-traps.[782] Protocol III forbids the use of incendiary weapons against civilians and military targets located within concentrations of civilians,[783] and Protocol IV forbids the use of blinding laser weapons.[784]

1126   Thus there exists a range of instruments under international law that prohibit the use of certain conventional weapons in whole or in part. The prohibited use of these weapons, however, appears not to be subject to criminal sanction under customary international law. It is true that these are acts that normally go hand-in-hand with concrete danger to life and limb. But the Conventions are binding on only a small number of states.[785] At the Rome Conference, the question of whether to criminalize the use of certain conventional weapons was – as discussed above – controversial.[786] Where the criminality of the use of conventional weapons under customary international law is in question, a careful examination of international prohibitions and criminality in each specific case is therefore indispensable. Only if the state parties to the ICC Statute decide to adopt a prohibited list as called for under Article 8(2)(b)(xx) of the ICC Statute will greater clarity be achieved.

Intersessional Meeting from 19 to 30 January held in Zutphen, UN Doc. A/AC.249/1998/L.13; *Report of the Preparatory Committee on the Establishment of an International Criminal Court, Draft Statute and Final Act*, UN Doc. A/Conf.183/2/Add.1 (1998). All listed documents are reprinted in M.C. Bassiouni (ed.), *The Statute of the ICC – A Documentary History* (1998). See also C.K. Hall, 91 *American Journal of International Law* (1997), pp. 177 et seq.; C.K. Hall, 92 *American Journal of International Law* (1998), pp. 125 et seq. and pp. 331 et seq.

[780] 1342 *UNTS* (1980), p. 137.

[781] *Protocol on Non-Detectable Fragments (Protocol I)* of 10 October 1980, 1342 *UNTS* (1980), p. 168.

[782] *Protocol on Prohibitions or Restrictions on the Use of Mines, Booby-Traps and Other Devices (Protocol II)*, 1342 *UNTS* (1980), p. 168, amended version, 3 May 1996, see <http://www.icrc.org/ihl>. The amended version of the Protocol permits the use of landmines only under narrow circumstances. A complete prohibition on the use of landmines is contained in Art. 1(1)(a) of the *Convention on the Prohibition of the Use, Stockpiling, Production and Transfer of Anti-Personnel Mines and on their Destruction* of 18 September 1997, 2056 *UNTS* (1999), p. 241. However, important states like the United States have not yet acceded to this Convention.

[783] *Protocol on Prohibitions or Restrictions on the Use of Incendiary Weapons (Protocol III)* of 10 October 1980, 1342 *UNTS* (1980), p. 171.

[784] *Protocol on Blinding Laser Weapons (Protocol IV)* of 13 October 1995, 2024 *UNTS* (1998), p. 167.

[785] The UN Weapons Convention is currently binding on 94 states, Protocol I to the Convention on 88 states, Protocol II on 80 states (68 states in its amended form as of 3 May 1997), Protocol III on 85 states and Protocol IV on 67 states (as of October 2004).

[786] See marginal no. 1098 and M. Cottier, in O. Triffterer (ed.), *Commentary on the Rome Statute of the International Criminal Court* (1999), Art. 8, marginal no. 188.

IV. Non-International Conflict (Customary International Law)

The ICC Statute contains no prohibition on weapons in non-international armed con- **1127** flict,[787] because states considered their sovereignty to be particularly threatened in this area.[788] By contrast, under customary international law the use of certain weapons is criminal even in non-international armed conflict. As usual in the law of war crimes, to prove an offense under customary international law one must show, first of all, the existence of an international legal prohibition, and second of all, that it is subject to criminal sanction under customary international law.

International law was at first very restrained in regard to prohibitions on the use of **1128** weapons in non-international conflict. Important regulations such as the poison gas prohibition in Article 23(a) of the Hague Regulations and the Poison Gas Protocol of 1925 were only applicable to international conflict. Nor do the Geneva Conventions or Additional Protocol II contain any prohibitions on weapons in civil wars.

More recent treaties are right to no longer exercise this restraint. A prohibition on the **1129** use of biological weapons in non-international conflicts arises from the Biotoxin Weapons Convention of 1972. Because state parties to this Convention are prohibited from developing, producing or stockpiling biological weapons under any circumstances, they may not be used in civil wars. This is underlined in paragraph 9 of the preamble to the Convention, in which the treaty parties state their decision "to exclude completely the possibility of [biological agents] being used as weapons." The Chemical Weapons Convention of 1993 also prohibits the use of chemical weapons in all types of conflicts;[789] the use of chemical weapons in non-international conflicts is prohibited under customary international law.[790]

In addition, a trend is emerging toward prohibiting other means of warfare in non- **1130** international conflict. The revised Protocol II to the UN Weapons Convention, which prohibits the use of landmines, is also applicable to non-international armed conflict.[791] The same is true of the *Convention on the Prohibition of the Use, Stockpiling, Production and Transfer of Anti-Personnel Mines and on their Destruction* of 18 September 1997.[792] Through the change in Article 1 of the UN Weapons Convention of 21 December 2001, this Convention and its protocols became applicable to non-international armed conflict. However, this amendment has not yet entered into force.[793]

---

[787] For a critical view, see A. Cassese, 10 *European Journal of International Law* (1999), p. 144 at pp. 152 et seq.; A. Cassese, *International Criminal Law* (2003), pp. 61 et seq.; C. Kress, 30 *Israel Yearbook on Human Rights* (2001), p. 103 at p. 136.

[788] On the controversy over this, see P. Kirsch and J.T. Holmes, 93 *American Journal of International Law* (1999), p. 2 at p. 7; C. Kress, 30 *Israel Yearbook on Human Rights* (2001), p. 103 at p. 136.

[789] The Chemical Weapons Convention also refers, in paragraph 5 of its preamble, to the goal of completely ending the use of chemical weapons.

[790] *Prosecutor* v. *Tadić*, ICTY (Appeals Chamber), decision of 2 October 1995, paras. 120 et seq.

[791] See Art. 1(2) of the *Protocol on Prohibitions or Restrictions on the Use of Mines, Booby-Traps and Other Devices (Protocol II)*, as amended on 3 May 1996, see <http://www.icrc.org/ihl>.

[792] 2056 *UNTS* (1999), p. 241. Art. 1(1)(a) of the Convention prohibits the use of mines under any circumstances, including in non-international armed conflicts.

[793] Under the UN Weapons Convention, Art. 8(1)(b) in conjunction with Art. 5(1), an amendment takes effect six months after the 20th ratification of the amendment. By April 2003, only 9 states had ratified the amendment.

1131   If a prohibition on a specific weapon can be shown to exist for non-international armed conflict, proving that it is subject to criminal sanction under customary international law presents little problem. Violations of weapons prohibitions are usually especially grave, and often their criminality in international conflicts is unquestioned; the requirements for the prohibition's criminal status under customary international law are thus satisfied.[794] The criminal status of the use of poison, chemical and biological weapons and so-called dum dum bullets is therefore assured in non-international as well as international conflict. Consequently, the (German) Code of Crimes Against International Law [*Völkerstrafgesetzbuch, VStGB*] makes the use of these weapons a criminal offense, regardless of the type of conflict.[795]

1132   A mental element is required under customary international law. Negligence is not sufficient.[796]

G. War Crimes Against Humanitarian Operations

1133   Evan T. Bloom: Protecting Peacekeepers: The Convention on the Safety of United Nations and Associated Personnel, 89 *American Journal of International Law* (1995), pp. 621 et seq.; M.-Christiane Bourloyannis-Vrailas: Crimes Against United Nations and Associated Personnel, in Gabrielle Kirk McDonald and Olivia Swaak-Goldman (eds.), *Substantive and Procedural Aspects of International Criminal Law, The Experience of International and National Courts*, Vol. 1 (2000), pp. 337 et seq.; Zdzisaw Galicki: Atteintes à la securité du personnel des Nations Unies et des personells associés, in Hervé Ascensio, Emmanuel Decaux and Alain Pellet (eds.), *Droit International Pénal* (2000), pp. 493 et seq.

1134   Article 8(2)(b)(iii) of the ICC Statute covers

"intentionally directing attacks against personnel, installations, material, units or vehicles involved in a humanitarian assistance or peacekeeping mission in accordance with the Charter of the United Nations, as long as they are entitled to the protection given to civilians or civilian objects under the international law of armed conflict."[797]

Article 8(2)(e)(iii) of the ICC Statute contains an identical provision for non-international armed conflicts. The provisions are a response to numerous attacks on UN and associated personnel in recent decades[798] that particularly affect the interests of the international community, and additionally threaten to lessen the willingness to participate in aid missions. The offense embodies customary international law.

---

[794] See marginal nos. 803 et seq. However, where the criminality of use of certain conventional weapons is concerned, the reservations expressed in marginal no. 1126 apply accordingly.

[795] See (German) Code of Crimes Against International Law [*Völkerstrafgesetzbuch, VStGB*], Sec. 12(1) and Explanatory Memorandum of the (German) Code of Crimes Against International Law, *BT-Drs.* 14/8524, pp. 35 et seq.

[796] For details on the requirements of the mental element, see marginal nos. 294 et seq., esp. 304 et seq.

[797] The Elements of Crimes basically limit themselves to a repetition of the requirements of the offense.

[798] See M.-C. Bourloyannis-Vrailas, in G. Kirk McDonald and O. Swaak-Goldman (eds.), *Substantive and Procedural Aspects of International Criminal Law,* Vol. 1 (2000), pp. 337 et seq.

The offense largely overlaps with criminal attacks on civilians and civilian objects[799] **1135**
and with war crimes against persons. Thus the offenses have mainly symbolic character
and prevent gaps in criminality in certain marginal areas.[800]

Article 71(2) of Additional Protocol I demands that participants in relief operations be respected **1136**
and protected. In contrast, the Geneva Conventions contain no specific protective provisions for
members of UN peacekeeping missions. The ICC Statute is the first multilateral treaty that expressly defines attacks on UN and associated personnel as war crimes.[801] The number of attacks
on UN personnel has dramatically increased since the early 1990s.[802] Under the influence of these
attacks on UN operations, in 1994 the General Assembly unanimously adopted the *Convention on
the Safety of United Nations and Associated Personnel,*[803] which went into force on 15 January
1999. Under the influence of this treaty, an offense entitled "Crimes Against United Nations and
Associated Personnel" was adopted into Article 19 of the *Draft Code of Crimes Against the Peace
and Security of Mankind,* drafted in 1996 by the UN International Law Commission. However,
this was not considered a war crime, but a separate type of crime against the peace and security of
mankind.[804] The UN International Law Commission emphasized that attacks on UN personnel
were violent crimes of extraordinary gravity that had serious consequences not only for the victims,
but for the entire international community. Such attacks could cause a gradual decline in the willingness of individuals to co-operate in peacekeeping and humanitarian operations and the willingness of states to make personnel available.[805]

Article 8(2)(b)(iii) of the ICC Statute covers two different methods of commission – at- **1137**
tacks on humanitarian relief missions and attacks on peacekeeping missions. The ICC
Statute refrains from more clearly defining these criteria. The concept of peacekeeping is
described as follows in the UN Secretary-General's 1992 *Agenda for Peace*:

"Peace-keeping is the deployment of a United Nations presence in the field, hitherto with the consent of all the parties concerned, normally involving United Nations military and/or police person-

---

[799] See D. Frank, in R.S. Lee (ed.), *The International Criminal Court, Elements of Crimes and Rules
of Procedure and Evidence* (2001), p. 145.

[800] The offense primarily prevents non-military attacks on members of such missions from going
unpunished because the victims – due for example to their nationality – might not be protected persons within the meaning of Geneva Convention IV, so that the offenses in ICC Statute, Art. 8(2)(a),
could not be applied.

[801] See D. Frank, in R.S. Lee (ed.), *The International Criminal Court, Elements of Crimes and Rules
of Procedure and Evidence* (2001), p. 145.

[802] While the number of deaths among UN personnel totalled 1074 by March 1994, in 1993
alone, 202 UN staff members were killed. In Somalia and the Yugoslavia conflict, especially, large
numbers of attacks occurred; thus in late 1994, Bosnian-Serb troops held 400 UN employees hostage,
see M.-C. Bourloyannis-Vrailas, in G. Kirk McDonald and O. Swaak-Goldman (eds.), *Substantive
and Procedural Aspects of International Criminal Law,* Vol. 1 (2000), p. 337 at p. 338, fns. 6 et seq.

[803] 2051 *UNTS* (1999), p. 391. On this treaty, see Z. Galicki, in H. Ascensio, E. Decaux and A.
Pellet (eds.), *Droit International Pénal* (2000), pp. 493 et seq.; E. Bloom, 89 *American Journal of International Law* (1995), pp. 621 et seq.; M.-C. Bourloyannis-Vrailas, in G. Kirk McDonald and O.
Swaak-Goldman (eds.), *Substantive and Procedural Aspects of International Criminal Law,* Vol. 1
(2000), p. 337 at pp. 339 et seq.

[804] See J. Allain and J.R.W.D. Jones, 8 *European Journal of International Law* (1997), pp. 100 et
seq.

[805] *Draft Code* 1996, commentary on Art. 19, para. 2.

nel and frequently civilians as well. Peace-keeping is a technique that expands the possibilities for both the prevention of conflict and the making of peace."[806]

1138   Peacekeeping thus includes operations generally consisting of the temporary deployment of military personnel in order to prevent the outbreak of hostilities in tense situations in which large-scale military operations are not, or are no longer, taking place. A peacekeeping mission can also consist of mere observers. In any case, the members of such a mission must be neutral and may not participate in hostilities beyond a necessary degree of self-defense. The concept of peacekeeping must thus be distinguished from compulsory UN military measures under Chapter VII of the UN Charter, which are decided upon by the Security Council and include the employment of military force.[807]

1139   As to the meaning of humanitarian relief missions, conclusions can be drawn from Articles 70 and 71 of Additional Protocol I. Article 70(1), sentence 1, of Additional Protocol I provides:

> "If the civilian population of any territory under the control of a Party to the conflict, other than occupied territory, is not adequately provided with . . . supplies . . . relief actions which are humanitarian and impartial in character and conducted without any adverse distinction shall be undertaken, subject to the agreement of the Parties concerned in such relief actions."

1140   Humanitarian relief missions, therefore, are primarily concerned with getting supplies to the population, especially victims of armed conflicts. This does not include long-term measures involving development aid. Humanitarian relief missions must be impartial in granting aid.[808] They may not use violence, outside of necessary self-defense.[809] Such missions are usually carried out by non-governmental and inter-state organizations, including subsidiaries of the United Nations such as UNHCR, UNICEF, UNESCO and the Food and Agriculture Organization (FAO). Humanitarian activities by the Red Cross and Red Crescent are also protected by Article 8(2)(b)(xxiv) of the ICC Statute.[810]

1141   Attacks within the meaning of this offense are not only military operations under Article 49(1) of Additional Protocol I. Any type of use of force against humanitarian relief organizations and peacekeeping missions is covered. This derives from the underlying *Convention on the Safety of United Nations and Associated Personnel.* Article 9 of the Convention obligates the treaty parties, among other things, to criminalize killing, kidnapping and other attacks on the life and freedom of UN personnel,[811] as well as violent

---

[806] UN Secretary-General, *Agenda for Peace* of 17 June 1992, UN Doc. A/47/277 – S/24111, para. 20.

[807] B.-O. Bryde, in B. Simma (ed.), *The Charter of the United Nations*, Vol. 1, 2nd edn. (2002), Art. 44, marginal nos. 1 and 8; M. Bothe, in B. Simma (ed.), *The Charter of the United Nations*, Vol. 1, 2nd edn. (2002), Peace-Keeping, marginal nos. 72 et seq.

[808] K. Kittichaisaree, *International Criminal Law* (2001), p. 161.

[809] M. Cottier, in O. Triffterer (ed.), *Commentary on the Rome Statute of the International Criminal Court* (1999), Art. 8, marginal no. 33.

[810] M. Cottier, in O. Triffterer (ed.), *Commentary on the Rome Statute of the International Criminal Court* (1999), Art. 8, marginal no. 34.

[811] Art. 1 of the Convention defines UN personnel as the following: "Persons engaged or deployed by the Secretary-General of the United Nations as members of the military, police or civilian components of a United Nations operation . . .. Other officials and experts on mission of the United Nations

attacks endangering life or freedom against official bases, private accommodations or transport of UN personnel. The list in Article 9 can be used to clarify the term "attack."[812]

Attacks on humanitarian relief and peacekeeping missions are criminal under Article **1142** 8(2)(b)(iii) of the ICC Statute only as long as such missions are "entitled to the protection given to civilians or civilian objects under the international law of armed conflict." Article 51(3) of Additional Protocol I indicates that civilians are only protected if they do not directly participate in hostilities. Under Article 52(2) of Additional Protocol I, civilian objects are protected as long as they are not used for military purposes. For the offense in Article 8(2)(b)(iii) of the ICC Statute, therefore, humanitarian and peacekeeping missions are not protected if their members participate in hostilities. If they merely exercise self-defense, they do not lose their civilian status.

As to the mental element, Article 30 of the ICC Statute applies.[813] **1143**

H. Multiplicity of Offenses

War crimes can at the same time satisfy the definitions of genocide and of crimes against **1144** humanity.[814] The offenses remain simultaneously applicable, because none of them is a *lex specialis*. A conviction for all crimes is thus always required in order to adequately express the wrong.

There is little case law on the concurrent relationship of specific war crimes with one **1145** another. The Yugoslavia Tribunal did establish that Article 2 of the ICTY Statute represents a *lex specialis* in relation to Article 3 of the Statute;[815] however, this is not transferable without more to the war crimes provisions of the ICC Statute. For details, see the discussions of the various offenses above.[816]

If the same perpetrator commits various war crimes in various places and at various **1146** times, these are generally independent acts, each of which can be prosecuted separately. While the linkage of various criminal acts to the same genocidal intent or to the same attack on a civilian population can turn these acts into one comprehensive crime of genocide or crime against humanity, the connection with the same armed conflict alone is not enough to turn separate war crimes into one comprehensive "overall crime."[817]

---

or its specialized agencies or the International Atomic Energy Agency who are present in an official capacity in the area where a United Nations operation is being conducted." Associated persons are also protected, which under Art. 1(b) of the Convention includes persons assigned by a government or an inter-state organization with the approval of the responsible UN organ, engaged by the UN Secretary-General, a special UN agency or the International Atomic Energy Agency, or deployed with the approval of the UN Secretary-General or a UN special agency to conduct support activities to fulfill a UN mandate.

[812] See also K. Kittichaisaree, *International Criminal Law* (2001), pp. 160 et seq.; M. Cottier, in O. Triffterer (ed.), *Commentary on the Rome Statute of the International Criminal Court* (1999), Art. 8, marginal no. 48, expresses doubts.

[813] On the general requirements of the mental element, see marginal nos. 294 et seq., esp. 304 et seq.

[814] See marginal nos. 528 et seq.

[815] *Prosecutor* v. *Mucić* et al., ICTY (Appeals Chamber), judgment of 20 February 2001, paras. 414 et seq.

[816] See, e.g., marginal nos. 904, 922 et seq., 1029, 1061, 1078, 1087.

[817] See also marginal no. 523.

Part Six: The Crime of Aggression

1147 Stanimir A. Alexandrov: *Self-Defense Against the Use of Force in International Law* (1996); M. Cherif Bassiouni and Benjamin B. Ferencz: The Crime Against Peace, in M. Cherif Bassiouni (ed.), *International Criminal Law*, Vol. 1, 2nd edn. (1999), pp. 313 et seq.; Bengt Broms: The Definition of Aggression, 154 *Recueil des Cours* (1977), Vol. 1, pp. 229 et seq.; Ian Brownlie: *International Law and the Use of Force by States* (1963); Thomas Bruha: *Die Definition der Aggression* (1980); Allegra Carrol Carpenter: The International Criminal Court and the Crime of Aggression, 64 *Nordic Journal of International Law* (1995), pp. 223 et seq.; Antonio Cassese: *International Criminal Law* (2003), pp. 111 et seq.; Yoram Dinstein: *War, Aggression and Self-Defence*, 3rd edn. (2001); Yoram Dinstein: The Distinctions between War Crimes and Crimes Against Peace, 24 *Israel Yearbook on Human Rights* (1994), pp. 1 et seq.; Joachim von Elbe: The Evolution of the Concept of the Just War in International Law, 33 *American Journal of International Law* (1939), pp. 665 et seq.; Paula Escarameia: The ICC and the Security Council on Aggression: Overlapping Competencies?, in Mauro Politi and Giuseppe Nesi (eds.), *The International Criminal Court and the Crime of Aggression* (2004), pp. 133 et seq.; Benjamin B. Ferencz: *Defining International Aggression: The Search for World Peace, A Documentary History and Analysis* (1975); Benjamin B. Ferencz: The Crime of Aggression, in Gabrielle Kirk McDonald and Olivia Swaak-Goldman (eds.), *Substantive and Procedural Aspects of International Criminal Law, The Experience of International and National Courts*, Vol. 1 (2000), pp. 33 et seq.; Benjamin B. Ferencz: Aggression, in Rudolf Bernhardt (ed.), *Encyclopedia of Public International Law*, Vol. 1 (1992), pp. 58 et seq.; Benjamin B. Ferencz: Can Aggression Be Deterred by Law? in 10 *Pace International Law Review* (1999), pp. 341 et seq.; George A. Finch: The Nuremberg Trial and International Law, 41 *American Journal of International Law* (1947), pp. 20 et seq.; Giorgio Gaja: The Long Journey towards Repressing Aggression, in Antonio Cassese, Paola Gaeta and John R.W.D. Jones (eds.), *The Rome Statute of the International Criminal Court: A Commentary*, Vol. 1 (2002), pp. 427 et seq.; Pietro Gargiulo: States' Obligations of Cooperation and the Role of the Security Council, in Flavia Lattanzi and William A. Schabas (eds.), *Essays on the Rome Statute of the International Criminal Court*, Vol. 1 (1999), pp. 67 et seq.; Stefan Glaser: Culpabilité en Droit International Pénal, 99 *Recueil des Cours* (1960), Vol. 1, pp. 465 et seq.; Richard L. Griffiths: International Law, the Crime of Aggression and the Ius Ad Bellum, 2 *International Criminal Law Review* (2002), pp. 301 et seq.; Frederik Harhoff: Unauthorized Humanitarian Interventions, Armed Violence in the Name of Humanity?, 70 *Nordic Journal of International Law* (2001), pp. 65 et seq.; Justin Hogan-Doran and Bibi T. van Ginkel: Aggression as a Crime under International Law and the Prosecution of Individuals by the proposed International Criminal Court, 43 *Netherlands International Law Review* (1996), pp. 321 et seq.; Martin Hummrich: *Der völkerrechtliche Straftatbestand der Aggression – Historische Entwicklung, Geltung und Definition im Hinblick auf das Statut des Internationalen Strafgerichtshofes* (2001); Hans-Heinrich Jescheck: *Die Verantwortlichkeit der Staatsorgane nach Völkerstrafrecht, Eine Studie zu den Nürnberger Prozessen* (1952); Hans-Peter Kaul: The Crime of Aggression: Definitional Options for the Way Forward, in Mauro Politi and Giuseppe Nesi (eds.), *The International Criminal Court and the Crime of Aggression* (2004), pp. 97 et seq.; Kriangsak Kittichaisaree: *International Criminal Law* (2001), pp. 206 et seq.; Claus Kress: The Iraqi Special Tribunal and the Crime of Aggression, in 2 *Journal of International Criminal Justice* (2004), pp. 347 et seq.; Josef L. Kunz: Bellum Iustum and Bellum Legale, 45 *American Journal of International Law* (1951), pp. 528 et seq.; Peter Malanczuk: Monroe Doctrine, in Rudolf Bernhardt (ed.), *Encyclopedia of Public*

International Law, Vol. 3 (1997), pp. 460 et seq.; Hilaire McCoubrey and Nigel D. White: *International Law and Armed Conflict* (1992); Werner Meng: War, in Rudolf Bernhardt (ed.), *Encyclopedia of Public International Law*, Vol. 4 (2000), pp. 1334 et seq.; Hermann Meyer-Lindenberg: Saavedra Lamas Treaty (1933), in Rudolf Bernhardt (ed.), *Encyclopedia of Public International Law*, Vol. 4 (2000), pp. 273 et seq.; Irina Kaye Müller-Schieke: Defining the Crime of Aggression Under the Statute of the International Criminal Court, 14 *Leiden Journal of International Law* (2001), pp. 409 et seq.; Fritz Münch: War, Laws of, History, in Rudolf Bernhardt (ed.), *Encyclopedia of Public International Law*, Vol. 4 (2000), pp. 1386 et seq.; Mauro Politi: The Debate within the Preparatory Commission for the International Criminal Court, in Mauro Politi and Giuseppe Nesi (eds.), *The International Criminal Court and the Crime of Aggression* (2004), pp. 43 et seq.; Albrecht Randelzhofer: Use of Force, in Rudolf Bernhardt (ed.), *Encyclopedia of Public International Law*, Vol. 4 (2000), pp. 1246 et seq.; Ahmed M. Rifaat: *International Aggression: A Study of the Legal Concept its Developments and Definition in International Law* (1979); William A. Schabas: A Origins of the Criminalization of Aggression: How Crimes against Peace Became the "Supreme International Crime," in Mauro Politi and Giuseppe Nesi (eds.), *The International Criminal Court and the Crime of Aggression* (2004), pp. 17 et seq.; F.B. Schick: The Nuremberg Trial and the International Law of the Future, 41 *American Journal of International Law* (1947), pp. 770 et seq.; Matthias Schuster: The Rome Statute and the Crime of Aggression: A Gordian Knot in Search for a Sword, 14 *Criminal Law Forum* (2003), pp. 1 et seq.; Julius Stone: Hopes and Loopholes in the 1974 Definition of Aggression, 71 *American Journal of International Law* (1977), pp. 224 et seq.; Cynthia D. Wallace: Kellogg-Briand Pact (1928), in Rudolf Bernhardt (ed.), *Encyclopedia of Public International Law*, Vol. 3 (1997), pp. 76 et seq.; Gerd Westdickenberg and Oliver Fixson: Das Verbrechen der Aggression im Römischen Statut des Internationalen Strafgerichtshofs, in Jochen Frowein et al. (eds.), *Festschrift für Eitel* (2003), pp. 483 et seq.; Quincy Wright: Legal Positivism and the Nuremberg Judgment, 42 *American Journal of International Law* (1948), pp. 405 et seq.; Herman von Hebel and Darryl Robinson: Crimes within the Jurisdiction of the Court, in Roy S. Lee (ed.), *The International Criminal Court, The Making of the Rome Statute* (1999), pp. 81 et seq.; Antonio Yáñez- Barnuevo: The Exercise of the International Criminal Court's Jurisdiction over the Crime of Aggression: Short Term and Long Term Prospects, in Mauro Politi and Giuseppe Nesi (eds.), *The International Criminal Court and the Crime of Aggression* (2004), pp. 109 et seq.; Andreas Zimmermann: ICC Statute, Article 5, in Otto Triffterer (ed.), *Commentary on the Rome Statute of the International Criminal Court – Observer's Notes, Article by Article* (1999), pp. 97 et seq.

The criminalization of aggression directly affects state sovereignty, and thus it is not surprising that both the definition of the crime of aggression and the requirements for criminal prosecution before the International Criminal Court were extremely controversial at the negotiations on the ICC Statute. Ultimately, no agreement could be reached on the requirements of the crime of aggression or the role of the Security Council in prosecuting such crimes. In view of this situation, many delegations hoped to prevent the crime of aggression from being completely omitted from the ICC Statute and thus not regulated at all for the foreseeable future.   **1148**

The result was a compromise that is laid down in Article 5(1)(d), (2) of the ICC Statute.[1] On the one hand, this provision gives the ICC jurisdiction to try the crime of aggression, and thus recognizes the crime as such. On the other hand, the Court cannot exercise this authority until the crime of aggression is defined and its relationship to the   **1149**

---

[1] For more on the negotiations, see G. Gaja, in A. Cassese, P. Gaeta and J.R.W.D. Jones (eds.), *The Rome Statute of the International Criminal Court*, Vol. 1 (2002), p. 427 at pp. 430 et seq.; H. von Hebel and D. Robinson, in R.S. Lee (ed.), *The International Criminal Court, The Making of the Rome Statute* (1999), pp. 81 et seq.

UN Charter clarified. Under the ICC Statute, aggression is thus a crime in "abeyance."[2] Independently of this, the question arises whether and to what extent acts of aggression are criminal under customary international law.

1150 The following text deals first of all with the international legal prohibition of aggression (A). It then examines whether and to what extent violations of this prohibition are punishable under customary international law; here it will be shown that only aggressive war is directly criminalized under international law (B). The outlook for international legal policy (C) completes the analysis.

A. The Prohibition of Aggression Under International Law

I. Developments Prior to World War II

1151 The proscription of war under international law, which is a requirement for individual criminal liability, looks back on only a short history.[3] In the 19th and early 20th centuries, war was considered a legitimate political tool. Every sovereign state was free to wage war in pursuit of its interests.[4] International legal limitations concerned only the methods and means of waging war, so-called *jus in bello*,[5] but not the right to wage war itself, *jus ad bellum*. The state's unlimited right to wage war was first cautiously called into question in the course of the Hague Peace Conferences of 1899 and 1907, without resulting in a clear prohibition. Under Article 1 of the Hague *Convention for the Pacific Settlement of International Disputes* of 1899[6] and 1907,[7] the parties obligated themselves to settle conflicts peacefully as far as possible. Article 2 of the Convention introduced a mediation process before any resort to weapons, to be undertaken, however, only when circumstances permitted.

---

[2] According to C. Tomuschat, 73 *Die Friedens-Warte* (1998), p. 335 at p. 337. For criticism of the approach taken in the ICC Statute, see M. Schuster, 14 *Criminal Law Forum* (2003), p. 1 at p. 17; R. Wedgwood, 10 *European Journal of International Law* (1999), p. 93 at p. 105.

[3] However, in ancient Rome, the international law of war was already bound by conditions. The doctrine of just war developed in the Middle Ages; only a just war was permissible. With the emergence of state structures, however, this doctrine was ever more restricted. See generally, S.A. Alexandrov, *Self-Defense Against the Use of Force in International Law* (1996), pp. 1 et seq.; M.C. Bassiouni and B.B. Ferencz, in M.C. Bassiouni (ed.), *International Criminal Law*, Vol. 1, 2nd edn. (1999), pp. 313 et seq.; Y. Dinstein, *War, Aggression and Self-Defence*, 3rd edn. (2001), pp. 59 et seq.; J. von Elbe, 33 *American Journal of International Law* (1939), pp. 665 et seq.; J.L. Kunz, 45 *American Journal of International Law* (1951), p. 528 at pp. 529 et seq.

[4] See, e.g., Y. Dinstein, *War, Aggression and Self-Defence*, 3rd edn. (2001), pp. 71 et seq.; J. von Elbe, 33 *American Journal of International Law* (1939), p. 665 at pp. 682 et seq.; W. Meng, in R. Bernhardt (ed.), *Encyclopedia of Public International Law*, Vol. 4 (2000), pp. 1334 et seq.; see also S.A. Alexandrov, *Self-Defense Against the Use of Force in International Law* (1996), pp. 9 et seq.

[5] On developments in this regard, see F. Münch, in R. Bernhardt (ed.), *Encyclopedia of Public International Law*, Vol. 4 (2000), pp. 1386 et seq.

[6] Reprinted at J.B. Scott, *The Hague Peace Conferences of 1899 and 1907*, Vol. II: Documents (1909), pp. 80 et seq.

[7] Reprinted at J.B. Scott, *The Hague Peace Conferences of 1899 and 1907*, Vol. II: Documents (1909), pp. 308 et seq. On the Hague Peace Conference, see A. Randelzhofer, in R. Bernhardt (ed.), *Encyclopedia of Public International Law*, Vol. 4 (2000), p. 1246 at p. 1247.

After World War I, the international community attempted further to restrict war as an instru-   **1152**
ment of politics. The preamble to the *Covenant of the League of Nations*[8] emphasized the treaty
parties' duty "not to resort to war," in order to ensure international peace and security. In Article
10 of the Covenant, the parties agreed to respect "the territorial integrity and existing political independence" of states. To settle disputes that could lead to war, an arbitration system was introduced that – depending on the character of the dispute – provided for a decision by either a court
of arbitration or the League of Nations Council.[9] If a state complied with the decision of an arbitrator, no war could be waged against it. The same was true of a unanimous decision of the Council. In any case, three months had to have passed between the decision of the arbitrator or the
Council and the beginning of hostilities.[10] If a state refused to comply with the dispute settlement
system, Article 16 of the Covenant provided for imposition of mainly economic sanctions. Overall,
however, the prohibition of war in the *Covenant of the League of Nations* was incomplete. Not even
aggressive war was subject to an unconditional prohibition.[11] The *Covenant of the League of Nations* also reflected a traditional concept of war, which in particular required the state's intent to
bring about a state of war.[12] Thus states could avoid their obligations under the Covenant by
claiming, for example, that the conflict lacked *animus bellegerendi* and thus was not a war in the
formal sense.[13]

The deficiencies of the *Covenant of the League of Nations* were to be corrected by the   **1153**
Geneva Protocol of 2 October 1924,[14] which provided in Article 2 for a comprehensive
ban on war. Article 10 of the Protocol described states that violated the provisions of the
Protocol as aggressors. At the same time, the dispute settlement system of the Covenant
was considerably expanded and a system of collective security added (see Article 11). But
lacking a sufficient number of ratifications, the Geneva Protocol never entered into
force.

The system for prevention of war in the *Covenant of the League of Nations* was ex-   **1154**
panded on a regional level. In the *Treaties of Locarno*,[15] Germany and France, as well as
Germany and Belgium, agreed to solve conflicts peacefully in their mutual relations. The
use of force would only be permissible in exercise of the right of self-defense and as part
of League of Nations sanctions.[16]

---

[8] Reprinted at Sir G. Butler, *A Handbook to the League of Nations* (1919), pp. 49 et seq.

[9] See *Covenant of the League of Nations*, Arts. 13 and 15. A decision by an arbitrator was mainly
considered in disputes over legal questions. The League of Nations Council was to decide mainly political conflicts.

[10] *Covenant of the League of Nations*, Art. 12(1) sentence 2.

[11] See I. Brownlie, *Principles of Public International Law*, 6th edn. (2003), p. 697 and I. Brownlie,
International Law and the Use of Force by States (1963), pp. 55 et seq.

[12] See I. Brownlie, *International Law and the Use of Force by States* (1963), pp. 26 et seq.

[13] See I. Brownlie, *International Law and the Use of Force by States* (1963), pp. 59 et seq. and
pp. 384 et seq.

[14] *Protocol on the Pacific Settlement of International Disputes,* International Legislation II (1922–
1924), pp. 1378 et seq. See B. Broms, 154 *Recueil des Cours* (1977), Vol. 1, pp. 306 et seq.

[15] The *Treaties of Locarno* of 16 October 1925, 54 *UNTS* (1949), p. 290, consist of a treaty signed
by Germany, Belgium, France, Great Britain, and Italy, in which Germany, France, and Belgium
agreed to mutually renounce war and to an obligatory arbitration process. This treaty was supplemented by arbitration accords between Germany and Belgium and Germany and France, and two arbitration treaties between Germany and Poland and Germany and Czechoslovakia. See B. Broms, 154
Recueil des Cours (1977), Vol. 1, pp. 307 et seq.

[16] See Art. 2 of the *Treaties of Locarno* of 16 October 1925, 54 *UNTS* (1949), p. 290.

1155   A decisive step towards a comprehensive ban on war was taken with the so-called
Kellogg-Briand Pact of 27 August 1928,[17] which remains in force.[18] In the preamble of
the pact, the state parties declared their belief "that the time has come when a frank renunciation of war as an instrument of national policy should be made." This renunciation was formulated in the treaty's provisions. However, the Kellogg-Briand Pact also
had several weak points: Like the *Covenant of the League of Nations*, the treaty based its
prohibition of warfare on an overly narrow, formal concept of war.[19] Further, the use of
belligerent force remained permissible as part of collective measures by the League of Nations, since war was only renounced as a tool of national, not international, policy.[20] In
addition, through declarations submitted when the treaty was signed, the parties made
clear that the treaty did not limit their right to self-defense. Because the Kellogg-Briand
Pact itself contained no definition of lawful self-defense measures, this left open the danger of misuse of the right of self-defense.[21]

1156   In this context, the United States believed that the right of self-defense made it possible for it to
uphold[22] the so-called Monroe Doctrine.[23] The United Kingdom claimed such an interpretation
for certain British spheres of interest.[24] With this in mind, the view is sometimes voiced that the
ban on war in the Kellogg-Briand Pact was so limited that it placed no legally binding obligation
on the state parties.[25] It is more convincing to see these interpretations as a mere reference to the
right of self-defense, which leaves the legal duty untouched.[26] Whether this broad interpretation
of the right of self-defense advanced by the contracting states would have been covered by the pact
is doubtful, but need not be determined here.

---

[17] *Treaty for the Renunciation of War as an Instrument of National Policy* of 27 August 1928. The
treaty text can be found at <http://www.yale.edu/lawweb/avalon/imt/kbpact.htm>. On the history of
this treaty, see C.D. Wallace, in R. Bernhardt (ed.), *Encyclopedia of Public International Law*, Vol. 3
(1997), pp. 76 et seq.

[18] See I. Brownlie, *International Law and the Use of Force by States* (1963), p. 75 at pp. 113 et seq.;
R.L. Griffiths, 2 *International Criminal Law Review* (2002), p. 301 at p. 304; A. Randelzhofer, in R.
Bernhardt (ed.), *Encyclopedia of Public International Law*, Vol. 4 (2000), p. 1246 at p. 1248.

[19] See H. McCoubrey and N.D. White, *International Law and Armed Conflict* (1992), p. 22; however, for a contrasting view, see I. Brownlie, *International Law and the Use of Force by States* (1963),
pp. 84 et seq.

[20] See Y. Dinstein, *War, Aggression and Self-Defence*, 3rd edn. (2001), p. 79.

[21] See B. Broms, 154 *Recueil des Cours* (1977), Vol. 1, pp. 308 et seq.; I. Brownlie, *International
Law and the Use of Force by States* (1963), pp. 235 et seq.; Y. Dinstein, *War, Aggression and Self-Defence*, 3rd edn. (2001), pp. 78 et seq.

[22] See I. Brownlie, *International Law and the Use of Force by States* (1963), pp. 245 et seq., which
points out that the United States declared no official reservations, and that only the report of the Sen-
ate Foreign Relations Committee referred to the Monroe Doctrine.

[23] The Monroe Doctrine was formulated by the American President James Monroe in a speech to
the US Congress on 2 December 1823. The occasion was the continuing colonial efforts of European
powers in North and South America. The United States opposed this by declaring that they would
exercise self-defense not only against direct attacks on their own territory, but against any European
interventions on the American continent. Other states as a result also claimed a right of self-defense
even if their own territory was not directly affected by military action. See P. Malanczuk, in R.
Bernhardt (ed.), *Encyclopedia of Public International Law*, Vol. 3 (1997), pp. 460 et seq.

[24] See I. Brownlie, *International Law and the Use of Force by States* (1963), pp. 235 et seq.; C.D.
Wallace, in R. Bernhardt (ed.), *Encyclopedia of Public International Law*, Vol. 3 (1997), p. 76 at p. 78.

[25] See C. Schmitt, in H. Quaritsch (ed.), *Das internationalrechtliche Verbrechen des Angriffskrieges
und der Grundsatz "Nullum crimen, nulla poena sine lege"* (1994), pp. 45 et seq., with additional citations.

[26] See I. Brownlie, *International Law and the Use of Force by States* (1963), pp. 244 et seq.

By 1939, 63 of 67 states had ratified the Kellogg-Briand Pact, giving it near-universal **1157** applicability.[27] The pact was often affirmed by state practice[28] and formed the basis for other treaties involving bilateral and multilateral prohibitions of war.[29] Despite the fact that the Kellogg-Briand Pact could not prevent the outbreak of World War II, waged by aggressive regimes that deliberately ignored their obligations under international law, there is little doubt that by the end of the 1930s, international law's position toward war had changed dramatically: Far from being seen as a legitimate political tool, aggressive war was now considerably restricted, if not completely outlawed.

II. Current Status

Following World War II, the prohibition of aggression was significantly expanded in the **1158** UN Charter. The Charter liberated itself from the traditional concept of war, which – as discussed above – left room for abuse by states. In Article 2(4), the Charter prohibits "the threat or use of force against the territorial integrity or political independence of any state, or in any other manner inconsistent with the purposes of the United Nations." The most important exception to this prohibition on the use of force is regulated by Article 51 of the Charter, which recognizes the right of member states to defend themselves against armed attack individually or collectively as long as the Security Council does not take necessary measures. Additionally, the Charter created a system of collective security that granted the Security Council a broad monopoly of force. In case of a threat to the peace, breach of the peace, or act of aggression (Article 39), the Security Council is authorized by Article 42 to take military measures.[30] The Security Council can also authorize individual states or groups of states to use military force.[31]

---

[27] Only four of the states in existence before World War II (Argentina, Bolivia, El Salvador, and Uruguay) were not parties to the Kellogg-Briand Pact, see I. Brownlie, *International Law and the Use of Force by States* (1963), p. 75, fn. 2. However, these states were bound by the *Saavedra Lamas Treaty* of 10 October 1933, 163 *LNTS*, p. 393, in a manner similar to the state parties to the *Kellogg-Briand Pact*, see H. Meyer-Lindenberg, in R. Bernhardt (ed.), *Encyclopedia of Public International Law*, Vol. 4 (2000), pp. 273 et seq.; A. Randelzhofer, in R. Bernhardt (ed.), *Encyclopedia of Public International Law*, Vol. IV (2000), p. 1246 at p. 1248.

[28] An example is the so-called Stimson Doctrine. On the occasion of the Japanese invasion of Manchuria (1931), the American Secretary of State, Henry Stimson, declared that the United States would not recognize territorial changes in contravention of the Kellogg-Briand Pact. This idea was adopted by League of Nations resolutions and international treaties. The Stimson Doctrine is today considered customary international law and obligates states not to recognize violent changes in other states' territory that occur contrary to international law, see C.D. Wallace, in R. Bernhardt (ed.), *Encyclopedia of Public International Law*, Vol. 3 (1997), p. 76 at p. 78.

[29] In addition to the aforementioned *Saavedra Lamas Treaty* (see marginal no. 1157, fn. 27), numerous regional treaties subsequently affirmed the Kellogg-Briand Pact, see citations in I. Brownlie, *International Law and the Use of Force by States* (1963), p. 76, fn. 1. The pact was also referred to within the League of Nations, not least at the start of World War II. Finally, in 1945 it formed the legal basis for Art. 6(a) of the Nuremberg Charter, see I. Brownlie, *International Law and the Use of Force by States* (1963), pp. 76 et seq. Art. 2(4) of the UN Charter is also based on the principles in the pact, see C.D. Wallace, in R. Bernhardt (ed.), *Encyclopedia of Public International Law*, Vol. 3 (1997), p. 76 at p. 78.

[30] In addition to military operations, which may normally only be considered as a last resort, the Security Council may also require other measures, make recommendations, and impose non-military, especially economic, sanctions; for details, see M.N. Shaw, *International Law*, 5th edn. (2003), pp. 1124 et seq.

[31] See M.N. Shaw, *International Law*, 5th edn. (2003), pp. 1133 et seq.

1159   The UN Charter employs three closely-related concepts in connection with aggressive
acts: Article 2(4) of the UN Charter prohibits the threat or use of force; Article 39 of the
Charter grants the Security Council the right, where acts of aggression occur, to take
measures in accordance with Chapter VII of the Charter; and Article 51 recognizes the
right of self-defense against armed attack. The exact meaning of the concepts used in the
UN Charter and their relationship to one another are subject to dispute.[32]

1160   The term "act of aggression" as used in Article 39 of the UN Charter was explained
in the annex to UN General Assembly Resolution 3314 (XXIX) on 14 December 1974
(the so-called UN Definition of Aggression).[33] Under Article 1 of the UN Definition of
Aggression, an act of aggression is "the use of armed force by a state against the sovereignty, territorial integrity or political independence of another state." Article 3 lists examples[34] of acts of aggression, including attack by the armed forces, occupation and
bombardment, sea blockades and support for armed bands in other countries. Thus the
term "act of aggression" also includes acts of lesser intensity and magnitude than war.
The same is true of the concept of force in Article 2(4) of the UN Charter.[35] The prohibition on use of force is violated even if a state supports a rebel group in another state
through weapons supply or logistical aid.[36] The threat of such force is also forbidden by
Article 2(4).

B. Criminal Responsibility Under Customary International Law (War of Aggression)

1161   The prohibition on aggression in international law comprises, as shown above, the prohi-

---

[32] Particularly since the invasion of Iraq in 2003 by a coalition of states led by the United States of
America, the exact extent of the prohibition of the use of force in international relations has been the
subject of extensive debate, see, e.g., Attorney-General of the United Kingdom, 52 *International and
Comparative Law Quarterly* (2003), pp. 811 et seq.; I.H. Daalder, 16 *Leiden Journal of International
Law* (2003), pp. 171 et seq.; R.A. Falk, 97 *American Journal of International Law* (2003), pp. 607 et
seq.; R.N. Gardner, 97 *American Journal of International Law* (2003), pp. 585 et seq.; Legal Depart-
ment of the Ministry of Foreign Affairs of the Russian Federation, 52 *International and Comparative
Law Quarterly* (2003), pp. 1059 et seq.; W.M. Reissman, 97 *American Journal of International Law*
(2003), pp. 83 et seq.; M. Sapiro, 97 *American Journal of International Law* (2003), pp. 599 et seq.;
J.E. Stromseth, 97 *American Journal of International Law* (2003), pp. 628 et seq.; W.H. Taft IV and
T.F. Buchwald, 97 *American Journal of International Law* (2003), pp. 557 et seq.; C. Tomuschat, 58
Die Friedens-Warte (2003), pp. 141 et seq.; J. Yoo, 97 *American Journal of International Law* (2003),
pp. 563 et seq.; see also the references cited in marginal no. 1172, fn. 71.

[33] On the UN Definition of Aggression, see J. Stone, 71 *American Journal of International Law*
(1977), pp. 224 et seq.

[34] See UN Definition of Aggression, Art. 4.

[35] M.N. Shaw, *International Law*, 5th edn. (2003), p. 1018; A. Randelzhofer, in B. Simma (ed.),
The Charter of the United Nations, 2nd edn. (2002), Art. 2(4), marginal nos. 22 et seq. However, there
is disagreement on whether the prohibition on violence also includes political and economic sanctions,
see A.C. Carpenter, 64 *Nordic Journal of International Law* (1995), p. 223 at p. 230; R.L. Griffiths,
2 *International Criminal Law Review* (2002), p. 301 at p. 317; A. Randelzhofer, in B. Simma (ed.),
The Charter of the United Nations, 2nd edn. (2002), Art. 2(4), marginal nos. 17 et seq.

[36] *Nicaragua* v. *USA*, ICJ, judgment of 27 June 1986 (Case Concerning Military and Paramilitary
Activities in and Against Nicaragua), *ICJ Rep.* 1986, p. 14, paras. 106 et seq. On this decision, see
M.C. Bassiouni and B.B. Ferencz, in M.C. Bassiouni (ed.), *International Criminal Law*, Vol. 1, 2nd
edn. (1999), pp. 334 et seq.; see also C. Gray, 14 *European Journal of International Law* (2003),
pp. 867 et seq.

bition of aggressive war, though that is not the full extent of the prohibition. The following seeks to determine whether violations of the prohibition of aggression under international law lead to direct criminal liability under international law, and which violations this applies to. We will show that a zone of criminal responsibility does exist, but is plainly narrower than the scope of what is forbidden by international law. Only aggressive war, as a particularly grave and obvious form of aggression, is criminalized under customary international law.

I. Nuremberg and the Criminality of Aggressive War

Article 6(a) of the Nuremberg Charter declared a crime against peace the "planning,   **1162**
preparation, initiation or waging of a war of aggression, or a war in violation of international treaties, agreements or assurances, or participation in a common plan or conspiracy for the accomplishment of any of the foregoing." This was the first time an international treaty established individual liability under international criminal law for waging a war of aggression.[37] At the Nuremberg trial of the major war criminals, all 22 defendants were charged with crimes against peace, and twelve[38] were convicted of this crime. The wording of Article 6(a) of the Nuremberg Charter was copied in Article 5(a) of the Tokyo Charter. At the Tokyo trial, 28 defendants were charged with crimes against peace and 25 were convicted.[39] Article II(1)(a) of Control Council Law No. 10 followed Article 6(a) of the Nuremberg Charter in regulating crimes against peace. At the Nuremberg follow-up trials, a number of additional indictments for crimes against peace were brought on this basis,[40] but only two other defendants were convicted.[41]

Punishment of those responsible on the Axis side for crimes against peace encoun-   **1163**
tered considerable criticism. In particular, it was argued that crimes against peace were applied *ex post facto*, and thus violated principles of justice.[42] The critics are correct that

---

[37] On the history of this provision see W.A. Schabas, in M. Politi and G. Nesi, *The International Criminal Court and the Crime of Aggression* (2004), p. 17 at pp. 22 et seq.

[38] Namely, Hermann W. Göring, Rudolf Hess, Joachim von Ribbentrop, Wilhelm Keitel, Alfred Rosenberg, Wilhelm Frick, Walther Funk, Karl Dönitz, Erich Raeder, Alfred Jodl, Arthur Seys-Inquart and Konstantin von Neurath.

[39] See P. Osten, *Der Tokioter Kriegsverbrecherprozess und die japanische Rechtswissenschaft* (2003), p. 30 and marginal nos. 15 et seq.

[40] Indictments for crimes against peace were brought at US Military Tribunal Nuremberg, judgment of 30 July 1948 (*Krauch* et al., so-called IG Farben Trial), in *Trials of War Criminals* VIII, pp. 1081 et seq., US Military Tribunal Nuremberg, judgment of 31 July 1948 (*Krupp* et al., so-called Krupp Trial), in *Trials of War Criminals* IX, pp. 1327 et seq., US Military Tribunal Nuremberg, judgment of 14 April 1949 (*von Weizsäcker* et al., so-called Ministries Trial), in *Trials of War Criminals* XIV, pp. 308 et seq., and US Military Tribunal Nuremberg, judgment of 28 October 1948 (*Wilhelm von Leeb* et al., so-called High Command Trial), in *Trials of War Criminals* XI, pp. 462 et seq. See generally, PCNICC/2002/WGCA/L.1, paras. 118 et seq.

[41] See US Military Tribunal Nuremberg, judgment of 14 April 1949 (*von Weizsäcker* et al., so-called Ministries Trial), in *Trials of War Criminals* XIV, pp. 308 et seq. Wilhelm Keppler and Hans Heinrich Lammers were convicted. The convictions of Ernst von Weizsäcker and Ernst Wörmann, who were also originally convicted of crimes against peace, were overturned on appeal. See generally PCNICC/2002/WGCA/L.1, paras. 209, 225.

[42] For thorough discussion of the criticism at the time, see G.A. Finch, 41 *American Journal of International Law* (1947), pp. 25 et seq.; F.B. Schick, 41 *American Journal of International Law* (1947), pp. 770 et seq.; Q. Wright, 42 *American Journal of International Law* (1948), pp. 405 et seq.

waging war was not explicitly criminalized prior to the outbreak of World War II. As discussed above, war was widely proscribed, but no provision called for criminal prosecution of those responsible.[43] The Nuremberg Tribunal justified the critical step from prohibiting aggressive war to criminalizing it with substantive arguments: given the grave consequences, waging an aggressive war was the most serious of all crimes. To enforce the prohibition of war, those responsible had to be punished. Crimes under international law, said the Tribunal, were not committed by states themselves, but by people, who needed to be held accountable.[44] The Tribunal thus concluded, from the fact that waging an aggressive war deserved and needed punishment, that it was in fact criminal.

1164   This argument was plausible. Even in the period before World War II, there had long been efforts to criminalize aggressive war. Article 227 of the Versailles Treaty, for example, provided for prosecution of the German Kaiser for unleashing World War I.[45] The aforementioned Geneva Protocol of 2 October 1924 defined aggressive war as an international crime,[46] a formulation that was taken up by League of Nations resolutions[47] and the 6th Pan-American Conference.[48] The stage had thus been set for assigning individual criminal responsibility for aggressive war, as a logical consequence[49] of the proscription of war even before World War II. Any residual doubt as to the lawfulness of criminalizing aggressive war can be eliminated from today's point of view by the fact that even *ex post facto* prosecution would have been permissible: the *ex post facto* prohibition does not prevent holding state leaders accountable for crimes they commit against international law.[50]

1165   Today, the Charters of the Nuremberg and Tokyo Tribunals, and the Tribunals' judgments that clarified the offense, form the basis for the criminalization of aggressive war.[51] The offenses in the Charters, and above all the Nuremberg judgment, are the starting points for the established *opinio juris* of the international community that waging aggressive war is criminal. In UN General Assembly Resolution 95(I) of 11 December 1946, the criminality of waging aggressive war was expressly "affirmed." The international community thus expressed the view that this offense was valid generally, and not merely in regard to the Axis powers in World War II.[52] Later, Article 5(2), sentence 1, of the UN Definition of Aggression and Principle 1(2) of the so-called Friendly

---

For a summary from today's point of view, see S. Jung, *Die Rechtsprobleme der Nürnberger Prozesse* (1992), pp. 137 et seq.

[43] See also marginal no. 27.

[44] IMT, judgment of 1 October 1946, in *The Trial of German Major War Criminals. Proceedings of the International Military Tribunal Sitting at Nuremberg, Germany*, Part 22, p. 447.

[45] For thorough discussion, see Y. Dinstein, *War, Aggression and Self-Defence*, 3rd edn. (2001), p. 106. See also marginal nos. 6 et seq.

[46] Preamble, para. 3. However, this protocol never went into force; see marginal no. 1153.

[47] Citations in I. Brownlie, *International Law and the Use of Force by States* (1963), pp. 71 et seq.

[48] Citations in I. Brownlie, *International Law and the Use of Force by States* (1963), pp. 73 et seq.

[49] See G. Dahm, J. Delbrück and R. Wolfrum, *Völkerrecht*, Vol. I/3, 2nd edn. (2002), p. 1035.

[50] See *European Convention for the Protection of Human Rights and Fundamental Freedoms*, Art. 7(2), and *International Covenant on Civil and Political Rights*, Art. 15(2); see also marginal no. 28.

[51] R.L. Griffiths, 2 *International Criminal Law Review* (2002), p. 301 at p. 308.

[52] See I. Brownlie, *International Law and the Use of Force of States* (1963), p. 190; G. Westdickenberg and O. Fixson, in J. Frowein et al. (eds.), *Festschrift für Eitel* (2003), p. 483 at pp. 487 et seq.

Relations Declaration[53] explicitly defined aggressive war as a crime against international peace. In 1991 and 1996 the International Law Commission submitted drafts, each of which contained the crime of aggression.[54] Finally, the inclusion of the crime of aggression in the ICC Statute is an expression of a belief in its criminality under customary international law.[55]

The Nuremberg and Tokyo trials embodied the state practice that is necessary for the creation of customary international law,[56] confirmed by states' official statements, for example in connection with the UN Definition of Aggression. The fact that no other trials have occurred involving the waging of aggressive war does not contradict this, since the fact that criminal norms have been violated with impunity does not call their validity into question.[57] Thus the objections that, for example, the Yugoslavia Tribunal was given no jurisdiction to prosecute aggressive war are unconvincing.[58]   **1166**

In summary, it may be said that aggressive war is criminal under customary international law.[59] The scope of the offense must be determined on the basis of the only prece-   **1167**

---

[53] *Declaration on Principles of International Law concerning Friendly Relations and Co-operation among States in accordance with the Charter of the United Nations*, UN Doc. A/RES/2625 of 24 October 1970.

[54] See 1991 *Draft Code*, Arts. 15 et seq., and 1996 *Draft Code*, Art. 16. The 1991 draft contains a far-reaching provision, essentially based on the UN Definition of Aggression of 1974, and thus follows on the 1954 draft, see J. Hogan-Doran and B.T. van Ginkel, 43 *Netherlands International Law Review* (1996), p. 321 at p. 335; G. Westdickenberg and O. Fixson, in J. Frowein et al. (eds.), *Festschrift für Eitel* (2003) p. 483 at pp. 491 et seq. Art. 16 of the 1996 *Draft Code*, in contrast, followed a more restrictive concept on the basis of the Nuremberg model, and thus affirmed the scope of punishable aggression recognized since the end of World War II, see *Yearbook of the International Law Commission* 1996 II/2, p. 43; M.C. Bassiouni and B.B. Ferencz, in M.C. Bassiouni (ed.), *International Criminal Law*, Vol. 1, 2nd edn. (1999), p. 313 at pp. 337 et seq.; G. Westdickenberg and O. Fixson, in J. Frowein et al. (eds.), *Festschrift für Eitel* (2003), p. 483 at pp. 491 et seq.

[55] Similarly, G. Gaja, in A. Cassese, P. Gaeta and J.R.W.D. Jones (eds.), *The Rome Statute of the International Criminal Court*, Vol. 1 (2002), p. 427 at p. 431.

[56] See A.C. Carpenter, 64 *Nordic Journal of International Law* (1995), p. 223 at pp. 225 et seq.; M. Hummrich, *Der völkerrechtliche Straftatbestand der Aggression* (2001), pp. 128 et seq., esp. p. 137, which includes the Nuremberg successor trials as independent state practice and thus sees in the period from 1945 to 1949 "a certain element of repetition" (p. 130). As a result, Hummrich comes to the conclusion that "the practice of the Nuremberg and Tokyo Tribunals and the accompanying *opinio juris* of the international community at the end of World War II created new customary international law"; see M. Hummrich, *Der völkerrechtliche Straftatbestand der Aggression* (2001), p. 139.

[57] See also I. Brownlie, *International Law and the Use of Force by States* (1963), p. 175. Verbal acts have been granted decisive significance by the ICTY, see *Prosecutor* v. *Tadić*, ICTY (Appeals Chamber), decision of 2 October 1995, paras. 96 et seq., in order to establish the core norms of international humanitarian law in intrastate armed conflicts. For the Appeals Chamber, official statements by states and the content of national military manuals were enough to show sufficient practice for the emergence of customary international law.

[58] But see C. Tomuschat, in Y. Dinstein and M. Tabory (eds.), *War Crimes in International Law* (1996), p. 41 at p. 53; C. Tomuschat, *Europäische Grundrechte-Zeitschrift* 1998, p. 1 at p. 5. G. Gaja, in A. Cassese, P. Gaeta and J.R.W.D. Jones (eds.), *The Rome Statute of the International Criminal Court*, Vol. 1 (2002), p. 427 at p. 430, in contrast, notes correctly that the ICTY and the ICTR were created as a response to crimes against humanity and war crimes, and thus the absence of the crime of aggression is not surprising.

[59] For similar views, see Y. Dinstein, *War, Aggression and Self-Defence*, 3rd edn. (2001), p. 109 at pp. 113 et seq.; Y. Dinstein, 24 *Israel Yearbook on Human Rights* (1994), p. 1 at p. 2; R.L. Griffiths, 2 *International Criminal Law Review* (2002), p. 301 at p. 308; I.K. Müller-Schieke, 14 *Leiden Journal of International Law* (2001), p. 409 at pp. 414 et seq.; but see, for an opposing view, H.-H. Jescheck,

dents to date, the Nuremberg and Tokyo judgments.[60] However, there is no evidence that acts of aggression not reaching the level of intensity of aggressive war are criminal under customary international law.[61] State practice is insufficient to show this. Further, the tough negotiations on the ICC Statute indicate[62] that no general *opinio juris* exists in this area.

II. Material Elements

1. Aggressive War

1168 Article 6(a) of the Nuremberg Charter criminalized the planning, preparation, initiation or waging of a war of aggression, or a war in violation of international treaties, agreements or assurances. This creates the impression that crimes against peace could be accomplished through either wars of aggression or wars that violate international treaties. The Nuremberg Tribunal discussed the crime of aggressive war thoroughly and, on the subject of waging war in violation of international treaties, noted only that this did not need to be considered in depth, as aggressive war had already been proven.[63] From this it can be inferred that even in the view of the Nuremberg Tribunal, two different subsidiary offenses make up the crime against peace. However, the offense should not be split in this way between aggressive war, on the one hand, and waging war in violation of international treaties, on the other. Aggressive war is criminalized as a war prohibited under international law.[64] In this vein, Control Council Law No. 10 speaks of "wars of aggression in violation of international laws and treaties."

1169 Thus from a terminological standpoint, an "aggressive" war can only be found to exist if the war is contrary to international law. This violation is based on the international legal situation that prevails at the time of the offense; thus by definition, no aggressive war exists in cases of United Nations measures under Chapter VII of the UN Charter or self-defense under Article 51 of the Charter.[65]

Goltdammer's Archiv für Strafrecht 1981, p. 49 at pp. 53 et seq.; W.G. Grewe, in K. Hailbronner, G. Ress and T. Stein (eds.), *Festschrift für Doehring* (1989), p. 229 at pp. 242 et seq.; C. Tomuschat, in Y. Dinstein and M. Tabory (eds.), *War Crimes in International Law* (1996), p. 41 at p. 53.

[60] *Draft Code* 1996, commentary on Art. 16: "(5) . . . The Charter and Judgement of the Nuremberg Tribunal are the main sources of authority with regard to individual criminal responsibility for acts of aggression." See also A.C. Carpenter, 64 *Nordic Journal of International Law* (1995), p. 223 at pp. 225 et seq.; R.L. Griffiths, 2 *International Criminal Law Review* (2002), p. 301 at p. 314; M. Schuster, 14 *Criminal Law Forum* (2003), p. 1 at pp. 10 et seq.

[61] For a different view, see A. Cassese, *International Criminal Law* (2003), p. 113, who refers to the UN Definition of Aggression in determining applicable customary law.

[62] See marginal nos. 1184 et seq. In *R v Jones* et al., 4 *All England Law Reports* (2004), p. 956 at p. 970, the English Court of Appeals held that the crime of aggression was not a crime under English law as there was "no firmly established rule of international law which establishes a crime of aggression which can be translated into domestic law as a crime in domestic law." The Court of Appeals based this argument on the lack of consensus among the states parties to the ICC Statute as to the role of the Security Council of the United Nations. The Court's finding is questionable as the debate on the role of the Security Council relates to the exercise of jurisdiction by the ICC and not to the question of whether aggressive war is a crime under current international law.

[63] IMT, judgment of 1 October 1946, in *The Trial of German Major War Criminals. Proceedings of the International Military Tribunal Sitting at Nuremberg, Germany*, Part 22, p. 445.

[64] H.-H. Jescheck, *Die Verantwortlichkeit der Staatsorgane nach Völkerstrafrecht* (1952), p. 348, states that the definition of aggressive war is "nothing but a popular expression of a war prohibited under international law."

[65] See R.L. Griffiths, 2 *International Criminal Law Review* (2002), p. 301 at pp. 320 et seq.

The illegality of a war under international law is not in itself sufficient to make it an **1170** aggressive war, as the precedents of Nuremberg and Tokyo show. The wars condemned after World War II aimed to totally or partially annex the territory of the countries involved or to subjugate these countries. Characteristic of the situations criminalized as wars of aggression after World War II was the attackers' aim to subjugate another state and to use its resources for the benefit of the attacking state. Only on this basis was customary international law created.[66] Thus an additional aggressive element is necessary to distinguish a war of aggression from other wars that contravene international law. The aggressive aims of a war are generally determined by the government waging the war and can be proven, for example, through statements by the political leadership;[67] it is not necessary that the perpetrator him or herself set the aggressive aims of the war or have a hand in forming them.

By virtue of their very aims, therefore, so-called humanitarian interventions to pre- **1171** vent genocide or serious human rights violations[68] are not included in the definition of the crime. Nor are military operations to rescue a country's own nationals.[69]

Whether the actions of the "Coalition of the Willing" against Iraq could be justified **1172** under international law as intervention to eliminate a regime that violated human rights is doubtful. The United States and Great Britain relied mainly on prior UN Security Council resolutions to justify their actions.[70] This argument is controversial.[71] However,

---

[66] The fact that the Tribunals have also classified some situations as aggressive war in cases where this assessment was dubious is a different issue and does not call into question the formulated elements of the crime of aggressive war. On various doubtful cases, see, e.g., H.-H. Jescheck, *Die Verantwortlichkeit der Staatsorgane nach Völkerstrafrecht* (1952), pp. 351 et seq., and marginal nos. 27 et seq.

[67] Thus the Nuremberg Tribunal found that Hitler's "Mein Kampf" already contained an "unmistakable attitude of aggression," which would continue to mark the German Reich and was judged to constitute preparation of aggressive war, see IMT, judgment of 1 October 1946, in *The Trial of German Major War Criminals. Proceedings of the International Military Tribunal Sitting at Nuremberg, Germany*, Part 22, pp. 422 et seq. The Tribunal saw the four secret conferences held by Hitler and his top functionaries between 1937 and 1939 as important evidence of German attack plans. At these planning sessions, Hitler informed his followers of his belligerent intentions and made clear his regime's aggressive aims, IMT, judgment of 1 October 1946, in *The Trial of German Major War Criminals. Proceedings of the International Military Tribunal Sitting at Nuremberg, Germany*, Part 22, pp. 423 et seq.

[68] On humanitarian intervention generally, see S.A. Alexandrov, *Self-Defense Against the Use of Force in International Law* (1996), pp. 204 et seq.; T.J. Farer, 25 *Human Rights Quarterly* (2003), pp. 382 et seq.; R.L. Griffiths, 2 *International Criminal Law Review* (2002), p. 301 at pp. 338 et seq. On the NATO military operation against the Federal Republic of Yugoslavia (Kosovo) in early 1999, see V.D. Degan, in L.C. Vohrah et al. (eds.), *Man's Inhumanity to Man* (2003), pp. 232 et seq.; F. Harhoff, 70 *Nordic Journal of International Law* (2001), pp. 65 et seq.; R. Kolb, 85 *International Review of the Red Cross* (2003), pp. 119 et seq.; R. Zacklin, in L.C. Vohrah et al. (eds.), *Man's Inhumanity to Man* (2003), pp. 935 et seq.; K. Zemanek, in L.C. Vohrah et al. (eds.), *Man's Inhumanity to Man* (2003), pp. 953 et seq.

[69] A state's right to rescue its own nationals without permission of the state in which they are located has in the past been repeatedly based on the right to self-defense under Article 51 of the UN Charter. However, this is questionable; for discussion, see S.A. Alexandrov, *Self-Defense Against the Use of Force in International Law* (1996), pp. 188 et seq., pp. 202 et seq.

[70] See C. Greenwood, 4 *San Diego International Law Journal* (2003), p. 7 at pp. 26 et seq.

[71] On this issue and other justifications advanced by the United States, see, e.g., M. Bothe, 14 *European Journal of International Law* (2003), pp. 227 et seq.; E. de Wet, *Humanitäres Völkerrecht-*

it was not a criminal war of aggression even if one agrees that the action was contrary to international law. For the Allies were not interested in annexing or subjugating Iraq. The war lacked the specific aggressive element necessary under customary international law for a war to be one of aggression.

1173   Not every belligerent use of military force is an aggressive "war." Instead, a use of force must reach a certain degree and intensity in order to qualify as war.[72] To determine the necessary degree of military force, recourse must be had mainly to the Nuremberg judgments. These decisions refrained from creating abstract definitions of aggressive war, but crucial criteria can be inferred from the case-related discussions. The German attacks on neighboring states that were tried at Nuremberg were generally waged by large armies on broad fronts; they led to total or partial occupation of the victimized state. The offense of aggressive war requires use of a similar degree of military force.

1174   The initiation of hostilities of a certain intensity is necessary for war to be present, but not an express declaration of war. The formal concept of war, based on the will of the parties to create a state of war, had already proved unworkable in the period prior to World War II. The Nuremberg Tribunal viewed the German Reich's occupation of Denmark as an aggressive war,[73] even though both the German and the Danish governments both insisted, following the Wehrmacht invasion of Denmark, that no state of war existed.[74] The Tokyo Charter expressly provided that a declaration of war was irrelevant, thus abandoning the traditional concept of war.[75]

2. Other Acts of Aggression

1175   The definition of the term "war of aggression" also conclusively defines the scope of acts of aggression criminalized under customary international law. The threshold for criminal responsibility is thus high. Acts of aggression of lesser intensity are not criminal even if they violate Article 2(4) of the UN Charter or trigger the right of self-defense under Article 51. Many aggressive acts mentioned in the UN Definition of Aggression thus incur no criminal liability under customary international law. One may deplore this narrow limitation of the offense from the standpoint of international legal policy; however, the international community lacks both the *opinio juris* and the state practice necessary for broader criminalization under customary international law.[76] It remains to be seen if this

---

Informationsschriften (2003), pp. 233 et seq.; M. Sapiro, 97 *American Journal of International Law*, pp. 599 et seq.; S.P. Shamra, 43 *Indian Journal of International Law* (2003), pp. 215 et seq.; A.D. Sofaer, 14 *European Journal of International Law* (2003), pp. 209 et seq.; R. Wedgwood, 97 *American Journal of International Law* (2003), pp. 576 et seq.; see also the references cited in marginal no. 1159, fn. 32, above.

[72] See also R.L. Griffiths, 2 *International Criminal Law Review* (2002), p. 301 at pp. 319 et seq.; G. Westdickenberg and O. Fixson, in J. Frowein et al. (eds.), *Festschrift für Eitel* (2003), p. 483 at p. 508.

[73] IMT, judgment of 1 October 1946, in *The Trial of German Major War Criminals. Proceedings of the International Military Tribunal Sitting at Nuremberg, Germany*, Part 22, p. 437.

[74] See I. Brownlie, *International Law and the Use of Force by States* (1963), p. 211 at p. 389.

[75] Tokyo Charter, Art. 5(a): "declared or undeclared war of aggression." Art. 6(a) of the Nuremberg Charter did not yet contain this wording.

[76] For discussion of these questions, see G. Westdickenberg and O. Fixson, in J. Frowein et al. (eds.), *Festschrift für Eitel* (2003), p. 483 at pp. 505 et seq.

criminal liability will be expanded in the course of negotiations over the crime of aggression in the ICC Statute.[77]

3. Perpetrators

In accordance with the principles of Nuremberg and Tokyo, the crime of aggression is **1176** correctly classified today as a "leadership crime."[78] Neither the Nuremberg and Tokyo Statutes nor Control Council Law No. 10 contained explicit limitations on the class of perpetrators.[79] But it can be inferred from the judgments at Nuremberg and Tokyo that only political or military leaders were considered perpetrators of crimes against peace.[80] Thus at the Nuremberg trial of the major war criminals, important high-ranking representatives of the German government, military and Nazi Party were tried and convicted for their participation in a war of aggression. The class of perpetrators of the crime of aggressive war is thus limited to a relatively small group of military and political leaders.[81] The crucial element is the possibility of effective control or leadership, not legal position.[82] The perpetrator must not necessarily make the actual decisions on war and peace, but must take part in activities of major significance in preparing, initiating or waging a war of aggression.[83]

---

[77] On the UN Definition of Aggression, see marginal no. 1160.

[78] See G. Westdickenberg and O. Fixson, in J. Frowein et al. (eds.), *Festschrift für Eitel* (2003), p. 483 at p. 503. From the negotiations on the ICC Statute, see the final discussion paper by the coordinator of 11 July 2002 (PCNICC/2002/WGCA/RT. 1/Rev. 2), according to which the issue is one of a person "being in a position effectively to exercise control over or to direct the political or military action of a State."

[79] See Nuremberg Charter, Art. 6(a), Tokyo Charter, Art. 5(a), and Control Council Law No. 10, Art. II(1)(a).

[80] For a summary, see E. Brand, 26 *British Yearbook of International Law* (1949), p. 414 at pp. 419 et seq.

[81] At the so-called High Command Trial, the twelfth Nuremberg follow-up trial, the American Military Tribunal stated: "As we have pointed out, war whether it be lawful or unlawful is the implementation of a national policy. If the policy under which it is initiated is criminal in its intent and purpose it is so because the individuals at the policy-making level had a criminal intent and purpose in determining the policy. If war is the means by which the criminal objective is to be attained then the waging of the war is but an implementation of the policy, and the criminality which attaches to the waging of an aggressive war should be confined to those who participate in it at the policy level," US Military Tribunal Nuremberg, judgment of 28 October 1948 (*von Leeb* et al., so-called High Command Trial), in *Trials of War Criminals* XI, p. 462 at p. 486.

[82] For discussion, see Y. Dinstein, *War, Aggression and Self-Defence*, 3rd edn. (2001), pp. 121 et seq.; Y. Dinstein, 24 *Israel Yearbook on Human Rights* (1994), p. 1 at pp. 4 et seq.; G. Gaja, in A. Cassese, P. Gaeta and J.R.W.D. Jones (eds.), *The Rome Statute of the International Criminal Court*, Vol. 1 (2002), p. 427 at pp. 437 et seq.; R.L. Griffiths, 2 *International Criminal Law Review* (2002), p. 301 at pp. 368 et seq.; I.K. Müller-Schieke, 14 *Leiden Journal of International Law* (2001), p. 409 at pp. 419 et seq.; G. Westdickenberg and O. Fixson, in J. Frowein et al. (eds.), *Festschrift für Eitel* (2003), p. 483 at pp. 503 et seq.

[83] See also Y. Dinstein, *War, Aggression and Self-Defence*, 3rd edn. (2001), pp. 122 et seq.; E. Brand, 26 *British Yearbook of International Law* (1949), p. 414 at pp. 420 et seq. In the current negotiations on the crime of aggression under the ICC Statute, there is also consensus that perpetrators of the crime of aggression can only be the political and military leaders of a state, see PCNICC/2002/L.1/Rev.1, p. 22. Customary international law has thus been affirmed to this extent.

1177 Of interest for the limitation of the offense is, first of all, the conviction of General Wilhelm Keitel by the Nuremberg Tribunal. As head of the Wehrmacht High Command, Keitel, according to the International Military Tribunal itself, possessed no command authority over individual sections of the Wehrmacht, but was involved in the planning of attacks and military operations. This sufficed to convict him.[84] The commander of the German submarine fleet and later commander of the navy, Admiral Karl Dönitz, was also convicted for participating in aggressive war. The Tribunal here based its decision on the fact that his importance to the German war effort was considerable and that Hitler regularly asked him for advice.[85] Defendant Baldur von Schirach, on the other hand, was acquitted. The Tribunal found that, as Reich Youth Leader, he had not been directly involved in the preparations for war.[86] The former Reichsbank president and minister Hjalmar Schacht was also acquitted. He only participated in Germany's rearmament, the Tribunal found, which was not in itself a crime.[87] Also, he did not belong to "the inner circle around Hitler which was most closely involved with this common plan [the occupation of Austria and Czechoslovakia]."[88]

4. Criminal Acts

1178 Under Article 6(a) of the Nuremberg Charter, the planning, preparation, initiation or waging of a war of aggression is criminal. In addition, conspiracy to wage a war of aggression is criminalized, but this was interpreted very restrictively by the Nuremberg Tribunal and gained no independent significance.[89] The Charter of the Tokyo Tribunal and Control Council Law No. 10 adopted the wording of the Nuremberg Charter.[90] The proscribed acts of the offense are essentially oriented toward the development stages of the crime, from planning to preparation to initiating and finally waging a war of aggression. The fact that participation after the start of a war of aggression suffices is expressed by the part of the offense involving "waging" an aggressive war. This position has also been established by precedents. Thus the conviction of Dönitz by the Nuremberg Tribunal for crimes against peace was based on his participation in the waging of the war; he was not involved in its planning, preparation or initiation.[91]

---

[84] IMT, judgment of 1 October 1946, in *The Trial of German Major War Criminals. Proceedings of the International Military Tribunal Sitting at Nuremberg, Germany*, Part 22, pp. 491 et seq.

[85] IMT, judgment of 1 October 1946, in *The Trial of German Major War Criminals. Proceedings of the International Military Tribunal Sitting at Nuremberg, Germany*, Part 22, p. 507.

[86] IMT, judgment of 1 October 1946, in *The Trial of German Major War Criminals. Proceedings of the International Military Tribunal Sitting at Nuremberg, Germany*, Part 22, p. 511.

[87] IMT, judgment of 1 October 1946, in *The Trial of German Major War Criminals. Proceedings of the International Military Tribunal Sitting at Nuremberg, Germany*, Part 22, pp. 504 et seq.

[88] IMT, judgment of 1 October 1946, in *The Trial of German Major War Criminals. Proceedings of the International Military Tribunal Sitting at Nuremberg, Germany*, Part 22, p. 506.

[89] See H.-H. Jescheck, *Die Verantwortlichkeit der Staatsorgane nach Völkerstrafrecht* (1952), p. 352.

[90] Tokyo Charter, Art. 5(a): "Crimes against Peace: Namely, the planning, preparation, initiation, or waging of a declared or undeclared war of aggression, or a war in violation of international law, treaties, agreements or assurances, or participation in a common plan or conspiracy for the accomplishment of any of the foregoing." In contrast, see CCL No. 10, Art. II(1)(a): "Crimes against Peace. Initiation of invasions of other countries and wars of aggression in violation of international laws and treaties, including but not limited to planning, preparation, initiation or waging a war of aggression, or a war of violation of international treaties, agreements or assurances, or participation in a common plan or conspiracy for the accomplishment of any of the foregoing."

[91] IMT, judgment of 1 October 1946, in *The Trial of German Major War Criminals. Proceedings of the International Military Tribunal Sitting at Nuremberg, Germany*, Part 22, p. 507.

This conviction has been criticized because Dönitz had no opportunity to stop the **1179** war.[92] The criticism is correct, in that the starting point for criminal liability for aggressive war lies in its initiation, for which a perpetrator who is involved only in the waging of the war bears no direct responsibility. At the same time, criminal liability does seem justified here, as the perpetrator was part of the overall plan of the aggressive war at the highest levels and worsened the existing wrong.

Planning and preparation of a war of aggression are only criminal if they actually re- **1180** sult in the initiation of hostilities. A narrowly-limited exception is made for the largely non-violent occupation of a country that occurs in the shadow of massive military superiority. This can be derived from the Nuremberg judgment. The Nuremberg Tribunal described the occupations of Denmark and Luxemburg as aggressive wars, even though these states were subjugated without the use of significant military force.[93] The occupations of Czechoslovakia and Austria were only termed "aggressive action" by the Tribunal and were examined as part of the planning of aggression.[94] These aggressive actions served as evidence of the aggressive policies of the German Reich, but were not themselves a basis of liability.[95]

III. Mental Element

The planning, preparation, initiation or waging of aggressive war must be committed in- **1181** tentionally.[96] In particular, the perpetrator must be aware of the aggressive aims of the war, but nevertheless continue to work on its planning, initiation or waging. If the perpetrator acts despite knowledge of the aims of the war, he or she adopts these aims as his or her own's and acts with *animus aggressionis*.[97] Purpose on the part of the perpetrator is not necessary and was not required by the Nuremberg Court.[98]

---

[92] H.-H. Jescheck, *Die Verantwortlichkeit der Staatsorgane nach Völkerstrafrecht* (1952), pp. 353 et seq.

[93] See IMT, judgment of 1 October 1946, in *The Trial of German Major War Criminals. Proceedings of the International Military Tribunal Sitting at Nuremberg, Germany*, Part 22, pp. 437 et seq. See also CCL No. 10, Art. II(1)(a).

[94] See IMT, judgment of 1 October 1946, in *The Trial of German Major War Criminals. Proceedings of the International Military Tribunal Sitting at Nuremberg, Germany*, Part 22, p. 493 and p. 519.

[95] This became especially clear in regard to the defendant Kaltenbrunner, who was directly involved in the occupation of Austria. Because it saw no proof of the defendant's participation in other planning for war, the Court acquitted him of this and explained, "The Anschluss [of Austria], although it was an aggressive act, is not charged as an aggressive war," see IMT, judgment of 1 October 1946, in *The Trial of German Major War Criminals. Proceedings of the International Military Tribunal Sitting at Nuremberg, Germany*, Part 22, p. 493; for a comment, see I.K. Müller-Schieke, 14 *Leiden Journal of International Law* (2001), p. 409 at pp. 417 et seq.

[96] See Y. Dinstein, *War, Aggression and Self-Defence*, 3rd edn. (2001), p. 124.

[97] For proof of the mental element, the Nuremberg Tribunal relied primarily on the fact that the defendants had acted despite being thoroughly informed of Hitler's plans; see IMT, judgment of 1 October 1946, in *The Trial of German Major War Criminals. Proceedings of the International Military Tribunal Sitting at Nuremberg, Germany*, Part 22, p. 425 and pp. 489 et seq., pp. 491 et seq., also pp. 495 et seq., and p. 499, p. 507, pp. 523 et seq. and p. 526. In regard to the defendant Schacht, the Nuremberg Tribunal commented: "The case against Schacht therefore depends on the inference that Schacht did in fact know of the Nazi aggressive plans." (p. 506). The same was true of its comments in the judgment against Bormann: "The evidence does not show that Bormann knew of Hitler's plans to

IV. Jurisdiction

1182 The authority to try aggressive war should lie with an international criminal court. As long as no relevant expansion of the ICC Statute occurs,[99] the possibility remains of creating an *ac hoc* tribunal through the UN Security Council, which could hold trials based on the customary international law in force at the time of the offense.

1183 Another question is the extent to which states have the authority to prosecute people for the crime of aggression. This authority is unquestioned if it involves the participation of a country's own nationals in a war begun by that state.[100] Under the general principles of criminal sanction, a state must also be granted the authority to prosecute participation in an aggressive war waged against that state, even though one may have certain reservations about such an approach, given the lack of neutrality on the part of the victim state. Nor is prosecution by third states an ideal solution, given the political nature of the crime of aggressive war. Before a trial is held, in any case, the UN Security Council or General Assembly should have already made the basic determination that an aggressive war has occurred.[101]

C. The Crime of Aggression in the ICC Statute – Prospects

1184 The continuing negotiations on the definition of the crime of aggression in the ICC Statute are of great significance to international legal policy. In its final act, the Rome Conference authorized the Preparatory Commission to prepare a proposal for consideration by the Review Conference. In 2002, the Assembly of States Parties to the ICC Statute established a Special Working Group to continue the work of the Preparatory Commission.[102] The proposal should also establish the conditions under which jurisdiction may be exercised.[103]

---

prepare, initiate or wage aggressive wars. . . . Nor can knowledge be conclusively inferred from the positions he held." (p. 527). The defendant Streicher was acquitted of the charge of crimes against peace, because the Court found no evidence that he knew of the government's political plans. (p. 501). Summarized in A. Cassese, *International Criminal Law* (2003), p. 115.

[98] See also Y. Dinstein, *War, Aggression and Self-Defence*, 3rd edn. (2001), p. 126; R.L. Griffiths, 2 *International Criminal Law Review* (2002), p. 301 at pp. 369 et seq.; J. Hogan-Doran and B.T. van Ginkel, 43 *Netherlands International Law Review* (1996), p. 321 at pp. 337 et seq.; A. Cassese, *International Criminal Law* (2003), pp. 115 et seq., raises doubts; however, on the requirement of intent, see S. Glaser, 99 *Recueil des Cours* (1960), p. 465 at pp. 504 et seq.

[99] See marginal no. 1184.

[100] For example, the Iraqi Special Tribunal has jurisdiction over the crimes of "abuse of position and the pursuit of policies that may lead to threat of war or the use of the armed forces of Iraq against an Arab Country," see Statute of the Iraqi Special Tribunal, Art. 14(c). This provision is based on Iraqi criminal law; on this, see C Kress, 2 *Journal of International Criminal Justice* (2004), pp. 347 et seq.

[101] On the authority of the General Assembly in ensuring peace, see M.N. Shaw, *International Law*, 5th edn. (2003), p. 1105.

[102] See ICC-ASP/1/Fes. 1 Continuity of work in respect of the crime of aggression.

[103] For discussion on the work of the Preparatory Commission on the offense of aggression until now, see R.L. Griffiths, 2 *International Criminal Law Review* (2002), p. 301 at pp. 364 et seq.; M. Schuster, 14 *Criminal Law Forum* (2003), p. 1 at pp. 19 et seq.

Under Article 123(1) of the ICC Statute, a Review Conference may be convened no earlier than **1185**
seven years after the ICC Statute enters into force (that is, on 1 July 2009) to consider the adoption of such a provision. A change in regard to the crime of aggression can only go into effect,
according to Article 121(5) of the Statute, for those states that accept the amendment.

Rapid agreement on the offense of aggression cannot be expected.[104] Both the definition **1186**
of the crime of aggression and the role of the Security Council in the prosecution of such
crimes remain in dispute.[105]

I. Definition of the Crime of Aggression

The discussion on the limits of the criminality of aggression is of great political conse- **1187**
quence.[106] Especially controversial is the issue of whether the crime of aggression should

---

[104] See P. Gargiulo, in F. Lattanzi and W.A. Schabas (eds.), *Essays on the Rome Statute*, Vol. 1
(1999), p. 100: "highly unlikely"; K. Kittichaisaree, *International Criminal Law* (2001), p. 217:
"doubtful"; A. Cassese, 10 *European Journal of International Law* (1999), p. 144 at p. 147: "at least not
in the near future." See also A. Yáñez-Barnuevo, in M. Politi and G. Nesi (eds.), *The International
Criminal Court and the Crime of Aggression* (2004), pp. 109 et seq.

[105] The current state of the discussion is reflected in the Definition of the crime of aggression and
conditions for the exercise of jurisdiction, Proceedings of the Preparatory Commission at its ninth session (18-19 April 2002), UN Doc. PCNICC/2002/L.1/Rev.1, pp. 17 et seq. In 1999, the Preparatory
Commission summarized the proposals of state parties, see *Compilation of proposals on the crime of Ag-
gression submitted at the Preparatory Commission on the Establishment of an International Criminal Court
(1996–1998), the United Nations Diplomatic Conference of Plenipotentiaries on the Establishment of an
International Criminal Court (1998) and the Preparatory Commission for the International Criminal
Court (1999)*, UN Doc. PCNICC/1999/INF/2. The discussion continues in the framework of the
Special Working Group on the Crime of Aggression of the ICC ICC/ASP/3/25, Annex II. See also
Proceedings of the Preparatory Commission at its first, second and third sessions (16–26 February, 26 July–
13 August and 29 November–17 December 1999), UN Doc. PCNICC/ 1999/L.5/Rev.1, pp. 27 et
seq.; *Proceedings of the Preparatory Commission at its fourth session* (13–31 March 2000), UN Doc.
PCNICC/2000/L.1/Rev.1, pp. 37 et seq.; *Proceedings of the Preparatory Commission at its fifth session*
(12–30 June 2000), UN Doc. PCNICC/2000/L.3/Rev.1, pp. 8 et seq.; *Proceedings of the Preparatory
Commission at its sixth session* (27 November–8 December 2000), UN Doc. PCNICC/2000/ L.4/
Rev.1, pp. 13 et seq.; *Proceedings of the Preparatory Commission at its seventh session* (26 February–
9 March 2001), UN Doc. PCNICC/2001/L.1/Rev.1, pp. 17 et seq.; *Proceedings of the Preparatory
Commission at its eighth session* (24 September–5 October 2001), UN Doc. PCNICC/2001/L.3/Rev.1,
pp. 13 et seq.; On the state of the discussion before the Rome Conference (1998), see *Report of the
Preparatory Committee on the Establishment of an International Criminal Court, Addendum, Draft Statute for the International Criminal Court*, UN Doc. A/CONF.183/2/Add. 1 of 14 April 1998, pp. 12 et
seq.; see also G. Gaja, in A. Cassese, P. Gaeta and J.R.W.D. Jones (eds.), *The Rome Statute of the International Criminal Court*, Vol. 1 (2002), p. 427 at pp. 435 et seq.; H.-P. Kaul, in M. Politi and G. Nesi
(eds.), *The International Criminal Court and the Crime of Aggression* (2004), pp. 97 et seq.; I.K.
Müller-Schieke, 14 *Leiden Journal of International Law* (2001), p. 409 at p. 410; H. von Hebel and D.
Robinson, in R.S. Lee (ed.), *The International Criminal Court, The Making of the Rome Statute* (1999),
p. 79 at pp. 81 et seq.; M. Politi, in M. Politi and G. Nesi (eds.), *The International Criminal Court and
the Crime of Aggression* (2004), pp. 43 et seq.; A. Zimmermann, in O. Triffterer (ed.), *Commentary on
the Rome Statute of the International Criminal Court* (1999), Art. 5, marginal nos. 17 et seq.

[106] For an introductory survey, see *Preliminary list of possible issues relating to the crime of aggression,
Discussion Paper proposed by the Coordinator* (29 March 2001), UN Doc. PCNICC/2000/WGCA/
RT.1, pp. 1 et seq.

go beyond what is currently criminal under customary international law to include other acts of aggression of lesser intensity. The advocates of an expansion of criminal liability propose, in particular, basing the offense on the acts listed in Article 3 of the UN Definition of Aggression, so that, for example, even sea blockades contrary to international law could be punished.[107] Such an expansion of criminality is legally possible, but would make it far more difficult to build consensus.[108]

II. The Role of the UN Security Council

1188 A further point of contention in the negotiations is the role of the Security Council in ICC prosecution of the crime of aggression.[109] Under Article 24 of the UN Charter, the Security Council has primary responsibility for maintaining world peace. Broad agreement exists that the Security Council should be given priority in determining whether a war of aggression has occurred. The ICC should thus, as a rule, only prosecute aggression if the Security Council has already dealt with the situation and made such a determination.[110]

---

[107] In this vein, see, e.g., the proposal by the Arab states, UN Doc. PCNICC/1999/DP.11. The 1991 *Draft Code* established the definition in Art. 3 of the UN Definition of Aggression as the basis of the offense, and thus turned the structure of the definition of aggression on its head – as emphasized by G. Westdickenberg and O. Fixson, in J. Frowein et al. (eds.), *Festschrift für Eitel* (2003), p. 483 at pp. 491 et seq. – since it only defines aggressive war as a crime. For a limitation of the offense to areas criminalized under customary international law, see, e.g., Russia's proposal, UN Doc. PCNICC/1999/DP.12, which refers only to waging or preparing a war of aggression; for general discussion, see also Germany's proposal, UN Doc. PCNICC/2000/WGCA/DP.4, paras. 13 et seq.

[108] The main aim of the Rome Conference was to achieve the broadest possible acceptance of the ICC by mainly adopting into the Statute provisions recognized under customary international law, see M.H. Arsanjani, 93 *American Journal of International Law* (1999), p. 22 at p. 25; H.-P. Kaul, in M. Politi and G. Nesi (eds.), *The International Criminal Court and the Crime of Aggression* (2004), pp. 97 et seq.

[109] Based on proposals by state parties, the Preparatory Commission also drafted possible options for a provision on the role of the Security Council. See *Proceedings of the Preparatory Commission at its first, second and third sessions* (16–26 February, 26 July–13 August and 29 November–17 December 1999), UN Doc. PCNICC/1999/L.5/Rev.1, pp. 27 et seq.; *Proceedings of the Preparatory Commission at its fourth session* (13–31 March 2000), UN Doc. PCNICC/2000/L.1/Rev.1, pp. 39 et seq.; *Proceedings of the Preparatory Commission at its fifth session* (12–30 June 2000), UN Doc. PCNICC/2000/L.3/Rev.1, pp. 10 et seq.; *Proceedings of the Preparatory Commission at its sixth session* (27 November–8 December 2000), UN Doc. PCNICC/2000/L.4/Rev.1, pp. 15 et seq.; *Proceedings of the Preparatory Commission at its seventh session* (26 February–9 March 2001), UN Doc. PCNICC/2001/L.1/Rev.1, pp. 19 et seq.; *Proceedings of the Preparatory Commission at its eighth session* (8–24 September 2001), UN Doc. PCNICC/2001/L.3/Rev.1, pp. 15 et seq.; *Proceedings of the Preparatory Commission at its ninth session* (8–19 April 2002), UN Doc. PCNICC/2002/L.1/Rev.1, pp. 19 et seq. See also G. Gaja, in A. Cassese, P. Gaeta and J.R.W.D. Jones (eds.), *The Rome Statute of the International Criminal Court*, Vol. 1 (2002), p. 427 at p. 433; R.L. Griffiths, 2 *International Criminal Law Review* (2002), p. 301 at pp. 310 et seq.

[110] The PCNICC documents all speak of a "primary responsibility of the Security Council," see *Proceedings of the Preparatory Commission at its first, second and third sessions* (16–26 February, 26 July–13 August and 29 November–17 December 1999), UN Doc. PCNICC/ 1999/L.5/Rev.1, p. 30; *Proceedings of the Preparatory Commission at its fourth session* (13–31 March 2000), UN Doc. PCNICC/2000/L.1/Rev.1, p. 41; *Proceedings of the Preparatory Commission at its fifth session* (12–30 June 2000), UN Doc. PCNICC/2000/L.3/Rev.1, p. 12; *Proceedings of the Preparatory Commission at its sixth session*

Disagreement exists over whether the ICC should take action even if the Security **1189** Council, for political reasons, refuses to make a determination on the occurrence of an aggressive war.[111] To prevent the Security Council from blockading the ICC, it has been proposed that the ICC should be able to begin investigations even without a Security Council decision after a certain period of time. It would also be possible in such cases to assign the decision to another organ,[112] such as the UN General Assembly or the International Criminal Court.[113] Which proposal will prevail in the end remains uncertain.

(27 November–8 December 2000), UN Doc. PCNICC/2000/L.4/Rev.1, p. 17; *Proceedings of the Preparatory Commission at its seventh session* (26 February–9 March 2001), UN Doc. PCNICC/2001/L.1/ Rev.1, p. 21; *Proceedings of the Preparatory Commission at its eighth session* (24 September–5 October 2001), UN Doc. PCNICC/2001/L.3/Rev.1, p. 17; *Proceedings of the Preparatory Commission at its ninth session* (8–19 April 2002), UN Doc. PCNICC/2002/L.1/Rev.1, p. 23.

[111] The proposal by the UN Human Rights Commission in Art. 23(2) of the *ILC Draft Statute of the International Criminal Court* (1994), UN Doc. A/CN.4/L.491/Rev.2, p. 17, provided that the ICC would not become involved without a prior determination by the Security Council. This would grant the Security Council at least decision-making authority with procedural priority. Whether this would be accompanied by substantive authority to make the final decision is unclear; see G. Westdickenberg and O. Fixson, in J. Frowein et al. (eds.), *Festschrift für Eitel* (2003), p. 483 at pp. 494 et seq.

[112] See generally, G. Westdickenberg and O. Fixson, in J. Frowein et al. (eds.), *Festschrift für Eitel* (2003), p. 483 at pp. 517 et seq.

[113] See *Proceedings of the Preparatory Commission at its ninth session* (8–19 April 2002), UN Doc. PCNICC/2002/L.1/Rev.1, p. 18.

Appendix 1:
Materials

A. ICC Statute
(Rome Statute of the International Criminal Court)
[Extract]

Preamble

The States Parties to this Statute,

Conscious that all peoples are united by common bonds, their cultures pieced together in a shared heritage, and concerned that this delicate mosaic may be shattered at any time,

Mindful that during this century millions of children, women and men have been victims of unimaginable atrocities that deeply shock the conscience of humanity,

Recognizing that such grave crimes threaten the peace, security and well-being of the world,

Affirming that the most serious crimes of concern to the international community as a whole must not go unpunished and that their effective prosecution must be ensured by taking measures at the national level and by enhancing international cooperation,

Determined to put an end to impunity for the perpetrators of these crimes and thus to contribute to the prevention of such crimes,

Recalling that it is the duty of every State to exercise its criminal jurisdiction over those responsible for international crimes,

Reaffirming the Purposes and Principles of the Charter of the United Nations, and in particular that all States shall refrain from the threat or use of force against the territorial integrity or political independence of any State, or in any other manner inconsistent with the Purposes of the United Nations,

Emphasizing in this connection that nothing in this Statute shall be taken as authorizing any State Party to intervene in an armed conflict or in the internal affairs of any State,

Determined to these ends and for the sake of present and future generations, to establish an independent permanent International Criminal Court in relationship with the United Nations system, with jurisdiction over the most serious crimes of concern to the international community as a whole,

Emphasizing that the International Criminal Court established under this Statute shall be complementary to national criminal jurisdictions,

Resolved to guarantee lasting respect for and the enforcement of international justice,

Have agreed as follows

Part 1
Establishment of the Court

Article 1
The Court

An International Criminal Court ("the Court") is hereby established. It shall be a permanent institution and shall have the power to exercise its jurisdiction over persons for the most serious crimes of international concern, as referred to in this Statute, and shall be complementary to national criminal jurisdictions. The jurisdiction and functioning of the Court shall be governed by the provisions of this Statute.

Article 2
Relationship of the Court with the United Nations

The Court shall be brought into relationship with the United Nations through an agreement to be approved by the Assembly of States Parties to this Statute and thereafter concluded by the President of the Court on its behalf.

Article 3
Seat of the Court

1. The seat of the Court shall be established at The Hague in the Netherlands ("the host State").
2. The Court shall enter into a headquarters agreement with the host State, to be approved by the Assembly of States Parties and thereafter concluded by the President of the Court on its behalf.
3. The Court may sit elsewhere, whenever it considers it desirable, as provided in this Statute.

Article 4
Legal status and powers of the Court

1. The Court shall have international legal personality. It shall also have such legal capacity as may be necessary for the exercise of its functions and the fulfilment of its purposes.
2. The Court may exercise its functions and powers, as provided in this Statute, on the territory of any State Party and, by special agreement, on the territory of any other State.

Part 2
Jurisdiction, Admissibility and Applicable Law

Article 5
Crimes within the jurisdiction of the Court

1. The jurisdiction of the Court shall be limited to the most serious crimes of concern to the international community as a whole. The Court has jurisdiction in accordance with this Statute with respect to the following crimes:
   (a) The crime of genocide;
   (b) Crimes against humanity;
   (c) War crimes;
   (d) The crime of aggression.
2. The Court shall exercise jurisdiction over the crime of aggression once a provision is adopted in accordance with articles 121 and 123 defining the crime and setting out the conditions under which the Court shall exercise jurisdiction with respect to this crime. Such a provision shall be consistent with the relevant provisions of the Charter of the United Nations.

Article 6
Genocide

For the purpose of this Statute, "genocide" means any of the following acts committed with intent to destroy, in whole or in part, a national, ethnical, racial or religious group, as such:
(a) Killing members of the group;
(b) Causing serious bodily or mental harm to members of the group;
(c) Deliberately inflicting on the group conditions of life calculated to bring about its physical destruction in whole or in part;
(d) Imposing measures intended to prevent births within the group;
(e) Forcibly transferring children of the group to another group.

Article 7
Crimes against humanity

1. For the purpose of this Statute, "crime against humanity" means any of the following acts when committed as part of a widespread or systematic attack directed against any civilian population, with knowledge of the attack:
   (a) Murder;
   (b) Extermination;
   (c) Enslavement;
   (d) Deportation or forcible transfer of population;
   (e) Imprisonment or other severe deprivation of physical liberty in violation of fundamental rules of international law;
   (f) Torture;
   (g) Rape, sexual slavery, enforced prostitution, forced pregnancy, enforced sterilization, or any other form of sexual violence of comparable gravity;
   (h) Persecution against any identifiable group or collectivity on political, racial, national, ethnic, cultural, religious, gender as defined in paragraph 3, or other grounds that are universally recognized as impermissible under international law, in connection with any act referred to in this paragraph or any crime within the jurisdiction of the Court;
   (i) Enforced disappearance of persons;
   (j) The crime of apartheid;
   (k) Other inhumane acts of a similar character intentionally causing great suffering, or serious injury to body or to mental or physical health.
2. For the purpose of paragraph 1:
   (a) "Attack directed against any civilian population" means a course of conduct involving the multiple commission of acts referred to in paragraph 1 against any civilian population, pursuant to or in furtherance of a State or organizational policy to commit such attack;
   (b) "Extermination" includes the intentional infliction of conditions of life, *inter alia* the deprivation of access to food and medicine, calculated to bring about the destruction of part of a population;

(c) "Enslavement" means the exercise of any or all of the powers attaching to the right of ownership over a person and includes the exercise of such power in the course of trafficking in persons, in particular women and children;

(d) "Deportation or forcible transfer of population" means forced displacement of the persons concerned by expulsion or other coercive acts from the area in which they are lawfully present, without grounds permitted under international law;

(e) "Torture" means the intentional infliction of severe pain or suffering, whether physical or mental, upon a person in the custody or under the control of the accused; except that torture shall not include pain or suffering arising only from, inherent in or incidental to, lawful sanctions;

(f) "Forced pregnancy" means the unlawful confinement of a woman forcibly made pregnant, with the intent of affecting the ethnic composition of any population or carrying out other grave violations of international law. This definition shall not in any way be interpreted as affecting national laws relating to pregnancy;

(g) "Persecution" means the intentional and severe deprivation of fundamental rights contrary to international law by reason of the identity of the group or collectivity;

(h) "The crime of apartheid" means inhumane acts of a character similar to those referred to in paragraph 1, committed in the context of an institutionalized regime of systematic oppression and domination by one racial group over any other racial group or groups and committed with the intention of maintaining that regime;

(i) "Enforced disappearance of persons" means the arrest, detention or abduction of persons by, or with the authorization, support or acquiescence of, a State or a political organization, followed by a refusal to acknowledge that deprivation of freedom or to give information on the fate or whereabouts of those persons, with the intention of removing them from the protection of the law for a prolonged period of time.

3. For the purpose of this Statute, it is understood that the term "gender" refers to the two sexes, male and female, within the context of society. The term "gender" does not indicate any meaning different from the above.

Article 8
War crimes

1. The Court shall have jurisdiction in respect of war crimes in particular when committed as part of a plan or policy or as part of a large-scale commission of such crimes.

2. For the purpose of this Statute, "war crimes" means:

(a) Grave breaches of the Geneva Conventions of 12 August 1949, namely, any of the following acts against persons or property protected under the provisions of the relevant Geneva Convention:

    (i) Wilful killing;

    (ii) Torture or inhuman treatment, including biological experiments;

    (iii) Wilfully causing great suffering, or serious injury to body or health;

    (iv) Extensive destruction and appropriation of property, not justified by military necessity and carried out unlawfully and wantonly;

    (v) Compelling a prisoner of war or other protected person to serve in the forces of a hostile Power;

    (vi) Wilfully depriving a prisoner of war or other protected person of the rights of fair and regular trial;

    (vii) Unlawful deportation or transfer or unlawful confinement;

    (viii) Taking of hostages.

(b) Other serious violations of the laws and customs applicable in international armed conflict, within the established framework of international law, namely, any of the following acts:

    (i) Intentionally directing attacks against the civilian population as such or against individual civilians not taking direct part in hostilities;

(ii) Intentionally directing attacks against civilian objects, that is, objects which are not military objectives;

(iii) Intentionally directing attacks against personnel, installations, material, units or vehicles involved in a humanitarian assistance or peacekeeping mission in accordance with the Charter of the United Nations, as long as they are entitled to the protection given to civilians or civilian objects under the international law of armed conflict;

(iv) Intentionally launching an attack in the knowledge that such attack will cause incidental loss of life or injury to civilians or damage to civilian objects or widespread, long-term and severe damage to the natural environment which would be clearly excessive in relation to the concrete and direct overall military advantage anticipated;

(v)   Attacking or bombarding, by whatever means, towns, villages, dwellings or buildings which are undefended and which are not military objectives;

(vi) Killing or wounding a combatant who, having laid down his arms or having no longer means of defence, has surrendered at discretion;

(vii) Making improper use of a flag of truce, of the flag or of the military insignia and uniform of the enemy or of the United Nations, as well as of the distinctive emblems of the Geneva Conventions, resulting in death or serious personal injury;

(viii) The transfer, directly or indirectly, by the Occupying Power of parts of its own civilian population into the territory it occupies, or the deportation or transfer of all or parts of the population of the occupied territory within or outside this territory;

(ix) Intentionally directing attacks against buildings dedicated to religion, education, art, science or charitable purposes, historic monuments, hospitals and places where the sick and wounded are collected, provided they are not military objectives;

(x)   Subjecting persons who are in the power of an adverse party to physical mutilation or to medical or scientific experiments of any kind which are neither justified by the medical, dental or hospital treatment of the person concerned nor carried out in his or her interest, and which cause death to or seriously endanger the health of such person or persons;

(xi) Killing or wounding treacherously individuals belonging to the hostile nation or army;

(xii) Declaring that no quarter will be given;

(xiii) Destroying or seizing the enemy's property unless such destruction or seizure be imperatively demanded by the necessities of war;

(xiv) Declaring abolished, suspended or inadmissible in a court of law the rights and actions of the nationals of the hostile party;

(xv) Compelling the nationals of the hostile party to take part in the operations of war directed against their own country, even if they were in the belligerent's service before the commencement of the war;

(xvi) Pillaging a town or place, even when taken by assault;

(xvii) Employing poison or poisoned weapons;

(xviii) Employing asphyxiating, poisonous or other gases, and all analogous liquids, materials or devices;

(xix) Employing bullets which expand or flatten easily in the human body, such as bullets with a hard envelope which does not entirely cover the core or is pierced with incisions;

(xx) Employing weapons, projectiles and material and methods of warfare which are of a nature to cause superfluous injury or unnecessary suffering or which are inherently indiscriminate in violation of the international law of armed conflict, provided that such weapons, projectiles and material and methods of warfare are the subject of a comprehensive prohibition and are included in an annex to this Statute, by an amendment in accordance with the relevant provisions set forth in articles 121 and 123;

(xxi) Committing outrages upon personal dignity, in particular humiliating and degrading treatment;

(xxii) Committing rape, sexual slavery, enforced prostitution, forced pregnancy, as defined in article 7, paragraph 2 (f), enforced sterilization, or any other form of sexual violence also constituting a grave breach of the Geneva Conventions;

(xxiii) Utilizing the presence of a civilian or other protected person to render certain points, areas or military forces immune from military operations;

(xxiv) Intentionally directing attacks against buildings, material, medical units and transport, and personnel using the distinctive emblems of the Geneva Conventions in conformity with international law;

(xxv) Intentionally using starvation of civilians as a method of warfare by depriving them of objects indispensable to their survival, including wilfully impeding relief supplies as provided for under the Geneva Conventions;

(xxvi) Conscripting or enlisting children under the age of fifteen years into the national armed forces or using them to participate actively in hostilities.

(c) In the case of an armed conflict not of an international character, serious violations of article 3 common to the four Geneva Conventions of 12 August 1949, namely, any of the following acts committed against persons taking no active part in the hostilities, including members of armed forces who have laid down their arms and those placed *hors de combat* by sickness, wounds, detention or any other cause:

(i) Violence to life and person, in particular murder of all kinds, mutilation, cruel treatment and torture;

(ii) Committing outrages upon personal dignity, in particular humiliating and degrading treatment;

(iii) Taking of hostages;

(iv) The passing of sentences and the carrying out of executions without previous judgement pronounced by a regularly constituted court, affording all judicial guarantees which are generally recognized as indispensable.

(d) Paragraph 2 (c) applies to armed conflicts not of an international character and thus does not apply to situations of internal disturbances and tensions, such as riots, isolated and sporadic acts of violence or other acts of a similar nature.

(e) Other serious violations of the laws and customs applicable in armed conflicts not of an international character, within the established framework of international law, namely, any of the following acts:

(i) Intentionally directing attacks against the civilian population as such or against individual civilians not taking direct part in hostilities;

(ii) Intentionally directing attacks against buildings, material, medical units and transport, and personnel using the distinctive emblems of the Geneva Conventions in conformity with international law;

(iii) Intentionally directing attacks against personnel, installations, material, units or vehicles involved in a humanitarian assistance or peacekeeping mission in accordance with the Charter of the United Nations, as long as they are entitled to the protection given to civilians or civilian objects under the international law of armed conflict;

(iv) Intentionally directing attacks against buildings dedicated to religion, education, art, science or charitable purposes, historic monuments, hospitals and places where the sick and wounded are collected, provided they are not military objectives;

(v) Pillaging a town or place, even when taken by assault;

(vi) Committing rape, sexual slavery, enforced prostitution, forced pregnancy, as defined in article 7, paragraph 2 (f), enforced sterilization, and any other form of sexual violence also constituting a serious violation of article 3 common to the four Geneva Conventions;

(vii) Conscripting or enlisting children under the age of fifteen years into armed forces or groups or using them to participate actively in hostilities;

(viii) Ordering the displacement of the civilian population for reasons related to the conflict, unless the security of the civilians involved or imperative military reasons so demand;

(ix) Killing or wounding treacherously a combatant adversary;

(x) Declaring that no quarter will be given;

(xi) Subjecting persons who are in the power of another party to the conflict to physical mutilation or to medical or scientific experiments of any kind which are neither justified by the medical, dental or hospital treatment of the person concerned nor carried out in his or her interest, and which cause death to or seriously endanger the health of such person or persons;

(xii) Destroying or seizing the property of an adversary unless such destruction or seizure be imperatively demanded by the necessities of the conflict.

(f) Paragraph 2 (e) applies to armed conflicts not of an international character and thus does not apply to situations of internal disturbances and tensions, such as riots, isolated and sporadic acts of violence or other acts of a similar nature. It applies to armed conflicts that take place in the territory of a State when there is protracted armed conflict between governmental authorities and organized armed groups or between such groups.

3. Nothing in paragraph 2 (c) and (e) shall affect the responsibility of a Government to maintain or re-establish law and order in the State or to defend the unity and territorial integrity of the State, by all legitimate means.

Article 9
Elements of Crimes

1. Elements of Crimes shall assist the Court in the interpretation and application of articles 6, 7 and 8. They shall be adopted by a two-thirds majority of the members of the Assembly of States Parties.

2. Amendments to the Elements of Crimes may be proposed by:
   (a) Any State Party;
   (b) The judges acting by an absolute majority;
   (c) The Prosecutor.
   Such amendments shall be adopted by a two-thirds majority of the members of the Assembly of States Parties.

3. The Elements of Crimes and amendments thereto shall be consistent with this Statute.

Article 10
Nothing in this Part shall be interpreted as limiting or prejudicing in any way existing or devel-

oping rules of international law for purposes other than this Statute.

Article 11
Jurisdiction ratione temporis

1. The Court has jurisdiction only with respect to crimes committed after the entry into force of this Statute.
2. If a State becomes a Party to this Statute after its entry into force, the Court may exercise its jurisdiction only with respect to crimes committed after the entry into force of this Statute for that State, unless that State has made a declaration under article 12, paragraph 3.

Article 12
Preconditions to the exercise of jurisdiction

1. A State which becomes a Party to this Statute thereby accepts the jurisdiction of the Court with respect to the crimes referred to in article 5.
2. In the case of article 13, paragraph (a) or (c), the Court may exercise its jurisdiction if one or more of the following States are Parties to this Statute or have accepted the jurisdiction of the Court in accordance with paragraph 3:
   (a) The State on the territory of which the conduct in question occurred or, if the crime was committed on board a vessel or aircraft, the State of registration of that vessel or aircraft;
   (b) The State of which the person accused of the crime is a national.
3. If the acceptance of a State which is not a Party to this Statute is required under paragraph 2, that State may, by declaration lodged with the Registrar, accept the exercise of jurisdiction by the Court with respect to the crime in question. The accepting State shall cooperate with the Court without any delay or exception in accordance with Part 9.

Article 13
Exercise of jurisdiction

The Court may exercise its jurisdiction with respect to a crime referred to in article 5 in accordance with the provisions of this Statute if:
(a) A situation in which one or more of such crimes appears to have been committed is referred to the Prosecutor by a State Party in accordance with article 14;
(b) A situation in which one or more of such crimes appears to have been committed is referred to the Prosecutor by the Security Council acting under Chapter VII of the Charter of the United Nations; or
(c) The Prosecutor has initiated an investigation in respect of such a crime in accordance with article 15.

Article 14
Referral of a situation by a State Party

1. A State Party may refer to the Prosecutor a situation in which one or more crimes within the jurisdiction of the Court appear to have been committed requesting the Prosecutor to investigate the situation for the purpose of determining whether one or more specific persons should be charged with the commission of such crimes.
2. As far as possible, a referral shall specify the relevant circumstances and be accompanied by such supporting documentation as is available to the State referring the situation.

Article 15
Prosecutor

1. The Prosecutor may initiate investigations *proprio motu* on the basis of information on crimes within the jurisdiction of the Court.
2. The Prosecutor shall analyse the seriousness of the information received. For this purpose, he or she may seek additional information from States, organs of the United Nations, intergovernmental or non-governmental organizations, or other reliable sources that he or she deems appropriate, and may receive written or oral testimony at the seat of the Court.
3. If the Prosecutor concludes that there is a reasonable basis to proceed with an investigation, he or she shall submit to the Pre-Trial Chamber a request for authorization of an investigation, together with any supporting material collected. Victims may make representations to the Pre-Trial Chamber, in accordance with the Rules of Procedure and Evidence.
4. –6. (...)

Article 16
Deferral of investigation or prosecution

No investigation or prosecution may be commenced or proceeded with under this Statute for a period of 12 months after the Security Council, in a resolution adopted under Chapter VII of the Charter of the United Nations, has requested the Court to that effect; that request may be renewed by the Council under the same conditions.

Article 17
Issues of admissibility

1. Having regard to paragraph 10 of the Preamble and article 1, the Court shall determine that a case is inadmissible where:
   (a) The case is being investigated or prosecuted by a State which has jurisdiction over it, unless the State is unwilling or unable genuinely to carry out the investigation or prosecution;
   (b) The case has been investigated by a State which has jurisdiction over it and the State has decided not to prosecute the person concerned, unless the decision resulted from the unwillingness or inability of the State genuinely to prosecute;
   (c) The person concerned has already been tried for conduct which is the subject of the complaint, and a trial by the Court is not permitted under article 20, paragraph 3;
   (d) The case is not of sufficient gravity to justify further action by the Court.
2. In order to determine unwillingness in a particular case, the Court shall consider, having regard to the principles of due process recognized by international law, whether one or more of the following exist, as applicable:
   (a) The proceedings were or are being undertaken or the national decision was made for the purpose of shielding the person concerned from criminal responsibility for crimes within the jurisdiction of the Court referred to in article 5;
   (b) There has been an unjustified delay in the proceedings which in the circumstances is inconsistent with an intent to bring the person concerned to justice;
   (c) The proceedings were not or are not being conducted independently or impartially, and they were or are being con-

ducted in a manner which, in the circumstances, is inconsistent with an intent to bring the person concerned to justice.
3. In order to determine inability in a particular case, the Court shall consider whether, due to a total or substantial collapse or unavailability of its national judicial system, the State is unable to obtain the accused or the necessary evidence and testimony or otherwise unable to carry out its proceedings.

Article 20
Ne bis in idem

1. Except as provided in this Statute, no person shall be tried before the Court with respect to conduct which formed the basis of crimes for which the person has been convicted or acquitted by the Court.
2. No person shall be tried by another court for a crime referred to in article 5 for which that person has already been convicted or acquitted by the Court.
3. No person who has been tried by another court for conduct also proscribed under article 6, 7 or 8 shall be tried by the Court with respect to the same conduct unless the proceedings in the other court:
   (a) Were for the purpose of shielding the person concerned from criminal responsibility for crimes within the jurisdiction of the Court; or
   (b) Otherwise were not conducted independently or impartially in accordance with the norms of due process recognized by international law and were conducted in a manner which, in the circumstances, was inconsistent with an intent to bring the person concerned to justice.

Article 21
Applicable law

1. The Court shall apply:
   (a) In the first place, this Statute, Elements of Crimes and its Rules of Procedure and Evidence;
   (b) In the second place, where appropriate, applicable treaties and the principles and rules of international law, including the established principles of the international law of armed conflict;

(c) Failing that, general principles of law derived by the Court from national laws of legal systems of the world including, as appropriate, the national laws of States that would normally exercise jurisdiction over the crime, provided that those principles are not inconsistent with this Statute and with international law and internationally recognized norms and standards.

2. The Court may apply principles and rules of law as interpreted in its previous decisions.

3. The application and interpretation of law pursuant to this article must be consistent with internationally recognized human rights, and be without any adverse distinction founded on grounds such as gender as defined in article 7, paragraph 3, age, race, colour, language, religion or belief, political or other opinion, national, ethnic or social origin, wealth, birth or other status.

Part 3
General Principles of Criminal Law

Article 22
Nullum crimen sine lege

1. A person shall not be criminally responsible under this Statute unless the conduct in question constitutes, at the time it takes place, a crime within the jurisdiction of the Court.

2. The definition of a crime shall be strictly construed and shall not be extended by analogy. In case of ambiguity, the definition shall be interpreted in favour of the person being investigated, prosecuted or convicted.

3. This article shall not affect the characterization of any conduct as criminal under international law independently of this Statute.

Article 23
Nulla poena sine lege

A person convicted by the Court may be punished only in accordance with this Statute.

Article 24
Non-retroactivity ratione personae

1. No person shall be criminally responsible under this Statute for conduct prior to the entry into force of the Statute.

2. In the event of a change in the law applicable to a given case prior to a final judgement, the law more favourable to the person being investigated, prosecuted or convicted shall apply.

Article 25
Individual criminal responsibility

1. The Court shall have jurisdiction over natural persons pursuant to this Statute.

2. A person who commits a crime within the jurisdiction of the Court shall be individually responsible and liable for punishment in accordance with this Statute.

3. In accordance with this Statute, a person shall be criminally responsible and liable for punishment for a crime within the jurisdiction of the Court if that person:

(a) Commits such a crime, whether as an individual, jointly with another or through another person, regardless of whether that other person is criminally responsible;

(b) Orders, solicits or induces the commission of such a crime which in fact occurs or is attempted;

(c) For the purpose of facilitating the commission of such a crime, aids, abets or otherwise assists in its commission or its attempted commission, including providing the means for its commission;

(d) In any other way contributes to the commission or attempted commission of such crime by a group of persons acting with a common purpose. Such contribution shall be intentional and shall either:

(i) Be made with the aim of furthering the criminal activity or criminal purpose of the group, where such activity or purpose involves the commission of a crime within the jurisdiction of the Court; or

(ii) Be made in the knowledge of the intention of the group to commit the crime;

(e) In respect of the crime of genocide, directly and publicly incites others to commit genocide;

(f) Attempts to commit such a crime by taking action that commences its execution by means of a substantial step, but the crime does not occur because of circumstances independent of the person's intentions. However, a person who abandons the effort to commit the crime or otherwise prevents the completion of the crime shall not be liable for punishment under this Statute for the attempt to commit that crime if that person completely and voluntarily gave up the criminal purpose.

4. No provision in this Statute relating to individual criminal responsibility shall affect the responsibility of States under international law.

Article 26
Exclusion of jurisdiction over persons under eighteen

The Court shall have no jurisdiction over any person who was under the age of 18 at the time of the alleged commission of a crime.

Article 27
Irrelevance of official capacity

1. This Statute shall apply equally to all persons without any distinction based on official capacity. In particular, official capacity as a Head of State or Government, a member of a Government or parliament, an elected representative or a government official shall in no case exempt a person from criminal responsibility under this Statute, nor shall it, in and of itself, constitute a ground for reduction of sentence.
2. Immunities or special procedural rules which may attach to the official capacity of a person, whether under national or international law, shall not bar the Court from exercising its jurisdiction over such a person.

Article 28
Responsibility of commanders and other superiors

In addition to other grounds of criminal responsibility under this Statute for crimes within the jurisdiction of the Court:

(a) A military commander or person effectively acting as a military commander shall be criminally responsible for crimes within the jurisdiction of the Court committed by forces under his or her effective command and control, or effective authority and control as the case may be, as a result of his or her failure to exercise control properly over such forces, where:

(i) That military commander or person either knew or, owing to the circumstances at the time, should have known that the forces were committing or about to commit such crimes; and

(ii) That military commander or person failed to take all necessary and reasonable measures within his or her power to prevent or repress their commission or to submit the matter to the competent authorities for investigation and prosecution.

(b) With respect to superior and subordinate relationships not described in paragraph (a), a superior shall be criminally responsible for crimes within the jurisdiction of the Court committed by subordinates under his or her effective authority and control, as a result of his or her failure to exercise control properly over such subordinates, where:

(i) The superior either knew, or consciously disregarded information which clearly indicated, that the subordinates were committing or about to commit such crimes;

(ii) The crimes concerned activities that were within the effective responsibility and control of the superior; and

(iii) The superior failed to take all necessary and reasonable measures within his or her power to prevent or repress their commission or to submit the matter to the competent authorities for investigation and prosecution.

Article 29
Non-applicability of statute of limitations

The crimes within the jurisdiction of the Court shall not be subject to any statute of limitations.

Article 30
Mental element

1. Unless otherwise provided, a person shall be criminally responsible and liable for punishment for a crime within the jurisdiction of the Court only if the material elements are committed with intent and knowledge.
2. For the purposes of this article, a person has intent where:

(a) In relation to conduct, that person means to engage in the conduct;

(b) In relation to a consequence, that person means to cause that consequence or is aware that it will occur in the ordinary course of events.

3. For the purposes of this article, "knowledge" means awareness that a circumstance exists or a consequence will occur in the ordinary course of events. "Know" and "knowingly" shall be construed accordingly.

Article 31
Grounds for excluding criminal responsibility

1. In addition to other grounds for excluding criminal responsibility provided for in this Statute, a person shall not be criminally responsible if, at the time of that person's conduct:

(a) The person suffers from a mental disease or defect that destroys that person's capacity to appreciate the unlawfulness or nature of his or her conduct, or capacity to control his or her conduct to conform to the requirements of law;

(b) The person is in a state of intoxication that destroys that person's capacity to appreciate the unlawfulness or nature of his or her conduct, or capacity to control his or her conduct to conform to the requirements of law, unless the person has become voluntarily intoxicated under such circumstances that the person knew, or disregarded the risk, that, as a result of the intoxication, he or she was likely to engage in conduct constituting a crime within the jurisdiction of the Court;

(c) The person acts reasonably to defend himself or herself or another person or, in the case of war crimes, property which is essential for the survival of the person or another person or property which is essential for accomplishing a military mission, against an imminent and unlawful use of force in a manner proportionate to the degree of danger to the person or the other person or property protected. The fact that the person was involved in a defensive operation conducted by forces shall not in itself constitute a ground for excluding criminal responsibility under this subparagraph;

(d) The conduct which is alleged to constitute a crime within the jurisdiction of the Court has been caused by duress resulting from a threat of imminent death or of continuing or imminent serious bodily harm against that person or another person, and the person acts necessarily and reasonably to avoid this threat, provided that the person does not intend to cause a greater harm than the one sought to be avoided. Such a threat may either be:

(i) Made by other persons; or

(ii) Constituted by other circumstances beyond that person's control.

2. The Court shall determine the applicability of the grounds for excluding criminal responsibility provided for in this Statute to the case before it.

3. At trial, the Court may consider a ground for excluding criminal responsibility other than those referred to in paragraph 1 where such a ground is derived from applicable law as set forth in article 21. The procedures relating to the consideration of such a ground shall be provided for in the Rules of Procedure and Evidence.

Article 32
Mistake of fact or mistake of law

1. A mistake of fact shall be a ground for excluding criminal responsibility only if it negates the mental element required by the crime.

2. A mistake of law as to whether a particular type of conduct is a crime within the jurisdiction of the Court shall not be a ground for excluding criminal responsibility. A mistake of law may, however, be a ground for excluding criminal responsibility if it negates the mental element required by such a crime, or as provided for in article 33.

Article 33
Superior orders and prescription of law

1. The fact that a crime within the jurisdiction of the Court has been committed by a person pursuant to an order of a Government or of a superior, whether military or civilian, shall not relieve that person of criminal responsibility unless:

    (a) The person was under a legal obligation to obey orders of the Government or the superior in question;

    (b) The person did not know that the order was unlawful; and

    (c) The order was not manifestly unlawful.

2. For the purposes of this article, orders to commit genocide or crimes against humanity are manifestly unlawful.

B. ICTY Statute
(Statute of the International Criminal Tribunal for the Former Yugoslavia) [Extract]

Article 1
Competence of the International Tribunal

The International Tribunal shall have the power to prosecute persons responsible for serious violations of international humanitarian law committed in the territory of the former Yugoslavia since 1991 in accordance with the provisions of the present Statute.

Article 2
Grave breaches of the Geneva Conventions of 1949

The International Tribunal shall have the power to prosecute persons committing or ordering to be committed grave breaches of the Geneva Conventions of 12 August 1949, namely the following acts against persons or property protected under the provisions of the relevant Geneva Convention:
a) wilful killing;
b) torture or inhuman treatment, including biological experiments;
c) wilfully causing great suffering or serious injury to body or health;
d) extensive destruction and appropriation of property, not justified by military necessity and carried out unlawfully and wantonly;
e) compelling a prisoner of war or a civilian to serve in the forces of a hostile power;
f) wilfully depriving a prisoner of war or a civilian of the rights of fair and regular trial;
g) unlawful deportation or transfer or unlawful confinement of a civilian;
h) taking civilians as hostages.

Article 3
Violations of the laws or customs of war

The International Tribunal shall have the power to prosecute persons violating the laws or customs of war. Such violations shall include, but not be limited to:
a) employment of poisonous weapons or other weapons calculated to cause unnecessary suffering;
b) wanton destruction of cities, towns or villages, or devastation not justified by military necessity;
c) attack, or bombardment, by whatever means, of undefended towns, villages, dwellings, or buildings;
d) seizure of, destruction or wilful damage done to institutions dedicated to religion, charity and education, the arts and sciences, historic monuments and works of art and science;
e) plunder of public or private property.

Article 4
Genocide

1. The International Tribunal shall have the power to prosecute persons committing genocide as defined in paragraph 2 of this article or of committing any of the other acts enumerated in paragraph 3 of this article.
2. Genocide means any of the following acts committed with intent to destroy, in whole or in part, a national, ethnical, racial or religious group, as such:
   a) killing members of the group;
   b) causing serious bodily or mental harm to members of the group;
   c) deliberately inflicting on the group conditions of life calculated to bring about its physical destruction in whole or in part;
   d) imposing measures intended to prevent births within the group;
   e) forcibly transferring children of the group to another group.
3. The following acts shall be punishable:
   a) genocide;
   b) conspiracy to commit genocide;
   c) direct and public incitement to commit genocide;
   d) attempt to commit genocide;
   e) complicity in genocide.

Article 5
Crimes against humanity

The International Tribunal shall have the power to prosecute persons responsible for the following crimes when committed in armed conflict, whether international or internal in character, and directed against any civilian population:
a) murder;
b) extermination;
c) enslavement;
d) deportation;
e) imprisonment;
f) torture;
g) rape;
h) persecutions on political, racial and religious grounds;
i) other inhumane acts.

Article 7
Individual criminal responsibility

1. A person who planned, instigated, ordered, committed or otherwise aided and abetted in the planning, preparation or execution of a crime referred to in articles 2 to 5 of the present Statute, shall be individually responsible for the crime.
2. The official position of any accused person, whether as Head of State or Government or as a responsible Government official, shall not relieve such person of criminal responsibility nor mitigate punishment.
3. The fact that any of the acts referred to in articles 2 to 5 of the present Statute was committed by a subordinate does not relieve his superior of criminal responsibility if he knew or had reason to know that the subordinate was about to commit such acts or had done

so and the superior failed to take the necessary and reasonable measures to prevent such acts or to punish the perpetrators thereof.
4. The fact that an accused person acted pursuant to an order of a Government or of a superior shall not relieve him of criminal responsibility, but may be considered in mitigation of punishment if the International Tribunal determines that justice so requires.

Article 8
Territorial and temporal jurisdiction

The territorial jurisdiction of the International Tribunal shall extend to the territory of the former Socialist Federal Republic of Yugoslavia, including its land surface, airspace and territorial waters. The temporal jurisdiction of the International Tribunal shall extend to a period beginning on 1 January 1991.

Article 9
Concurrent jurisdiction

1. The International Tribunal and national courts shall have concurrent jurisdiction to prosecute persons for serious violations of international humanitarian law committed in the territory of the former Yugoslavia since 1 January 1991.
2. The International Tribunal shall have primacy over national courts. At any stage of the procedure, the International Tribunal may formally request national courts to defer to the competence of the International Tribunal in accordance with the present Statute and the Rules of Procedure and Evidence of the International Tribunal.

C. ICTR Statute
(Statute of the International Criminal Tribunal for Rwanda)
[Extract]

Article 1
Competence of the International Tribunal for Rwanda

The International Tribunal for Rwanda shall have the power to prosecute persons responsible for serious violations of international humanitarian law committed in the territory of Rwanda and Rwandan citizens responsible for such violations committed in the territory of neighbouring States, between 1 January 1994 and 31 December 1994, in accordance with the provisions of the present Statute.

Article 2
Genocide

1. The International Tribunal for Rwanda shall have the power to prosecute persons committing genocide as defined in paragraph 2 of this Article or of committing any of the other acts enumerated in paragraph 3 of this Article.
2. Genocide means any of the following acts committed with intent to destroy, in whole or in part, a national, ethnical, racial or religious group, as such:
   a) Killing members of the group;
   b) Causing serious bodily or mental harm to members of the group;
   c) Deliberately inflicting on the group conditions of life calculated to bring about its physical destruction in whole or in part;
   d) Imposing measures intended to prevent births within the group;
   e) Forcibly transferring children of the group to another group.
3. The following acts shall be punishable:
   a) Genocide;
   b) Conspiracy to commit genocide;
   c) Direct and public incitement to commit genocide;
   d) Attempt to commit genocide;
   e) Complicity in genocide.

Article 3
Crimes against Humanity

The International Tribunal for Rwanda shall have the power to prosecute persons responsible for the following crimes when committed as part of a widespread or systematic attack against any civilian population on national, political, ethnic, racial or religious grounds:
a) Murder;
b) Extermination;
c) Enslavement;
d) Deportation;
e) Imprisonment;
f) Torture;
g) Rape;
h) Persecutions on political, racial and religious grounds;
i) Other inhumane acts.

Article 4
Violations of Article 3 common to the Geneva Conventions and of Additional Protocol II

The International Tribunal for Rwanda shall have the power to prosecute persons committing or ordering to be committed serious violations of Article 3 common to the Geneva Conventions of 12 August 1949 for the Protection of War Victims, and of Additional Protocol II thereto of 8 June 1977. These violations shall include, but shall not be limited to:
a) Violence to life, health and physical or mental well-being of persons, in particular murder as well as cruel treatment such as torture, mutilation or any form of corporal punishment;
b) Collective punishments;
c) Taking of hostages;
d) Acts of terrorism;
e) Outrages upon personal dignity, in particular humiliating and degrading treatment, rape, enforced prostitution and any form of indecent assault;
f) Pillage;

g) The passing of sentences and the carrying out of executions without previous judgement pronounced by a regularly constituted court, affording all the judicial guarantees which are recognized as indispensable by civilised peoples;

h) Threats to commit any of the foregoing acts.

Article 6
Individual Criminal Responsibility

1. A person who planned, instigated, ordered, committed or otherwise aided and abetted in the planning, preparation or execution of a crime referred to in articles 2 to 4 of the present Statute, shall be individually responsible for the crime.

2. The official position of any accused person, whether as Head of State or Government or as a responsible government official, shall not relieve such person of criminal responsibility nor mitigate punishment.

3. The fact that any of the acts referred to in articles 2 to 4 of the present Statute was committed by a subordinate does not relieve his or her superior of criminal responsibility if he or she knew or had reason to know that the subordinate was about to commit such acts or had done so and the superior failed to take the necessary and reasonable measures to prevent such acts or to punish the perpetrators thereof.

4. The fact that an accused person acted pursuant to an order of a Government or of a superior shall not relieve him or her of criminal responsibility, but may be considered in mitigation of punishment if the International Tribunal for Rwanda determines that justice so requires.

Article 7
Territorial and temporal jurisdiction

The territorial jurisdiction of the International Tribunal for Rwanda shall extend to the territory of Rwanda including its land surface and airspace as well as to the territory of neighbouring States in respect of serious violations of international humanitarian law committed by Rwandan citizens. The temporal jurisdiction of the International Tribunal for Rwanda shall extend to a period beginning on 1 January 1994 and ending on 31 December 1994.

Article 8
Concurrent jurisdiction

1. The International Tribunal for Rwanda and national courts shall have concurrent jurisdiction to prosecute persons for serious violations of international humanitarian law committed in the territory of Rwanda and Rwandan citizens for such violations committed in the territory of the neighbouring States, between 1 January 1994 and 31 December 1994.

2. The International Tribunal for Rwanda shall have the primacy over the national courts of all States. At any stage of the procedure, the International Tribunal for Rwanda may formally request national courts to defer to its competence in accordance with the present Statute and the Rules of Procedure and Evidence of the International Tribunal for Rwanda.

D. London Agreement
(Agreement for the Prosecution and Punishment of the Major War Criminals of the European Axis)
[Extract]

Agreement by the Government of the United States of America, the Provisional Government of the French Republic, the Government of the United Kingdom of Great Britain and Northern Ireland and the Government of the Union of Soviet Socialist Republics for the Prosecution and Punishment of the Major War Criminals of the European Axis

Whereas the United Nations have from time to time made declarations of their intention that War Criminals shall be brought to justice;

And whereas the Moscow Declaration of the 30th October 1943 on German atrocities in Occupied Europe stated that those German Officers and men and members of the Nazi Party who have been responsible for or have taken a consenting part in atrocities and crimes will be sent back to the countries in which their abominable deeds were done in order that they may be judged and punished according to the laws of these liberated countries and of the free Governments that will be created therein;

And whereas this Declaration was stated to be without prejudice to the case of major criminals whose offenses have no particular geographical location and who will be punished by the joint decision of the Governments of the Allies;

Now therefore the Government of the United States of America, the Provisional Government of the French Republic, the Government of the United Kingdom of Great Britain and Northern Ireland and the Government of the Union of Soviet Socialist Republics (hereinafter called "the Signatories") acting in the interests of all the United Nations and by their representatives duly authorized thereto have concluded this Agreement.

Article 1

There shall be established after consultation with the Control Council for Germany an International Military Tribunal for the trial of war criminals whose offenses have no particular geographical location whether they be accused individually or in their capacity as members of the organizations or groups or in both capacities.

E. Nuremberg Charter
(Charter of the International Military Tribunal)
[Extract]

Article 6

The Tribunal established by the Agreement referred to in Article 1 hereof for the trial and punishment of the major war criminals of the European Axis countries shall have the power to try and punish persons who, acting in the interests of the European Axis countries, whether as individuals or as members of organizations, committed any of the following crimes.

The following acts, or any of them, are crimes coming within the jurisdiction of the Tribunal for which there shall be individual responsibility:

a) *Crimes against Peace:* namely, planning, preparation, initiation or waging of a war of aggression, or a war in violation of international treaties, agreements or assurances, or participation in a common plan or conspiracy for the accomplishment of any of the foregoing;

b) *War Crimes:* namely, violations of the laws or customs of war. Such violations shall include, but not be limited to, murder, ill-treatment or deportation to slave labor or for any purpose of civilian population of or in occupied territory, murder or ill-treatment of prisoners of war or persons on the seas, killing of hostages, plunder of public or private property, wanton destruction of cities, towns or villages, or devastation not justified by military necessity;

c) *Crimes against Humanity:* namely, murder, extermination, enslavement, deportation, and other inhumane acts committed against any civilian population, before or during the war, or persecutions on political, racial or religious grounds in execution of or in connection with any crime within the jurisdiction of the Tribunal, whether or not in violation of the domestic law of the country where perpetrated.

Leaders, organizers, instigators and accomplices participating in the formulation or execution of a common plan or conspiracy to commit any of the foregoing crimes are responsible for all acts performed by any persons in execution of such plan.

Article 7

The official position of the defendants, whether as Heads of State or responsible officials in Government Departments, shall not be considered as freeing them from responsibility or mitigating punishment.

Article 8

The fact that the Defendant acted pursuant to order of his Government or of a superior shall not free him from responsibility, but may be considered in mitigation of punishment if the Tribunal determines that justice so requires.

F. Tokyo Charter
(Charter of the International Military Tribunal for the Far East)
[Extract]

Article 5
Jurisdiction Over Persons and Offences

The Tribunal shall have the power to try and punish Far Eastern war criminals who as individuals or as members of organizations are charged with offences which include Crimes against Peace.

The following acts, or any of them, are crimes coming within the jurisdiction of the Tribunal for which there shall be individual responsibility:

a) *Crimes against Peace:* Namely, the planning, preparation, initiation or waging of a declared or undeclared war of aggression, or a war in violation of international law, treaties, agreements or assurances, or participation in a common plan or conspiracy for the accomplishment of any of the foregoing;

b) *Conventional War Crimes:* Namely, violations of the laws or customs of war;

c) *Crimes against Humanity:* Namely, murder, extermination, enslavement, deportation, and other inhumane acts committed against any civilian population, before or during the war, or persecutions on political or racial grounds in execution of or in connection with any crime within the jurisdiction of the Tribunal, whether or not in violation of the domestic law of the country where perpetrated. Leaders, organizers, instigators and accomplices participating in the formulation or execution of a common plan or conspiracy to commit any of the foregoing crimes are responsible for all acts performed by any person in execution of such plan.

Article 6
Responsibility of Accused

Neither the official position, at any time, of an accused, nor the fact that an accused acted pursuant to order of his government or of a superior shall, of itself, be sufficient to free such accused from responsibility for any crime with which he is charged, but such circumstances may be considered in mitigation of punishment if the Tribunal determines that justice so requires.

G. CCL No. 10

(Allied Control Council Law No. 10, Punishment of Persons Guilty of War Crimes, Crimes Against Peace and Against Humanity)
[Extract]

Article II

1. Each of the following acts is recognized as a crime:

   (a) *Crimes against Peace.* Initiation of invasions of other countries and wars of aggression in violation of international laws and treaties, including but not limited to planning, preparation, initiation or waging a war of aggression, or a war in violation of international treaties, agreements or assurances, or participation in a common plan or conspiracy for the accomplishment of any of the foregoing.

   (b) *War Crimes.* Atrocities or offenses against persons or property, constituting violations of the laws or customs of war, including but not limited to murder, ill-treatment or deportation to slave labour or for any other purpose, of civilian population from occupied territory, murder or ill-treatment of prisoners of war or persons on the seas, killing of hostages, plunder of public or private property, wanton destruction of cities, towns or villages, or devastation not justified by military necessity.

   (c) *Crimes against Humanity.* Atrocities and offenses, including but not limited to murder, extermination, enslavement, deportation, imprisonment, torture, rape, or other inhumane acts committed against any civilian population, or persecutions on political, racial or religious grounds whether or not in violation of the domestic laws of the country where perpetrated.

   (d) Membership in categories of a criminal group or organization declared criminal by the International Military Tribunal.

2. Any person without regard to nationality or the capacity in which he acted, is deemed to have committed a crime as defined in paragraph 1 of this Article, if he was

   (a) a principal or;

   (b) was an accessory to the commission of any such crime or ordered or abetted the same or;

   (c) took a consenting part therein or;

   (d) was connected with plans or enterprises involving its commission or;

   (e) was a member of any organization or group connected with the commission of any such crime or;

   (f) with reference to paragraph 1(a), if he held a high political, civil or military (including General Staff) position in Germany or in one of its Allies, co-belligerents or satellites or held high position in the financial, industrial or economic life of any such country.

3. Any persons found guilty of any of the crimes above mentioned may upon conviction be punished as shall be determined by the tribunal to be just. Such punishment may consist of one or more of the following:

   (a) Death.

   (b) Imprisonment for life or a term of years, with or without hard labor.

   (c) Fine, and imprisonment with or without hard labour, in lieu thereof.

   (d) Forfeiture of property.

   (e) Restitution of property wrongfully acquired.

   (f) Deprivation of some or all civil rights.

   Any property declared to be forfeited or the restitution of which is ordered by the Tribunal shall be delivered to the Control Council for Germany, which shall decide on its disposal.

4. (a) The official position of any person, whether as Head of State or as a responsible official in a Government Department, does not free him from responsibility for a crime or entitle him to mitigation of punishment.

(b) The fact that any person acted pursuant to the order of his Government or of a superior does not free him from responsibility for a crime, but may be considered in mitigation.

In any trial or prosecution for a crime herein referred to, the accused shall not be entitled to the benefits of any statute of limitation in respect of the period from 30 January 1933 to 1 July 1945, nor shall any immunity, pardon or amnesty granted under the Nazi regime be admitted as a bar to trial or punishment.

H. Nuremberg Principles

Principle I

Any person who commits an act which constitutes a crime under international law is responsible therefore and liable to punishment.

Principle II

The fact that internal law does not impose a penalty for an act which constitutes a crime under international law does not relieve the person who committed the act from responsibility under international law.

Principle III

The fact that a person who committed an act which constitutes a crime under international law acted as Head of State or responsible government official does not relieve him from responsibility under international law.

Principle IV

The fact that a person acted pursuant to order of his Government or of a superior does not relieve him from responsibility under international law, provided a moral choice was in fact possible to him.

Principle V

Any person charged with a crime under international law has the right to a fair trial on the facts and law.

Principle VI

The crimes hereinafter set out are punishable as crimes under international law:

(a) *Crimes against peace:*
   (i) Planning, preparation, initiation or waging of a war of aggression or a war in violation of international treaties, agreements or assurances;
   (ii) Participation in a common plan or conspiracy for the accomplishment of any of the acts mentioned under (i).
(b) *War Crimes:* Violations of the laws or customs of war which include, but are not limited to, murder, ill-treatment or deportation to slave-labour or for any other purpose of the civilian population of or in occupied territory, murder or ill-treatment of prisoners of war or persons on the seas, killing of hostages, plunder of public or private property, wanton destruction of cities, towns, or villages, or devastation not justified by military necessity.
(c) *Crimes against humanity:* Murder, extermination, enslavement, deportation and other inhumane acts done against any civilian population, or persecutions on political, racial, or religious grounds, when such acts are done or such persecutions are carried on in execution of or in connection with any crime against peace or any war crime.

Principle VII

Complicity in the commission of a crime against peace, a war crime, or a crime against humanity as set forth in Principle VI is a crime under international law.

I. (German) Code of Crimes Against International Law
(*Völkerstrafgesetzbuch, VStGB*)

Part 1[1]
General provisions

Section 1
Scope of application

This Act shall apply to all criminal offences against international law designated under this Act, to serious criminal offences[2] designated therein even when the offence was committed abroad and bears no relation to Germany.[3]

Section 2
Application of the general law

The general criminal law shall apply to offences pursuant to this Act so far as this Act does not make special provision in sections 1 and 3 to 5.

Section 3
Acting upon orders

Whoever commits an offence pursuant to sections 8 to 14 in execution of a military order or of an order comparable in its actual binding effect shall have acted without guilt so far as the

---

[1] Unofficial translation by Brian Duffet, reprinted by kind permission of the German Federal Ministry of Justice.

[2] In German law the term "serious criminal offence" (*Verbrechen*) is used to denote criminal offences (*Straftaten*) that are punishable with not less than one year of imprisonment. Mitigating (and aggravating) circumstances – as set out for instance in section 8(5) – are to be disregarded in this respect. As a result, all criminal offences in the CCIL are "serious criminal offences" (*Verbrechen*) with the sole exception of those in sections 13 and 14. Please note that the terminological differentiation between "criminal offences" (*Straftaten*) and "serious criminal offences" (*Verbrechen*) is, for technical reasons, not reflected everywhere in this translation.

[3] See also Sec. 153f of the (German) Code of Criminal Procedure, reprinted at marginal no. 265, fn. 470.

perpetrator does not realise that the order is unlawful and so far as it is also not manifestly unlawful.

Section 4
Responsibility of military commanders and other superiors

(1) A military commander or civilian superior who omits to prevent his or her subordinate from committing an offence pursuant to this Act shall be punished in the same way as a perpetrator of the offence committed by that subordinate. Section 13 subsection (2) of the Criminal Code shall not apply in this case.

(2) Any person effectively giving orders or exercising command and control in a unit shall be deemed equivalent to a military commander. Any person effectively exercising command and control in a civil organisation or in an enterprise shall be deemed equivalent to a civilian superior.

Section 5
Non-applicability of statute of limitations

The prosecution of serious criminal offences pursuant to this Act and the execution of sentences imposed on their account shall not be subject to any statute of limitations.

Part 2
Crimes against international law

Chapter 1
Genocide and crimes against humanity

Section 6
Genocide

(1) Whoever with the intent to destroy, in whole or in part, a national, racial, religious or ethnic group as such
   1. kills a member of the group,

2. causes serious bodily or mental harm to a member of the group, especially of the kind referred to in section 226 of the Criminal Code,

3. inflicts on the group conditions of life calculated to bring about its physical destruction in whole or in part,

4. imposes measures intended to prevent births within the group,

5. forcibly transfers a child of the group to another group

shall be punished with imprisonment for life.

(2) In less serious cases referred to under subsection (1), numbers 2 to 5, the punishment shall be imprisonment for not less than five years .

Section 7
Crimes against humanity

(1) Whoever, as part of a widespread or systematic attack directed against any civilian population,

1. kills a person,

2. inflicts, with the intent of destroying a population in whole or in part, conditions of life on that population or on parts thereof, being conditions calculated to bring about its physical destruction in whole or in part,

3. traffics in persons, particularly in women or children, or whoever enslaves a person in another way and in doing so arrogates to himself a right of ownership over that person,

4. deports or forcibly transfers, by expulsion or other coercive acts, a person lawfully present in an area to another State or another area in contravention of a general rule of international law,

5. tortures a person in his or her custody or otherwise under his or her control by causing that person substantial physical or mental harm or suffering where such harm or suffering does not arise only from sanctions that are compatible with international law,

6. sexually coerces, rapes, forces into prostitution or deprives a person of his or her reproductive capacity, or confines a woman forcibly made pregnant with the intent of affecting the ethnic composition of any population,

7. causes a person's enforced disappearance, with the intention of removing him or her from the protection of the law for a prolonged period of time,

   (a) by abducting that person on behalf of or with the approval of a State or a political organisation, or by otherwise severely depriving such person of his or her physical liberty, followed by a failure immediately to give truthful information, upon inquiry, on that person's fate and whereabouts, or

   (b) by refusing, on behalf of a State or of a political organisation or in contravention of a legal duty, to give information immediately on the fate and whereabouts of the person deprived of his or her physical liberty under the circumstances referred to under letter (a) above, or by giving false information thereon,

8. causes another person severe physical or mental harm, especially of the kind referred to in section 226 of the Criminal Code,

9. severely deprives, in contravention of a general rule of international law, a person of his or her physical liberty, or

10. persecutes an identifiable group or collectivity by depriving such group or collectivity of fundamental human rights, or by substantially restricting the same, on political, racial, national, ethnic, cultural or religious, gender or other grounds that are recognised as impermissible under the general rules of international law

shall be punished, in the cases referred to under numbers 1 and 2, with imprisonment for life, in the cases referred to under numbers 3 to 7, with imprisonment for not less than five years, and, in the cases referred to under numbers 8 to 10, with imprisonment for not less than three years.

(2) In less serious cases under subsection (1), number 2, the punishment shall be imprisonment for not less than five years, in less serious cases under subsection (1), numbers 3 to 7, imprisonment for not less than two years, and in less serious cases under sub-

section (1), numbers 8 and 9, imprisonment for not less than one year.

(3) Where the perpetrator causes the death of a person through an offence pursuant to subsection (1), numbers 3 to 10, the punishment shall be imprisonment for life or for not less than ten years in cases under subsection (1), numbers 3 to 7, and imprisonment for not less than five years in cases under subsection (1), numbers 8 to 10.

(4) In less serious cases under subsection (3) the punishment for an offence pursuant to subsection (1), numbers 3 to 7, shall be imprisonment for not less than five years, and for an offence pursuant to subsection (1), numbers 8 to 10, imprisonment for not less than three years.

(5) Whoever commits a crime pursuant to subsection (1) with the intention of maintaining an institutionalised regime of systematic oppression and domination by one racial group over any other shall be punished with imprisonment for not less than five years so far as the offence is not punishable more severely pursuant to subsection (1) or subsection (3). In less serious cases the punishment shall be imprisonment for not less than three years so far as the offence is not punishable more severely pursuant to subsection (2) or subsection (4).

Chapter 2
War crimes

Section 8
War crimes against persons

(1) Whoever in connection with an international armed conflict or with an armed conflict not of an international character
1. kills a person who is to be protected under international humanitarian law,
2. takes hostage a person who is to be protected under international humanitarian law,
3. treats a person who is to be protected under international humanitarian law cruelly or inhumanly by causing him or her substantial physical or mental harm or suffering, especially by torturing or mutilating that person,

4. sexually coerces, rapes, forces into prostitution or deprives a person who is to be protected under international humanitarian law of his or her reproductive capacity, or confines a woman forcibly made pregnant with the intent of affecting the ethnic composition of any population,
5. conscripts children under the age of fifteen years into the armed forces, or enlists them in the armed forces or in armed groups, or uses them to participate actively in hostilities,
6. deports or forcibly transfers, by expulsion or other coercive acts, a person who is to be protected under international humanitarian law and lawfully present in an area to another State or another area in contravention of a general rule of international law,
7. imposes on, or executes a substantial sentence, in particular the death penalty or imprisonment, in respect of a person who is to be protected under international humanitarian law, without that person having been sentenced in a fair and regular trial affording the legal guarantees required by international law,
8. exposes a person who is to be protected under international humanitarian law to the risk of death or of serious injury to health
    (a) by carrying out experiments on such a person, being a person who has not previously given his or her voluntary and express consent, or where the experiments concerned are neither medically necessary nor carried out in his or her interest,
    (b) by taking body tissue or organs from such a person for transplantation purposes so far as it does not constitute removal of blood or skin for therapeutic purposes in conformity with generally recognised medical principles and the person concerned has previously not given his or her voluntary and express consent, or
    (c) by using treatment methods that are not medically recognised on

such person, without this being necessary from a medical point of view and without the person concerned having previously given his or her voluntary and express consent,

9. treats a person who is to be protected under international humanitarian law in a gravely humiliating or degrading manner

shall be punished, in the cases referred to under number 1, with imprisonment for life, in the cases referred to under number 2, with imprisonment for not less than five years, in the cases referred to under numbers 3 to 5, with imprisonment for not less than three years, in the cases referred to under numbers 6 to 8, with imprisonment for not less than two years, and, in the cases referred to under number 9, with imprisonment for not less than one year.

(2) Whoever in connection with an international armed conflict or with an armed conflict not of an international character, wounds a member of the adverse armed forces or a combatant of the adverse party after the latter has surrendered unconditionally or is otherwise placed hors de combat shall be punished with imprisonment for not less than three years.

(3) Whoever in connection with an international armed conflict

1. unlawfully holds as a prisoner or unjustifiably delays the return home of a protected person within the meaning of subsection (6), number 1,

2. transfers, as a member of an Occupying Power, parts of its own civilian population into the occupied territory,

3. compels a protected person within the meaning of subsection (6), number 1, by force or threat of appreciable harm to serve in the forces of a hostile Power or

4. compels a national of the adverse party by force or threat of appreciable harm to take part in the operations of war directed against his or her own country

shall be punished with imprisonment for not less than two years.

(4) Where the perpetrator causes the death of the victim through an offence pursuant to subsection (1), numbers 2 to 6, the punishment shall, in the cases referred to under subsection (1), number 2, be imprisonment for life or imprisonment for not less than ten years, in the cases referred to under subsection (1), numbers 3 to 5, imprisonment for not less than five years, and, in the cases referred to under subsection (1), number 6, imprisonment for not less than three years. Where an act referred to under subsection (1), number 8, causes death or serious harm to health, the punishment shall be imprisonment for not less than three years.

(5) In less serious cases referred to under subsection (1), number 2, the punishment shall be imprisonment for not less than two years, in less serious cases referred to under subsection (1), numbers 3 and 4, and under subsection (2) the punishment shall be imprisonment for not less than one year, in less serious cases referred to under subsection (1), number 6, and under subsection (3), number 1, the punishment shall be imprisonment from six months to five years.

(6) Persons who are to be protected under international humanitarian law shall be

1. in an international armed conflict: persons protected for the purposes of the Geneva Conventions and of the Protocol Additional to the Geneva Conventions (Protocol I) (...), namely the wounded, the sick, the shipwrecked, prisoners of war and civilians;

2. in an armed conflict not of an international character: the wounded, the sick, the shipwrecked as well as persons taking no active part in the hostilities who are in the power of the adverse party;

3. in an international armed conflict and in an armed conflict not of an international character: members of armed forces and combatants of the adverse party, both of whom have laid down their arms or have no other means of defence.

Section 9
War crimes against property and other rights

(1) Whoever in connection with an international armed conflict or with an armed conflict not of an international character pillages or, unless this is imperatively demanded by the necessities of the armed conflict, otherwise extensively destroys, appropriates or seizes property of the adverse party contrary to international law, such property being in the power of the perpetrator's party, shall be punished with imprisonment from one to ten years.

(2) Whoever in connection with an international armed conflict and contrary to international law declares the rights and actions of all, or of a substantial proportion of, the nationals of the hostile party abolished, suspended or inadmissible in a court of law shall be punished with imprisonment from one to ten years.

Section 10
War crimes against humanitarian operations and emblems

(1) Whoever in connection with an international armed conflict or with an armed conflict not of an international character
   1. directs an attack against personnel, installations, material, units or vehicles involved in a humanitarian assistance or peacekeeping mission in accordance with the Charter of the United Nations, as long as they are entitled to the protection given to civilians or civilian objects under international humanitarian law, or
   2. directs an attack against personnel, buildings, material, medical units and transport, using the distinctive emblems of the Geneva Conventions in conformity with international humanitarian law

shall be punished with imprisonment for not less than three years. In less serious cases, particularly where the attack does not take place by military means, the punishment shall be imprisonment for not less than one year.

(2) Whoever in connection with an international armed conflict or with an armed conflict not of an international character makes improper use of the distinctive emblems of the Geneva Conventions, of the flag of truce, of the flag or of the military insignia or of the uniform of the enemy or of the United Nations, thereby causing a person's death or serious personal injury (section 226 of the Criminal Code) shall be punished with imprisonment for not less than five years.

Section 11
War crimes consisting in the use of prohibited methods of warfare

(1) Whoever in connection with an international armed conflict or with an armed conflict not of an international character
   1. directs an attack by military means against the civilian population as such or against individual civilians not taking direct part in hostilities,
   2. directs an attack by military means against civilian objects, so long as these objects are protected as such by international humanitarian law, namely buildings dedicated to religion, education, art, science or charitable purposes, historic monuments, hospitals and places where the sick and wounded are collected, or against undefended towns, villages, dwellings or buildings, or against demilitarised zones, or against works and installations containing dangerous forces,
   3. carries out an attack by military means and definitely anticipates that the attack will cause death or injury to civilians or damage to civilian objects on a scale out of proportion to the concrete and direct overall military advantage anticipated,
   4. uses a person who is to be protected under international humanitarian law as a shield to restrain a hostile party from undertaking operations of war against certain targets,
   5. uses starvation of civilians as a method of warfare by depriving them of objects indispensable to their survival or impedes relief supplies in contravention of international humanitarian law,

6. orders or threatens, as a commander, that no quarter will be given, or
7. treacherously kills or wounds a member of the hostile armed forces or a combatant of the adverse party

shall be punished with imprisonment for not less than three years. In less serious cases under number 2 the punishment shall be imprisonment for not less than one year.

(2) Where the perpetrator causes the death or serious injury of a civilian (section 226 of the Criminal Code) or of a person who is to be protected under international humanitarian law through an offence pursuant to subsection (1), numbers 1 to 6, he shall be punished with imprisonment for not less than five years. Where the perpetrator intentionally causes death, the punishment shall be imprisonment for life or for not less than ten years.

(3) Whoever in connection with an international armed conflict carries out an attack by military means and definitely anticipates that the attack will cause widespread, long-term and severe damage to the natural environment on a scale out of proportion to the concrete and direct overall military advantage anticipated shall be punished with imprisonment for not less than three years.

Section 12
War crimes consisting in employment of prohibited means of warfare

(1) Whoever in connection with an international armed conflict or with an armed conflict not of an international character
1. employs poison or poisoned weapons,
2. employs biological or chemical weapons or
3. employs bullets which expand or flatten easily in the human body, in particular bullets with a hard envelope which does not entirely cover the core or is pierced with incisions

shall be punished with imprisonment for not less than three years.

(2) Where the perpetrator causes the death or serious injury (section 226 of the Criminal Code) of a civilian or of a person protected under international humanitarian law through an offence pursuant to subsection (1), he shall be punished with imprisonment

for not less than five years. Where the perpetrator intentionally causes death, the punishment shall be imprisonment for life or for not less than ten years.

Chapter 3
Other crimes

Section 13
Violation of the duty of supervision

(1) A military commander who intentionally or negligently omits properly to supervise a subordinate under his or her command or under his or her effective control shall be punished for violation of the duty of supervision if the subordinate commits an offence pursuant to this Act, where the imminent commission of such an offence was discernible to the commander and he or she could have prevented it.

(2) A civilian superior who intentionally or negligently omits properly to supervise a subordinate under his or her authority or under his or her effective control shall be punished for violation of the duty of supervision if the subordinate commits an offence pursuant to this Act, where the imminent commission of such an offence was discernible to the superior without more and he or she could have prevented it.

(3) Section 4 subsection (2) shall apply mutatis mutandis.

(4) Intentional violation of the duty of supervision shall be punished with imprisonment for not more than five years, and negligent violation of the duty of supervision shall be punished with imprisonment for not more than three years.

Section 14
Omission to report a crime

(1) A military commander or a civilian superior who omits immediately to draw the attention of the agency responsible for the investigation or prosecution of any offence pursuant to this Act, to such an offence committed by a subordinate, shall be punished with imprisonment for not more than five years.

(2) Section 4 subsection (2) shall apply mutatis mutandis.

Appendix 2:
Table of Cases

Table of Cases

The figures below refer to marginal numbers, including footnotes within them.

A. Yugoslavia Tribunal

Aleksovski

ICTY (Trial Chamber I), judgment of 25 June 1999, case no. IT-95-14/1-T:	320, 362, 372, 394, 846, 905, 920, 922
ICTY (Appeals Chamber), judgment of 24 March 2000, case no. IT-95-14/1-A:	87, 149, 158, 363, 372, 378, 390, 809, 840, 869, 871, 922

Banović

ICTY (Trial Chambers III), judgment of 28 October 2003, case no. IT-02-65/1-T:	465, 468

Blaškić

ICTY (Trial Chamber I), judgment of 3 March 2000, case no. IT-95-14-T:	320, 358, 362, 372, 377, 389-390, 394, 542, 647, 649, 655-657, 659, 661, 663, 669, 671, 675, 677, 737, 739, 741, 743, 745, 767, 840, 857, 870, 876, 878, 904-905, 958-959, 962, 996, 1017, 1091, 1095
ICTY (Appeals Chamber), judgment (on the Request of the Republic Croatia for Review of the Decision of Trial Chamber II of 18 July 1997) of 29 October 1997, case no. IT-95-14:	511-512, 515-516
ICTY (Appeals Chamber), judgment of 29 July 2004, case no. IT-95-14-A:	324, 330, 334, 361-362, 375, 383, 392, 540, 870

Češić

ICTY (Trial Chamber), judgment of 11 March 2004, case no. IT-95-10/1-S:	377, 468, 538

Mucić et al. ("Čelebići")

ICTY (Trial Chamber II), judgment of 16 November 1998, case no. IT-96-21-T:	91, 159, 270, 273, 290, 295-296, 334, 342, 369, 372, 375, 377-378, 384, 390-393, 464-466, 492, 505, 712-713, 719, 725-726, 822, 846-847, 865, 871, 875-876, 878, 885, 887-889, 891-892, 903-905, 910, 952-953, 989, 995
ICTY (Appeals Chamber), judgment of 20 February 2001, case no. IT-96-21-A:	149-150, 320, 372, 375, 377, 383, 390, 464, 466-468, 534-536, 542, 871, 1145

Deronjić
ICTY (Trial Chamber II), judgment of 30 March 2004, case no. IT-02-61-S: 85, 95

Erdemović
ICTY (Appeals Chamber), judgment of 7 October 1997, case no. IT-96-22-A: 423, 429-432, 434, 457, 645

Furundžija
ICTY (Trial Chamber II), judgment of 10 December 1998, case no. IT-95-17/1-T: 123, 134, 140, 144, 146, 152, 154, 361, 515-516, 553, 712, 715-716, 719, 725-726, 822, 889, 910, 923

ICTY (Appeals Chamber), judgment of 21 July 2000, case no. IT-95-17/1-A: 347, 712, 716

Galić
ICTY (Trial Chamber I), judgment of 5 December 2003, case no. IT-98-29-T: 538, 666, 768, 1018, 1020-1022

Hadžihasanović
ICTY (Appeals Chamber), decision on Interlocutory Appeal Challenging Jurisdiction in Relation to Command Responsibility of 16 July 2003, case no. IT-01-47-AR72:   372, 386

Jelisić
ICTY (Trial Chamber I), judgment of 14 December 1999, case no. IT-95-10-T: 92, 566, 569, 578, 606, 615-616, 618, 620-621, 647, 649, 657, 669, 675, 677

ICTY (Appeals Chamber I), judgment of 5 July 2001, case no. IT-95-10-A: 91, 535, 538, 606, 615-616, 618, 622, 769

Jokić
ICTY (Trial Chamber I), judgment of 18 March 2004, case no. IT-01-42/1-S: 85

Karadžić and Mladić
ICTY (Trial Chamber), Review of the Indictments Pursuant to Rule 61 of the Rules of Procedure and Evidence of 11 July 1996, case no. IT-95-5/18-R61:   595, 597, 604-605, 622

Kordić and Čerkez
ICTY (Trial Chamber III), judgment of 26 February 2001, case no. IT-95-14/2-T: 149, 210, 358, 381, 408-409, 419, 491, 505, 647, 649, 659, 666, 669, 671, 675, 677, 706, 737, 739-741, 743-745, 767, 769, 857, 875, 892, 1000-1001

Krstić
ICTY (Trial Chamber I), judgment of 2 August 2001, case no. IT-98-33-T: 133, 235, 357-358, 371, 491, 538, 698

ICTY (Appeals Chamber), judgment of 19   535, 538-539
April 2004, case no. IT-98-33-A:

Krnojelac
ICTY (Trial Chamber II), judgment of 15   342, 361-362, 659, 666, 669, 675, 685, 687,
March 2002, case no. IT-97-25-T: 689, 692, 698-699, 706-708, 716, 719, 737,
                                               740-741, 771, 933

ICTY (Appeals Chamber), judgment of 17   349, 363, 383
September 2003, case no. IT-97-25-A:

Kunarac et al.
ICTY (Trial Chamber II), judgment of 22 Feb-   647-648, 653, 655-656, 666, 669-670, 685,
ruary 2001, case no. IT-96-23/-23/1-T: 687, 689, 692, 712, 716, 718-719, 725, 727-
                                               728, 769, 888-889, 919-921

ICTY (Appeals Chamber), judgment of 12   531, 535, 537-539, 641, 647, 651, 656, 666,
June 2002, case no. IT-96-23/-23/1-A: 670, 685-689, 712-713, 716, 719, 725-726,
                                               769, 771, 809, 847, 888, 890

Kupreškić et al.   52, 85, 123, 149, 296, 334, 479-480, 484,
ICTY (Trial Chamber II), judgment of 14   535, 538, 542, 647, 649-650, 659, 663, 665-
January 2000, case no. IT-95-16-T: 666, 669, 671, 675-677, 737, 739, 741, 743-
                                               745, 766-767, 795, 813, 1027, 1053

ICTY (Appeals Chamber), judgment of 23 Oc-   348, 538, 769
tober 2001, case no. IT-95-16-A:

Kvočka et al.
ICTY (Trial Chamber I), judgment of 2 No-   342, 345-347, 358-359, 361-362, 474, 539,
vember 2001, case no. IT-98-30/1-T: 669, 675, 677, 713, 715-716, 719, 725-726,
                                               737, 739, 741, 767, 771, 904

Milošević
ICTY (Trial Chamber III), decision of 8 No-   522
vember 2001, case no. IT-02-54:

Mrđja
ICTY (Trial Chamber), judgment of 31 March   429
2004, case no. IT-02-59-S:

Naletilić and Martinović
ICTY (Trial Chamber I), judgment of 31   85, 357-359, 361, 371, 534-535, 540, 651-
March 2003, case no. IT-98-34-T: 652, 703, 738, 822, 832, 840, 865, 871, 875,
                                               891, 903-905, 927, 965, 967, 996, 1000-1001,
                                               1004

D. Nikolić
ICTY (Trial Chamber II), judgment of 18 De-   95, 539
cember 2003, case no. IT-94-2-S:

Simić
ICTY (Trial Chamber II), judgment of 17 Oc-   666, 737, 739, 745
tober 2003, case no. IT-95-9-T

Stakić
ICTY (Trial Chamber II), judgment of 31 July   330, 335, 351-352, 357, 390, 491, 538-540,
2003, case no. IT-97-24-T: 653, 676, 700, 702, 737, 741, 878

Tadić
ICTY (Trial Chamber), decision on the Prose-   46, 808
cutor's Motion Requesting Protective Measures
for Victims and Witnesses of 10 August 1995,
case no. IT-94-1:

ICTY (Appeals Chamber), decision on the De-   52, 79, 92, 127-131, 156-157, 159, 171, 652,
fence Motion for Interlocutory Appeal on Ju-   806-810, 813-814, 822, 827, 842-845, 847,
risdiction of 2 October 1995, case no.   868, 922, 994, 1054, 1129, 1166
IT-94-1-A:

ICTY (Trial Chamber II), judgment of 7 May   327, 362, 492, 647-649, 652, 654-656, 659-
1997, case no. IT-94-1-T: 660, 663, 669, 671, 737, 739-741, 743, 746,
                                                748, 767, 829, 838, 847, 851, 855, 865

ICTY (Appeals Chamber), judgment of 15 July   52, 144, 146, 150-151, 158, 160, 257, 334,
1999, case no. IT-94-1-A: 338, 342, 345-352, 363, 503, 641, 669, 671,
                                                838-840, 869

ICTY (Appeals Chamber), judgment on Alle-   74, 665
gations of Contempt Against Prior Council of
31 January 2000, case no. IT-94-1-A-R77:

Todorović
ICTY (Trial Chamber I), judgment of 31 July   464
2001, case no. IT-95-9/1-S:

Vasiljević
ICTY (Trial Chamber II), judgment of 29 No-   320, 346-347, 363, 531, 533, 678, 681-682,
vember 2002, case no. IT-98-32-T: 737, 741, 768, 847, 857

ICTY (Appeals Chamber), judgment of 25   361, 363
February 2004, case no. IT-98-32-A

B. Rwanda Tribunal

Akayesu
ICTR (Trial Chamber I), judgment of 2 Sep-   55, 214, 361, 372, 505, 535, 538, 562, 566,
tember 1998, case no. ICTR-96-4-T: 569, 571, 574-576, 580-582, 584, 586, 588,
                                                590-592, 595, 597, 603, 615-616, 622-624,
                                                626-627, 647, 653, 655-656, 659, 675, 677,
                                                679, 682, 712, 716, 719, 725-726, 734, 748,
                                                809, 814, 828, 848, 878, 889, 891, 923, 983

ICTR (Appeals Chamber), judgment of 1 June   358, 641, 671, 849, 851
2001, case no. ICTR-96-4-A:

Bagilishema
ICTR (Trial Chamber I), judgment of 7 June   577, 588, 616, 618, 622, 651, 657, 659, 677,
2001, case no. ICTR-95-1A-T: 679, 682, 767

ICTR (Appeals Chamber II), judgment of 3   382-384
July 2002, case no. ICTR-95-1A-A:

Kajelijeli
ICTR (Trial Chamber II), judgment of 1 De-   345, 653, 681
cember 2003, case no. ICTR-98-44A-T:

Kambanda
ICTR (Trial Chamber I), judgment of 4 Sep-   214, 372, 379, 521, 626
tember 1998, case no. ICTR-97-23-S:

ICTR (Appeals Chamber), judgment of 19 Oc-   214, 626
tober 2000, case no. ICTR-97-23-A:

Kamuhanda
ICTR (Trial Chamber II), judgment of 22   357, 362, 377, 386, 535, 537, 577, 621, 666,
January 2004, case no. ICTR-98-54A-T: 681

Kanyabashi
ICTR (Trial Chamber II), decision on the De-   814
fence Motion on Jurisdiction of 18 June 1997,
case no. ICTR-96-15-T:

Kayishema and Ruzindana
ICTR (Trial Chamber II), judgment of 21 May   335, 372, 379, 390, 538, 576, 581, 584, 590-
1999, case no. ICTR-95-1-T: 592, 595, 603, 606, 615-616, 618, 621-622,
                                                 630, 647, 651, 656, 659, 677, 679-682, 767-
                                                 768, 848, 852, 1017

Musema
ICTR (Trial Chamber I), judgment of 27   334, 377, 379, 577, 653, 675-677, 679-680,
January 2000, case no. ICTR-96-13-T: 682, 725, 767, 887, 920

ICTR (Appeals Chamber), judgment of 16   531, 534, 537-538, 631, 769
November 2001, case no. ICTR-96-13-A:

Ntagerura et al. (Cyangugu)
ICTR (Trial Chamber III), judgment of 25   375
February 2004, case no. ICTR-99-46-T:

Nahimana et al.
ICTR (Trial Chamber I), judgment of 3 De-   379, 625, 740
cember 2003, case no. ICTR-96-11-T:

Ntakirutimana, E. and G.
ICTR (Trial Chamber I), judgment of 21 Feb-   378, 534, 538, 681
ruary 2003, case no. ICTR-96-10-T/ICTR-96-
17-T:

Niyitegeka
ICTR (Trial Chamber I), judgment of 16 May   87, 626
2003, case no. ICTR-96-14-T:

Ruggiu
ICTR (Trial Chamber I), judgment of 1 June   623, 625-627
2000, case no. ICTR-97-32-I:

Rutaganda
ICTR (Trial Chamber I), judgment of 6 De-   491, 577, 616, 653, 675, 677, 679-680, 682,
cember 1999, case no. ICTR-96-3-T: 809, 983

Semanza
ICTR (Trial Chamber III), judgment of 15   357-358, 361-362, 372, 375, 534, 577, 621-
May 2003, case no. ICTR-97-20-T: 622, 653, 666, 677, 681, 716, 737

Serushago
ICTR (Trial Chamber I), judgment of 5 Feb-   372
ruary 1999, case no. ICTR-98-39-S:

C. International Military Tribunal (Nuremberg)

IMT, judgment of 1 October 1946, in *The*   15, 22-27, 92, 295, 340, 455-456, 484, 489,
Trial of German Major War Criminals. Proceed- 517, 521, 561, 659, 691, 742, 753, 790, 801,
ings of the International Military Tribunal sitting 1163-1170, 1174-1181
at Nuremberg, Germany, Part 22 (22nd August,
1946 to 1st October, 1946):

D. International Military Tribunal for the Far East (Tokyo)

International Military Tribunal for the Far   15-16, 30-33, 637, 801, 1162, 1165-1167,
East, judgment of 12 November 1948, in John   1170, 1174, 1176
Pritchard and Sonia M. Zaide (eds.), *The Tokyo*
War Crimes Trial, Vols. 1-22 (1981):

E. Permanent Court of International Justice/International Court of Justice

Permanent Court of International Justice,   172
judgment of 7 September 1927 (France v. Turkey), in *Publications of the Permanent Court of*
International Justice, Series A: Collection of
Judgements, No. 10, The Case of the S.S. "Lotus":

ICJ, Advisory Opinion of 28 May 1951 (Reser-   42, 562, 566
vation to the Convention on the Prevention
and Punishment of Genocide), in *ICJ Reports*
1951, paras. 23 et seq.:

ICJ, judgment of 27 June 1986 (Nicaragua v.   838, 1160
USA), in *ICJ Reports* 1986, paras. 14 et seq.:

ICJ, decision of 14 April 1991 (Case Concern-   183
ing Questions of Interpretation and Application of the 1971 Montreal Convention Arising
from Aerial Incident at Lockerbie, Libyan Arab
Jamahiriya v. United Kingdom), in *ICJ Reports*
1992, paras. 3 et seq.:

ICJ, judgment of 11 July 1996 (Case Concern-   99, 174
ing Application of the Convention on the Prevention and Punishment of the Crime of
Genocide, Bosnia and Herzegovina v. Yugoslavia), in *ICJ Reports* 1996, paras. 13 et seq.:

ICJ, Advisory Opinion of 8 July 1996 (Case   1104, 1118
Concerning the Legality of the Threat or Use
of Nuclear Weapons), in *ICJ Reports* 1996, pp.
226 et seq.:

ICJ, judgment of 12 December 1996 (Case   158
concerning Oil Platforms, Iran v. USA), in *ICJ
Reports* 1996, paras. 803 et seq.:

ICJ, judgment of 14 February 2002 (Case   171-172, 235, 513, 515, 519, 525
Concerning the Arrest Warrant of 11 April
2000, DR Congo v. Belgium), available at
<http://www.icj-cij.org/icjwww/idocket/
iCOBE/icobejudgment/icobe_ijudgment_
20020214.PDF>

F. US Military Tribunals at Nuremberg

Karl Brandt et al. (so-called Medical Trial)
US Military Tribunal Nuremberg, judgment of   38, 372, 436, 489, 508, 733, 767, 900
20 August 1947, in *Trials of War Criminals be-
fore the Nuremberg Military Tribunals under
Control Council Law No. 10*, Vol. II, pp. 171 et
seq.:

Erhard Milch
US Military Tribunal Nuremberg, judgment of   38, 482, 508, 691, 900
17 April 1947, in *Trials of War Criminals before
the Nuremberg Military Tribunals under Control
Council Law No. 10*, Vol. II, pp. 773 et seq.:

Josef Altstötter et al. (so-called Justice Trial)
US Military Tribunal Nuremberg, judgment of   38, 753, 940-941
4 December 1947, in *Trials of War Criminals
before the Nuremberg Military Tribunals under
Control Council Law No. 10*, Vol. III, pp. 954
et seq.:

Oswald Pohl et al.
US Military Tribunal Nuremberg, judgment of   38, 382, 489
3 November 1947, in *Trials of War Criminals before the Nuremberg Military Tribunals under Control Council Law No. 10*, Vol. V, pp. 958 et seq.:

Friedrich Flick et al.
US Military Tribunal Nuremberg, judgment of   38, 424, 743
22 December 1947, in *Trials of War Criminals before the Nuremberg Military Tribunals under Control Council Law No. 10*, Vol. VI, 1187 et seq.:

Carl Krauch et al. (so-called IG Farben Trial)
US Military Tribunal Nuremberg, judgment of   38, 482, 743, 1162
29 July 1948, in *Trials of War Criminals before the Nuremberg Military Tribunals under Control Council Law No. 10*, Vol. VIII, pp. 1081 et seq.:

Wilhelm List et al. (so-called Hostages Trial)
US Military Tribunal Nuremberg, judgment of   38, 372, 382, 455, 959
19 February 1948, in *Trials of War Criminals before the Nuremberg Military Tribunals under Control Council Law No. 10*, Vol. XI, pp. 1230 et seq.:

Ulrich Greifelt et al. (so-called RuSHA Trial)
US Military Tribunal Nuremberg, judgment of   38
10 March 1948, in *Trials of War Criminals before the Nuremberg Military Tribunals under Control Council Law No. 10*, Vol. V, pp. 88 et seq.:

Otto Ohlendorf et al. (so-called Einsatzgruppen Trial)
US Military Tribunal Nuremberg, judgment of   38, 295, 377, 455
10 April 1948, in *Trials of War Criminals before the Nuremberg Military Tribunals under Control Council Law No. 10*, Vol. IV, pp. 411 et seq.:

Alfred Krupp et al. (so-called Krupp Trial)
US Military Tribunal Nuremberg judgment of   38, 1162
31 July 1948, in *Trials of War Criminals before the Nuremberg Military Tribunals under Control Council Law No. 10*, Vol. IX, pp. 1327 et seq.:

Wilhelm von Leeb et al. (so-called High Command Trial)
US Military Tribunal Nuremberg, judgment of   38, 372, 455, 489, 508, 1162, 1176
28 October 1948, in *Trials of War Criminals*
before the Nuremberg Military Tribunals under
Control Council Law No. 10, Vol. XI, pp. 462
et seq.:

Ernst von Weizsäcker et al. (so-called Ministries Trial)
US Military Tribunal Nuremberg, judgment of   38, 378, 925, 1162
11 April 1949, in *Trials of War Criminals before*
the Nuremberg Military Tribunals under Control
Council Law No. 10, Vol. XIV, pp. 308 et seq.

G. Inter-American Court of Human Rights

Inter-American Court of Human Rights, judg-   181
ment of 29 July 1988 (Velázquez Rodriguez),
in 28 *ILM* (1989), pp. 291 et seq.:

H. National Courts

I. Australia

Ivan Polyukhovich
High Court, judgment of 14 August 1991, in   43
91 *ILR* (1993), pp. 1 et seq.:

II. Canada

Imre Finta
Ontario High Court of Justice, judgment of 25   43, 155, 640
May 1990, in 82 *ILR* (1990), pp. 424 et seq.

Ontario Court of Appeal, judgment of 20 April   43, 155, 640
1992, in 98 *ILR* (1994), pp. 520 et seq.:

Supreme Court of Canada, judgment of 24   43, 155, 640
March 1994, in 104 *ILR* (1997), pp. 284 et
seq.:

Kurt Meyer (so-called Abbaye Ardenne Trial)
Canadian Military Court Aurich, judgment of   883, 1074, 1077
28 December 1945, in UNWCC, *Law Reports*
of Trials of War Criminals, Vol. IV, pp. 97 et
seq.:

III. France

Klaus Barbie
Cour de Cassation, judgment of 6 October   43, 155
1983, in 78 *ILR* (1988), pp. 124 et seq.:

Cour de Cassation, judgment of 26 January   43, 155, 553
1984, in 78 *ILR* (1988), pp. 126 et seq.:

Cour de Cassation, judgment of 20 December   43, 155, 640
1985, in 78 *ILR* (1988), pp. 136 et seq.:

Cour de Cassation, judgment of 3 June 1988,   43, 155, 640
in 100 *ILR* (1995), pp. 331 et seq.:

Paul Touvier
Cour de Appelle de Paris, judgment of 13 April   155
1992, in 100 *ILR* (1995), pp. 338 et seq.:

Cour de Cassation, judgment of 27 November   155
1992, in 100 ILR (1995), pp. 357 et seq.:

Moammar Qaddafi
Cour de Cassation, judgment of 13 March   525
2001, in *Bulletin des arrets de la Cour de Cassa-*
tion (2001), pp. 218 et seq.:

IV. Great Britain

Heinz Eck et al. (so-called Peleus Trial)
British Military Court Hamburg, judgment of   1074
20 October 1945, in UNWCC, *Law Reports of*
Trials of War Criminals, Vol. I, pp. 1 et seq.:

Erich Heyer et al. (so-called Essen Lynching
Trial)
British Military Court Essen, judgment of 10   852
May 1946, in UNWCC, *Law Reports of Trials*
of War Criminals, Vol. I, pp. 88 et seq.:

Kurt Student
British Military Court Lueneburg, judgment of   1091
10 May 1946, in UNWCC, *Law Reports of*
Trials of War Criminals, Vol. IV, pp. 118 et
seq.:

Max Wielen (so-called Stalag Luft III Trial)
British Military Court Hamburg, judgment of   883
3 September 1947, in UNWCC, *Law Reports*
of Trials of War Crimes Criminals, Vol. XI, pp.
30 et seq.:

Augusto Pinochet
High Court of Justice, judgment of 28 October 1998, in 38 *ILM* (1999), pp. 68 et seq.:   519

House of Lords, judgment of 25 November 1998, in 37 *ILM* (1998), pp. 1302 et seq.:   519

House of Lords, judgment of 24 March 1999, in 38 *ILM* (1999), 581 et seq.:   519

V. Israel

Adolf Eichmann
District Court of Jerusalem, judgment of 12 December 1961, in 36 *ILR* (1968), pp. 18 et seq.:   43, 155, 566, 595, 640

Supreme Court, judgment of 29 May 1962, in 36 *ILR* (1968), pp. 277 et seq.:   43, 155, 640

VI. Netherlands

Pieter Menten
Supreme Court, judgment of 13 January 1981, in 75 *ILR* (1987), pp. 362 et seq.:   659

VII. Nigeria

Pius Nwaoga
Supreme Court of Nigeria, judgment of 3 March 1972, in 52 *ILR* (1979), pp. 494 et seq.:   1059

VIII. Poland

Rudolf Höß
Supreme National Tribunal of Poland, judgment of 29 March 1947, in UNWCC, *Law Reports of Trials of War Criminals*, Vol. VII, pp. 11 et seq.:   900

IX. Spain

Augusto Pinochet
Audiencia Nacional, judgment of 5 November 1998, available at <http://www.ua.es/up/pinochet/documentos/chile.html>:   572, 580, 618

X. United States of America

Tomoyuki Yamashita
US Military Commission Manila, judgment of 4 February 1946, in UNWCC, *Law Reports of Trials of War Criminals*, Vol. IV, pp. 1 et seq.:   372

Shigeru Sawada
US Military Commission Shanghai, judgment   940
of 15 April 1946, in UNWCC, *Law Reports of*
Trials of War Criminals, Vol. V, pp. 1 et seq.:

Anton Dostler
US Military Commission Rome, judgment of   1074
12 October 1945, in UNWCC, *Law Reports of*
Trials of War Criminals, Vol. I, pp. 22 et seq.:

John (Ivan) Demjanjuk
Court of Appeals, judgment of 31 October   155
1985, in 79 *ILR* (1989), pp. 534 et seq.:

J. German Courts

I. Supreme Court in the British Occupied Zone

Judgment of 25 May 1948, case no. Sts 1/48,   652
in 1 *OGHSt*, pp. 6 et seq.:

Judgment of 22 June 1948, case no. Sts 5/48,   652
in 1 *OGHSt*, pp. 19 et seq.:

Judgment of 27 July 1948, case no. Sts 19/48,   650
in 1 *OGHSt*, pp. 45 et seq.:

Judgment of 28 September 1948, case no. Sts   652
32/48, in 1 *OGHSt*, pp. 91 et seq.:

Judgment of 19 October 1948, case no. Sts 56/   652
48, in 1 *OGHSt*, pp. 105 et seq.:

Judgment of 26 October 1948, case no. Sts 57/   652
48, in 1 *OGHSt*, pp. 122 et seq.:

Judgment of 2 November 1948, case no. Sts   652
64/48, in 1 *OGHSt*, pp. 141 et seq.:

Judgment of 22 February 1949, case no. Sts   430
89/48, in 1 *OGHSt*, pp. 310 et seq.:

Judgment of 5 March 1949, case no. Sts 19/49,   483
in 1 *OGHSt*, pp. 322 et seq.:

Judgment of 18 October 1949, case no. Sts   650
309/49, in 2 *OGHSt*, pp. 231 et seq.:

Judgment of 12 December 1949, case no. Sts   290
365/49, in 2 *OGHSt*, pp. 291 et seq.:

II. Federal Constitutional Court (Bundesverfassungsgericht)

Decision of 31 March 1987, case no. 2 BvM 2/   237
86, in 75 *BVerfGE*, pp. 1 et seq.:

Decision of 12 December 2000, case no. 2 BvR   236, 242
1290/99, in *Neue Juristische Wochenschrift*
2001, pp. 1848 et seq.:

III. Federal Supreme Court (Bundesgerichtshof)

Decision of 13 February 1994, case no. 1 BGs   242
100/94, in *Neue Zeitschrift für Strafrecht* 1994,
pp. 232 et seq.:

Judgment of 20 March 1995, case no. 5 StR   242
111/94, in 41 *BGHSt*, pp. 101 et seq.:

Decision of 11 December 1998, case no. 2 ARs   242
499/98, in *Neue Zeitschrift für Strafrecht* 1999,
pp. 236 et seq.:

Judgment of 30 April 1999, case no. 3 StR   236, 242, 264, 630
215/98, in 45 *BGHSt*, pp. 64 et seq.:

Judgment of 21 February 2001, case no. 3 StR   180, 236, 242
372/00, in 46 *BGHSt*, pp. 292 et seq.:

Judgment of 21 February 2001, case no. 3 StR   616
244/00, in *Neue Juristische Wochenschrift* 2001,
pp. 2732 et seq.:

IV. Other Courts

Federal Social Security Court (Bundessozial-
gericht)
Judgment of 14 December 1978, case no. Az 1   824
RA 73/77, in 47 *BSGE*, pp. 263 et seq.:

Bavarian Highest Regional Court (Bayerisches
Oberstes Landesgericht)
Judgment of 23 May 1997, case no. 3 St 20/   242
96, in *Neue Juristische Wochenschrift* 1998, p.
392:

District Court of Cologne (Landgericht Köln)
Judgment of 9 July 1980, case no. 31-18/80, in   263
Neue Zeitschrift für Strafrecht 1981, 263 pp.
261:

V. Supreme Court of the German Democratic Republic

Hans Globke
Judgment of 23 July 1963, in *Neue Justiz* 1963,   640
pp. 449 et seq.:

Horst Fischer
Judgment of 25 March 1966, in *Neue Justiz*   640
1966, pp. 193 et seq.:

Appendix 3:
Table of Statutes and International Instruments

Table of Statutes and International Instruments

The figures below refer to marginal numbers, including footnotes within them.

I. Statutes of International Courts and Tribunals, and Control Council Law No. 10

1. Control Council Law No. 10:

34-39, 144, 146, 155, 239, 247, 489
Art. II: 36
Art. II(1)(a): 341, 487, 1162, 1168, 1176, 1178, 1180
Art. II(1)(c): 637-638, 659, 666, 675, 678, 684, 696, 704, 710, 722-723, 736, 747, 766
Art. II(2): 341, 487
Art. II(4)(a): 516
Art. II(4)(b): 455-456
Art. III: 36

2. ICC Statute:

5, 56, 66-70, 125-128, 138-141, 158-159, 166, 184, 186, 192, 196, 199, 201-204, 216-219, 221-223, 235-236, 243-245, 251, 266, 269, 275-277, 290, 298, 307, 311-312, 331, 354, 362, 405-406, 436, 460, 465, 468, 478, 486, 492, 497, 507, 518, 524, 642, 654, 796, 1055, 1098, 1148, 1167, 1176, 1182, 1184-1189
Preamble: 74, 77-79, 87, 100, 178, 186, 199
Art. 1: 79, 119-121, 199, 217
Art. 2: 121
Art. 3: 121
Art. 5: 120, 280
Art. 5(1): 69, 94, 120, 201
Art. 5(1), Sentence 1: 74, 79, 994, 1006
Art. 5(1), Sentence 2: 121
Art. 5(1)(d): 201, 1149, 1165
Art. 5(2): 62, 201, 1149
Art. 6: 69, 138, 201, 222, 277-278, 280, 311, 313, 324, 329, 336, 548, 550, 562, 564, 586, 607-609
Art. 6(a): 254, 587-589, 613, 675
Art. 6(b): 254, 587-588, 590-592
Art. 6(c): 587-588, 593-596, 612
Art. 6(d): 587-588, 597, 612
Art. 6(e): 254, 564, 587-588, 598-603, 614
Art. 7: 69, 138, 201, 222, 255, 277, 280, 326,

336, 643, 690, 769
Art. 7(1): 278, 318, 327, 644, 646-657, 669, 672, 761, 767
Art. 7(1)(a): 334, 675-677, 875
Art. 7(1)(b): 335, 504, 678-682
Art. 7(1)(c): 684-689, 690, 693, 933
Art. 7(1)(d): 696-703, 964
Art. 7(1)(e): 704-708
Art. 7(1)(f): 710-720, 888
Art. 7(1)(g): 324, 722-734
- Alt. 1: 723-727
- Alt. 2: 728
- Alt. 3: 729-730
- Alt. 4: 482, 731-732
- Alt. 5: 733
- Alt. 6: 734, 915
Art. 7(1)(h): 324, 671, 736-751
Art. 7(1)(i): 753-757
Art. 7(1)(j): 759-765
Art. 7(1)(k): 290, 311-312, 766-768
Art. 7(2)(a): 646-665
Art. 7(2)(b): 311, 504, 679-682
Art. 7(2)(c): 685-689, 934
Art. 7(2)(d): 697-703
Art. 7(2)(e): 311, 711-720
Art. 7(2)(f): 311, 324, 482, 731-732
Art. 7(2)(g): 736-751
Art. 7(2)(h): 311, 761, 765
Art. 7(2)(i): 311, 754-757
Art. 7(3): 736, 751
Art. 8: 69, 138, 201, 222, 277, 280, 312-313, 326-327, 336, 412, 819, 833, 836,
Art. 8(1): 328, 548-549, 769, 801, 850
Art. 8(2): 257-258, 805, 820, 858, 934-935, 937, 955, 1019, 1022, 1048, 1053, 1073, 1088, 1095, 1127
Art. 8(2)(a): 291, 309, 819, 867, 1022, 1092, 1135
Art. 8(2)(a)(i): 257, 311, 315, 334, 675, 857, 867, 875-878
Art. 8(2)(a)(ii): 289, 867, 886, 911
- Alt. 1: 887-890
- Alt. 2: 898-906
Art. 8(2)(a)(iii): 311-312, 857, 867, 886, 891-894, 904, 911, 1087
Art. 8(2)(a)(iv): 311, 320, 481, 867, 986

- Alt. 1: 1000-1004
- Alt. 2 : 987-999
Art. 8(2)(a)(v): 924-928, 937
Art. 8(2)(a)(vi): 311, 446, 857, 867, 938-943
Art. 8(2)(a)(vii): 867
- Alt. 1: 964-967
- Alt. 2: 964-967
- Alt. 3: 950, 955
Art. 8(2)(a)(viii): 324, 867, 958-962
Art. 8(2)(b): 278, 819, 997, 1106
Art. 8(2)(b)(i): 311, 1008, 1015-1018, 1021, 1040, 1045, 1087
Art. 8(2)(b)(ii): 311, 986, 1000, 1008, 1024-1026, 1029, 1040, 1045, 1051
Art. 8(2)(b)(iii): 311, 440, 819, 986, 1008, 1040, 1134-1143
Art. 8(2)(b)(iv): 309, 311, 986, 1008, 1019, 1040-1047
Art. 8(2)(b)(v): 986, 1049, 1053
Art. 8(2)(b)(vi): 257, 858, 879-884, 1078
Art. 8(2)(b)(vii): 321, 1061-1072
Art. 8(2)(b)(viii)
- Alt. 1: 971-976
- Alt. 2: 964-967
Art. 8(2)(b)(ix): 311, 986, 1008, 1029-1034
Art. 8(2)(b)(x): 89, 874, 886
- Alt. 1. 895-897
- Alt. 2: 899-902
Art. 8(2)(b)(xi): 311, 324, 1054-1058, 1061
Art. 8(2)(b)(xii): 883, 1013, 1074-1079
Art. 8(2)(b)(xiii): 986
- Alt. 1: 1001-1004
- Alt. 2: 987-999
Art. 8(2)(b)(xiv): 986, 1005-1007
Art. 8(2)(b)(xv): 924, 929-931
Art. 8(2)(b)(xvi): 986, 999
Art. 8(2)(b)(xvii): 1098, 1106, 1114
Art. 8(2)(b)(xviii): 1098-1099, 1105, 1107-1110, 1114
Art. 8(2)(b)(xix): 1098-1099, 1111-1113, 1114, 1125
Art. 8(2)(b)(xx): 1098-1099, 1106, 1108, 1114, 1116, 1126
Art. 8(2)(b)(xxi): 911, 917-923, 934, 937
Art. 8(2)(b)(xxii): 908-916, 922-923
Art. 8(2)(b)(xxiii): 1014, 1090-1094
Art. 8(2)(b)(xxiv): 311, 986, 1008, 1035-1038, 1040
Art. 8(2)(b)(xxv): 288, 311, 504, 1014, 1081-1087
Art. 8(2)(b)(xxvi): 291, 321, 978-985
Art. 8(2)(c): 278, 815, 819, 873
Art. 8(2)(c)(i): 884, 886
- Alt. 1: 257, 334, 675, 875-878,
- Alt. 2: 895-897

- Alt. 3: 894, 903-906
- Alt. 4: 887-890
Art. 8(2)(c)(ii): 911, 917-923, 934, 937
Art. 8(2)(c)(iii): 324, 958-962
Art. 8(2)(c)(iv): 942, 944-949
Art. 8(2)(d): 825-826
Art. 8(2)(e): 815, 819
Art. 8(2)(e)(i): 311, 1008, 1015-1018, 1021, 1040
Art. 8(2)(e)(ii): 311, 986, 1008, 1035-1038, 1040
Art. 8(2)(e)(iii): 311, 819, 986, 1008, 1040, 1134-1143
Art. 8(2)(e)(iv): 311, 986, 1008, 1033, 1040
Art. 8(2)(e)(v): 986-999
Art. 8(2)(e)(vi): 908-916, 923
Art. 8(2)(e)(vii): 978-985
Art. 8(2)(e)(viii): 700, 968-970
Art. 8(2)(e)(ix): 311, 324, 1059-1060
Art. 8(2)(e)(x): 1074-1079
Art. 8(2)(e)(xi): 886
- Alt. 1: 895-897
- Alt. 2: 899-902
Art. 8(2)(e)(xii): 481, 986
- Alt. 1: 1001-1004
- Alt. 2: 987-999
Art. 8(2)(f): 825-830
Art. 9: 67, 316
Art. 9(1): 138
Art. 9(3): 138, 166
Art. 10: 125, 140, 228, 805
Art. 11: 95, 201
Art. 12: 64, 201
Art. 12(2): 64
Art. 12(3): 201
Art. 13: 64, 204
Art. 13(a): 204
Art. 13(b): 64, 201
Art. 14: 204
Arts. 14 et seq.: 120
Art. 15(1): 65
Art. 16: 66, 202
Art. 17: 199, 204, 218
Art. 17(1)(a): 226
Art. 17(1)(b): 192
Art. 17(2)(a): 192
Art. 17(3): 226
Art. 20: 218, 546
Art. 20(1): 284
Art. 20(3): 546
Art. 21: 164-167, 269, 310, 314, 406, 478
Art. 21(1): 166, 314
Art. 21(2): 149, 167
Art. 21(3): 161
Art. 22: 93-95, 251

Art. 22(1): 95, 282
Art. 22(2): 94, 307
Art. 22(3): 75, 94
Art. 23: 91, 93, 95, 251
Art. 24: 93, 95, 251
Art. 24(1): 282
Art. 24(2): 95
Art. 25: 251, 277
Art. 25(1): 97
Art. 25(2): 277, 371
Art. 25(3): 277, 343-366, 371
Art. 25(3)(a):
  - Alt. 1: 345
  - Alt. 2: 346
  - Alt. 3: 343, 353-355
Art. 25(3)(b): 356, 501
  - Alt. 1: 357
  - Alt. 2: 358-359
  - Alt. 3: 358-359
Art. 25(3)(c): 324, 360-363, 501
Art. 25(3)(d): 343, 352, 360, 364-366, 490, 501
Art. 25(3)(e): 343, 356, 498, 623-627
Art. 25(3)(f): 486, 493-501, 1054
Art. 25(4): 99
Art. 26: 66, 201, 251, 284, 355, 547
Art. 27: 251, 512, 523
Art. 27(1): 282, 515-519
Art. 27(2): 284, 522, 552
Art. 28: 251, 261-262, 277, 288, 320, 369-400, 504
Art. 28(a): 373, 377
Art. 28(a)(i): 320, 384, 387
Art. 28(a)(ii): 386-394
Art. 28(b): 373, 378-380
Art. 28(b)(i): 385, 387
Art. 28(b)(ii): 380
Art. 28(b)(iii): 386-394
Art. 29: 251, 284, 553
Art. 30: 251-252, 275, 277, 280-281, 287, 290, 295, 297-336, 366, 381, 385, 400, 436, 565, 596, 608, 610-611, 615, 627, 644, 669, 676, 682, 689, 703, 708, 718, 727, 732, 745, 757, 765, 768, 854, 878, 882, 890, 897, 902, 906, 913, 916, 921, 927, 931, 943, 954, 957, 962, 967, 969, 976, 985, 989, 996, 1004, 1007, 1018, 1026, 1028, 1034, 1047, 1052, 1058, 1065, 1067, 1071, 1079, 1086, 1094, 1102, 1110, 1113, 1143
Art. 31: 251, 275, 277, 282, 406, 437
Art. 31(1): 282, 314, 478
Art. 31(1)(a): 464-468, 472
Art. 31(1)(b): 470-476
Art. 31(1)(c): 408-419

Art. 31(1)(d): 423-434
Art. 31(3): 282, 406, 478
Art. 32: 251, 282, 436-447
Art. 32(1): 438-442
Art. 32(2): 438, 443-447, 462
Art. 33: 251, 282, 443, 447, 460-462
Art. 34: 203
Arts. 34 et seq.: 120
Art. 48(4): 465
Art. 51(3): 138
Art. 51(5): 166
Arts. 53 et seq.: 120, 204
Art. 54(1)(a): 276
Art. 56(2)(c): 465
Art. 61: 204
Arts. 62 et seq.: 120, 204
Art. 66(2): 276
Art. 67(1)(i): 276
Art. 70: 74, 218
Art. 77: 91, 204
Art. 78(1): 344, 462, 468
Art. 78(3): 529, 543
Arts. 81 et seq.: 120
Arts. 86 et seq.: 107, 120
Art. 93(1)(b), (c), (2): 465
Art. 98: 523-524
Art. 100(1)(a): 465
Art. 100(1)(d): 465
Arts. 103 et seq.: 120, 204
Art. 112: 67
Art. 121: 1098, 1115, 1185
Art. 123: 74, 1098, 1185
Art. 126: 66, 95

3. ICC Rules of Procedure and Evidence:

  67, 124, 138, 166, 204, 465
Rule 70: 726
Rule 145(1)(c): 344
Rule 145(2)(b): 338

4. ICTR Statute:

  47, 62, 142, 150, 158, 267, 295, 344, 403, 490, 523, 529, 553, 642, 923
Art. 1: 211
Art. 1(1): 345
Art. 2: 55
Art. 2(2): 562
Art. 2(3)(b): 347, 489
Art. 2(3)(c): 623
Art. 2(3)(d): 494
Art. 3: 55, 641, 654, 659, 666, 671, 673
Art. 3(a): 675, 677, 875
Art. 3(b): 678, 944

Art. 3(c): 684
Art. 3(d): 696
Art. 3(e): 704
Art. 3(f): 710
Art. 3(g): 722-723
Art. 3(h): 736, 747
Art. 3(i): 766
Art. 4: 55, 211, 812, 848
Art. 4(a): 887, 895, 903
Art. 4(b): 944
Art. 4(c): 956
Art. 4(e): 910, 917, 922
Art. 4(f): 986
Art. 4(g): 812, 944
Art. 6(1): 342, 357, 487
Art. 6(2): 516
Art. 6(3): 372, 382, 387-388
Art. 6(4): 457
Art. 8: 46
Art. 8(1): 198
Art. 8(2): 198
Art. 9(2)(a): 218
Art. 13(3): 54
Art. 13(4): 54
Art. 15(3): 54

5. ICTY Statute:

    47, 62, 142, 150, 158, 160, 267, 295, 344,
    346, 403, 490, 492, 523, 529, 553, 811-
    812, 910, 923
Art. 1: 206
Art. 1(1): 345
Art. 2: 51, 206, 320, 1145
Art. 2(a): 295, 875
Art. 2(b): 296, 887, 895, 903
Art. 2(c): 295, 891
Art. 2(d): 986, 1004
Art. 2(e): 924
Art. 2(f): 938
Art. 2(g), Alt. 1: 964
Art. 2(h): 956
Art. 3: 51, 206, 335, 806, 922, 994, 1020,
    1145
Art. 3(a): 1100, 1114
Art. 3(b): 481
Art. 3(c): 1049
Art. 3(d): 1001, 1030
Art. 3(e): 986
Art. 4: 51, 206
Art. 4(2): 295, 562
Art. 4(3)(b): 489
Art. 4(3)(c): 623
Art. 4(3)(d): 494
Art. 5: 51-52, 206, 641, 654, 659, 666, 671,
    673

Art. 5(a): 296, 675, 677
Art. 5(b): 678
Art. 5(c): 684
Art. 5(d): 696
Art. 5(e): 704
Art. 5(f): 710
Art. 5(g): 722-723, 909
Art. 5(h): 736, 744, 747
Art. 5(i): 766-767
Art. 6: 206
Art. 7: 206
Art. 7(1): 334, 342-343, 346-347, 357, 487,
    492, 503
Art. 7(2): 516
Art. 7(3): 372, 382, 386-388
Art. 7(4): 403, 457
Art. 8: 206
Art. 9: 46
Art. 9(1): 198
Art. 9(2): 198
Art. 10(2)(a): 218
Art. 11: 207
Art. 15: 208
Arts. 15 et seq.: 53
Arts. 18 et seq.: 208
Art. 25: 208
Art. 77: 74
Art. 91: 74

6. ICTY Rules of Procedure and Evidence:

    53, 118, 208
Rule 2: 662
Rule 53: 210
Rule 67(A)(ii)(b): 273, 464
Rule 87: 529
Rule 96: 482
Rule 101: 529

7. Nuremberg Charter:

    5, 15, 17-29, 32, 62, 144-145, 198, 239,
    247, 267, 269-270, 295, 344, 372, 402,
    487, 489-490, 529, 553, 773
Art. 2: 22
Art. 6: 198, 345, 487
Art. 6(a): 19, 23, 27, 83, 340, 487, 1157,
    1162, 1165, 1168, 1174, 1176, 1178
Art. 6(b): 8, 19, 481, 801, 959
Art. 6(c): 19, 23, 340, 635, 641, 659, 666,
    673, 675, 677-678, 684, 690, 696, 722,
    736, 747, 766
Art. 7: 21, 516
Art. 8: 21, 455
Art. 9: 97

Art. 10: 20, 97
Art. 14: 22
Arts. 16 et seq.: 53
Art. 26: 22

8. Statute of the Special Court for Sierra Leone:

   143, 978
Art. 2(g): 722
Art. 10: 189

9. Tokyo Charter:

   16, 30-33, 144-145, 372, 487, 553
Art. 3: 32
Art. 5: 32, 345
Art. 5(a): 340, 487, 1162, 1165, 1174, 1176,
   1178
Art. 5(b): 801
Art. 5(c): 637, 675, 678, 684, 696, 736, 747,
   766
Art. 6: 516, 455
Art. 8: 32

II. International Treaties and Conventions

1. African (Banjul) Charter on Human and Peoples' Rights of 27 June 1981:

Art. 12(2): 700
Art. 12(4): 701
Art. 12(5): 701

2. Agreement on the Privileges and Immunities of the International Criminal Court of 9 September 2002:

   67, 513

3. American Convention on Human Rights of 22 November 1969

Art. 22(3): 700
Art. 22(4): 700-701
Art. 22(6): 701
Art. 22(9): 701
Arts. 33, 44 et seq.: 111

4. Convention Against Illicit Traffic in Narcotic Drugs and Psychotropic Substances of 20 December 1988:

   62, 100

5. Convention Against Torture and Other Cruel, Inhuman or Degrading Treatment or Punishment of 10 December 1984:

   62
Art. 1(1): 711-720, 888-889
Art. 4: 218
Art. 4(1): 100
Art. 7: 179

6. Convention Against Transnational Organized Crime of 15 November 2000:

Art. 3(a): 694

7. Convention for the Protection of Cultural Property in the Event of an Armed Conflict of 14 May 1954:

   788, 1033, 1055
Art. 1: 1031
Art. 4(1): 1031
Art. 4(2): 1031
Art. 8: 1031

8. Convention for the Suppression of the Traffic in Persons and of the Exploitation of the Prostitution of Others of 21 March 1950:

   693

9. Convention for the Suppression of Unlawful Acts Against the Safety of Civil Aviation of 23 September 1971:

   100

10. Convention for the Suppression of Unlawful Acts Against the Safety of Maritime Navigation of 10 March 1988:

   100

11. Convention for the Suppression of Unlawful Seizure of Aircraft of 16 December 1970:

   100

12. Convention on Offenses and Certain Other Acts Committed on Board Aircraft of 14 September 1963:

   100

13. Convention on Psychotropic Substances of 21 February 1971:

100

14. Convention on Prohibitions or Restrictions on the Use of Certain Conventional Weapons Which May be Deemed to be Excessively Injurious or to Have Indiscriminate Effects of 10 October 1980 (UN Weapons Convention):

788, 1097, 1125-1126
Art. 1: 1130
Art. 5(1), Art. 8(1): 1130

15. Convention on Special Missions of 8 December 1969:

Arts. 21, 31: 513

16. Convention on the Elimination of all Forms of Discrimination Against Women of 18 December 1979:

Art. 1: 751
Art. 6: 693

17. Convention on the High Seas of 29 April 1958:

100

18. Convention on the Prevention and Punishment of Crimes against Internationally Protected Persons, including Diplomatic Agents of 14 December 1973:

100

19. Convention on the Prevention and Punishment of the Crime of Genocide of 9 December 1948:

42, 58, 147, 184, 240, 557, 559-560, 577, 581, 583, 586, 594, 599
Art. II: 345, 562, 571, 585, 590
Art. III(b): 489
Art. III(c): 623
Art. III(d): 494
Art. IV: 179, 516
Art. VI: 174

20. Convention on the Prohibition of Military or Any Other Hostile Use of Environmental Modification Techniques (ENMOD) of 10 December 1976:

Art. I: 1043-1044

21. Convention on the Prohibition of the Development, Production and Stockpiling of Bacteriological (Biological) and Toxin Weapons and on Their Destruction of 10 April 1972:

788, 1097, 1106, 1129
Preamble: 1122, 1129
Art. 1: 1122

22. Convention on the Prohibition of the Development, Production, Stockpiling and Use of Chemical Weapons and on Their Destruction of 13 January 1993:

788, 1106, 1119
Preamble: 1129
Art. 1(1)(c): 1119
Art. 1(5): 1107
Art. 2(2): 1104
Art. 2(7): 1107
Art. 7(1)(a): 1120

23. Convention on the Prohibition of the Use, Stockpiling, Production and Transfer of Anti-Personnel Mines and on Their Destruction of 18 September 1997:

788
Art. 1(1)(a): 1125, 1130

24. Convention on the Rights of the Child of 20 November 1989:

Art. 11: 693
Art. 38(3): 979

25. Convention on the Safety of United Nations and Associated Personnel of 9 December 1994:

819, 1073, 1136, 1141
Art. 1: 1141
Art. 9: 1141

26. Convention pour la Création d'une Cour Pénale Internationale of 16 November 1937:

27. Convention (I) for the Pacific Settlement of International Disputes of 29 July 1899:

Arts. 1, 2: 1151

28. Convention (II) for the Pacific Settlement of International Disputes of 8 October 1907:

Arts. 1, 2: 1151

29. Convention (II) with Respect to the Laws and Customs of War on Land of 29 July 1899:

141, 636, 787

30. Convention (III) Relative to the Opening of Hostilities of 18 October 1907:

774

31. Convention (IV) respecting the Laws and Customs of War on Land of 18 October 1907:

636, 787, 791
Art. 3, Sentence 2: 849

32. Convention (X) for the Adaptation to Maritime Warfare of the Principles of the Geneva Convention of 18 October 1907:

783

33. Covenant of the League of Nations of 28 June 1919:

1152-1155
Art. 10: 1152
Art. 12(1): 1152
Arts. 13, 15: 1152
Art. 16: 1152

34. Declaration on the Use of Bullets Which Expand or Flatten Easily in the Human Body of 29 July 1899:

1111

35. Declaration Renouncing the Use, in Times of War, of Explosive Projectiles under 400 Grammes Weight of 29 November / 11 December 1868 (St. Petersburg Declaration):

786, 1097

36. European Convention on the Non-Applicability of Statutory Limitations to Crimes Against Humanity and War Crimes of 25 January 1974:

553

37. European Convention on the Protection of Human Rights and Fundamental Freedoms of 4 November 1950:

938
Art. 1: 181
Art. 4(3): 690
Art. 7: 91
Art. 7(2): 1164
Art. 13: 181
Arts. 32 et seq.: 111

38. European Convention on the Suppression of Terrorism of 27 January 1977:

100

39. (Geneva) Convention for the Amelioration of the Condition of the Wounded and Sick in Armies in the Field of 22 August 1864:

782

40. (Geneva) Convention for the Amelioration of the Condition of the Wounded and Sick in Armies in the Field of 6 July 1906:

783, 797

41. (Geneva) Convention for the Amelioration of the Condition of the Wounded and Sick in Armies in the Field of 27 July 1929:

783

42. (Geneva) Convention Relative to Treatment of Prisoners of War of 27 July 1929:

783

43. Geneva Conventions of 12 August 1949:

42, 141, 147, 174, 180, 183, 240, 247, 264, 783-785, 790, 798, 804, 808-810, 817, 819, 857, 860-873, 876-878, 887, 891, 898, 903, 908, 910, 915, 1010, 1050, 1055, 1068, 1090, 1092, 1094, 1128, 1136

44. (Geneva) Convention for the Amelioration of the Condition of the Wounded and Sick in Armed Forces in the Field of 12 August 1949 (Geneva Convention I):

42, 783
Art. 1: 784
Art. 2: 824
Art. 2(1): 831
Art. 2(2): 832
Art. 3: 127, 180, 648-649, 784-785, 793, 811-816, 819, 825, 828-829, 857, 871-872, 875, 878, 884, 887, 895-896, 903, 905, 908, 915, 922, 932, 948, 959-960, 983
Art. 3(1): 872
Art. 3(1)(a): 875
Art. 3(1)(c): 918
Art. 3(1)(d): 944, 946-947
Art. 13: 861, 864
Art. 13(4), (5): 863
Art. 19: 990, 1030
Art. 19(1): 1003
Art. 20: 990, 1030
Arts. 21 to 23: 1030
Arts. 24 to 26: 863
Arts. 24 to 27: 1035
Art. 28: 951
Art. 32: 951
Arts. 33 to 36: 990
Art. 36: 1035
Art. 38: 1038, 1068
Arts. 39 to 44: 1035
Art. 49(1): 257, 798
Art. 50: 875, 990, 999
Art. 63: 790

45. (Geneva) Convention for the Amelioration of the Condition of the Wounded, Sick and Shipwrecked Members of Armed Forces at Sea of 12 August 1949 (Geneva Convention II):

42, 783
Art. 2: see Art. 2 Geneva Convention I
Art. 3: see Art. 3 Geneva Convention I
Art. 12: 905
Art. 13: 861, 864
Art. 13(4), (5): 863
Art. 18(2): 852
Arts. 22 to 24: 1030
Arts. 22 to 28: 990
Art. 35: 1030
Art. 36: 951
Art. 37: 951
Art. 38: 990
Art. 39: 990

Arts. 42 to 44: 1035
Art. 50(1): 257, 798
Art. 50(2): 798
Art. 50(3): 799
Art. 51: 875, 990, 999
Art. 62: 790

46. (Geneva) Convention Relative to the Treatment of Prisoners of War of 12 August 1949 (Geneva Convention III):

42, 783, 955
Art. 2: see Art. 2 Geneva Convention I
Art. 3: see Art. 3 Geneva Convention I
Art. 4: 861
Art. 4A: 864
Art. 4A(2): 838
Art. 4A(4), (5): 863
Art. 13: 898, 905, 932
Art. 13(1): 895
Art. 15: 810
Art. 18: 991
Art. 20: 905
Art. 21: 951
Art. 22: 951
Art. 23(1): 1090
Art. 26: 810
Art. 46: 905
Arts. 49 et seq.: 927, 935-936
Art. 50(f) 927
Art. 84(2) 939
Art. 86: 939
Art. 87(3): 939
Art. 99: 91
Art. 99(1): 939
Art. 99(3): 939
Art. 100: 939
Art. 102: 939
Art. 104: 939
Art. 105(1): 939
Art. 105(4): 939
Art. 106: 939
Art. 109(1): 956
Art. 118(1): 951, 956
Art. 129: 179
Art. 129(1): 257, 357, 798
Art. 129(2): 798
Art. 129(3): 799
Art. 130: 857, 875, 924, 938, 991
Art. 142: 790

47. (Geneva) Convention Relative to the Protection of Civilian Persons in Time of War of 12 August 1949 (Geneva Convention IV):

42, 648, 783, 865-866, 1135

Art. 2: see Art. 2 Geneva Convention I
Art. 3: see Art. 3 Geneva Convention I
Art. 4(1): 865, 1017
Art. 5: 866, 952
Art. 13: 861
Art. 14: 1030
Art. 18: 990, 1030, 1035
Art. 19: 1030, 1035
Art. 20: 1035
Art. 21: 990, 1035
Art. 22: 990, 1035
Art. 23: 1082, 1085
Art. 27: 905, 932, 952
Art. 27(1): 918
Art. 27(2): 729, 909
Art. 28: 1090
Art. 29: 850-851
Art. 32: 895, 905
Art. 33: 939
Art. 34(4): 959
Art. 35(1): 956
Arts. 41 to 43: 952
Art. 45: 965
Art. 45(1), (2): 966
Art. 45(3): 966
Art. 45(4): 966
Art. 49: 700, 965, 974
Art. 49(1): 966
Art. 49(2): 966, 968
Art. 49(3): 966
Art. 49(6): 972
Art. 51: 927, 935-936
Art. 53: 1000, 1003, 1082
Art. 55: 1082
Art. 57: 998
Arts. 59 to 62: 1085
Art. 67: 939
Art. 68: 939
Art. 71(2): 939
Art. 72(1): 939
Art. 72(2): 939
Art. 72(4): 939
Art. 73: 939
Art. 78: 952
Art. 97: 991
Art. 117(3): 939
Art. 134: 956
Art. 146: 179, 183, 218
Art. 146(1): 257, 357, 798
Art. 146(2): 798
Art. 146(3): 799
Art. 147: 315, 696, 875, 924, 938, 950, 959, 964, 990, 999
Art. 158: 790

48. ICJ Statute of 26 June 1945:

Art. 38(1): 123
Art. 38(1)(a): 123
Art. 38(1)(b): 123, 128, 164, 269
Art. 38(1)(c): 123, 166, 269
Art. 38(1)(d): 123

49. ILO Convention (No. 29) Concerning Forced or Compulsory Labor of 28 June 1930:

Art. 2: 690

50. ILO Convention (No. 105) Concerning the Abolition of Forced Labour of 25 June 1957:

Art. 1: 690

51. Inter-American Convention on the Forced Disappearance of Persons of 9 June 1994:

Art. II: 753

52. International Convention Against the Taking of Hostages of 17 December 1979:

Art. 1(1): 962

53. International Convention on the Elimination of All Forms of Racial Discrimination of 7 March 1966:

Art. 1: 765

54. International Convention for the Suppression of Counterfeiting of 20 April 1929:

100

55. International Convention for the Suppression of Terrorist Bombings of 15 December 1997:

Art. 2(3)(c): 364

56. International Convention on the Suppression and Punishment of the Crime of Apartheid of 30 November 1973 (UN Apartheid Convention):

639
Art. I: 760
Art. II: 761-762
Art. III: 760

57. International Covenant on Civil and Political Rights of 16 December 1966:

739, 938
Art. 2: 739
Art. 8(3): 690
Art. 12(3): 700
Art. 12(4): 701
Art. 13: 701
Art. 15: 91, 1164
Art. 15(2): 1164
Arts. 28 et seq.: 111

58. London Agreement of 8 August 1945:

15, 17, 145
Art. 1: 198
Art. 4: 198

59. Optional Protocol to the Convention on the Rights of the Child of 25 May 2000:

111, 979

60. Optional Protocol to the International Covenant on Civil and Political Rights of 16 December 1966:

111

61. Protocol Additional to the Geneva Conventions of 12 August 1949, and Relating to the Protection of Victims of International Armed Conflicts (Protocol I) of 8 June 1977 (Additional Protocol I):

42, 147, 257, 648, 783, 785, 790, 793, 811, 938, 1010, 1035, 1046, 1050, 1055, 1068, 1090, 1092, 1094
Art. 1(2): 791
Art. 1(4): 785, 825, 836
Art. 11: 898
Art. 11(2)(a), (b): 895
Art. 11(4): 799, 857, 895, 902
Art. 12: 1030
Arts. 12 et seq.: 1036
Art. 15: 1036
Art. 18: 1036
Art. 23: 1036
Art. 24: 1036
Art. 35(2): 1097, 1114, 1116
Art. 35(3): 1041-1044, 1046
Art. 37: 1054-1055, 1063
Art. 37(1): 1054
Art. 37(1)(d): 1062, 1070

Art. 37(2): 1056
Art. 38(2): 1062, 1070
Art. 39(2): 1062, 1066
Art. 39(3): 1056
Art. 40: 1074, 1077
Art. 41: 879
Art. 41(2): 881
Art. 43: 925, 981
Art. 43(2): 792, 863
Art. 43(3): 1050
Art. 44(3): 1060
Art. 45(3): 866
Art. 48: 1009
Art. 49 : 1051
Art. 49(1): 1017, 1025, 1141
Art. 49(2): 1032
Art. 49(3): 1017
Art. 50(1): 1017
Art. 50(2): 1017
Art. 50(3): 647, 1017
Arts. 50 et seq.: 1010
Art. 51: 1017
Art. 51(2): 1016, 1019, 1021
Art. 51(3): 1017, 1142
Art. 51(4): 1041, 1114
Art. 51(4)(b): 1097, 1117
Art. 51(5)(b): 1046
Art. 51(7): 1090, 1093
Art. 52(1): 1024-1025, 1027
Art. 52(2): 1025, 1142
Art. 52(3): 1025
Art. 53(a): 998, 1031
Art. 53(b): 998
Art. 54: 1081
Art. 54(2): 1084-1085
Art. 54(3): 1084
Art. 54(5): 1084-1085
Art. 55(1): 1041-1042
Art. 57(2): 1011
Art. 57(2)(a)(iii): 1046
Art. 57(3): 1011
Art. 59(1): 1049
Art. 59(2)(a) to (d): 1050
Art. 59(3): 1050
Art. 69: 1082, 1085
Art. 70: 1082, 1085, 1139
Art. 71: 1082, 1139
Art. 71(1): 1139
Art. 71(2): 1136
Art. 75: 866
Art. 75(1): 905
Art. 75(2): 909
Art. 75(2)(b): 729, 918, 922
Art. 75(2)(c): 959
Art. 75(3), (4): 939

Art. 76(1): 729, 909
Art. 77(2): 979, 984
Art. 78: 975
Art. 85: 1022
Art. 85(1): 257
Art. 85(3): 857-858, 1020
Art. 85(3)(a): 1016, 1018
Art. 85(3)(b): 1041
Art. 85(3)(e): 879, 882
Art. 85(3)(f): 1062
Art. 85(4): 857, 967, 1030
Art. 85(4)(a): 964, 972, 974
Art. 85(4)(b): 955-957
Art. 85(4)(d): 1031
Art. 85(4)(e): 938
Arts. 85 et seq.: 799
Art. 86(1): 506-507
Art. 86(2): 382
Art. 87: 391
Art. 87(4)(a): 696

62. Annex I to Additional Protocol I:

Art. 3: 1036, 1068
Arts. 5 to 8: 1036

63. Protocol Additional to the Geneva Conventions of 12 August 1949, and Relating to the Protection of Victims of Non-International Armed Conflicts (Protocol II) of 8 June 1977 (Additional Protocol II):

42, 147, 257, 783, 785, 790, 793, 811, 813, 815, 825, 1010, 1027, 1055, 1074, 1128
Art. 1(1): 828
Art. 1(2): 826
Art. 4(1): 872, 905, 932, 983
Art. 4(2): 812
Art. 4(2)(a): 895
Art. 4(2)(c): 959
Art. 4(2)(d): 932
Art. 4(2)(e): 729, 909, 918, 922
Art. 4(2)(f): 812
Art. 4(3)(c): 979, 981, 984
Art. 5(2)(e): 895
Art. 6: 812
Art. 6(2): 946-947
Art. 6(4): 948
Art. 6(5): 189
Art. 7(2): 905
Art. 11: 1033
Art. 11(1): 1037
Art. 12: 1037
Art. 13(2): 1016, 1019,1021

Art. 14: 1088-1089
Art. 16: 99, 1033
Art. 17: 696
Art. 17(1): 700, 968
Art. 17(2): 968

64. Protocol for the Prohibition of the Use in War of Asphyxiating, Poisonous or Other Gases, and of Bacteriological Methods of Warfare of 17 June 1925 (Poison Gas Protocol):

787, 1097, 1107-1109, 1118, 1122, 1128

65. Protocol No. 4 of the European Convention for the Protection of Human Rights and Fundamental Freedoms of 16 September 1963:

Art. 2(3): 700
Art. 3: 701
Art. 4: 701
Art. 7(2): 1164

66. Protocol on Blinding Laser Weapons of 13 October 1995 (UN Weapons Protocol IV):

788, 1097, 1125-1126

67. Protocol on Non-Detectable Fragments of 10 October 1980 (UN Weapons Protocol I):

788, 1097, 1125-1126

68. Protocol on Prohibitions or Restrictions on the Use of Incendiary Weapons of 10 October 1980 (UN Weapons Protocol III):

788, 1097, 1125-1126

69. Protocol on Prohibitions or Restrictions on the Use of Mines, Booby-Traps and Other Devices of 10 October 1980 (UN Weapons Protocol II):

788, 1097, 1125-1126
Art. 1(2): 1130

70. Protocol to Prevent, Suppress and Punish Trafficking in Persons, Especially Women and Children of 15 November 2000:

Art. 3(a): 694

71. Regulation Concerning the Laws and Customs of War on Land of 18 October 1907 (Hague Regulations):

147, 787, 1033, 1055
Section II, Chapter 1: 787
Art. 22: 787
Art. 23, Sentence 2: 929
Art. 23(a): 1100, 1105, 1118, 1128
Art. 23(b): 1054
Art. 23(c): 879, 883
Art. 23(d): 1074
Art. 23(e): 1114, 1116
Art. 23(f): 1062
Art. 23(g): 999, 1001, 1082, 1097
Art. 23(h): 924, 1005-1006
Art. 24: 1056
Art. 25: 1049
Art. 27: 1030
Art. 32, Sentence 2: 1064
Art. 42: 973
Art. 43: 1082
Art. 46: 959
Art. 46(2): 998
Art. 47: 998
Art. 52: 926
Art. 53: 997
Art. 53(2): 998
Art. 56: 1030

72. Saavedra Lamas Treaty of 10 October 1933:

1157

73. Second Protocol to the Convention for the Protection of Cultural Property in the Event of an Armed Conflict of 26 March 1999:

Art. 6(a): 1031
Art. 15(1): 1031

74. Single Convention on Narcotic Drugs of 30 March 1961:

100

75. Slavery Convention of 25 September 1926; amended by Protocol of 7 December 1953:

685
Art. 1: 686

76. South Pacific Nuclear Free Zone Treaty of 6 August 1985:

1118

77. Supplementary Convention on the Abolition of Slavery, the Slave Trade and Institutions and Practices Similar to Slavery of 7 September 1956:

236, 685
Art. 1(a), (b): 686
Art. 7: 686

78. Treaty Banning Nuclear Weapons Tests in the Atmosphere, Outer Space and Under Water of 5 August 1963:

1118

79. Treaty Between the United States of America and the Union of Soviet Socialist Republics on the Elimination of Their Intermediate-Range and Shorter-Range Missiles of 8 December 1987 (INF Treaty):

1118

80. Treaty for the Prohibition of Nuclear Weapons in Latin America of 14 February 1967:

1118

81. Treaties of Locarno of 16 October 1925:

1154
Art. 2: 1154

82. Treaty of Versailles of 28 June 1919:

6-14
Art. 227(1): 6, 1164
Art. 227(2): 7
Art. 228(1): 7
Art. 228(2): 7
Art. 229(1): 7
Art. 229(2): 7, 800
Art. 230: 7

83. Treaty on the Non-Proliferation of Nuclear Weapons of 1 July 1968:

1118

84. Treaty on Principles Governing the Activities of States in the Exploration and Use of Outer Space, Including the Moon and Other Celestial Bodies (Outer Space Treaty) of 27 January 1967:

1118

85. Treaty on the Final Settlement with Respect to Germany of 12 September 1990 (2+4 Treaty):

   1118

86. Treaty on the Prohibition of the Emplacement of Nuclear Weapons and Other Weapons of Mass Destruction on the Sea-Bed and the Ocean-Floor and in the Subsoil Thereof (Sea Bed Treaty) of 11 February 1971:

   1118

87. Treaty on the Reduction and Limitation of American and Soviet Strategic Offensive Arms of 31 July 1991 (START-I Treaty):

   1118

88. Treaty Providing for the Renunciation of War as an Instrument of National Policy (Kellogg-Briand-Pact) of 27 August 1928:

   23, 1155-1157

89. UN Charter of 26 June 1945:

Art. 1: 739
Art. 1(1): 78
Art. 2(4): 1157-1160, 1175
Art. 2(6): 78
Art. 2(7): 172
Art. 7(2): 46
Art. 11: 78
Art. 12: 78
Art. 13(1)(a): 41
Art. 18: 78
Art. 24: 1188
Art. 25: 46
Art. 29: 46
Art. 39: 78, 1158-1160
Chapter VII: 46, 54, 64, 78, 201-202, 204, 523, 1138, 1160, 1169
Art. 42: 1158
Art. 51: 419, 1158-1159, 1169, 1171, 1175
Art. 55: 739

90. United Nations Convention on the Non-Applicability of Statutory Limitations to War Crimes and Crimes Against Humanity of 16 November 1968:

   553, 639
Art. 1(b): 760

91. United Nations Convention on the Law of the Sea of 10 December 1982:

   100

92. Vienna Convention on Consular Relations of 24 April 1963:

Arts. 41, 43: 513
Art. 53(4): 513

93. Vienna Convention on Diplomatic Relations of 18 April 1961:

Arts. 31, 39: 513
Art. 39(2): 513

94. Vienna Convention on the Law of Treaties of 23 May 1969:

Art. 31: 158
Art. 32: 158-159

III. National Legislation

1. German Legislation

a) Act to Introduce the Code of Crimes Against International Law [Gesetz zur Einführung des Völkerstrafgesetzbuches] of 26 June 2002:

Art. 3: 265

b) Basic Law [Grundgesetz, GG]:

Art. 16(2): 243
Art. 25: 222
Art. 26(1): 263

c) Code of Crimes Against International Law [Völkerstrafgesetzbuch, VStGB] of 26 June 2002:

   156, 235, 238-265, 820, 955, 1027
Sec. 1: 250, 264-265
Sec. 2: 250-253, 307
Sec. 3: 250, 253
Sec. 4: 253, 261-264
Sec. 5: 250, 253
Sec. 6: 254
Sec. 7: 255
Sec. 7(1) No. 3: 236
Sec. 7(1) No. 4: 697
Sec. 7(1) No. 5: 236
Sec. 7(1) No. 10: 744

Sec. 8: 256
Sec. 8(1) No. 1: 257
Sec. 8(1) Nos. 1 to 9: 259
Sec. 8(1) No. 6: 968
Sec. 8(3): 259
Sec. 8(3) Nos. 1 to 4: 259
Sec. 8(3) No. 3: 924, 926
Sec. 8(6): 259
Sec. 9: 256, 259
Sec. 9(1): 236, 1000-1001
Sec. 9(2): 1006
Sec. 10: 256, 259
Sec. 10(2): 1073
Sec. 11: 256, 260, 815
Sec. 11(1) Nos. 1 to 7: 260
Sec. 11(1) No. 2: 1053
Sec. 11(1) No. 4: 1095
Sec. 11(1) No. 5: 1088
Sec. 11(1) No. 6: 1076
Sec. 12: 256, 260, 815
Sec. 12(1) Nos. 1 to 3: 260, 1131
Sec. 12(1) No. 1: 1105
Sec. 12(1) No. 2: 1105, 1109
Sec. 13: 253, 261-262, 264
Sec. 14: 253, 261-262, 264

d) Code of Criminal Procedure [Strafprozess-
ordnung, StPO]:

Sec. 153f: 265

e) Criminal Code [Strafgesetzbuch, StGB]:

250, 253
Sec. 6 No. 1 old version: 264
Sec. 6 No. 9: 264
Sec. 13: 252
Sec. 15 : 252
Sec. 20: 467
Secs. 80, 80a: 263
Sec. 220a old version: 232, 254, 630

f) ICC Statute Ratification Act [IStGH-
Statutsgesetz] of 4 December 2000:

243

g) ICC Statute Implementation Act [Gesetz zur
Ausführung des Römischen Statuts des Internationalen Strafgerichtshofes] of 21 June
2002:

243

h) Law on Prosecution of War Crimes and
Misdemeanors [Gesetz zur Verfolgung von
Kriegsverbrechen und Kriegsvergehen] of 18
December 1919:

Sec. 1: 11

i) Military Criminal Code [Wehrstrafgesetz,
WStG]:

Sec. 6: 434

j) Reich Criminal Code [Reichsstrafgesetzbuch,
RStGB]:

Sec. 9: 7

2. Other National Legislation

a) American Servicemembers' Protection Act of
2 August 2002 (USA):

66

b) Crimes Against Humanity and War Crimes
Act 2000 (Canada):

Sec. 4: 223

c) East German Criminal Code (East Germany):

640

d) English Draft Criminal Code Bill (United
Kingdom):

Sec. 18(b)(ii): 306
Sec. 18(c): 330

e) Finnish Criminal Code:

Chapter 11: 228

f) International Crimes and International
Criminal Court Act 2000 (New Zealand):

Sec. 9: 223

g) Lieber Code of 24 April 1863 (USA):

781
Art. 35: 1030
Art. 44: 796

h) Loi du 16 juin 1993 relative à la répression des infractions graves aux conventions internationales de Genève du 12 août 1949 et aux protocoles I et II du 8 juin 1977, additionnels à ces conventions (Belgium):

798

i) Model Penal Code (USA):

Sec. 2.02(1): 297
Sec. 2.02(2)(c): 330
Sec. 2.06: 354, 363
Sec. 2.08: 474
Sec. 3.02: 421
Sec. 4.01: 467
Sec. 5.01: 495

j) Rules of Courts-Martial (USA):

Rule 916(h): 429
Rule 916(k): 474

k) South African Constitution:

Sec. 232: 222

l) Spanish Criminal Code:

Art. 20(2): 474

m) Statute of the Iraqi Special Tribunal:

Art. 14(c): 1183

n) War Crimes Act of 1996 (USA):

798

IV. Drafts and Principles

1. Draft Agreement between the United Nations and the Royal Government of Cambodia Concerning the Prosecution under Cambodian Law of Crimes Committed During the Period of Democratic Kampuchea of 17 March 2003:

46

2. Draft Articles on State Responsibility for Internationally Wrongful Acts of 1976 (ILC):

Art. 19(4): 97

3. Draft Articles on Responsibility of States for Internationally Wrongful Acts of 2001 (ILC):

Art. 1: 97
Arts. 30 et seq.: 98
Art. 58: 99

4. Draft Code 1954 (ILC):

41, 59, 1165
Art. 1: 77
Art. 2(11): 639, 665, 749, 751

5. Draft Code 1991 (ILC):

41, 152, 673
Art. 3: 342
Art. 6: 185
Arts. 15 et seq.: 74, 1165, 1187
Art. 20: 760, 764
Art. 21: 113, 639, 663, 673, 749, 751

6. Draft Code 1996 (ILC):

41, 152, 362, 673
Art. 1: 77
Art. 9: 185
Art. 12: 218
Art. 14: 403
Art. 16: 1165
Art. 18: 639, 642, 654-658, 673
Art. 18(a): 675
Art. 18(b): 679
Art. 18(e): 737, 739, 749
Art. 18(f): 760, 763-764
Art. 18(g): 696, 698, 753
Art. 18(h): 706
Art. 18(j): 729
Art. 18(k): 766-767
Art. 19: 1136

7. Draft ICC Statute of 14 April 1998:

60, 474, 476, 751
Art. 5: 982
Art. 23: 362
Art. 23(7)(e): 486
Art. 28: 286, 288, 507
Art. 28(3): 290
Art. 29(4): 331
Art. 30: 445
Art. 31(1): 423
Art. 31(1)(d): 429, 433
Art. 32(2): 462
Art. 33: 479
Art. 34: 406

8. Draft Statute 1994 (ILC):

41, 59, 276
Art. 20(e): 62
Art. 23(2): 1189

9. Nuremberg Principles of 1950 (ILC):

41, 144, 239
Principle I: 178
Principle III : 516
Principle IV: 455
Principle VII: 340

10. Princeton Principles:

Principle 1(1): 171
Principle 6: 553
Principle 7: 189

11. Protocol on the Pacific Settlement of International Disputes of 2 October 1924 (Geneva Protocol):

1153, 1164
Art. 2: 1153
Art. 10: 1153
Art. 11: 1153

12. Treaty of Sèvres of 10 August 1920:

14

V. Resolutions of the UN Security Council and of the UN General Assembly

13. UN General Assembly Resolution 95(I) of 11 December 1946:

41, 150, 1165

14. UN General Assembly Resolution 96(I) of 11 December 1946:

561, 566, 583

15. Universal Declaration of Human Rights of 10 December 1948:

739

16. UN General Assembly Resolution 2625 (XXVI) of 24 October 1970 (Friendly Relations Declaration):

Principle 1(2): 1165

17. UN General Assembly Resolution 3314 (XXIX) of 14 December 1974 (UN Definition of Aggression):

58, 1160, 1165-1167, 1175
Art. 1: 1160
Art. 3: 1160, 1187
Art. 4: 1160
Art. 5(2), Sentence 1: 1165

18. UN General Assembly Resolution 47/133 of 18 December 1992 (Declaration on the Protection of All Persons from Enforced Disappearances):

754

19. UN Security Council Resolution 808 of 22 February 1993:

49, 78

20. UN Security Council Resolution 827 of 25 May 1993:

50, 206

21. UN Security Council Resolution 955 of 8 November 1994:

54, 78, 211, 812

22. UN Security Council Resolution 1422 of 12 July 2002:

66, 202

23. UN Security Council Resolution 1487 of 12 June 2003:

66, 202

24. UN Security Council Resolution 1373 of 28 September 2001:

78

Appendix 4:
Index

Index

The figures below refer to marginal numbers, including footnotes within them.

abduction, 738
abortion, 731, 900
accessorial liability, 343
acknowledgment and truth finding functions, see
    also *purposes of punishment*, 88
acting under orders, see *superior orders*
actus reus, see *theory of crimes under international
    law - material elements*
Additional Protocol I (1977), see also table of stat-
    utes, 799, 825
Additional Protocol II (1977), see also table of
    statutes, 811, 815, 825-826
Additional Protocols to the Geneva Conventions
    (1977), see also table of statutes, 42, 147,
    785, 793
age of criminal responsibility, 547
aggression, crime of, see also *aggression, war of*,
    1147-1189
  act of aggression (UN Charter, Art. 39), 1160
  context of organized violence, 83
  customary international law, 1161-1181,
    1187
  (German) Code of Crimes Against Interna-
    tional Law, 253
  ICC Statute, 62, 1149, 1184-1189
  jurisdiction, 1182-1183
  as a leadership crime, 1176
  lower intensity act of violence, 1167, 1175
  mental element, 1181
  Nuremberg Charter, 19, 1162
  Nuremberg judgment, 27
  perpetrators, 1176
  prohibiton of aggression, 1151-1161
  prosecution by ICC, 1149, 1182, 1184, 1188
  prosecution by third states, 1183
  and the Security Council, 1186, 1188-1189
  support of armed bands, 1160
  UN definition, 1160, 1166, 1175
aggression, war of, see also *aggression, crime of*,
    1161-1181
  aggressive element, 1170, 1172
  attempt, 1180
  criminality, 1148
  definition, 1168-1174
  execution, 1178-1179
  introduction, 1178
  planning, 1178, 1180

aggression (cont.)
  preparation, 1178, 1180
  violation of international law, 1169
aid organizations, 863
aiding and abetting, see *individual criminal re-
    sponsibility - aiding and abetting*
air traffic, crimes against, 100
Allied Control Council, 35
American Civil War, 781, 828
ammunition, use of prohibited, 1098, 1111-1113
  customary international law, 1125-1126
  mental element, 1113
  non-international conflict, 1125-1126
  particular danger, 1113
amnesty, see also *duty to prosecute*, 188-192
apartheid, 758-765
  institutionalized regime, 763
  legislative measures, 762
  material elements, 761-764
  mental element, 765
  Rome conference, 760
  symbolic significance of the offense, 760
appropriation, 987-988
armchair perpetrator, 338
armed attack (UN Charter, Art. 2(4)), 1159-1160
armed conflict, 822-832
armed forces, 863, 924-926, 929-930, 981, 1050,
    1072
Armenians, 14, 555, 636
assistance in commission of a crime, see *individual
    criminal responsibility - assistance*
attacks on 11 September 2001, see also *terrorism*,
    664, 794
attack, military, 1017, 1025, 1032, 1035, 1045
  purposeful action, 1018, 1025, 1028, 1034,
    1038
attacks on aid missions, 1008, 1133-1143
  customary international law, 1134
  mental element, 1143
  origin of the norm, 1136
  practical significance, 1135
  right to protection, 1142
attacks on civilian objects, 1024-1028
  customary international law, 1027
  international conflict, 1024
  mental element, 1026, 1028
  non-international conflict, 1027-1028
  object of attack, 1025

attacks on civilian populations, 1015-1018
material elements, 1017
mental element, 1018
non-international conflict, 1015
rules of international humanitarian law, 1017
attacks on non-military targets, 1008-1011
customary international law, 1009
limits of the prohibition, 1011
origin of the norm, 1009-1010
relationship to other crimes of attack, 1010
attacks on specially protected objects, 1029-1034
customary international law, 1029, 1033
mental element, 1034
non-international conflict, 1033
attacks on persons and objects bearing protective
emblems, 1035-1038
mental element, 1038
non-international conflict, 1035
attacks on undefended non-military objects,
1008, 1049-1053
definition, 1050-1051
mental element, 1052
non-international conflict, 1053
protective purpose, 1049
attacks on UN missions, 1008, 1070, 1133-1143
customary international law, 1134
mental element, 1143
origin of the norm, 1136
practical significance, 1135
right to protection, 1142
attempt, 493-499
abandonment, 496, 500-501
customary international law, 494
material elements, 495
mitigation of punishment, 497
participation in, 497
practical significance, 499
aut dedere aut judicare, 183, 185, 798

Barbie, Klaus, 640
binding effect of court decisions, 149, 167
biological experiments, see *medical and scientific
experiments*
biological weapons, use of, 1098, 1106, 1109,
1122-1124
customary international law, 1123-1124
mental element, 1124
non-international conflict, 1131
blinding laser weapons, 1125
bombardment, 1160

causality, 290
causing suffering or bodily injury, 885, 891-894
consequences, 891

causing suffering or bodily injury (cont.)
difference from other crimes, 892
mental element, 893
non-international conflict, 894
by omission, 505
chain of inducements, 358
chemical weapons, use of, 1098, 1106, 1108,
1119-1121
customary international law, 1119, 1129
jurisdiction of ICC, 1120
mental element, 1121
non-international conflict, 1129, 1131
child soldiers, use of, 977-985
age limit, 979, 985
auxiliary activities, 982-983
customary international law, 978-979
enlistment, 981
material elements, 981-984
mental element, 985
non-international conflict, 978, 981
protective purpose, 980
voluntary participation, 981, 984
churches, 1030-1031
circumstances, 291-292
circumstances, contextual, see *theory of crimes
under international law - contextual element*
civil war, see *non-international conflict*
civilians, 863, 866, 873, 877, 896, 935, 952, 960,
983, 1008-1009, 1015-1017, 1045,
1053, 1057, 1059, 1081-1082, 1088,
1090-1095
protection of property, 991
using for service, 927
Control Council Law No. 10, see also table of
statutes, 35-39, 146, 155, 1162, 1168
Cold War, 4, 40-44
collateral damage, 1011, 1044
collective punishment, 939, 946, 952
collision of duties, 483
colonial domination, 836
combatants, 792, 877, 880, 1009, 1057, 1059,
1075
unlawful, 866
command responsibility, see *superior responsibility*
*Commission des Responsabilités des Auteurs de la
Guerre et Sanctions*, 8
compelling military service, 924-928
definition, 925-927
integration into armed forces, 926
mental element, 928
non-international conflict, 924
protective purpose, 925
compelling participation in military operations,
see also *compelling military service*, 924,
929-931

compelling participation in military operations
    (cont.)
  mental element, 931
  protective purpose, 929
  support activities, 930
complicity, see *individual criminal responsibility -
    joint perpetration*
confinement, unlawful, 950-954
  maintaining confinement, 953
  mental element, 954
  non-international conflict, 950
  on political, ethnic etc. grounds, 952
  protected persons, 951
  violation of procedural rights, 952-953
concursus delictorum, see *multiplicity of offenses*
confiscation, see *expropriation*
consent, 482
conspiracy, 340, 343, 364, 488-490
  aggression, 489, 1178
  crimes against humanity, 489
  customary international law, 489
  genocide, 489
  Nuremberg Charter, 487
  war crimes, 489
context of organized violence, 81-84, 278, 292,
    327, 646, 846-847
  as object of the mental element, 325-329
contextual element, see *theory of crimes under in-
    ternational law - contextual element*
concentration camps, 556, 594, 733
core crimes, 74
counterfeiting, 100
crimes against peace, see *aggression, crime of*
crimes against humanity, 632-771
  accessorial requirements, lack of, 637, 641
  actual prosecution, 640
  applicability in peacetime, 647
  attack on a civilian population, 646-671
  attack, widespread or systematic, 652-657
  catch-all provision, 766-768
  CCL No. 10, 36, 637-638
  civilian population as object, 647
  context of organized violence, see also con-
    textual element, 82, 645
  contextual element, 644, 646-671
  customary international law, 639, 641, 666-
    667, 669
  discriminatory motives, 671
  and genocide, 633
  (German) Code of Crimes Against Interna-
    tional Law, 255
  history, 635-643
  ICTR Statute, 641
  ICTY Statute, 641
  individual acts, 644, 672-768

crimes against humanity (cont.)
  and international humanitarian law, 648-650
  isolated act of violence, 660
  manifestations, 633-634
  mental element, 327, 644, 669
  murder-type crimes, 672-673
  non-state actors, 668
  Nuremberg Charter, 19, 635
  organization, definition of, 663
  "other inhumane acts", 766-768
  perpetrators, 668
  persecution-type crimes, see also *persecution*,
    672-673
  planning and preparation, 491-492
  policy element, 656, 658-667
  political opponents, 678
  protected rights, 645
  protection of own nationals, 635, 647
  Rome Conference, 643
  state, definition of, 662
  structure of offense, 644
  systematic attack, 656
  Tokyo Charter, 637
  tolerating attacks, 665
  widespread attack, 654-655
crimes against peace, see *aggression, crime of*
crimes under international law, see also *theory of
    crimes under international law*
  aggression, 1147-1189
  concept, 72, 272
  crimes against humanity, 632-771
  genocide, 554-631
  war crimes, 772-1146
cross-border criminality, 103
cultural facilities, 1029
cultural property, 998, 1030-1031
customary international law (generally), 16, 29,
    47, 75, 128-133, 135, 139, 166, 790
  opinio juris, 128, 130, 133, 142, 154-157,
    1165, 1175
  relationship to ICC Statute, 139, 141
  relationship to international treaty law, 127
  state practice, 128-129, 133, 154-157, 813-
    814, 1166, 1175

death penalty, imposition of, as war crime, see
    also *punishment without regular trial*, 939
defenses, see *theory of crimes under international
    law - defenses* and *grounds for excluding
    responsibility*
delay in repatriation, 955-957
  of civilians, 955-956
  customary international law, 955
  mental element, 957
  non-international conflict, 955

delay in repatriation (cont.)
  of prisoners of war, 955-956
  similar rules, 955
denying quarter, 1013, 1074-1079
  commander, 1076
  customary international law, 1074
  declaration, 1076
  mental element, 1079
  and prohibition on weapons, 1075
  relationship to other offenses, 1078
  threat of, 1076
deportation, 695-703, 963-970
  as crime against humanity, 695-703
  customary international law, 702
  definition, 697-699, 965
  forcible nature, 699
  justifications under international law, 700,
    966
  lawfulness of residence, 701
  material elements, 697-699
  mental element, 703, 967
  non-international conflict, 968-970
  World War II, 964
deprivation of liberty, see *imprisonment*
destruction of agriculture, 1085, 1089
destruction of property, 986, 1000-1004
  extent, 1003
  justification, 1003
  material elements, 1002-1003
  mental element, 1004
  object, 1003
  scope, 1001
  structure, 1001
destructive conditions of life, see *genocide - in-
    flicting destructive conditions of life*
deterrence, see also *purposes of punishment*, 86
direct enforcement of international criminal law,
    194-196
disproportionate incidental damage, causing of,
    1008, 1039-1048
  customary international law, 1042, 1048
  mental element, 1047
  non-international conflict, 1048
dolus eventualis, see *mental element - dolus eventu-
    alis*
domestic legality, irrelevance of, 21
Dönitz, Karl, 1177
double jeopardy, prohibition of, 546
dum dum bullets, 1111, 1125, 1131
Dunant, Henry, 782
duress, see also *necessity and duress*, 404, 420-434
duty to prosecute, 177-187
  aggression, 185
  crimes against humanity, 184-187
  general amnesty, 189

duty to prosecute (cont.)
  Geneva Conventions (1949), 180, 183
  genocide, 184-187
  human rights, 181
  state of commission, 179-181
  third states, 182-187
  truth commissions, 188-192
  war crimes, 183

economic sanctions, 824
effective control test, 838
Eichmann, Adolf, 338, 640
Einsatzgruppen Trial, see *Nuremberg follow-up
    trials*
Elements of Crimes, 124, 138, 159, 166
encroachments on rights, 986, 1005-1007
  mental element, 1007
  protective purpose, 1006
  scope, 1006
enemy flags, insignia, and uniforms, misuse of,
    1066-1067
enforced disappearance, 752-757
  at the behest or with approval, 755
  definition, 754
  deprivation of liberty, 755
  mental element, 757
  refusal to give information, 756
  Rome conference, 753
enforced prostitution, see also *sexual violence*, 729-
    730, 914
  attack on dignity, 909-910
enforced sterilization, 733, 914
enslavement, 683-694, 933
  customary international law, 685
  functional definition, 686
  mental element, 689
  during the Nazi period, 691
environmental damage, 1040
  customary international law, 1042
  definition, 1043
  long-term damage, 1043-1044
"ethnic cleansing", 48, 595, 604-605
expropriation, 987-999
  definition, 988
  extent of, 994-995
  justifications, 997-999
  mental element, 996
  objects of, 990-991
extermination, see also *genocide - inflicting destruc-
    tive conditions of life*, 678-682
  "indirect" causing of death, 680
  material elements, 679-681
  mental element, 682
extraterritorial jurisdiction, rules on, 108

flag of truce, misuse of, 1064-1065
fragmentation weapons, 1125
forced pregnancy, see also *sexual violence*, 731-
    732, 914
    mental element, 732
forced labor, 595, 690-692, 926-927, 935-937
    severity, 937
forum shopping, 176
forcible transfer of population, see *deportation*

general principles of international criminal law,
    266-553
    development, 267-270
    ICC Statute, 269-270
general principles of law, 26, 134-135, 166
Geneva, law of, 782-785, 789, 820, 874
Geneva Convention (1864), see also table of stat-
    utes, 8, 782
Geneva Convention (1906), see also table of stat-
    utes, 797
Geneva Conventions (1949), see also table of stat-
    utes, 42, 183, 783
    common article 3, see also table of statutes,
        784-785, 793, 811-812, 815, 825, 872,
        884, 887, 895, 903, 908, 918, 932, 959-
        960, 983
    grave breaches, 798, 809-810, 817, 867, 898,
        903, 908, 924, 938, 950, 959, 986
    protected persons, 860-873
    protective emblems, 1035, 1068
    scope of conventions, 864
genocide, 69, 554-631
    causing serious bodily or mental harm, 590-
        592
    context of a manifest pattern of similar con-
        duct, 550
    context of organized violence, 82, 564, 606-
        609
    and crimes against humanity, 631
    cultural, 564, 568, 599
    customary international law, 562
    ethnic groups, 571, 581
    forcibly transferring children, 598-603
    (German) Code of Crimes Against Interna-
        tional Law, 254, 1001
    history, 560-562
    imposing measures to prevent births, 597
    inflicting destructive conditions of life, 593-
        596
    intent to destroy, 565, 615-622
    killing, 589
    manifestations, 555-559
    material elements, 564, 571-609
    mental element, 329, 565, 610-622
    national groups, 571, 580

genocide (cont.)
    objective constitution of group, 573-579
    planning and preparation, 492
    political groups, 562, 580
    protected groups, 571-586
    protected rights, 563, 566-570
    racial groups, 571, 582
    religious groups, 571, 583-584
    separate acts, 564, 587-605
    social groups, 562, 580
    stable groups, 575, 577, 586
    structure of crime, 563-565
    subjective construction of group, 573-579
    substantial part of the group, 621
    and war crimes, 631
Genocide Convention (1948), see also table of
    statutes, 42, 58, 557, 559, 560, 566, 571,
    577, 581, 583, 586, 594, 599, 623
(German) Code of Crimes against International
    Law, see also table of statutes, 238-265,
    926, 1053, 1073, 1095, 1131
    aims, 246-248
    aggression, 263
    crimes against humanity, 255
    genocide, 254
    general principles, 250-253
    history, 239-245
    legal situation before entering into force, 247
    superior responsibility, 261-262
    structure, 249
    universal jurisdiction, 264-265
    war crimes, 256-260, 798, 815, 820
Göring, Hermann, 22
grave breaches, see *Geneva Conventions - grave
    breaches*
grounds for excluding responsibility, 277, 282-
    283, 401-484
    ICC Statute, 405-406
    ICTY and ICTR practice, 403
    Nuremberg Charter, 402
    outside the ICC Statute, 477-484
    practical significance, 402-404
guerrilla wars, 828, 1060

The Hague, law of, 786-789, 817, 820
Hague Convention for the Protection of Cultural
    Property (1954), see also table of statutes,
    788, 1031, 1033
Hague Peace Conferences, 1151
Hague Regulations (1907), see also table of stat-
    utes, 8, 147, 787
High Command Trial, see *Nuremberg follow-up
    trials*
Hitler, Adolf, 556
Holocaust, 3, 555-556, 594, 678

hors de combat, 872-873, 879-884, 1072, 1077
  intent to surrender, 881
  non-international conflict, 884
  unconsciousness, wounding or sickness, 881
hospital ships, 990, 1037
hospitals, 990, 998, 1000, 1030-1031, 1037
Hostages Trial, see *Nuremberg follow-up trials*
hostage taking, 958-962
  coercive intent, 962
  definition, 960-961
  justification, 959
  killing of hostages, 959
  mental element, 962
  non-international conflict, 958
  protected persons, 960
human dignity, 570, 904, 909, 918
human rights, 78, 102, 109-117, 181, 187
  criminalization of violations, 115
  and international criminal law, 109-117
human shields, use of, 1014, 1090-1095
  customary international law, 1095
  definition, 1092-1093
  intent to use, 1094
  mental element, 1094
  non-international conflict, 1095
  protective purpose, 1091
human trafficking, 693-694
humanitarian intervention, 1171
humanitarian relief missions, see also *attacks on aid missions*, 1139-1140
humiliating and degrading treatment, 917-923
  consequences, 920
  definition, 919-920
  human dignity, 918
  mental element, 921
  by omission, 920
  as a preliminary stage of torture, 920
  relationship to crimes of sexual violence, 923
  relationship to offenses of mistreatment, 922
  severity, 919

ICC Rules of Procedure and Evidence, see also table of statutes, 124, 166
ICC states parties, 66
ICC Statute, see also table of statutes, 66, 68-70, 138-141
  deficiencies in the international criminal law of war, 815
  drafts, 58-59, 185
  relationship to customary international law, 139, 141
  significance, 68-70
ICTR Statute, see also table of statutes
  relationship to customary international law, 142

ICTY Statute, see also table of statutes
  relationship to customary international law, 142
IG Farben trial, see *Nuremberg follow-up trials*
ignorance of the law, see *mistake - ignorance of the law*
immunity, 509-526, 552
  basic concepts, 511
  customary international law, 515, 522
  domestic criminal courts, 519, 525
  heads of state and government, foreign ministers, diplomats, 520-525
  obstacle to prosecution, 521
  ratione materiae, 512, 515-519
  ratione personae, 513
  scope, 512-514
implementation of international criminal law, domestic, 215-265
  forms, 230-234
  necessity, 217-219
  options, 220-229
imprisonment, 704-708
  violation of fundamental rules of international law, 706
  material elements, 704-707
  mental element, 708
improper use of insignia, 1012, 1061-1073
  customary international law, 1061, 1073
  mental element, 1065, 1067, 1069, 1071
  non-international conflict, 1073
  and the prohibition on perfidy, 1061
  protective purpose, 1063
  serious consequences, 1072
  treachery, 1063
incapacitating agents, 1104
incendiary weapons, 1125
incitement to genocide, 356, 623-627
  material elements, 626
  mental element, 627
  practical significance, 624-625
indirect enforcement of international criminal law, 194-196
individual criminal responsibility, 274, 337-366
  aiding and abetting, 343, 361-363
  assistance, 360-366
  assisting commission of group crime, 364-366
  CCL No. 10, 341
  customary international law, 339-342
  ICC Statute, 343-344
  ICTY jurisprudence, 342
  individual commission, 343, 345
  inducement, 343, 358-359
  instigation, 358-359
  International Law Commission, 342
  joint commission, see also *joint criminal enterprise*, 343, 346-352

individual criminal responsibility (cont.)
    Nuremberg Charter, 340
    ordering, 343, 357
    perpetration-by-means, 343, 353-355
inducement, see *individual criminal responsibility - inducement*
inhuman or cruel treatment, 885, 903-906
    as catch-all provision, 904
    definition, 904-905
    mental element, 906
    violation of dignity, 904-905
instigation, see *individual criminal responsibility - instigation*
intent, see *mental element - intent*
International Committee of the Red Cross, 782, 811
international conflict, 823, 833-841
    inter-state conflict as international conflict, 834
    intra-state conflict with indirect participation of third state, 837
    intra-state conflict with international character, 835
    United Nations as party to conflict, 834
International Court of Justice, 40
international crimes, 100-104
International Criminal Court, see also *Rome Conference*, 56-70, 201-205
    assembly of states parties, 66-67
    jurisdiction, 63-64, 201
    procedure, 120, 204
    relationship to UN Security Council, 201-202, 204
    structure, 203
international criminal procedure, 118-121, 545
international element of crimes under international law, 81-84, 278, 292
international humanitarian law (generally), 161, 391, 775-816
    addressees, 795, 810, 849
    basic principles, 792
    challenges, 793
    criminalization of violations, 803
    as customary international law, 790-791
    development outside of Europe, 778
    domestic criminal law, 795
    individuals as addressees, 810
    origins, 776-783
    police action, 824
    requirements for application, 808, 822
    scope of application in regard to type of conflict, 816, 833
    use of force, absence of, 831
international law associations, 136
International Law Commission, see *United Nations - International Law Commission*

interpretation, 158-163
    in conformity with customary law, 160
    in conformity with prohibitions of international law, 161
    of customary international law, 163
    domestic context, 235-237
    methods, 159
inter-state conflict, 823-825
intoxication, 469-476
    customary international law, 471
    definition, 472
    general principles of law, 471
    voluntary intoxication, 473-476
intra-state conflict, 823, 825-830
    comparability with interstate conflict, 830
    disturbances and tensions, 826
    occupation of part of the state territory, 828
    parties to the conflict, 827, 830
    protracted conflict, 829
    threshold of intensity, 825
Iraq war, 1091, 1172

joint criminal enterprise, 347-352
    categories, 349-351
    common plan, 348
judicial assistance and co-operation, international, 105, 107
jus ad bellum, 1151
jus in bello, see also *international humanitarian law*, 775, 1151
Justice Trial, see also *Nuremberg follow-up trials*, 940-941

Keitel, Wilhelm, 1177
Kellogg-Briand Pact, see also table of statutes, 23, 1155-1157
killing, see also *extermination* and *genocide - inflicting destructive conditions of life*, 589, 674-677, 875-878
    acting with premeditation, 677
    causality, 876
    of combatants, 859, 877
    as crime against humanity, 674-677
    as genocide, 589
    as grave breach of the Geneva Conventions, 875
    indirect, 680
    material elements, 675, 876
    mental element, 676, 878
    non-international conflict, 875
    by omission, 505
    of persons *hors de combat*, 879-884
    as war crime, 875-878
knowledge, see *mental element - knowledge*

League of Nations, 57, 1152-1155, 1164
    proscription of war, 1152

Leipzig war crimes trials, 10-12
levée en masse, 863
Lieber Code, see also table of statutes, 781, 797, 1030
like-minded states, 61, 243
limited warfare, 1009
Locarno, treaties of, see also table of statutes, 1154
London Agreement, see also table of statutes, 15, 17

maritime navigation, crimes against, 100
Martens Clause, 636, 791
material elements, see *theory of crimes under international law-material elements*
means of determining law, see *sources of law and means of determining law*
means of warfare, use of prohibited, 786, 820, 1096-1132
    catch-all offense, 1114-1115
    customary international law, 1099, 1106, 1116-1132
    development, 1097
    ICC Statute, 1098
    international conflict, 1100-1126
    mental element under customary international law, 1132
    non-international conflict, 815, 1099, 1127-1132
    political compromise, 1098, 1106
    prohibited list, 1098, 1115, 1126
medical aircraft, 990
medical personnel, 863, 1037, 1050
medical and scientific experiments, 885, 898-902
    endangering the victim, 898, 901
    medical indications, 898, 900-901
    mental element, 902
Medical Trial, see *Nuremberg follow-up trials*
membership in criminal organizations, 20
mens rea, see *mental element*
mental disease or defect, 463-468
    diminished capacity, 468
    evidence, 465
    practical significance, 464
mental element, 281, 293-336, 610-622, 669-671, 676, 682, 689, 703, 708, 718-720, 727, 732, 745-751, 757, 765, 768, 854-858, 878, 882, 890, 893, 897, 902, 906, 913, 916, 921, 928, 931, 943, 949, 954, 957, 962, 967, 969, 976, 985, 996, 1004, 1007, 1018, 1026, 1028, 1034, 1038, 1047, 1052, 1058, 1065, 1067, 1069, 1071, 1079, 1086, 1094, 1110, 1113, 1121, 1124, 1132, 1143, 1181
    circumstances, 308-309
    cognitive element, 299
    consequences, 306
    contextual element, 325-329
    criminal conduct, 305

mental element (cont.)
    customary international law, 313-315
    departures from the standard requirements, 310-324
    dolus eventualis, 330-336
    Elements of Crimes, 313-316
    expanded liability, 319-322
    general, 296
    ICC Statute, 298-324
    ICC Statute and customary international law, 311-315, 857-858, 878, 962, 985, 1065
    intent, 304-307
    intent to engage in conduct, 305
    knowledge, 304-309
    narrowed liability, 323-324
    points of reference, 299
    purpose, 324, 329, 363, 565, 569, 597, 600, 605, 610, 613, 615-622, 627, 629, 633, 682, 732, 754, 757, 765, 921, 951, 962, 968, 989, 1058, 1065, 1067, 1079, 1086, 1094, 1181
    recklessness, 296, 330-336, 857-858, 878, 882, 893, 902, 943, 949, 976, 996, 1004
    specific intent, 296, 324, 329, 565, 569, 600, 610, 613, 615-622, 627, 629, 633, 921, 1058
    standard requirements, 304-309
    superior responsibility, 320
    voluntative element, 299
    wantonness, 320, 986, 996
    wilfulness, 320, 857-858, 875, 882, 893, 902, 943, 976
mental harm and suffering, 892
methods of warfare, use of prohibited, 786, 820, 1008-1095
    and destruction of property, 1000
    means of warfare, 1012-1014
    non-international conflict, 815
    structure, 1008, 1012-1014
military chaplains, 863, 1037, 1050
military justice, codes of, 796
military necessity, 481, 997-999, 1003, 1101
military target, 1025, 1030-1032
militias, 838, 849, 863
Milošević, Slobodan, 210
mines, 1125
Ministries Trial, see *Nuremberg follow-up trials*
Mistake, 435-447
    customary international law, 438
    and duress, 447
    about factual requirements of defense, 442
    ignorance of the law, 436, 443-447
    mistake of fact, 436, 439-442
    mistake of law, 436, 443-447
    about normative elements, 440, 446
    superior orders, 443, 447

mistreatment, 885-906
mixed conflicts, 842-843
modes of liability, see *individual criminal responsibility*
Monroe Doctrine, 1156
monuments, attacks on, 1030
Moscow Declaration (1943), 18
multiplicity of offenses, 527-543, 628-631, 769-771, 1144-1146
    Čelebići test, 535-540
    cumulative charging, 543
    ICC Statute, 529
    lex specialis, 537, 769, 1144-1145
    overall sentence, 542-543
    practical significance, 530
    relationship between core crimes, 538, 631, 769, 1144
    relationship between individual acts, 539, 628-630, 770, 1145-1146
    same conduct, 531-540
    separate conduct, 531-533
    single sentence, 542-543
murder, see *killing*
mustard gas, 900
mutilation, 885, 892, 895-897
    definition, 895
    mental element, 897
    victims, 896

narcotics trafficking, 100, 103
nationality, 868
nationality principle, 108
ne bis in idem principle, 546, 939
necessity and duress, 420-434
    balancing of interests, 431
    customary international law, 423
    danger induced by perpetrator, 432-433
    duty to assume danger, 434
    ICC Statute, 423
    killing of innocent civilians, 429
    mental element, 430
    necessary and reasonable measures, 428-429
    practical significance, 424
    threat to life or limb, 426-427
    voluntary exposure to danger, 433
negligence, 296, 382-385, 1121, 1124, 1132
nemo tenetur principle, 946
non-international conflict, 784-785, 823, 827
    minimum standards, 784
non-intervention principle, 172, 811
nuclear weapons, use of, 1098, 1118
nulla poena sine lege, see *principle of legality*
nullum crimen sine lege, see *principle of legality*
Nuremberg Charter, see also table of statutes, 15, 198, 1165

Nuremberg follow-up trials, see also table of cases, 37-38, 1162
Nuremberg principles, see also table of statutes, 5, 15-16, 29, 41, 1165
Nuremberg Trial of the Major War Criminals, see also table of cases, 5, 22-24, 559, 561, 678, 801, 1162-1166, 1165, 1168, 1170, 1173, 1177

obstacles to prosecution, see *requirements for prosecution*
occupation, 832, 971-974, 997, 1006, 1082, 1160
    limited duration, 973
    without armed force, 832
official capacity, irrelevance of, 21, 515-519
omissions, 502-508
    customary international law, 505, 508
    ICTY and ICTR case law, 505
ordering, see *individual criminal responsibility - ordering*
outrages upon personal dignity, see *humiliating and degrading treatment*
overall control test, 839

participation, see *individual criminal responsibility*
peacekeeping, 1137-1138
perfidious killing or wounding, 1012, 1054-1060
    abuse of trust, 1056, 1058
    customary international law, 1054
    international conflict, 1054-1058
    material elements, 1055-1057
    mental element, 1058
    non-international conflict, 1059
    protected persons, 1057, 1059
    war at sea, 1056
persecution, 735-751
    definition, 736-744
    definition of group, 738
    through deprivation of rights, 739-743
    gender-specific, 751
    homosexuality, 751
    in the ICC Statute, 744
    manifestations, 740
    material elements, 738-744
    mental element, 745-751
    motives, 745-751
    during the Nazi period, 742
    relationship to other crimes, 771
    severe nature, 741-742
    through violation of property rights, 743
personality principle, 64, 108
pillage, 986-989, 994
    no justification, 998
    objects, 993

planning and preparation, 491-492
poison, use of, 1098, 1100-1106
    definition, 1103-1104
    incidental effect, 1104
    mental element, 1102
    non-international conflict, 1131
    prohibition, 1101
poison gas, use of, 1098, 1105, 1107-1110
    and the definition of poison, 1105
    mental element, 1110
    non-international conflict, 1131
    special rule, 1105
Poison Gas Protocol, see also table of statutes, 1107-1109, 1128
poisoned weapons, see *poison*
power plants, 1025
power to prosecute, see also *universal jurisdiction*, 168-170
    competing jurisdictions, 175-176
    limitations under international law, 172-173
Preparatory Commission, 67, 1184
Preparatory Committee, 59
preventing births, 597
prevention, see also *purposes of punishment*, 87
principle of complementarity, 199, 217
principle of legality, 90-95, 586, 939, 1104
principle of proportionality, 1011, 1046, 1049, 1091
principle of vicarious administration of justice, 108
prisoners of war, 776, 810, 838, 862, 877, 883, 892, 896, 935, 938-939, 951, 1050
    duty to provide food, 810
    protection of property, 991
    recruitment of, 925
    use for service, 927
procedural law, 118-121
    of the ICC, 120
    of the ICTY, 53
property, attacks on, 986-1004
protected persons, 861-874, 876-877, 891, 938, 950-952, 983, 1090-1092
    mental element, 309
    modern conflicts, 869-871
    non-international conflicts, 872-873
protected values in international criminal law, 77-80
protection principle, 108
protective emblems, 1036, 1068, 1070
    authorization to bear, 1037
punishment without regular trial, 938-949
    acquittal, 942
    execution of sentence, 942
    mental element, 943, 949
    non-international conflict, 944-949

punishment without regular trial (cont.)
    participation, 945
    practical significance, 940
    victim's suicide, 942
purposes of punishment, 85-88

"racial hygiene", 733
racial segregation and racial discrimination, see *apartheid*
rape, see also *sexual violence*, 723-727, 892, 912-913
    attack on honor, 909
    coercive element, 725
    as crime against humanity, 723-727
    definition, 724, 912
    as genocide, 590-591, 595, 597
    mental element, 272, 913
    as war crime, 912-913
recklessness, see *mental element-recklessness*
Red Crescent, see *protective emblems*
Red Cross, see *protective emblems*
Red Lion and Red Sun, see *protective emblems*
Red Star of David, see *protective emblems*
Reichsgericht, 10-12
reprisal, 479-480
requirements for prosecution, 284, 544-553
responsibility under international law, 97-99
retribution, see *purposes of punishment*, 86
retroactivity prohibition, 25, 28, 91, 946
right to a defense, 939, 946
right to fair trial, 866, 938, 946-947
right to wage war, see *jus ad bellum*
Rome Conference, 60-66
ruses of war, 1056
Rwanda conflict, 54, 558, 812
    domestic prosecution, 213
    non-international conflict, 812
Rwanda Tribunal, 4-5, 54-55, 211-214, 559, 802
    creation, 54, 211
    jurisdiction, 55, 211, 812
    practice, 211
    procedure, 212
    status of trials, 214
    structure, 212

"scorched-earth" tactics, 1085
sea blockades, 1160, 1187
Security Council, see *United Nations - Security Council*
self-defense, 407-419
    customary international law, 408
    defensible interests, 412-415
    defensive intent, 417
    mental element, 417
    self-defense measures, 416
    self-defense situation, 410-415

sentencing law, 541-543

Sèvres, Treaty of, see also table of statutes, 14

sexual slavery, see also *sexual violence*, 728

sexual violence, see also *rape*, 721-734, 907-916
   attack on honor, 909
   catch-all offense, 734, 915
   as crime against humanity, 721-734
   as genocide, 590-591
   as grave breach of Geneva Conventions, 908, 915
   mental element, 916
   as outrage upon personal dignity, 910
   practical significance, 909
   as war crime, 907-916

shipwrecked persons, 864

sick or wounded persons, 864, 951

Sierra Leone, Special Court for, 143

slavery, 932-934
   as outrage upon personal dignity, 934

Solferino, battle of, 782

solitary confinement, 892

sources of law and means of determining law, 123-157
   Additional Protocols to the Geneva Conventions (1977), 147
   Control Council Law No. 10, 146
   customary international law, 128-133
   decisions of domestic courts, 154-155
   decisions of international courts, 148
   domestic legislation, 156
   Elements of Crimes, 138
   general principles of law, 134-135
   Genocide Convention (1948), 147
   Hague Regulations (1907), 147
   hierarchy in the ICC Statute, 164-166
   International Law Commission, 152
   international legal doctrine, 123
   international treaties, 126-127
   interpretation, 158-163
   ICC Statute, 138-141
   ICC Rules of Procedure and Evidence, 138
   ICTY Statute, 142,
   ICTR Statute, 142,
   military manuals, 157
   Nuremberg Charter, 144-145
   scholarly associations, 153
   Tokyo Charter, 144
   UN General Assembly, 150
   UN Security Council, 150
   UN Secretary-General, 151

sovereignty, 79, 98, 112, 825, 829, 1148

St. Petersburg Declaration (1868), see also table of statutes, 786

stare decisis doctrine, 167

starvation of the civilian population, 1014, 1080-1088
   customary international law, 1081, 1088
   definition, 1083, 1089
   mental element, 1086
   non-international conflict, 1088
   by omission, 1085
   relationship to other offenses, 1087
   ways of committing, 1084

state practice, see *customary international law - state practice*

state responsibility, 97-99

states' right of self-defense, 418-419, 1154-1156, 1158-1159, 1169

statute of limitations, exclusion of, 551-553
   customary international law, 553

subjects of international law, 2, 98

superior orders, 21, 404, 448-462
   absolute liability principle, 452, 456, 461-462
   CCL No. 10, 455
   and crimes against humanity, 461
   customary international law, 454, 458, 460
   and genocide, 461
   ICC Statute, 460-462
   ICTY and ICTR Statutes, 457
   manifest illegality of the order, 453, 456, 459, 461
   manifest illegality principle, 453, 456, 458-462
   and mistake of law, 443, 447
   in mitigation of sentence, 454
   Nuremberg Charter, 21, 455
   post World War II trials, 455
   practical significance, 449, 457
   respondeat superior principle, 451
   Tokyo Charter, 455
   and war crimes, 461

superior responsibility, 368-400
   causality, 393, 399
   civilian superiors, 369, 374, 378-380
   customary international law, 372
   doctrinal classification, 371
   effective control, 375, 379-380, 394
   failure to take necessary measures, 386-394
   (German) Code of Crimes Against International Law, 261-262
   mental element, 320, 381-385, 400
   military commanders, 377
   non-reporting of crimes, 398
   practical significance, 370, 372
   superior-subordinate relationship, 374-376
   violation of duty of supervision, 395-400

supplying the civilian population, 1082

supranational criminal law, 105-106

Supreme Court in the British Occupied Zone, 39, 155, 638

teargas, use of, 1104
territoriality principle, 64
terror against a civilian population, 1019-1023
    material elements, 1020
    non-international conflict, 1019
    relationship to other war crimes, 1022
terrorism, 74, 100, 663-664, 794
theory of crimes under international law, 272-277
    concept of crimes under international law, 275-277
    contextual element, 278, 292
    defenses, 273, 282-283
    ICC Statute, 275-277
    material elements, 273, 280, 285-292
    mental element, 273, 281, 293-336
    two-pronged concept of crime under Common Law, 277
third states, 174-175, 200
Thirty Years' War, 779
Tokyo Charter, see also table of statutes, 32, 1162, 1165
Tokyo Trial, 16, 30-33, 801, 1162
torture, 100, 709-720, 885, 887-890, 904-905
    as crime against humanity, 709-720
    definition, 711-716, 888
    definition under international law, 712
    lawful sanctions, 717
    mental element, 718, 890
    mental suffering, 715
    official capacity, 711, 888
    by omission, 505
    purposes of torture, 711, 718-720, 889
    as war crime, 887-890
transfer of children, 598-603
transfer of own civilian population, 971-976
    conduct of occupying power, 974
    indirect, 974
    mental element, 976
    non-international conflict, 971
    private settlement, 974
    protective purpose, 972-973
    sending of children, 975
    use of force, 973
treaty-based crimes, 100
truth commissions, see also duties to prosecute, 192
tu quoque, 484

United Nations, 45-46, 60, 78
    compulsory military measures, 1138
    Economic and Social Council, 561
    General Assembly, 5, 40-41, 58-59, 561, 566, 583, 1183, 1189
    Human Rights Committee, 713
    International Law Commission, 40-41, 58-59, 639, 642, 1136, 1165

United Nations (cont.)
    prohibition on aggression, see aggression, crime of - UN definition
    protective emblems, 1070
    Secretary-General, 49, 561
    Security Council, 49-50, 63, 65, 201-202, 204, 559, 642, 1158-1159, 1182-1183, 1188-1189
United Nations War Crimes Commission (UNWCC), 18, 34
UN Weapons Convention (1980), see also table of statutes, 788
United States and ICC, 66, 524
universal jurisdiction, 171-176
    crimes against humanity, 174
    (German) Code of Crimes Against International Law, 264-265
    genocide, 174
    mandatory, 183
    war crimes, 174
universality principle, see also universal jurisdiction, 108
unnecessary suffering, prohibition on causing, 792, 1097-1098, 1114-1115, 1117

Versailles Peace Treaty, see also table of statutes, 6, 800, 1164
victors' justice, 25
volunteer corps, 838, 849, 863

wantonness, see mental element - wantonness
war, declaration of, 1174
war, definition of, 822, 824, 1152, 1155
war crimes, see also international humanitarian law, 772-1146
    as accessory to international humanitarian law, 775-810
    act's nexus to conflict, 846-853
    approval by parties to the conflict, 851
    categories, 819
    context of organized violence, 83, 846-853
    criminalization, criteria for, 806-810, 814
    under customary international law, 805-810, 813-816, 821, 882, 902, 917, 924, 936, 950, 955, 971, 978-979, 1015, 1029, 1033, 1042, 1053-1054, 1066, 1073-1074, 1081, 1088, 1095, 1105-1106, 1116-1132, 1127, 1129, 1131-1132, 1134
    definition, 773
    (German) Code of Crimes Against International Law, 256-260
    historical development, 774-802
    against humanitarian operations, 820, 1133-1143

war crimes (cont.)
  ICC Statute, 5, 805, 819
  ICTY jurisdiction, 806-810
  inconsistency with international humanitar-
    ian law, 808
  mental element, 854-858
  necessity and duress, 433
  in non-international conflicts (generally),
    811-816
  Nuremberg Charter, 19
  outside the ICC Statute, 805, 815
  perpetrator's awareness of the conflict, 327,
    855-856
  perpetrator's connection to a party to the con-
    flict, 848-852
  perpetrator's private motive, 853
  against persons, 820, 859-985
  planning and preparation, 492
  private persons as perpetrators, 851-852
  prohibition of means of warfare, see *means of
    warfare, use of prohibited*
  prohibition of methods of warfare, see *meth-
    ods of warfare, use of prohibited*
  against property and other rights, 820, 986-
    1007
  protected interests, 817-818
  protection of individuals, 817
  protection of world peace, 818
  relationship to the crime of aggression, 773
  relationship to international humanitarian
    law, 804, 808

war crimes (cont.)
  scope of provisions, 822, 831
  serious violations of international humanitar-
    ian law, 809, 814, 994-995
  structure of the norms, 804
  temporal scope, 844-845
  territorial scope, 844-845
  and terrorism, 794
  threshold clause, 328, 549
war in violation of international treaties, 1168
wars of national liberation, 785, 793, 836
weapons with indiscriminate effect, 1097-1098,
    1106, 1114-1115, 1117-1118
weapons of mass destruction, 1098, 1106
William II of Hohenzollern, 6-7, 9
wilfulness, see *mental element*
wilful killing, see *killing*
wrongful act under international law, 99
World War I, 6-14,
World War II, 556, 1091, 1163

Yugoslavia conflict, 48-49, 558, 1091
Yugoslavia Tribunal, 4-5, 45, 48-53, 206-210,
    559, 802
  creation, 206
  jurisdiction, 206
  procedure, 208
  structure, 207
  status of trials, 209-210

Appendix 5:
International Criminal Law in the World Wide Web

International Criminal Law in the World Wide Web

A. Statutes and International Instruments

ICC Statute
http://www.un.org/law/icc/statute/romefra.htm

ICC Rules of Procedure and Evidence
http://www.icc-cpi.int/library/about/officialjournal/Rules_of_Proc_and_Evid_070704-EN.pdf

ICC Elements of Crimes
http://www.icc-cpi.int/library/about/officialjournal/Elements_of_Crimes_120704EN.pdf

ICTY Statute, ICTY Rules of Procedure and Evidence
http://www.un.org/icty/legaldoc/index.htm

ICTR Statute, ICTR Rules of Procedure and Evidence
http://www.ictr.org/default.htm

Nuremberg Charter, IMT Rules of Procedure
http://www.yale.edu/lawweb/avalon/imt/imt.htm

International Humanitarian Law (Hague Regulations, Geneva Conventions and Additional Protocols, and other Treaties and Conventions)
http://www.icrc.org/ihl

Genocide Convention
http://www.unhchr.ch/html/menu3/b/p_genoci.htm

International Law Commission, Drafts and Commentaries
http://www.un.org/law/ilc/convents.htm

B. International Criminal Courts and Tribunals

International Criminal Court
www.icc-cpi.int

Yugoslavia Tribunal[1]
www.un.org/icty

Rwanda Tribunal[2]
www.ictr.org

Special Court for Sierra Leone
www.sc-sl.org

C. Other Useful Links

(Non-Governmental) Coalition for the International Criminal Court
http://www.iccnow.org

International Committee of the Red Cross
http://www.icrc.org

Amnesty International
http://web.amnesty.org/web/web.nsf/pages/ICChome

Links to Domestic Legislation Implementing the ICC Statute
http://www.legal.coe.int/criminal/icc
http://www.iuscrim.mpg.de/forsch/straf/projekte/natstraf2_mat.html

---

[1] Website includes all judgments rendered at the Tribunal.
[2] Website includes all judgments rendered at the Tribunal.